# Contents

**II** **Key to map symbols**

**III** **Sandwiches on the move** – we peel back the cellophane wrappers

**IV** **Service areas on motorways and primary routes**

**VIII** **Route planning maps**

**XIV** **Distances and journey times**

**1** **Road maps of Britain**

**315** **Urban approach maps**

| | | |
|---|---|---|
| 315 **Bristol** *approaches* | 320 **Glasgow** *approaches* | 327 **Manchester** *approaches* |
| 316 **Birmingham** *approaches* | 321 **Leeds** *approaches* | 328 **Newcastle** *approaches* |
| 318 **Cardiff** *approaches* | 322 **London** *approaches* | 329 **Nottingham** *approaches* |
| 319 **Edinburgh** *approaches* | 326 **Liverpool** *approaches* | 330 **Sheffield** *approaches* |

**331** **Town plans**

331 Aberdeen, Aberystwyth, Ashford, Ayr, Bangor
332 Barrow-in-Furness, Bath, Berwick-upon-Tweed, Birmingham, Blackpool
333 Bournemouth, Bradford, Brighton, Bristol, Bury St Edmunds
334 Cambridge, Canterbury, Cardiff, Carlisle, Chelmsford, Cheltenham
335 Chester, Chichester, Colchester, Coventry, Derby, Dorchester
336 Dumfries, Dundee, Durham, Edinburgh, Exeter
337 Fort William, Glasgow, Gloucester, Grimsby, Hanley
338 Harrogate, Holyhead, Hull, Inverness, Ipswich, Kendal
339 King's Lynn, Leeds, Lancaster, Leicester, Lewes
340 London
342 Lincoln, Liverpool, Llandudno, Llanelli, Luton
343 Macclesfield, Manchester, Maidstone, Merthyr Tydfil, Middlesbrough
344 Milton Keynes, Newcastle, Newport, Newquay, Newtown, Northampton
345 Norwich, Nottingham, Oban, Oxford, Perth, Peterborough
346 Plymouth, Poole, Portsmouth, Preston, Reading, St Andrews
347 Salisbury, Scarborough, Shrewsbury, Sheffield, Southampton
348 Southend-on-Sea, Stirling, Stoke, Stratford-upon-Avon, Sunderland, Swansea
349 Swindon, Taunton, Telford, Torquay, Truro, Wick
350 Winchester, Windsor, Wolverhampton, Worcester, Wrexham, York

**351** **Index to town plans**

**367** **Index to road maps of Britain**

**Inside back cover: County and unitary authority boundaries**

**www.philips-maps.co.uk**

First published in 1994 by Philip's,
a division of Octopus Publishing Group Ltd
www.octopusbooks.co.uk
Endeavour House, 189 Shaftesbury Avenue,
London WC2H 8JY
An Hachette UK Company
www.hachette.co.uk

Second edition 2012
First impression 2012

ISBN 978-1-84907-234-2

Cartography by Philip's

Data for the speed cameras provided by **PocketGPSWorld.com Ltd**.

Information for National Parks, Areas of Outstanding Natural Beauty, National Trails and Country Parks in Wales supplied by the Countryside Council for Wales.

Information for National Parks, Areas of Outstanding Natural Beauty, National Trails and Country Parks in England supplied by Natural England. Data for Regional Parks, Long Distance Footpaths and Country Parks in Scotland provided by Scottish Natural Heritage.

Information for Forest Parks supplied by the Forestry Commission

Information for the RSPB reserves provided by the RSPB

Gaelic name forms used in the Western Isles provided by Comhairle nan Eilean.

Data for the National Nature Reserves in England provided by Natural England. Data for the National Nature Reserves in Wales provided by Countryside Council for Wales. Darparwyd data'n ymwneud â Gwarchodfeydd Natur Cenedlaethol Cymru gan Gyngor Cefn Gwlad Cymru.

Information on the location of National Nature Reserves in Scotland was provided by Scottish Natural Heritage.

Data for National Scenic Areas in Scotland provided by the Scottish Executive Office. Crown copyright material is reproduced with the permission of the Controller of HMSO and the Queen's Printer for Scotland. Licence number C02W0003960.

Printed in China

## Road map symbols

Motorway

Motorway junctions – full access, restricted access

Toll motorway

**Pease Pottage Services** Motorway service area

Motorway under construction

Primary route – dual, single carriageway, services – under construction, narrow

**Cardiff** Primary destination

Numbered junctions – full, restricted access

A road – dual, single carriageway – under construction, narrow

B road – dual, single carriageway – under construction, narrow

Minor road – dual, single carriageway

Drive or track

Urban side roads

Roundabout, multi-level junction

Distance in miles

Tunnel

Toll, steep gradient – points downhill

Speed camera – single, multiple

**CLEVELAND WAY** National trail – England and Wales

**GREAT GLEN WAY** Long distance footpath – Scotland

**YATTON** Railway with station, level crossing, tunnel

**ROPLEY** Preserved railway with level crossing, station, tunnel

Tramway

National boundary

County or unitary authority boundary

Car ferry, catamaran

Passenger ferry, catamaran

**CALAIS 1:30** Ferry destination, journey time – hours: minutes

Hovercraft

Internal ferry – car, passenger

Principal airport, other airport or airfield

**MENDIP HILLS** Area of outstanding natural beauty, National Forest – England and Wales, **Forest park, National park, National scenic area** – Scotland, **Regional park**

Woodland

Beach – sand, shingle

**KENNET AND AVON CANAL** Navigable river or canal

Lock, flight of locks, canal bridge number

Viewpoint, spot height – in metres ▲ 965

Linear antiquity

**P&R** Park and ride

**29** Adjoining page number

**SY 70 / 80** Ordnance Survey National Grid reference – see inside back cover

### Road map scale 1: 112 903 or 1.78 miles to 1 inch

0    1    2    3 miles

0    1    2    3    4    5 km

### Road map scale (Isle of Man and parts of Scotland)
1: 225 806 or 3.56 miles to 1 inch

0    1    2    3    4    5    6 miles

0  1  2  3  4  5  6  7  8  9  10 km

## Tourist information

| | | | |
|---|---|---|---|
| BYLAND ABBEY | ✠ Abbey or priory | HOLTON HEATH | National nature reserve |
| WOODHENGE | Ancient monument | | ⚓ Marina |
| SEALIFE CENTRE | Aquarium or dolphinarium | NAT MARITIME MUSEUM | Maritime or military museum |
| CITY MUSEUM AND ART GALLERY | Art collection or museum | SILVERSTONE | Motor racing circuit |
| TATE ST IVES | Art gallery | CUMBERLAND PENCIL MUSEUM | Museum |
| 1644 | Battle site and date | | Ⓟ Picnic area |
| ABBOTSBURY SWANNERY | Bird sanctuary or aviary | WEST SOMERSET RAILWAY | Preserved railway |
| | Camping site | THIRSK | Racecourse |
| | Caravan site | LEAHILL TURRET | Roman antiquity |
| BAMBURGH CASTLE | Castle | BOYTON MARSHES | RSPB reserve |
| YORK MINSTER | ✝ Cathedral | THRIGBY HALL | Safari park |
| SANDHAM MEMORIAL CHAPEL | Church of interest | FREEPORT BRAINTREE | Shopping village |
| SEVEN SISTERS | Country park – England and Wales | MILLENNIUM STADIUM | Sports venue |
| LOCHORE MEADOWS | – Scotland | ALTON TOWERS | Theme park |
| ROYAL BATH & WEST SHOWGROUND | County show ground | | ℹ Tourist information centre – open all year |
| MONK PARK FARM | Farm park | | ℹ – open seasonally |
| HILLIER GARDENS AND ARBORETUM | Garden, arboretum | NATIONAL RAILWAY MUSEUM | Transport collection |
| ST ANDREWS | Golf course – 18-hole | LEVANT MINE | World heritage site |
| TYNTESFIELD | Historic house | HELMSLEY | △ Youth hostel |
| SS GREAT BRITAIN | Historic ship | MARWELL | Zoo |
| HATFIELD HOUSE | House and garden | SUTTON BANK VISITOR CENTRE | ● Other place of interest |
| MUSEUM OF DARTMOOR LIFE | Local museum | GLENFIDDICH DISTILLERY | |

## Approach map symbols

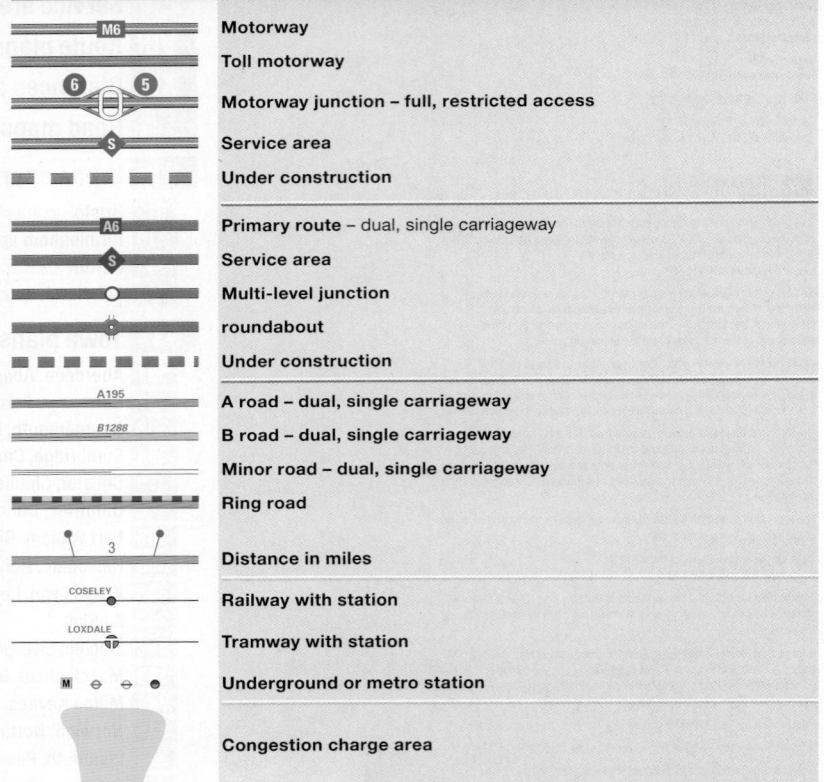

**M6** Motorway

Toll motorway

Motorway junction – full, restricted access

**S** Service area

Under construction

**A6** Primary route – dual, single carriageway

**S** Service area

Multi-level junction

roundabout

Under construction

**A195** A road – dual, single carriageway

**B1288** B road – dual, single carriageway

Minor road – dual, single carriageway

Ring road

Distance in miles  3

**COSELEY** Railway with station

**LOXDALE** Tramway with station

**M** Underground or metro station

Congestion charge area

## Speed Cameras

Fixed camera locations are shown using the ⑳ symbol. In congested areas the ⑳ symbol is used to show that there are two or more cameras on the road indicated.

Due to the restrictions of scale the camera locations are only approximate and cannot indicate the operating direction of the camera. Mobile camera sites, and cameras located on roads not included on the mapping are not shown. Where two or more cameras are shown on the same road, drivers are warned that this may indicate that a SPEC system is in operation. These cameras use the time taken to drive between the two camera positions to calculate the speed of the vehicle. At the time of going to press, some local authorities were considering decommissioning their speed cameras.

# Sandwiches on the move

## The Philip's team peels back the cellophane wrapper and reveals more than you probably want to see

By Stephen Mesquita,
Philip's Correspondent
on the Road

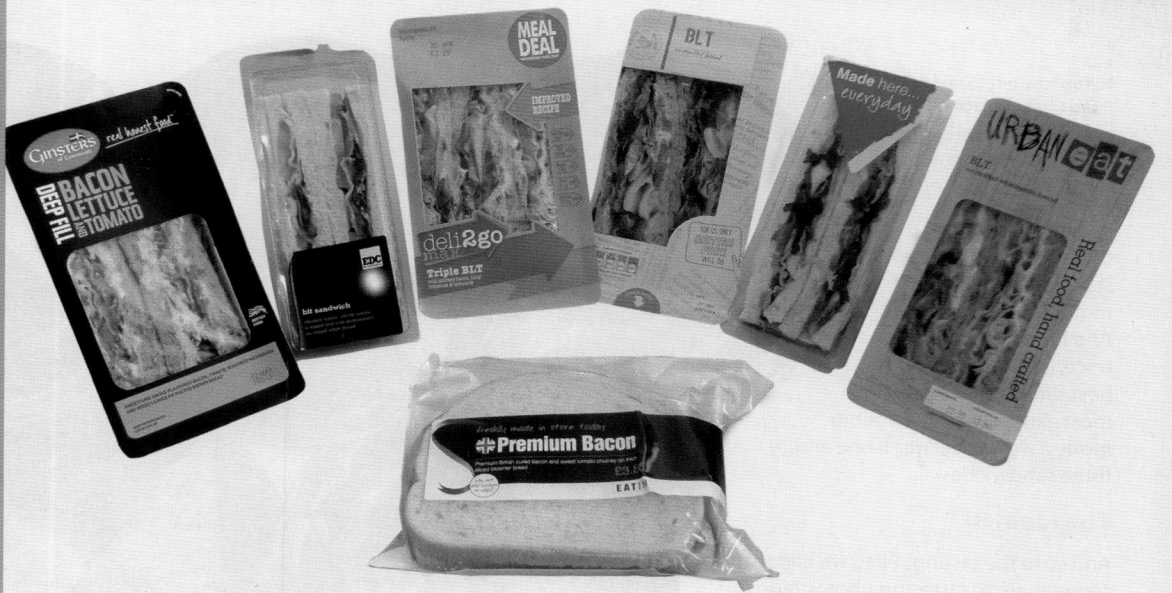

### Grabbing a sandwich – the ultimate impulse purchase

**W**e've probably all done it. You're on a car journey. You stop off at a petrol station or motorway service area. It's been a long time since your last meal. You haven't got time to stop for a proper meal. So you grab a sandwich.

Notice the word 'grab'. You don't stop, think, carefully inspect the wares, read the nutritional information on the packaging (if supplied – we'll return to that theme later) and take a rational decision. It's what the retail experts call an impulse purchase.

And we can say at the outset – it's probably not going to be one of your better impulse purchases.

So it was, on a fine spring day, that the Philip's sandwich tasting team met at Milton Keynes for a morning of recreational sandwich tasting. Milton Keynes had been hand-picked from a cast of thousands because it had petrol stations from four petrol companies and motorway service areas run by the three main operators all quickly and easily accessible.

This was the plan: we would 'grab a sandwich' at each, throw them in the back of the car and retreat to a suitable location to celebrate the gastronomic delights of our purchases.

### Seven BLTs in quick succession – a challenge

One other word of explanation. Motorway service areas offer a more diverse shopping and eating experience than they used to. There is usually a newsagent, a coffee shop as well as a restaurant, all offering sandwiches. In this survey, we picked the sandwiches from the restaurant.

To make the survey as fair as possible, we chose sandwiches with the same filling – or its nearest equivalent – at each stop. And there wasn't really a choice when it came to choosing which sandwich. It had to be a BLT.

It was a daunting challenge. I enjoy a BLT as much as the next man. When the pangs of hunger strike, BLT offers a seductive mix of the fresh and healthy (the tomato and lettuce) with something a bit naughty and tasty (the bacon). But seven BLTs in quick succession – now that's what I call devotion to duty.

### Touring the hotspots of Milton Keynes

It's a terrible confession for an atlas publisher to make, but if you ever have to visit seven petrol stations and service areas to buy seven BLTs in quick succession, sat nav is just the job. There are lots of things that an atlas can do that a sat nav can't – but putting in 'nearest petrol station' and getting the name up on the screen isn't one of them.

So off we went to spend £24.05 on seven BLTs. The first thing to say is that, with one exception, the seven people who served us were pleasant and helpful. We were offered trade ups to meal deals, we had smiles and thank you's. We asked for and got seven receipts without it causing a problem, the sun was shining and all was right in the world.

### Price – not always an indication of quality or value

But that was as far as the pleasant experience went. First there was the price. We fast discovered that you don't always get what you pay for. Our BLTs varied in price from £2.99 to £3.99. If you happen to buy a BLT every day for lunch and don't want to spend an extra £365 a year, our advice would be to search out the best deal –

| | Price | Sell-by date on 30 April | Number of sandwiches | Description on package | Tester's comments | Nutritional info | Marks out of 10 |
|---|---|---|---|---|---|---|---|
| **Texaco** | £2.99 | 2 May | 2 | 'Deep Fill. Sweetcure Smoke Flavoured Bacon, Tomato, Seasoned Mayonnaise and Mixed Leaves on Malted Brown Bread' | Bread soggy yet tasted stale; main taste was mayo; bacon chewy | 34 ingredients • 439 calories fat 18.1gm • salt 2.42gm | 5 |
| **Total** | £2.99 | 2 May | 2 | 'BLT on malted wheatgrain bread. Real food, hand crafted' | Soggy; too much mayo; bacon tasted cheap | 45 ingredients • 460 calories fat 27.4gm • salt 1.50gm | 5.5 |
| **Road Chef** | £3.99 | 1 May | 2 | 'BLT Sandwich made here everyday' | Bitter lettuce with grey edges; white bread; very unpleasant taste | None | 2 |
| **BP** | £3.25 | 1 May | 2 | 'BLT on malted bread. For us only British Pork will do' | Decent sandwich – bacon quite tasty; mayo nice; bread a bit soggy; lettuce perhaps past its best but all in all edible | Approximately 40 ingredients 465 calories fat 20.8gm • salt 2.53gm | 6 |
| **Moto** | £3.69 | 1 May | 2 | 'BLT sandwich: smoked bacon, sliced tomato and mixed leaf with mayonnaise on sliced white bread' | White bread; tasteless old lettuce; bacon unpleasant | None | 2 |
| **Shell** | £3.29 | 30 Apr | 3 | 'Improved recipe: Triple BLT with smokey bacon, juicy tomatoes and lettuce dip' | Three sandwiches plus trade up to £3.99 lunch but salty; tomatoes and lettuce looked past their best; bacon unappetising | 49 ingredients • 791 calories fat 48.2gm • salt 5.1gm | 4 |
| **Welcome Break** | £3.85 | 1 May | 1 | Premium British cured bacon and sweet tomato chutney on thick sliced bloomer bread | Disgusting – two bits of stale round white bread with a bit of tasteless bacon and ketchup | None | 1 |

▶ **Top row**, left to right
Road Chef • Texaco • Moto • BP
▶ **Bottom row**, left to right
Shell • Total • Welcome Break

and, not surprisingly, these come from petrol stations rather than motorway service areas. And it's not just about price, it's about value. Our best sandwich was not the most expensive – and, for our money, we got between one and three sandwiches.

## The ideal BLT

And so to the tasting. First, we had to find somewhere to taste and photograph our BLTs. Where better than the coach terminal off the M1 at Milton Keynes? It's a glamorous life, this sandwich tasting.

On the way, we had thought about what you would expect from the perfect BLT if you were making it at home. It goes without saying that you'd want fresh, good-quality ingredients – especially the bacon. Even if you bought these from a shop, it should be possible to source a tasty, ripe tomato, a piece of lettuce and one rasher of decent bacon for around 60p – offering a reasonable mark up on a £3.99 sandwich.

But it's only fair to admit that the home-made sandwich has one huge advantage that the packaged sandwich can never offer. It can be eaten immediately. Our pack-aged sandwiches mostly had a sell-by date of 48 to 72 hours after the start of the day we bought them. By this time neither the bread nor what goes inside it will be at its best.

## Never open up a packaged sandwich

And now, the votes. Tasting these seven BLTs in quick succession could never be described as a pleasant experience. It was made less pleasant by having to open up the sandwiches and examine the contents. When you come face to face with the ingredients, the whole business of sandwich eating becomes rather less than appetising.

The results of our survey are presented here in word and pictures – and we will let them speak for themselves.

## Finally, a health warning

Map making is our area of expertise at Philip's, not nutrition. But we thought it would be informative to offer you at least the headlines from the back of the boxes. Four out of the seven sandwiches came with a full list of ingredients.

The pack with three sandwiches contained nearly 40% of a woman's guideline intake of calories, nearly 70% of the guideline intake of fat and almost the entire daily guideline for salt. Even the two-sandwich packs had nearly a quarter of a woman's daily calories, over a third of fat and up to 40% for salt.

It is perhaps revealing that the three sandwiches which came without the contents list were the three made from white bread.

## A telling moment

The team were quite hungry by the time they came to do the tasting. We took only one bite from each BLT. There was only one sandwich which we came back to at the end and took another bite from because the taste was enjoyable. Next time I think I'm going to stick to egg mayo.

---

# Service areas on motorways and primary routes

## Symbols

- 🛏 Accommodation
- 👶 Baby change
- 💈 Barber shop
- €$ Bureau de change
- 💷 Cash machine
- 🌉 Footbridge
- ⛽ Fuel
- 🖥 Meeting room
- 🅿 Free parking
- 🚿 Showers
- 🚻 Toilets
- ♿ Disabled toilets
- ♿ RADAR key scheme
- 🚛 Truckstop
- 🚿 Truck wash
- ((•)) Free WiFi
- 💼 Work space
- ✉ Address
- ☎ Telephone number
- @ e-mail address
- 🖥 website
- 🕐 Details of shops and catering outlets that are normally open 24 hours are listed at the end of each entry. Other listed outlets may not be open 24 hours.

## England

### A1 Grantham South — Moto
🚻👶♿ ((•))
A1 at Colsterworth • Northbound and southbound 155 E8 SK93822366
Costa • ⛽ Esso • 🛏 Travelodge • 🅿 2hrs
✉ A1 Colsterworth, Grantham NG33 5JR ☎ 01476 861006

### A1 Grantham North — Moto
🚻👶♿ ((•))
A1, 3 miles North of Grantham • Northbound and southbound 155 B7 SK88863988
Burger King • Costa • Eat In • EDC • WH Smith ⛽ BP • 🛏 Travelodge • 🅿 2hrs
✉ Gonerby Moor, Grantham NG32 2AB ☎ 01476 563451

### A1 Scotch Corner — Moto
🚻👶 ((•))
A1, 6 miles North of Catterick • Northbound and southbound 224 D4 NZ21670542
Burger King • Costa • M&S Simply Food • WH Smith ⛽ Esso • 🛏 Travelodge 🅿 2hrs
✉ Middleton Tyas Lane, Scotch Corner, Richmond DL10 6PQ
☎ 01325 377719

### A14 Cambridge — Extra
💷🚻🚛((•))
A14, 4 miles from northern end of M11 • Northbound and southbound 123 D7 TL35856537
KFC • Le Petit Four • M&S Simply Food • McDonald's • WH Smith ⛽ Shell
🛏 Days Inn 🅿 2 hrs
✉ Boxworth, Cambridge CB3 8WU
🕐 Forecourt outlets open 24 hrs

### A38 Saltash — Moto
🚻 ((•))
A38 Carkeel Roundabout • Eastbound and westbound 7 C8 SX41186015
Costa ⛽ BP 🛏 Travelodge 🅿 2hrs
✉ Carkeel Roundabout, Saltash PL12 6LF ☎ 07827 978664

### A50 Derby South – westbound — Welcome Break
💷🚻👶♿ 🖥((•))
A50 Junctions 1-2 • Westbound 153 C8 SK42463021
Burger King • Eat In • WH Smith ⛽ Shell 🛏 Days Inn
✉ Shardlow, Derby DE72 2WW
☎ 01332 794194 @ derby.enquiry@welcomebreak.co.uk
🖥 www.welcomebreak.co.uk
🕐 WH Smith and forecourt outlet open 24 hrs

### A50 Derby South – eastbound — Welcome Break
💷🚻👶♿ 🖥((•))
A50 Junctions 1-2 • Eastbound 153 C8 SK42673024
Burger King • Coffee Nation • Eat In • WH Smith ⛽ Shell, LPG available
✉ Shardlow, Derby DE72 2WW
☎ 01332 794194 @ derby.enquiry@welcomebreak.co.uk
🖥 www.welcomebreak.co.uk
🕐 WH Smith and forecourt outlet open 24 hrs

### A1(M) Baldock — Extra MSA
💷🚻👶♿ 🖥🚛((•))
A1(M) J10 • Northbound and southbound 104 D4 TL23443661
KFC Le Petit Four • M&S Simply Food • McDonald's • Starbucks ⛽ Shell 🛏 Days Inn 🅿 2hrs
✉ A1(M), Junction 10, Baldock, Hertfordshire SG7 5TR
🖥 www.extraservices.co.uk
🕐 Forecourt shop, McDonald's and Starbucks open 24 hrs

### A1(M) Peterborough — Extra MSA
💷🚻🚛((•))
A1(M) J17 • Northbound and southbound 138 E2 TL13939395
Costa • KFC • Le Petit Four • M&S Simply Food • McDonald's • WH Smith ⛽ Shell, LPG 🛏 Days Inn 🅿 2hrs

### Great North Road, Haddon, Peterborough PE7 8UQ
🖥 www.extraservices.co.uk
🕐 Forecourt shop open 24 hrs

### A1(M) Blyth — Moto
🚻👶♿ 🚿((•))
A1(M) Junction 34 • Northbound and southbound 187 D10 SK62568827
Burger King • Costa • EDC • M&S Simply Food • WH Smith ⛽ Esso 🛏 Travelodge
✉ Hill Top Roundabout, Blyth S81 8HG ☎ 01909 591841
🖥 www.moto-way.co.uk

### A1(M) Wetherby — Moto
💷🚻👶♿ 🚿🚛🚿((•))
A1(M): J46 • Northbound and southbound 206 C4 SE41525025
Burger King • Costa • M&S Simply Food • Upper Crust • West Cornish Pasty • WH Smith ⛽ BP 🛏 Days Inn 🅿 2 hrs
✉ Kirk Deighton, North Yorkshire LS22 5GT ☎ 01937 545080
🖥 www.moto-way.co.uk
🕐 Forecourt outlets open 24 hrs

### A1(M) Durham — RoadChef
💷🚻👶♿ 🖥((•))
A1(M) J61 • Northbound and southbound 234 D2 NZ30843718
The Burger Company • Costa • Restbite! • WH Smith ⛽ Total 🛏 Days Inn 🅿 2 hrs

### Tursdale Road, Bowburn, County Durham DH6 5NP ☎ 0191 377 9222
🖥 www.roadchef.com
🕐 Fast food outlet and forecourt shop open 24 hrs

### A1(M) Washington — Moto
💷🚻👶♿ 🖥((•))🚛
A1(M) just north of J64 • Northbound and southbound 243 F7 NZ28375506
Burger King • Costa • EDC • WH Smith ⛽ BP 🛏 Travelodge 🅿 2 hrs
✉ Portobello, Birtley, County Durham DH3 2SJ ☎ 0191 410 3436 🖥 www.moto-way.co.uk
🕐 WH Smith and forecourt outlets open 24 hrs.

### M1 London Gateway — Welcome Break
💷🚻👶♿ 🖥((•))🚛
M1 between J2 and J4 • Northbound and southbound 85 G11 TQ20269369
Burger King • Eat In • Starbucks • Waitrose • WH Smith ⛽ Shell, LPG available 🛏 Days Hotel 🅿 2 hrs
✉ M1 J2/4, Mill Hill, London NW7 3HB
☎ 0208 906 0611 @ lgw.enquiry@welcomebreak.co.uk
🖥 www.welcomebreak.co.uk
🕐 WH Smith open 24 hrs

### M1 Toddington — Moto
M1, 1 mile south of J12 • Northbound and southbound 103 F10 TL03092878
*Burger King • Costa • EDC • Krispy Kreme • M&S Simply Food • Starbucks • West Cornish Pasty (northbound) • WH Smith • BP, LPG available • Travelodge* 2 hrs
Toddington, Bedfordshire LU5 6HR • 01525 878400
www.moto-way.co.uk
Forecourt outlets open 24 hrs

### M1 Newport Pagnell — Welcome Break
M1, north of J14 • Northbound and southbound 103 C7 SP85834351
*Eat In • KFC • Starbucks • Waitrose • WH Smith • Shell • Days Inn* 2 hrs
M1 Motorway, J14/15, Newport Pagnell, Buckinghamshire MK16 8DS • 01908 217722 • newport.enquiry@welcomebreak.co.uk
www.welcomebreak.co.uk
WH Smith and forecourt shop open 24 hrs.

### M1 Northampton — RoadChef
M1 J15A • Northbound and southbound 120 F4 SP72285732
*The Burger Company (northbound) • Costa • Hot Food Co (southbound) • McDonald's (southbound) • Restbite! (northbound) • WH Smith • BP, LPG available* 2 hrs
M1 Junction 15A, Northampton, Northamptonshire NN4 9QY • 01604 831888
www.roadchef.com
WH Smith, forecourt shop and (southbound) McDonald's open 24 hrs

### M1 Watford Gap — RoadChef
M1 between J16 and J17 • Northbound and southbound 119 D11 SP59956802
**Northbound:** *Costa • Cotton Traders • Hot Food Co • McDonald's • WH Smith* **Southbound:** *The Burger Company • Costa • Restbite! • WH Smith • Shell • Days Inn (southbound)* 2 hrs
M1 Motorway, Northamptonshire NN6 7UZ • 01327 879001
www.roadchef.com

### M1 Leicester Forest East — Welcome Break
M1 between J21 and J21A • Northbound and southbound 135 C10 SK53860267
*Waitrose • WH Smith • Burger King • Eat In • KFC • Starbucks • BP, LPG available • Days Inn* 2 hrs
Leicester Forest East, M1, Leicester, Leicestershire LE3 3GB • 0116 238 6801
lfe.enquiry@welcomebreak.co.uk
www.welcomebreak.co.uk
Eat In and WH Smith open 24 hrs

### M1 Leicester — Eurogarages
M1 just off J22 • Northbound and southbound 153 G9 SK47651111
*Burger King • Coffee Nation • BP, LPG available*
Littleshaw Lane, Markfield LE67 9PP • 01530 244706
www.eurogarages.com

### M1 Donington Park — Moto
M1 J23A • Northbound and southbound 153 E9 SK46712513
*Burger King • Costa • EDC • M&S Simply Food • WH Smith • BP • Travelodge* 2 hrs
Castle Donington, Derby, East Midlands DE74 2TN • 01509 672220
www.moto-way.co.uk
Forecourt shop and WH Smith open 24 hrs

### M1 Trowell — Moto
M1 between J25 and J26 • Northbound and southbound 171 G7 SK49354073
*Burger King • Costa • EDC • M&S Simply Food • WH Smith • BP* 2 hrs
Ilkeston, Trowell, Nottinghamshire NG9 3PL • 01159 320291
www.moto-way.co.uk
WH Smith and forecourt outlets are open 24 hrs.

### M1 Tibshelf – northbound — RoadChef
M1, 2 miles north of J28 • 170 C6 SK44856031
*The Burger Company • Costa • Restbite! • WH Smith • Shell • Days Inn* 2 hrs
Newton Wood Lane, Newton, Alfreton DE55 5TZ • 01773 876600
www.roadchef.com • WH Smith and forecourt shop open 24 hrs

### M1 Tibshelf – southbound — RoadChef
M1, 2 miles north of J28 • 170 C6 SK44856031
*Costa • McDonald's • Restbite! • WH Smith • Shell • Days Inn* 2 hrs
Newton Wood Lane, Newton, Alfreton DE55 5TZ • 01773 876600
www.roadchef.com
WH Smith, forecourt shop and McDonald's open 24 hrs

### M1 Woodall — Welcome Break
M1, 2.5 miles north of J30 • Northbound and southbound 187 E7 SK47928006
*WH Smith • Burger King • Eat In • KFC • Starbucks • Shell, LPG available • Days Inn* 2 hrs
M1 Motorway, Sheffield, South Yorkshire S26 7XR • 0114 248 7992
woodall.enquiry@welcomebreak.co.uk • www.welcomebreak.co.uk
Eat In, WH Smith and forecourt outlets open 24 hrs.

### M1 Woolley Edge — Moto
M1, just north of J38 • Northbound and southbound 197 E10 SE29841400
*Burger King • Costa • EDC • M&S Simply Food • WH Smith • BP • Travelodge* 2 hrs
West Bretton, Wakefield, West Yorkshire WF4 4LQ • 01924 830371
www.moto-way.co.uk
WH Smith and forecourt outlets open 24 hrs

### M2 Medway — Moto
M2 between J4 and J5 • Eastbound and westbound 69 G10 TQ81756344
*Burger King • Costa • WH Smith • BP, LPG available • Travelodge* 2 hrs
M2, Rainham, Gillingham, Kent ME8 8PQ • 01634 236900
www.moto-way.co.uk
WH Smith and forecourt shop open 24 hrs

### M3 Fleet — Welcome Break
M3 between J4A/J5 • Eastbound and westbound 49 B9 SU79885583
*Waitrose • WH Smith • Burger King • Eat In • KFC • Starbucks • Shell, LPG available (southbound only) • Days Inn* 2 hrs
Fleet, Hampshire GU51 1AA • 01252 788 500
fleet.enquiry@welcomebreak.co.uk
www.welcomebreak.co.uk
Eat In and WH Smith open 24 hrs

### M3 Winchester — Moto
M3, 4 miles north of J9 • Northbound and southbound 48 F4 SU52303550
*Burger King • Costa • EDC • Hot Food Co • Krispy Kreme • WH Smith • BP • Days Inn* 2 hrs
Shroner Wood, Winchester, Hampshire SO21 1PP • 01962 791140
www.moto-way.co.uk
Forecourt outlets open 24 hrs

### M4 Heston — Moto
M4 1 mile east of J3 • Eastbound and westbound 66 D6 TQ11777778
*Burger King • Costa • EDC (westbound) • Krispy Kreme • WH Smith • BP, LPG (westbound) • Travelodge* 2 hrs
Phoenix Way, Heston, Hounslow, London TW5 9NB • 0208 590 2101
www.moto-way.co.uk
WH Smith open 24 hrs

### M4 Reading – eastbound — Moto
M4 Junctions 11-12 • Eastbound 65 E7 SU67177012
*Burger King • Costa • EDC • Krispy Kreme • M&S Simply Food • West Cornish Pasty • WH Smith • BP, LPG available • Travelodge* 2 hrs
Burghfield, Reading RG30 3UQ • 01189 566966
www.moto-way.co.uk
WH Smith and forecourt outlets open 24 hrs

### M4 Reading – westbound — Moto
M4 Junctions 11-12 • Westbound 65 F7 SU67046985
*Burger King • Costa • EDC • Krispy Kreme • M&S Simply Food • Upper Crust • West Cornish Pasty • WH Smith • BP, LPG available • Travelodge* 2 hrs
Burghfield, Reading RG30 3UQ • 01189 566966
www.moto-way.co.uk
WH Smith and forecourt outlets open 24 hrs

### M4 Chieveley — Moto
M4 J13 • Eastbound and westbound 64 E3 SU48157268
*Burger King • Costa • EDC • Krispy Kreme • M&S Simply Food • West Cornish Pasty • WH Smith • BP, LPG available • Travelodge* 2 hrs
Oxford Road, Hermitage, Thatcham, Berkshire, RG18 9XX • 01635 248024 • www.moto-way.co.uk
WH Smith open 24 hrs

### M4 Membury — Welcome Break
M4, 4 miles west of J14 • Eastbound and westbound 63 D10 SU30847601
*Waitrose • WH Smith • Burger King • Eat In • KFC • Starbucks • BP, LPG available (eastbound) • Days Inn* 2 hrs
Woodlands Road, Membury, near Lambourn, Berkshire RG17 7TZ • 01488 674360 • membury.enquiry@welcomebreak.co.uk
www.welcomebreak.co.uk
Eat In, WH Smith and forecourt shop open 24 hrs

### M4 Leigh Delamere — Moto
M4 just west of J17 • Eastbound and westbound 61 D11 ST89077899
*Burger King • Costa • EDC • Krispy Kreme • M&S Simply Food • West Cornish Pasty • WH Smith • BP, LPG available • Travelodge* 2 hrs
Chippenham, Wiltshire SN14 6LB • 01666 837691 (eastbound); 01666 842015 (westbound)
www.moto.co.uk
WH Smith and shop and coffee shops in the forecourt are open 24 hrs

### M5 Frankley — Moto
M5 J3 • Northbound and southbound 133 G9 SO98938120
*Burger King • Costa • EDC • M&S Simply Food • WH Smith • Esso • Travelodge (southbound only)*
2 hrs • Illey Lane, Birmingham, West Midlands B32 4AR • 0121 550 3131
www.moto-way.co.uk
Coffee Nation and WH Smith open 24 hrs

### M5 Strensham – southbound — RoadChef
M5 southbound, just before J8 • Southbound only 99 D8 SO90413993
*Costa • Cotton Traders • Hot Food Co • McDonald's • Soho Coffee Company • WH Smith • BP, LPG available* 2 hrs
M5 Motorway, Lower Strensham, Worcestershire WR8 9LJ • 01684 290577
www.roadchef.com
McDonald's and forecourt outlet open 24 hrs

### M5 Strensham – northbound — RoadChef
M5, 1 mile north of J8 • Northbound only 99 C7 SO89344072
*Costa • Cotton Traders • Hot Food Co • McDonald's • Pizza Hut Express • Subway • Starbucks • WH Smith • Texaco, LPG available • Days Inn* 2 hrs
M5 Motorway, Lower Strensham, Worcestershire WR8 9LJ • 01684 293004
www.roadchef.com
McDonald's and forecourt outlets open 24 hrs

### M5 Michaelwood — Welcome Break
M5, just north of J14 • Northbound and southbound 80 F2 ST70409541
*WH Smith • Burger King • Eat In • KFC • Starbucks • BP, Ecotricity charge point • Days Inn* 2 hrs
Lower Wick, Dursley, Gloucestershire GL11 6DD • 01454 260631 • michaelwood.enquiry@welcomebreak.co.uk
www.welcomebreak.co.uk
WH Smith and forecourt shop open 24 hrs

### M5 Gordano — Welcome Break
M5 J19 • Northbound and southbound 60 D4 ST50977563
*Burger King • Eat In • KFC • Starbucks • Waitrose • WH Smith • Shell, LPG available • Days Inn* 2 hrs
Portbury, Bristol BS20 7XG • 01275 373624 • gordano.enquiry@welcomebreak.co.uk
www.welcomebreak.co.uk
WH Smith open 24 hrs

### M5 Sedgemoor Southbound — RoadChef
M5, 7 miles south of J21 43 C11 ST35815259
*The Burger Company • Costa • Restbite! • WH Smith • Total • Days Inn* 2 hrs
M5 Southbound Rooksbridge, Axbridge, Somerset BS24 0JL • 01934 750888
www.roadchef.com
Forecourt shop open 24 hrs

### M5 Sedgemoor Northbound — Welcome Break
M5, 3 miles north of J22 43 C11 ST35815259
*Burger King • Eat In • KFC • Starbucks • Waitrose • WH Smith • Shell, Ecotricity charge point • Days Inn* 2 hrs
M5 Motorway Northbound, Bridgwater, Somerset BS24 0JL • 01934 750730
sedgemoor.enquiry@welcomebreak.co.uk
www.welcomebreak.co.uk
WH Smith and shop on forecourt are open 24 hrs.

### M5 Bridgwater — Moto
M5, J24 • Northbound and southbound 43 G10 ST30403441
*Burger King • Costa • EDC • West Cornish Pasty • WH Smith • BP • Travelodge* 2 hrs
Huntsworth Business Park, Bridgwater, Somerset TA6 6TS • 01278 456800
www.moto-way.co.uk
WH Smith and forecourt shop open 24 hrs

### M5 Taunton Deane — RoadChef
M5 between J25 and J26 • Northbound and southbound 28 C2 ST19592035
*The Burger Company • Costa • Restbite! • WH Smith • Shell • Days Inn* 2 hrs
Trull, Taunton, Somerset TA3 7PF • 01823 271111
www.roadchef.com
Forecourt outlets are open 24 hrs

### A38/M5 Tiverton — Moto
M5 Junction 27 • Northbound and southbound 27 E8 ST04901386
*Costa • Burger King • Shell, LPG available • Travelodge* 2 hrs. No HGVs
Tiverton EX16 7HD • 01884 829423
www.moto-way.co.uk

### M5 Cullompton — Extra MSA
M5, J28 • Northbound and southbound 27 F8 ST02660798
*Costa • McDonald's • WH Smith • Shell* 2 hrs
Old Station Yard, Station Road, Cullompton, Devon EX15 1NS • 01522 523737
www.extraservices.co.uk
WH Smith and forecourt shop open 24 hrs

### M5 Exeter — Moto
M5 J30 • Northbound and southbound 14 C5 SX96779180
*Burger King • Costa • Harry Ramsden • M&S Simply Food • West Cornish Pasty • WH Smith • BP • Travelodge* 2 hrs
Sandygate, Exeter, Devon EX2 7HF • 01392 436266
www.moto-way.co.uk
WH Smith open 24 hrs

### M6 Corley — Welcome Break
M6, 2.5 miles west of J3 • Eastbound and westbound 134 F6 SP30898604
*Burger King • Eat In • KFC • Starbucks • Waitrose • WH Smith • Shell, LPG available • Days Inn* 2 hrs
Highfield Lane, Corley, Staffordshire CV7 8NR • 01676 540111 • corleyenquiry@welcomebreak.co.uk
www.welcomebreak.co.uk
WH Smith open 24 hrs

### M6 Norton Canes — Road Chef
M6 Toll between JT6 and JT7 • Eastbound and westbound 133 B10 SK02290745
*The Burger Company • Costa • Restbite! • WH Smith • BP, LPG available • Days Inn* 2 hrs
Betty's Lane, Norton Canes, Cannock, Staffordshire WS11 9UX • 01543 272540
www.roadchef.co.uk
WH Smith and forecourt shop open 24 hrs

### M6 Hilton Park — Moto
M6 J10A and J11 • Northbound and southbound 133 C9 SJ96200500
*Burger King • Costa • EDC • M&S Simply Food • WH Smith • BP • Travelodge* 2 hrs
Essington, Wolverhampton, Staffordshire WV11 2AT • 01922 412237
www.moto-way.co.uk
Coffee shops in forecourt and WH Smith are open 24 hrs

### M6 Stafford – northbound — Moto
M6, 3 miles north of J14 • Northbound only 151 C7 SJ88613186
*Burger King • Costa • EDC • Krispy Kreme • M&S Simply Food • WH Smith • BP, LPG available • Travelodge* 2 hrs
Stone, Staffordshire ST15 0EU • 01785 811188
www.moto-way.co.uk
Forecourt outlets open 24 hrs

### M6 Stafford – southbound — RoadChef
M6, 7.5 miles south of J15 • Southbound only 151 C7 SJ89243065
*The Burger Company • Costa • Restbite! • WH Smith • Esso, LPG available • Days Inn* 2 hrs
M6 Southbound, Stone, Staffordshire ST15 0EU • 01785 826300
www.roadchef.com

### M6 Keele — Welcome Break
M6, 6 miles north of J15 • Northbound and southbound 168 G4 SJ80624406
*Burger King • Eat In • KFC • Starbucks • Waitrose • WH Smith • Shell, LPG available (southbound)* 2 hrs
Three Mile Lane, Keele, Newcastle under Lyme, Staffordshire ST5 5HG • 01782 634230 • keele.enquiry@welcomebreak.co.uk
www.welcomebreak.co.uk
Eat In and WH Smith open 24 hrs

### M6 Sandbach — RoadChef
M6, just south of J17 • Northbound and southbound 168 C3 SK02290745
**Northbound:** *Costa • Restbite! • WH Smith* **Southbound:** *Costa • Hot Food Co • McDonald's • WH Smith • Esso* 2 hrs
M6 Northbound, Sandbach, Cheshire CW11 2FZ • 01270 767134
www.roadchef.co.uk
Forecourt outlets and (southbound) McDonald's open 24 hrs

### M6 Knutsford — Moto
M6, between J18 and J19 • Northbound and southbound 184 F2 SJ73267826
*Burger King • Costa • EDC • Krispy Kreme • M&S Simply Food • West Cornish Pasty (southbound) • WH Smith • BP, LPG available • Travelodge* 2 hrs
Northwich Road, Knutsford, Cheshire WA16 0TL • 01565 634167 • www.moto-way.co.uk
Forecourt shop open 24 hrs

### M6 Charnock Richard — Welcome Break
M6, 2.5 miles north of J27 • Northbound and southbound 194 E4 SD54411521
*Burger King • Eat In • KFC • Starbucks • WH Smith • Shell • Days Inn* 2 hrs
Mill Lane, Chorley, Lancashire PR7 5LR • 01257 791746
charnock.enquiry@welcomebreak.co.uk
www.welcomebreak.co.uk
Eat In and WH Smith open 24 hrs.

**M6 Lancaster (Forton)** Moto

M6 south of J33 • Northbound and southbound **202 C6** SD50145198

*Burger King • Costa • Eat In • M&S Simply Food • West Cornish Pasty (northbound) • WH Smith BP, LPG available Travelodge* 2 hrs

White Carr Lane, Bay Horse, Lancaster, Lancashire LA2 9DU

01524 791775

www.moto-way.co.uk

WH Smith and forecourt shop are open 24 hrs

**M6 Burton-in-Kendal** Moto

M6 between J35 and J36 • Northbound only **211 D10** SD52207617

*Burger King • Costa • EDC • WH Smith BP Travelodge* 2 hrs

Burton West, Carnforth, Lancashire LA6 1JF 01524 781234

www.moto-way.co.uk

**M6 Killington Lake** RoadChef

M6 just south of J37 • Southbound only **221 G11** SD58779111

*The Burger Company • Costa • Restbite! • WH Smith BP Days Inn* 2 hrs

M6 Southbound, near Kendal, Cumbria LA8 0NW 01539 620739

www.roadchef.com

WH Smith and forecourt shop open 24 hrs

**M6 Tebay – northbound** Westmorland

M6, just north of J38 • Northbound only **222 D2** NY60510626

*Butcher's counter • cafe and coffee shop • farm shop • forecourt shop • takeaway snack bar Total, LPG available Westmorland Hotel* Yes

M6, Old Tebay, Cumbria CA10 3ZA

01539 624511

www.westmorland.com

Petrol forecourt shop and takeaway open 24 hours

**M6 Tebay – southbound** Westmorland

M6, 4.5 miles south of J39 • Southbound only **222 D2** NY60790650

*Butcher's counter • cafe and coffee shop • farm shop • forecourt shop • takeaway snack bar Total, LPG available*

Yes M6, Old Tebay, Cumbria CA10 3SB 01539 624511

www.westmorland.com

Petrol forecourt shop and takeaway open 24 hours

**M6 Southwaite** Moto

M6 Junctions 41-42 • Northbound and southbound **230 B4** NY44164523

*Burger King • Costa • EDC • M&S Simply Food • West Cornish Pasty (southbound) • WH Smith BP Travelodge* 2 hrs

Broadfield Road, Carlisle CA4 0NT

01697 473476

www.moto-way.co.uk

WH Smith and outlets on the forecourts are open 24 hours

**M11 Birchanger Green** Welcome Break

M11 at J8/J8a • Northbound and southbound **105 G10** TL51202149

*Burger King • Eat In • KFC • Starbucks • Waitrose • WH Smith Shell, LPG available Days Hotel* 2 hrs

Old Dunmow Road, Bishop's Stortford, Hertfordshire CM23 5QZ

01279 653388

www.welcomebreak.co.uk

WH Smith open 24 hrs

**M18 Doncaster North** Moto

M18 J5, at the western end of the M180 • Northbound and southbound **199 E7** SE66791104

*Burger King • Costa • EDC • WH Smith BP, LPG available Travelodge*

2 hrs Hatfield, Doncaster, South Yorkshire DN8 5GS

02920 891141

www.moto-way.co.uk

WH Smith open 24 hrs

**M20 Maidstone** RoadChef

M20 J8 **53 C10** TQ82455523

*Costa • McDonald's • Restbite! • WH Smith Esso Days Inn* 2 hrs

M20 J8, Hollingbourne, Maidstone, Kent ME17 1SS

01622 631100

www.roadchef.com

McDonald's, WH Smith and forecourt outlets open 24 hrs

**M20 Stop24 (Folkestone)** Stop 24

M20 J11 **54 F6** TR13283729

*Coffee Stop • Haldane Express • Julian Graves • Just Spuds • KFC • Starbucks • WH Smith • Wimpy Shell, LPG available* 2 hrs

Junction 11 M20, Stanford Intersection, Stanford, Kent CT21 4BL

01303 760273

info@stop24.co.uk

www.stop24.co.uk

Forecourt outlets open 24 hrs.

**M23 Pease Pottage** Moto

M23 J11 • Northbound and southbound **51 G9** TQ26183310

*Burger King • Costa • EDC • Krispy Kreme • M&S Simply Food • West Cornish Pasty • WH Smith BP, LPG available*

2 hrs Brighton Road, Pease Pottage, Crawley, West Sussex RH11 9AE 01293 562852

www.moto-way.co.uk

WH Smith and forecourt outlets open 24 hrs

**M25 Clacket Lane** RoadChef

M25 between J5 and J6 • Eastbound and westbound **52 C2** TQ42335457

*Costa • Hot Food Co • McDonald's • WH Smith Total Days Inn* 2hrs

M25 Westbound, Westerham, Kent TN16 2ER 01959 565577

www.roadchef.com

McDonald's open 24 hrs

**M25 Cobham** Extra MSA

M25 J9-10 • Clockwise and anti-clockwise TQ11345768

*Eat In • KFC • M&S Simply Food • McDonald's • Starbucks • WH Smith Shell, LPG available Days Inn*

2 hrs www.extraservices.co.uk

*Forecourt outlets open 24 hrs*

**M25 South Mimms** Welcome Break

M25 J23 and A1(M) J1 • Clockwise and anti-clockwise **86 E2** TL23000023

*Burger King • Eat In • KFC • Starbucks • Waitrose • WH Smith BP, Ecotricity charge point Days Inn* 2 hrs

Bignells Corner, Potters Bar, Hertfordshire EN6 3QQ

01707 621001 mimms.enquiry @welcomebreak.co.uk

www.welcomebreak.co.uk

Eat In, WH Smith and forecourt outlets open 24 hrs

**M25 Thurrock** Moto

M25, signposted from J30/J31 • Clockwise and anti-clockwise **68 C5** TQ57837947

*Burger King • Costa • EDC • Krispy Kreme • M&S Simply Food • WH Smith Esso Travelodge* 2 hrs

Arterial Road, West Thurrock, Grays, Essex RM16 3BG

01708 865487

www.moto-way.co.uk

WH Smith and forecourt outlet open 24 hrs

**M27 Rownhams** RoadChef

M27, between J3 and J4 • Eastbound and westbound **32 D5** SU38791769

*The Burger Company (westbound) • Costa • Restbite! • WH Smith Esso Days Inn (westbound)* 2 hrs

M27 Southbound, Southampton, Hampshire SO16 8AP

02380 734480

www.roadchef.com

The outlets in the forecourts are open 24 hrs

**M40 Beaconsfield** Extra MSA

M40 J2 • Eastbound and westbound **66 B3** SU95098897

*KFC • Le Petit Four • M&S Simply Food • McDonald's • Presto • Starbucks • WH Smith Shell, LPG available Etap Hotel* 2 hrs

A355 Windsor Drive, Beaconsfield, Buckinghamshire HP9 2SE

www.extraservices.co.uk

McDonald's and forecourt outlet open 24 hrs

**M40 Oxford** Welcome Break

M40 J8A • Northbound and southbound **83 E10** SP62440479

*Burger King • Eat In • KFC • Starbucks • Waitrose • WH Smith BP Days Inn* 2 hrs M40 Junction 8A, Waterstock, Oxfordshire OX33 1JN

01865 877000 oxford.enquiry@ welcomebreak.co.uk

www.welcomebreak.co.uk

McDonald's and Starbucks open 24 hours

**M40 Cherwell Valley** Moto

M40 J10 • Northbound and southbound **101 F10** SP55162822

*Burger King • Costa • EDC • Krispy Kreme • M&S Simply Food • West Cornish Pasty • WH Smith Esso Travelodge*

2 hrs Northampton Road, Ardley, Bicester, Oxfordshire OX27 7RD 01869 346060

www.moto-way.co.uk

WH Smith open 24 hrs

**M40 Warwick South** Welcome Break

M40 between J12 and J13 • Southbound **118 F6** SP34075801

*Burger King • Eat In • KFC • Starbucks • Waitrose • WH Smith BP, LPG available Days Inn*

2 hrs Banbury Road, Ashorne, Warwick CV35 0AA 01926 651681

warwicksouth.enquiry @welcomebreak.co.uk

www.welcomebreak.co.uk

Eat In, WH Smith and forecourt outlets open 24 hrs.

**M40 Warwick North** Welcome Break

M40 between J12 and J13 • Northbound **118 F6** SP33885770

*Burger King • Eat In • KFC • Starbucks • Waitrose • WH Smith BP, LPG available Days Inn*

2 hrs Banbury Road, Ashorne, Warwick CV35 0AA 01926 650681

warwicknorth.enquiry @welcomebreak.co.uk

www.welcomebreak.co.uk

Eat In and WH Smith open 24 hrs

**M42 Hopwood Park** Welcome Break

M42 Junction 2 • Eastbound and westbound **117 C10** SP03637389

*Burger King • Eat In • KFC • Starbucks • Waitrose • WH Smith Shell, LPG available* 2 hrs Redditch Road, Alvechurch B48 7AU 0121 4474000

hopwood.enquiry @welcomebreak.co.uk

www.welcomebreak.co.uk

**M42 Tamworth** Moto

M42, just north of J10 • Northbound and southbound **134 C4** SK24440112

*Burger King • Costa • EDC • M&S Simply Food • WH Smith Esso Travelodge*

2 hrs Green Lane, Tamworth, Staffordshire B77 5PS

01827 260120

www.moto-way.co.uk

WH Smith and forecourt outlets are open 24 hrs.

**M48 Severn View** Moto

M48 J1 • Eastbound and westbound **60 B5** ST57118959

*Burger King • Costa • Krispy Kreme • WH Smith BP Travelodge* 2 hrs

Aust, South Gloucestershire BS35 4BH 01454 623851

www.moto-way.co.uk

Forecourt outlets open 24 hrs

**M54 Telford** Welcome Break

M54 J4 • Eastbound and westbound **132 B4** SJ73050890

*Burger King • Eat In • Starbucks • WH Smith Shell, LPG available Days Inn* 2 hrs Priorslee Road, Shifnal, Telford, Shropshire TF11 8TG 01952 238400

telford.enquiry @welcomebreak.co.uk

www.welcomebreak.co.uk

WH Smith and shop on forecourt open 24 hrs.

**M56 Chester** RoadChef

M56 J14 • Eastbound and westbound **183 G7** SJ46537491

*Costa • Cotton Traders • Hot Food Co • McDonald's • WH Smith Shell Days Inn* 2 hrs

Elton, Chester, Cheshire CH2 4QZ

01928 728500

www.roadchef.com

Costa and McDonald's open 24 hrs

**M61 Rivington – northbound** Euro Garages

M61 between J6 and J8 • Northbound and southbound **194 E6** SD62111168

*Burger King • Spar • Starbucks • Subway BP* 2 hrs M61, Horwich, Bolton, Lancashire BL6 5UZ

01254 56070

enquiries@eurogarages.com

www.eurogarages.com

Forecourt outlets open 24 hrs

**M61 Rivington – southbound** Euro Garages

M61 between J8 and J6 • Northbound and southbound **194 E6** SD62111168

*Burger King • Spar • Starbucks • Subway BP Rivington Lodge* 2 hrs

M61, Horwich, Bolton, Lancashire BL6 5UZ 01254 56070

enquiries@eurogarages.com

www.eurogarages.com

Forecourt outlets open 24 hrs

**M62 Burtonwood** Welcome Break

M62 J8 • Eastbound and westbound **183 C9** SJ57749129

*KFC • Starbucks • WH Smith Shell*

2 hrs M62 Great Sankey, Warrington, Cheshire WA5 3AX

01925 651656

burtonwood.enquiry @welcomebreak.co.uk

www.welcomebreak.co.uk

WH Smith open 24 hrs.

**M62 Birch – eastbound** Moto

M62 1.5 miles east of J18 • Eastbound and westbound **195 F10** SD84700797

*Burger King • Costa • EDC • Krispy Kreme • M&S Simply Food • WH Smith BP Travelodge* 2 hrs

Heywood, Lancashire OL10 2HQ

0161 643 0911

www.moto-way.co.uk

WH Smith is open 24 hrs.

**M62 Birch – westbound** Moto

M62 1.5 miles east of J18 • Eastbound and westbound **195 F10** SD84700797

*Burger King • Costa • EDC • Krispy Kreme • M&S Simply Food • WH Smith BP Travelodge* 2 hrs

Heywood, Lancashire OL10 2HQ

0161 643 0911

www.moto-way.co.uk

WH Smith is open 24 hrs.

**M62 Hartshead Moor** Welcome Break

M62, between J25 and J26 • Eastbound and westbound **197 C7** SE16892413

*Burger King • Eat In • KFC • Starbucks • WH Smith Shell Days Inn* 2 hrs

Clifton, Brighouse, West Yorkshire HD6 4JX 01274 876584

hartshead.enquiry @welcomebreak.co.uk

www.welcomebreak.co.uk

Eat In and WH Smith open 24 hrs

**M62 Ferrybridge** Moto

M62 Junction 33. Also A1(M) J40 (northbound) or J41 (southbound) • Northbound and southbound **198 C3** SE48512262

*Burger King • Costa • EDC • M&S Simply Food • WH Smith BP Travelodge*

2 hrs Ferrybridge, Knottingly, West Yorkshire WF11 0AF

01977 672767

www.moto-way.co.uk

Coffee Nation and WH Smith open 24 hrs

**M65 Blackburn with Darwen** Extra MSA

M65 J4. • Eastbound and westbound **195 C7** SD68592414

*Co-op • Le Petit Four • McDonald's Shell, LPG Travelodge* 2 hrs

Darwen Motorway Services Area, Darwen, Lancashire BB3 0AT

www.extraservices.co.uk

Forecourt shop is open 24 hrs.

## Scotland

**A1 Edinburgh** Moto

A1 City Bypass, Old Craighall junction • Northbound and southbound **280 G6** NT33777084

*Costa Esso Travelodge*

A1 City Bypass, Old Craighall Junction, Musselburgh EH21 8RE

01316 653507

**M9 Stirling** Moto

M9 J9 • Northbound and southbound **278 D6** NS80438870

*Burger King • Costa • EDC • WH Smith BP Travelodge* 2 hrs

Pirnhall, Stirling FK7 8EU

01786 813614

www.moto-way.co.uk

WH Smith is open 24 hrs.

**M74 Bothwell** RoadChef

M74, south of J4 • southbound only **268 D4** NS70855980

*Costa • Restbite! • WH Smith BP*

2hrs M74 Southbound, Bothwell, Lanarkshire G71 8BG

01698 854123

www.roadchef.com

Forecourt shop is open 24 hrs.

**M74 Hamilton** RoadChef

M74, 1 mile north of J6 • northbound only **268 D4** NS72525672

*Costa • Restbite! • WH Smith BP Days Inn* 2hrs M74 Northbound, Hamilton, South Lanarkshire ML3 6JW

01698 282176

www.roadchef.com

Forecourt shop is open 24hrs

**M74 Happendon** Cairn Lodge

M74 between J11 and J12 on B7078 • Northbound and southbound **259 C8** NS85243364

*Coffee shop • restaurant • retail shop Shell* 2hrs Cairn Lodge, Douglas, Lanark, South Lanarkshire ML11 0RJ 01555 851880

Forecourt shop open 24 hrs

**A74(M) Abington** Welcome Break

A74(M) J13 • Northbound and southbound **259 D10** NS93022505

*Burger King • Eat In • Starbucks • WH Smith Shell, LPG available Days Inn* 2 hrs Abington, Biggar, South Lanarkshire ML12 6RG

01864 502637

abington.enquiry @welcomebreak.co.uk

www.welcomebreak.co.uk

Eat In open 24 hrs. Tourist information office

**A74(M) Annandale Water** Road Chef

A74(M) J16 • Northbound and southbound **248 E4** NY10389261

*The Burger Company • Costa • Restbite! • WH Smith BP Days Inn* 2hrs

Johnstone Bridge, near Lockerbie, Dumfries and Galloway DG11 1HD

01576 470870

www.roadchef.com

Restbite and forecourt shop are open 24 hrs.

**A74(M) Gretna Green** Welcome Break

A74(M), just north of J22 • Northbound and southbound **239 D8** NY30476872

*Burger King • Eat In • KFC • Starbucks • WH Smith BP, LPG available Days Inn* 2 hrs

M74A Trunk Road, Gretna Green, Dumfries and Galloway DG16 5HQ

01461 337567

gretna.enquiry @welcomebreak.co.uk

www.welcomebreak.co.uk

Eat In open 24 hrs

## M80 Old Inns

M80 · Eastbound and Westbound
**278 F5** NS77187671
*Shell Select · Old Inns Cafe · Silk
Cottage Cantonese buffet and takeaway* ⛽ *Shell* ✉ Castlecary Road,
Cumbernauld G68 0BJ
📞 0843 2590190 (filling station)
🖥 www.shell.co.uk ·
www.oldinnscafe.com

## M90 Kinross                    Moto

M90 J6 · Northbound and
southbound **286 G5** NO10800282
*Burger King · Costa · EDC · WH Smith*
⛽ *Esso* 🛏 *Travelodge* 🅿 2 hrs
✉ M90, Kinross, Perth and Kinross
KY13 7NQ 📞 01577 863123
🖥 www.moto-way.co.uk
🌙 WH Smith and forecourt shop
open 24 hrs

## Wales

## M4 Magor                    RoadChef

M4 J23A · Eastbound and
westbound **60 B2** ST42068796
*Costa · McDonald's · Restbite! ·
WH Smith* ⛽ *Esso* 🛏 *Days Inn*
🅿 2 hours ✉ M4 Magor, Caldicot,
Monmouthshire NP26 3YL
📞 01633 881515
@ info@firstmotorway.co.uk
🖥 www.roadchef.com
🌙 McDonald's open 24 hrs

## M4 Cardiff Gate
Welcome Break

M4 J30 · Eastbound and
westbound **59 C8** ST21658283
*Burger King · Starbucks · Waitrose ·
WH Smith* ⛽ *Total, LPG available*
🅿 2 hrs ✉ Cardiff Gate Business Park,
Cardiff, South Glamorgan CF23 8RA
📞 01758 822102 @ cardiff.enquiry
@welcomebreak.co.uk
🖥 www.welcomebreak.co.uk
🌙 Forecourt shop open 24 hrs

## M4 Cardiff West                Moto

M4, off J33 · Eastbound and
westbound **58 D5** ST09417967
*Burger King · Costa · Krispy Kreme ·
WH Smith* ⛽ *Esso* 🛏 *Travelodge*
🅿 2 hrs ✉ Pontyclun, Mid
Glamorgan CF72 8SA
📞 02920 891141
🖥 www.moto-way.co.uk
🌙 WH Smith is open 24 hrs.

## M4 Sarn Park Welcome Break

M4 J36 · Eastbound and
westbound **58 C2** SS90688290
*Burger King · Cafe Primo · WH Smith*
⛽ *Shell* 🛏 *Days Inn* 🅿 2 hrs
✉ M4 Motorway, Junction 36,
Sarn Park, Bridgend CF32 9RW
📞 01656 655332 @ sarn.enquiry
@welcomebreak.co.uk
🖥 www.welcomebreak.co.uk
🌙 WH Smith and forecourt shop
open 24 hrs.

## M4 Swansea                    Moto

M4 at J47 · Eastbound and
westbound **75 F10** SS62159969
*Burger King · Costa · WH Smith* ⛽ *BP*
🛏 *Travelodge* 🅿 2 hrs
✉ Penllergaer, Swansea, West
Glamorgan SA4 1GT
📞 01792 896222
🖥 www.moto-way.co.uk
🌙 Forecourt outlets open 24 hrs.

## M4 Pont Abraham RoadChef

M4 J49 · Eastbound and
westbound **75 D9** SN57470743
*Costa · Restbite! · WH Smith* ⛽ *Texaco*
🅿 2 hours ✉ Llanedi, Pontarddulais,
Swansea SA4 0FU 📞 01792 884 663
🖥 www.roadchef.com
🌙 Forecourt outlets open 24 hrs

● Primary route service area
● Motorway service area

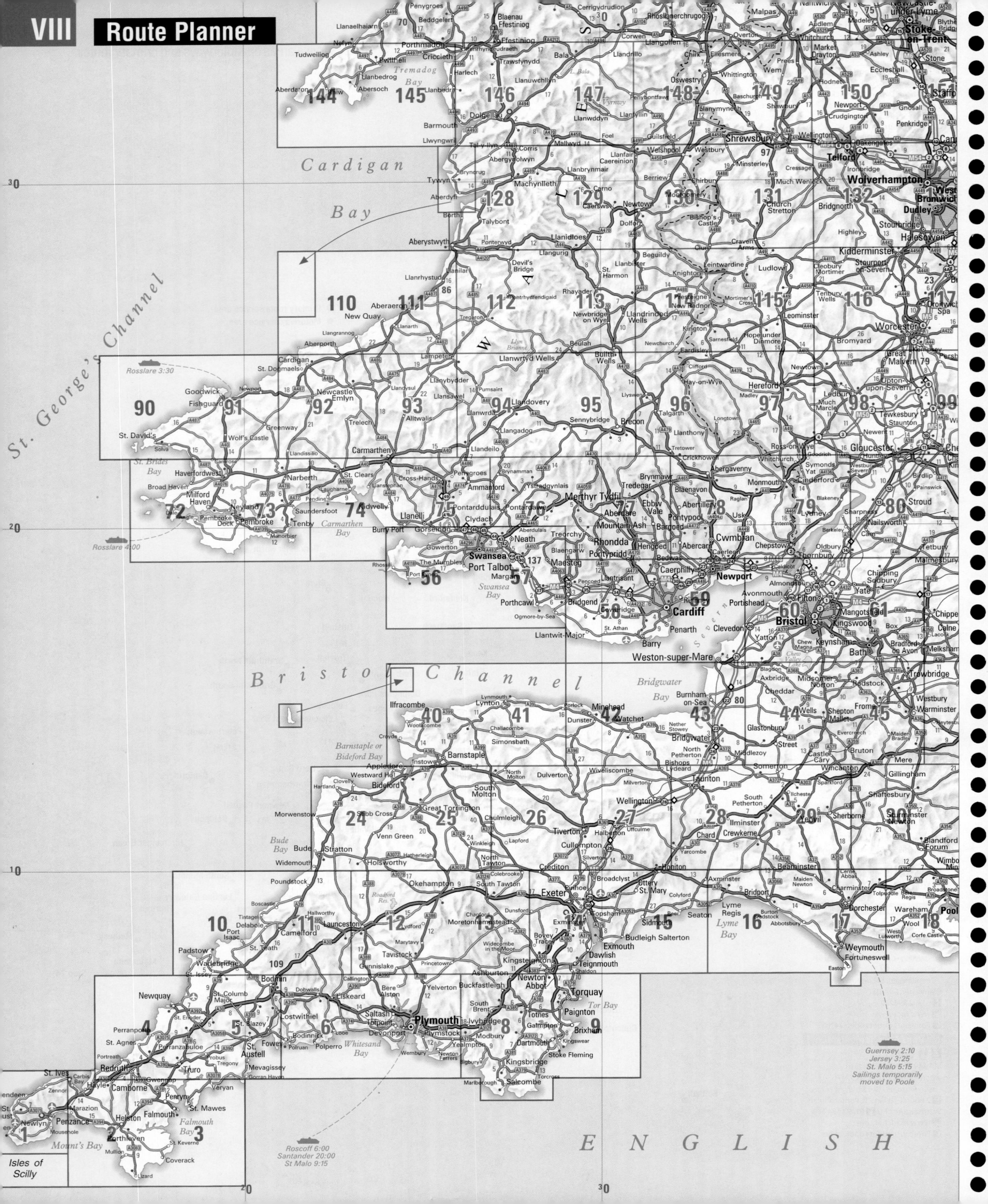
Cardigan
Bay
St. George's Channel
Bristol Channel
ENGLISH
Tremadog Bay
Carmarthen Bay
Swansea Bay
Bridgwater Bay
Barnstaple or Bideford Bay
Bude Bay
Lyme Bay
Tor Bay
Whitesand Bay
Falmouth Bay
Mount's Bay
Isles of Scilly
Rosslare 3:30
Rosslare 4:00
Roscoff 6:00
Santander 20:00
St Malo 9:15
Guernsey 2:10
Jersey 3:25
St. Malo 5:15
Sailings temporarily moved to Poole
Shrewsbury
Telford
Wolverhampton
Dudley
Kidderminster
Worcester
Hereford
Gloucester
Aberystwyth
Carmarthen
Swansea
Port Talbot
Merthyr Tydfil
Newport
Cardiff
Bristol
Weston-super-Mare
Bath
Taunton
Exeter
Plymouth
Torquay
Dorchester
Weymouth
Penzance
Truro
Newquay
Barnstaple
Stoke-on-Trent
Newcastle-under-Lyme

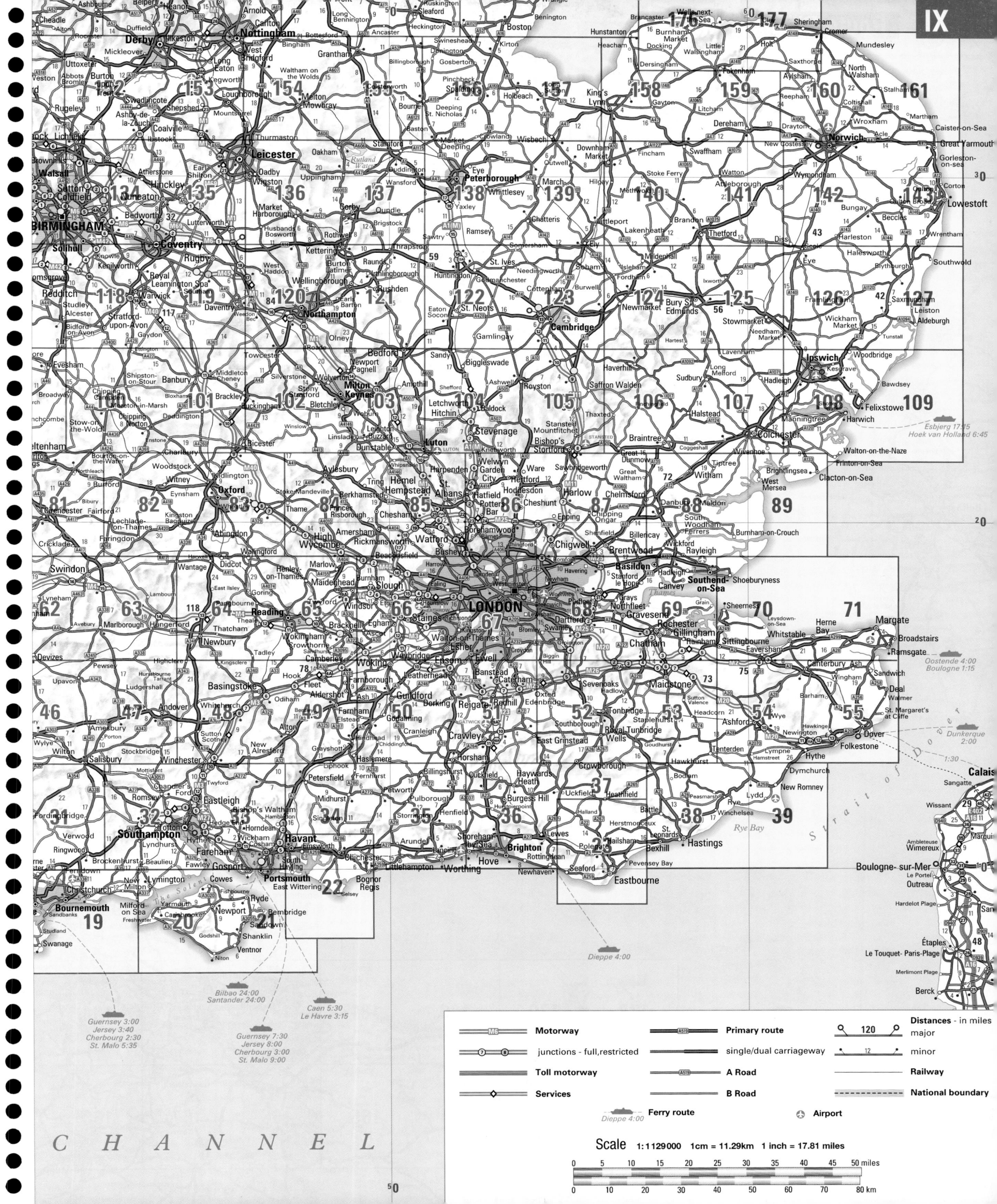

C H A N N E L

**Scale** 1:1129000  1cm = 11.29km  1 inch = 17.81 miles

| | Motorway | | | Primary route | | | Distances - in miles |
|---|---|---|---|---|---|---|---|
| | junctions - full, restricted | | | single/dual carriageway | | | major |
| | Toll motorway | | | A Road | | | minor |
| | Services | | | B Road | | | Railway |
| | Ferry route | | | Airport | | | National boundary |

*Dieppe 4:00*

Edinburgh
Glasgow
Greenock
Paisley
Clydebank
Motherwell
Hamilton
East Kilbride
Kilmarnock
Irvine
Ayr
Prestwick
Troon
Girvan
Stranraer
Newton Stewart
Dumfries
Lockerbie
Moffat
Hawick
Jedburgh
Galashiels
Carlisle
Brampton
Hexham
Penrith
Keswick
Cockermouth
Workington
Whitehaven
Maryport
Kendal
Windermere
Ambleside
Barrow-in-Furness
Lancaster
Morecambe
Fleetwood
Blackpool
Preston
Blackburn
Burnley
Southport
Bolton
Wigan
Manchester
Salford
Oldham
Stockport
Liverpool
Birkenhead
St. Helens
Warrington
Chester
Wrexham
Crewe
Stoke-on-Trent
Holyhead
Bangor
Caernarfon
Colwyn Bay
Rhyl
Belfast
Bangor
Larne
Newtownards
Downpatrick
Newcastle
Douglas
Ramsey
Peel
Castletown
Isle of Man
Arran
Campbeltown
North Channel
Firth of Clyde
Solway Firth
Luce Bay
Wigtown Bay
Morecambe Bay
Liverpool Bay
Caernarfon Bay
IRISH SEA
Anglesey
Larne 2:00
Troon 2:00
Liverpool 8:00
Douglas 2:55
Belfast 2:55
Dublin 2:55
Belfast 8:00
Dublin 7:30
Dublin 1:49
Dun Laoghaire 2:00
254
255
256
257
258
259
260
261
262
263
266
267
268
269
270
271
272
273
236
237
238
239
240
241
244
245
246
248
249
250
251
228
229
230
231
232
220
221
222
223
192
210
212
213
203
204
193
194
195
178
180
181
184
162
163
164
165
166
167

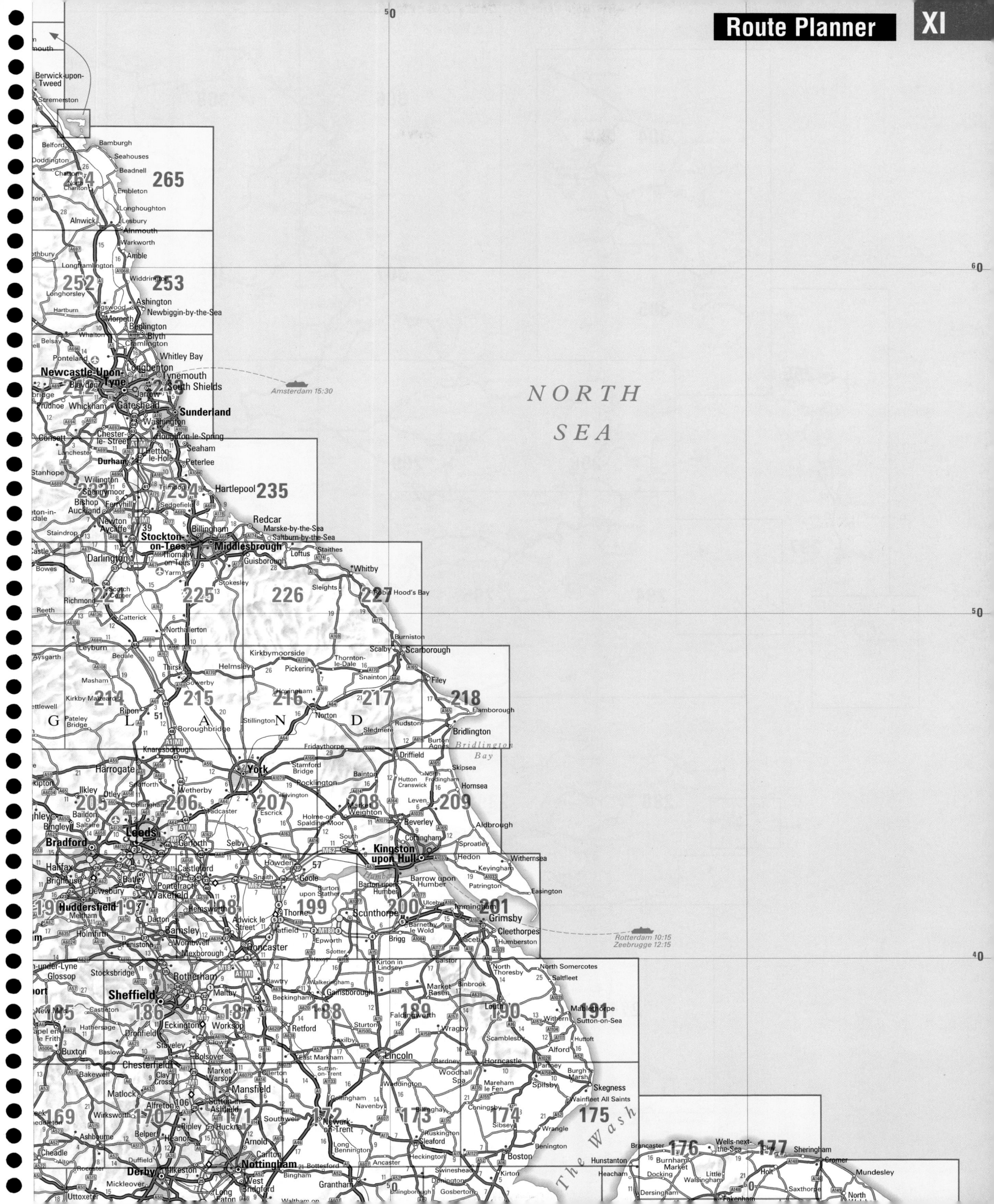

NORTH

SEA

Amsterdam 15:30

Rotterdam 10:15
Zeebrugge 12:15

*The Wash*

*Bridlington Bay*

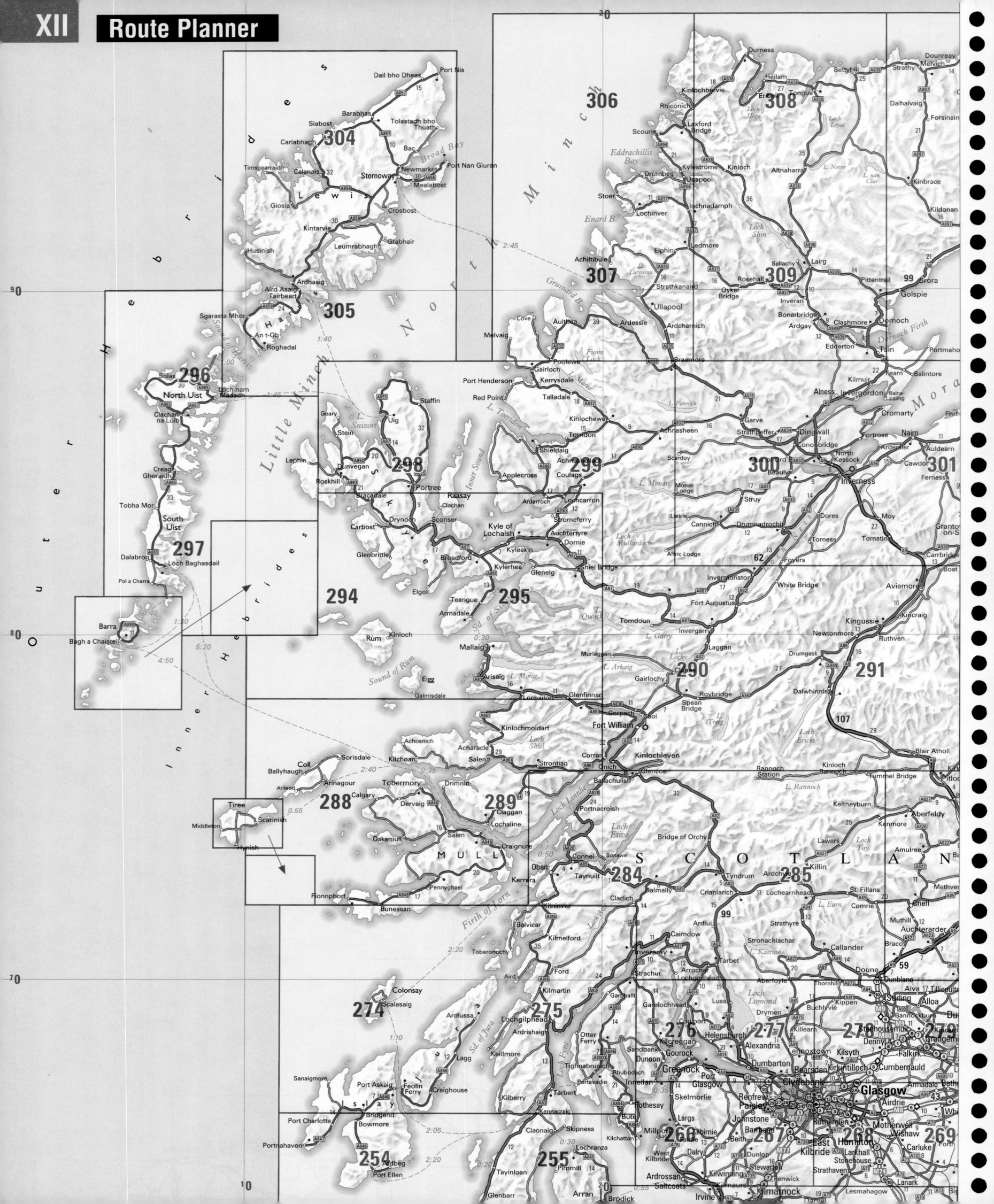

Outer Hebrides
Inner Hebrides
North Minch
Little Minch
SCOTLAND
304
305
306
307
308
309
296
297
298
299
300
301
294
295
290
291
288
289
284
285
274
275
276
277
278
254
255
266
267
268
269
Port Nis
Dail bho Dheas
Barabhas
Siabost
Tolastadh bho Thuath
Carlabhagh
Bac
Broad Bay
Timsgearraidh
Calanais
Stornoway
Newmarket
Port Nan Giuran
Mealabost
Lewis
Giosla
Crosbost
Kintarvie
Leumrabhagh
Grabhair
Husinish
Ardhasig
Aird Asaig
Tairbeart
Harris
Sgarasta Mhor
An t-Ob
Roghadal
Sound of Harris
Solas
North Uist
Loch nam Madadh
Clachan na Luib
Creag Ghoraidh
Tobha Mor
South Uist
Dalabrog
Loch Baghasdail
Pol a Charra
Barra
Bagh a Chaisteil
Durness
Heilam
Tongue
Kinlochbervie
Rhiconich
Laxford Bridge
Scourie
Eddrachillis Bay
Drumbeg
Kylestrome
Kinloch
Altnaharra
Unapool
Stoer
Inchnadamph
Lochinver
Enard B.
Ledmore
Elphin
Achiltibuie
Strathkanaird
Oykel Bridge
Rosehall
Lairg
Sallachy
Inveran
Ullapool
Gruinard B.
Ardessie
Ardcharnich
Braemore
Aultbea
Cove
Melvaig
Poolewe
Gairloch
Kerrysdale
Port Henderson
Red Point
Talladale
Loch Maree
Kinlochewe
Torridon
L. Torridon
Shieldaig
Achnasheen
Garve
Strathpeffer
Dingwall
Conon Bridge
Muir of Ord
Beauly
North Kessock
Inverness
Alness
Invergordon
Cromarty
Fortrose
Nairn
Auldearn
Ardersier
Cawdor
Ferness
Bettyhill
Strathy
Melvich
Dounreay
Dalhalvaig
Forsinain
Kinbrace
Kildonan
Pittentrail
Brora
Golspie
Dornoch
Clashmore
Bonarbridge
Ardgay
Edderton
Tain
Dornoch Firth
Portmahomack
Kilmuir
Balintore
Moray Firth
Staffin
Geary
Uig
Stein
Snizort
Lephin
Dunvegan
Roskhill
Portree
Bracadale
Skye
Raasay
Clachan
Drynoch
Sconser
Carbost
Glenbrittle
Broadford
Elgol
Kyle of Lochalsh
Kyleakin
Kylerhea
Applecross
Achnashellach
Coulags
Lochcarron
Ardarroch
Stromeferry
Auchtertyre
Dornie
Glenelg
Shiel Bridge
Inner Sound
Scardoy
L. Monar
Monar Lodge
Struy
Latrie
Cannich
Drumnadrochit
Loch Mullardoch
Affric Lodge
Loch Ness
Dores
Torness
Foyers
Moy
Tomatin
Carrbridge
Invermoriston
Fort Augustus
White Bridge
Aviemore
Teangue
Armadale
Rùm
Kinloch
Mallaig
Sound of Rùm
Eigg
Galmisdale
Arisaig
L. Morar
Lochailort
Glenfinnan
Tomdoun
L. Quoich
L. Garry
Invergarry
Laggan
Murlaggan
L. Arkaig
Loch Lochy
Gairlochy
Spean Bridge
Roybridge
Corpach
Caol
Fort William
Kinlochmoidart
Loch Shiel
Acharacle
Salen
Strontian
Corran
Onich
Kinlochleven
Glencoe
Ballachulish
Kingussie
Newtonmore
Kincraig
Ruthven
Drumgask
Dalwhinnie
Loch Ericht
Blair Atholl
Rannoch Station
L. Rannoch
Kinloch Rannoch
Tummel Bridge
Keltneyburn
Aberfeldy
Kenmore
Loch Tay
Amulree
Lawers
Killin
Coll
Sorisdale
Ballyhaugh
Arinagour
Arileod
Achosnich
Kilchoan
Tobermory
Calgary
Dervaig
Drimnin
Tiree
Scarinish
Middleton
Hynish
Claggan
Lochaline
Craignure
Oskamull
Mull
Fionnphort
Bunessan
Pennyghael
Kerrera
Oban
Connel
Bonawe
Taynuilt
Loch Linnhe
Portnacroish
Loch Etive
Bridge of Orchy
Tyndrum
Dalmally
Cladich
Crianlarich
Lochearnhead
St. Fillans
Comrie
Crieff
Kilninver
Firth of Lorn
Balvicar
Kilmelford
Toberonochy
Ardlui
Strathyre
Callander
Cairndow
Inveraray
Loch Awe
Arrochar
Tarbet
Stronachlachar
L. Katrine
Aberfoyle
Doune
Dunblane
Ford
Aird
Strachur
Kilmartin
Loch Lomond
Luss
Garelochhead
Drymen
Buchlyvie
Kippen
Stirling
Alloa
Colonsay
Scalasaig
Ardlussa
Jura
Sd. of Jura
Lochgilphead
Ardrishaig
Kilmore
Lagg
Otter Ferry
Loch Fyne
Tighnabruaich
Portavadie
Kilberry
Tarbert
Kennacraig
Claonaig
Skipness
Lochranza
Arran
Pirnmill
Tayinloan
Glenbarr
Brodick
Sanaigmore
Port Askaig
Feolin Ferry
Craighouse
Islay
Port Charlotte
Bridgend
Bowmore
Portnahaven
Ardbeg
Port Ellen
Dunoon
Sandbank
Kilcreggan
Helensburgh
Gourock
Greenock
Port Glasgow
Dumbarton
Alexandria
Balloch
Clydebank
Bearsden
Glasgow
Renfrew
Paisley
Johnstone
Barrhead
Rutherglen
East Kilbride
Hamilton
Motherwell
Wishaw
Airdrie
Coatbridge
Cumbernauld
Kilsyth
Kirkintilloch
Lennoxtown
Denny
Falkirk
Grangemouth
Larkhall
Stonehouse
Carluke
Lanark
Strathaven
Lesmahagow
Rothesay
Bute
Innellan
Skelmorlie
Largs
Millport
Kilbirnie
Dalry
Beith
Dunlop
Stewarton
Kilwinning
Kilmaurs
Kilmarnock
Fenwick
West Kilbride
Ardrossan
Saltcoats
Irvine
Kilchattan

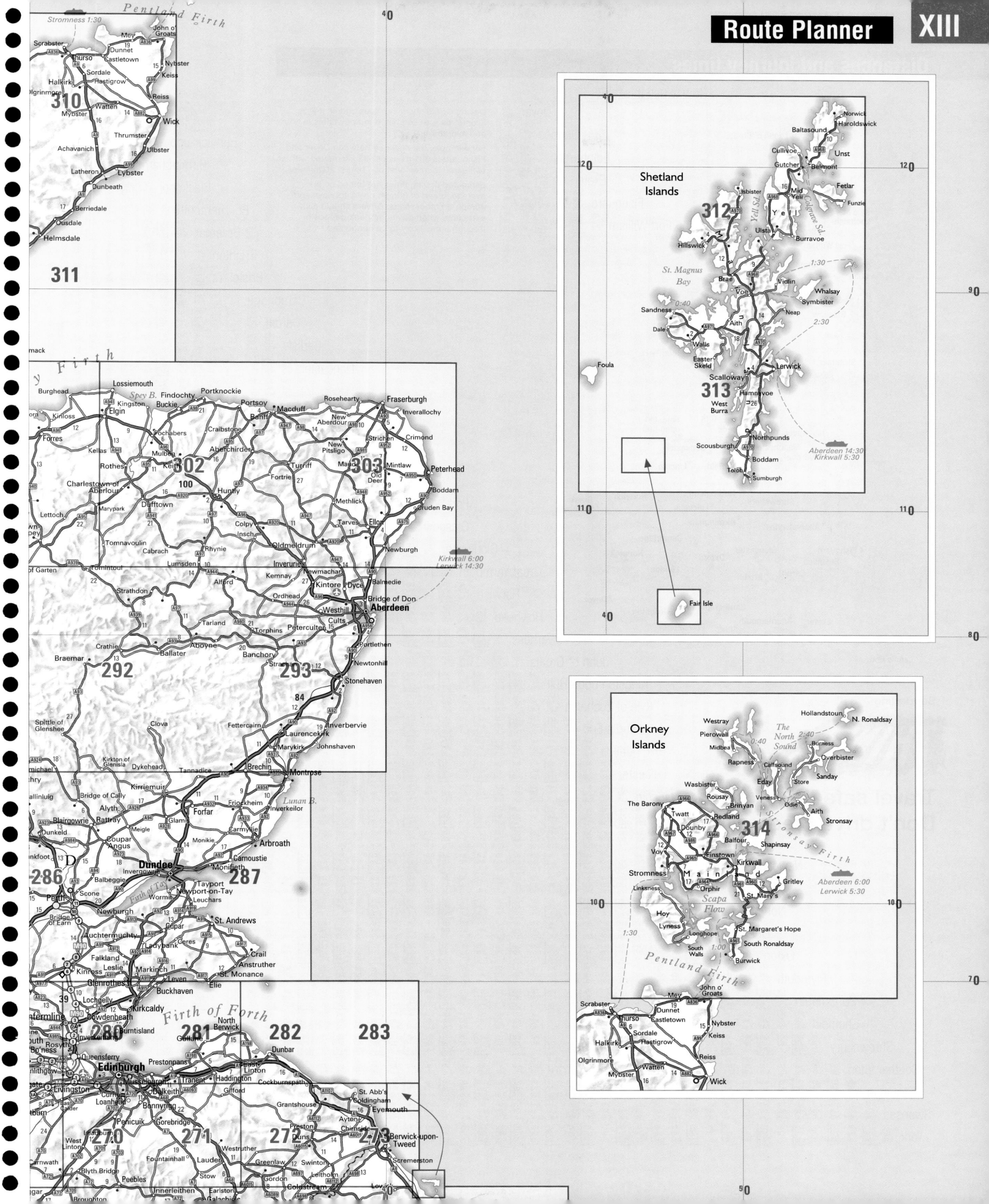

Shetland Islands
Orkney Islands
Aberdeen
Dundee
Edinburgh
Firth of Forth
Pentland Firth
Lerwick
Kirkwall

## Distances and journey times

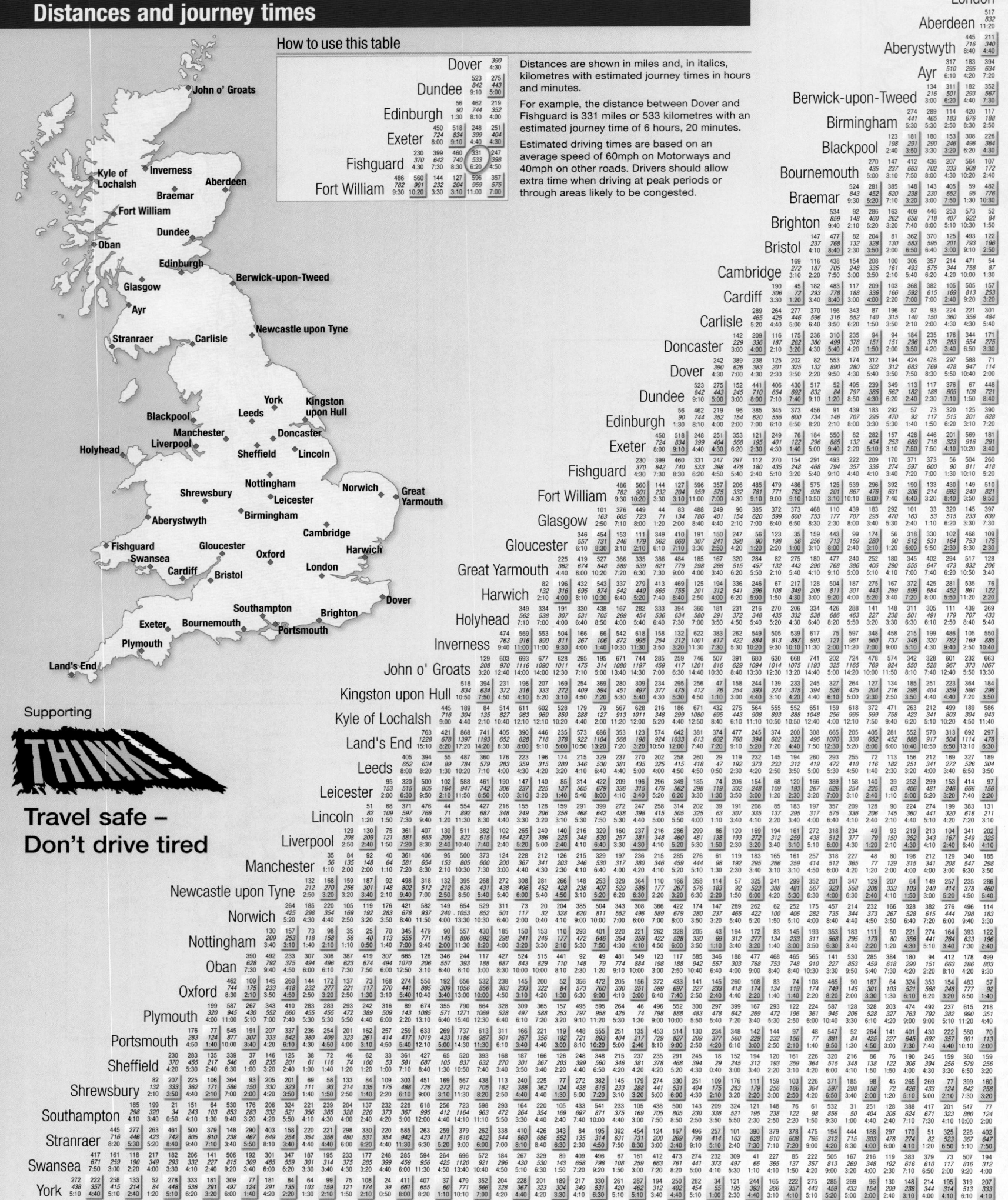

### How to use this table

| | Fishguard | Exeter | Edinburgh | Dundee | Dover | |
|---|---|---|---|---|---|---|
| Dover | | | | | | 390 / 4:30 |
| Dundee | | | | | 523 / 842 / 9:10 | 275 / 443 / 5:00 |
| Edinburgh | | | | 56 / 90 / 1:30 | 462 / 744 / 8:10 | 219 / 352 / 4:00 |
| Exeter | | | 450 / 724 / 8:00 | 518 / 834 / 9:10 | 248 / 399 / 4:40 | 251 / 404 / 4:30 |
| Fishguard | | 230 / 370 / 4:30 | 399 / 642 / 7:30 | 460 / 740 / 8:30 | 331 / 533 / 6:20 | 247 / 398 / 4:50 |
| Fort William | 486 / 782 / 9:30 | 560 / 901 / 10:20 | 144 / 232 / 3:30 | 127 / 204 / 3:10 | 596 / 959 / 11:00 | 357 / 575 / 7:00 |

Distances are shown in miles and, in italics, kilometres with estimated journey times in hours and minutes.

For example, the distance between Dover and Fishguard is 331 miles or 533 kilometres with an estimated journey time of 6 hours, 20 minutes.

Estimated driving times are based on an average speed of 60mph on Motorways and 40mph on other roads. Drivers should allow extra time when driving at peak periods or through areas likely to be congested.

| | Swansea | Stranraer | Southampton | Shrewsbury | Sheffield | Portsmouth | Plymouth | Oxford | Oban | Nottingham | Norwich | Newcastle upon Tyne | Manchester | Liverpool | Lincoln | Leicester | Leeds | Land's End | Kyle of Lochalsh | Kingston upon Hull | John o' Groats | Inverness | Holyhead | Harwich | Great Yarmouth | Gloucester | Glasgow | Fort William | Fishguard | Exeter | Edinburgh | Dundee | Dover | Doncaster | Carlisle | Cardiff | Cambridge | Bristol | Brighton | Braemar | Bournemouth | Blackpool | Birmingham | Berwick-upon-Tweed | Ayr | Aberystwyth | Aberdeen | London |
|---|---|---|---|---|---|---|---|---|---|---|---|---|---|---|---|---|---|---|---|---|---|---|---|---|---|---|---|---|---|---|---|---|---|---|---|---|---|---|---|---|---|---|---|---|---|---|---|---|
| London | | | | | | | | | | | | | | | | | | | | | | | | | | | | | | | | | | | | | | | | | | | | | | | | |
| Aberdeen | | | | | | | | | | | | | | | | | | | | | | | | | | | | | | | | | | | | | | | | | | | | | | | | 517 / 832 / 11:20 |
| Aberystwyth | | | | | | | | | | | | | | | | | | | | | | | | | | | | | | | | | | | | | | | | | | | | | | | 445 / 716 / 8:40 | 211 / 340 / 4:40 |
| Ayr | | | | | | | | | | | | | | | | | | | | | | | | | | | | | | | | | | | | | | | | | | | | | | 317 / 510 / 6:10 | 183 / 295 / 4:20 | 394 / 634 / 7:20 |
| Berwick-upon-Tweed | | | | | | | | | | | | | | | | | | | | | | | | | | | | | | | | | | | | | | | | | | | | | 134 / 216 / 3:00 | 311 / 501 / 6:20 | 182 / 293 / 4:40 | 352 / 567 / 7:30 |
| Birmingham | | | | | | | | | | | | | | | | | | | | | | | | | | | | | | | | | | | | | | | | | | | | 274 / 441 / 5:30 | 289 / 465 / 5:30 | 114 / 183 / 2:50 | 420 / 676 / 8:30 | 117 / 188 / 2:50 |
| Blackpool | | | | | | | | | | | | | | | | | | | | | | | | | | | | | | | | | | | | | | | | | | | 123 / 198 / 2:40 | 181 / 291 / 3:50 | 180 / 290 / 3:30 | 153 / 246 / 3:20 | 308 / 496 / 6:20 | 226 / 364 / 4:30 |
| Bournemouth | | | | | | | | | | | | | | | | | | | | | | | | | | | | | | | | | | | | | | | | | | 270 / 435 / 5:00 | 147 / 237 / 3:10 | 412 / 663 / 7:50 | 436 / 702 / 8:00 | 207 / 333 / 4:30 | 564 / 908 / 10:20 | 107 / 172 / 2:40 |
| Braemar | | | | | | | | | | | | | | | | | | | | | | | | | | | | | | | | | | | | | | | | | 524 / 843 / 9:30 | 281 / 452 / 5:20 | 385 / 620 / 7:10 | 148 / 238 / 3:20 | 143 / 230 / 3:00 | 405 / 652 / 7:50 | 59 / 95 / 1:30 | 482 / 776 / 10:30 |
| Brighton | | | | | | | | | | | | | | | | | | | | | | | | | | | | | | | | | | | | | | | | 534 / 859 / 9:40 | 92 / 148 / 2:10 | 286 / 460 / 5:20 | 163 / 262 / 3:20 | 409 / 658 / 7:40 | 446 / 718 / 8:00 | 253 / 407 / 5:10 | 573 / 922 / 10:30 | 52 / 84 / 1:50 |
| Bristol | | | | | | | | | | | | | | | | | | | | | | | | | | | | | | | | | | | | | | | 147 / 237 / 4:10 | 477 / 768 / 8:40 | 82 / 132 / 2:30 | 204 / 328 / 3:50 | 81 / 130 / 2:00 | 362 / 583 / 6:50 | 370 / 595 / 6:40 | 125 / 201 / 3:00 | 493 / 793 / 9:10 | 122 / 196 / 2:50 |
| Cambridge | | | | | | | | | | | | | | | | | | | | | | | | | | | | | | | | | | | | | | 169 / 272 / 3:10 | 116 / 187 / 2:20 | 438 / 705 / 7:50 | 154 / 248 / 3:00 | 208 / 335 / 3:50 | 100 / 161 / 2:10 | 306 / 493 / 5:40 | 357 / 575 / 6:20 | 214 / 344 / 4:20 | 471 / 758 / 10:00 | 54 / 87 / 1:30 |
| Cardiff | | | | | | | | | | | | | | | | | | | | | | | | | | | | | | | | | | | | | 190 / 306 / 3:30 | 45 / 72 / 1:20 | 182 / 293 / 3:40 | 483 / 778 / 8:40 | 117 / 188 / 3:00 | 209 / 336 / 4:00 | 103 / 166 / 2:20 | 368 / 592 / 7:00 | 382 / 615 / 7:00 | 105 / 169 / 2:40 | 505 / 813 / 9:20 | 157 / 253 / 3:20 |
| Carlisle | | | | | | | | | | | | | | | | | | | | | | | | | | | | | | | | | | | | 289 / 465 / 5:20 | 264 / 425 / 4:40 | 277 / 446 / 5:00 | 370 / 596 / 6:40 | 196 / 316 / 3:50 | 343 / 552 / 6:20 | 87 / 140 / 1:50 | 196 / 315 / 3:50 | 87 / 140 / 2:10 | 93 / 150 / 2:00 | 224 / 360 / 4:30 | 221 / 356 / 4:30 | 301 / 484 / 5:40 |
| Doncaster | | | | | | | | | | | | | | | | | | | | | | | | | | | | | | | | | | | 142 / 229 / 3:00 | 209 / 336 / 4:00 | 116 / 187 / 2:10 | 175 / 282 / 3:20 | 236 / 380 / 4:30 | 310 / 499 / 5:40 | 235 / 378 / 4:20 | 94 / 151 / 1:50 | 94 / 151 / 2:00 | 184 / 296 / 3:50 | 235 / 378 / 4:20 | 176 / 283 / 3:40 | 344 / 554 / 6:50 | 171 / 275 / 3:30 |
| Dover | | | | | | | | | | | | | | | | | | | | | | | | | | | | | | | | | | 242 / 390 / 4:30 | 389 / 626 / 7:00 | 238 / 383 / 4:30 | 125 / 201 / 2:30 | 202 / 325 / 3:50 | 82 / 132 / 2:20 | 553 / 890 / 9:50 | 174 / 280 / 4:30 | 312 / 502 / 5:40 | 194 / 312 / 3:50 | 424 / 683 / 7:50 | 478 / 769 / 8:30 | 297 / 478 / 5:50 | 588 / 947 / 10:40 | 71 / 114 / 2:00 |
| Dundee | | | | | | | | | | | | | | | | | | | | | | | | | | | | | | | | | 523 / 842 / 9:10 | 275 / 443 / 5:00 | 152 / 245 / 3:00 | 441 / 710 / 8:00 | 406 / 654 / 7:10 | 430 / 692 / 7:40 | 517 / 832 / 9:10 | 52 / 84 / 1:20 | 495 / 797 / 8:50 | 239 / 385 / 4:30 | 349 / 562 / 6:20 | 113 / 182 / 2:40 | 117 / 188 / 2:30 | 376 / 605 / 7:10 | 67 / 108 / 1:50 | 448 / 721 / 8:40 |
| Edinburgh | | | | | | | | | | | | | | | | | | | | | | | | | | | | | | | | 56 / 90 / 1:30 | 462 / 744 / 8:10 | 219 / 352 / 4:00 | 96 / 154 / 2:00 | 385 / 620 / 7:00 | 345 / 555 / 6:10 | 373 / 600 / 6:50 | 456 / 734 / 8:20 | 91 / 146 / 2:10 | 439 / 707 / 8:00 | 183 / 295 / 3:30 | 292 / 470 / 5:30 | 57 / 92 / 1:40 | 73 / 117 / 1:50 | 320 / 515 / 6:20 | 125 / 201 / 3:10 | 390 / 628 / 7:20 |
| Exeter | | | | | | | | | | | | | | | | | | | | | | | | | | | | | | | 450 / 724 / 8:00 | 518 / 834 / 9:10 | 248 / 399 / 4:40 | 251 / 404 / 4:30 | 353 / 568 / 6:20 | 121 / 195 / 2:30 | 249 / 401 / 4:30 | 76 / 122 / 1:40 | 184 / 296 / 5:00 | 550 / 885 / 9:40 | 82 / 132 / 2:20 | 282 / 454 / 5:10 | 157 / 253 / 3:10 | 428 / 689 / 7:50 | 446 / 718 / 7:50 | 201 / 323 / 4:10 | 569 / 916 / 10:20 | 181 / 291 / 3:40 |
| Fishguard | | | | | | | | | | | | | | | | | | | | | | | | | | | | | | 230 / 370 / 4:30 | 399 / 642 / 7:30 | 460 / 740 / 8:30 | 331 / 533 / 6:20 | 247 / 398 / 4:50 | 297 / 478 / 5:40 | 112 / 180 / 2:40 | 270 / 435 / 5:10 | 154 / 248 / 3:20 | 291 / 468 / 5:40 | 493 / 794 / 9:10 | 222 / 357 / 4:40 | 209 / 336 / 4:10 | 170 / 274 / 3:40 | 371 / 597 / 7:20 | 373 / 600 / 7:00 | 56 / 90 / 1:30 | 504 / 811 / 10:10 | 260 / 418 / 5:20 |
| Fort William | | | | | | | | | | | | | | | | | | | | | | | | | | | | | 486 / 782 / 9:30 | 560 / 901 / 10:20 | 144 / 232 / 3:30 | 127 / 204 / 3:10 | 596 / 959 / 11:00 | 357 / 575 / 7:00 | 206 / 332 / 4:30 | 485 / 781 / 9:10 | 479 / 771 / 9:00 | 486 / 782 / 9:10 | 575 / 926 / 10:50 | 125 / 201 / 3:10 | 539 / 867 / 10:10 | 296 / 476 / 6:00 | 392 / 631 / 7:40 | 190 / 306 / 4:40 | 133 / 214 / 3:20 | 430 / 692 / 8:40 | 149 / 240 / 3:50 | 510 / 821 / 9:50 |
| Glasgow | | | | | | | | | | | | | | | | | | | | | | | | | | | | 101 / 163 / 2:50 | 376 / 605 / 7:10 | 449 / 723 / 8:00 | 44 / 71 / 1:20 | 83 / 134 / 2:00 | 488 / 786 / 8:40 | 249 / 401 / 4:40 | 96 / 154 / 2:10 | 385 / 620 / 7:00 | 372 / 599 / 6:40 | 373 / 600 / 6:50 | 468 / 753 / 8:30 | 110 / 177 / 2:30 | 439 / 707 / 8:00 | 183 / 295 / 3:40 | 292 / 470 / 5:30 | 101 / 163 / 2:40 | 33 / 53 / 1:10 | 320 / 515 / 6:20 | 145 / 233 / 3:30 | 397 / 639 / 7:30 |
| Gloucester | | | | | | | | | | | | | | | | | | | | | | | | | | | 346 / 557 / 6:10 | 454 / 731 / 8:30 | 153 / 246 / 3:10 | 111 / 179 / 2:10 | 349 / 562 / 6:10 | 410 / 660 / 7:10 | 191 / 307 / 3:30 | 150 / 241 / 2:50 | 247 / 398 / 4:20 | 56 / 90 / 1:20 | 123 / 198 / 2:20 | 35 / 56 / 1:00 | 159 / 256 / 3:10 | 443 / 713 / 8:00 | 99 / 159 / 2:40 | 174 / 280 / 3:10 | 56 / 90 / 1:20 | 318 / 512 / 6:00 | 330 / 531 / 5:50 | 102 / 164 / 2:30 | 468 / 753 / 8:30 | 109 / 175 / 2:30 |
| Great Yarmouth | | | | | | | | | | | | | | | | | | | | | | | | | | 225 / 362 / 4:40 | 419 / 674 / 8:00 | 527 / 848 / 10:20 | 366 / 589 / 7:20 | 335 / 539 / 6:30 | 386 / 621 / 7:30 | 484 / 779 / 9:00 | 185 / 298 / 4:00 | 167 / 269 / 3:40 | 320 / 515 / 6:20 | 284 / 457 / 5:50 | 82 / 132 / 2:10 | 275 / 443 / 5:40 | 180 / 290 / 4:10 | 477 / 768 / 9:10 | 240 / 386 / 5:00 | 252 / 406 / 5:10 | 180 / 290 / 4:10 | 345 / 555 / 7:00 | 402 / 647 / 7:40 | 294 / 473 / 6:20 | 517 / 832 / 10:50 | 128 / 206 / 3:40 |
| Harwich | | | | | | | | | | | | | | | | | | | | | | | | | 82 / 132 / 2:10 | 196 / 316 / 4:00 | 432 / 695 / 8:10 | 543 / 874 / 10:30 | 337 / 542 / 6:40 | 279 / 449 / 5:20 | 413 / 665 / 7:40 | 469 / 755 / 8:40 | 125 / 201 / 2:50 | 194 / 312 / 4:00 | 336 / 541 / 6:20 | 246 / 396 / 5:00 | 67 / 108 / 1:50 | 217 / 349 / 4:30 | 128 / 206 / 3:00 | 504 / 811 / 9:20 | 187 / 301 / 4:00 | 275 / 443 / 5:20 | 167 / 269 / 3:40 | 372 / 599 / 7:20 | 425 / 684 / 8:00 | 281 / 452 / 5:50 | 535 / 861 / 11:20 | 76 / 122 / 2:20 |
| Holyhead | | | | | | | | | | | | | | | | | | | | | | | | 349 / 562 / 7:10 | 334 / 538 / 7:00 | 191 / 307 / 4:00 | 330 / 531 / 6:40 | 438 / 705 / 8:50 | 167 / 269 / 4:00 | 282 / 454 / 5:40 | 333 / 536 / 6:40 | 394 / 634 / 7:30 | 360 / 580 / 7:00 | 181 / 291 / 3:50 | 231 / 372 / 4:50 | 216 / 348 / 5:40 | 270 / 435 / 5:20 | 206 / 332 / 4:30 | 334 / 538 / 6:40 | 426 / 686 / 8:20 | 288 / 463 / 5:50 | 141 / 227 / 3:20 | 148 / 238 / 3:30 | 311 / 501 / 6:30 | 305 / 491 / 6:10 | 111 / 179 / 2:50 | 439 / 707 / 8:40 | 269 / 433 / 5:40 |
| Inverness | | | | | | | | | | | | | | | | | | | | | | | 474 / 763 / 9:40 | 569 / 916 / 11:00 | 553 / 890 / 11:00 | 504 / 811 / 9:30 | 166 / 267 / 4:00 | 66 / 106 / 1:40 | 542 / 872 / 10:30 | 618 / 995 / 11:30 | 158 / 254 / 3:50 | 132 / 212 / 3:20 | 622 / 1001 / 11:30 | 383 / 617 / 7:30 | 262 / 422 / 5:30 | 549 / 884 / 10:20 | 505 / 813 / 9:30 | 539 / 867 / 10:10 | 617 / 993 / 11:30 | 75 / 121 / 2:00 | 597 / 961 / 11:20 | 348 / 560 / 7:00 | 458 / 737 / 9:00 | 215 / 346 / 5:10 | 199 / 320 / 4:30 | 486 / 782 / 9:40 | 105 / 169 / 2:50 | 550 / 885 / 10:40 |
| John o' Groats | | | | | | | | | | | | | | | | | | | | | | 129 / 208 / 3:20 | 603 / 970 / 12:40 | 693 / 1116 / 14:00 | 677 / 1090 / 14:00 | 628 / 1011 / 12:30 | 295 / 475 / 7:10 | 195 / 314 / 5:00 | 671 / 1080 / 13:40 | 744 / 1197 / 14:30 | 285 / 459 / 7:00 | 259 / 417 / 6:30 | 746 / 1201 / 14:40 | 507 / 816 / 10:30 | 391 / 629 / 8:40 | 680 / 1094 / 13:30 | 630 / 1014 / 12:30 | 668 / 1075 / 13:20 | 741 / 1193 / 14:40 | 202 / 325 / 5:00 | 724 / 1165 / 14:20 | 478 / 769 / 10:00 | 574 / 924 / 11:50 | 342 / 550 / 8:10 | 328 / 528 / 7:40 | 601 / 967 / 12:40 | 232 / 373 / 5:50 | 663 / 1067 / 13:30 |
| Kingston upon Hull | | | | | | | | | | | | | | | | | | | | | 518 / 834 / 10:50 | 394 / 634 / 7:50 | 231 / 372 / 4:50 | 196 / 316 / 4:10 | 207 / 333 / 5:20 | 169 / 272 / 3:10 | 254 / 409 / 4:50 | 369 / 594 / 7:20 | 280 / 451 / 5:30 | 309 / 497 / 5:40 | 234 / 377 / 4:30 | 295 / 475 / 5:30 | 256 / 412 / 4:50 | 47 / 76 / 1:10 | 158 / 254 / 3:00 | 244 / 393 / 4:40 | 139 / 224 / 3:10 | 233 / 375 / 4:20 | 245 / 394 / 4:40 | 327 / 526 / 6:10 | 264 / 425 / 5:00 | 127 / 204 / 2:30 | 134 / 216 / 2:50 | 185 / 298 / 3:50 | 251 / 404 / 4:40 | 223 / 359 / 4:40 | 364 / 586 / 7:20 | 184 / 296 / 3:50 |
| Kyle of Lochalsh | | | | | | | | | | | | | | | | | | | | 445 / 716 / 9:00 | 189 / 304 / 4:40 | 84 / 135 / 2:10 | 514 / 827 / 10:40 | 611 / 983 / 12:10 | 602 / 969 / 12:10 | 528 / 850 / 10:20 | 179 / 288 / 4:40 | 79 / 127 / 2:00 | 567 / 913 / 11:20 | 628 / 1011 / 12:00 | 216 / 348 / 5:20 | 186 / 299 / 4:40 | 671 / 1080 / 12:50 | 432 / 695 / 8:40 | 275 / 443 / 6:10 | 564 / 908 / 11:10 | 555 / 893 / 10:50 | 552 / 888 / 10:50 | 651 / 1048 / 12:40 | 159 / 256 / 4:00 | 618 / 995 / 12:10 | 372 / 599 / 7:50 | 471 / 758 / 9:40 | 263 / 423 / 6:20 | 212 / 341 / 5:10 | 499 / 803 / 10:20 | 189 / 304 / 4:50 | 586 / 943 / 11:40 |
| Land's End | | | | | | | | | | | | | | | | | | | 763 / 1228 / 15:10 | 421 / 678 / 8:20 | 868 / 1397 / 17:20 | 741 / 1193 / 14:20 | 405 / 652 / 8:30 | 390 / 628 / 8:00 | 446 / 718 / 9:10 | 235 / 378 / 5:00 | 573 / 922 / 10:50 | 686 / 1104 / 13:20 | 353 / 568 / 7:20 | 123 / 198 / 3:20 | 574 / 924 / 10:50 | 642 / 1033 / 12:00 | 381 / 613 / 7:40 | 374 / 602 / 7:20 | 477 / 768 / 9:10 | 245 / 394 / 5:20 | 374 / 602 / 7:20 | 200 / 322 / 4:40 | 308 / 496 / 7:50 | 665 / 1070 / 12:30 | 205 / 330 / 5:20 | 405 / 652 / 8:00 | 281 / 452 / 6:00 | 552 / 888 / 10:40 | 570 / 917 / 10:50 | 313 / 504 / 6:50 | 692 / 1114 / 13:10 | 297 / 478 / 6:30 |
| Leeds | | | | | | | | | | | | | | | | | | 405 / 652 / 8:00 | 394 / 634 / 8:20 | 55 / 89 / 1:30 | 487 / 784 / 10:20 | 360 / 579 / 7:10 | 176 / 283 / 4:00 | 223 / 359 / 4:30 | 196 / 315 / 4:20 | 174 / 280 / 3:20 | 215 / 346 / 4:10 | 329 / 530 / 6:40 | 237 / 381 / 4:40 | 270 / 435 / 5:00 | 202 / 325 / 4:00 | 258 / 415 / 4:50 | 260 / 418 / 4:50 | 29 / 47 / 0:50 | 119 / 192 / 2:30 | 232 / 373 / 4:20 | 145 / 233 / 2:50 | 194 / 312 / 3:50 | 260 / 419 / 5:00 | 293 / 472 / 5:30 | 255 / 410 / 4:50 | 72 / 116 / 1:40 | 113 / 182 / 2:30 | 156 / 251 / 3:20 | 212 / 341 / 4:00 | 169 / 272 / 3:40 | 327 / 526 / 6:50 | 189 / 304 / 3:50 |
| Leicester | | | | | | | | | | | | | | | | | 95 / 153 / 2:00 | 320 / 515 / 6:30 | 500 / 805 / 9:50 | 102 / 164 / 2:10 | 588 / 947 / 11:50 | 461 / 742 / 8:50 | 190 / 306 / 4:00 | 147 / 237 / 3:10 | 140 / 225 / 3:20 | 85 / 137 / 1:40 | 314 / 505 / 5:40 | 422 / 679 / 8:00 | 209 / 336 / 4:10 | 196 / 315 / 3:40 | 296 / 476 / 5:20 | 349 / 562 / 6:20 | 185 / 298 / 3:30 | 74 / 119 / 1:30 | 206 / 332 / 3:50 | 154 / 248 / 3:00 | 68 / 109 / 1:20 | 120 / 193 / 2:30 | 166 / 267 / 3:20 | 389 / 626 / 7:00 | 158 / 254 / 3:10 | 140 / 225 / 2:40 | 39 / 63 / 1:10 | 252 / 406 / 5:00 | 299 / 481 / 5:20 | 153 / 246 / 3:20 | 414 / 666 / 7:40 | 97 / 156 / 2:20 |
| Lincoln | | | | | | | | | | | | | | | | 51 / 82 / 1:20 | 68 / 109 / 1:50 | 371 / 597 / 7:30 | 476 / 766 / 9:40 | 44 / 71 / 1:20 | 554 / 892 / 11:30 | 427 / 687 / 8:30 | 216 / 348 / 4:40 | 155 / 249 / 3:30 | 128 / 206 / 3:20 | 159 / 256 / 3:10 | 291 / 468 / 5:30 | 399 / 642 / 7:50 | 272 / 438 / 5:30 | 247 / 398 / 4:40 | 258 / 415 / 5:00 | 314 / 505 / 5:50 | 202 / 325 / 4:00 | 39 / 63 / 1:10 | 191 / 307 / 3:40 | 208 / 335 / 4:10 | 85 / 137 / 2:20 | 183 / 295 / 3:40 | 197 / 317 / 4:00 | 357 / 575 / 6:40 | 209 / 336 / 4:10 | 128 / 206 / 2:40 | 90 / 145 / 2:10 | 224 / 360 / 4:40 | 274 / 441 / 5:10 | 199 / 320 / 4:20 | 383 / 616 / 7:20 | 131 / 211 / 3:10 |
| Liverpool | | | | | | | | | | | | | | | 129 / 208 / 2:50 | 130 / 209 / 2:40 | 75 / 121 / 1:50 | 361 / 581 / 7:20 | 407 / 655 / 8:30 | 130 / 209 / 2:40 | 511 / 822 / 10:40 | 382 / 615 / 7:40 | 102 / 164 / 2:40 | 265 / 427 / 5:20 | 240 / 386 / 5:00 | 140 / 225 / 2:40 | 216 / 348 / 4:10 | 329 / 530 / 6:40 | 160 / 257 / 3:30 | 237 / 381 / 4:30 | 216 / 348 / 4:10 | 286 / 460 / 5:20 | 299 / 481 / 5:30 | 86 / 138 / 1:50 | 120 / 193 / 2:30 | 169 / 272 / 3:20 | 194 / 312 / 3:40 | 161 / 259 / 3:10 | 272 / 438 / 5:10 | 318 / 512 / 6:00 | 234 / 377 / 4:30 | 49 / 79 / 1:20 | 93 / 150 / 2:10 | 219 / 352 / 4:30 | 213 / 343 / 4:10 | 104 / 167 / 2:40 | 341 / 549 / 6:40 | 202 / 325 / 4:10 |
| Manchester | | | | | | | | | | | | | | 35 / 56 / 1:10 | 84 / 135 / 2:00 | 92 / 148 / 2:00 | 40 / 64 / 1:10 | 361 / 581 / 7:20 | 406 / 654 / 8:30 | 95 / 153 / 2:10 | 500 / 805 / 10:30 | 373 / 600 / 7:30 | 124 / 200 / 3:00 | 228 / 367 / 4:40 | 212 / 341 / 4:30 | 126 / 203 / 2:30 | 215 / 346 / 4:10 | 329 / 530 / 6:40 | 197 / 317 / 4:00 | 236 / 380 / 4:20 | 215 / 346 / 4:10 | 285 / 459 / 5:20 | 276 / 444 / 5:10 | 61 / 98 / 1:30 | 119 / 192 / 2:30 | 183 / 295 / 3:40 | 165 / 266 / 3:10 | 161 / 259 / 3:10 | 257 / 414 / 4:50 | 318 / 512 / 6:00 | 227 / 365 / 4:20 | 48 / 77 / 1:20 | 80 / 129 / 2:00 | 196 / 315 / 4:00 | 212 / 341 / 4:00 | 129 / 208 / 3:00 | 340 / 547 / 6:30 | 185 / 298 / 3:50 |
| Newcastle upon Tyne | | | | | | | | | | | | | 132 / 212 / 2:50 | 168 / 270 / 3:20 | 159 / 256 / 3:20 | 187 / 301 / 3:40 | 92 / 148 / 2:10 | 498 / 802 / 9:40 | 318 / 512 / 7:00 | 132 / 212 / 2:50 | 395 / 636 / 8:50 | 268 / 431 / 5:40 | 272 / 438 / 5:40 | 308 / 496 / 6:00 | 281 / 452 / 5:40 | 266 / 428 / 4:50 | 148 / 238 / 3:10 | 253 / 407 / 5:20 | 329 / 529 / 6:20 | 364 / 586 / 6:30 | 110 / 177 / 2:20 | 166 / 267 / 3:20 | 358 / 576 / 6:30 | 114 / 183 / 2:20 | 57 / 92 / 1:50 | 325 / 523 / 6:00 | 241 / 388 / 4:20 | 299 / 481 / 5:30 | 352 / 567 / 6:30 | 201 / 323 / 4:00 | 347 / 558 / 6:30 | 129 / 208 / 2:40 | 207 / 333 / 4:10 | 64 / 103 / 1:50 | 149 / 240 / 3:00 | 257 / 414 / 5:20 | 235 / 378 / 4:50 | 286 / 460 / 5:40 |
| Norwich | | | | | | | | | | | | 264 / 425 / 5:20 | 185 / 298 / 4:30 | 220 / 354 / 4:40 | 105 / 169 / 2:50 | 119 / 192 / 3:20 | 176 / 283 / 3:50 | 421 / 678 / 8:40 | 582 / 937 / 11:50 | 149 / 240 / 4:00 | 654 / 1053 / 13:30 | 529 / 852 / 10:30 | 311 / 501 / 6:40 | 73 / 117 / 2:00 | 20 / 32 / 0:40 | 204 / 328 / 4:10 | 385 / 620 / 9:00 | 504 / 811 / 10:00 | 343 / 552 / 7:00 | 308 / 496 / 6:00 | 366 / 589 / 7:00 | 422 / 679 / 8:00 | 174 / 280 / 3:50 | 147 / 237 / 3:20 | 289 / 465 / 5:40 | 262 / 422 / 5:20 | 62 / 100 / 1:50 | 252 / 406 / 5:10 | 175 / 282 / 4:00 | 457 / 735 / 8:40 | 214 / 344 / 4:40 | 232 / 373 / 4:50 | 166 / 267 / 3:50 | 328 / 528 / 6:40 | 382 / 615 / 7:20 | 276 / 444 / 6:00 | 496 / 798 / 9:40 | 114 / 183 / 3:30 |
| Nottingham | | | | | | | | | | | 130 / 209 / 3:40 | 157 / 253 / 3:10 | 73 / 118 / 1:40 | 98 / 158 / 2:10 | 35 / 56 / 1:10 | 25 / 40 / 0:50 | 70 / 113 / 1:40 | 345 / 555 / 7:00 | 479 / 771 / 9:40 | 90 / 145 / 2:00 | 557 / 896 / 11:30 | 430 / 692 / 8:20 | 185 / 298 / 4:00 | 150 / 241 / 3:20 | 153 / 246 / 3:30 | 110 / 177 / 2:10 | 293 / 472 / 5:30 | 401 / 646 / 7:50 | 220 / 354 / 4:30 | 221 / 356 / 4:10 | 262 / 422 / 4:50 | 328 / 528 / 6:00 | 205 / 330 / 3:50 | 43 / 69 / 1:10 | 194 / 312 / 3:40 | 172 / 277 / 3:20 | 83 / 134 / 1:40 | 145 / 233 / 3:00 | 193 / 311 / 3:50 | 353 / 568 / 6:30 | 183 / 295 / 3:40 | 111 / 179 / 2:20 | 50 / 80 / 1:20 | 221 / 356 / 4:30 | 274 / 441 / 5:10 | 164 / 264 / 3:40 | 393 / 633 / 7:30 | 122 / 196 / 2:40 |
| Oban | | | | | | | | | | 390 / 628 / 7:30 | 492 / 792 / 9:40 | 233 / 375 / 4:50 | 307 / 494 / 6:00 | 308 / 496 / 6:10 | 387 / 623 / 7:30 | 419 / 674 / 7:50 | 307 / 494 / 6:00 | 665 / 1070 / 12:50 | 128 / 206 / 3:10 | 346 / 557 / 6:40 | 244 / 393 / 6:10 | 117 / 188 / 3:00 | 427 / 687 / 8:30 | 524 / 843 / 10:00 | 515 / 829 / 10:00 | 441 / 710 / 8:10 | 92 / 148 / 2:30 | 49 / 79 / 1:20 | 481 / 774 / 9:10 | 549 / 884 / 10:00 | 123 / 198 / 3:00 | 117 / 188 / 2:50 | 585 / 942 / 10:40 | 346 / 557 / 6:40 | 188 / 303 / 4:00 | 477 / 768 / 9:00 | 468 / 753 / 8:40 | 465 / 748 / 8:40 | 565 / 910 / 10:30 | 141 / 227 / 3:30 | 530 / 853 / 9:50 | 285 / 459 / 5:40 | 384 / 618 / 7:30 | 180 / 290 / 4:20 | 94 / 151 / 2:20 | 412 / 663 / 8:10 | 178 / 286 / 4:20 | 499 / 803 / 9:30 |
| Oxford | | | | | | | | | 462 / 744 / 8:30 | 109 / 175 / 2:10 | 145 / 233 / 3:50 | 260 / 418 / 4:50 | 144 / 232 / 2:50 | 172 / 277 / 3:20 | 137 / 221 / 2:50 | 73 / 117 / 1:30 | 168 / 270 / 3:10 | 274 / 441 / 5:40 | 550 / 885 / 10:40 | 192 / 309 / 3:40 | 656 / 1056 / 13:00 | 532 / 856 / 10:00 | 238 / 383 / 4:50 | 145 / 233 / 3:10 | 200 / 322 / 4:20 | 52 / 84 / 1:30 | 356 / 573 / 6:30 | 472 / 760 / 9:00 | 205 / 330 / 4:10 | 156 / 251 / 3:00 | 372 / 599 / 6:40 | 433 / 697 / 7:40 | 141 / 227 / 2:50 | 145 / 233 / 2:40 | 260 / 418 / 4:40 | 108 / 174 / 2:20 | 83 / 134 / 1:40 | 74 / 119 / 1:40 | 108 / 174 / 2:20 | 465 / 749 / 8:20 | 90 / 145 / 2:00 | 187 / 301 / 3:30 | 64 / 103 / 1:30 | 324 / 521 / 6:10 | 353 / 568 / 6:20 | 154 / 248 / 3:20 | 483 / 777 / 8:50 | 57 / 92 / 1:40 |
| Plymouth | | | | | | | | 199 / 320 / 4:00 | 587 / 945 / 11:00 | 267 / 430 / 5:10 | 343 / 552 / 7:00 | 410 / 660 / 7:40 | 283 / 455 / 5:30 | 283 / 455 / 5:30 | 293 / 472 / 5:50 | 242 / 389 / 4:40 | 316 / 509 / 6:00 | 89 / 143 / 2:20 | 674 / 1085 / 13:10 | 355 / 571 / 6:40 | 790 / 1271 / 15:40 | 664 / 1069 / 12:30 | 328 / 528 / 6:40 | 309 / 497 / 6:10 | 365 / 588 / 7:20 | 157 / 253 / 3:20 | 495 / 797 / 9:10 | 595 / 958 / 11:20 | 264 / 425 / 5:30 | 46 / 74 / 1:30 | 496 / 798 / 9:00 | 552 / 888 / 10:00 | 300 / 483 / 5:50 | 297 / 478 / 5:40 | 399 / 642 / 7:20 | 167 / 269 / 3:40 | 293 / 472 / 5:30 | 122 / 196 / 2:50 | 224 / 361 / 6:00 | 587 / 945 / 10:40 | 128 / 206 / 3:30 | 328 / 528 / 6:10 | 203 / 327 / 4:20 | 474 / 763 / 9:00 | 492 / 792 / 9:00 | 237 / 382 / 5:10 | 615 / 990 / 11:20 | 218 / 351 / 4:40 |
| Portsmouth | | | | | | | 176 / 283 / 4:50 | 77 / 124 / 1:40 | 545 / 877 / 10:00 | 191 / 307 / 3:40 | 207 / 333 / 4:20 | 337 / 542 / 6:10 | 236 / 380 / 4:30 | 254 / 409 / 4:50 | 201 / 323 / 4:00 | 162 / 261 / 3:10 | 257 / 414 / 4:50 | 259 / 417 / 5:40 | 633 / 1019 / 12:10 | 269 / 433 / 5:00 | 737 / 1186 / 14:30 | 613 / 987 / 11:30 | 311 / 501 / 6:10 | 166 / 267 / 3:40 | 221 / 356 / 4:40 | 119 / 192 / 3:00 | 448 / 721 / 8:10 | 555 / 893 / 10:20 | 251 / 404 / 5:00 | 135 / 217 / 2:40 | 453 / 729 / 8:10 | 514 / 827 / 9:00 | 130 / 209 / 2:50 | 234 / 377 / 4:20 | 348 / 560 / 6:10 | 142 / 229 / 3:00 | 144 / 232 / 2:50 | 97 / 156 / 2:10 | 48 / 77 / 1:40 | 547 / 881 / 9:50 | 52 / 84 / 1:30 | 264 / 425 / 4:50 | 141 / 227 / 3:00 | 401 / 645 / 7:30 | 430 / 692 / 7:40 | 222 / 357 / 4:40 | 560 / 901 / 10:10 | 70 / 113 / 2:00 |
| Sheffield | | | | | | 230 / 370 / 4:20 | 283 / 455 / 5:30 | 135 / 217 / 2:40 | 339 / 546 / 6:30 | 37 / 60 / 1:00 | 146 / 235 / 3:20 | 125 / 201 / 2:40 | 38 / 61 / 1:00 | 72 / 116 / 1:40 | 46 / 74 / 1:20 | 62 / 100 / 1:20 | 33 / 53 / 1:00 | 361 / 581 / 7:10 | 427 / 687 / 8:40 | 65 / 105 / 1:30 | 520 / 837 / 10:50 | 393 / 632 / 7:40 | 168 / 270 / 3:40 | 187 / 301 / 3:50 | 166 / 267 / 3:40 | 126 / 203 / 2:20 | 248 / 399 / 4:40 | 348 / 560 / 6:50 | 215 / 346 / 4:20 | 237 / 381 / 4:20 | 235 / 378 / 4:20 | 291 / 468 / 5:20 | 245 / 394 / 4:30 | 18 / 29 / 0:40 | 152 / 245 / 3:00 | 194 / 312 / 3:40 | 120 / 193 / 2:20 | 161 / 259 / 3:10 | 226 / 364 / 4:20 | 320 / 515 / 6:00 | 216 / 348 / 4:10 | 86 / 138 / 1:50 | 76 / 122 / 1:50 | 190 / 306 / 4:00 | 245 / 394 / 4:30 | 159 / 256 / 3:30 | 360 / 579 / 6:50 | 159 / 256 / 3:20 |
| Shrewsbury | | | | | 82 / 132 / 2:10 | 207 / 333 / 3:50 | 225 / 362 / 4:40 | 106 / 171 / 2:10 | 364 / 586 / 7:00 | 93 / 150 / 2:00 | 205 / 330 / 4:20 | 201 / 323 / 3:50 | 69 / 111 / 1:40 | 58 / 93 / 1:50 | 133 / 214 / 2:50 | 84 / 135 / 1:40 | 109 / 175 / 2:20 | 303 / 488 / 6:10 | 451 / 726 / 9:00 | 169 / 272 / 3:10 | 567 / 912 / 11:30 | 438 / 705 / 8:20 | 113 / 182 / 2:50 | 240 / 386 / 4:40 | 225 / 362 / 4:40 | 77 / 124 / 1:30 | 272 / 438 / 5:00 | 382 / 615 / 7:20 | 145 / 233 / 3:10 | 179 / 288 / 3:20 | 274 / 441 / 5:00 | 330 / 531 / 6:00 | 251 / 404 / 4:30 | 109 / 175 / 2:10 | 176 / 283 / 3:20 | 111 / 179 / 2:20 | 159 / 256 / 3:00 | 103 / 166 / 2:50 | 226 / 364 / 4:20 | 371 / 597 / 6:50 | 185 / 298 / 3:40 | 98 / 158 / 2:00 | 45 / 72 / 1:20 | 265 / 426 / 5:10 | 269 / 433 / 5:00 | 77 / 124 / 2:10 | 399 / 642 / 7:30 | 160 / 258 / 3:20 |
| Southampton | | | | 185 / 298 / 4:10 | 199 / 320 / 3:40 | 21 / 34 / 0:50 | 151 / 243 / 4:10 | 64 / 103 / 1:30 | 530 / 853 / 9:40 | 176 / 283 / 3:20 | 206 / 332 / 4:20 | 324 / 521 / 5:50 | 221 / 356 / 4:10 | 239 / 385 / 4:30 | 204 / 328 / 4:00 | 137 / 220 / 2:40 | 232 / 373 / 4:20 | 228 / 367 / 5:00 | 618 / 995 / 12:00 | 256 / 412 / 4:40 | 723 / 1164 / 14:10 | 598 / 963 / 11:10 | 293 / 472 / 5:50 | 164 / 264 / 3:30 | 220 / 354 / 4:40 | 105 / 169 / 2:40 | 433 / 697 / 7:40 | 541 / 871 / 10:00 | 233 / 375 / 4:40 | 105 / 169 / 3:00 | 438 / 705 / 7:50 | 500 / 805 / 8:50 | 143 / 230 / 2:50 | 209 / 336 / 3:50 | 324 / 521 / 5:50 | 121 / 195 / 2:30 | 148 / 238 / 2:50 | 76 / 122 / 2:20 | 61 / 98 / 1:50 | 532 / 856 / 9:30 | 31 / 50 / 1:00 | 251 / 404 / 4:40 | 128 / 206 / 2:40 | 388 / 624 / 7:10 | 417 / 671 / 7:30 | 201 / 323 / 4:10 | 547 / 880 / 10:00 | 77 / 124 / 2:00 |
| Stranraer | | | 445 / 716 / 8:20 | 277 / 446 / 5:30 | 263 / 423 / 5:20 | 461 / 742 / 8:40 | 500 / 805 / 9:40 | 379 / 610 / 7:10 | 148 / 238 / 3:40 | 290 / 467 / 5:50 | 403 / 649 / 8:10 | 158 / 254 / 3:40 | 220 / 354 / 4:40 | 221 / 356 / 4:40 | 298 / 480 / 6:00 | 330 / 531 / 6:20 | 220 / 354 / 4:40 | 585 / 942 / 11:30 | 263 / 423 / 6:30 | 259 / 417 / 5:20 | 379 / 610 / 9:00 | 262 / 422 / 6:00 | 338 / 544 / 7:00 | 410 / 660 / 8:10 | 426 / 686 / 8:40 | 343 / 552 / 6:30 | 84 / 135 / 2:30 | 195 / 314 / 4:50 | 392 / 631 / 7:50 | 454 / 731 / 8:30 | 124 / 200 / 3:00 | 167 / 269 / 3:40 | 496 / 798 / 9:10 | 257 / 414 / 5:10 | 101 / 163 / 2:40 | 390 / 628 / 7:30 | 379 / 610 / 7:10 | 378 / 608 / 7:20 | 475 / 765 / 9:00 | 194 / 312 / 4:20 | 444 / 715 / 8:30 | 188 / 303 / 4:00 | 297 / 478 / 6:00 | 170 / 274 / 4:10 | 51 / 82 / 1:20 | 325 / 523 / 6:50 | 228 / 367 / 5:10 | 402 / 647 / 7:50 |
| Swansea | | 417 / 671 / 7:50 | 161 / 259 / 3:00 | 118 / 190 / 2:20 | 217 / 349 / 4:00 | 182 / 293 / 3:30 | 206 / 332 / 4:10 | 141 / 227 / 2:40 | 506 / 815 / 9:20 | 192 / 309 / 3:40 | 301 / 485 / 6:00 | 347 / 559 / 6:20 | 187 / 301 / 3:30 | 195 / 314 / 3:40 | 233 / 375 / 4:30 | 177 / 285 / 3:20 | 248 / 399 / 4:40 | 285 / 459 / 6:00 | 594 / 956 / 11:30 | 264 / 425 / 4:50 | 696 / 1120 / 13:40 | 572 / 921 / 10:40 | 184 / 296 / 4:50 | 267 / 430 / 5:10 | 329 / 530 / 6:30 | 89 / 143 / 1:50 | 409 / 658 / 7:20 | 496 / 798 / 9:20 | 67 / 108 / 1:50 | 161 / 259 / 3:00 | 412 / 663 / 7:20 | 473 / 761 / 8:20 | 274 / 441 / 5:00 | 232 / 373 / 4:10 | 309 / 497 / 5:30 | 41 / 66 / 1:10 | 227 / 365 / 4:10 | 85 / 137 / 1:50 | 222 / 357 / 4:20 | 505 / 813 / 9:00 | 167 / 269 / 3:20 | 216 / 348 / 4:00 | 119 / 192 / 2:30 | 383 / 616 / 7:10 | 379 / 610 / 6:50 | 73 / 117 / 2:00 | 507 / 816 / 9:20 | 194 / 312 / 4:00 |
| York | 272 / 438 / 5:10 | 222 / 357 / 4:40 | 258 / 415 / 5:10 | 133 / 214 / 2:40 | 52 / 84 / 1:20 | 278 / 448 / 5:10 | 333 / 536 / 6:20 | 181 / 291 / 3:20 | 309 / 497 / 6:00 | 77 / 124 / 1:40 | 181 / 291 / 4:20 | 84 / 135 / 2:20 | 64 / 103 / 1:30 | 99 / 159 / 2:10 | 75 / 121 / 1:50 | 108 / 174 / 2:10 | 24 / 39 / 0:50 | 411 / 661 / 8:00 | 407 / 655 / 8:20 | 37 / 60 / 1:10 | 479 / 771 / 10:10 | 352 / 566 / 7:00 | 204 / 328 / 4:20 | 228 / 367 / 4:40 | 201 / 323 / 4:20 | 189 / 304 / 3:30 | 217 / 349 / 4:10 | 330 / 531 / 6:30 | 261 / 420 / 5:10 | 287 / 462 / 5:10 | 194 / 312 / 3:40 | 250 / 402 / 4:40 | 282 / 454 / 5:10 | 34 / 55 / 1:00 | 121 / 195 / 2:30 | 244 / 393 / 4:40 | 165 / 266 / 3:10 | 222 / 357 / 4:10 | 275 / 443 / 5:10 | 285 / 459 / 5:20 | 269 / 433 / 5:00 | 96 / 154 / 2:00 | 130 / 209 / 2:40 | 148 / 238 / 3:10 | 214 / 344 / 4:00 | 195 / 314 / 4:10 | 319 / 513 / 6:10 | 207 / 333 / 4:10 |

Supporting

THINK!

**Travel safe – Don't drive tired**

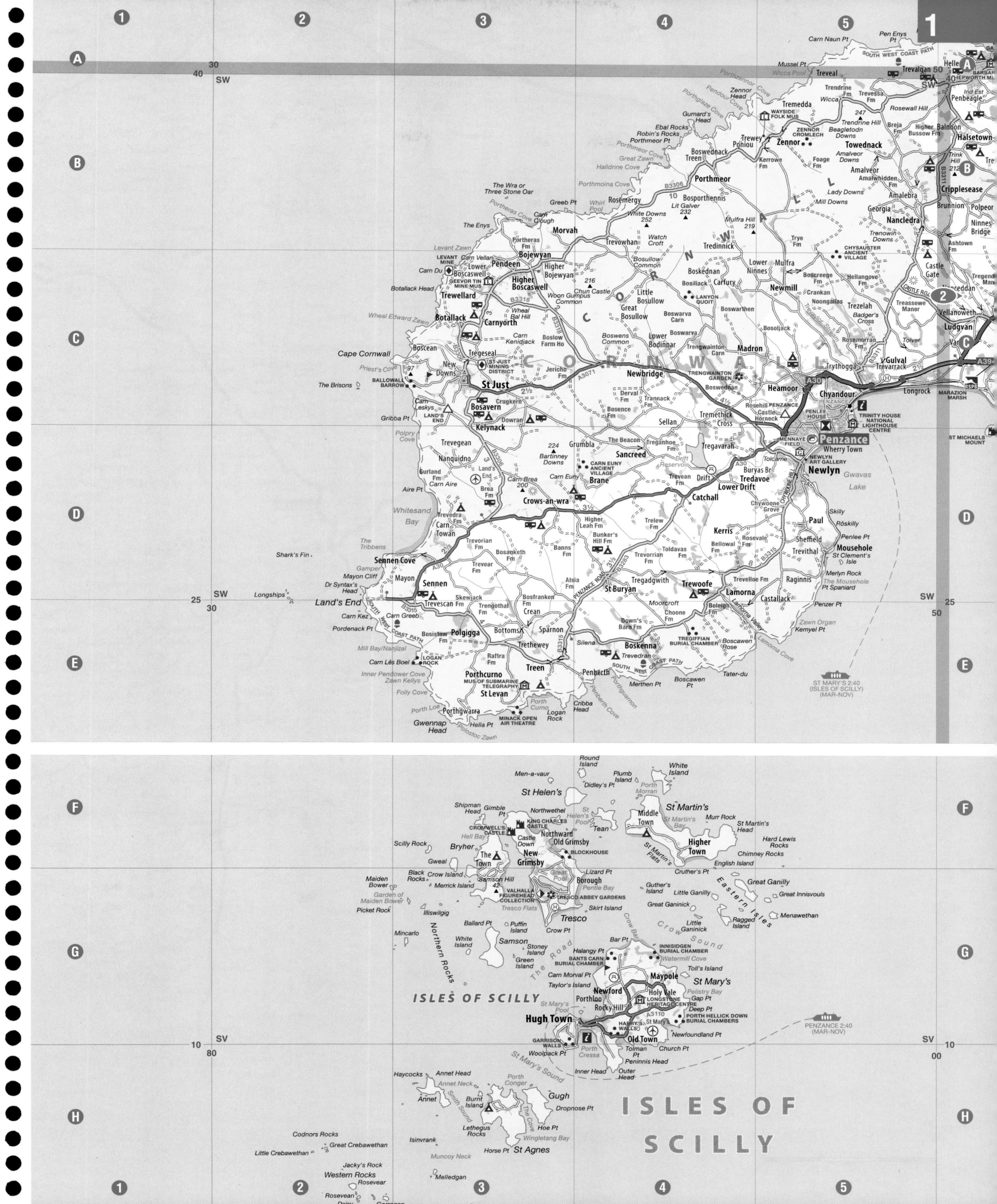

1
2
3
4
5
A
B
C
D
E
F
G
H
30
40
SW
25
50
Carn Naun Pt
Pen Enys Pt
SOUTH WEST COAST PATH
Mussel Pt
Wicca Pool
Treveal
Trevalgan
Helle
Porthzennor Cove
Zennor Head
Pendour Cove
Porthglaze Cove
Tremedda
Trendrine Fm
Trevessa Fm
Wicca
Gurnard's Head
WAYSIDE FOLK MUS
ZENNOR CROMLECH
Beagletodn Downs
Tredrine Hill
Rosewall Hill
Ind Est
Penbeagle
Ebal Rocks
Robin's Rocks
Porthmeor Pt
Trewey
Poniou
Zennor
Towednack
Breja Fm
Higher Bussow Fm
Balnoon
Halsetown
Porthmeor Cove
Great Zawn
Halldrine Cove
Boswednack
Treen
Kerrowe Fm
Foage Fm
Amalveor Downs
Amalveor
Amalwhidden Fm
Trink Hill
Porthmoina Cove
B3306
Porthmeor
Bosporthennis
Lit Galver
Lady Downs
Mill Downs
Amalebra
Cripplesease
The Wra or Three Stone Oar
Greeb Pt
Whirl Pool
Rosemergy
White Downs
Brunnion
Polpeor
Portheras Cove
Carn Clough
Mulfra Hill
Georgia
Nancledra
Ninnes Bridge
The Enys
Portheras Fm
Morvah
Watch Croft
Trye Fm
Trenowin Downs
Levant Zawn
Trevowhan
Tredinnick
CHYSAUSTER ANCIENT VILLAGE
Ashtown Fm
LEVANT MINE
Carn Vellan
Bojewyan
Pendeen
Lower Ninnes
Mulfra
Carn Du
Lower Boscaswell
Higher Bojewyan
Bosullow Common
Boskednan
Boscreege Fm
Hellangove Fm
Castle Gate
Botallack Head
GEEVOR TIN MINE MUS
Higher Boscaswell
Chun Castle
Bosiliack
Carfury
Newmill
Crankan
Nanceddan
Trewellard
Woon Gumpus Common
Little Bosullow
LANYON QUOIT
Noongallas
Trezelah
Treassowe Manor
Wheal Bal Hill
B3318
Great Bosullow
Boswarva Carn
Boswarthen
Badger's Cross
Vellanoweth
Wheal Edward Zawn
Botallack
Carnyorth
Ludgvan
Carn Kenidjack
Boslow Farm Ho
Boswens Common
Lower Bodinnar
Boswarva
Bosoljack
Rosemorran Fm
Tolver
Boscean
Tregeseal
Trengwainton Carn
Madron
Cape Cornwall
Priest's Cove
ST JUST MINING DISTRICT
C O R N W A L L
Gulval
Trevarrack
Trythogga
A39
The Brisons
BALLOWALL BARROW
New Downs
St Just
Jericho Fm
A3071
Newbridge
TRENGWAINTON GARDEN
Boswednan
A30
Heamoor
Chyandour
Longrock
MARAZION MARSH
Carn Leskys
Bosavern
Grugkern
Derval Fm
Trannack Fm
Rosehill
Castle Horneck
PENZANCE
PENLEE HOUSE
TRINITY HOUSE NATIONAL LIGHTHOUSE CENTRE
Gribba Pt
LAND'S END
Dowran
Bosence Fm
Tremethick Cross
Kelynack
Sellan
MENNAYE FIELD
Penzance
ST MICHAELS MOUNT
Polpry Cove
Trevegean
Grumbla
The Beacon
Treganhoe Fm
Tregavarah
Wherry Town
Bartinney Downs
Sancreed
Drift Reservoir
Tolcarne
NEWLYN ART GALLERY
Nanquidno
Land's End
CARN EUNY ANCIENT VILLAGE
Gwavas Lake
Gurland Fm
Carn Aire
Carn Brea
Carn Euny
Trevean Fm
Drift
Buryas Br
Tredavoe
Newlyn
Brane
Lower Drift
Aire Pt
Brea Fm
Chywoone Grove
Skilly
Crows-an-wra
Catchall
Whitesand Bay
Trevedra Fm
Paul
Rôskilly
Carn Towan
Higher Leah Fm
Trelew Fm
Kerris
Pemlee Pt
The Tribbens
Trevorian Fm
Bosanketh Fm
Bunker's Hill Fm
Sheffield
Mousehole
Banns Fm
Rosevale Fm
Bellowal Fm
Trevithal
St Clement's Isle
Shark's Fin
Sennen Cove
Trevear Fm
Trevorrian Fm
Toldavas Fm
Gamper
Mayon Cliff
Mayon
A30
Tregadgwith
Trevelloe Fm
Merlyn Rock
The Mousehole
Pt Spaniard
Dr Syntax's Head
Sennen
Alsia Fm
PENZANCE ROAD
B3283
St Buryan
Trewoofe
Lamorna
Raginnis
Longships
Land's End
Trevescan Fm
Skewjack
Bosfranken Fm
Crean
Moorcroft
Castallack
Trengothal Fm
Boleigh Fm
Penzer Pt
Carn Kez
Carn Greeb
Choone Fm
Pordenack Pt
SOUTH WEST COAST PATH
Bosistow Fm
Polgigga
Bottoms
Sparnon
Down's Barn Fm
Lamorna Valley
Zawn Organ
Kemyel Pt
Mill Bay/Nanjizal
Trethewey
B3315
Silena
Boskenna
Trevedran
TREGIFFIAN BURIAL CHAMBER
Boscawen Rose
Lamorna Cove
Carn Les Boel
LOGAN ROCK
Raftra Fm
Treen
Inner Pendower Cove
Zawn Kellys
Porthcurno
MUS OF SUBMARINE TELEGRAPHY
Penberth
SOUTH WEST COAST PATH
Merthen Pt
Boscawen Pt
Tater-du
ST MARY'S 2:40 (ISLES OF SCILLY) (MAR-NOV)
Folly Cove
St Levan
Porth Curno
Logan Rock
Cribba Head
Penberth Cove
Porthguarnon
Porth Loe
Porthgwarra
MINACK OPEN AIR THEATRE
Gwennap Head
Hella Pt
Polostoc Zawn
Round Island
Men-a-vaur
Plumb Island
White Island
Didley's Pt
St Helen's
Porth Morran
Shipman Head
Gimble Pt
Northwethel
St Helen's Pool
Middle Town
St Martin's
Murr Rock
St Martin's Head
CROMWELL'S CASTLE
KING CHARLES CASTLE
Tean
St Martin's Bay
Hell Bay
Castle Down
Northward
Old Grimsby
Higher Town
Hard Lewis Rocks
Scilly Rock
Bryher
St Martin's Flats
Chimney Rocks
The Town
New Grimsby
BLOCKHOUSE
Gweal
English Island
Maiden Bower
Black Rocks
Crow Island
Samson Hill
Lizard Pt
Great Pool
Borough
Pentle Bay
Cruther's Pt
Guther's Island
Great Ganilly
Merrick Island
VALHALLA FIGUREHEAD COLLECTION
TRESCO ABBEY GARDENS
Little Ganilly
Great Innisvouls
Garden of Maiden Bower
Eastern Isles
Picket Rock
Tresco Flats
Skirt Island
Great Ganinick
Menawethan
Illiswilgig
Tresco
Ragged Island
Ballard Pt
Puffin Island
Crow Pt
Little Ganinick
Mincarlo
Northern Rocks
Crow Sound
White Island
Samson
Stoney Island
Bar Pt
Halangy Pt
INNISIDGEN BURIAL CHAMBER
BANTS CARN BURIAL CHAMBER
Watermill Cove
Green Island
The Road
Toll's Island
Carn Morval Pt
Maypole
St Mary's
Taylor's Island
ISLES OF SCILLY
Newford
Holy Vale
Pelistry Bay
St Mary's Pool
Porthloo
Rocky Hill
LONGSTONE HERITAGE CENTRE
Gap Pt
Deep Pt
Hugh Town
PORTH HELLICK DOWN BURIAL CHAMBERS
A3110
HARRY'S WALLS
St Mary's
PENZANCE 2:40 (MAR-NOV)
GARRISON WALLS
Old Town
Newfoundland Pt
SV
10
80
00
Woolpack Pt
Porth Cressa
Tolman Pt
Church Pt
Peninnis Head
St Mary's Sound
Inner Head
Outer Head
Haycocks
Annet Head
Porth Conger
Annet Neck
Gugh
Annet
Burnt Island
Smith Sound
Dropnose Pt
ISLES OF SCILLY
The Cove
Hoe Pt
Lethegus Rocks
Wingletang Bay
Codnors Rocks
Isinvrank
Little Crebawethan
Great Crebawethan
Horse Pt
St Agnes
Muncoy Neck
Jacky's Rock
Western Rocks
Melledgan
Rosevear
Rosevean
Daisy
Gorregan

2
St Ives
ST IVES BAY
Carbis Bay
Halsetown
Lelant
Hayle
Copperhouse
Phillack
Gwithian
Camborne
Tuckingmill
Pool
Carnbrea
Carnkie
Lanner
Gwennap
Four Lanes
Troon
Barripper
Roseworthy
Connor Downs
Kehelland
Nancemellin
Roscroggan
Treswithian
Praze-an-Beeble
Crowan
Leedstown
Fraddam
St Erth
St Erth Praze
Canon's Town
Crowlas
Ludgvan
Nancledra
Cripplesease
Townshend
Godolphin Cross
Drym
Releath
Nancegollan
Wendron
Porkellis
Stithians
Penmarth
Carnkie
Rame
Longdowns
Constantine
Gweek
Helston
Crowntown
Sithney
Breage
Ashton
Germoe
Praa Sands
Rinsey
Porthleven
Marazion
Perranuthnoe
Goldsithney
St Hilary
Relubbus
Trescowe
Mawgan
Garras
St Martin
Gunwalloe
Berepper
Cury
Cross Lanes
Mullion
Mullion Cove
Penhale
Goonhilly Downs
Traboe
Kuggar
Ruan Minor
St Ruan
Cadgwith
Grade
Lizard
Lizard Point
Landewednack
Church Cove
Predannack Wollas
MOUNT'S BAY
C O R N W A L L
A30
A394
A3083
B3280
B3302
B3304
B3297
B3293
B3296
SW
0 1 2 3 miles
0 1 2 3 4 5 km

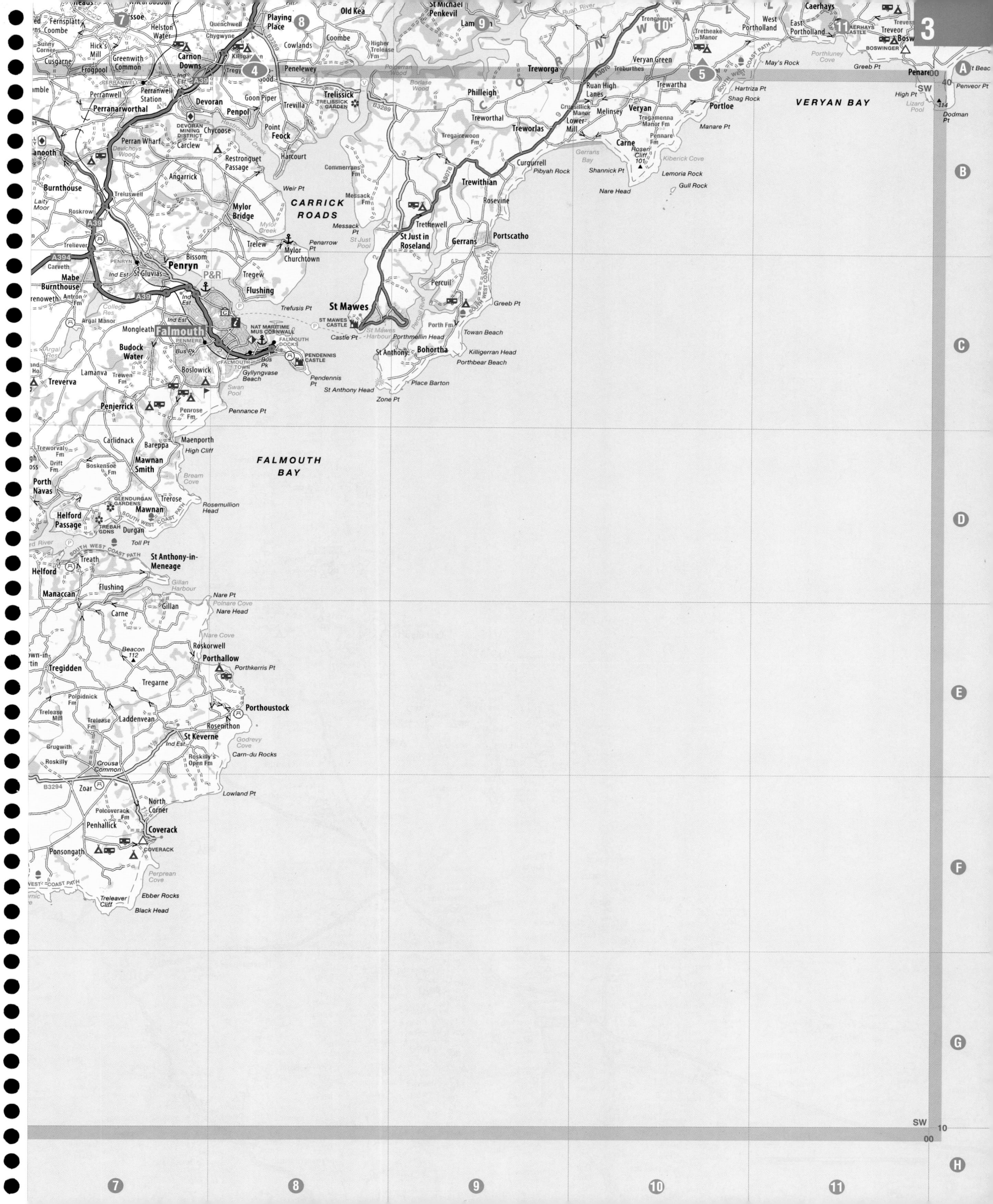
Fernsplatt
Coombe
Helston Water
Quenchwell
Chygwyne
Playing Place
Old Kea
St Michael Penkevil
Lamorran
Ruan River
Trengrouse
Tretheake Manor
West Portholland
East Portholland
Caerhays
Treveor
Sunny Corner
Hick's Mill
Cusgarne
Greenwith Common
Frogpool
Carnon Downs
Killiganoon
Cowlands
Coombe
Higher Trelease Fm
Penelewey
Polgerran Wood
Borlase Wood
Treworga
Veryan Green
Treburthes
May's Rock
Portholland Cove
Greeb Pt
Penare
Penveor Pt
Perranwell
Perranwell Station
Perranarworthal
Devoran
Goon Piper
Penpol
Trevilla
Trelissick
TRELISSICK GARDEN
Philleigh
Ruan High Lanes
Trewartha
Hartriza Pt
Shag Rock
VERYAN BAY
High Pt
Lizard Pool
Dodman Pt
DEVORAN MINING DISTRICT
Chycoose
Point
Feock
Restronguet Creek
Treworthal
Treworlas
Crugsillick Manor
Lower Mill
Melinsey
Veryan
Tregamenna Manor Fm
Portloe
Manare Pt
Perran Wharf
Devichoys Wood
Carclew
Tregairewoon Fm
Carne
Pennare Fm
Restronguet Passage
Harcourt
Commerrans Fm
Curgurrell
Pibyah Rock
Gerrans Bay
Rosen Cliff
Kiberick Cove
Shannick Pt
Lemoria Rock
Gull Rock
Nare Head
Burnthouse
Angarrick
Weir Pt
CARRICK ROADS
Messack Fm
Trewithian
Rosevine
Laity Moor
Treluswell
Roskrow
Mylor Bridge
Mylor Creek
Messack Pt
Tretheweli
St Just in Roseland
Gerrans
Portscatho
St Just Pool
Penarrow Pt
Treliever
Trelew
Mylor Churchtown
Bissom
Penryn
Carveth
St Gluvias
Ind Est
Tregew
Mabe Burnthouse
Percuil
Antron Fm
Flushing
Trefusis Pt
St Mawes
Greeb Pt
College Res
Argal Manor
Ind Est
ST MAWES CASTLE
Porth Fm
Towan Beach
Mongleath
Falmouth
NAT MARITIME MUS CORNWALL
Castle Pt
St Mawes Harbour
Porthmellin Head
FALMOUTH DOCKS
Budock Water
PENMERE
Bus Pk
PENDENNIS CASTLE
St Anthony
Bohortha
Killigerran Head
Porthbear Beach
Lamanva
Boslowick
FALMOUTH TOWN
Gyllyngvase Beach
Pendennis Pt
Treverva
Trewen Fm
St Anthony Head
Place Barton
Zone Pt
Swan Pool
Penjerrick
Penrose Fm
Pennance Pt
Carlidnack
Bareppa
Maenporth
High Cliff
Treworval Fm
Drift Fm
Boskensoe Fm
Mawnan Smith
FALMOUTH BAY
Bream Cove
Porth Navas
GLENDURGAN GARDENS
Trerose
Mawnan
Rosemullion Head
Helford Passage
TREBAH GDNS
Durgan
Toll Pt
SOUTH WEST COAST PATH
Treath
St Anthony-in-Meneage
Helford
Flushing
Gillan Harbour
Manaccan
Nare Pt
Polnare Cove
Gillan
Nare Head
Carne
Nare Cove
Beacon 112
Roskorwell
Porthallow
Porthkerris Pt
Tregidden
Tregarne
Polpidnick
Trelease Mill
Trelease Fm
Laddenvean
Porthoustock
Rosenithon
St Keverne
Ind Est
Godrevy Cove
Grugwith
Roskilly's Open Fm
Carn-du Rocks
Roskilly
Crousa Common
B3294
Zoar
Lowland Pt
North Corner
Polcoverack Fm
Penhallick
Coverack
COVERACK
Ponsongath
Perprean Cove
Treleaver Cliff
Ebber Rocks
Black Head
A39
A394
A3078
B3289
SW
7
8
9
10
11
A
B
C
D
E
F
G
H

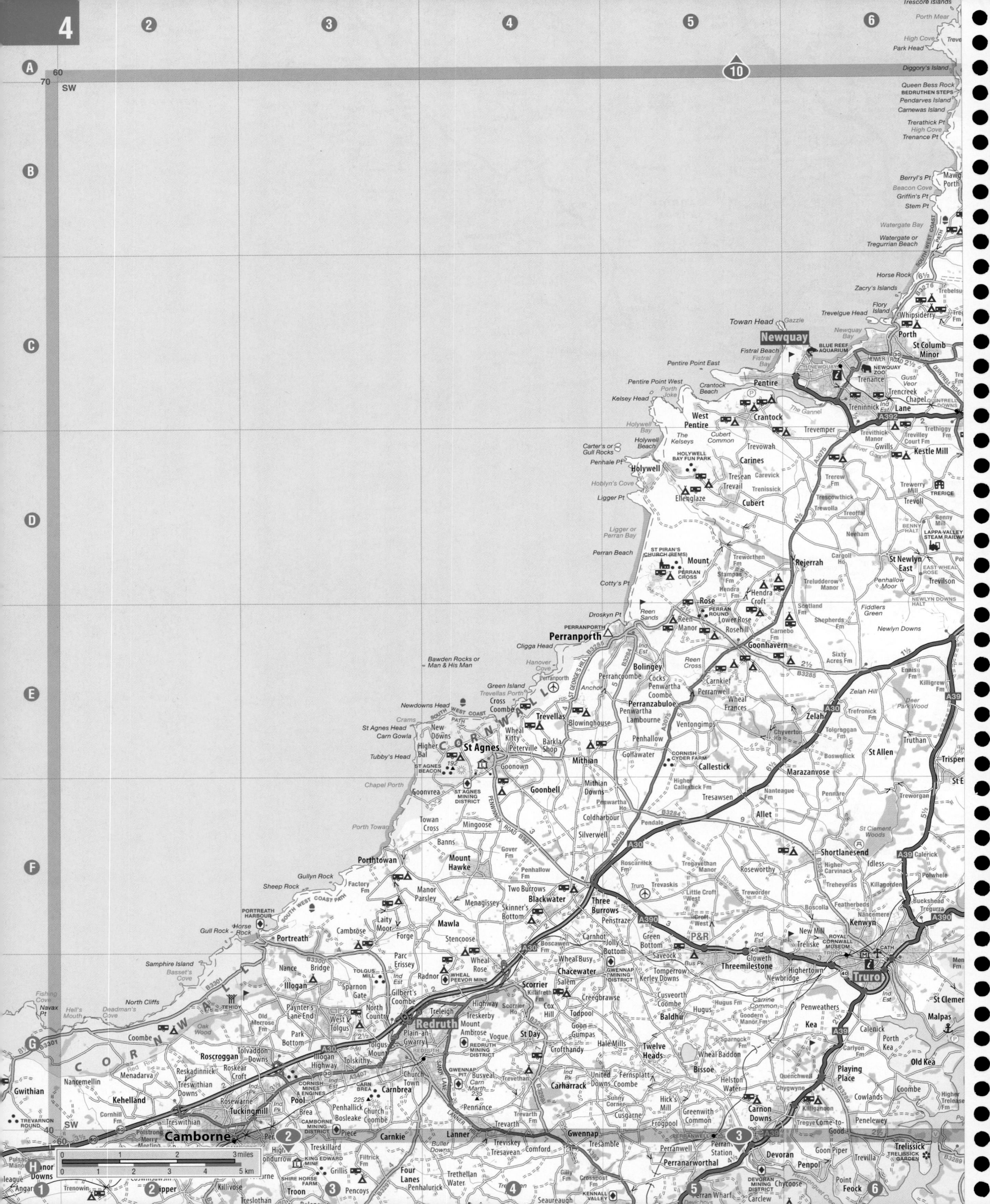
4
2
3
4
5
6
A
B
C
D
E
F
G
H
60
70
SW
10
Tresco Islands
Porth Mear
High Cove
Park Head
Diggory's Island
Queen Bess Rock
BEDRUTHEN STEPS
Pendarves Island
Carnewas Island
Trerathick Pt
High Cove
Trenance Pt
Berryl's Pt
Mawgan Porth
Beacon Cove
Griffin's Pt
Stem Pt
Watergate Bay
Watergate or Tregurrian Beach
SOUTH WEST COAST PATH
Horse Rock
Zacry's Islands
B3276
Flory Island
Trevelgue Head
Whipsiderry
Towan Head
Gazzle
Newquay Bay
Newquay
Porth
St Columb Minor
Fistral Beach
Fistral Bay
BLUE REEF AQUARIUM
NEWQUAY ZOO
HENVER ROAD
QUINTRELL ROAD
Pentire Point East
Pentire Point West
Pentire
Trenance
Gusti Veor
Trencreek
Chapel
QUINTRELL DOWNS
Kelsey Head
Porth Joke
Crantock Beach
Treninnick
Lane
A392
West Pentire
Crantock
The Gannel
Trevemper
Holywell Bay
Holywell Beach
The Kelseys
Cubert Common
Trevithick Manor
Treviiley Court Fm
Trethiggy Fm
Carter's or Gull Rocks
HOLYWELL BAY FUN PARK
Trevowah
Carines
A3075
Gwills
River Gannel
Kestle Mill
Penhale Pt
Holywell
Tresean
Carevick
Trevail
Trenissick
Trerew Fm
Trewerry Mill
TRERICE
Hoblyn's Cove
Ligger Pt
Ellenglaze
Cubert
Trescowthick
Trevolla
Trewolla
Treoffal
BENNY HALT
Benny Mill
LAPPA VALLEY STEAM RAILWAY
Ligger or Perran Bay
Perran Beach
Neeham
ST PIRAN'S CHURCH (REMS)
Mount
PERRAN CROSS
Treworthen Fm
Rejerrah
Cargoll Ho
St Newlyn East
EAST WHEAL ROSE
Stampas Fm
Hendra Fm
Hendra Croft
Treludderow Manor
Penhallow Moor
Trevilson
NEWLYN DOWNS HALT
Cotty's Pt
Reen Sands
Rose
PERRAN ROUND
Scotland Ho
Fiddlers Green
Droskyn Pt
Reen Manor
Lower Rose
Rosehill
Shepherds Fm
Newlyn Downs
PERRANPORTH HARBOUR
Perranporth
Carnebo Fm
Goonhavern
Cligga Head
Ind Est
Bawden Rocks or Man & His Man
Hanover Cove
B3285
ST GEORGE'S HILL
Bolingey
Reen Cross
Sixty Acres Fm
Perranporth
Perrancoombe
Cocks
Penwartha Coombe
Carnkief
Perranwell
Ennis Fm
Killigrew Fm
Green Island
Trevellas Porth
Anchor
Wheal Frances
Zelah Hill
Newdowns Head
Cross Coombe
SOUTH WEST COAST PATH
Trevellas
Blowinghouse
Perranzabuloe
Penwartha Lambourne
Deer Park Wood
Trefronick Fm
A39
Crams
St Agnes Head
Carn Gowla
New Downs
Wheal Kitty
Barkla Shop
Ventongimps
Zelah
Chyverton Ho
Tolgroggan Fm
Truthan
CORNWALL
Higher Bal
St Agnes
Peterville
Penhallow
Tubby's Head
ST AGNES BEACON
Goonown
Mithian
Gollawater
CORNISH CYDER FARM
Callestick
St Allen
Boswellick
Trispen
Chapel Porth
Goonvrea
ST AGNES MINING DISTRICT
PENWINNICK ROAD
Goonbell
Mithian Downs
Higher Callestick Fm
Marazanvose
Tresawsen
Nanteague Fm
Pennare
Treworgan
Penwartha Ho
Coldharbour
B3284
Allet
Porth Towan
Towan Cross
Mingoose
Pendale
St Clement Woods
Silverwell
A30
Banns
Gover Fm
Porthtowan
Mount Hawke
Roscarnick Fm
Tregavethan Manor
Shortlanesend
Calerick
Gullyn Rock
Penhallow Fm
Roseworthy
Higher Carvinack
Idless
Polwhele
Sheep Rock
Factory Fm
Two Burrows
Truro
Trevaskis
Little Croft West
Trehevaras
Killagorden
Manor Parsley
Blackwater
Three Burrows
Treworder
River Kenwyn
Buckshead
Tregurra
PORTREATH HARBOUR
Menagissey
Skinner's Bottom
Penstraze
A390
Croft West
Boscolla
Featherbeds
Nancemere
Laity Moor
Mawla
Kenwyn
Horse Rock
Gull Rock
Portreath
Cambrose
Forge
Stencoose
Boscawen Fm
Carnhot
Jolly's Bottom
Green Bottom
P&R
Ind Est
New Mill
Treliske
ROYAL CORNWALL MUSEUM
Samphire Island
Basset's Cove
B3300
Nance
Bridge
TOLGUS MILL
Parc Erissey
Wheal Rose
Wheal Busy
Chacewater
GWENNAP MINING DISTRICT
Saveock
Bus Pk
Gloweth
Threemilestone
Highertown
Truro
Illogan
Sparnon Gate
Radnor
WHEAL PEEVOR MINE
Scorrier
Killifreth Fm
Salem
Tomperrow
Kerley Downs
Newbridge
Fishing Cove
Navax Pt
Hell's Mouth
Deadman's Cove
North Cliffs
TEHIDY
Gilbert's Coombe
Creegbrawse
Cusgarne Coombe
Cusveorth Coombe
Carrine Common
Penweathers
Malpas
Old Merrose Fm
Paynter's Lane End
North Country
West Tolgus
Treleigh
Highway
Cox Hill
Todpool
Baldhu
Hugus
Hugus Fm
Goodern Manor Fm
Kea
St Clement
Oak Wood
Redruth
Mount Ambrose
Treskerby
Goon Gumpas
Coombe
Park Bottom
Plain-an-Gwarry
Vogue
St Day
Hale Mills
Twelve Heads
Sparnock Fm
Porth Kea
Calenick
B3301
Roscroggan
Tolvaddon Downs
Illogan Highway
Tolgus Mount
REDRUTH MINING DISTRICT
Crofthandy
Wheal Baddon
Carlyon Fm
Old Kea
C O R N W A L L
Menadarva
Reskadinnick
Roskear Croft
Tolskithy
A3047
Church Town
Bissoe
Quenchwell
Playing Place
Gwithian
Nancemellin
Treswithian Downs
CORNISH MINES & ENGINES
Carnbrea
GWENNAP PIT
Busveal
Carn Marth
Trevethan
United Downs
Fernsplatt Coombe
Carharrack
Helston Water
Chygwyne
Coombe
Kehelland
Rosewarne
Pool
CARN BREA
SANDY LANE
Carnon Downs
Killiganoon
Cowlands
Higher Trelease
Cornhill Fm
Tuckingmill
Brea
Penhallick
Bosleake
Church Coombe
Pennance
Sunny Corner
Hick's Mill
Greenwith Common
Trevarth Fm
Cusgarne
Frogpool
Tregye
Come-to-Good
Penelewey
TREVARNON ROUND
Treswithian
CAMBORNE MINING DISTRICT
Trevarth
Camborne
Piece
Carnkie
Lanner
Gwennap
Perranwell
Trelissick
TRELISSICK GARDEN
Treskillard
Buller Downs
Treviskey
Tresavean
Comford
Tresamble
Perranwell
Perran Station
Devoran
Goon Piper
Trevilla
B3289
Pulsack Manor
Downs
KING EDWARD MINE
Grillis
Filtrick Fm
Four Lanes
Trethellan Water
Perranarworthal
Penpol
Point
Feock
Angarrack
Trenowin
Killivose
SHIRE HORSE FARM
Troon
Pencoys
Penhalurick
Crosspost Fm
DEVORAN MINING DISTRICT
Chycoose
Treslothan
Seureaugh
KENNALL VALE
Carclew
0 1 2 3 miles
0 1 2 3 4 5 km

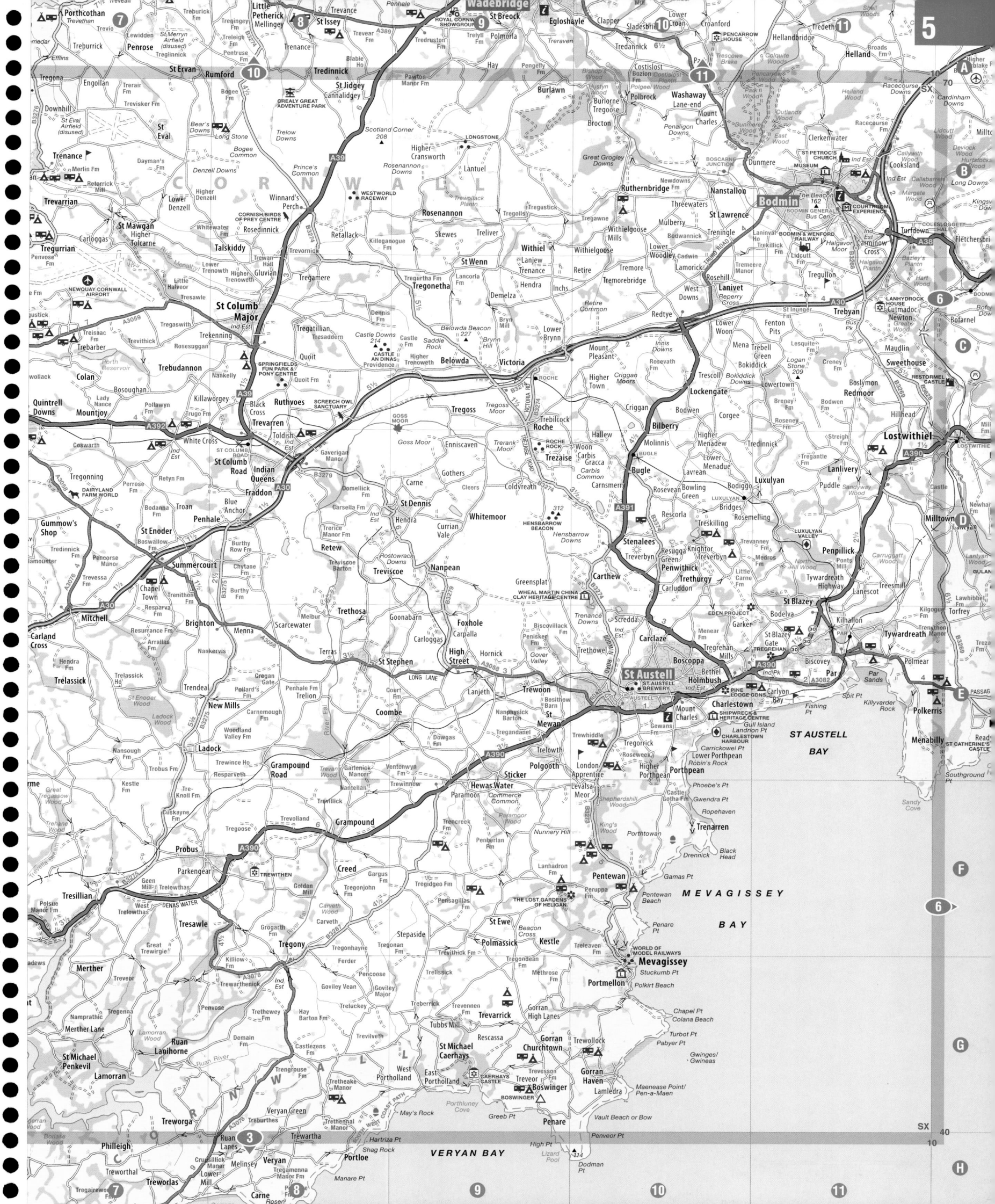
CORNWALL
Wadebridge
Bodmin
St Austell
Lostwithiel
St Columb Major
Mevagissey
ST AUSTELL BAY
MEVAGISSEY BAY
VERYAN BAY
Summercourt
Grampound
Tregony
Par
Charlestown
Gorran Haven
Veryan
Probus
Indian Queens
Roche
Bugle
St Dennis
Newquay Cornwall Airport
The Lost Gardens of Heligan
Eden Project

Cardinham Moor
Hard Head
Redhill Downs
Colliford Lake
Bunning's Park
Lord's Park Fm
Westerlake Fm
Sparretts Fm
THE HURLERS STONE CIRCLES
Marsh
Upton Cross
Dunslea
Ley Mill
Caradon Town
Browda
Trewoodle
Golberdon
Colvannick Tor
Carburrow Tor
Colliford Downs
Craddock Moor
Minions
CARADON MINING DISTRICT
Caradon Hill 369
Downgate
Tokenbury Manor
Scrawsdon Fm
Higher Carblake
Praze
Millpool
St Bellarmin's Tor
Maidenwell
Letter Moor
Redhill Downs
Draynes Common
Siblyback Lake
Crylla Fm
Gonamena
Pensilva
Racecourse Downs
Bodmin
Tragg
Warleggan Down
Whitebarrow Fm
Mutton's Downs
Wortha
Trekeivesteps
Commonmoor
Darite
Tokenbury Corner
Ind Est
Charaton Cross
Bicton Wood
Trevigro
Haye Fm
SX
Cardinham Downs
Fore Downs
Hobb's Hill
282
Northwood
Draynes
Carpuan
GOLITHA FALLS
KING DONIERT'S INSCRIBED STONE
Higher Tremarcoombe
Crow's Nest
Middlehill
Redland Fm
Bicton Manor
Appledore
Cardinham
Milltown
Treslea Downs
Pantersbridge
Warleggan
Berry Down
Tremaddock
Trenant
Treworrick
Trecarne
TRETHEVY QUOIT
St Cleer
Tremar
Newton Fm
Rosecraddoc Manor
Wayland
Woolston
Frogwell
Callywith Wood
Cooksland
Old Cardinham Castle
Mount
Lestow Fm
Goonzion Downs
St Neot
Treverbyn
Treverbyn Mill
CARNGLAZE SLATE CAVERNS
Lamprettten Ho
Gang
St Ive
Merryhue
Thornton
Parkfield
St Ive Cross
Dunnerdake Fm
Durnaford Fm
Long Downs
Higher Hill Fm
Welltown
Lower Hill
Trenay
Trethinnick Fm
Treleathick
Penhawger Fm
Trebeigh Wood
Ludcott Fm
Kingswood Downs
Pinsla Park
Tawna Downs
Tredinnick
Carnglaze Caverns
Ley
Woodland Fm
Ashford Br
Bokenna Wood
Treworgey Manor
Venton Veor
Woodhill Manor
Trengrove Fm
Venton Ho
Hendrabridge
Merrymeet
Westdown Wood
Hammett
Crendle Downs
Turfdown
Fletchersbridge
Holtroad Downs
Twelvewoods
East Tuelmenna
High Wood
Trembraze
Addington
Trehunsey Br
Quethiock
Bodmin Parkway
Drawbridge
Doublebois
A38
Old Park
Penkestle Downs
Hall Downs
Dobwalls
Ind Est
Liskeard
Stony Br
Pengover Green
Tregondale Fm
Hepwell Br
Goodmerry Fm
Leigh Fm
Moorswater
Looe Mills
Bus Pk
Bodithiel Fm
Middle Taphouse
Treburgie
Trelwith Ind Est
Lanhydrock House
Newbridge Wood
Tencreek Fm
Pounda
Trehunist
Trebrown
Cutmadoc
Newton
Bofarnel Downs
West Taphouse
Tithe Hall Fm
Gelly Fm
Trevelmond
Boduel
Camellion
Roseland
Trewint
Bofarnel
Bedwindle Fm
Cripstone Fm
East Taphouse
St Pinnock
COOMBE
LISKEARD
Tregrill
Lambest
Penpoll
Blunts
A390
Babbington
Connon
Cliver Wood
Scawns Fm
Lodge Hill
Menheniot
Fairy Cross
Trewindle
Braddock
Penfrane Manor
Trussel Br
Bodway
Doddycross
Pathada Wood
Sweethouse
RESTORMEL CASTLE
C O R N W A L L
Crickapit Mill
Trevillis Wood
Trethawle Fm
Lower Clicker
MENHENIOT
Coldrenick
Trehurst
Tilland
Molenick
Tideford Cross
Druid's Hill
Wilton Fm
West Trevillies
Lametton Mill
MUSIC MACHINES
Roselyon
St Keyne
Hillhead
Sandylake
Brooks
Beara Fm
Deerpark Wood
Woodlay Fm
Herodsfoot
Great Trethew
Horningtops
Berry Fm
Cutmere
Lostwithiel
Millham Fm
Beacon Hill
Coombe Fm
Trebarret
Polmartin Fm
Hollowpark
Canakey Wood
Lean Park Fm
Trebrownbridge Wood
Catchfrench Manor
Budge's Shop
Kernow Mill
Tideford
Bethany
LOSTWITHIEL
Bridgend
Polpiece
208
Bury Down
Trewidland
Fursdon
Bylane End
Bawdoe Fm
Couch's Mill
Netherton
Black Down
Windsor Wood
CAUSELAND
Landlooe Br
Pensipple
Castle
Tawell Fm
Botallick
Abovetown
Tremadart Wood
Landare Fm
Churchbridge
Polvean Cross
Polvean Wood
Duloe
Lower Trenode
Wilton Fm
Trerulefoot
Bake Manor
Newham Fm
St Winnow
Winnick
Bocaddon
Penquite Fm
Trefanny Hill
Westnorth Fm
Wringworthy
Lydcott Wood
Bake Wood
Widegates
Shortacross
Hessenford
Milltown
Lantyan
Ribby Fm
Lerryn
LANREATH FOLK & FARM MUSEUM
Tregarrick Mill
Tredinnick
Highercliff
Tregarlandbridge
Tregarland
Bin Down
SANDPLACE
Sandplace
Morval
Cleese Fm
Trelowia
Minard Fm
Polbathic
Great Wood
Trevollard
Lanreath
East Court Wood
Puffiland Fm
Bokenver Wood
No Man's Land
Keveral Wood
Carcoe Fm
Narkurs
GULANT
Penquite Cliff
Wooda Fm
Treire Fm
Court Wood
Muchlarnick
Hall Wood
Snowden's Bridge
Milcombe
Great Tree
Treesmill
Lawhibbet Fm
St Veep
Haye Fm
Tregarrick Fm
Lancare Fm
Pelynt
Ten Acre Wood
Watergate
Trenant Wood
St Martin
MONKEY SANCTUARY
Penhale Fm
Seaton
Kilgogue Fm
Torfrey
Trenython Manor
Golant
Trefrawl
Trelay Fm
Catherinepark Wood
Kiln Wood
Trelawne Manor
Ind Est
Millendreath
Plaidy
Bodigga Cliff
Colmer Rocks
Downderry
SOUTH WEST COAST PATH
Tywardreath
Penpoll
Peakswater
Polveithan Fm
Bake Fm
Penkelly
Barcelona
Trad Est
LOOE
Shutta
East Looe
Trezare Fm
Mixtow
Lanteglos Highway
Trenewan
Polean Fm
Polmear
Whitecross
Trevedda Fm
Trethake Fm
West Watergate
POLPERRO ROAD
West Looe
LOOE MUSEUM
Looe
Hannafore
Looe Bay
Hannafore Pt
Passage Lane
Polkerris
Bodinnick
Pont
Tremeer Fm
Great Tratford
Great Kellow Fm
Tencreek
Portlooe
Carneggan Fm
Frogmore Fm
Lansallos
Carey Park
Porthallow
Vardere Rock
Fowey
Readymoney
ST CATHERINE'S CASTLE
Menabilly
Polruan
Churchtown Fm
Pont Pill
West Coombe
Crumplehorn
Brent
HERITAGE MUSEUM
Talland
Talland Bay
Portnadler Bay
St George's or Looe Island
WHITSAND
Coombe Hawne
Washing Rocks
Blackbottle Rock
Lantic Bay
Pencarrow Head
Lantivet Bay
Shag Rock
Hard Hd 132
Polperro
Chapel Cliff
Downend Pt
Southground Pt
Sandy Cove
A
B
C
D
E
F
G
H
1
2
3
4
5
6
11
12
70
10
40
SX
0 1 2 3 miles
0 1 2 3 4 5 km

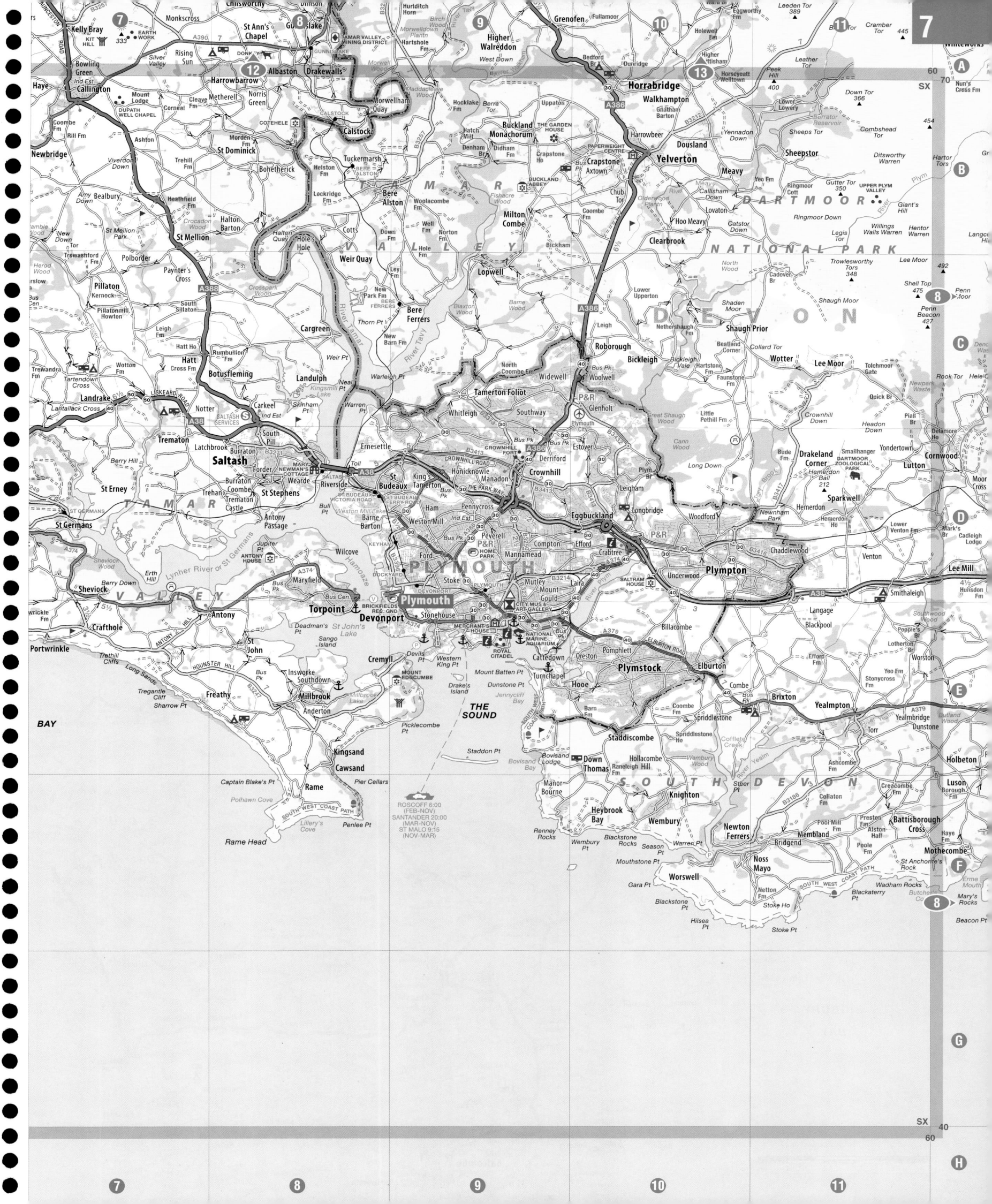
Kelly Bray
Monkscross
St Ann's Chapel
Gunnislake
Higher Walreddon
Grenofen
Horrabridge
Walkhampton
Bowling Green
Rising Sun
Harrowbarrow
Albaston
Drakewalls
Haye
Callington
Metherell
Norris Green
Morwellham Quay
Calstock
Cotehele
Buckland Monachorum
Yelverton
Dousland
Sheepstor
Newbridge
St Dominick
Bohetherick
Tuckermarsh
Bere Alston
Crapstone
Meavy
Milton Combe
Clearbrook
Hoo Meavy
St Mellion
Halton Barton
Weir Quay
Lopwell
DARTMOOR NATIONAL PARK
DEVON
Pillaton
Cargreen
Bere Ferrers
Shaugh Prior
Roborough
Bickleigh
Hatt
Botusfleming
Landulph
Wotter
Lee Moor
Landrake
Notter
Tamerton Foliot
Woolwell
Whitleigh
Southway
Glenholt
Tremator
Saltash
Ernesettle
Derriford
Crownhill
Estover
St Budeaux
King's Tamerton
Honicknowle
Manadon
Leigham
Drakeland Corner
Sparkwell
Cornwood
Lutton
St Erney
St Stephens
Trematon Castle
Ham
Pennycross
Eggbuckland
Longbridge
Woodford
St Germans
Antony Passage
Barne Barton
Weston Mill
Peverell
Compton
Efford
Crabtree
Wilcove
Ford
PLYMOUTH
Mannamead
Chaddlewood
Plympton
Underwood
Sheviock
Maryfield
Stoke
Mutley
Laira
Mount Gould
Lee Mill
Smithaleigh
Torpoint
Devonport
Plymouth
Stonehouse
Antony
Crafthole
Portwrinkle
St John
Cremyll
Langage
Billacombe
Pomphlett
Oreston
Plymstock
Elburton
Turnchapel
Hooe
Freathy
Millbrook
Anderton
Mount Edgcumbe
THE SOUND
Drake's Island
Brixton
Yealmpton
Staddiscombe
Spriddlestone
Kingsand
Cawsand
Rame
Rame Head
Down Thomas
Hollacombe Hill
Knighton
SOUTH DEVON
Heybrook Bay
Wembury
Newton Ferrers
Noss Mayo
Membland
Bridgend
Worswell
Battisborough Cross
Mothecombe
Holbeton
BAY
ROSCOFF 6:00 (FEB-NOV)
SANTANDER 20:00 (MAR-NOV)
ST MALO 9:15 (NOV-MAR)
A38
A386
A388
A374
A379
A390
B3416
SX
7
8
9
10
11
A
B
C
D
E
F
G
H

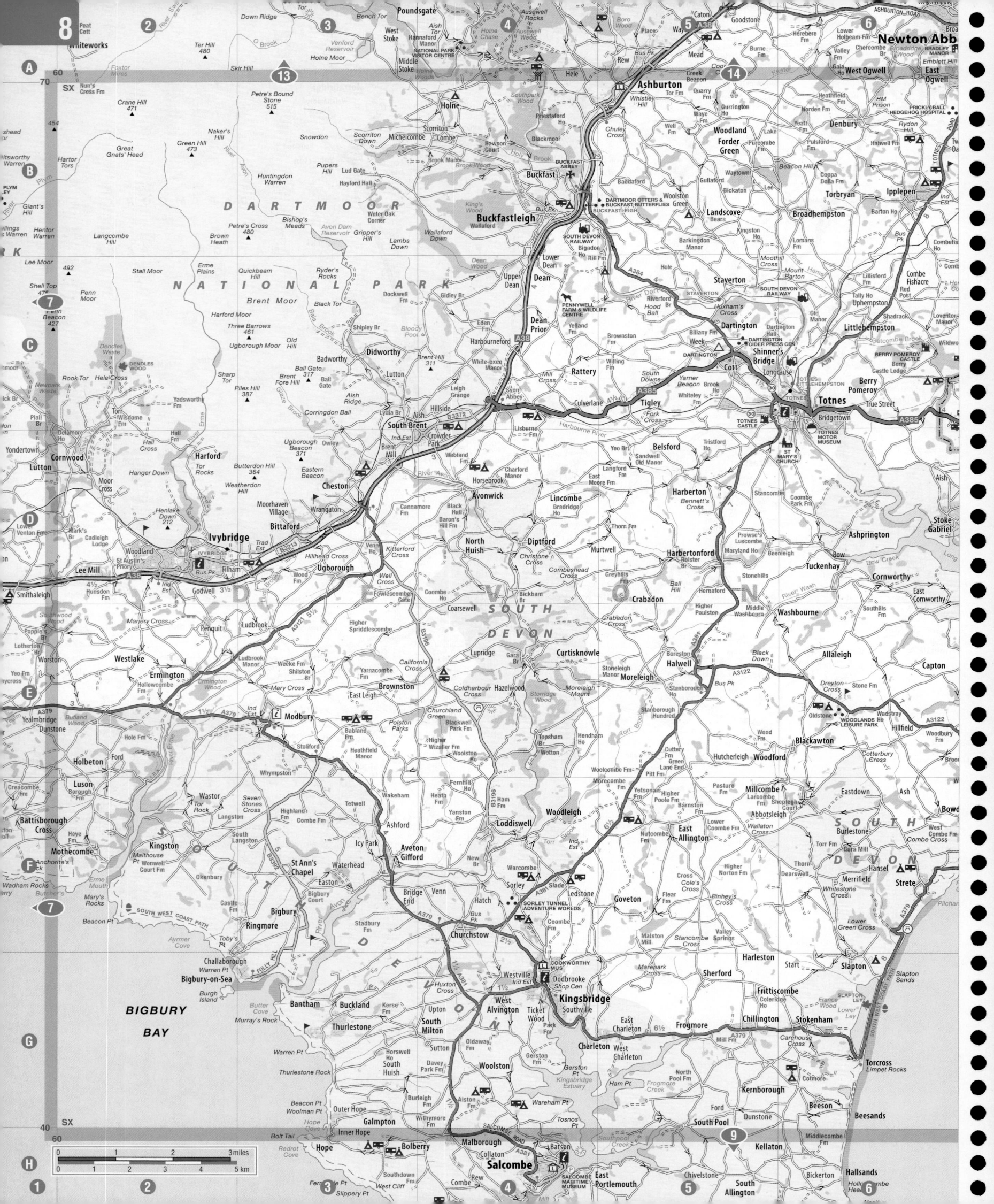
DARTMOOR
NATIONAL PARK
SOUTH DEVON
BIGBURY BAY
Newton Abbot
Ashburton
Buckfastleigh
Buckfast
Totnes
Ivybridge
Kingsbridge
Salcombe
Modbury
South Brent
Dartington
Ipplepen
Denbury
Poundsgate
Holne
Whiteworks
Down Ridge
Bench Tor
West Stoke
Middle Stoke
Hannaford Manor
NATIONAL PARK VISITOR CENTRE
Ausewell Rocks
Goodstone
Caton
Place
Rew
Mead
Burne Fm
Herebere Fm
Lower Holbeam Fm
Chercombe
Valley Fm
West Ogwell
East Ogwell
Emblett Hill
Ter Hill 480
Skir Hill
Holne Moor
Venford Reservoir
Foxtor Mires
Hele
Nun's Cross Fm
Crane Hill 471
Petre's Bound Stone 515
Naker's Hill
Green Hill 473
Great Gnats' Head
Hartor Tors
Snowdon
Scorriton Down
Scorriton
Michelcombe
Combe
Hawson Court
Priestaford Ho
Blackmoor
BUCKFAST ABBEY
Whistley Hill
Tor Fm
Quarry Fm
Gurrington Ho
Chuley Cross
Waye Fm
Woodland
Forder Green
Well Fm
Lake
Purcombe Fm
Pulsford Fm
Yeatt Fm
Norden Fm
Heathfield Fm
HM Prison
PRICKLY BALL HEDGEHOG HOSPITAL
Rydon Hill
Halwell Fm
Brook Manor
Huntingdon Warren
Pupers Hill
Lud Gate
Hayford Hall
Baddaford
Woolston Green
Waytown
Gullaford
Bickaton
Beacon Hill
Coppa Dolla Fm
Torbryan
Landscove
Beara
Broadhempston
Barton Ho
DARTMOOR OTTERS & BUCKFAST BUTTERFLIES
Petre's Cross 480
Bishop's Meads
Water Oak Corner
Avon Dam Reservoir
Gripper's Hill
Lambs Down
Wallaford Down
Wallaford
SOUTH DEVON RAILWAY
Bigadon Ho
Rill Fm
Kingston Ho
Barkingdon Manor
Lomans Fm
Moothill Cross
Mount Barton
Hole
Staverton
Lillisford Fm
Combe Fishacre
Red Post
Tally Ho
Upphempston
Langcombe Hill
Brown Heath
Lee Moor
Stall Moor
Erme Plains
Quickbeam Hill
Ryder's Rocks
Dean Wood
Upper Dean
Lower Dean
Dean
Shell Top
Penn Moor
Penn Beacon 427
Brent Moor
Black Tor
Dockwell Fm
Gidley Br
PENNYWELL FARM & WILDLIFE CENTRE
Riverford Br
Hood Ball
Huxham's Cross
Harford Moor
Three Barrows 461
Ugborough Moor
Old Hill
Shipley Br
Bloody Pool
Eden Fm
Dean Prior
Yelland Fm
Brownston Fm
Billany Fm
Week
DARTINGTON
Dartington Hall
DARTINGTON CIDER PRESS CEN
Shinner's Bridge
Cott
Old Manor
Littlehempston
Shadrack
Loventor Manor
Dendles Waste
DENDLES WOOD
Badworthy
Didworthy
Brent Hill 311
Harbourneford
White-oxen Manor
Willing Fm
South Downs
Yarner Beacon
Brook Ho
Longcause
Berry Pomeroy
BERRY POMEROY CASTLE
Castle Lodge
Ball Gate 317
Ball Gate
Brent Fore Hill
Sharp Tor
Rook Tor
Hele Cross
Lutton
Mill Cross
Rattery
Piles Hill 387
Aish Ridge
Leigh Grange
Syon Abbey
Culverlane
Tigley
Whiteley Fm
Bridgetown
True Street
Yadsworthy Fm
Torr
Wisdome Fm
Corringdon Ball
Lydia Br
Aish
Hillside
Lisburne Fm
Fork Cross
Harbourne River
TOTNES CASTLE
TOTNES MOTOR MUSEUM
Delamore Ho
Hall Fm
Hall Cross
Ugborough Beacon 371
Owley
Brent Mill
Crowder Park
Webland Fm
Charford Manor
Horsebrook
Yeo Br
Sandwell Old Manor
Langford Fm
Belsford
Tristford Ho
ST MARY'S CHURCH
Yondertown
Cornwood
Lutton
Harford
Tor Rocks
Hanger Down
Butterdon Hill 364
Weatherdon Hill
Eastern Beacon
Cheston
Avonwick
East Moore Fm
Lincombe
Bradridge Ho
Harberton
Bennett's Cross
Stancombe
Coombe Park Fm
Aish
Moor Cross
Moorhaven Village
Bittaford
Wrangaton
Cannamore Fm
Black Hall
Baron's Hill Fm
Thorn Fm
Stoke Gabriel
Lower Venton Fm
Mark's Br
Cadleigh Lodge
Henlake Down 212
Woodland
St Austin's Priory
Filham
Trad Est
Lee Mill
Hunsdon Fm
Godwell
Ugborough
Hillhead Cross
Venn Ho
Kitterford Cross
North Huish
Diptford
Christone Cross
Murtwell
Harbertonford
Rolster Br
Prowse's Luscombe
Maryland Ho
Beenleigh
Ashprington
Bow
Bow Creek
Tuckenhay
Smithaleigh
Southwood Wood
Popple's Br
Marjery Cross
Penquit
Ludbrook
Wood Fm
Well Cross
Fowlescombe Gate
Coombe Ho
Coarsewell
Bickham Br
Combeshead Cross
Greyhills Fm
Ball Hill
Crabadon
Hernaford
Higher Poulston
Middle Washbourn
Washbourne
Stonehills
Cornworthy
East Cornworthy
Southhills Fm
Lotherton Br
Worston
Higher Spriddlescombe
Crabadon Cross
Westlake
Ermington
Ermington Wood
Ludbrook Manor
Weeke Fm
Shilston Br
California Cross
Yarnacombe Fm
Lupridge
Gara Br
Curtisknowle
Stoneleigh Manor
Moreleigh
Boreston
Halwell
Black Down
Allaleigh
Capton
Yeo Fm
Hollowcombe Fm
Mary Cross
Brownston
Coldharbour Cross
Hazelwood
Moreleigh Mount
Stanborough Ho
Bus Pk
Dreyton Cross
Stone Fm
Yealmbridge
Dunstone
Butland Wood
East Leigh
Churchland Green
Blackwell Park Fm
Storridge Wood
Stanborough Hundred
Oldstone
WOODLANDS LEISURE PARK
Wadstray
Hillfield
Woodbury Fm
Hole Fm
Babland Fm
Polston Parks
Higher Wizaller Fm
Woolston Ho
Topsham Br
Wotton
Hendham Ho
Cuttery Fm
Green Lane End
Wood Fm
Blackawton
Cotterbury Cross
Holbeton
Ford
Stoliford
Heathfield Manor
Whympston
Woolcombe Fm
Pitt Fm
Hutcherleigh
Woodford
Luson
Creacombe Fm
Morecombe Fm
Yetsonais Fm
Higher Poole Fm
Pasture Fm
Millcombe
Larcombe Fm
Shepleigh Court
Eastdown
Ash
Battisborough Cross
Wastor
Tor Rock
Seven Stones Cross
Langston
Highland Fm
Combe Fm
Tetwell
Wakeham
Fernhill Ho
Heath Fm
Ham Fm
Yanston Fm
Barnston Fm
Abbotsleigh
Woodleigh
Loddiswell
Nutcombe Fm
East Allington
Lower Coombe Fm
Wallaton Cross
Burlestone
Haye Fm
Mothecombe
Kingston
South Langston
Ashford
Icy Park
Aveton Gifford
Torr Fm
Gara Mill
Malthouse Pt
Wonwell Court Fm
St Ann's Chapel
Waterhead
New Br
Anchorite's Rock
Okenbury
Easton
Warcombe
Sorley
Slade
Ledstone
Higher Norton Fm
Thorn
Dearswell
Merrifield
Whitestone Cross
Hansel
Strete
Wadham Rocks
Erme Mouth
Mary's Rocks
Castle Fm
Bigbury Court
Bridge End
Venn
Hatch
SORLEY TUNNEL ADVENTURE WORLDS
Goveton
Cross Cole's Cross
Flear Fm
Pinhey's Cross
Pilchard
SOUTH WEST COAST PATH
Beacon Pt
Bigbury
Ringmore
Stadbury Fm
Churchstow
Coombe Fm
Malston Mill
Stancombe Cross
Valley Springs
Lower Green Cross
Toby's Pt
Aymer Cove
Challaborough
Warren Pt
Bigbury-on-Sea
Burgh Island
Huxton Cross
Westville
COOKWORTHY MUS
Dodbrooke
Shop Cen
Marepark Cross
Sherford
Harleston
Start
Slapton
Slapton Sands
Frittiscombe
Coleridge Ho
SLAPTON LEY
France Wood
Lower Ley
Butter Cove
Murray's Rock
Bantham
Buckland
Kerse Fm
Upton
West Alvington
Ticket Wood
Kingsbridge
Southville
Park Fm
East Charleton
Frogmore
Chillington
Stokenham
Thurlestone
South Milton
Oldaway Fm
Charleton
West Charleton
Mill Fm
Carehouse Cross
Torcross
Limpet Rocks
Warren Pt
Thurlestone Rock
Horswell Ho
South Huish
Sutton
Davey Park Fm
Gerston Fm
Gerston Pt
Kingsbridge Estuary
Woolston
Ham Pt
Fromgore Creek
North Pool Fm
Kernborough
Cotmore
Beacon Pt
Woolman Pt
Outer Hope
Burleigh Fm
Alston Fm
Wareham Pt
Beeson
Hope Cove
Galmpton
Withymore Fm
Tosnos Pt
Ford
South Pool
Dunstone
Beesands
Bolt Tail
Inner Hope
Hope
Bolberry
Malborough
SALCOMBE ROAD
Collaton
Batson
Southpool Creek
Middlecombe Fm
Kellaton
Redrot Cove
Salcombe
SALCOMBE MARITIME MUSEUM
East Portlemouth
Chivelstone
South Allington
Bickerton
Hallsands
Southdown Fm
Combe
Rew
West Cliff
Slippery Pt
SX
A
B
C
D
E
F
G
H
1
2
3
4
5
6
7
9
13
14
60
70
40
A38
A384
A385
A381
A3121
A379
A3122
B3372
B3213
B3196
B3392
0 1 2 3 miles
0 1 2 3 4 5 km

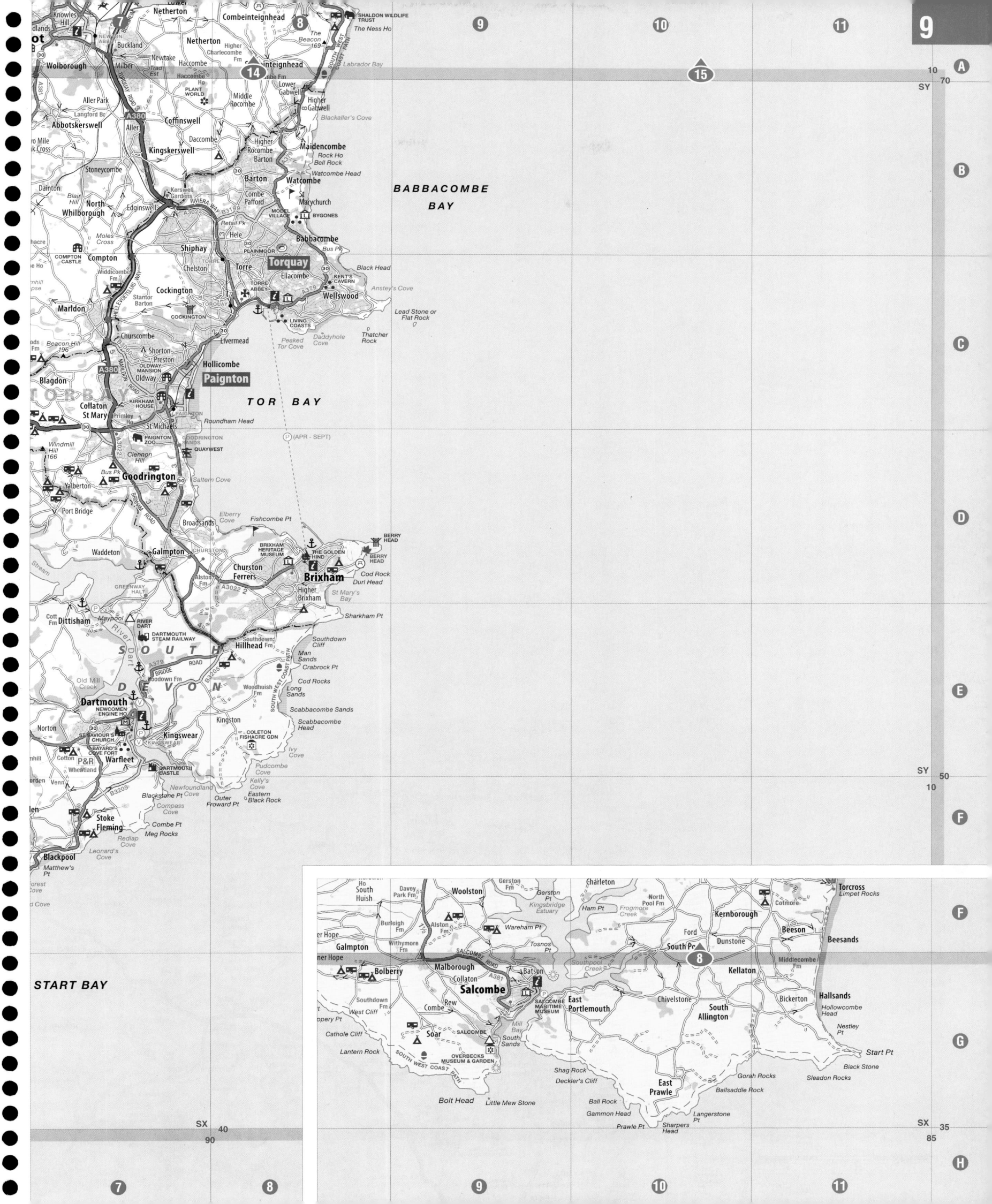
BABBACOMBE
BAY
TOR BAY
START BAY
Torquay
Paignton
Brixham
Dartmouth
Salcombe
Kingswear
Goodrington
Babbacombe
Watcombe
Maidencombe
Shiphay
Torre
Cockington
Marldon
Compton
Abbotskerswell
Kingskerswell
Coffinswell
Wolborough
Netherton
Combeinteignhead
Wellswood
Ellacombe
Livermead
Hollicombe
Preston
Churscombe
Blagdon
Collaton St Mary
Galmpton
Churston Ferrers
Higher Brixham
Broadsands
Hillhead
Dittisham
Kingston
Warfleet
Stoke Fleming
Blackpool
Norton
Waddeton
Yalberton
Port Bridge
Berry Head
Sharkham Pt
Scabbacombe Sands
Scabbacombe Head
Roundham Head
Hope's Nose
Black Head
Anstey's Cove
Lead Stone or Flat Rock
Thatcher Rock
Daddyhole Cove
Peaked Tor Cove
Saltern Cove
Elberry Cove
Fishcombe Pt
Labrador Bay
The Ness Ho
SOUTH DEVON
Woolston
Charleton
Kernborough
Torcross
Beeson
Beesands
Dunstone
Kellaton
Hallsands
Start Pt
Marlborough
Bolberry
Soar
Batson
East Portlemouth
Chivelstone
South Allington
East Prawle
Bolt Head
Little Mew Stone
Prawle Pt
Gammon Head
Ball Rock
Sharpers Head
Langerstone Pt
Gorah Rocks
Ballsaddle Rock
Sleadon Rocks
Black Stone
Bickerton
Ford
Collaton
Rew
Combe
Galmpton
South Huish
Shag Rock
Deckler's Cliff
Lantern Rock
Cathole Cliff
SX
SY
70
50
35
85
90
40
10

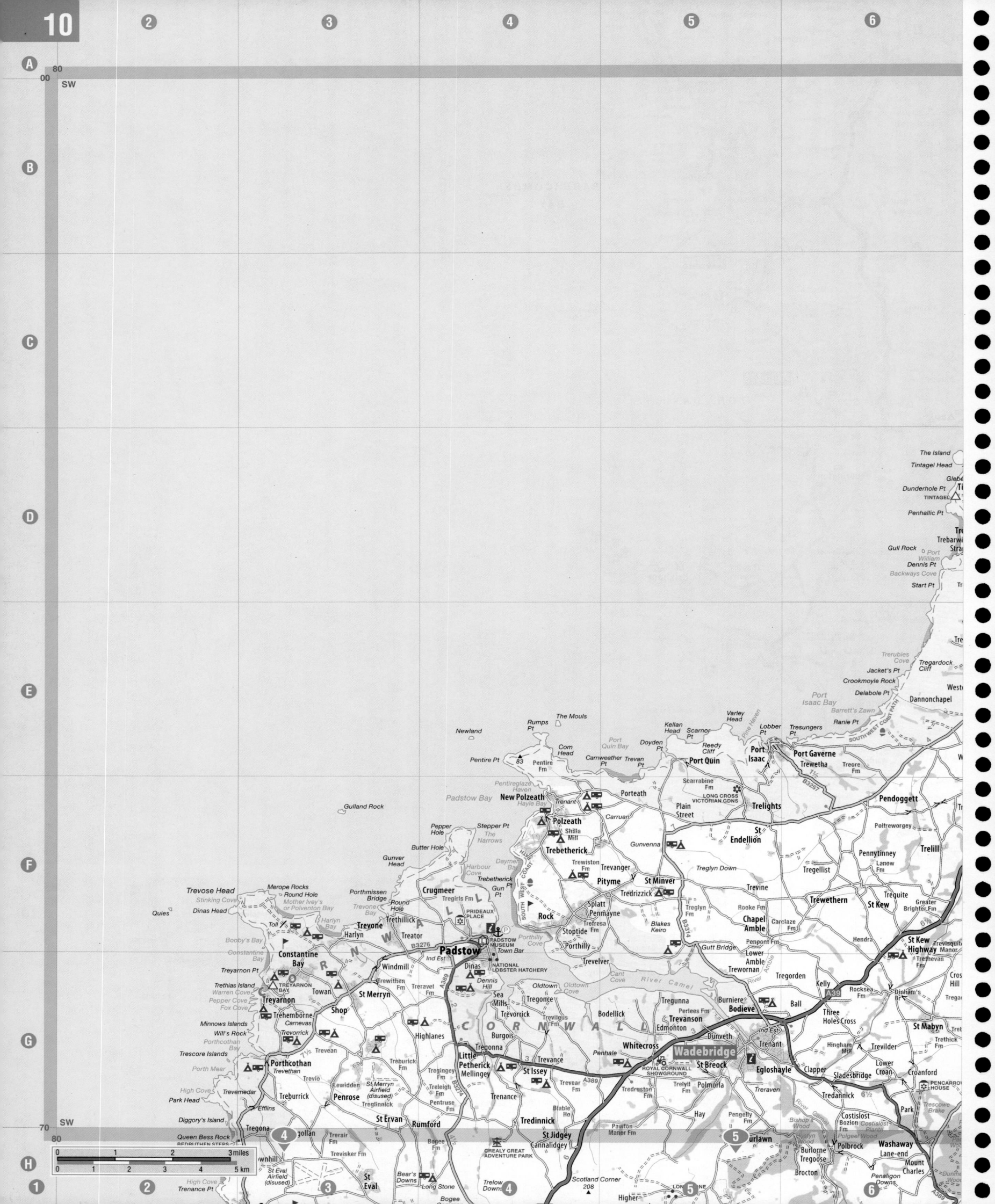

2
3
4
5
6
A
B
C
D
E
F
G
H
1
80
00
SW
70
The Island
Tintagel Head
Dunderhole Pt
TINTAGEL
Penhallic Pt
Trebarwith
Gull Rock
Port William
Dennis Pt
Backways Cove
Start Pt
Trerubies Cove
Tregardock Cliff
Jacket's Pt
Crookmoyle Rock
Delabole Pt
Dannonchapel
Port Isaac Bay
Barrett's Zawn
Ranie Pt
SOUTH WEST COAST PATH
Tresungers Pt
Lobber Pt
Varley Head
Pine Haven
Kellan Head
Scarnor Pt
Reedy Cliff
Doyden Pt
Port Quin Bay
Trevan Pt
Carnweather Pt
Com Head
The Mouls
Rumps Pt
Newland
Pentire Pt
83
Pentire Fm
Port Isaac
Port Gaverne
Trewetha
Treore Fm
B3267
Port Quin
Scarrabine Fm
LONG CROSS VICTORIAN GDNS
Trelights
Plain Street
Porteath
Pentireglaze Haven
Padstow Bay
New Polzeath
Trenant
Hayle Bay
Polzeath
Carruan
Shilla Mill
Trebetherick
Gulland Rock
Pepper Hole
Stepper Pt
The Narrows
Butter Hole
St Endellion
Gunvenna
Pendoggett
Poltreworgey
Trelill
Pennytinney
Lanow Fm
Tregellist
Treglyn Down
Gunver Head
Harbour Cove
Daymer Bay
Trebetherick Pt
Trewiston Fm
Trevanger
Pityme
St Minver
Tredrizzick
Trevine
Trewethern
St Kew
Trequite
Greater Brighter Fm
Trevose Head
Stinking Cove
Merope Rocks
Round Hole
Mother Ivey's or Polventon Bay
Porthmissen Bridge
Crugmeer
Tregirls Fm
Gun Pt
Quies
Dinas Head
Trevone Bay
Round Hole
Trethillick
PRIDEAUX PLACE
SOUTH WEST COAST
Rock
Splatt
Penmayne
Treglyn Fm
Rooke Fm
Chapel Amble
Carclaze Fm
Blakes Keiro
Trefresa Fm
Stoptide
Porthilly
Toll
Harlyn Bay
Trevone
Harlyn
Treator
PADSTOW MUSEUM
Town Bar
Porthilly Cove
Booby's Bay
Constantine Bay
Constantine Bay
B3276
Padstow
Ind Est
Windmill
NATIONAL LOBSTER HATCHERY
Trevelver
Gutt Bridge
B3314
Penpont Fm
Lower Amble
Trewornan
Tregorden
Hendra
St Kew Highway
Trevisquite Manor
Trethevan Fm
Treyarnon Pt
Trethias Island
Warren Cove
TREYARNON BAY
Pepper Cove
Fox Cove
Treyarnon
Towan
Trewithen Fm
St Merryn
Trevarel Fm
Dinas
Dennis Hill
A389
Cant Cove
River Camel
Oldtown
Oldtown Cove
Sea Mills
Tregonce
Trevorrick
Treviglus Fm
Kelly
A39
Rocksea Fm
Dinham's Br
Cross Hill
Ball
Three Holes Cross
St Mabyn
Trethick Fm
Burniere
Bodieve
Tregunna
Perlees Fm
Trevanson
Edmonton
Bodellick
Minnows Islands
Will's Rock
Porthcothan Bay
Trehemborne
Carnevas
Shop
Trevorrick
Trevean
Highlanes
CORNWALL
Burgois
Tregonna
Trevance
Dunveth
Ind Est
Trenant
Whitecross
Wadebridge
Penhale
ROYAL CORNWALL SHOWGROUND
St Breock
Egloshayle
Clapper
Hingham Mill
Trevilder
Lower Croan
Croanford
Sladesbridge
PENCARROW HOUSE
Trescore Islands
Porthcothan
Trevethan
Porth Mear
Trevio
Treburick Fm
Little Petherick
Mellingey
St Issey
Trevear Fm
A389
Tredruston Fm
Trelyll Fm
Polmorla
Treraven
Tredannick
High Cove
Trevemedar
Park Head
Treburrick
Efflins
Lewidden
St Merryn Airfield (disused)
Treglinnick
Penrose
Treleigh Fm
Pentruse Fm
Trenance
Blable Ho
Hay
Pengelly Fm
River Camel
Bishop's Wood
Costislost
Bozion Fm
Polgeel Wood
Park
Trescowe Brake
Diggory's Island
Tregona
St Ervan
Rumford
Tredinnick
Pawton Manor Fm
St Jidgey
Queen Bess Rock
BEDRUTHEN STEPS
Trerair Fm
Bogee Fm
CREALY GREAT ADVENTURE PARK
Cannalidgey
Burlawn
Burlorne Tregoose
Polbrock
Washaway
Lane-end
Mount Charles
Trevisker Fm
Brocton
St Eval Airfield (disused)
St Eval
Bear's Downs
Long Stone
Trelow Downs
Scotland Corner
208
Higher
Penaligon Downs
High Cove
Trenance Pt
Bogee
0 1 2 3 miles
0 1 2 3 4 5 km

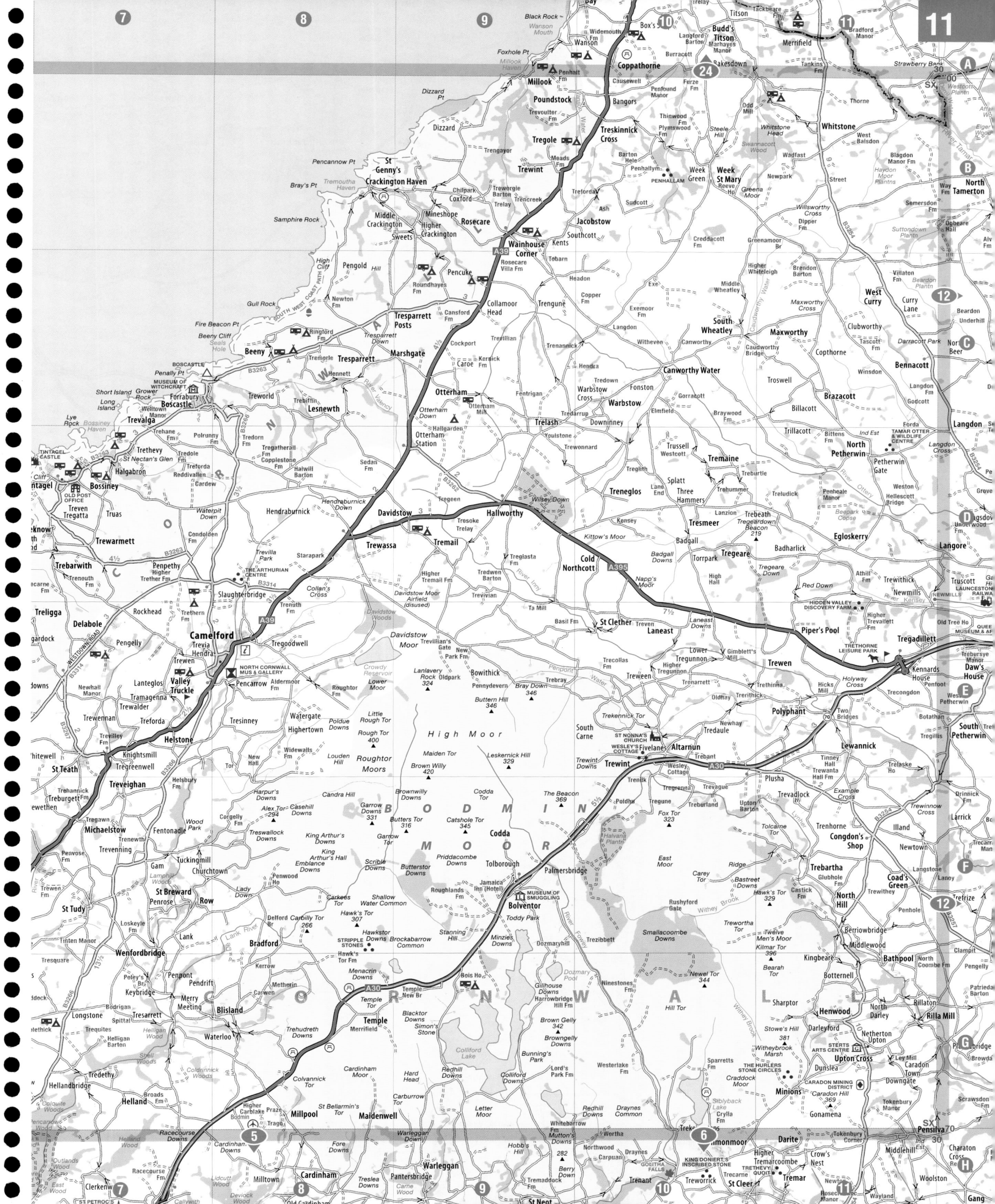

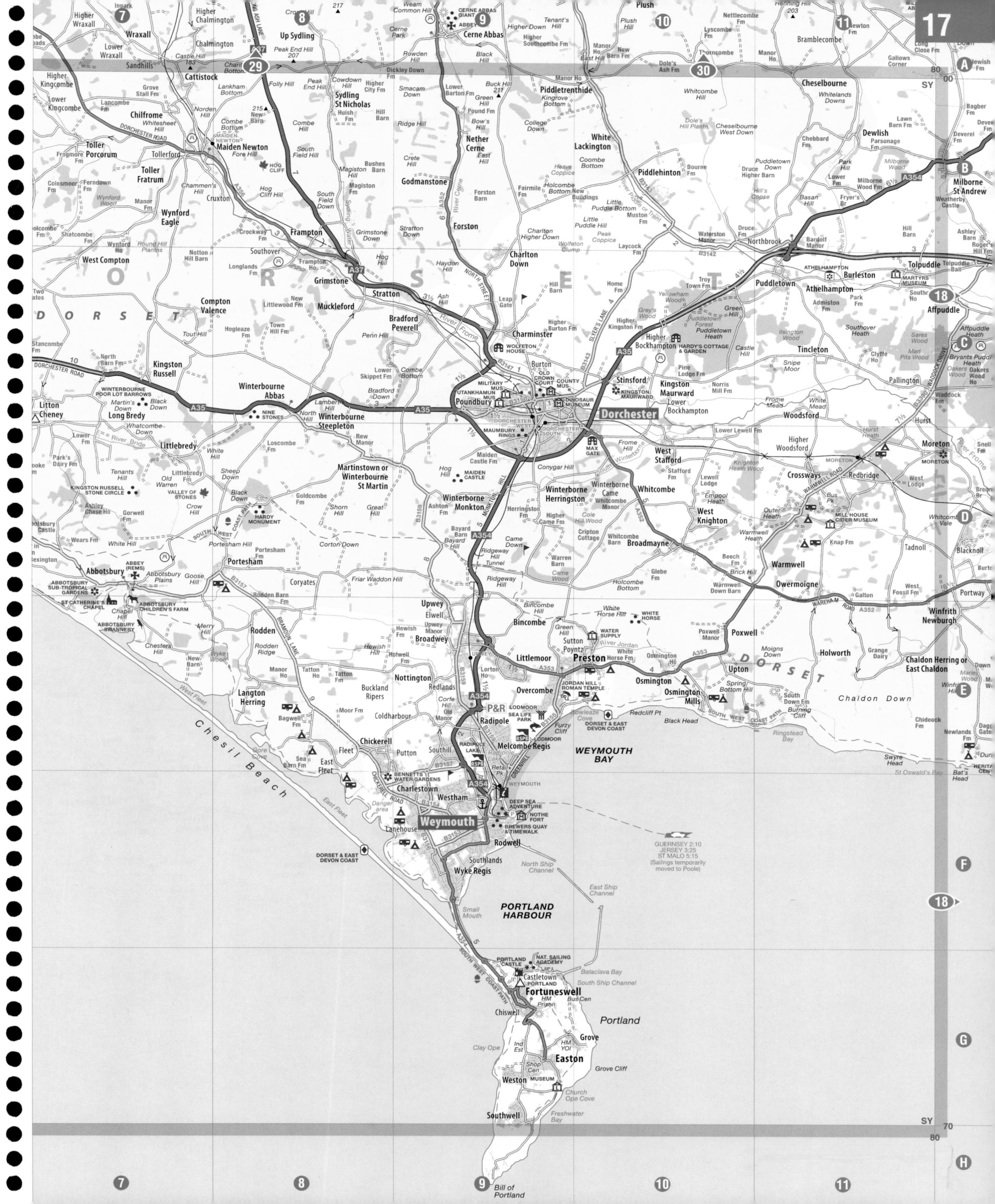
Higher Wraxall
Wraxall
Lower Wraxall
Higher Chalmington
Chalmington
Up Sydling
Cerne Abbas
Plush
Bramblecombe
Sandhills
Cattistock
Higher Kingcombe
Lower Kingcombe
Chilfrome
Sydling St Nicholas
Piddletrenthide
Cheselbourne
Dewlish
Maiden Newton
Toller Porcorum
Tollerford
Toller Fratrum
Nether Cerne
White Lackington
Piddlehinton
Godmanstone
Milborne St Andrew
Cruxton
Wynford Eagle
Forston
Frampton
Southover
West Compton
Charlton Down
Grimstone
Stratton
Muckleford
Compton Valence
Bradford Peverell
Puddletown
Athelhampton
Burleston
Tolpuddle
Affpuddle
DORSET
Charminster
Kingston Russell
Winterbourne Abbas
Burton
Stinsford
Kingston Maurward
Higher Bockhampton
Lower Bockhampton
Tincleton
Pallington
Litton Cheney
Long Bredy
Winterbourne Steepleton
Poundbury
Dorchester
Woodsford
Littlebredy
Martinstown or Winterbourne St Martin
West Stafford
Moreton
Crossways
Redbridge
Whitcombe
Winterbourne Herringston
Winterborne Monkton
West Knighton
Broadmayne
Warmwell
Abbotsbury
Portesham
Coryates
Upwey
Owermoigne
Poxwell
Winfrith Newburgh
Rodden
Broadwey
Bincombe
Littlemoor
Preston
Sutton Poyntz
Osmington
Osmington Mills
Upton
Holworth
Chaldon Herring or East Chaldon
Chaldon Down
Langton Herring
Nottington
Overcombe
Radipole
Melcombe Regis
WEYMOUTH BAY
Chickerell
Fleet
East Fleet
Charlestown
Westham
Weymouth
Lanehouse
Rodwell
Southlands
Wyke Regis
Chesil Beach
PORTLAND HARBOUR
Castletown
Fortuneswell
Chiswell
Portland
Grove
Easton
Weston
Southwell
Bill of Portland
GUERNSEY 2:10
JERSEY 3:25
ST MALO 5:15
(Sailings temporarily moved to Poole)
A35
A37
A352
A353
A354
A356
B3157
B3159
SY
80
70
00

Milton Abbas
Higher Whatcombe
Whatcombe
Lower Whatcombe
Shapwick
Tadden
Hound Hill
Merry Field Hill
Pilford
Canford Bottom
Colehill
Long Close Fm
Hewish Fm
Winterborne Whitechurch
Charlton Down
Field Dairy Fm
Moorcourt Fm
Sturminster Marshall
Chilbridge
Hillbutts
Barford Fm
Wimborne Minster
Leigh
Little Canford
Oakley
Canford Magna
Merley
Cowgrove
Deverel Down
North Down
Bagber Fm
Lawn Barn Fm
Deverel Fm
Almer
Stag Gate
East Almer Fm
Newton Peveril
Lion Lodge
Charborough Park
Bushes Fm
Mapperton
Huish
Winterborne Kingston
Winterborne Zelston
Anderson Manor
Anderson
Marsh Br
Henbury
Lambs Green
Ashington
Sleight
East End
Knoll Fm
Rushcombe Bottom
Dullar Fm
Combe Almer
Green Fields Fm
High Wood
Brock Hill
Corfe Mullen
Bere Down
Foxpound
Milborne St Andrew
Weatherby Castle
Dairy Ho
Botany Bay Barn
Bloxworth Down
West Park Fm
Barrow Hill
Hill View
Corfe Hills
Broadstone
POOLE
Bearwood
Canford Heath
East Field Fm
Muddox Barrow Fm
West Morden
Morden
Lytchett Ho
Lytchett Matravers
Poor Common
Roke Fm
Ashley Barn
Roger's Hill Fm
Hill Barn
Town's End
Bere Wood
Bloxworth Ho
Dolman's Hill
Bartom's Hill
Lodge Hill
Tolpuddle
Tolpuddle Ball
Martyrs Museum
Bere Regis
Black Hill
Shitterton
Woodbury Hill
Bloxworth
Newport
East Bloxworth
Whitefield
Morden Mill
East Morden
Whitmore Bottom
Beacon Hill
Upton Heath
Lytchett Heath
Canford Heath
Hillbourne
Waterloo
Bus Pk
Tower Park Leisure Complex
Turners Puddle
Dodding's Fm
Lower Woodbury Fm
Woodlake
Oak Hill
Black Heath
Sherford
Park Corner
Slepe
Bere Fm
Post Green
Lytchett Minster
Creekmoor
Upton
Newtown
Oakdale
Affpuddle
Hollow Oak
Throop
Briants Puddle
Affpuddle Heath
Chamberlayne's Fm
Lane End
Bere Heath
Sugar Hill
Wareham Forest
Morden Park
Sherford Br
Farmer Palmer's
Organford
Pike's Fm
Lytchett Bay
Hamworthy
Turlin Moor
Holes Bay
Stanley Green
Sterte
Longfleet
Branksome
Ashley Road
Bryants Puddle Heath
Oakers Wood
Throop Heath
Chamberlayne's Heath
Warren
Philliols Fm
Stroud Br
Decoy Heath
Morden Bog
Gore Heath
Holton Heath
East Holton
Rockley Sands
Lake
Poole
Parkstone
Lilliput
Pallington
Waddock Fm
Tonerspuddle Heath
Warren Heath
Gallows Hill
Clouds Hill
Clouds Hill
Bere Heath
Trent Vale Fm
Trigon Hill
Great Ovens Hill
Holton Heath
Wood Bar Looe
Lower Hamworthy
DORSET
Hurst
Moreton
Snelling Fm
Bovington Heath
Wool Heath
South Heath
Budden's Fm
Cold Harbour
Northport Heath
Sandford
Keysworth Fm
Keysworth Pt
Gold Pt
Patchins Pt
Poole Harbour
Wareham Channel
Main Channel
Cranes Moor
Longthorns Fm
Monkey World
Bovington Camp
The Tank Museum
Woolbridge Heath
Great Plantn
Trigon Fm
Carey Heath
Northport
Arne Bay
Shipstal Pt
Maryland
The Villa
Brownsea Island
West Lodge
Broomhill Br
Stokeford Heath
Wareham
Priory of Lady St Mary
Museum
Ind Est
Swineham Pt
Arne Toy Mus
Arne
Arne Reed Beds
RSPB
Fitzworth Pt
Furzey Island
North Haven Pt
Sandbanks
Whitcombe Vale
Tout Hill
East Burton
Wool
Bindon Abbey (Rems)
Stokeford
Binnegar Hall
Binnegar
Worgret Heath
Rushton
Worgret
Ridge
Middlebere Fm
Nath Pt
Green Island
South Deep
South Haven Pt
Tadnoll
Blacknoll
Knighton Heath
Giddy Green
Braytown
Quarr Hill
East Stoke
River Frome
Holmebridge
Holme Priory
East Holme
Stoborough
Stoborough Heath
Hartland Moor
Slepe Fm
Cleavel Pt
Newton Bay
Brand's Bay
Shell Bay
West Burton Fm
New Buildings
Woodstreet Fm
Highwood Heath
Cole Wood
West Holme
Danger area
Doreys Fm
Stoborough Green
Hartland Stud
Hartland Moor
Wytch Fm
Newton
Goathorn Plantn
Drove Island
Studland Beach & Nature Reserve
West Fossil Fm
Portway
East Knighton
Highwood
Oil Terminal
Wytch Heath
Newton Heath
Rempstone Heath
Greenlands Fm
Little Sea
Winfrith Newburgh
Coombe Wood
Coombe Keynes
Coombe Heath
West Holme Heath
Holme Heath
Creech Bottom
Middlebere Heath
Studland Bay
Hurst Mill
Grange Barn
Creech Heath
Furzebrook Ho
Furzebrook
Norden Heath
Bushey
Studland & Godlingston Heath
The Agglestone
Redend Pt
Chaldon Herring or East Chaldon
Vine's Down Bldgs
Shaggs
Park Lodge
Home Fm
Povington Heath
Grange Heath
Creech
Blue Pool
Norden
P&R
Lower Bushey Fm
Higher Bushey Fm
Godlington Heath
Black Down
Winfrith Hill
Marley Wood
Marley Wood House
Belhuish Ho
Park Wood
Whiteway
East Creech
Knowle Hill
Corfe Castle
Rollington Fm
Rempstone Hall
Studland
Down
Lulworth Castle
Burngate Fm
East Lulworth
Great Wood
Stonehill Down
Barneston Manor
Cocknowle
Model Village & Garden
Corfe Castle
Little Woolgarston
Woolgarston
Ailwood Fm
Chideock Fm
Newlands Fm
Daggers Gate
Lulworth Camp
Danger Area
Povington Hill
West Creech Hill
Purbeck Hills
Grange Arch
Animal Sanctuary
Church Knowle
West Bucknowle
Town's End
Swanage Railway
Valley Road
Knitson Fm
New Buildings
Godlingston Manor
Ulwell
Swyre Head
Dungy Head
West Lulworth
Lulworth Cove
Heritage Centre
Whiteway Hill
Tyneham
Steeple
Blackmanston Fm
Bradle Fm
West Orchard Fm
Blashenwell Fm
Lynch Fm
Harman's Cross
New Swanage
St Oswald's Bay
Bat's Head
Bindon Hill
Mupe Bay
Worbarrow Bay
Gad Cliff
Worbarrow
Kimmeridge
Smedmore Hill
Orchard Hill Fm
Kingston
West Street
Dunshay Manor
New Barn
Herston Halt
Swanage
Swanage Bay
Brandy Bay
Kimmeridge Bay
Hobarrow Bay
Swyre Head
Coombe Bottom
Compact Fm
Langton Matravers
Herston
Peveril Pt
Durlston Bay
Swalland Fm
South West Coast Path
Kimmeridge Ledges
Westhill Fm
Acton
Eastington Fm
Houns-tout Cliff
Renscombe Fm
California Fm
Durlston
Durlston Head
Rope Lake Head
Egmont Pt
Worth Matravers
Tilly Whim Caves
Anvil Pt
Chapman's Pool
Blackers Hole
Seacombe Cliff
Dorset & East Devon Coast
St Aldhelm's or St Alban's Head
A31
A35
A350
A351
A352
A354
A3049
B3075
B3070
B3071
B3069
B3351
B3369
B3390
SY
0 1 2 3 miles
0 1 2 3 4 5 km

Ferndown
Trickett's Cross
West Parley
Dudsbury
Longham
Parley Cross
Parley Green
Bear Cross
Kinson
Ensbury
Northbourne
Muscliff
Red Hill
East Howe
BOURNEMOUTH
Charminster
Moordown
Turbary Common
Ensbury Park
Talbot Village
Winton
Wallisdown
Rossmore
Bourne Valley
Talbot Heath
Talbot Woods
Queen's Park
Meyrick Park
Springbourne
Westbourne
Branksome Park
West Cliff
Bournemouth
Boscombe
Southbourne
Pokesdown
West Southbourne
Tuckton
Iford
Littledown
Holdenhurst
Blackwater
West Hurn
Hurn
Merritown
BOURNEMOUTH AIRPORT
Jumpers Green
Jumpers Common
St Catherine's Hill
Christchurch
Purewell
Somerford
Wick
Stanpit
Mudeford
Friars Cliff
Hengistbury Head
Christchurch Harbour
Sopley
Winkton
Burton
Avon
Ripley
North Ripley
Shirley
Bransgore
Neacroft
Godwinscroft
Hinton
Walkford
Highcliffe
HIGHCLIFFE CASTLE
Barton on Sea
Old Milton
New Milton
Ashley
Golden Hill
Bashley
Wootton
Sway
Hordle
Everton
Downton
Milford on Sea
Keyhaven
Lymore
Pennington
Lymington
Buckland
Mount Pleasant
Battramsley
Setley
DORSET
HANTS
CHRISTCHURCH BAY
POOLE BAY
Canford Cliffs
Branksome Chine
Flag Head Chine
Poole Head
Handfast Point or The Foreland
The Pinnacles
DORSET & EAST DEVON COAST
Ballard Pt
GUERNSEY 3:00 (APR-OCT)
JERSEY 3:00 (APR-OCT)
ST MALO 5:30 (MAY-SEPT)
CHERBOURG 2:30 (MAY-SEPT)
Totland
Hatherwood Pt
Alum Bay
CHAIR LIFT
THE NEEDLES PARK
The Needles
THE NEEDLES OLD BATTERY
Scratchell's Bay
Main Bench
Hurst Beach
20

Lymington
Newport
Cowes
East Cowes
Yarmouth
Freshwater
Totland
Newbridge
Calbourne
Shalfleet
Brighstone
Shorwell
Godshill
Niton
Whitwell
Blackgang
Chale
Wroxall
Milford on Sea
Keyhaven
Beaulieu Heath
Exbury
Lepe
Blackfield
Calshot
Hill Head
THE
ISLE OF WIGHT
St Catherine's Down
Brighstone Bay
Compton Bay
Totland Bay
Colwell Bay
Newtown Bay
Thorness Bay
Gurnard Bay
Osborne Bay
Cowes Roads
Needles
St Catherine's Pt
St Lawrence
Sandford
Arreton
Rookley
Carisbrooke
Gunville
Parkhurst
Whippingham
Wootton Bridge
Porchfield
Newtown
Hamstead
Ningwood
Wellow
Thorley
Afton
Brook
Mottistone
Limerstone
Kingston
Chillerton
Gatcombe
Blackwater
Downend
Horringford
Merstone
Roud
Southford
Kingates
Bierley
Pyle
Chale Green
Little Atherfield
Yafford
Thorncross
Moortown
Hulverstone
Shalcombe
Norton
Norton Green
Colwell
Weston Manor
Pound Green
Freshwater Bay
Pennington
Lower Pennington
Woodside
Walhampton
Boldre
Pilley
Portmore
Norleywood
South Baddesley
East End
Setley
Battramsley
Buckland
Everton
Lymore
Hatchet Gate
East Boldre
Bucklers Hard
Langley
West Common
SZ
1
2
3
4
5
6
A
B
C
D
E
F
G
H
32
33
19
0 1 2 3 miles
0 1 2 3 4 5 km

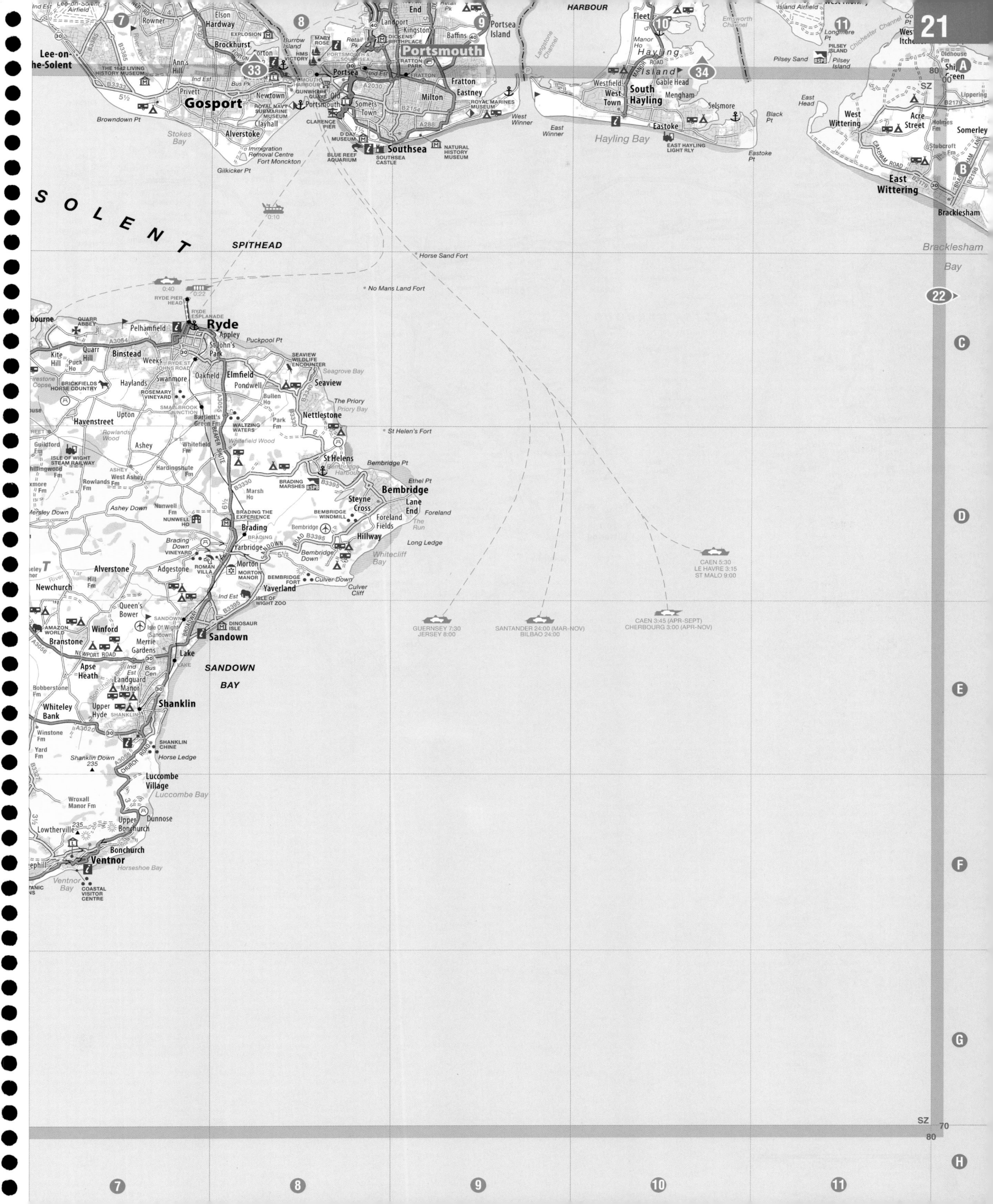
Lee-on-the-Solent
Rowner
Elson
Hardway
Brockhurst
Ann's Hill
Privett
Gosport
Newtown
Alverstoke
Clayhall
Browndown Pt
Stokes Bay
Gilkicker Pt
Fort Monckton
Immigration Removal Centre
THE 1642 LIVING HISTORY MUSEUM
EXPLOSION
Burrow Island
HMS VICTORY
MARY ROSE
ROYAL NAVY SUBMARINE MUSEUM
Portsmouth
Portsea
Landport
Kingston
DICKENS' BIRTHPLACE
Fratton
Baffins
Portsea Island
Milton
Eastney
Somers Town
Old Portsmouth
Southsea
SOUTHSEA CASTLE
BLUE REEF AQUARIUM
CLARENCE PIER
D DAY MUSEUM
NATURAL HISTORY MUSEUM
ROYAL MARINES MUSEUM
West Winner
East Winner
HARBOUR
Langstone Channel
Emsworth Channel
Fleet
Manor Ho
Hayling Island
Gable Head
Westfield
West Town
South Hayling
Mengham
Selsmore
Eastoke
Eastoke Pt
Black Pt
Hayling Bay
EAST HAYLING LIGHT RLY
Pilsey Sand
PILSEY ISLAND
Longmere Pt
Chichester Channel
East Head
West Wittering
Acre Street
Holmes Fm
Somerley
Stubcroft Fm
East Wittering
Bracklesham
Bracklesham Bay
Oldhouse Fm
Lipperlng
CAKEHAM ROAD
SOLENT
SPITHEAD
Horse Sand Fort
No Mans Land Fort
St Helen's Fort
RYDE PIER HEAD
RYDE ESPLANADE
Ryde
Appley
Puckpool Pt
St John's Park
Pelhamfield
QUARR ABBEY
Quarr Hill
Kite Hill
Binstead
Weeks
Puck Ho
Firestone Copse
BRICKFIELDS HORSE COUNTRY
Haylands
Swanmore
ROSEMARY VINEYARD
Oakfield
Elmfield
Pondwell
SEAVIEW WILDLIFE ENCOUNTER
Seagrove Bay
Seaview
The Priory
Priory Bay
Bullen Ho
Nettlestone
Park Fm
WALTZING WATERS
SMALLBROOK JUNCTION
Bartlett's Green Fm
Upton
Havenstreet
Rowlands Wood
Whitefield Wood
Whitefield Fm
Ashey
Guildford Fm
ISLE OF WIGHT STEAM RAILWAY
Hardingshute Fm
ASHEY West Ashey
Rowlands Fm
St Helens
Bembridge Pt
Bembridge Harbour
BRADING MARSHES
Marsh Ho
Ethel Pt
Bembridge
Lane End
Foreland
Steyne Cross
Foreland Fields
BEMBRIDGE WINDMILL
The Run
Long Ledge
Hillway
Ashey Down
Nunwell Fm
NUNWELL HO
BRADING THE EXPERIENCE
Brading
Brading Down
VINEYARD
Yarbridge
ROMAN VILLA
Morton
MORTON MANOR
Bembridge Down
Whitecliff Bay
BEMBRIDGE FORT
Culver Down
Culver Cliff
Yaverland
ISLE OF WIGHT ZOO
DINOSAUR ISLE
Alverstone
Adgestone
Hill Fm
Newchurch
Queen's Bower
AMAZON WORLD
Winford
Branstone
Isle Of Wight (Sandown)
Merrie Gardens
NEWPORT ROAD
Sandown
Lake
SANDOWN BAY
Apse Heath
Landguard Manor
Bobberstone Fm
Whiteley Bank
Upper Hyde
Shanklin
Winstone Fm
Yard Fm
SHANKLIN CHINE
Horse Ledge
Shanklin Down 235
CHURCH ROAD
Luccombe Village
Luccombe Bay
Wroxall Manor Fm
Dunnose
Upper Bonchurch
Lowtherville
Bonchurch
Ventnor
Horseshoe Bay
Ventnor Bay
COASTAL VISITOR CENTRE
CAEN 5:30
LE HAVRE 3:15
ST MALO 9:00
GUERNSEY 7:30
JERSEY 8:00
SANTANDER 24:00 (MAR-NOV)
BILBAO 24:00
CAEN 3:45 (APR-SEPT)
CHERBOURG 3:00 (APR-NOV)
SZ
7
8
9
10
11
A
B
C
D
E
F
G
H
22

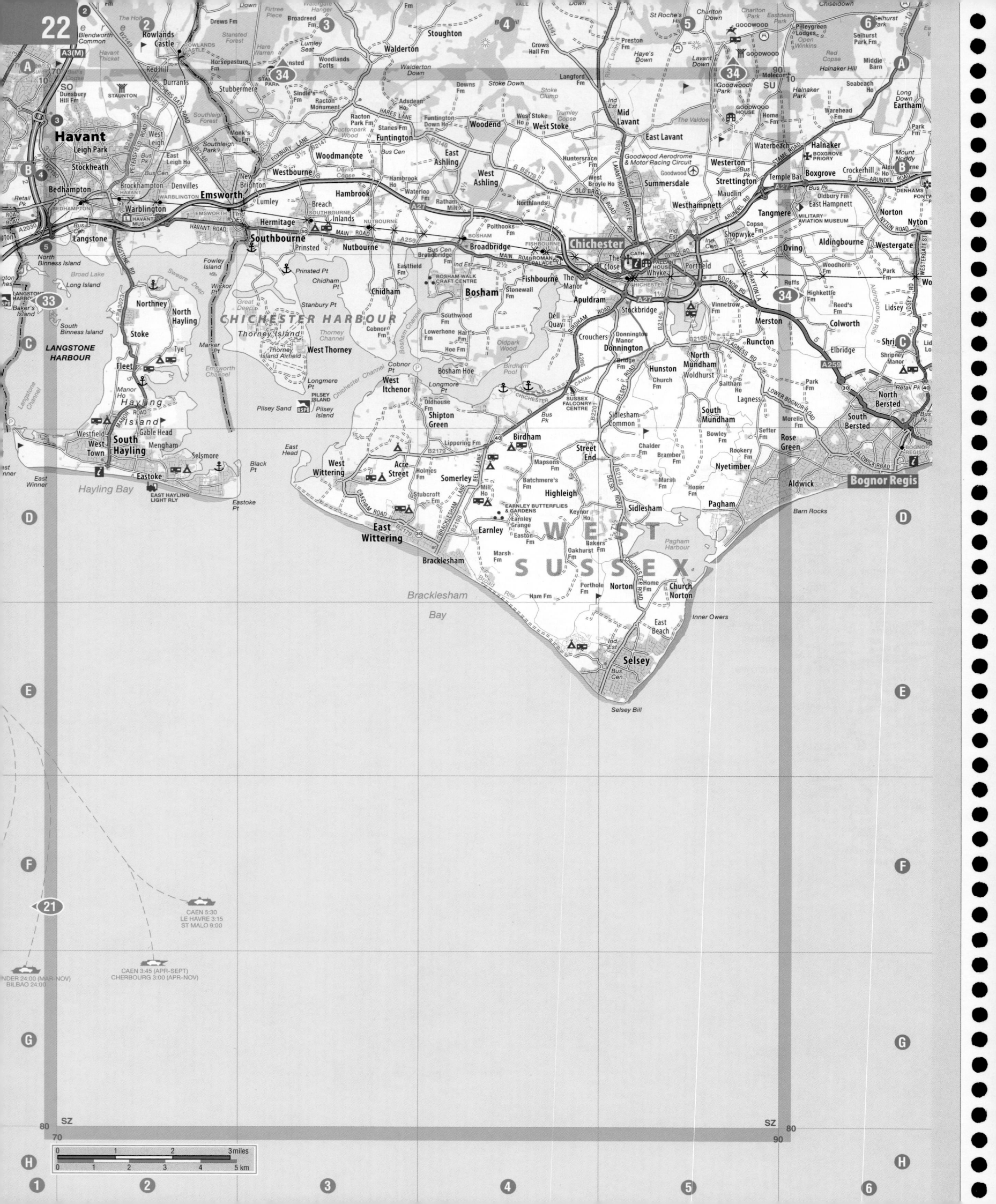

Rowlands Castle
Havant
Leigh Park
Stockheath
Bedhampton
Warblington
Emsworth
Langstone
Westbourne
Southbourne
Hermitage
Nutbourne
Woodmancote
Funtington
Stoughton
Walderton
East Ashling
West Ashling
Woodend
West Stoke
Mid Lavant
East Lavant
Goodwood Aerodrome & Motor Racing Circuit
Summersdale
Westerton
Strettington
Westhampnett
Halnaker
Boxgrove
Tangmere
Oving
Aldingbourne
Westergate
Norton
Nyton
Eartham
Chichester
Fishbourne
Broadbridge
Bosham
Chidham
Apuldram
Stockbridge
Donnington
Hunston
North Mundham
Runcton
Merston
Colworth
North Bersted
South Bersted
Bognor Regis
Aldwick
Rose Green
Nyetimber
Pagham
South Mundham
Sidlesham
Highleigh
Birdham
Somerley
Earnley
West Itchenor
Shipton Green
West Wittering
East Wittering
Bracklesham
Bracklesham Bay
WEST SUSSEX
Norton
Church Norton
East Beach
Selsey
Selsey Bill
Pagham Harbour
CHICHESTER HARBOUR
Thorney Island
West Thorney
LANGSTONE HARBOUR
Northney
North Hayling
Stoke
Fleet
Hayling Island
South Hayling
West Town
Eastoke
Mengham
Hayling Bay
CAEN 5:30
LE HAVRE 3:15
ST MALO 9:00
CAEN 3:45 (APR-SEPT)
CHERBOURG 3:00 (APR-NOV)
BILBAO 24:00
0 1 2 3 miles
0 1 2 3 4 5 km

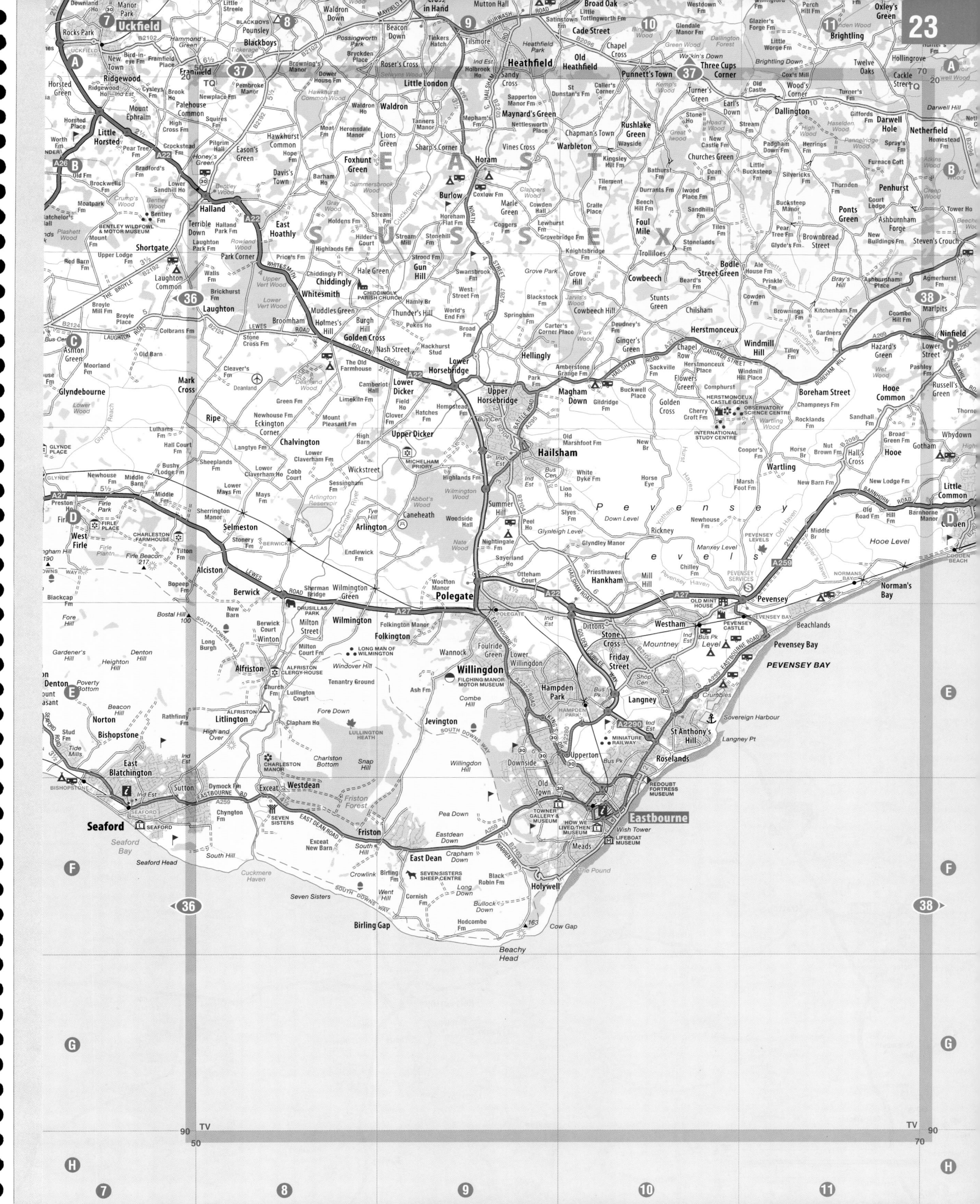

Downland Ho
Manor Park
Little Streele
Waldron Down
Cross in Hand
Mutton Hall
Broad Oak
Little Tottingworth Fm
Westdown Fm
Perch Hill Fm
Oxley's Green
Uckfield
Blackboys
Pounsley
Possingworth Park
Beacon Down
Tinkers Hatch
Tilsmore
Satinstown Fm
Cade Street
Glendale Manor Fm
Glazier's Forge Fm
Brightling
Hollingrove
Rocks Park
Hammond's Green
Bird-in-eye Fm
Framfield Place
New Town
Framfield
Browning's Manor
Bryckden Place
Roser's Cross
Heathfield Park
Heathfield
Holbrook Ho
Old Heathfield
Chapel Cross
Punnett's Town
Three Cups Corner
Little Worge Fm
Brightling Down
Twelve Oaks
Cackle Street
Ridgewood
Horsted Green
Cysleys Fm
Brook Ho
Palehouse Common
Newplace Fm
Pembroke Manor
Dower House Fm
Hawkhurst Common Wood
Little London
Sandy Cross
Sapperton Manor Fm
St Dunstan's Fm
Caller's Corner
Turner's Green
Old Castle
Wood's Corner
Earl's Down
Mount Ephraim
Squires Fm
Waldron Ho
Waldron
Tanners Manor
Maynard's Green
Nettlesworth Place
Stone Ho
Dallington
Darwell Hill
Horsted Place
Little Horsted
High Cross Fm
Moat Fm
Heronsdale Manor
Lions Green
Mephams Fm
Chapman's Town
Rushlake Green
Wayside
New Castle Fm
Stream Fm
Padgham Down Fm
Herrings Fm
Giffords Fm
Darwell Hole
Netherfield
Homestead Fm
Worth Fm
Pear Tree Fm
Crockstead Fm
Pilgrim Hall
Hawkhurst Common
Sharp's Corner
Vines Cross
Warbleton
Kingsley Hill Fm
Churches Green
Spray's Fm
Honey's Green
Eason's Green
Hope Fm
Foxhunt Green
Horam
Furnace Cott
Old Fm
Brockwells Fm
Bradford's Fm
Davis's Town
Barham Ho
Summersbrook Wood
Bathurst Fm
Dean Fm
Little Bucksteep Fm
Silverlicks Fm
Penhurst
Lower Sandhill Ho
Halland
Bentley Wood
Burlow
Coxlow Fm
Tilement Fm
Durrants Fm
Iwood Place Fm
Thornden Fm
Court Lodge
Tower Ho
Moatpark Fm
Crump's Wood
Bentley Fm
Bentley Wildfowl & Motor Museum
Gray Wood
Holdens Fm
Stream Fm
Cuckmere River
Horeham Flat Fm
Marle Green
Cowden Hall
Crafle Place
Beech Hill Fm
Sandhills Fm
Bucksteep Manor
Ponts Green
Ashburnham Forge
Plashett Wood
Mount Fm
Terrible Down
Halland Park Fm
East Hoathly
Hilder's Court
Stream Mill
Stonehill Fm
Coggers Fm
Lewhurst Fm
Grovebridge Fm
Foul Mile
Tiles Fm
Pear Tree Fm
Brownbread Street
New Buildings Fm
Steven's Crouch
Laughton Park Fm
Rowland Wood
Highlands Fm
Strood Fm
Knightsbridge Fm
Trolliloes
Stonelands Fm
Glyde's Fm
Shortgate
Upper Lodge Fm
Red Barn Fm
Park Corner
Price's Fm
Whitesmith
Gun Hill
Swansbrook Fm
Grove Park
Grove Hill
Cowbeech
Street Green
Bodle Street Green
Ale House Fm
Beard's Fm
Prinkle Fm
Bray's Hill
Ashburnham Place
Agmerhurst Fm
Laughton Common
Walls Fm
Upper Vert Wood
Chiddingly Pl
Chiddingly
Hale Green
Chiddingly Parish Church
West Street Fm
Hamly Br
The Broyle
Brickhurst Fm
Lower Vert Wood
Whitesmith
Blackstock Fm
Jarvis's Wood
Stunts Green
Chilsham
Cowden Fm
Brownings Fm
Kitchenham Fm
Marlpits
Broyle Mill Fm
Broyle Place
Laughton
Muddles Green
Thunder's Hill
World's End Fm
Springham Fm
Cowbeech Hill
Coombe Hill Fm
Holmes's Hill
Burgh Hill
Pekes Ho
Carter's Corner Place
Deudney's Fm
Ginger's Green
Herstmonceux
Bus Centre
Colbrans Fm
Laughton Road
Lewes Road
Broomham
Golden Cross
Broad Fm
Park Wood
Gardner Street
Windmill Hill
Gardners Fm
Hazard's Green
Ninfield
Ashton Green
Old Barn
Stone Cross Fm
Nash Street
Hackhurst Stud
Lower Horsebridge
Hellingly
Chapel Row
Tilley Fm
Lower Street
Moorland Fm
Cleaver's Fm
The Old Farmhouse
Deanland
Deanland Wood
Camberlot Hall
Amberstone Grange Fm
Herstmonceux Place
Sackville Fm
Windmill Hill Place
Wet Wood
Pashley Fm
Russell's Green
Glyndebourne
Mark Cross
Green Fm
Lower Dicker
Field Ho
Upper Horsebridge
Park Fm
Magham Down
Buckwell Place
Flowers Green
Comphurst
Boreham Street
Hooe Common
Lower Wood
Limekiln Fm
Hempstead Fm
Gildridge Fm
Golden Cross
Herstmonceux Castle Gdns
Observatory Science Centre
Champneys Fm
Ripe
Newhouse Fm
Eckington Corner
Mount Pleasant Fm
Clover Fm
Hatches Fm
Cherry Croft Fm
Warbling Wood
Rocklands Fm
Sandhall Fm
Thorne
Luthams Fm
Chalvington
High Barn
Upper Dicker
Old Marshfoot Fm
International Study Centre
Broad Green Fm
Whydown
Glynde Place
Hall Court Fm
Langtye Fm
Lower Claverham Fm
Michelham Priory
Hailsham
New Br
Cooper's Fm
Horse Br
Nut Brown Fm
Hall's Cross
Hooe
Gotham
Sheeplands Fm
Bushy Lodge Fm
Wickstreet
Ind Est
Bus Cen
Wartling
Lower Claverham Ho
Cobb Court
Highlands Fm
White Dyke Fm
Horse Eye
Marsh Foot Fm
New Barn Fm
New Lodge Fm
Little Common
Glynde
Newhouse Fm
Middle Barn
Lower Mays Fm
Sessingham Fm
Wilmington Wood
Lion Ho
Preston Ho
Middle Fm
Firle Park
Mays Fm
Arlington Reservoir
Abbot's Wood
Summer Hill
Pevensey
Old Road Fm
Hill Fm
Barnhorne Manor
Firle Place
Sherrington Manor
Tye Hill
Caneheath
Slyes Fm
Down Level
Newhouse Fm
Middle Br
Cooden
West Firle
Charleston Farmhouse
Selmeston
Arlington
Woodside Hall
Peel Ho
Glynleigh Level
Rickney
Pevensey Levels
Hooe Level
Stonery Fm
Berwick
Nate Wood
Nightingale Fm
Glyndley Manor
Manxey Level
Levels
Cooden Beach
Firle Plantn
Firle Beacon 217
Tilton Fm
Endlewick Fm
Sayerland Ho
Chilley Fm
A259
Alciston
Otteham Court
Priesthawes Fm
Mill Hill
Pevensey Haven
Normans Bay
Bopeep Fm
Lewes Road
Wilmington Green
Wootton Manor
Hankham
Pevensey Services
Norman's Bay
Blackcap Fm
Berwick
Sherman Bridge
Drusillas Park
Polegate
Old Mint House
Pevensey
Pevensey Bay
Fore Hill
Bostal Hill 100
New Barn
Wilmington
Folkington Manor
Ind Est
Westham
Pevensey Castle
Beachlands
Berwick Court
Milton Street
Folkington
Ditton's
Stone Cross
Mountney
Bus Pk
Level
Pevensey Bay
Long Burgh
Winton
Eastbourne Road
PEVENSEY BAY
Gardener's Hill
Denton Hill
Milton Court Fm
Long Man of Wilmington
Wannock
Foulride Green
Lower Willingdon
Friday Street
Heighton Hill
Alfriston
Alfriston Clergy House
Windover Hill
Willingdon
Filching Manor Motor Museum
Hampden Park
Shop Cen
Langney
Crumbles
Denton
Poverty Bottom
Church Fm
Tenantry Ground
Ash Fm
Sovereign Harbour
Lullington Court
Combe Hill
Hampden Park
Beacon Hill
Norton
Rathfinny Fm
Alfriston
Litlington
Clapham Ho
Fore Down
Jevington
A2290
Ind Est
St Anthony's Hill
Langney Pt
Stud Fm
Bishopstone
High and Over
Lullington Heath
South Downs Way
Miniature Railway
Tide Mills
Ind Est
Charleston Manor
Charlston Bottom
Snap Hill
Willingdon Hill
Downside
Upperton
Bus Pk
Roselands
East Blatchington
Westdean
Old Town
Redoubt Fortress Museum
Bishopstone
Sutton
Dymock Fm
Exceat
Friston Forest
Ind Est
Eastbourne
Towner Gallery & Museum
How We Lived Then Museum
Seaford
Chyngton Fm
Seven Sisters
East Dean Road
Pea Down
Wish Tower
Seaford
Seaford Bay
Friston
Eastdean Down
Meads
Lifeboat Museum
Seaford Head
South Hill
Exceat New Barn
South Hill
East Dean
Crapham Down
Warren Hill
Cuckmere Haven
Crowlink
Birling Fm
Seven Sisters Sheep Centre
Black Robin Fm
Holywell
The Pound
Seven Sisters
Went Hill
Long Down
Cornish Fm
Bullock Down
Birling Gap
Hodcombe Fm
163
Cow Gap
Beachy Head
EAST SUSSEX
Pevensey Levels
TQ
TV
36
37
38
A
B
C
D
E
F
G
H
7
8
9
10
11

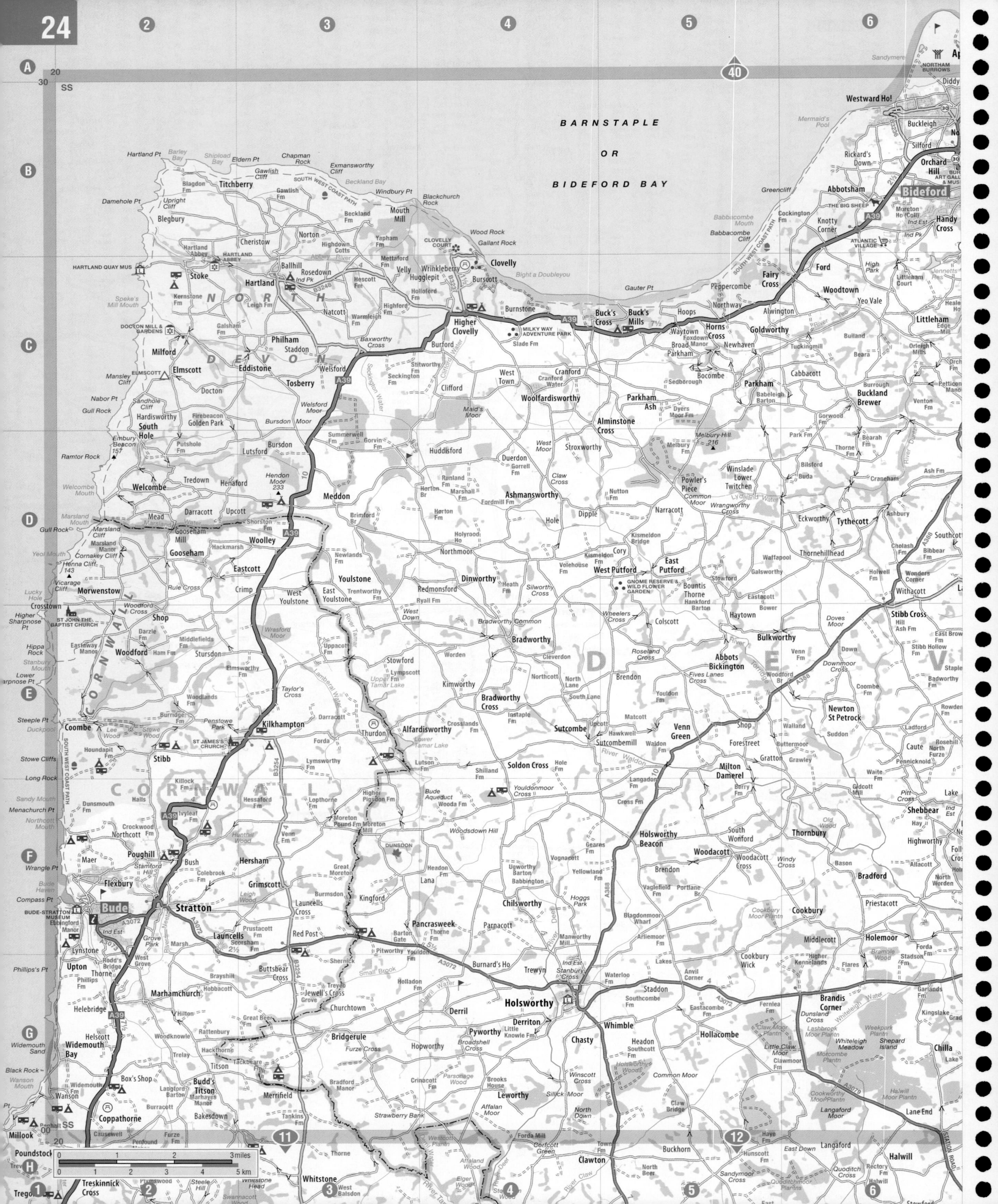
BARNSTAPLE
OR
BIDEFORD BAY
Hartland Pt
Barley Bay
Shipload Bay
Eldern Pt
Chapman Rock
Exmansworthy Cliff
Gawlish Cliff
Beckland Bay
Windbury Pt
Blackchurch Rock
Damehole Pt
Blagdon Fm
Titchberry
Upright Cliff
Blegbury
Gawlish Fm
SOUTH WEST COAST PATH
Beckland Fm
Mouth Mill
Wood Rock
Gallant Rock
Clovelly
Clovelly Court
Cheristow
Norton
Yapham Fm
Highdown Cotts
Hartland Abbey
Hartland Quay Mus
Stoke
Ballhill
Rosedown
Hartland
Ind Pk
Mettaford Fm
Velly
Wrinkleberry
Hugglepit
Burscott
Bight a Doubleyou
Speke's Mill Mouth
Kernstone Fm
NORTH
Leigh Fm
Hescott Fm
Holloford Fm
Highford Fm
Natcott
Warmleigh Fm
Docton Mill & Gardens
Galsham Fm
Philham
Staddon
Baxworthy Cross
Higher Clovelly
Burnstone
Milky Way Adventure Park
Slade Fm
A39
Buck's Cross
Buck's Mills
Gauter Pt
Milford
Elmscott
DEVON
Eddistone
Welsford
Tosberry
Burford
Stitworthy Fm
Seckington Fm
Mansley Cliff
Docton
Nabor Pt
Gull Rock
Sandhole Cliff
Hardisworthy
South Hole
Firebeacon
Golden Park
Welsford Moor
Bursdon Moor
Clifford
West Town
Cranford
Cranford Water
Woolfardisworthy
Maid's Moor
Embury Beacon 157
Ramtor Rock
Putshole Fm
Lutsford
Bursdon
Summerwell Fm
Gorvin Fm
Huddisford
Welcombe Mouth
Welcombe
Tredown
Henaford
Hendon Moor 233
Meddon
Marsland Mouth
Mead
Darracott
Upcott
Gull Rock
Marsland Cliff
Gooseham Mill
Shorston Fm
Woolley
Brimford Br
Horton Fm
Holywood Ho
Northmoor
Norton Br
Runland Fm
Marshall Fm
Fordmill Fm
Duerdon
Gorrell Fm
West Moor
Claw Cross
Stroxworthy
Ashmansworthy
Nutton Fm
Dipple
Hole
Yeol Mouth
Henna Cliff 143
Cornakey Cliff
Marsland Manor
Gooseham
Hackmarsh
Eastcott
Newlands Fm
Youlstone
Dinworthy
Vicarage Cliff
Morwenstow
Lucky Hole
Crosstown
St John the Baptist Church
Rule Cross
Crimp
West Youlstone
East Youlstone
Trentworthy Fm
Redmonsford
Ryall Fm
Heath Fm
Silworthy Cross
Volehouse Fm
Kismeldon Fm
Cory
West Putford
East Putford
Kismeldon Bridge
Gnome Reserve & Wild Flower Garden
Higher Sharpnose Pt
Woodford Cross
Shop
Hippa Rock
Darzie Fm
Middlefields Fm
Wrasford Moor
West Down
Bradworthy Common
Bradworthy
Eastaway Manor
Woodford
Ham Fm
Sturdson
Uppacott Fm
Stowford
Worden
Cleverdon
Stanbury Mouth
Lower Sharpnose Pt
Elmsworthy Fm
Lympscott Fm
Upper Tamar Lake
Taylor's Cross
Kimworthy
Northcott
North Lane
South Lane
Bradworthy Cross
Instaple Fm
Woodlands Fm
Steeple Pt
Duckpool
Coombe
Lee Wood
Stowe Wood
Burridge Fm
Penstowe Park
Kilkhampton
Darracott
Thurdon
Alfardisworthy
Crosslands Fm
Lower Tamar Lake
Sutcombe
Upcott
Hawkwell
Sutcombemill
St James's Church
Houndapit Fm
Stowe Cliffs
Stibb
Forda
Lymsworthy Fm
Lutsor Fm
Shilland Fm
Soldon Cross
Hole Fm
River Waldon
Long Rock
CORNWALL
Killock Fm
B3254
Halls
Hessaford Fm
Lopthorne Fm
Higher Pigsdon Fm
Bude Aqueduct
Wooda Fm
Youldonmoor Cross
Langadon Fm
Sandy Mouth
Dunsmouth Fm
Menachurch Pt
Northcott Mouth
Ivyleaf Fm
Crockwood Fm
Northcott
Moreton Pound Fm
Moreton Mill
Venn Fm
Huntfill Wood
Woodsdown Hill
Dunsdon
Poughill
Bush
Hersham
Maer
Wrangle Pt
Stamford Hill
Colebrook Fm
Great Moreton
Headon Fm
Lana
Ugworthy Barton
Babbington
Vognacott
Yellowland Fm
Gearns Fm
Bude Haven
Flexbury
Compass Pt
Grimscott
Burmsdon
Launcells Cross
Kingford
Leigh Wood
Chilsworthy
Hoggs Park
Bude
Stratton
Bude-Stratton Museum
Ebbingford Manor
Ind Est
A3072
A3073
Prustacott Fm
Launcells
Scorsham Fm
Red Post
Pancrasweek
Thorne Fm
Barton Gate
Parnacott
Manworthy Mill
River Deer
Lynstone
Grove Park
Marsh
West Grove
Shernick
Pitworthy
Youldon Fm
Burnard's Ho
Trewyn
Ind Est
Stanbury Cross
Phillips's Pt
Upton
Rodd's Bridge
Thorne
Phillips Fm
Brayshill
Buttsbear Cross
Small Brook
Holladon Fm
Derril Water
Marhamchurch
Hobbacott
Treyeo
Jewell's Cross
Grove
Churchtown
Derril
Holsworthy
Helebridge
Hilton
Great Beer
Derriton
Pyworthy
Little Knowle Fm
Rattenbury
Bridgerule
Broadshell Cross
Hopworthy
Widemouth Sand
Helscott Fm
Widemouth Bay
Woodknowle
Trelay
Hackthorne
Furze Cross
Titson
Tackbeare Fm
Budd's Titson
Marhayes Manor
Parsonage Wood
Brooks House
Black Rock
Box's Shop
Leworthy
Widemouth Fm
Langford Barton
Bradford Manor
Crinacott Fm
Wanson Mouth
Wanson
Burracott
Merrifield
Affalan Moor
Coppathorne
Bakesdown
Tankins Fm
Strawberry Bank
Millook
Causewell
Penfound
Furze Fm
Poundstock
Thorne
Whitstone
Westcott Plantn
Affaland Wood
Elger Wood
Trevi
Tregol
Treskinnick Cross
Plymswood
Steele Hill
Whitstone Head
Swannacott Wood
West Balsdon
River Tamar
Stacey Wood
Sandymere
Northam Burrows
Diddy
Westward Ho!
Mermaid's Pool
Buckleigh
Silford
Rickard's Down
Orchard Hill
Bideford
Greencliff
Abbotsham
The Big Sheep
Moreton Ho (Coll)
Ind Est
Handy Cross
Cockington Fm
Knotty Corner
Babbacombe Mouth
Babbacombe Cliff
Atlantic Village
Ind Pk
Fairy Cross
Ford
High Park
Littleham Court
Peppercombe
Northway
Woodtown
Yeo Vale
Alwington
Hoops
Littleham
Waytown
Horns Cross
Foxdown Manor
Broad Parkham
Goldworthy
River Yeo
Bulland
Tuckingmill
Beara
Orleigh Mills
Newhaven
Bocombe
Sedborough
Parkham
Cabbacott
Burrough Manor
Buckland Brewer
Venton Fm
Parkham Ash
Dyers Moor Fm
Alminstone Cross
Babeleigh Barton
Gorwood Fm
Melbury Hill 216
Melbury Fm
Park Fm
Thorne Fm
Bearah Fm
Bilsford
Buda
Ash Fm
Winslade
Lower Twitchen
Powler's Piece
Common Moor
Wrangworthy Cross
Craneham
Narracott
Eckworthy
Tythecott
Ashbury
Southcott
Cholash Fm
Bibbear Fm
Waffapool
Thornehillhead
Galsworthy
Stowford
Holwell Fm
Wonders Corner
Withacott
Bountis Thorne
Hankford Barton
Eastacott
Bower
Stibb Cross
Hill
Ash Fm
Wheelers Cross
Colscott
Haytown
Doves Moor
Bulkworthy
East Brow
Stibb Hollow Fm
Roseland Cross
Abbots Bickington
DEVON
Venn Fm
Down
Downmoor Cross
Staple
Brendon
Fives Lanes Cross
Woodford Br
A388
Badworthy Fm
Youldon Fm
Matcott
Coombe Fm
Newton St Petrock
Rowden Fm
Venn Green
Shop
Walland
Ladford
Forestreet
Suddon
Buttermoor
Caute
Rosehill
North Furze
Waldon Fm
Gratton
Grawley
Pennicknold
Milton Damerel
Waite Fm
Berry Fm
Oldcott Mill
Pitt Cross
Lake
Cross Fm
Shebbear
Hay
Old Wood
Holsworthy Beacon
South Wonford
Thornbury
Highworthy
Woodacott
Woodacott Cross
Windy Cross
Bason
Allacott
Brendon
Bradford
Vaglefield Fm
Portlane Br
North Worden
Priestacott
Cookbury Moor Plantn
Cookbury
Blagdonmoor Wharf
Arliemoor Fm
Middlecott
Holemoor
Forda Fm
Lakes
Cookbury Wick
Higher Kennelands
Flares
Bramble Wood
Stadson Fm
Waterloo Fm
Anvil Corner
Staddon
Garlands Fm
Brandis Corner
Southcombe Fm
Eastacombe Fm
Fernlea Fm
Dunsland Cross
Kingslake
Whimble
Lashbrook Moor Plantn
Weekpark Plantn
Chasty
Headon
Southcott Fm
Hollacombe
Claw Moor Plantn
Little Claw Moor
Whiteleigh Meadow
Shepard Island
Chilla
Holsworthy Woods
Clawmoor Fm
Morcombe Plantn
Winscott Cross
Common Moor
Sillick Moor
Claw Bridge
Cookworthy Moor Plantn
Halwill Moor Plantn
North Down
Langaford Moor
Lane End
Forda Mill
Corfcott Green
Town Fm
Haye Fm
Langaford
Clawton
Buckhorn
Hunscott Fm
East Down
Halwill
North Beer
Sandymoor Cross
Quoditch Cross
Rectory Fm
Halwill
River Claw
Station Road
A3079
A386
SS
20
30
00
40
11
12
0 1 2 3 miles
0 1 2 3 4 5 km

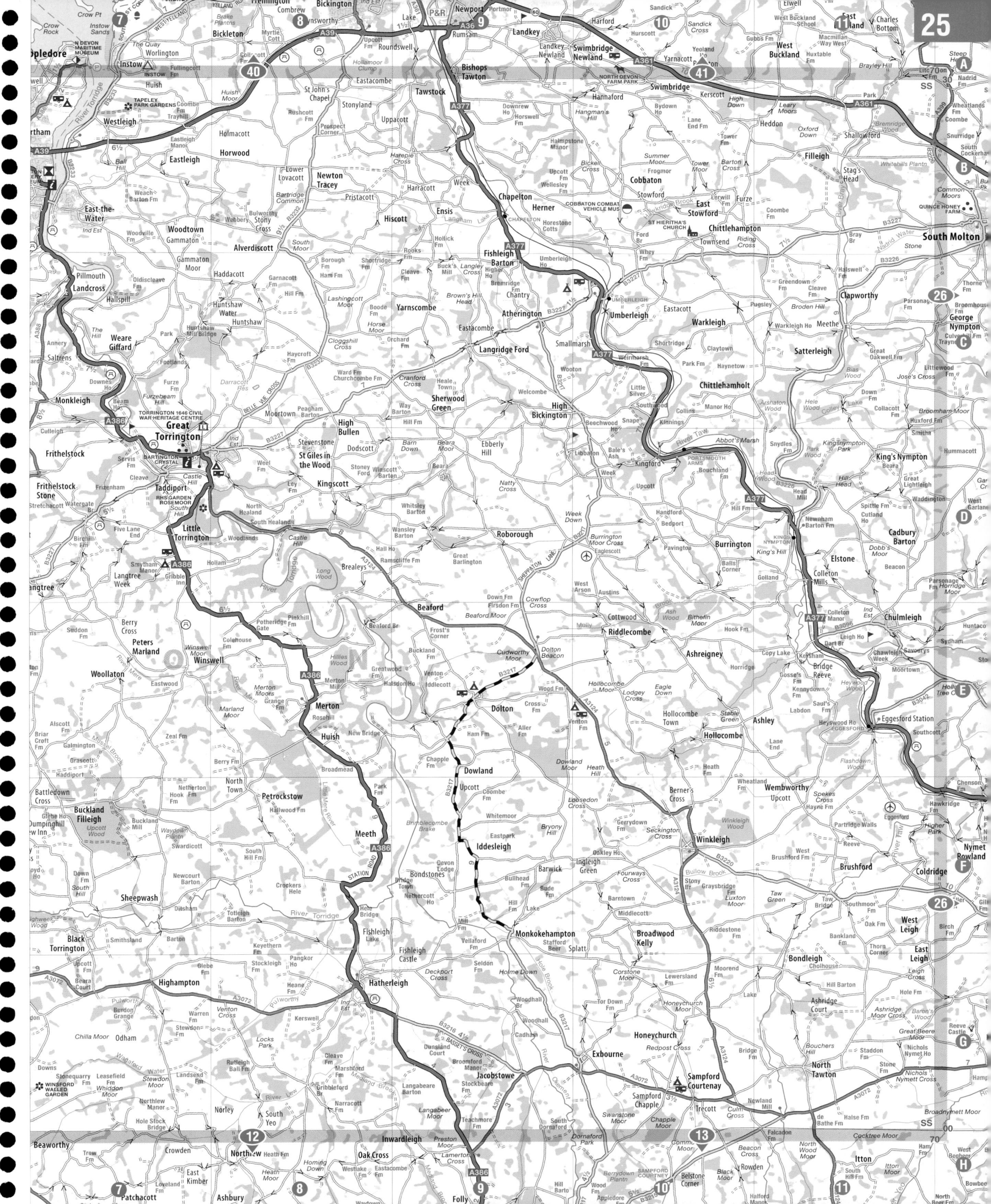

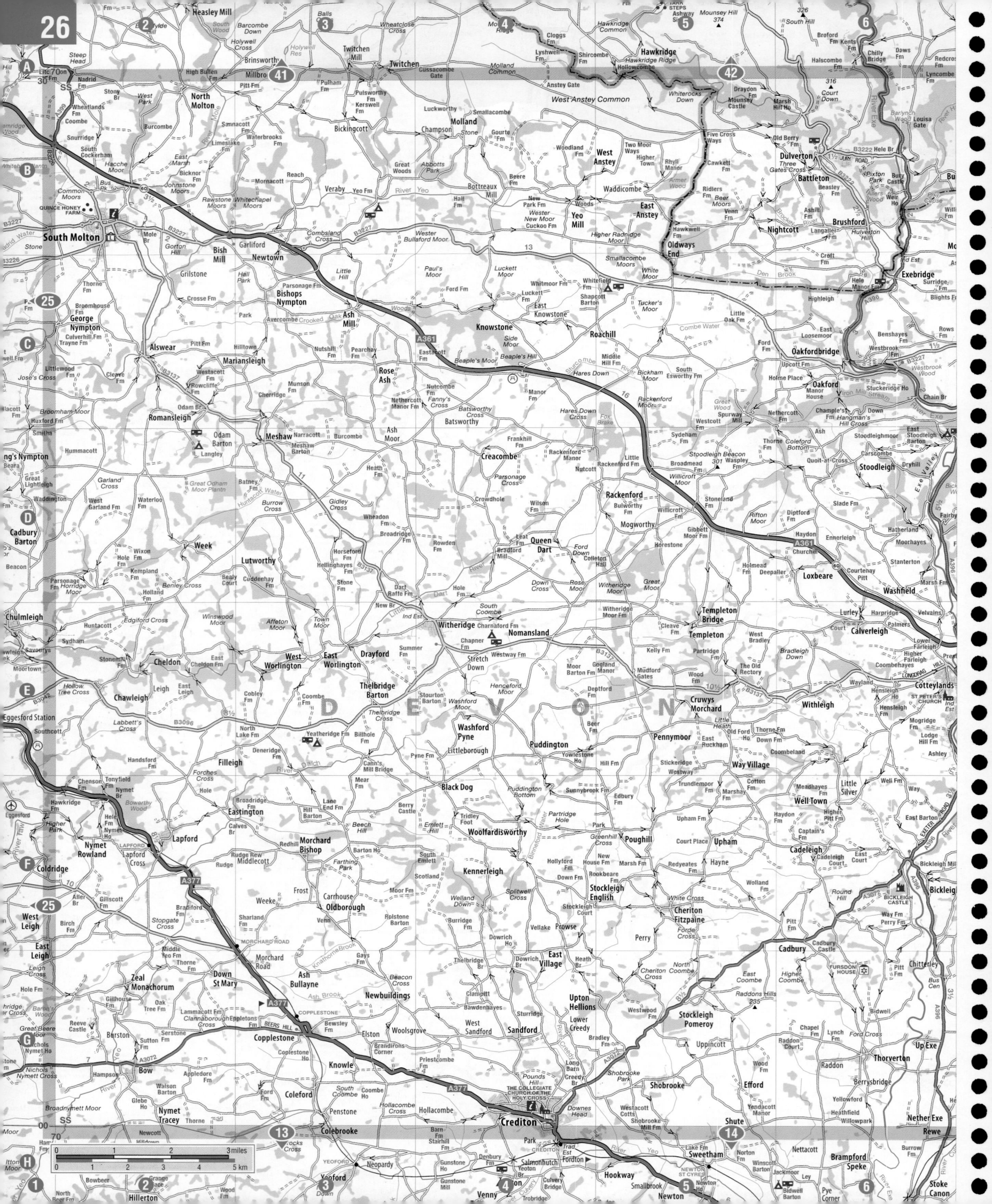
Heasley Mill
Barcombe Down
Holywell Cross
Balls Cross
Wheatclose Cross
Molland Ridge
Cloggs
Lyshwell
Hawkridge Common
Tarr Steps
Ashway Side
Mounsey Hill
374
South Hill
Broford Fm
Kents Fm
Chilly Bridge
Daws Fm
Redcross
Steep Head
Brinsworthy
Holywell Res
Twitchen Mill
Twitchen
Cussacombe Gate
Molland Common
Shircombe
Hollowcombe
Hawkridge
Hawkridge Ridge
Halscombe Fm
Lyncombe
Nadrid Fm
High Bullen
Millbrook
41
42
Pulham Fm
Pulsworthy Fm
Kerswell Fm
Anstey Gate
West Anstey Common
Whiterocks Down
Draydon Fm
Mounsey Castle
Marsh Hill Ho
316
Court Down
River Exe
Stony Br
West Park
North Molton
Pitt Fm
Wheatlands Fm
Coombe
Burcombe
Sannacott Fm
Waterbrooks Fm
Luckworthy
Smallacombe
Molland
Champson
Bickingcott
Stone
Gourte Fm
Five Cross Ways
Old Berry Fm
Barlynch Wood
Louisa Gate
Snurridge
South Cockerham
East Marsh
Limeslake Fm
Great Woods
Abbotts Park
Woodland Fm
West Anstey
Two Moor Ways
Higher Town
Rhyll Manor
Cawkett Fm
Dulverton
Three Gates Cross
Hele Br
Hacche Moor
Bicknor Fm
Johnstone Moors
Reach
Mornacott
Veraby
Yeo Fm
River Yeo
Bottreaux Mill
Beere Fm
Armer Wood
Battleton
Beasley Fm
Pixton Park
Bury Castle
Weir Ho
Common Moors
Quince Honey Farm
Rawstone Moors
Whitechapel Moors
Hall Fm
New Park Fm
Woods
Waddicombe
East Anstey
Ridlers Fm
Beer Moors
Venn Fm
Ashill Fm
Brushford
South Molton
Mole Br
Gorton Hill
Combsland Cross
Wester Bullaford Moor
Wester New Moor
Cuckoo Fm
Yeo Mill
Higher Radnidge Moor
Hawkwell Fm
Oldways End
Nightcott
Langaller Fm
Hulverton Hill
Stone
Bish Mill
Garliford
Newtown
Smallacombe Moors
White Moor
Croft Fm
Den Brook
Exebridge
Hele Manor Fm
Grilstone
Hall Park
Little Hill
Paul's Moor
Luckett Moor
Surridge
Thorne Fm
Parsonage Fm
Bishops Nympton
Ford Fm
Whitmoor Fm
Whitefield Fm
Shapcott Barton
Tucker's Moor
Highleigh
Blights Fm
25
Crosse Fm
Luckett Fm
East Knowstone
Broomhouse Fm
George Nympton
Culverhill Fm
Trayne Fm
Park
Avercombe
Crooked Oak
Ash Mill
Woods
Knowstone
Roachill
Little Oak Fm
Combe Water
East Loosemoor
Benshayes Fm
Rows Fm
Alswear
Pitt Fm
Hilltown
Nutshill Fm
Pearchay Fm
Eastacott Fm
A361
Side Moor
Beaple's Hill
Beaple's Moor
Middle Hill Fm
Ford Fm
Oakfordbridge
Westbrook Fm
Marianslieigh
Rose Ash
Hares Down
Bickham Moor
South Esworthy Fm
Upcott Fm
Holme Place
Oakford
Westbrook Wood
Littlewood Fm
Jose's Cross
Cleave Fm
Westacott Fm
Rowcliffe Fm
Cherridge
Munson Fm
Nutcombe Fm
Nethercott Manor Fm
Fanny's Cross
Manor Fm
Rackenford Moor
Spurway Mill
Manor House
Stuckeridge Ho
Chain Br
Broomham Moor
Huxford Fm
Romansleigh
Odam Br
Odam Barton
Batsworthy Cross
Batsworthy
Hares Down Cross
Fox Brake
Westcott Fm
Nethercott Fm
Chample's Fm
Hangman's Hill Cross
River Exe
Smitha
Narracott
Meshaw
Meshaw Barton
Burcombe
Ash Moor
Langley
Frankhill Fm
Sydeham Fm
Ash
Stoodleighmoor
East Stoodleigh Barton
Hummacott
Creacombe
Rackenford Manor
Little Rackenford Fm
Stoodleigh Beacon
301
Waspley Fm
Thorne Fm
Coleford Bottom
Carscombe
Quoit-at-Cross
Stoodleigh
Dryhill
Exe Valley
King's Nympton
Great Lightleigh
Garland Cross
Great Odham Moor Plantn
Batney Fm
Heath Fm
Parsonage Cross
Nutcott
Broadmead Fm
Willicroft Moor
Waddington
West Garland Fm
Waterloo Fm
Huntacott Water
Burrow Cross
Gidley Cross
Crowdhole
Rackenford
Bulworthy Fm
Willscroft Fm
Stoneland Fm
Rifton Moor
Diptford Fm
Slade Fm
Cadbury Barton
Wheadon Fm
Broadridge Fm
Wilson Fm
Mogworthy
Gibbett Moor Fm
Haydon
Churchill
Hatherland
Moorhayes
Fairby
Week
Lutworthy
Horseford Fm
Hellinghayes Fm
Rowden Fm
Leat Fm
Queen Dart
Bradford Mill
Ford Down
Colleton Hall
Horestone
Ennerleigh
Beacon
Wixon Fm
Hole Fm
Kempland Fm
Holland Fm
Benley Cross
Bealy Court
Cuddenhay Fm
Stone Fm
Dart Raffe Fm
Hole Fm
Down Cross
Rose Moor
Witheridge Moor
Great Moor
Holmead Fm
Deepaller
Loxbeare
Courtenay Pitt
Stanterton
Washfield
Marsh Fm
Parsonage Fm
Horridge Moor
New Br
Ind Est
South Coombe
Witheridge Moor Fm
Templeton Bridge
Lurley
Harpridge
Velvains
Chulmleigh
Huntacott
Edgiford Cross
Winswood Moor
Affeton Moor
Town Moor
Witheridge
Charnaford Fm
Nomansland
Chapner Fm
Cleave Fm
Templeton
Court
Calverleigh
Palmers
Lower Farleigh
Sydham
Savourys
Stonemoor
Cheldon
East Cheldon Fm
West Worlington
East Worlington
Drayford
Summer Fm
Stretch Down
Westway Fm
West Bradley
Kelly Fm
Partridge Fm
Bradleigh Down
Higher Farleigh
Coombehayes
Moortown
Moor Barton Fm
Gogland Manor
Mudford Gates
Wood Fm
The Old Rectory
Longdrag Hill
Hollow Tree Cross
Chawleigh
Leigh
East Leigh
Cobley Fm
Coombe Fm
Thelbridge Barton
Stourton Barton
Henceford Moor
Deptford Fm
Cruwys Morchard
Wayland
Cotteylands
Withleigh
St Peter's Church
Hensleigh Fm
Eggesford Station
D
E
V
O
N
Labbett's Cross
Washford Moor
Thelbridge Cross
Washford Pyne
Beer Fm
Little Heath
Old Ford Ho
Thorne Fm
Mogridge Fm
Lodge Hill Fm
Southcott
North Lake Fm
Yeatheridge Fm
Billhole Fm
Puddington
Pennymoor
East Ruckham
Down Fm
Ashley
Handsford Fm
Filleigh
Denerige Fm
Pyne Fm
Littleborough
Yowlestone Ho
Hill Fm
Stickeridge
Westway
Coombeland
Chenson Fm
Tonyfield Fm
Nymet Br
Forches Cross
Cann's Mill Bridge
Way Village
Mear Fm
Black Dog
Puddington Bottom
Sunnybrook Fm
Trundlemoor Fm
Cotton Fm
Marshay Fm
Meadhayes Fm
Little Silver
Well Fm
Hawkridge Fm
Bowerthy Wood
Hole
Broadridge Fm
Eastington
Lane End Fm
Berry Castle
Tridley Foot
Edbury Fm
Well Town
Way
Eggesford
Hele Fm
Nymet Ho
Higher Park
Calves Br
Hill Barton
Beech Hill
Emlett Hill
Woolfardisworthy
Partridge Hole
Upham Fm
Haydon Fm
Higher Pitt Fm
East Barton
Nymet Rowland
Lapford
Lapford Cross
Redhill
Morchard Bishop
Barton Ho
Park
Greenhill Cross
Poughill
Court Place
Upham
Captain's Fm
Cadeleigh
Rudge Rew
Middlecott
Rudge
Farthing Park
South Emlett
Hollyford Fm
New House Fm
Marsh Fm
Redyeates Fm
Hayne
Cadeleigh Court
East Court
Bickleigh Mill
Coldridge
A377
Scotland
Kennerleigh
Down Fm
Rookbeare Fm
Stockleigh English
White Cross
Wolland Fm
Round Hill
Bickleigh Castle
Bickleigh
Aller Br
Gillscott Fm
Frost
Carrhouse
Oldborough
Moor Fm
Welland Down
Splitwell Cross
Cheriton Fitzpaine
Way Fm
Perry Fm
West Leigh
Birch Fm
Bradiford Fm
Stopgate Cross
Weeke
Sharland Fm
Venn
Rolstone Barton
Burridge Fm
Vellake
Prowse
Stockleigh Court
Forde Cross
Pitt Fm
East Leigh
Morchard Road
Dowrich Ho
Perry
Cadbury
Cadbury Castle
Leigh Cross
Middle Yeo Fm
Thorne Fm
Morchard Road
Knathorne Brook
Gays Fm
Thelbridge Br
Dowrich Br
East Village
Heath Br
North Coombe
Cheriton Cross
East Coombe
Higher Coombe
Fursdon House
Pitt Fm
Chitterley
Hole Fm
Zeal Monachorum
Down St Mary
Ash Bullayne
Beacon Cross
Clampitt
Raddons Hills
235
Bus Cen
Oak Tree Fm
Ash Brook
Newbuildings
Bawdenhayes
Upton Hellions
Gillhouse Fm
Lammacott Fm
Clannaborough Cross
Eppletons Fm
Copplestone
Sturridge
Westwood Fm
Stockleigh Pomeroy
Bidwell
Reeve Castle
Serstone Fm
Beers Hill
Bewsley Fm
Woolsgrove
West Sandford
Sandford
Lower Creedy
Chapel Fm
Lynch Fm
Ford Cross
Up Exe
Great Beere
Nichols Nymet Ho
Burston
Sutton Fm
A3072
Copplestone
Elston
Brandirons Corner
Bradley Fm
Uppincott
Raddon Court
Thorverton
Nichols Nymett Cross
Hampson
Bow
Appledore Fm
Copplestone Ho
Knowle
Priestcombe Fm
Pounds Hill
Long Barn
Creedy Br
Shobrooke Park
Shobrooke
Wood Fm
Efford
Raddon
Berrysbridge
Walson Barton
Ford Fm
Coleford
South Coombe
Coombe Ho
The Collegiate Church of the Holy Cross
Downes Head
Westacott Cotts
Yendacott Manor
Yellowford
Broadnymett Moor
Glebe Ho
Nymet Tracey
Thorne
Penstone
Hollacombe Cross
Hollacombe
Crediton
Shobrooke Mill Fm
Shute
Heathfield
Willowpark
Nether Exe
Newcott
Colebrooke
13
Park
14
Rewe
Hamlyn
Barn Fm
Stairhill Fm
Crediton
Trad Est
Lake Fm
Sweetham
Norton Fm
Nettacott
Brampford Speke
Burrow Fm
Itton Moor
Frocks Cross
Yeoford
Neopardy
Gunstone Ho
Denbury Fm
Yeoton
Salmonhutch
Fordton
Hookway
Winscott Barton
Jackmoor
Newton St Cyres
Smallbrook
Bidwell Barton
Ley
Pye Corner
Stoke Canon
Bowbeer
Grange Ho
Hillerton
Yeoford Down
Gunstone Mill
Venny
Culvery Bridge
Trobridge
Newton
North Beer Fm
0 1 2 3 miles
0 1 2 3 4 5 km

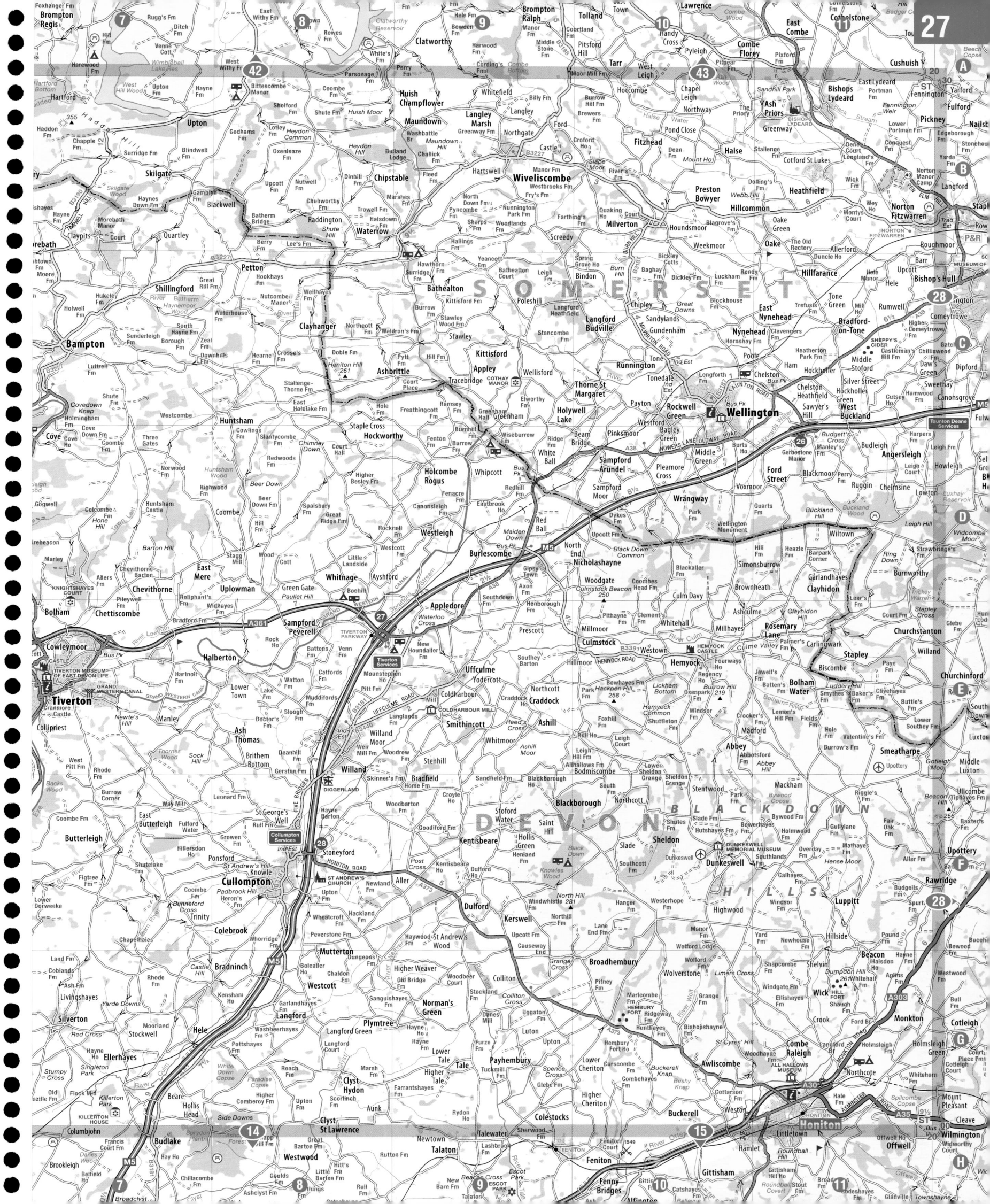
Brompton Regis
Harewood Fm
Hartford
Upton
Skilgate
Blackwell
Bampton
Huntsham
Cove
Bolham
Chettiscombe
Chevithorne
Cowleymoor
Tiverton
Halberton
Ash Thomas
Manley
Uplowman
East Mere
Sampford Peverell
Petton
Shillingford
Clayhanger
Raddington
Waterrow
Chipstable
Huish Champflower
Maundown
Clatworthy
Brompton Ralph
Tolland
Langley Marsh
Langley
Northgate
Wiveliscombe
Castle
Ford
Fitzhead
Milverton
Halse
Ash Priors
Bishops Lydeard
Cotford St Lukes
Heathfield
Hillcommon
Preston Bowyer
Oake
Norton Fitzwarren
Hillfarrance
Bradford-on-Tone
Nynehead
East Nynehead
Langford Budville
Runnington
Tonedale
Wellington
Rockwell Green
Westford
Thorne St Margaret
Holywell Lake
Greenham
Appley
Kittisford
Stawley
Ashbrittle
Bathealton
Hockworthy
Holcombe Rogus
Whipcott
Westleigh
Burlescombe
Whitnage
Appledore
Nicholashayne
Culmstock
Hemyock
Clayhidon
Churchstanton
Stapley
Rosemary Lane
West Buckland
Angersleigh
Ford Street
Wrangway
Sampford Arundel
Bishop's Hull
Upottery
Luppitt
Dunkeswell
Sheldon
Blackborough
Kentisbeare
Craddock
Ashill
Smithincott
Uffculme
Willand
Cullompton
Butterleigh
Bradninch
Silverton
Ellerhayes
Hele
Langford
Plymtree
Payhembury
Broadhembury
Kerswell
Dulford
Awliscombe
Combe Raleigh
Honiton
Buckerell
Feniton
Talaton
Clyst Hydon
Clyst St Lawrence
Westwood
Budlake
Colebrook
Beacon
Monkton
Cotleigh
Wilmington
Offwell
Gittisham
Fenny Bridges
Smeatharpe
Wick
Abbey
SOMERSET
DEVON
BLACKDOWN HILLS
Taunton Deane Services
Tiverton Services
Cullompton Services
M5
A38
A361
A373
A30
A35
42
43
28
27
26
14
15

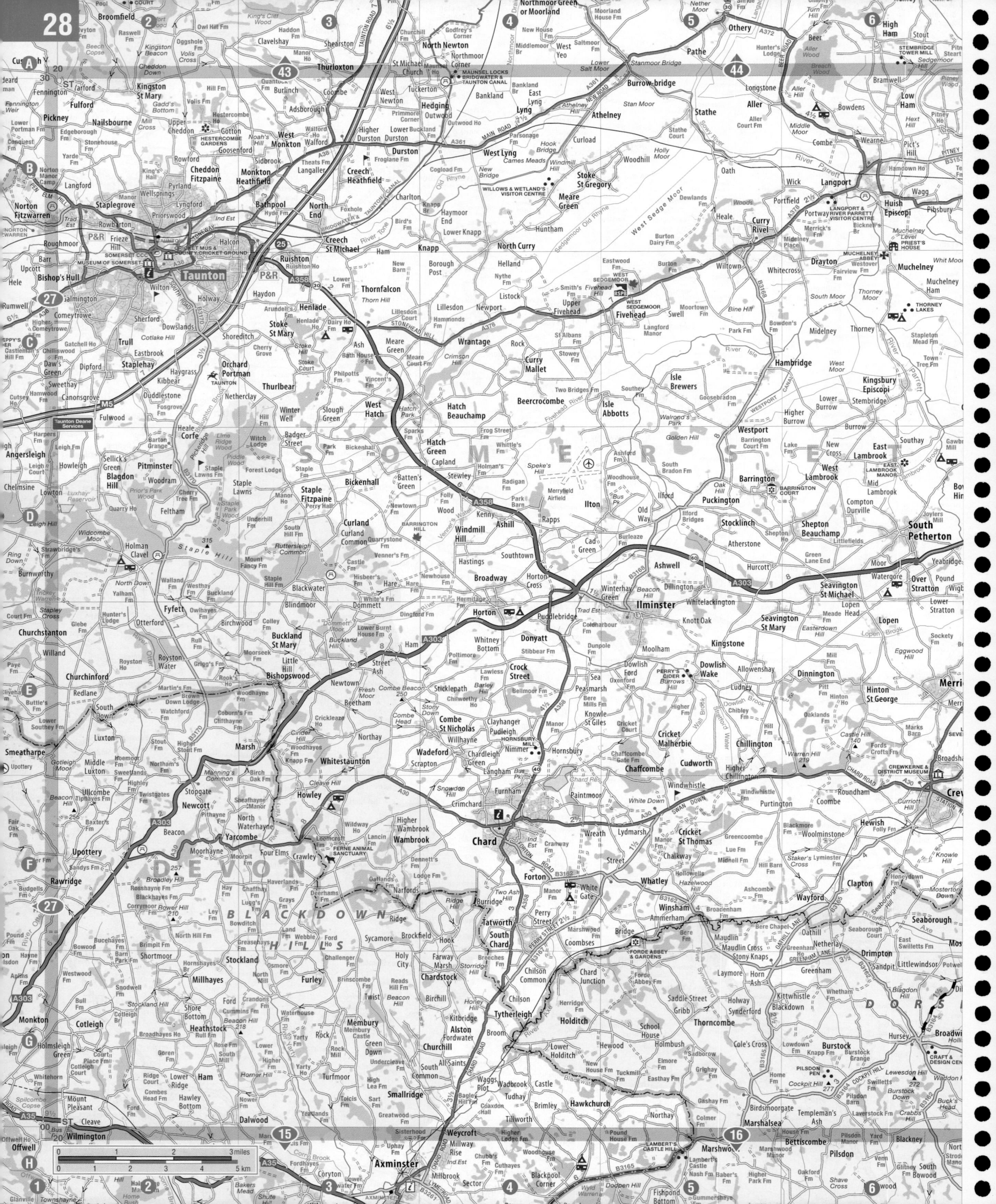

43
44
Taunton
27
Broomfield
Clavelshay
Shearston
North Newton
Northmoor Green or Moorland
Othery
High Ham
Thurloxton
Kingston St Mary
Burlinch
Burrow-bridge
Athelney
Fulford
Pickney
Nailsbourne
Cheddon
West Monkton
Walford
Hedging
Lyng
Aller
Durston
West Lyng
Stathe
Norton Fitzwarren
Staplegrove
Cheddon Fitzpaine
Monkton Heathfield
Creech Heathfield
Stoke St Gregory
Langport
Bathpool
North End
Meare Green
Curry Rivel
Huish Episcopi
Creech St Michael
Knapp
North Curry
Drayton
Muchelney
Bishop's Hull
Ruishton
Henlade
Thornfalcon
Fivehead
Stoke St Mary
Trull
Staplehay
Wrantage
Curry Mallet
Hambridge
Orchard Portman
Thurlbear
Isle Brewers
Kingsbury Episcopi
West Hatch
Hatch Beauchamp
Beercrocombe
Isle Abbotts
Westport
Heale Corfe
Angersleigh
Pitminster
Blagdon Hill
Hatch Green
East Lambrook
SOMERSET
Staple Fitzpaine
Bickenhall
Barrington
Puckington
Ilton
Stocklinch
Shepton Beauchamp
South Petherton
Curland
Ashill
Windmill Hill
Holman Clavel
Staple Hill
Ashwell
Broadway
Horton
Ilminster
Seavington St Michael
Over Stratton
Churchstanton
Buckland St Mary
Donyatt
Seavington St Mary
Lopen
Kingstone
Churchinford
Bishopswood
Crock Street
Dowlish Wake
Dinnington
Hinton St George
Combe St Nicholas
Cricket Malherbie
Chillington
Marsh
Wadeford
Chaffcombe
Cudworth
Whitestaunton
Howley
Chard
Upottery
Yarcombe
Wambrook
Cricket St Thomas
Forton
Whatley
Wayford
Clapton
Rawridge
DEVON
BLACKDOWN HILLS
Winsham
Seaborough
Stockland
Millhayes
Furley
Chardstock
Tatworth
South Chard
Drimpton
Monkton
Cotleigh
Membury
Churchill
Tytherleigh
Holditch
Thorncombe
Burstock
Broadwindsor
DORSET
Dalwood
Hawkchurch
Marshalsea
Bettiscombe
Pilsdon
Wilmington
Offwell
Axminster
Marshwood
15
16

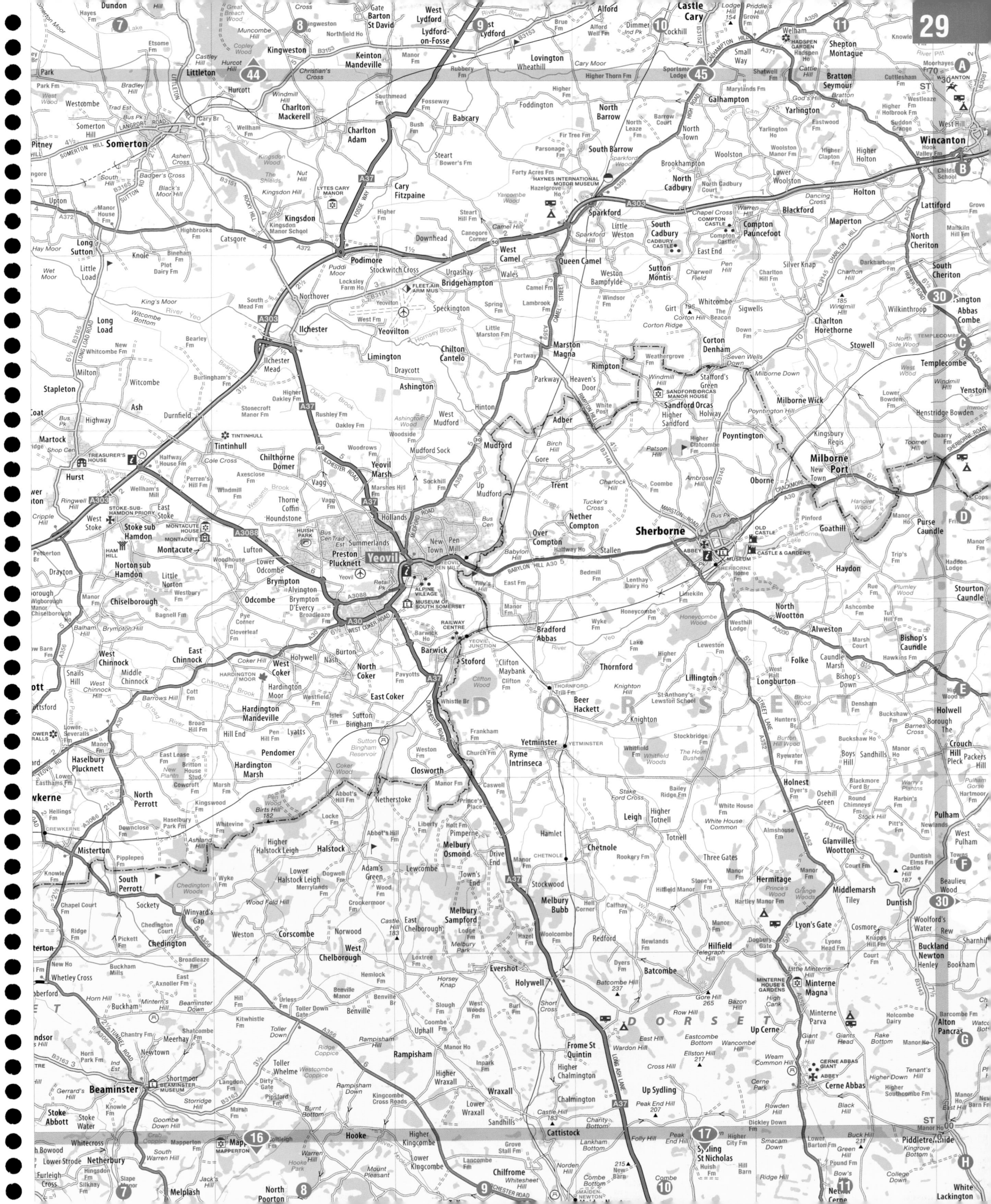
29
Dundon
Hayes Fm
Great Breach Wood
Barton St David
West Lydford
Lydford-on-Fosse
Alford
Castle Cary
Welham
Shepton Montague
Kingweston
Keinton Mandeville
Lovington
Wheathill
Littleton
Somerton
Charlton Mackerell
Charlton Adam
Babcary
Foddington
North Barrow
South Barrow
Galhampton
Yarlington
Bratton Seymour
Wincanton
Pitney
Long Sutton
Upton
Kingsdon
Lytes Cary Manor
Cary Fitzpaine
Sparkford
Haynes International Motor Museum
North Cadbury
South Cadbury
Compton Pauncefoot
Blackford
Maperton
Holton
Lattiford
North Cheriton
South Cheriton
Podimore
West Camel
Queen Camel
Sutton Montis
Little Load
Long Load
Knole
Bridgehampton
Fleet Air Arm Mus
Yeovilton
Speckington
Ilchester
Northover
Limington
Chilton Cantelo
Marston Magna
Rimpton
Corton Denham
Charlton Horethorne
Stowell
Templecombe
Abbas Combe
Henstridge Bowden
Yenston
Ashington
Draycott
Stapleton
Witcombe
Ash
Martock
Tintinhull
Chilthorne Domer
Mudford
Sandford Orcas
Milborne Wick
Milborne Port
Yeovil Marsh
Hurst
Treasurer's House
Stoke sub Hamdon
Montacute
Norton sub Hamdon
Lufton
Preston Plucknett
Yeovil
Thorne Coffin
Houndstone
Trent
Nether Compton
Over Compton
Sherborne
Purse Caundle
Goathill
Haydon
Odcombe
Brympton
Chiselborough
West Chinnock
Middle Chinnock
East Chinnock
West Coker
East Coker
North Coker
Barwick
Stoford
Bradford Abbas
Thornford
North Wootton
Alweston
Folke
Bishop's Caundle
Lillington
Longburton
Beer Hackett
Hardington Mandeville
Hardington Marsh
Sutton Bingham
Closworth
Yetminster
Ryme Intrinseca
Haselbury Plucknett
North Perrott
Pendomer
Crewkerne
Misterton
South Perrott
Halstock
Melbury Osmond
Chetnole
Leigh
Holnest
Hermitage
Glanvilles Wootton
Pulham
Middlemarsh
Stockwood
Melbury Bubb
Melbury Sampford
Evershot
Batcombe
Hilfield
Minterne Magna
Chedington
Corscombe
West Chelborough
East Chelborough
Holywell
Frome St Quintin
Up Cerne
Cerne Abbas
Buckland Newton
Alton Pancras
Beaminster
Rampisham
Toller Whelme
Wraxall
Up Sydling
Chalmington
Cattistock
Sydling St Nicholas
Hooke
Netherbury
Melplash
Chilfrome
Piddletrenthide
White Lackington
D O R S E T
A37
A303
A30
A359
A356
A3088
A352
A3030
44
45
30
16
17
7
8
9
10
11
A
B
C
D
E
F
G
H

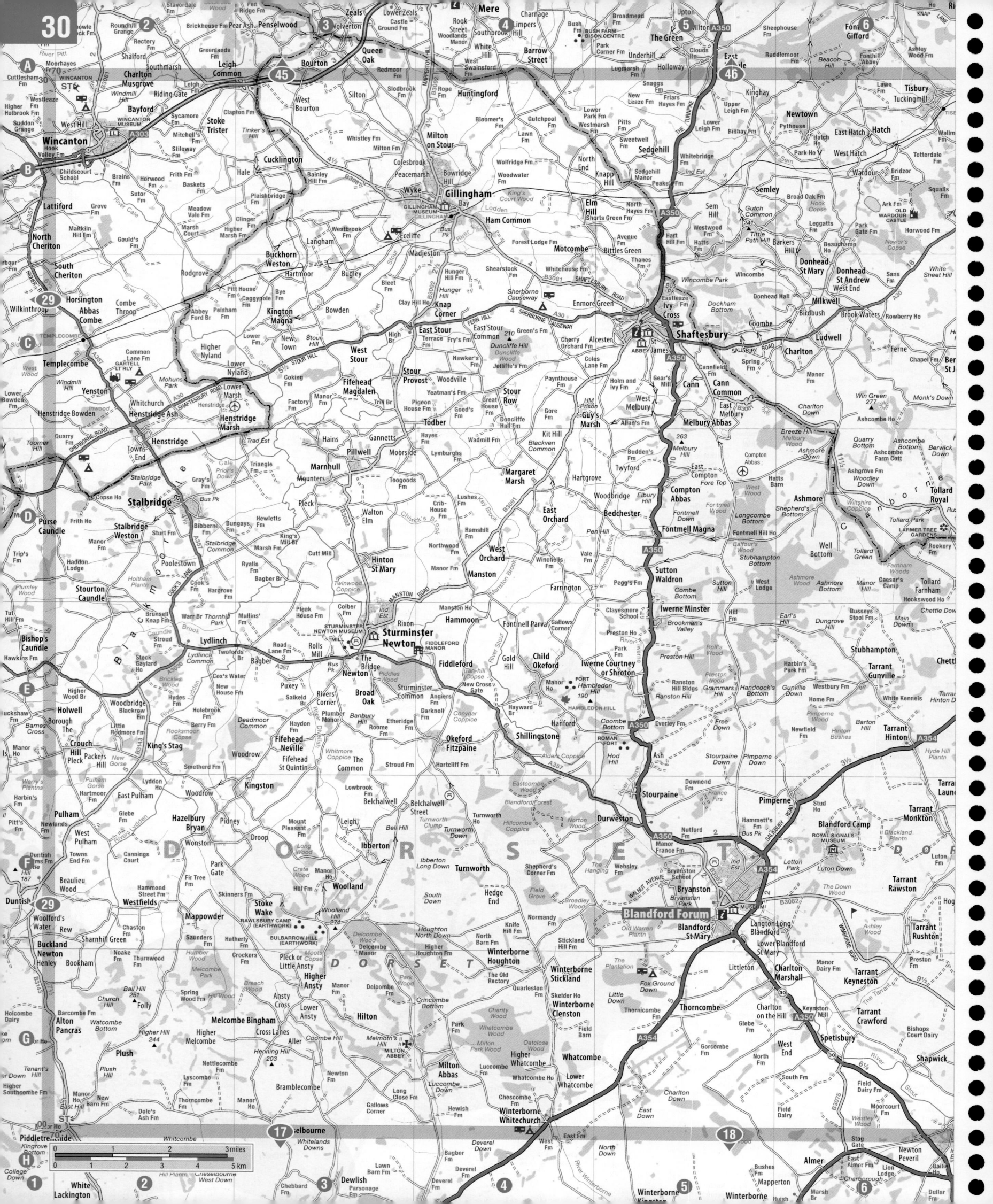
Zeals
Mere
Penselwood
Bourton
Queen Oak
Charlton Musgrove
Leigh Common
Wincanton
Bayford
Stoke Trister
Cucklington
Milton on Stour
Huntingford
Gillingham
Wyke
Ham Common
Motcombe
Sedgehill
Semley
Tisbury
Tuckingmill
Newtown
Hatch
East Hatch
West Hatch
The Green
Upton
Milton
Barrow Street
Charnage
Shaftesbury
Enmore Green
Ivy Cross
St James
Melbury Abbas
Cann
Cann Common
Donhead St Mary
Donhead St Andrew
Milkwell
Ludwell
Charlton
Berwick St John
Lattiford
North Cheriton
South Cheriton
Horsington
Abbas Combe
Templecombe
Yenston
Henstridge Ash
Henstridge Marsh
Henstridge
Kington Magna
Buckhorn Weston
East Stour
West Stour
Stour Provost
Fifehead Magdalen
Todber
Stour Row
Marnhull
Pillwell
Stalbridge
Stalbridge Weston
Purse Caundle
Stourton Caundle
Bishop's Caundle
Margaret Marsh
East Orchard
West Orchard
Hinton St Mary
Manston
Bedchester
Fontmell Magna
Sutton Waldron
Iwerne Minster
Compton Abbas
Ashmore
Tollard Royal
Sturminster Newton
Fiddleford
Child Okeford
Iwerne Courtney or Shroton
Shillingstone
Okeford Fitzpaine
Lydlinch
King's Stag
Fifehead Neville
Hazelbury Bryan
Kingston
Ibberton
Woolland
Turnworth
Durweston
Stourpaine
Pimperne
Blandford Camp
Tarrant Gunville
Tarrant Hinton
Tarrant Monkton
Tarrant Rawston
Tarrant Rushton
Tarrant Keyneston
Tarrant Crawford
Blandford Forum
Blandford St Mary
Bryanston
Langton Long Blandford
Charlton Marshall
Spetisbury
Shapwick
Winterborne Stickland
Winterborne Clenston
Winterborne Houghton
Winterborne Whitechurch
Whatcombe
Milton Abbas
Hilton
Higher Ansty
Melcombe Bingham
Mappowder
Buckland Newton
Alton Pancras
Plush
Pulham
Westfields
Holwell
Dewlish
Almer
DORSET
0 1 2 3 miles
0 1 2 3 4 5 km

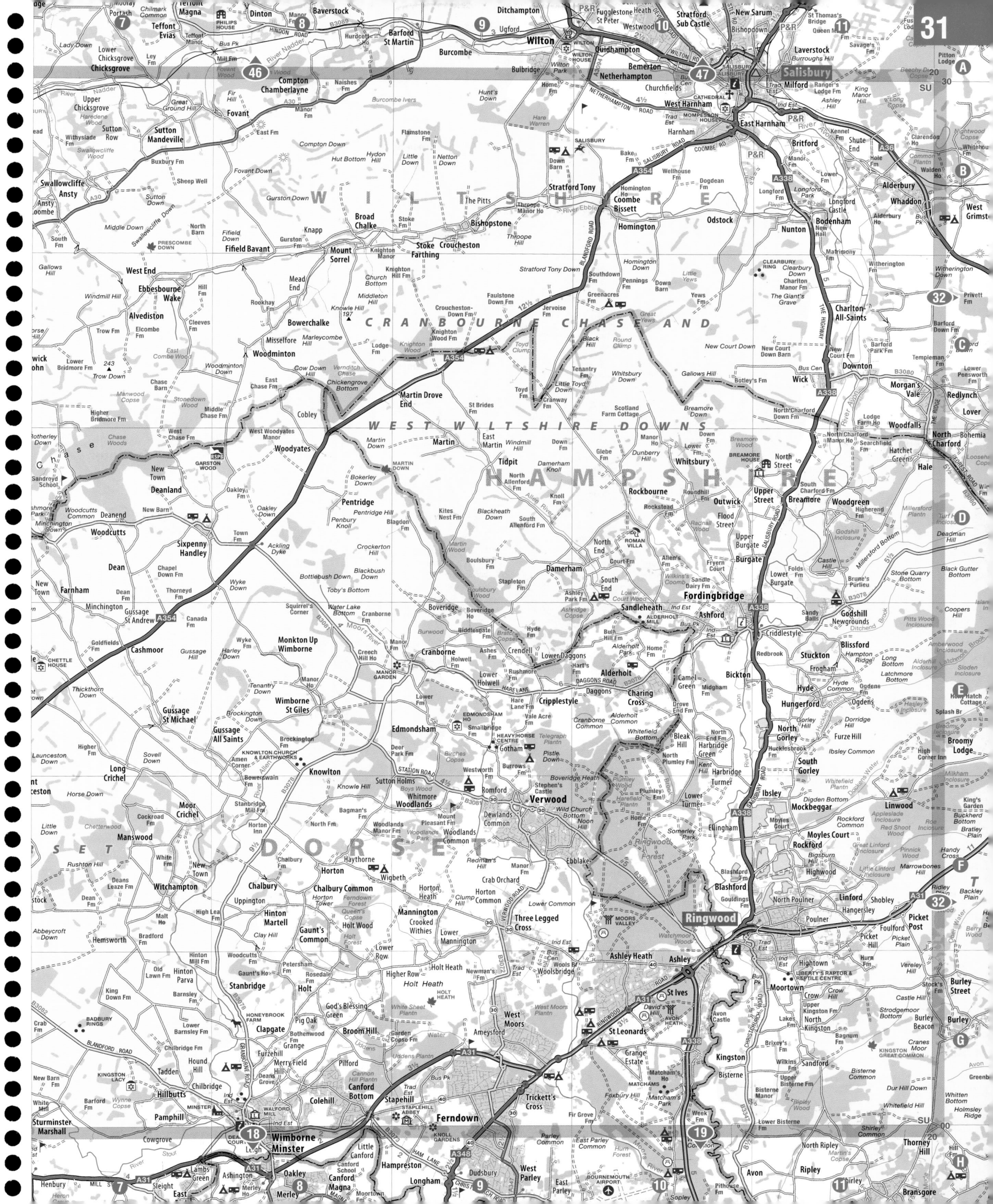

Portash
Teffont Magna
Dinton
Baverstock
Ditchampton
Fugglestone St Peter
Stratford Sub Castle
New Sarum
St Thomas's Bridge
Teffont Evias
Barford St Martin
Ugford
Wilton
Quidhampton
Bishopdown
Laverstock
Lady Down
Lower Chicksgrove
Chicksgrove
Burcombe
Bemerton
Netherhampton
Salisbury
Compton Chamberlayne
Bulbridge
Churchfields
Milford
West Harnham
East Harnham
Upper Chicksgrove
Fovant
Sutton Row
Sutton Mandeville
Harnham
Britford
Shute End
Alderbury
Whaddon
Swallowcliffe
Ansty
Stratford Tony
Coombe Bissett
Homington
Odstock
Nunton
Bodenham
Broad Chalke
Bishopstone
Knapp
Croucheston
Stoke Farthing
Mount Sorrel
Fifield Bavant
West End
Ebbesbourne Wake
Alvediston
Bowerchalke
Misselfore
Woodminton
Charlton-All-Saints
Downton
Wick
Morgan's Vale
Redlynch
Lover
Woodfalls
North Charford
Hale
WILTSHIRE
CRANBOURNE CHASE AND
WEST WILTSHIRE DOWNS
HAMPSHIRE
DORSET
Martin Drove End
Cobley
Woodyates
Martin
East Martin
Tidpit
Whitsbury
North Street
New Town
Deanland
Pentridge
Rockbourne
Upper Street
Breamore
Woodgreen
Outwick
Flood Street
Woodcutts
Sixpenny Handley
North End
Damerham
South End
Upper Burgate
Burgate
Lower Burgate
Dean
Farnham
Minchington
Gussage St Andrew
Fordingbridge
Sandleheath
Ashford
Godshill
Criddlestyle
Cashmoor
Monkton Up Wimborne
Cranborne
Crendell
Lower Daggons
Alderholt
Stuckton
Blissford
Frogham
Bickton
Hyde
Hungerford
Ogdens
Charing Cross
Daggons
Cripplestyle
Wimborne St Giles
Gussage St Michael
Gussage All Saints
Edmondsham
Gotham
Bleak Hill
Harbridge Green
North Gorley
South Gorley
Broomy Lodge
Long Crichel
Knowlton
Sutton Holms
Woodlands
Romford
Verwood
Dewlands Common
Harbridge
Turmer
Lower Turmer
Ibsley
Mockbeggar
Linwood
Moor Crichel
Manswood
Ellingham
Moyles Court
Rockford
Witchampton
Chalbury
Horton
Wigbeth
Chalbury Common
Hinton Martell
Gaunt's Common
Mannington
Three Legged Cross
Blashford
Ringwood
Linford
Hangersley
North Poulner
Poulner
Picket Post
Hemsworth
Ashley Heath
Ashley
St Ives
Hightown
Moortown
Burley Street
Stanbridge
Holt
Clapgate
Broom Hill
West Moors
Ameysford
St Leonards
Burley
Kingston
Sandford
Hillbutts
Pamphill
Colehill
Stapehill
Ferndown
Tricketts Cross
Sturminster Marshall
Wimborne Minster
Canford Bottom
Hampreston
Dudsbury
West Parley
Longham
Ashington
Oakley
Merley
Canford Magna
East Parley
North Ripley
Ripley
Avon
Thorney Hill
Bransgore
Henbury
Sleight
East

47
48
31
19
20
West Winterslow
Pitton
West Tytherley
East Tytherley
Bossington
Horsebridge
King's Somborne
Somborne
Ashley
Sparsholt
Farley
East Grimstead
West Dean
Lockerley
Mottisfont
Dunbridge
East Dean
Alderbury
Whaddon
West Grimstead
Michelmersh
Timsbury
Braishfield
Pucknall
Hursley
Standon
Whiteparish
Newton
Sherfield English
Awbridge
Kent's Oak
Romsey
Abbotswood
Ampfield
Chandler's Ford
Eastleigh
Redlynch
Morgan's Vale
Woodfalls
North Charford
Hale
Landford
Plaitford
West Wellow
Canada
Nomansland
North Baddesley
Chilworth
Rownhams
Nursling
Bramshaw
Wigley
Ower
Totton
Calmore
Cadnam
Brook
Fritham
Bassett
Swaythling
SOUTHAMPTON
Southampton
Shirley
Millbrook
Eling
Netley Marsh
Ashurst
Woodlands
Stoney Cross
Minstead
Marchwood
Hythe
Dibden
Dibden Purlieu
Lyndhurst
Emery Down
Bank
Burley
Burley Street
Brockenhurst
Beaulieu
Hardley
Holbury
Hill Top
Exbury
Bucklers Hard
East Boldre
Setley
Battramsley
Sway
Pilley
Bransgore
Picket Post
Linwood
Woolston
Northam
Itchen
Portswood
THE NEW FOREST
NATIONAL PARK
0 1 2 3 miles
0 1 2 3 4 5 km

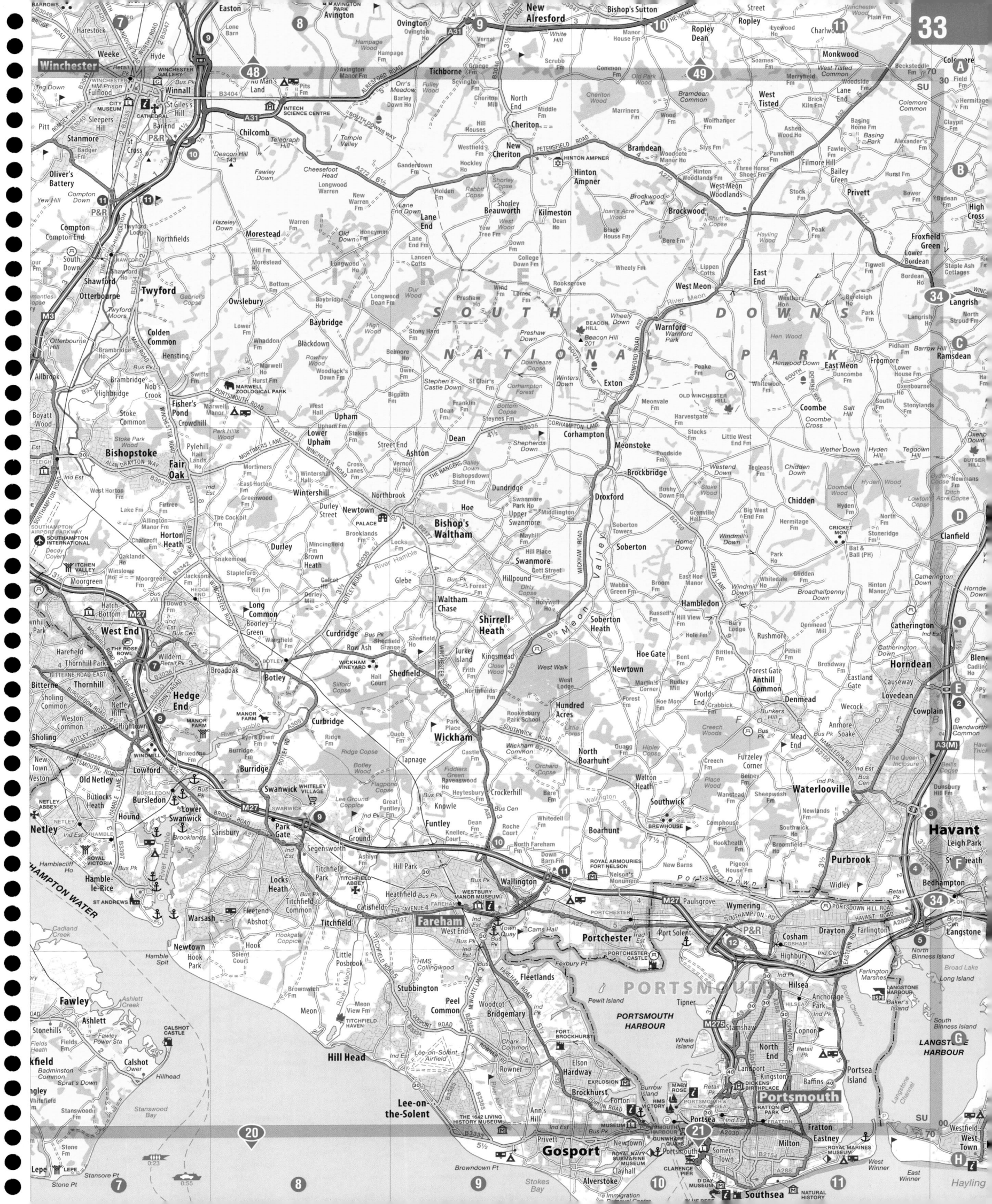
Winchester
Easton
Avington
Ovington
New Alresford
Bishop's Sutton
Ropley
Ropley Dean
Charlwood
Harestock
Weeke
Hyde
Winnall
Tichborne
Chilcomb
Cheriton
New Cheriton
Bramdean
Hinton Ampner
West Tisted
Monkwood
Colemore
Stanmore
St Cross
Oliver's Battery
Compton
Compton End
Bishopstoke
Twyford
Shawford
Otterbourne
Morestead
Owslebury
Baybridge
Beauworth
Kilmeston
Lane End
Brockwood
West Meon
East End
Privett
Froxfield Green
Langrish
Ramsdean
SOUTH DOWNS NATIONAL PARK
Warnford
Exton
East Meon
Colden Common
Fisher's Pond
Upham
Lower Upham
Dean
Ashton
Corhampton
Meonstoke
Brockbridge
Droxford
Chidden
Coombe
Fair Oak
Horton Heath
Durley
Bishop's Waltham
Newtown
Soberton
Swanmore
Hillpound
Clanfield
Waltham Chase
Shirrell Heath
Hambledon
Catherington
Horndean
West End
Hedge End
Botley
Curdridge
Shedfield
Curbridge
Wickham
Hundred Acres
Hoe Gate
Denmead
Anthill Common
Cowplain
Lovedean
Waterlooville
Havant
Bedhampton
Purbrook
Widley
Netley
Hamble-le-Rice
Bursledon
Lower Swanwick
Swanwick
Sarisbury
Park Gate
Locks Heath
Titchfield
Fareham
Funtley
Knowle
Boarhunt
Southwick
North Boarhunt
Portchester
Cosham
Drayton
Farlington
Hilsea
Warsash
Newtown
Stubbington
Hill Head
Lee-on-the-Solent
Bridgemary
Fleetlands
Gosport
Portsmouth
PORTSMOUTH
PORTSMOUTH HARBOUR
Southsea
Fratton
Eastney
Milton
Portsea Island
LANGSTONE HARBOUR
Fawley
Ashlett
Calshot
SOUTHAMPTON WATER
Hayling
M3
M27
M275
A3(M)
A31
A32
A27
48
49
20
21
34
7
8
9
10
11
A
B
C
D
E
F
G
H
SU
70
00

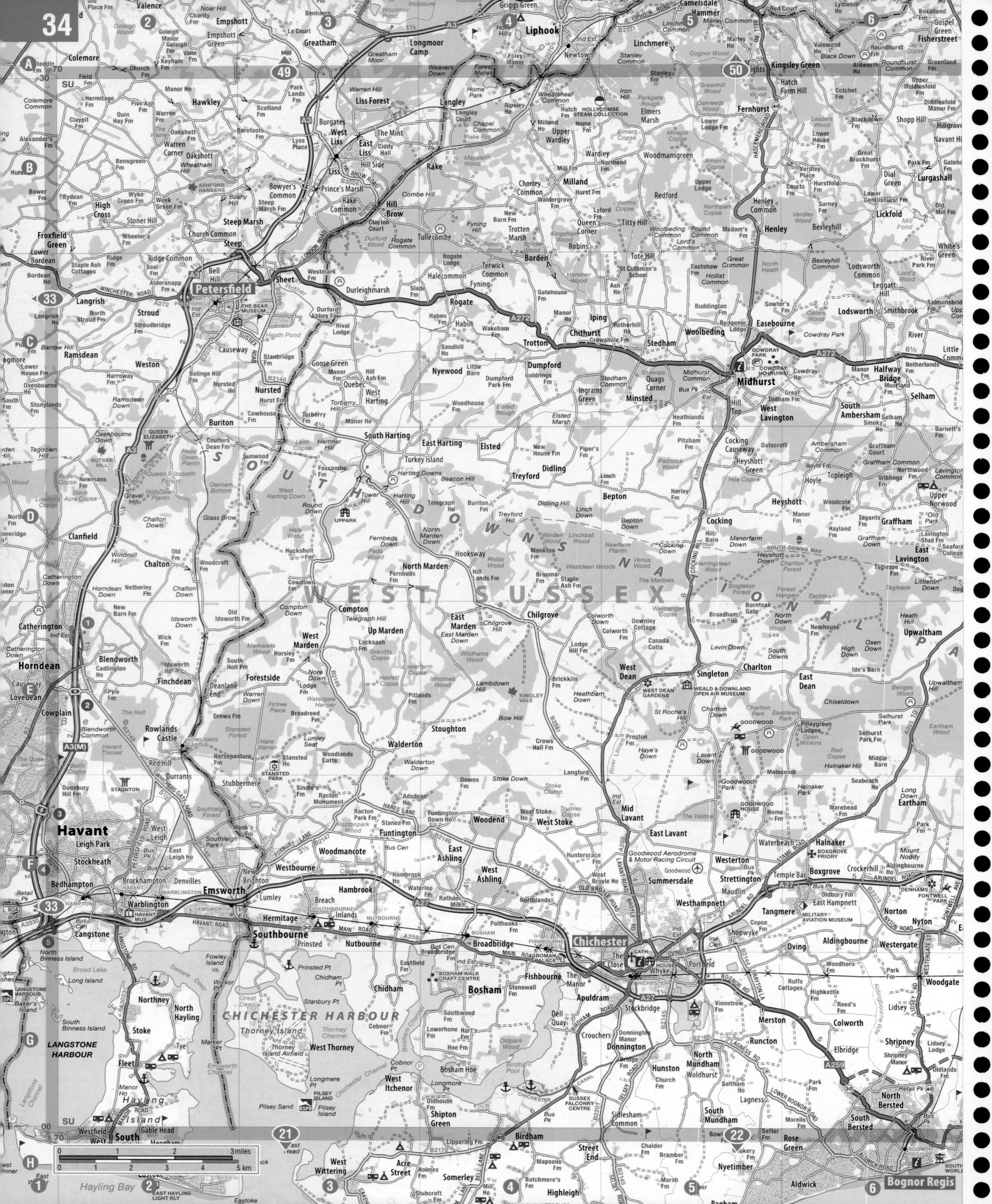

Liphook
Petersfield
Midhurst
Chichester
Havant
Emsworth
Bognor Regis
WEST SUSSEX
SOUTH DOWNS NATIONAL PARK
CHICHESTER HARBOUR
LANGSTONE HARBOUR
Hayling Bay
Liss
West Liss
East Liss
Liss Forest
Greatham
Empshott
Hawkley
Steep
Steep Marsh
Sheet
Langrish
Stroud
Ramsdean
Buriton
Nursted
Rogate
Trotton
Iping
Chithurst
Stedham
Woolbeding
Easebourne
Fernhurst
Henley
Lodsworth
Selham
South Harting
East Harting
Elsted
Treyford
Didling
Bepton
Cocking
Heyshott
Graffham
West Lavington
Clanfield
Chalton
Horndean
Cowplain
Rowlands Castle
Compton
West Marden
North Marden
East Marden
Up Marden
Chilgrove
Singleton
Charlton
West Dean
East Dean
Upwaltham
Eartham
Stoughton
Walderton
Funtington
West Stoke
Mid Lavant
East Lavant
Boxgrove
Halnaker
Westhampnett
Tangmere
Oving
Aldingbourne
Westergate
Woodgate
Bosham
Fishbourne
Apuldram
Southbourne
Nutbourne
Westbourne
Hermitage
Langstone
Northney
North Hayling
Stoke
West Thorney
Donnington
Hunston
North Mundham
South Mundham
Merston
Runcton
Colworth
Shripney
North Bersted
South Bersted
Birdham
West Wittering
Itchenor
Aldwick
Nyetimber
Bedhampton
Warblington
Leigh Park
Stockheath
Blendworth
Finchdean
Forestside
Woodmancote
Waterbeach
Westerton
Strettington
Summersdale
Crockerhill
Norton
Nyton
A3
A3(M)
A27
A272
A286
A259
A29
33
49
50
21
22
3 miles
5 km

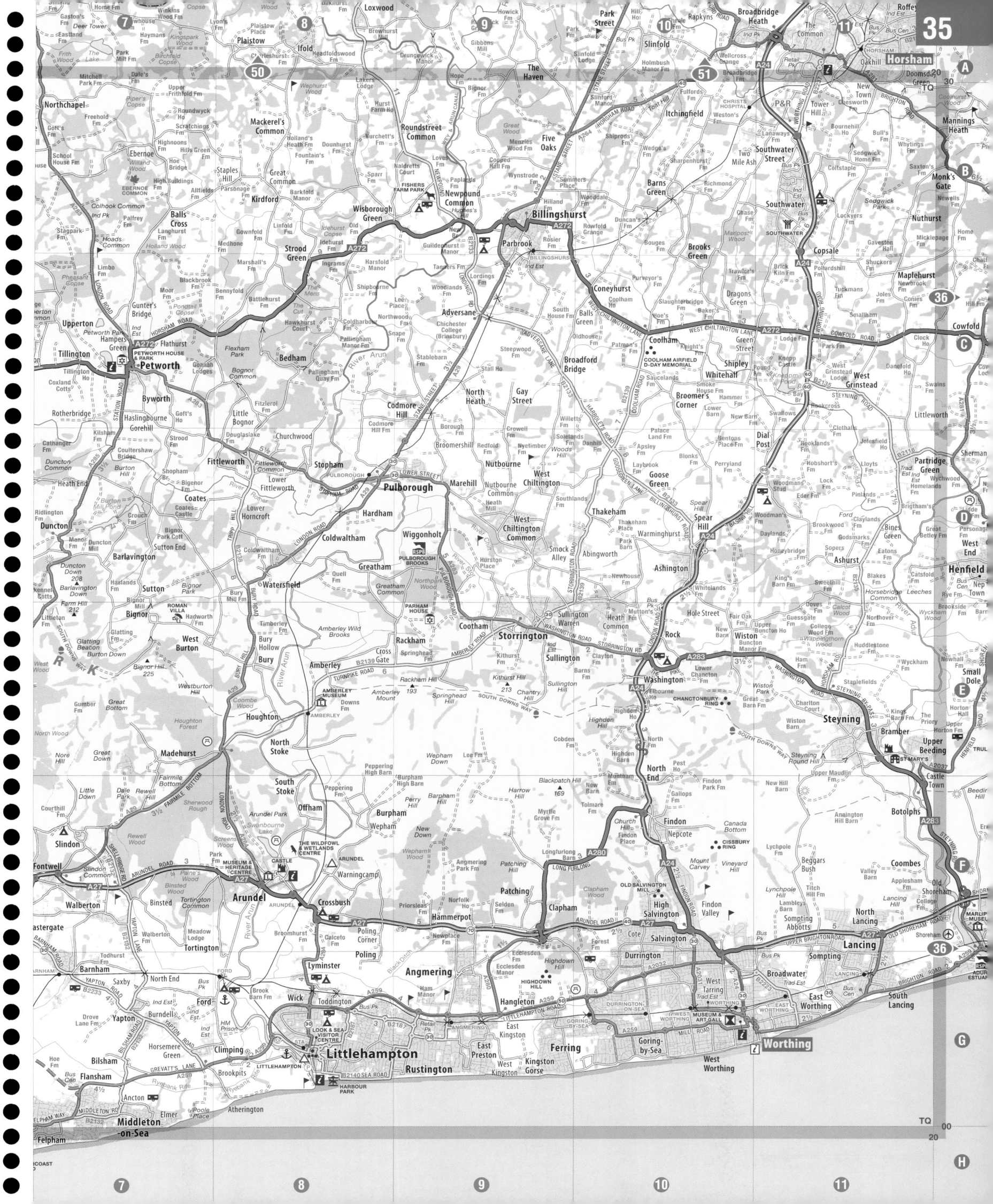

Horsham
Loxwood
Plaistow
Ifold
Park Street
Slinfold
Rapkyns
Broadbridge Heath
The Common
Roffey
50
51
The Haven
Northchapel
Mackerel's Common
Roundstreet Common
Five Oaks
Itchingfield
Tower Hill
Mannings Heath
Ebernoe
Staples Hill
Great Common
Kirdford
Barns Green
Southwater Street
Two Mile Ash
Monk's Gate
Balls Cross
Wisborough Green
Newpound Common
Billingshurst
Southwater
Nuthurst
Parbrook
Strood Green
Copsale
Brooks Green
Maplehurst
Coneyhurst
Dragons Green
36
Gunter's Bridge
Upperton
Adversane
Balls Green
Coolham
Cowfold
Tillington
Petworth
Flathurst
Bedham
Broadford Bridge
Green Street
Shipley
Whitehall
West Grinstead
Byworth
Codmore Hill
North Heath
Gay Street
Broomer's Corner
Little Bognor
Littleworth
Churchwood
Dial Post
Fittleworth
Stopham
Pulborough
Marehill
Nutbourne
West Chiltington
Goose Green
Partridge Green
Coates
Hardham
Thakeham
Spear Hill
Duncton
Coldwaltham
Wiggonholt
West Chiltington Common
Warminghurst
Barlavington
Greatham
Smock Alley
Abingworth
Ashington
Ashurst
West End
Henfield
Sutton
Watersfield
Bignor
West Burton
Cootham
Storrington
Sullington Warren
Heath Common
Rock
Hole Street
Rackham
Bury
Amberley
Cross Gate
Sullington
Washington
Wiston
Small Dole
Houghton
Steyning
Bramber
Madehurst
North Stoke
Upper Beeding
South Stoke
North End
Castle Town
Offham
Burpham
Wepham
Findon
Nepcote
Botolphs
Slindon
Fontwell
Arundel
Warningcamp
Crossbush
Patching
Clapham
High Salvington
Findon Valley
Coombes
Old Shoreham
Walberton
Binsted
Hammerpot
Sompting Abbotts
North Lancing
Tortington
Poling
Poling Corner
Cote
Salvington
Durrington
Lancing
Sompting
Barnham
Lyminster
Angmering
Broadwater
Wick
Toddington
Hangleton
West Tarring
East Worthing
South Lancing
Yapton
Ford
East Kingston
Worthing
Littlehampton
East Preston
Ferring
Goring-by-Sea
Bilsham
Climping
Rustington
West Kingston
Kingston Gorse
West Worthing
Flansham
Ancton
Atherington
Middleton-on-Sea
Elmer
Felpham
A B C D E F G H
7 8 9 10 11
TQ
20
00

Horsham
51
52
35
Balcombe
Handcross
Highbrook
Chelwood Gate
Ashdown Forest
Wych Cross
Ardingly
Mannings Heath
Ashfold Crossways
Staplefield
Slaugham
Horsted Keynes
Danehill
Nutley
Monk's Gate
Lower Beeding
Brook Street
Nuthurst
Warninglid
Whitemans Green
Cuckfield
Lindfield
Sheffield Green
Crabtree
Maplehurst
Bolney
Haywards Heath
Scayne's Hill
Splayne's Green
Fletching
Cowfold
Ansty
Chownes Mead
Bolnore
Crosspost
Grisling Common
Fletching Common
Kent Street
Red House Common
Newick
Littleworth
Twineham Green
Abbotsford
North Chailey
Sharpsbridge
Twineham
Hickstead
Wineham
Wivelsfield
Wivelsfield Green
Burgess Hill
Chailey
Shermanbury
World's End
Partridge Green
Sayers Common
South Street
Spithurst
Henfield
Hurstpierpoint
Hurst Wickham
Plumpton Green
Blackstone
Albourne
Albourne Green
Keymer
Ditchling
Barcombe Cross
Hassocks
Streat
East Chiltington
Chiltington
Woodmancote
Barcombe
Clayton
Westmeston
Plumpton
Cooksbridge
Hamsey
Small Dole
Poynings
Pyecombe
Offham
Saddlescombe
Fulking
Edburton
South Malling
Upper Beeding
Wallands Park
Lewes
Bramber
Southover
Stanmer
Patcham
Falmer
Kingston near Lewes
Botolphs
BRIGHTON AND HOVE
Coldean
Westdene
Hollingbury
Withdean
Beddingham
Mile Oak
Hangleton
West Blatchington
Moulsecoomb
Iford
Portslade
Bevendean
Preston
Hove
Woodingdean
Rodmell
Southwick
Kingston by Sea
Southease
Shoreham-by-Sea
Portslade-by-Sea
Aldrington
Whitehawk
Kemp Town
Roedean
South Lancing
Brighton
Ovingdean
Telscombe
Piddinghoe
Tarring Neville
Rottingdean
Saltdean
Brighton Marina
Telscombe Cliffs
Newhaven
Peacehaven
Peacehaven Heights
0 1 2 3 miles
0 1 2 3 4 5 km
TQ
A B C D E F G H
1 2 3 4 5 6

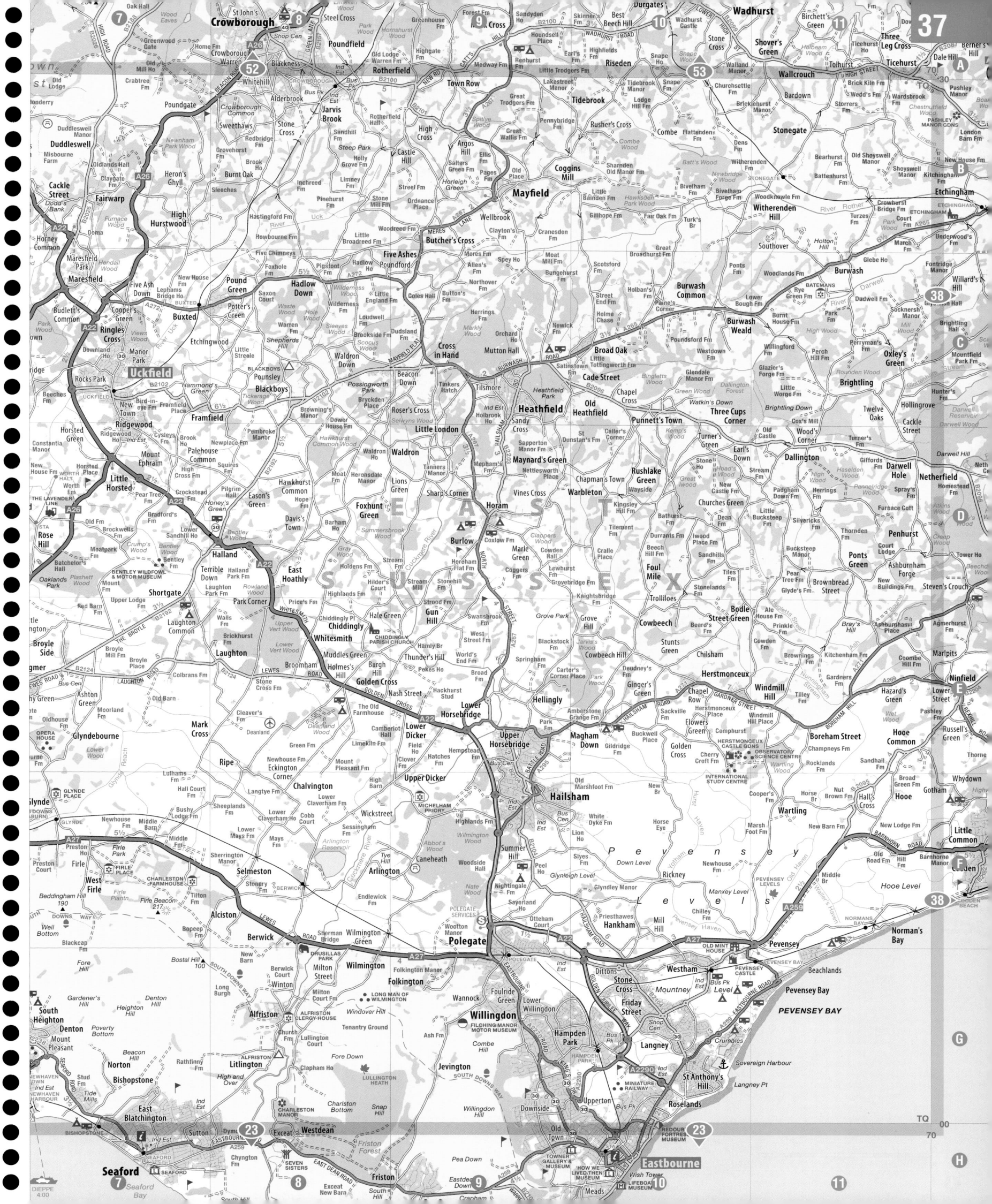

Crowborough
Wadhurst
Rotherfield
Town Row
Jarvis Brook
Poundfield
Tidebrook
Riseden
Stonegate
Ticehurst
Wallcrouch
Shover's Green
Three Leg Cross
Dale Hill
Duddleswell
Poundgate
Crowborough Warren
Whitehill
Alderbrook
Stone Cross
High Cross
Argos Hill
Castle Hill
Mayfield
Coggins Mill
Witherenden Hill
Etchingham
Burwash
Burwash Common
Burwash Weald
Fairwarp
Cackle Street
Heron's Ghyll
High Hurstwood
Maresfield
Five Ash Down
Pound Green
Hadlow Down
Five Ashes
Butcher's Cross
Buxted
Ringles Cross
Uckfield
Rocks Park
Etchingwood
Pounsley
Blackboys
Waldron Down
Cross in Hand
Broad Oak
Heathfield
Old Heathfield
Cade Street
Punnett's Town
Three Cups Corner
Brightling
Oxley's Green
Framfield
Ridgewood
Little London
Waldron
Maynard's Green
Rushlake Green
Dallington
Darwell Hole
Netherfield
Little Horsted
Horam
Warbleton
Vines Cross
Foxhunt Green
Burlow
Marle Green
Foul Mile
Trolliloes
Penhurst
Ponts Green
Halland
East Hoathly
Shortgate
Laughton
Chiddingly
Whitesmith
Gun Hill
Cowbeech
Bodle Street Green
Herstmonceux
Windmill Hill
Ninfield
Golden Cross
Lower Horsebridge
Upper Horsebridge
Hellingly
Magham Down
Boreham Street
Hooe Common
Lower Dicker
Upper Dicker
Hailsham
Hooe
Wartling
Glyndebourne
Mark Cross
Ripe
Chalvington
Arlington
Selmeston
Alciston
Berwick
Polegate
Wilmington
Pevensey
Westham
Stone Cross
Norman's Bay
Pevensey Bay
PEVENSEY BAY
Willingdon
Folkington
Alfriston
Hampden Park
Langney
St Anthony's Hill
Roselands
Jevington
Friston
Westdean
Exceat
Seaford
East Blatchington
Bishopstone
Norton
Sutton
Eastbourne
South Heighton
Denton
Firle
West Firle
Glynde
E A S T S U S S E X
P e v e n s e y L e v e l s
Hooe Level

Hawkhurst
Gill's Green
Beal's Green
Iden Green
Beacon Hill
West Cross
C M BOOTH COLLECTION OF HISTORIC VEHICLES
Rolvenden
Rolvenden Layne
Small Hythe
SMALLHYTHE PLACE
Reading Street
Appledore Heath
Flimwell
Little Pix Hall Fm
Siseley Fm
Slip Mill
High Street
Park Fm
Woodsden
Gun Green
Pipsden
Standen Street
Dingleden
Kemsdale Ho
Merrington Place
Great Maytham
Cornhill
Bulleign
Leg Cross
Berner's Hill
Dale Hill
Seacox Heath
Elm Hill Ho
Hensill Ho
Highgate
Four Throws
Field Green
Spongden Ho
Hope Ho
Springhill Fm
Wassall Ho
Lowden Fm
Friezingham Fm
Britcher Fm
Hillgate Fm
Great Job's Cross
Peening Quarter
Ringden Fm
Delmonden Ho
Pashley Manor
PASHLEY MANOR GDNS
Wardsbrook Fm
Brookgate Fm
Horns Corner
The Moor
Alderden Manor
Beeches Fm
Kensham Fm
Sandhurst
Linkhill
Lamberden
KENT & EAST SUSSEX RAILWAY
Mayham Fm
Potman's Heath
Plastre Court
Kingsgate Ho
Black Barn
Odiam Fm
Stone
Swiftsden
London Barn Fm
Conghurst Fm
Stone House Fm
Hoad's Fm
Hexden Fm
Heronden Fm
Frogs Hill
Newenden
Isle of Oxney
Moon's Green
Maytham Wharf
Wittersham
Wittersham Manor
Holman's Fm
Stone in Oxney
The Stocks
Great Prawls Fm
Sandhurst Cross
Three Gates Fm
New House Fm
Burgh Wood
Cooper's Corner
Hurst Green
Burgh Hill
Kitchingham Fm
Etchingham
Haremere Hall
Little Iridge Fm
Boarsney Fm
Bourne Fm
Old Place Fm
Marsh Quarter Fm
South Park
Elms Fm
Lower Northlands Fm
Kent Ditch
Gate Ct
Northiam
River Rother
Rother Levels
Blackbrook Fm
Ham Green
Newbridge Fm
Cliff Marsh Fm
Wet Level
Iridge Place
Clinsett's Fm
Silver Hill
Bodiam
BODIAM CASTLE
Bodiam Br
Dixter Wood
GREAT DIXTER
FARM WORLD
Knelle Wood
Bellhurst Fm
Bugsell Mill Fm
Squibs Fm
Ockham Ho
Bush Barn
Beech House Fm
Haiselman's Fm
New Ho
Park Fm
Moat Fm
Higham Ho
Snagshall
Ewhurst Green
Quarry Fm
Northbridge Street
ROTHER VALLEY RLY CENTRE
Salehurst
Robertsbridge
Fontridge Manor
Willard's Hill
Underwood's Fm
Sogg's Ho
Sempstead Wood
Tufton Place
BRICKWALL HOUSE
Mill Corner
Glebe Ho
Goteley Manor
Woodgate Ho
Gooseley Fm
Four Oaks
Beckley
Clayhill
King's Bank
Flackley Ash
Peasmarsh
New House Fm
Corkwood Fm
Moat Fm
Old House Fm
Forstal Fm
Baron's Grange
Bosney Fm
Boonshill
Iden
Iden Wood
Mockbeggar
Houghton Green
Park Fm
Fowlbrook Wood
Hollow Wall Fm
Watts Hill Fm
Collier's Green
Gate Fm
Lordine Court
Horns Cross
Great Stent Fm
Stockhurst Fm
Weaver's Fm
Woodlands Fm
Peasmarsh Place
Lea Fm
Rye Foreign
Bowler's Town
Saltbarn Fm
Playden
East Guldeford
Brightling Hall
Glottenham Manor
Scalands Wood
Walter's Fm
Lordship Wood
Handsel Fm
Staplecross
The Grange
Stockwood Fm
Maplestone Fm
Tilebarn Fm
Gate Fm
Beckley Woods
Leasam Ho
Rye
Oxley's Green
Mountfield Park Fm
Tunstall Fm
Taylor's Cott
Newpond Fm
John's Cross
Poppinghole Fm
Swaile's Green
The Beacon
Brede Green Cott
Gate Cottage
Beckley Furnace
Groves
Partridge Fm
Dew Fm
Clayton Fm
EAST SUSSEX
Black House Fm
YPRES TOWER
Hunter's Fm
Hollingrove
Baldwin's Fm
Mountfield Court
Cripp's Corner
Footland Fm
Chitcombe
Brede High Wood
Conster Manor
Ludley Fm
Hayes Fm
TREASURY OF MECHANICAL MUSIC
Tillingham Fm
Cackle Street
Darwell Reservoir
Darwell Wood
Mountfield
Vinehall Street
Great Sanders School
Streetfield Wood
Powdermill Res
Goatham Green
Broad Oak
Broadland Row
Great Sowdens Wood
Newman's Fm
Udimore
Gillshaw Fm
Codborough Fm
Watlands
HERITAGE CENTRE & TOWN MODEL
Darwell Hill
Crowhurst Wood
Crowhurst Fm
Jacob's Fm
Hurst Wood
Steephill Wood
Cackle Street
Rye Marsh Fm
Rye Harbour
Darwell Hole
Netherfield
Netherfield Court
Eastlands Fm
Woodmans Green
Sedlescombe
Brede Barn Fm
Brook Lodge Fm
Brede
Pickdick Fm
Great Park Wood
Court Fm
Cock Marling
Float Fm
CAMBER CASTLE
Homestead Fm
Spray's Fm
Eatenden Wood
Burnthouse Wood
Wood's Place
Canadia
Stonelink Fm
WINCHELSEA
Ferry Br
Brede Level
Castle Fm
Nook Beach
Furnace Cott
Atkins Wood
Netherfield Place
Whatlington
Petley Wood
Sedlescombe Street
Pestalozzi Children's Village
Rocks Fm
Crowham Manor
Brook Fm
Winchelsea
Penhurst
Court Lodge
Kingswell Fm
Le Rette Fm
Gate Fm
Bus Pk
Little Park Fm
Beanford Fm
Randall's Fm
Platnix Fm
Doleham Fm
Lidham Hill
Stocks Fm
Broad Street
Icklesham
Crutches Fm
Ind Pk
WINCHELSEA COURT MUSEUM
Wickham Manor
Battle
Beech Fm
Coarsebarn Fm
Marley Ho
Battle Barn Fm
Great Buckhurst Fm
Yew Tree Ho
Guestling Thorn
Manor Fm
Elms Fm
Winchelsea Beach
Ashburnham Forge
Tower Ho
Beechdown Wood
NORTH TRADE ROAD
BATTLE ABBEY
Kent Street
Great Wood
Ireland's Fm
Oak Wood
Copshall
Knockbridge Fm
Pett Level
New Buildings Fm
Steven's Crouch
Tellis Coppice
Tower Hill
Starr's Green
Branshill Fm
Norton's Fm
Westfield
Pannel
Pannel Fm
Great Park Fm
Telham
Little Hemingfold Fm
Whiteland Wood
Claremont School
Rodger's Fm
Three Oaks
Agmerhurst Fm
Parkgate Manor
Peppering Eye Fm
Loose Fm
Beauport Park
Lankhurst Fm
Eastlands Fm
Fraysland Fm
Church Fm
Guestling Wood
French Court Fm
Pett
Catsfield
Catsfield Manor
Millers Fm
Telham Hill
Telham Place
Pye's Fm
Breadsell Fm
Maplehurst Wood
Hole Fm
Coghurst Hall
Guestling Green
New Barn Fm
Lunsford
Marlpits
Coombe Hill Fm
Catsfield Stream
FORE WOOD
CROWHURST
Baldslow
Bachelor's Bump
Friar's Hill
Marsham Sewer
Wakehams Fm
Cliff End
Ninfield
Catsfield Place
Crowhurst
Park Fm
Holmhurst St Mary
Hazel Ct
Ivy Ho
The Hall
Cherry Garden Fm
Hazard's Green
Lower Street
Hurst Wood
Henley's Down
Nashes Fm
Queensway
Silverhill Park
St Helen's
Fairlight
Mallydams Wood
Stonelynk Fm
Fairlight Cove
Pashley Fm
Watermill
Hill House Fm
Green Street
Lower Willing Fm
Hollington
St Helen's Wood
Ore
Fairlight Pl
Fire Hills
Hooe Common
Russell's Green
Potmans Place
Sprays Wood
Park Wood
Lunsford's Cross
Byne's Fm
Adam's Fm
Upper Willing Fm
Silverhill
Bohemia
Broomsgrove
Clive Vale
Belmont
HASTINGS
Fairlight Glen
Covehurst Bay
Thorne Fm
Cole Wood
Acton's Fm
Blacklands
West Hill
ST CLEMENTS CAVE
Broad Green Fm
Whydown
Hooe
The Highlands
Preston Hall
Worsham Fm
Pebsham Fm
Harley Shute
ST LEONARDS WARRIOR SQ
SHIPWRECK HERITAGE CENTRE
Ecclesbourne Glen
Gotham
Highwoods
Sidley
Glenleigh Park
Bulverhythe
WEST ST LEONARDS
UNDERWATER WORLD
Old Town
Hastings
New Lodge Fm
Old Town
Pebsham
Little Common
KING OFFA WAY
Ret Pk
Glyne Gap
West Marina
St Leonards
MARINA
Barnhorne Manor
COLLINGTON
Galley Hill
Cooden
COODEN DRIVE
MUS
BEXHILL
My Lord's Rock
Hooe Level
DELAWARR PAVILION
Bexhill
COODEN BEACH
Norman's Bay
A21
A229
A268
A28
A265
A2100
A259
A271
A2036
A269
B2089
B2244
B2165
B2088
B2082
B2096
B2204
B2095
B2093
B2092
53
54
37
TQ
70
00
0
1
2
3 miles
4
5 km
A
B
C
D
E
F
G
H
1
2
3
4
5
6

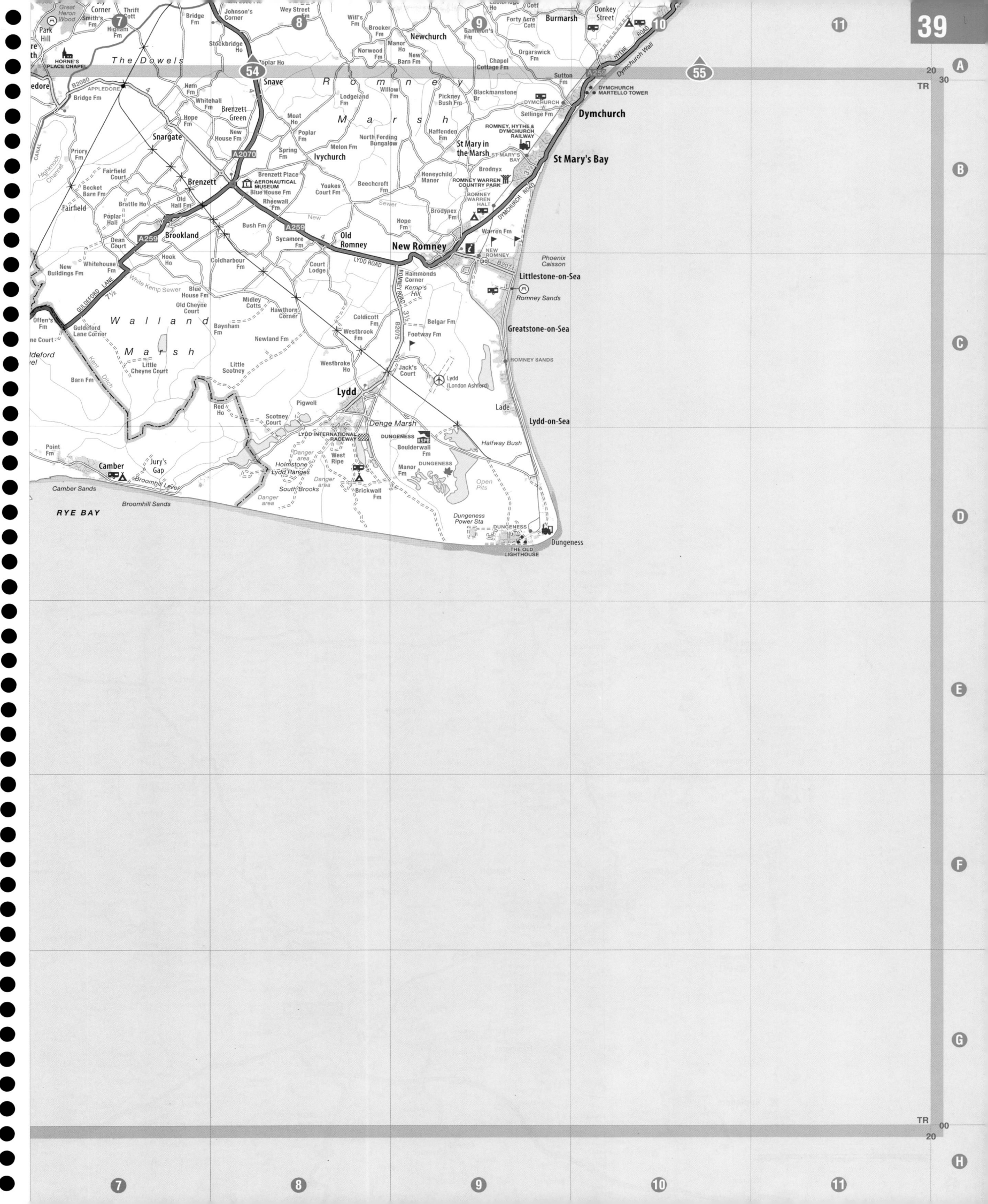
39
7
8
9
10
11
54
55
A
B
C
D
E
F
G
H
TR
20
30
00
Burmarsh
Donkey Street
Newchurch
Snave
Romney Marsh
The Dowels
HORNE'S PLACE CHAPEL
Park Hill
Corner
Thrift Cott
Higham Fm
Bridge Fm
Johnson's Corner
Wey Street Fm
Will's Fm
Brooker Fm
Gammon's Fm
Forty Acre Cott
Stockbridge Ho
Poplar Ho
Manor Ho
Norwood Fm
New Barn Fm
Orgarswick Fm
Chapel Cottage Fm
Sutton Fm
HYTHE ROAD
Dymchurch Wall
A259
B2080
APPLEDORE
Bridge Fm
Ham Fm
Whitehall Fm
Brenzett Green
Hope Fm
New House Fm
Moat Ho
Lodgeland Fm
Willow Fm
Pickney Bush Fm
Blackmanstone Br
DYMCHURCH MARTELLO TOWER
DYMCHURCH
Dymchurch
Selling Fm
ROMNEY, HYTHE & DYMCHURCH RAILWAY
Haffenden Fm
St Mary in the Marsh
ST MARY'S BAY
St Mary's Bay
Snargate
A2070
Spring Fm
Poplar Fm
Melon Fm
North Fording Bungalow
Ivychurch
Priory Fm
Fairfield Court
Brenzett
Brenzett Place
AERONAUTICAL MUSEUM
Blue House Fm
Yoakes Court Fm
Beechcroft Fm
Honeychild Manor
Brodnyx
ROMNEY WARREN COUNTRY PARK
ROMNEY WARREN HALT
Becket Barn Fm
Fairfield
Brattle Ho
Old Hall Fm
Rheewall Fm
Sewer
New
Poplar Hall
Brodynex Fm
DYMCHURCH ROAD
Hope Fm
Dean Court
Brookland
Bush Fm
Sycamore Fm
Old Romney
New Romney
Warren Fm
NEW ROMNEY
Phoenix Caisson
B2071
Littlestone-on-Sea
Romney Sands
New Buildings Fm
Whitehouse Fm
Hook Ho
Coldharbour Fm
Court Lodge
LYDD ROAD
Hammonds Corner
Kemp's Hill
ROMNEY ROAD
White Kemp Sewer
GULDEFORD LANE
Blue House Fm
Old Cheyne Court
Midley Cotts
Hawthorn Corner
Coldicott Fm
Belgar Fm
Greatstone-on-Sea
Walland Marsh
Offen's Fm
Guldeford Lane Corner
Baynham Fm
Westbrook Fm
Footway Fm
B2075
Newland Fm
Kent Ditch
Little Cheyne Court
Little Scotney
Westbroke Ho
Jack's Court
ROMNEY SANDS
Lydd (London Ashford)
Barn Fm
Lydd
Pigwell
Lade
Lydd-on-Sea
Red Ho
Scotney Court
Denge Marsh
LYDD INTERNATIONAL RACEWAY
DUNGENESS
RSPB
Boulderwall Fm
Halfway Bush
Point Fm
Camber
Jury's Gap
Danger area
Holmstone
Lydd Ranges
West Ripe
Manor Fm
DUNGENESS
Broomhill Level
South Brooks
Brickwall Fm
Open Pits
Camber Sands
Broomhill Sands
RYE BAY
Dungeness Power Sta
THE OLD LIGHTHOUSE
Dungeness

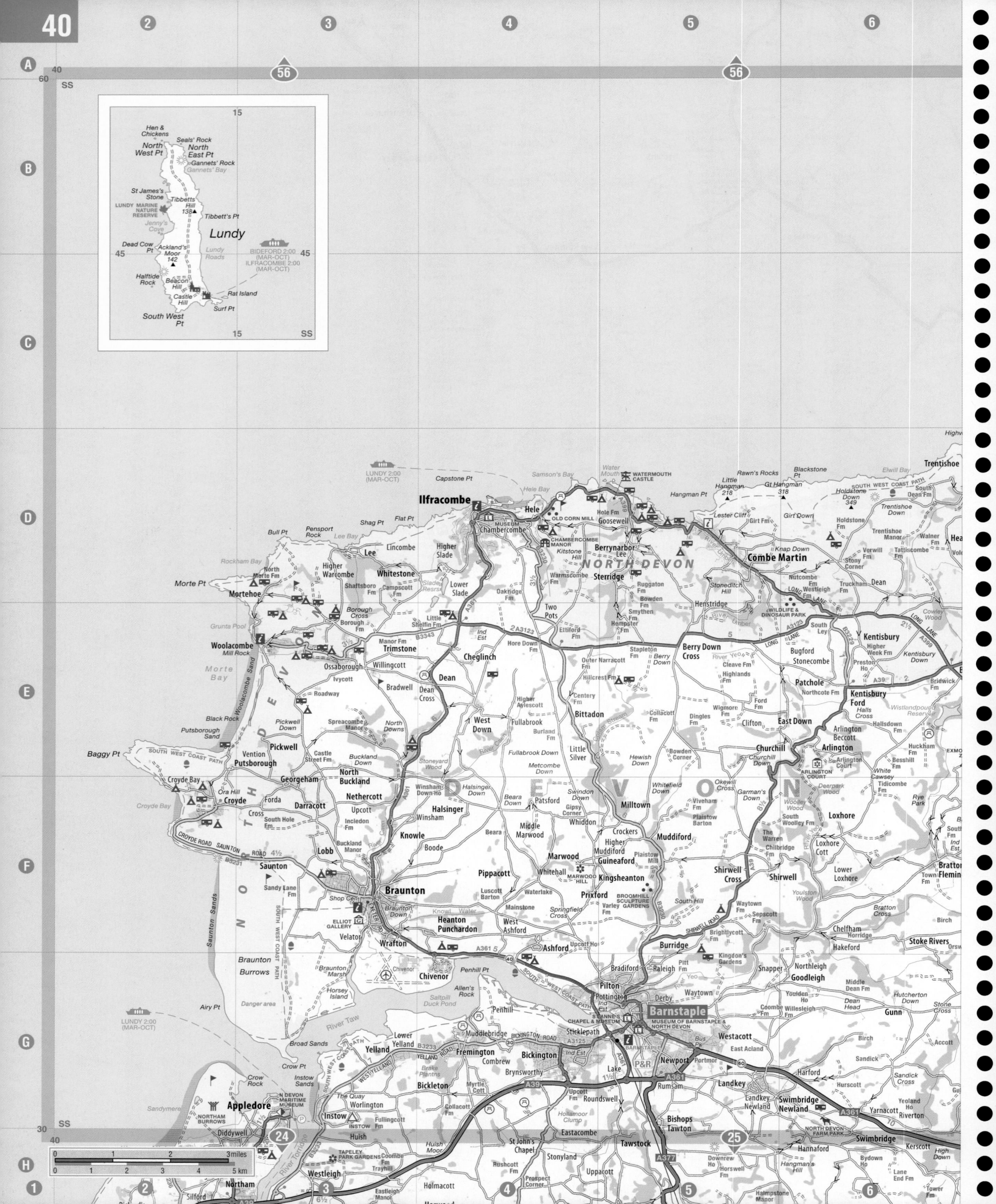
2
3
4
5
6
A
B
C
D
E
F
G
H
1
56
56
SS
Hen & Chickens
Seals' Rock
North West Pt
North East Pt
Gannets' Rock
Gannets' Bay
St James's Stone
Tibbetts Hill 138
LUNDY MARINE NATURE RESERVE
Tibbett's Pt
Jenny's Cove
Lundy
Dead Cow Pt
Ackland's Moor 142
Lundy Roads
BIDEFORD 2:00 (MAR-OCT)
ILFRACOMBE 2:00 (MAR-OCT)
Halftide Rock
Beacon Hill
Castle Hill
Rat Island
Surf Pt
South West Pt
15
45
LUNDY 2:00 (MAR-OCT)
Capstone Pt
Samson's Bay
Hele Bay
Water Mouth
WATERMOUTH CASTLE
Rawn's Rocks
Little Hangman 218
Gt Hangman 318
Blackstone Pt
Elwill Bay
Trentishoe
Hangman Pt
Ilfracombe
Hele
OLD CORN MILL
Hole Fm
Goosewell
MUSEUM
Chambercombe
CHAMBERCOMBE MANOR
Kitstone Hill
Berrynarbor
Lee
NORTH DEVON
Sterridge
Lester Cliff
Girt Fm
Girt Down
Holdstone Down 349
SOUTH WEST COAST PATH
South Dean Fm
Trentishoe Down
Holdstone Fm
Trentishoe Manor
Walner Fm
Knap Down
Verwill Fm
Tattiscombe Fm
Combe Martin
Stony Corner
Nutcombe Fm
Westleigh Fm
Truckham Fm
Dean
Stoneditch Hill
Henstridge
WILDLIFE & DINOSAUR PARK
Shag Pt
Flat Pt
Bull Pt
Pensport Rock
Lee Bay
Lee
Lincombe
Higher Slade
Rockham Bay
Higher Warcombe
Whitestone
North Morte Fm
Morte Pt
Mortehoe
Shaftsboro Fm
Campscott Fm
Slade Resrs
Lower Slade
Oakridge Fm
Warmscombe Fm
Ruggaton Fm
Bowden Fm
Smythen Fm
Hempster Fm
Two Pots
Borough Cross
Borough Fm
Little Shelfin Fm
Grunta Pool
Woolacombe
Mill Rock
Manor Fm
Trimstone
Ind Est
2A3123
Ettiford Fm
LONG LANE
South Ley
Kentisbury
Higher Week Fm
Kentisbury Down
Morte Bay
Woolacombe Sand
Ossaborough
Willingcott
Hore Down Fm
Cheglinch
Outer Narracott Fm
Stapleton Fm
Berry Down
Berry Down Cross
Cleave Fm
Highlands Fm
Bugford
Stonecombe
Preston Fm
Ivycott
Roadway
Bradwell
Dean
Dean Cross
Hillcrest Fm
Centery Fm
Patchole
Northcote Fm
Bridwick Fm
Kentisbury Ford
Halls Cross
Wistlandpound Reservoir
Black Rock
Pickwell Down
Spreacombe Manor
North Downs
West Down
Higher Aylescott
Fullabrook
Burland Fm
Bittadon
Collacott Fm
Dingles Fm
Wigmore Fm
Ford Fm
Clifton
East Down
Arlington Beccott
Hallsdown Fm
Putsborough Sand
Baggy Pt
Vention
Pickwell
Putsborough
Castle Street Fm
Buckland Down
Fullabrook Down
Little Silver
Hewish Down
Bowden Corner
Churchill
Churchill Down
Arlington
Arlington Court
Huckham Fm
Besshill Fm
Croyde Bay
Ora Hill
Croyde
Georgeham
North Buckland
Stoneyard Wood
Metcombe Down
ARLINGTON COURT
White Cawsey
Tidicombe Fm
Croyde Bay
Forda
Darracott
Nethercott
Winsham Down Ho
Halsinger Down
Beara Down
Patsford
Swindon Down
Gipsy Corner
Whitefield Down
Okewill Cross
Garman's Down
Viveham Fm
Plaistow Barton
Deerpark Wood
Woolley Wood
Rye Park
Cross
South Hole Fm
Upcott
Incledon Fm
Halsinger
Winsham
Milltown
South Woolley Fm
Loxhore
CROYDE ROAD
SAUNTON ROAD
Buckland Manor
Knowle
Boode
Beara
Middle Marwood
Whiddon
Crockers
Higher Muddiford
Muddiford
The Warren
Chilbridge Fm
Loxhore Cott
Saunton
Lobb
Marwood
Guineaford
Plaistow Mill
Whitehall
MARWOOD HILL
Kingsheanton
Shirwell Cross
Shirwell
Lower Loxhore
Bratton Fleming
Town Fm
Sandy Lane Fm
Braunton
Shop Centre
Pippacott
Luscott Barton
Waterlake
Prixford
BROOMHILL SCULPTURE GARDENS
South Hill
Waytown Fm
Sepscott Fm
Youlston Wood
Bratton Cross
Saunton Sands
ELLIOT GALLERY
Braunton Down
Heanton Punchardon
Knowl Water
Mainstone
West Ashford
Springfield Cross
Varley Fm
SHIRWELL ROAD
Brightlycott Fm
Chelfham
Horridge
Birch
SOUTH WEST COAST PATH
Velator
Wrafton
A361
Ashford
Upcott Ho
Burridge
Kingdon's Gardens
Hakeford
Stoke Rivers
Braunton Burrows
Braunton Marsh
Chivenor
Penhill Pt
Bradiford
Raleigh
Pitt Fm
Snapper
Northleigh
Goodleigh
Horsey Island
Allen's Rock
Saltpill Duck Pond
Pilton
Pottington
Ind Est
Derby
Waytown
Middle Dean Fm
Hutcherton Down
Airly Pt
Danger area
Penhill
ST ANNE'S CHAPEL & MUSEUM
Barnstaple
MUSEUM OF BARNSTAPLE & NORTH DEVON
Youlden Ho
Coombe Fm
Willesleigh Fm
Dean Head
Gunn
Stone Cross
LUNDY 2:00 (MAR-OCT)
River Taw
Broad Sands
Muddlebridge
BICKINGTON ROAD
Sticklepath
Westacott
East Acland
Birch
Accott
Yelland
Lower Yelland
Fremington
Bickington
Ind Est
Newport
Portmore
Sandick
Crow Pt
Combrew
Brake Plantns
Brynsworthy
Lake
Harford
Sandick Cross
Crow Rock
Instow Sands
Bickleton
Myrtle Cott
Rumsam
Landkey
Hurscott
N DEVON MARITIME MUSEUM
Appledore
The Quay
Worlington
Collacott Fm
Upcott Fm
Roundswell
Landkey Newland
Swimbridge Newland
Yarnacott
Yeoland Ho
Riverton
Sandymere
NORTHAM BURROWS
Instow
Fullingcott Fm
Hollamoor Clump
Bishops Tawton
NORTH DEVON FARM PARK
Swimbridge
Diddywell
24
25
Huish
Eastacombe
St John's Chapel
Tawstock
Hannaford
Kerscott
High Down
0 1 2 3 miles
0 1 2 3 4 5 km
TAPELEY PARK GARDENS
Coombe Fm
Huish Moor
Rushcott Fm
Stonyland
Downrew Ho
Horswell Fm
Hangman's Hill
Bydown Ho
Lane End Fm
Westleigh
Trayhill
Uppacott
Northam
Holmacott
Prospect Corner
Eastleigh Manor
Silford
Halmpstone Manor
Tower Fm

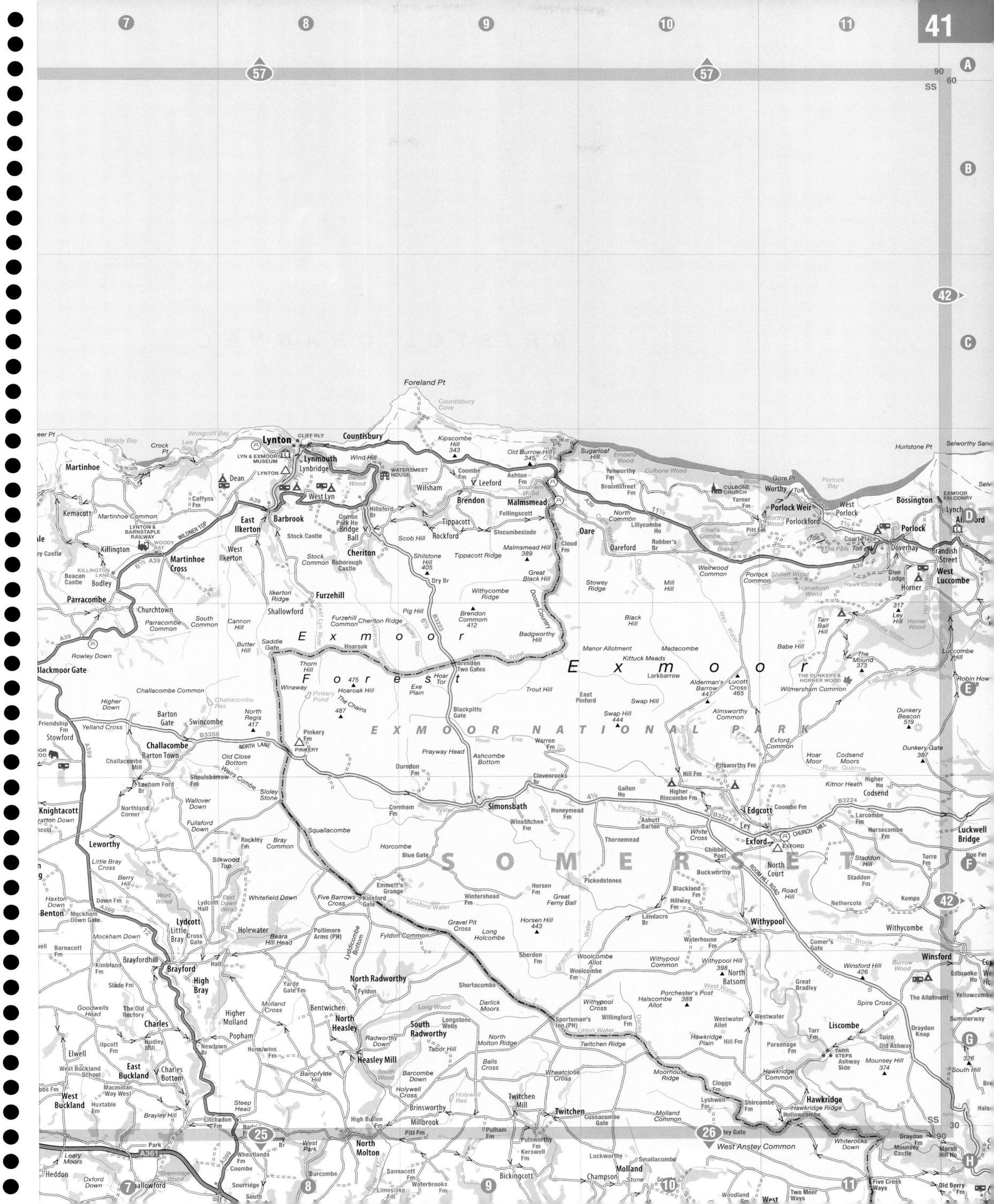

7
8
9
10
11
57
57
42
42
25
26
A
B
C
D
E
F
G
H
90
60
SS
SS
30
90
Foreland Pt
Countisbury Cove
Woody Bay
Wringcliff Bay
Crock Pt
Lee Bay
Lynton
CLIFF RLY
Countisbury
LYN & EXMOOR MUSEUM
Lynmouth
Lynbridge
LYNTON
Wind Hill
Kipscombe Hill 343
Old Burrow Hill 345
Sugarloaf Hill
Embelle Wood
Culbone Wood
Hurlstone Pt
Selworthy Sand
Martinhoe
Dean
Barton Wood
WATERSMEET HOUSE
Coombe Fm
Leeford
Ashton Fm
Yenworthy Fm
CULBONE CHURCH
Gore Pt
Porlock Bay
Caffyns Fm
West Lyn
Wilsham
Brendon
Malmsmead
Broomstreet Fm
Worthy
Porlock Weir
Bossington
EXMOOR FALCONRY
Lynch
Kemacott
Martinhoe Common
East Ilkerton
Barbrook
Combe Park Ho
Hillsford Br
Fellingscott
North Common
Yarner Fm
West Porlock
Porlockford
LYNTON & BARNSTAPLE RAILWAY
WOODY BAY
WILDNER TOP
Stock Castle
Bridge Ball
Tippacott
Rockford
Slocombeslade
Oare
Lillycombe Ho
Pitt Fm
Porlock
Killington
Scob Hill
Shilstone Hill 405
Tippacott Ridge
Malmsmead Hill 389
Cloud Fm
Oareford
Robber's Br
Smalla Combe
Westcott Brake
Court Place
Doverhay
Brandish Street
Martinhoe Cross
West Ilkerton
Cheriton
Stock Common
Roborough Castle
Great Black Hill
Weirwood Common
Porlock Common
Shillett Wood
Glen Lodge
West Luccombe
KILLINGTON LANE
Beacon Castle
Bodley
Dry Br
Stowey Ridge
Mill Hill
Homebush Wood
Hawk Combe
Horner
Furzehill
Withycombe Ridge
Paracombe
Ilkerton Ridge
Churchtown
Shallowford
Pig Hill
Brendon Common 412
Doone Country
317 Ley Hill
Horner Wood
Tarr Ball Hill
Parracombe Common
South Common
Cannon Hill
Furzehill Common
Cheriton Ridge
Black Hill
Butter Hill
Saddle Gate
Hoaroak
Badgworthy Hill
Manor Allotment
Madacombe
Babe Hill
Rowley Down
Exmoor Forest
Hoccombe Water
Kittuck Meads
The Mound 373
Luccombe Hill
Blackmoor Gate
Thorn Hill
Brendon Two Gates
Exmoor
Larkbarrow
Alderman's Barrow 447
Lucott Cross 465
THE DUNKERY & HORNER WOOD
Robin How
Winaway
475 Hoaroak Hill
Hoar Tor
Exe Plain
Trout Hill
East Pinford
Swap Hill
Wilmersham Common
Challacombe Common
Challacombe Res
Pinkery Pond
The Chains 487
Blackpitts Gate
Swap Hill 444
Almsworthy Common
Dunkery Beacon 519
Higher Down
Barton Gate
North Regis 417
EXMOOR NATIONAL PARK
Friendship Fm
Yelland Cross
Swincombe
Pinkery Fm
River Exe
Warren Fm
Exford Common
Dunkery Gate 387
Stowford
Challacombe
B3358
NORTH LANE
PINKERY
Prayway Head
Ashcombe Bottom
Hoar Moor
Codsend Moors
River Quarme
Barton Town
Old Close Bottom
Challacombe Mill
Weirs Combe
Duredon Fm
Pitsworthy Fm
Hill Fm
Kitnor Heath
Higher Ho
Codsend
Leeham Ford Br
Shoulsbarrow Fm
Sloley Stone
Clovenrocks Br
Gallon Ho
Higher Riscombe Fm
Northland Corner
Wallover Down
Cornham Fm
Barle Water
Simonsbath
Honeymead Fm
Pennycombe Water
Edgcott
Coombe Fm
B3224
Larcombe Fm
Knightacott
Fullaford Down
Squallacombe
Winstitchen Fm
Ashott Barton
Ley
CHURCH HILL
Horsecombe Fm
Luckwell Bridge
Rockley Fm
Bray Common
Thornemead
White Cross
Exford
EXFORD
Leworthy
Horcombe
Chibbet Post
Staddon Hill
Torre Fm
Hoe Fm
Little Bray Cross
Silkwood Top
Blue Gate
SOMERSET
North Court
Berry Hill
River Bray
Pickedstones
Buckworthy
ROOM HILL ROAD
Staddon Fm
Wort Wood
Emmett's Grange
Horsen Fm
Blackland Fm
Road Hill
Haxton Down
Whitefield Down
Five Barrows Cross
Kinsford Gate
Wintershead Fm
Great Ferny Ball
Hillway Fm
Nethercote
Kemps
Benton
Down Fm
Lydcott Hall
East Down Wood
Kinsford Water
Landacre Br
Withypool
Mockham Down Gate
A399
Lydcott
Little Bray
Cross Gate
Holewater
Poltimore Arms (PH)
Gravel Pit Cross
Long Holcombe
Horsen Hill 443
River Barle
Withycombe
Mockham Down
Beara Hill Head
Lydiacombe Bottom
Fyldon Common
Waterhouse Fm
Comer's Gate
Winn Brook
Barnacott Fm
Kimbland Fm
Brayfordhill
Brayford
Hall
Sherdon Fm
Woolcombe Allot
Withypool Common
Withypool Hill 398
North Batsom
Winsford Hill 426
Burrow Wood
Winsford
High Bray
Yarde Gate Fm
North Radworthy
Fyldon
Shortacombe
Woolcombe Fm
Great Bradley
Edbrooke Ho
Slade Fm
Goodwells Head
The Old Rectory
Molland Cross
Bentwichen
Long Wood
Darlick Moors
Withypool Cross
Halscombe Allot
Porchester's Post 388
The Allotment
Higher Molland
North Heasley
Spire Cross
Yellowcombe
Charles
South Radworthy
Longstone Wells
Sportsman's Inn (PH)
Willingford Fm
Westwater Allot
Westwater Fm
Liscombe
Summerway
Hudley Mill
Popham
Radworthy Down
North Molton Ridge
Litton Water
Hawkridge Plain
Hill Fm
Draydon Knap
Upcott Fm
Newtown Br
Hunniwins Fm
Tabor Hill
Twitchen Ridge
Danes Brook
Tarr Fm
Parsonage Fm
TARR STEPS
Ashway Side
Spire
Old Ashway
326 South Hill
Elwell
Heasley Mill
West Buckland School
East Buckland
Charles Bottom
Bampfylde Hill
South Wood
Balls Cross
Moorhouse Ridge
Hawkridge Common
Mounsey Hill 374
Macmillan Way West
Barcombe Down
Wheatclose Cross
Cloggs Fm
West Buckland
Huxtable Fm
Holywell Cross
Holywell Res
Twitchen Mill
Lyshwell Fm
Shircombe Fm
Hawkridge
Hawkridge Ridge
Hollowcombe
Brayley Hill
Steep Head
Brinsworthy
Twitchen
Molland Common
Litchadon Fm
High Bullen Fm
Millbrook
Cussacombe Gate
Pitt Fm
Pulham Fm
Whitecrocks Down
Draydon Fm
Mounsey Castle
Marsh Hill Ho
Park
A361
Wheatlands Fm
Coombe
West Park
North Molton
Pulsworthy Fm
Kerswell Fm
West Anstey Common
Leary Moors
Bremridge Wood
Burcombe
Sannacott Fm
Luckworthy
Smallacombe
Molland
Heddon
Oxford Down
Snurridge
River Mole
Waterbrooks Fm
Bickingcott
Champson
Stone
Five Cross Ways
Old Berry Fm
South
Limeslake
Woodland
West
Two Moor Ways

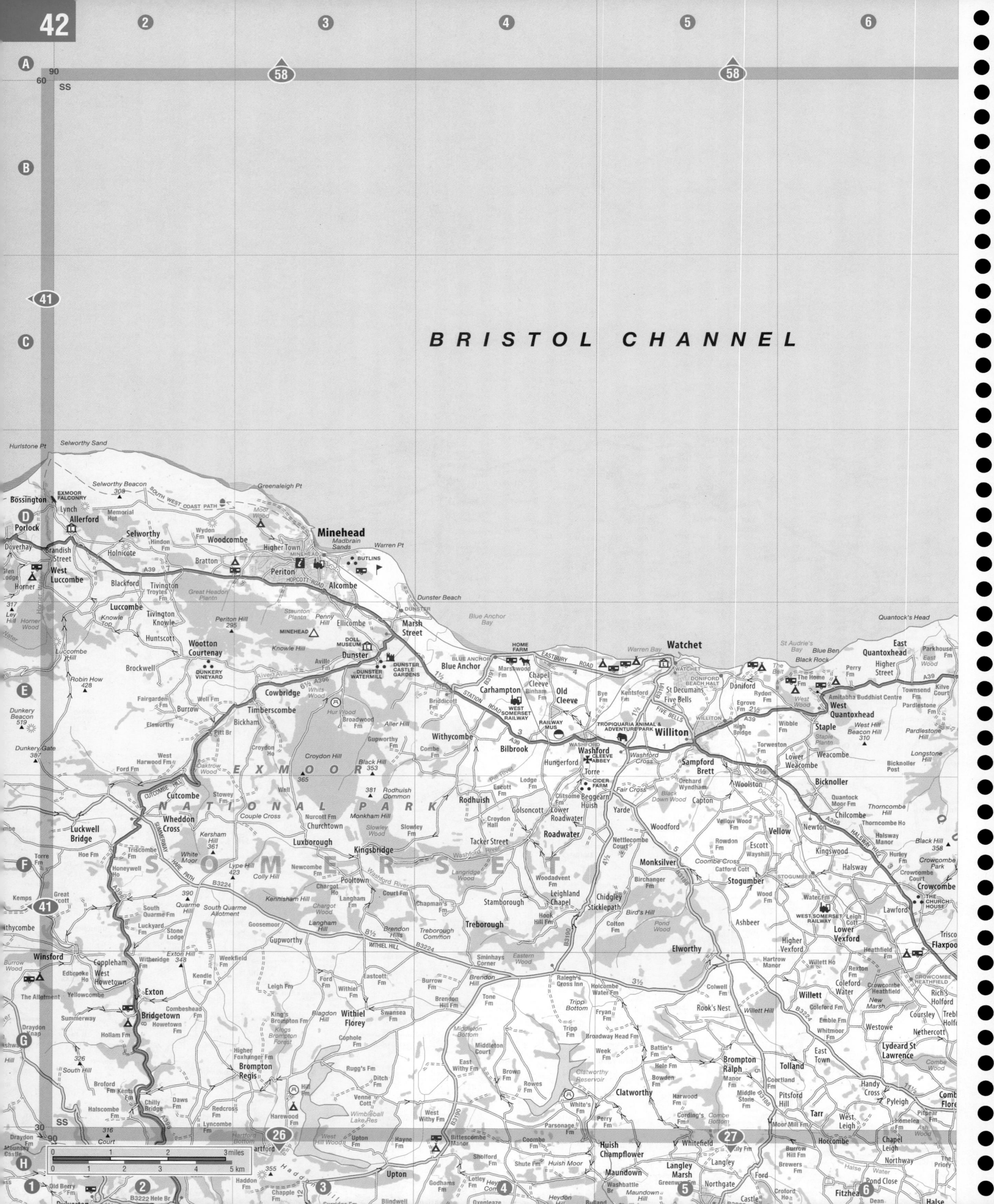
BRISTOL CHANNEL
EXMOOR NATIONAL PARK
SOMERSET
Hurlstone Pt
Selworthy Sand
Selworthy Beacon 308
Greenaleigh Pt
SOUTH WEST COAST PATH
Bossington
EXMOOR FALCONRY
Lynch
Allerford
Porlock
Selworthy
Woodcombe
Minehead
Madbrain Sands
Warren Pt
BUTLINS
Higher Town
Bratton
Periton
Alcombe
West Luccombe
Horner
Blackford
Tivington
Luccombe
Great Headon Plantn
Dunster Beach
Blue Anchor Bay
Periton Hill 295
Ellicombe
Marsh Street
MINEHEAD
Knowle Hill
DOLL MUSEUM
Dunster
DUNSTER CASTLE GARDENS
DUNSTER WATERMILL
Wootton Courtenay
DUNKERY VINEYARD
Brockwell
Robin How 428
Dunkery Beacon 519
Dunkery Gate 387
Cowbridge
Timberscombe
Burrow
Elsworthy
Bickham
Croydon Hill
Black Hill 353
Cutcombe
Wheddon Cross
Luckwell Bridge
Luxborough
Kingsbridge
Churchtown
Pooltown
Blue Anchor
HOME FARM
Carhampton
WEST SOMERSET RAILWAY
Chapel Cleeve
Old Cleeve
Withycombe
Bilbrook
Washford
CLEEVE ABBEY
TROPIQUARIA ANIMAL & ADVENTURE PARK
Watchet
Warren Bay
St Decumans
Five Bells
Doniford
Williton
Sampford Brett
Rodhuish
Hungerford
Torre
Beggearn Huish
Roadwater
Lower Roadwater
Golsoncott
Yarde
Woodford
Capton
Monksilver
Stogumber
Elworthy
Leighland Chapel
Treborough
Stamborough
Chidgley
Sticklepath
Brendon Hill
Quantock's Head
St Audrie's Bay
East Quantoxhead
West Quantoxhead
Staple
Weacombe
Bicknoller
Woolston
Yellow
Newton
Chilcombe
Kingswood
Halsway
Crowcombe
Lawford
Lower Vexford
Higher Vexford
Flaxpool
Willett
Coleford Water
Lydeard St Lawrence
Tolland
Brompton Ralph
Pitsford Hill
Clatworthy
Clatworthy Reservoir
Huish Champflower
Maundown
Langley Marsh
Langley
Northgate
Winsford
Exton
Bridgetown
Withiel Florey
Brompton Regis
Upton
Hoccombe
Chapel Leigh
Pyleigh
Handy Cross
Fitzhead
Halse
58
41
26
27
SS
0 1 2 3 miles
0 1 2 3 4 5 km

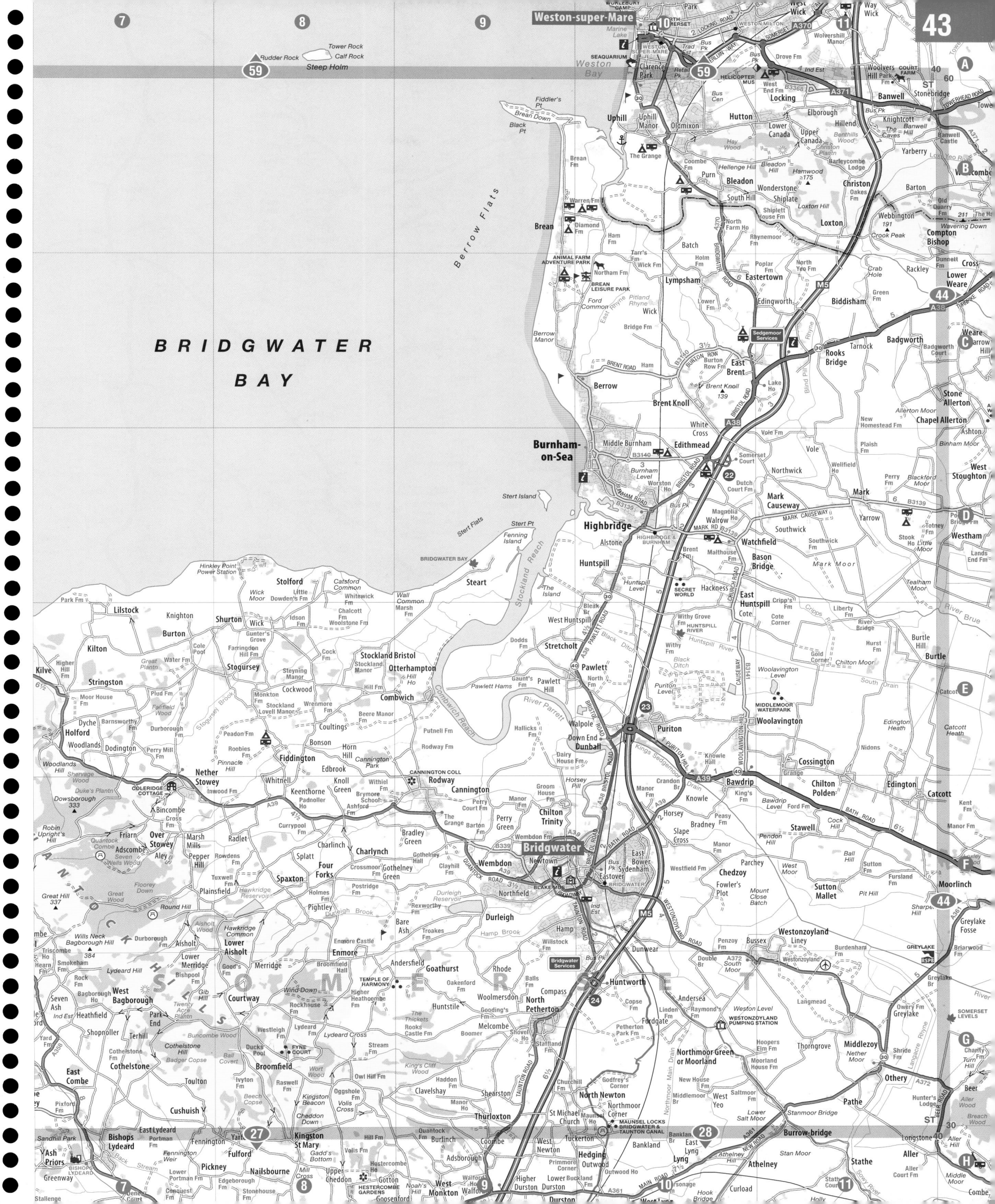
Weston-super-Mare
BRIDGWATER
BAY
Steep Holm
Berrow Flats
Burnham-on-Sea
Highbridge
Bridgwater
Uphill
Brean
Berrow
Brent Knoll
East Brent
Lympsham
Bleadon
Hutton
Locking
Banwell
Loxton
Christon
Compton Bishop
Edingworth
Eastertown
Biddisham
Rooks Bridge
Badgworth
Mark
Mark Causeway
Watchfield
Huntspill
East Huntspill
Pawlett
Puriton
Woolavington
Cossington
Chilton Polden
Edington
Catcott
Bawdrip
Stolford
Stogursey
Otterhampton
Combwich
Cannington
Nether Stowey
Holford
Kilton
Lilstock
Stringston
Fiddington
Spaxton
Durleigh
North Petherton
Westonzoyland
Middlezoy
Othery
Burrow-bridge
Thurloxton
North Newton
Cothelstone
Broomfield
Kingston St Mary
Bishops Lydeard
Sedgemoor Services
Bridgwater Services
QUANTOCK HILLS
SOMERSET
M5
A38
A39
A372
B3139
B3140

Cheddar
Wells
Glastonbury
Street
Shepton Mallet
Castle Cary
Wedmore
Mendip Hills
Axbridge
Westbury-sub-Mendip
Chewton Mendip
Compton Martin
Blagdon
Somerset Levels
0 1 2 3 miles
0 1 2 3 4 5 km

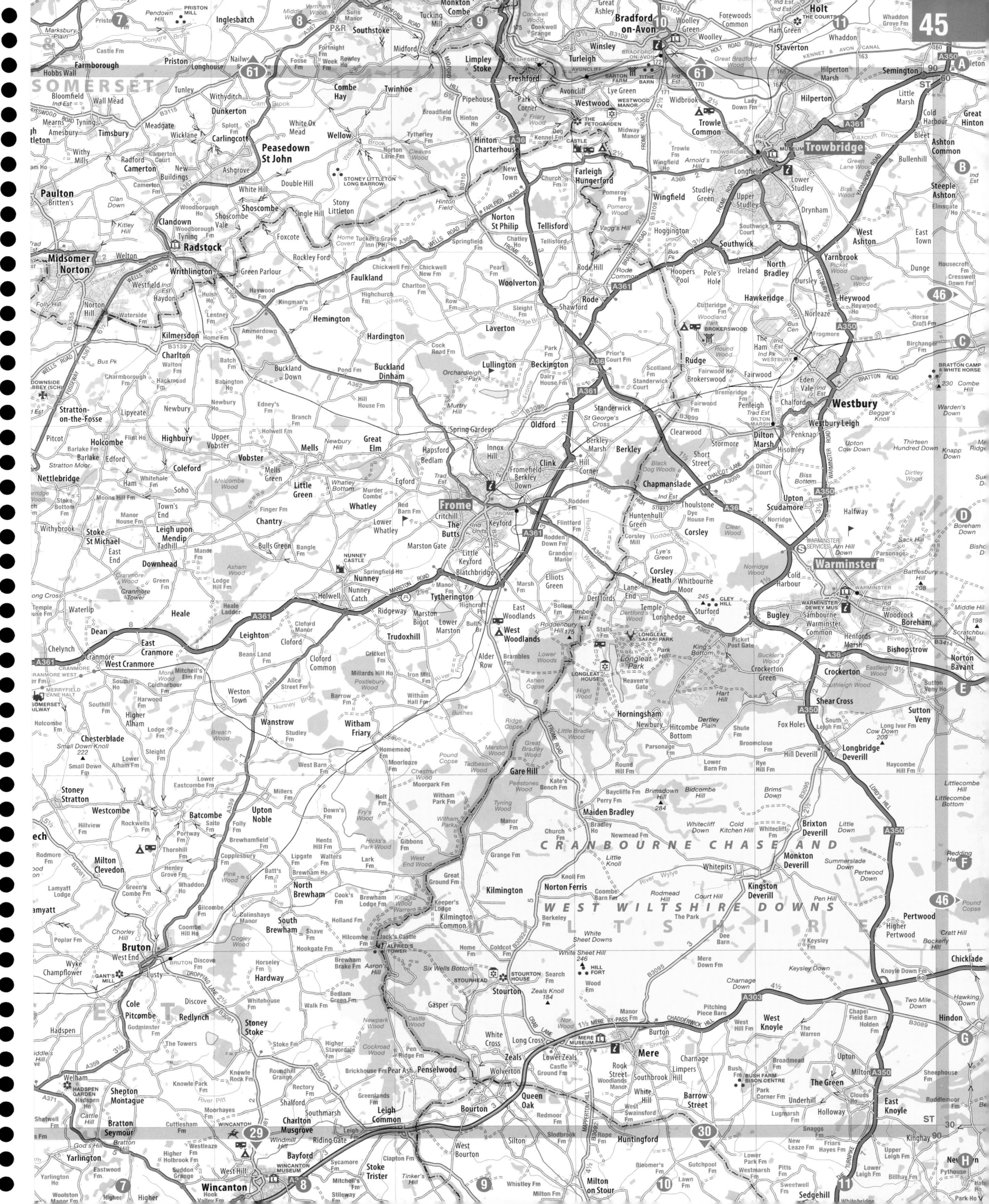
SOMERSET
CRANBOURNE CHASE AND
WEST WILTSHIRE DOWNS
WILTSHIRE
Bradford on-Avon
Trowbridge
Westbury
Warminster
Frome
Radstock
Midsomer Norton
Paulton
Peasedown St John
Timsbury
Farmborough
Priston
Inglesbatch
Southstoke
Midford
Limpley Stoke
Freshford
Monkton Combe
Tucking Mill
Winsley
Turleigh
Avoncliff
Westwood
Holt
Staverton
Hilperton
Semington
Wellow
Combe Hay
Twinhoe
Dunkerton
Camerton
Shoscombe
Single Hill
Foxcote
Clandown
Writhlington
Kilmersdon
Hemington
Faulkland
Hardington
Buckland Dinham
Lullington
Beckington
Laverton
Woolverton
Rode
Tellisford
Norton St Philip
Hinton Charterhouse
Farleigh Hungerford
Wingfield
North Bradley
Yarnbrook
West Ashton
Southwick
Heywood
Hawkeridge
Dilton Marsh
Westbury Leigh
Chapmanslade
Berkley
Standerwick
Oldford
Upton Scudamore
Corsley
Corsley Heath
Chalford
Rudge
Mells
Great Elm
Vobster
Coleford
Holcombe
Highbury
Nettlebridge
Stratton-on-the-Fosse
Chantry
Whatley
Little Green
Leigh upon Mendip
Stoke St Michael
Downhead
Nunney
Nunney Catch
Marston Gate
Tytherington
Trudoxhill
Leighton
Cloford
East Woodlands
West Woodlands
Longleat Park
Horningsham
Crockerton
Shear Cross
Sutton Veny
Longbridge Deverill
Brixton Deverill
Monkton Deverill
Kingston Deverill
Maiden Bradley
Gare Hill
Witham Friary
Wanstrow
Cranmore
East Cranmore
West Cranmore
Dean
Heale
Batcombe
Upton Noble
Milton Clevedon
North Brewham
South Brewham
Bruton
Kilmington
Kilmington Common
Norton Ferris
Stourton
Stourhead
Zeals
Mere
Penselwood
Wolverton
Bourton
Queen Oak
Charlton Musgrove
Wincanton
Bayford
Stoke Trister
Shepton Montague
Pitcombe
Cole
Redlynch
Stoney Stoke
Huntingford
West Knoyle
East Knoyle
Hindon
Chicklade
Pertwood
The Green
Bugley
Boreham
Bishopstrow
Norton Bavant
A350
A36
A361
A362
A366
A303
A359
A371
B3092
B3095
B3098
B3109
B3110
61
29
30
46
A
B
C
D
E
F
G
H
7
8
9
10
11

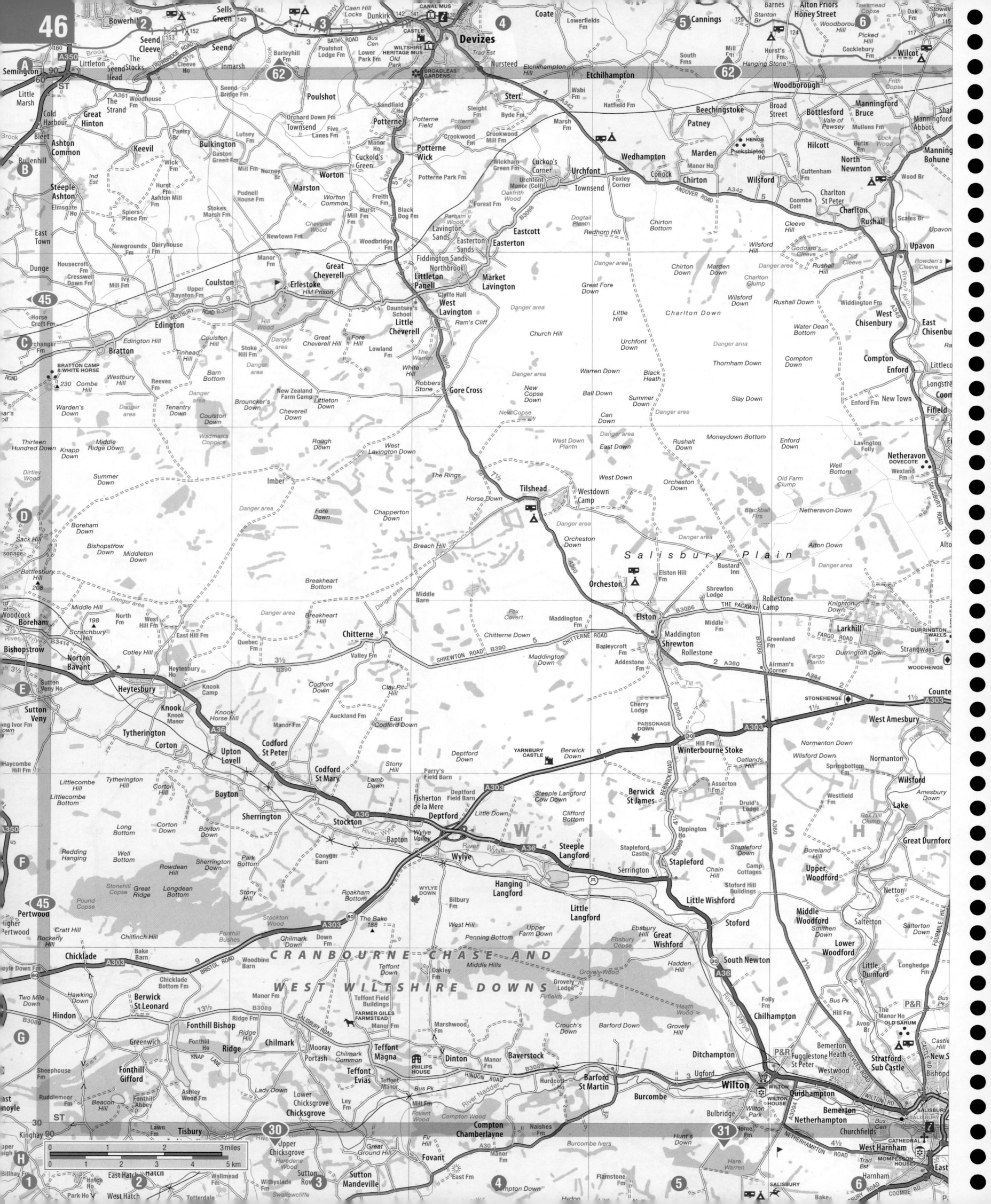
Devizes
Bowerhill
Sells Green
Seend Cleeve
Seend
Semington
Littleton
Seend Head
Inmarsh
Caen Hill Locks
Dunkirk
CANAL MUS
WILTSHIRE HERITAGE MUS
BROADLEAS GARDENS
Coate
Cannings
Nursteed
Etchilhampton
Stert
Poulshot
Potterne
Potterne Wick
Worton
Marston
Keevil
Bulkington
Great Hinton
Ashton Common
Steeple Ashton
Little Marsh
Cold Harbour
Bleet
Urchfont
Wedhampton
Chirton
Marden
Patney
Beechingstoke
Woodborough
Broad Street
Bottlesford
Manningford Bruce
Wilsford
Conock
Charlton
Rushall
Upavon
North Newnton
Hilcott
Eastcott
Easterton
Market Lavington
Littleton Panell
West Lavington
Little Cheverell
Great Cheverell
Erlestoke
Coulston
Edington
Bratton
BRATTON CAMP & WHITE HORSE
Gore Cross
Salisbury Plain
Tilshead
Westdown Camp
Orcheston
Elston
Shrewton
Maddington
Rollestone
Larkhill
Durrington Walls
Strangways
Woodhenge
Stonehenge
West Amesbury
Winterbourne Stoke
Berwick St James
Stapleford
Steeple Langford
Hanging Langford
Little Langford
Great Wishford
Little Wishford
Stoford
South Newton
Chilhampton
Ditchampton
Wilton
Quidhampton
Bemerton
Netherhampton
Fugglestone St Peter
West Harnham
Harnham
Salisbury
Stratford sub Castle
Old Sarum
Upper Woodford
Middle Woodford
Lower Woodford
Wilsford
Lake
Great Durnford
Little Durnford
Netton
Salterton
Enford
Compton
Fifield
Netheravon
West Chisenbury
East Chisenbury
Chitterne
Imber
Heytesbury
Knook
Tytherington
Corton
Sutton Veny
Bishopstrow
Norton Bavant
Boreham
Upton Lovell
Codford St Peter
Codford St Mary
Boyton
Sherrington
Stockton
Deptford
Fisherton de la Mere
Bapton
Wylye
YARNBURY CASTLE
CRANBOURNE CHASE AND WEST WILTSHIRE DOWNS
WILTSHIRE
Chicklade
Hindon
Berwick St Leonard
Fonthill Bishop
Ridge
Chilmark
Teffont Magna
Teffont Evias
Dinton
PHILIPS HOUSE
Baverstock
Barford St Martin
Burcombe
Compton Chamberlayne
Fonthill Gifford
Chicksgrove
Tisbury
Sutton Mandeville
Fovant
Pertwood
Greenwich
Burcombe Ivers
A350
A36
A303
A360
A342
A345
A3094
B3098
B3086
B3083
B3089
B3390
B3414
62
45
30
31
0 1 2 3 miles
0 1 2 3 4 5 km

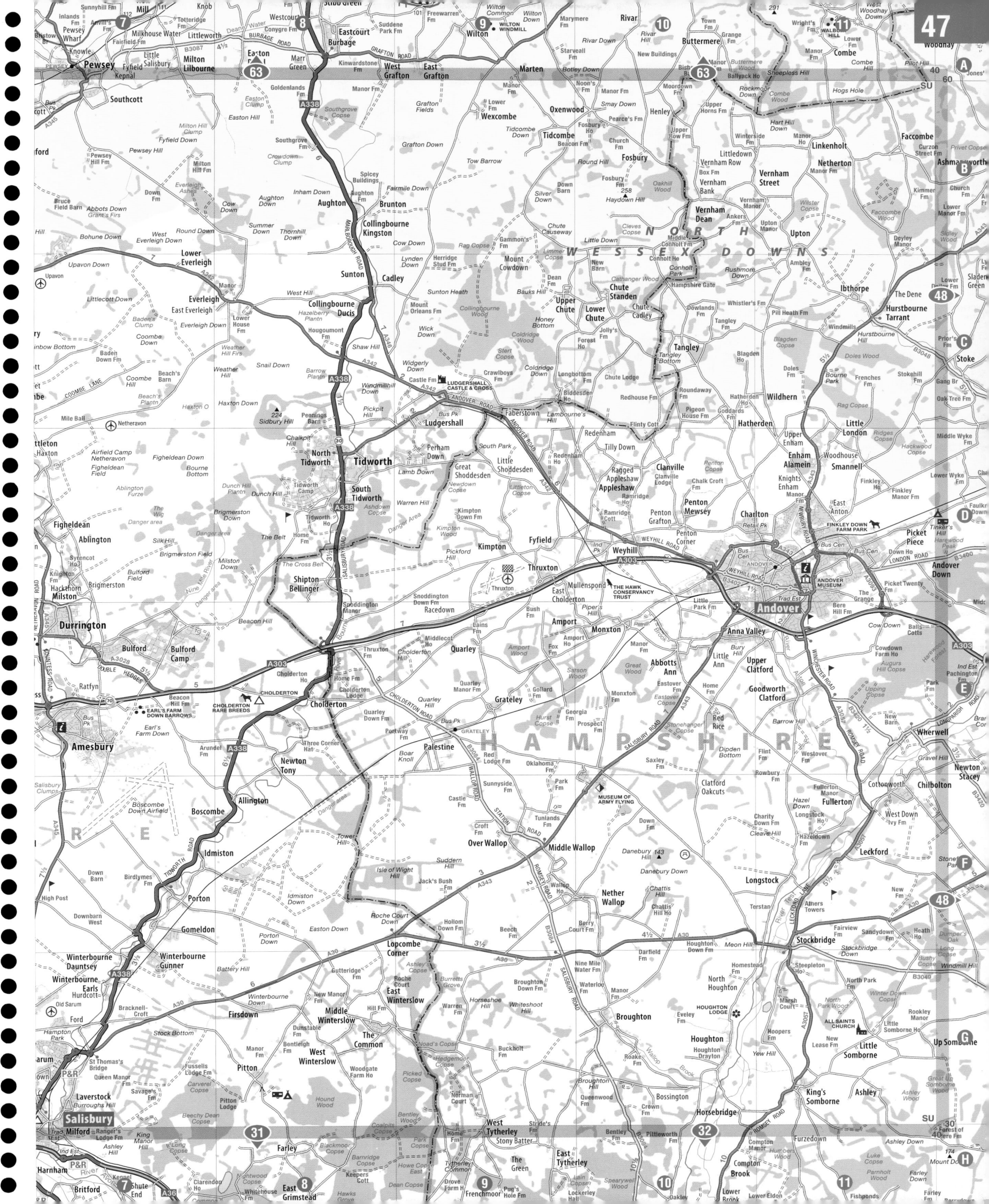

47
Pewsey
Milton Lilbourne
Easton Royal
Burbage
Eastcourt
Wilton
Wilton Windmill
Marten
West Grafton
East Grafton
Rivar
Buttermere
Combe
Oxenwood
Tidcombe
Fosbury
Henley
Linkenholt
Faccombe
Netherton
Vernham Street
Vernham Dean
Upton
Southcott
Wexcombe
Aughton
Brunton
Collingbourne Kingston
Collingbourne Ducis
Sunton
Cadley
Lower Everleigh
Everleigh
East Everleigh
Chute Standen
Upper Chute
Lower Chute
Chute Cadley
Tangley
Ibthorpe
Hurstbourne Tarrant
The Dene
Stoke
NORTH WESSEX DOWNS
Ludgershall
Ludgershall Castle & Cross
Faberstown
Wildhern
Hatherden
Little London
North Tidworth
Tidworth
South Tidworth
Perham Down
Great Shoddesden
Little Shoddesden
Ragged Appleshaw
Appleshaw
Clanville
Enham Alamein
Smannell
Knights Enham
Penton Mewsey
Penton Grafton
Charlton
Finkley Down Farm Park
Picket Piece
Figheldean
Ablington
Kimpton
Fyfield
Weyhill
Thruxton
Mullenspond
East Cholderton
The Hawk Conservancy Trust
Andover
Andover Museum
Andover Down
Shipton Bellinger
Milston
Durrington
Bulford
Bulford Camp
Amport
Monxton
Anna Valley
Quarley
Abbotts Ann
Little Ann
Upper Clatford
Goodworth Clatford
Ratfyn
Cholderton
Cholderton Rare Breeds
Earl's Farm Down Barrows
Amesbury
Grateley
Palestine
Newton Tony
HAMPSHIRE
Red Rice
Wherwell
Newton Stacey
Chilbolton
Clatford Oakcuts
Fullerton
Cottonworth
Allington
Boscombe
Museum of Army Flying
Over Wallop
Middle Wallop
Leckford
Idmiston
Danebury Hill
Longstock
Nether Wallop
Porton
Gomeldon
Stockbridge
Lopcombe Corner
Winterbourne Dauntsey
Winterbourne Gunner
Winterbourne Earls
Hurdcott
East Winterslow
Middle Winterslow
Firsdown
Old Sarum
Ford
Broughton
Houghton
North Houghton
Houghton Lodge
All Saints Church
Little Somborne
The Common
West Winterslow
Pitton
Laverstock
Salisbury
Milford
Bossington
Horsebridge
King's Somborne
Ashley
West Tytherley
Stony Batter
East Tytherley
Farley
Harnham
Britford
East Grimstead
Frenchmoor
Compton
Brook
Furzedown

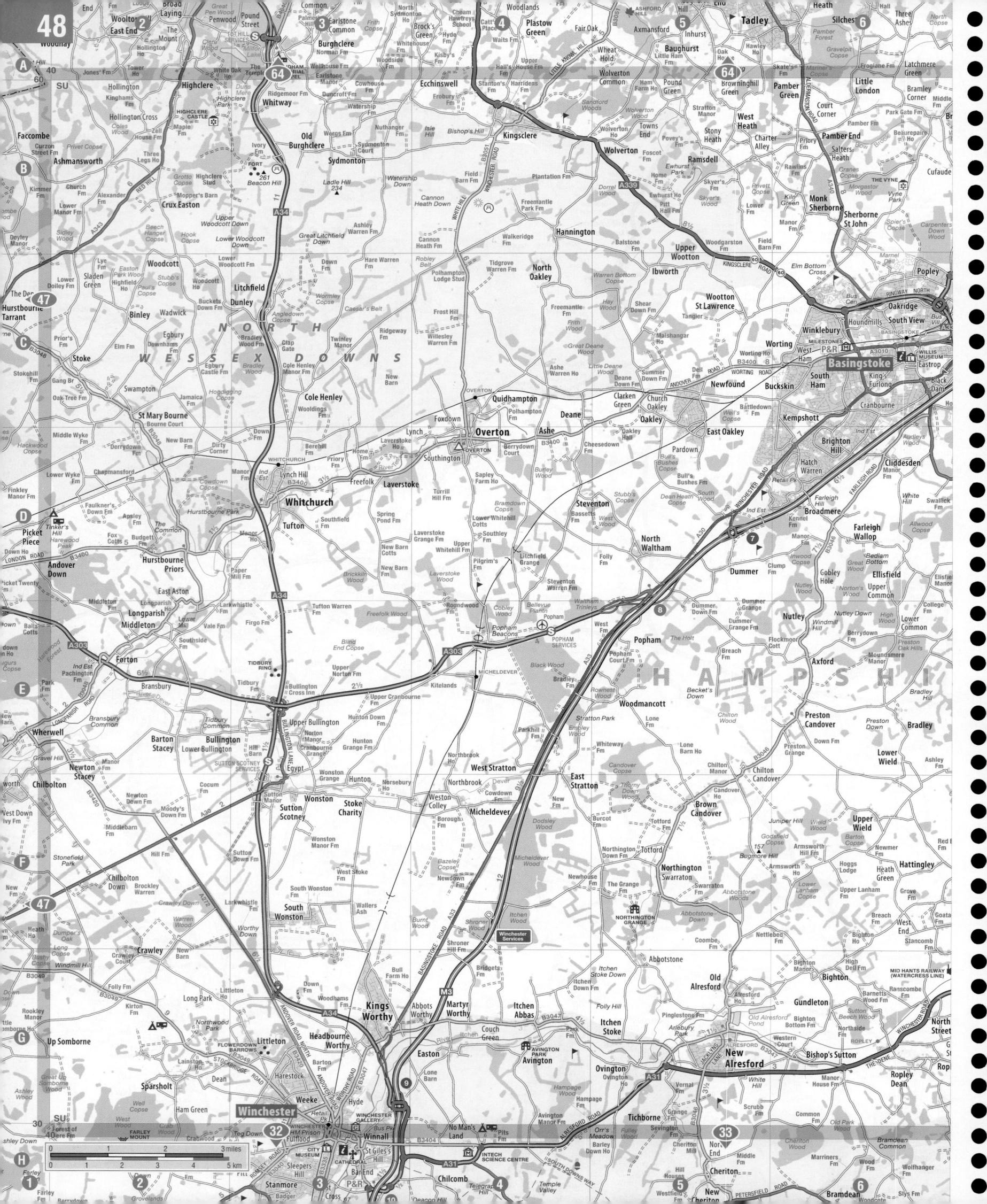
Highclere
Whitway
Burghclere
Kingsclere
Wolverton
Tadley
Baughurst
Ramsdell
Pamber Green
Pamber End
Little London
Monk Sherborne
Sherborne St John
Sydmonton
Old Burghclere
Ecchinswell
Faccombe
Ashmansworth
Crux Easton
Woodcott
Litchfield
Dunley
Binley
Hannington
North Oakley
Ibworth
Upper Wootton
Wootton St Lawrence
Popley
Oakridge
South View
Winklebury
Worting
Basingstoke
South Ham
Buckskin
Kempshott
Brighton Hill
Hatch Warren
Cliddesden
Farleigh Wallop
Ellisfield
Newfound
Oakley
Church Oakley
East Oakley
Deane
Ashe
Overton
Quidhampton
Laverstoke
Freefolk
Whitchurch
Tufton
St Mary Bourne
Stoke
Hurstbourne Priors
Hurstbourne Tarrant
Andover Down
Picket Piece
Longparish
Middleton
Forton
Bransbury
Wherwell
Barton Stacey
Bullington
Newton Stacey
Chilbolton
Sutton Scotney
Wonston
Stoke Charity
Hunton
Micheldever
West Stratton
East Stratton
Steventon
North Waltham
Dummer
Popham
Woodmancott
Axford
Nutley
Preston Candover
Chilton Candover
Brown Candover
Bradley
Lower Wield
Upper Wield
Northington
Swarraton
Abbotstone
Old Alresford
New Alresford
Bighton
Gundleton
Hattingley
Bishop's Sutton
Ropley Dean
Tichborne
Cheriton
Itchen Abbas
Itchen Stoke
Avington
Easton
Kings Worthy
Abbots Worthy
Martyr Worthy
Headbourne Worthy
Littleton
Crawley
South Wonston
Up Somborne
Sparsholt
Weeke
Harestock
Winchester
Winnall
Chilcomb
Stanmore
Ovington
Bramdean
HAMPSHI
NORTH WESSEX DOWNS
Winchester Services

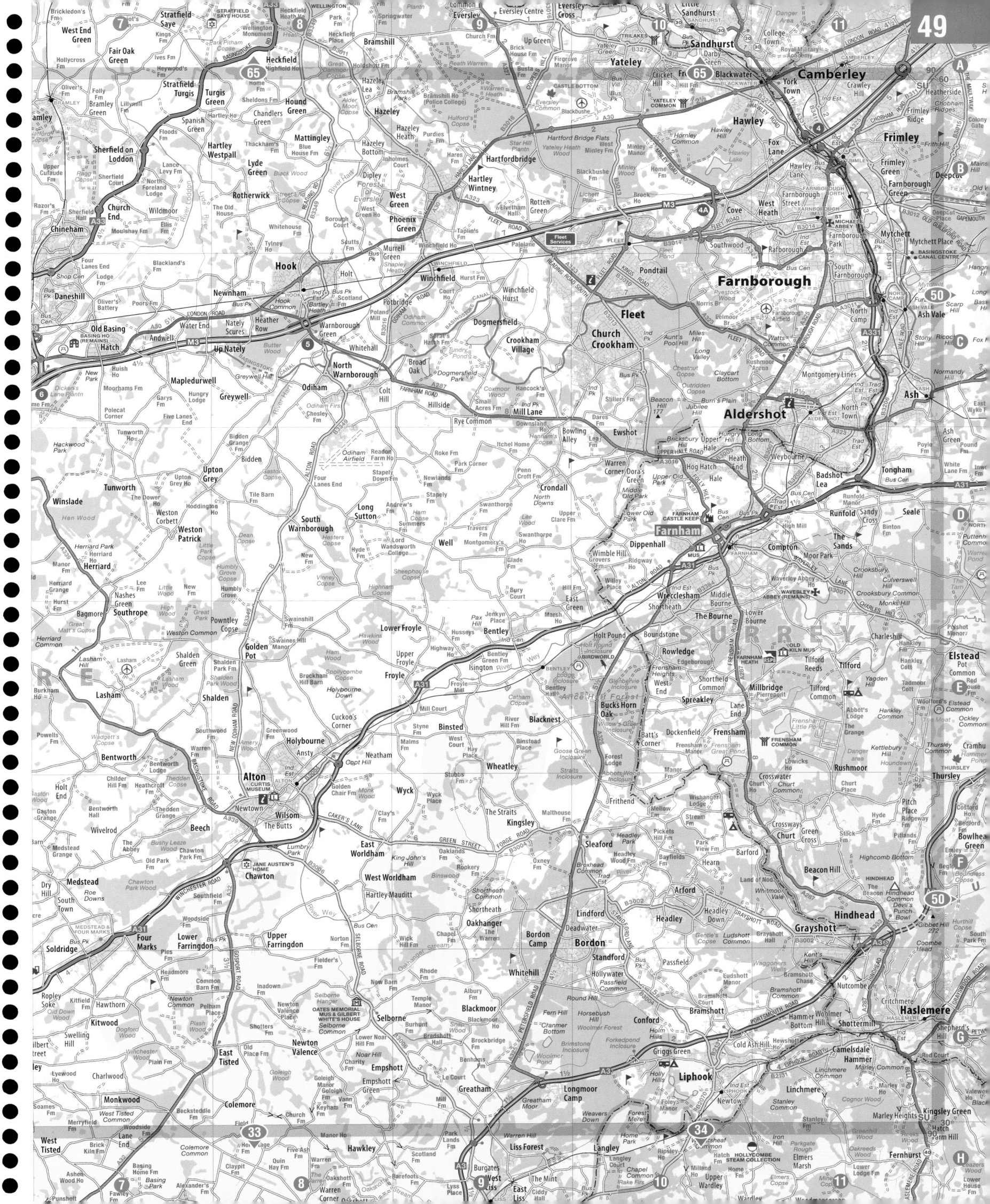

Stratfield Saye
West End Green
Fair Oak Green
Heckfield
Bramshill
Eversley
Eversley Centre
Eversley Cross
Little Sandhurst
Sandhurst
Yateley
Blackwater
Camberley
York Town
Crawley Hill
Heatherside
Frimley
Frimley Green
Deepcut
Mytchett
Mytchett Place
Farnborough
Cove
West Heath
Fleet
Church Crookham
Hawley
Stratfield Turgis
Turgis Green
Hound Green
Chandlers Green
Mattingley
Hazeley
Hazeley Heath
Hazeley Bottom
Hartfordbridge
Hartley Wintney
Sherfield on Loddon
Hartley Westpall
Lyde Green
Rotherwick
West Green
Phoenix Green
Chineham
Church End
Wildmoor
Hook
Newnham
Winchfield
Winchfield Hurst
Daneshill
Old Basing
Basing Ho (Remains)
Hatch
Andwell
Water End
Nately Scures
Heather Row
Up Nately
Warnborough Green
North Warnborough
Odiham
Dogmersfield
Crookham Village
Broad Oak
Mapledurwell
Greywell
Colt Hill
Hillside
Rye Common
Mill Lane
Ewshot
Bowling Alley
Aldershot
Ash
Ash Vale
Tongham
Badshot Lea
Runfold
Seale
Upper Hale
Hale
Heath End
Weybourne
Hog Hatch
Crondall
Upton Grey
Tunworth
Winslade
Weston Corbett
Weston Patrick
Long Sutton
South Warnborough
Well
Farnham
Dippenhall
Compton
The Sands
Moor Park
Herriard
Nashes Green
Southrope
Bagmore
Powntley Copse
Golden Pot
Lower Froyle
Upper Froyle
Froyle
Bentley
Isington
Wrecclesham
Shortheath
The Bourne
Middle Bourne
Lower Bourne
Boundstone
Rowledge
Charleshill
Elstead
Tilford
Tilford Reeds
Tilford Common
Millbridge
Spreakley
Frensham
Dockenfield
Batt's Corner
Bucks Horn Oak
Blacknest
Binsted
Holybourne
Lasham
Shalden
Shalden Green
Bentworth
Alton
Newtown
Wilsom
The Butts
Beech
Chawton
Medstead
Wyck
Wheatley
Kingsley
East Worldham
West Worldham
Hartley Mauditt
Sleaford
Headley
Arford
Lindford
Bordon
Bordon Camp
Standford
Whitehill
Oakhanger
Grayshott
Hindhead
Beacon Hill
Churt
Rushmoor
Thursley
Haslemere
Shottermill
Camelsdale
Hammer
Linchmere
Four Marks
Lower Farringdon
Upper Farringdon
Soldridge
Ropley Soke
Hawthorn
Kitwood
Newton Valence
Selborne
Empshott
Empshott Green
Blackmoor
Greatham
Longmoor Camp
Conford
Bramshott
Liphook
Griggs Green
East Tisted
Colemore
Monkwood
Charlwood
Hawkley
West Tisted
Liss Forest
Langley
West Liss
East Liss
Burgates
Kingsley Green
Fernhurst
Marley Heights
SURREY

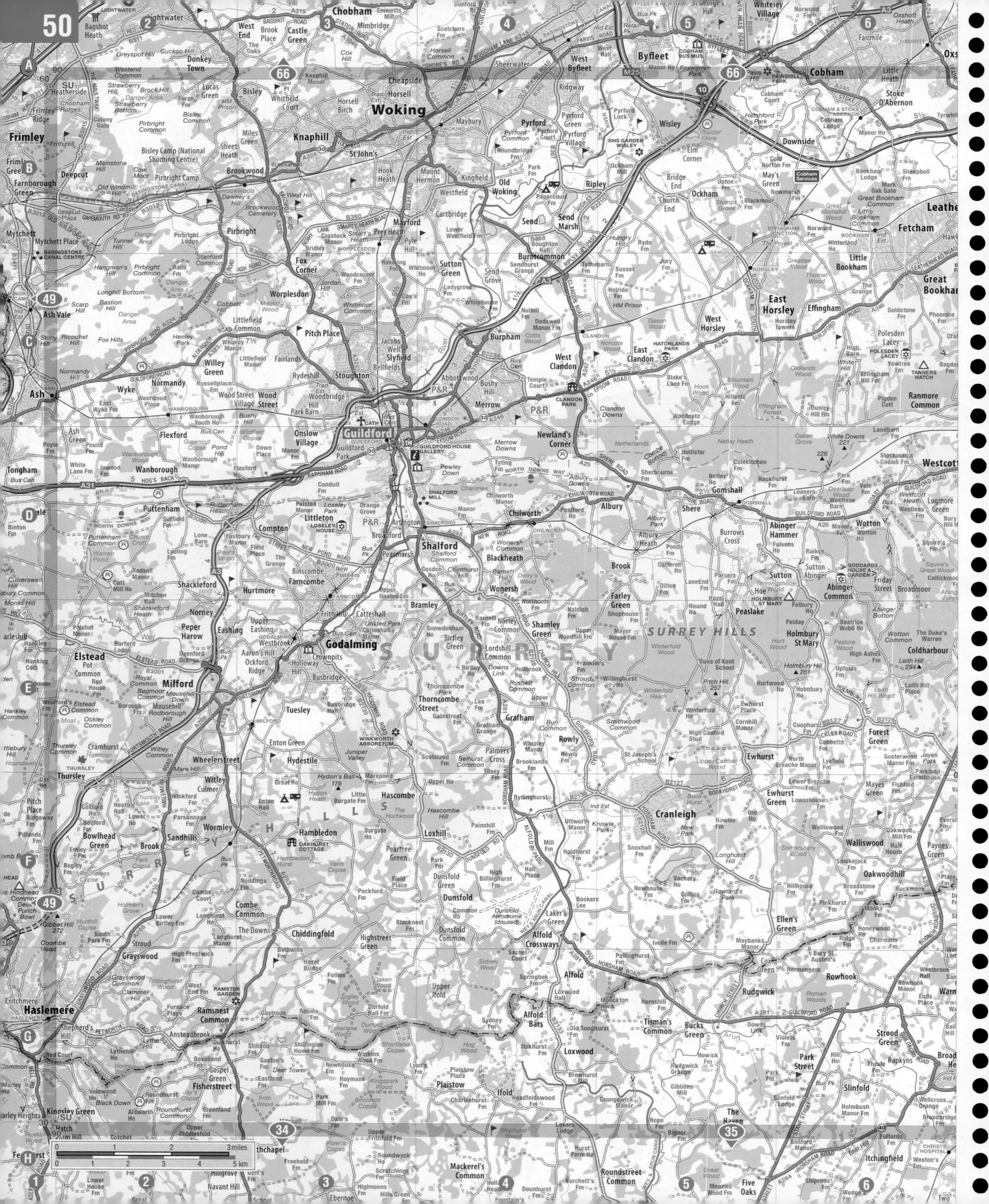
Bagshot Heath
Lightwater
Chobham
West End
Brook Place
Castle Green
Mimbridge
Byfleet
Whiteley Village
Oxshott Heath
Donkey Town
Bisley
Whitfield Court
Horsell
Cheapside
Woking
Sheerwater
West Byfleet
Cobham
Little Heath
Stoke D'Abernon
Frimley
Frimley Ridge
Heatherside
Knaphill
St John's
Maybury
Pyrford
Pyrford Green
Pyrford Village
Wisley
RHS GARDEN WISLEY
Downside
Deepcut
Brookwood
Hook Heath
Mount Hermon
Kingfield
Westfield
Old Woking
Ripley
Ockham
Bridge End
Church End
Farnborough Green
Mytchett
Mytchett Place
BASINGSTOKE CANAL CENTRE
Pirbright
Mayford
Prey Heath
Pyle Hill
Send
Send Marsh
Burntcommon
Fetcham
Leatherhead
Effingham Junction
Little Bookham
Great Bookham
Fox Corner
Worplesdon
Sutton Green
Send Grove
East Horsley
West Horsley
Effingham
Ash Vale
Pitch Place
Jacobs Well
Slyfield
Burpham
West Clandon
East Clandon
HATCHLANDS PARK
CLANDON PARK
POLESDEN LACEY
Ranmore Common
Willey Green
Normandy
Fairlands
Rydeshill
Stoughton
Bellfields
Abbotswood
Merrow
Ash
Wyke
Wood Street Village
Park Barn
Guildford
GUILDFORD HOUSE GALLERY
Onslow Village
Newland's Corner
Flexford
Wanborough
Tongham
Puttenham
Compton
Littleton
LOSELEY HOUSE
Artington
Shalford
Chilworth
Albury
Gomshall
Shere
Westcott
Abinger Hammer
Wotton
Blackheath
Wonersh
Brook
Farley Green
Sutton Abinger
Abinger Common
GODDARDS HOUSE & GARDEN
Holmbury St Mary
Peaslake
Shackleford
Hurtmore
Farncombe
Bramley
Norney
Peper Harow
Eashing
Catteshall
Godalming
Shamley Green
SURREY HILLS
SURREY
Elstead
Milford
Busbridge
Tuesley
Thorncombe Street
Grafham
Rowly
Ewhurst
Forest Green
Coldharbour
Leith Hill
Thursley
Witley
Wheelerstreet
Hydestile
WINKWORTH ARBORETUM
Enton Green
Hascombe
Cranleigh
Ewhurst Green
Walliswood
Oakwoodhill
Bowlhead Green
Brook
Sandhills
Wormley
Hambledon
OAKHURST COTTAGE
Loxhill
Dunsfold
Alfold Crossways
Ellen's Green
Hindhead Common
Gibbet Hill
Chiddingfold
Grayswood
Combe Common
Alfold
Rudgwick
Rowhook
Haslemere
Ramsnest Common
RAMSTER GARDEN
Alfold Bars
Tisman's Common
Bucks Green
Loxwood
Strood Green
Shepherd's Hill
Fisherstreet
Plaistow
Ifold
Slinfold
Broadbridge Heath
Kingsley Green
Lower Roundhurst
Upper Diddlesfold
Rapkyns
The Haven
Itchingfield
Mackerel's Common
Roundstreet Common
Five Oaks
Fernhurst
Lower Lodge
Navant Hill
Northchapel
0 1 2 3 miles
0 1 2 3 4 5 km

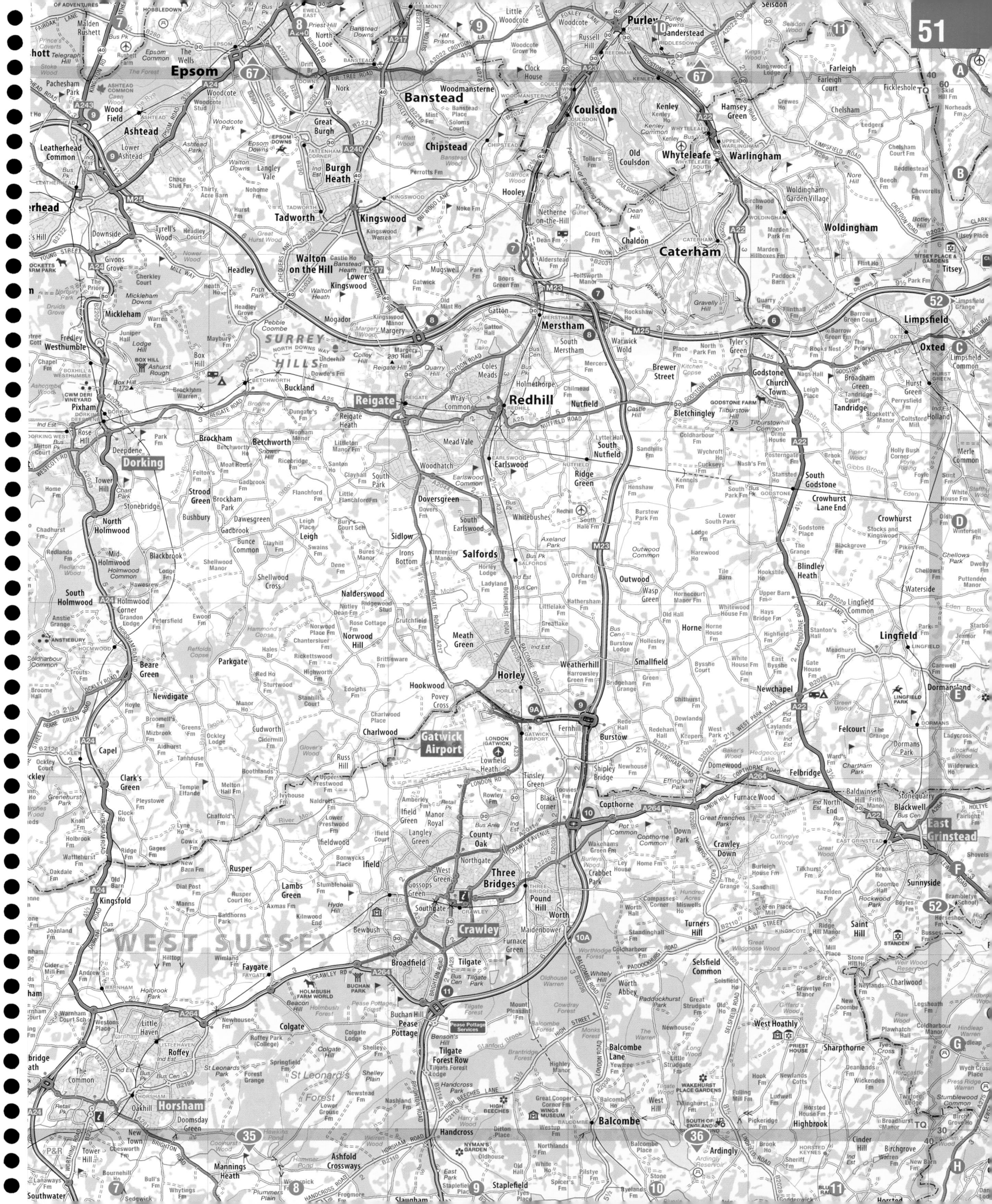
Epsom
Banstead
Purley
Ashtead
Woodcote
Coulsdon
Whyteleafe
Warlingham
Chipstead
Burgh Heath
Tadworth
Kingswood
Hooley
Caterham
Woldingham
Leatherhead
Walton on the Hill
Headley
Mickleham
Merstham
Limpsfield
Oxted
SURREY HILLS
Reigate
Redhill
Nutfield
Bletchingley
Godstone
Tandridge
Dorking
Brockham
Betchworth
Earlswood
South Nutfield
South Godstone
Crowhurst
Leigh
Sidlow
Salfords
Outwood
Lingfield
Horley
Smallfield
Gatwick Airport
Charlwood
Burstow
Copthorne
Felbridge
East Grinstead
Dormansland
Capel
Kingsfold
Rusper
Ifield
Three Bridges
Crawley
Pound Hill
Worth
Turners Hill
West Hoathly
Sharpthorne
WEST SUSSEX
Faygate
Colgate
Pease Pottage
Handcross
Balcombe
Ardingly
Horsham
Roffey
Mannings Heath
Highbrook
Saint Hill
Sunnyside
Titsey
Chelsham
Farleigh
Kenley
Old Coulsdon
Chaldon
Lingfield Park
Wakehurst Place Gardens
Nymans Garden
High Beeches
Pease Pottage Services

Leaves Green
Downe
Badger's Mount
Halstead
Shoreham
Knockholt Pound
Biggin Hill
Cudham
Knockholt
Otford
Kemsing
Heaverham
Wrotham
Stansted
Vigo Village
Fairseat
Trottiscliffe
Tatsfield
South Street
Chevening
Dunton Green
Seal
Borough Green
Platt
Ightham
Riverhead
Chipstead
Longford
Sundridge
Brasted
Sevenoaks
Titsey
Westerham
Limpsfield
Oxted
Brasted Chart
Ivy Hatch
Plaxtol
Stone Street
Crouch
Ide Hill
Toy's Hill
Sevenoaks Weald
Hubbard's Hill
Underriver
Shipbourne
Crockham Hill
Hurst Green
Oakhurst
Hildenborough
Hadlow
Golden Green
KENT DOWNS
Four Elms
Pootings
Marlpit Hill
Edenbridge
Crouch House Green
Leigh
Chiddingstone Causeway
Tonbridge
Tudeley
Five Oak Green
KENT
Chiddingstone
Hever
Penshurst
Lingfield
Marsh Green
Dormansland
Markbeech
Bidborough
Southborough
Pembury
HIGH WEALD
Speldhurst
Fordcombe
Cowden
Lullenden
Blackham
Rusthall
Langton Green
Royal Tunbridge Wells
East Grinstead
Hammerwood
Ashurst
Groombridge
Frant
Bells Yew Green
Sunnyside
Ashurst Wood
Hartfield
Withyham
Eridge Green
Forest Row
Upper Hartfield
EAST SUSSEX
Coleman's Hatch
Friar's Gate
Boarshead
Crowborough
Wych Cross
Chelwood Gate
Rotherfield
Mark Cross
Wadhurst
Durgates
Town Row
Tidebrook
Jarvis Brook
Ashdown Forest
M25
M26
A21
A26
A25
A264
A22
68
51
36
37
0 1 2 3 miles
0 1 2 3 4 5 km

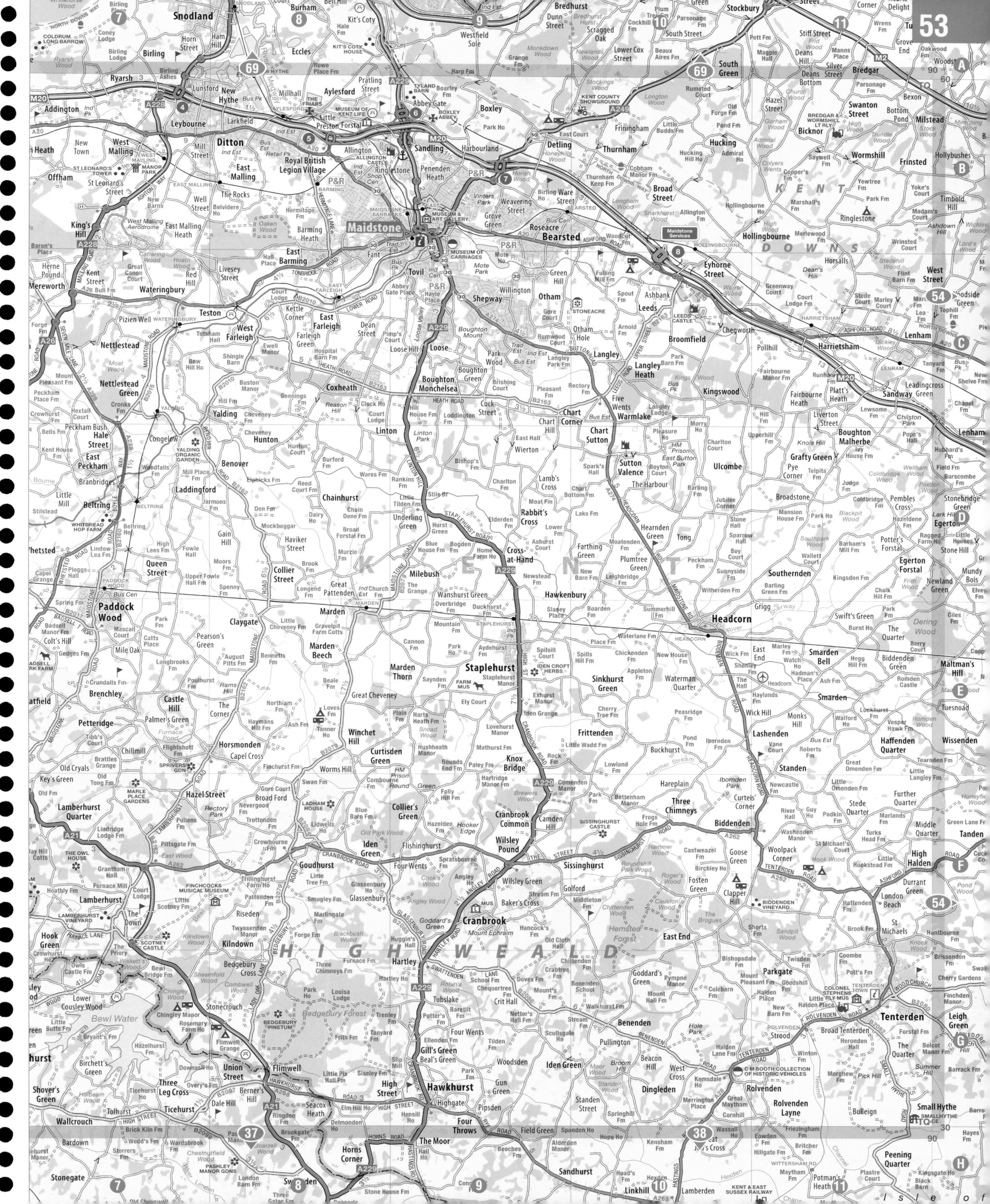

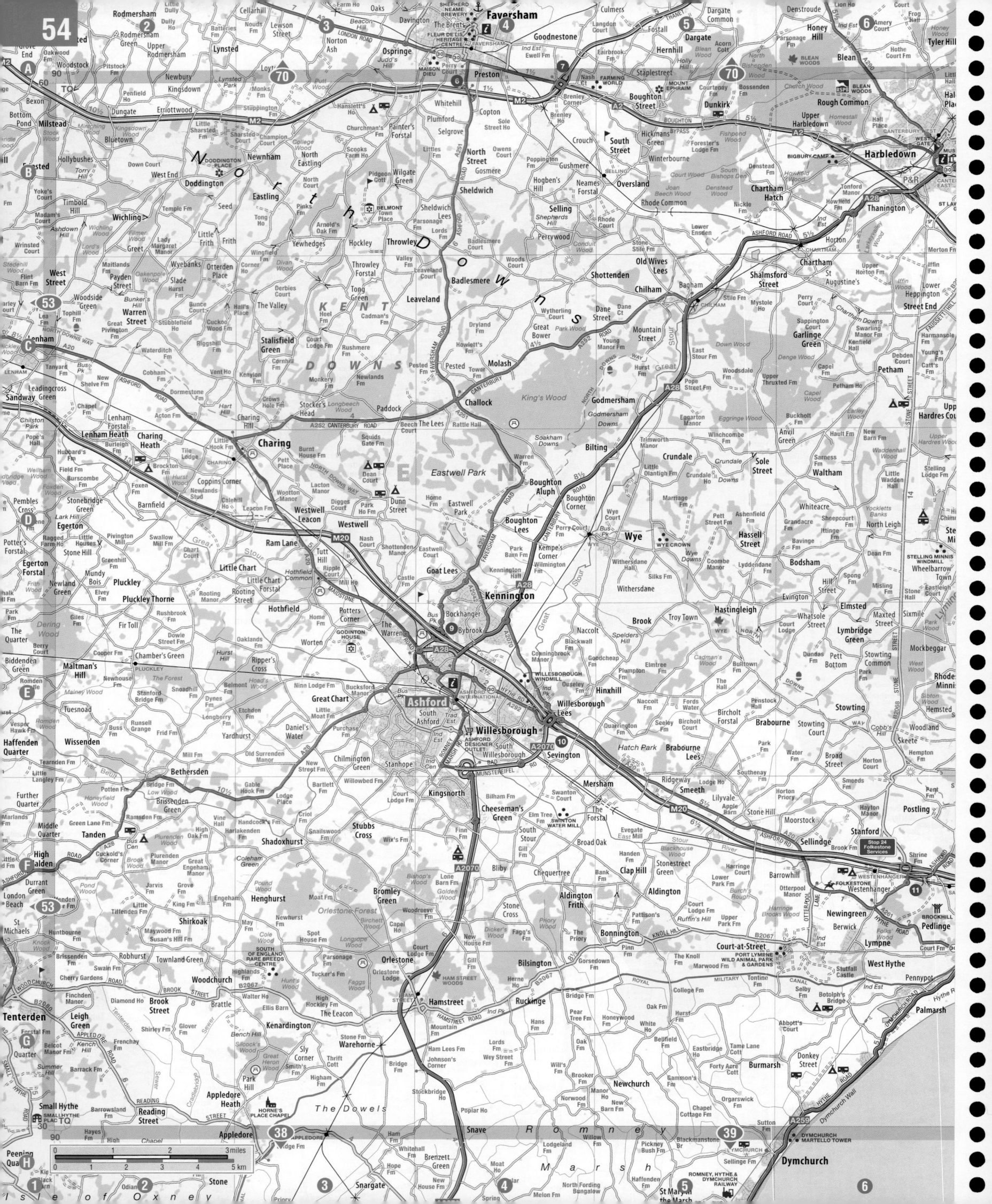
Faversham
Rodmersham
Lynsted
Ospringe
Davington
Goodnestone
Dargate
Hernhill
Honey Hill
Blean
Tyler Hill
Preston
Staplestreet
Boughton Street
Dunkirk
Rough Common
Harbledown
Upper Harbledown
Milstead
Newnham
Doddington
Eastling
North Downs
North Street
Sheldwich
Selling
Oversland
South Street
Chartham Hatch
Thanington
Chartham
Wichling
Throwley
Badlesmere
Leaveland
Shottenden
Old Wives Lees
Chilham
Bagham
Shalmsford Street
Lenham
Molash
Challock
Godmersham
Petham
Garlinge Green
Charing
Charing Heath
Lenham Heath
Westwell
Eastwell Park
Boughton Aluph
Boughton Lees
Crundale
Wye
Waltham
Egerton
Pluckley
Pluckley Thorne
Little Chart
Hothfield
Kennington
Bybrook
Ashford
South Ashford
Willesborough
Willesborough Lees
Hinxhill
Brook
Hastingleigh
Elmsted
Brabourne
Stowting
Great Chart
Bethersden
Kingsnorth
Mersham
Smeeth
Sellindge
Stanford
Postling
Shadoxhurst
Stubbs Cross
Aldington
Bonnington
Lympne
Court-at-Street
West Hythe
Pedlinge
Orlestone
Hamstreet
Ruckinge
Bilsington
Woodchurch
Tenterden
Kenardington
Warehorne
Appledore
Appledore Heath
Newchurch
Burmarsh
Dymchurch
Palmarsh
Snargate
Snave
Romney Marsh
Isle of Oxney
KENT
DOWNS
M2
M20
A2
A20
A28
A251
A252
A2070
A259
Eastwell Park
King's Wood
Orlestone Forest
0 1 2 3 miles
0 1 2 3 4 5 km

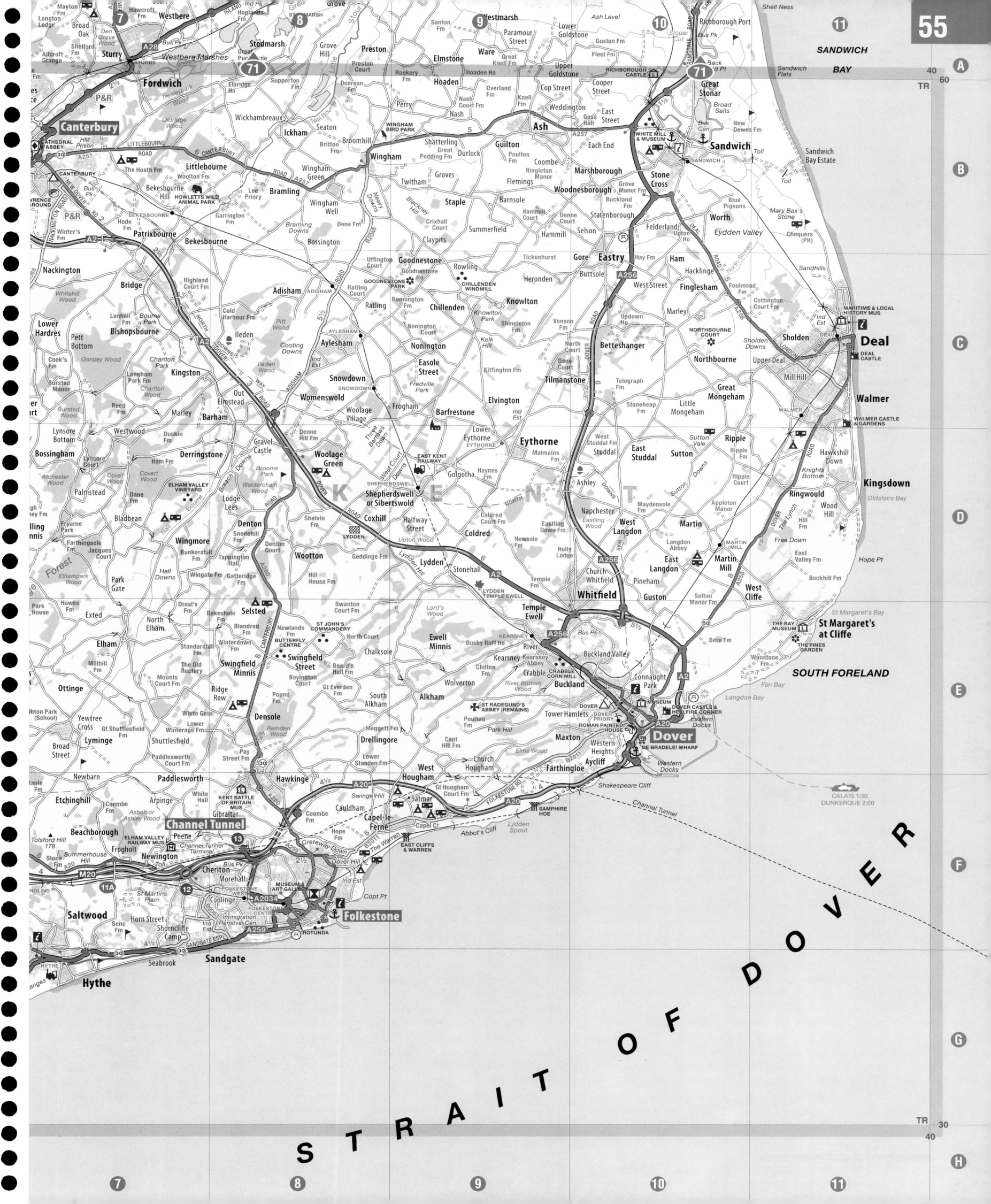
SANDWICH BAY
Shell Ness
Sandwich Flats
Richborough Port
Stonar Cut
Back Pt
Great Stonar
Broad Salts
New Downs Fm
Sandwich
Sandwich Bay Estate
Toll
WHITE MILL & MUSEUM
RICHBOROUGH CASTLE
Stone Cross
Worth
Blue Pigeons
Mary Bax's Stone
Chequers (PH)
Lydden Valley
North Stream
Sandhills
Deal
DEAL CASTLE
MARITIME & LOCAL HISTORY MUS
Sholden
Sholden Downs
Upper Deal
Mill Hill
Walmer
WALMER CASTLE & GARDENS
Hawkshill Down
Knights Bottom
Kingsdown
Oldstairs Bay
Ringwould
Wood Hill
Hill Fm
Free Down
East Valley Fm
Hope Pt
Bockhill Fm
St Margaret's Bay
St Margaret's at Cliffe
THE BAY MUSEUM
THE PINES GARDEN
SOUTH FORELAND
Fan Bay
Langdon Bay
Bere Fm
Wanstone Fm
West Cliffe
Martin Mill
Martin
East Langdon
Langdon Abbey
Guston
Pineham
Solton Manor Fm
Whitfield
Church Whitfield
Temple Ewell
Temple Fm
Buckland Valley
Connaught Park
Dover
DOVER CASTLE & HELLFIRE CORNER
Eastern Docks
Western Docks
DE BRADELEI WHARF
MUSEUM
DOVER PRIORY
ROMAN PAINTED HOUSE
Western Heights
Maxton
Tower Hamlets
Aycliff
Farthingloe
Shakespeare Cliff
Channel Tunnel
CALAIS 1:30
DUNKERQUE 2:00
SAMPHIRE HOE
Lydden Spout
Abbot's Cliff
Capel-le-Ferne
EAST CLIFFS & WARREN
The Warren
Capel Ct
Folkestone
Copt Pt
Dover Hill
MUSEUM & ART GALLERY
ROTUNDA
Sandgate
Seabrook
Hythe
Saltwood
Cheriton
Morehall
Newington
Channel Tunnel
Channel Tunnel Terminal
Peene
Frogholt
Beachborough
ELHAM VALLEY RAILWAY MUS
KENT BATTLE OF BRITAIN MUS
Gibraltar
Arpinge
White Hall
Etchinghill
Newbarn
Paddlesworth
Hawkinge
Densole
Swingfield Minnis
Swingfield Street
ST JOHN'S COMMANDERY
BUTTERFLY CENTRE
Alkham
Drellingore
West Hougham
Church Hougham
Crabble
CRABBLE CORN MILL
Buckland
River
Kearsney
Kearsney Abbey
ST RADEGUND'S ABBEY (REMAINS)
Ewell Minnis
Lydden
Stonehall
LYDDEN TEMPLE EWELL
Coldred
Shepherdswell or Sibertswold
Coxhill
EAST KENT RAILWAY
Eythorne
Barfrestone
Elvington
Tilmanstone
Betteshanger
Northbourne
NORTHBOURNE COURT
Great Mongeham
Little Mongeham
Ripple
Sutton
East Studdal
Studdal
West Studdal Fm
Ashley
Napchester
West Langdon
Eastry
Gore
Buttsole
Ham
Finglesham
Marley
Hacklinge
Knowlton
Chillenden
CHILLENDEN WINDMILL
Goodnestone
GOODNESTONE PARK
Rowling
Nonington
Easole Street
Snowdown
Womenswold
Aylesham
Adisham
Ratling
Staple
Barnsole
Woodnesborough
Marshborough
Ash
Guilton
Wingham
WINGHAM BIRD PARK
Ickham
Wickhambreaux
Seaton
Preston
Elmstone
Hoaden
Westmarsh
Ware
Stodmarsh
Grove
Fordwich
Sturry
Westbere
Westbere Marshes
Canterbury
CATHEDRAL & ABBEY
Littlebourne
Bekesbourne
Patrixbourne
HOWLETTS WILD ANIMAL PARK
Bramling
Nackington
Bridge
Bishopsbourne
Kingston
Barham
Derringstone
Denton
Wootton
Selsted
Elham
Ottinge
Lyminge
KENT
STRAIT OF DOVER
TR
40
60
30
7
8
9
10
11
A
B
C
D
E
F
G
H
A2
A20
A256
A258
A257
A260
A259
M20
B2011
71

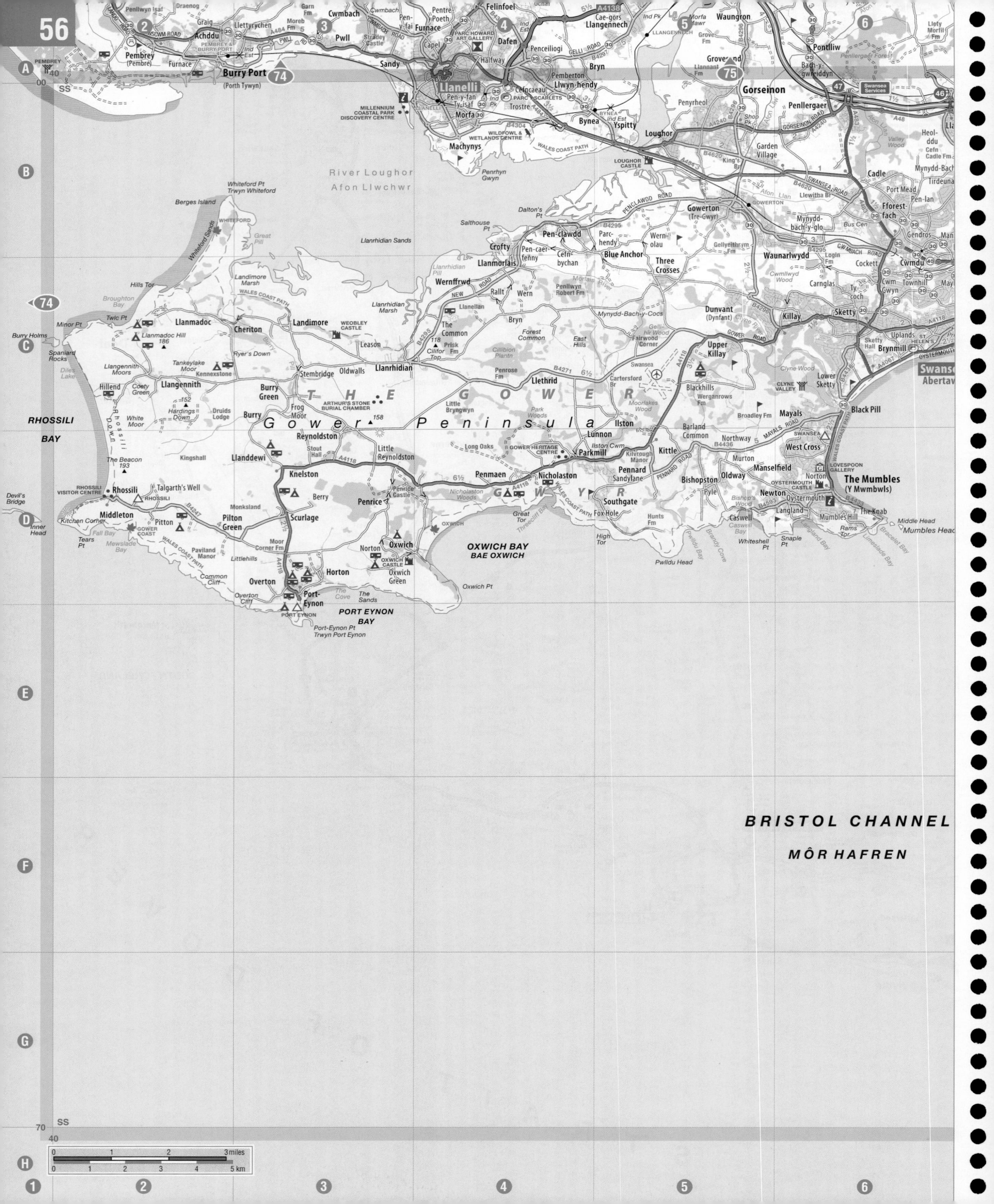
Gower Peninsula
THE GOWER
GŴYR
RHOSSILI BAY
OXWICH BAY
BAE OXWICH
PORT EYNON BAY
BRISTOL CHANNEL
MÔR HAFREN
River Loughor
Afon Llwchwr
Llanelli
Swansea
The Mumbles
(Y Mwmbwls)
Burry Port
Gorseinon
Gowerton
Loughor

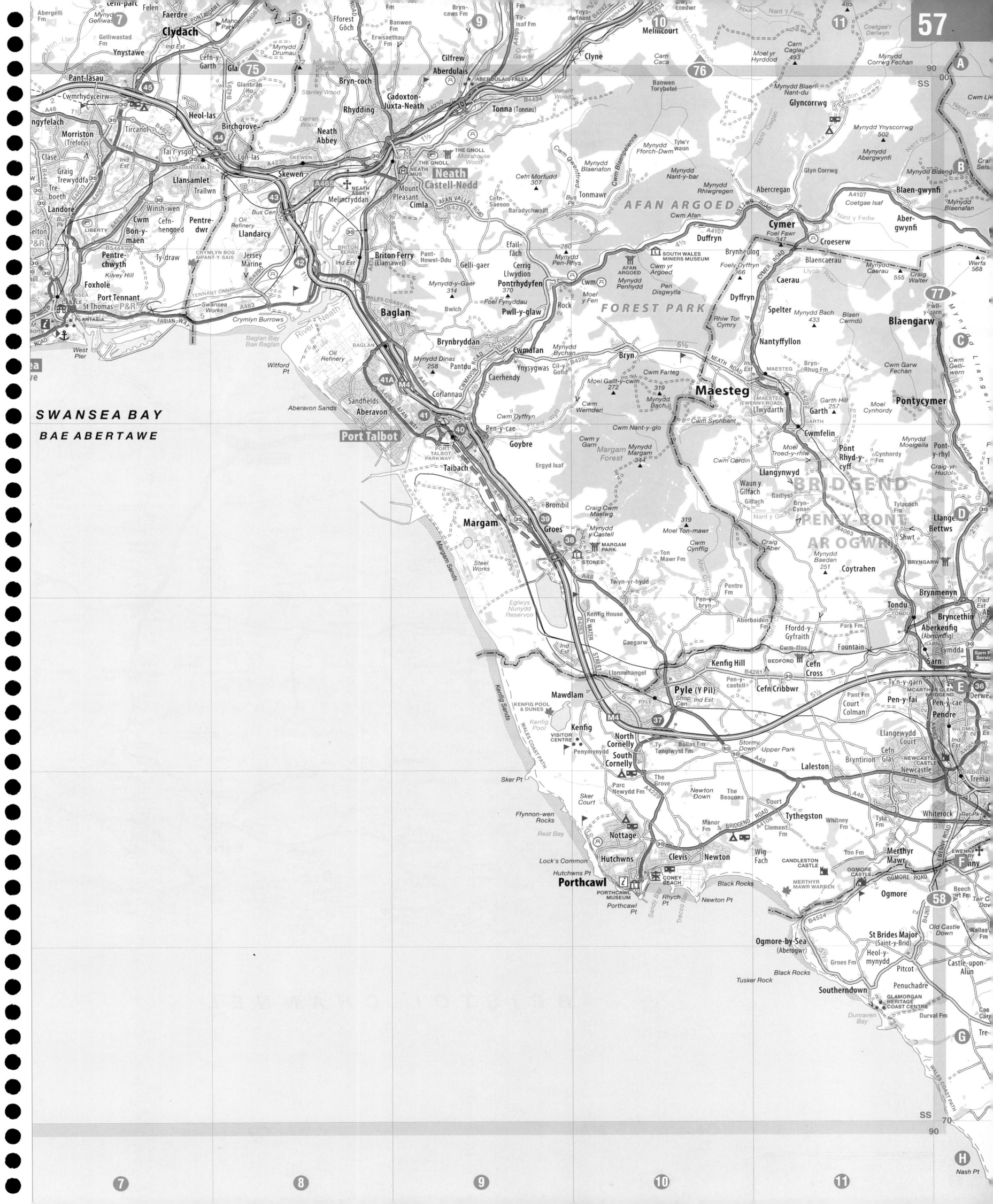

SWANSEA BAY
BAE ABERTAWE
Clydach
Felen
Faerdre
Ynystawe
Pant-lasau
Cwmrhydyceirw
Morriston (Treforys)
Heol-las
Birchgrove
Llansamlet
Trallwn
Tircanol
Tai'r-ysgol
Lon-las
Skewen
Glanbran Ho
Clase
Graig Trewyddfa
Tre-boeth
Landore
Winsh-wen
Cwm
Bon-y-maen
Cefn-hengoed
Pentre-dwr
Llandarcy
Pentre-chwyth
Ty-draw
Kilvey Hill
Foxhole
Port Tennant
St Thomas
Jersey Marine
Crymlyn Burrows
Swansea Works
West Pier
Baglan Bay
Bae Baglan
Witford Pt
Aberavon Sands
Sandfields
Aberavon
Port Talbot
Taibach
Margam
Margam Sands
Steel Works
Eglwys Nunydd Reservoir
Kenfig Sands
Kenfig Pool
KENFIG POOL & DUNES
Kenfig
Mawdlam
Sker Pt
Sker Court
Ffynnon-wen Rocks
Rest Bay
Lock's Common
Hutchwns Pt
Porthcawl
PORTHCAWL MUSEUM
Porthcawl Pt
Nottage
Hutchwns
Clevis
Newton
CONEY BEACH
Sandy Bay
Trecco Bay
Rhych Pt
Newton Pt
Black Rocks
North Cornelly
South Cornelly
Pyle (Y Pil)
Kenfig Hill
Cefn Cribbwr
Cefn Cross
Neath
Castell-Nedd
NEATH ABBEY
Neath Abbey
Melincryddan
Mount Pleasant
Cimla
Briton Ferry (Llansawel)
Baglan
Brynbryddan
Cwmafan
Pontrhydyfen
Pwll-y-glaw
Cadoxton-Juxta-Neath
Rhydding
Bryn-coch
Aberdulais
Cilfrew
Tonna (Tonnau)
Melincourt
Clyne
AFAN ARGOED
FOREST PARK
SOUTH WALES MINERS MUSEUM
Cymer
Croeserw
Duffryn
Dyffryn
Caerau
Spelter
Nantyffyllon
Maesteg
Llwydarth
Garth
Cwmfelin
Bryn
Goybre
Brombil
Groes
MARGAM PARK
Glyncorrwg
Abercregan
Blaen-gwynfi
Aber-gwynfi
Blaengarw
Pontycymer
Llangeinor
Llangynwyd
BRIDGEND
PEN-Y-BONT AR OGWR
Coytrahen
Tondu
Brynmenyn
Bryncethin
Aberkenfig (Abercynffig)
Sarn
Pen-y-fai
Pendre
Laleston
Newcastle
Tythegston
Merthyr Mawr
Ogmore
Ogmore-by-Sea (Aberogwr)
St Brides Major (Saint-y-Brid)
Southerndown
Dunraven Bay
GLAMORGAN HERITAGE COAST CENTRE
CANDLESTON CASTLE
MERTHYR MAWR WARREN
OGMORE CASTLE
Tusker Rock
Nash Pt
M4
A48
A4107
A4063

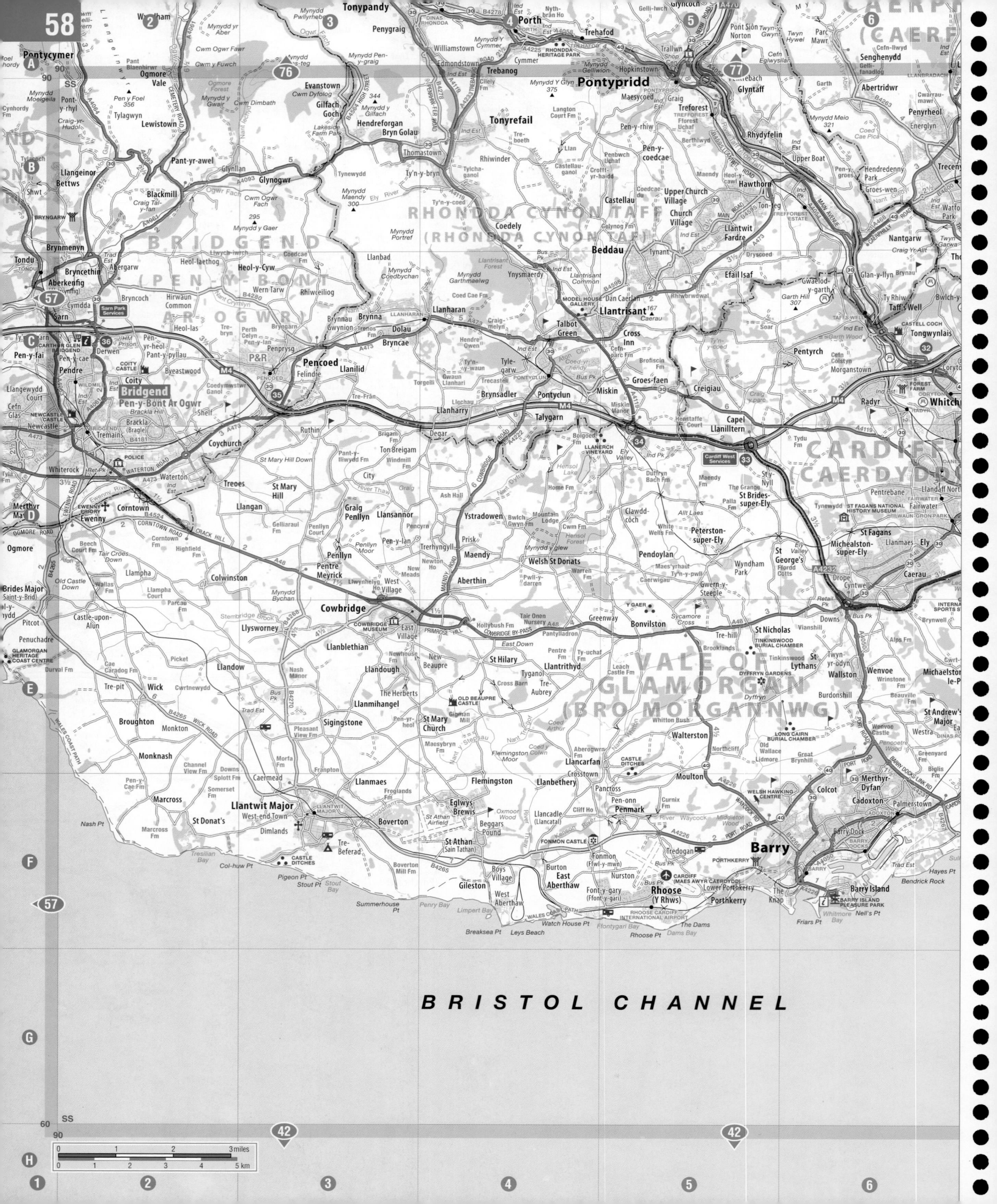
Pontycymer
Ogmore Vale
Lewistown
Tonypandy
Penygraig
Porth
Trehafod
Williamstown
Edmondstown
Trebanog
Cymmer
Pontypridd
Hopkinstown
Glyncoch
Pont Siôn Norton
Trallwn
Treforest
Glyntaff
Rhydyfelin
Senghenydd
Abertridwr
Penyrheol
Energlyn
Evanstown
Gilfach Goch
Hendreforgan
Bryn Golau
Thomastown
Tonyrefail
Tynewydd
Ty'n-y-bryn
Glynogwr
Blackmill
Llangeinor
Bettws
Pant-yr-awel
Glynllan
RHONDDA CYNON TAFF
(RHONDDA CYNON TAF)
Coedely
Beddau
Castellau
Upper Church Village
Church Village
Llantwit Fardre
Efail Isaf
Hawthorn
Ton-teg
Nantgarw
Taff's Well
Tongwynlais
Pentyrch
Creigiau
Radyr
BRIDGEND
(PEN-Y-BONT AR OGWR)
Brynmenyn
Bryncethin
Aberkenfig
Tondu
Sarn
Heol-laethog
Heol-y-Cyw
Wern Tarw
Bryncoch
Hirwaun Common
Heol-las
Llanharan
Brynna
Dolau
Bryncae
Talbot Green
Llantrisant
Cross Inn
Pencoed
Felindre
Llanilid
Pen-y-fai
Derwen
Pendre
Coity
Bridgend
Pen-y-Bont Ar Ogwr
Brackla
Tremains
Coychurch
Shelf
Byeastwood
Penprysg
Ruthin
Llanharry
Brynsadler
Pontyclun
Talygarn
Miskin
Groes-faen
Capel Llanilltern
Tyle-garw
Degar
Whiterock
Waterton
Treoes
St Mary Hill
Llangan
Ewenny
Corntown
Ogmore
Graig Penllyn
Llansannor
Penllyn
Pen-y-lan
Ystradowen
Maendy
Aberthin
Welsh St Donats
Prisk
Pendoylan
Peterston-super-Ely
St Brides-super-Ely
St George's
Wyndham Park
Michaelston-super-Ely
St Fagans
Ely
Caerau
Culverhouse
CARDIFF
(CAERDYDD)
Llandaff North
Fairwater
Colwinston
Llampha
Pentre Meyrick
West Village
Cowbridge
Llysworney
Llanblethian
Landough
Llandow
East Village
Newbeaupre
St Hilary
Llantrithyd
Bonvilston
Greenway
Tre-hill
St Nicholas
Wallston
Wenvoe
St Lythans
VALE OF GLAMORGAN
(BRO MORGANNWG)
Tre-pit
Wick
Broughton
Monkton
Monknash
Marcross
St Donat's
Llantwit Major
West-end Town
Dimlands
Tre-Beferad
Boverton
Llanmaes
Llanmihangel
Sigingstone
St Mary Church
Flemingston
Llancarfan
Llanbethery
Walterston
Moulton
Colcot
Cadoxton
Merthyr-Dyfan
Palmerstown
Eglwys Brewis
Beggars Pound
St Athan
(Sain Tathan)
Llancadle
Penmark
Fonmon
Barry
Barry Island
Rhoose
(Y Rhws)
Porthkerry
The Knap
Gileston
Boys Village
West Aberthaw
East Aberthaw
Font-y-gary
Nash Pt
Breaksea Pt
Rhoose Pt
Friars Pt
BRISTOL CHANNEL
M4
A48
A4226
57
76
77
42
0 1 2 3 miles
0 1 2 3 4 5 km
A B C D E F G H
1 2 3 4 5 6

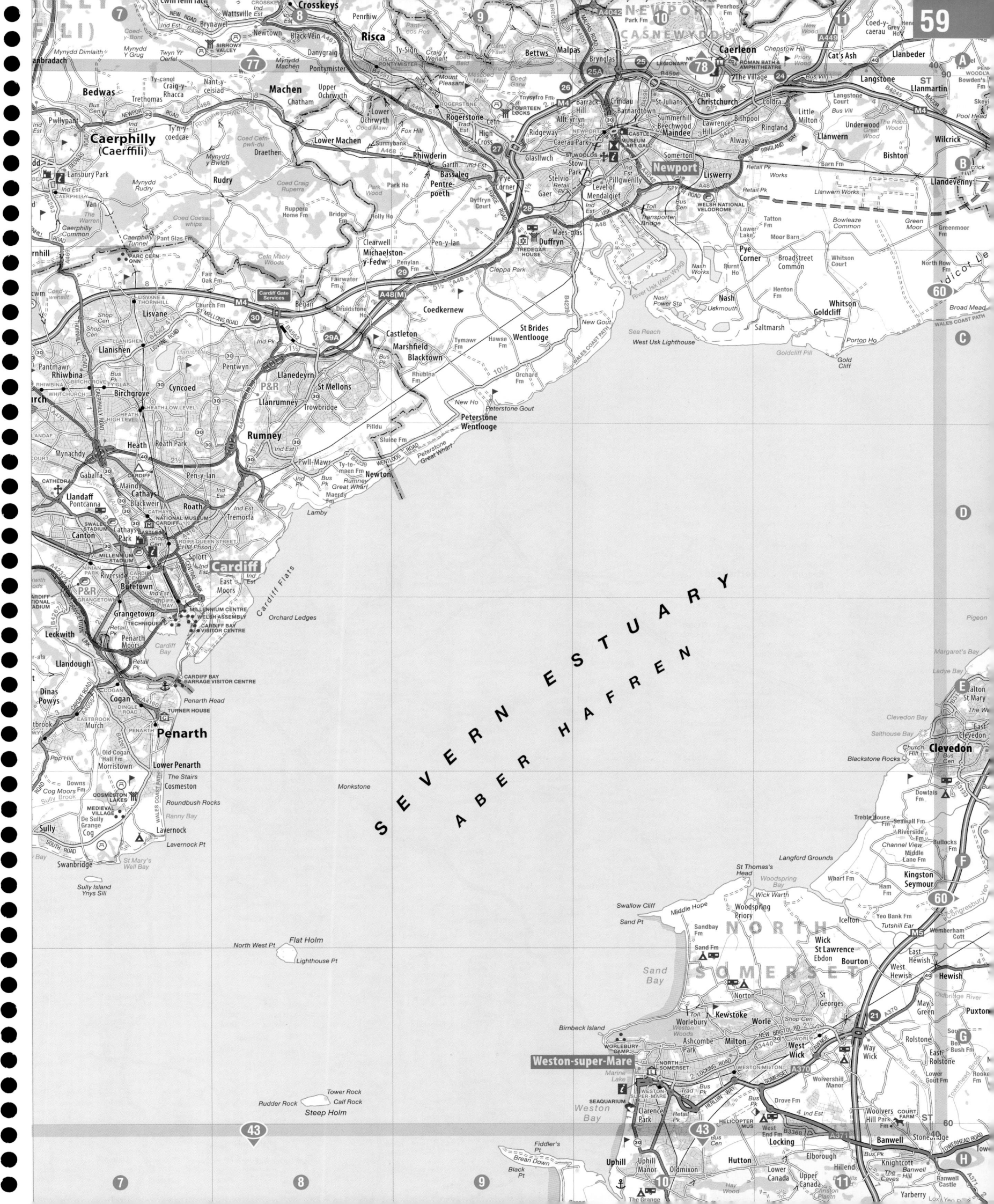
SEVERN ESTUARY
ABER HAFREN
NORTH SOMERSET
Crosskeys
Risca
Penrhiw
Wattsville
Brynawel
Newtown
Black Vein
Danygraig
Pontymister
Ty-Sign
NEWPORT
CASNEWYDD
Caerleon
Cat's Ash
Llanbeder
Coed-y-caerau
Bettws
Malpas
Brynglas
Langstone
Llanmartin
Bedwas
Trethomas
Machen
Chatham
Upper Ochrwyth
Lower Ochrwyth
Rogerstone
High Cross
Cefn
Ridgeway
Allt-yr-yn
Barrack Hill
Crindau
Barnardtown
St Julians
Christchurch
Summerhill
Beechwood
Maindee
Lawrence Hill
Bishpool
Coldra
Ringland
Little Milton
Underwood
Llanwern
Wilcrick
Bishton
Alway
Caerphilly
(Caerffili)
Pwllypant
Draethen
Lower Machen
Rhiwderin
Bassaleg
Garth
Pentre-poeth
Lansbury Park
Rudry
Van
Caerphilly Common
Pye Corner
Glasllwch
Caerau Park
Stow Park
Stelvio
Gaer
Level of Mendalgief
Pillgwenlly
Somerton
Newport
Liswerry
Llandevenny
Maes-glas
Duffryn
Tredegar House
Cleppa Park
Clearwell
Michaelston-y-Fedw
Pen-y-lan
Transporter Bridge
Welsh National Velodrome
Pye Corner
Broadstreet Common
Nash
Goldcliff
Whitson
Saltmarsh
Lisvane
Llanishen
Pentwyn
Cyncoed
Coedkernew
Castleton
Marshfield
Blacktown
St Brides Wentlooge
Llanedeyrn
St Mellons
Llanrumney
Trowbridge
Rumney
Rhiwbina
Birchgrove
Heath
Roath Park
Mynachdy
Gabalfa
Maindy
Cathays
Llandaff
Pontcanna
Blackweir
Roath
Tremorfa
Pen-y-lan
Pwll-Mawr
Newton
Lamby
Peterstone Wentlooge
Canton
Cathays Park
Riverside
Splott
Cardiff
East Moors
Butetown
Grangetown
Leckwith
Penarth Moors
Llandough
Dinas Powys
Cogan
Murch
Penarth
Lower Penarth
Cosmeston
Lavernock
Sully
Swanbridge
Sully Island
Ynys Sili
Cardiff Flats
Orchard Ledges
Monkstone
Flat Holm
Steep Holm
Clevedon
Kingston Seymour
Woodspring Priory
Wick St Lawrence
Ebdon
Bourton
West Hewish
Hewish
Kewstoke
Worlebury
Worle
St Georges
Milton
Ashcombe Park
West Wick
Weston-super-Mare
Sand Bay
Weston Bay
Uphill
Oldmixon
Hutton
Locking
Banwell
Clarence Park
Lower Canada
Upper Canada
Elborough
Hillend
Yarberry

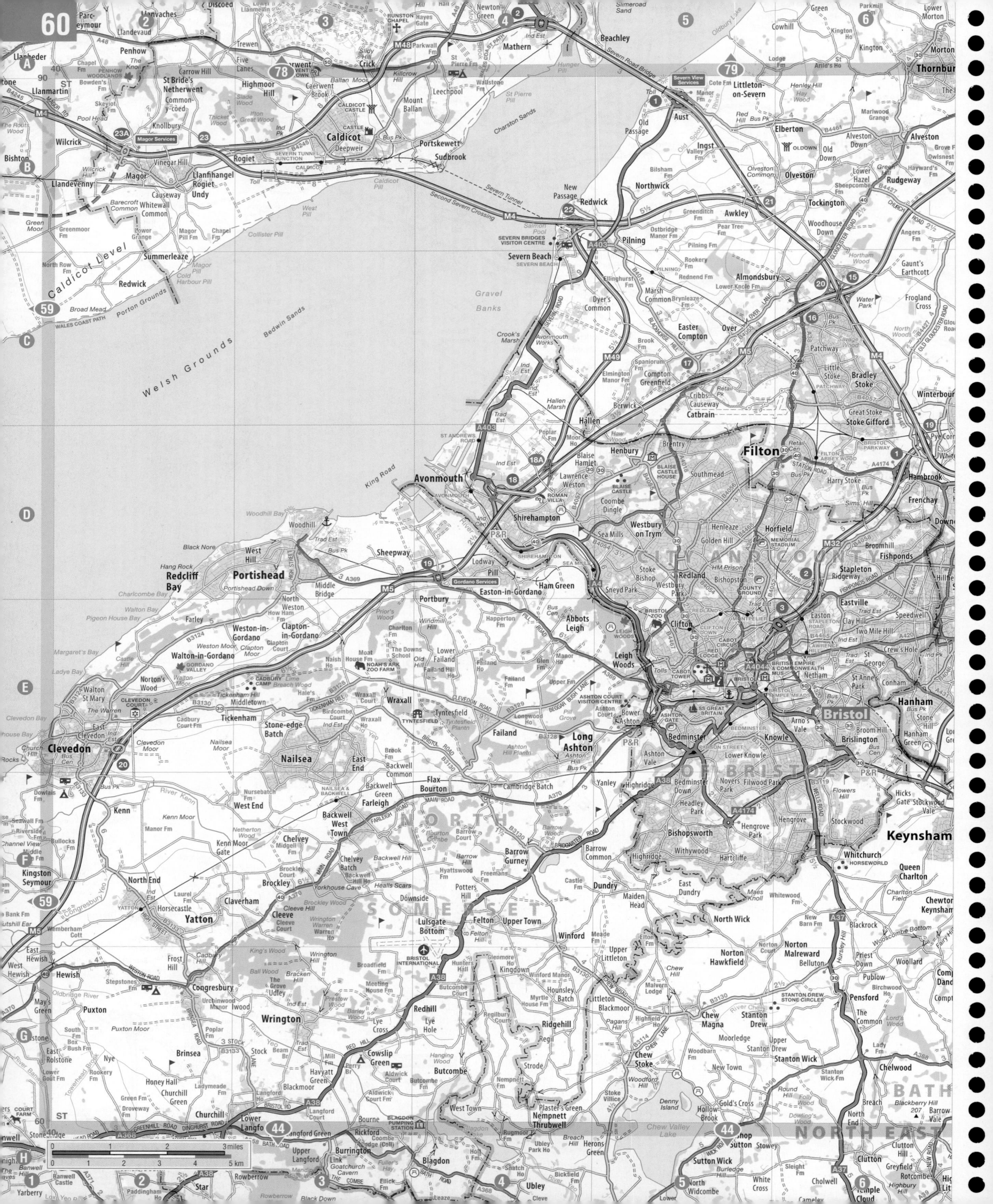
Caldicot
Rogiet
Magor
Undy
Sudbrook
Portskewett
Caerwent
Crick
Mathern
Beachley
Aust
Littleton-on-Severn
Elberton
Olveston
Alveston
Thornbury
Rudgeway
Tockington
Awkley
Northwick
Redwick
Pilning
New Passage
Severn Beach
Almondsbury
Easter Compton
Over
Patchway
Bradley Stoke
Little Stoke
Winterbourne
Stoke Gifford
Filton
Hallen
Henbury
Avonmouth
Shirehampton
Lawrence Weston
Coombe Dingle
Westbury on Trym
Horfield
Southmead
Henleaze
Stapleton
Fishponds
Frenchay
Hambrook
Harry Stoke
Redland
Clifton
Eastville
Easton
Speedwell
Two Mile Hill
St George
Conham
Hanham
Brislington
Knowle
Bedminster
Bishopsworth
Withywood
Hengrove
Stockwood
Keynsham
Whitchurch
Queen Charlton
Bristol
CITY AND COUNTY OF BRISTOL
Portishead
Portbury
Pill
Easton-in-Gordano
Ham Green
Abbots Leigh
Leigh Woods
Long Ashton
Failand
Wraxall
Tyntesfield
Nailsea
Backwell
Flax Bourton
Barrow Gurney
Dundry
Felton
Winford
Chew Magna
Chew Stoke
Pensford
Stanton Drew
Norton Malreward
Norton Hawkfield
Chelwood
Clutton
Sutton Wick
Blagdon
Ubley
Butcombe
Wrington
Congresbury
Yatton
Claverham
Cleeve
Brockley
Kenn
Clevedon
Tickenham
Walton-in-Gordano
Weston-in-Gordano
Clapton-in-Gordano
Redcliff Bay
Kingston Seymour
Puxton
Hewish
Churchill
Langford
Redhill
Lulsgate Bottom
Bristol International
Welsh Grounds
Severn Road Bridge
Second Severn Crossing
NORTH SOMERSET
BATH AND NORTH EAST
Chew Valley Lake
Gordano Services
Severn View Services
Magor Services
78
79
59
44
M4
M5
M48
M49
M32
A38
A37
A369
A370
A403
A4174
0 1 2 3 miles
0 1 2 3 4 5 km

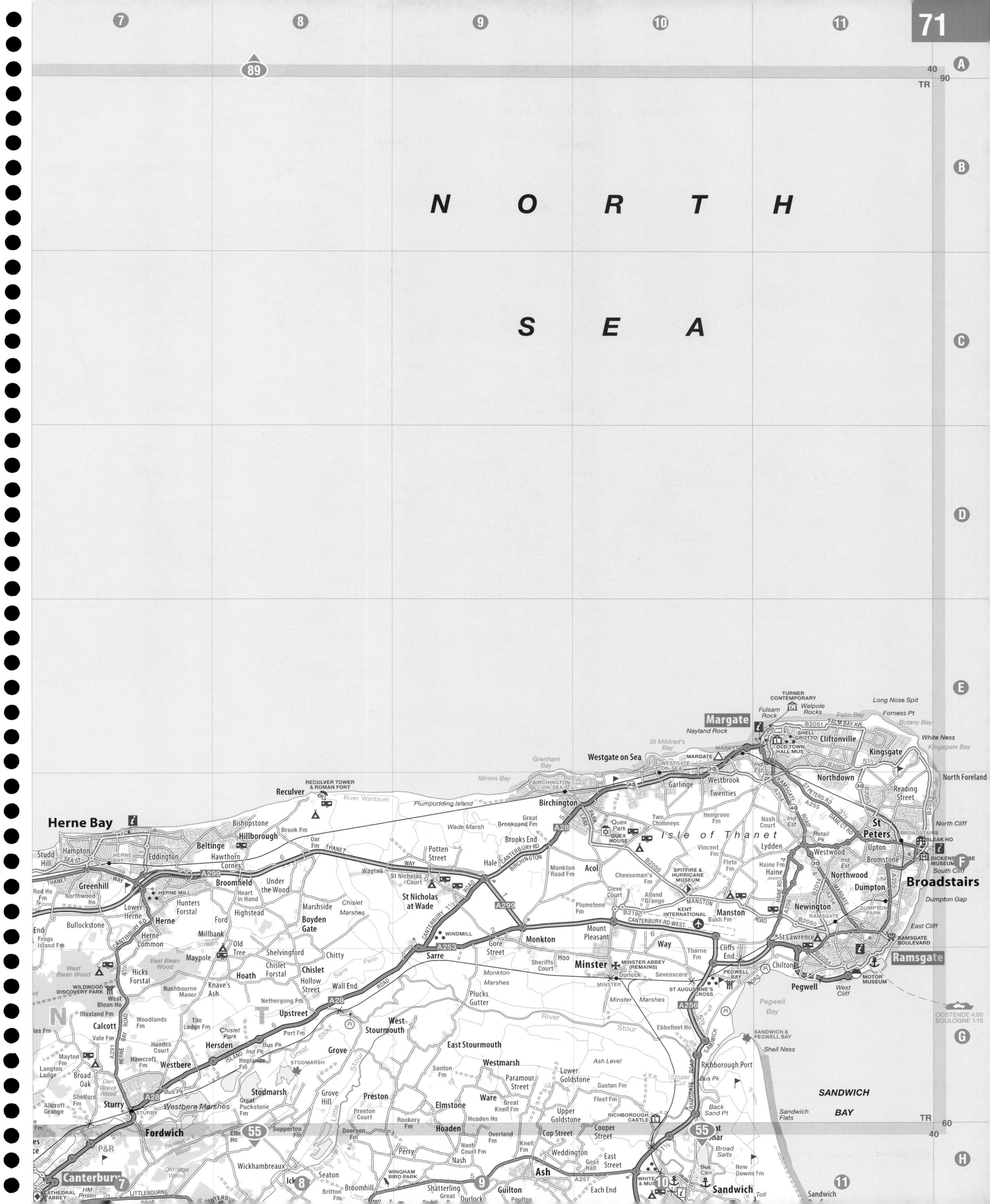

NORTH

SEA

Margate

TURNER CONTEMPORARY
Fulsam Rock
Walpole Rocks
Long Nose Spit
Forness Pt
Palm Bay
Botany Bay
Nayland Rock
Cliftonville
SHELL GROTTO
OLD TOWN HALL MUS
Kingsgate
White Ness
Kingsgate Bay
St Mildred's Bay
Westgate on Sea
Grenham Bay
WESTGATE ON SEA
MARGATE
Northdown
Reading Street
North Foreland

Minnis Bay
Garlinge
Westbrook
Twenties

Reculver
RECULVER TOWER & ROMAN FORT
River Wantsum
Plumpudding Island
Wade Marsh
BIRCHINGTON ON SEA
Birchington
Hengrove
Quex Park
QUEX HOUSE
Two Chimneys
Isle of Thanet
Nash Court
St Peters
BROADSTAIRS
North Cliff

Herne Bay
Bishopstone
Brook Fm
Oar Fm
Hillborough
Great Brooksend Fm
Brooks End
Cleve Court
Vincent
Lydden
BLEAK HO
DICKENS HOUSE MUSEUM
SE

Beltinge
Hawthorn Corner
Potten Street
Hale
CANTERBURY RD
Monkton Road Fm
Acol
Cheeseman's
SPITFIRE & HURRICANE MUSEUM
Flete
Haine Fm
Haine
Westwood
Upton
Bromstone
Broadstairs

Studd Hill
Hampton
SEA ST
Eddington
Herne
Highstead
St Nicholas at Wade
Alland Grange
Northwood
Dumpton
Dumpton Gap

Greenhill
Broomfield
Under the Wood
Marshside
Chislet Marshes
Plumstone Fm
MANSTON
Newington
East Cliff

Red Ho Fm
Northwood Ho
Lower Herne
Herne Mill
Heart in Hand
Boyden Gate
Chitty
KENT INTERNATIONAL
Manston
Bush Fm
St Lawrence
RAMSGATE BOULEVARD
MOTOR MUSEUM

Bullockstone
Herne Common
Millbank
Shelvingford
Chislet Forstal
Sarre
Gore Street
Mount Pleasant
Way
Thorne
Cliffs End
Chilton
Ramsgate

West Blean Wood
Hicks Forstal
Maypole
Old Tree
Hoath
Hollow Street
Wall End
Sheriffs Court
Hoo
Minster
MINSTER ABBEY (REMAINS)
Durlock
Sevenscore
PEGWELL BAY
Pegwell
West Cliff

Wildwood
WILDWOOD DISCOVERY PARK
Blaxland Fm
Woodlands Fm
Knave's Ash
Rushbourne Manor
Nethergong Fm
Upstreet
Port Fm
Plucks Gutter
Monkton Marshes
Minster Marshes
ST AUGUSTINE'S CROSS
Pegwell Bay

OOSTENDE 4:00
BOULOGNE 1:15

Calcott
Tile Lodge Fm
West Stourmouth
River Stour
Ebbsfleet Ho
SANDWICH & PEGWELL BAY
Shell Ness

Sturry
Hersden
Grove
East Stourmouth
Westmarsh
Ash Level
Richborough Port
Sandwich Flats

Westbere
Hoades Court
Stodmarsh
STODMARSH
Grove Hill
Preston
Ware
Paramour Street
Lower Goldstone
Guston Fm
RICHBOROUGH CASTLE
SANDWICH

Broad Oak
Shelford
Westbere Marshes
Puckstone Fm
Preston Court
Rookery Fm
Upper Goldstone
Back Sand Pt
BAY

Fordwich
Supperton Fm
Hoaden
Overland
Cop Street
Cooper Street

Canterbury
CATHEDRAL
ABBEY
HM PRISON
Wickhambreaux
WINGHAM BIRD PARK
Shatterling
Guilton
Ash
Each End
East Street
Sandwich
Toll

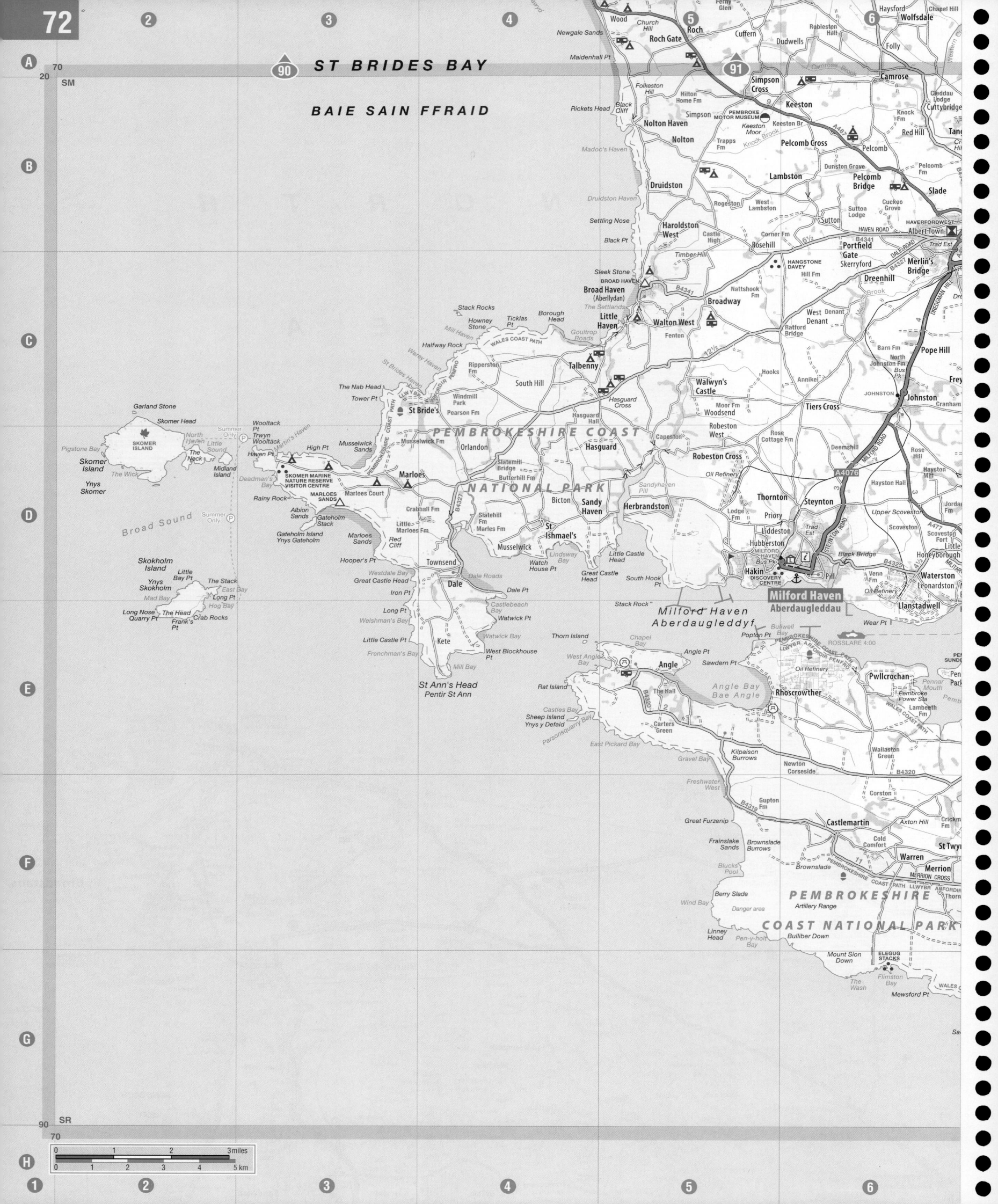
ST BRIDES BAY
BAIE SAIN FFRAID
90
91
Wood
Church Hill
Roch Gate
Roch
Newgale Sands
Maidenhall Pt
Cuffern
Dudwells
Robleston Hall
Haysford
Wolfsdale
Folly
Camrose
Simpson Cross
Keeston
Folkeston Hill
Hilton Home Fm
Simpson
PEMBROKE MOTOR MUSEUM
Keeston Moor
Keeston Br
Rickets Head
Black Cliff
Nolton Haven
Nolton
Trapps Fm
Pelcomb Cross
Pelcomb
Knock Fm
Red Hill
Cleddau Lodge
Cuttybridge
Madoc's Haven
Dunston Grove
Lambston
Pelcomb Bridge
Slade
Druidston
Druidston Haven
Rogeston
West Lambston
Sutton
Sutton Lodge
Cuckoo Grove
Settling Nose
Haroldston West
Castle High
Corner Fm
Rosehill
HAVERFORDWEST
Albert Town
Black Pt
Timber Hill
Portfield Gate
Skerryford
Merlin's Bridge
HANGSTONE DAVEY
Hill Fm
Dreenhill
Sleek Stone
BROAD HAVEN
Broad Haven (Aberllydan)
The Settlands
Nattshook Fm
Broadway
Stack Rocks
Howney Stone
Ticklas Pt
Borough Head
Little Haven
Walton West
West Denant
Denant
Ratford Bridge
Goultrop Roads
Fenton
Mill Haven
Halfway Rock
WALES COAST PATH
Talbenny
Barn Fm
Pope Hill
North Johnston Fm
Ripperston Fm
South Hill
Walwyn's Castle
Hooks
Annikel
St Brides Haven
The Nab Head
Tower Pt
Windmill Park
Pearson Fm
Hasguard Cross
JOHNSTON
Johnston
St Bride's
Moor Fm
Woodsend
Tiers Cross
Hasguard Hall
Garland Stone
Skomer Head
North Haven
Summer Only
Wooltack Pt
Trwyn Wooltack
Martin's Haven
PEMBROKESHIRE COAST
NATIONAL PARK
Robeston West
Capeston
Hasguard
Rose Cottage Fm
Deemshill
Rose Hill
SKOMER ISLAND
Pigstone Bay
Little Sound
The Neck
Haven Pt
High Pt
Musselwick Sands
Musselwick Fm
Orlandon
Robeston Cross
Skomer Island
Midland Island
Oil Refinery
Hayston Mill
The Wick
Deadman's Bay
SKOMER MARINE NATURE RESERVE VISITOR CENTRE
Marloes
Statemill Bridge
Butterhill Fm
Hayston Hall
Ynys Skomer
MARLOES SANDS
Marloes Court
Sandyhaven Pill
Thornton
Steynton
Rainy Rock
Bicton
Sandy Haven
Herbrandston
Crabhall Fm
Upper Scoveston
Broad Sound
Summer Only
Albion Sands
Gateholm Stack
Statehill Fm
Marles Fm
Lodge Fm
Priory
Scoveston
Little Marloes Fm
St Ishmael's
Liddeston
Trad Est
Scoveston Fort
Gateholm Island
Ynys Gateholm
Marloes Sands
Red Cliff
Musselwick
Hubberston
Skokholm Island
Hooper's Pt
Townsend
Lindsway Bay
Little Castle Head
MILFORD HAVEN
Black Bridge
Honeyborough
Watch House Pt
Hakin
DISCOVERY CENTRE
Pill
Little Bay Pt
Westdale Bay
Dale Roads
Great Castle Head
South Hook Pt
Venn Fm
Waterston
Ynys Skokholm
The Stack
East Bay
Great Castle Head
Dale
Dale Pt
Milford Haven
Aberdaugleddau
Leonardston
Oil Refinery
Mad Bay
Long Pt
Iron Pt
Hog Bay
Stack Rock
Castlebeach Bay
Llanstadwell
Long Nose
Quarry Pt
The Head
Crab Rocks
Frank's Pt
Long Pt
Watwick Pt
Milford Haven
Aberdaugleddyf
Welshman's Bay
Bullwell Bay
Wear Pt
Popton Pt
ROSSLARE 4:00
Little Castle Pt
Kete
Watwick Bay
Thorn Island
Chapel Bay
Frenchman's Bay
West Blockhouse Pt
West Angle Bay
Angle Pt
PEMBROKESHIRE COAST PATH
LLWYBR ARFORDIR PENFRO
Mill Bay
Angle
Sawdern Pt
Oil Refinery
Pwllcrochan
St Ann's Head
Pentir St Ann
Rat Island
Angle Bay
Bae Angle
Pennar Mouth
The Hall
Rhoscrowther
Pembroke Power Sta
Lambeeth Fm
Castles Bay
Sheep Island
Ynys y Defaid
Carters Green
Parsonsquarry Bay
East Pickard Bay
Wallaston Green
Gravel Bay
Kilpaison Burrows
Newton Corseside
B4320
Freshwater West
Corston
Gupton Fm
Great Furzenip
Castlemartin
Axton Hill
Frainslake Sands
Brownslade Burrows
Cold Comfort
Warren
Merrion
MERRION CROSS
Blucks Pool
Brownslade
Berry Slade
PEMBROKESHIRE
Artillery Range
Wind Bay
Danger area
COAST NATIONAL PARK
Linney Head
Pen-y-holt Bay
Bulliber Down
Mount Sion Down
ELEGUG STACKS
Flimston Bay
The Wash
Mewsford Pt
A487
A4076
A477
B4341
B4327
B4325
B4319
B4320
HAVEN ROAD
DALE ROAD
MILFORD ROAD
STEYNTON ROAD
SM
SR
0 1 2 3 miles
0 1 2 3 4 5 km

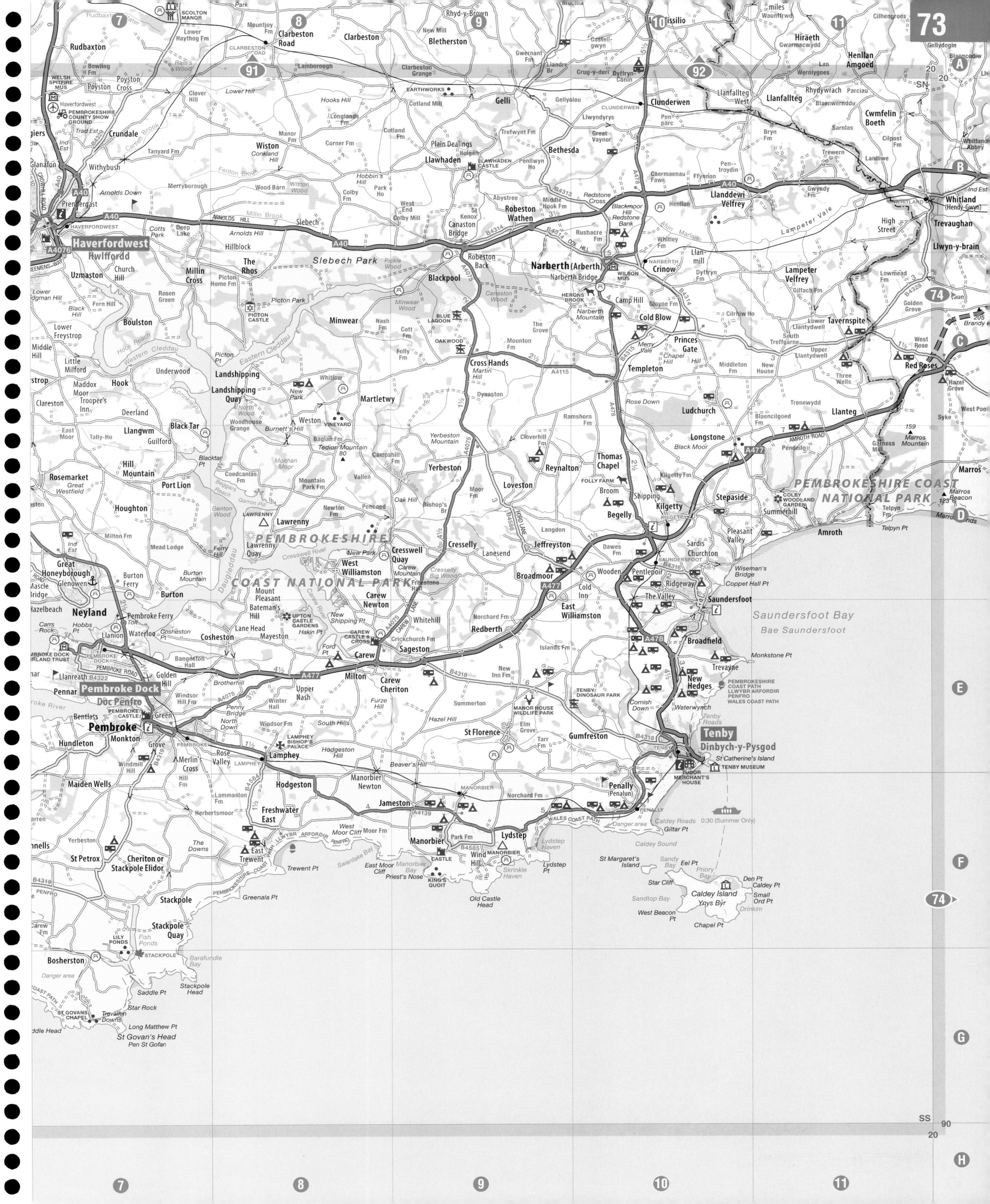

Rudbaxton
Scolton Manor
Clarbeston Road
Clarbeston
Rhyd-y-Brown
New Mill
Bletherston
Llandissilio
Hiraeth
Henllan Amgoed
Gwernant Fm
Crug-y-deri
Dyffryn-Conin
Lamborough
Clarbeston Grange
Earthworks
Cotland Mill
Gelli
Clunderwen
Llanfallteg West
Llanfallteg
Rhydywrach
Cwmfelin Boeth
Poyston Cross
Welsh Spitfire Mus
Pembrokeshire County Show Ground
Crundale
Wiston
Hooks Hill
Plain Dealings
Llawhaden
Llawhaden Castle
Bethesda
Great Vaynor
Withybush
Tanyard Fm
Merryborough
Wood Barn
Colby Fm
Robeston Wathen
Canaston Bridge
Llanddewi Velfrey
Whitland (Hendy-Gwyn)
Trevaughan
Prendergast
Haverfordwest
Hwlffordd
Arnolds Down
Arnolds Hill
Slebech
Slebech Park
Cotts Park
Deep Lake
Hillblock
The Rhos
Millin Cross
Picton Castle
Picton Park
Robeston Back
Blackpool
Narberth (Arberth)
Narberth Bridge
Crinow
Lampeter Velfrey
Llwyn-y-brain
Uzmaston
Church Hill
Boulston
Minwear
Blue Lagoon
Oakwood
Camp Hill
Cold Blow
Princes Gate
Taverspite
Red Roses
Cross Hands
Templeton
Landshipping
Landshipping Quay
Martletwy
Hook
Llangwm
Black Tar
Ludchurch
Longstone
Llanteg
Yerbeston
Reynalton
Thomas Chapel
Loveston
Kilgetty
Begelly
Stepaside
Amroth
Marros
Pembrokeshire Coast National Park
Colby Woodland Garden
Rosemarket
Hill Mountain
Port Lion
Houghton
Lawrenny
Lawrenny Quay
Cresswell Quay
West Williamston
Cresselly
Jeffreyston
Broadmoor
Saundersfoot
Saundersfoot Bay
Bae Saundersfoot
Sardis
Pleasant Valley
Wiseman's Bridge
Pentlepoir
Ridgeway
The Valley
Neyland
Burton
Carew Newton
Carew
Upton Castle Gardens
Carew Castle & Cross
Cosheston
Mayeston
Whitehill
Redberth
East Williamston
Sageston
Milton
Carew Cheriton
Broadfield
Trevayne
New Hedges
Pembroke Dock
Doc Penfro
Pembroke
Monkton
Lamphey
Lamphey Bishop's Palace
Hodgeston
St Florence
Gumfreston
Manor House Wildlife Park
Tenby Dinosaur Park
Tenby
Dinbych-y-Pysgod
Tudor Merchant's House
Tenby Museum
St Catherine's Island
Penally (Penalun)
Jameston
Manorbier
Manorbier Newton
Lydstep
Freshwater East
East Trewent
Maiden Wells
Hundleton
St Petrox
Cheriton or Stackpole Elidor
Stackpole
Stackpole Quay
Bosherston
Stack Rocks
St Govan's Head
Pen St Gofan
Caldey Island
Ynys Bŷr
Caldey Sound
Caldey Roads
0:30 (Summer Only)
Pembrokeshire Coast Path
Llwybr Arfordir Penfro
Wales Coast Path
A40
A477
A478
A4075
A4076
B4318
B4585
A4139
SS
90
20
7
8
9
10
11
A
B
C
D
E
F
G
H
74
91
92

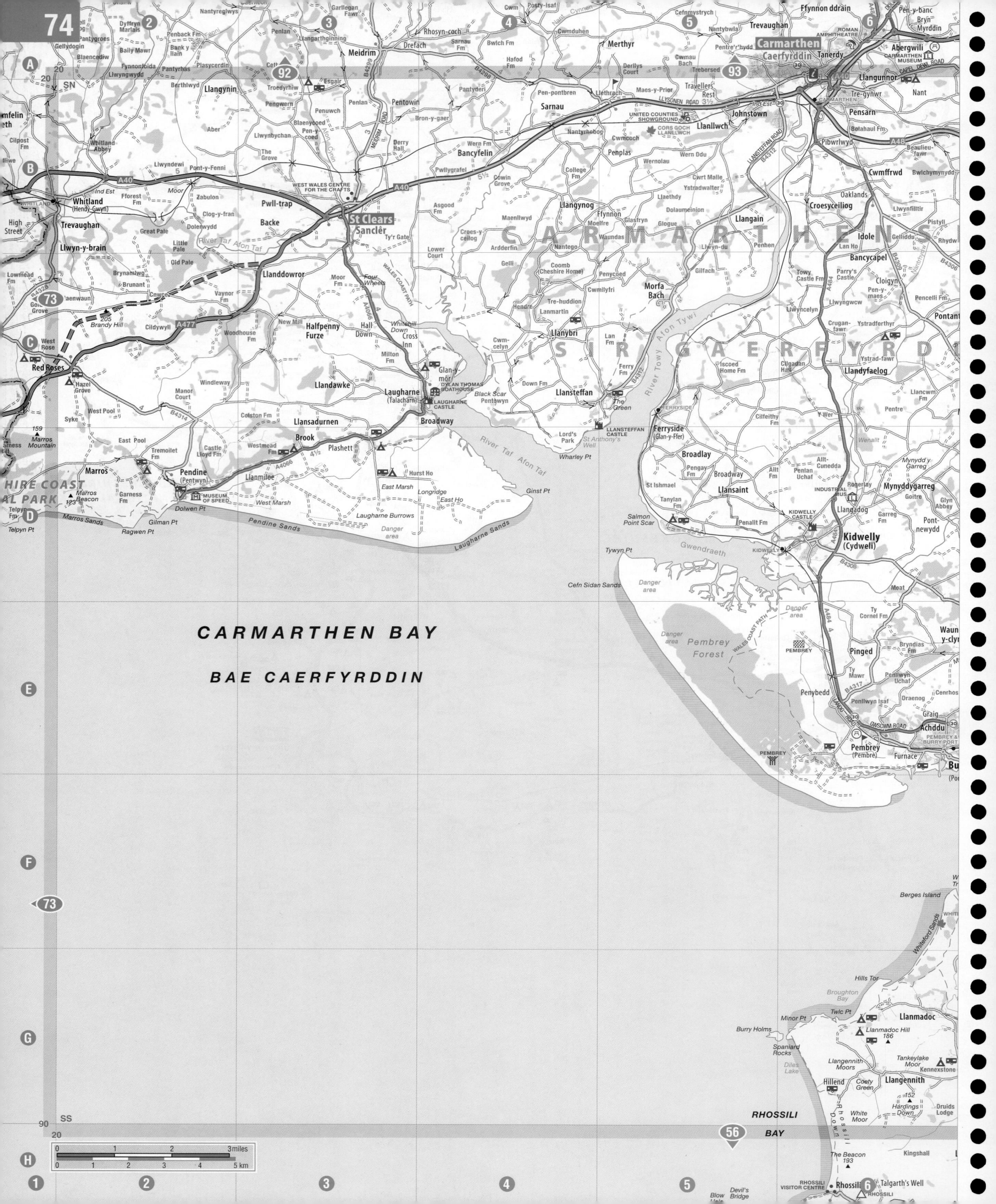
CARMARTHEN BAY
BAE CAERFYRDDIN
CARMARTHENSHIRE
(SIR GAERFYRDDIN)
Carmarthen
Caerfyrddin
Abergwili
Tanerdy
Llangunnor
Johnstown
Llanllwch
Sarnau
Merthyr
Meidrim
Drefach
Trevaughan
Whitland
(Hendy-Gwyn)
Llangynin
Pwll-trap
Backe
St Clears
Sanclêr
Bancyfelin
Llangynog
Llangain
Croesyceiliog
Idole
Bancycapel
Cwmffrwd
Pensarn
Llanddowror
Halfpenny Furze
Llandawke
Laugharne
(Talacharn)
Broadway
Llansadurnen
Brook
Plashett
Pendine
(Pentywn)
Marros
Red Roses
Llanybri
Llansteffan
Morfa Bach
Ferryside
(Glan-y-Fferi)
Broadlay
Llansaint
Llandyfaelog
Kidwelly
(Cydweli)
Mynyddygarreg
Pinged
Pembrey
(Pembre)
Penybedd
Achddu
Furnace
Pembrey Forest
Cefn Sidan Sands
Pendine Sands
Laugharne Burrows
Marros Sands
River Taf
Afon Taf
River Towy
Afon Tywi
Gwendraeth
Llanmadoc
Llangennith
RHOSSILI BAY
Rhossili
Whiteford Sands
Burry Holms
Talgarth's Well
A40
A477
A4066
A484
B4312
WALES COAST PATH
92
93
73
56
1
2
3
4
5
6
A
B
C
D
E
F
G
H
SN
SS
0 1 2 3 miles
0 1 2 3 4 5 km

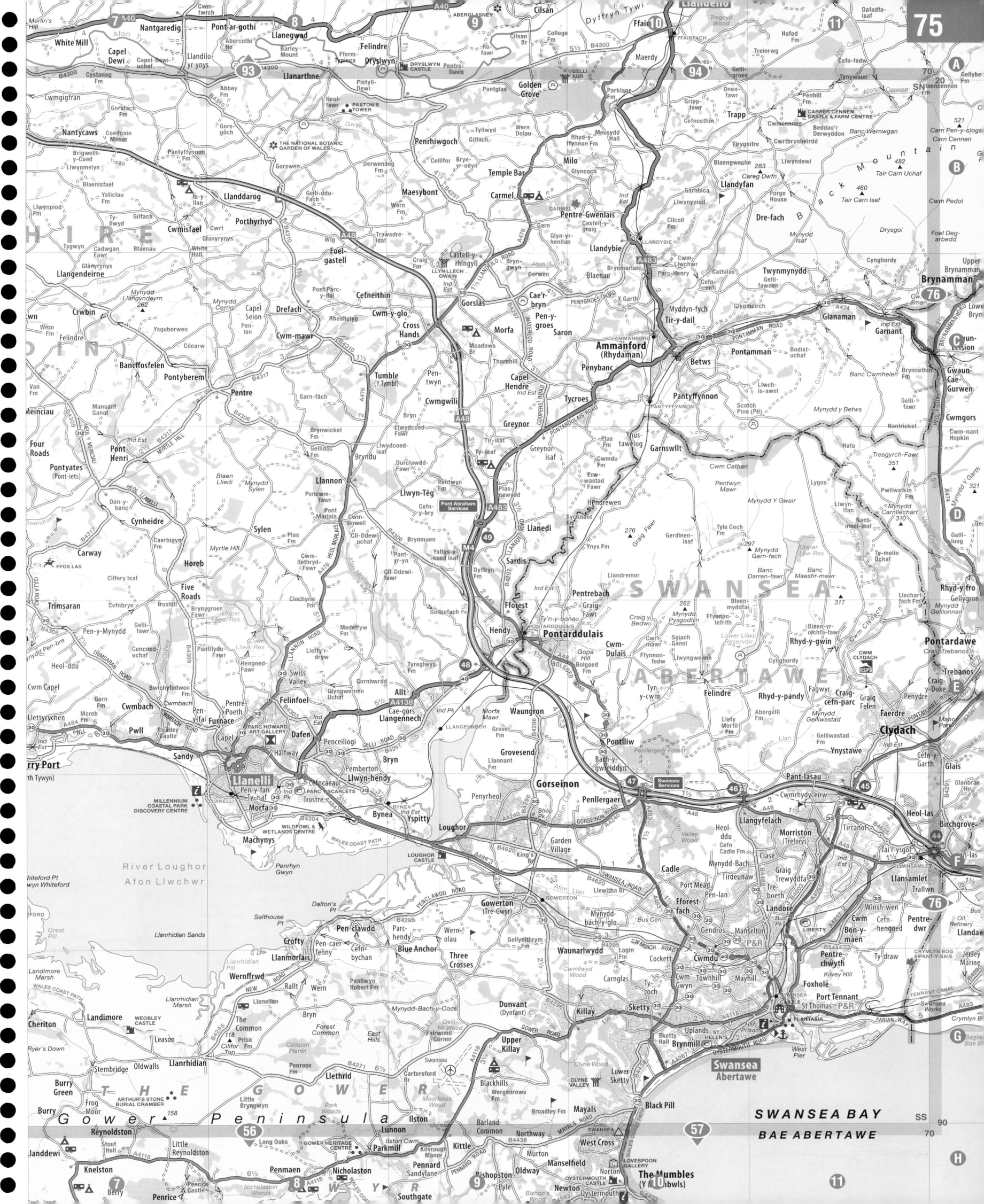

Nantgaredig
Pont-ar-gothi
Llanegwad
Dyffryn Tywi
Llandeilo
Ffairfach
White Mill
Capel Dewi
Felindre
Dryslwyn
DRYSLWYN CASTLE
Llanarthne
Golden Grove
Maerdy
Trapp
CARREG CENNEN CASTLE & FARM CENTRE
Nantycaws
THE NATIONAL BOTANIC GARDEN OF WALES
PAXTON'S TOWER
Penrhiwgoch
Temple Bar
Milo
Carmel
Llanddarog
Porthyrhyd
Maesybont
Pentre-Gwenlais
Llandyfan
Dre-fach
Black Mountain
Cwmisfael
Foel-gastell
Llandybie
Llangendeirne
Cefneithin
Gorslas
Blaenau
Twynmynydd
Brynamman
Crwbin
Drefach
Cwm-y-glo
Cross Hands
Morfa
Saron
Ammanford (Rhydaman)
Tir-y-dail
Glanaman
Garnant
Cwm-mawr
Bancffosfelen
Pontyberem
Tumble (Y Tymbl)
Capel Hendre
Penybanc
Betws
Pontamman
Gwaun-Cae-Gurwen
Pentre
Cwmgwili
Tycroes
Pantyffynnon
Greynor
Cwmgors
Four Roads
Pont-Henri
Pontyates (Pont-iets)
Llannon
Llwyn-Têg
Garnswllt
Pont Abraham Services
Cynheidre
Sylen
Llanedi
SWANSEA
Carway
Horeb
Sardis
Five Roads
Trimsaran
Fforest
Pentrebach
Hendy
Pontarddulais
Cwm-Dulais
Rhyd-y-gwin
Pontardawe
Swiss Valley
Felinfoel
Allt
Llangennech
Felindre
Rhyd-y-pandy
Craig-cefn-parc
Clydach
Cwmbach
Pwll
Furnace
Dafen
Waungron
Pontlliw
Ynystawe
Sandy
Llanelli
Bryn
Llwyn-hendy
Gorseinon
Penllergaer
Pant-lasau
Burry Port
Morfa
Bynea
Yspitty
Loughor
Llangyfelach
Morriston (Treforys)
Machynys
Garden Village
Llansamlet
River Loughor
Afon Llwchwr
Cadle
Fforest-fach
Landore
Gowerton (Tre-Gwyr)
Pen-clawdd
Crofty
Llanmorlais
Blue Anchor
Three Crosses
Waunarlwydd
Cwmdu
Pentre-chwyth
Foxhole
Port Tennant
Wernffrwd
Dunvant (Dynfant)
Killay
Sketty
Cheriton
Landimore
WEOBLEY CASTLE
Llanrhidian
Upper Killay
Brynmill
Swansea Abertawe
Burry Green
THE GOWER
Gower Peninsula
Black Pill
Mayals
SWANSEA BAY
BAE ABERTAWE
Reynoldston
Ilston
Kittle
West Cross
Knelston
Penmaen
Nicholaston
Parkmill
Bishopston
Oldway
Newton
The Mumbles (Y Mwmbwls)
Southgate

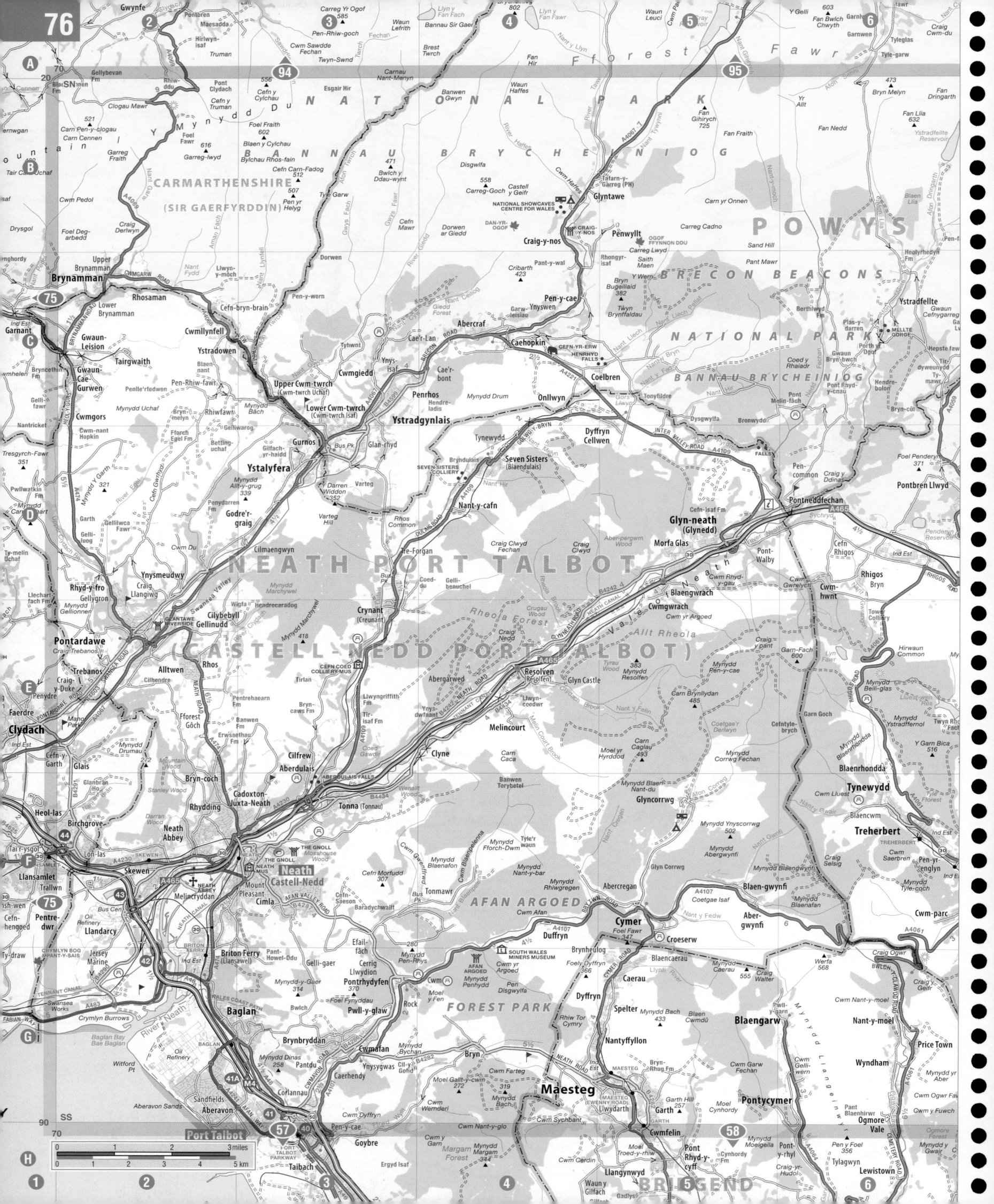
Brynamman
Rhosaman
Garnant
Gwaun-Cae-Gurwen
Cwmllynfell
Ystradowen
Upper Cwm-twrch
Lower Cwm-twrch
Ystradgynlais
Ystalyfera
Gurnos
Abercraf
Caehopkin
Coelbren
Onllwyn
Craig-y-nos
Glyntawe
Penwyllt
Pen-y-cae
Dyffryn Cellwen
Seven Sisters (Blaendulais)
Nant-y-cafn
Glyn-neath (Glynedd)
Pontneddfechan
Ystradfellte
Morfa Glas
Blaengwrach
Cwmgwrach
Crynant (Creunant)
Rhyd-y-fro
Pontardawe
Trebanos
Alltwen
Rhos
Cilybebyll
Gellinudd
Resolven (Resolfen)
Glyn Castle
Melincourt
Clyne
Cilfrew
Aberdulais
Tonna (Tonnau)
Cadoxton-Juxta-Neath
Rhydding
Bryn-coch
Neath Abbey
Neath
Castell-Nedd
Skewen
Llansamlet
Clydach
Birchgrove
Llandarcy
Briton Ferry (Llansawel)
Baglan
Pontrhydyfen
Cymer
Croeserw
Duffryn
Glyncorrwg
Abercregan
Blaen-gwynfi
Treherbert
Tynewydd
Blaenrhondda
Rhigos
Cwm-hwnt
Maesteg
Caerau
Nantyffyllon
Blaengarw
Pontycymer
Garth
Llwydarth
Cwmfelin
Port Talbot
Aberavon
Sandfields
Taibach
Goytre
Cwmafan
Bryn
Nant-y-moel
Price Town
Wyndham
Ogmore Vale
Lewistown
BRIDGEND
CARMARTHENSHIRE (SIR GAERFYRDDIN)
POWYS
NEATH PORT TALBOT (CASTELL-NEDD PORT TALBOT)
BANNAU BRYCHEINIOG NATIONAL PARK
BRECON BEACONS NATIONAL PARK
Fforest Fawr
Y Mynydd Du
AFAN ARGOED FOREST PARK
Rheola Forest
Vale of Neath
NATIONAL SHOWCAVES CENTRE FOR WALES
DAN-YR-OGOF
SOUTH WALES MINERS MUSEUM
CEFN COED COLLIERY MUS
ABERDULAIS FALLS
THE GNOLL
94
95
75
57
58
0 1 2 3 miles
0 1 2 3 4 5 km

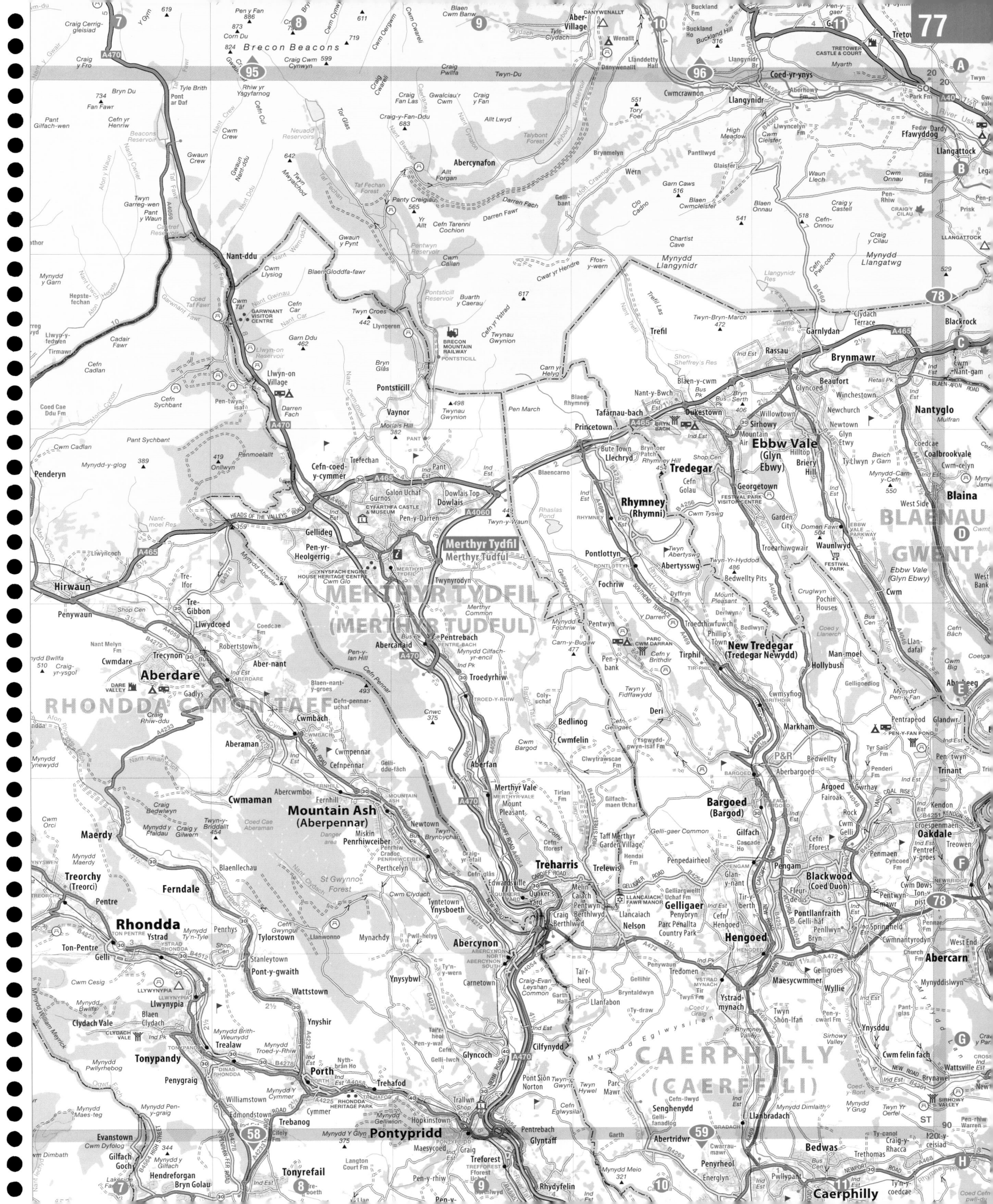
Brecon Beacons
Aber-Village
Tretower
TRETOWER CASTLE & COURT
Coed-yr-ynys
Cwmcrawnon
Llangynidr
Ffawyddog
Llangattock
Abercynafon
Taf Fechan Forest
Talybont Forest
Brynmelyn
Pantllwyd
Wern
Garn Caws
Blaen Cwmcleisfer
Chartist Cave
Mynydd Llangynidr
Mynydd Llangatwg
Nant-ddu
Cwm Llysiog
Blaen Gloddfa-fawr
Cwm Callan
Pontsticill Reservoir
Buarth y Caerau
Cwm Taf
GARWNANT VISITOR CENTRE
Twyn Croes
Llyngeren
BRECON MOUNTAIN RAILWAY
Twynau Gwynion
Trefil
Twyn-Bryn-March
Garnlydan
Clydach Terrace
Blackrock
Rassau
Brynmawr
Beaufort
Glyncoed
Winchestown
Nantyglo
Llwyn-on Village
Pontsticill
Vaynor
Darren Fach
Pen-twyn-isaf
Cefn Sychbant
Cadair Fawr
Cefn Cadlan
Llwyn-y-fedwen
Tirmawr
Pen March
Blaen-Rhymney
Tafarnau-bach
Dukestown
Nant-y-Bwch
Blaen-y-cwm
Princetown
Sirhowy
Willowtown
Ebbw Vale (Glyn Ebwy)
Newchurch
Newtown
Glyn Etwy
Mulfran
Coedcae
Coalbrookvale
Hilltop
Briery Hill
Ty Llwyn
Bwich y Garn
Mynydd-Carn-y-Cefn
Blaina
Cwm-celyn
Bute Town
Llechryd
Rhymney Hill
Tredegar
Cefn Golau
Shop Cen
Georgetown
FESTIVAL PARK VISITOR CENTRE
Penderyn
Mynydd-y-glog
Onllwyn
Penmoelallt
Pant Sychbant
Cwm Cadlan
Cefn-coed-y-cymmer
Trefechan
Morlais Hill
Pant
Dowlais Top
Dowlais
Galon Uchaf
Gurnos
CYFARTHFA CASTLE & MUSEUM
Pen-y-Darren
Twyn-y-Waun
Blaencarno
Rhaslas Pond
Rhymney (Rhymni)
Cwm Tyswg
Garden City
Domen Fawr
Troedrhiwgwair
Waunlwyd
FESTIVAL PARK
West Side
BLAENAU GWENT
Ebbw Vale (Glyn Ebwy)
Cwm
HEADS OF THE VALLEYS ROAD
Gellideg
Pen-yr-Heolgerrig
YNYSFACH ENGINE HOUSE HERITAGE CENTRE
Cwm Glo
Merthyr Tydfil
Merthyr Tudful
Twynyrodyn
Pontlottyn
Twyn Abertysswg
Abertysswg
Twyn-Yr-Hyddod
Bedwellty Pits
MERTHYR TYDFIL (MERTHYR TUDFUL)
Hirwaun
Llwyncoch
Tre-Ifor
Tre-Gibbon
Penywaun
Llwydcoed
Coedcae Fm
Robertstown
Merthyr Common
Fochriw
Mynydd Fochriw
Pentwyn
Dyffryn
Mount Pleasant
Derlwyn
Bedlwyn
Cruglwyn
Pochin Houses
Y Darren
Troedrhiwfuwch
Phillip's Town
New Tredegar (Tredegar Newydd)
Tirphil
Coed y Llanerch
Man-moel
Hollybush
Llan-dafal
Cwm Big
Abertillery
Pentrebach
Abercanaid
Mynydd Cilfach-yr-encil
Pen-y-lan Hill
Cefn Pennar
Troedyrhiw
Trecynon
Cwmdare
Aberdare
Aber-nant
DARE VALLEY
Gadlys
RHONDDA CYNON TAFF
Craig Rhiw-ddu
Blaen-nant-y-groes
Cefn-pennar-uchaf
Cwmbach
Carn-y-Bugaw
Pen-y-bank
PARC CWM DARRAN
Cefn y Brithdir
Twyn y Fidffawydd
Cwmsyfiog
BRITHDIR
Deri
Markham
Pentrapeod
Glandwr
PEN-Y-FAN POND
Cwmpennar
Cefnpennar
Cwmbwrla
Aberaman
Gelli-ddu-fâch
Cwm Bargod
Cwmfelin
Bedlinog
Aberfan
Clwytrawscae Fm
Ysgwydd-gwyn-isaf Fm
Trinant
Pen-twyn
Bedwellty
Aberbargoed
Penderi
Cwmaman
Abercwmboi
Fernhill
Mountain Ash (Aberpennar)
Merthyr Vale
Mount Pleasant
Tirlan Fm
Gilfach-maen Uchaf
Bargoed (Bargod)
Argoed
Fairoak
Gwrhay
Rock
Cwm Gelli
Kendon
Croespenmaen
Oakdale
Treowen
Craig Bedwlwyn
Mynydd y Ffaldau
Craig y Gilwern
Twyn-y-Briddallt
Coed Cae Aberaman
Newtown
Twyn Brynbychan
Miskin
Penrhiwceiber
Perthcelyn
Cwm-Cothi
Cefn-fforest
Taff Merthyr Garden Village
Gelli-gaer Common
Gilfach
Cascade
Cefn Fforest
Penmaen
Pentref-y-groes
Maerdy
Cwm Orci
Mynydd Maerdy
Treorchy (Treorci)
Ferndale
Blaenllechau
St Gwynno Forest
Cwm Clydach
Edwardsville
Treharris
Trelewis
Penpedairheol
Glan-y-nant
Pengam
Blackwood (Coed Duon)
Cwm Dows
Pentwyn-mawr
Pentre
Rhondda
Ystrad
Ton-Pentre
Gelli
Penrhys
Tylorstown
Llanwonno
Mynachdy
Tyntetown
Ynysboeth
Quakers Yard
Craig Berthlwyd
Nelson
Llancaiach
LLANCAIACH FAWR MANOR
Gelligaer
Penybryn
Parc Penallta Country Park
Tir-y-berth
Cefn Hengoed
Hengoed
Fleur-de-lis
Pontllanfraith
Gelli-haf
Penllwyn
Bryn
Springfield
Cwmnantyrodyn
West End
Abercarn
Cwm Cesig
LLWYNYPIA
Llwynypia
Blaen Clydach
Clydach Vale
Stanleytown
Pont-y-gwaith
Wattstown
Ynyshir
Ynysybwl
Abercynon
Carnetown
Craig-Evan Leyshan Common
Tai'r-heol
Llanfabon
Bryntaldwyn
Ystrad Mynach
Tredomen
Maesycwmmer
Gelligroes
Wyllie
Mynyddislwyn
Twyn Shôn-Ifan
Pen-y-cwarl Fm
Sirhowy Valley
Ynysddu
Trealaw
Tonypandy
Mynydd Pwllyrhebog
Penygraig
Porth
Trehafod
RHONDDA HERITAGE PARK
Glyncoch
Cilfynydd
Mynydd Eglwysilan
CAERPHILLY (CAERFFILI)
Cwm felin fach
Wattsville
Brynawel
Williamstown
Edmondstown
Trebanog
Cymmer
Hopkinstown
Trallwn
Pont Siôn Norton
Twyn Hywel
Parc Mawr
Senghenydd
Llanbradach
Mynydd Dimlaith
Mynydd Y Grug
Twyn Yr Oerfel
Evanstown
Cwm Dyfolog
Gilfach Goch
Hendreforgan
Bryn Golau
Tonyrefail
Pontypridd
Maesycoed
Graig
Treforest
Pentrebach
Glyntaff
Abertridwr
Penyrheol
Energlyn
Bedwas
Trethomas
Craig-y-Rhacca
Pwllypant
Caerphilly
Rhydyfelin
Langton Court Fm
Pen-y-rhiw
Mynydd Meio

78
BRECON BEACONS
NATIONAL PARK
BANNAU BRYCHEINIOG
MONMOUTHSHIRE
(SIR FYNWY)
BLAENAU GWENT
TORFAEN
(TOR-FAEN)
NEWPORT
CASNEWYDD
Abergavenny
Y Fenni
Crickhowell
(Crug Hywel)
Llangattock
Llangenny
Cwrt-y-gollen
Glangrwyney
Gilwern
Govilon
Llanelly
Clydach
Blackrock
Llanelly Hill
Nantyglo
Blaina
Coalbrookvale
Brynmawr
Blaenavon
Forge Side
Garn-yr-erw
Cwmavon
Varteg
Abersychan
Garndiffaith
Talywain
Abertillery
Six Bells
Aberbeeg
Cwmtillery
East Bank
Llanhilleth
Brynithel
St Illtyd
Pontypool
Trevethin
Wainfelin
Penygarn
Griffithstown
New Inn
Sebastopol
Pontnewydd
Croesyceiliog
Cwmbran
Llanyrafon
Oakfield
Llantarnam
Henllys
Crumlin
Newbridge
Oakdale
Abercarn
Cwmcarn
Pontywaun
Crosskeys
Risca
Rogerstone
Malpas
Bettws
Caerleon
Christchurch
Llanfoist
Llanellen
Llanover
Mamhilad
Penperlleni
Goetre
Little Mill
Monkswood
Glascoed
Usk
Llanbadoc
Llangybi
Llantrisant
Llanfrechfa
Ponthir
Llanhennock
Tredunnock
Newbridge-on-Usk
Llanvaches
Penhow
Llanmartin
Raglan
Llandenny
Kemeys Commander
Bettws Newydd
Llanarth
Coed Morgan
Llanvapley
Llantilio Crossenny
Llanvetherine
Llantilio Pertholey
Mardy
Llanddewi Skirrid
Llanfihangel Crucorney
Pandy
Llangattock Lingoed
Stanton
Twyn
Llanbedr
Sugar Loaf 596
Blorenge Carn 561
Table Mountain 451
A40
A465
A4042
A472
A449
A467
M4
B4598
B4246
77
96
97
59
60
2
3
4
5
6
A
B
C
D
E
F
G
H
SO
ST
20
90
0 1 2 3 miles
0 1 2 3 4 5 km

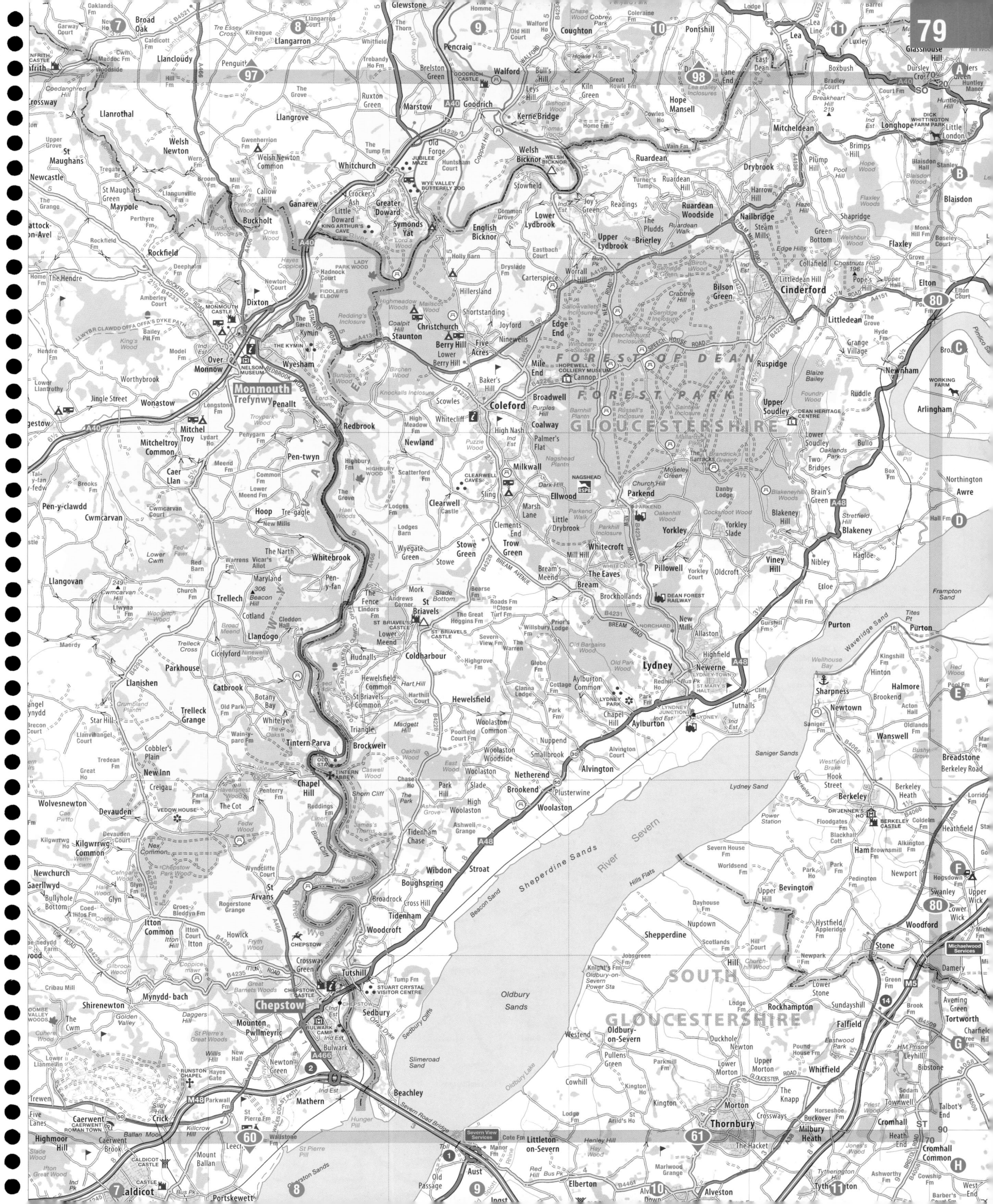

Glewstone
Broad Oak
Llangarron
Pencraig
Coughton
Pontshill
Lea
Llancloudy
Walford
Goodrich Castle
Mitcheldean
Longhope
Llanrothal
Marstow
Goodrich
Kerne Bridge
Hope Mansell
Llangrove
Welsh Newton
Whitchurch
Welsh Bicknor
Ruardean
Drybrook
St Maughans
Newcastle
Maypole
Ganarew
Symonds Yat
English Bicknor
Lower Lydbrook
Upper Lydbrook
Brierley
Ruardean Woodside
Nailbridge
Blaisdon
Flaxley
Buckholt
Rockfield
Dixton
Monmouth
Trefynwy
Cinderford
Elton
Littledean
Christchurch
Staunton
Berry Hill
Five Acres
Edge End
Forest of Dean
Forest Park
Gloucestershire
Ruspidge
Newnham
Over Monnow
Wyesham
Mile End
Cannop
Coleford
Broadwell
Upper Soudley
Arlingham
Wonastow
Penallt
Redbrook
Coalway
Mitchel Troy
Mitcheltroy Common
Newland
Milkwall
Parkend
Awre
Pen-y-clawdd
Cwmcarvan
Hoop
Clearwell
Ellwood
Yorkley
Blakeney
Whitebrook
Trow Green
Whitecroft
Pillowell
Viney Hill
Llangovan
Trellech
St Briavels
Bream
Llandogo
Coldharbour
Lydney
Newerne
Purton
Parkhouse
Llanishen
Catbrook
Hewelsfield
Aylburton
Sharpness
Trelleck Grange
Tintern Parva
Brockweir
Alvington
Wanswell
New Inn
Chapel Hill
Netherend
Brookend
Woolaston
Berkeley
Wolvesnewton
Devauden
Kilgwrrwg Common
Ham
Newchurch
St Arvans
Wibdon
Stroat
Boughspring
Bevington
Tidenham
Woodcroft
River Severn
River Wye
Shepperdine
Stone
Woodford
Itton Common
Tutshill
Chepstow
Sedbury
Oldbury Sands
South Gloucestershire
Rockhampton
Tortworth
Shirenewton
Mynydd-bach
Mounton
Pwllmeyric
Bulwark
Oldbury-on-Severn
Falfield
Whitfield
Newton Green
Beachley
Mathern
Thornbury
Crick
Caerwent
Littleton-on-Severn
Highmoor Hill
Aust
Elberton
Alveston
Portskewett
Caldicot
Severn View Services
Michaelwood Services

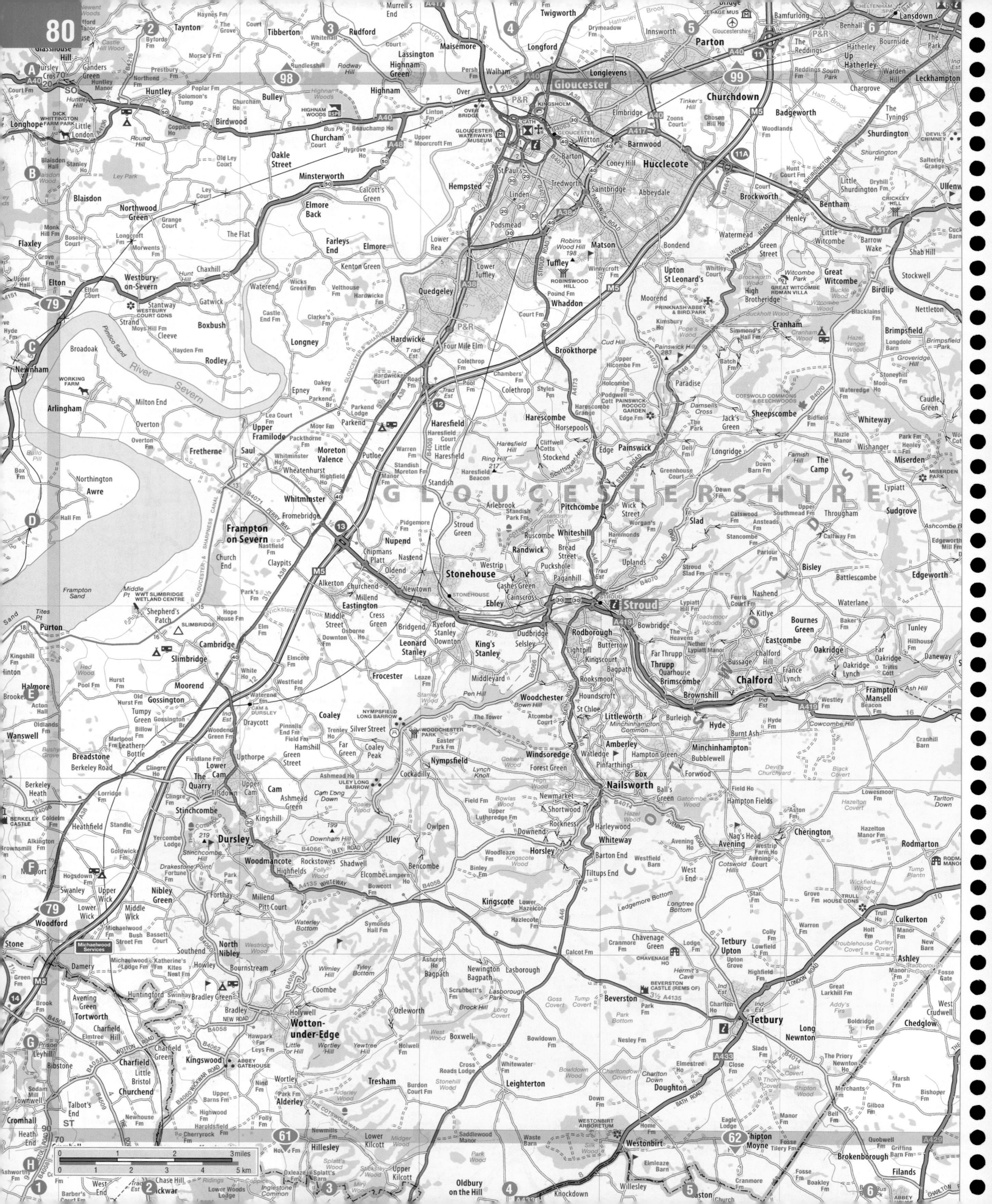

GLOUCESTERSHIRE
Gloucester
Stroud
River Severn
Taynton
Tibberton
Rudford
Maisemore
Twigworth
Longford
Innsworth
Parton
Bamfurlong
Benhall
Lansdown
Huntley
Highnam
Over
Longlevens
Churchdown
Leckhampton
Up Hatherley
Longhope
Birdwood
Churcham
Kingsholm
Elmbridge
Barnwood
Badgeworth
Shurdington
Hucclecote
Hempsted
Minsterworth
Oakle Street
Blaisdon
Northwood Green
Elmore Back
Linden
Tredworth
Saintbridge
Abbeydale
Brockworth
Bentham
Podsmead
Matson
Tuffley
Lower Tuffley
Quedgeley
Whaddon
Flaxley
Elton
Westbury-on-Severn
Chaxhill
Farleys End
Elmore
Upton St Leonard's
Great Witcombe
Birdlip
Stockwell
Boxbush
Longney
Hardwicke
Four Mile Elm
Brookthorpe
Cranham
Brimpsfield
Rodley
Newnham
Broadoak
Arlingham
Milton End
Epney
Haresfield
Harescombe
Paradise
Sheepscombe
Whiteway
Overton
Fretherne
Saul
Upper Framilode
Moreton Valence
Putloe
Painswick
Edge
Longridge
Miserden
The Camp
Awre
Northington
Whitminster
Standish
Pitchcombe
Wick Street
Throughan
Sudgrove
Lypiatt
Frampton on Severn
Frampton Sand
Nupend
Stroud Green
Whiteshill
Slad
Bisley
Edgeworth
Stonehouse
Westrip
Randwick
Ruscombe
Paganhill
Uplands
Nashend
Waterlane
Purton
Slimbridge
Cambridge
Eastington
Ebley
Cainscross
Rodborough
Bowbridge
Bournes Green
Eastcombe
Oakridge
Tunley
Daneway
Leonard Stanley
King's Stanley
Frocester
Middleyard
Selsley
Thrupp
Brimscombe
Chalford
Frampton Mansell
Moorend
Gossington
Woodchester
Houndscroft
Brownshill
Hyde
Wanswell
Breadstone
Coaley
Draycott
Silver Street
Littleworth
Amberley
Minchinhampton
Lower Cam
Cam
Upper Cam
Nympsfield
Windsoredge
Forest Green
Box
Nailsworth
Forwood
Stinchcombe
Dursley
Kingshill
Uley
Owlpen
Horsley
Newmarket
Shortwood
Whiteway
Avening
Cherington
Rodmarton
Woodmancote
Nibley Green
North Nibley
Kingscote
Tiltups End
Woodford
Culkerton
Tetbury Upton
Ashley
Damery
Tortworth
Bagpath
Newington Bagpath
Beverston
Tetbury
Long Newnton
Chedglow
Wotton-under-Edge
Charfield
Kingswood
Boxwell
Leighterton
Doughton
Tresham
Alderley
Hillesley
Westonbirt
Shipton Moyne
Brokenborough
Filands
Cromhall
Upper Kilcott
Lower Kilcott
Oldbury on the Hill
Willesley
Knockdown

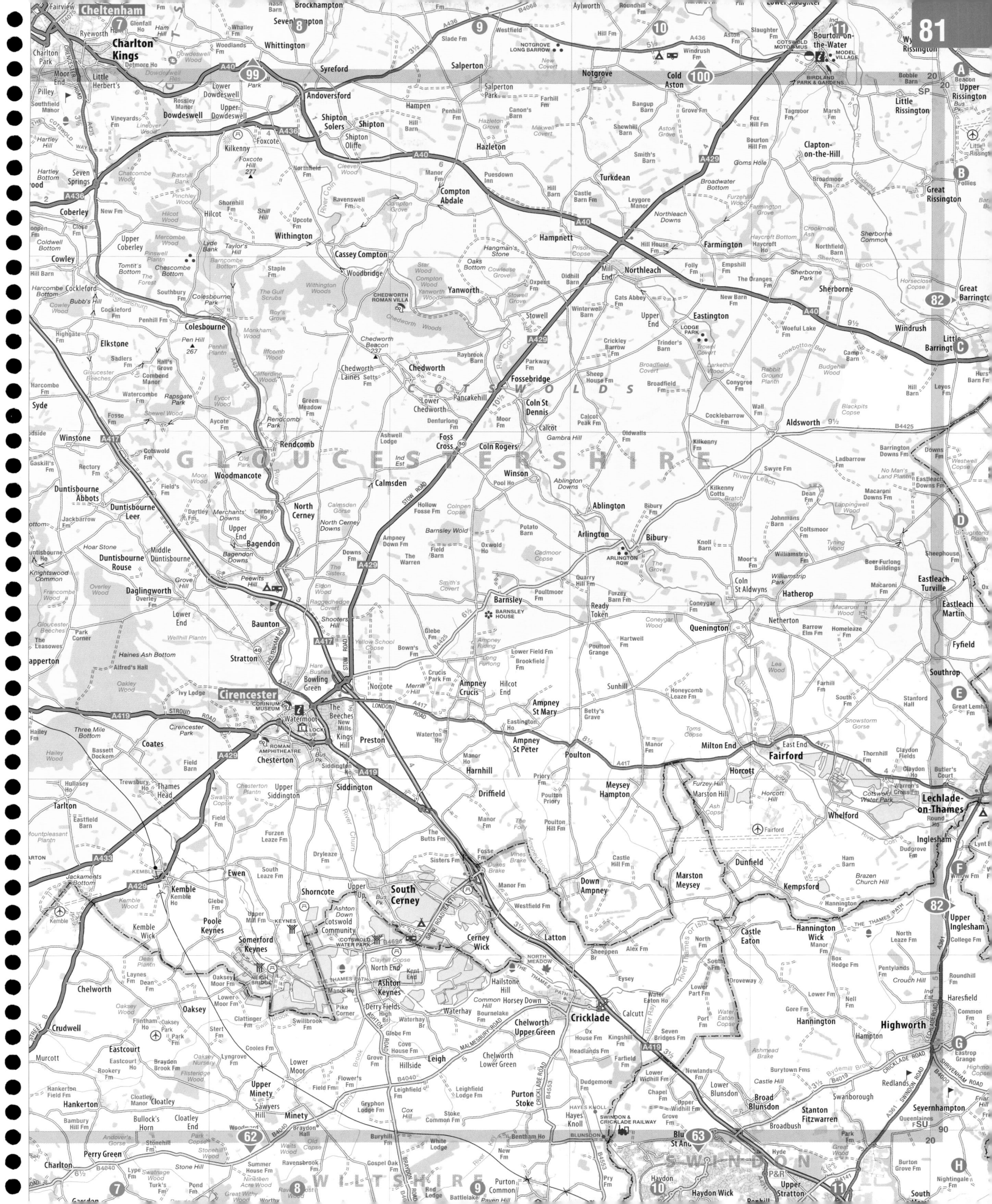
Cheltenham
Charlton Kings
Whittington
Syreford
Andoversford
Dowdeswell
Shipton Solers
Shipton
Shipton Oliffe
Salperton
Hazleton
Notgrove
Cold Aston
Turkdean
Bourton-on-the-Water
Upper Rissington
Little Rissington
Clapton-on-the-Hill
Great Rissington
Compton Abdale
Hampnett
Northleach
Farmington
Sherborne
Great Barrington
Windrush
Eastington
Coberley
Cowley
Colesbourne
Elkstone
Withington
Cassey Compton
Chedworth
Yanworth
Stowell
Fossebridge
Coln St Dennis
Calcot
Aldsworth
COTSWOLDS
GLOUCESTERSHIRE
Syde
Winstone
Rendcomb
Woodmancote
Calmsden
Foss Cross
Coln Rogers
Winson
Duntisbourne Abbots
Duntisbourne Leer
Duntisbourne Rouse
Middle Duntisbourne
North Cerney
Bagendon
Ablington
Arlington
Bibury
Hatherop
Coln St Aldwyns
Eastleach Turville
Eastleach Martin
Daglingworth
Barnsley
Ready Token
Quenington
Netherton
Fyfield
Southrop
Baunton
Stratton
Cirencester
Bowling Green
Norcote
Ampney Crucis
Ampney St Mary
Ampney St Peter
Sunhill
Poulton
Milton End
Fairford
Horcott
Coates
Chesterton
Preston
Siddington
Harnhill
Driffield
Meysey Hampton
Lechlade-on-Thames
Whelford
Inglesham
Tarlton
Ewen
Kemble
Kemble Wick
Poole Keynes
Somerford Keynes
Shorncote
South Cerney
Cerney Wick
Latton
Down Ampney
Marston Meysey
Dunfield
Kempsford
Castle Eaton
Hannington Wick
Upper Inglesham
Ashton Keynes
North End
Chelworth
Oaksey
Crudwell
Hailstone Hill
Cricklade
Calcutt
Hannington
Highworth
Leigh
Chelworth Upper Green
Chelworth Lower Green
Eastcourt
Hankerton
Upper Minety
Minety
Purton Stoke
Hayes Knoll
Broad Blunsdon
Lower Blunsdon
Stanton Fitzwarren
Sevenhampton
Perry Green
Charlton
SWINDON
WILTSHIRE
Haydon Wick
Upper Stratton
A40
A436
A429
A417
A419
A433
A435
B4425
B4040
B4019
A361
99
100
62
63
82

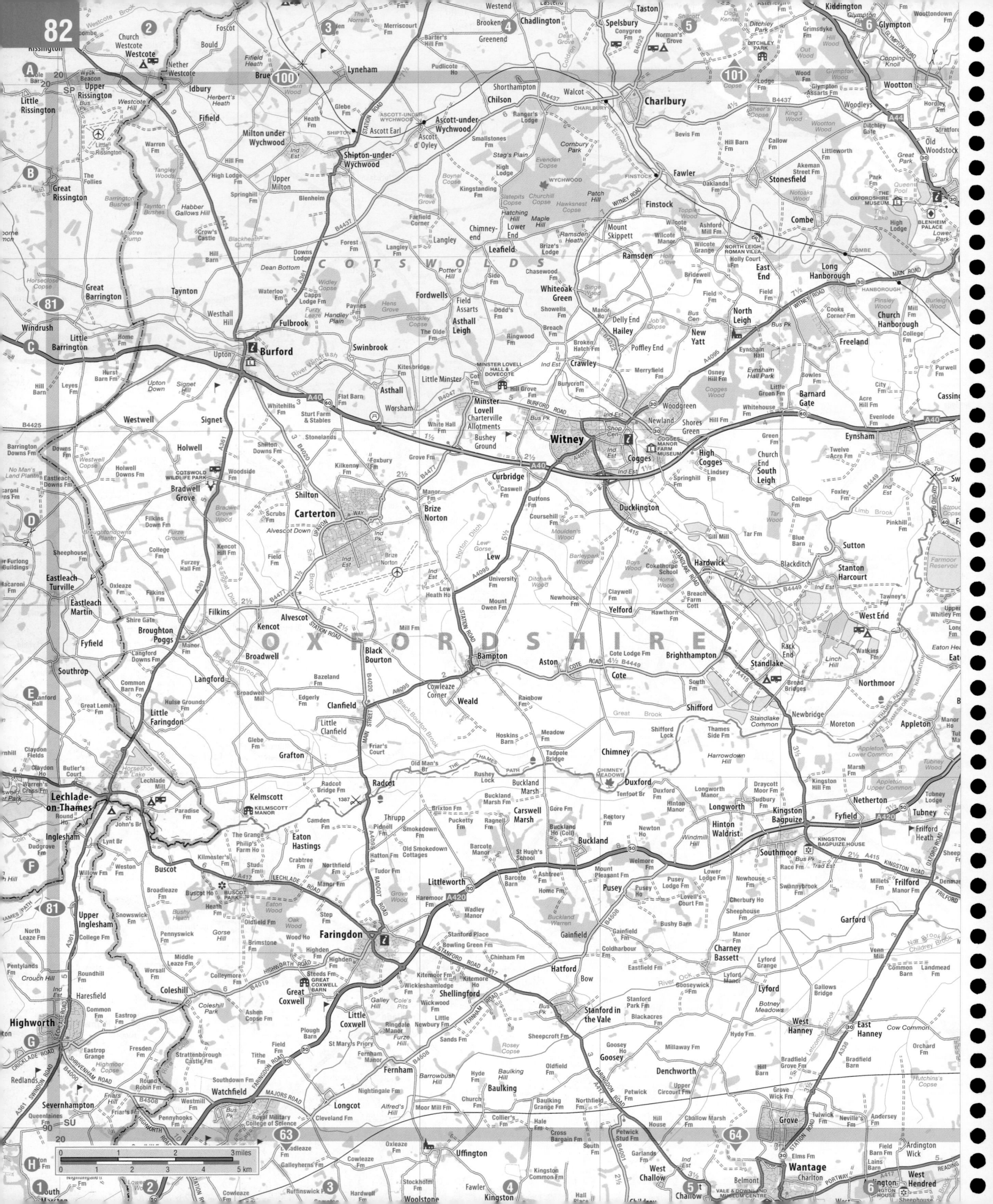
82
Church Westcote
Westcote
Nether Westcote
Foscot
Bould
Idbury
Fifield
Fifield Heath
Bruern
Lyneham
Merriscourt Fm
Pudlicote Ho
Westend
Brookend
Chadlington
Greenend
Taston
Spelsbury
Conygree Fm
Norman's Grove
Dean Grove
Ditchley Park
Grimsdyke Fm
Kiddington
Glympton
Wootton
Copping Knoll
Charlbury
Shorthampton
Chilson
Walcot
Ranger's Lodge
Wyck Beacon
Upper Rissington
Little Rissington
Westcote Hill
Herbert's Heath
Milton under Wychwood
Ascott Earl
Ascott-under-Wychwood
Ascott d'Oyley
Shipton-under-Wychwood
Smallstones Fm
Stag's Plain
Cornbury Park
Evenden Copse
Bevis Fm
Hill Barn Fm
Callow Fm
Stonesfield
Fawler
Finstock
Littleworth Fm
Akeman Street Fm
Woodleys
Ditchley Gate
Old Woodstock
Great Park
Great Rissington
The Follies
Barrington Bushes
Tangley Woods
Taynton Bushes
Habber Gallows Hill
Upper Milton
Blenheim
Springhill Fm
High Lodge Fm
Hill Fm
Warren Fm
Kingstanding Fm
High Lodge
Wychwood
Slatepits Copse
Churchill Copse
Hawksnest Copse
Patch Hill
Hatching Hill
Maple Hill
Lower End
Chimney-end
Langley
Farfield Corner
Forest Fm
Crow's Castle
Hill Barn
Downs Lodge
Dean Bottom
Mount Skippett
Ramsden
Ramsden Heath
Wilcote Manor
Wilcote Grange
North Leigh Roman Villa
Holly Court Fm
Combe
Long Hanborough
Blenheim Palace
Oxfordshire Museum
Leafield
Brize's Lodge
Chasewood Fm
COTSWOLDS
Potter's Hill
Side Fm
Whiteoak Green
Fordwells
Field Assarts
Asthall Leigh
Dodd's Fm
Showells Fm
Widley Copse
Capps Lodge Fm
Waterloo Fm
Taynton
Great Barrington
Westhall Hill
Fulbrook
Paynes Fm
Handley Plain
Hens Grove
Stockley Copse
The Olde Fm
Ringwood Fm
Beach Fm
Broken Hatch Fm
Delly End
Hailey
Poffley End
Bus Cen
New Yatt
North Leigh
East End
Field Fm
Bridewell Fm
Cooks Corner Fm
Church Hanborough
Freeland
Windrush
Little Barrington
Home Fm
Burford
Upton
Swinbrook
River Windrush
Kitesbridge Fm
Little Minster
Minster Lovell Hall & Dovecote
Hill Grove Fm
Crawley
Merryfield Fm
Burycroft Fm
Eynsham Hall
Eynsham Hall Park
Osney Hill Fm
Cogges Wood
Bowles Fm
Barnard Gate
Purwell Fm
Cassington
Hill Barn
Leyes Fm
Hurst Barn Fm
Upton Down
Signet Hill
Asthall
Flat Barn Fm
Worsham
Minster Lovell
Charterville Allotments
Bushey Ground
White Hall Fm
Woodgreen
Newland
Shores Green
Witney
Cogges
Cogges Manor Farm Museum
Whitehouse Fm
Hill Fm
Evenlode Fm
Eynsham
Twelve Acre Fm
Westwell
Signet
Whitehills Fm
Sturt Farm & Stables
Stonelands
Barrington Downs Fm
Downs Fm
Westwell Copse
Holwell
Holwell Downs Fm
Shilton Downs Fm
Kilkenny Fm
Foxbury Fm
Grove Fm
Curbridge
Caswell Fm
High Cogges
Lindsey Fm
Springhill Fm
Church End
South Leigh
Foxley Fm
Cotswold Wildlife Park
Woodside Fm
Bradwell Grove
Shilton
Carterton
Manor Fm
Brize Norton
Duttons Fm
Coursehill Fm
Ducklington
College Fm
Tar Fm
Pinkhill Fm
Sutton
Stanton Harcourt
Farmoor Reservoir
Filkins Down Fm
Scrubs Fm
Alvescot Down
Furze Ground
Broughtondowns Plantn
Moulden's Wood
Gill Mill
Blue Barn
Blackditch
Sheephouse Fm
College Fm
Furzey Hall Fm
Field Fm
Brize Norton
Lew Gorse
Lew
Barleypark Wood
Boys Wood
Cokethorpe School
Hardwick
Eastleach Turville
Kencot Hill Fm
Oxleaze Fm
Filkins Fm
University Fm
Ditcham Wood
Home Wood
Breach Farm Cott
Tawney's Fm
Eastleach Martin
Lew Heath Ho
Mount Owen Fm
Newhouse Fm
Claywell Fm
Yelford
Hawthorn Fm
West End
Shire Gate
Filkins
Kencot
Alvescot
Mill Fm
Broughton Poggs
Fyfield
Langford Downs Fm
Broadwell
Black Bourton
Bampton
Aston
Cote Lodge Fm
Brighthampton
Rack End
Standlake
Watkins Fm
Linch Hill
OXFORDSHIRE
Southrop
Common Barn Fm
Langford
Bazeland Fm
Cowleaze Corner
Weald
Cote
Broad Bridges
Northmoor
Great Lemhill Fm
Broadwell Mill
Edgerly Fm
Clanfield
Rainbow Fm
South Fm
Shifford
Hulse Grounds Fm
Little Faringdon
Little Clanfield
Great Brook
Standlake Common
Newbridge
Moreton
Appleton
Claydon Fields
Glebe Fm
Grafton
Friar's Court
Hoskins Barn
Meadow Fm
Tadpole Bridge
Shifford Lock
Thames Side Fm
Chimney
Harrowdown Hill
Appleton Lower Common
Claydon Ho
Butler's Court
Horseshoe Lake
Lechlade Mill
Old Man's Br
Thames Path
Rushey Lock
Buckland Marsh
Chimney Meadows
Duxford
Marsh Fm
Tubney Wood
Lechlade-on-Thames
Kelmscott
Kelmscott Manor
Radcot Bridge Fm
Radcot
Buckland Marsh Fm
Tenfoot Br
Duxford Fm
Longworth Manor
Draycott Moor Fm
Sudbury Fm
Kingston Hill Fm
Netherton
Tubney Lodge
Paradise Fm
Camden Fm
Thrupp
Brixton Fm
Carswell Marsh
Gore Fm
Hinton Manor
Longworth
Kingston Bagpuize
Fyfield
Tubney
Frilford Heath
Inglesham
St John's Br
The Grange
Philip's Farm Ho
Eaton Hastings
Pidnell Fm
Smokedown Fm
Old Smokedown Cottages
Puckety Fm
Ragnell Fm
Rectory Fm
Buckland Ho (Coll)
Newton Ho
Windmill Hill
Hinton Waldrist
Kingston Bagpuize House
Dudgrove Fm
Lynt Br
Weston Fm
Kilmester's Fm
Stud Fm
Crabtree Fm
Northfield Fm
Hatton Fm
Barcote Manor
St Hugh's School
Buckland
Welmore Fm
Southmoor
Race Fm
Buscot
Willow Fm
Tudor Fm
Littleworth
Ashtree Fm
Mount Pleasant Fm
Lower Lodge Fm
Newhouse Fm
Swannybrook Fm
Millets Fm
Frilford
Frilford Manor Fm
Broadleaze Fm
Buscot Ho
Buscot Park
Manor Fm
Grove Wood
Haremoor Fm
Barcote Barn
Home Fm
Pusey
Pusey Ho
Pusey Lodge Fm
Lovell's Court Fm
Cherbury Ho
Sheephouse Fm
Upper Inglesham
Snowswick Fm
Heath Fm
Bushy Heath
Eaton Wood
Oldfield Fm
Oak Wood
Step Fm
Wadley Manor
Buckland Warren
Bushy Barn
Garford
North Leaze Fm
College Fm
Pennyswick Fm
Gorse Hill
Brimstone Fm
Wood Ho
Faringdon
Stanford Place
Bowling Green Fm
Gainfield
Gainfield Fm
Manor Fm
Charney Bassett
Coldharbour Fm
Lyford Grange
Venn Mill
Common Barn
Landmead Fm
Childrey Brook
Pentylands Fm
Crouch Hill
Roundhill Fm
Middle Leaze Fm
Worsall Fm
Highden Fm
Colleymore Fm
Chinham Fm
Eastfield Fm
Lyford Manor
Lyford
Gallows Bridge
Haresfield
Coleshill
Steeds Fm
Great Coxwell Barn
Great Coxwell
Kitemoor Fm
Kitemore Ho
Wicklesham Lodge
Shellingford
Hatford
Bow
River Ock
Gooseywick Fm
Common Fm
Eastrop Fm
Coleshill Park
Ashen Copse Fm
Galley Hill
Cole's Pits
Wickwood Fm
Little Newbury Fm
Little Coxwell
Stanford Park Fm
Stanford in the Vale
Blackacres Fm
Botney Meadows
Highworth
Plough Barn
Ringdale Manor
Furze Hill
Sands Fm
Sheepcroft Fm
West Hanney
East Hanney
Cow Common
Hyde Fm
Eastrop Grange
Highmoor Copse
Fresden Fm
Strattenborough Castle Fm
Tithe Fm
Field Fm
St Mary's Priory
Fernham Manor
Rosey Copse
Goosey Ho
Goosey
Millaway Fm
Bradfield Grove Fm
Bradfield Barn
Orchard Fm
Redlands
Round Robin Fm
Southdown Fm
Fernham
Barrowbush Hill
Hyde Fm
Baulking Hill
Baulking
Oldfield Fm
Denchworth
Hill Barn
Hutchins's Copse
Watchfield
Nightingale Fm
Upper Circourt Fm
Petwick Fm
Grove Wick Fm
Severnhampton
Friars Hill
Westmill Fm
Longcot
Alfred's Hill
Moor Mill Fm
Church Fm
Baulking Grange Fm
Northfield Fm
Grove
Tulwick Fm
Neville's Fm
Andersey Fm
Queenlaines Fm
Friar's Fm
Pennyhooks Fm
Royal Military College of Science
Cleveland Fm
Collier's Fm
Hale Fm
Cross Bargain Fm
Petwick Stud Fm
Hill House
Challow Marsh Fm
Eadleaze Fm
Oxleaze Fm
Uffington
Galleyherns Fm
Cowleaze Fm
South Fm
Garlands Fm
West Challow
Elms Fm
Field Barn Fm
Lains Barn
Ardington Wick
Wantage
Charlton
Kingston Common Fm
Belmont
Vale & Downland Museum Centre
Fawler
Kingston
Woolstone
Stockholm Fm
Hardwell Fm
Ruffinswick Fm
West Hendred
Sheephouse
0 1 2 3 miles
0 1 2 3 4 5 km

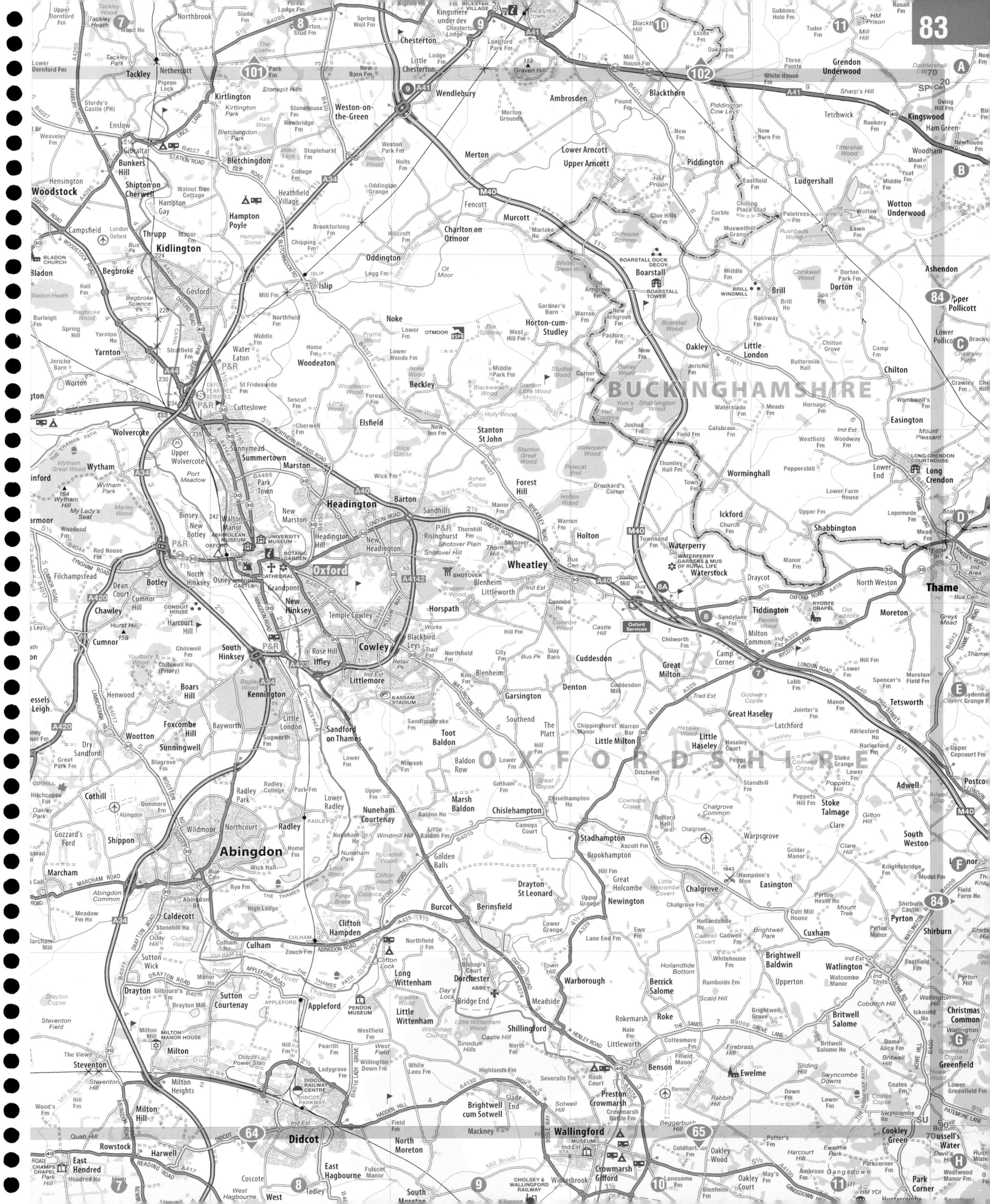
Oxford
Abingdon
Didcot
Wallingford
Thame
Kidlington
Bicester
Woodstock
Headington
Cowley
Wheatley
BUCKINGHAMSHIRE
OXFORDSHIRE
Dorchester
Benson
Watlington
Chalgrove
Long Crendon
Brill
Islip
101
102
64
65
84

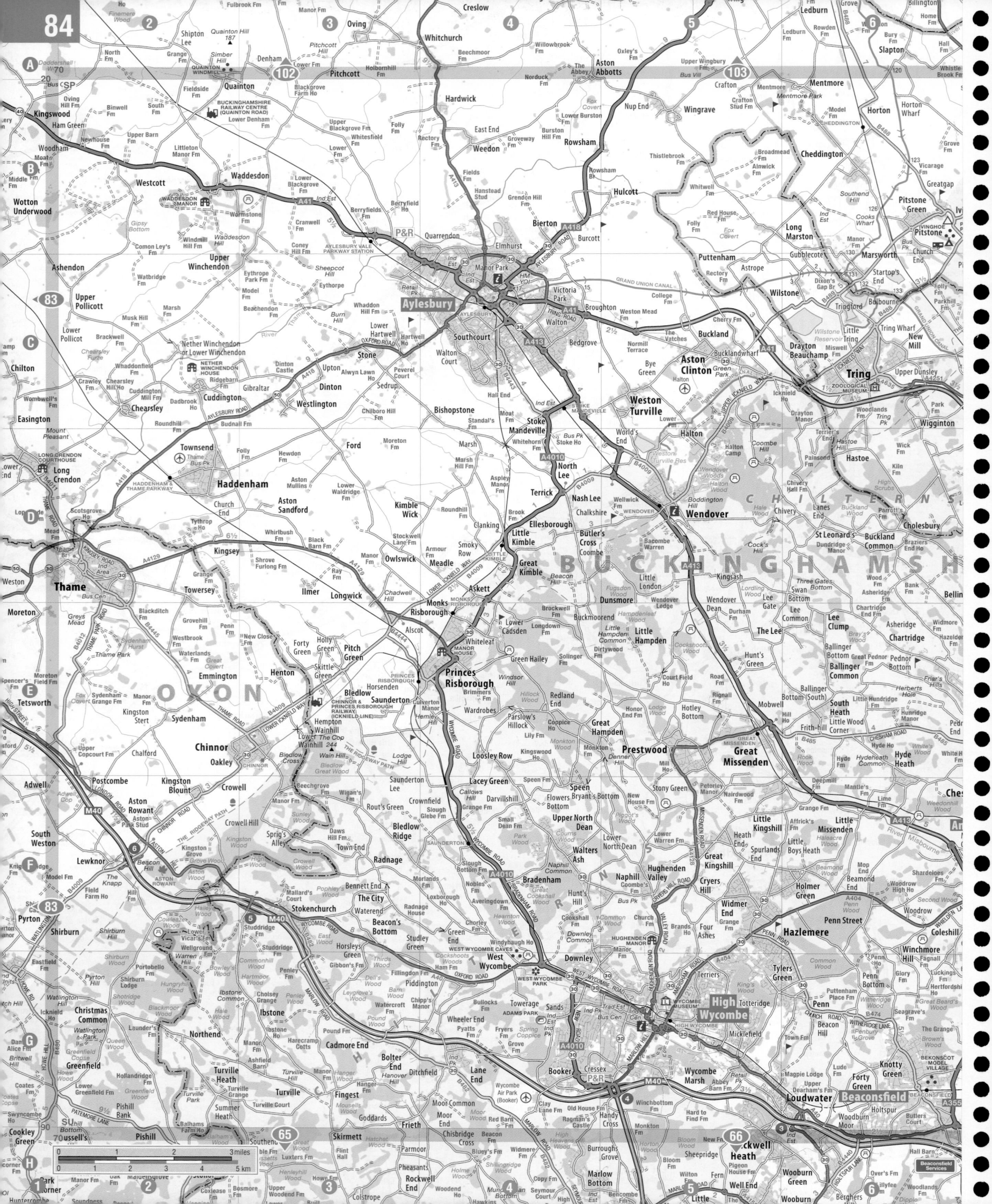

Creslow
Oving
Whitchurch
Shipton Lee
Quainton Hill 187
Denham
Pitchcott
Aston Abbotts
Ledburn
Slapton
Quainton
Buckinghamshire Railway Centre (Quainton Road)
Hardwick
Kingswood
Ham Green
Nup End
Wingrave
Mentmore
Crafton
Horton
Woodham
Waddesdon
Westcott
Waddesdon Manor
Wotton Underwood
East End
Weedon
Rowsham
Cheddington
Hulcott
Bierton
Quarrendon
Pitstone Green
Pitstone
Long Marston
Puttenham
Marsworth
Upper Winchendon
Ashendon
Aylesbury
Aylesbury Vale Parkway Station
Manor Park
Elmhurst
Victoria Park
Broughton
Walton
Southcourt
Bedgrove
Wilstone
Tringford
Upper Pollicott
Lower Pollicott
Nether Winchendon or Lower Winchendon
Nether Winchendon House
Stone
Dinton
Buckland
Aston Clinton
Bucklandwharf
Drayton Beauchamp
Tring
Chilton
Cuddington
Chearsley
Gibraltar
Westlington
Bishopstone
Weston Turville
Halton
Wigginton
Easington
Long Crendon
Long Crendon Courthouse
Stoke Mandeville
World's End
Townsend
Haddenham
Haddenham & Thame Parkway
Ford
Aston Sandford
Terrick
Nash Lee
Wendover
Hastoe
Chivery
Cholesbury
Kimble Wick
Ellesborough
Little Kimble
Great Kimble
Butler's Cross
St Leonard's
Buckland Common
Thame
Kingsey
Towersey
Owlswick
Meadle
Longwick
Ilmer
Askett
Monks Risborough
Dunsmore
Little London
Kingsash
Wendover Dean
Lee Gate
Moreton
Alscot
Whiteleaf
Lower Cadsden
Little Hampden
The Lee
Lee Clump
Chartridge
Ballinger Common
Pitch Green
Forty Green
Henton
Emmington
Princes Risborough
Green Hailey
Hunt's Green
OXON
Tetsworth
Bledlow
Saunderton
Chinnor & Princes Risborough Railway (Icknield Line)
Horsenden
Kingston Stert
Sydenham
Chinnor
Oakley
Redland End
Great Hampden
Prestwood
Great Missenden
South Heath
Frith-hill
Hyde Heath
Adwell
Postcombe
Kingston Blount
Crowell
Loosley Row
Lacey Green
Speen
Aston Rowant
Darvillshill
Saunderton Lee
Crownfield
Rout's Green
Bledlow Ridge
Upper North Dean
Little Kingshill
Little Missenden
South Weston
Lewknor
Radnage
Walters Ash
Great Kingshill
Pyrton
Shirburn
Stokenchurch
The City
Beacon's Bottom
Bradenham
Naphill
Hughenden Valley
Cryers Hill
Holmer Green
Widmer End
Penn Street
Hazlemere
Studley Green
West Wycombe
West Wycombe Park
Downley
Hughenden Manor
Four Ashes
Winchmore Hill
Coleshill
Christmas Common
Ibstone
Piddington
Towerage
Sands
High Wycombe
Terriers
Tylers Green
Penn
Northend
Cadmore End
Bolter End
Wheeler End
Lane End
Booker
Cressex
Micklefield
Wycombe Marsh
Beacon Hill
Knotty Green
Forty Green
Greenfield
Turville Heath
Turville
Fingest
Frieth
Moor Common
Loudwater
Beaconsfield
Pishill
Pishill Bank
Skirmett
Parmoor
Pheasants
Rockwell End
Goddards
Chisbridge Cross
Handy Cross
Marlow Bottom
Burroughs Grove
Wooburn Green
Wooburn
Holtspur
Flackwell Heath
Sheepridge
Well End
BUCKINGHAMSHIRE
CHILTERNS
THE RIDGEWAY PATH
LOWER ICKNIELD WAY
UPPER ICKNIELD WAY
GRAND UNION CANAL
M40
A41
A413
A418
A4010
A4129
A355
102
103
83
65
66
0 1 2 3 miles
0 1 2 3 4 5 km

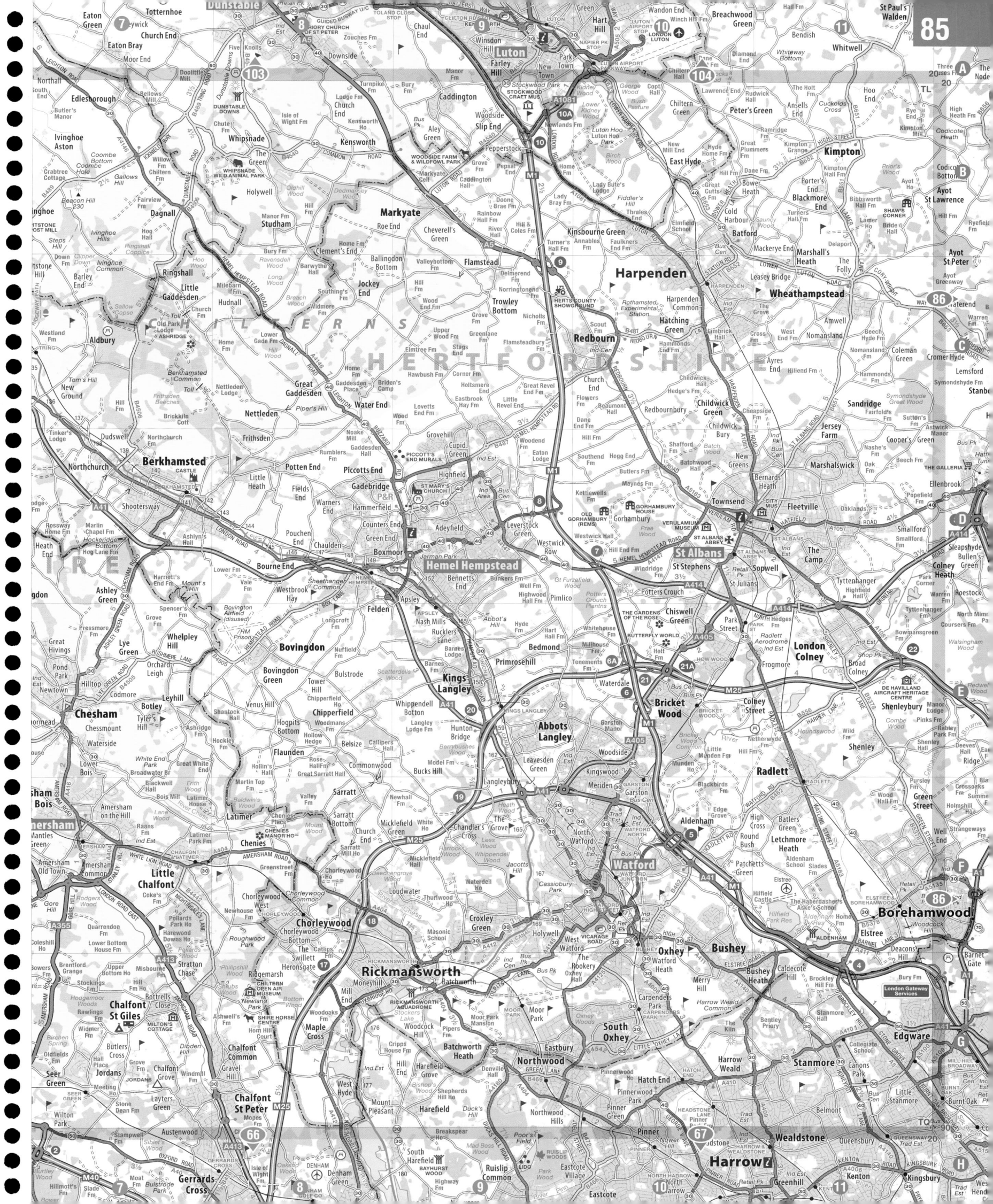
HERTFORDSHIRE
CHILTERNS
Dunstable
Luton
Harpenden
Wheathampstead
Redbourn
Markyate
Caddington
Kensworth
Whipsnade
Studham
Flamstead
Kimpton
Batford
Berkhamsted
Northchurch
Hemel Hempstead
St Albans
Fleetville
London Colney
Kings Langley
Abbots Langley
Bricket Wood
Radlett
Shenley
Watford
Bushey
Oxhey
South Oxhey
Borehamwood
Elstree
Edgware
Stanmore
Harrow
Wealdstone
Pinner
Northwood
Rickmansworth
Chorleywood
Chalfont St Giles
Chalfont St Peter
Little Chalfont
Amersham
Chesham
Bovingdon
Aldbury
Great Gaddesden
Nettleden
Potten End
Leverstock Green
Chiswell Green
St Stephens
Sopwell
Colney Heath
Sandridge
Marshalswick
Ruislip Common
Harefield
Denham
Gerrards Cross
Kenton
Kingsbury
M1
M25
A41
A5
A414
A405
103
104
66
67
86

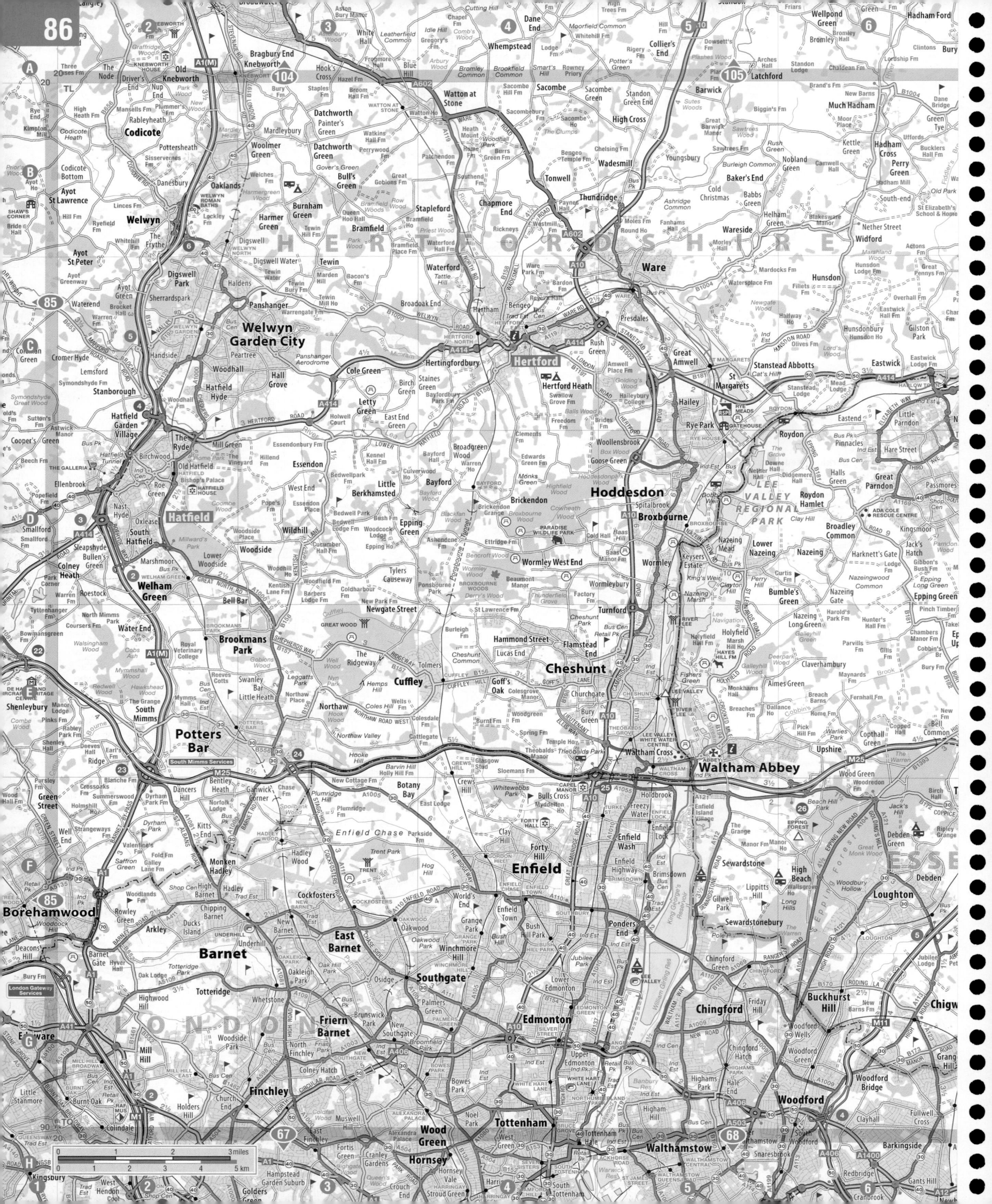

Knebworth
Bragbury End
Old Knebworth
Watton at Stone
Whempstead
Dane End
Collier's End
Latchford
Wellpond Green
Hadham Ford
Bury Green
Codicote
Rableyheath
Datchworth
Datchworth Green
Mardleybury
Woolmer Green
Sacombe
Sacombe Green
High Cross
Barwick
Much Hadham
Standon Green End
Kettle Green
Hadham Cross
Perry Green
Wadesmill
Tonwell
Youngsbury
Baker's End
Nobland Green
Welwyn
Oaklands
Burnham Green
Bull's Green
Stapleford
Chapmore End
Thundridge
Cold Christmas
Babbs Green
Helham Green
Wareside
Widford
Ayot St Lawrence
Ayot St Peter
Harmer Green
Bramfield
Waterford
HERTFORDSHIRE
Digswell
Digswell Water
Digswell Park
Tewin
Ware
Hunsdon
Welwyn Garden City
Panshanger
Sherrardspark
Haldens
Waterend
Broadoak End
Hertingfordbury
Bengeo
Hertford
Presdales
Great Amwell
Stanstead Abbotts
St Margarets
Eastwick
Gilston Park
Hunsdonbury
Cole Green
Letty Green
Birch Green
Hertford Heath
Rush Green
Hailey
Rye Park
Roydon
Little Parndon
Hare Street
Eastend
Hatfield
Hatfield Garden Village
The Ryde
Mill Green
Essendon
Little Berkhamsted
Bayford
Brickendon
Hoddesdon
Broxbourne
Woollensbrook
Goose Green
Great Parndon
Roydon Hamlet
Lee Valley Regional Park
Nast Hyde
Oxlease
South Hatfield
Welham Green
Epping Green
Wormley West End
Wormley
Nazeing
Lower Nazeing
Broadley Common
Harknett's Gate
Epping Long Green
Brookmans Park
Cuffley
Newgate Street
Turnford
Cheshunt
Hammond Street
Goff's Oak
Flamstead End
Waltham Cross
Waltham Abbey
Upshire
Potters Bar
South Mimms
Shenley
Borehamwood
Enfield
Forty Hill
Crews Hill
Botany Bay
Hadley Wood
Monken Hadley
Cockfosters
High Barnet
Barnet
East Barnet
Arkley
Chingford
Sewardstone
High Beach
Loughton
Buckhurst Hill
Chigwell
Edmonton
Southgate
Friern Barnet
Whetstone
Totteridge
Edgware
Mill Hill
Finchley
Tottenham
Walthamstow
Woodford
Wood Green
Hornsey
Kingsbury
Woodford Bridge
Barkingside
LONDON
ESSEX
Enfield Chase
M25
A1(M)
A10
M11
M1
0 1 2 3 miles
0 1 2 3 4 5 km

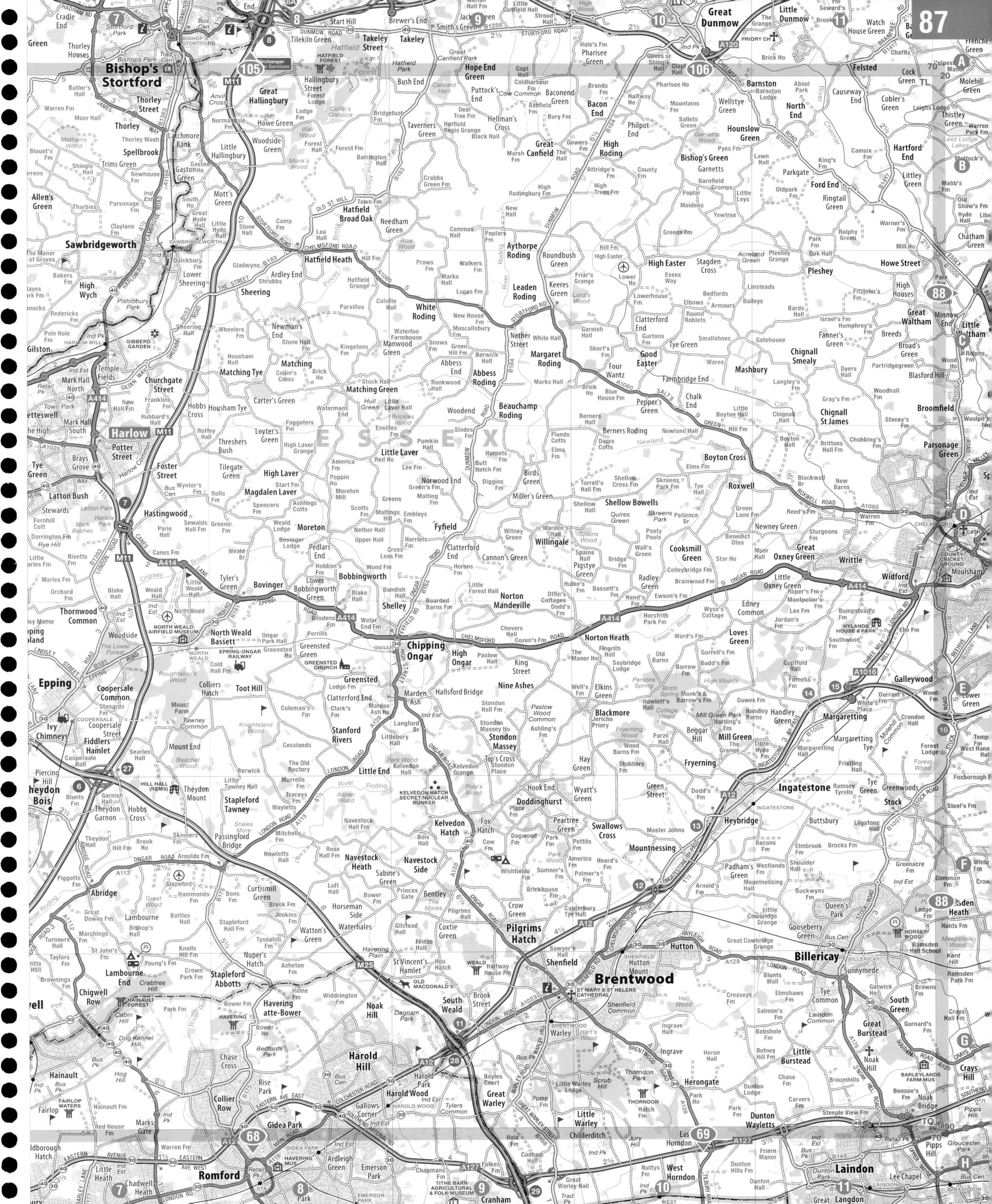
Bishop's Stortford
Great Dunmow
Little Dunmow
Takeley
Takeley Street
Tilekiln Green
Great Canfield
Hatfield Forest
Hatfield Broad Oak
Hatfield Heath
Great Hallingbury
Little Hallingbury
Thorley
Thorley Street
Spellbrook
Sawbridgeworth
High Wych
Sheering
Lower Sheering
Harlow
Potter Street
Churchgate Street
Matching
Matching Tye
Matching Green
Aythorpe Roding
Leaden Roding
White Roding
Abbess Roding
Beauchamp Roding
Margaret Roding
Good Easter
High Easter
Pleshey
High Roding
Felsted
Barnston
Great Waltham
Little Waltham
Chignall Smealy
Chignall St James
Broomfield
Mashbury
Roxwell
Boyton Cross
Writtle
Widford
Chelmsford
Willingale
Fyfield
Moreton
Bobbingworth
Shelley
Chipping Ongar
High Ongar
Norton Mandeville
Norton Heath
Little Laver
High Laver
Magdalen Laver
Foster Street
Hastingwood
North Weald Bassett
Epping
Coopersale Common
Toot Hill
Stanford Rivers
Greensted
Marden Ash
Blackmore
Stondon Massey
Doddinghurst
Kelvedon Hatch
Navestock Heath
Navestock Side
Fryerning
Ingatestone
Mill Green
Margaretting
Galleywood
Stock
Mountnessing
Hutton
Shenfield
Brentwood
Billericay
Pilgrims Hatch
South Weald
Harold Hill
Harold Wood
Gidea Park
Romford
Havering-atte-Bower
Stapleford Abbotts
Stapleford Tawney
Abridge
Lambourne End
Chigwell Row
Hainault
Collier Row
Noak Hill
Great Warley
Little Warley
Herongate
Ingrave
Dunton Wayletts
Little Burstead
Great Burstead
Laindon
West Horndon
Cranham
Theydon Bois
Ivy Chimneys
Fiddlers Hamlet
ESSEX
M11
M25
A12
A414
A127
A120

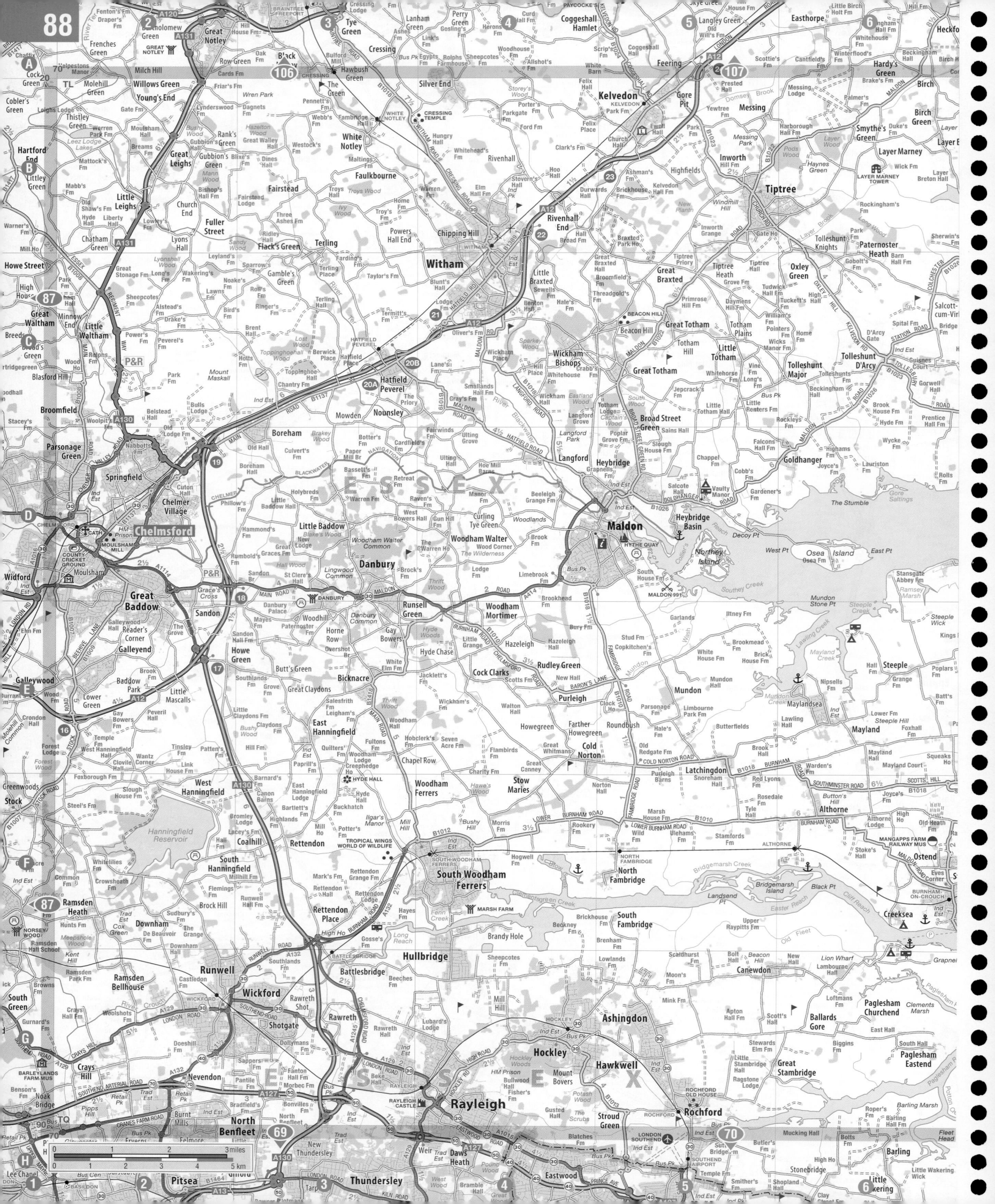
Great Notley
Tye Green
Cressing
Coggeshall Hamlet
Feering
Kelvedon
Messing
Tiptree
Layer Marney
Silver End
White Notley
Faulkbourne
Terling
Witham
Rivenhall
Little Leighs
Fuller Street
Great Leighs
Fairstead
Great Braxted
Little Braxted
Wickham Bishops
Great Totham
Little Totham
Tolleshunt Major
Tolleshunt D'Arcy
Great Waltham
Little Waltham
Broomfield
Springfield
Chelmer Village
Chelmsford
Moulsham
Great Baddow
Boreham
Hatfield Peverel
Nounsley
Langford
Heybridge
Heybridge Basin
Maldon
Northey Island
Osea Island
Goldhanger
Little Baddow
Danbury
Woodham Walter
Sandon
Runsell Green
Woodham Mortimer
Hazeleigh
Purleigh
Cock Clarks
Galleywood
Bicknacre
East Hanningfield
West Hanningfield
Hanningfield Reservoir
Stock
Woodham Ferrers
Stow Maries
Cold Norton
Latchingdon
Mundon
Maylandsea
Mayland
Steeple
Althorne
South Woodham Ferrers
North Fambridge
South Fambridge
Creeksea
Rettendon
Rettendon Place
Runwell
Wickford
Shotgate
Battlesbridge
Hullbridge
Rawreth
Canewdon
Ashingdon
Hockley
Hawkwell
Rochford
Rayleigh
Paglesham Churchend
Paglesham Eastend
Great Stambridge
Ballards Gore
Barling
Crays Hill
Nevendon
North Benfleet
Pitsea
Thundersley
Eastwood
Ramsden Heath
Ramsden Bellhouse
Downham
ESSEX
0 1 2 3 miles
0 1 2 3 4 5 km

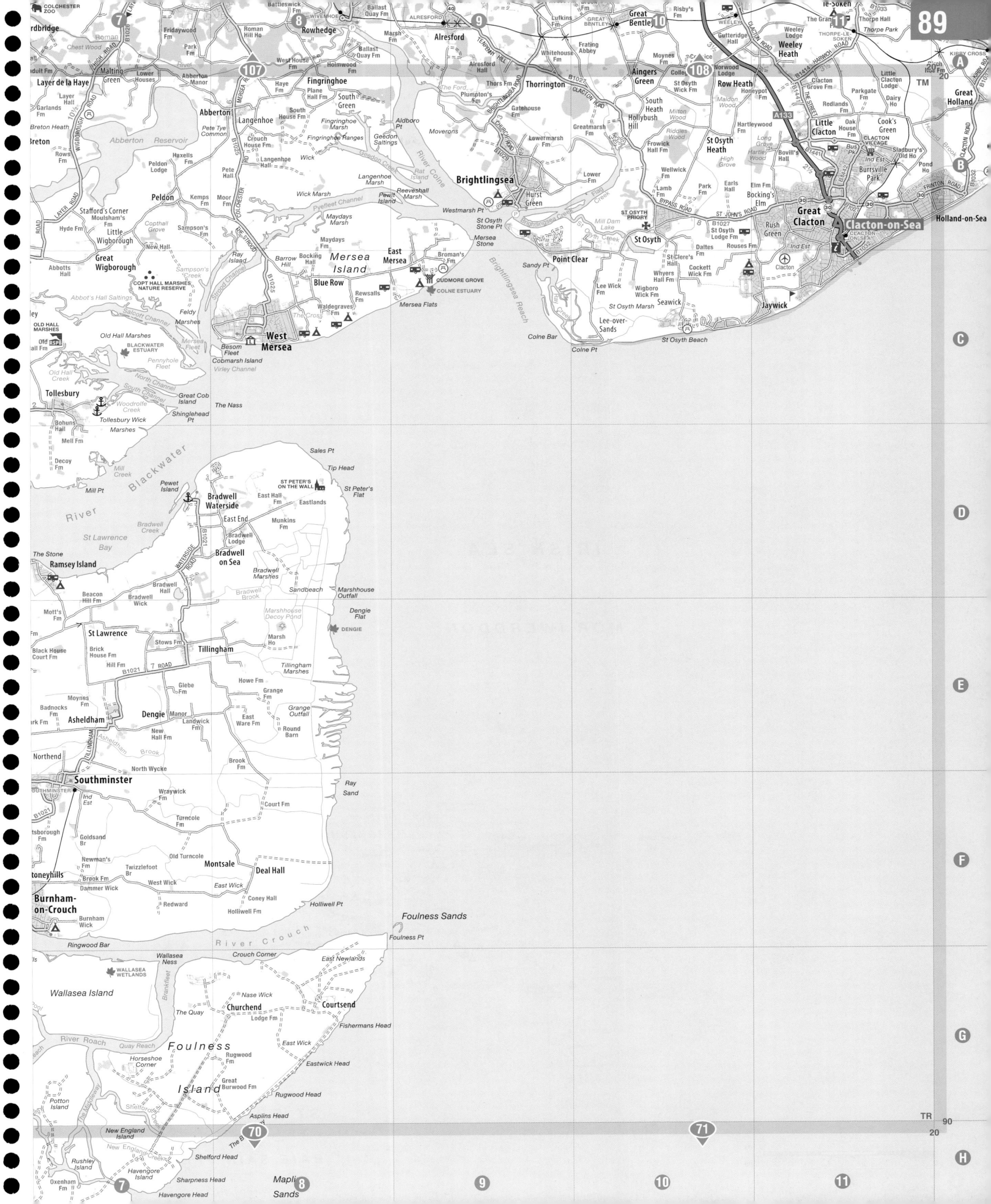

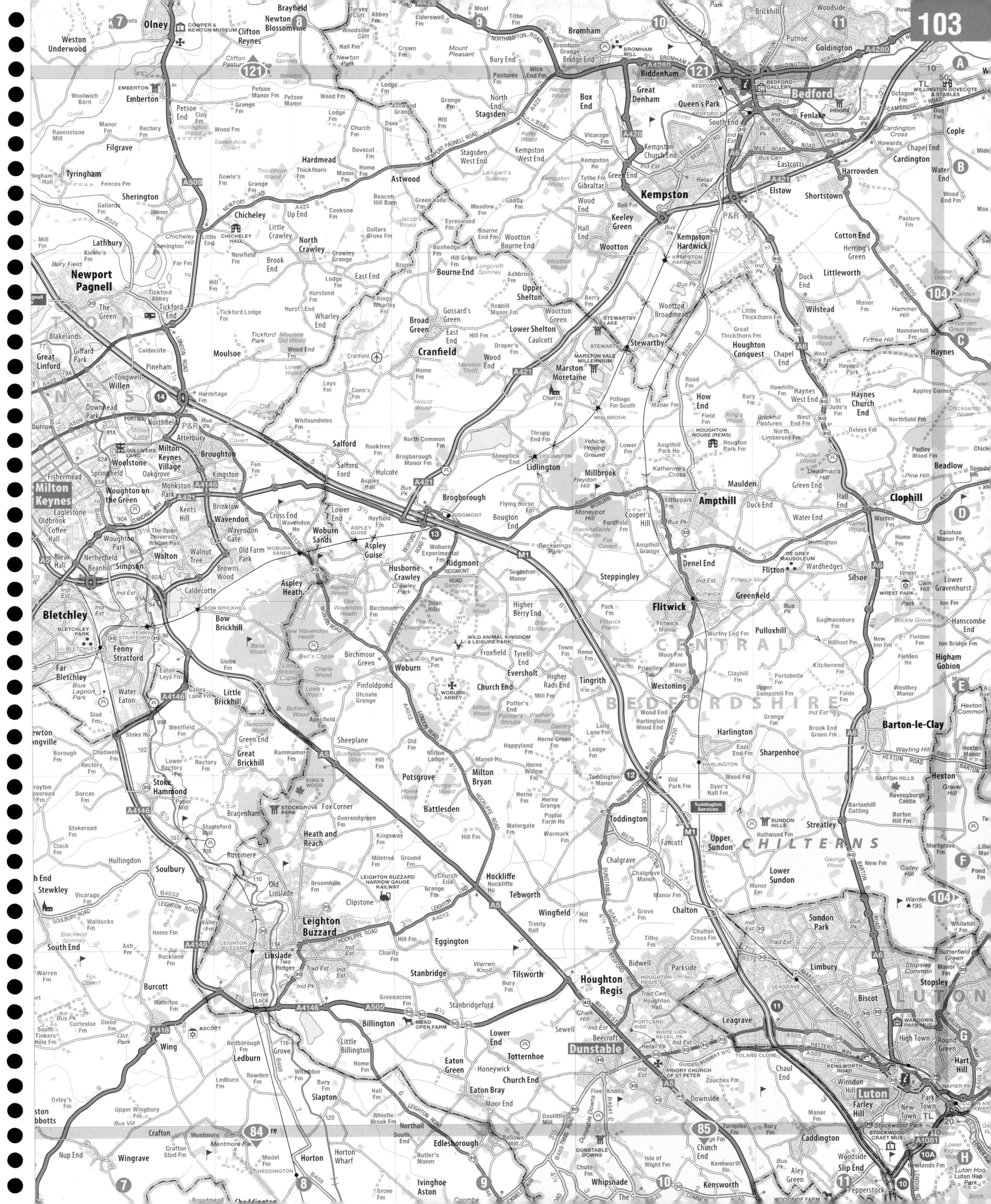
Olney
Weston Underwood
Emberton
Newton Blossomville
Clifton Reynes
Brayfield
Turvey
Bromham
Biddenham
Bedford
Putnoe
Goldington
Renhold
Great Denham
Queen's Park
Fenlake
Kempston
Elstow
Cardington
Cople
Harrowden
Shortstown
Filgrave
Tyringham
Sherington
Chicheley
Hardmead
Astwood
Stagsden
North Crawley
Lathbury
Newport Pagnell
Cranfield
Wootton
Kempston Hardwick
Wilstead
Cotton End
Haynes
Stewartby
Marston Moretaine
Lower Shelton
Upper Shelton
Moulsoe
Great Linford
Willen
Milton Keynes Village
Broughton
Kingston
Salford
Brogborough
Lidlington
Ridgmont
Millbrook
Ampthill
Maulden
Clophill
Houghton Conquest
Woughton on the Green
Wavendon
Woburn Sands
Aspley Guise
Aspley Heath
Husborne Crawley
Milton Keynes
Bletchley
Fenny Stratford
Far Bletchley
Bow Brickhill
Little Brickhill
Woburn
Birchmoor Green
Eversholt
Steppingley
Flitwick
Flitton
Silsoe
Pulloxhill
Westoning
Tingrith
Harlington
Sharpenhoe
Barton-le-Clay
Toddington
Great Brickhill
Stoke Hammond
Potsgrove
Milton Bryan
Battlesden
Heath and Reach
Soulbury
Stewkley
Leighton Buzzard
Linslade
Hockliffe
Tebworth
Chalton
Chalgrave
Upper Sundon
Lower Sundon
Streatley
Sundon Park
Limbury
Leagrave
Luton
Houghton Regis
Dunstable
Tilsworth
Stanbridge
Eggington
Billington
Wing
Ledburn
Slapton
Eaton Bray
Edlesborough
Totternhoe
Kensworth
Caddington
Whipsnade
Ivinghoe Aston
Wingrave
CENTRAL BEDFORDSHIRE
CHILTERNS
M1
A5
A6
A421
A428
A507
A4146

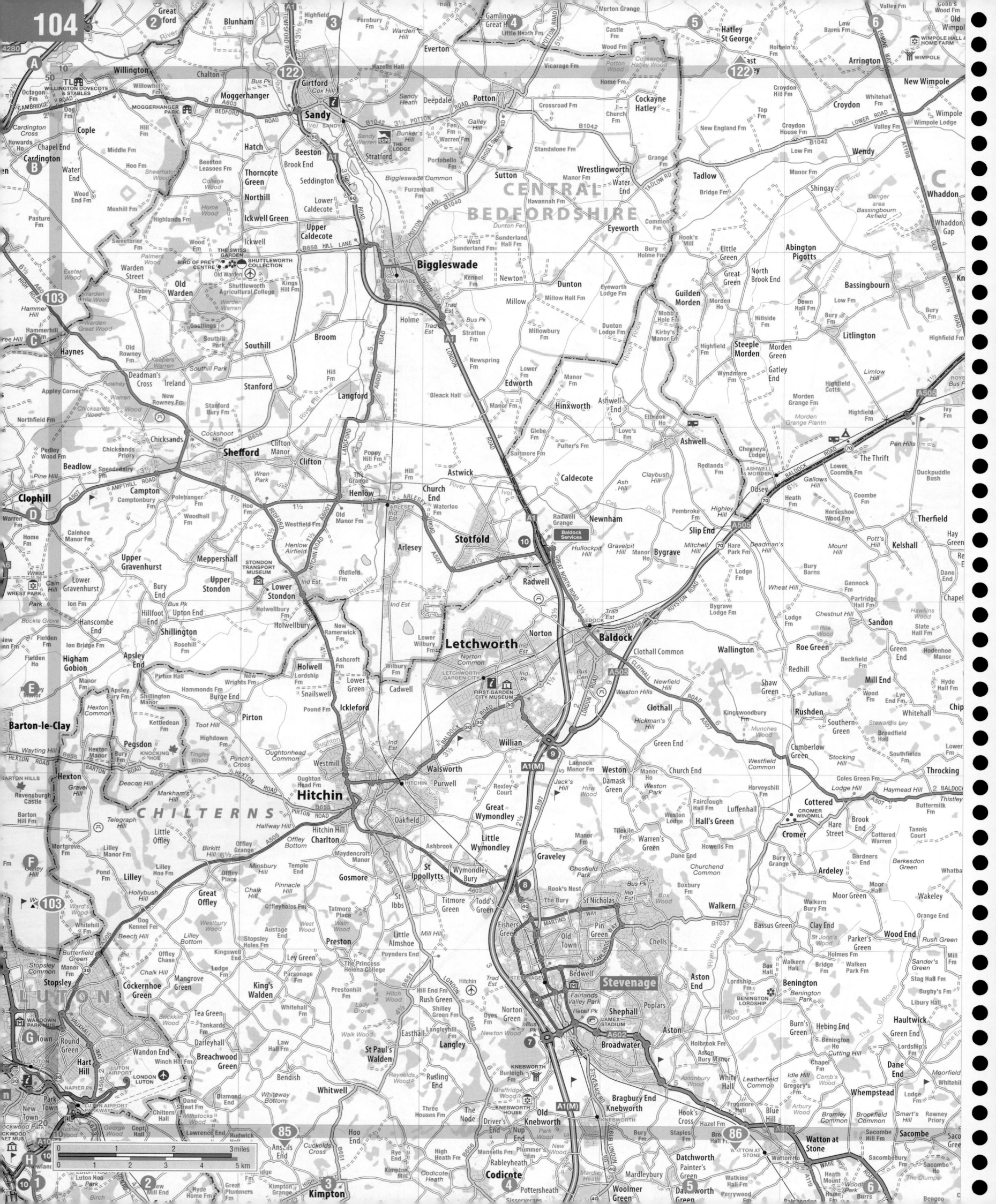

Great Barford
Blunham
Tempsford Road
Highfield Fm
Fernbury Fm
Warden Hill
Everton
Gamlingay Great Heath
Little Heath Fm
Potton Road
Merton Grange
Castle Fm
Wood Fm
Potton Wood
Cockayne Hatley Wood
Hatley St George
East Hatley
Low Barns Fm
Valley Fm
Cobb's Wood Fm
Old Wimpole
Wimpole Hall & Home Farm
Wimpole
Arrington
Ermine Way
Willington
Willington Dovecote & Stables
Chalton
Moggerhanger
Moggerhanger Park
Girtford
Cox Hill
Sandy
Hazells Hall
Sandy Heath
Deepdale
Potton
Home Fm
Vicarage Fm
Crossroad Fm
Cockayne Hatley
Church Fm
Holbein's Fm
Croydon Hill Fm
Croydon
Whitehall Fm
New Wimpole
Wimpole Lodge
Octagon Fm
Cambridge Road
Cardington Cross
Howards Ho
Cople
Chapel End
Cardington
Hatch
Beeston
Beeston Leasoes Fm
Brook End
Thorncote Green
Sandy Warren
RSPB The Lodge
Bunker's Hill
Warren Fm
Fen Fm
Galley Hill
Stratford
Portobello Fm
Biggleswade Road
Standalone Fm
Top Fm
New England Fm
Croydon House Fm
Valley Fm
Lower Road
Low Fm
Wendy
Middle Fm
Hoo Fm
Sheerhatch Wood
College Wood
Seddington
Biggleswade Common
Furzenhall Fm
Sutton
Wrestlingworth
Manor Fm
Water End
Tadlow Road
Grange Fm
Tadlow
Bridge Fm
Manor Fm
Shingay
Whaddon
Water End
Wood End Fm
Northill
Home Wood
Lower Caldecote
Moxhill Fm
Highlands Fm
Ickwell Green
Upper Caldecote
Central Bedfordshire
Havannah Fm
Dunton Fen
Common Fm
Danger area Bassingbourn Airfield
Whaddon Gap
Pasture Fm
Sweetbrier Fm
Wood Fm
Ickwell
The Swiss Garden
Shuttleworth Collection
Bird of Prey Centre
Old Warden
Hill Lane
Sunderland Hall Fm
West Sunderland Fm
Eyeworth
Bury Holme Fm
Hook's Mill
Little Green
Abington Pigotts
Exeter Wood
Warden Street
Palmers Wood
Biggleswade
Kennel Fm
Newton
Dunton
Eyeworth Lodge Fm
Guilden Morden
Great Green
North Brook End
Bassingbourn
Old Warden
Shuttleworth Agricultural College
Kings Hill Fm
Abbey Fm
Warden Warren
Millow
Millow Hall Fm
Morden Ho
Down Hall Fm
Low Fm
Bury Fm
Hammer Hill
Warden Little Wood
Warden Great Wood
Holme
Trad Est
Bus Pk
Stratton Fm
Millowbury Fm
Dunton Lodge Fm
Mobb's Hole Fm
Kirby's Manor Fm
Hillside Fm
Hammerhill Fm
Haynes
Gastlings
Southill Park
Southill
Broom
Highfield Fm
Steeple Morden
Morden Green
Litlington
Highfield Fm
Old Rowney Fm
Keepers Warren
Southill Park
Newspring Fm
Lower Fm
Gatley End
Wyndmere Fm
Limlow Hill
Deadman's Cross
Ireland
Stanford
Hill Fm
Edworth
Manor Fm
Ashwell End
Highfield Cotts
Apply Corner
Rowney Warren
New Rowney Fm
Langford
Bleack Hall
Hinxworth
Morden Grange Fm
Morden Grange Plantn
Highfield Fm
Chicksands Wood
Stanford Bury Fm
Manor Fm
Elbrook Ho
Ashwell
Pen Hills
Northfield Fm
Cockshoot Hill
Chicksands
Clifton Manor
Poppy Hill Fm
Glebe Fm
Pulter's Fm
Love's Fm
Cheyneys Lodge
Lower Coombe Fm
The Thrift
Pedley Wood Fm
Chicksands Priory
Shefford
Clifton
Saltmore Fm
Redlands Fm
Ashwell & Morden
Duckpuddle Bush
Beadlow
Pine Hill
Speedsearly
Ampthill Road
Campton
Wren Park
The Grange
Hill Fm
Astwick
Caldecote
Ash Hill
Claybush Hill
Odsey
Gallows Hill
Clophill
Camptonbury Fm
Polehanger Fm
Henlow
Arlesey Road
Church End
Waterloo Fm
Heath Fm
Coombe Fm
Woodhall Fm
Hoo Fm
Westfield Fm
Old Manor Fm
Radwell Grange
Newnham
Pembroke Fm
Highley Hill
Horseshoe Wood Fm
Therfield
Cainhoe Manor Fm
Henlow Airfield
Hitchin Road
Stotfold
Baldock Services
Slip End
Home Fm
Arlesey
Hullockpit Hill
Gravelpit Hill
Manor Ho
Bygrave
Mitchell Hill
Hare Park Fm
Deadman's Hill
Mount Hill
Pott's Hill
Kelshall
Hay Green
Upper Gravenhurst
Meppershall
Stondon Transport Museum
Oldfield Fm
Radwell
Great North Road
Lodge Fm
Bury Barns
Dane End
Wrest Park
Lower Gravenhurst
Upper Stondon
Lower Stondon
Bury End
Ind Est
River Hiz
Wheat Hill
Gannock Fm
Partridge Hall Fm
Chapel
Ion Fm
Bus Pk
Upton End
Hillfoot End
Holwellbury Fm
Ind Est
Trad Est
Royston Road
Bygrave Lodge Fm
Chestnut Hill
Hawkins Wood
Buckle Grove
Hanscombe End
Holwellbury
New Ramerwick Fm
Lower Wilbury Fm
Letchworth
Norton
Baldock
Lodge Fm
Roe Wood
Sandon
Slate Hall Fm
Fielden Fm
Ion Bridge Fm
Shillington
Rosehill Fm
Ashcroft Fm
Norton Common
Ind Est
Clothall Common
Wallington
Roe Green
Green End
Hodenhoe Manor
Higham Gobion
Apsley End
Holwell
Lordship Fm
Lower Green
Wilbury Fm
Letchworth Garden City
First Garden City Museum
Ind Pk
Bus Cen
London Road
Newfield Hill
Weston Hills
Redhill
Beckfield Fm
Mill End
Hyde Hall Fm
Pirton Hall
New Wrights Fm
Cadwell
Clothall
Shaw Green
Julians
Wood Fm
Lye End Fm
Apsley Bury Fm
Hammonds Fm
Burge End
Snailswell
Hickman's Hill
Kingswoodbury Fm
Munches Wood
Whitehall
Chip
Hexton Common
Shillington Manor
Pound Fm
Ickleford
Rushden
Southern Green
Steward's Ley
Broadfield Hall
Barton-le-Clay
Kettledean Fm
Pirton
Green End
Toot Hill
Willian
Highdown Fm
Pegsdon
Knocking Hoe
Tingley Wood
Oughtonhead Common
Westfield Common
Cumberlow Green
Southfields Fm
Stocking Hill
Lower
Waylting Hill
Hexton Manor
Bury Fm
Punch's Cross
Westmill
Walsworth
Lannock Manor Fm
Weston
Church End
Throcking
Hexton Road
Barton Road
Deacon Hill
Hexton
Gravel Hill
Oughton Head Fm
Hitchin
Purwell
Roxley Court
Jack's Hill
Weston Park
Damask Green
Harveyshill Fm
Coles Green Fm
Lodge Hill
Haymead Hill
Baldock
Thistley
Barton Hills
Ravensburgh Castle
Markham's Hill
Chilterns
Pirton Road
Great Wymondley
Faircough Hall Fm
Luffenhall
Weston Lodge
Hall's Green
Cottered
Cromer Windmill
Buttermilk Fm
Barton Hill Fm
Telegraph Hill
Halfway Hill
Hitchin Hill
Oakfield
Charlton
Little Wymondley
Tilekiln Fm
Warren's Green
Cromer
Hare Street
Brook End
Cottered Warren
Tannis Court
Mortgrove Fm
Little Offley
Birkitt Hill
Offley Grange
Offley Bottom
Maydencroft Manor
Ashbrook
Manor Fm
Howells Fm
Dane End
Bury Grange
Gardners End
Berkesdon Green
Lilley Manor Fm
Minsbury Hill
Temple End
St Ippollytts
Wymondley Bury
Graveley
Chesfield Park
Churchend Common
Ardeley
Pond Fm
Lilley
Lilley Hoo Fm
Offley Place
Gosmore
Rook's Nest
Boxbury Fm
Moor Hall
Hollybush Hill
Great Offley
Chalk Hill
Pinnacle Hill
St Ibbs
Titmore Green
Todd's Green
The Bury
St Nicholas
Bus Pk
Ind Est
Box Wood
Moor Green
Wakeley
Offleyholes Fm
Tatmore Place
Wain Wood
Fishers Green
Martins Way
Walkern
Walkern Bury Fm
Orange End
Dog Kennel Fm
Westbury Wood
West Wood
Old Town
Pin Green
Bassus Green
Clay End
Wood End
Whitehill Fm
Beech Hill
Little Bottom
Stopsley Holes Fm
Austage End
Preston
Little Almshoe
Mill Hill
Chells
St John's Wood
Parker's Green
Rush Green
Butterfield Green
Offley Chase
Kingswell End
Ley Green
Poynders End
Holmes Fm
Mill Fm
Stopsley Common
Chalk Hill
Lodge Fm
The Princess Helena College
Fairlands Way
Box Hall
Walkern Hall
Bridge Fm
Walkern Park Fm
Sander's Green
Stopsley
Manor Fm
Cockernhoe Green
Mangrove Green
King's Walden
Parsonage Fm
Prestonhill Fm
Hill End Fm
Rush Green
Hitchin
Trad Est
Stevenage
Bedwell
Aston End
Lordship Fm
Benington
Benington Park
Stag Hall Fm
Bugby's Fm
Luton
Warden Hill
Whitehall Fm
Hitch Wood
Lady Grove
Shilley Green Fm
Fairlands Valley Park
Shephall
Poplars
Benington Lordship
Libury Hall
Wardown Park Mus
Vauxhall Way
Tea Green
Tankards Fm
Brickkiln Wood
Walk Wood
Langleyhill Fm
Dyes Fm
Norton Green
Retail Pk
Lamex Stadium
Hitch Wood
Burn's Green
Hebing End
Haultwick
Round Green
Darleyhall
Eastahall
Langley
Newton Wood
Bus Pk
A602
Broadwater
Aston
Holbrook Fm
Benington Ho
Cutting Hill
Green End
Hart Hill
Wandon End
Law Hall Fm
St Paul's Walden
Aston Bury Manor
Lordship's Fm
Breachwood Green
Winch Hill Fm
Luton Airport
London Luton
Bendish
Rusling End
Knebworth Park
Burleigh Fm
Chapel Fm
Idle Hill
Gregory's Fm
Comb's Wood
Dane End
Moorfield
Whitehill
Napier Pk
Park Town
New Town
Whitewoy Bottom
Diamond End
Whitwell
Reynolds Wood
Graffridge Wood
Knebworth House
Bragbury End
Knebworth
Astonbury Wood
White Hall
Leatherfield Common
Frogmore Hall
Arbury Wood
Whempstead
Lodge Fm
Luton Airport Parkway
Dane Street Fm
Withstocks Wood
Chiltern Hall
George Wood
Three Houses Fm
The Node
Driver's End
Old Knebworth
Hook's Cross
Hazel Fm
Blue Hill
Bromley Common
Brookfield Common
Smart's Hill
Rowney Priory
Copt Hall
Lawrence End
Rudwick Hall
Ansells End
Cuckolds Cross
Hoo End
Rye End
High Heath Fm
Nup End
Mansells Fm
Plummer's Fm
New Wood
Park Wood
Bury Fm
Staples Fm
Watton at Stone
Sacombe
Sacombe Hill Fm
Sacombe Green
Kimpton Mill
Codicote Heath
Rableyheath
Datchworth
Painter's Green
Watton Ho
Ware Road
Sacombebury Fm
Sacombe Ho
Heath Mount Sch
Woodhall Park
The Clumps
Luton Hoo
Mill End
Hyde
Hyde Home Fm
Great Plummers Fm
Kimpton Grange
Kimpton
Codicote
Pottersheath
Mardley Heath
Mardleybury
Woolmer Green
Datchworth
Watkins Hall Fm
Perrywood
Burrs
Begoon
0 1 2 3 miles
0 1 2 3 4 5 km

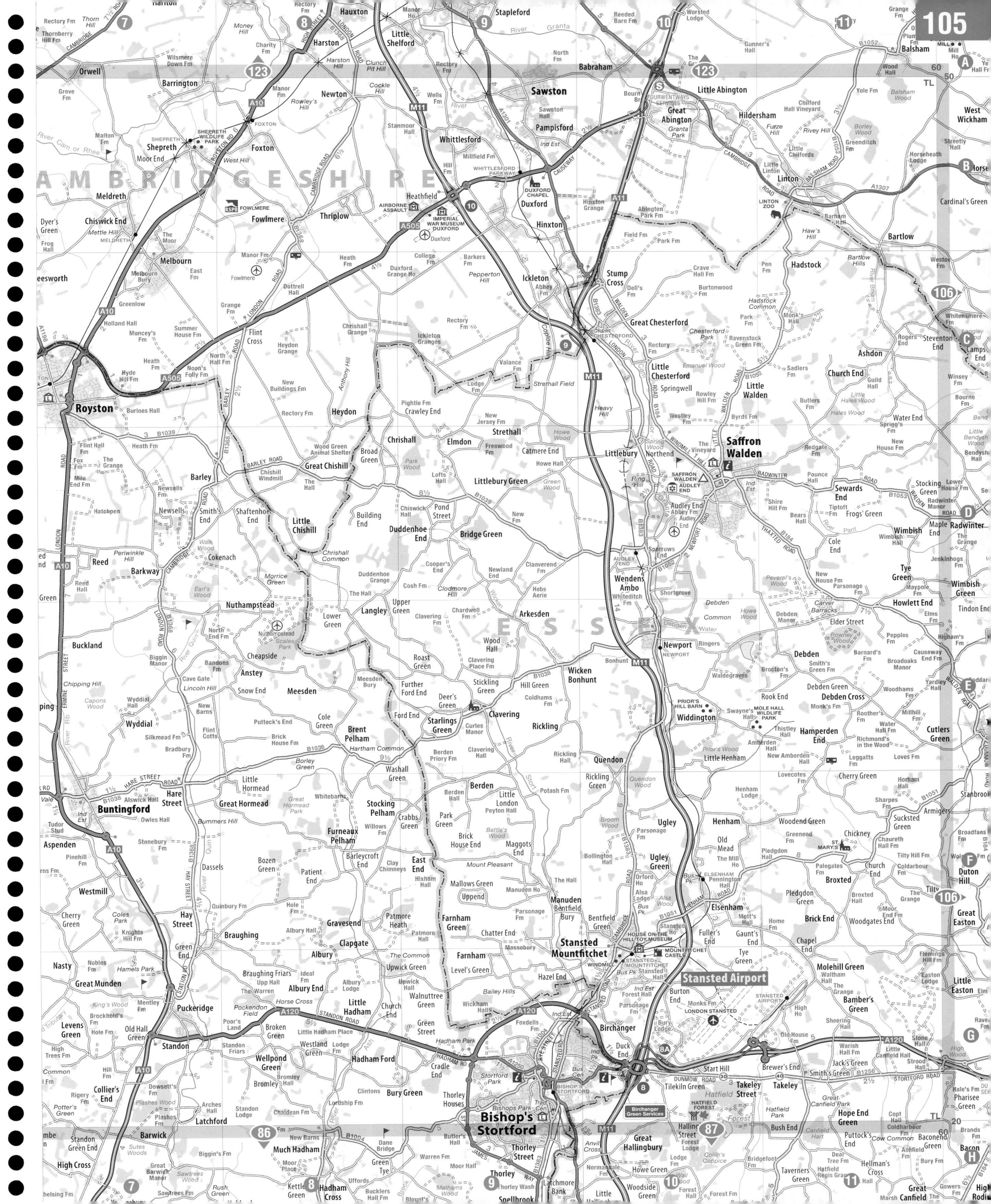
CAMBRIDGESHIRE
ESSEX
Stapleford
Hauxton
Little Shelford
Harston
Orwell
Barrington
Newton
Babraham
Sawston
Little Abington
Great Abington
Hildersham
Balsham
West Wickham
Shepreth
Foxton
Whittlesford
Pampisford
Meldreth
Fowlmere
Thriplow
Heathfield
Duxford
Hinxton
Linton
Cardinal's Green
Chiswick End
Melbourn
Ickleton
Stump Cross
Hadstock
Bartlow
Great Chesterford
Little Chesterford
Ashdon
Church End
Royston
Heydon
Chrishall
Elmdon
Strethall
Littlebury
Saffron Walden
Little Walden
Springwell
Great Chishill
Barley
Littlebury Green
Audley End
Sewards End
Radwinter
Wimbish
Little Chishill
Duddenhoe End
Bridge Green
Reed
Barkway
Cokenach
Wendens Ambo
Nuthampstead
Langley
Arkesden
Newport
Debden
Howlett End
Buckland
Anstey
Meesden
Wicken Bonhunt
Clavering
Starlings Green
Wyddial
Brent Pelham
Rickling
Widdington
Hamperden End
Cutlers Green
Debden Cross
Quendon
Little Henham
Buntingford
Hare Street
Great Hormead
Stocking Pelham
Berden
Henham
Ugley
Ugley Green
Aspenden
Furneaux Pelham
East End
Broxted
Westmill
Manuden
Elsenham
Hay Street
Braughing
Gravesend
Clapgate
Farnham Green
Farnham
Stansted Mountfitchet
Stansted Airport
Albury
Albury End
Molehill Green
Little Easton
Great Munden
Nasty
Puckeridge
Little Hadham
Birchanger
Levens Green
Standon
Hadham Ford
Takeley
Takeley Street
Bishop's Stortford
Thorley Street
Great Hallingbury
Barwick
Latchford
Much Hadham
High Cross
Hatfield Forest
Great Canfield
M11
A10
A505
A120
A11
A1307
B1368
B1383
B1039
B1038
B1036
B1051
B1052
B1053
B1256
B1004
123
86
87
106

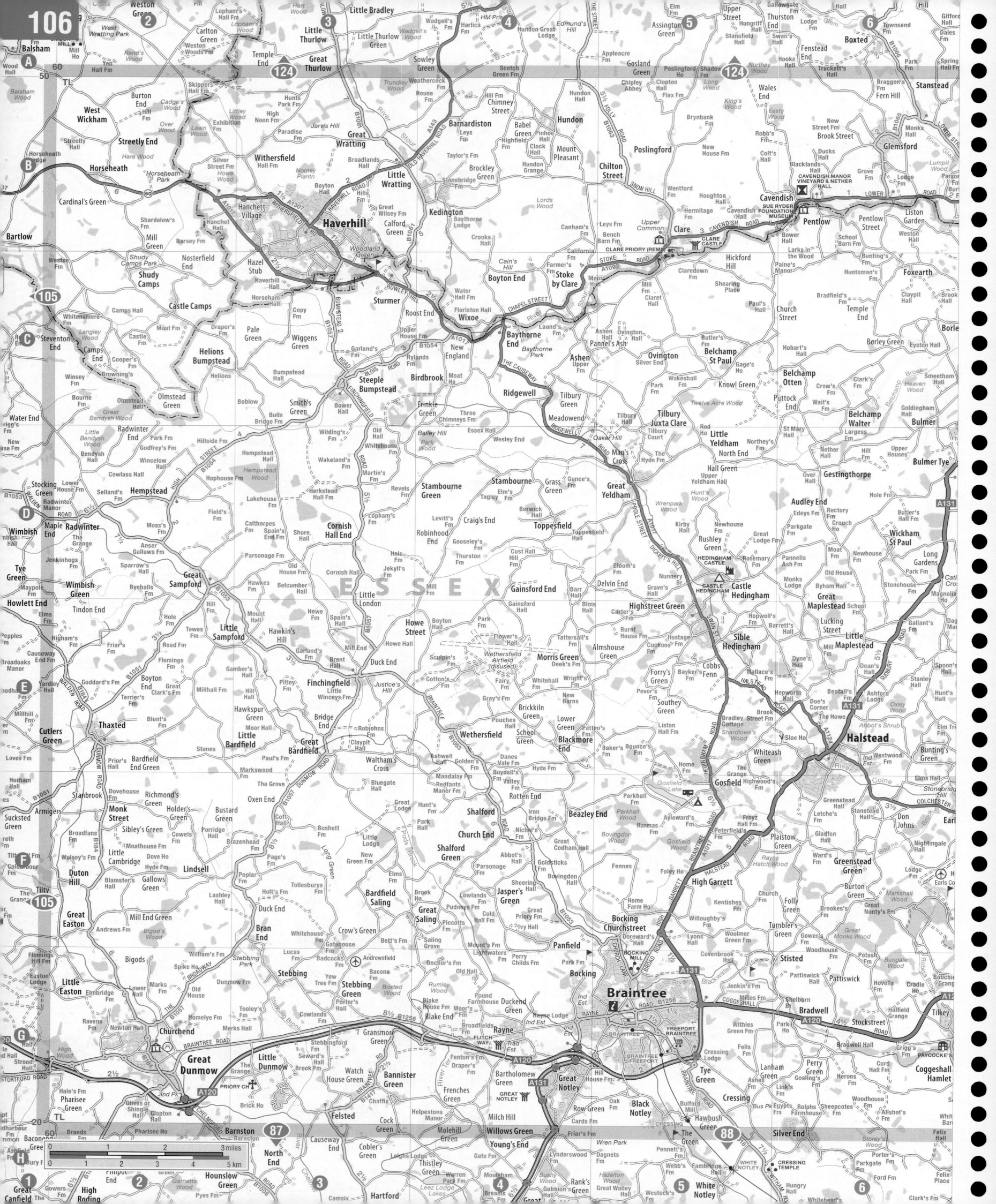
Balsham
Weston Green
Little Bradley
Little Thurlow
Great Thurlow
Carlton Green
Temple End
Sowley Green
Hundon Great Lodge
Assington Green
Upper Street
Thurston End
Boxted
124
West Wickham
Burton End
Streetly End
Withersfield
Great Wratting
Little Wratting
Barnardiston
Chimney Street
Babel Green
Hundon
Chilton Street
Poslingford
Glemsford
Horseheath
Cardinal's Green
Hanchett Village
Haverhill
Kedington
Calford Green
Brockley Green
Mount Pleasant
Wentford
Houghton Hall
Cavendish
CAVENDISH MANOR VINEYARD & NETHER HALL
SUE RYDER FOUNDATION MUSEUM
Pentlow
Pentlow Street
Liston Garden
Bartlow
Shudy Camps
Hazel Stub
Nosterfield End
Clare
CLARE PRIORY (REMS)
CLARE CASTLE
Hickford Hill
Boyton End
Stoke by Clare
Foxearth
105
Castle Camps
Sturmer
Roost End
Wixoe
Water Hall Fm
Church Street
Temple End
Steventon End
Camps End
Pale Green
Helions Bumpstead
Wiggens Green
New England
Baythorne End
Ashen
Ovington
Belchamp St Paul
Borley Green
Steeple Bumpstead
Birdbrook
Ridgewell
Tilbury Green
Belchamp Otten
Knowl Green
Puttock End
Olmstead Green
Smith's Green
Frinkle Green
Meadowend
Tilbury Juxta Clare
Belchamp Walter
Bulmer
Water End
Radwinter End
Little Yeldham
North End
Bulmer Tye
Stocking Green
Hempstead
Stambourne Green
Stambourne
Grass Green
Great Yeldham
Gestingthorpe
Audley End
Wimbish
Radwinter
Cornish Hall End
Robinhood End
Toppesfield
Craig's End
Rushley Green
Wickham St Paul
Tye Green
Great Sampford
ESSEX
Little London
Gainsford End
Delvin End
HEDINGHAM CASTLE
Castle Hedingham
Long Gardens
Wimbish Green
Howlett End
Tindon End
Highstreet Green
Great Maplestead
Little Sampford
Hawkin's Hill
Howe Street
Almshouse Green
Sible Hedingham
Lucking Street
Little Maplestead
Morris Green
Duck End
Finchingfield
Forry's Green
Cobbs Fenn
Boyton End
Thaxted
Cutlers Green
Hawkspur Green
Bridge End
Brickkiln Green
Lower Green
Southey Green
Little Bardfield
Great Bardfield
Wethersfield
School Green
Blackmore End
Halstead
Whiteash Green
Richmond's Green
Holder's Green
Bustard Green
Oxen End
Waltham's Cross
Gosfield
Stanbrook
Armigers
Monk Street
Sibley's Green
Shalford
Beazley End
Church End
Suckstead Green
Little Cambridge
Duton Hill
Lindsell
Gallows Green
Shalford Green
Greenstead Green
High Garrett
Plaistow Green
Tilty
Great Easton
Mill End Green
Duck End
Bardfield Saling
Jasper's Green
Great Saling
Bocking Churchstreet
Folly Green
Burton Green
Bran End
Crow's Green
Panfield
Tumbler's Green
Bigods
Stebbing
Stebbing Green
Bocking
Stisted
Pattiswick
Little Easton
Braintree
Bradwell
Stockstreet
Tilkey
Churchend
Great Dunmow
Little Dunmow
Gransmore Green
Rayne
Duckend Green
Blake End
FREEPORT BRAINTREE
Bannister Green
Watch House Green
Bartholomew Green
Great Notley
Tye Green
Lanham Green
Perry Green
Coggeshall Hamlet
Pharisee Green
Felsted
Frenches Green
Black Notley
Cressing
Milch Hill
Hawbush Green
Barnston
87
Willows Green
Silver End
88
Causeway End
North End
Young's End
The Green
Great Canfield
High Roding
Hounslow Green
Hartford
White Notley
CRESSING TEMPLE
0 1 2 3 miles
0 1 2 3 4 5 km

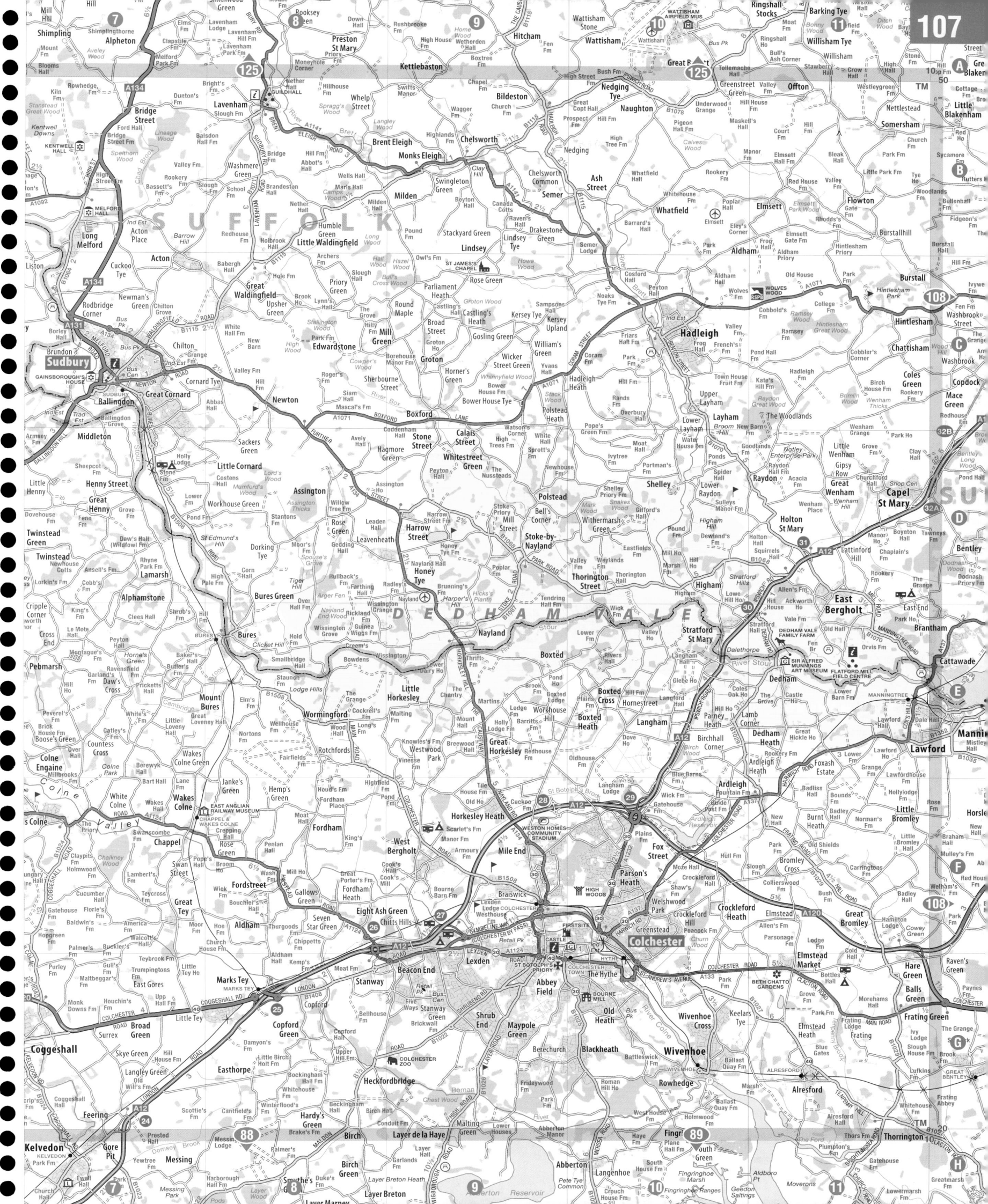
SUFFOLK
DEDHAM VALE
Sudbury
Colchester
Hadleigh
Lavenham
Long Melford
Coggeshall
Kelvedon
Wivenhoe
Alresford
Lawford
Dedham
East Bergholt
Capel St Mary
Ardleigh
Nayland
Boxford
Bures
Great Cornard
Ballingdon
Acton
Chelsworth
Monks Eleigh
Brent Eleigh
Kettlebaston
Bildeston
Hitcham
Wattisham
Nedging Tye
Naughton
Whatfield
Elmsett
Offton
Somersham
Little Blakenham
Aldham
Burstall
Hintlesham
Chattisham
Washbrook
Copdock
Raydon
Layham
Shelley
Polstead
Stoke-by-Nayland
Higham
Stratford St Mary
Langham
Boxted
Great Horkesley
Little Horkesley
Wormingford
Mount Bures
Wakes Colne
Colne Engaine
Chappel
Fordham
West Bergholt
Aldham
Marks Tey
Stanway
Lexden
Copford
Eight Ash Green
Mile End
Fox Street
Parson's Heath
Elmstead Market
Frating Green
Great Bromley
Little Bromley
Abberton
Layer de la Haye
Birch
Messing
Feering
Heckfordbridge
Rowhedge
Thorrington
Mistley
Manningtree
Brantham
Bentley
Holton St Mary
Great Wenham
Assington
Newton
Edwardstone
Groton
Milden
Lindsey
Kersey
Semer
Little Waldingfield
Great Waldingfield
Chilton
Middleton
Henny Street
Lamarsh
Alphamstone
Pebmarsh
Twinstead
Shimpling
Alpheton
Preston St Mary
Nedging
Ash Street
Flowton
Cattawade
Colchester Zoo
Abberton Reservoir
River Stour
River Colne
Colne Valley
A12
A120
A134
A131
A1071
A1141
A137
A133
B1508
B1068
B1070
B1029
B1027
B1025
B1026
B1022
B1024
B1115
B1078
B1087
125
108
88
89
7
8
9
10
11
24
25
26
27
28
29
30
31
32A
32B

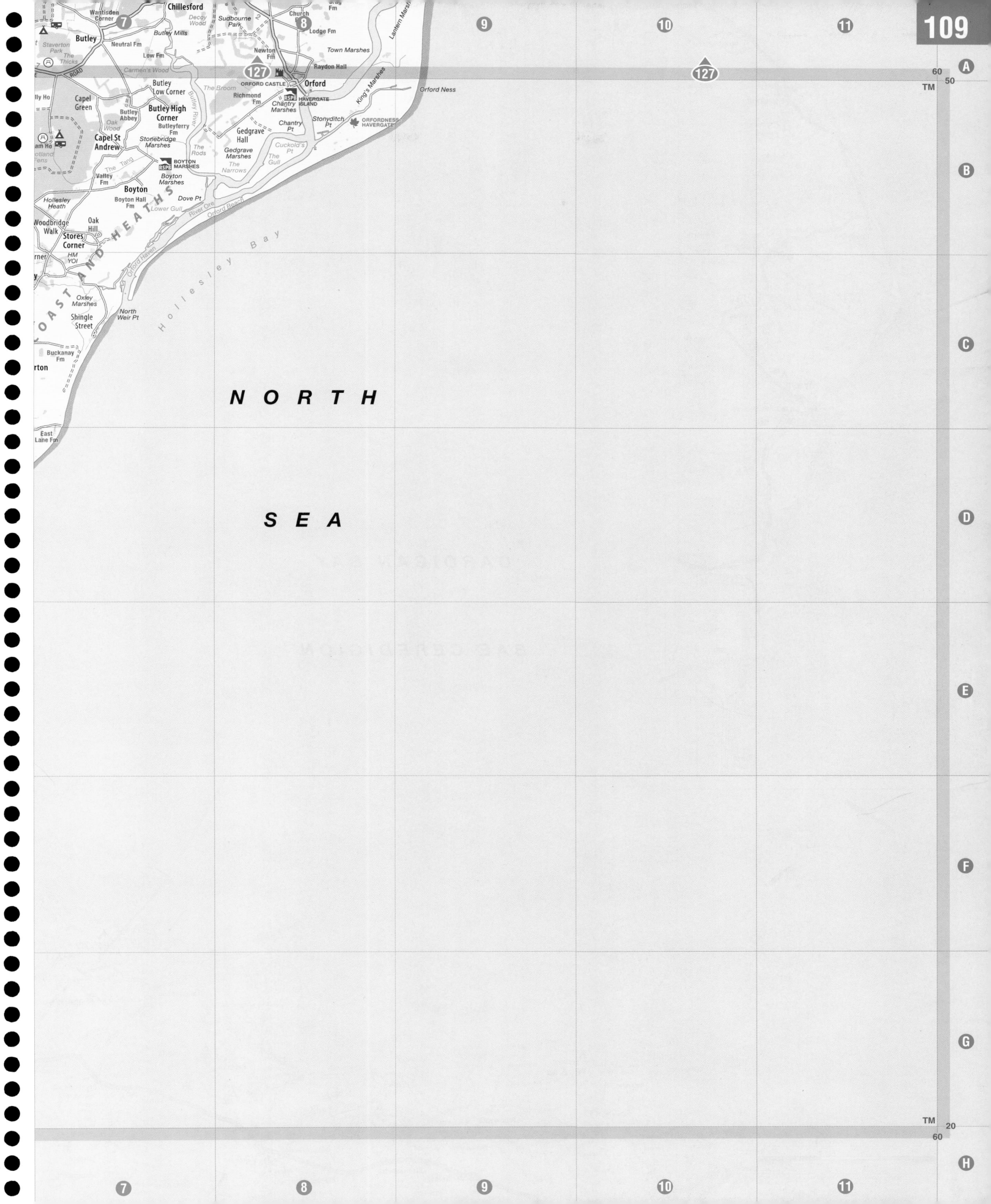

NORTH

SEA

Chillesford
Wantisden
Corner
7
Butley
Butley Mills
Neutral Fm
Low Fm
Staverton
Park
The Thicks
Decoy
Wood
Sudbourne
Park
Church
8
Newton
Fm
Lodge Fm
Town Marshes
Raydon Hall
Carmen's Wood
ROAD
127
ORFORD CASTLE
Orford
127
60
50
TM
Butley
Low Corner
The Broom
Richmond
Fm
King's Marshes
Orford Ness
Butley
Abbey
Capel
Green
Butley High
Corner
Butleyferry
Fm
Chantry
Marshes
Stonyditch
Pt
ORFORDNESS
HAVERGATE
HAVERGATE
ISLAND
Oak
Wood
Butley River
Gedgrave
Hall
Chantry
Pt
Capel St
Andrew
Stonebridge
Marshes
Gedgrave
Marshes
Cuckold's
Pt
The
Rods
The
Gull
BOYTON
MARSHES
The Narrows
The Tang
Boyton
Marshes
Boyton
Dove Pt
Valley
Fm
Boyton Hall
Fm
Lower Gull
River Ore
Hollesley
Heath
Oak
Hill
Orford Beach
Woodbridge
Walk
Stores
Corner
COAST AND HEATHS
Orford Haven
Hollesley Bay
HM
YOI
Oxley
Marshes
North
Weir Pt
Shingle
Street
Buckanay
Fm
East
Lane Fm
9
10
11
A
B
C
D
E
F
G
H
TM
20
60
7
8
9
10
11

CARDIGAN BAY
BAE CEREDIGION
Friog
Llwyngwril
Rhoslefain
Llanegryn
Peniarth
Bryncrug
Rhyd-yr-onen
Tywyn
Pendre
NARROW GAUGE RAILWAY MUSEUM
Neptune Hall
Caethle
Aberdovey
(Aberdyfi)
Aberdovey Bar
Ynyslas
Ynys Tachwedd
Borth Sands
Aberleri
Borth
(Y Borth)
Cardigan Island
Mwnt
Aberporth
Parcllyn
Tresaith
Penbryn
Llangrannog
Pontgarreg
Penmorfa
Brynhoffnant
Sarnau
Felinwynt
Rhosygadair Newydd
Blaenannerch
Tremain
Blaenporth
Tan-y-groes
Glynarthen
Cwmcoednerth
Glasgoed
Gwbert
Y Ferwig
Cippyn
Cemaes Head
Carreg Lydan
Trwyn Crou
Ynys-Lochtyn
Traeth-yr-ynys
Carreg y Nodwydd
0 1 2 3 miles
0 1 2 3 4 5 km

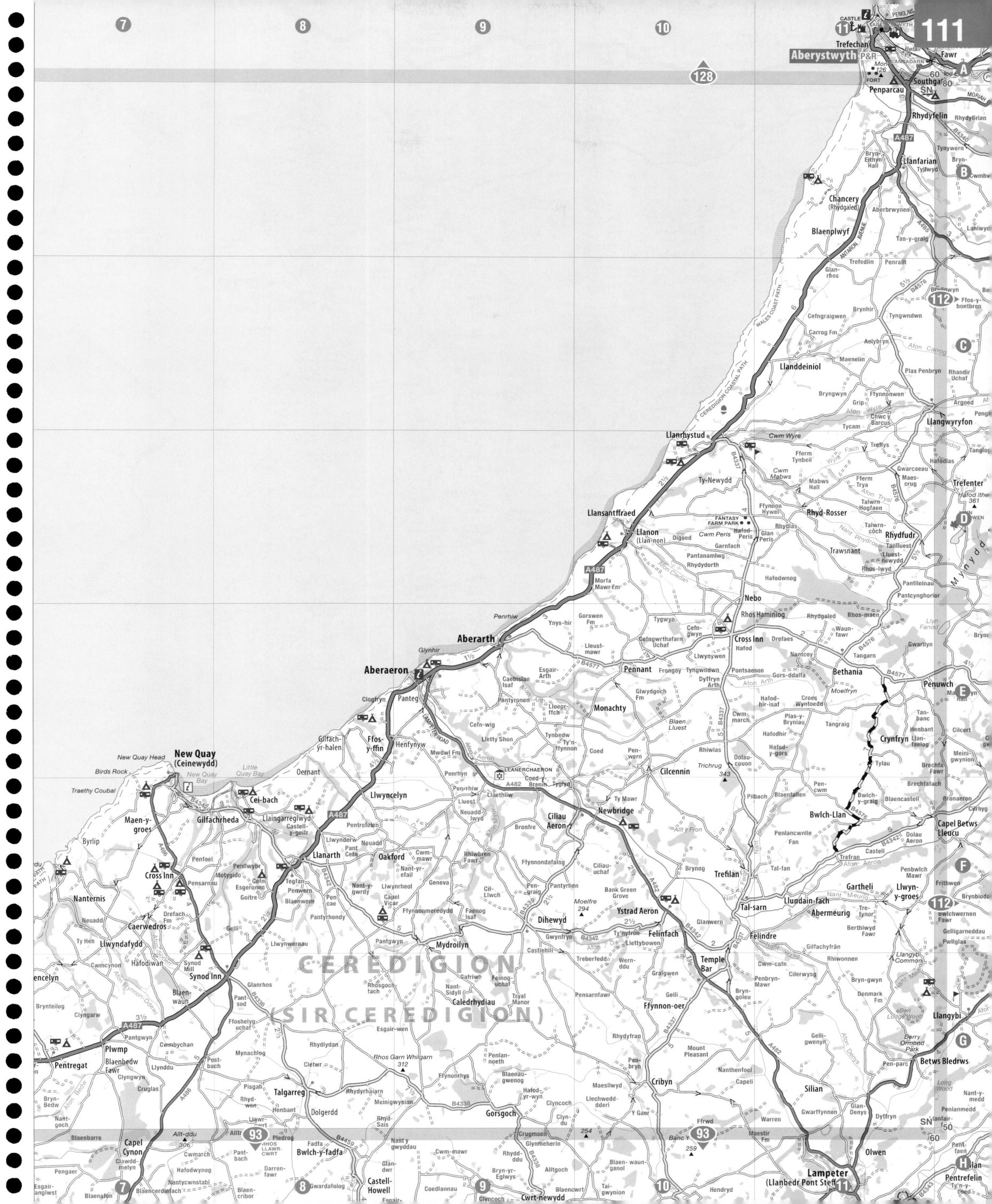

111
7
8
9
10
11
128
93
112
A
B
C
D
E
F
G
H
Aberystwyth
Trefechan
Penparcau
Southgate
Rhydyfelin
Llanfarian
Chancery (Rhydgaled)
Blaenplwyf
Aberbrwynen
Tan-y-graig
Trefedlin
Penrallt
Glan-rhos
Brynhir
Tyngwndwn
Cefngraigwen
Carrog Fm
Aelybryn
Afon Carrog
Llanddeiniol
Maenelin
Plas Penbryn
Rhandir Uchaf
Bryngwyn
Ffynnonwen
Argoed
Grip
Afon Wyre
Chwc y Barcus
Tycam
Llangwyryfon
Llanrhystud
Cwm Wyre
Fferm Tynbeil
Trefenter
Ty-Newydd
Cwm Mabws
Mabws Hall
Fferm Trya
Maes-crug
Gwarcaeau
Hafodlas
Ffynnon Hywel
Rhyd-Rosser
Rhydfudr
Llansantffraed
Llanon (Llan-non)
Digoed
Cwm Peris
Fantasy Farm Park
Hafod-Peris
Glan Peris
Trawsnant
Garnfach
Pantanamlwg
Rhydydorth
Afon Cledan
Hafodwnog
Pantlleinau
Pantcynghorior
Morfa Mawr Fm
Nebo
Rhos Haminiog
Rhydgaled
Rhos-maen
Mynydd
Penrhiw
Aberarth
Ynys-hir
Gorswen Fm
Tygwyn
Cefn-gwyn
Cross Inn
Hafod
Drefaes
Waun-fawr
Llyn Fanod
Lleust-mawr
Cefngwrthafarn Uchaf
Llwynywen
Nantcoy
Tangarn
Gwarllyn
Glynhir
Aberaeron
Pennant
Frongoy
Tyngwndwn
Pontsaeson
Gors-ddalfa
Bethania
Penuwch
Esgair-Arth
Caebislan Isaf
Glwydgoch Fm
Dyffryn Arth
Afon Arth
Moelfryn
Cilgeirfan
Panteg
Pantyronen
Lloegr-ffch
Monachty
Hafod-hir-isaf
Croes Wyntoedd
Tan-banc
Henbant
Crynfryn
Cilcert
Ffos-y-ffin
Henfynyw
Cefn-wig
Lletty Shon
Tynbedw
Ty'n-ffynnon
Coed
Blaen Lluest
Cwm-march
Plas-y-Bryniau
Hafodhir
Tangraig
Rhiwlas
Hafod-y-gors
Tylau
Brechfa Fawr
Meini-gwynion
Mwdwl Fm
Afon Aeron
Llanerchaeron
Coed-y-Brenin
Tyglyn
Pen-wern
Cilcennin
Trichrug
Dolau-couon
Pen-cwm
Brechtafach
Gilfach-yr-halen
Oernant
Little Quay Bay
New Quay Head
New Quay (Ceinewydd)
New Quay Bay
Birds Rock
Traethy Coubal
Cei-bach
Llwyncelyn
Penrhyn
Pen-rhiw
Llaethliw
Ty Mawr
Newbridge
Pilbach
Blaenfallen
Bwlch-y-graig
Blaencastell
Bronaeron
Bwlch-Llan
Capel Betws Lleucu
Gilfachrheda
Maen-y-groes
Llaingarreglwyd
Castell-y-geifr
Pentrefelen
Lluest
Neuadd-lwyd
Ciliau Aeron
Bronfre
Allt y Fron
Dolau Aeron
Byrlip
Llanarth
Llwynderw
Pant Cefn
Neuadd
Oakford
Cwm-mawr
Rhiwbren Fawr
Fynnondafalog
Penlancwnile Fan
Castell
Trefran
Afon Aeron
Penfoel
Penllwybr
Cefn Esgeronen
Motygido
Tegfan
Penwern
Nant-yr-efail
Llwynrheol
Geneva
Ciliau-uchaf
Brynog
Trefilan
Tal-fan
Penbwlch Mawr
Gartheli
Llwyn-y-groes
Frithwen
Cross Inn
Pensarnau
Goitre
Blaenwern
Nant-y-gwrdy
Capel Vicar
Pen-cae
Cil-Llwch
Pen-graig
Pantyrhen
Moelfre
Bank Green Grove
Tal-sarn
Lludain-fach
Abermeurig
Tre-fynor
Nanternis
Drefach Fm
Pantyrhendy
Ffynnonmeredydd
Faenog Isaf
Ystrad Aeron
Berthlwyd Fawr
Bwichwernen Fawr
Neuadd
Caerwedros
Gelli
Dihewyd
Glanwern
Gelligarneddau
Ty Hen
Llwyndafydd
Llwynwernau
Pantgwyn
Mydroilyn
Gwynfryn
Ty'nyfron
Felinfach
Lletty bowen
Felindre
Gilfachyfrân
Pwllglas
Cwmcynon
Hafodiwan
Synod Mill
Synod Inn
Castlehill
Treberfedd
Wern-ddu
Temple Bar
Rhiwonnen
Llangybi Common
CEREDIGION
(SIR CEREDIGION)
Glanrhos
Rhosgoch-fach
Gafriw
Feinog-uchaf
Nant-Sidyll
Caledrhydiau
Tryal Manor
Pensarnfawr
Graigwen
Cwm-cafn
Cilerwysg
Penbryn-Mawr
Bryn-gwyn
Denmark Fm
Llangybi
Blaen-waun
Pant-sod
Gelli
Ffynnon-oer
Bryn-goleu
Brynteilog
Clyngarw
Ffoshelyg-uchaf
Rhydlydan
Esgair-wen
Rhydyfran
Derry Ormond Park
Pantgwyn
Cwmbychan
Penlan-noeth
Pen-bryn
Mount Pleasant
Gelli-gwenyn
Afon Denys
Betws Bledrws
Pentregat
Plwmp
Blaenbedw Fawr
Llynddu
Post-bach
Mynachlog
Cletwr
Rhos Garn Whilgarn
Ffynonrhys
Blaenau-gwenog
Nanthenfoel
Pen-parc
Long Wood
Clyngwyn
Cruglas
Pisgah
Talgarreg
Rhydyrhaiarn
Hafod-yr-wyn
Maesllwyd
Cribyn
Capeli
Silian
Nant-y-medd
Bryn-Bedw
Rhyd-wen
Henbant
Dolgerdd
Meinigwynion
Gorsgoch
Clyncoch
Llechwedd-dderi
Y Gaer
Glan-Denys
Gwarffynnon
Dyffryn
Penianmedd
Nant-goch
Blaenbarre
Allt-ddu
Llawr-cwrt
Pledrog
Rhyd-Sais
Clyn-du
Ffrwd
Warren
Capel Cynon
Cwmarch
Pant-bach
Fadfa
Bwlch-y-fadfa
Nant y gwyddau
Cwm-mawr
Crugmaen
Glynmeherin
Banc Y
Maestir Fm
Olwen
Pengaer
Clawdd-melyn
Hafodwynog
Darren-fawr
Glan-dwr
Rhydd-ddu
Bryn-yr-Eglwys
Alltgoch
Blaen-waun-ganol
Pentrefelin
Esgair-anglwst
Nantycwnstabl
Blaencerdinfach
Blaenafon
Blaen-cribor
Gwardafolog
Castell-Howell
Coedlannau
Clyncoch
Cwrt-newydd
Blaencwrt
Tai-gwynion
Hendryd
Lampeter (Llanbedr Pont Steffan)
WALES COAST PATH
CEREDIGION COASTAL PATH
ANTARON AVENUE
LAMPETER ROAD
A487
A482
A486
A485
B4577
B4576
B4337
B4342
B4338
B4459
B4343
B4340

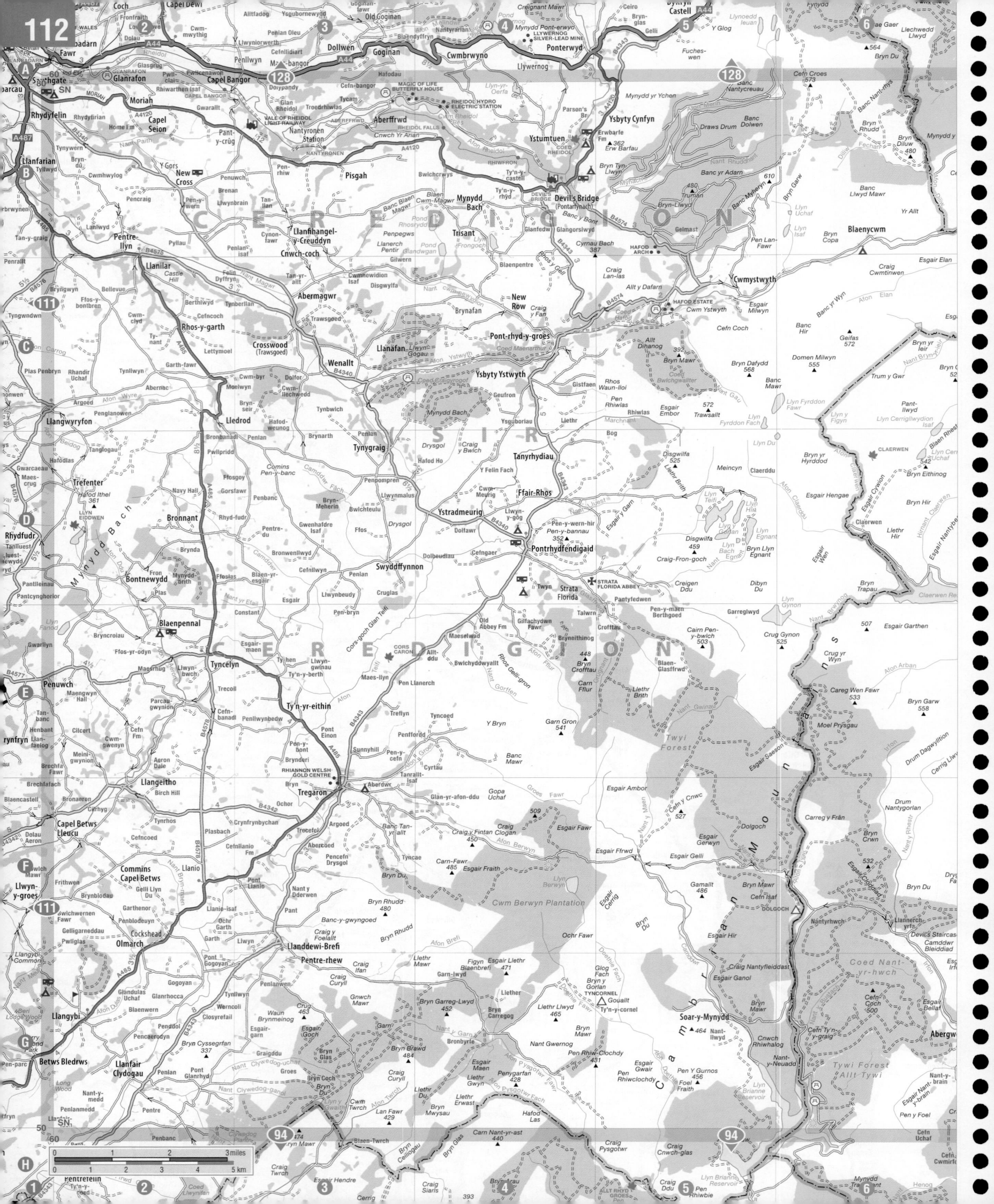
CEREDIGION
SIR CEREDIGION
Aberffrwd
Devil's Bridge (Pontarfynach)
Ponterwyd
Goginan
Capel Bangor
Llanfarian
Llanilar
Pontrhydfendigaid
Strata Florida
Tregaron
Llangeitho
Llanddewi-Brefi
Ysbyty Ystwyth
Cwmystwyth
Tyncelyn
Penuwch
Bontnewydd
Blaenpennal
Swyddffynnon
Ystradmeurig
Ffair-Rhos
Tanyrhydiau
Llangwyryfon
Trefenter
Lledrod
Abermagwr
Crosswood (Trawsgoed)
Wenallt
Llanafan
Pont-rhyd-y-groes
Llangybi
Betws Bledrws
Llanfair Clydogau
Olmarch
Cwm Berwyn Plantation
Twyi Forest
Cambrian Mountains
Soar-y-Mynydd
Blaenycwm
0 1 2 3 miles
0 1 2 3 4 5 km

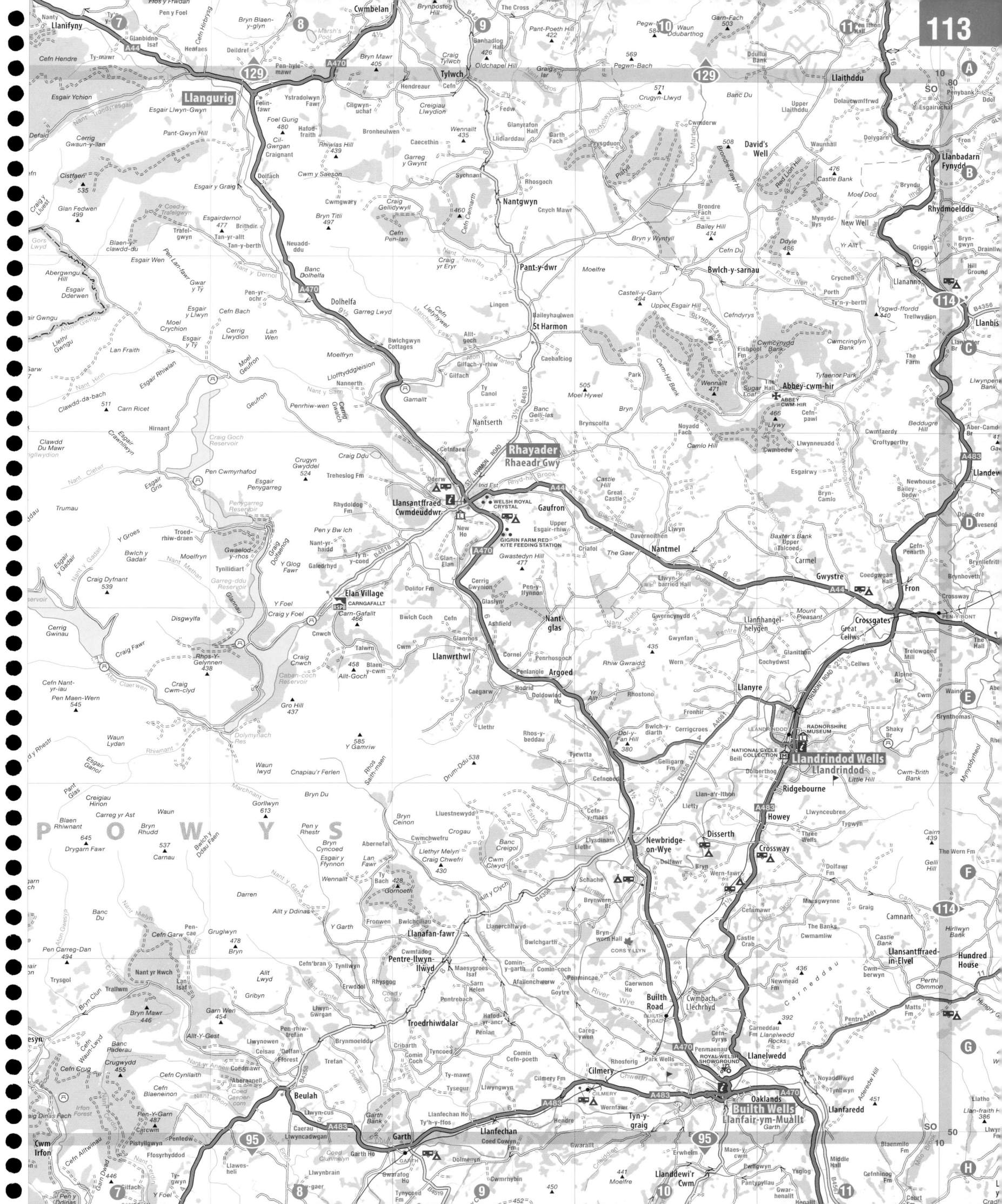
Llanifyny
Cwmbelan
Llangurig
Esgair Ychion
Esgair Llwyn-Gwyn
Pant-Gwyn Hill
Cerrig Gwaun-y-llan
Cistfaen 535
Glan Fedwen 499
Fedwen
Foel Gurig 480
Cil-Gwrgan
Craignant
Dolfach
Esgair y Graig
Esgairdernol 477
Tan-y-allt
Tan-y-berth
Trafel-gwyn
Brithdir
Neuadd-ddu
Banc Dolhelfa
Dolhelfa
Garreg Lwyd
Ystradolwyn Fawr
Cilgwyn-uchaf
Hafod-fraith
Rhiwlas Hill 439
Cwm y Saeson
Cwmgwary
Bryn Titli 497
Bronheulwen
Caecethin
Wennallt 435
Garreg y Gwynt
Craig Gellidywyll
Cefn Pen-lan
Bryn Mawr 405
Hendreaur
Cefn
Tylwch
Craig Tylwch
Creigiau Llwydion
Oldchapel Hill
Banhadlog Hall
The Cross
Pant-Poeth Hill 422
Brynposteg Hill
Glanyrafon Halt
Llidiarddau
Garth Fach
Sychnant
Rhosgoch
Nantgwyn
Cnych Mawr
Craig yr Eryr
Pant-y-dwr
Moelfre
Lingen
St Harmon
Baileyhaulwen
Caebalcoig
Bwlchgwyn Cottages
Gilfach
Gamallt
Nannerth
Moelfryn
Penrhiw-wen
Nantserth
Ty Canol
Banc Gelli-las
Moel Hywel 505
Park
Bryn
Brynscolfa
Rhayader
Rhaeadr Gwy
Cefnfaes
Craig Ddu
Crugyn Gwyddel 524
Treheslog Fm
Llansantffraed Cwmdeuddwr
Gaufron
Upper Esgair-rhiw
Gigrin Farm Red Kite Feeding Station
Welsh Royal Crystal
Castle Hill
Great Castle
Llwyn
Davernoithen
The Gaer
Nantmel
Llwyn-barried Hall
Gwastedyn Hill 477
Cerrig Gwynion
Pen-y-Ffynnon
Glan-Elan
Rhydoldog Fm
Pen y Bw Ich
Nant-yr-haidd
Galedrhyd
Ty'n-y-coed
Doliför Fm
Elan Village
Carngafallt
Carn-Gafallt 466
Cnwch
Craig y Foel
Y Foel
Y Glog Fawr
Craig Dolfaenog
Gwaelod-y-rhos
Tynllidiart
Moelfryn
Troed-rhiw-draen
Craig Goch Reservoir
Penygarreg Reservoir
Garreg-ddu Reservoir
Caban-coch Reservoir
Dolymynach Res
Hirnant
Carn Ricet
Clawdd-da-bach
Esgair Rhiwlan
Moel Geufron
Geufron
Lan Fraith
Clawdd Du Mawr
Esgair Crawnllwyn
Pen Cwmyrhafod
Esgair Penygarreg
Esgair Gris
Trumau
Y Groes
Bwlch y Gadair
Esgair y Gadair
Craig Dyfnant 539
Cerrig Gwinau
Disgwylfa
Craig Fawr
Rhos-Y-Gelynnen 438
Craig Cwm-clyd
Cefn Nant-yr-iau
Pen Maen-Wern 545
Waun Lydan
Esgair Ganol
Gro Hill 437
Craig Cnwch
Allt-Goch
Talwrn
Blaen-y-cwm
Bwlch Coch
Cwm
Glanrhos
Llanwrthwl
Ashfield
Glaslyn
Nant-glas
Cornel
Penrhoscoch
Penlanole
Argoed
Caegarw
Hodrid
Doldowlod Ho
Llethr
Rhos-y-beddau
Y Gamriw 585
Waun lwyd
Cnapiau'r Ferlen
Drum-Ddu 538
Tycwtta
Gorllwyn 613
Bryn Du
Pant Glas
Creigiau Hirion
Carreg yr Ast
Waun
Blaen Rhiwnant
P O W Y S
Bryn Rhudd
645 Drygarn Fawr
537 Carnau
Bwlch y Ddau Faen
Pen y Rhestr
Bryn Cyncoed
Esgair y Ffynnon
Wennallt
Lan Fawr
Abernefal
Bryn Ceinon
Lluestnewydd
Crogau
Cwmchwefru
Llethyr Melyn
Craig Chwefri 430
Cwm Clwyd
Banc Creigol
Ty Bach 428
Gornoeth
Darren
Allt y Ddinas
Banc Du
Y Garth
Fronwen
Bwlchciliau
Llanafan-fawr
Llanerchllwyd
Bwlchgarth
Pentre-Llwyn-llwyd
Cwmfadog
Tynllwyn
Cefn'bran
Maesygroes Isaf
Sarn Helen
Rhysgog
Erwdodol
Pentrebach
Troedrhiwdalar
Hafod-yr-ancr
Penlan
Cribarth
Tyncoed
Comin Coch
Trefan
Llwyn-Gwrgan
Brynmoeldda
Ty-mawr
Tysegur
Llwyngwyn
Cilmery
Cilmery Fm
Beulah
Garth
Garth Bank
Llanfechan
Llanfechan Ho
Ty'h-y-ffos
Coed Cowyn
Hendre
Tyn-y-graig
Wernfawr
Gwaralit
Dolmenyn
Cwmrhybin
Llwynbrain
Llawes-heli
Garth Ho
Caerau
Llwyncadwgan
Penfedw
Pistyllgwyn
Ffosyrhyddod
Cefn Alltwinau
Garn Dwad
Cilfach
Y Foel
Beulah
Cefn Blaeneinon
Cefn Cynllaith
Crugwydd 455
Cefn Crug
Banc Paderau
Allt-Y-Gest
Garn Wen 454
Bryn Mawr 446
Llwynowen
Celsau
Pen-rhiw-trefan
Coedmawr
Aberannell
Irfon Forest
Pen-Y-Garn 487
Carcwm
Gribyn
Allt Lwyd
Lan Isaf
Nant yr Hwch
Trallwm
Trysgol
Bryn Clun
Pen Carreg-Dan 494
Cefn Garw
Pen-cae
Gruglwyn
478 Bryn
Cwm Irfon
Moelfre
Llanddewi'r Cwm
Erwhelm
Maes-y-cwm
Pwllgwyn
Pantypyllau
Ysglog
Gwar-henallt
Builth Wells
Llanfair-ym-Muallt
Oaklands
Llanelwedd
Royal Welsh Showground
Park Wells
Rhosferig
Penmaenau
Cefn-dyrys
Builth Road
Cwmbach-Llechrhyd
Caerwnon Ho
Goytre
Afallenchwerw
Comin-coch
Comin-y-garth
Penmincae
Bryn-wern Hall
Cors y Llyn
Brynwern
Schache
Newbridge-on-Wye
Dolfawr
Llysdinam
Llethr
Cefn-y-maes
Cefncoed
Dol-y-Fan Hill 380
Bwlch-y-diarth
Cerrigcroes
Fronhir
Rhostono
Rhiw Gwraidd
Wern
Gwynfan
Gwerncynydd
Llanfihangel-helygen
Llanyre
Cochydwst
Glanithon
Crossgates
Great Cellws
Gwystre
Fron
Coedgwgan Hall
Carmel
Baxter's Bank
Upper Talcoed
Llandrindod Wells
Llandrindod
Radnorshire Museum
National Cycle Collection
Gelligarn Fm
Beili
Dolberthog
Little Hill
Ridgebourne
Howey
Llwynceubren
Tygwyn
Three Wells
Disserth
Bryn
Crossway
Wern-fawr
Cefnmawr
Maesgwynne
The Banks
Cwmamliw
Castle Crab
Newmead Fm
Carneddau
Carneddau Fm
Llanelwedd Rocks
Graig
Camnant
Castle Bank
Llansantffraed-in-Elvel
Cwm-berwyn
Hundred House
Perthi Common
Hirllwyn Bank
Matts Fm
Noyaddllwyd
Tynllwyn
Llanfaredd
Blaenmilo Fm
Middle Hall
Cefnhinog Fm
Llathog
Llan-fraith 386
Abbey-cwm-hir
Abbey Cwm-Hir
Cefn-pawl
Llwyneuadd
Cwmbedw
Camlo Hill
Noyadd Fach
Wennallt 471
Sugar Loaf
The Hall
Fishpool Fm
Cwmcynydd Bank
Cwmcringlyn Bank
Tyfaenor Park
The Farm
Castell-y-Garn 494
Upper Esgair Hill
Glyndŵr's Way
Cefndyrys
Bwlch-y-sarnau
Cefn Du
Bryn y Wyntyll
Bailey Hill 474
Brondre Fach
Dyke 486
Mynydd-llys
New Well
Yr Allt
Crychell
Porth
Ty'n-y-berth
Ysgwd-ffordd 440
Trellwydion
Llanbis
Llananno
Criggin
Rhydmoelddu
Llanbadarn Fynydd
Moel Dod
Castle Bank 476
Waunhall
David's Well
Cwmderw
Rhysgduon
Pistyll
Crugyn-Llwyd 571
Pegwn-Bach 569
Banc Du
Upper Llaithddu
Llaithddu
Dolaucwmffrwd
Penybank
Esgairuchaf
Dolygarn
Pen Ithon Hall
Garn-Fach 503
Waun Ddubarthog
Pegwn Mawr 584
Ddulas Bank
Cwmfaerdy
Croftyperthy
Beddugre Hill
Esgairwy
Bryn-Camlo
Newhouse
Bailey-bedw
Cefn-Penarth
Mount Pleasant
Trelowgoed Mill
Cellws
Alpine Br
Cwm
Shaky Br
Cwm-brith Bank
Mynydd-hiroel
Cairn 439
The Wern Fm
Gelli Hill
Llandewi
Crossway
Pen-y-bont
The Hall
A44
A470
A483
A4081
A481
B4518
B4358
B4356
B4519
B4567
129
114
95
7
8
9
10
11
A
B
C
D
E
F
G
H
SO

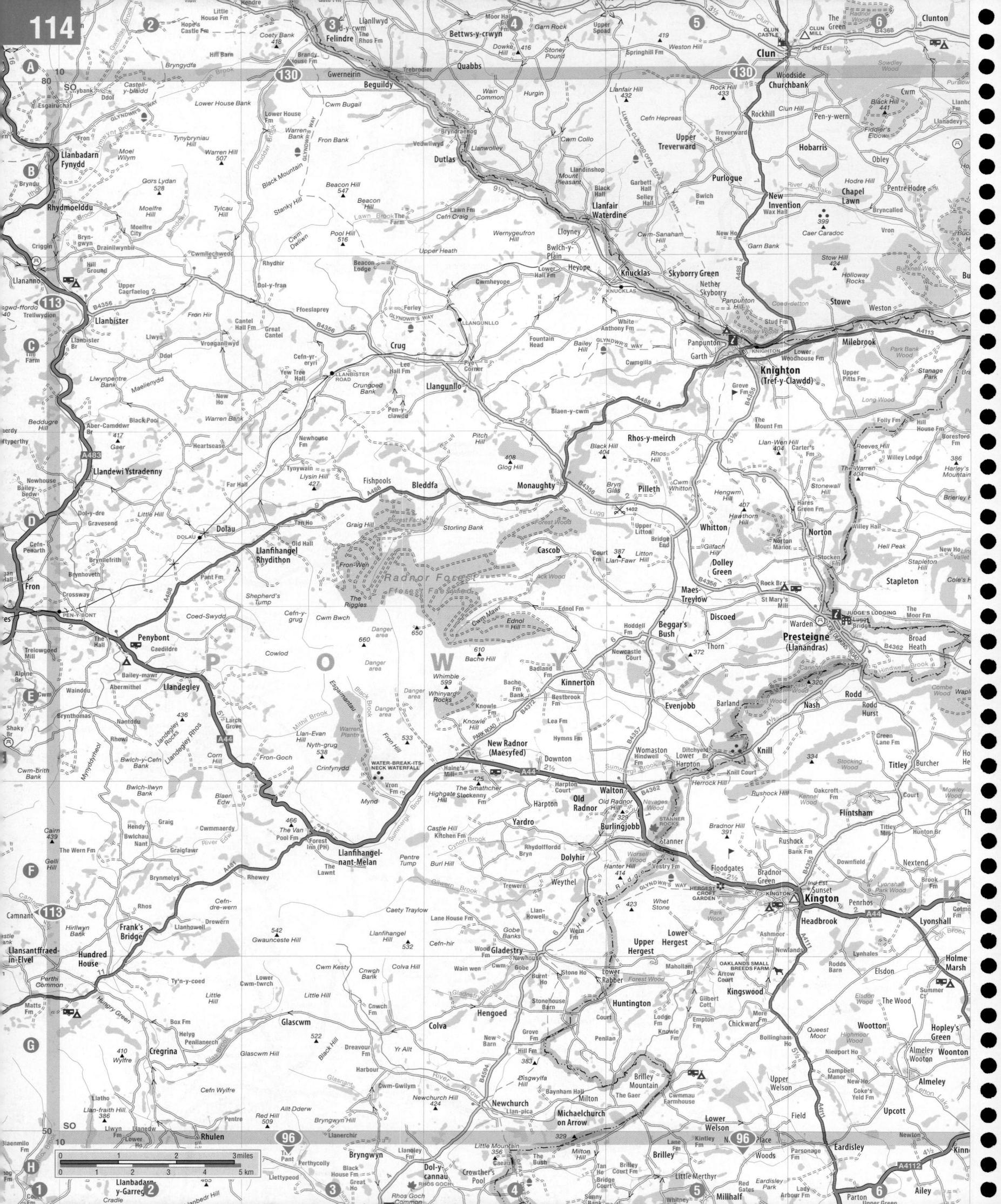
Felindre
Bettws-y-crwyn
Clun
Clunton
Beguildy
Quabbs
Gwerneirin
Trebrodier
Woodside
Churchbank
Rockhill
Pen-y-wern
Hobarris
Llanbadarn Fynydd
Dutlas
Upper Treverward
Purlogue
Chapel Lawn
New Invention
Rhydmoelddu
Llanfair Waterdine
Caer Caradoc
Knucklas
Skyborry Green
Heyope
Lloyney
Stowe
Weston
Llanbister
Crug
Llangunllo
Knighton (Tref-y-Clawdd)
Milebrook
Panpunton
Garth
Rhos-y-meirch
Llandewi Ystradenny
Bleddfa
Monaughty
Pilleth
Whitton
Norton
Dolau
Llanfihangel Rhydithon
Cascob
Radnor Forest
Fforest Faesyfed
Dolley Green
Stapleton
Maes-Treylow
Fron
Discoed
Presteigne (Llanandras)
Penybont
Beggar's Bush
Broad Heath
Llandegley
Kinnerton
Evenjobb
Nash
Rodd
P O W Y S
New Radnor (Maesyfed)
Knill
Titley
Walton
Old Radnor
Burlingjobb
Llanfihangel-nant-Melan
Yardro
Dolyhir
Stanner
Floodgates
Kington
Flintsham
Headbrook
Lyonshall
Frank's Bridge
Hundred House
Llansantffraed-in-Elvel
Gladestry
Upper Hergest
Lower Hergest
Kingswood
Holme Marsh
Huntington
Hengoed
Glascwm
Colva
Cregrina
Wootton
Hopley's Green
Almeley Wooton
Almeley
Brilley Mountain
Newchurch
Michaelchurch on Arrow
Lower Welson
Upper Welson
Field
Upcott
Rhulen
Bryngwyn
Dol-y-cannau
Crowther's Pool
Brilley
Eardisley
Llanbadarn-y-Garreg
Millhalf
Ailey
A488
A483
A44
A481
A4113
A4111
A4112
B4355
B4356
B4362
B4357
B4372
B4594
B4368
113
130
96
SO
0 1 2 3 miles
0 1 2 3 4 5 km

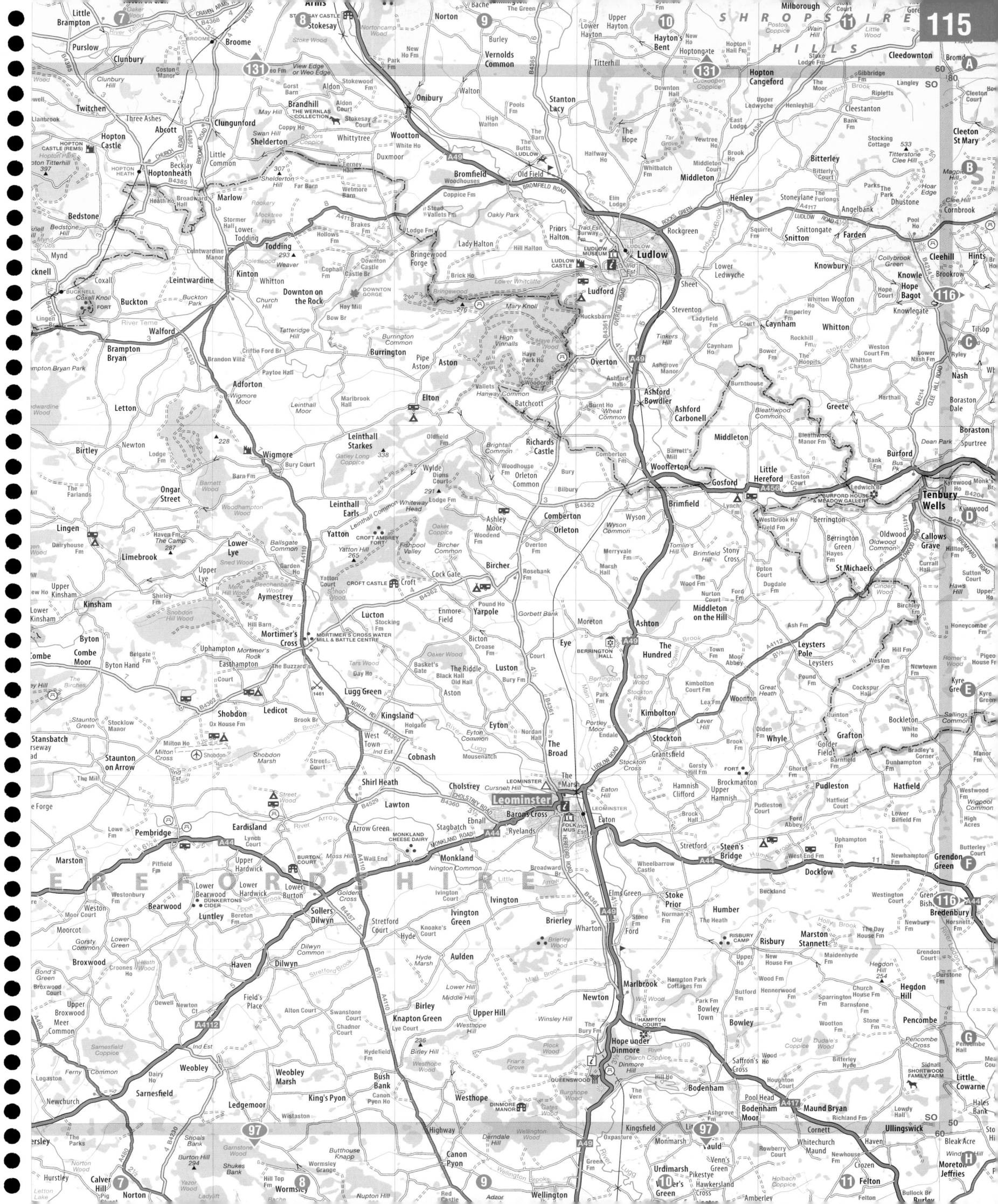

SHROPSHIRE HILLS
HEREFORDSHIRE
Little Brampton
Purslow
Clunbury
Twitchen
Hopton Castle
Hoptonheath
Bedstone
Bucknell
Coxall
Buckton
Walford
Brampton Bryan
Letton
Birtley
Lingen
Limebrook
Kinsham
Byton
Combe
Combe Moor
Stansbatch
Staunton on Arrow
Pembridge
Marston
Bearwood
Broxwood
Broome
Aston
Clungunford
Abcott
Beckjay
Shelderton
Marlow
Leintwardine
Kinton
Todding
Downton on the Rock
Burrington
Adforton
Wigmore
Ongar Street
Lower Lye
Upper Lye
Aymestrey
Mortimer's Cross
Shobdon
Ledicot
Eardisland
Lower Bearwood
Lower Hardwick
Lower Burton
Luntley
Haven
Dilwyn
Sollers Dilwyn
Field's Place
Weobley
Weobley Marsh
Sarnesfield
Ledgemoor
King's Pyon
Stokesay
Aldon
Brandhill
Stokesay Castle
Onibury
Norton
Vernolds Common
Walton
Wootton
Whittytree
Duxmoor
Bromfield
Stanton Lacy
Ludlow
Ludford
Lady Halton
Priors Halton
Bringewood Forge
Elton
Leinthall Starkes
Leinthall Earls
Yatton
Croft
Croft Castle
Lucton
Kingsland
Cobnash
Shirl Heath
Lawton
Monkland
Stretford Court
Ivington
Ivington Green
Birley
Knapton Green
Upper Hill
Bush Bank
Westhope
Canon Pyon
Wellington
Highway
Aston
Pipe Aston
Richards Castle
Orleton
Comberton
Bircher
Yarpole
Eyton
Luston
Eye
Moreton
Ashton
The Broad
Cholstrey
Leominster
Barons Cross
Ebnall
Stagbatch
Ryelands
Eaton
Brierley
Wharton
Newton
Marlbrook
Hope under Dinmore
Bodenham
Bodenham Moor
Maund Bryan
Kingsfield
Vauld
Urdimarsh
Pikestye
Hawkersland
Amberley
Felton
Overton
Ashford Bowdler
Ashford Carbonell
Woofferton
Brimfield
Middleton on the Hill
The Hundred
Kimbolton
Stockton
Grantsfield
Hamnish Clifford
Steen's Bridge
Stretford
Stoke Prior
Humber
Risbury
Marston Stannett
Pudleston
Hatfield
Docklow
Bowley
Hegdon Hill
Pencombe
Little Cowarne
Ullingswick
Middleton
Henley
Rockgreen
Sheet
Caynham
Knowbury
Middleton
Little Hereford
Gosford
Tenbury Wells
Berrington
Oldwood
St Michaels
Leysters Pole
Leysters
Woonton
Whyle
Grafton
Hopton Cangeford
Cleedownton
Cleestanton
Bitterley
Angelbank
Farden
Cleehill
Hints
Knowle
Hope Bagot
Whitton
Greete
Nash
Boraston
Burford
Callows Grave
Bredenbury
Grendon Green
Moreton Jeffries
Bleak Acre
Hopton Heath
Lower Ledwyche
Steventon
A49
A44
A4113
A4110
A4112
A456
A417
A4117
B4361
B4362
B4360
B4529
B4457
B4230
131
97
116
A
B
C
D
E
F
G
H
SO
60
50

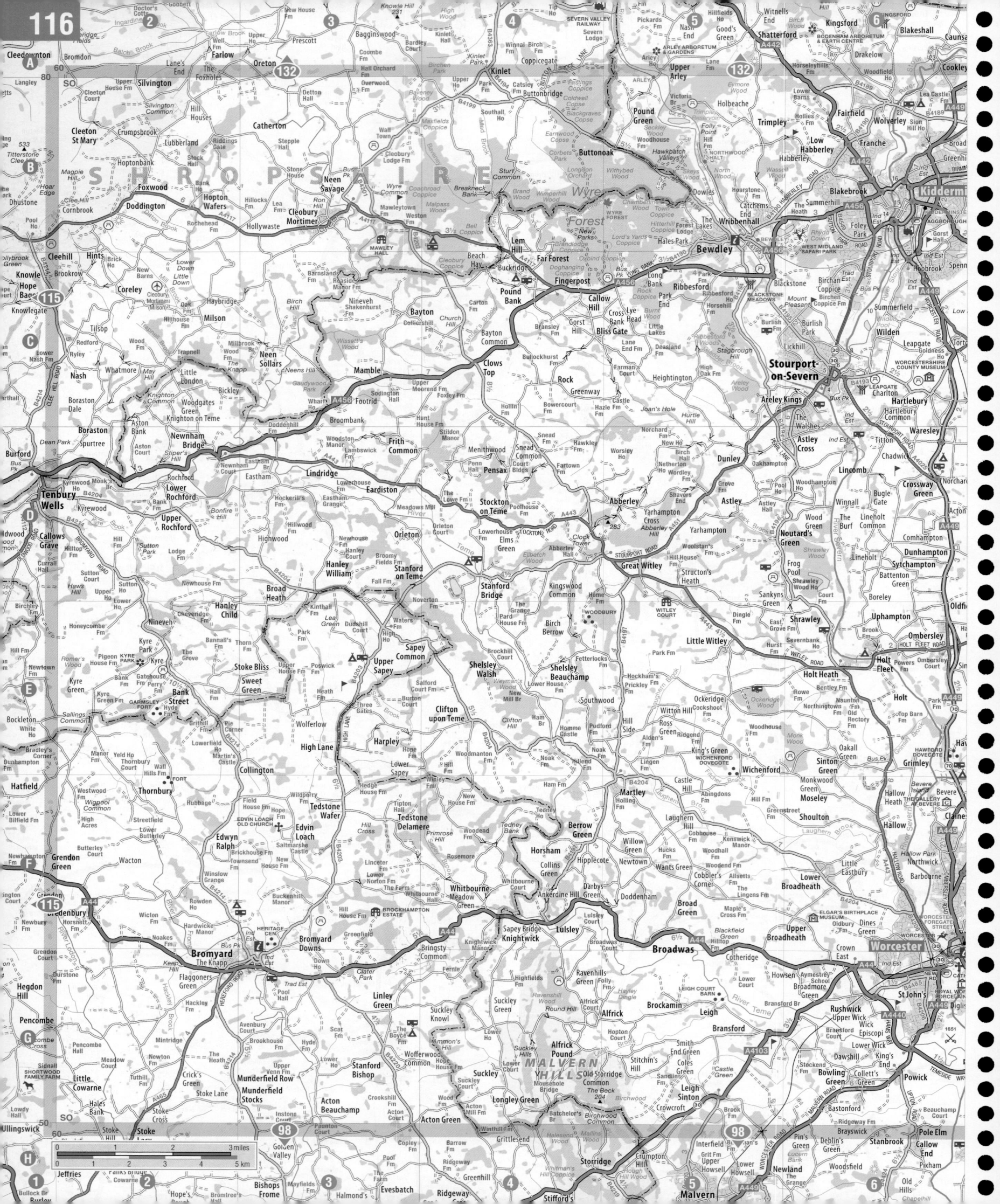
SHROPSHIRE
132
115
98
Cleedownton
Bromdon
Farlow
Oreton
Prescott
Baggingswood
Kinlet
Coppicegate
Buttonbridge
Upper Arley
Shatterford
Kingsford
Blakeshall
Silvington
Catherton
Cleeton St Mary
Crumpsbrook
Lubberland
Hoptonbank
Neen Savage
Sturt Common
Buttonoak
Pound Green
Trimpley
Wolverley
Low Habberley
Franche
Foxwood
Doddington
Hopton Wafers
Cleobury Mortimer
Hollywaste
Wyre Forest
Blakebrook
Kidderminster
Bewdley
Wribbenhall
Far Forest
Lem Hill
Cleehill
Hints
Coreley
Knowle
Hope Bagot
Knowlegate
Milson
Bayton
Pound Bank
Fingerpost
Callow Hill
Bliss Gate
Ribbesford
Blackstone
Tilsop
Nash
Whatmore
Neen Sollars
Mamble
Clows Top
Rock
Greenway
Heightington
Stourport-on-Severn
Areley Kings
Hartlebury
Boraston Dale
Boraston
Little London
Bickley
Woodgates Green
Knighton on Teme
Footrid
Broombank
Newnham Bridge
Frith Common
Menithwood
Pensax
Snead Common
Dunley
Astley Cross
Waresley
Burford
Tenbury Wells
Kyrewood
Lower Rochford
Rochford
Eastham
Lindridge
Eardiston
Stockton on Teme
Abberley
Astley
Lincomb
Crossway Green
Upper Rochford
Callows Grave
Highwood
Orleton
Elms Green
Great Witley
Yarhampton
Noutard's Green
Hanley William
Stanford on Teme
Broad Heath
Stanford Bridge
Kingswood Common
Dunhampton
Sytchampton
Hanley Child
Nineveh
Kyre Park
Kyre
Stoke Bliss
Sweet Green
Upper Sapey
Sapey Common
Shelsley Walsh
Shelsley Beauchamp
Birch Berrow
Little Witley
Shrawley
Ombersley
Holt Heath
Holt Fleet
Holt
Kyre Green
Bank Street
Wolferlow
Clifton upon Teme
Harpley
High Lane
Southwood
Hill Side
Ockeridge
Wichenford
Sinton Green
Grimley
Hatfield
Thornbury
Collington
Tedstone Wafer
Tedstone Delamere
Edvin Loach
Martley
Castle Hill
Moseley
Shoulton
Hallow
Edwyn Ralph
Grendon Green
Wacton
Horsham
Berrow Green
Hipplecote
Newtown
Wants Green
Broad Green
Lower Broadheath
Bredenbury
Whitbourne
Ankerdine Hill
Doddenham
Upper Broadheath
Bromyard
Bromyard Downs
Knightwick
Lulsley
Broadwas
Worcester
Hegdon Hill
Pencombe
Linley Green
Suckley
Alfrick
Brockamin
Leigh
St John's
Rushwick
Little Cowarne
Munderfield Row
Munderfield Stocks
Stanford Bishop
Longley Green
Alfrick Pound
Bransford
Powick
Malvern Hills
Stoke Lacy
Acton Beauchamp
Acton Green
Leigh Sinton
Stoke Cross
Grittlesend
Storridge
Callow End
Stanbrook
Pole Elm
Evesbatch
Bishops Frome
Malvern
Ridgeway Cross
Newland
Jeffries
Halmond's Frome
0 1 2 3 miles
0 1 2 3 4 5 km

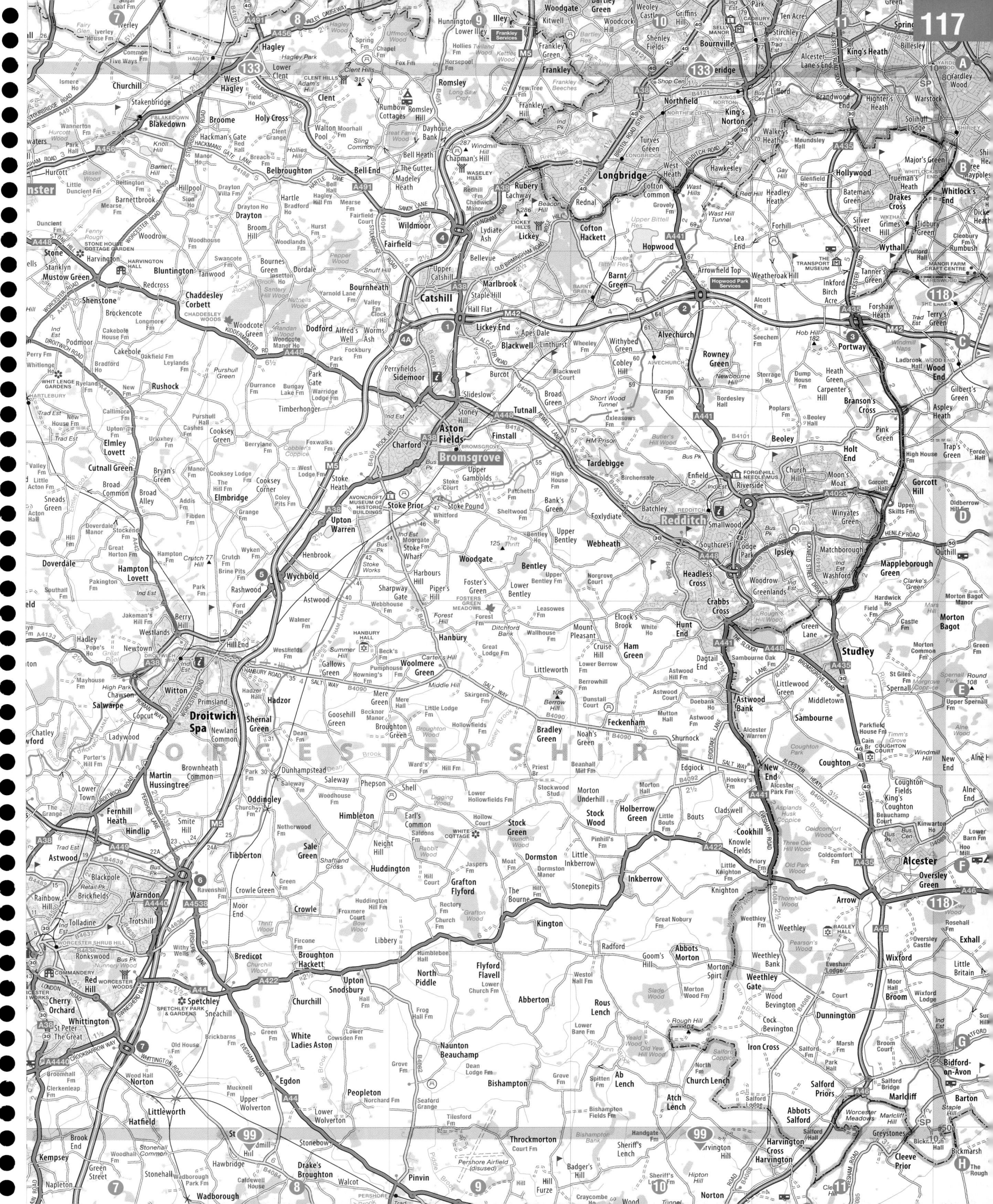

WORCESTERSHIRE
Iverley
Hagley
West Hagley
Churchill
Stakenbridge
Blakedown
Broome
Clent
Holy Cross
Romsley
Illey
Frankley
Woodgate
Bartley Green
Weoley Castle
Griffins Hill
Bournville
King's Heath
Northfield
King's Norton
Longbridge
Rubery
Rednal
Cofton Hackett
Hopwood
Hollywood
Whitlock's End
Wythall
Belbroughton
Bell End
Wildmoor
Fairfield
Drayton
Harvington
Stone
Mustow Green
Shenstone
Bluntington
Chaddesley Corbett
Catshill
Marlbrook
Barnt Green
Alvechurch
Portway
Dodford
Lickey End
Blackwell
Rowney Green
Bromsgrove
Aston Fields
Sidemoor
Charford
Finstall
Tutnall
Tardebigge
Beoley
Holt End
Rushock
Elmley Lovett
Cutnall Green
Stoke Prior
Upton Warren
Redditch
Webheath
Ipsley
Headless Cross
Mappleborough Green
Doverdale
Hampton Lovett
Wychbold
Woodgate
Bentley
Crabbs Cross
Studley
Morton Bagot
Hanbury
Droitwich Spa
Witton
Salwarpe
Hadzor
Feckenham
Astwood Bank
Sambourne
Coughton
Martin Hussingtree
Oddingley
Himbleton
Stock Green
Inkberrow
Alcester
Arrow
Tibberton
Warndon
Crowle
Kington
Abbots Morton
Wixford
Spetchley
Whittington
Upton Snodsbury
North Piddle
Flyford Flavell
Abberton
Rous Lench
Weethley Gate
Dunnington
Norton
Egdon
Peopleton
Bishampton
Ab Lench
Church Lench
Atch Lench
Salford Priors
Abbots Salford
Bidford-on-Avon
Marlcliff
Harvington
Cleeve Prior
Kempsey
Drake's Broughton
Pinvin
Throckmorton
M5
M42
A38
A441
A448
A435
A422
A44
A4538
A46
133
118
99

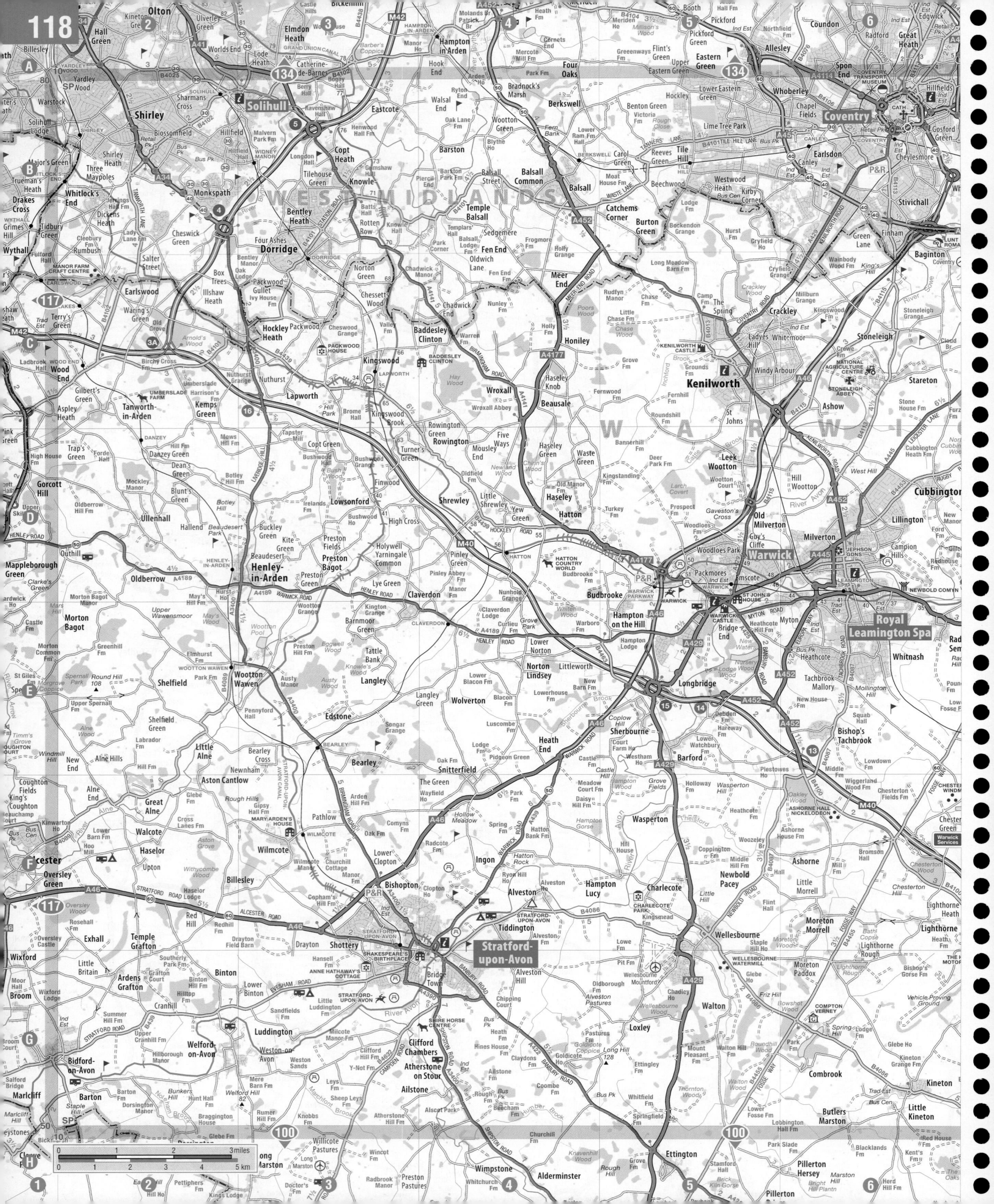

Olton
Hall Green
Elmdon Heath
Hampton in Arden
Balsall Common
Berkswell
Allesley
Coundon
Coventry
Solihull
Shirley
Eastcote
Barston
Four Oaks
Eastern Green
Tile Hill
Earlsdon
Canley
Cheylesmore
Stivichall
Finham
Baginton
WEST MIDLANDS
Monkspath
Knowle
Bentley Heath
Dorridge
Temple Balsall
Fen End
Meer End
Burton Green
Catchems Corner
Earlswood
Hockley Heath
Baddesley Clinton
Honiley
Crackley
Kenilworth
Stoneleigh
Stareton
Ashow
Kingswood
Lapworth
Wroxall
Beausale
Haseley Knob
Tanworth-in-Arden
Kemps Green
Rowington
Shrewley
Haseley
Hatton
Leek Wootton
Cubbington
Lillington
Old Milverton
Milverton
Warwick
Royal Leamington Spa
Whitnash
Henley-in-Arden
Oldberrow
Preston Bagot
Claverdon
Budbrooke
Hampton on the Hill
Myton
Bishop's Tachbrook
Morton Bagot
Wootton Wawen
Langley
Norton Lindsey
Longbridge
Wolverton
Edstone
Sherbourne
Barford
Snitterfield
Bearley
Aston Cantlow
Great Alne
Wasperton
Ashorne
Walcote
Haselor
Wilmcote
Ingon
Alveston
Hampton Lucy
Charlecote
Newbold Pacey
Moreton Morrell
Bishopton
Tiddington
Wellesbourne
Stratford-upon-Avon
Shottery
Drayton
Binton
Exhall
Temple Grafton
Ardens Grafton
Wixford
Broom
Bidford-on-Avon
Welford-on-Avon
Luddington
Weston-on-Avon
Clifford Chambers
Atherstone on Stour
Ailstone
Alveston Hill
Loxley
Walton
Combrook
Kineton
Little Kineton
Butlers Marston
Ettington
Wimpstone
Alderminster
Pillerton Hersey
Marlcliff
Barton
M42
M40
A46
A452
A429
A3400
A4177

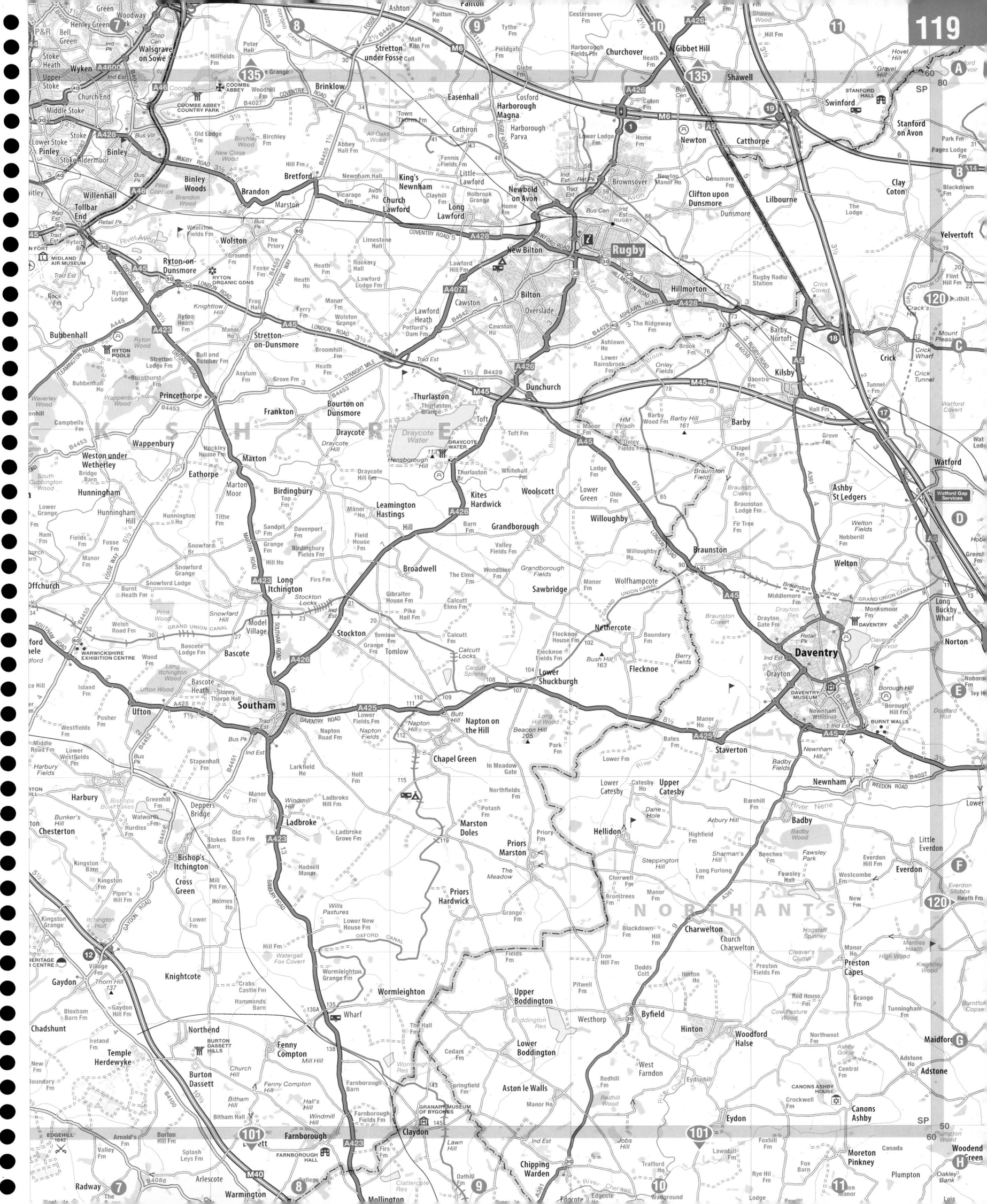
Walsgrave on Sowe
Wyken
Binley
Binley Woods
Willenhall
Tollbar End
Brinklow
Easenhall
Harborough Magna
Churchover
Gibbet Hill
Shawell
Swinford
Stanford on Avon
Newton
Catthorpe
Brownsover
Clifton upon Dunsmore
Lilbourne
Clay Coton
Yelvertoft
Newbold on Avon
Long Lawford
Church Lawford
King's Newnham
Bretford
Brandon
Wolston
Ryton-on-Dunsmore
Rugby
New Bilton
Bilton
Overslade
Hillmorton
Barby Nortoft
Crick
Kilsby
Stretton-on-Dunsmore
Bubbenhall
Princethorpe
Frankton
Bourton on Dunsmore
Thurlaston
Draycote
Dunchurch
Barby
Wappenbury
Weston under Wetherley
Eathorpe
Marton
Birdingbury
Leamington Hastings
Kites Hardwick
Woolscott
Grandborough
Willoughby
Braunston
Welton
Ashby St Ledgers
Watford
Hunningham
Broadwell
Sawbridge
Wolfhampcote
Long Itchington
Stockton
Nethercote
Flecknoe
Daventry
Long Buckby Wharf
Norton
Lower Shuckburgh
Bascote
Southam
Ufton
Napton on the Hill
Staverton
Chapel Green
Upper Catesby
Newnham
Harbury
Ladbroke
Marston Doles
Hellidon
Badby
Chesterton
Bishop's Itchington
Priors Marston
Priors Hardwick
Everdon
Charwelton
Preston Capes
Gaydon
Knightcote
Wormleighton
Upper Boddington
Byfield
Hinton
Woodford Halse
Maidford
Chadshunt
Northend
Fenny Compton
Lower Boddington
Aston le Walls
Adstone
Temple Herdewyke
Burton Dassett
Canons Ashby
Eydon
Farnborough
Claydon
Chipping Warden
Moreton Pinkney
Radway
Warmington
NORTHANTS
M6
M45
M40
A45
A423
A426
A425
A5
SP

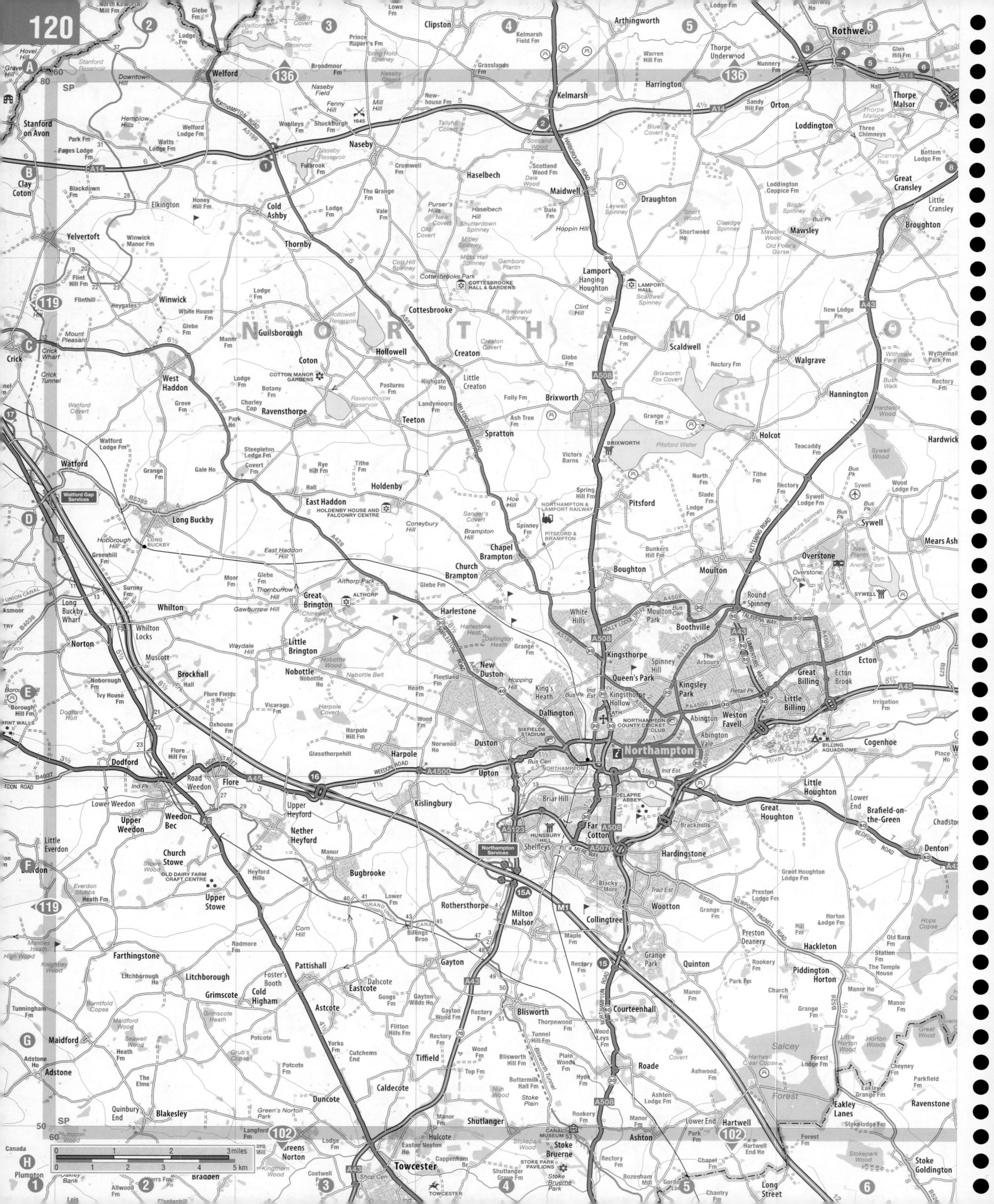

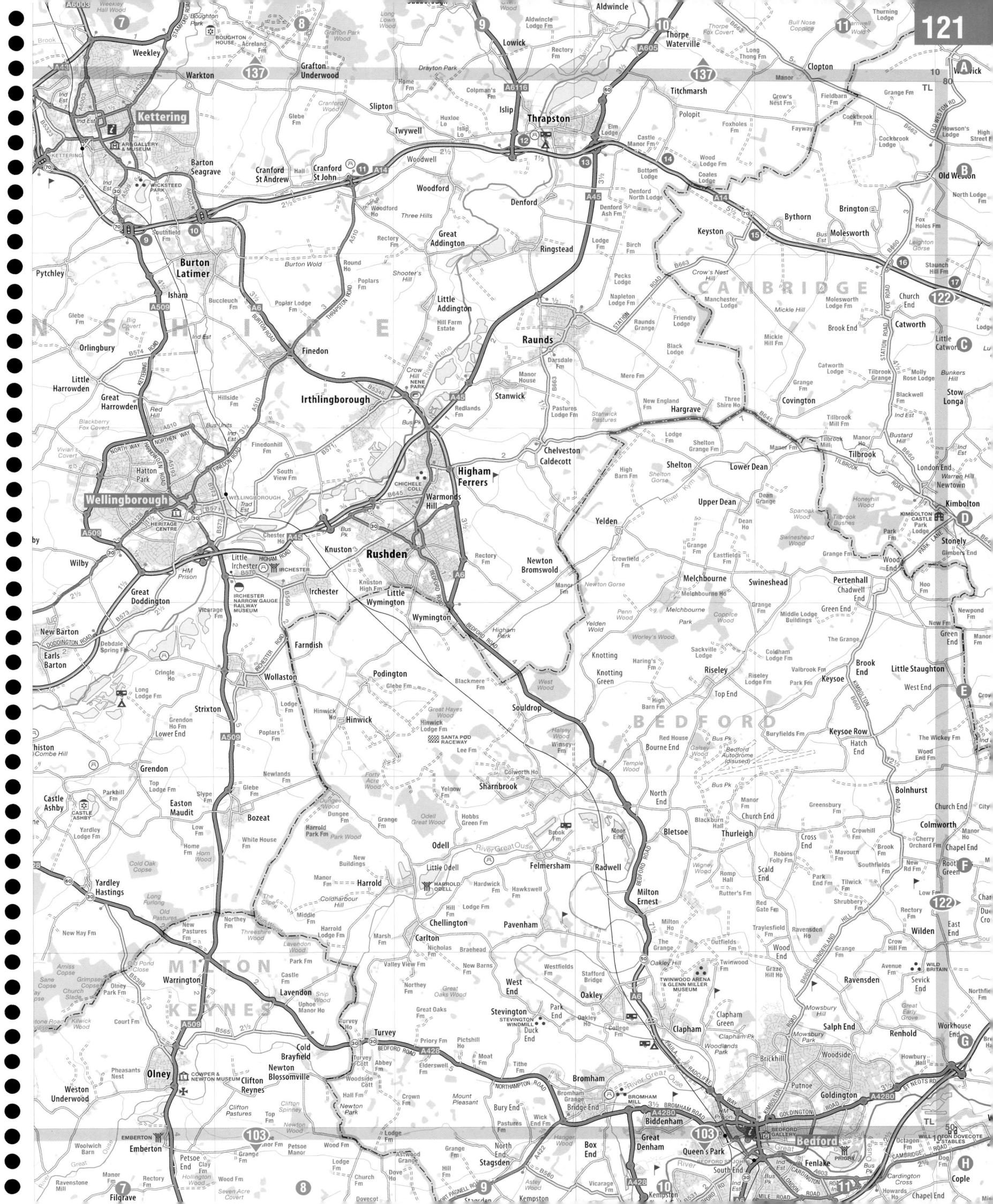
Kettering
Wellingborough
Rushden
Higham Ferrers
Irthlingborough
Thrapston
Raunds
Bedford
Olney
Burton Latimer
Finedon
Kimbolton
Weekley
Warkton
Barton Seagrave
Cranford St Andrew
Cranford St John
Woodford
Denford
Great Addington
Little Addington
Ringstead
Stanwick
Chelveston
Caldecott
Isham
Orlingbury
Little Harrowden
Great Harrowden
Pytchley
Wilby
Great Doddington
Earls Barton
Little Irchester
Irchester
Knuston
Wymington
Little Wymington
Farndish
Podington
Wollaston
Strixton
Grendon
Easton Maudit
Bozeat
Castle Ashby
Yardley Hastings
Hinwick
Souldrop
Sharnbrook
Odell
Harrold
Felmersham
Radwell
Milton Ernest
Pavenham
Carlton
Chellington
Turvey
Lavendon
Warrington
Cold Brayfield
Newton Blossomville
Clifton Reynes
Emberton
Weston Underwood
Stevington
Oakley
Clapham
Bromham
Biddenham
Great Denham
Kempston
Stagsden
Lowick
Islip
Slipton
Twywell
Titchmarsh
Thorpe Waterville
Aldwincle
Clopton
Keyston
Bythorn
Brington
Molesworth
Catworth
Covington
Hargrave
Shelton
Lower Dean
Upper Dean
Yelden
Tilbrook
Melchbourne
Swineshead
Pertenhall
Riseley
Keysoe
Keysoe Row
Bolnhurst
Colmworth
Thurleigh
Bletsoe
Ravensden
Wilden
Renhold
Salph End
Goldington
Putnoe
Brickhill
Queen's Park
Newton Bromswold
Stonely
Little Staughton
CAMBRIDGE
BEDFORD
MILTON KEYNES
A14
A45
A6
A509
A428
A4280
A603
A605
A6116
B645
B660
B663
137
122
103

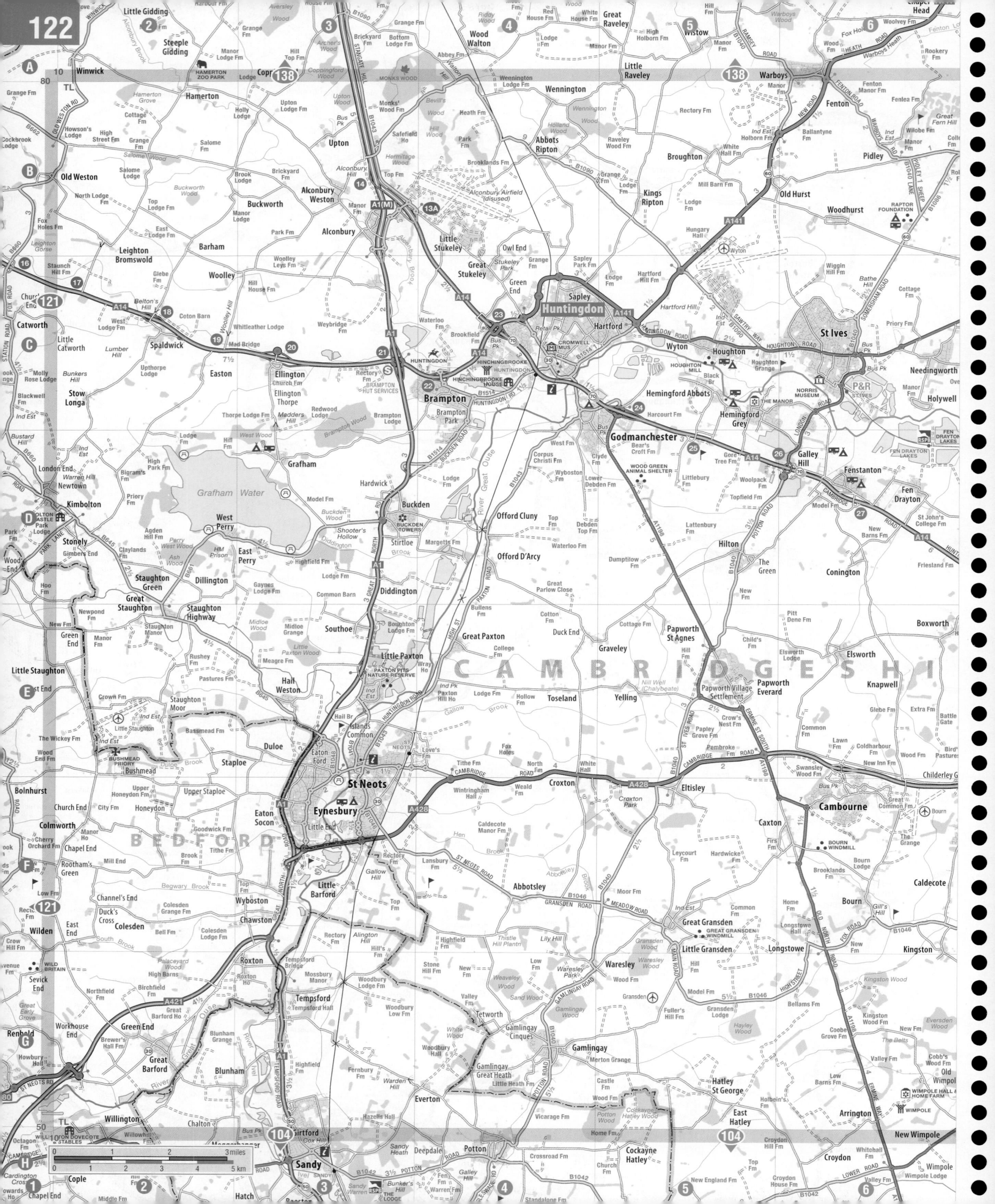
Little Gidding
Steeple Gidding
Winwick
Hamerton
Copmanford
Wood Walton
Great Raveley
Little Raveley
Wistow
Warboys
Wennington
Abbots Ripton
Broughton
Fenton
Pidley
Old Weston
Upton
Alconbury Weston
Alconbury
Buckworth
Barham
Kings Ripton
Old Hurst
Woodhurst
Leighton Bromswold
Woolley
Little Stukeley
Great Stukeley
Owl End
Green End
Sapley
Huntingdon
Hartford
Wyton
Houghton
St Ives
Needingworth
Holywell
Catworth
Little Catworth
Spaldwick
Easton
Stow Longa
Ellington
Ellington Thorpe
Brampton
Hemingford Abbots
Hemingford Grey
Godmanchester
Galley Hill
Fenstanton
Fen Drayton
Grafham
Grafham Water
Kimbolton
Newtown
Hardwick
Buckden
Offord Cluny
Offord D'Arcy
West Perry
East Perry
Stonely
Staughton Green
Dillington
Great Staughton
Staughton Highway
Diddington
Southoe
Great Paxton
Hilton
Conington
Boxworth
Papworth St Agnes
Graveley
Duck End
Little Paxton
Elsworth
Little Staughton
Hail Weston
Toseland
Yelling
Papworth Village Settlement
Papworth Everard
Knapwell
CAMBRIDGESHI
Duloe
Staploe
Bushmead
St Neots
Eaton Socon
Eynesbury
Croxton
Eltisley
Cambourne
Childerley G
Bolnhurst
Upper Staploe
Colmworth
Honeydon
BEDFORD
Caxton
Caldecote
Abbotsley
Little Barford
Great Gransden
Little Gransden
Longstowe
Bourn
Kingston
Wyboston
Chawston
Colesden
Wilden
Roxton
Tempsford
Waresley
Tetworth
Gamlingay
Gamlingay Cinques
Gamlingay Great Heath
Green End
Great Barford
Blunham
Everton
Hatley St George
East Hatley
Arrington
Willington
Sandy
Potton
Deepdale
Cockayne Hatley
Croydon
New Wimpole
Wimpole
Cople
Chapel End
Hatch
A1(M)
A1
A14
A141
A428
A1198
A421
B1040
B1046
B1042
138
104
121

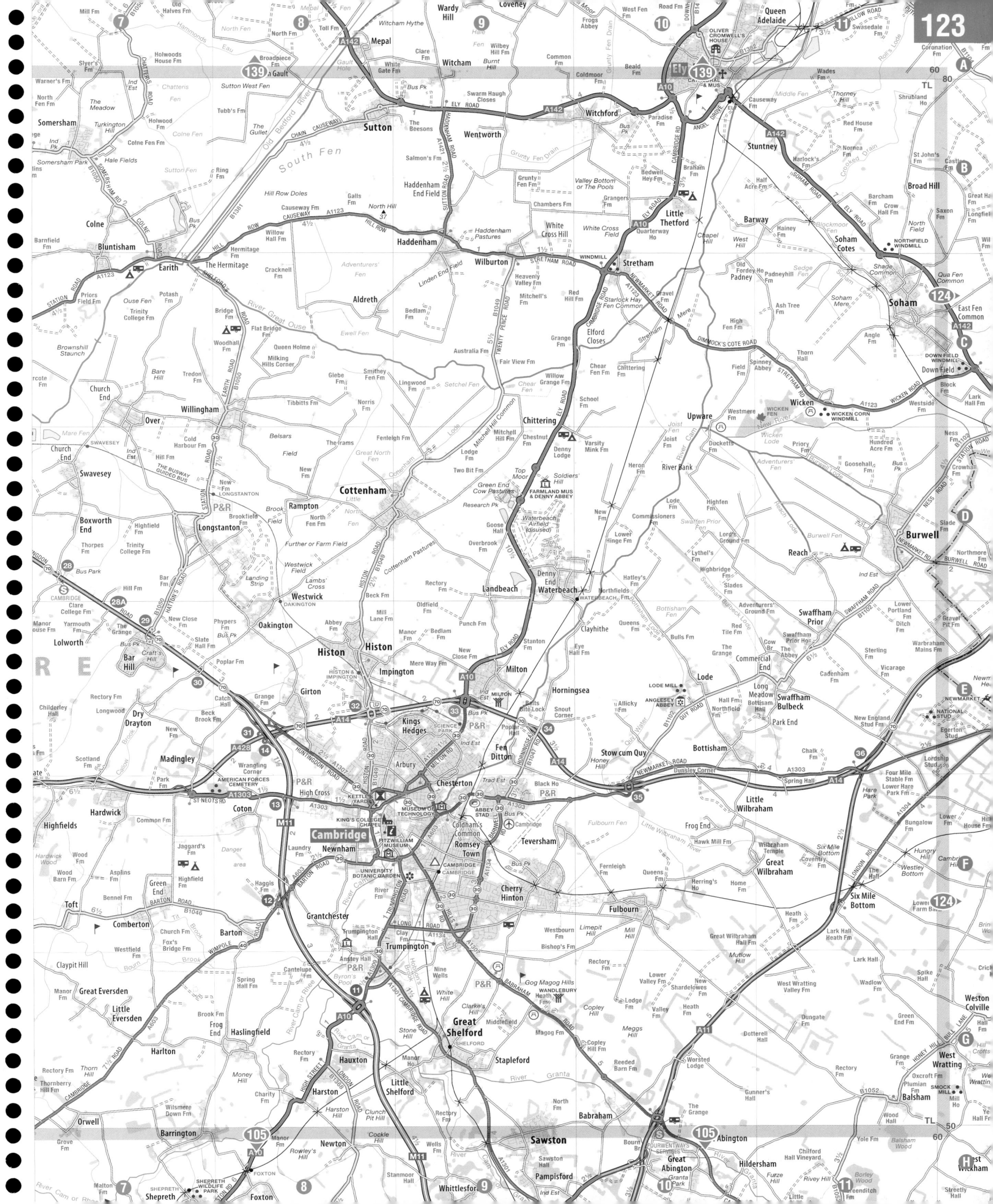
Mill Fm
Old Halves Fm
Mepal
Wardy Hill
Coveney
Frogs Abbey
West Fen Fm
Road Fm
Queen Adelaide
Oliver Cromwell's House
Witcham Hythe
Toll Fm
North Fen
Holwoods House Fm
Broadpiece Fm
Gault
Clare Fm
White Gate Fm
Witcham
Wilbey Hill Fm
Burnt Hill
Common Fm
Coldmoor Fm
Beald Fm
Ely
Cathedral & Mus
Wades Fm
Coronation Fm
Warner's Fm
Ind Est
Chatteris Fen
Sutton West Fen
Bus Pk
Swarm Haugh Closes
Middle Fen
Thorney Hill
Shrubland Ho
North Fen Fm
The Meadow
Tubb's Fm
Sutton
The Beesons
Wentworth
Witchford
Paradise Fm
Causeway Fm
Red House Fm
Somersham
Turkington Hill
Holwood Fm
Colne Fen
The Gullet
Chain Causeway
Angel Drove
Stuntney
Colne Fen Fm
Salmon's Fm
Grunty Fen Drain
Nornea Fm
St John's Fm
Somersham Park
Hale Fields
South Fen
Sutton Fen
Ring Fm
Braham Fm
Bedwell Hey Fm
Harlock's Fm
Haddenham End Field
Grunty Fen Fm
Valley Bottom or The Pools
Half Acre Fm
Broad Hill
Hill Row Doles
Galls Fm
Causeway Fm
North Hill
Chambers Fm
Grangers Fm
Little Thetford
Barcham Fm
Crow Hall Fm
Colne
Haddenham Pastures
White Cross Hill
White Cross Field
Quarterway Ho
Barway
Hainey Fm
Blackmoor Fen
North Field
Barnfield Fm
Willow Hall Fm
Haddenham
Soham Cotes
Northfield Windmill
Bluntisham
Hermitage Fm
Wilburton
Windmill
Stretham
Chapel Hill
West Hill
Earith
The Hermitage
Cracknell Fm
Adventurers' Fen
Linden End Field
Heavenly Valley Fm
Red Hill Fm
Old Fordey Ho
Padney
Padneyhill Fm
Sedge Fen
Shade Common
Qua Fen Common
Priors Field Fm
Ouse Fen
Potash Fm
Aldreth
Mitchell's Fm
Starlock Hay Fen Common
Gravel Fm
Soham
Trinity College Fm
Bridge Fm
Bedlam Fm
Mere
Ash Tree Fm
Soham Mere
East Fen Common
River Great Ouse
Flat Bridge Fm
Ewell Fen
Elford Closes
High Fen Fm
Brownshill Staunch
Woodhall Fm
Queen Holme
Milking Hills Corner
Australia Fm
Grange Fm
Dimmock's Cote Road
Angle Fm
Thorn Hall
Down Field Windmill
Down Field
Fair View Fm
Chear Fen Fm
Chittering Fm
Field Fm
Spinney Abbey
Bare Hill
Tredon Fm
Glebe Fm
Smithey Fen Fm
Lingwood Fm
Setchel Fen
Chear Fen
Willow Grange Fm
Church End
Willingham
Tibbitts Fm
Norris Fm
School Fm
Wicken
Wicken Fen
Wicken Corn Windmill
Westmere Fm
Block Fm
Lark Hall Fm
Westside Fm
Over
Mare Fen
Chittering
Upware
New River
Swavesey
Church End
Ind Est
Cold Harbour Fm
Belsars Field
The Irams
Fenleigh Fm
Mitchell Hill Fm
Chestnut Fm
Denny Lodge
Varsity Mink Fm
Joist Fen
Wicken Lode
Hundred Acre Fm
Priory Fm
Ness Fm
Hill Fm
The Busway Guided Bus
Great North Fen
Lodge Fm
Adventurers' Fen
Gooseball Fm
Crowhall Fm
New Fm
Longstanton
Cottenham
Two Bit Fm
Top Moor
Soldiers' Hill
Heron Fm
River Bank
Bus Pk
Green End
Cow Pastures
Farmland Mus & Denny Abbey
Research Pk
Swavesey
P&R
Brookfield Fm
Rampton
Lode Fm
Highfen Fm
Reach Lode
Boxworth End
Highfield Fm
North Fen Fm
Waterbeach Airfield (disused)
New Fm
Commissioners Fm
Swaffen Prior Fen
Lord's Ground Fm
Burwell Fen
Burwell
Slade Fm
Thorpes Fm
Trinity College Fm
Further or Farm Field
Goose Hall
Overbrook Fm
Lower Hinge Fm
Lythel's Fm
Reach
Northmore Fm
Bus Park
Westwick Field
Lambs' Cross
Cottenham Pastures
Denny End
Highbridge Fm
Ind Est
Landing Strip
Bar Fm
Rectory Fm
Landbeach
Waterbeach
Hatley's Fm
Slades Fm
Hill Fm
Cambridge
Westwick
Dakington
Beck Fm
Oldfield Fm
Northfields Fm
Adventurers' Ground Fm
Swaffham Prior
Lower Portland Fm
Clare College Fm
Mill Lane Fm
Punch Fm
Bottisham Fen
Ditch Fm
Gravel Pit Fm
Manor House Fm
Yarmouth Fm
The Grange
New Close Fm
Phypers Fm
Oakington
Abbey Fm
Queens Fm
Red Tile Fm
Lolworth
Slate Hall Fm
Bus Pk
Manor Fm
Bedlam Fm
Stanton Fm
Clayhithe
Bulls Fm
Swaffham Prior Ho
Warbraham Mains Fm
Bar Hill
Craft's Hill
Histon
New Close Fm
Eye Hall Fm
Cow Hall
The Abbey
Sterling Fm
Poplar Fm
Mere Way Fm
Milton
The Grange
Commercial End
Cadenham Fm
Vicarage Fm
Rectory Fm
Catch Hall
Impington
Histon & Impington
Horningsea
Lode
Lode Mill
Anglesey Abbey
Long Meadow
Swaffham Bulbeck
Childerley Hall
Longwood
Dry Drayton
Girton
Grange Fm
Milton
Kings Hedges
Science Park
Balls Bite Lock
Snout Corner
Allicky Fm
Hall Fm
Northfield Fm
Bottisham Hall
Park End
New England Stud Fm
National Stud
Newmarket
Egerton Stud
Beck Brook Fm
New Fm
Ind Est
Poplar Hall
Fen Ditton
Stow cum Quy
Honey Hill
Bottisham
Chalk Fm
Lordship Stud
Scotland Fm
Madingley
Wrangling Corner
Arbury
Chesterton
Newmarket Road
Dunsley Corner
Spring Hall
Four Mile Stable Fm
Lower Hare Park Fm
Hare Park
Park Fm
American Forces Cemetery
High Cross
Kettle's Yard
Trad Est
Black Ho
Little Wilbraham
Hardwick
Highfields
Common Fm
Coton
King's College Chapel
Museum of Technology
Abbey Stad
Coldham's Common
Fulbourn Fen
Little Wilbraham River
Frog End
Bungalow Fm
Lower Fm
Hill House Fm
Cambridge
Newnham
Fitzwilliam Museum
Romsey Town
Teversham
Hawk Mill Fm
Wilbraham Temple
Six Mile Bottom
Hungry Hill
Westley Bottom
Jaggard's Fm
Danger area
Laundry Fm
Wood Fm
Wood Barn Fm
Asplins Fm
Highfield Fm
Haggis Fm
University Botanic Garden
Great Wilbraham
Coventry Fm
The Hall
Green End
River Fm
Cherry Hinton
Fernleigh Fm
Queens Fm
Herring's Ho
Home Fm
Toft
Bennel Fm
Barton
Grantchester
Fulbourn
Heath Fm
Lower Farm Barn
Comberton
Church Fm
Fox's Bridge Fm
Trumpington Hall
Clay Fm
Trumpington
Westbourn Fm
Bishop's Fm
Limepit Hill
Mill Hill
Great Wilbraham Hall Fm
Lark Hall Heath Fm
Westfield Fm
Anstey Hall
Rectory Fm
Mutlow Hill
Lark Hall
Claypit Hill
Cantelupe Fm
Byron's Pool
Nine Wells
Gog Magog Hills
Wandlebury
Lower Valley Fm
New Shardelowes Fm
West Wratting Valley Fm
Spike Hall
Wadlow Fm
Manor Fm
Great Eversden
Spring Hall Fm
White Hill
Clarke's Hill
Copley Hill
Lodge Fm
Valley Fm
Heath Fm
Dungate Fm
Green End Fm
Weston Colville
Little Eversden
Brook Fm
Frog End
Haslingfield
Stone Hill
Great Shelford
Middlefield
Magog Fm
Meggs Hill
Dotterell Hall
Harlton
Rectory Fm
Hauxton
Manor Ho
Shelford
Stapleford
Copley Hill Fm
Reeded Barn Fm
Worsted Lodge
Rectory Fm
Grange Fm
West Wratting
Oxcroft Fm
Plumian Fm
Rectory Fm
Thorn Hill
Thornberry Hill Fm
Money Hill
Harston
Little Shelford
River Granta
Gunner's Hall
Balsham
Smock Mill
Charity Fm
Wilsmere Down Fm
Harston Hill
Clunch Pit Hill
Rectory Fm
North Fm
Babraham
The Grange
Wood Hall
Orwell
Barrington
Newton
Cockle Hill
Manor Fm
Rowley's Hill
Wells Fm
Sawston
Abington
Fourwentways Services
Yole Fm
Balsham Wood
Grove Fm
Chilford Hall Vineyard
Hildersham
West Wickham
Sawston Hall
Pampisford
Great Abington
Little Abington
Granta Park
Furze Hill
Rivey Hill
Borley Wood
Malton Fm
Shepreth
Shepreth Wildlife Park
Foxton
Stanmoor Hall
Whittlesford
Ind Est
Streetly Hall

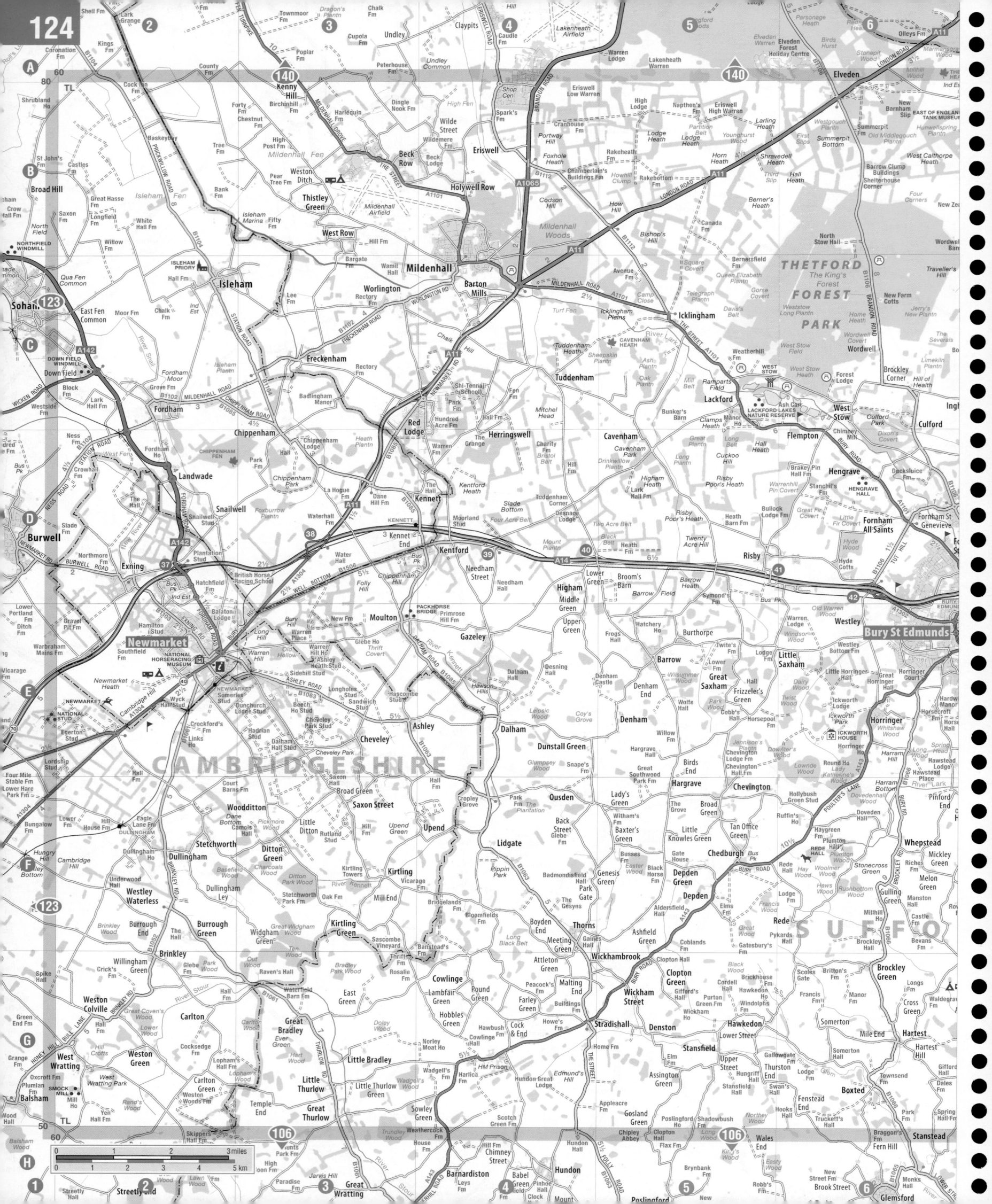

140
106
123
CAMBRIDGESHIRE
SUFFO
THETFORD FOREST PARK
The King's Forest
Mildenhall
Newmarket
Bury St Edmunds
Isleham
Soham
Fordham
Chippenham
Landwade
Snailwell
Exning
Burwell
Kennett
Kentford
Red Lodge
Freckenham
Worlington
Barton Mills
Eriswell
Holywell Row
Beck Row
West Row
Thistley Green
Kenny Hill
Icklingham
Tuddenham
Herringswell
Cavenham
Lackford
West Stow
Flempton
Culford
Hengrave
Fornham All Saints
Risby
Higham
Barrow
Moulton
Gazeley
Dalham
Denham
Ousden
Great Saxham
Little Saxham
Westley
Horringer
Chevington
Hargrave
Chedburgh
Depden
Rede
Whepstead
Hartest
Boxted
Stansfield
Hawkedon
Wickhambrook
Stradishall
Denston
Lidgate
Cowlinge
Kirtling
Cheveley
Ashley
Woodditton
Saxon Street
Stetchworth
Dullingham
Brinkley
Carlton
Weston Colville
West Wratting
Balsham
Great Bradley
Little Bradley
Little Thurlow
Great Thurlow
Barnardiston
Hundon
Great Wratting
Stanstead
Glemsford
Lakenheath Airfield
Mildenhall Airfield
Elveden
A11
A14
A142
A1101
A1065
A143
A1304
A1302
B1085
B1063
B1106
B1102
B1104
B1506
B1061
B1052
B1066
0 1 2 3 miles
0 1 2 3 4 5 km

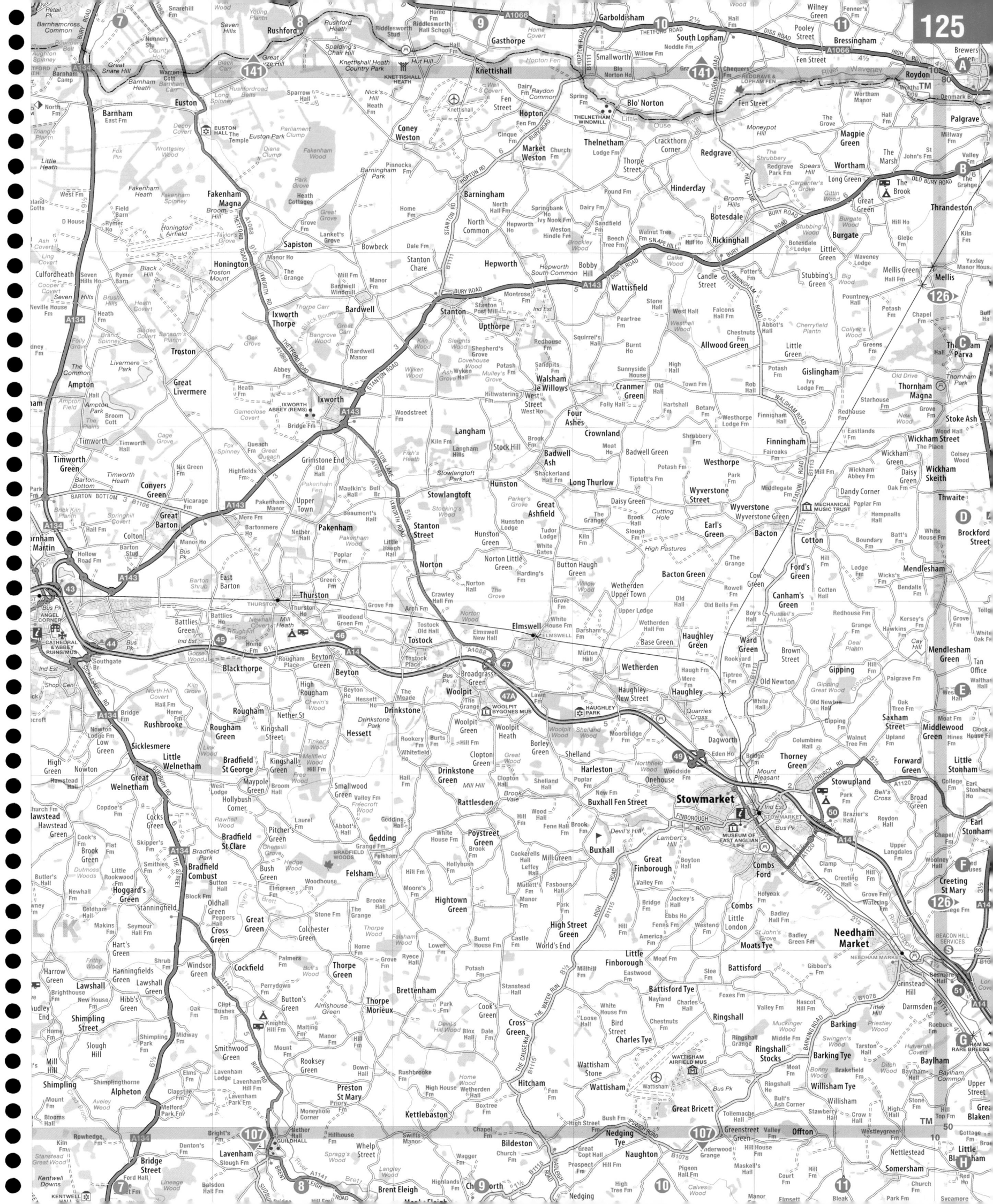
Rushford
Gasthorpe
Garboldisham
South Lopham
Bressingham
Roydon
Barnham
Euston
Knettishall
Blo' Norton
Fen Street
Palgrave
Coney Weston
Hopton
Thelnetham
Redgrave
Magpie Green
Market Weston
Thorpe Street
Wortham
Hinderclay
Botesdale
Rickinghall
Burgate
Thrandeston
Fakenham Magna
Barningham
North Common
Sapiston
Honington
Bowbeck
Stanton Chare
Hepworth
Bobby Hill
Wattisfield
Candle Street
Stubbing's Green
Mellis Green
Mellis
Ixworth Thorpe
Bardwell
Stanton
Upthorpe
Allwood Green
Little Green
Gislingham
Troston
Walsham le Willows
Cranmer Green
Thornham Parva
Thornham Magna
Ampton
Great Livermere
Ixworth
Four Ashes
Crownland
Stoke Ash
Langham
Stock Hill
Badwell Ash
Badwell Green
Westhorpe
Finningham
Wickham Street
Timworth Green
Conyers Green
Grimstone End
Stowlangtoft
Hunston
Long Thurlow
Wyverstone Street
Wyverstone
Wyverstone Green
Wickham Skeith
Thwaite
Great Barton
Pakenham
Upper Town
Stanton Street
Great Ashfield
Hunston Green
Earl's Green
Bacton
Cotton
Brockford Street
Norton
Norton Little Green
Button Haugh Green
Bacton Green
Mendlesham
Ford's Green
Canham's Green
East Barton
Thurston
Wetherden Upper Town
Cow Green
Elmswell
Tostock
Haughley Green
Ward Green
Brown Street
Mendlesham Green
Blackthorpe
Beyton
Woolpit
Wetherden
Haughley New Street
Haughley
Gipping
Old Newton
Rougham
Drinkstone
Hessett
Saxham Street
Middlewood Green
Rushbrooke
Rougham Green
Kingshall Street
Woolpit Green
Woolpit Heath
Borley Green
Shelland
Dagworth
Sicklesmere
Little Welnetham
Bradfield St George
Kingshall Green
Drinkstone Green
Clopton Green
Harleston
Thorney Green
Forward Green
Little Stonham
Great Welnetham
Smallwood Green
Rattlesden
Buxhall Fen Street
Stowmarket
Stowupland
Broad Green
Earl Stonham
Bradfield St Clare
Gedding
Poystreet Green
Buxhall
Great Finborough
Combs Ford
Bradfield Combust
Felsham
Hogmand's Green
Hightown Green
Creeting St Mary
Combs
Little London
Needham Market
Great Green
Cross Green
High Street Green
World's End
Moats Tye
Lawshall
Cockfield
Thorpe Green
Little Finborough
Battisford
Brettenham
Thorpe Morieux
Battisford Tye
Ringshall
Barking
Shimpling Street
Cross Green
Bird Street
Charles Tye
Ringshall Stocks
Barking Tye
Baylham
Alpheton
Shimpling
Rooksey Green
Preston St Mary
Hitcham
Wattisham Stone
Wattisham
Willisham Tye
Kettlebaston
Great Bricett
Lavenham
Bildeston
Nedging Tye
Naughton
Offton
Bridge Street
Brent Eleigh
Somersham
Little Blakenham
A1066
A134
A143
A14
A1088
A1120
B1113
B1115
A1141
141
107
126

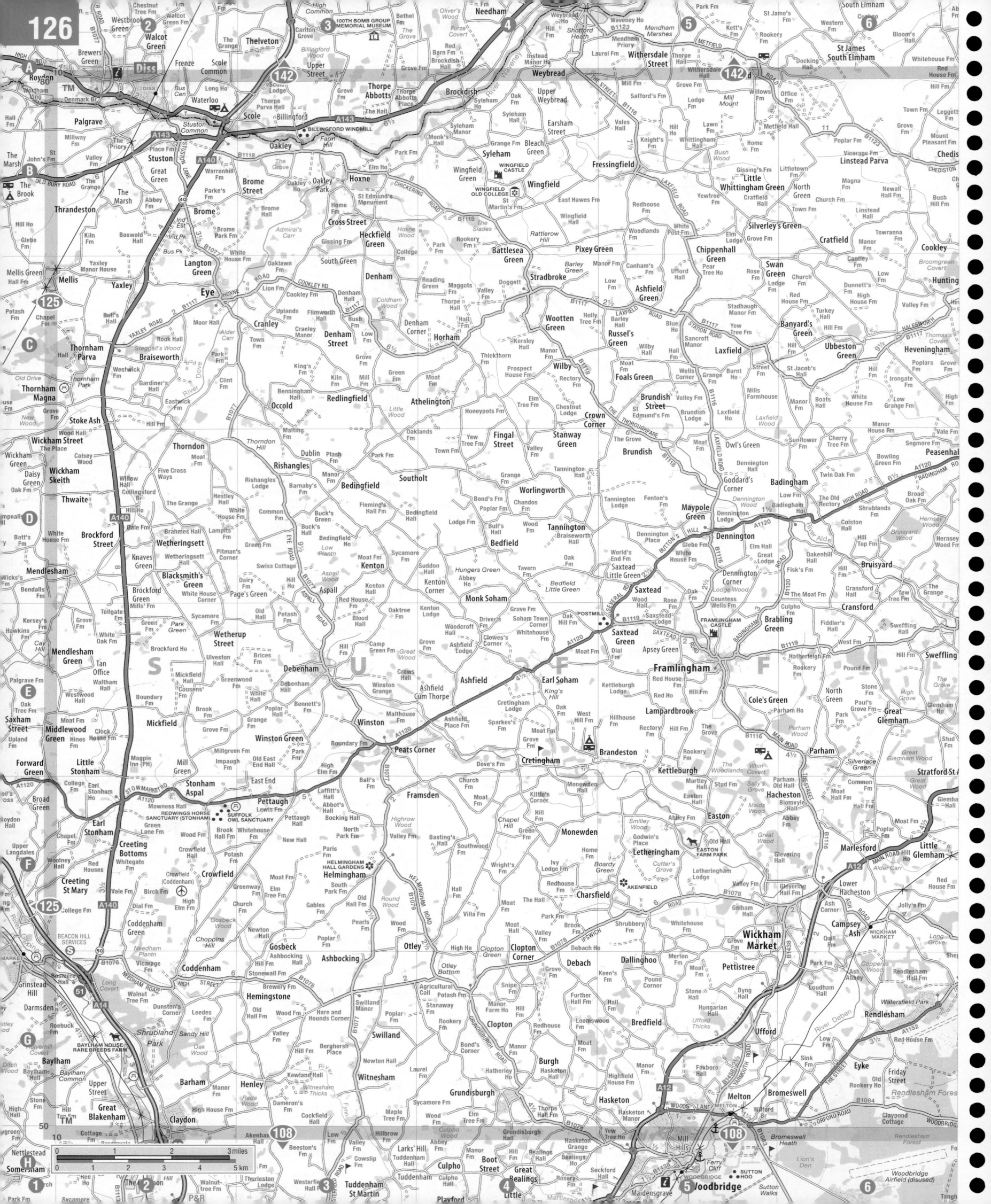
Diss
Eye
Stradbroke
Framlingham
Debenham
Wickham Market
Woodbridge
Laxfield
Fressingfield
Hoxne
Scole
Mellis
Brandeston
Helmingham
Otley
Grundisburgh
Wetheringsett
Mendlesham
Stowmarket Road
FRAMLINGHAM CASTLE
HELMINGHAM HALL GARDENS
EASTON FARM PARK
BAYLHAM HOUSE RARE BREEDS FARM
REDWINGS HORSE SANCTUARY (STONHAM)
SUFFOLK OWL SANCTUARY
100TH BOMB GROUP MEMORIAL MUSEUM
BILLINGFORD WINDMILL
WINGFIELD CASTLE
WINGFIELD OLD COLLEGE
0 1 2 3 miles
0 1 2 3 4 5 km

127
Covehithe
Frostenden
Stoven
Westhall
Brampton
Mill Common
Uggeshall
South Cove
Cove Bottom
Clay Common
Frostenden Corner
Rumburgh
Spexhall
Wissett
Broadway
Halesworth
Holton
Wangford
Reydon Smear
Reydon
Southwold
SOUTHWOLD MUSEUM
Sole Bay
Gunhill Cliff
Blyford
Wenhaston
Mells
Blythburgh
Blackheath
Walberswick
The Flats
HEN REEDBED NATURE RESERVE
Walpole
Bramfield
Thorington
Sibton Green
High Street
Darsham
Dunwich
DUNWICH UNDERWATER EXPLORATION MUSEUM
Dunwich Cliffs
Dunwich Forest
Westleton
Hemp Green
Sibton
Yoxford
Middleton
Middleton Moor
Theberton
Eastbridge
Minsmere Level
MINSMERE
The Sluice
Rotten End
North Green
Curlew Green
Kelsale
Carlton
Rendham
Saxmundham
LEISTON ABBEY
Sizewell
Leiston
LONG SHOP MUSEUM
Knodishall
Coldfair Green
Aldringham
Thorpe Ness
Thorpeness
Benhall Green
Benhall Street
Sternfield
Friday Street
Farnham
Friston
Gromford
Snape
SNAPE MALTINGS
Blaxhall
Iken
Aldeburgh
THE RED HOUSE
NORTH WARREN
Fort Green
Slaughden
Aldeburgh Bay
Tunstall
Tunstall Forest
High Street
Sudbourne
Chillesford
Butley
Orford
Orford Ness
HAVERGATE ISLAND
ORFORDNESS HAVERGATE
Capel Green
Butley High Corner
Gedgrave Hall
SUFFOLK COAST AND HEATHS
A12
A144
A1094
B1125
B1122
B1119
B1121
B1069
B1078
B1084
B1387
B1126
B1123
143
109
TM
60
80
50
7
8
9
10
11
A
B
C
D
E
F
G
H

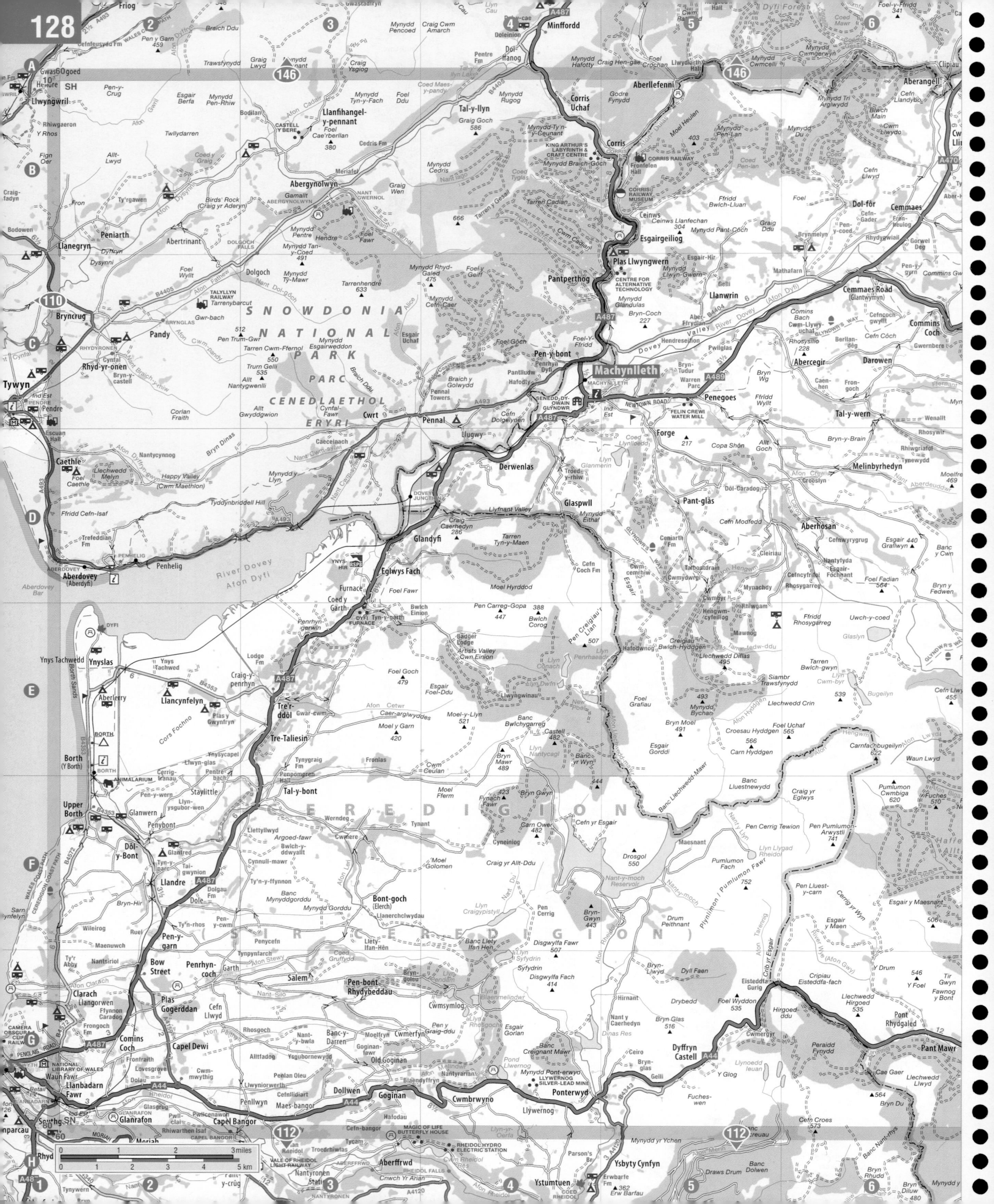
SNOWDONIA NATIONAL PARK
PARC CENEDLAETHOL ERYRI
CEREDIGION
(SIR CEREDIGION)
Machynlleth
Tywyn
Aberdovey (Aberdyfi)
Borth (Y Borth)
Upper Borth
Ynyslas
Llwyngwril
Llanegryn
Bryncrug
Rhyd-yr-onen
Pendre
Caethle
Abergynolwyn
Llanfihangel-y-pennant
Tal-y-llyn
Minffordd
Corris Uchaf
Corris
Aberllefenni
Esgairgeiliog
Plas Llwyngwern
Pantperthog
Llanwrin
Pen-y-bont
Pennal
Cwrt
Llugwy
Derwenlas
Glaspwll
Glandyfi
Eglwys Fach
Furnace
Penhelig
Forge
Penegoes
Tal-y-wern
Melinbyrhedyn
Pant-glâs
Aberhosan
Abercegir
Darowen
Cemmaes
Cemmaes Road (Glantwymyn)
Commins Coch
Dol-fôr
Aberangell
Clipiau
Tre'r-ddôl
Tre-Taliesin
Llancynfelyn
Tal-y-bont
Dôl-y-Bont
Llandre
Bow Street
Penrhyn-coch
Pen-y-garn
Clarach
Salem
Pen-bont Rhydybeddau
Capel Dewi
Comins Coch
Plas Gogerddan
Llanbadarn Fawr
Waun Fawr
Glanrafon
Capel Bangor
Dollwen
Goginan
Cwmbrwyno
Ponterwyd
Dyffryn Castell
Ysbyty Cynfyn
Ystumtuen
Aberffrwd
Bont-goch (Elerch)
Cwmsymlog
Pant Mawr
River Dovey
Afon Dyfi
Nant-y-moch Reservoir
Pumlumon Fach
Plynlimon / Pumlumon Fawr
752
Pen Pumlumon Arwystli
741
Drosgol
550
A487
A493
A44
A470
A489
B4405
B4404
B4353
B4572
146
110
112
1
2
3
4
5
6
A
B
C
D
E
F
G
H
SH
SN
0 1 2 3 miles
0 1 2 3 4 5 km

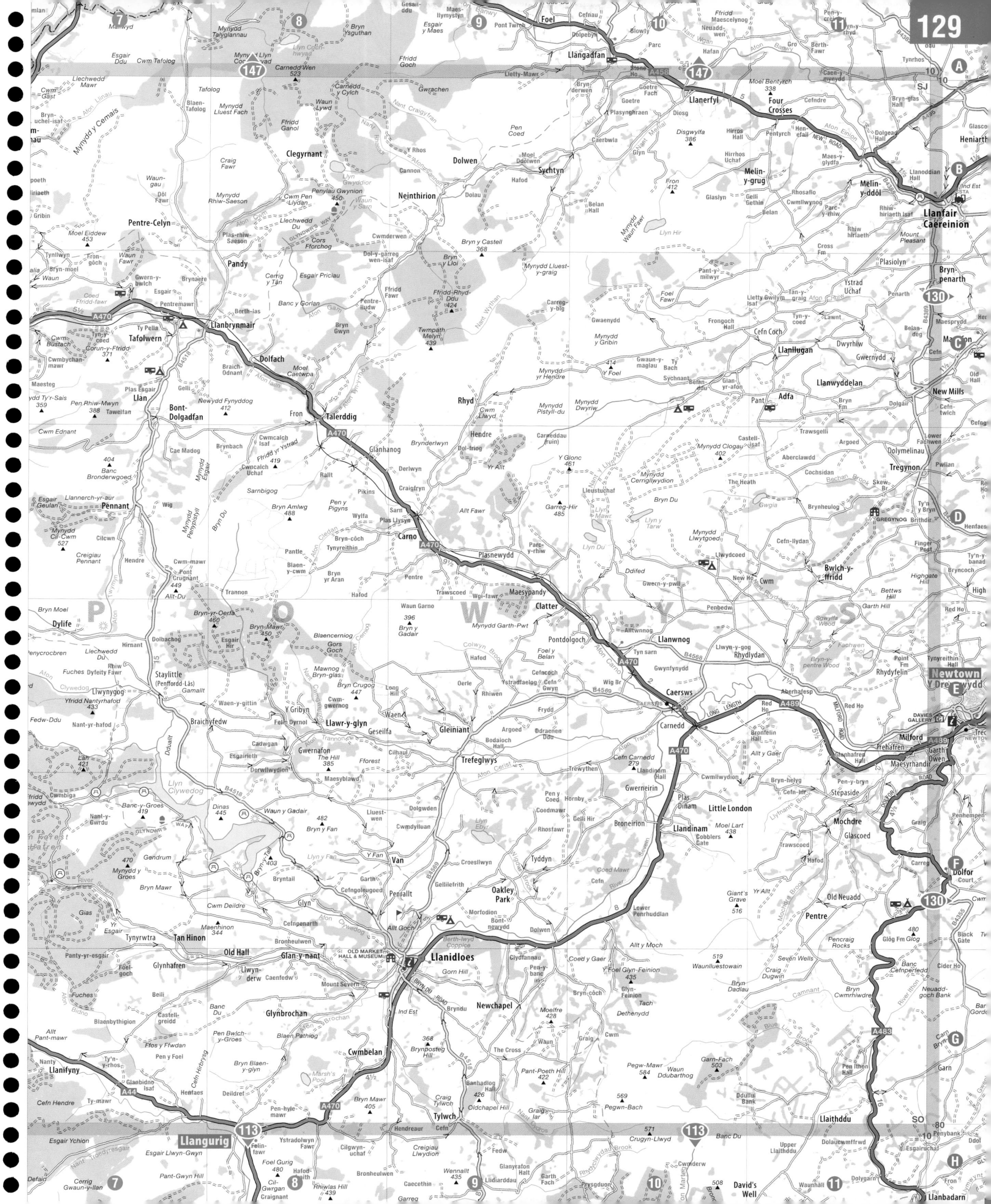
Mallwyd
Mynydd Tafylgannau
Bryn Ysguthan
Egsair y Maes
Maes-llymystyn
Pont Twrch
Foel
Cefnau
Dolpebyll
Blowty
Ffridd Maescelynog
Neuadd-wen
Parc
Gro
Berth-Fawr
Tynrhos
Esgair Ddu
Cwm Tafolog
Mynydd Llyn Coch-hwyad
Carnedd Wen 523
Ffridd Goch
Llangadfan
Llety-Mawr
Stone Ho
A458
Hafan
Llanerfyl
Moel Bentyrch 338
Four Crosses
Cefndre
Bryn-glas Hall
Llechwedd Mawr
Cwm Gast
Tafolog
Blaen-Tafolog
Mynydd Lluest Fach
Carnedd y Cylch
Gwrachen
Nant Craigyfran
Bryn-derwen
Goetre
Goetre Fach
Plasynghraen
Diosg
Disgwylfa 386
Hirros Hall
Pentyrch
Hen-efail
Dolgead Hall
Heniarth
Mynydd y Cemais
Ffridd Ganol
Waun Lwyd
Pen Coed
Caerbwla
Glyn
Hirrhos Uchaf
Melin-y-grug
Maes-y-glydfa
Clegyrnant
Craig Fawr
Y Rhos
Dolwen
Moel Ddolwen
Sychtyn
Cannon
Hafod
Fron 412
Llanoddian Hall
Melin-y-ddôl
Llanfair Caereinion
Waun-gau
Dôl Fawr
Mynydd Rhiw-Saeson
Llyn Gwyddior
Penylau Gwynion 450
Neinthirion
Dolau
Belan Hall
Glaslyn
Gelli Gethin
Cwmllwynog
Rhosaflo
Parc-y-rhiw
Rhiw-hiriaeth Isaf
Rhiw hiriaeth
Mount Pleasant
Cwm Pen Llydan
Llechwedd Du
Pentre-Celyn
Moel Eiddew 453
Plas-rhiw-Saeson
Cors Fforchog
Cwmderwen
Mynydd Waun Fawr
Llyn Hir
Belan
Tynllwyn
Fron-goch
Waun Fawr
Bryn-moel
Waun
Pandy
Cerrig y Tân
Esgair Priciau
Dol-y-garreg wen-isaf
Bryn y Lloi
Bryn y Castell 368
Mynydd Lluest-y-graig
Cross Fm
Plasiolyn
Pant-y-milwyr
Bryn-penarth
Gwern-y-bwlch
Esgair
Brynaere
Coed Ffridd-fawr
Banc y Gorlan
Ffridd Fawr
Pentre-llwdw
Ffridd-Rhyd-Ddu 424
Carreg-y-big
Foel Fawr
Tan-y-graig
Llettty Gwilym Isaf
Ystrad Uchaf
Penarth
Pentremawr
Berth-las
A470
Llanbrynmair
Ty Pella
Tafolwern
Cwm Bustach
Tyn-y-coed
Corun-y-Ffridd 371
Cwmbychan-mawr
Bryn Gwyn
Twmpath Melyn 439
Nant Wythan
Gwaenydd
Mynydd y Gribin
Frongoch Hall
Cefn Coch
Tyn-y-coed
Lawnt
Llanllugan
Dwyrhiw
Gwernydd
Belan-deg
Maesprydd
B4518
Braich-Odnant
Dolfach
Moel Caetwpa
Afon Iaen
Mynydd yr Hendre
414 Y Foel
Gwaun-y-maglau
Ty Bach
Sychnant
Belan-ddu
Glan-yr-afon
Pant
Adfa
Llanwyddelan
New Mills
Maesteg
Plas Esgair
Llan
Gelli
Pen Rhiw-Mwyn 388
Taweltan
Mynydd Ty'r-Sais 359
Bont-Dolgadfan
Newydd Fynyddog 412
Fron
Talerddig
Rhyd
Cwm Llwyd
Mynydd Pistyll-du
Mynydd Dwyriw
Bryn Fm
Dolgair
Cefn-twlch
Cwm Ednant
Cae Madog
Brynbach
Cwmcalch Isaf
Ffridd yr Ystrad 419
Mynydd Esgair
Glanhanog
Brynderlwyn
Hendre
Dol-friog
Carneddau (ruin)
Y Glonc 461
Castell-isaf
Mynydd Clogau 402
Trawsgelli
Argoed
Lower Fachwen
Dolymelinau
404 Banc Bronderwgoed
Cwmcalch Uchaf
Rallt
Derlwyn
Yr Allt
Mynydd Cerriglwydion
Aberclawdd
Cochsidan
Bechan Brook
Tregynon
Pwllan
Sarnbigog
Pikins
Craigfryn
Lleustuchaf
The Heath
Skew Br
Esgair Geulan
Llannerch-yr-aur
Pennant
Wig
Mynydd Penypistyll
Bryn Du
Bryn Amlwg 488
Pen y Pigyns
Sarn
Allt Fawr
Garreg-Hir 485
Llyn Mawr
Bryn Du
Gwgia
Brynheulog
Ty'n y Bryn
Brithdir
GREGYNOG
Mynydd Cil-Cwm 527
Cilcwn
Wylfa
Plas Llysyn
Carno
Bryn-côch
Tynyreithin
Llyn y Tarw
Mynydd Llwytgoed
Cefn-llydan
Finger Post
Hendre
Creigiau Pennant
Pantle
Blaen-y-cwm
Plasnewydd
Parc-y-rhiw
Llyn Du
Llwydcoed
Ddifed
Gwern-y-pwll
New Ho
Cwm
Bwlch-y-ffridd
Highgate Hill
Bryncoch
Cwm-mawr
Pont Crugnant
449
Allt-Du
Bryn yr Aran
Pentre
Trawscoed
Wgi-fawr
Maesypandy
Bettws Hill
Trannon
Hafod
Waun Garno
Clatter
Penbedw
Garth Hill
Red Ho
Bryn Moel
Dylife
P
O
W
Y
S
Bryn-yr-Oerfa 460
Bryn-Mawr 450
Blaencerniog
396 Bryn y Gadair
Mynydd Garth-Pwt
Alltwnnog
Llanwnog
Llwyn-y-gog
Rhydlydan
Sgwyfla Wood
Fachwen Pool
Penycrocbren
Llechwedd Du
Hirnant
Dolbachog
Esgair Hir
Gors Goch
Pontdolgoch
Foel y Belan
Tyn sarn
B4568
Bryn-y-pentre Wood
Point Fm
Tynyreithin Hall
Newtown
Y Drenewydd
Fuches Dyfeity Fawr
Rhiw
Staylittle (Penffordd-Lâs)
Mawnog Bryn-glas
Hafod
Cefncoch
Cefn Gwyn
Gwynfynydd
Rhydyfelin
Clywedog
Llwynygog
Gamallt
Bryn Crugog 447
Long Hill
Oerle
Ystradfaelog
Wig Br
B4569
Caersws
Aberhafesp
Red Ho
Yfridd Nantyrhafod 433
Waen-y-gittin
Cwm-gwernog
Rhiwen
Fedw-Ddu
Y Gribyn
Nant-yr-hafod
Braichyfedw
Felin Dyrnol
Llawr-y-glyn
Waen
Gleiniant
Frydd
Carnedd
LONG LENGTH
A489
Red Ho
DAVIES GALLERY
Geseilfa
Argoed
Dolgwlen
Bodaioch Hall
Bronfelin Hall
Allt y Gaer
Frehafren
Milford
Garth Owen
Maesyrhandir
Cadwgan
Gwernafon
The Hill 385
Cilhaul
Fforest
Trefeglwys
Cefn Carnedd 279
Llandinam Hall
Cwmllwydion
Trewythen
Penycrocbren
Lan 421
Esgairieth
Derwlwydion
Maesyblawd
Gwerneirin
Bryn-helyg
Cefn-Ilr
Pen-y-bryn
Stepaside
Dinas 445
Waun y Gadair
Pen y Coed
Hornby
Plas Dinam
Little London
Cwmbiga
Banc-y-Groes 419
Llyn Clywedog
Nant-y-Gwrdu
482 Bryn y Fan
Lluest-wen
Cwmdylluan
Coedmawr
Gelli Hir
Broneirion
Llandinam
Moel Lart 438
Cobblers Gate
Mochdre
Glascoed
Penhempen
Llyn Ebyr
Rhosfawr
Trawscoed
Hafod
470 Mynydd y Groes
Gendrum
Bryn-y-Tail 403
Llyn y Fan
Y Fan
Van
Tyddyn
Yr Allt
Carreg
Dolfor
Bryn Mawr
Bryntail
Garth
Cefngoleugoed
Penrallt
Croesllwyn
Oakley Park
Coed Mawr
Cefn
Giant's Grave 516
Old Neuadd
Gellilefrith
Pentre
Gias
Cwm Deildre
Glyn
Morfodion
Bont-newydd
Lower Penrhuddlan
Yr Esgair
Tynyrwtra
Maenhinon 344
Tan Hinon
Cefnpenarth
Allt Goch
Dolwen
Allt y Moch
480 Glôg Fm Glôg
Black Gate
Bronheulwen
Berth-lwyd Coppice
Pencraig Rocks
Panty-yr-esgair
Old Hall
Glan-y-nant
OLD MARKET HALL & MUSEUM
Llanidloes
Clydfannau
Coed y Gaer
519 Waunllluestowain
Seven Wells
Banc Cefnperfedd
Cider Ho
Glynhafren
Foel-goch
Llwyn-derw
Caenfedw
Gorn Hill
Pen-y-banc
Y Foel Glyn-Feinion 435
Craig Dugwin
Mount Severn
Glyn-Feinion
Tach
Bryn Dadlau
Bryn Cwmrhiwdre
Neuadd-goch Bank
Fuches
Beili
Castell-greidd
Banc Du
Glynbrochan
Ind Est
Bryndu
Newchapel
Moelfre 428
Dethenydd
Blaenbythigion
Pen Bwlch-y-Groes
Blaen Pathiog
Waun
Cwm
Blue Lins Brook
A483
Allt Pant-mawr
Ffos y Ffwdan
Pen y Foel
368 Brynposteg Hill
The Cross
Carn Bryn
Nanty
Llanifyny
Tyn-y-rhos
Cefn Hirbrysg
Bryn Blaen-y-glyn
Cwmbelan
Pegw-Mawr 584
Waun Ddubarthog
Garn-Fach 503
Pen Ithon Hall
Garn
Glanbidno Isaf
A44
Henfaes
Deildref
Marsh's Pool
Banhadlog Hall
Pant-Poeth Hill 422
Cefn Hendre
Ty-mawr
Pen-hyle-mawr
A470
Bryn Mawr 405
Craig Tylwch
426 Oldchapel Hill
569 Pegwn-Bach
Dolfflu Bank
Tylwch
Graig-lar
Llaithddu
SO
Esgair Ychion
Llangurig
113
Ystradolwyn Fawr
Hendreraur
Cefn
571 Crugyn-Llwyd
Banc Du
Penybank
Esgair Llwyn-Gwyn
Felin-fawr
Cilgwyn-uchaf
Creigiau Llwydion
Fedw
Upper Llaithddu
Dolauewmffrwd
Esgairiuchaf
Foel Gurig 480
Hafod-aith
Bronheulwen
Glanyrafon Halt
Garth Fach
Cwmderw
Defaid
Cerrig Gwaun-y-llan
Pant-Gwyn Hill
Cil-Gwrgan
Craignant
Rhiwlas Hill 439
Caecethin
Wennallt 435
Llidiarddau
Prysgduon
508
David's Well
Waunhall
Dolygarn
Fron
Llanbadarn
Garreg
Afon Clywedog
River Severn
GLYNDŴR'S WAY
A
B
C
D
E
F
G
H
7
8
9
10
11
147
130

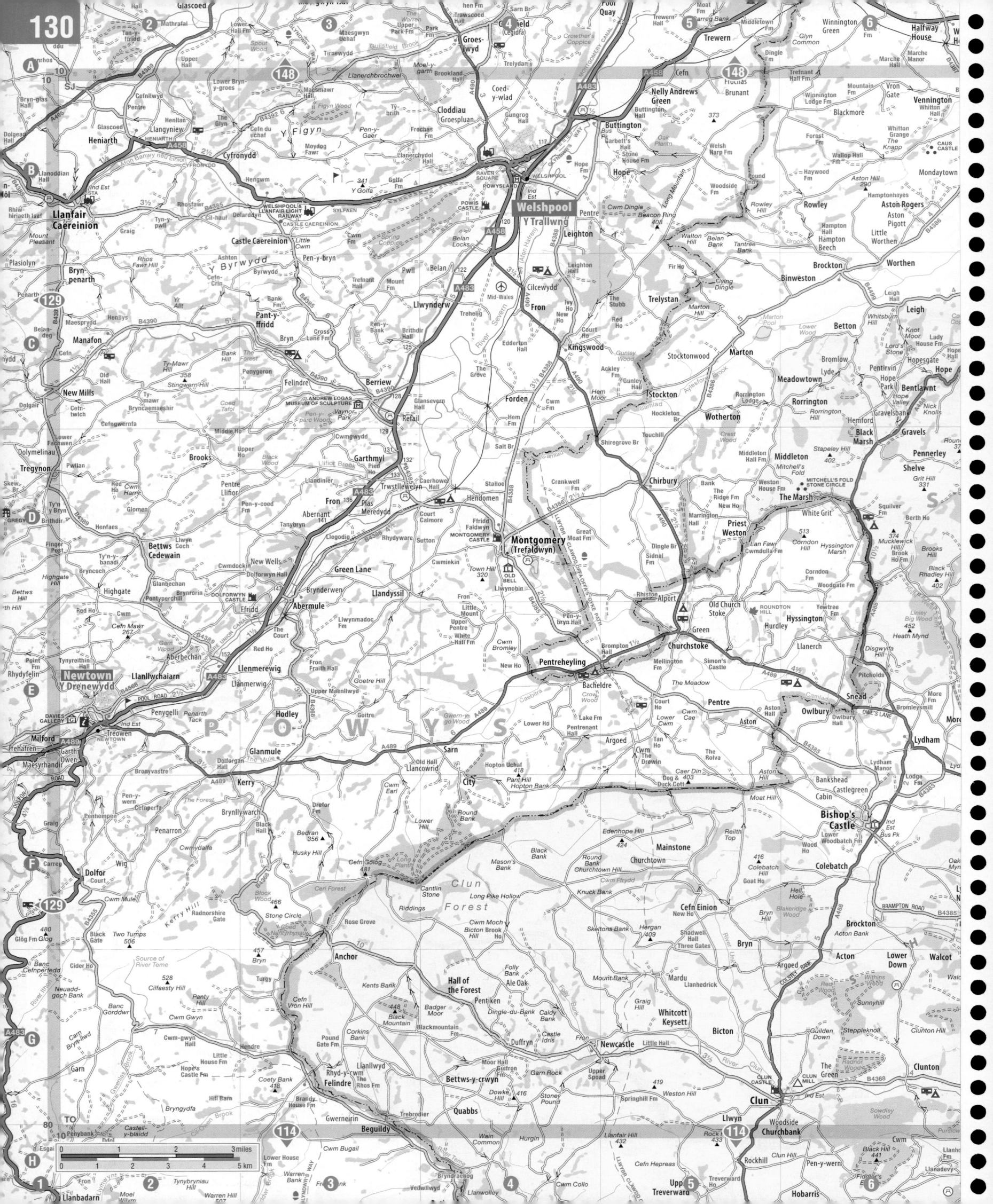

Glascoed
Mathrafal
Groes-lwyd
Quay
Trewern
Winnington Green
Halfway House
148
Llanerchbrochwel
Brookland Hall
Coed-y-wlad
Cefn
Nelly Andrews Green
Buttington
Vennington
Heniarth
Cyfronydd
Cloddiau
Groespluan
Y Figyn
Welshpool Y Trallwng
Llanfair Caereinion
Welshpool & Llanfair Light Railway
Castle Caereinion
Powis Castle
Leighton
Hope
Rowley
Aston Rogers
Bryn-penarth
Y Byrwydd
Pwll
Belan
Cilcewydd
Fron
Trelystan
Binweston
Brockton
Worthen
129
Pant-y-ffridd
Llwynderw
Manafon
Bryn
Berriew
Kingswood
Stocktonwood
Marton
Betton
Leigh
New Mills
Felindre
Forden
Stockton
Meadowtown
Rorrington
Hope
Bentlawnt
Andrew Logas Museum of Sculpture
Refail
Wotherton
Black Marsh
Gravels
Brooks
Garthmyl
Shiregrove Br
Middleton
Pennerley
Tregynon
Trwstllewelyn
Hendomen
Chirbury
Shelve
Fron
The Marsh
Abernant
Montgomery (Trefaldwyn)
Priest Weston
Bettws Cedewain
New Wells
Green Lane
Llandyssil
Abermule
Alport
Old Church Stoke
Hyssington
Churchstoke
Newtown Y Drenewydd
Llanllwchaiarn
Llenmerewig
Pentreheyling
Bacheldre
Hurdley
Llanerch
Hodley
POWYS
Sarn
Pentre
Aston
Owlbury
Snead
Milford
Treowen
Glanmule
Kerry
City
Argoed
Lydham
Dolfor
Bishop's Castle
Castlegreen
Mainstone
Churchtown
Colebatch
Clun Forest
Cefn Einion
Brockton
Anchor
Hall of the Forest
Bryn
Acton
Lower Down
Walcot
Whitcott Keysett
Bicton
Newcastle
Rhyd-y-cwm
Felindre
Bettws-y-crwyn
Clun
Clunton
Quabbs
Beguildy
Llwyn
Woodside
Churchbank
114
0 1 2 3 miles
0 1 2 3 4 5 km
Llanbadarn

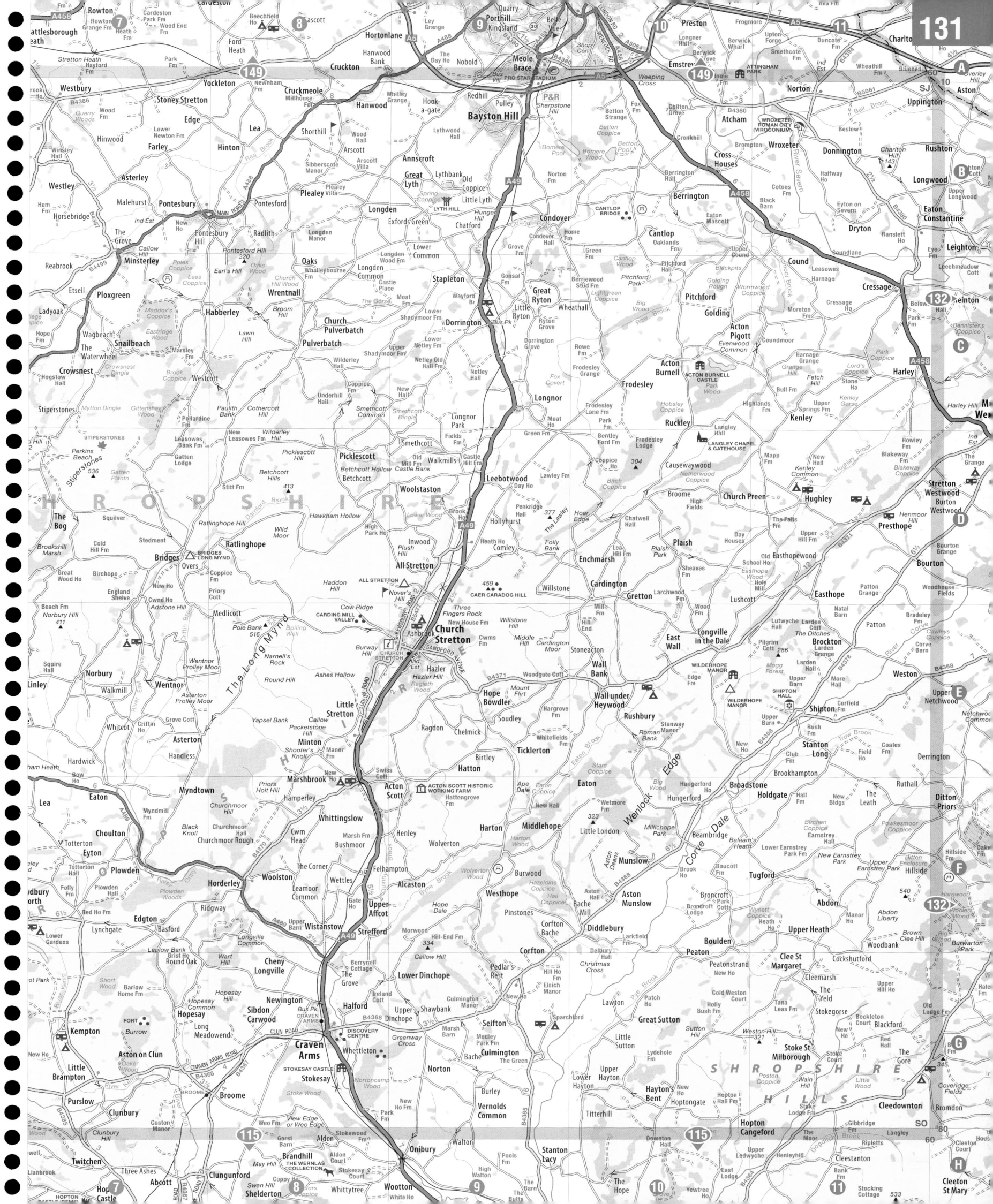
Rowton
Cardeston
Quarry
Porthill
Kingsland
Belle Vue
Preston
Charlton
Westbury
Yockleton
Cruckmeole
Cruckton
Hanwood
Meole Brace
Bayston Hill
Emstrey
Atcham
Norton
Uppington
Aston
Wroxeter
Donnington
Rushton
Longwood
Eaton Constantine
Dryton
Leighton
Cound
Cressage
Harley
Kenley
Stoney Stretton
Edge
Farley
Hinton
Lea
Shorthill
Arscott
Annscroft
Great Lyth
Lyth Hill
Pulley
Condover
Berrington
Cantlop
Cross Houses
Asterley
Westley
Pontesbury
Pontesbury Hill
Pontesford
Pontesford Hill
Minsterley
Plealey
Longden
Exfords Green
Chatford
Radlith
Oaks
Longden Common
Stapleton
Great Ryton
Little Ryton
Dorrington
Wheathall
Pitchford
Golding
Acton Pigott
Acton Burnell
Acton Burnell Castle
Frodesley
Ruckley
Longnor
Plox Green
Habberley
Wrentnall
Church Pulverbatch
Pulverbatch
Snailbeach
Crowsnest
Westcott
Stiperstones
Pickle Scott
Smethcott
Woolstaston
Leebotwood
Langley Chapel & Gatehouse
Church Preen
Hughley
Presthope
Stretton Westwood
Bourton
Easthope
The Bog
Bridges
Ratlinghope
Long Mynd
Hollyhurst
Plaish
Enchmarsh
Cardington
Gretton
Willstone
All Stretton
Caer Caradog Hill
Church Stretton
Carding Mill Valley
Medlicott
Longville in the Dale
East Wall
Wall Bank
Wall under Heywood
Rushbury
Brockton
Weston
Shipton
Wilderhope Manor
Norbury
Wentnor
Linley
Little Stretton
Hope Bowdler
Ticklerton
Minton
Asterton
Myndtown
Marshbrook
Acton Scott
Acton Scott Historic Working Farm
Hatton
Eaton
Wenlock Edge
Stanton Long
Broadstone
Holdgate
Ditton Priors
Lea
Choulton
Eyton
Plowden
Horderley
Woolston
Whittingslow
Harton
Middlehope
Corve Dale
Munslow
Aston Munslow
Tugford
Abdon
Wistanstow
Upper Affcot
Strefford
Diddlebury
Corfton
Peaton
Clee St Margaret
Upper Heath
Edgton
Lydbury North
Cheney Longville
Lower Dinchope
Hopesay
Sibdon Carwood
Halford
Craven Arms
Seifton
Culmington
Great Sutton
Stoke St Milborough
Kempton
Aston on Clun
Little Brampton
Stokesay
Stokesay Castle
Norton
Vernolds Common
Purslow
Clunbury
Broome
Aldon
Onibury
Stanton Lacy
Hayton's Bent
Hopton Cangeford
Cleedownton
Twitchen
Clungunford
Abcott
Wootton
Shelderton
Cleeton St Mary
SHROPSHIRE
SHROPSHIRE HILLS
A5
A49
A458
A488
A489
B4368
B4371
B4370
B4385
149
132
115
7
8
9
10
11
A
B
C
D
E
F
G
H
SJ
SO
60
80

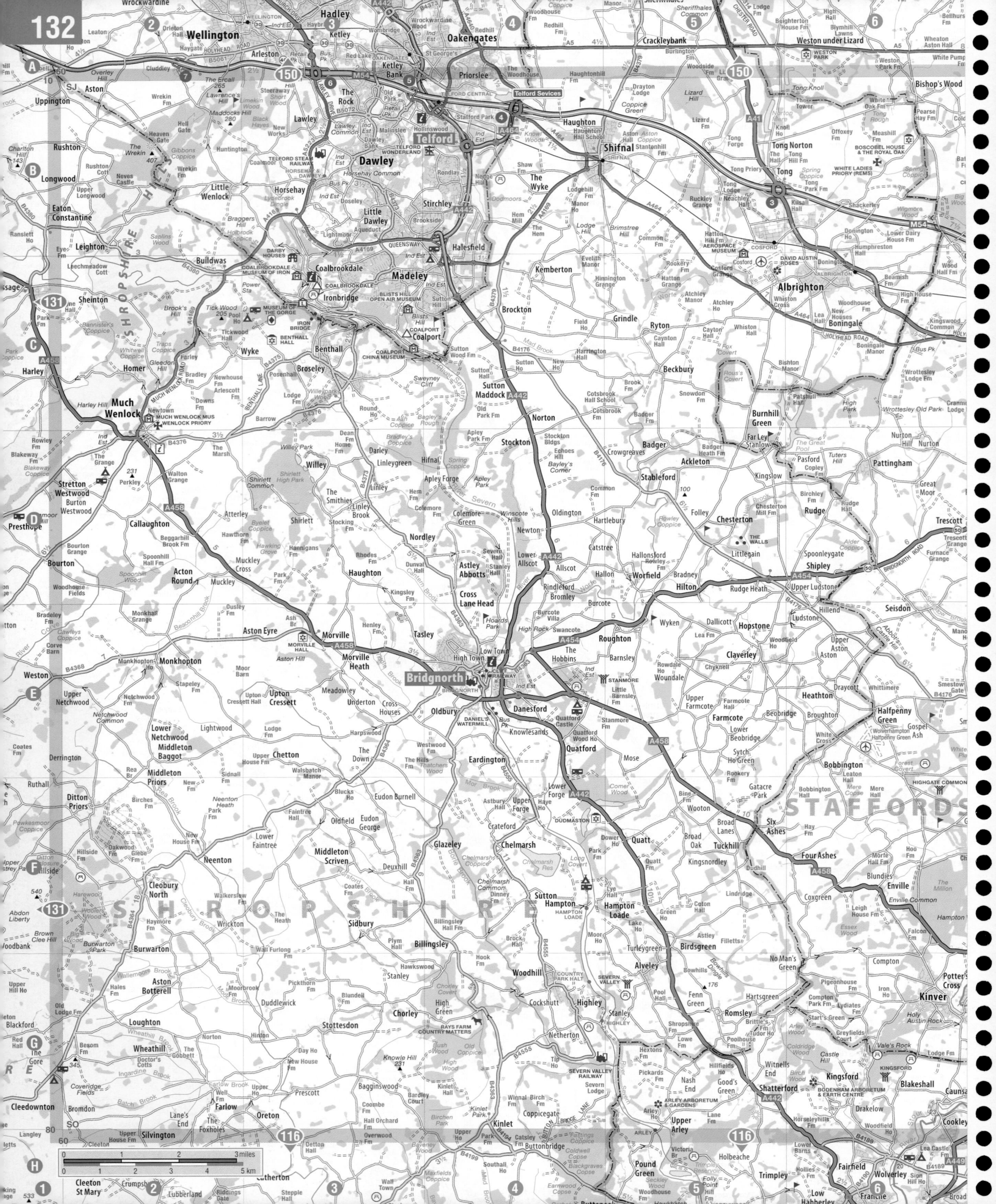
Wellington
Oakengates
Telford
Dawley
Shifnal
Madeley
Ironbridge
Albrighton
Much Wenlock
Bridgnorth
Kinver
SHROPSHIRE
STAFFORDS
131
150
116

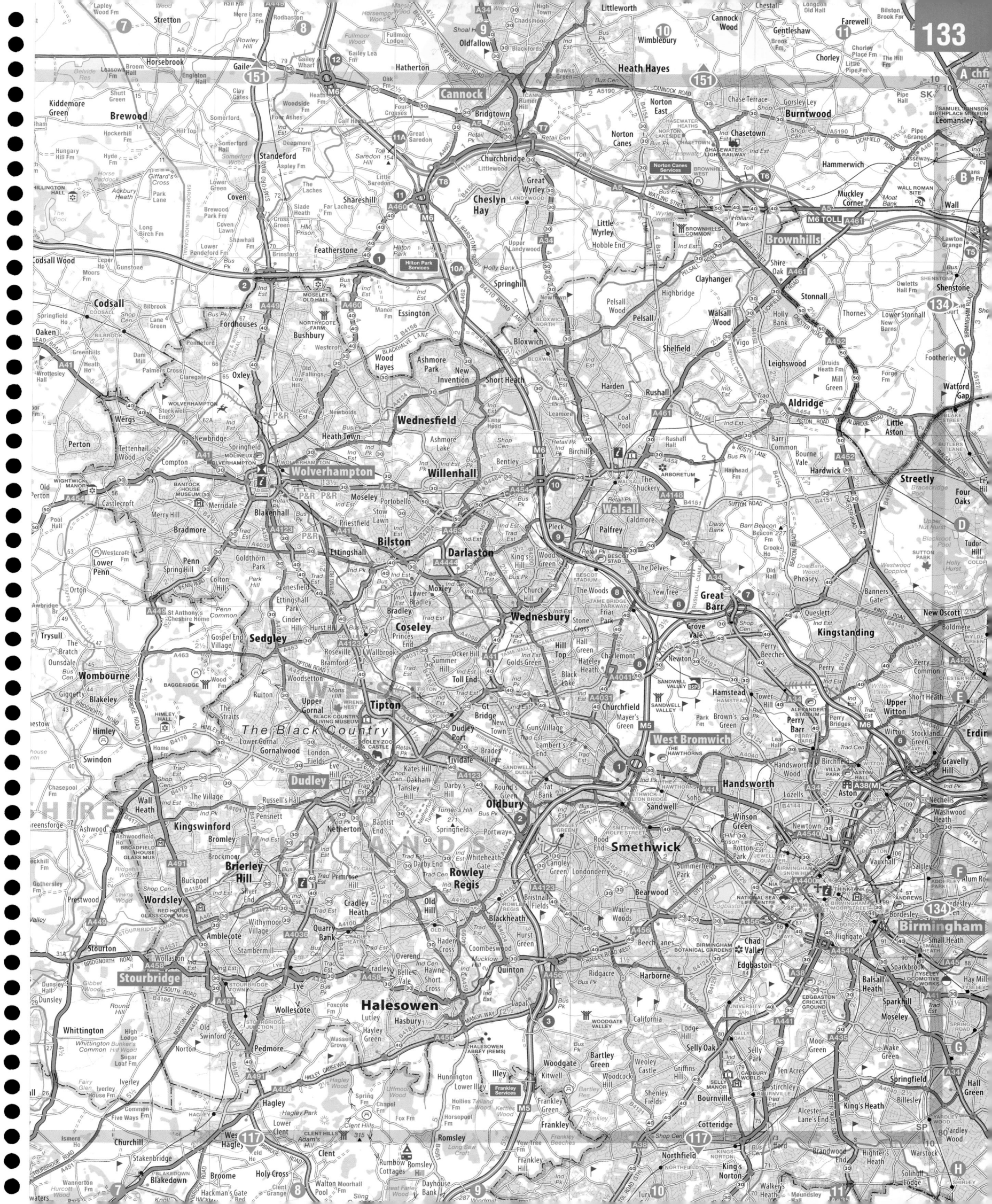
Cannock
Wolverhampton
Walsall
Brownhills
West Bromwich
Dudley
Stourbridge
Halesowen
Birmingham
Heath Hayes
Burntwood
Chasetown
Norton Canes
Bridgtown
Cheslyn Hay
Great Wyrley
Churchbridge
Hednesford
Brewood
Codsall
Wednesfield
Willenhall
Bilston
Darlaston
Wednesbury
Tipton
Sedgley
Coseley
Bloxwich
Pelsall
Aldridge
Streetly
Great Barr
Kingstanding
Handsworth
Smethwick
Oldbury
Rowley Regis
Brierley Hill
Kingswinford
Wordsley
Wombourne
Amblecote
Lye
Cradley Heath
Harborne
Edgbaston
Aston
Selly Oak
Bournville
Northfield
King's Norton
Moseley
Sparkhill
Hagley
Romsley
Frankley
The Black Country
WEST MIDLANDS
Hilton Park Services
Norton Canes Services
Frankley Services
M6 TOLL
M6
M5
A5
A41
A449
A452
A461
A34
A38
A456
A4123
151
134
117

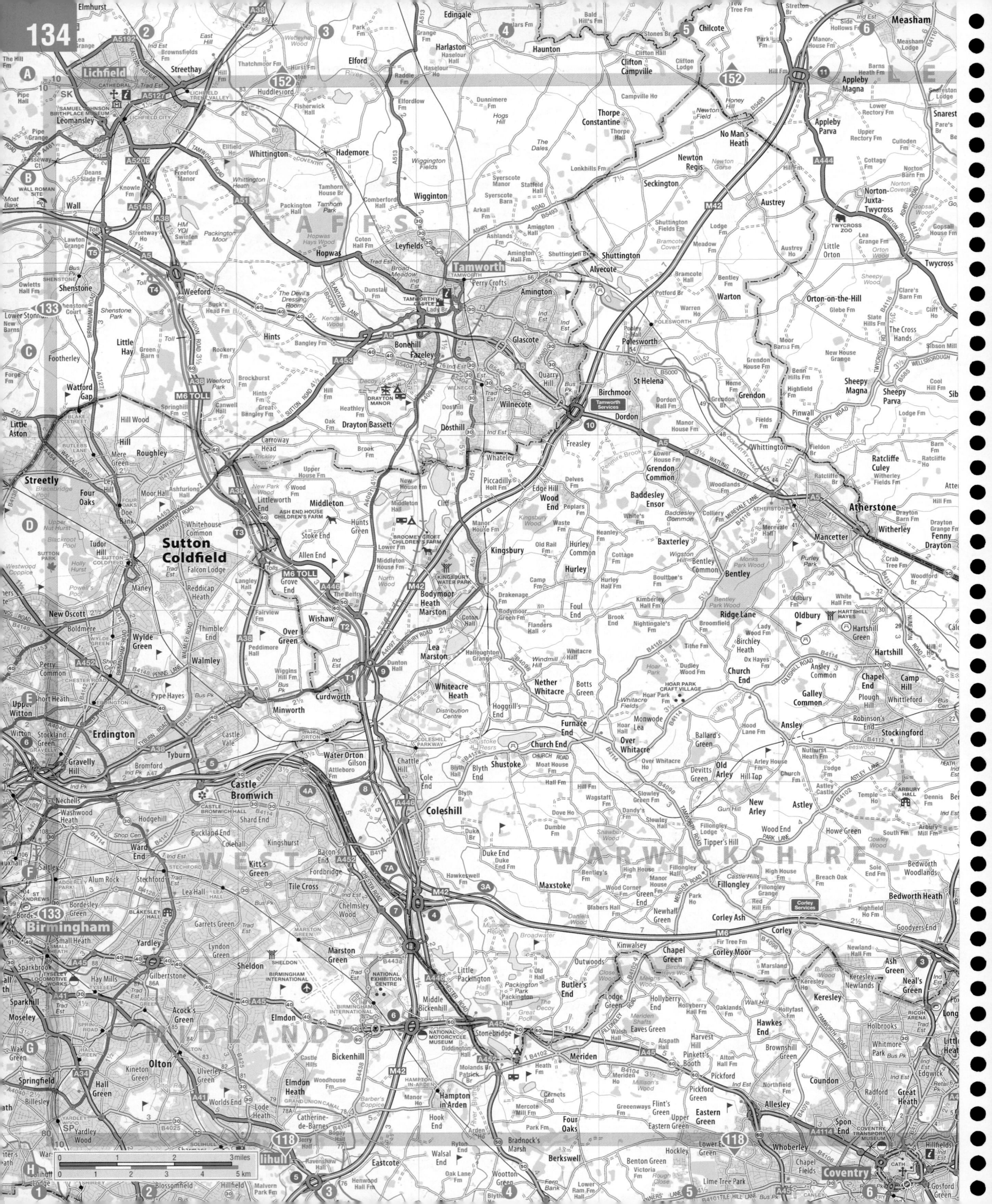
Lichfield
Elmhurst
Streethay
Huddlesford
Whittington
Hademore
Elford
Edingale
Harlaston
Haunton
Chilcote
Measham
Clifton Campville
Appleby Magna
Appleby Parva
Thorpe Constantine
No Man's Heath
Newton Regis
Seckington
Austrey
Norton-Juxta-Twycross
Twycross
Leomansley
Wall
Shenstone
Weeford
Hopwas
Wigginton
Leyfields
Tamworth
Amington
Glascote
Shuttington
Alvecote
Warton
Orton-on-the-Hill
Polesworth
St Helena
Birchmoor
Dordon
Grendon
Sheepy Magna
Sheepy Parva
Pinwall
Hints
Bonehill
Fazeley
Wilnecote
Drayton Bassett
Dosthill
Little Hay
Footherley
Watford Gap
Little Aston
Hill
Roughley
Streetly
Four Oaks
Sutton Coldfield
Middleton
Kingsbury
Hurley
Baxterley
Bentley
Atherstone
Mancetter
Witherley
Fenny Drayton
Ratcliffe Culey
Whittington
Grendon Common
Baddesley Ensor
Wood End
Freasley
New Oscott
Wylde Green
Walmley
Wishaw
Over Green
Bodymoor Heath
Marston
Lea Marston
Ridge Lane
Oldbury
Hartshill
Nether Whitacre
Whiteacre Heath
Curdworth
Minworth
Erdington
Pype Hayes
Tyburn
Castle Vale
Water Orton
Coleshill
Church End
Over Whitacre
Shustoke
Furnace End
Old Arley
New Arley
Ansley
Astley
Galley Common
Stockingford
Castle Bromwich
Hodgehill
Shard End
Kingshurst
Fordbridge
Tile Cross
Chelmsley Wood
Maxstoke
Fillongley
Corley Ash
Corley
Bedworth Heath
Birmingham
Yardley
Sheldon
Marston Green
Elmdon
Bickenhill
Sparkhill
Moseley
Olton
Acock's Green
Meriden
Hampton in Arden
Berkswell
Allesley
Coventry
Coundon
Keresley
Ash Green
Chapel Green
Kinwalsey
Little Packington
Middle Bickenhill
Stonebridge
Eastern Green
Catherine-de-Barnes
Hockley Heath
Eastcote
Balsall Common
Four Oaks
S T A F F S
W A R W I C K S H I R E
W E S T
M I D L A N D S
M42
M6
M6 TOLL
A5
A38
A45
A446
A452
152
133
118
0 1 2 3 miles
0 1 2 3 4 5 km

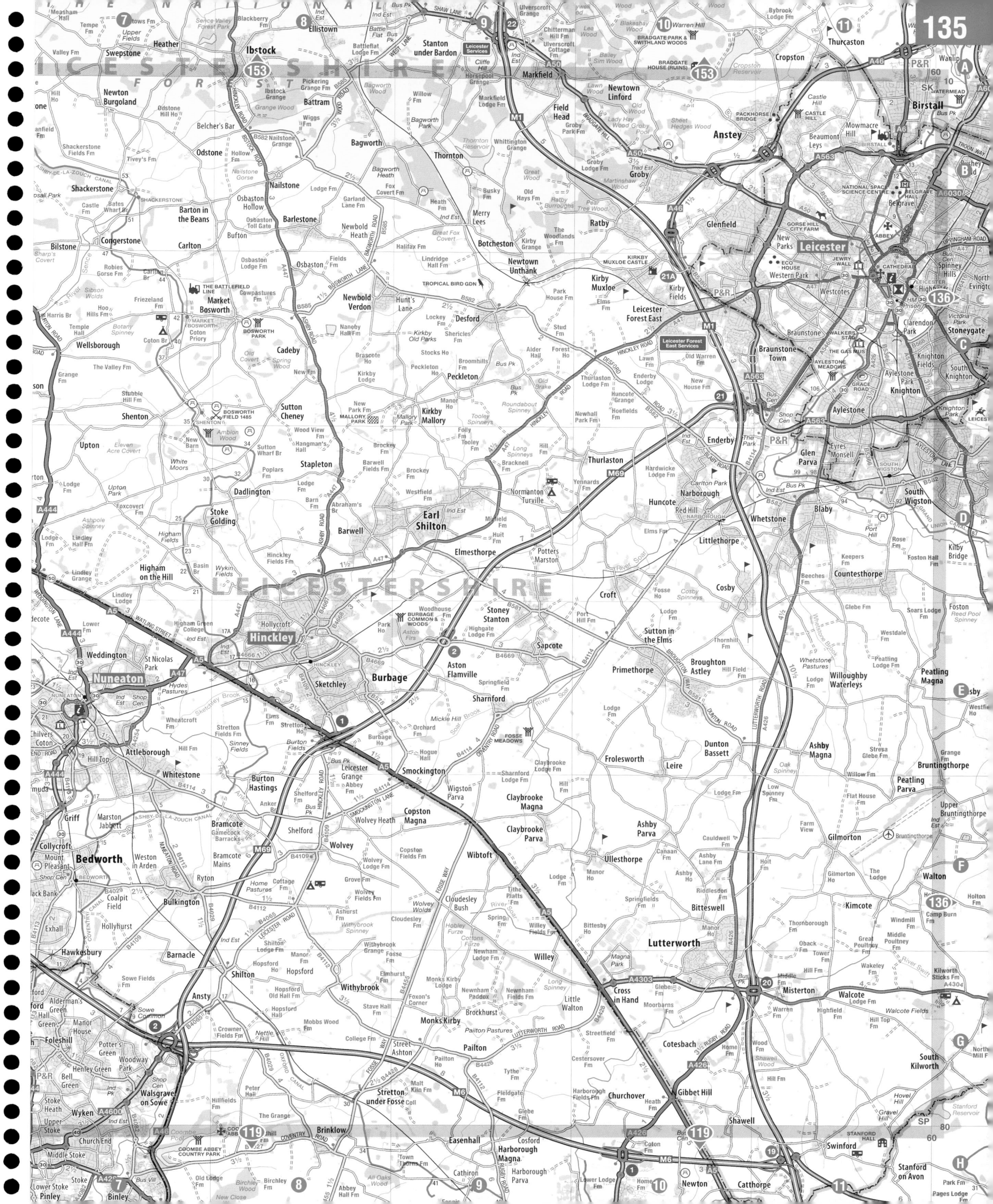
LEICESTERSHIRE
Ibstock
Ellistown
Stanton under Bardon
Markfield
Newtown Linford
Anstey
Thurcaston
Cropston
Birstall
Leicester
Belgrave
Glenfield
Kirby Muxloe
Leicester Forest East
Braunstone Town
Aylestone
Knighton
Stoneygate
Wigston
South Wigston
Glen Parva
Blaby
Enderby
Narborough
Whetstone
Littlethorpe
Cosby
Countesthorpe
Huncote
Thurlaston
Croft
Stoney Stanton
Sapcote
Broughton Astley
Primethorpe
Sutton in the Elms
Dunton Bassett
Leire
Frolesworth
Ashby Magna
Peatling Magna
Willoughby Waterleys
Bruntingthorpe
Peatling Parva
Gilmorton
Ashby Parva
Ullesthorpe
Bitteswell
Lutterworth
Kimcote
Walton
Misterton
Walcote
Cotesbach
Gibbet Hill
Shawell
South Kilworth
Swinford
Stanford on Avon
Catthorpe
Newton
Churchover
Pailton
Monks Kirby
Little Walton
Cross in Hand
Willey
Wibtoft
Claybrooke Magna
Claybrooke Parva
Copston Magna
Wolvey
Wigston Parva
Smockington
Sharnford
Aston Flamville
Burbage
Sketchley
Hinckley
Barwell
Earl Shilton
Elmesthorpe
Stapleton
Kirkby Mallory
Peckleton
Desford
Newbold Verdon
Barlestone
Nailstone
Bagworth
Thornton
Botcheston
Ratby
Groby
Field Head
Market Bosworth
Cadeby
Sutton Cheney
Shenton
Upton
Dadlington
Stoke Golding
Higham on the Hill
Wellsborough
Congerstone
Carlton
Shackerstone
Barton in the Beans
Odstone
Osbaston
Newton Burgoland
Swepstone
Heather
Nuneaton
Weddington
Attleborough
Whitestone
Burton Hastings
Bulkington
Bedworth
Hawkesbury
Barnacle
Shilton
Ansty
Withybrook
Wyken
Walsgrave on Sowe
Brinklow
Easenhall
Harborough Magna
Stretton under Fosse
Binley
Pinley
M1
M69
M6
A5
A47
A426
A4303

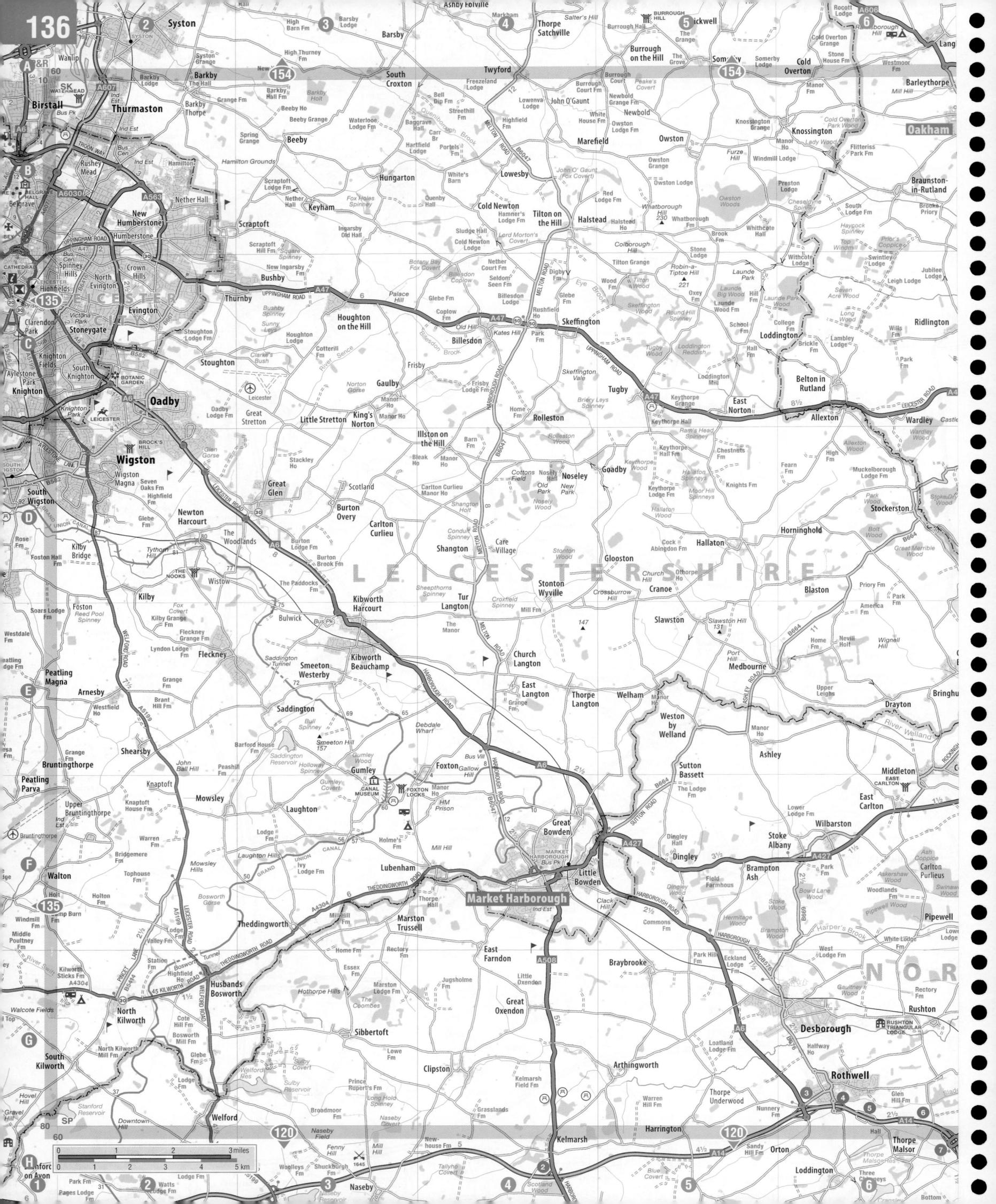
136
Syston
Barsby
Thorpe Satchville
Burrough on the Hill
Somerby
Cold Overton
Barleythorpe
Oakham
Birstall
Thurmaston
Barkby
Barkby Thorpe
South Croxton
Twyford
John O'Gaunt
Newbold
Marefield
Owston
Knossington
Beeby
Hungarton
Keyham
Lowesby
Cold Newton
Tilton on the Hill
Halstead
Braunston-in-Rutland
New Humberstone
Humberstone
Scraptoft
Bushby
Thurnby
Evington
Stoneygate
LEICESTER
Houghton on the Hill
Billesdon
Skeffington
Loddington
Ridlington
Stoughton
Oadby
Knighton
Gaulby
Frisby
Tugby
East Norton
Belton in Rutland
Allexton
Wardley
Great Stretton
Little Stretton
King's Norton
Illston on the Hill
Rolleston
Wigston
South Wigston
Great Glen
Noseley
Goadby
Newton Harcourt
Burton Overy
Carlton Curlieu
Scotland
Stockerston
Horninghold
Kilby
Wistow
Shangton
Hallaton
Glooston
LEICESTERSHIRE
Stonton Wyville
Cranoe
Blaston
Kibworth Harcourt
Tur Langton
Slawston
Fleckney
Bulwick
Kibworth Beauchamp
Smeeton Westerby
Church Langton
Medbourne
Peatling Magna
Arnesby
East Langton
Thorpe Langton
Welham
Weston by Welland
Drayton
Saddington
Shearsby
Bruntingthorpe
Gumley
Foxton
Sutton Bassett
Ashley
Middleton
Peatling Parva
Knaptoft
Mowsley
Laughton
Great Bowden
East Carlton
Upper Bruntingthorpe
Dingley
Stoke Albany
Wilbarston
Walton
Lubenham
Little Bowden
Brampton Ash
Market Harborough
Marston Trussell
Theddingworth
East Farndon
Pipewell
Braybrooke
Husbands Bosworth
North Kilworth
Great Oxendon
Rushton
Desborough
Sibbertoft
South Kilworth
Clipston
Arthingworth
Rothwell
Thorpe Underwood
Welford
Harrington
Kelmarsh
Orton
Thorpe Malsor
Naseby
Loddington
NOR
A47
A6
A427
A508
A14
A4304
A5199
B664
B6047
154
135
120
0 1 2 3 miles
0 1 2 3 4 5 km

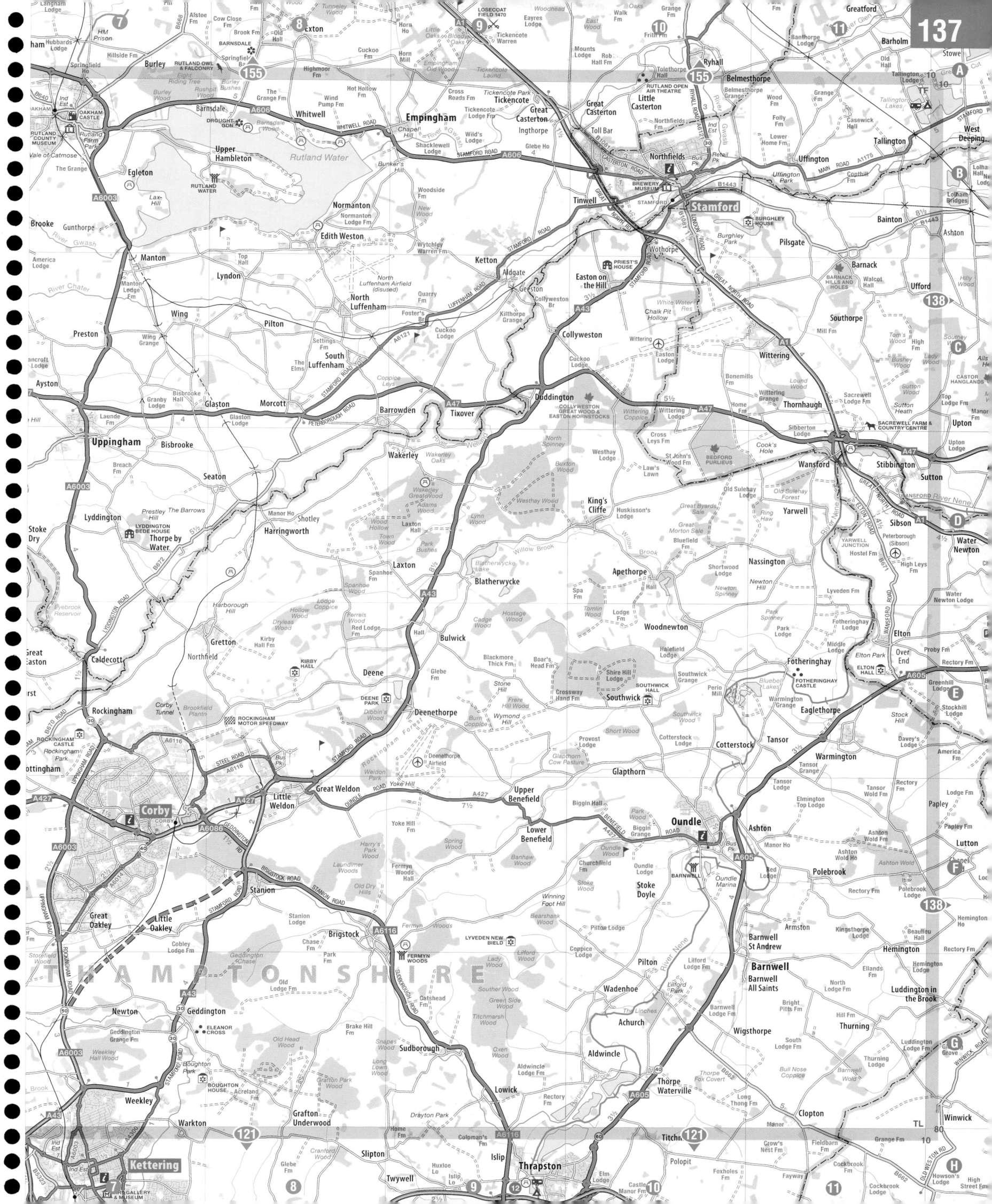
Burley
Exton
Greatford
Barholm
Stowe
Ryhall
Belmesthorpe
Little Casterton
Great Casterton
Tickencote
Empingham
Whitwell
Barnsdale
Oakham
Egleton
Upper Hambleton
Rutland Water
Normanton
Edith Weston
Tinwell
Stamford
Northfields
Uffington
Tallington
West Deeping
Bainton
Ashton
Pilsgate
Barnack
Ufford
Southorpe
Wothorpe
Easton on the Hill
Ketton
Aldgate
Geeston
Collyweston
Wittering
Thornhaugh
Manton
Lyndon
North Luffenham
South Luffenham
Wing
Pilton
Preston
Ayston
Glaston
Morcott
Barrowden
Tixover
Duddington
Uppingham
Bisbrooke
Seaton
Wakerley
Lyddington
Thorpe by Water
Harringworth
Laxton
Blatherwycke
King's Cliffe
Apethorpe
Nassington
Yarwell
Wansford
Stibbington
Sutton
Sibson
Water Newton
Upton
Woodnewton
Fotheringhay
Elton
Over End
Bulwick
Deene
Deenethorpe
Gretton
Caldecott
Rockingham
Southwick
Eaglethorpe
Tansor
Cotterstock
Warmington
Glapthorn
Great Weldon
Little Weldon
Corby
Upper Benefield
Lower Benefield
Oundle
Ashton
Polebrook
Stanion
Great Oakley
Little Oakley
Brigstock
Stoke Doyle
Barnwell St Andrew
Barnwell
Barnwell All Saints
Hemington
Luddington in the Brook
Pilton
Wadenhoe
Achurch
Aldwincle
Thurning
Wigsthorpe
Newton
Geddington
Sudborough
Lowick
Thorpe Waterville
Clopton
Weekley
Warkton
Grafton Underwood
Slipton
Twywell
Islip
Thrapston
Titchmarsh
Polopit
Kettering
Winwick
NORTHAMPTONSHIRE
Rockingham Motor Speedway
Burghley House
Kirby Hall
Deene Park
Fotheringhay Castle
Elton Hall
Lyveden New Bield
Boughton House
Eleanor Cross
Sacrewell Farm & Country Centre
Bedford Purlieus
A1
A47
A43
A606
A6003
A6121
A427
A6116
A605
A6086
B1443
B1081
B672
B670
B662
B671
155
121
138

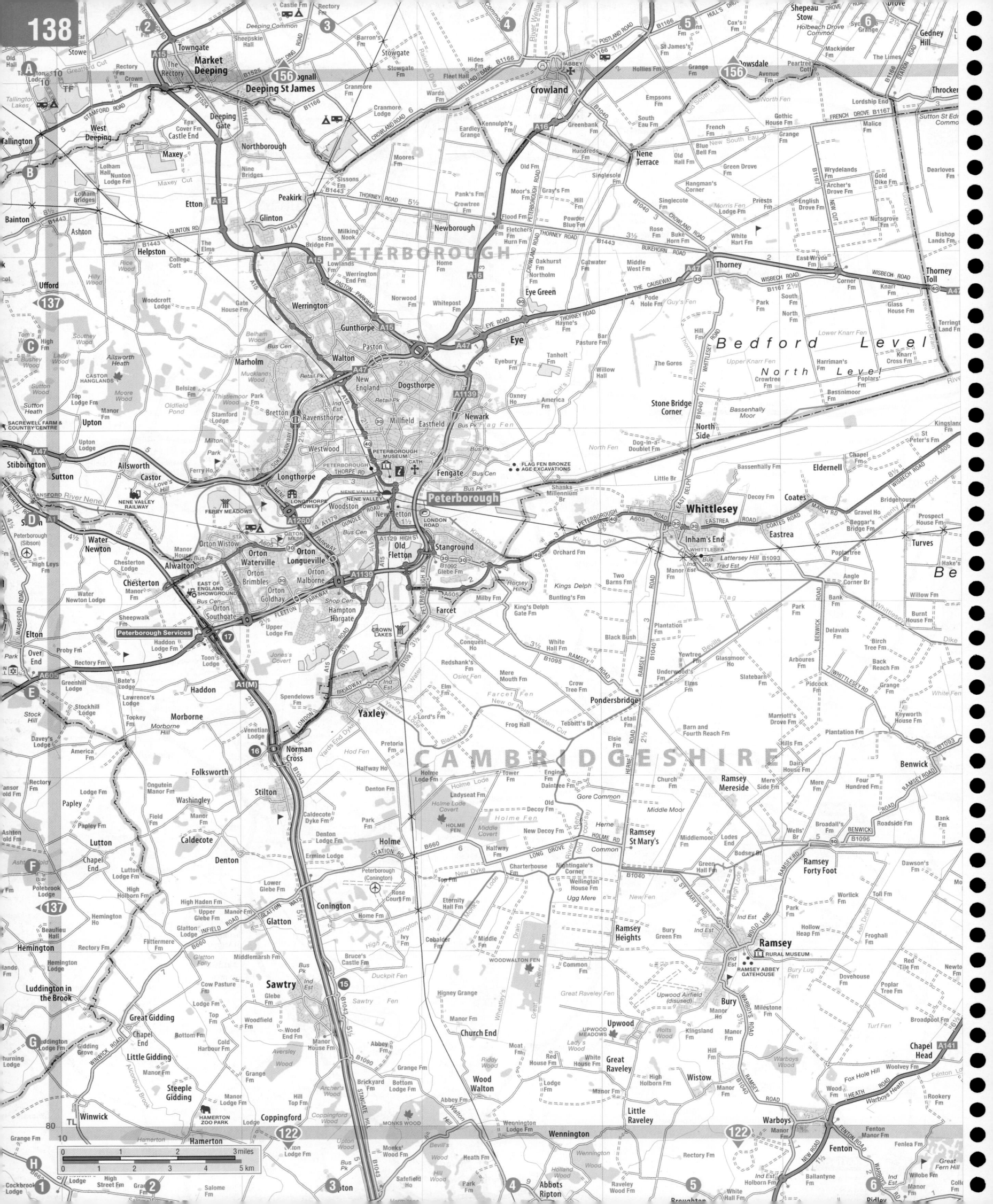

156
137
122
Market Deeping
Deeping St James
Crowland
West Deeping
Deeping Gate
Northborough
Maxey
Peakirk
Etton
Glinton
Newborough
Helpston
Bainton
Ashton
Ufford
Thorney
Thorney Toll
Eye
Eye Green
PETERBOROUGH
Werrington
Gunthorpe
Paston
Walton
Marholm
New England
Dogsthorpe
Newark
Ravensthorpe
Millfield
Eastfield
Bretton
Westwood
Longthorpe
Fengate
Peterborough
Woodston
Old Fletton
Stanground
Orton Waterville
Orton Longueville
Orton Wistow
Alwalton
Chesterton
Castor
Ailsworth
Sutton
Stibbington
Upton
Water Newton
Hampton Hargate
Farcet
Yaxley
Haddon
Morborne
Norman Cross
Folksworth
Stilton
Caldecote
Denton
Lutton
Glatton
Conington
Holme
Sawtry
Great Gidding
Little Gidding
Steeple Gidding
Winwick
Hamerton
Coppingford
Hemington
Luddington in the Brook
Whittlesey
Inham's End
Eastrea
Coates
Turves
Pondersbridge
Ramsey
Ramsey St Mary's
Ramsey Heights
Ramsey Mereside
Ramsey Forty Foot
Benwick
Upwood
Great Raveley
Little Raveley
Wistow
Bury
Warboys
Church End
Wood Walton
Wennington
Abbots Ripton
Chapel Head
Fenton
Bedford Level
North Level
CAMBRIDGESHIRE
Peterborough Services
0 1 2 3 miles
0 1 2 3 4 5 km

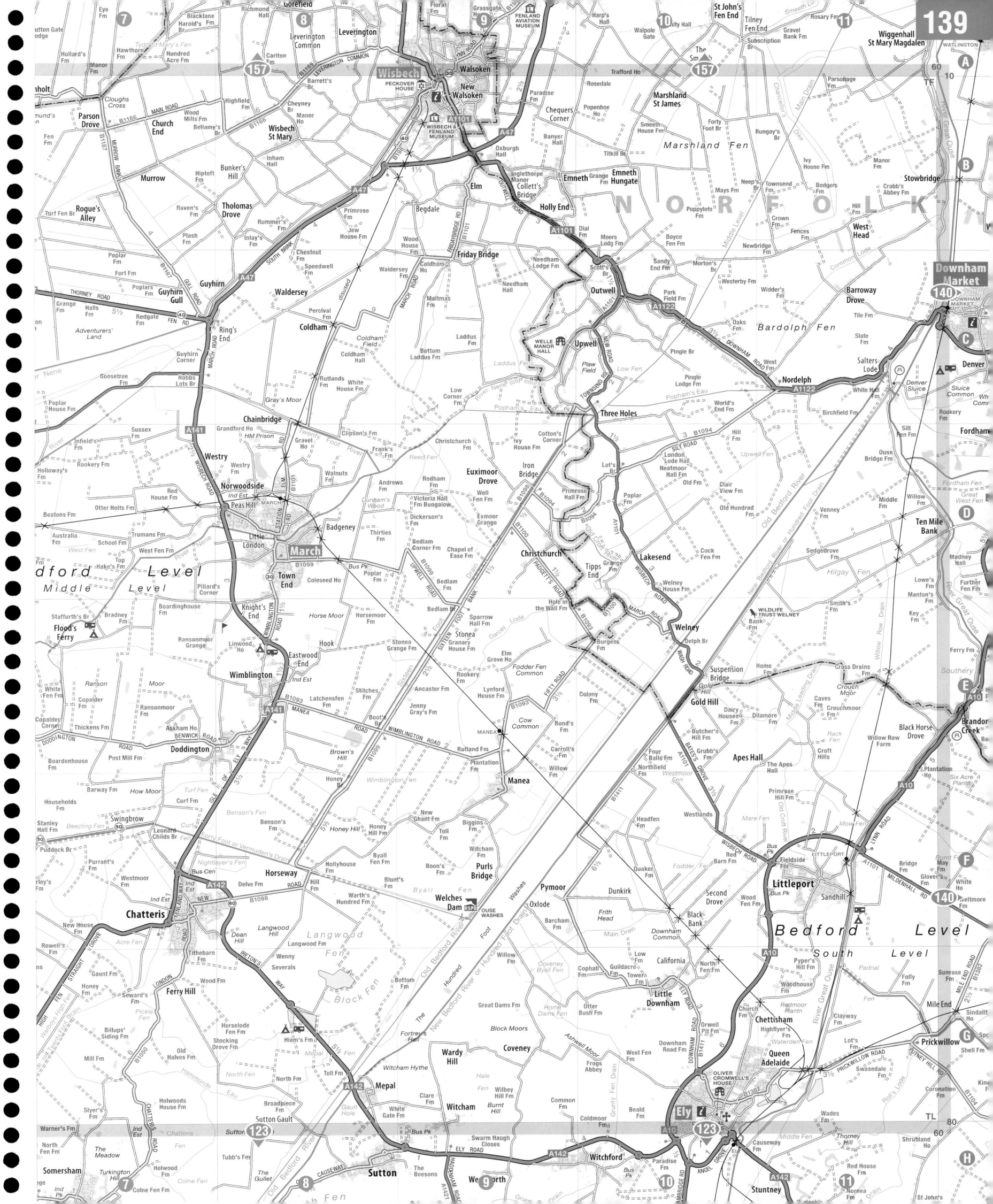
Wisbech
March
Chatteris
Ely
Downham Market
Littleport
Upwell
Outwell
Welney
Manea
Doddington
Wimblington
Sutton
Witchford
N O R F O L K
Marshland Fen
Bedford Level
Middle Level
Bedford South Level
Bardolph Fen
Nordelph
Denver
Emneth
Elm
Leverington
Walsoken
Coldham
Guyhirn
Chainbridge
Westry
Three Holes
Christchurch
Lakesend
Pymoor
Mepal
Witcham
Coveney
Wardy Hill
Little Downham
Queen Adelaide
Prickwillow
Stuntney
Somersham
Ferry Hill
Horseway
Welches Dam
Purls Bridge
Stowbridge
Wiggenhall St Mary Magdalen
Marshland St James
Ten Mile Bank
Brandon Creek
Apes Hall
Gold Hill
Suspension Bridge
Chettisham
Mile End
Holly End
Friday Bridge
Murrow
Parson Drove
Church End
Wisbech St Mary
Tholomas Drove
Rogue's Alley
Norwoodside
Peas Hill
Town End
Knight's End
Eastwood End
Flood's Ferry
Stonea
Hook
Badgeney
Salters Lode
Barroway Drove
West Head
Emneth Hungate
Fenland Aviation Museum
Peckover House
Wisbech & Fenland Museum
Welle Manor Hall
Oliver Cromwell's House
Wildlife Trust Welney
OUSE WASHES
A47
A141
A142
A10
A1101
A1122
157
123
140

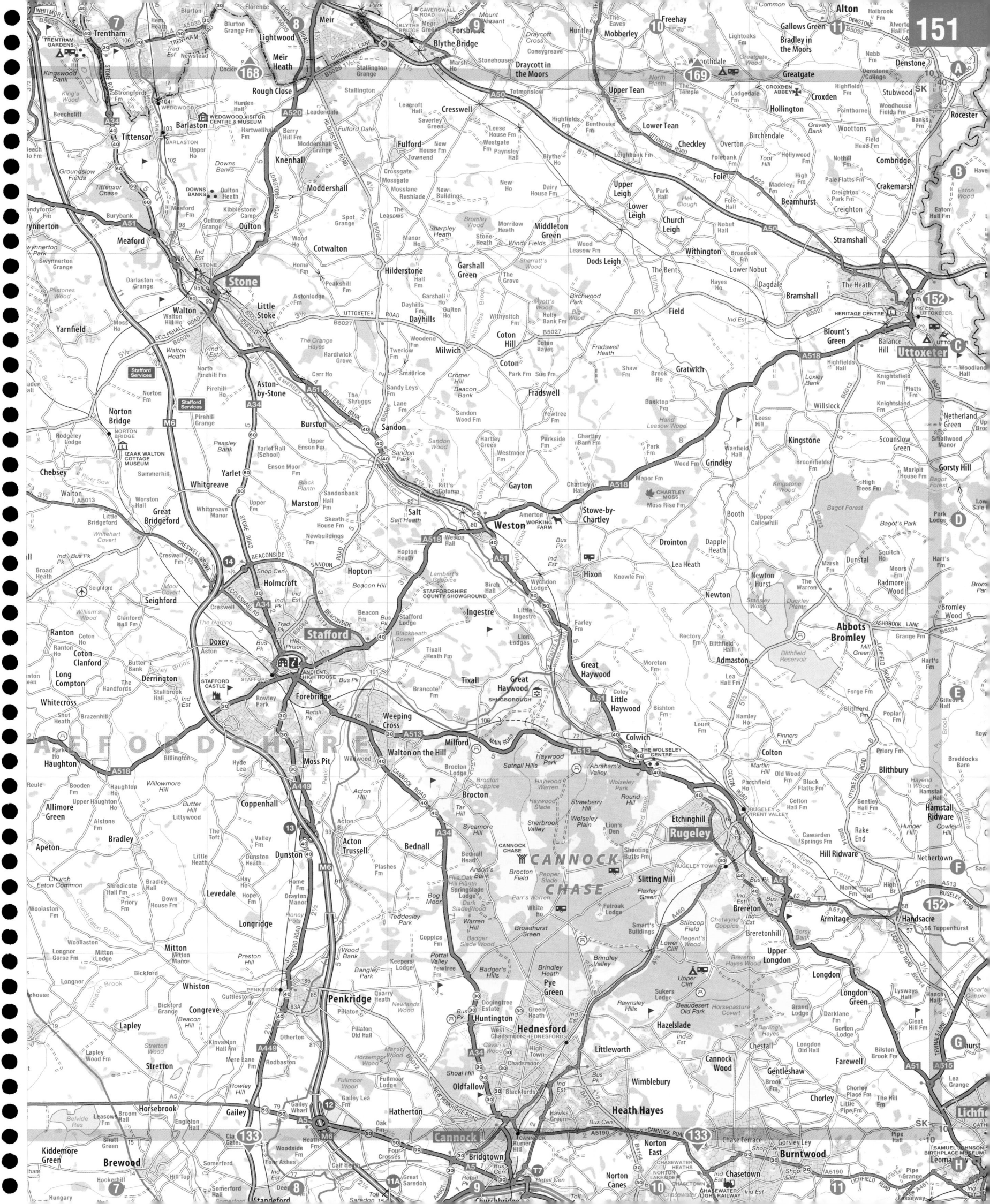
Trentham
Trentham Gardens
Blurton
Florence
Meir
Lightwood
Meir Heath
Rough Close
Caverswall Road
Forsbrook
Blythe Bridge
Draycott in the Moors
Huntley
Mobberley
Freehay
Alton
Gallows Green
Bradley in the Moors
Denstone
Woodhouse
Greatgate
Upper Tean
Croxden
Hollington
Stubwood
Rocester
Lower Tean
Checkley
Cresswell
Barlaston
Wedgwood Visitor Centre & Museum
Tittensor
Fulford
Knenhall
Moddershall
Oulton
Meaford
Stone
Cotwalton
Hilderstone
Garshall Green
Middleton Green
Upper Leigh
Lower Leigh
Church Leigh
Withington
Dods Leigh
Fole
Combridge
Crakemarsh
Beamhurst
Stramshall
The Heath
Bramshall
Walton
Little Stoke
Dayhills
Milwich
Coton Hill
Coton
Field
Blount's Green
Uttoxeter
Yarnfield
Aston-by-Stone
Fradswell
Gratwich
Burston
Sandon
Norton Bridge
Izaak Walton Cottage Museum
Chebsey
Yarlet
Whitgreave
Marston
Salt
Weston
Stowe-by-Chartley
Grindley
Kingstone
Gayton
Great Bridgeford
Hopton
Drointon
Hixon
Holmcroft
Seighford
Ingestre
Stafford
Stafford Castle
Doxey
Derrington
Newton
Abbots Bromley
Tixall
Great Haywood
Little Haywood
Admaston
Weeping Cross
Milford
Walton on the Hill
Colwich
Haughton
Moss Pit
Coppenhall
Brocton
Cannock Chase
Etchinghill
Rugeley
Bradley
Dunston
Acton Trussell
Bednall
Slitting Mill
Brereton
Armitage
Handsacre
Levedale
Longridge
Penkridge
Huntington
Hednesford
Pye Green
Upper Longdon
Longdon
Hazelslade
Whiston
Congreve
Lapley
Stretton
Littleworth
Cannock Wood
Gentleshaw
Farewell
Chorley
Wimblebury
Heath Hayes
Gailey
Horsebrook
Hatherton
Cannock
Bridgtown
Norton East
Burntwood
Chasetown
Brewood
Kiddemore Green
Norton Canes
Staffordshire

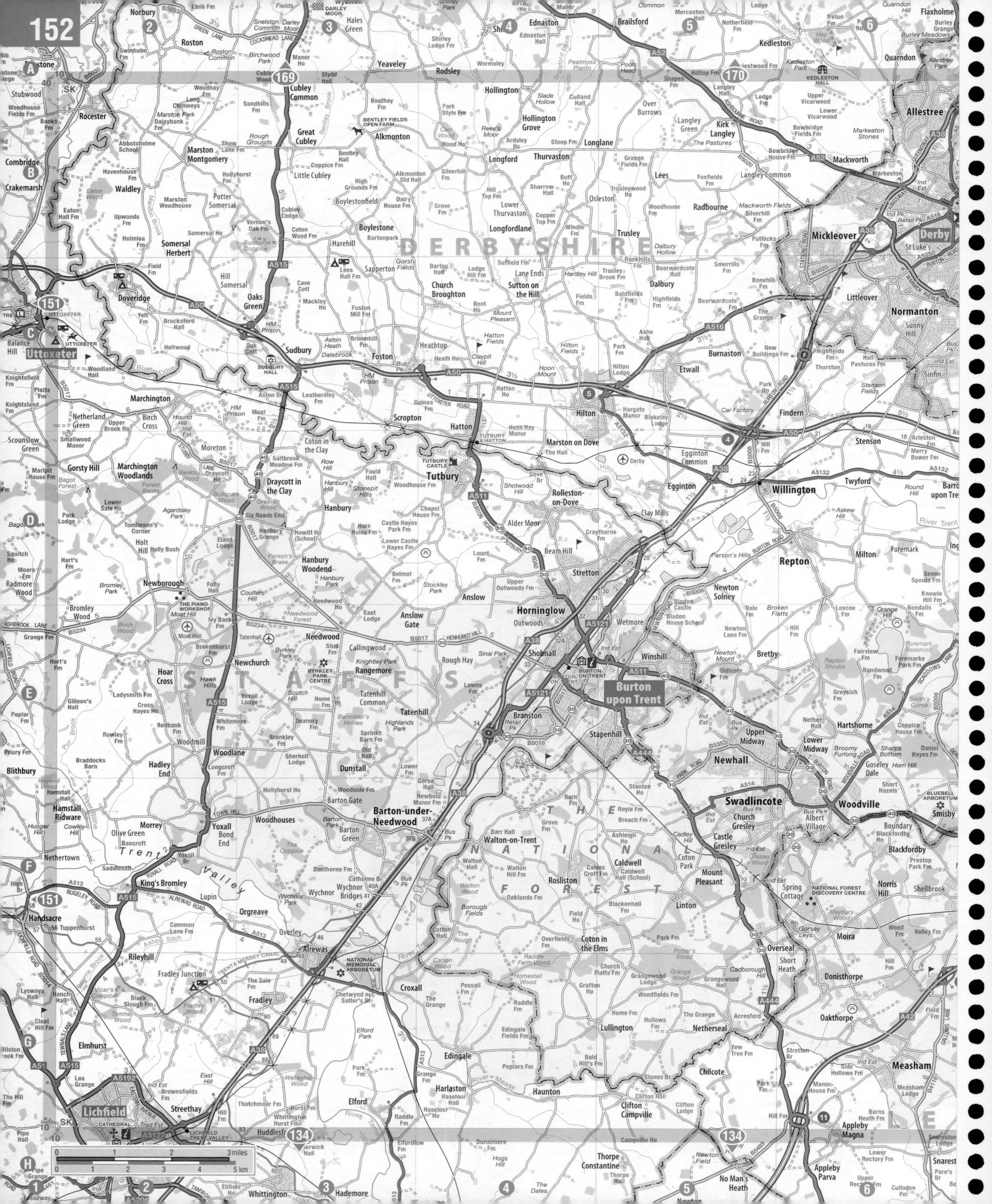
DERBYSHIRE
STAFFS
THE NATIONAL FOREST
Norbury
Roston
Rocester
Stubwood
Cubley Common
Great Cubley
Alkmonton
Yeaveley
Rodsley
Hollington
Ednaston
Brailsford
Kedleston
Quarndon
Flaxholme
Allestree
Mackworth
Langley Common
Kirk Langley
Longlane
Thurvaston
Longford
Marston Montgomery
Waldley
Somersal Herbert
Doveridge
Uttoxeter
Sudbury
Foston
Boylestone
Sapperton
Church Broughton
Sutton on the Hill
Dalbury
Trusley
Radbourne
Lees
Mickleover
Derby
Littleover
Normanton
Etwall
Burnaston
Hilton
Findern
Stenson
Willington
Twyford
Repton
Milton
Egginton
Marston on Dove
Hatton
Scropton
Tutbury
Marchington
Marchington Woodlands
Draycott in the Clay
Hanbury
Rolleston-on-Dove
Stretton
Horninglow
Anslow
Needwood
Newborough
Hoar Cross
Newchurch
Rangemore
Tatenhill
Burton upon Trent
Winshill
Branston
Stapenhill
Newhall
Swadlincote
Woodville
Hartshorne
Barton-under-Needwood
Walton-on-Trent
Rosliston
Caldwell
Linton
Coton in the Elms
Overseal
Moira
Donisthorpe
Oakthorpe
Measham
Lullington
Netherseal
Chilcote
Clifton Campville
Edingale
Croxall
Alrewas
Fradley
Orgreave
King's Bromley
Yoxall
Handsacre
Elmhurst
Lichfield
Streethay
Elford
Harlaston
Haunton
Thorpe Constantine
No Man's Heath
Appleby Magna
Appleby Parva
Whittington
Hademore
Blithbury
Hamstall Ridware
Woodlane
Hadley End
Dunstall
Wychnor
A50
A38
A515
A511
A444
A513
A52
A5121
A5132
1 2 3 miles
1 2 3 4 5 km

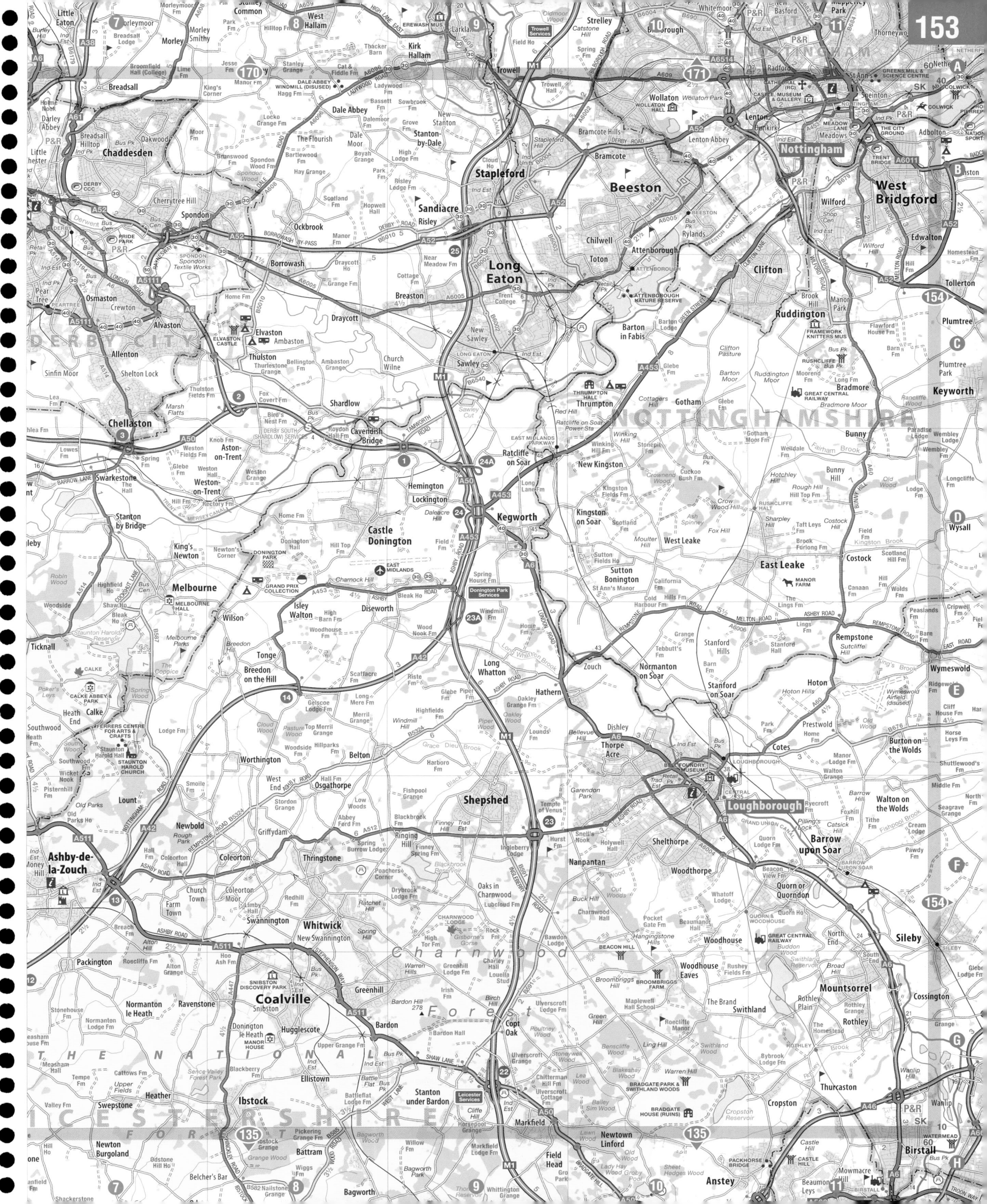

NOTTINGHAM
Nottingham
West Bridgford
Beeston
Stapleford
Long Eaton
Chaddesden
Spondon
Borrowash
Breaston
Draycott
Sandiacre
Risley
Ockbrook
Dale Abbey
Stanton-by-Dale
Trowell
Wollaton
Bramcote
Chilwell
Attenborough
Toton
Clifton
Ruddington
Wilford
Edwalton
Tollerton
Plumtree
Keyworth
Bradmore
Bunny
Gotham
Thrumpton
Barton in Fabis
Sawley
Shardlow
Cavendish Bridge
Elvaston
Ambaston
Thulston
Alvaston
Osmaston
Crewton
Allenton
Chellaston
Aston-on-Trent
Weston-on-Trent
Swarkestone
Stanton by Bridge
King's Newton
Melbourne
Wilson
Castle Donington
Hemington
Lockington
Kegworth
Ratcliffe on Soar
New Kingston
Kingston on Soar
West Leake
East Leake
Costock
Sutton Bonington
Isley Walton
Diseworth
Tonge
Breedon on the Hill
Long Whatton
Hathern
Zouch
Normanton on Soar
Stanford on Soar
Rempstone
Wymeswold
Hoton
Prestwold
Cotes
Burton on the Wolds
Dishley
Thorpe Acre
Loughborough
Shepshed
Belton
Osgathorpe
Worthington
Griffydam
Coleorton
Newbold
Thringstone
Whitwick
Swannington
Coalville
Greenhill
Hugglescote
Ibstock
Heather
Bardon
Markfield
Stanton under Bardon
Copt Oak
Nanpantan
Shelthorpe
Woodthorpe
Quorn or Quorndon
Barrow upon Soar
Walton on the Wolds
Woodhouse
Woodhouse Eaves
Swithland
Mountsorrel
Rothley
Sileby
Cossington
Thurcaston
Cropston
Anstey
Newtown Linford
Birstall
Ashby-de-la-Zouch
Packington
Ravenstone
Normanton le Heath
Calke
Ticknall
Lount
Swepstone
Newton Burgoland
Battram
Bagworth
Ellistown
Charnwood Forest
DERBY CITY
NOTTINGHAMSHIRE
LEICESTERSHIRE
THE NATIONAL FOREST
M1
A52
A6
A453
A42
A50
A511
A512
A60
A46

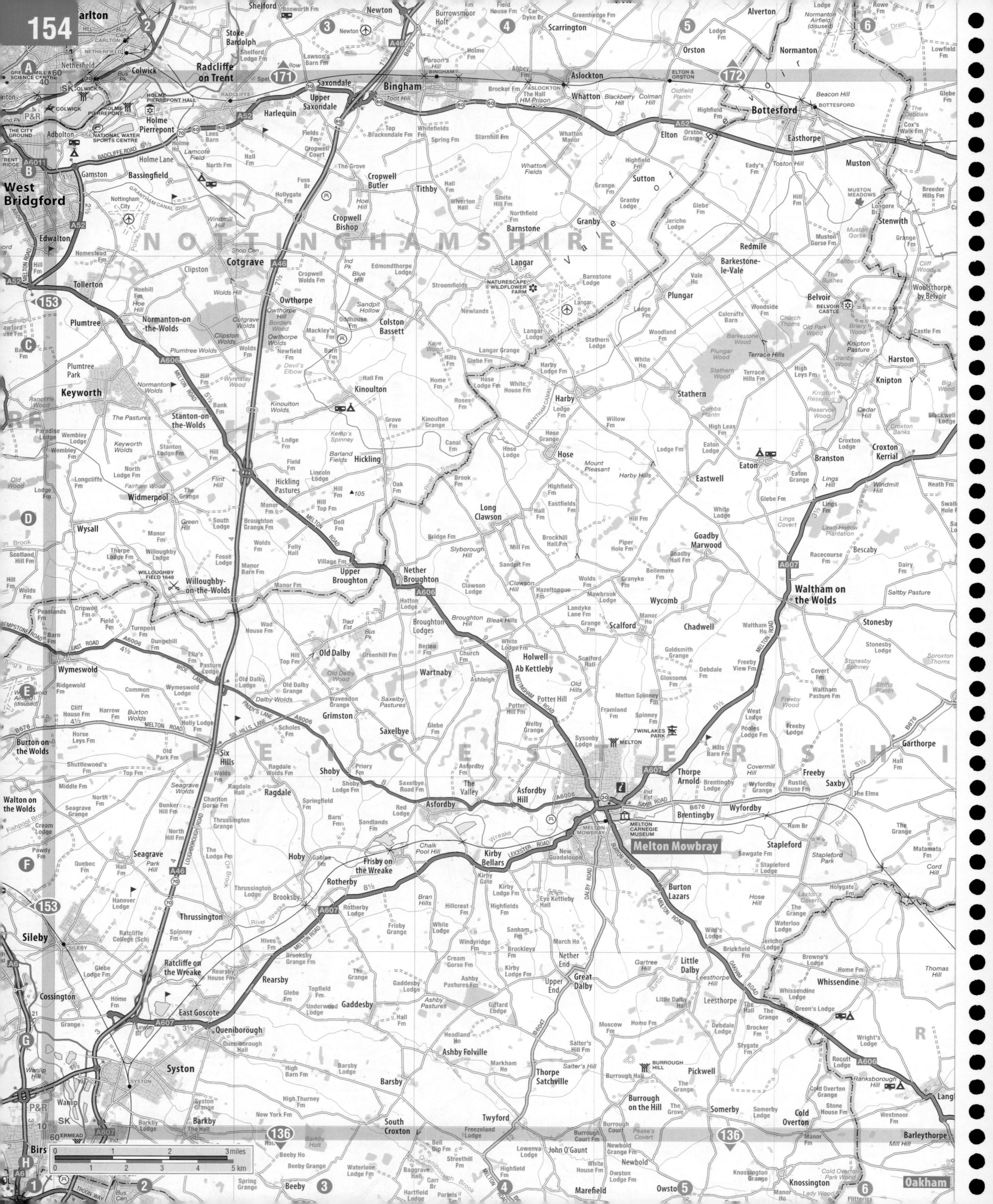

Carlton
Netherfield
Colwick
Shelford
Newton
Stoke Bardolph
Radcliffe on Trent
Saxondale
Upper Saxondale
Bingham
Aslockton
Whatton
Orston
Alverton
Normanton
Elton
Bottesford
Easthorpe
Muston
Holme Pierrepont
Adbolton
Harlequin
Gamston
Bassingfield
West Bridgford
Edwalton
Tollerton
Cotgrave
Clipston
Cropwell Butler
Cropwell Bishop
Tithby
Barnstone
Granby
Sutton
Redmile
Barkestone-le-Vale
Langar
Plungar
Belvoir
Woolsthorpe by Belvoir
Stenwith
NOTTINGHAMSHIRE
Vale of Belvoir
Owthorpe
Colston Bassett
Kinoulton
Plumtree
Normanton-on-the-Wolds
Keyworth
Stanton-on-the-Wolds
Hickling
Harby
Stathern
Hose
Eastwell
Eaton
Branston
Harston
Knipton
Croxton Kerrial
Widmerpool
Wysall
Long Clawson
Goadby Marwood
Willoughby-on-the-Wolds
Upper Broughton
Nether Broughton
Wycomb
Chadwell
Waltham on the Wolds
Stonesby
Scalford
Wymeswold
Old Dalby
Holwell
Ab Kettleby
Wartnaby
Grimston
Saxelbye
Burton on the Wolds
Six Hills
Shoby
Asfordby
Asfordby Hill
Thorpe Arnold
Brentingby
Wyfordby
Freeby
Saxby
Garthorpe
LEICESTERSHIRE
Melton Mowbray
Walton on the Wolds
Seagrave
Ragdale
Hoby
Frisby on the Wreake
Kirby Bellars
Rotherby
Brooksby
Burton Lazars
Stapleford
Thrussington
Sileby
Ratcliffe on the Wreake
Rearsby
Cossington
East Goscote
Queniborough
Gaddesby
Little Dalby
Great Dalby
Upper End
Leesthorpe
Whissendine
Syston
Ashby Folville
Thorpe Satchville
Pickwell
Barsby
Burrough on the Hill
Somerby
Cold Overton
Barkby
South Croxton
Twyford
John O'Gaunt
Newbold
Marefield
Knossington
Barleythorpe
Beeby
Oakham
A46
A52
A606
A607
A6006
B676
B6047
171
172
153
136
A
B
C
D
E
F
G
H
1
2
3
4
5
6
0 1 2 3 miles
0 1 2 3 4 5 km

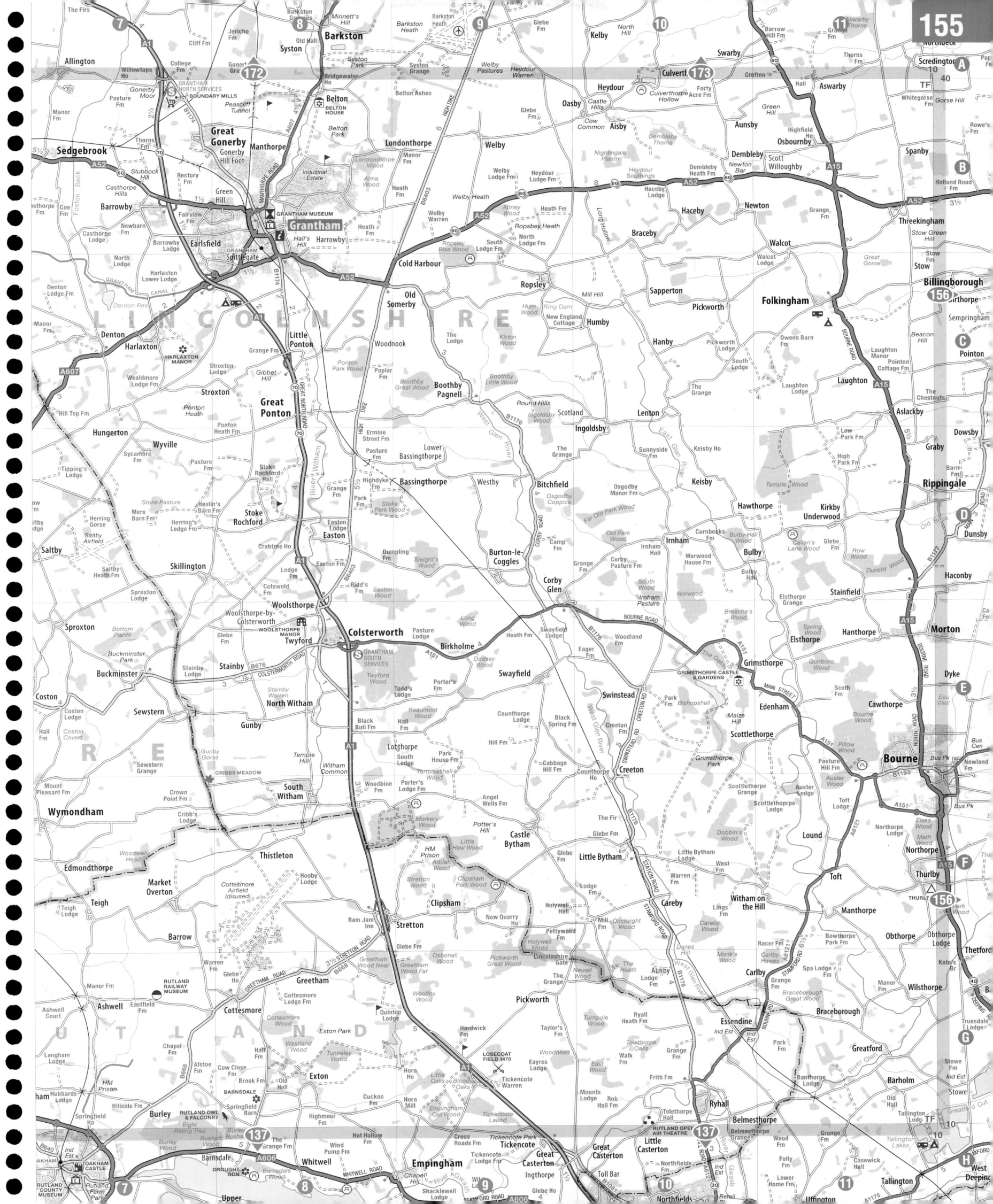

Barkston
Syston
Allington
Sedgebrook
Great Gonerby
Manthorpe
Belton
Belton House
Londonthorpe
Welby
Kelby
Heydour
Oasby
Aisby
Culverthorpe
Swarby
Aswarby
Aunsby
Osbournby
Dembleby
Scott Willoughby
Scredington
Spanby
Threekingham
Barrowby
Grantham
Grantham Museum
Harrowby
Earlsfield
Spittlegate
Cold Harbour
Ropsley
Haceby
Newton
Braceby
Walcot
Sapperton
Pickworth
Folkingham
Billingborough
Birthorpe
Sempringham
Pointon
LINCOLNSHIRE
Denton
Harlaxton
Harlaxton Manor
Old Somerby
Little Ponton
Woodnook
Humby
Hanby
Laughton
Stroxton
Great Ponton
Boothby Pagnell
Ingoldsby
Scotland
Lenton
Aslackby
Dowsby
Graby
Hungerton
Wyville
Lower Bassingthorpe
Bassingthorpe
Westby
Bitchfield
Keisby
Rippingale
Stoke Rochford
Easton
Burton-le-Coggles
Irnham
Bulby
Hawthorpe
Kirkby Underwood
Dunsby
Saltby
Skillington
Corby Glen
Haconby
Stainfield
Sproxton
Woolsthorpe
Woolsthorpe-by-Colsterworth
Woolsthorpe Manor
Colsterworth
Twyford
Birkholme
Swayfield
Grimsthorpe
Grimsthorpe Castle & Gardens
Elsthorpe
Hanthorpe
Morton
Buckminster
Stainby
Coston
Sewstern
North Witham
Gunby
Swinstead
Edenham
Cawthorpe
Dyke
Scottlethorpe
Bourne
Creeton
South Witham
Wymondham
Castle Bytham
Little Bytham
Lound
Northorpe
Thurlby
Edmondthorpe
Thistleton
Market Overton
Teigh
Clipsham
Careby
Witham on the Hill
Toft
Mantorpe
Barrow
Stretton
Obthorpe
Thetford
Greetham
Carlby
Wilsthorpe
Ashwell
Rutland Railway Museum
Cottesmore
Pickworth
Aunby
Braceborough
Essendine
Greatford
Exton
Barholm
Losecoat Field 1470
Ryhall
Belmesthorpe
Burley
Rutland Owl & Falconry
Tickencote
Great Casterton
Little Casterton
Rutland Open Air Theatre
Tallington
Whitwell
Empingham
Oakham
Oakham Castle
Rutland County Museum
Barnsdale
Toll Bar
West Deeping
Uffington
Northfields
Upper
Ingthorpe
RUTLAND
A1
A52
A15
A151
A607
A606
B1176
172
173
156
137
7
8
9
10
11
A
B
C
D
E
F
G
H
TF

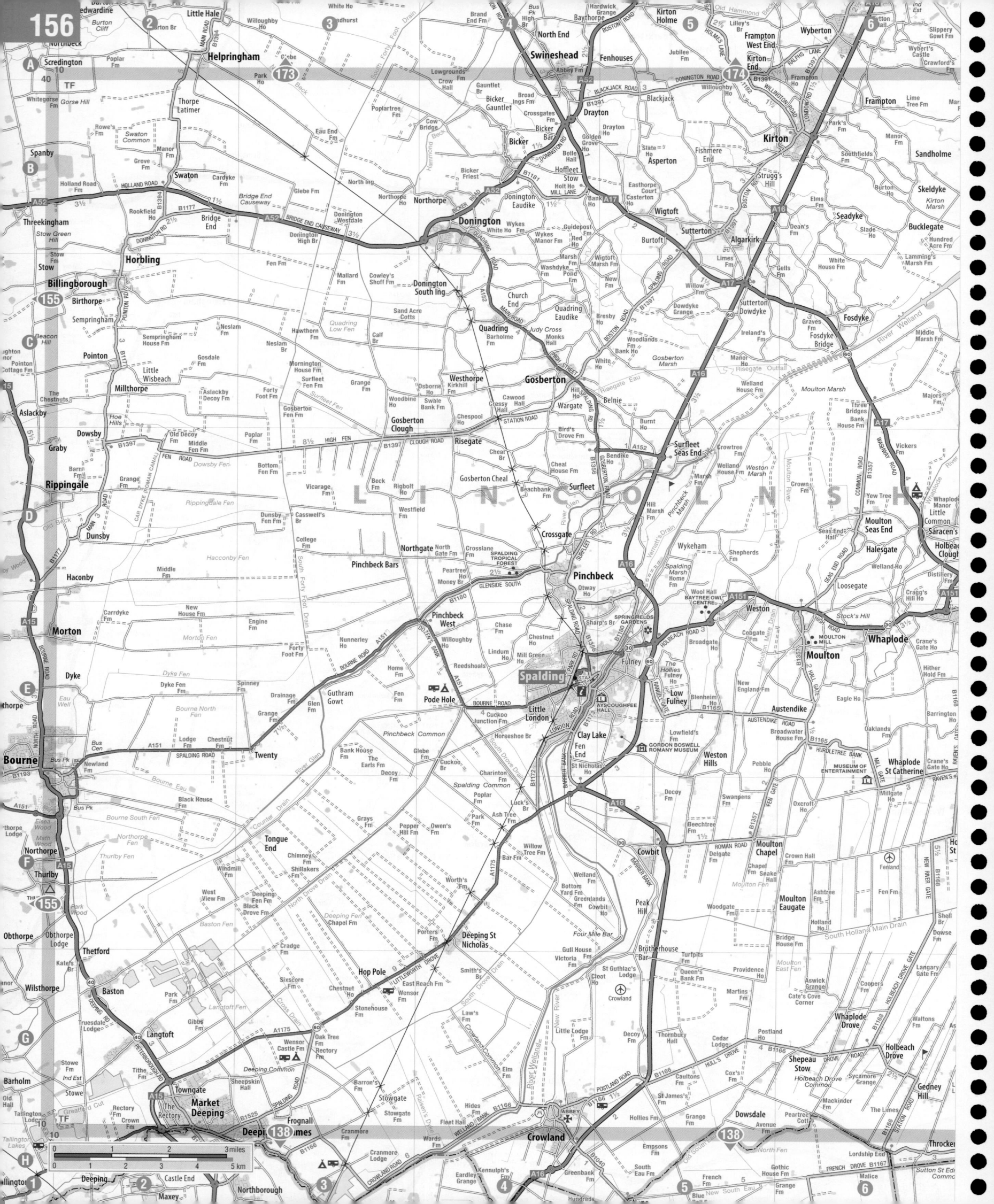

Helpringham
Little Hale
Swineshead
North End
Fenhouses
Kirton Holme
Frampton West End
Kirton End
Wyberton
Scredington
Thorpe Latimer
Bicker Gauntlet
Bicker
Drayton
Blackjack
Frampton
Kirton
Spanby
Swaton
Asperton
Fishmere End
Sandholme
Skeldyke
Threekingham
Bridge End
Donington
Northorpe
Donington Eaudike
Wigtoft
Sutterton
Algarkirk
Seadyke
Bucklegate
Horbling
Stow
Billingborough
Birthorpe
Sempringham
Donington South Ing
Church End
Quadring Eaudike
Sutterton Dowdyke
Fosdyke
Fosdyke Bridge
Quadring
Pointon
Little Wisbeach
Millthorpe
Westhorpe
Gosberton
Aslackby
Gosberton Clough
Wargate
Belnie
Dowsby
Graby
Risegate
Surfleet Seas End
Rippingale
Gosberton Cheal
Surfleet
L I N C O L N S H I R E
Dunsby
Crossgate
Northgate
Pinchbeck Bars
Pinchbeck
Moulton Seas End
Halesgate
Haconby
Loosegate
Weston
Pinchbeck West
Whaplode
Moulton
Morton
Dyke
Spalding
Fulney
Low Fulney
Pode Hole
Guthram Gowt
Little London
Austendike
Twenty
Clay Lake
Fen End
Weston Hills
Whaplode St Catherine
Bourne
Tongue End
Cowbit
Moulton Chapel
Northorpe
Thurlby
Peak Hill
Moulton Eaugate
Deeping St Nicholas
Obthorpe
Thetford
Brotherhouse Bar
Hop Pole
Baston
Wilsthorpe
Whaplode Drove
Langtoft
Shepeau Stow
Holbeach Drove
Market Deeping
Towngate
Barholm
Stowgate
Crowland
Dowsdale
Gedney Hill
Deeping St James
Frognall
Deeping
Castle End
Maxey
Northborough
Throckenholt
173
174
138
155
0 1 2 3 miles
0 1 2 3 4 5 km

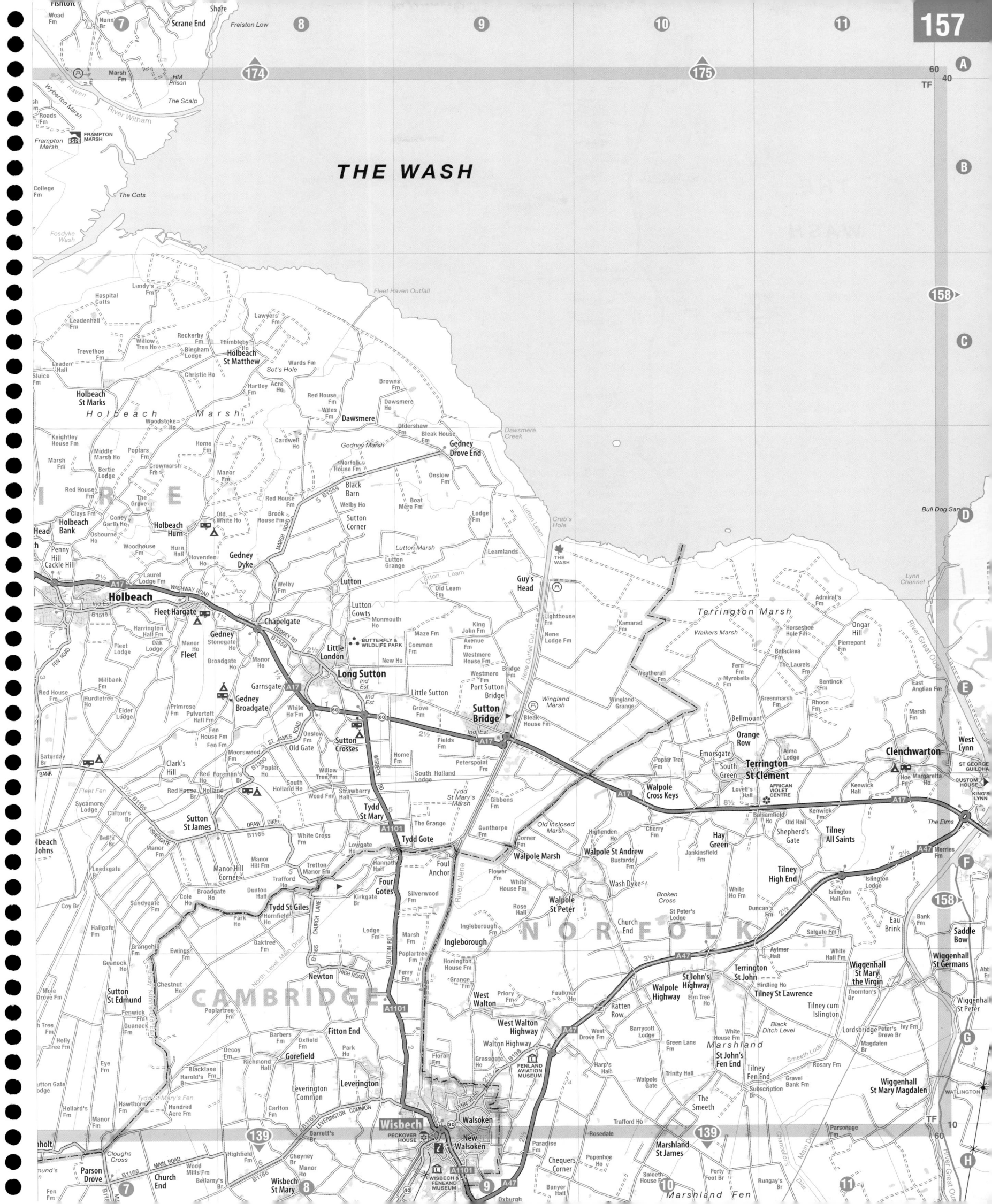
THE WASH
Scrane End
Freiston Low
HM Prison
The Scalp
River Witham
Wyberton Marsh
Frampton Marsh
FRAMPTON MARSH
College Fm
The Cots
Fosdyke Wash
Fleet Haven Outfall
Lundy's Fm
Hospital Cotts
Leadenhall Fm
Trevethoe Fm
Leaden Hall
Sluice Fm
Reckerby Fm
Willow Tree Ho
Bingham Lodge
Thimbleby Ho
Holbeach St Matthew
Lawyers' Fm
Wards Fm
Sot's Hole
Christie Ho
Hartley Fm
Acre Ho
Browns Fm
Red House Fm
Wiles Fm
Dawsmere Ho
Dawsmere
Holbeach St Marks
Holbeach Marsh
Woodstoke Ho
Keightley House Fm
Middle Marsh Ho
Poplars Fm
Home Fm
Cardwell Ho
Oldershaw Fm
Bleak House Fm
Gedney Marsh
Gedney Drove End
Dawsmere Creek
Marsh Fm
Bertie Lodge
Crowmarsh Fm
Manor Fm
Norfolk House Fm
Onslow Fm
Red House Fm
The Grove
Black Barn
Welby Ho
Boat Mere Fm
Red House Fm
Clays Fm
Holbeach Bank
Coney Garth Ho
Old White Ho
Brook House Fm
Holbeach Hurn
Sutton Corner
Lodge Fm
Crab's Hole
Lutton Leam
Bull Dog Sand
Osbourne Ho
Penny Hill
Cackle Hill
Woodhouse Fm
Hurn Hall
Hovenden Ho
Gedney Dyke
Lutton Marsh
Lutton Grange
Leamlands
THE WASH
Lynn Channel
Laurel Lodge Fm
Welby Fm
Lutton
Old Leam Fm
Guy's Head
Holbeach
Fleet Hargate
Chapelgate
Lutton Gowts
Monmouth Ho
Lighthouse Fm
Nene Lodge Fm
Kamarad Fm
Terrington Marsh
Walkers Marsh
Admiral's Fm
Ongar Hill
Horseshoe Hole Fm
Pierrepont Fm
Harrington Hall Fm
Gedney
Stonegate Ho
Oak Lodge
Fleet Lodge
Manor Ho
Fleet
BUTTERFLY & WILDLIFE PARK
Little London
Maze Fm
King John Fm
Avenue Fm
Common Fm
Westmere House Fm
New Ho
Long Sutton
Broadgate Ho
Manor Ho
Millbank Fm
Garnsgate
Hurdletree Ho
Elder Lodge
Red House Fm
Gedney Broadgate
Primrose Fm
Puiverfoft Hall Fm
White Ho Fm
Little Sutton
Westmere Fm
Port Sutton Bridge
Bridge Fm
Grove Fm
Sutton Bridge
Bleak House Fm
Wingland Marsh
Wingland Grange
Weatherall Fm
Fern Fm
Myrobella Fm
Balaclava Fm
The Laurels Fm
Bentinck Fm
Greenmarsh Fm
Rhoon Fm
East Anglian Fm
Marsh Fm
Bellmount
Orange Row
Fen House Fm
Fen Fm
Moorswood Fm
Onslow Fm
Old Gate
Sutton Crosses
Fields Fm
Home Fm
Peterspoint Fm
Poplar Tree Fm
Emorsgate
South Green
Terrington St Clement
Alma Lodge
Clenchwarton
West Lynn
Saturday Br
Clark's Hill
Red Ho
Foreman's Br
Poplar Ho
South Holland Ho
Willow Tree Fm
South Holland Lodge
Walpole Cross Keys
Lovell's Hall
AFRICAN VIOLET CENTRE
Kenwick Hall
Hoe Fm
Margaretta Ho
ST GEORGE GUILDHA
CUSTOM HOUSE
KING'S LYNN
Fleet Fen
Sycamore Lodge
Clifton's Br
Red House Br
Holland Ho
Wood Fm
Strawberry Hall
Tydd St Mary
Tydd St Mary's Marsh
Gibbons Fm
Balsamfield Ho
Old Hall
Kenwick Fm
Shepherd's Gate
Tilney All Saints
The Elms
Sutton St James
Bell's Br
White Cross Fm
The Grange
Gunthorpe Fm
Old Inclosed Marsh
Highenden Ho
Cherry Fm
Hay Green
Jankinsfield Fm
Merries Fm
Holbeach St Johns
Manor Fm
Leedsgate Ho
Manor Hill Fm
Manor Hill Corner
Lowgate Ho
Tydd Gote
Corner Fm
Walpole Marsh
Walpole St Andrew
Bustards Fm
Tretton Manor Fm
Hannath Hall
Foul Anchor
Wash Dyke
Tilney High End
Islington Lodge
Islington Hall Fm
Trafford Ho
Dunton Hall
Four Gotes
Flower Fm
White House Fm
Coy Br
Sandygate Fm
Broadgate Ho
Cole Ho
Kirkgate Br
Silverwood Fm
Broken Cross
White Ho Fm
Duncan's Fm
Tydd St Giles
Hornfield Ho
Park Ho
Rose Hall
Walpole St Peter
St Peter's Lodge
Eau Brink
Bank Fm
Saddle Bow
Hallgate Fm
Grangehill Fm
Ewings Fm
Oaktree Fm
Lodge Fm
Ingleborough Fm
Church End
NORFOLK
Salgate Fm
Marsh Fm
Ingleborough
Aylmer Hall
White Hall Fm
Wiggenhall St Germans
Guanock Ho
Poplartree Fm
Honington House Fm
Terrington St John
Wiggenhall St Mary the Virgin
Newton
Ferry Fm
Grange Fm
St John's Highway
Hirdling Ho
Mole Drove Fm
Chestnut Ho
CAMBRIDGE
Walpole Highway
Tilney St Lawrence
Thornton's Br
Sutton St Edmund
West Walton
Priory Fm
Faulkner Ho
Ratten Row
Elm Tree Ho
Tilney cum Islington
Wiggenhall St Peter
Fenwick Fm
Guanock Fm
Poplartree Fm
West Walton Highway
West Drove Fm
Barrycott Lodge
Black Ditch Level
Lordsbridge
Peter's Drove Br
Ivy Fm
Magdalen Br
Holly Tree Fm
Barbers Fm
Oxfield Fm
Fitton End
Walton Highway
White House Fm
Green Lane Fm
Marshland
Park Ho
Decoy Fm
Gorefield
Floral Fm
Grassgate Ho
FENLAND AVIATION MUSEUM
Harp's Hall
St John's Fen End
Smeeth Lode
Rosary Fm
Eye Fm
Richmond Hall
Blacklane Fm
Harold's Br
Trinity Hall
Tilney Fen End
Walpole Gate
Gravel Bank Fm
Wiggenhall St Mary Magdalen
Tydd St Mary's Fen
Leverington Common
Leverington
Subscription Br
WATLINGTON
Holland's Fm
Hawthorn Fm
Hundred Acre Fm
Carlton Fm
The Smeeth
Manor Fm
Wisbech
Walsoken
Trafford Ho
PECKOVER HOUSE
Barrett's Br
New Walsoken
Rosedale
Parsonage Fm
Cloughs Cross
Highfield Fm
Cheyney Br
Manor Ho
Paradise Fm
Chequers Corner
Popenhoe Ho
Marshland St James
Forty Foot Br
Parson Drove
Church End
Wood Mills Fm
Bellamy's Br
Wisbech St Mary
WISBECH & FENLAND MUSEUM
Banyer Hall
Smeeth House Fm
Rungay's Br
Fen Fm
Oxburgh
Marshland Fen
River Nene
Nene Outfall Cut
River Great Ouse
North Level Main Drain
Main Drain
Chancellor's Dike
A17
A47
A1101
B1359
B1390
B1165
B1166
B1169
B1198
B1515
WASHWAY ROAD
GEDNEY RD
MARSH ROAD
ST JAMES ROAD
FEN ROAD
DRAW DIKE
CHURCH LANE
SUTTON RD
WISBECH RD
HIGH ROAD
MAIN ROAD
LEVERINGTON COMMON
LYNN ROAD
FISHERGATE
174
175
158
139
7
8
9
10
11
A
B
C
D
E
F
G
H
TF
60
40
10

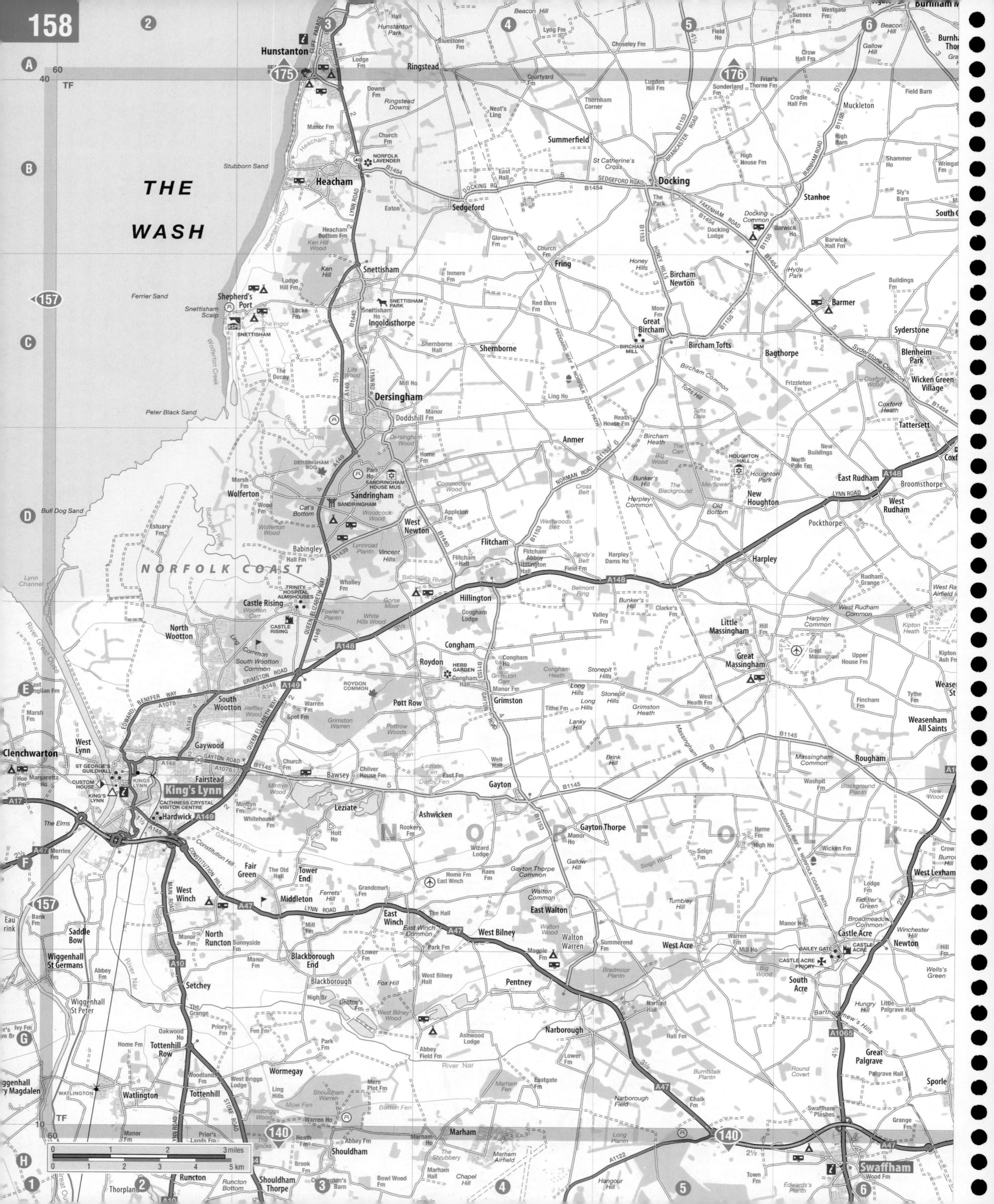
THE WASH
NORFOLK COAST
NORFOLK
Hunstanton
Heacham
Snettisham
Shepherd's Port
Ingoldisthorpe
Dersingham
Sandringham
Wolferton
Babingley
Castle Rising
North Wootton
South Wootton
Gaywood
King's Lynn
West Lynn
Clenchwarton
Hardwick
Fairstead
Ringstead
Sedgeford
Docking
Stanhoe
Summerfield
Fring
Shernborne
Great Bircham
Bircham Tofts
Bircham Newton
Bagthorpe
Barmer
Syderstone
Blenheim Park
Wicken Green Village
Tattersett
Anmer
New Houghton
East Rudham
West Rudham
Pockthorpe
Broomsthorpe
Harpley
West Newton
Flitcham
Hillington
Congham
Roydon
Grimston
Pott Row
Little Massingham
Great Massingham
Weasenham All Saints
Rougham
Bawsey
Leziate
Ashwicken
Gayton
Gayton Thorpe
West Lexham
Castle Acre
Newton
South Acre
West Acre
East Walton
West Bilney
East Winch
West Winch
Middleton
Tower End
Fair Green
North Runcton
Setchey
Blackborough End
Pentney
Narborough
Great Palgrave
Sporle
Swaffham
Marham
Shouldham
Shouldham Thorpe
Wormegay
Tottenhill
Tottenhill Row
Watlington
Runcton
Saddle Bow
Wiggenhall St Germans
Wiggenhall St Peter
Muckleton
Sandringham House Mus
Norfolk Lavender
Castle Acre Priory
Houghton Hall
A148
A149
A47
A10
A1065
A1076
A1078
B1145
B1153
B1154
B1155
B1439
B1440
B1454
A17
A1122
175
176
157
140
Peddars Way & Norfolk Coast Path
TF
0 1 2 3 miles
0 1 2 3 4 5 km

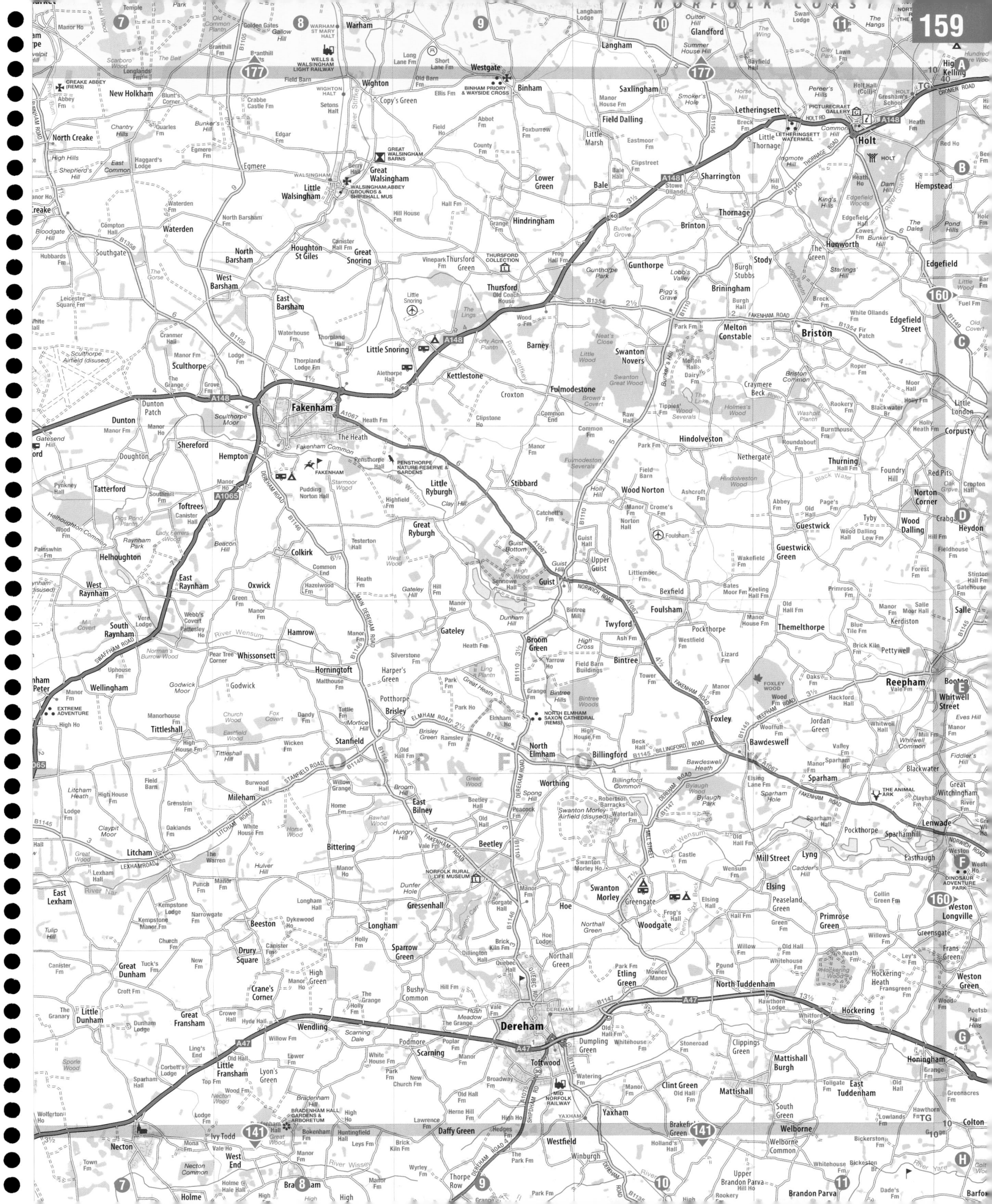

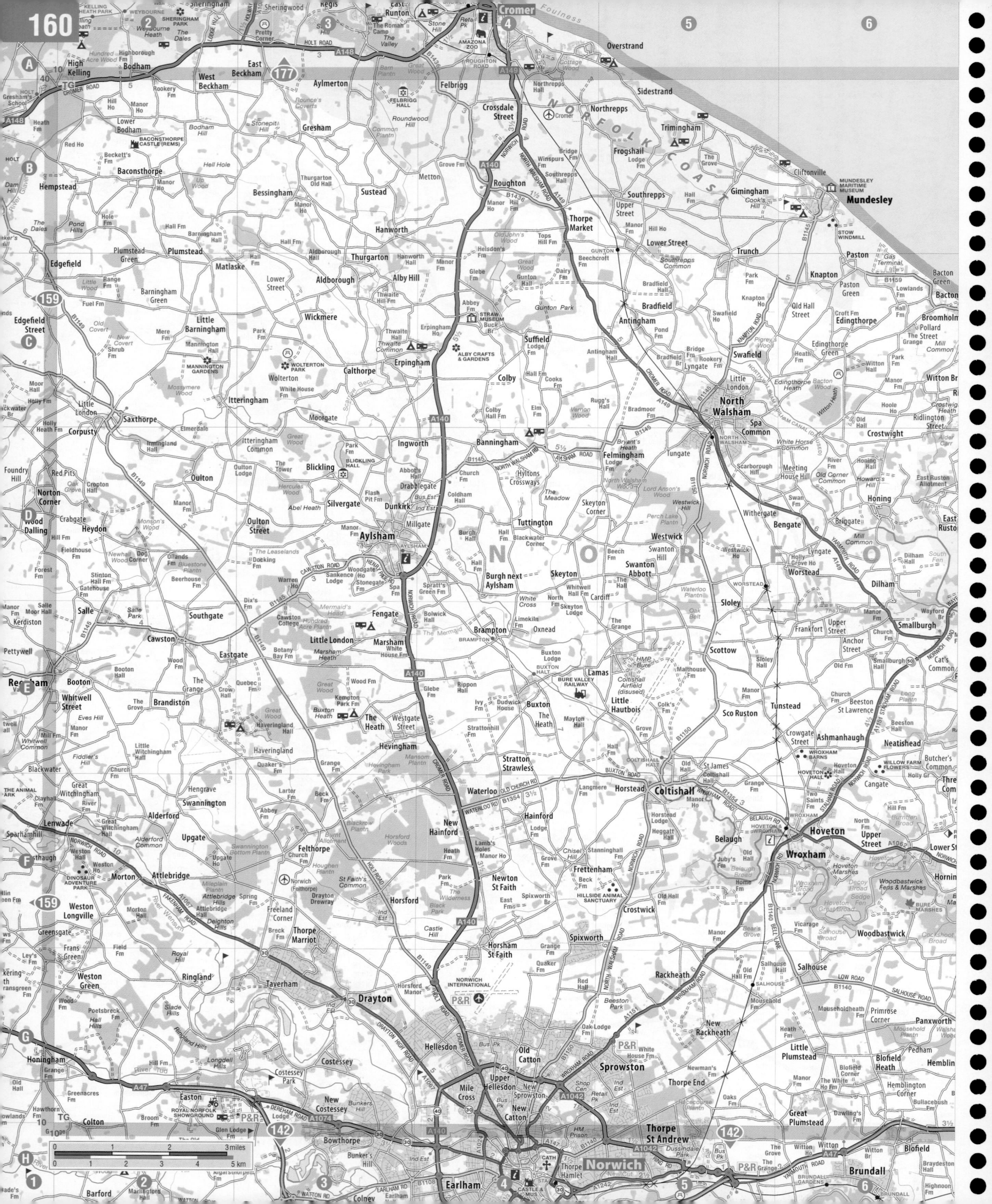

Cromer
Overstrand
Sidestrand
Northrepps
Trimingham
Mundesley
Gimingham
Southrepps
Thorpe Market
Roughton
Felbrigg
Aylmerton
Gresham
Bodham
High Kelling
West Beckham
East Beckham
Baconsthorpe
Hempstead
Bessingham
Sustead
Metton
Hanworth
Thurgarton
Plumstead
Matlaske
Edgefield
Edgefield Street
Aldborough
Alby Hill
Wickmere
Little Barningham
Barningham Green
Erpingham
Calthorpe
Wolterton
Itteringham
Saxthorpe
Corpusty
Little London
Colby
Suffield
Antingham
Bradfield
Trunch
Knapton
Paston
Bacton
Edingthorpe
Swafield
North Walsham
Spa Common
Crostwight
Honing
Felmingham
Banningham
Ingworth
Blickling
Moorgate
Oulton
Oulton Street
Heydon
Wood Dalling
Norton Corner
Aylsham
Millgate
Dunkirk
Drabblegate
Silvergate
Tuttington
Skeyton
Burgh next Aylsham
Westwick
Swanton Abbott
Worstead
Dilham
Smallburgh
Sloley
Scottow
Cawston
Salle
Southgate
Eastgate
Marsham
Little London
Brampton
Oxnead
Lamas
Buxton
Little Hautbois
Tunstead
Sco Ruston
Ashmanhaugh
Neatishead
Hevingham
Haveringland
Brandiston
Booton
Whitwell Street
Reepham
Swannington
Alderford
Upgate
Felthorpe
Attlebridge
Morton
Weston Longville
Lenwade
Great Witchingham
Stratton Strawless
Waterloo
Horstead
Coltishall
Hainford
Newton St Faith
Frettenham
Crostwick
Belaugh
Hoveton
Wroxham
Horsford
Horsham St Faith
Spixworth
Rackheath
Salhouse
Woodbastwick
Thorpe Marriott
Taverham
Drayton
Ringland
Weston Green
Hellesdon
Old Catton
Sprowston
Costessey
New Costessey
Mile Cross
Upper Hellesdon
New Catton
Thorpe End
Little Plumstead
Great Plumstead
Blofield Heath
Pedham
Panxworth
Thorpe St Andrew
Norwich
Thorpe Hamlet
Earlham
Bowthorpe
Colton
Easton
Honingham
Barford
Colney
Brundall
Blofield
Witton
NORFOLK COAST
NORFOLK
Norwich International
A148
A149
A140
A1067
A47
A1151
A1042
A1074
B1145
B1149
B1150
B1354
B1436
B1159
B1140
177
159
142
0 1 2 3 miles
0 1 2 3 4 5 km

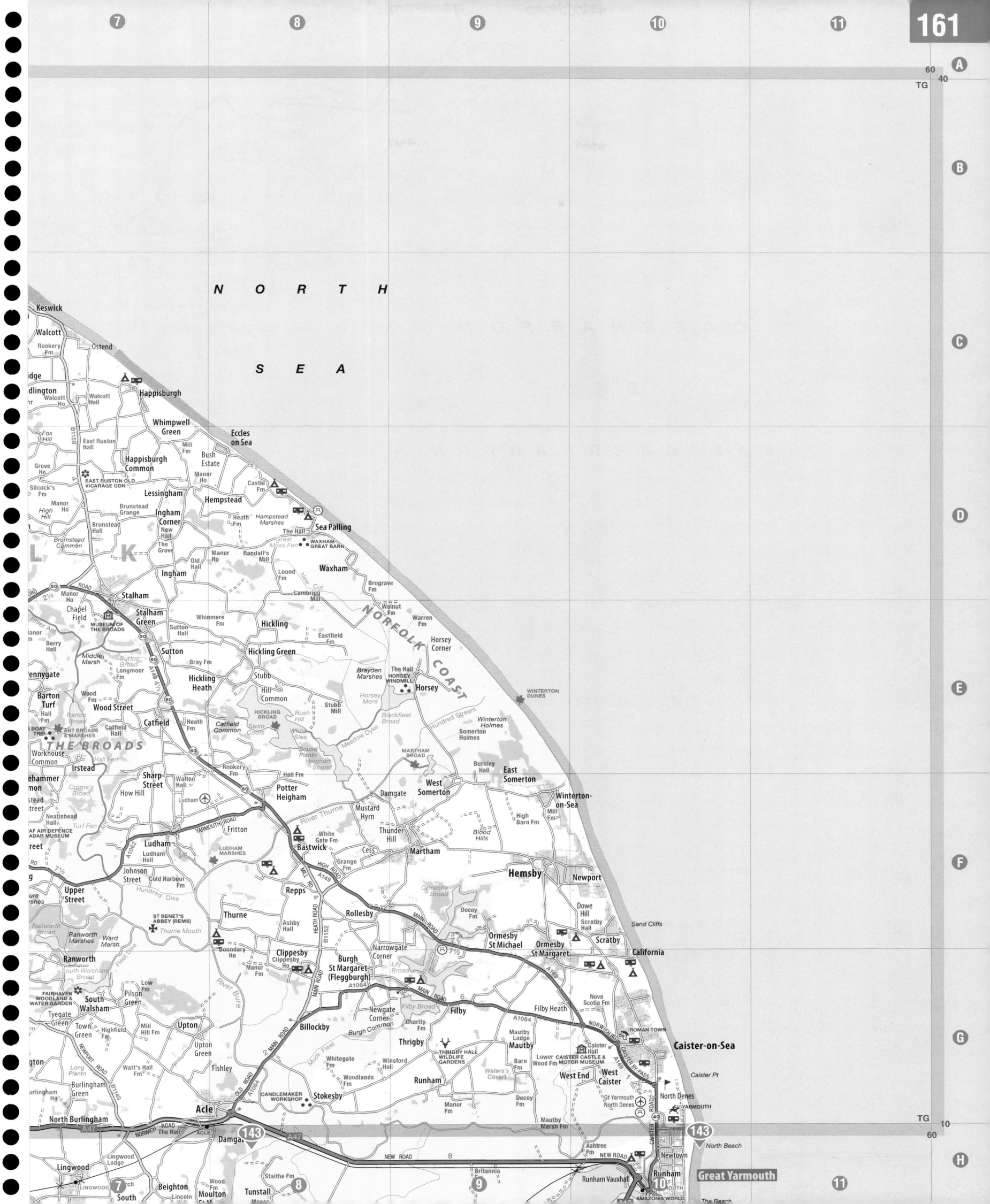
NORTH
SEA
Keswick
Walcott
Ostend
Happisburgh
Whimpwell Green
Eccles on Sea
Happisburgh Common
East Ruston Old Vicarage Gdn
Lessingham
Hempstead
Ingham Corner
Sea Palling
Hampstead Marshes
Waxham Great Barn
Waxham
Ingham
Stalham
Stalham Green
Museum of the Broads
Hickling
Norfolk Coast
Horsey Corner
Sutton
Hickling Green
Hickling Heath
Horsey
Horsey Windmill
Winterton Dunes
Wood Street
Catfield
Hickling Broad
Winterton Holmes
Somerton Holmes
The Broads
Martham Broad
East Somerton
West Somerton
Potter Heigham
Damgate
Winterton-on-Sea
Irstead
Sharp Street
How Hill
Ludham
Fritton
Bastwick
Thurne
Martham
Ludham Marshes
Hemsby
Newport
Repps
Johnson Street
Upper Street
St Benet's Abbey (Rems)
Rollesby
Ormesby St Michael
Ormesby St Margaret
Scratby
California
Sand Cliffs
Ranworth
Clippesby
Burgh St Margaret (Fleggburgh)
South Walsham
Pilson Green
Filby
Filby Heath
Billockby
Upton
Thrigby
Thrigby Hall Wildlife Gardens
Mautby
Caister Castle & Motor Museum
Caister-on-Sea
West End
West Caister
Caister Pt
Runham
Stokesby
Candlemaker Workshop
Acle
Fishley
North Burlingham
Burlingham Green
Damgate
North Denes
North Beach
Great Yarmouth
Newtown
Runham Vauxhall
Amazonia-World
Lingwood
Beighton
Tunstall
Moulton
South
A47
A149
A1064
A1062
B1152
B1159
B1140
143
TG

CAERNARFON
BAY
BAE CAERNARFON
178
144
145
Aberffraw
Llangadwaladr
Hermon
Bodorgan
Malltraeth
Llangaffo
Newborough
(Niwbwrch)
Pen-lon
Dwyran
ISLE OF ANGLESEY
YNYS MÔN
Malltraeth Sands
Newborough Forest
NEWBOROUGH WARREN & YNYS LLANDDWYN
Malltraeth Bay
Bae Malltraeth
Llanddwyn
Ynys Llanddwyn
Newborough Warren
Traeth Melynog
Llangwyfan-isaf
BARCLODIAD Y GAWRES BURIAL CHAMBER
Bethel
Capel Mawr
Trefdraeth
Porth Cwyfan
Porth China
Penrhyn
Braich-lwyd
Aber Ffraw Bay
Trefi
Bodowen
Porth-cadwaladr
Porth Twyn-mawr
TACLA TAID TRANSPORT MUSEUM
MODEL VILLAGE
BIRD WORLD
WALES COAST PATH
South Sands
Warren Fm
Caernarfon
CAERNARFON AIR MUSEUM
Morfa Dinlle
Dinas Dinlle
Llandwrog
Pontllyfni
Aberdesach
Afon Desach
WELSH LIFE
Tainlon
Clynnog-fawr
Capel Uchaf
ST BEUNO'S WELL
Cwmgwared
Gyrn-goch
Bryn-yr-eryr
Gyrn Goch 492
509 Bwlch Mawr
Morfa
Trwyn y Tâl
Gwydir
Trefor
522 Gyrn Ddu
297 Moel Penllechog
Moel Bronmoid 416
Pen-Y-Gaer 389
Cwm
Hedre-fawr
Trwyn y Gorlech
Cwm-coryn Fm
Llanaelhaearn
Moelfre
Bronmiod Fm
Cwm Cilio
Yr Eifl 564
TRE'R-CEIRI (FORT)
Porth y Nant
Penrhyn Glas
Mount Pleasant
Gelliau
Hafod
Llithfaen
Mynydd Carnguwch 359
Carnguwch Fawr
Moel Gwynus
Carnguwch Bach
Pont y Gydrhos
Brynbychan
Bryn Mawr
Cefn-caer-ferch
Pen-sarn
Penrhyn Bodeilas
Pistyll
Cefnydd
Moel Ty-Gwyn
Wern
Tir Bach
Gwyniasa
Ysgubor Plas
Tyddyn Cestyll
Cefn Isaf
Trallwyn Hall
Pencaenewydd
Llangybi
Lleyn Peninsula
LLEYN HISTORICAL MARITIME MUSEUM
Mynydd Nefyn
Carreg Ddu
Trwyn Porth Dinllaen
Porth Dinllaen
Borth Wen
Penrhyn Nefyn
Porth Nefyn
Morfa Nefyn
Nefyn
Aber Geirch
Llwyndyrys
Castell Gwgan
Garn Boduan 280
Edern
Fron
Pentreuchaf
Rhos-fawr
Y Ffôr
Rhyd-y-gwystl
Llanarmon
Chwilog
Tan-y-graig
Plasyngheidio
Rhos-y-llan
Penrhyn Cwmistir
Moelypenmaen
Llannerch
Bryn Rodyn
Tyn-rhos-fawr
Ty Du Isaf
Bryngwdyn
Pencraig
Glyncoed
Ynyslecí
0 1 2 3 miles
0 1 2 3 4 5 km

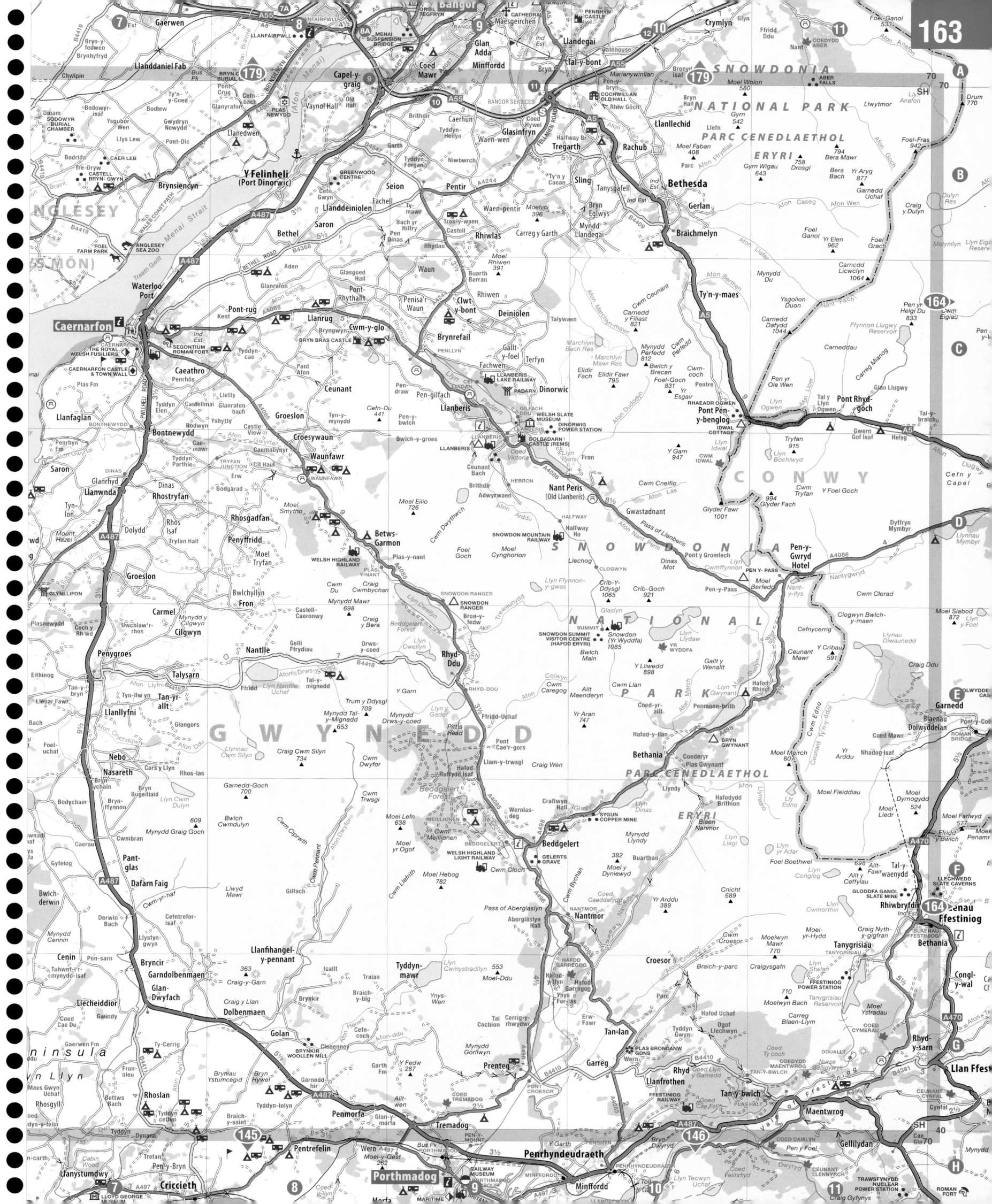
Bangor
Gaerwen
Llanfairpwll
Menai Suspension Bridge
Glan Adda
Minffordd
Maesgeirchen
Llandegai
Tal-y-bont
Crymlyn
Penrhyn Castle
Llanddaniel Fab
Capel-y-graig
Coed Mawr
SNOWDONIA
NATIONAL PARK
PARC CENEDLAETHOL
ERYRI
Moel Wnion 580
Vaynol Hall
Glasinfryn
Tregarth
Rachub
Llanllechid
Brynsiencyn
Y Felinheli (Port Dinorwic)
Seion
Pentir
Sling
Bethesda
Gerlan
Braichmelyn
ANGLESEY
(YS MÔN)
Menai Strait
Anglesey Sea Zoo
Foel Farm Park
Llanddeiniolen
Saron
Bethel
Rhiwlas
Waun
Waterloo Port
Caernarfon
Caernarfon Castle & Town Wall
Segontium Roman Fort
Pont-rug
Llanrug
Cwm-y-glo
Clwt-y-bont
Deiniolen
Brynrefail
Ty'n-y-maes
Caeathro
Ceunant
Fachwen
Dinorwic
Llanberis
Llyn Padarn
Llanberis Lake Railway
Welsh Slate Museum
Dolbadarn Castle (rems)
Dinorwig Power Station
Llanfaglan
Bontnewydd
Groeslon
Croesywaun
Waunfawr
Pont Pen-y-benglog
Idwal Cottage
Pont Rhyd-goch
Tryfan 915
Glyder Fach 994
Glyder Fawr 1001
CONWY
Nant Peris (Old Llanberis)
Gwastadnant
Pass of Llanberis
Saron
Llanwnda
Rhostryfan
Rhosgadfan
Betws-Garmon
Welsh Highland Railway
Snowdon Mountain Railway
Pen-y-Gwryd Hotel
Pen-y-Pass
Dolydd
Penyffridd
Moel Tryfan
Groeslon
Carmel
Fron
Cilgwyn
Snowdon Ranger
Llyn Cwellyn
Snowdon Summit Visitor Centre (Hafod Eryri)
Snowdon (Yr Wyddfa) 1085
Crib-y-Ddysgl 1065
Crib-Goch 921
Y Lliwedd 898
Penygroes
Nantlle
Talysarn
Rhyd-Ddu
Llanllyfni
Tan-yr-allt
GWYNEDD
Nebo
Nasareth
Bethania
Craig Cwm Silyn 734
Garnedd-Goch 700
Beddgelert Forest
Beddgelert
Sygun Copper Mine
Moel Hebog 782
Pant-glas
Dafarn Faig
Bwlch-derwin
Nantmor
Pass of Aberglaslyn
Llanfihangel-y-pennant
Bryncir
Garndolbenmaen
Glan-Dwyfach
Dolbenmaen
Golan
Brynkir Woollen Mill
Tyddyn-mawr
Croesor
Tanygrisiau
Ffestiniog Power Station
Blaenau Ffestiniog
Llechwedd Slate Caverns
Rhiwbryfdir
Dolwyddelan
Garnedd
Tan-lan
Garreg
Rhyd
Llanfrothen
Tan-y-bwlch
Maentwrog
Prenteg
Tremadog
Penmorfa
Rhoslan
Llecheiddior
Pentrefelin
Criccieth
Llanystumdwy
Porthmadog
Penrhyndeudraeth
Minffordd
Gellilydan
Trawsfynydd Nuclear Power Station
A5
A55
A487
A4085
A4086
A498
A470
A496
A497
B4410
B4418
179
145
146
164

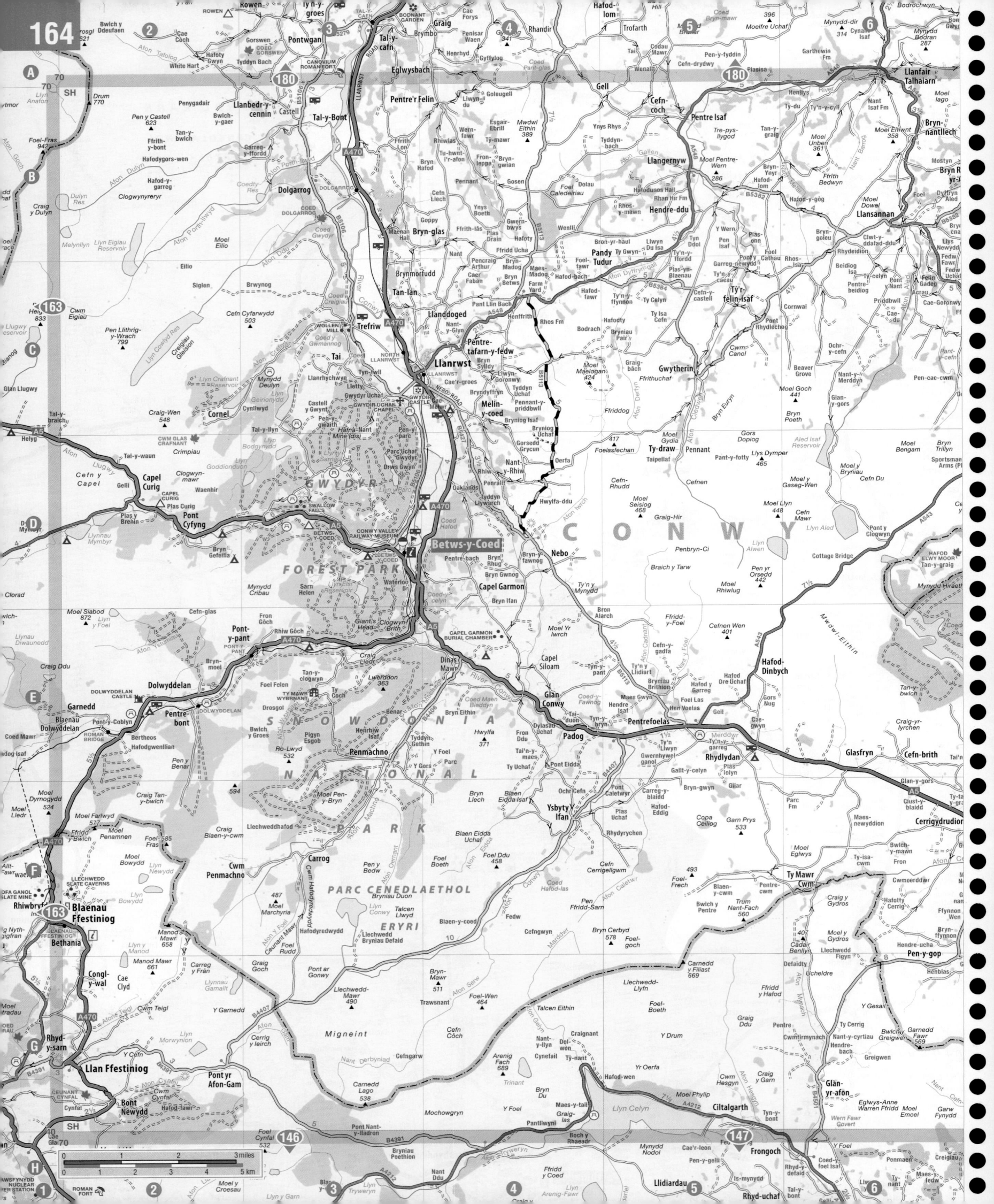
Rowen
Ty'n-y-groes
Tal-y-cafn
Bodnant Garden
Graig
Rhandir
Hafod-lom
Trofarth
Moelfre Uchaf
Mynydd-dir
Bodrochwyn
Bwlch y Ddeufaen
Pontwgan
Gorswen
Hafoty Gwyn
Tyddyn Bach
White Hart
Canovium Roman Fort
Eglwysbach
Gell
Cefn-coch
Pentre Isaf
Llanfair Talhaiarn
Drum
Penygadair
Llanbedr-y-cennin
Tal-y-Bont
Pentre'r Felin
Pen y Castell
Foel-Fras
Dolgarrog
Llangernyw
Bryn-nantllech
Clogwynyreryr
Melynllyn
Llyn Eigiau Reservoir
Moel Eilio
Eilio
Siglen
Brwynog
Bryn-glas
Brynmorfudd
Tan-lan
Llanddoged
Pandy Tudur
Hendre-ddu
Llansannan
Tŷ'r-felin-isaf
Cefn Cyfarwydd
Pen Llithrig-y-Wrach
Cwm Eigiau
Llugwy Reservoir
Trefriw
Pentre-tafarn-y-fedw
Llanrwst
Gwytherin
Tai
Llanrhychwyn
Gwydir Uchaf
Cornel
Craig-Wen
Tal-y-braich
Helyg
Tal-y-waun
Capel Curig
Cefn y Capel
Gelli
Plas Curig
Pont Cyfyng
Swallow Falls
Betws-y-Coed
Conwy Valley Railway Museum
Melin-y-coed
Ty-draw
Pennant
Foelasfechan
Nebo
CONWY
GWYDYR
FOREST PARK
Capel Garmon
Moel Siabod
Pont-y-pant
Dolwyddelan
Dolwyddelan Castle
Garnedd
Blaenau Dolwyddelan
Pentre-bont
Dinas Mawr
Capel Garmon Burial Chamber
Glan-Conwy
Padog
Pentrefoelas
Rhydlydan
Hafod-Dinbych
Glasfryn
Cefn-brith
Cerrigydrudion
Penmachno
SNOWDONIA
NATIONAL
PARK
Ysbyty Ifan
Cwm Penmachno
Carrog
PARC CENEDLAETHOL
ERYRI
Blaenau Ffestiniog
Llechwedd Slate Caverns
Rhiwbryfdir
Bethania
Congl-y-wal
Manod Mawr
Ty Mawr Cwm
Pen-y-gop
Rhyd-y-sarn
Llan Ffestiniog
Pont yr Afon-Gam
Bont Newydd
Migneint
Arenig Fach
Llyn Celyn
Ciltalgarth
Frongoch
Carnedd Lago
Mochowgryn
Pont Nant-y-lladron
Glan-yr-afon
Llidiardau
Rhyd-uchaf
miles
km

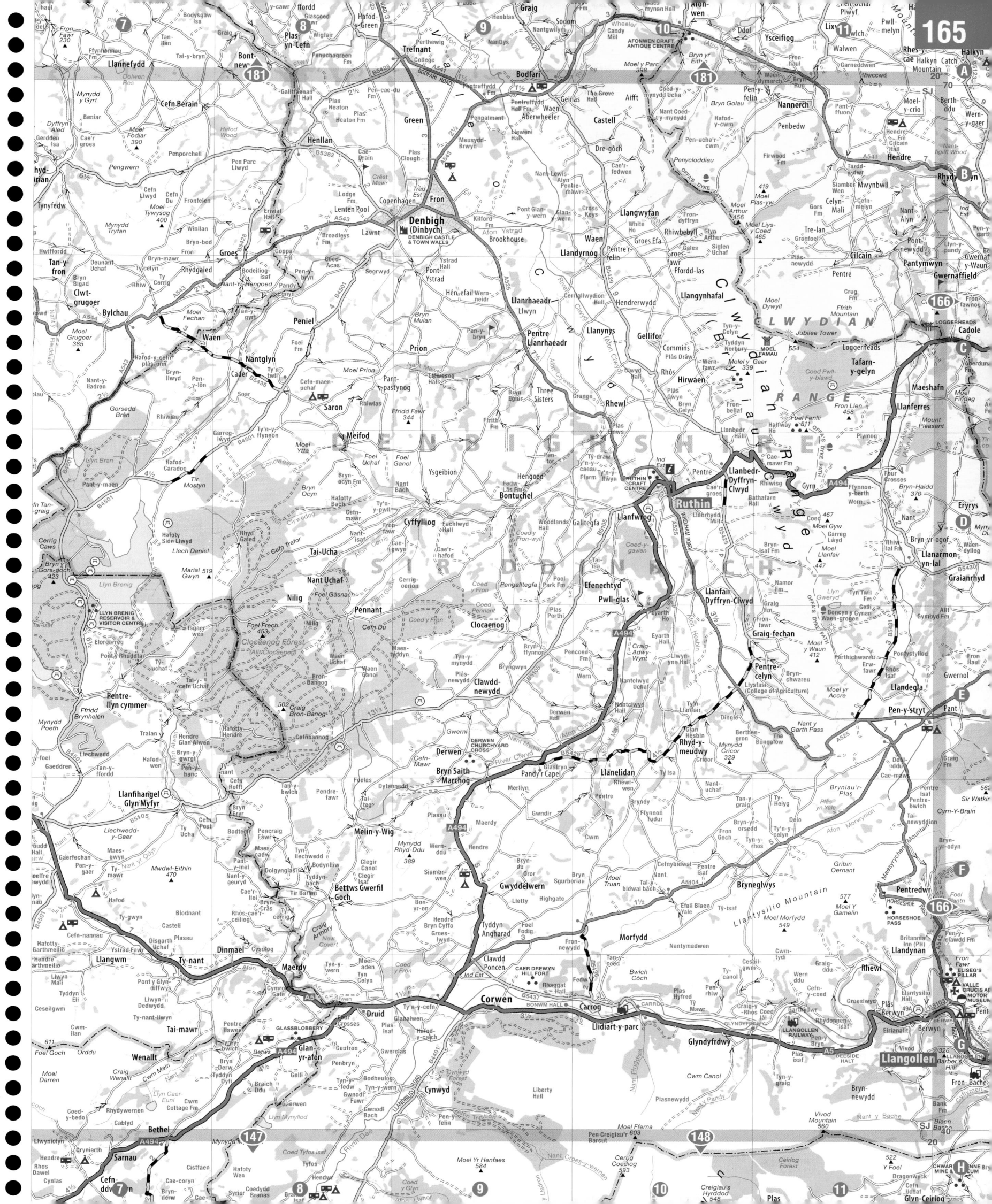

Llannefydd
Bont-newydd
Plas-yn-Cefn
Trefnant
Bodfari
Afon-wen
Ysceifiog
Halkyn
Cefn Berain
Henllan
Green
Aberwheeler
Castell
Nannerch
Denbigh (Dinbych)
DENBIGH CASTLE & TOWN WALLS
Fron
Lenten Pool
Copenhagen
Lawnt
Llangwyfan
Llandyrnog
Groes
Rhydgaled
Tan-y-fron
Clwt-grugoer
Bylchau
Waen
Nantglyn
Peniel
Prion
Llanrhaeadr
Pentre Llanrhaeadr
Llanynys
Gellifor
Hirwaen
Rhewl
Llangynhafal
Cilcain
Pantymwyn
Gwernaffield
Cadole
Tafarn-y-gelyn
Maeshafn
Llanferres
CLWYDIAN
RANGE
Jubilee Tower
Saron
Meifod
DENBIGHSHIRE
(SIR DDINBYCH)
Ruthin
Llanfwrog
Llanbedr-Dyffryn-Clwyd
Gyrn
Eryrys
Bontuchel
Cyffylliog
Tai-Ucha
Nant Uchaf
Nilig
Pennant
Clocaenog
Efenechtyd
Pwll-glas
Llanfair-Dyffryn-Clwyd
Llanarmon-yn-Ial
Graianrhyd
Graig-fechan
Pentre-celyn
Llandegla
Pen-y-stryt
Clocaenog Forest
Llyn Brenig
Pentre-llyn cymmer
Clawdd-newydd
Derwen
Bryn Saith Marchog
Rhyd-y-meudwy
Llanelidan
Llanfihangel Glyn Myfyr
Melin-y-Wig
Bettws Gwerfil Goch
Gwyddelwern
Bryneglwys
Pentredwr
Llantysilio Mountain
Morfydd
Llandynan
Ty-nant
Dinmael
Maerdy
Llangwm
Corwen
Carrog
Druid
Lidiart-y-parc
Glyndyfrdwy
Rhewl
Berwyn
Llangollen
Tai-mawr
Wenallt
Glan-yr-afon
Cynwyd
Bethel
Sarnau
Cefn-ddwysarn

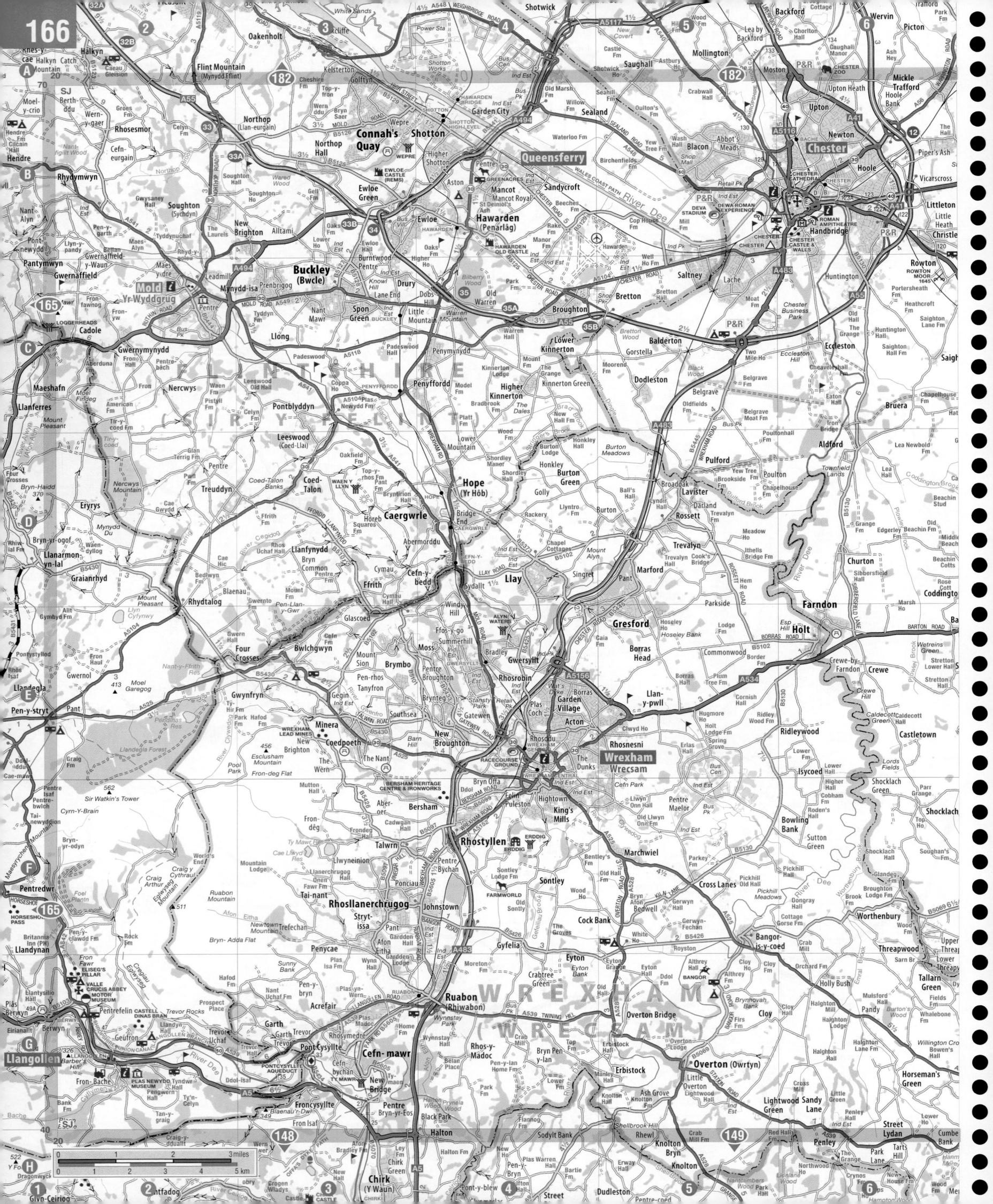
Halkyn
Oakenholt
Flint Mountain
(Mynydd Fflint)
Shotwick
Backford
Wervin
Picton
Mollington
Saughall
Sealand
Garden City
Connah's
Quay
Shotton
Northop
(Llan-eurgain)
Rhosesmor
Northop
Hall
Queensferry
Blacon
Chester
Newton
Upton
Hoole
Vicarscross
Littleton
Christleton
Rhydymwyn
Soughton
(Sychdyn)
Ewloe
Green
Ewloe
Hawarden
(Penarlâg)
Mancot
Sandycroft
River Dee
Handbridge
Rowton
New
Brighton
Buckley
(Bwcle)
Mold
Yr Wyddgrug
Mynydd-isa
Drury
Saltney
Lache
Bretton
Broughton
Huntington
Pantymwyn
Gwernaffield
Cadole
Gwernymynydd
Llong
Penymynydd
Lower
Kinnerton
Balderton
Eccleston
Dodleston
Higher
Kinnerton
Penyffordd
FLINTSHIRE
(SIR Y FFLINT)
Maeshafn
Llanferres
Nercwys
Pontblyddyn
Leeswood
(Coed-Llai)
Belgrave
Pulford
Aldford
Bruera
Treuddyn
Coed-
Talon
Hope
(Yr Hôb)
Burton
Green
Lavister
Rossett
Caergwrle
Eryrys
Llanarmon-
yn-Ial
Graianrhyd
Llanfynydd
Cefn-y-
bedd
Ffrith
Llay
Marford
Trevalyn
Churton
Farndon
Holt
Rhydtalog
Gresford
Four
Crosses
Bwlchgwyn
Brymbo
Gwersyllt
Rhosrobin
Borras
Head
Llandegla
Pen-y-stryt
Gwynfryn
Minera
Coedpoeth
Garden
Village
Acton
Llan-
y-pwll
Crewe
Wrexham
Wrecsam
Rhosnesni
Ridleyway
Castletown
Isycoed
Bersham
Rhostyllen
King's
Mills
Marchwiel
Sontley
Cross Lanes
Rhosllanerchrugog
Johnstown
Cock Bank
Bangor-
is-y-coed
Worthenbury
Threapwood
Llandynan
Gyfelia
Eyton
Ruabon
(Rhiwabon)
WREXHAM
(WRECSAM)
Overton Bridge
Cloy
Pandy
Garth
Trevor
Pont Cysyllte
Cefn-mawr
Llangollen
Erbistock
Overton (Owrtyn)
Horseman's
Green
Froncysyllte
Black Park
Halton
Lightwood
Green
Sandy
Lane
Penley
Chirk
(Y Waun)
Knolton
Dudleston
Street
Street
Lydan
0 1 2 3 miles
0 1 2 3 4 5 km
182
148
149
165

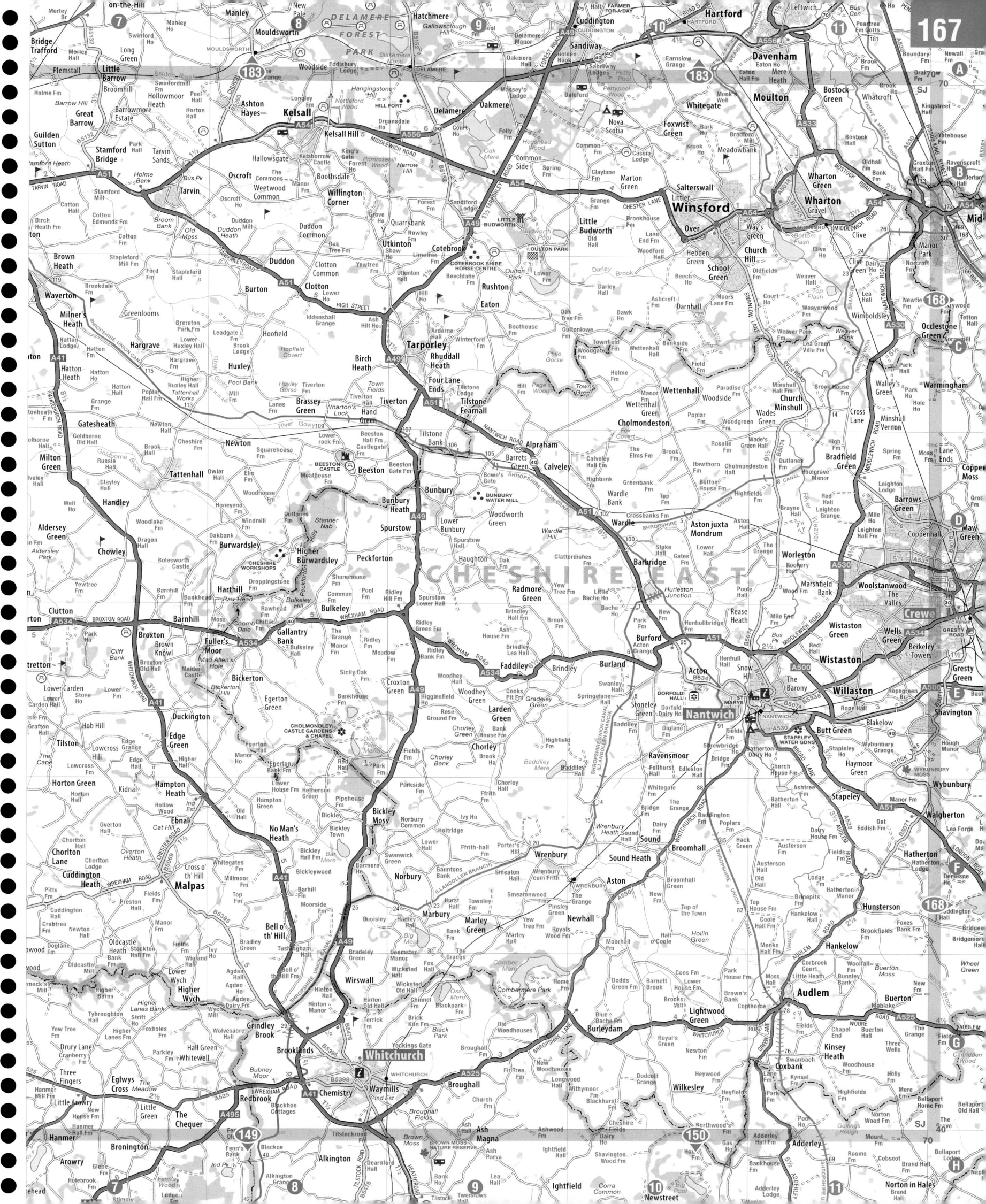
DELAMERE FOREST PARK
CHESHIRE EAST
Hartford
Davenham
Moulton
Winsford
Middlewich
Kelsall
Tarvin
Tarporley
Crewe
Nantwich
Malpas
Whitchurch
Audlem
Cuddington
Sandiway
Mouldsworth
Manley
Ashton Hayes
Delamere
Oakmere
Little Budworth
Cotebrook
Utkinton
Duddon
Clotton
Eaton
Rushton
Beeston
Bunbury
Peckforton
Burwardsley
Higher Burwardsley
Tattenhall
Handley
Chowley
Broxton
Barnhill
Bulkeley
Bickerton
Duckington
Edge Green
Hampton Heath
No Man's Heath
Norbury
Marbury
Wrenbury
Aston
Newhall
Sound Heath
Broomhall
Ravensmoor
Burland
Acton
Barbridge
Wardle
Calveley
Alpraham
Tilstone Fearnall
Tiverton
Cholmondeston
Wettenhall
Church Minshull
Warmingham
Worleston
Wistaston
Willaston
Shavington
Wybunbury
Stapeley
Walgherton
Hatherton
Hunsterton
Hankelow
Buerton
Coxbank
Adderley
Burleydam
Wilkesley
Wirswall
Ash Magna
Alkington
Broughall
Redbrook
Bronington
Hanmer
Waymills
Chemistry
Brooklands
Grindley Brook
Higher Wych
Cuddington Heath
Chorlton Lane
Horton Green
Tilston
Clutton
Aldersey Green
Milton Green
Waverton
Hargrave
Huxley
Gatesheath
Stamford Bridge
Great Barrow
Guilden Sutton
Little Barrow
Oscroft
Willington Corner
Duddon Common
Kelsall Hill
Nova Scotia
Whitegate
Foxwist Green
Salterswall
Over
Wharton
Wharton Green
Bostock Green
Clive
Church Hill
School Green
Darnhall
Wimboldsley
Occlestone Green
Bradfield Green
Barrows Green
Coppenhall
Woolstanwood
Wells Green
Gresty Green
Berkeley Towers
Faddiley
Brindley
Larden Green
Chorley
Cholmondley Castle Gardens & Chapel
Beeston Castle
Bunbury Water Mill
Cheshire Workshops
Oulton Park
Cotebrook Shire Horse Centre
Stapeley Water Gdns
Wybunbury Moss
Combermere Park
Brown Moss Nature Reserve
Lightwood Green
Bickley Moss
Bell o' th' Hill
Ebnal
Fuller's Moor
Gallantry Bank
Harthill
Spurstow
Bunbury Heath
Tilstone Bank
Four Lane Ends
Rhuddall Heath
Birch Heath
Brassey Green
Radmore Green
Hurleston Junction
Stoneley Green
Swanley
Baddiley
Sound
Newhall
Audlem
Kinsey Heath
SHROPSHIRE UNION CANAL
A49
A51
A54
A556
A534
A41
A530
A500
A525
A495
A533
B5074
183
149
150
168
SJ
70

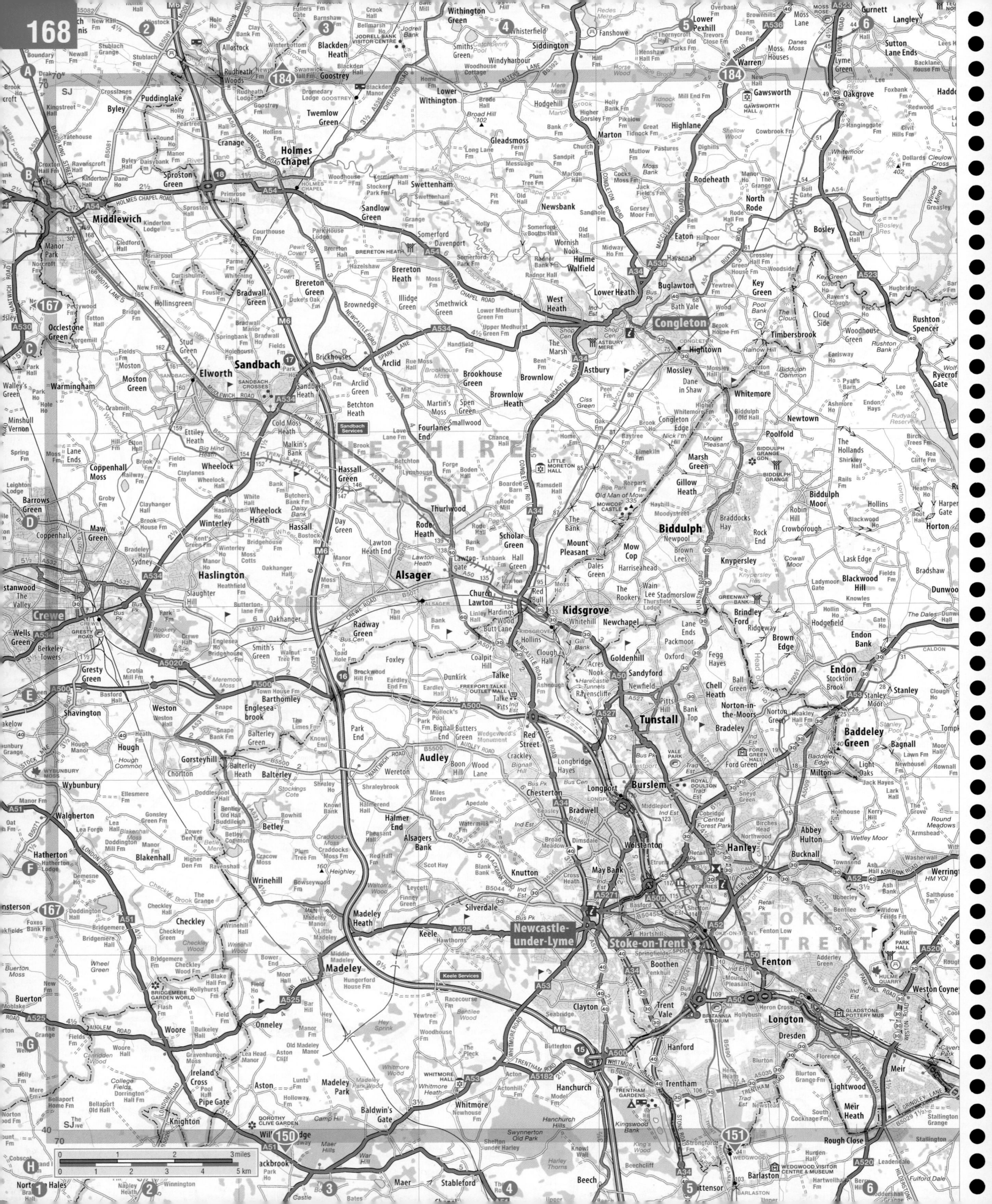

Middlewich
Holmes Chapel
Byley
Puddinglake
Cranage
Sproston Green
Goostrey
Lower Withington
Siddington
Withington Green
Gawsworth
Warren
Oakgrove
Swettenham
Gleadsmoss
Marton
Highlane
Rodeheath
North Rode
Bosley
Eaton
Sandlow Green
Somerford
Davenport
Brereton Heath
Newsbank
Hulme Walfield
West Heath
Lower Heath
Buglawton
Congleton
Key Green
Timbersbrook
Hightown
Mossley
Astbury
Brownlow
Brownlow Heath
Arclid
Brickhouses
Sandbach
Elworth
Occlestone Green
Warmingham
Moston Green
Sandbach Heath
Betchton Heath
Fourlanes End
Smallwood
Whitemore
Biddulph Moor
Poolfold
Marsh Green
Gillow Heath
Biddulph
Knypersley
Rushton Spencer
Ryecroft Gate
Wheelock
Wheelock Heath
Winterley
Hassall Green
Hassall
Coppenhall Moss
Maw Green
Thurlwood
Rode Heath
Scholar Green
Mow Cop
Mount Pleasant
Haslington
Alsager
Church Lawton
Kidsgrove
Newchapel
Brindley Ford
Brown Edge
Endon
Endon Bank
Crewe
Gresty Green
Radway Green
Talke
Talke Pits
Goldenhill
Sandyford
Tunstall
Chell Heath
Norton-in-the-Moors
Baddeley Green
Stanley
Shavington
Weston
Barthomley
Englesea-brook
Hough
Gorsteyhill
Balterley
Audley
Red Street
Burslem
Milton
Wybunbury
Walgherton
Hatherton
Betley
Halmer End
Alsagers Bank
Chesterton
Bradwell
Wolstanton
Hanley
Bucknall
Abbey Hulton
Blakenhall
Wrinehill
Madeley Heath
Silverdale
Knutton
May Bank
Checkley
Keele
Newcastle-under-Lyme
Stoke-on-Trent
Fenton
Madeley
Onneley
Woore
Buerton
Clayton
Trent Vale
Longton
Dresden
Meir
Ireland's Cross
Pipe Gate
Knighton
Aston
Madeley Park
Baldwin's Gate
Whitmore
Hanchurch
Hanford
Trentham
Lightwood
Meir Heath
Rough Close
Barlaston
Beech
Stableford
Maer
Weston Coyney
CHESHIRE EAST
STOKE-ON-TRENT
M6
A34
A50
A500
A53
A54
A51
A52
A525
A527
A533
A534
A536
A523
A520
A5020
A5182
184
167
150
151
Sandbach Services
Keele Services
0 1 2 3 miles
0 1 2 3 4 5 km

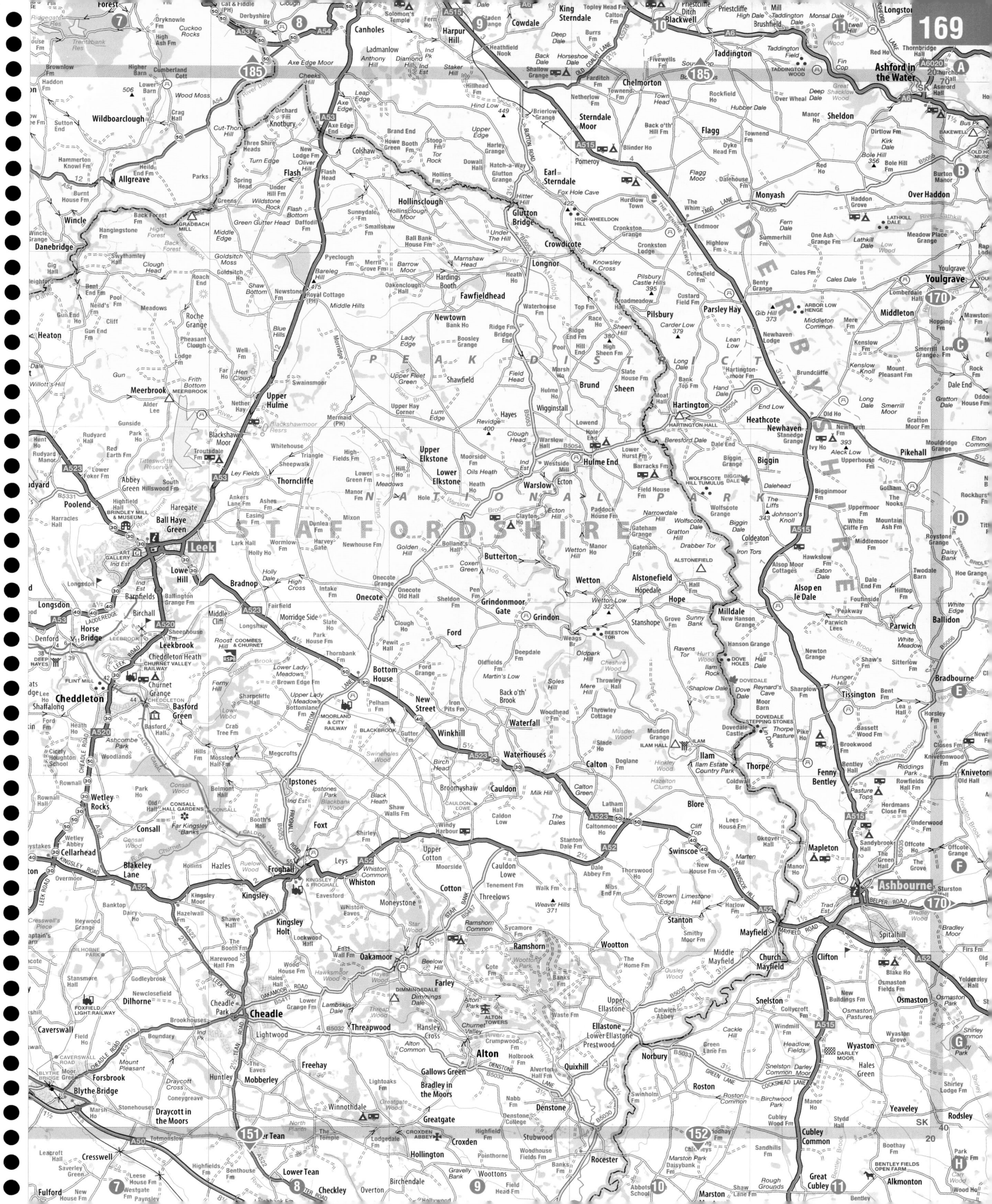
S T A F F O R D S H I R E
P E A K D I S T R I C T N A T I O N A L P A R K
D E R B Y S H I R E
Forest
Dryknowle
Cuckoo Rocks
Derbyshire Br
Canholes
Solomon's Temple
Harpur Hill
Cowdale
King Sterndale
Blackwell
Priestcliffe
Taddington
Longstone
Ashford in the Water
Axe Edge Moor
Ladmanlow
Anthony Hill
Diamond Hill
Staker Hill
Deep Dale
Back Dale
Horseshoe Dale
Chelmorton
Wildboarclough
Knotbury
Orchard Fm
Cut-Thorn Hill
Sterndale Moor
Flagg
Sheldon
Three Shire Heads
Colshaw
Brand End
Booth Fm
Stoop Fm
Upper Edge
Harley Grange
Allgreave
Flash
Earl Sterndale
Pomeroy
Monyash
Over Haddon
Hollinsclough
Glutton Bridge
Fox Hole Cave
Hurdlow Town
Wincle
Danebridge
Gradbach Mill
Crowdicote
Longnor
Hardings Booth
Fawfieldhead
Royal Cottage (PH)
Newstone
Pilsbury
Parsley Hay
Youlgrave
Middleton
Heaton
Roche Grange
Newtown
Arbor Low Henge
Hartington
Heathcote
Newhaven
Meerbrook
Upper Hulme
Shawfield
Sheen
Brund
Hulme End
Biggin
Pikehall
Tittesworth Reservoir
Thorncliffe
Upper Elkstone
Lower Elkstone
Warslow
Ecton
Leek
Ball Haye Green
Poolend
Haregate
Butterton
Wetton
Alstonefield
Hope
Alsop en le Dale
Parwich
Ballidon
Bradnop
Onecote
Grindon
Grindonmoor Gate
Milldale
Lowe Hill
Longsdon
Horse Bridge
Birchall
Cheddleton Heath
Leekbrook
Ford
Bottom House
New Street
Winkhill
Waterfall
Ilam
Thorpe
Fenny Bentley
Tissington
Bradbourne
Cheddleton
Basford Green
Waterhouses
Calton
Ipstones
Cauldon
Blore
Wetley Rocks
Consall
Foxt
Mapleton
Ashbourne
Cellarhead
Blakeley Lane
Froghall
Whiston
Kingsley
Cotton
Swinscoe
Mayfield
Kingsley Holt
Ramshorn
Wootton
Stanton
Clifton
Oakamoor
Farley
Church Mayfield
Snelston
Osmaston
Dilhorne
Cheadle
Caverswall
Threapwood
Alton
Ellastone
Wyaston
Norbury
Forsbrook
Blythe Bridge
Freehay
Mobberley
Gallows Green
Quixhill
Roston
Draycott in the Moors
Bradley in the Moors
Denstone
Yeaveley
Rodsley
Greatgate
Upper Tean
Croxden
Stubwood
Rocester
Cubley Common
Cresswell
Hollington
Lower Tean
Checkley
Great Cubley
Alkmonton
Fulford
Birchendale
Marston Montgomery
A6
A53
A54
A515
A523
A520
A52
A50
A522
A521
A6020
185
151
152
170
SK

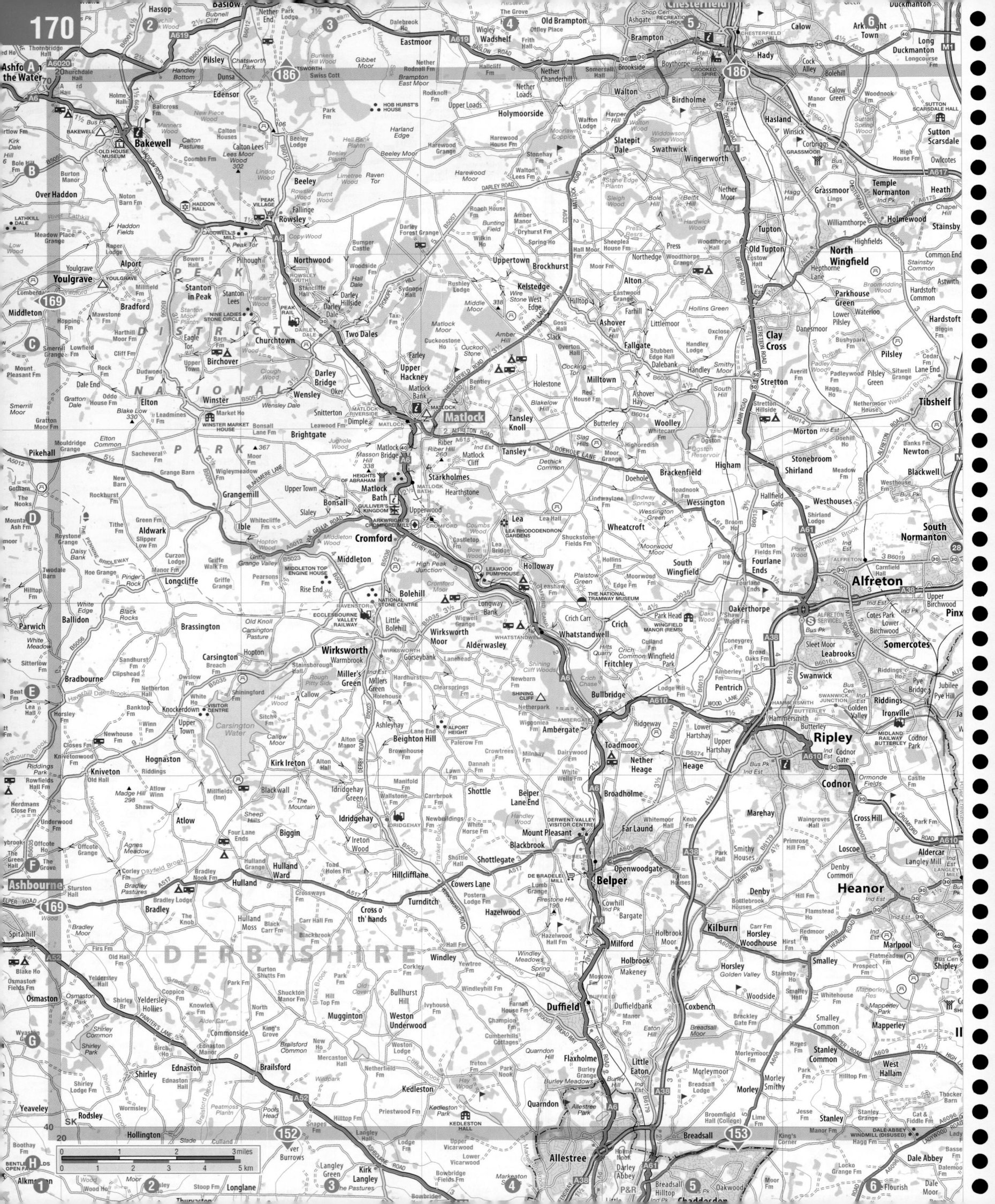
Hassop
Baslow
Chesterfield
Duckmanton
Calow
Arkwright Town
Long Duckmanton
Brampton
Old Brampton
Wadshelf
Eastmoor
Pilsley
Edensor
Bakewell
Holymoorside
Walton
Birdholme
Hady
Hasland
Sutton Scarsdale
Beeley
Rowsley
Over Haddon
Haddon Hall
Slatepit Dale
Swathwick
Wingerworth
Grassmoor
Temple Normanton
Heath
Holmewood
Northwood
Alport
Youlgrave
Stanton in Peak
Uppertown
Brockhurst
Kelstedge
Alton
Tupton
Old Tupton
North Wingfield
Middleton
Bradford
Darley Dale
Two Dales
Churchtown
Birchover
Ashover
Clay Cross
Fallgate
Darley Bridge
Wensley
Winster
Elton
Upper Hackney
Matlock
Matlock Bank
Milltown
Stretton
Tibshelf
Tansley Knoll
Woolley
Pilsley
Snitterton
Dimple
Brightgate
Tansley
Higham
Morton
Pikehall
Matlock Bridge
Starkholmes
Matlock Bath
Brackenfield
Shirland
Stonebroom
Blackwell
Grangemill
Bonsall
Wessington
Westhouses
Aldwark
Ible
Cromford
Lea
Wheatcroft
South Wingfield
South Normanton
Middleton
Holloway
Longcliffe
Alfreton
Bolehill
Fourlane Ends
Oakerthorpe
Ballidon
Brassington
Wirksworth
Crich
Whatstandwell
Alderwasley
Wirksworth Moor
Somercotes
Leabrooks
Carsington
Hopton
Fritchley
Swanwick
Riddings
Ironville
Bradbourne
Bullbridge
Ambergate
Ripley
Kirk Ireton
Hognaston
Beighton Hill
Toadmoor
Nether Heage
Heage
Codnor
Kniveton
Shottle
Belper Lane End
Broadholme
Marehay
Cross Hill
Atlow
Biggin
Idridgehay
Mount Pleasant
Far Laund
Blackbrook
Loscoe
Ashbourne
Hulland
Hulland Ward
Shottlegate
Belper
Openwoodgate
Heanor
Bradley
Turnditch
Cowers Lane
Hazelwood
Denby
Cross o' th' hands
Kilburn
Milford
Horsley Woodhouse
Marlpool
DERBYSHIRE
Windley
Holbrook
Horsley
Smalley
Shipley
Osmaston
Duffield
Coxbench
Woodside
Mugginton
Weston Underwood
Mapperley
Shirley
Ednaston
Brailsford
Commonside
Flaxholme
Little Eaton
Stanley Common
West Hallam
Kedleston
Quarndon
Morley
Yeaveley
Rodsley
Hollington
Stanley
Allestree
Breadsall
Kirk Langley
Dale Abbey
Longlane
Chaddesden
Oakwood
0 1 2 3 miles
0 1 2 3 4 5 km

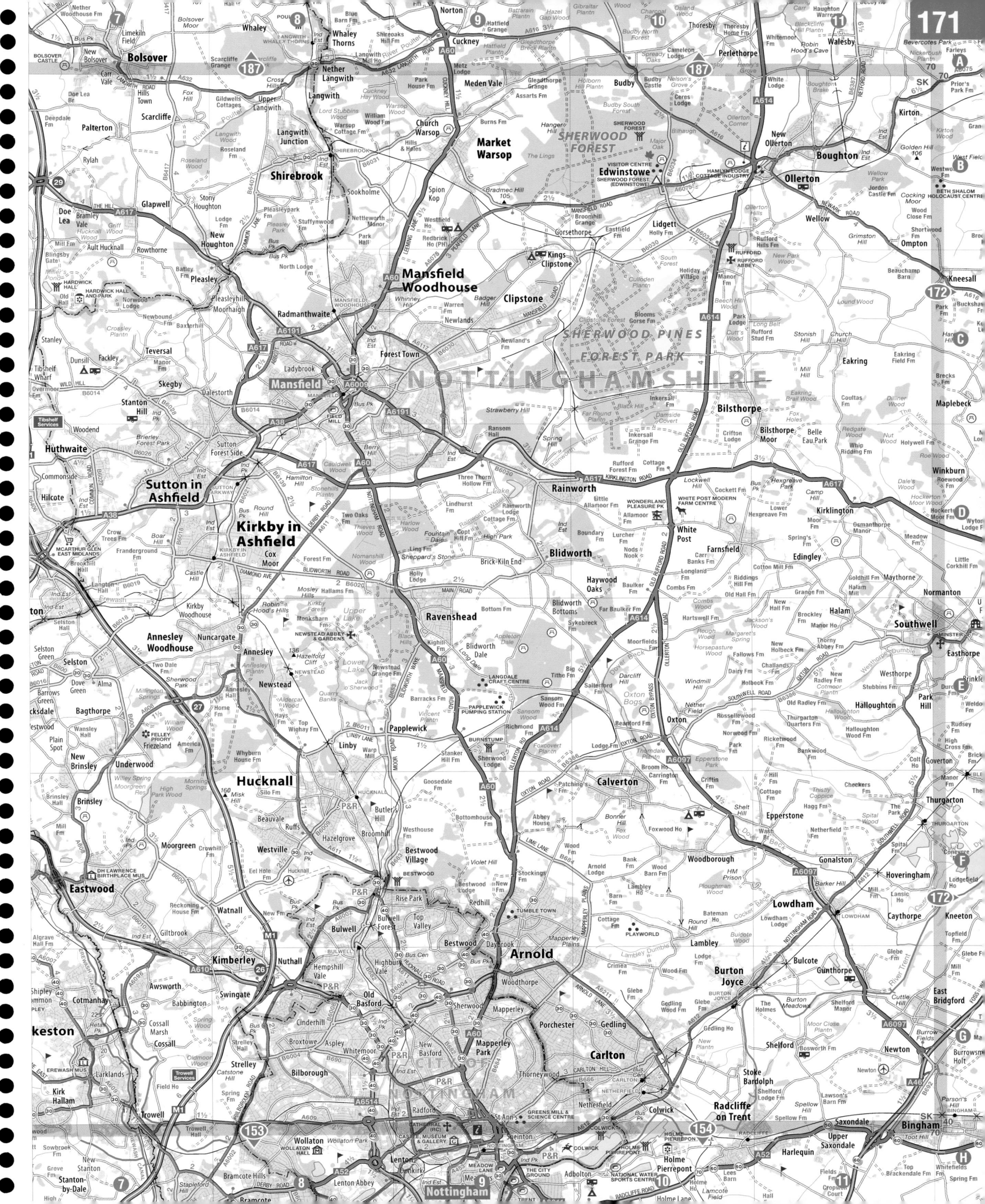

Bolsover
Whaley
Whaley Thorns
Nether Langwith
Langwith
Norton
Cuckney
Meden Vale
Budby
Thoresby
Perlethorpe
Walesby
Palterton
Scarcliffe
Church Warsop
Market Warsop
SHERWOOD FOREST
Edwinstowe
Boughton
Ollerton
Kirton
Shirebrook
Langwith Junction
Glapwell
New Houghton
Pleasley
Mansfield Woodhouse
Kings Clipstone
Clipstone
Lidgett
Wellow
Ompton
Kneesall
Radmanthwaite
Forest Town
SHERWOOD PINES FOREST PARK
NOTTINGHAMSHIRE
Teversal
Skegby
Mansfield
Eakring
Bilsthorpe
Maplebeck
Huthwaite
Sutton in Ashfield
Kirkby in Ashfield
Rainworth
Kirklington
Winkburn
Blidworth
Farnsfield
Edingley
White Post
Ravenshead
Normanton
Southwell
Halam
Annesley Woodhouse
Annesley
Newstead
Selston
Underwood
Hucknall
Papplewick
Linby
Calverton
Oxton
Halloughton
Epperstone
Thurgarton
Eastwood
Kimberley
Bulwell
Arnold
Woodborough
Lowdham
Gonalston
Hoveringham
Caythorpe
Lambley
Burton Joyce
Bulcote
Gunthorpe
East Bridgford
Cotmanhay
Ilkeston
Carlton
Gedling
Shelford
Newton
Bingham
Radcliffe on Trent
Holme Pierrepont
NOTTINGHAM
CITY OF NOTTINGHAM
Nottingham
Wollaton
Lenton
Trowell
Stapleford
Bramcote
Strelley
Bilborough
Kirk Hallam
Stanton-by-Dale
Saxondale
Upper Saxondale
Harlequin
187
153
154
172

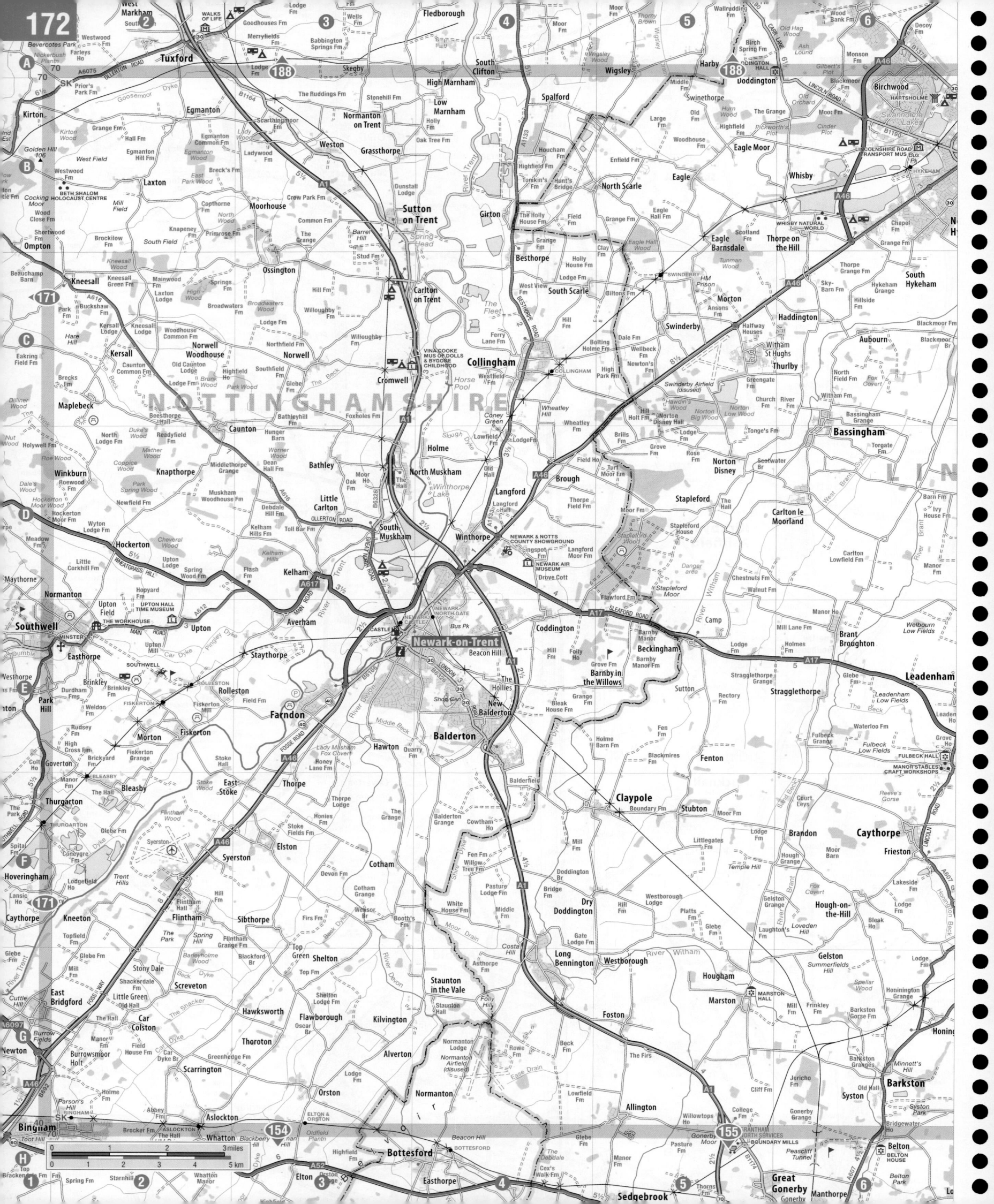

Tuxford
Markham
Fledborough
South Clifton
Wigsley
Harby
Doddington
Birchwood
Egmanton
High Marnham
Low Marnham
Normanton on Trent
Spalford
Kirton
Weston
Grassthorpe
Eagle Moor
Eagle
Whisby
Laxton
North Scarle
Moorhouse
Sutton on Trent
Girton
Ompton
Besthorpe
Eagle Barnsdale
Thorpe on the Hill
Ossington
Kneesall
Carlton on Trent
South Scarle
Morton
South Hykeham
Swinderby
Haddington
Kersall
Norwell Woodhouse
Norwell
Cromwell
Collingham
Witham St Hughs
Thurlby
Aubourn
NOTTINGHAMSHIRE
Maplebeck
Caunton
Holme
Bassingham
Winkburn
Knapthorpe
Bathley
North Muskham
Brough
Norton Disney
Little Carlton
Langford
Stapleford
Carlton le Moorland
Hockerton
South Muskham
Winthorpe
Kelham
Normanton
Southwell
Upton
Averham
Newark-on-Trent
Coddington
Beckingham
Barnby in the Willows
Brant Broughton
Leadenham
Easthorpe
Staythorpe
Rolleston
Farndon
Fiskerton
Morton
Balderton
New Balderton
Hawton
Stragglethorpe
Fenton
Claypole
Stubton
Thurgarton
Bleasby
East Stoke
Thorpe
Elston
Syerston
Cotham
Brandon
Caythorpe
Frieston
Hoveringham
Kneeton
Flintham
Sibthorpe
Dry Doddington
Hough-on-the-Hill
Shelton
Long Bennington
Westborough
Gelston
East Bridgford
Screveton
Staunton in the Vale
Hougham
Marston
Hawksworth
Flawborough
Kilvington
Foston
Car Colston
Thoroton
Alverton
Scarrington
Barkston
Orston
Normanton
Allington
Syston
Aslockton
Bingham
Whatton
Bottesford
Elton
Easthorpe
Sedgebrook
Great Gonerby
Manthorpe
3 miles
5 km

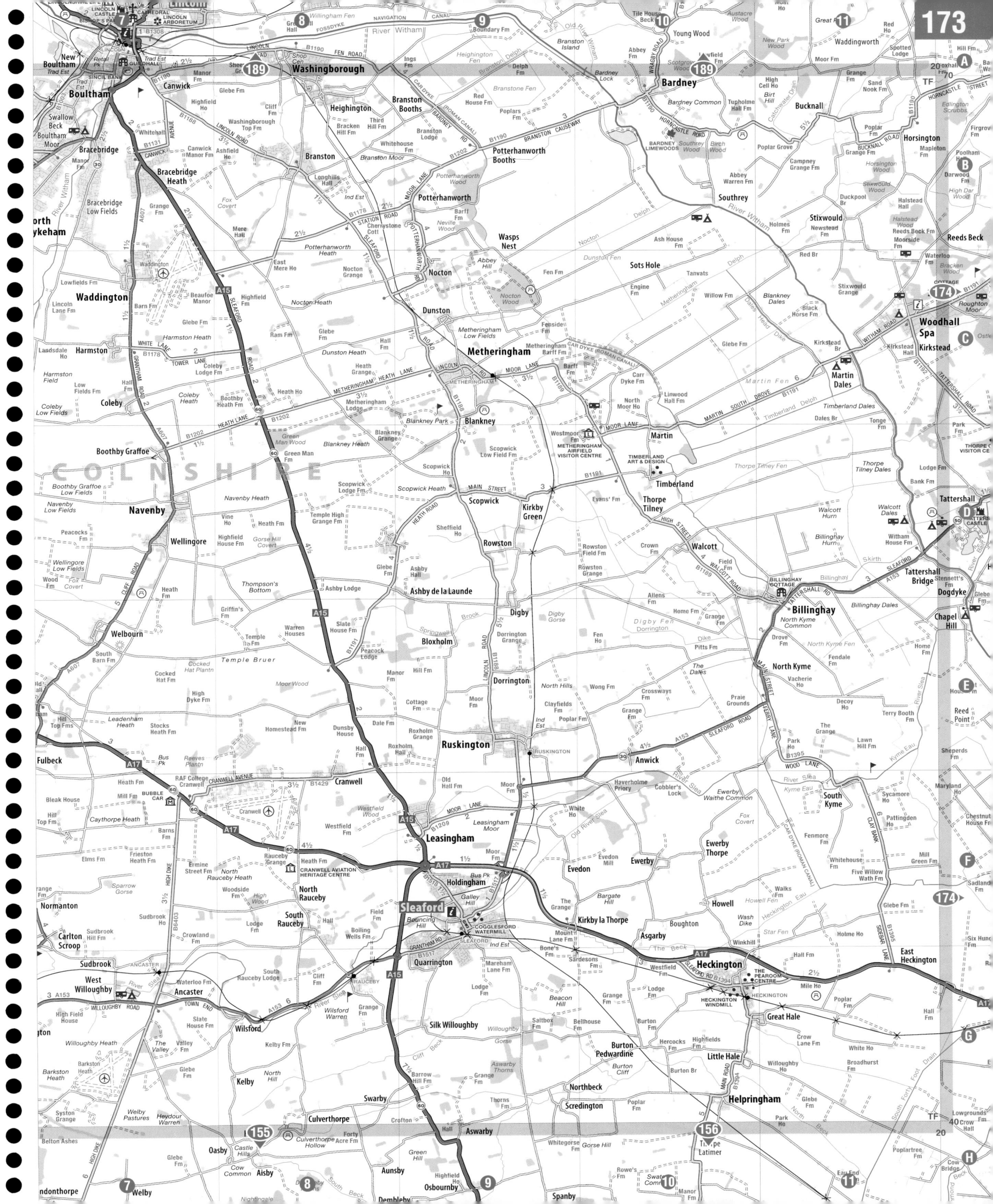
173
Lincoln
Lincoln Castle
Cathedral
Lincoln Arboretum
Boultham
New Boultham
Canwick
Washingborough
Heighington
Branston Booths
Branston
Bracebridge
Bracebridge Heath
Bracebridge Low Fields
Potterhanworth
Potterhanworth Booths
Nocton
Dunston
Metheringham
Waddington
Harmston
Coleby
Boothby Graffoe
Navenby
Wellingore
Welbourn
Blankney
Scopwick
Kirkby Green
Rowston
Ashby de la Launde
Digby
Bloxholm
Dorrington
Ruskington
Anwick
Fulbeck
Cranwell
Leasingham
Sleaford
Holdingham
North Rauceby
South Rauceby
Quarrington
Evedon
Ewerby
Kirkby la Thorpe
Asgarby
Heckington
Great Hale
Little Hale
Helpringham
Burton Pedwardine
Scredington
Northbeck
Silk Willoughby
Swarby
Culverthorpe
Aswarby
Kelby
Wilsford
Ancaster
West Willoughby
Sudbrook
Carlton Scroop
Normanton
Oasby
Aisby
Aunsby
Osbournby
Welby
Spanby
Dembleby
Bardney
Southrey
Bucknall
Horsington
Stixwould
Woodhall Spa
Kirkstead
Martin Dales
Martin
Timberland
Thorpe Tilney
Walcott
Billinghay
North Kyme
South Kyme
Tattershall
Tattershall Bridge
Dogdyke
Chapel Hill
Reeds Beck
East Heckington
Wasps Nest
Sots Hole
River Witham
River Slea
COLNSHIRE
A15
A17
A153
A607
B1188
B1189
B1191
B1202
Metheringham Airfield Visitor Centre
Cranwell Aviation Heritage Centre
Cogglesford Watermill
Heckington Windmill
The Pearoom Centre
Timberland Art & Design
Bardney Limewoods
Tattershall Castle
155
156
174
189
TF

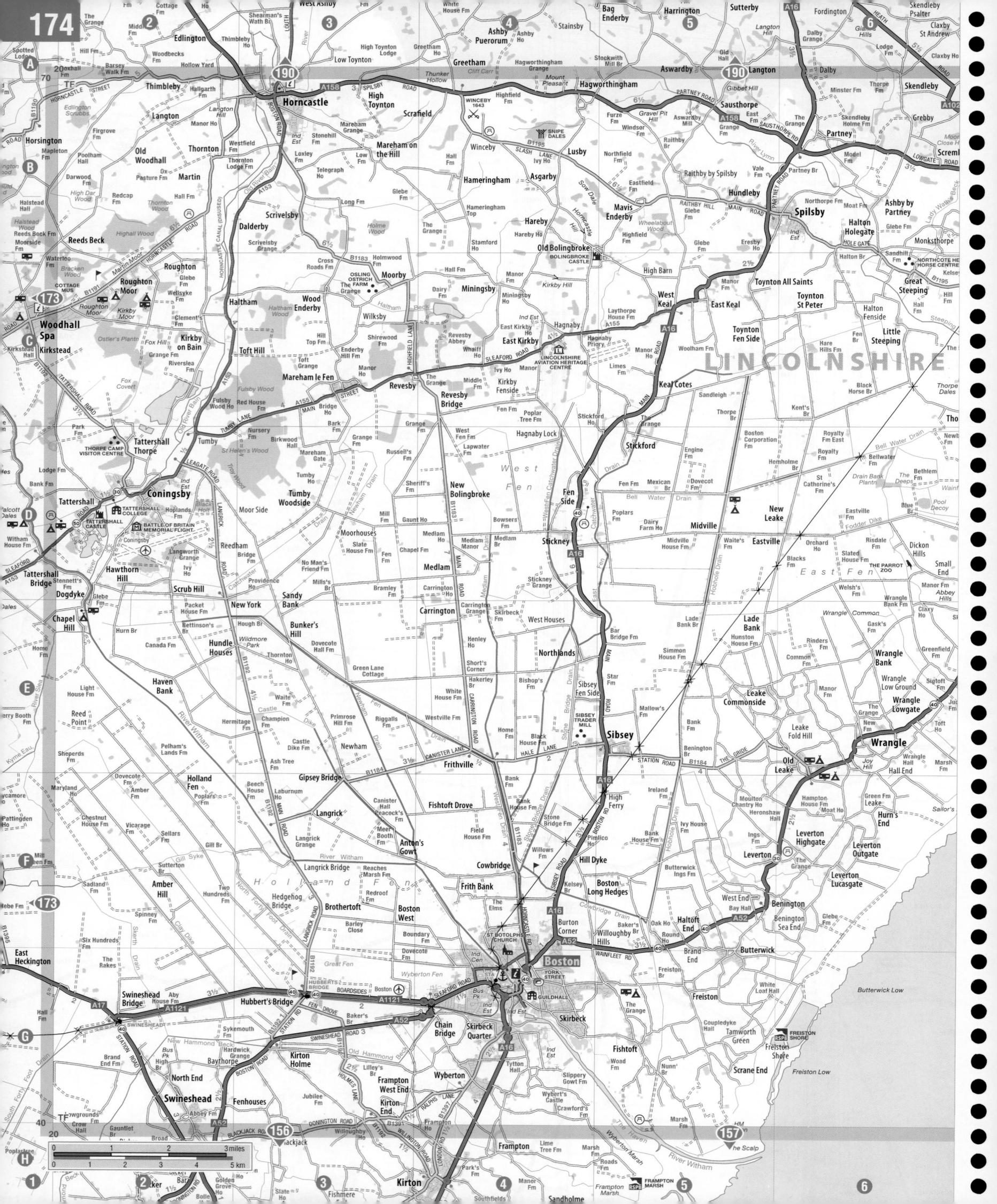

West Ashby
Bag Enderby
Harrington
Sutterby
Fordington
Skendleby Psalter
Edlington
Ashby Puerorum
Stainsby
Claxby St Andrew
Low Toynton
Greetham
Hagworthingham
Aswardby
Langton
Dalby
Thimbleby
Horncastle
High Toynton
Scrafield
Sausthorpe
Skendleby
Langton
Winceby
Mareham on the Hill
Lusby
Partney
Grebby
Horsington
Thornton
Old Woodhall
Martin
Hameringham
Asgarby
Raithby by Spilsby
Hundleby
Spilsby
Ashby by Partney
Mavis Enderby
Halton Holegate
Scrivelsby
Dalderby
Hareby
Monksthorpe
Reeds Beck
Old Bolingbroke
Roughton
Roughton Moor
Moorby
Miningsby
High Barn
Toynton All Saints
Great Steeping
Woodhall Spa
Haltham
Wood Enderby
Wilksby
West Keal
East Keal
Toynton St Peter
Kirkstead
Kirkby on Bain
Toft Hill
East Kirkby
Hagnaby
Toynton Fen Side
Little Steeping
Halton Fenside
LINCOLNSHIRE
Mareham le Fen
Revesby
Revesby Bridge
Kirkby Fenside
Keal Cotes
Sandleigh
Tattershall Thorpe
Tumby
Hagnaby Lock
Stickford
West Fen
Tattershall
Coningsby
Tumby Woodside
New Bolingbroke
Fen Side
New Leake
Moor Side
Midville
Eastville
Reedham
Medlam
Stickney
East Fen
Dickon Hills
Small End
Tattershall Bridge
Hawthorn Hill
Dogdyke
Scrub Hill
New York
Sandy Bank
Carrington
West Houses
Chapel Hill
Bunker's Hill
Lade Bank
Hundle Houses
Northlands
Wrangle Bank
Haven Bank
Sibsey Fen Side
Leake Commonside
Wrangle Lowgate
Reed Point
Newham
Frithville
Sibsey
Wrangle
Holland Fen
Gipsey Bridge
Old Leake
Langrick
Fishtoft Drove
High Ferry
Anton's Gowt
Hill Dyke
Leverton
Leverton Highgate
Leverton Outgate
Langrick Bridge
Cowbridge
Frith Bank
Boston Long Hedges
Leverton Lucasgate
Amber Hill
Brothertoft
Boston West
Hedgehog Bridge
Burton Corner
Willoughby Hills
Haltoft End
Benington
Benington Sea End
East Heckington
Boston
Brand End
Butterwick
Swineshead Bridge
Hubbert's Bridge
Freiston
Skirbeck
Chain Bridge
Skirbeck Quarter
Kirton Holme
Baythorpe
Fishtoft
Freiston Shore
North End
Frampton West End
Wyberton
Scrane End
Swineshead
Fenhouses
Kirton End
Frampton
Kirton
River Witham
The Haven
Butterwick Low
Freiston Low

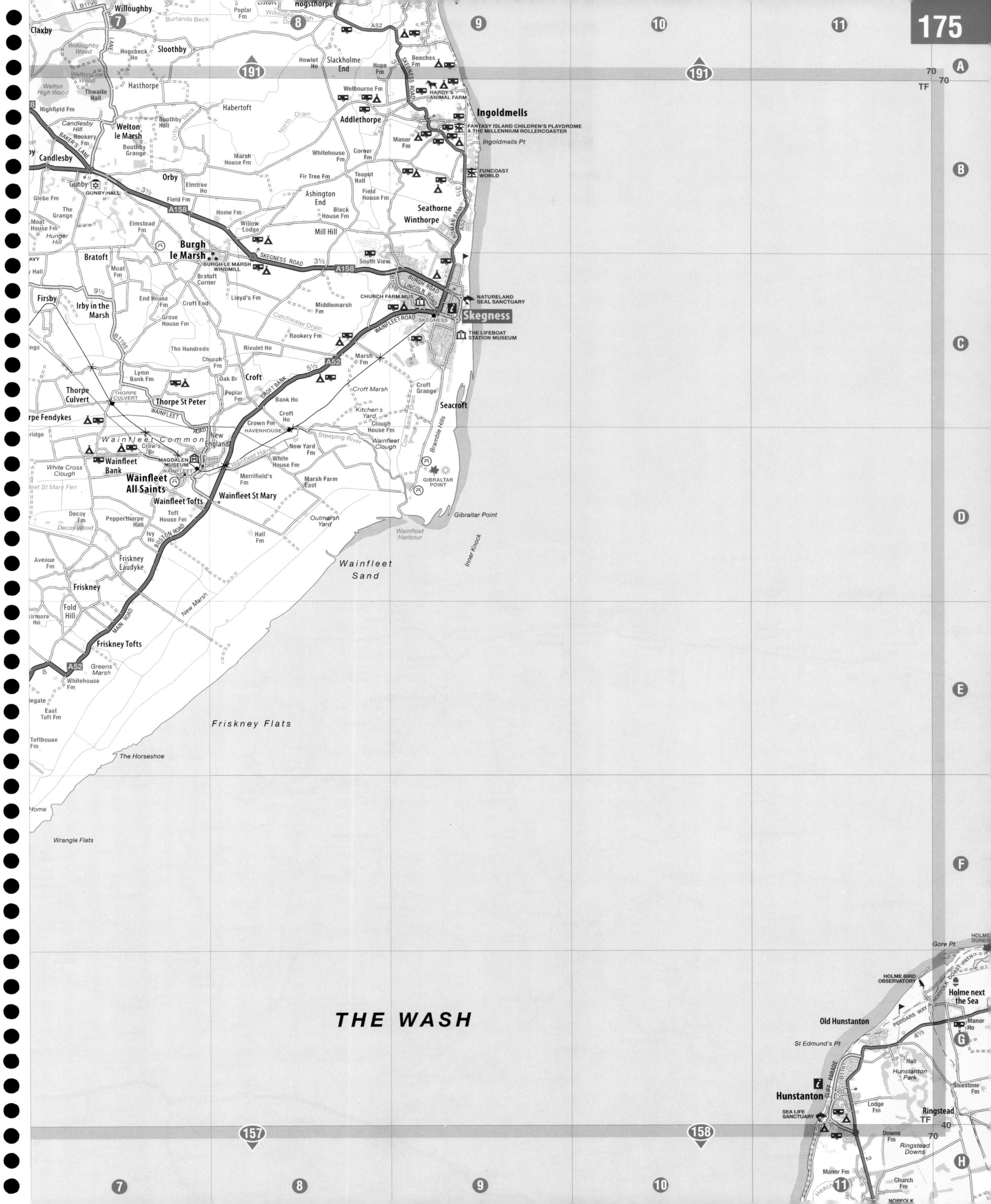

THE WASH

Willoughby
Claxby
7
Hogsthorpe
Sloothby
9
10
11

Willoughby Wood
Hogsbeck Ho
Howlet Ho
Slackholme End
Hope Fm
Beeches
191
191
70
TF
70

Highfield Fm
Welton le Marsh
Welbourne Fm
Hardy's Animal Farm
Ingoldmells
Fantasy Island Children's Playdrome & The Millennium Rollercoaster

Habertoft
Addlethorpe
Ingoldmells Pt

Candlesby
Welton le Marsh
Rookery
Boothby Grange
Whitehouse Fm
Corner Fm
Manor Fm
Seathorne
Winthorpe
Funcoast World

Orby
Fir Tree Fm
Teapot Hall
Field House Fm

Gunby
Gunby Hall
Glebe Fm
The Grange
Field Fm
Ashington End
Black House Fm
Mill Hill
A158

Bratoft
Burgh le Marsh
Burgh-le-Marsh Windmill
Skegness Road
A158
South View
Church Farm Mus
Natureland Seal Sanctuary

Firsby
Irby in the Marsh
Bratoft Corner
Lloyd's Fm
Middlemarsh Fm
Burgh Road
Lincoln Road
Wainfleet Road
Skegness
The Lifeboat Station Museum

Thorpe Culvert
The Hundreds
Croft
A52
Marsh Fm
Croft Marsh
Croft Grange
Seacroft

Thorpe St Peter
Croft
Oak Br
Bank Ho
Kitchen's Yard
Clough House Fm
Bramble Hills

Wainfleet Common
New England
Crown Fm
Havenhouse
Steeping River
Wainfleet Clough
Gibraltar Point

Wainfleet Bank
Magdalen Museum
Wainfleet
Merrifield's Fm
New Yard Fm
White House Fm
Marsh Farm East

Wainfleet All Saints
Wainfleet Tofts
Wainfleet St Mary
Outmarsh Yard
Gibraltar Point

Pepperthorpe Hall
Toft House Fm
Hall Fm
Wainfleet Harbour

Decoy Fm
Decoy Wood
Avenue Fm
Friskney Eaudyke
Ivy Ho
Boston Road

Wainfleet Sand

Friskney
Fold Hill

Inner Knock

Friskney Tofts
A52
Greens Marsh
Whitehouse Fm

East Toft Fm
New Marsh

Friskney Flats

Tofthouse Fm

The Horseshoe

Wrangle Flats

**THE WASH**

Gore Pt
Holme Dunes
Holme Bird Observatory
Holme next the Sea
Manor Ho
Old Hunstanton
Peddars Way
Norfolk Coast Path
St Edmund's Pt
G

Hunstanton
Sea Life Sanctuary
Lodge Fm
Hunstanton Park
Hall
Ringstead
Bluestone
TF
40
70

Downs
Ringstead Downs

Manor Fm
Church Fm
Norfolk
H

7
8
9
10
11

HOLKHAM BAY
BRANCASTER BAY
SCOLT HEAD ISLAND
Brancaster Harbour
Harbour Channel
Gore Pt
HOLME DUNES
HOLME BIRD OBSERVATORY
Holme next the Sea
NORFOLK COAST PATH
PEDDARS WAY
TITCHWELL MARSH
Thornham
Titchwell
Brancaster
Brancaster Staithe
Burnham Deepdale
BRANCASTER MILLENNIUM ACTIVITY CENTRE
Marsh Side
Brancaster Marsh
Deepdale Marsh
Norton Creek
Trowland Creek
Burnham Harbour
Norton Marsh
Burnham Norton
Gun Hill
Burnham Overy Staithe
Overy Marsh
Marsh House Fm
Burnham Overy Town
Holkham Meals
Burrow Gap
West Sands
High Cape
The Run
Bob Hall's Sand
Big Gap
Lodge Marsh
Holkham Gap
HOLKHAM
WELLS HARBOUR MINIATURE RAILWAY
Dale Hole
Holkham
Wells-Next-The-Sea
Warham Salt Marshes
East Fleet
Stonemeal Creek
STIFFKEY ROAD
COAST ROAD
PEDDARS WAY & NORFOLK COAST PATH
WELLS-NEXT-THE-SEA
THE MIDDEN
NORFOLK COAST
HIGH STREET
Manor Ho
Barrow Common
The Downs
Hawker's Hill Fm
Westgate
Burnham Market
WELLS ROAD
Leath Ho
Peterstone Fm
Howe Hill
Bone's Belt
HOLKHAM HALL
Holkham Park
The Temple
Lucas Hill Wood
Old Common Plantn
Golden Gates
Gallow Hill
Northgate Hall Fm
Warham
WARHAM ST MARY HALT
Hunstanton Park
Beacon Hill
Lyng Fm
Bluestone Fm
Choseley Fm
Field Ho
Sussex Fm
Westgate Fm
Beacon Hill
Gallow Hill
Burnham Thorpe
Gravelpit Hill
Manor Ho
Scarboro Wood
Longlands Fm
The Belt
Branthill Fm
Branthill Cotts
WELLS & WALSINGHAM LIGHT RAILWAY
Field Barn
Wighton
WIGHTON HALT
Ringstead
Courtyard Fm
Lugden Hill Fm
Crow Hall Fm
Sunderland Fm
Friar's Thorne Fm
Cradle Hall Fm
Muckleton
Field Barn
CREAKE ABBEY (REMS)
Abbey Fm
New Holkham
Blunt's Corner
Crabbe Castle Fm
Setons Halt
River Stiffkey
Downs Fm
Ringstead Downs
Thornham Corner
Neat's Ling
Church Fm
Summerfield
High Barn
BURNHAM ROAD
River Burn
North Creake
Chantry Hills
Quarles Fm
Bunker's Hill
Edgar Fm
Egmere Fm
NORFOLK LAVENDER
St Catherine's Cross
High House Fm
Shammer Ho
Wringate Fm
High Hills
Shepherd's Hill
East Common
Haggard's Lodge
Egmere
Berry Hall
Great Walsingham
WALSINGHAM
Little Walsingham
WALSINGHAM ABBEY GROUNDS & SHIREHALL MUSEUM
East Hall
DOCKING RD
SEDGEFORD ROAD
B1454
Docking
BRANCASTER ROAD
Stanhoe
Sly's Barn
Manor Ho
South Creake
Waterden Fm
North Barsham Fm
Eaton
Sedgeford
The Park
FAKENHAM ROAD
Docking Common
Docking Lodge
Barwick Ho
Bloodgate Hill
Compton Hall
Waterden
Glover's Fm
Church Fm
Fring
HONEY HILLS
Barwick Hall Fm
Hyde Park
Hubbards Fm
Southgate
North Barsham
Houghton St Giles
Canister Hall Fm
Great Snoring
Snettisham
Inmere Fm
Honey Hills
Bircham Newton
Buildings Fm
The Gorse
West Barsham
SNETTISHAM PARK
Red Barn Fm
Moor Fm
Great Bircham
Barmer
Leicester Square Fm
East Barsham
Ingoldisthorpe
Syderstone
White Hall
Cranmer Hall
Waterhouse Fm
Thorpland Hall
Shernborne Hall
Shernborne
BIRCHAM MILL
Bircham Tofts
Bagthorpe
Blenheim Park
Sculthorpe Airfield (disused)
Manor Fm
Sculthorpe
Lodge Fm
Little Snoring
Syderstone Common
Bircham Common
Tofts Hill
Frizzleton Fm
Coxford Wood
Wicken Green Village
The Grange
Grove Fm
Thorpland Lodge Fm
Mill Ho
Dersingham
Ling Ho
Manor Ho
Doddshill Fm
Tofts Dale
Coxford Heath
Heath House Fm
Tattersett
Dunton Patch
Dunton
A148
Fakenham
Sculthorpe Moor
Heath Fm
The Heath
Anmer
Gatesend Hill
Manor Fm
Coxford
Shereford
Hempton
Fakenham Common
Penshorpe Hall
The Carr
Big Wood
HOUGHTON HALL
North Pole Fm
New Buildings
Houghton Park
Doughton
FAKENHAM
Starmoor Wood
Bunker's Hill
The Mayflower
New Houghton
East Rudham
Broomsthorpe
Pynkney Hall
Tatterford
Southmill Fm
Manor Fm
Norton Hall
Commodore Wood
Cross Belt
Harpley Common
LYNN ROAD
West
A1065
A149
A1067
B1153
B1155
B1355
B1105
158
159
0 1 2 3 miles
0 1 2 3 4 5 km
TF
70
60
30

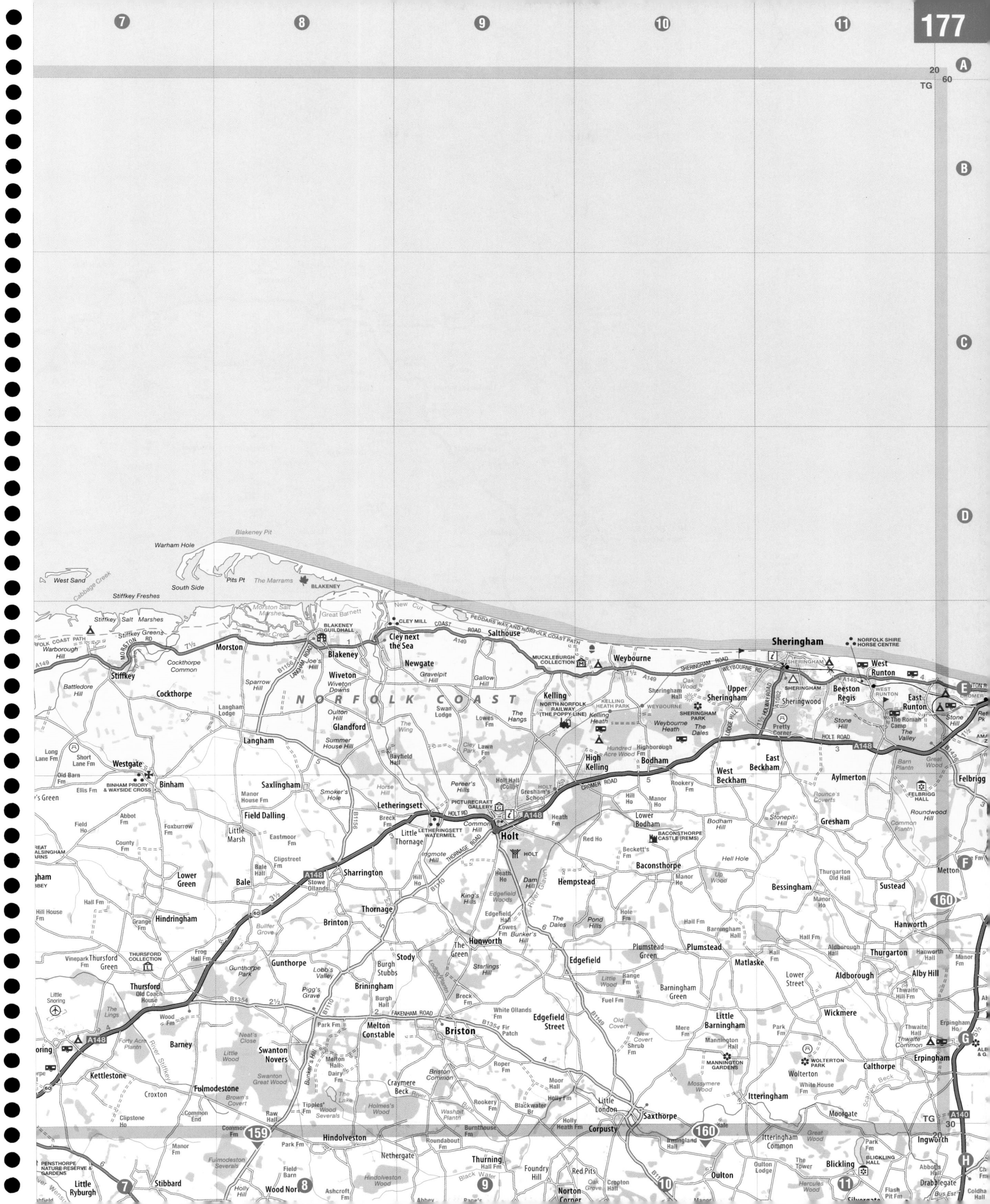

7  8  9  10  11

20
60
TG

A
B
C
D
E
F
G
H

Blakeney Pit

Warham Hole

West Sand  Cabbage Creek

Pits Pt  The Marrams

South Side

BLAKENEY

Stiffkey Freshes

Morston Salt Marshes

New Cut

Great Barnett

Stiffkey Salt Marshes

Agar Creek

COAST

ROAD

Salthouse

PEDDARS WAY AND NORFOLK COAST PATH

Warborough Hill

NORFOLK COAST PATH

MORSTON RD

Morston

CLEY MILL

BLAKENEY GUILDHALL

Blakeney

Cley next the Sea

Newgate

A149

MUCKLEBURGH COLLECTION

Weybourne

Sheringham

NORFOLK SHIRE HORSE CENTRE

West Runton

A149

Stiffkey

Cockthorpe Common

Sparrow Hill

Joe's Hill

Wiveton

Wiveton Downs

Gravelpit Hill

Gallow Hill

North Norfolk Railway (The Poppy Line)

Kelling Heath Park

KELLING HEATH PARK

Sheringham Heath

SHERINGHAM ROAD

WEYBOURNE RD

Upper Sheringham

SHERINGHAM

Sheringwood

Beeston Regis

WEST RUNTON

EAST RUNTON

CROMER

The Roman Camp

Stone Hill

Battledore Hill

Stiffkey

Cockthorpe

Langham Lodge

Oulton Hill

Glandford

The Wing

Swan Lodge

Lowes Fm

The Hangs

Kelling

Kelling Heath

Weybourne Heath

Sheringham Park

The Dales

Pretty Corner

HOLT ROAD

Stone Hill

AM/Z

Long Lane Fm

Short Lane Fm

Langham

Summer House Hill

Bayfield Hall

Cley Park Lawn

High Kelling

Hundred Acre Wood

Highborough Fm

Bodham

The Dales

West Beckham

East Beckham

Aylmerton

Barn Plantn

FELBRIGG HALL

Common Wood

Great Wood

Felbrigg

3

A148

Old Barn Fm

BINHAM PRIORY & WAYSIDE CROSS

Binham

Westgate

Saxlingham

Horse Hill

Pereer's Hills

Letheringsett

Holt Hall (Coll)

GRESHAM'S School

HOLT RD

Hill Ho

Manor Fm

Lower Bodham

Bodham Hill

Rookery Fm

Stonepit Hill

Rounce's Coverts

Gresham

Roundwood Fm

Common Plantn

Ellis Fm

's Green

Field Dalling

Little Marsh

Foxburrow Fm

Abbot Fm

County Fm

Eastmoor Fm

Breck Fm

Little Thornage

PICTURECRAFT GALLERY

LETHERINGSETT WATERMILL

HOLT RD

Common Hill

Holt

A148

Heath Fm

Red Ho

Beckett's Fm

BACONSTHORPE CASTLE (REMS)

Hell Hole

Thurgarton Old Hall

Field Ho

Grange Fm

GREAT WALSINGHAM BARNS

gham

ABBEY

Lower Green

Bale

Hindringham

Bale Hall

Clipstreet Fm

Sharrington

A148

Slowe Ollands

Ingmote Hill

THORNAGE ROAD

HOLT

Dam Fm

Hempstead

Hole Fm

Baconsthorpe

Manor Ho

Up Wood

Bessingham

Manor Ho

Sustead

160

Metton

Fm

Hill House Fm

Brinton

Hill Ho

B1110

Thornage

King's Hills

Edgefield Woods

River Glaven

Edgefield Hall

Lowes

Bunker's Hill

The Dales

Pond Hills

Hall Fm

Barningham Hall

Hall Fm

Thurgarton

Hanworth

Manor Fm

Vinepark

Thursford Green

THURSFORD COLLECTION

Hunworth

The Green

Stody

Starlings Hill

Edgefield

Plumstead Green

Plumstead

Matlaske

Aldborough

Alby Hill

Little Snoring

The Lings

Gunthorpe Park

Gunthorpe

Lobb's Valley

Burgh Stubbs

Briningham

Burgh Hall

Breck Fm

Little Wood

Range Fm

Barningham Green

Lower Street

Wickmere

Thwaite Hill Fm

Thwaite Ho

Erpingham

Thursford

Old Coach House

Frog Hall Fm

Pigg's Grave

B1354

2½

White Ollands Fm

Fir Patch

Edgefield Street

B1149

Old Covert

New Covert

Mere Fm

Little Barningham

Park Fm

Thwaite Common

Erpingham

ALE & G.

Little Ryburgh

Wood Fm

Neat's Close

Park Fm

FAKENHAM ROAD

Melton Constable

B1354

Briston

Roper Fm

MANNINGTON GARDENS

Mannington Hall

Park Fm

Wolterton

WOLTERTON PARK

Calthorpe

Erpingham

G.

Kettlestone

Barney

Little Wood

Swanton Novers

Swanton Great Wood

Melton Hall

Dairy Fm

Briston Common

Craymere Beck

Moor Hall

Rookery Fm

Blackwater Br

Holly Fm

Little London

Saxthorpe

160

Moorgate

TG

A140

Fulmodestone

Croxton

Clipstone Ho

A148

60

Common End

Brown's Covert

Tipples' Wood

Holmes's Wood

Wood Seavals

Washpit Plantn

Burnt Ho

Holly Heath Fm

Corpusty

B

Mannington Hall

Itteringham

White House Fm

Scarrow Beck

A140

159

Manor Fm

Fulmodeston Severals

Field Barn

Park Fm

Hindolveston

Nethergate

Thurning

Thurning Hall Fm

Foundry Hill

Red Pits

Black Water

Burgh

Irmingland Hall

160

Itteringham Common

Great Wood

Park Fm

Blickling

BLICKLING HALL

Ingworth

A140

H

PENSTHORPE NATURE RESERVE & GARDENS

Little Ryburgh

Stibbard

Holly Hill

Wood Nor

Ashcroft

Hindolveston Wood

Thurning

Oulton

Oulton Lodge

The Tower

Blickling

Hercules Wood

Abbots Hall

Flash Pit Fm

Drabblegate

Coldha

 ring

Manor Fm

Norton Corner

Cropton Hall

Oak Grove

Bus Est T

Silvergate

7  8  9  10  11

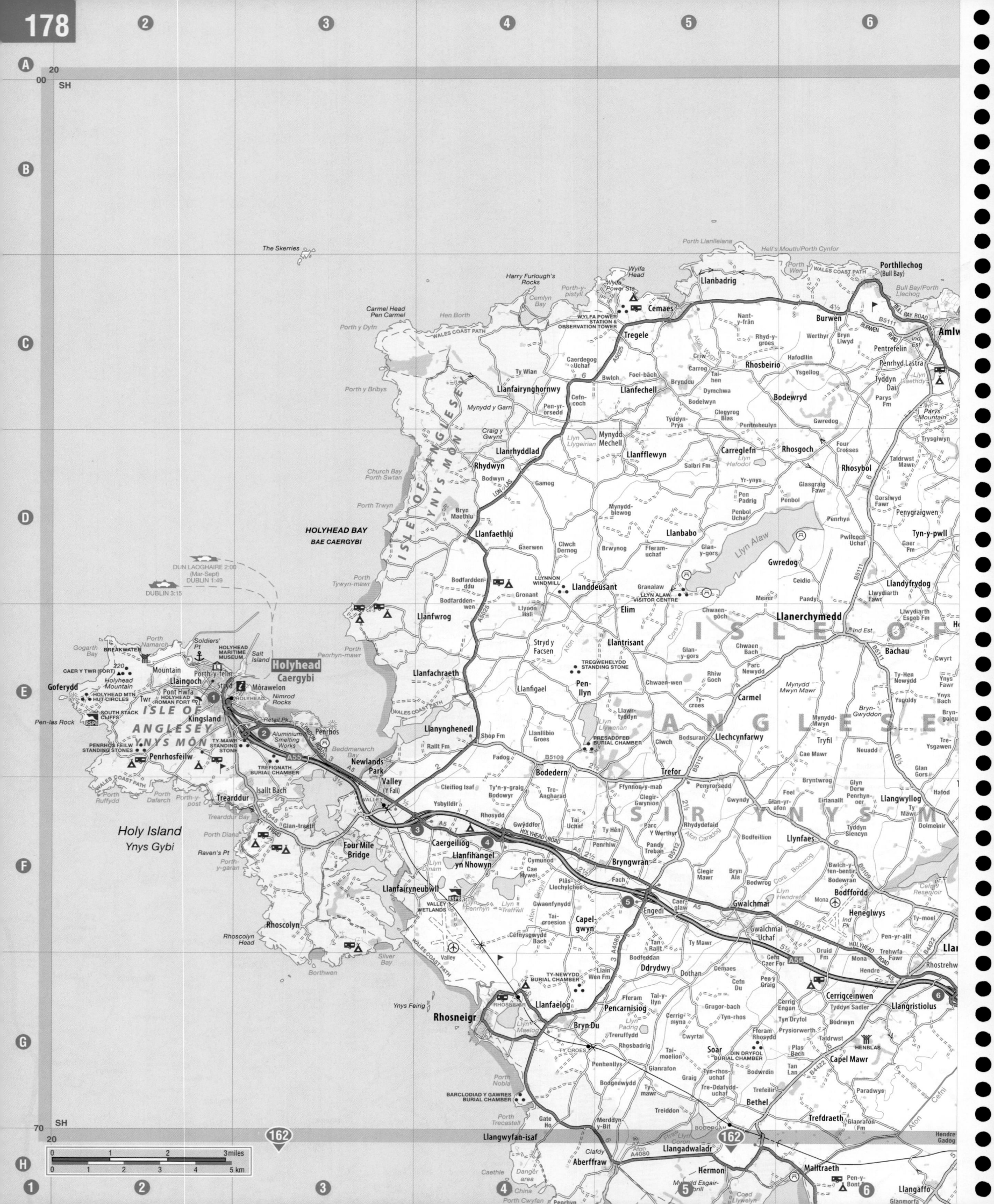

2
3
4
5
6
A
B
C
D
E
F
G
H
1
20
00
SH
The Skerries
Porth Llanlleiana
Hell's Mouth/Porth Cynfor
Wylfa Head
Harry Furlough's Rocks
Porth-y-pistyll
Cemlyn Bay
Wylfa Power Sta
Cemaes
WYLFA POWER STATION & OBSERVATION TOWER
Llanbadrig
Porth Wen
WALES COAST PATH
Porthllechog (Bull Bay)
Bull Bay/Porth Llechog
Burwen
Amlw
Carmel Head
Pen Carmel
Hen Borth
Porth y Dyfn
Tregele
Nant-y-frân
Rhyd-y-groes
Werthyr
Bryn Llwyd
Pentrefelin
Caerdegog Uchaf
Criw
Carrog
Tai-hen
Rhosbeirio
Hafodllin
Ysgellog
Penrhyd Lastra
Ty Wian
Bwlch
Foel-bâch
Brynddu
Llanfechell
Dymchwa
Bodewryd
Tyddyn Dai
Llanfairynghornwy
Cefn-coch
Pen-yr-orsedd
Porth y Bribys
Mynydd y Garn
Bodelwyn
Clegyrog Blas
Tyddyn-Prys
Pentreheulyn
Gwredog
Parys Fm
Parys Mountain
Craig y Gwynt
Llanrhyddlad
Llyn Llygeirian
Mynydd Mechell
Llanfflewyn
Carreglefn
Llyn Hafodol
Rhosgoch
Four Crosses
Trysglwyn
Church Bay
Porth Swtan
Rhydwyn
Bodwyn
Salbri Fm
Yr-ynys
Rhosybol
Taldrwst Mawr
ISLE OF ANGLESEY
YNYS MÔN
LÔN LAS
Gamog
Pen Padrig
Glasgraig Fawr
Penbol
Gorslwyd Fawr
Porth Trwyn
Bryn Maethlu
Mynydd-blewog
Penbol Uchaf
Penrhyn
Penygraigwen
HOLYHEAD BAY
BAE CAERGYBI
Llanfaethlu
Llanbabo
Pwllcoch Uchaf
Tyn-y-pwll
Gaerwen
Clwch Dernog
Brwynog
Fferam-uchaf
Glan-y-gors
Llyn Alaw
Gaer Fm
Gwredog
Llandyfrydog
DUN LAOGHAIRE 2:00 (Mar-Sept)
DUBLIN 1:49
DUBLIN 3:15
Porth Tywyn-mawr
Bodfardden-ddu
LLYNNON WINDMILL
Llanddeusant
Granalaw
LLYN ALAW VISITOR CENTRE
Ceidio
Bodfardden-wen
Gronant
Llynon Hall
Elim
Meinir
Pandy
Llwydiarth Fawr
Llwydiarth Esgob Fm
Chwaen-gôch
Llanerchymedd
Ind Est
Llanfwrog
A5025
Porth Namarch
Gogarth Bay
BREAKWATER
Soldiers' Pt
HOLYHEAD MARITIME MUSEUM
Salt Island
Holyhead
Caergybi
CAER Y TWR (FORT)
Holyhead Mountain
Mountain
Porth-y-felin
Stryd y Facsen
Afon Alaw
Llantrisant
Glan-y-gors
Chwaen Bach
Bachau
Cwyrt
Porth Penrhyn-mawr
Llanfachraeth
TREGWEHELYDD STANDING STONE
Rhiw Goch
Parc Newydd
Mynydd Mwyn Mawr
Ty-Hen Newydd
Ynys Fawr
Goferydd
HOLYHEAD MTN HUT CIRCLES
Llaingoch
Porth Hwfa
HOLYHEAD ROMAN FORT
Twr
Môrawelon
Nimrod Rocks
Llanfigael
Pen-llyn
Chwaen-wen
Carmel
Bryn-Gwyddon
Ysgoldy
Ynys Bach
SOUTH STACK CLIFFS
Pen-las Rock
Kingsland
Retail Pk
Llawr-tyddyn
Llyn Llywenan
Ty-croes
Penrhos
Llanynghenedl
Shop Fm
Llanllibio Groes
PRESADDFED BURIAL CHAMBER
Bodsuran
Llechcynfarwy
Mynydd-Mwyn
Tryfil
Bryn-goleu
Tre-Ysgawen
PENRHOS FEILW STANDING STONES
TY MAWR STANDING STONE
Aluminium Smelting Works
Beddmanarch Bay
Raillt Fm
Clwch
Cae Mawr
Neuadd
Penrhosfeilw
A55
Newlands Park
Fadog
B5109
Bodedern
Trefor
Glan Gors
TREFIGNATH BURIAL CHAMBER
Valley (Y Fali)
Cleifiog Isaf
Ty'n-y-graig Bodowyr
Tre-Angharad
Ffynnon-y-mab
Penyrorsedd
Bryntwrog
Glyn Derw Penrhyn-oer
Porth Ruffydd
Porth Dafarch
Porth-y-post
Trearddur
Isallt Bach
Ysbylldir
Clegir-Gwynion
Gwyndy
Glan-yr-afon
Foel
Eirianallt
Llangwyllog
Hafod
Trearddur Bay
Rhosydd
Gwyddfor
Tai Uchaf
Ty Hên
Parc Y Werthyr
Rhydydefaid
Tyddyn Sliencyn
Ty Mawr
Dolmeinir
Holy Island
Ynys Gybi
Porth Diana
Glan-traeth
Four Mile Bridge
Caergeiliog
HOLYHEAD ROAD
Penrhiw
Pandy Treban
Afon Caradog
Bodfeilion
Llynfaes
Raven's Pt
Porth-y-garan
Llanfihangel yn Nhowyn
Llyn Dinam
Cymunod
Cae Hywel
Bryngwran
Clegir Mawr
Bryn Ala
Bwlch-y-fen-bentir
Bodewran
Plâs-Llechylched
Fach
Bodwrog
Cors Bodwrog
Llyn Hendref
Bodffordd
Cefni Reservoir
Llanfairyneubwll
Llyn Penrhyn
VALLEY WETLANDS
Llyn Traffwll
Gwaenfynydd
Engedi
Caer-glaw
Gwalchmai
Mona
Heneglwys
Rhoscolyn
Tai-croesion
Capel-gwyn
Gwalchmai Uchaf
Ind Pk
Ty-moel
Rhoscolyn Head
Cefnysgwydd Bach
Tan Rallt
Ty Mawr
Druid Fm
Pen-yr-allt
Silver Bay
Borthwen
Valley
Bodfeddan
Ddrydwy
Dothan
Cemaes
Cefn Coch Fm
Mona
Trehwfa Fawr
Hendre
Rhostrehw
TY-NEWYDD BURIAL CHAMBER
Llain Wen Fm
Pen-y-Graig
Cefn Du
Cerrigceinwen
Llangristiolus
Ynys Feirig
Rhosneigr
Llanfaelog
Fferam
Tal-y-llyn
Pencarnisiog
Grugor-bach
Tyn-rhos
Cerrig Engan
Tyddyn Sadler
Tyn Dryfol
Bodrwyn
Llyn Maelog
Bryn Du
Llyn Padrig
Treruffydd
Cerrig-myna
Cwyrtai
Fferam Rhosydd
Prysiorwerth
Taldrwst
HENBLAS
TY CROES
Rhosbadrig
Tai-moelion
Soar
DIN DRYFOL BURIAL CHAMBER
Plas Bach
Capel Mawr
Penhenllys
Glanrafon
Tyn-rhos-uchaf
Tan Lan
B4422
Porth Nobla
Bodgedwydd
Graig
Bodwrdin
Paradwys
Ty-mawr
Tre-Ddafydd-uchaf
Trefeilir
Afon Cefni
BARCLODIAD Y GAWRES BURIAL CHAMBER
Treiddon
Bethel
Trefdraeth
Glanrafon Fm
SH
70
20
Porth Trecastell
Gate Ho
Merddyn-y-Bit
BODORGAN
Hendre Gadog
162
Llangwyfan-isaf
Clafdy
Afon Ffraw
Llyn Coron
A4080
Llangadwaladr
Aberffraw
Hermon
Malltraeth
Caethle
Danger area
China
Mynydd Esgair-ebrill
Coed Llywelyn
Pen-y-Bont
Llangaffo
Porth Cwyfan
Glanmorfa
0
1
2
3 miles
0
1
2
3
4
5 km

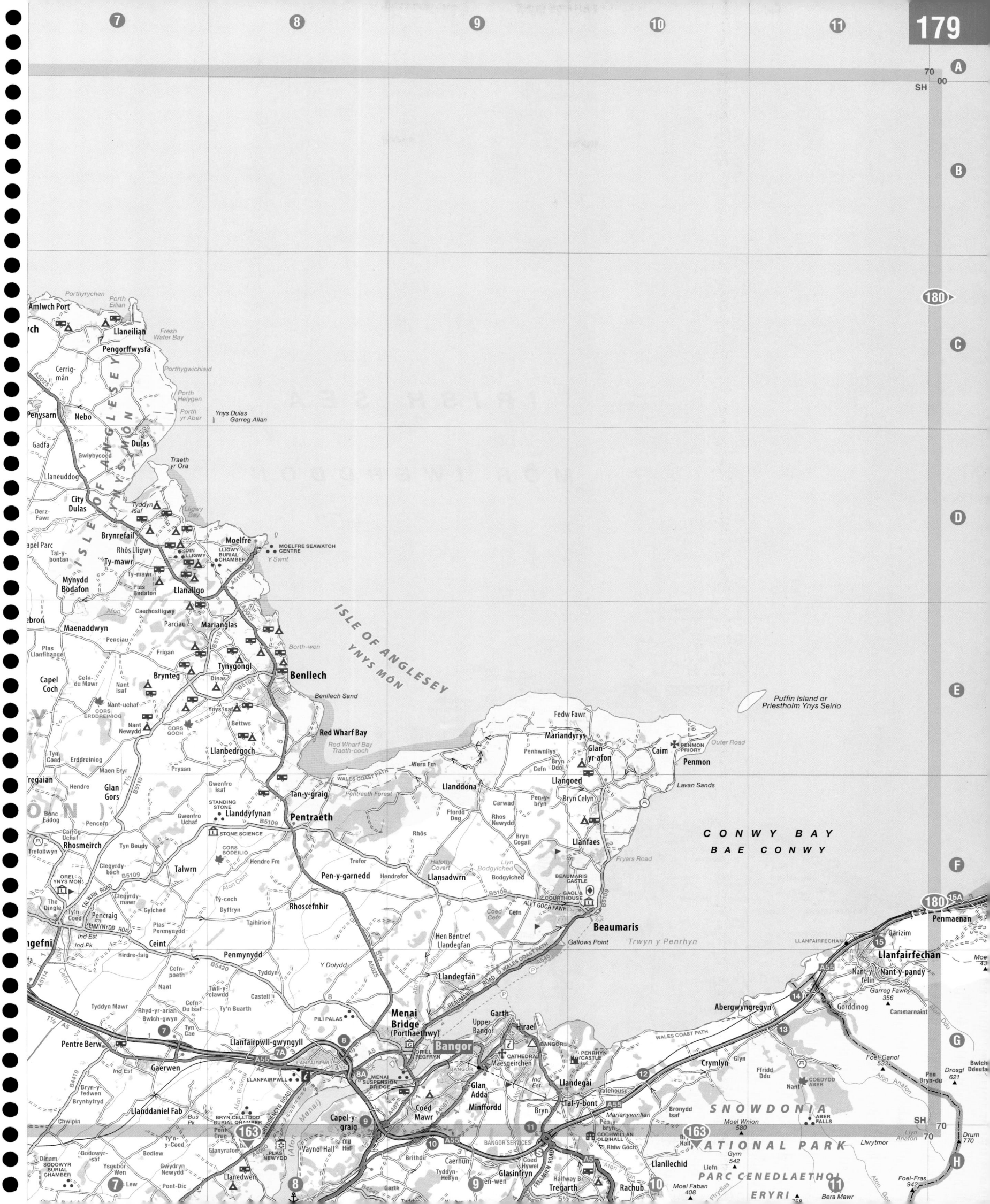

IRISH SEA
MÔR IWERDDON
ISLE OF ANGLESEY
YNYS MÔN
CONWY BAY
BAE CONWY
SNOWDONIA
NATIONAL PARK
PARC CENEDLAETHOL ERYRI
Amlwch Port
Llaneilian
Pengorffwysfa
Penysarn
Nebo
Dulas
City Dulas
Brynrefail
Moelfre
MOELFRE SEAWATCH CENTRE
Llanallgo
Marianglas
Benllech
Tynygongl
Brynteg
Red Wharf Bay
Llanbedrgoch
Tan-y-graig
Pentraeth
Llanddyfnan
Puffin Island or Priestholm Ynys Seirio
Penmon
Llanddona
Llangoed
Llanfaes
Beaumaris
Llansadwrn
Pen-y-garnedd
Rhoscefnhir
Talwrn
Rhosmeirch
Gaerwen
Pentre Berw
Llanfairpwll-gwyngyll
Menai Bridge (Porthaethwy)
Bangor
Llandegfan
Llandegai
Tal-y-bont
Abergwyngregyn
Llanfairfechan
Penmaenan
Llanllechid
Rachub
Tregarth
Glasinfryn
180
163

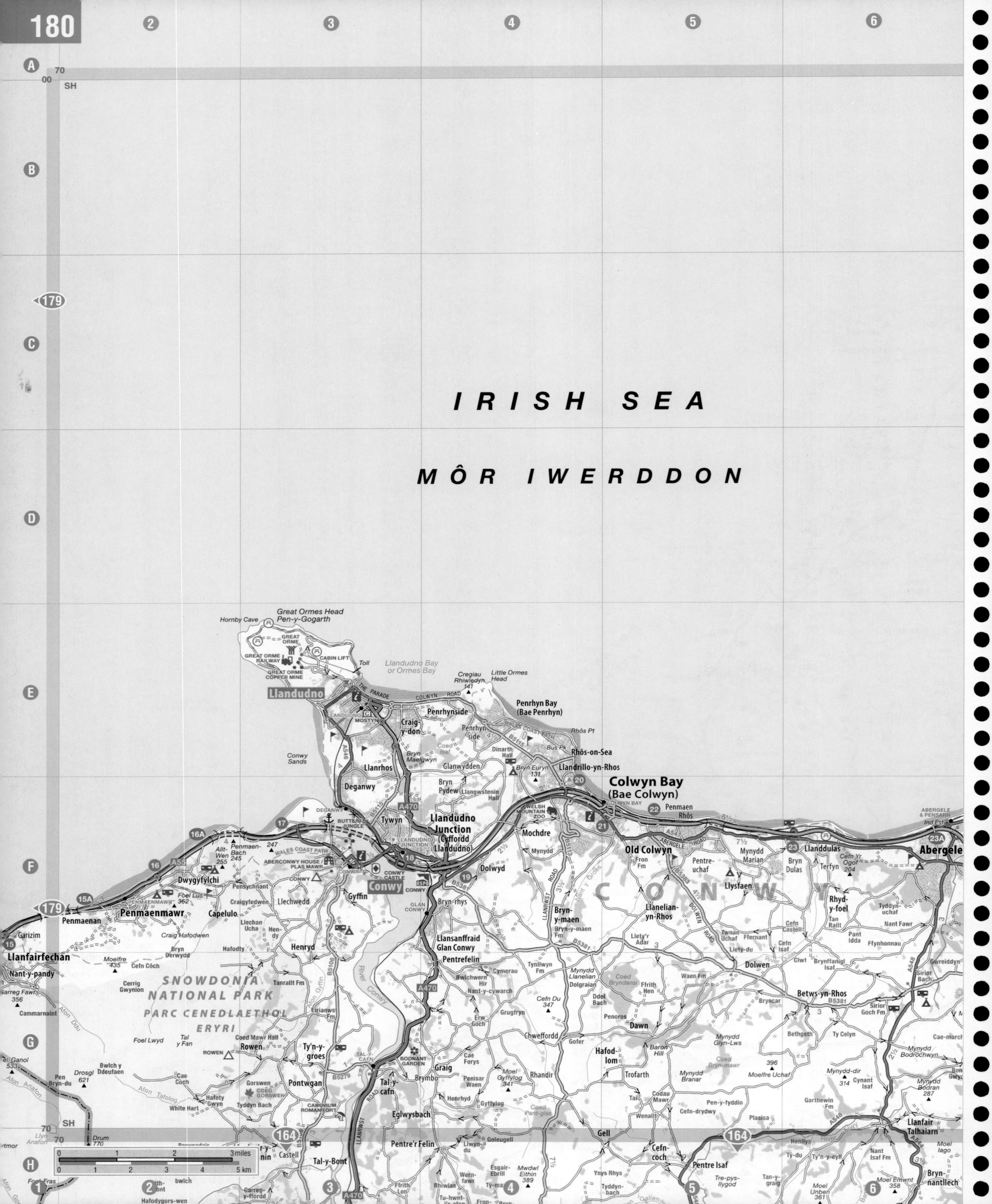
IRISH SEA
MÔR IWERDDON
Great Ormes Head
Pen-y-Gogarth
Llandudno
Colwyn Bay
(Bae Colwyn)
Conwy
Llandudno Junction
(Cyffordd Llandudno)
Abergele
Old Colwyn
Penmaenmawr
Llanfairfechan
SNOWDONIA NATIONAL PARK
PARC CENEDLAETHOL ERYRI
CONWY

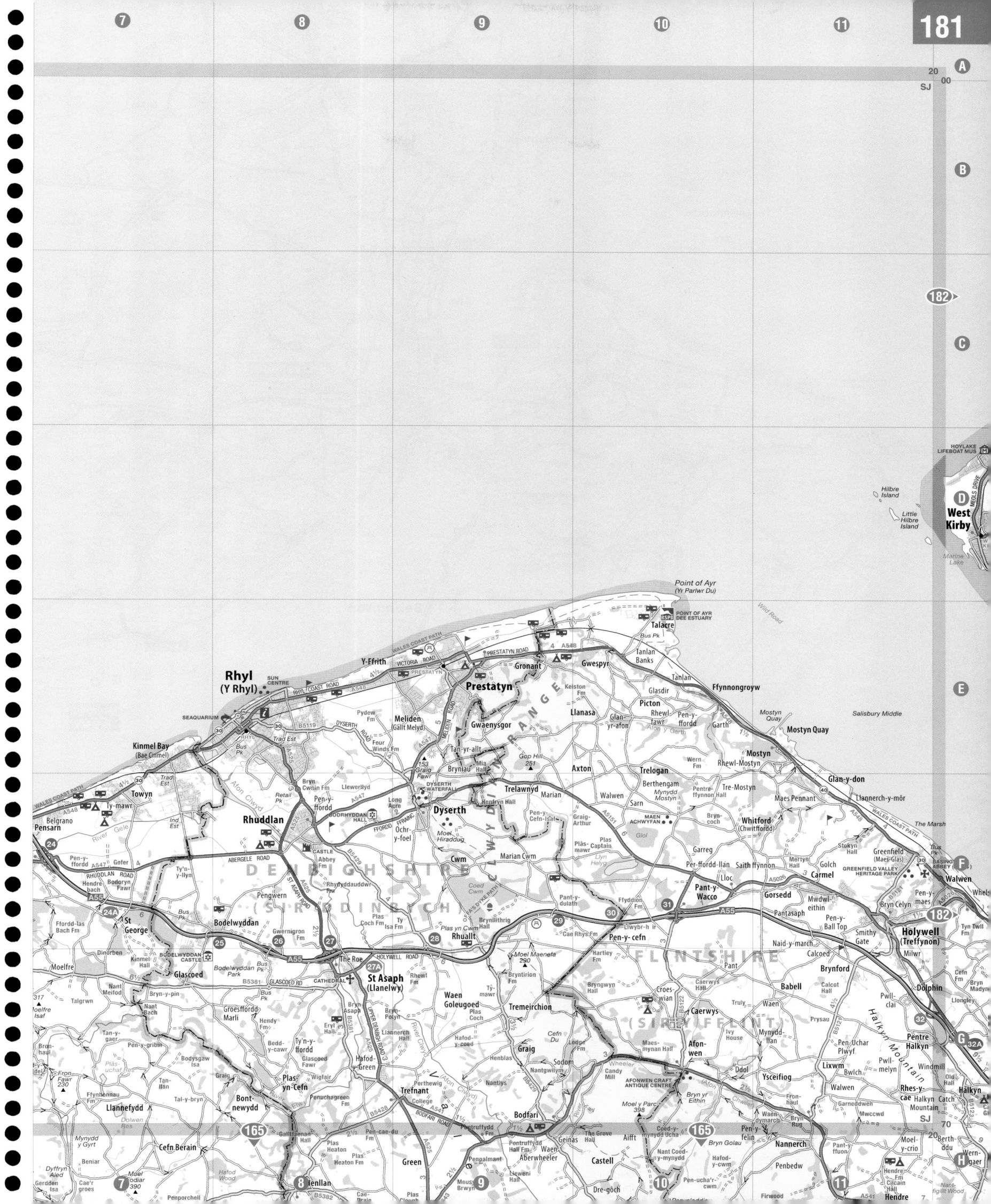
7
8
9
10
11
A
B
C
D
E
F
G
H
20
00
SJ
182
HOYLAKE LIFEBOAT MUS
Hilbre Island
Little Hilbre Island
West Kirby
MEOLS DRIVE
Marine Lake
Point of Ayr
(Yr Parlwr Du)
POINT OF AYR DEE ESTUARY
RSPB
Talacre
Bus Pk
Wild Road
Tanlan Banks
Tanlan
Ffynnongroyw
Gwespyr
Gronant
PRESTATYN ROAD
A548
WALES COAST PATH
Y-Ffrith
VICTORIA ROAD
PRESTATYN
Prestatyn
Rhyl
(Y Rhyl)
SUN CENTRE
RHYL COAST ROAD
SEAQUARIUM
Kinmel Bay
(Bae Cinmel)
Towyn
Ty-mawr
Belgrano
Pensarn
Trad Est
Retail Pk
Ind Est
Afon Clwyd
River Gele
Rhuddlan
CASTLE
Abbey Fm
ABERGELE ROAD
RHUDDLAN ROAD
Pen-y-ffordd
Gofer
Hendre-bach
Bodoryn Fawr
Ty'n-y-llyn
Meliden
(Gallt Melyd)
Pydew Fm
DYSERTH ROAD
Four Winds Fm
Bryn Cwnin Fm
Llewerllyd
Pen-y-ffordd
BODRHYDDAN HALL
Long Acre
FFRAINC
Ochr-y-foel
DYSERTH WATERFALL
Dyserth
Moel Hiraddug
Cwm
Graig Fawr
153
Bryniau
Mia Hall
Tan-yr-allt
Gwaenysgor
Gop Hill
251
Trelawnyd
Henfryn Hall
Marian
Marian Cwm
Pen-y-Cefn-isaf
CLWYDIAN RANGE
Kelston Fm
Llanasa
Glan-yr-afon
Glasdir
Picton
Rhewl-fawr
Pen-y-ffordd
Garth
Afon y Garth
Mostyn Quay
Mostyn
Salisbury Middle
Rhewl-Mostyn
Wern Fm
Trelogan
Berthengam
Mynydd Mostyn
Axton
Walwen
Sarn
Pentre-ffynnon Hall
Tre-Mostyn
MAEN ACHWYFAN
Glol
Graig-Arthur
Plâs-mawr
Plas Captain
Llyn Helyg
Bryn-coch
Whitford
(Chwitffordd)
Maes Pennant
Glan-y-don
Llannerch-y-môr
The Marsh
Garreg
Per-ffordd-llan
Saith ffynnon
Stokyn Hall
Mertyn Hall
Golch
Greenfield
(Maes-Glas)
BASINGWERK ABBEY
GREENFIELD VALLEY HERITAGE PARK
Carmel
Walwen
Lloc
Pant-y-Wacco
Gorsedd
Mwdwl-eithin
Pantasaph
Pen-y-maes
Bryn Celyn
Ffyddion Fm
Pant-y-dulath
Coed Cwm
OFFA'S DYKE PATH
DENBIGHSHIRE
(SIR DDINBYCH)
FLINTSHIRE
(SIR Y FFLINT)
Rhyddauddwr Fm
Pengwern
Bodelwyddan
Bus Pk
Plas Coch Fm
Ty Isa Fm
Plas yn Cwm
Brynllithrig Hall
Rhuallt
Cae Rhys Fm
Llwybr-h ir
Pen-y-cefn
Pen-y-Ball Top
Smithy Gate
Holywell
(Treffynon)
Naid-y-march
Calcoed
Milwr
Tyn Twll Fm
St George
Ffordd-las Bach Fm
Gwernigron Fm
BODELWYDDAN CASTLE
Bodelwyddan Park
Kinmel Hall
Dinorben
Moelfre
Glascoed
GLASCOED RD
The Roe
HOLYWELL ROAD
CATHEDRAL
St Asaph
(Llanelwy)
Rhewl Fm
Moel Maenefa
290
Bryntirion Fm
Hartley Fm
Pant
Brynford
Babell
Calcot Hall
Caerwys Hall
Dolphin
Cefn Fm
Bryn Madyn
Llongley
Bryn-y-pin
Nant Meifod
Nant Bach
Talgrwn
317
Moelfre Isaf
Groesffordd Marli
Hendy Fm
Eryl Hall
Bryn Asaph
Bryn-Polyn
UPPER DENBIGH ROAD
Llannerch Hall
River Clwyd
Waen Goleugoed
Plas Coch
Tŷ-mawr
Tremeirchion
Bryngwyn Hall
Croes-wian
Caerwys
Truly
Waen
Prysau
Pwll-clai
Halkyn Mountain
Pentre Halkyn
Tan-y-gaer
Pen-y-gribin
Bron-haul
Bodysgaw Isa
Plâs-uchaf Res
Bedd-y-cawr
Ty'n-y-rffordd
Glascoed Fawr
Hafod-y-coed
Henblas
Graig
Cefn Du
Lodge Fm
Sodom
Nantgwilym
Maes-mynan Hall
Afon-wen
Ivy House
Mynydd-llan
Pen Uchar Plwyf
Pwll-melyn
Windmill
Old Hall
Halkyn
Fron Fawr
230
Ffynnonnau Fm
Tan-llan
Tal-y-bryn
Graig
Plas-yn-Cefn
Wigfair
Hafod-Green
Perthewig
College
Trefnant
Nantlys
Wheeler
Candy Mill
AFONWEN CRAFT ANTIQUE CENTRE
Bryn yr Eithin
Ddol
Ysceifiog
Lixwm
Bwlch
Walwen
Rhes-y-cae
Halkyn Mountain
Catch
Llannefydd
Dolwen Res
Bont-newydd
River Elwy
Penuchagreen Fm
Bodfari
BODFARI ROAD
Moel y Parc
398
Fron-haul
Garneddwen
Mwccwd
Waen-dymarch
Bryn Rug
Mynydd y Gyrt
Beniar
Dyffryn Aled
Gerdden Isa
Cae'r groes
Moel Fodiar
390
Cefn Berain
Hafod Wood
Galltfaenan Hall
Henllan
Plas Heaton
Plas Heaton Fm
Pen-cae-du Fm
Green
Pontruffydd Fm
Pontruffydd Hall Fm
Penpalmant
Llewenl Hall
Meusy Brwyn
Waen Aberwheeler
Geinas
The Grove Hall
Aifft
Castell
Dre-gôch
Coed-y-mynydd Ucha
Nant Coed-y-mynydd
Bryn Golau
Hafod-y-cwm
Pen-ucha'r-cwm
Pen-y-felin
Nannerch
Penbedw
Pant-y-ffuon
Moel-y-crio
Berth-ddu
Wern-gaer
Hendre Fm
Cilcain Hall
Nant-figillt Wood
Hendre
Firwood
A55
A525
A547
A548
A5151
A5026
A541
B5119
B5381
B5429
B5428
B5382
B5122
24
24A
25
26
27
27A
28
29
30
31
32
32A
165

LIVERPOOL
BAY
Crosby Channel
Crosby
Little Crosby
Sefton
Thornton
Netherton
Melling
Blundellsands
Brighton le Sands
Great Crosby
Waterloo
Litherland
Orrell
Seaforth
Bootle
Aintree
Kirkby
Southdene
Fazakerley
Croxteth
Knowsley
Walton
Norris Green
West Derby
Kirkdale
Anfield
Everton
Liverpool
Kensington
Old Swan
Knotty Ash
Roby
Huyton
Edge Hill
Wavertree
Childwall
Toxteth
Princes Park
Dingle
Mossley Hill
Gateacre
Woolton
Aigburth
Allerton
Grassendale
Hunt's Cross
Garston
Liverpool Airport
MERSEYSIDE
BELFAST 8:00
DOUGLAS 4:15 (WINTER ONLY)
DUBLIN 7:30
DOUGLAS 2:30 (MARCH-NOV)
New Brighton
Wallasey
Liscard
Egremont
Leasowe
Moreton
Poulton
Bidston
Seacombe
Birkenhead
Claughton
Upton
Noctorum
Oxton
Tranmere
Rock Ferry
New Ferry
Prenton
Woodchurch
Arrowe Hill
Greasby
Frankby
Newton
Saughall Massie
East Hoyle Bank
Dove Point
Meols
Hoylake
West Kirby
Hilbre Island
Grange
Caldy
Irby
Thingwall
Landican
Storeton
Higher Bebington
Bebington
Port Sunlight
Bromborough Pool
Lower Bebington
Thurstaston
Pensby
Barnston
Brimstage
Heswall
Spital
Bromborough
Eastham
Eastham Ferry
River Mersey
Dawpool Bank
Gayton
Thornton Hough
Raby
Parkgate
Neston
Little Neston
Ness
Willaston
Hinderton
Hooton
Childer Thornton
Little Sutton
Overpool
Ellesmere Port
Stanlow
Stanlow Banks
Whitby
Great Sutton
CHESHIRE WEST & CHESTER
Ledsham
Capenhurst
Burton
Puddington
Two Mills
Thornton-le-Moors
Little Stanney
Backford
Mollington
Saughall
Shotwick
Sealand
Garden City
Shotton
Connah's Quay
Upton
Chester
Mickle Trafford
Hoole Bank
Holywell (Treffynon)
Bagillt
Flint (Y Fflint)
Mount Pleasant
Oakenholt
Flint Mountain (Mynydd Fflint)
Halkyn
Walwen
Whelston
Dolphin
Pentre Ffwrndan
Rockcliffe
Golftyn
0 1 2 3 miles
0 1 2 3 4 5 km

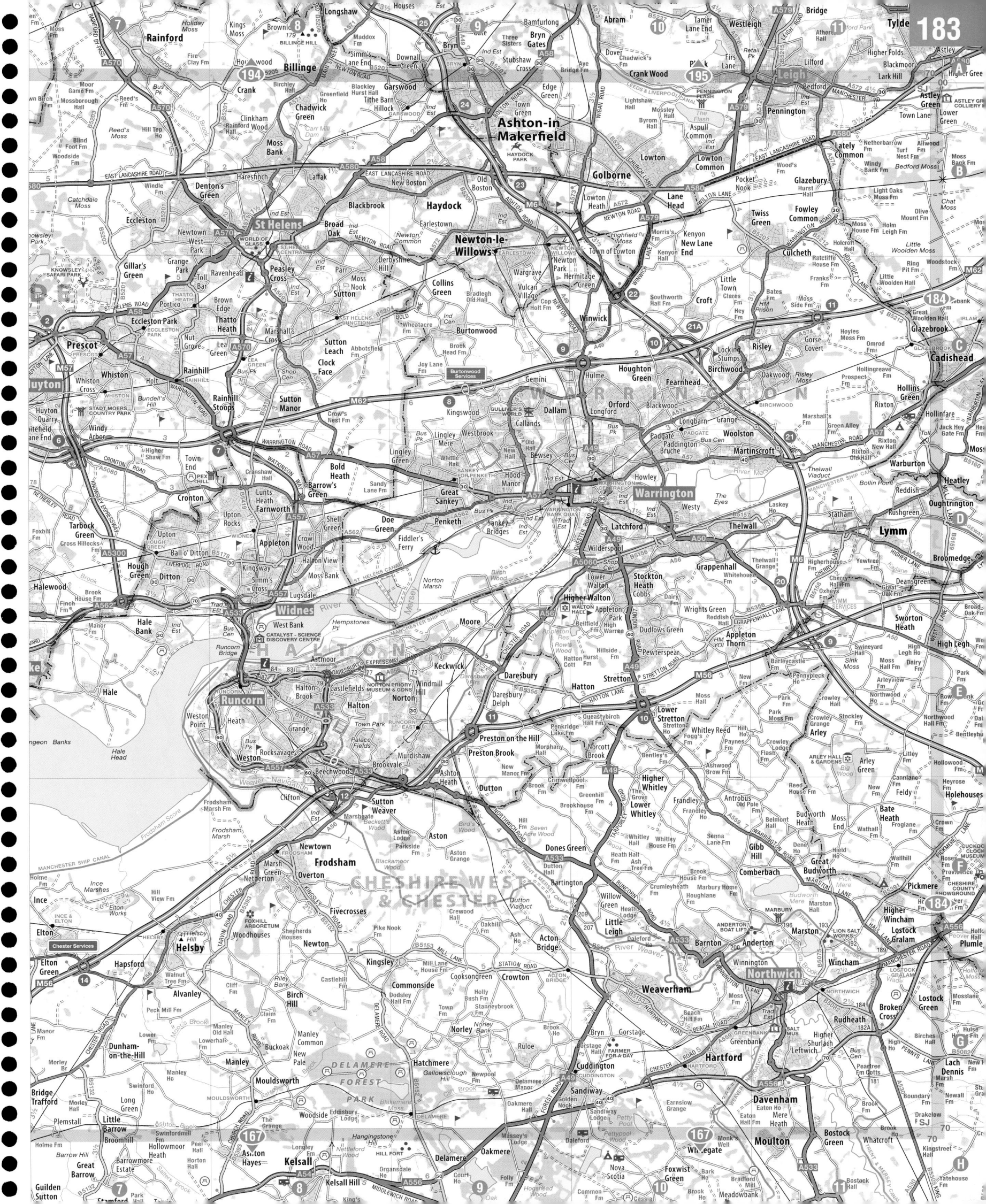
Tylde
Rainford
Billinge
Longshaw
Bryn
Bryn Gates
Bamfurlong
Abram
Westleigh
Bridge
Leigh
Ashton-in Makerfield
Golborne
Lowton
Lowton Common
Lately Common
Pennington
Astley
Crank
Garswood
Chadwick Green
Moss Bank
St Helens
Eccleston
Denton's Green
Haydock
Blackbrook
Newton-le-Willows
Earlestown
Lane Head
Glazebury
Culcheth
Twiss Green
Fowley Common
Kenyon
New Lane End
Croft
Winwick
Burtonwood
Collins Green
Sutton
Peasley Cross
Prescot
Whiston
Huyton
Rainhill
Rainhill Stoops
Thatto Heath
Eccleston Park
Clock Face
Sutton Manor
Houghton Green
Fearnhead
Birchwood
Risley
Cadishead
Glazebrook
WARRINGTON
Dallam
Orford
Longford
Kingswood
Westbrook
Callands
Woolston
Martinscroft
Padgate
Paddington
Warrington
Great Sankey
Penketh
Bold Heath
Barrow's Green
Farnworth
Cronton
Tarbock Green
Halewood
Hough Green
Ditton
Appleton
Widnes
Latchford
Thelwall
Lymm
Statham
Rixton
Warburton
Heatley
Oughtrington
Grappenhall
Stockton Heath
Wilderspool
Higher Walton
Lower Walton
Appleton Thorn
Moore
Hale
Hale Bank
HALTON
Runcorn
Weston
Weston Point
Halton
Norton
Castlefields
Murdishaw
Daresbury
Keckwick
Hatton
Stretton
Lower Stretton
Preston on the Hill
Preston Brook
Dutton
Higher Whitley
Lower Whitley
Antrobus
Arley
Great Budworth
Comberbach
Pickmere
Sutton Weaver
Aston
Frodsham
Helsby
Elton
Ince
CHESHIRE WEST & CHESTER
Newton
Kingsley
Crowton
Acton Bridge
Weaverham
Barnton
Anderton
Northwich
Marston
Wincham
Lostock Gralam
Hartford
Davenham
Moulton
Rudheath
Cuddington
Sandiway
Norley
Manley
Mouldsworth
Alvanley
Dunham-on-the-Hill
Delamere Forest Park
Hatchmere
Kelsall
Ashton Hayes
Delamere
Oakmere
Great Barrow
Little Barrow
Whitegate
Bostock Green
M6
M56
M62
M57
A580
A57
A49
A533
A556
A56
A50
A562
A557

Worsley
Swinton
Pendlebury
Salford
Eccles
Manchester
Trafford Park
Stretford
Old Trafford
Hulme
Ardwick
Gorton
Rusholme
Denton
Droylsden
Failsworth
Ashton
Dukinfield
Irlam
Urmston
Flixton
Cadishead
Partington
Carrington
Sale
Chorlton-cum-Hardy
Withington
Didsbury
Fallowfield
Levenshulme
Reddish
Stockport
Bredbury
Romiley
Altrincham
Timperley
Northenden
Wythenshawe
Gatley
Cheadle
Cheadle Hulme
Bramhall
Hazel Grove
Poynton
Lymm
Bowdon
Hale
Manchester Airport
Ashley
Styal
Handforth
Wilmslow
Knutsford
Alderley Edge
Mobberley
Prestbury
Bollington
Macclesfield
Hurdsfield
Chelford
Plumley
Lostock Gralam
Goostrey
Lower Withington
Siddington
Gawsworth
Marton
Tatton Park
Knutsford Services
0 1 2 3 miles
0 1 2 3 4 5 km

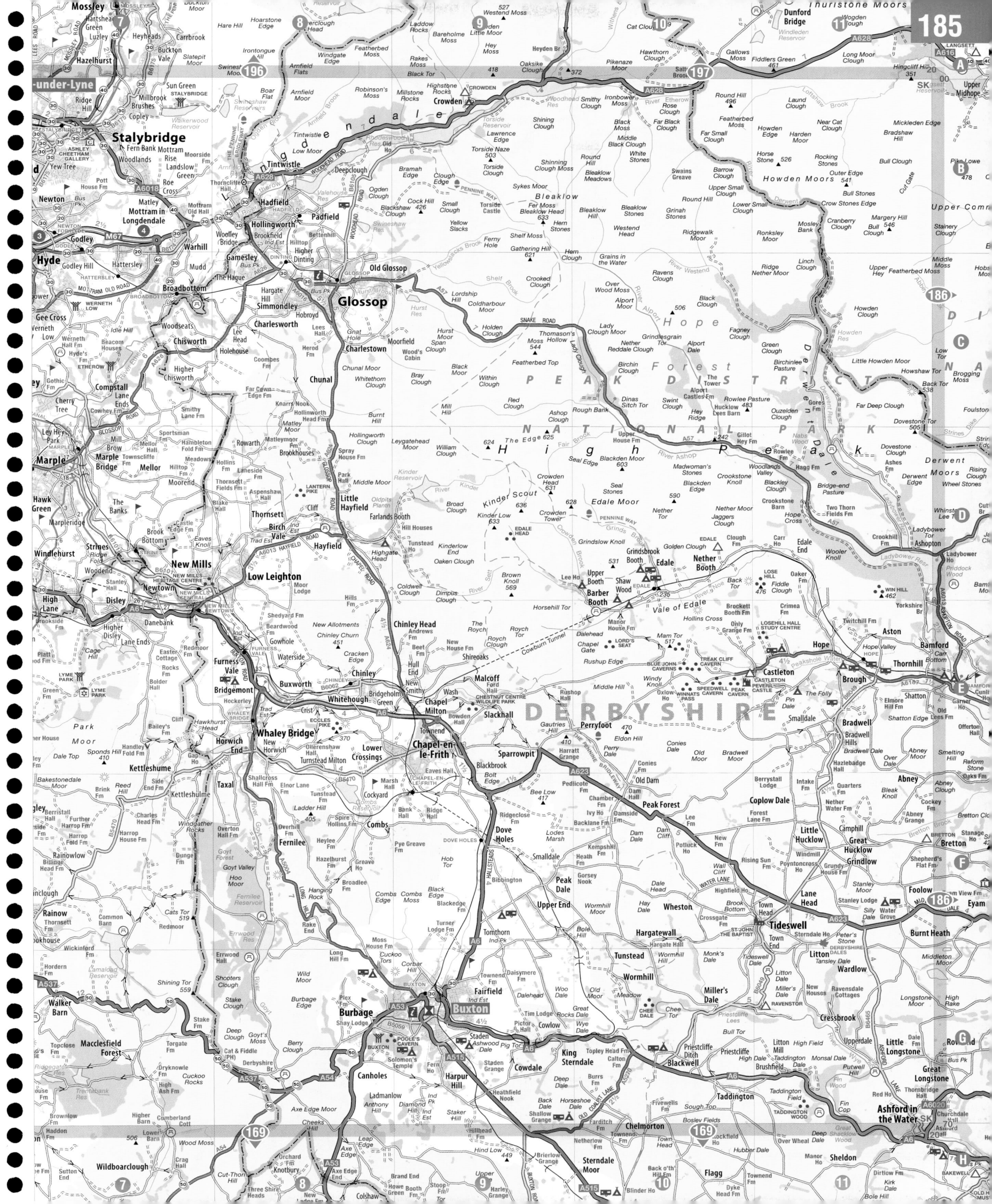
Mossley
Hazelhurst
Stalybridge
Dunford Bridge
Thurlstone Moors
Crowden
Longdendale
Tintwistle
Hadfield
Hollingworth
Padfield
Mottram in Longdendale
Hyde
Broadbottom
Gamesley
Old Glossop
Glossop
Simmondley
Charlesworth
Chisworth
Charlestown
Chunal
Compstall
Marple
Marple Bridge
Mellor
Little Hayfield
Hayfield
Birch Vale
Thornsett
New Mills
Low Leighton
Newtown
Disley
High Lane
Furness Vale
Bridgemont
Whaley Bridge
Chinley
Chinley Head
Buxworth
Chapel-en-le-Frith
Slackhall
Malcoff
Sparrowpit
Kettleshulme
Taxal
Combs
Dove Holes
Fernilee
Peak Forest
Perryfoot
Edale
Nether Booth
Barber Booth
Castleton
Hope
Aston
Thornhill
Bamford
Brough
Bradwell
Great Hucklow
Little Hucklow
Abney
Bretton
Foolow
Eyam
Tideswell
Litton
Wardlow
Cressbrook
Little Longstone
Great Longstone
Ashford in the Water
Sheldon
Taddington
Chelmorton
Blackwell
Wormhill
Tunstead
Hargatewall
Wheston
Upper End
Peak Dale
Fairfield
Buxton
Burbage
Harpur Hill
Cowdale
King Sterndale
Staden
Macclesfield Forest
Wildboarclough
Walker Barn
Rainow
Howden Moors
Derwent Moors
Bleaklow
Kinder Scout
Edale Moor
Featherbed Top
High Peak
Hope Forest
PEAK DISTRICT NATIONAL PARK
DERBYSHIRE
Vale of Edale
Snake Road
196
197
186
169

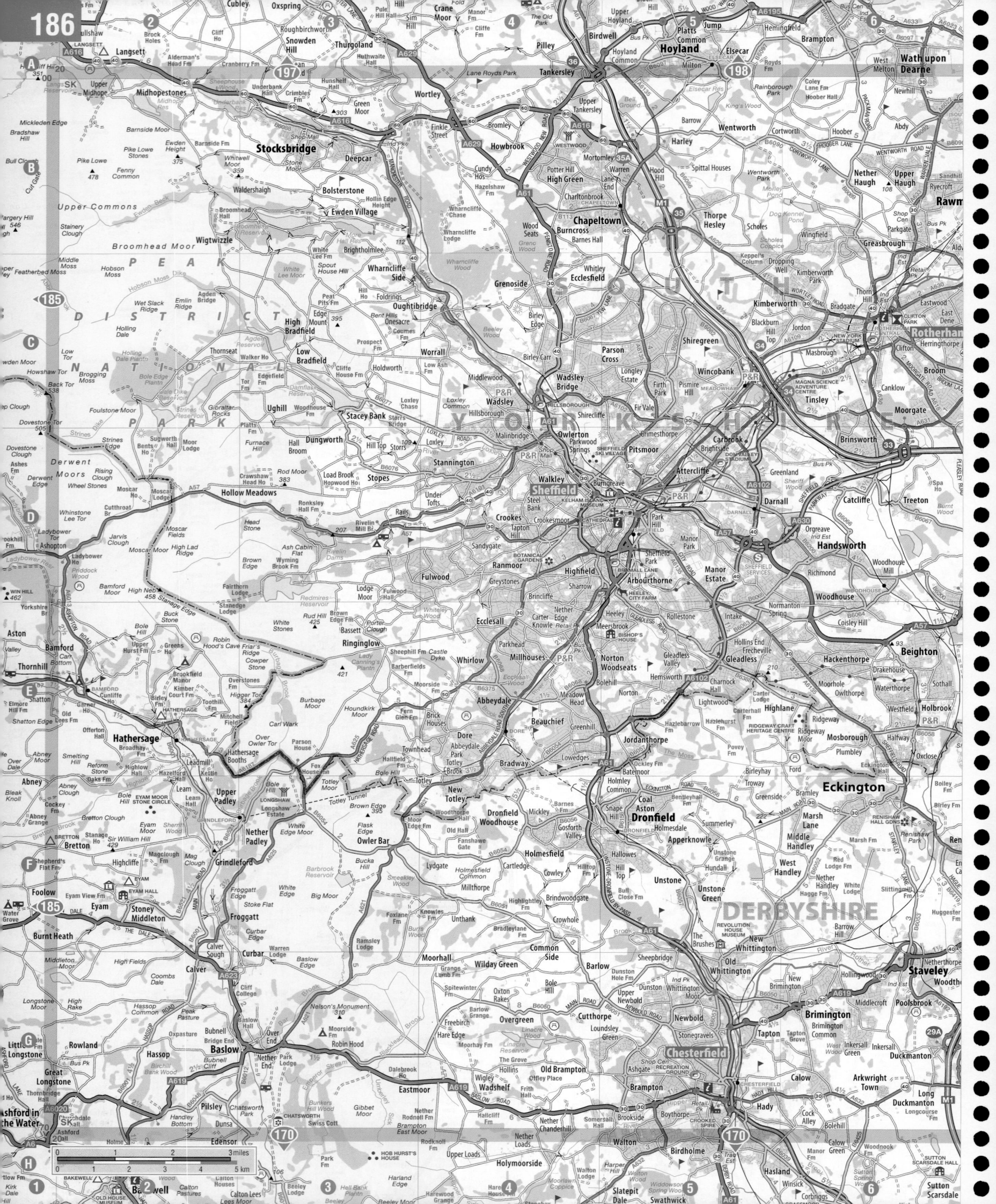
Langsett
Midhopestones
Stocksbridge
Deepcar
Bolsterstone
Ewden Village
Wortley
Thurgoland
Tankersley
Hoyland
Wath upon Dearne
Chapeltown
High Green
Ecclesfield
Grenoside
Oughtibridge
Wharncliffe Side
High Bradfield
Low Bradfield
Worrall
Wadsley Bridge
Shiregreen
Wincobank
Kimberworth
Rotherham
Tinsley
Brinsworth
Greasbrough
Wentworth
Stacey Bank
Dungworth
Stannington
Hillsborough
Owlerton
Pitsmoor
Attercliffe
Darnall
Sheffield
Crookes
Walkley
Ranmoor
Fulwood
Ecclesall
Handsworth
Woodhouse
Beighton
Hackenthorpe
Gleadless
Norton
Abbeydale
Dore
Totley
Bradway
Jordanthorpe
Eckington
Dronfield
Coal Aston
Unstone
Hathersage
Bamford
Thornhill
Upper Padley
Nether Padley
Grindleford
Froggatt
Curbar
Calver
Baslow
Eyam
Stoney Middleton
Foolow
Bretton
Abney
Hollow Meadows
Ringinglow
Whirlow
Beauchief
Owler Bar
Holmesfield
Apperknowle
West Handley
Middle Handley
Marsh Lane
Barlow
Old Whittington
New Whittington
Staveley
Brimington
Newbold
Chesterfield
Brampton
Tapton
Calow
Hady
Walton
Birdholme
Hasland
Holymoorside
Wadshelf
Old Brampton
Overgreen
Wigley
Pilsley
Edensor
Hassop
Rowland
Great Longstone
Little Longstone
Ashford in the Water
Bakewell
Beeley
P E A K  D I S T R I C T  N A T I O N A L  P A R K
S O U T H  Y O R K S H I R E
DERBYSHIRE
185
170
197
198

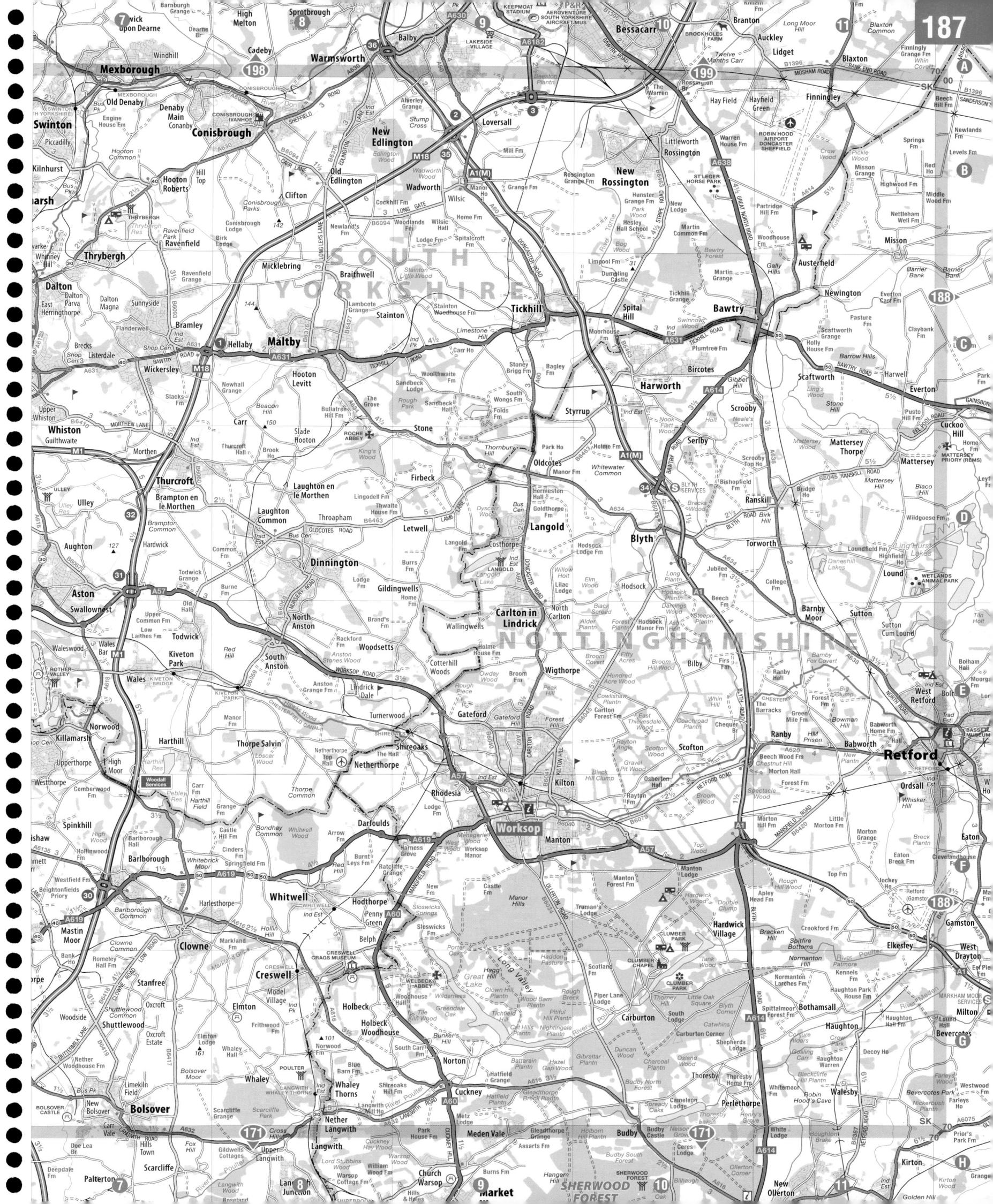

Mexborough
Swinton
Conisbrough
Denaby Main
Old Denaby
Warmsworth
Sprotbrough
High Melton
Cadeby
Balby
Bessacarr
Branton
Auckley
Lidget
Blaxton
Finningley
Loversall
New Edlington
Old Edlington
Wadworth
Hooton Roberts
Kilnhurst
Thrybergh
Ravenfield
Clifton
Micklebring
Braithwell
Stainton
Tickhill
Maltby
Hellaby
Bramley
Wickersley
Listerdale
Dalton
Sunnyside
Rossington
New Rossington
Bawtry
Austerfield
Misson
Newington
Scaftworth
Everton
Harworth
Bircotes
Styrrup
Scrooby
Serlby
Ranskill
Mattersey
Mattersey Thorpe
Hooton Levitt
Stone
Oldcotes
Carr
Whiston
Morthen
Thurcroft
Brampton en le Morthen
Ulley
Aughton
Aston
Swallownest
Laughton en le Morthen
Laughton Common
Firbeck
Letwell
Throapham
Dinnington
Gildingwells
Langold
Carlton in Lindrick
North Carlton
Blyth
Torworth
Hodsock
Barnby Moor
Sutton
Lound
North Anston
South Anston
Todwick
Kiveton Park
Wales
Woodsetts
Wallingwells
Wigthorpe
Bilby
Retford
West Retford
Ordsall
Babworth
Ranby
Scofton
Kilton
Worksop
Manton
Gateford
Shireoaks
Rhodesia
Netherthorpe
Thorpe Salvin
Harthill
Killamarsh
Norwood
Turnerwood
Darfoulds
Barlborough
Clowne
Whitwell
Creswell
Elmton
Holbeck
Norton
Cuckney
Carburton
Thoresby
Perlethorpe
Budby
Meden Vale
Bolsover
Shuttlewood
Stanfree
Oxcroft
Whaley
Whaley Thorns
Nether Langwith
Langwith
Upper Langwith
Scarcliffe
Palterton
Hardwick Village
Elkesley
Gamston
West Drayton
Milton
Bothamsall
Haughton
Walesby
Bevercotes
Markham Moor
Kirton
New Ollerton
Worksop
Clumber Park
Sherwood Forest
SOUTH YORKSHIRE
NOTTINGHAMSHIRE
M18
M1
A1(M)
A1
A57
A60
A614
A619
A631
A638
198
199
188
171

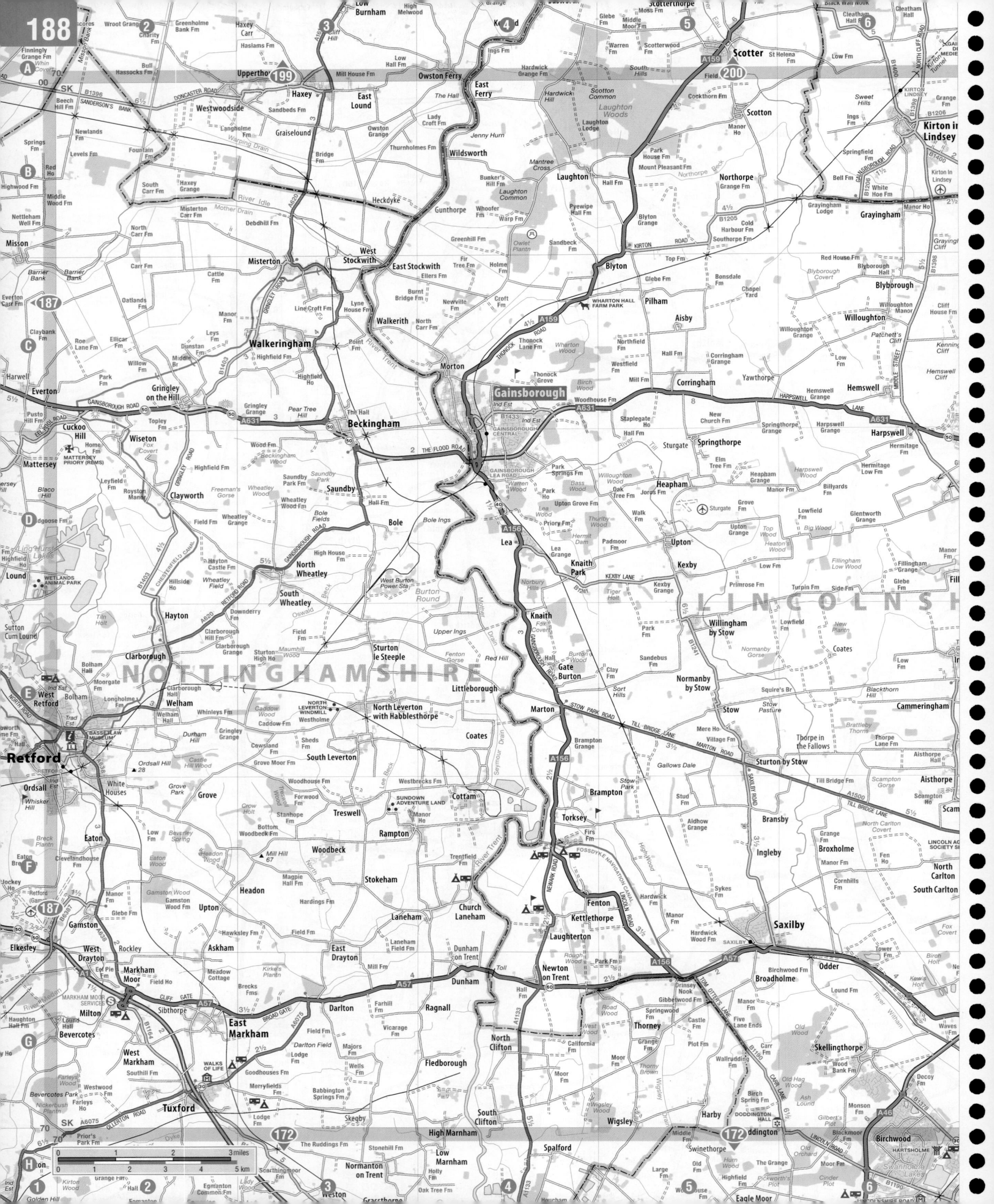
Gainsborough
Retford
Scotter
Kirton in Lindsey
Haxey
Misterton
Walkeringham
Beckingham
Blyton
Saxilby
Tuxford
East Markham
NOTTINGHAMSHIRE
LINCOLNSH
River Trent
187
199
200
172

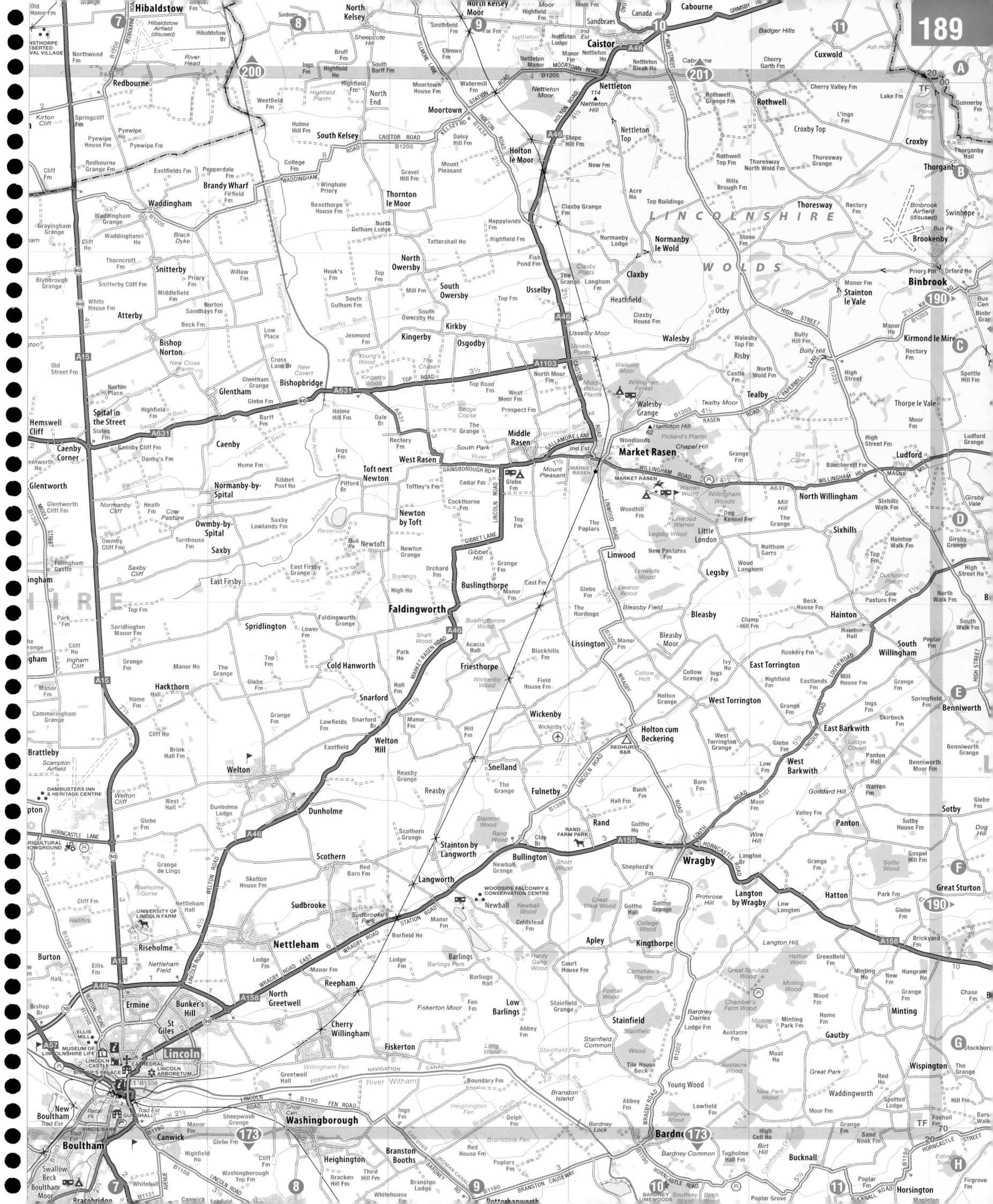
Hibaldstow
North Kelsey
Cabourne
Caistor
Nettleton
Redbourne
Rothwell
Moortown
South Kelsey
Croxby
Thorganby
Holton le Moor
Brandy Wharf
Thornton le Moor
Waddingham
Thoresway
Swinhope
LINCOLNSHIRE
WOLDS
Normanby le Wold
Brookenby
North Owersby
Snitterby
Claxby
Binbrook
South Owersby
Usselby
Stainton le Vale
Atterby
Kirkby
Kingerby
Osgodby
Walesby
Kirmond le Mire
Bishop Norton
Glentham
Bishopbridge
Tealby
Spital in the Street
Hemswell Cliff
Middle Rasen
Caenby
Caenby Corner
West Rasen
Market Rasen
Ludford
Toft next Newton
Glentworth
Normanby-by-Spital
North Willingham
Newton by Toft
Owmby-by-Spital
Sixhills
Saxby
Newtoft
Linwood
Little London
Legsby
Buslingthorpe
Faldingworth
Bleasby
Hainton
Spridlington
Lissington
South Willingham
Cold Hanworth
Friesthorpe
East Torrington
Hackthorn
Snarford
West Torrington
Wickenby
Holton cum Beckering
East Barkwith
Welton Hill
Benniworth
Brattleby
Snelland
West Barkwith
Welton
Fulnetby
Dunholme
Rand
Sotby
Panton
Stainton by Langworth
Scothern
Bullington
Wragby
Langworth
Langton by Wragby
Hatton
Great Sturton
Sudbrooke
Newball
Nettleham
Apley
Kingthorpe
Riseholme
Barlings
Burton
Reepham
Ermine
Bunker's Hill
North Greetwell
Low Barlings
Minting
St Giles
Cherry Willingham
Stainfield
Gautby
Lincoln
Fiskerton
Wispington
Young Wood
Waddingworth
New Boulthan
Washingborough
Bardney
Boultham
Canwick
Heighington
Branston Booths
Bucknall
Horsington
A15
A46
A631
A1103
A158
A57
B1205
B1203
B1225
B1399
B1202
B1190
B1188
B1131
B1398
B1200
7
8
9
10
11
200
201
190
173
A
B
C
D
E
F
G
H
TF
00
10
20
70

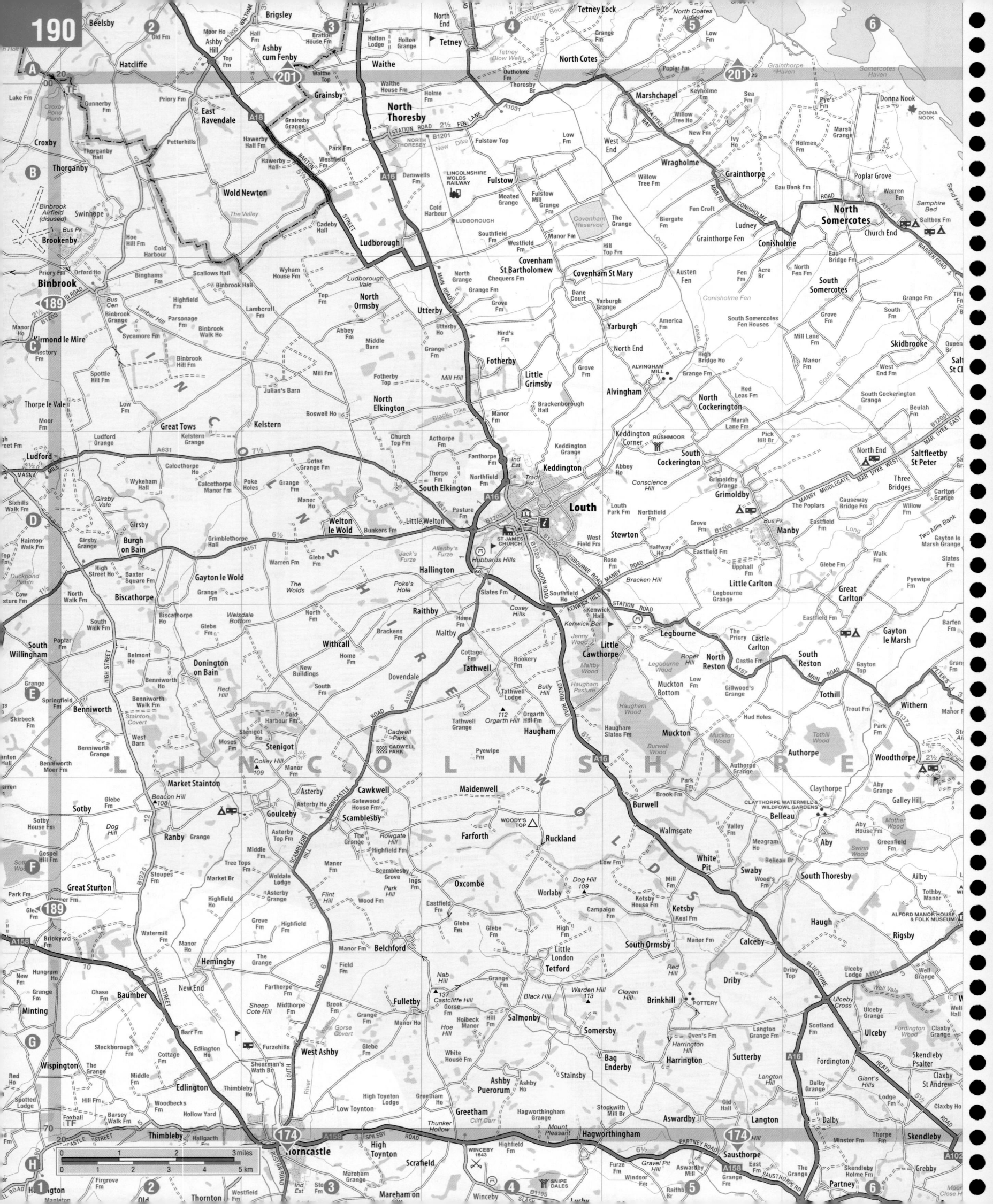
Beelsby
Brigsley
North End
Tetney Lock
North Coates Airfield
Ashby Hill
Ashby cum Fenby
Holton Le Clay
Tetney
Waithe
Hatcliffe
North Cotes
Grainsby
North Thoresby
Marshchapel
Donna Nook
East Ravendale
Croxby
Thorganby
Wold Newton
Fulstow
Wragholme
Grainthorpe
Poplar Grove
North Somercotes
Swinhope
Brookenby
Binbrook
Ludborough
Covenham St Bartholomew
Covenham St Mary
Conisholme
Ludney
Church End
North Ormsby
Utterby
South Somercotes
Kirmond le Mire
Yarburgh
Skidbrooke
Fotherby
Little Grimsby
Alvingham
North Elkington
North Cockerington
Thorpe le Vale
Kelstern
Great Tows
Keddington
South Cockerington
Ludford
Saltfleetby St Peter
South Elkington
Louth
Grimoldby
Welton le Wold
Burgh on Bain
Stewton
Manby
Gayton le Wold
Hallington
Little Carlton
Great Carlton
Biscathorpe
Raithby
Legbourne
Withcall
Maltby
Little Cawthorpe
Gayton le Marsh
South Willingham
Donington on Bain
Tathwell
North Reston
South Reston
Dovendale
Tothill
Withern
Benniworth
Haugham
Muckton
Stenigot
Authorpe
Woodthorpe
LINCOLNSHIRE
WOLDS
Market Stainton
Cawkwell
Maidenwell
Claythorpe
Sotby
Goulceby
Scamblesby
Burwell
Belleau
Ranby
Farforth
Ruckland
Aby
Walmsgate
White Pit
Swaby
South Thoresby
Great Sturton
Oxcombe
Worlaby
Ketsby
Haugh
Belchford
South Ormsby
Calceby
Rigsby
Hemingby
Tetford
Driby
Baumber
Fulletby
Brinkhill
Minting
Salmonby
Somersby
Ulceby
Wispington
West Ashby
Bag Enderby
Harrington
Sutterby
Edlington
Ashby Puerorum
Greetham
Aswardby
Langton
Thimbleby
Horncastle
High Toynton
Hagworthingham
Sausthorpe
Skendleby
Scrafield
Partney
Winceby
Mareham on
Old
Thornton
A16
A18
A153
A157
A158
A631
A1031
A1104
201
189
174
0 1 2 3 miles
0 1 2 3 4 5 km

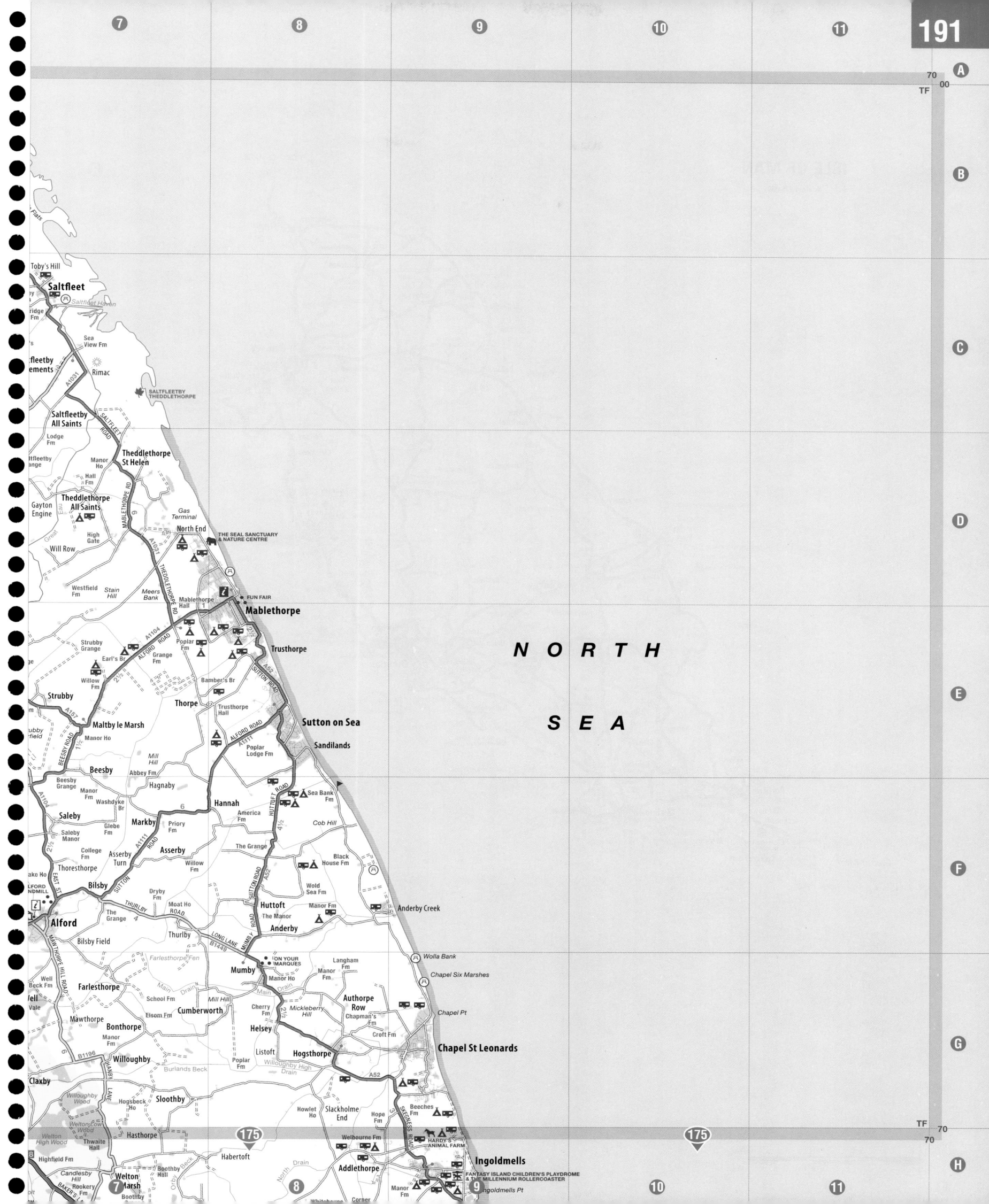

**NORTH**

**SEA**

Saltfleet
Toby's Hill
Saltfleet Haven
Sea View Fm
Rimac
fleetby ements
SALTFLEETBY THEDDLETHORPE
Saltfleetby All Saints
Lodge Fm
Theddlethorpe St Helen
Manor Ho
Hall
Gayton Engine
Theddlethorpe All Saints
Gas Terminal
North End
THE SEAL SANCTUARY & NATURE CENTRE
High Gate
Will Row
Westfield Fm
Stain Hill
Meers Bank
Mablethorpe Hall
FUN FAIR
**Mablethorpe**
Strubby Grange
Poplar Fm
Grange Fm
Trusthorpe
Earl's Br
Willow Fm
Bamber's Br
**Strubby**
**Thorpe**
Trusthorpe Hall
**Maltby le Marsh**
Manor Ho
**Sutton on Sea**
Mill Hill
Poplar Lodge Fm
Sandilands
**Beesby**
Abbey Fm
Beesby Grange
Manor Fm
Hagnaby
Washdyke Br
**Hannah**
Sea Bank Fm
**Saleby**
America Fm
Saleby Manor
Glebe Fm
**Markby**
Priory Fm
Cob Hill
College Fm
Asserby Turn
**Asserby**
Willow Fm
The Grange
Black House Fm
Thoresthorpe
**Bilsby**
Dryby Fm
Wold Sea Fm
 Anderby Creek
Moat Ho
Thurlby
**Huttoft**
Manor Fm
**Alford**
The Grange
Thurlby
**Anderby**
Bilsby Field
LONG LANE
B1449
Farlesthorpe Fen
ON YOUR MARQUES
Wolla Bank
Well Beck Fm
**Mumby**
Manor Ho
Langham Fm
Manor Fm
Chapel Six Marshes
**Farlesthorpe**
School Fm
Main Drain
Cherry Fm
Mickleberry Hill
**Authorpe Row**
Chapel Pt
Mawthorpe
Elsom Fm
Mill Hill
**Cumberworth**
Chapman's Fm
**Helsey**
Croft Fm
Manor Fm
**Bonthorpe**
Listoft
Poplar Fm
**Chapel St Leonards**
B1196
**Willoughby**
**Hogsthorpe**
Burlands Beck
Willoughby High Drain
A52
**Claxby**
Willoughby Wood
Hogsbeck Ho
**Sloothby**
Howlet Ho
Slackholme End
Hope Fm
Beeches Fm
Welton Low Welbo
Hasthorpe
175
Welbourne Fm
175
Welton High Wood
Thwaite Hall
Habertoft
HARDY'S ANIMAL FARM
**Ingoldmells**
Highfield Fm
Candlesby Hill Rookery
**Welton le Marsh**
Boothby Hall
**Addlethorpe**
FANTASY ISLAND CHILDREN'S PLAYDROME & THE MILLENNIUM ROLLERCOASTER
Bootlby
North Drain
Manor Fm
Ingoldmells Pt
BAKER'S
Whitehouse Corner

TF 00
TF 70
70

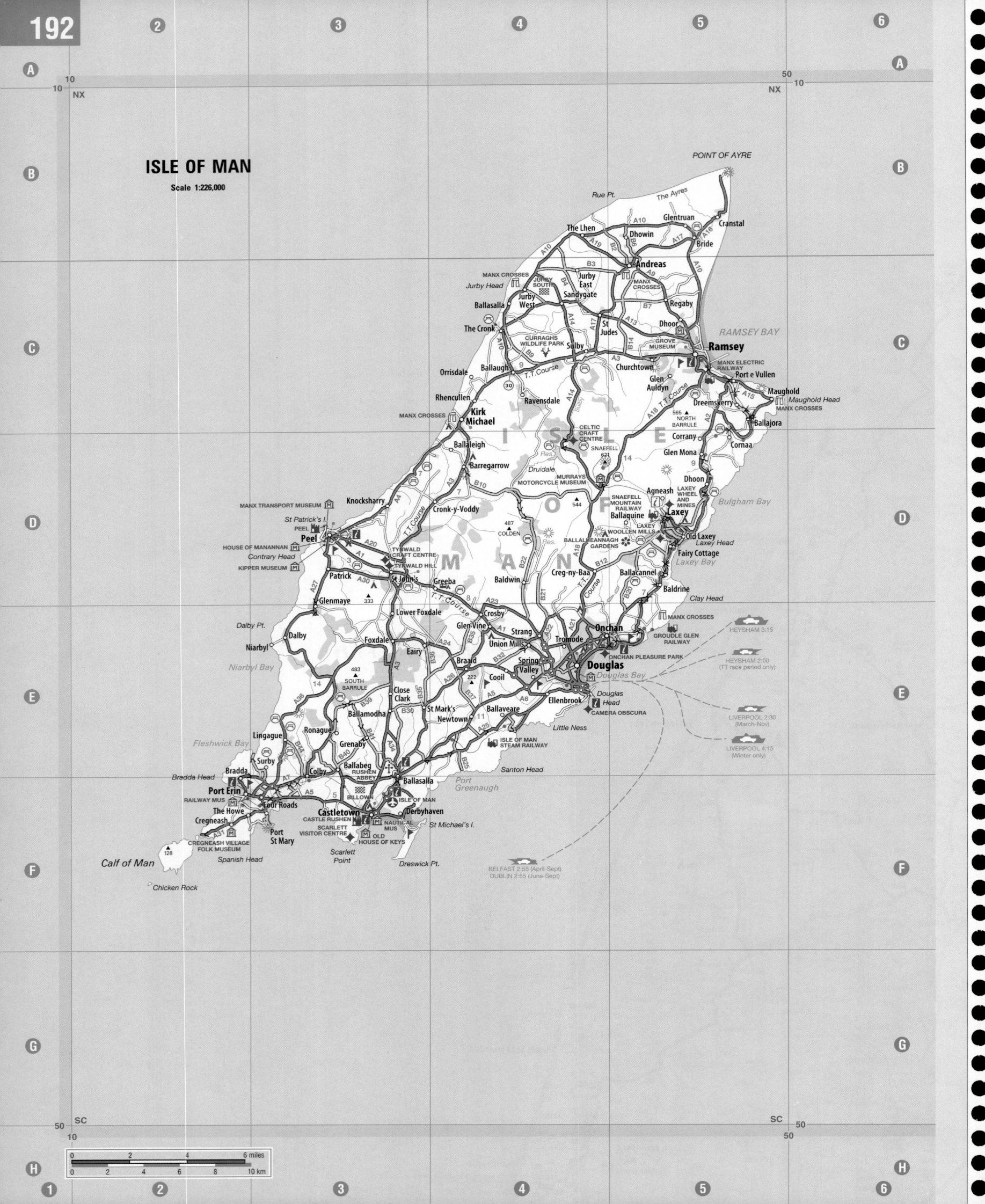

# ISLE OF MAN

Scale 1:226,000

POINT OF AYRE

Rue Pt.                    The Ayres

The Lhen          Glentruan     Cranstal

Dhowin        Bride

A10   A19   B2   B6   A17  A16

B3   A9

MANX CROSSES   Jurby   Andreas

Jurby Head      SOUTH   Jurby

Ballasalla   Jurby   East   MANX
West   Sandygate   CROSSES

The Cronk   B4   St   A13   Regaby   Dhoor   B7
Judes   A17

CURRAGHS   A14   A10   Churchtown   GROVE   RAMSEY BAY
WILDLIFE PARK   Sulby   A3   MUSEUM

Ballaugh   9   Ramsey

Orrisdale   T.T. Course   Glen   MANX ELECTRIC
Auldyn   RAILWAY

Rhencullen   Ravensdale   A14   A18   Dreemskerry   Port e Vullen
565   T.T. Course   A15   Maughold

MANX CROSSES   Kirk   CELTIC   NORTH   Maughold Head
Michael   CRAFT   BARRULE   MANX CROSSES
CENTRE   Corrany   Ballajora

Ballaleigh   SNAEFELL   E   Glen Mona   Cornaa
621   14   9

Barregarrow   Druidale   Dhoon

B10   MURRAYS   544   Agneash   LAXEY
MOTORCYCLE MUSEUM   SNAEFELL   WHEEL
MANX TRANSPORT MUSEUM   Knocksharry   MOUNTAIN   AND
RAILWAY   Ballaquine   MINES   Bulgham Bay

Cronk-y-Voddy   Laxey

St Patrick's I.   PEEL   487   LAXEY
HOUSE OF MANANNAN   COLDEN   BALLA MEANNAGH   WOOLLEN   Old Laxey
Contrary Head   Peel   GARDENS   MILLS   Laxey Head

KIPPER MUSEUM   A20   TYNWALD   B22   B12   Fairy Cottage
Patrick   CRAFT CENTRE   Creg-ny-Baa   Ballacannel   Laxey Bay
A1   TYNWALD HILL

Glenmaye   A30   St John's   Greeba   Baldwin   B21   Baldrine   Clay Head
333   A23   Course   B20

Dalby Pt.   Lower Foxdale   Crosby   T.T. Course

Niarbyl   Dalby   Glen Vine   A1   Onchan   GROUDLE GLEN
Strang   Tromode   RAILWAY   HEYSHAM 3:15

Niarbyl Bay   Foxdale   Union Mills   ONCHAN PLEASURE PARK   HEYSHAM 2:00
Eairy   A24   B32   Spring   Douglas   (TT race period only)
483   A3   Braaid   Valley

Close   Cooil   Douglas Bay
Clark   222   Ellenbrook   Douglas
SOUTH   A5   Head   LIVERPOOL 2:30
14   BARRULE   St Mark's   Ballaveare   CAMERA OBSCURA   (March-Nov)
Ballamodha   Newtown   11   A6

Lingague   B30   A25   Little Ness   LIVERPOOL 4:15
Ronague   ISLE OF MAN   (Winter only)
Fleshwick Bay   Grenaby   STEAM RAILWAY

Surby   Colby   Ballabeg   RUSHEN   Santon Head
Bradda   ABBEY   Port
Bradda Head   Ballasalla   Greenaugh
RAILWAY MUS   Port Erin   Four Roads   5   BILLOWN
The Howe   Castletown   ISLE OF MAN
Cregneash   128   CASTLE RUSHEN   Derbyhaven
Port   SCARLETT   NAUTICAL MUS   BELFAST 2:55 (April-Sept)
CREGNEASH VILLAGE   St Mary   VISITOR CENTRE   OLD   St Michael's I.   DUBLIN 2:55 (June-Sept)
FOLK MUSEUM   Spanish Head   Scarlett   HOUSE OF KEYS
Calf of Man   Point   Dreswick Pt.

Chicken Rock

10   NX                                        50   NX

I   S   L   E        O   F        M   A   N

RAMSEY BAY

0        2        4        6 miles
0    2    4    6    8    10 km

SC                                              SC

Blackpool International
Crusader Bank
North Hollow
Toy & Teddy Bear Mus
St Annes
Salter's Bank
Lytham St Anne's
Fairhaven
Ansdell
Hey Houses
Lytham
Lytham Windmill Museum
Church Scar
Fairhaven Lake
Westby
Peel
Great Marton Moss
Higher Ballam
Lower Ballam
Moss Side
Birks Fm
Saltcotes
Warton
Warton Bank
River Ribble
Hesketh Sands
Long Bank
Banks Sands
George's Brow
Great Bank
Ribble Marshes
Banks Marsh
Foulnaze
Marshside Sands
Crossens Marsh
Horse Bank
Angry Brow
Southport Sands
Marshside
Fiddler's Ferry
Banks
Crossens
Botanic Gardens Museum
Eco Visitor Centre
Churchtown
Meols Hall
Southport Model Railway Village
Southport
High Park
Blowick
Birkdale
Birkdale Sands
Brown Edge
Pool Hey
Carr Cross
Snape Green
Hillside
Birkdale Hills
Shirdley Hill
Scarisbrick
Bescar
Drummersdale
Ainsdale-on-Sea
Ainsdale
Ainsdale Hills
Ainsdale Sands
Woodvale
LANCS
Halsall Moss
Pinfold
Hurlston Green
Hurlston
Ainsdale Sand Dunes
Halsall
Primrose Hill
Formby Hills
Mad Wharf
Barton
Downholland Moss
Haskayne
Ormskirk
Freshfield
Formby
Formby Pt
Downholland Cross
Clieves Hills
Little Altcar
Great Altcar
Aughton Park
Cabin Hill
Taylor's Bank
Aughton
Town Green
North End
Lady Green
Carr Houses
Hightown
Ince Blundell
Lydiate
Formby Bank
Homer Green
Lunt
Maghull
Crosby Channel
Little Crosby
Sefton
Melling Mount
Melling
Thornton
Netherton
Blundellsands
Brighton le Sands
Great Crosby
Aintree
Waddicar
Westvale
Crosby
Waterloo

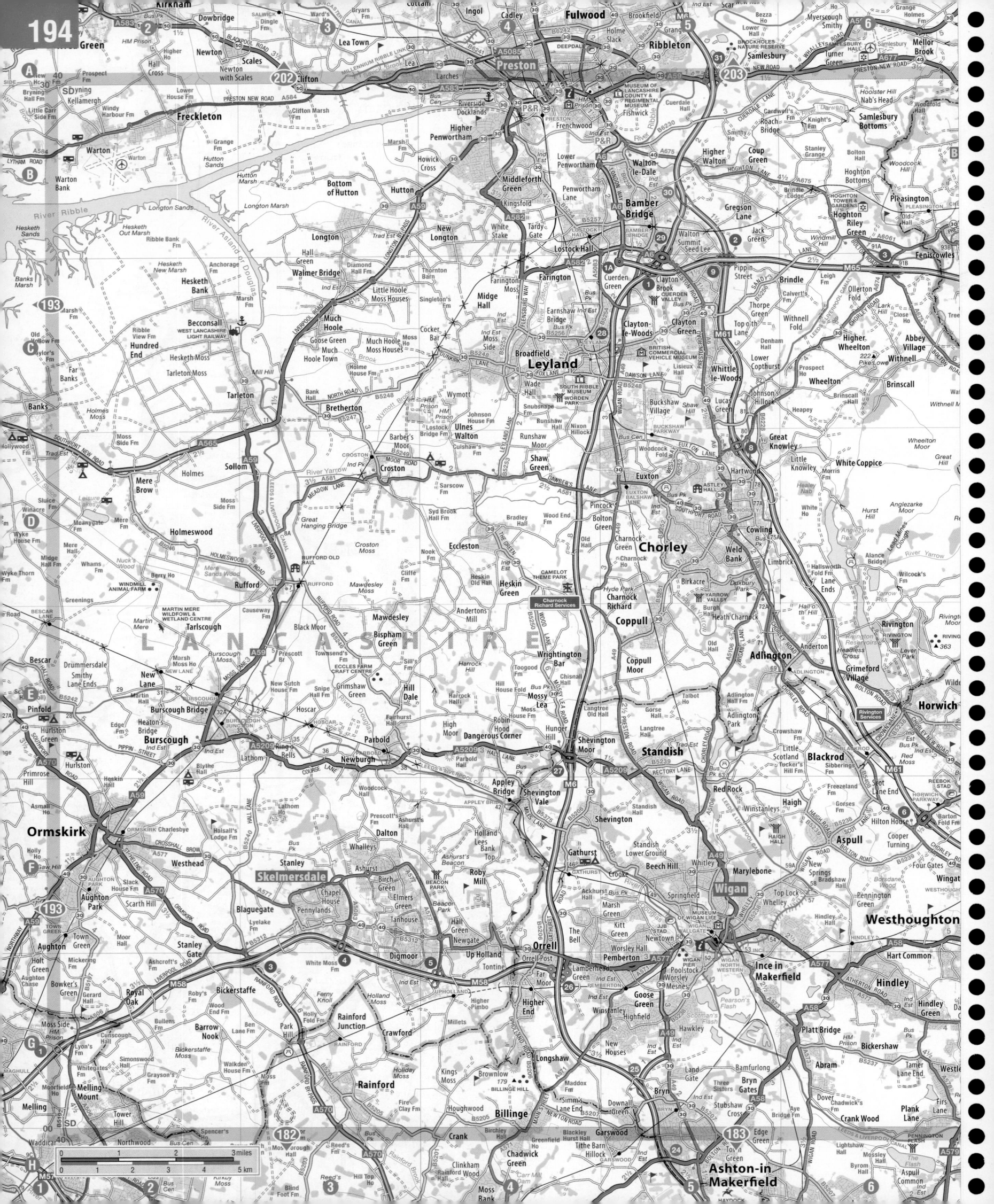

Kirkham
Dowbridge
Newton
Scales
Newton with Scales
Clifton
Freckleton
Warton
Warton Bank
Lea Town
Ingol
Cadley
Fulwood
Brookfield
Ribbleton
Samlesbury
Mellor Brook
Preston
Riverside Docklands
Higher Penwortham
Frenchwood
Fishwick
Samlesbury Bottoms
Walton-le-Dale
Higher Walton
Coup Green
Hoghton Bottoms
Pleasington
Bamber Bridge
Gregson Lane
Hoghton
Feniscowles
Hutton
Bottom of Hutton
Longton
New Longton
Middleforth Green
Kingsfold
Lostock Hall
Farington
Walmer Bridge
Hesketh Bank
Much Hoole
Becconsall
Hundred End
Tarleton
Leyland
Broadfield
Clayton-le-Woods
Clayton Green
Whittle-le-Woods
Wheelton
Brinscall
Abbey Village
Withnell
Higher Wheelton
Bretherton
Ulnes Walton
Banks
Mere Brow
Sollom
Croston
Euxton
Chorley
Hartwood
Great Knowley
Cowling
White Coppice
Holmeswood
Eccleston
Rufford
Heskin Green
Charnock Richard
Coppull
Adlington
Rivington
Horwich
Tarlscough
Mawdesley
Bispham Green
LANCASHIRE
Wrightington Bar
Burscough Bridge
Burscough
New Lane
Hill Dale
Parbold
Newburgh
Dangerous Corner
Shevington Moor
Standish
Blackrod
Appley Bridge
Shevington Vale
Shevington
Ormskirk
Westhead
Dalton
Skelmersdale
Gathurst
Beech Hill
Whitley
Marylebone
Wigan
Aspull
Westhoughton
Aughton Park
Aughton
Blaguegate
Digmoor
Up Holland
Orrell
Pemberton
Ince in Makerfield
Hindley
Hart Common
Bickerstaffe
Royal Oak
Rainford Junction
Crawford
Goose Green
Platt Bridge
Abram
Melling Mount
Melling
Rainford
Billinge
Bryn
Garswood
Ashton-in-Makerfield
Crank
Chadwick Green
Charnock Richard Services
Rivington Services

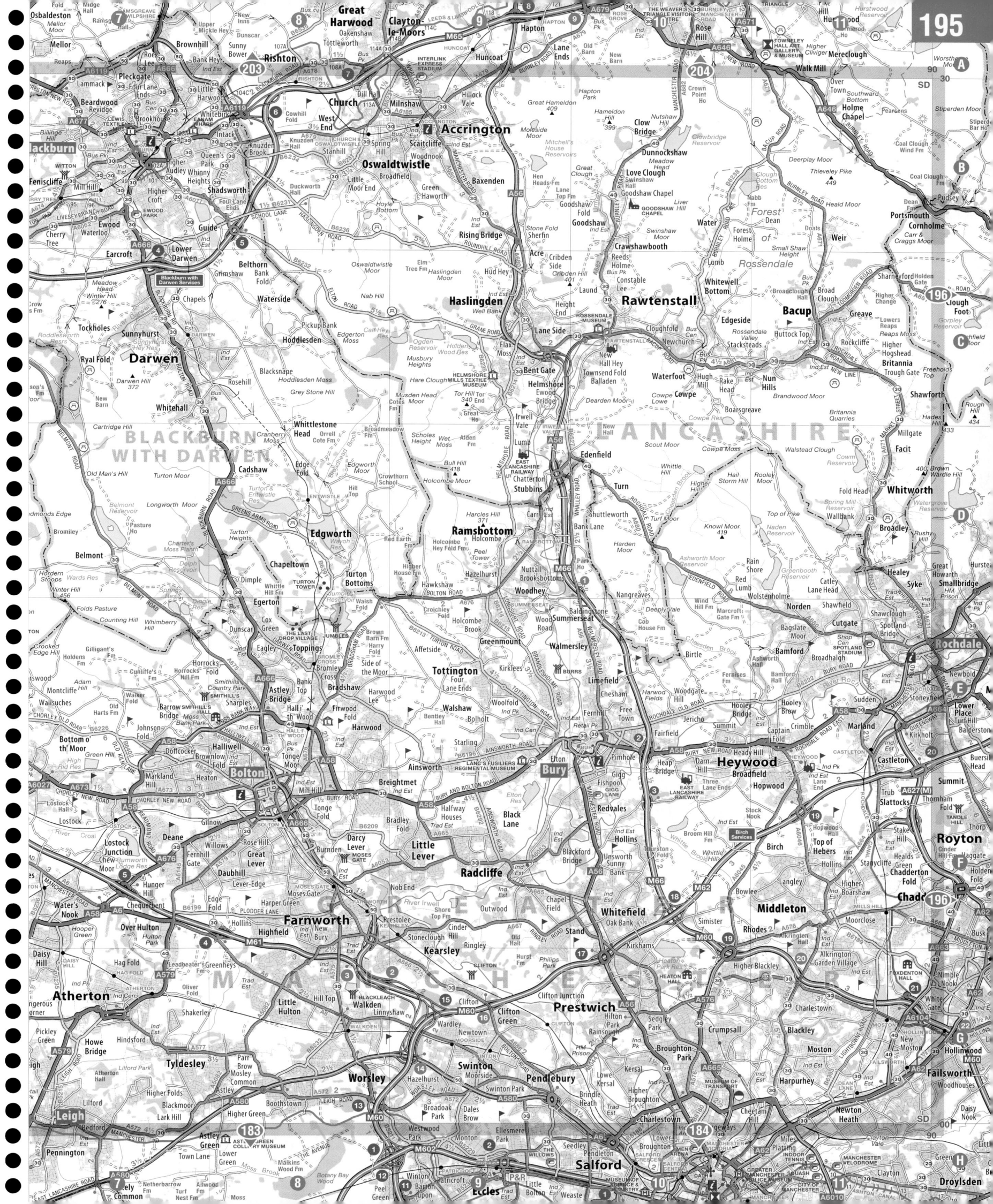
Great Harwood
Clayton-le-Moors
Rishton
Hapton
Huncoat
Rose Hill
Osbaldeston
Mellor
Brownhill
Pleckgate
Beardwood
Revidge
Blackburn
Feniscliffe
Mill Hill
Ewood
Cherry Tree
Waterloo
Earcroft
Lower Darwen
Guide
Shadsworth
Higher Croft
Whinny Heights
Queen's Park
Intack
Knuzden Brook
Church
West End
Accrington
Oswaldtwistle
Milnshaw
Scaitcliffe
Broadfield
Baxenden
Rising Bridge
Haslingden
Rawtenstall
Bacup
Dunnockshaw
Clow Bridge
Love Clough
Goodshaw Chapel
Goodshaw
Crawshawbooth
Water
Weir
Walk Mill
Holme Chapel
Portsmouth
Cornholme
Forest of Rossendale
Whitewell Bottom
Edgeside
Stacksteads
Newchurch
Waterfoot
Cowpe
Nun Hills
Shawforth
Britannia
Whitworth
Facit
Healey
Broadley
Lane Side
Bent Gate
Helmshore
Ewood Bridge
Edenfield
Turn
Stubbins
Chatterton
Ramsbottom
Holcombe
Shuttleworth
Bank Lane
Summerseat
Nuttall
Brooksbottoms
Woodhey
Hazelhurst
Walmersley
Limefield
Chesham
Fernhill
Pimhole
Heap Bridge
Heywood
Bamford
Norden
Cutgate
Rochdale
Castleton
Marland
Sudden
Royton
Summit
Middleton
Rhodes
Birch
Slattocks
Alkrington Garden Village
Chadderton
Failsworth
Hollinwood
Moston
Harpurhey
Blackley
Crumpsall
Clayton
Droylsden
Newton Heath
Darwen
Sunnyhurst
Tockholes
Belthorn
Waterside
Hoddlesden
Pickup Bank
Whitehall
Rosehill
Whittlestone Head
Cadshaw
Edgworth
Chapeltown
Turton Bottoms
Egerton
Dimple
Belmont
Cox Green
Eagley
Toppings
Bromley Cross
Bradshaw
Harwood
Astley Bridge
Sharples
Tottington
Walshaw
Woolfold
Greenmount
Bury
Elton
Ainsworth
Breightmet
Bolton
Halliwell
Heaton
Markland Hill
Doffcocker
Deane
Lostock
Lostock Junction
Daubhill
Great Lever
Darcy Lever
Little Lever
Radcliffe
Redvales
Hollins
Unsworth
Whitefield
Stand
Besses o' th' Barn
Simister
Prestwich
Kearsley
Farnworth
Highfield
Over Hulton
Little Hulton
Walkden
Atherton
Tyldesley
Leigh
Astley
Worsley
Swinton
Pendlebury
Clifton
Clifton Green
Kersal
Broughton Park
Salford
Eccles
Pennington
Westhoughton
GREATER MANCHESTER
LANCASHIRE
BLACKBURN WITH DARWEN
M65
M66
M62
M60
M61
M602
A56
A58
A666
A676
A580
A6
A62
A627(M)

Heptonstall Moor
Hebden Bridge
Heptonstall
Colden
Blackshaw Head
Charlestown
Mytholm
Mytholmroyd
Midgley
Pecket Well
Chiserley
Wainstalls
Booth
Luddenden
Luddenden Foot
Ogden
Causeway Foot
Queensbury
Illingworth
Ovenden
Pellon
Halifax
Clayton
Great Horton
Buttershaw
Shelf
Northowram
Hipperholme
Lightcliffe
Brighouse
Rastrick
Southowram
Elland
Stainland
Greetland
West Vale
Sowerby Bridge
Sowerby
Triangle
Ripponden
Rishworth
Barkisland
Cragg Vale
Todmorden
Walsden
Cornholme
Portsmouth
Lydgate
Eastwood
Mankinholes
Langfield Common
Shawforth
Whitworth
Facit
Wardle
Littleborough
Smallbridge
Rochdale
Milnrow
Newhey
Castleton
Royton
Shaw
Chadderton
Oldham
Failsworth
Hollinwood
Denshaw
Delph
Diggle
Dobcross
Uppermill
Greenfield
Mossley
Stalybridge
Droylsden
Marsden
Slaithwaite
Golcar
Meltham
Honley
Netherthong
Holmfirth
Holme
Linthwaite
Lindley
Huddersfield
Wessenden Moor
Saddleworth Moor
Black Hill
Crowden
PEAK DISTRICT NATIONAL PARK
GREATER MANCHESTER
M62
A58
A62
A635
A640
A672
A646
A629
195
204
205
184
185
0 1 2 3 miles
0 1 2 3 4 5 km

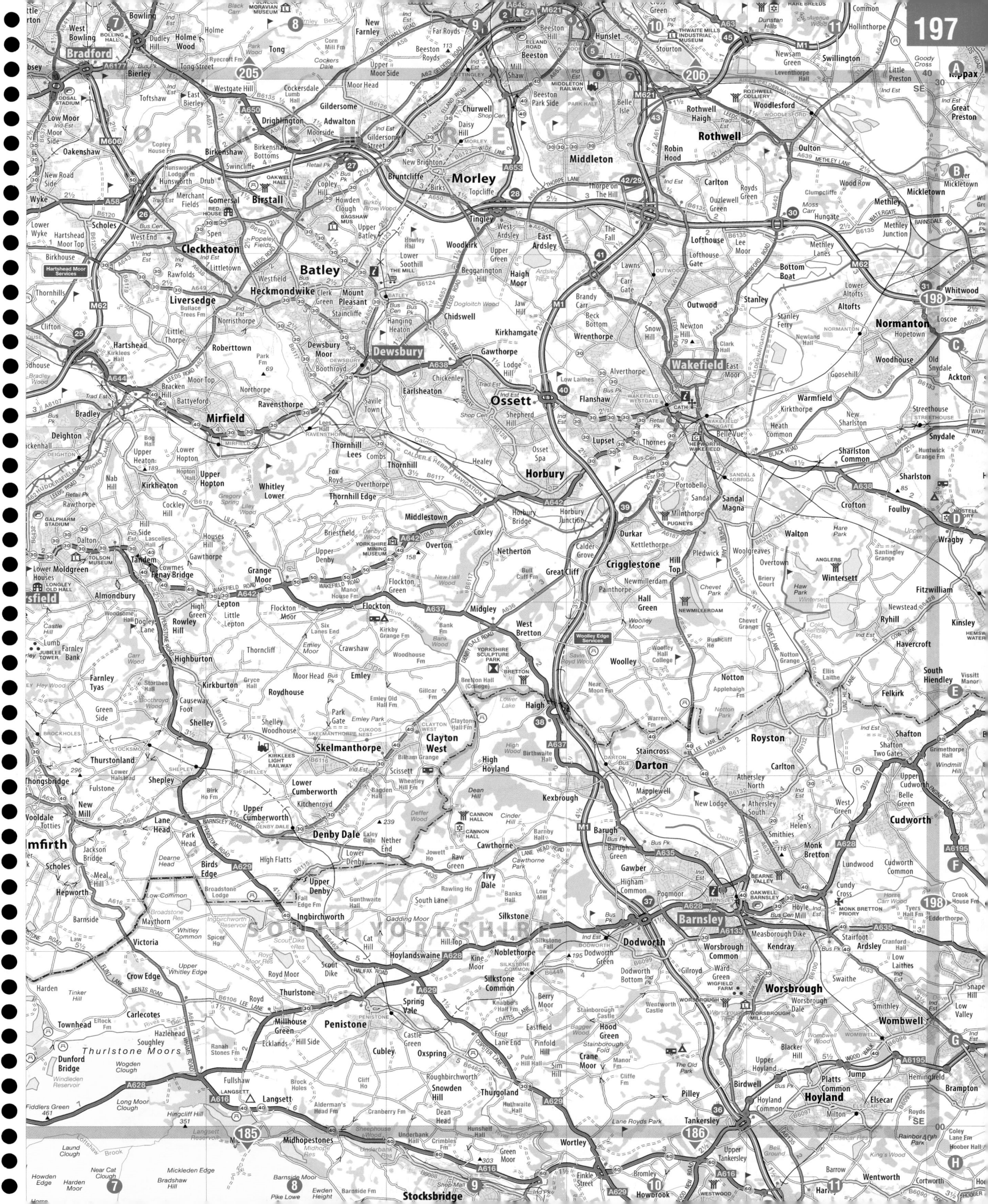

Bradford
Bowling
West Bowling
Tong
Farnley
Beeston
Hunslet
Stourton
Swillington
Kippax
Bierley
Tong Street
Westgate Hill
Cockersdale
Drighlington
Gildersome
Adwalton
Churwell
Morley
Middleton
Rothwell
Robin Hood
Oulton
Woodlesford
Great Preston
Birkenshaw
Birstall
Gomersal
Cleckheaton
Batley
Heckmondwike
Liversedge
Dewsbury
Ossett
Wakefield
Outwood
Stanley
Altofts
Normanton
Whitwood
Mirfield
Ravensthorpe
Earlsheaton
Horbury
Flanshaw
Lupset
Thornes
Sandal Magna
Crofton
Walton
Wragby
Netherton
Middlestown
Crigglestone
Durkar
Kirkburton
Emley
Skelmanthorpe
Clayton West
Darton
Royston
Cudworth
Shafton
Denby Dale
Barugh
Barnsley
Dodworth
Worsbrough
Wombwell
Hoyland
Silkstone
Penistone
Thurlstone
Holmfirth
Hepworth
Shepley
Langsett
Tankersley
Wortley
Stocksbridge
Thurlstone Moors
YORKSHIRE
SOUTH YORKSHIRE
M1
M62
M621
M606
A62
A58
A638
A642
A636
A637
A629
A628
A635
A616
A61
A6195
205
206
185
186
198

Micklefield
Roach Grange Fm
Packfield Bar
Steeton Hall
South Milford
Milford Lodge
Fryston Grange
Hagg Bush Fm
Owlet Hall
Thorpe Willoughby
Selby Abbey
East Common
Newlands Fm
Goody Cross
Prestor
Kippax
Ledston Luck
Ledston Park
Peckfield Lodge
206
Lumby
Hambleton
Brayton
207
Great Preston
Roman Ridge
Park House Fm
Ledsham
Monk Fryston
Monk Fryston Lodge
Brecks Fm
Hagg Ho
Gateforth Hall
Hambleton Hough
Burton Hall
Barlow Lodge
Commonside Fm
Ledston Hall
Ledston
Newfield Fm
Fairburn
Hillam
Bower's House Fm
Gateforth
Top House Fm
Burn
Henwick Hall
Barlow
Beckfield Fm
Burton Salmon
Burton Common Fm
Gateforth Wood
Primrose Hill
Burn Airfield
Allerton Bywater
Fairburn Ings
Northfield Fm
Chestercourt Hall Fm
Common Ho
Lower Mickletown
Mickletown
New Fryston
Poole
Yorkshire Garden World
Lodge Fm
Willow Grove Fm
Wheldale
Water Fryston
Park Ho
Birkin
West Haddlesey
Chapel Haddlesey
Chestercourt House Fm
Methley
Methley Junction
Airedale
Fryston Park
Brotherton
Byram Hall
Byram
Byram Fm
Eastfield House Fm
Quosquo Hall
Camblesforth
Castleford
Red Hill
Beal
NORTH
Sutton
Roall Manor Fm
Temple Manor
Temple Hirst
Kellington
Ferrybridge
Kellingley
Eggborough Power Sta
West Bank Ho
Hirst Courtney
Carlton
Cutsyke
Glass Houghton
Freeport Castleford
Hut Green
Whitwood
Thornfield Ho
Eggborough
Hensall
Coates Hall Fm
197
New Town
Knottingley
Whitley Bridge
Little Heck
Gowdall
Normanton
Hopetown
Loscoe
Pontefract
Ferrybridge Services
Stubbs Br
Kellington Common
Snaith
North Featherstone
Pontefract Monkhill
Pontefract Castle Museum
Farpark Fm
High Eggborough
Hollins Fm
Great Heck
Hill Fm
Gowdall Broach Fm
West Cowick
Woodhouse
Old Snydale
Ackton
Strawberry Hill
Park Lodge Fm
Pontefract
Grove Town
Hodgewood Fm
Cridling Stubbs
Whitley
Heck Hall Fm
Chequerfield
Carleton
Spring Lodge
Aire & Calder Navigation
Streethouse
Featherstone
Darrington
Scrombeck Fm
Whitley Thorpe
Balne Moor Cross Roads
Balne Moor
Pollington
Animal Fm
Snydale
YORKSHIRE
Norr Hall Fm
Huntwick Grange Fm
Purston Jaglin
Stapleton
Womersley
Stocking Green Fm
Balne
Pollington Br
Park Fm
West Hardwick
Ackworth Park Fm
Womersley Park
West End
Pollington Grange
Southfield Reservoir
Sharlston
East Hardwick
Stapleton Park
Castle Fm
Chapel Hill
Ash Tree Fm
Cross Hill
High Ackworth
Dawland Fm
Cherry Tree Fm
Balne Lodge
Topham
Eskholme
Plaice Hills Fm
Foulby
Nostell Priory
Hessle
Ackworth Grange
Little Smeaton
South End
Wentbridge
Walden Stubbs
Sykehouse
Wragby
Low Ackworth
Burnhill Ho
Stubbs Grange
Santingley Grange
Brakenhill
Kirk Smeaton
Wentbank Ho
Went Fm
Fenwick
Mawson Green
Moor Ho
Thorpe Audlin
Fenwick Hall
Went Br
Moat Hill Fm
West End
Ackworth Moor Top
Middle Field
Barnsdale Bar Services
Cliff Hill
Norton Priory
Norton Common Fm
Smallhedge Fm
Fitzwilliam
Lanes Fm
Thorpe Manor
Rogerthorpe Manor
Fenwick Grange
Newstead
Badsworth
Norton
Ladythorpe Fm
Jett Hall
Moseley Grange
Westfield Ho
Fosterhouses
Ryhill
Kinsley
Walton Wood Ho
Campsall
Moss
New House Fm
Hemsworth Water Park
Campsmount Home Fm
Askern
Havercroft
Elm Leys Fm
Royd Moor
Upton Beacon
Upton
Hawkhouse Green
Far Bank
Hemsworth
Wrangbrook
Instoneville
SOUTH
South Hiendley
Vissitt Manor
North Elmsall
Hollins Fm
Haywood
Braithwaite
Rushy Moor
Sutton
Skelbrooke
Robin Hood's Well
Burghwallis
Shirley Wood
Thorpe Grange
Wrancarr Ho
Trumfleet
Kirk Bramwith
South Bramwith
Stainforth
Shafton
Brierley
Moorthorpe
Burghwallis Grange
Owston
YORKSHIRE
Shafton Two Gates
Grimethorpe Hall
Windmill Hill
South Kirkby
South Elmsall
Hampole
Skellow
Carcroft
Owston Wood
Thorpe in Balne
Brierley Manor
Moorhouse
Ling Ho
Upper Cudworth
Tilts Hills
Sixteen Acre Plantn
Tilts
Barnby Dun
Belle Green
Moorhouse Common
Hampole Grange
Red Ho
Burntwood Hall
Hampole Wood
Adwick le Street
Shaftholme
Cudworth
Grimethorpe
Howell Wood
Hooton Pagnell Wood
Hall Villa
Almholme
Park Hill Grange
Warren Hill
West Haigh Wood
Howell Ho
Wink Ho
Frickley Hall
Lound Hill
Woodlands
Toll Bar
Dunsville
Houghton Lodge
Clayton
Hooton Pagnell
Kirk Sandall
Cudworth Common
Great Houghton
Bilham Grange
Pickburn
Brodsworth
Adwick Grange
Arksey
Wyndthorpe Hall
Little Park
Highfields
New Village
Green Lane Fm
Crook House Fm
Bilham House Fm
Brodsworth Hall
Long Sandall
Edenthorpe
Sandhill
Thurnscoe East
Scawthorpe
West Moor Fm
Edderthorpe
Little Houghton
Thurnscoe
Sunnyfields
Bentley
Wheatley Park
Armthorpe
Cranford Hall
Hickleton
Marr
Middlecliffe
Billingley
Scawsby
Wheatley Hills
West Moor Park
Low Laithes
Millhouses
Goldthorpe
Bella Wood
Marr Grange
Scawsby
Cusworth
Bentley Rise
Wheatley
Nutwell
Snape Hill
Darfield
Cusworth Hall Museum
St Leger Horse Park
Intake
Low Fm
Smithley
Low Valley
Highgate
Barnburgh
Melton Wood
Burntwood Grange
Cusworth Park
Doncaster
Sandall Beat Wood
Wombwell
Broomhill
Bolton upon Dearne
HM Prison Doncaster
Museum & Art Gal
Doncaster Racecourse
Cantley Common
Old Moor
Harlington
Toecroft Fm
Newton
Hyde Park
Doncaster Common
Cantley
Hexthorpe
Keepmoat Stadium
Aeroventure South Yorkshire Aircraft Mus
Branton
Barnburgh Grange
Sprotbrough
Scabba Wood
Hemingfield
Adwick upon Dearne
High Melton
Bessacarr
Brockholes Farm
Brampton
Dearne Br
Balby
Cadeby
Warmsworth
Lakeside Village
Twelve Months Carr
Elsecar
Windhill
West Melton
Wath upon Dearne
Mexborough
Royds Moor
Coley Lane Fm
Newhill
186
Conisbrough
187
Rossington
The Warren
Hay Field
Old Denaby
Denaby Main
Conanby
Alverley Grange
Engine House Fm
Stump Cross
Loversall
Conisbrough Ivanhoe
Swinton
Conisbrough
New Edlington
Wentworth
Cortworth
Hoober
Piccadilly
Warren House Fm
Rossington
0 1 2 3 miles
0 1 2 3 4 5 km
NORTH YORKSHIRE
SOUTH YORKSHIRE

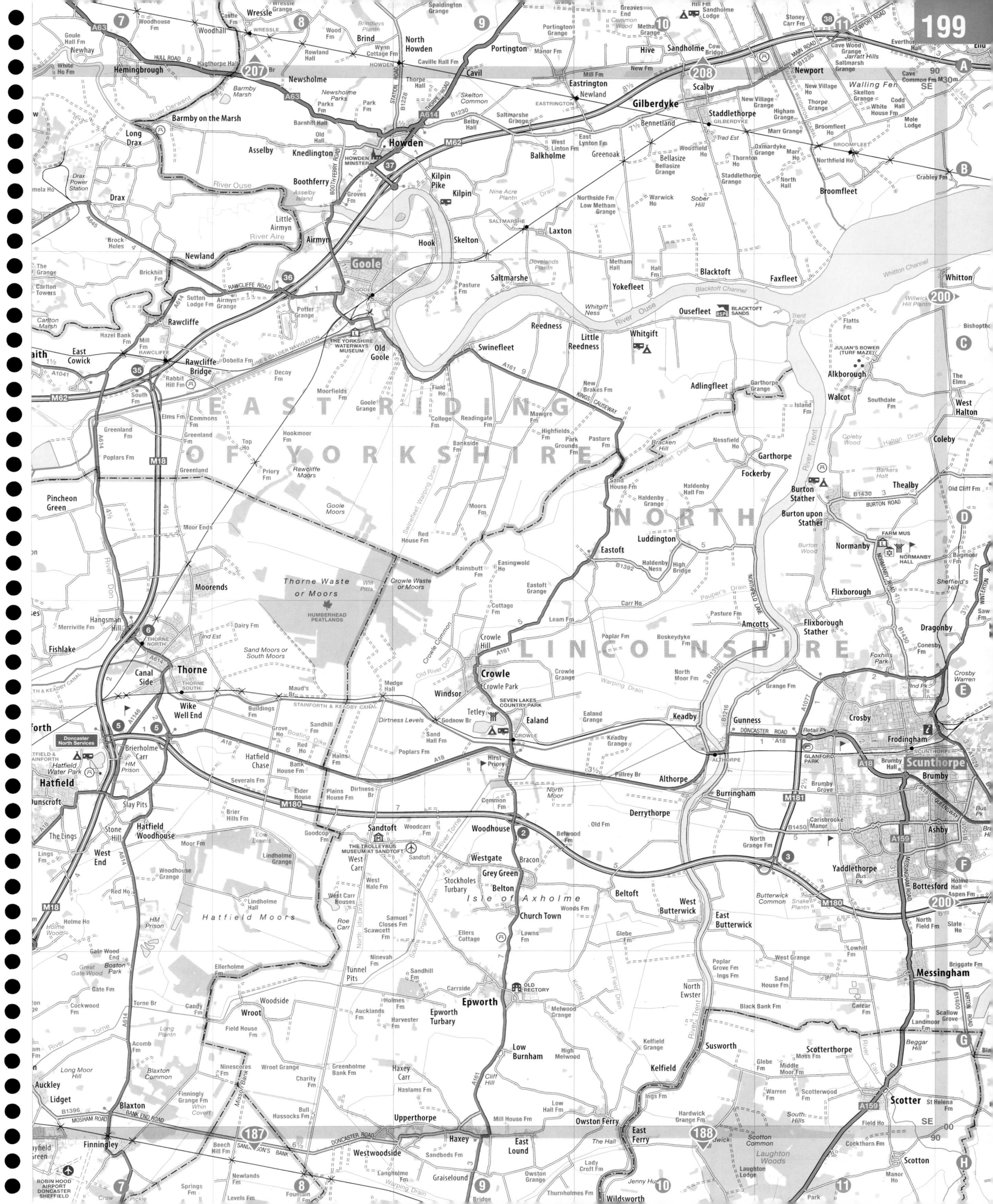
EAST RIDING OF YORKSHIRE
NORTH LINCOLNSHIRE
Hemingbrough
Newhay
Goule Hall Fm
Woodhall
Wressle
Brind
North Howden
Portington
Hive
Sandholme
Newport
Eastrington
Newland
Gilberdyke
Scalby
Staddlethorpe
Bennetland
Newsholme
Cavil
Barmby on the Marsh
Long Drax
Asselby
Knedlington
Howden
Kilpin Pike
Kilpin
Balkholme
Greenoak
Bellasize
Broomfleet
Drax
Boothferry
Little Airmyn
Airmyn
Hook
Skelton
Laxton
Newland
Goole
Saltmarshe
Yokefleet
Blacktoft
Faxfleet
Whitton
Rawcliffe
Rawcliffe Bridge
East Cowick
Old Goole
Swinefleet
Reedness
Little Reedness
Whitgift
Ousefleet
Adlingfleet
Alkborough
Walcot
West Halton
Coleby
Garthorpe
Fockerby
Thealby
Burton Stather
Burton upon Stather
Pincheon Green
Luddington
Eastoft
Normanby
Flixborough
Moorends
Thorne Waste or Moors
Crowle Waste or Moors
HUMBERHEAD PEATLANDS
Amcotts
Flixborough Stather
Dragonby
Fishlake
Thorne
Canal Side
Crowle
Crowle Park
Windsor
Wike Well End
Tetley
Ealand
Keadby
Gunness
Crosby
Frodingham
Scunthorpe
Brumby
Hatfield
Hatfield Chase
Althorpe
Burringham
Dunscroft
Slay Pits
Derrythorpe
Ashby
The Lings
Stone Hill
Hatfield Woodhouse
West End
Sandtoft
Woodhouse
Westgate
Bracon
Grey Green
Belton
Isle of Axholme
Beltoft
West Butterwick
East Butterwick
Yaddlethorpe
Bottesford
Church Town
Hatfield Moors
Tunnel Pits
Wroot
Epworth
Epworth Turbary
North Ewster
Messingham
Low Burnham
Kelfield
Susworth
Scotterthorpe
Auckley
Lidget
Blaxton
Upperthorpe
Haxey
East Lound
Owston Ferry
East Ferry
Scotter
Finningley
Westwoodside
Graiselound
Scotton
Wildsworth
ROBIN HOOD AIRPORT DONCASTER SHEFFIELD
Doncaster North Services
M62
M18
M180
M181
A63
A614
A161
A18
207
208
200
187
188

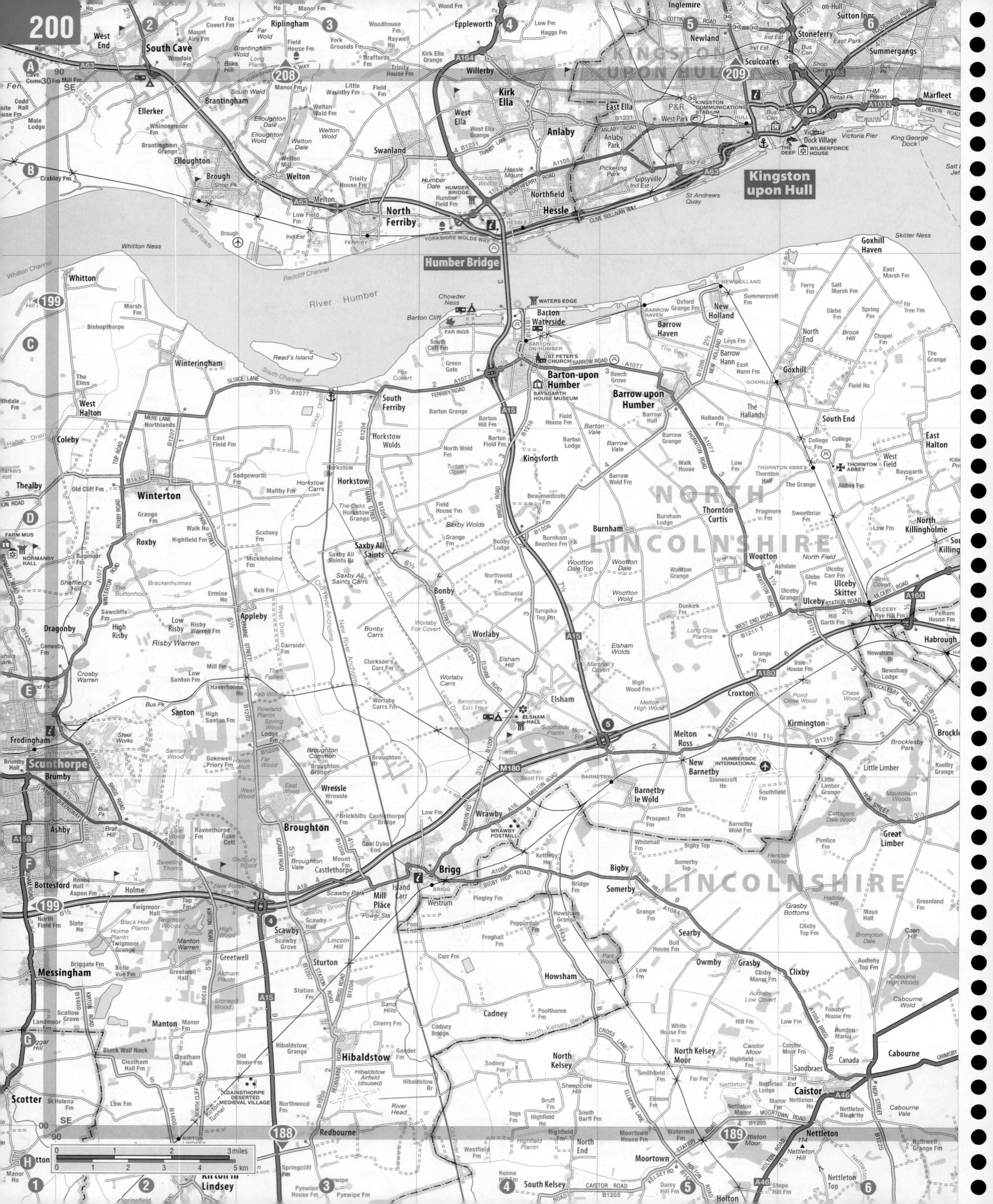
Kingston upon Hull
Humber Bridge
River Humber
NORTH LINCOLNSHIRE
LINCOLNSHIRE
Scunthorpe
Barton-upon Humber
Barrow upon Humber
Brigg
Caistor
Hessle
North Ferriby
South Cave
Winterton
Broughton
Hibaldstow
Messingham
Kirton in Lindsey
Humberside International
Elsham
Ulceby
Goxhill
New Holland
Immingham
Kirk Ella
Anlaby
Willerby
Brough
Welton
Swanland
Thornton Curtis
Wootton
Kirmington
Melton Ross
Barnetby le Wold
Wrawby
Bigby
Somerby
Searby
Grasby
Clixby
Howsham
Cadney
North Kelsey
Nettleton
South Kelsey
Moortown
Redbourne
Scawby
Bottesford
Ashby
Frodingham
Appleby
Roxby
Santon
Worlaby
Bonby
Saxby All Saints
Horkstow
South Ferriby
Winteringham
Whitton
West Halton
Coleby
Thealby
Dragonby
Croxton
Great Limber
Cabourne
Habrough
East Halton
North Killingholme
Kingsforth
Burnham
Barrow Haven
Barton Waterside
3 miles
5 km

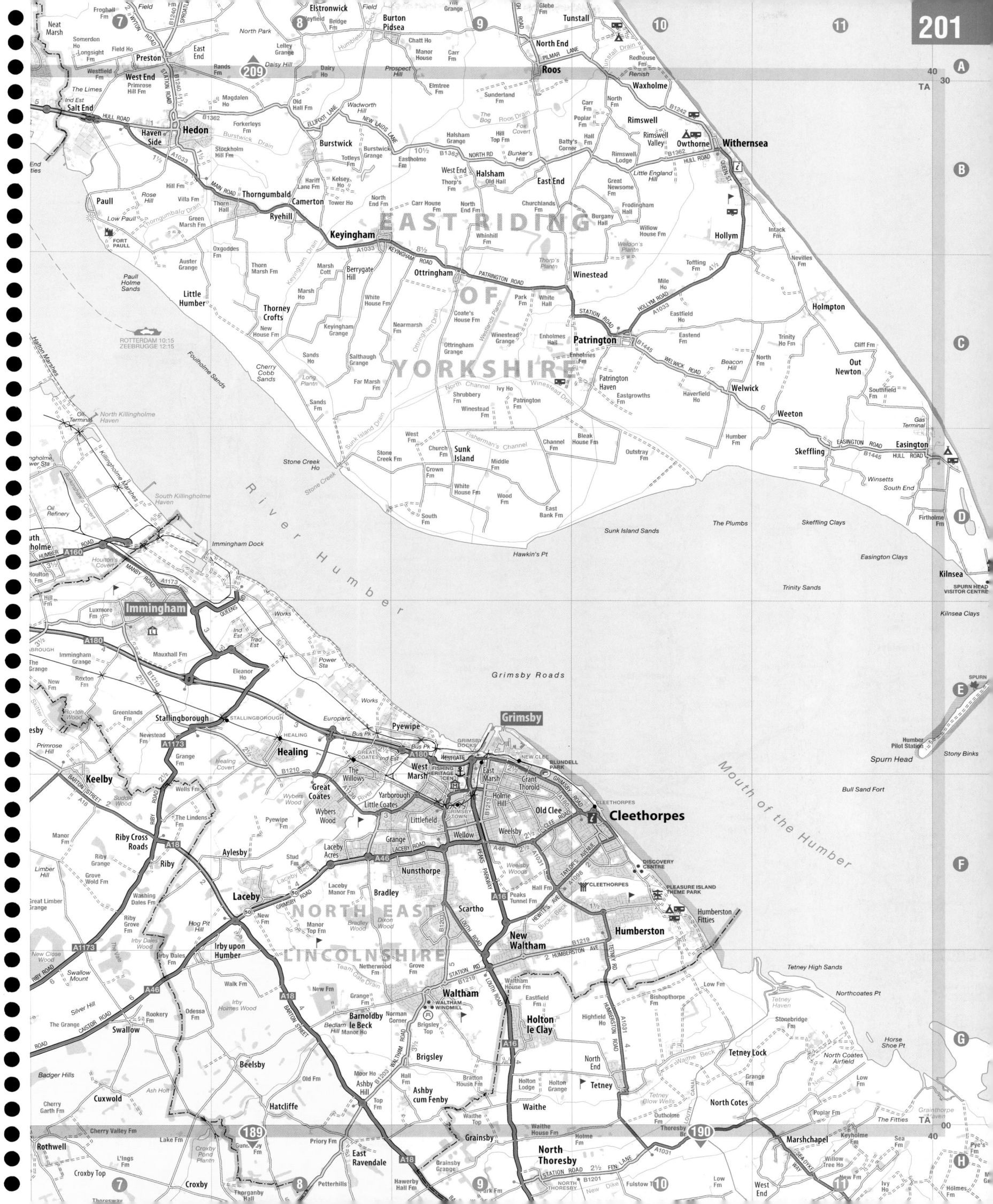

EAST RIDING OF YORKSHIRE
NORTH EAST LINCOLNSHIRE
River Humber
Mouth of the Humber
Grimsby Roads
Hedon
Haven Side
Salt End
Preston
West End
Elstronwick
Burton Pidsea
Tunstall
North End
Roos
Waxholme
Rimswell
Owthorne
Withernsea
Burstwick
Halsham
East End
Thorngumbald
Camerton
Ryehill
Paull
Keyingham
Ottringham
Winestead
Hollym
Patrington
Patrington Haven
Holmpton
Out Newton
Welwick
Weeton
Skeffling
Easington
Kilnsea
Spurn Head
Sunk Island
Little Humber
Thorney Crofts
Sunk Island Sands
Trinity Sands
Immingham
Immingham Dock
Stallingborough
Healing
Keelby
Riby
Riby Cross Roads
Aylesby
Laceby
Great Coates
Pyewipe
Grimsby
West Marsh
East Marsh
Grant Thorold
Cleethorpes
Old Clee
Weelsby
Littlefield
Wellow
Nunsthorpe
Bradley
Scartho
Humberston
Humberston Fitties
New Waltham
Waltham
Holton le Clay
Barnoldby le Beck
Brigsley
Ashby cum Fenby
Irby upon Humber
Swallow
Beelsby
Cuxwold
Hatcliffe
Waithe
Tetney
Tetney Lock
North Cotes
Marshchapel
Grainsby
North Thoresby
East Ravendale
Rothwell
Croxby
Croxby Top
Tetney High Sands
ROTTERDAM 10:15
ZEEBRUGGE 12:15
A1033
A180
A160
A1173
A18
A46
A16
A1031
B1362
B1445
B1242
B1210
B1219
B1203
209
189
190
7
8
9
10
11
A
B
C
D
E
F
G
H
TA
40
30
00

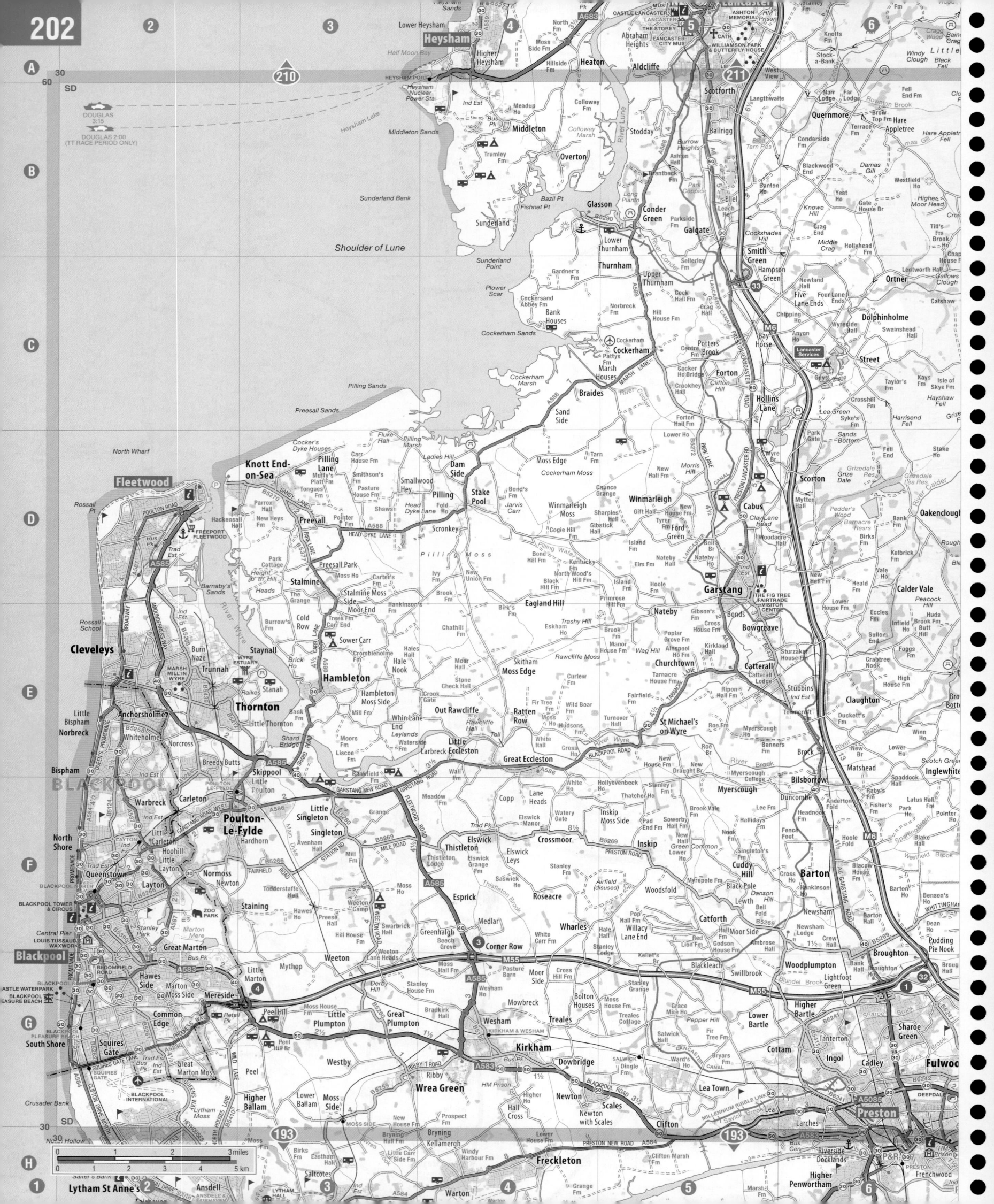
Heysham
Lower Heysham
Higher Heysham
Heysham Port
Heysham Nuclear Power Sta
Half Moon Bay
Heaton
Aldcliffe
Lancaster
Scotforth
Middleton
Middleton Sands
Heysham Lake
DOUGLAS 3:15
DOUGLAS 2:00 (TT RACE PERIOD ONLY)
Overton
Stodday
Bailrigg
Quernmore
Sunderland Bank
Sunderland
Glasson
Conder Green
Galgate
Shoulder of Lune
Thurnham
Upper Thurnham
Smith Green
Hampson Green
Ortner
Cockersand Abbey Fm
Bank Houses
Cockerham Sands
Cockerham
Dolphinholme
Bay Horse
Lancaster Services
Street
Forton
Pilling Sands
Braides
Hollins Lane
Preesall Sands
Sand Side
North Wharf
Knott End-on-Sea
Pilling Lane
Dam Side
Moss Edge
Cockerham Moss
Fleetwood
Pilling
Stake Pool
Winmarleigh
Scorton
Oakenclough
Preesall
Scronkey
Cabus
Pilling Moss
Stalmine
Preesall Park
Garstang
Calder Vale
Eagland Hill
Nateby
Cleveleys
Staynall
Hambleton
Bowgreave
Churchtown
Catterall
Thornton
Out Rawcliffe
Ratten Row
Claughton
Anchorsholme
Little Bispham
Norbreck
Little Thornton
Skitham
Moss Edge
St Michael's on Wyre
Bispham
Skippool
Little Eccleston
Great Eccleston
Brock
Inglewhite
BLACKPOOL
Carleton
Poulton-Le-Fylde
Myerscough
Bilsborrow
Warbreck
Little Singleton
Singleton
North Shore
Thistleton
Elswick
Crossmoor
Inskip
Cuddy Hill
Barton
Queenstown
Layton
Normoss
Esprick
Roseacre
Woodsfold
Staining
Catforth
Greenhalgh
Medlar
Wharles
Great Marton
Weeton
Corner Row
Broughton
Blackpool
Hawes Side
Little Marton
Mythop
Blackleach
Swillbrook
Woodplumpton
Mereside
Wesham
Mowbreck
Treales
Higher Bartle
Lower Bartle
Common Edge
Little Plumpton
Great Plumpton
Kirkham
Sharoe Green
Squires Gate
South Shore
Westby
Dowbridge
Ingol
Cottam
Cadley
Fulwood
Wrea Green
Ribby
Lea Town
Peel
Higher Ballam
Lower Ballam
Moss Side
Newton
Scales
Preston
Clifton
Larches
Bryning
Kellamergh
Freckleton
Lytham St Anne's
Ansdell
Saltcotes
Warton
Higher Penwortham
Frenchwood
Riverside Docklands
Crusader Bank
BLACKPOOL INTERNATIONAL
0 1 2 3 miles
0 1 2 3 4 5 km

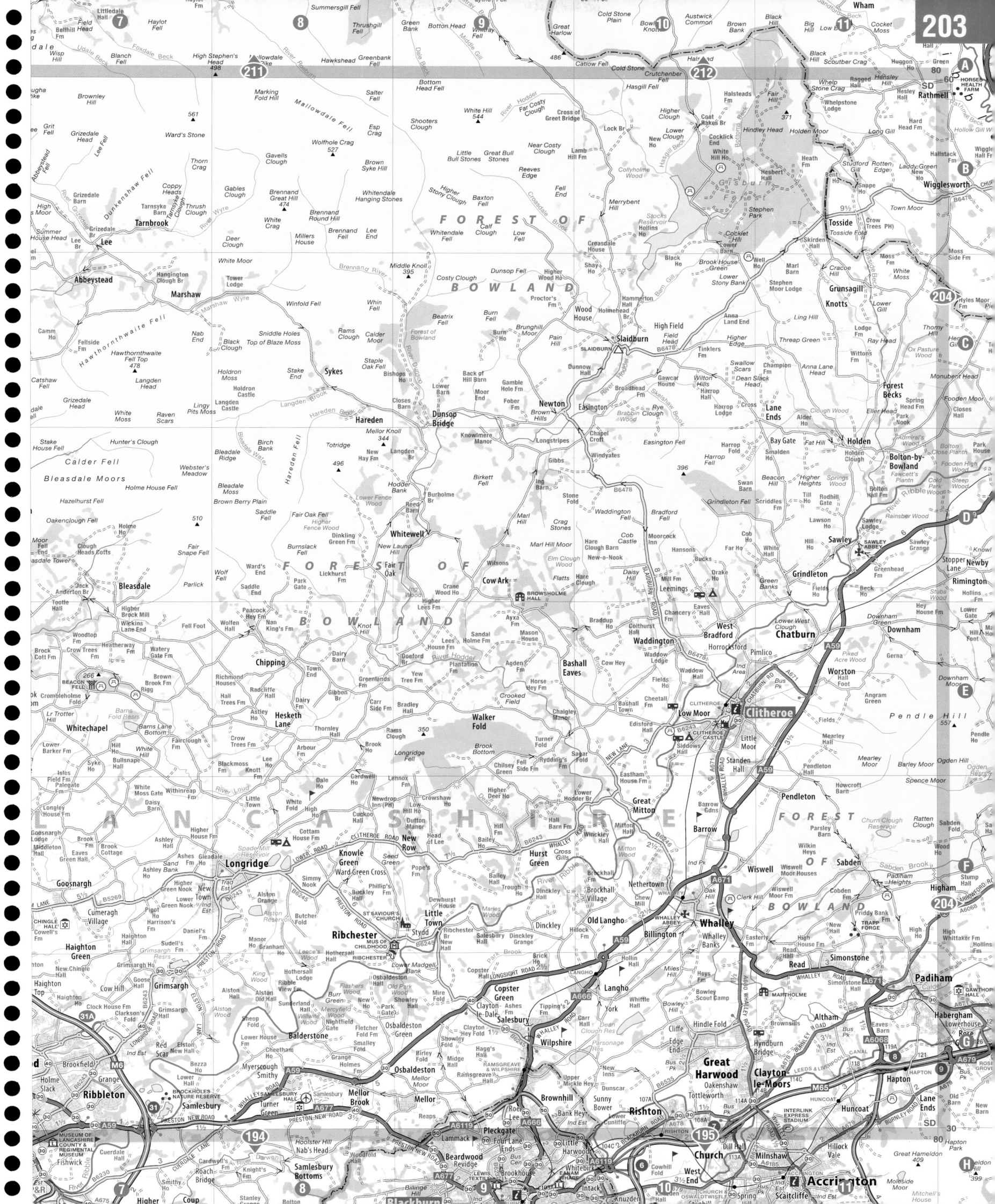
211
212
194
195
204
FOREST OF BOWLAND
LANCASHIRE
FOREST OF BOWLAND
Abbeystead
Marshaw
Tarnbrook
Lee
Sykes
Hareden
Dunsop Bridge
Newton
Slaidburn
Easington
Whitewell
Cow Ark
Chipping
Bleasdale
Hesketh Lane
Whitechapel
Longridge
Goosnargh
Ribchester
Grimsargh
Ribbleton
Samlesbury
Mellor Brook
Mellor
Osbaldeston
Balderstone
Salesbury
Wilpshire
Langho
Billington
Whalley
Clitheroe
Chatburn
West Bradford
Waddington
Grindleton
Sawley
Holden
Bolton-by-Bowland
Tosside
Wigglesworth
Rathmell
Grunsagill
Knotts
Forest Becks
Pendleton
Sabden
Read
Simonstone
Padiham
Altham
Clayton-le-Moors
Great Harwood
Rishton
Church
Accrington
Huncoat
Hapton
Great Mitton
Barrow
Wiswell
Higham
Whitebirk
Brownhill
Copster Green
Clayton-le-Dale
Bashall Eaves
Stydd
Little Town
Knowle Green
New Row
Hurst Green
Gisburn Forest
Pendle Hill
Stocks Reservoir

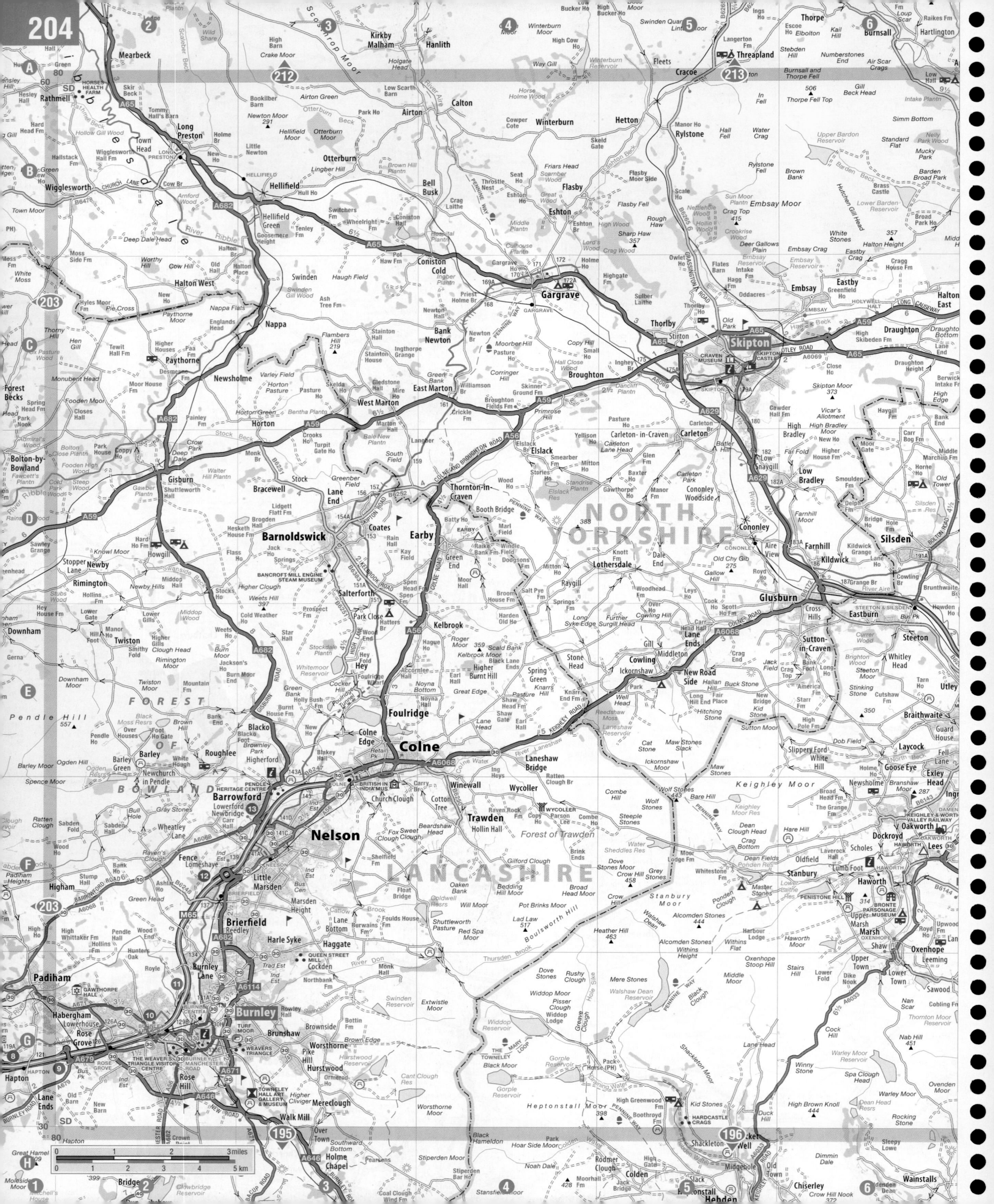

Mearbeck
Rathmell
Long Preston
Wigglesworth
Hellifield
Otterburn
Airton
Calton
Kirkby Malham
Hanlith
Winterburn
Hetton
Cracoe
Threapland
Rylstone
Flasby
Eshton
Gargrave
Coniston Cold
Bell Busk
Halton West
Nappa
Paythorne
Newsholme
Horton
West Marton
East Marton
Bank Newton
Thorlby
Stirton
Skipton
Embsay
Eastby
Draughton
Broughton
Elslack
Carleton
Carleton-in-Craven
Low Snaygill
Low Bradley
Cononley
Farnhill
Kildwick
Silsden
Gisburn
Bracewell
Barnoldswick
Lane End
Coates
Earby
Thornton-in-Craven
Booth Bridge
NORTH YORKSHIRE
Lothersdale
Glusburn
Cross Hills
Eastburn
Steeton
Sutton-in-Craven
Cowling
Middleton
Lane Ends
New Road Side
Kelbrook
Salterforth
Howgill
Rimington
Newby
Downham
Twiston
Hey
Foulridge
Colne
Laneshaw Bridge
Winewall
Wycoller
Trawden
Forest of Trawden
Blacko
Roughlee
Barley
Barrowford
Nelson
Pendle Hill
FOREST OF BOWLAND
LANCASHIRE
Fence
Higham
Little Marsden
Brierfield
Harle Syke
Haggate
Padiham
Habergham
Burnley
Burnley Lane
Brunshaw
Worsthorne
Hurstwood
Rose Hill
Hapton
Lane Ends
Walk Mill
Mereclough
Holme Chapel
Keighley Moor
Laycock
Goose Eye
Exley Head
Oakworth
Haworth
Oldfield
Stanbury
Oxenhope
Leeming
Colden
Heptonstall Moor
Utley
Braithwaite
A65
A59
A682
A56
A629
A6068
A646
A671
A6114
A679
M65
212
213
203
195
196

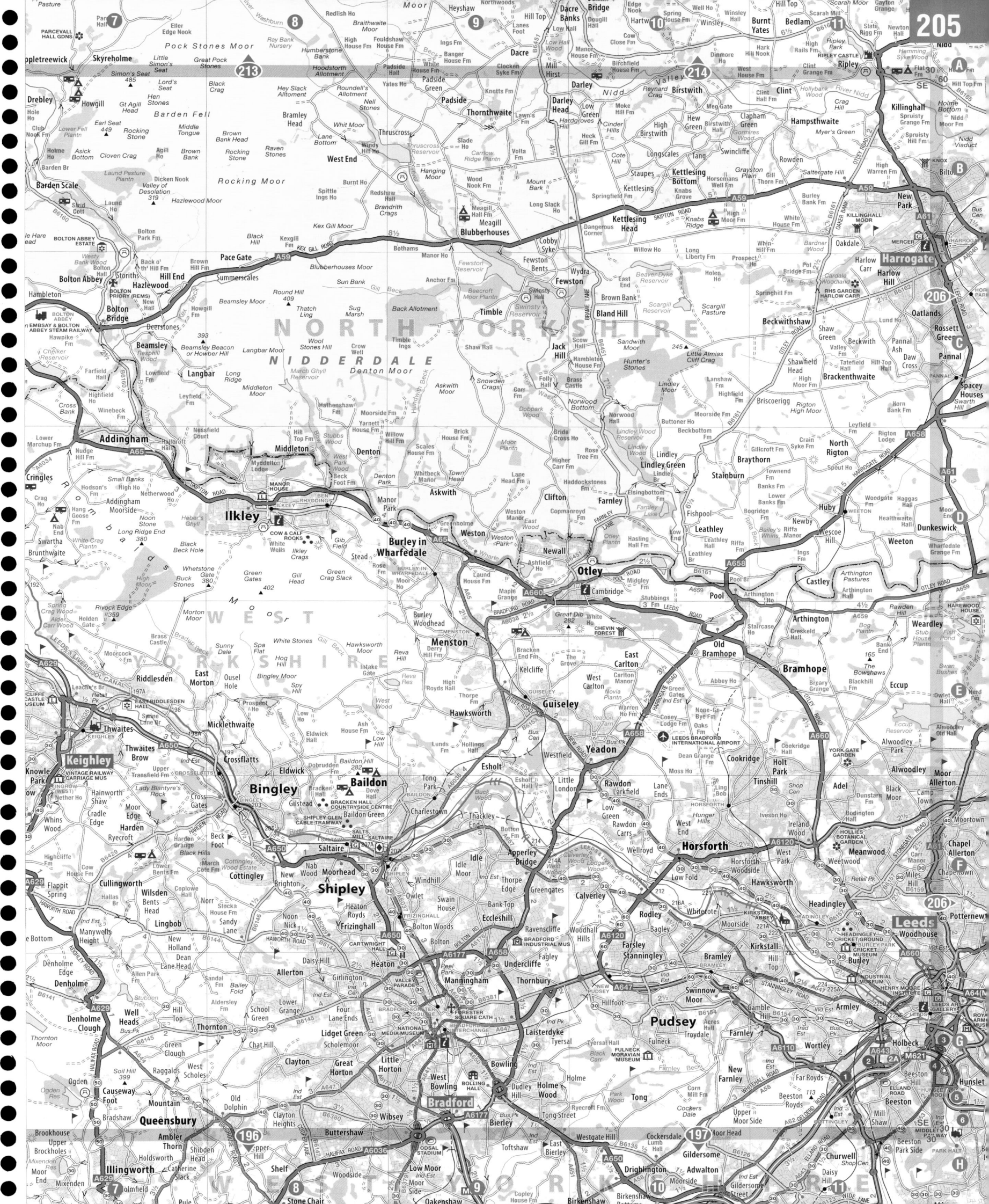
NORTH YORKSHIRE
NIDDERDALE
WEST YORKSHIRE
Harrogate
Leeds
Bradford
Keighley
Ilkley
Otley
Shipley
Bingley
Baildon
Guiseley
Yeadon
Horsforth
Pudsey
Queensbury
Burley in Wharfedale
Addingham
Menston
Pool
Bramhope
Ripley
Killinghall
Pannal
Harewood House
Bolton Abbey
Barden Fell
Rocking Moor
Denton Moor
Rombalds Moor
Blubberhouses
Kettlesing Head
Beckwithshaw
Pateley Bridge
Darley
Birstwith
Hampsthwaite
Burnt Yates
Bedlam
Farnley
Clifton
Stainburn
Huby
Weeton
Dunkeswick
Arthington
Castley
Cookridge
Tinshill
Adel
Alwoodley
Moor Allerton
Chapel Allerton
Headingley
Kirkstall
Bramley
Armley
Holbeck
Beeston
Hunslet
Farsley
Rodley
Calverley
Idle
Eccleshill
Thornbury
Heaton
Allerton
Thornton
Clayton
Wibsey
Bierley
Tong
Gildersome
Churwell
Drighlington
Illingworth
Cottingley
Cullingworth
Wilsden
Denholme
Harden
Riddlesden
Thwaites Brow
Crossflatts
Eldwick
Esholt
Rawdon
Apperley Bridge
Saltaire
Windhill
Lingbob
Mickelthwaite
Leeds Bradford International Airport
Skipton Road
Harrogate Road
Otley Road
Leeds & Liverpool Canal
213
214
206
196
197

Knaresborough
Harrogate
Wetherby
Leeds
Tadcaster
Garforth
Boston Spa
Collingham
Spofforth
Bramham
Sherburn in Elmet
Linton-on-Ouse
Newton on Ouse
Beningbrough
Green Hammerton
Kirk Hammerton
Marston Moor
Tockwith
Long Marston
Hutton Wandesley
Bilton in Ainsty
Rufforth
Askham Richard
Bilbrough
Healaugh
Wighill
Thorp Arch
Newton Kyme
Clifford
Aberford
Barwick in Elmet
Scholes
Thorner
Shadwell
Scarcroft
Bardsey
East Keswick
Harewood
Weardley
Wike
Sicklinghall
Kirkby Overblow
Pannal
Spacey Houses
Follifoot
Starbeck
Scotton
Scriven
Farnham
Ferrensby
Arkendale
Coneythorpe
Flaxby
Goldsborough
Allerton Mauleverer
Hopperton
Whixley
Cattal
Hunsingore
Walshford
Little Ribston
Cowthorpe
North Deighton
Kirk Deighton
Ingmanthorpe
Bickerton
Linton
Netherby
Dunkeswick
Weeton
Alwoodley
Moor Allerton
Chapel Allerton
Roundhay
Seacroft
Whitkirk
Halton
Colton
Manston
Swillington
Kippax
Micklefield
Ledsham
Ledston
Great Preston
Saxton
Barkston
Towton
Stutton
Ulleskelf
Church Fenton
Little Fenton
Biggin
Kirkby Wharfe
Bolton Percy
Oxton
Colton
Catterton
Hessay
Nun Monkton
Moor Monkton
Whixley
Tancred
Thorpe Underwood
Great Ouseburn
Little Ouseburn
Brearton
Killinghall
Bilton
High Harrogate
Woodlands
Oatlands
Rossett Green
Harlow Hill
Potternewton
Harehills
Sheepscar
Burmantofts
Osmondthorpe
Hunslet
Beeston
Rothwell
Oulton
Fairburn
Monk Fryston
Hillam
South Milford
Lumby
Newthorpe
Potterton
Kiddal Lane End
Sandhills
Wellington Hill
Gledhow
Lidgett Park
Park Villas
Moortown
Chapeltown
A1(M)
A59
A61
A64
A58
A659
A661
A658
A63
A642
A656
A162
A168
A1246
B1224
B1223
B1222
M1
M621
A6120
A64(M)
214
215
205
197
198
WEST YORKSHIRE
N O
0 1 2 3 miles
0 1 2 3 4 5 km

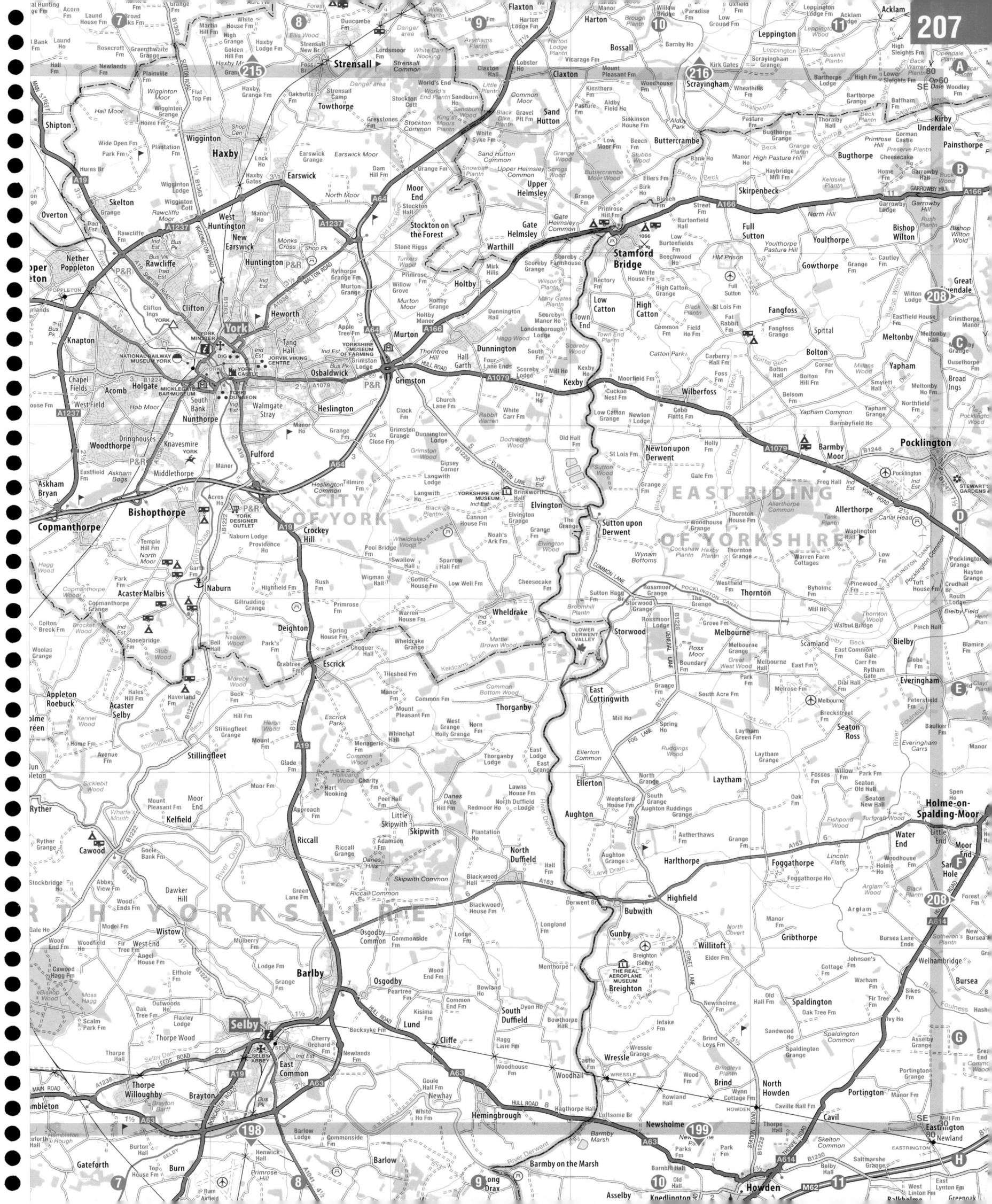
Strensall
Flaxton
Harton
Bossall
Claxton
Leppington
Acklam
Scrayingham
Haxby
Wigginton
Earswick
Shipton
Skelton
Overton
Moor End
Stockton on the Forest
Sand Hutton
Upper Helmsley
Gate Helmsley
Warthill
Buttercrambe
Skirpenbeck
Bugthorpe
Kirby Underdale
Painsthorpe
Full Sutton
Youlthorpe
Bishop Wilton
Stamford Bridge
Low Catton
High Catton
Gowthorpe
Fangfoss
Meltonby
Yapham
Bolton
Wilberfoss
Kexby
Pocklington
Barmby Moor
Allerthorpe
West Huntington
New Earswick
Huntington
Rawcliffe
Nether Poppleton
Clifton
Heworth
York
Holtby
Murton
Dunnington
Grimston
Osbaldwick
Knapton
Acomb
Holgate
Heslington
Woodthorpe
Dringhouses
Fulford
Askham Bryan
Bishopthorpe
Copmanthorpe
Crockey Hill
Elvington
Sutton upon Derwent
Newton upon Derwent
CITY OF YORK
EAST RIDING OF YORKSHIRE
Naburn
Acaster Malbis
Deighton
Wheldrake
Storwood
Melbourne
Thornton
Escrick
East Cottingwith
Thorganby
Bielby
Everingham
Seaton Ross
Appleton Roebuck
Acaster Selby
Stillingfleet
Kelfield
Ellerton
Laytham
Aughton
Holme-on-Spalding-Moor
Cawood
Riccall
Skipwith
North Duffield
Harlthorpe
Foggathorpe
Bubwith
Highfield
Wistow
Gunby
Willitoft
Gribthorpe
Barlby
Osgodby
Breighton
Spaldington
Selby
Lund
Cliffe
South Duffield
Wressle
Thorpe Willoughby
Brayton
Hemingbrough
North Howden
Portington
Cavil
Newsholme
Eastrington
Gateforth
Burn
Barlow
Barmby on the Marsh
Long Drax
Howden
Asselby
NORTH YORKSHIRE
A19
A64
A166
A1079
A1237
A163
A63
A614
B1363
B1228
B1222
B1223

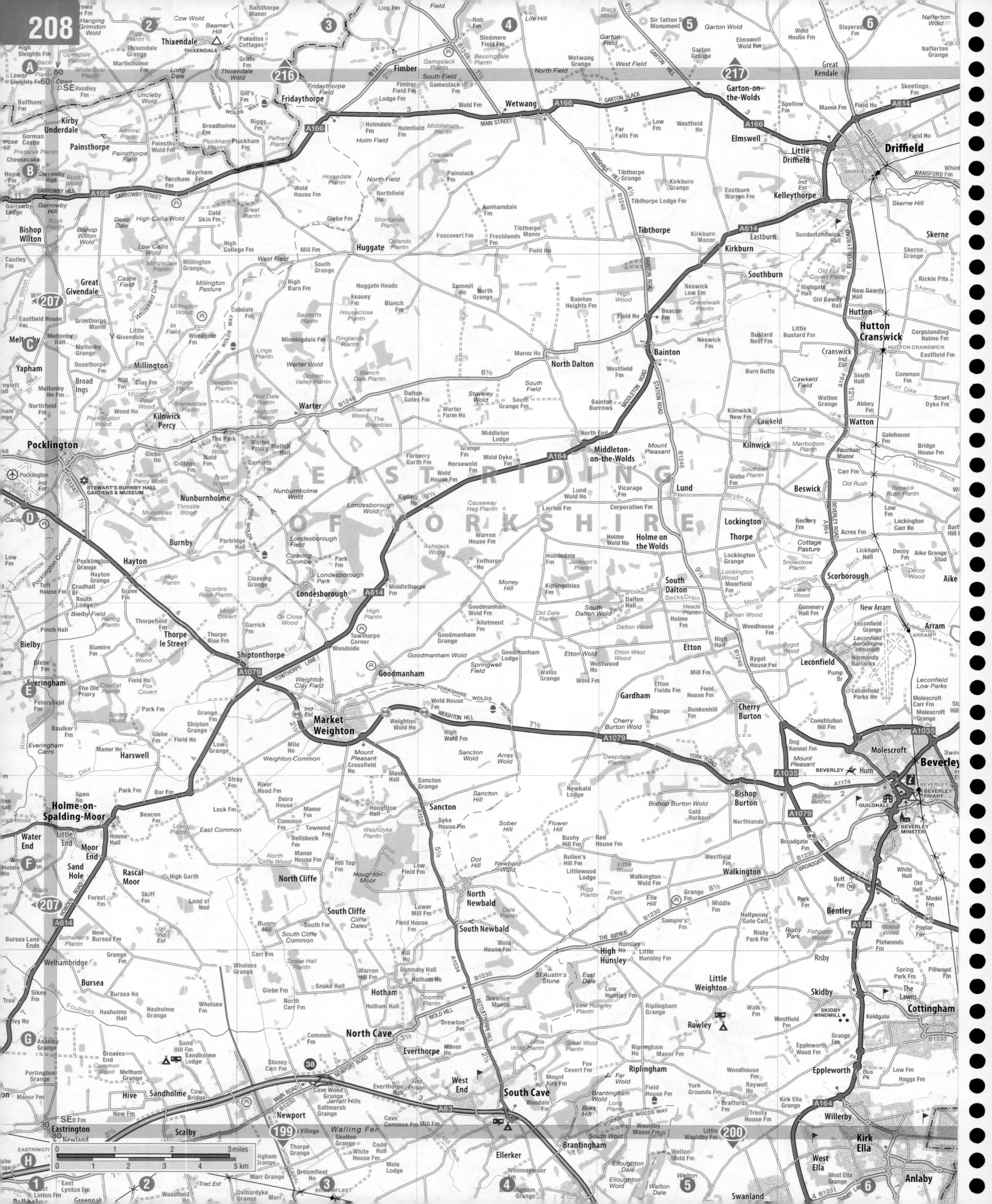

EAST RIDING OF YORKSHIRE
Thixendale
Fridaythorpe
Fimber
Wetwang
Garton-on-the-Wolds
Driffield
Little Driffield
Elmswell
Kelleythorpe
Kirby Underdale
Painsthorpe
Bishop Wilton
Great Givendale
Millington
Huggate
Tibthorpe
Kirkburn
Eastburn
Southburn
Skerne
Hutton
Hutton Cranswick
Bainton
North Dalton
Warter
Kilnwick Percy
Pocklington
Yapham
Meltonby
Nunburnholme
Burnby
Hayton
Londesborough
Middleton-on-the-Wolds
Lund
Kilnwick
Watton
Beswick
Lockington
Thorpe
Holme on the Wolds
South Dalton
Etton
Scorborough
Leconfield
Arram
Thorpe le Street
Shiptonthorpe
Goodmanham
Market Weighton
Everingham
Harswell
Holme-on-Spalding-Moor
Water End
Moor End
Sand Hole
Rascal Moor
Gardham
Cherry Burton
Bishop Burton
Molescroft
Beverley
Walkington
Bentley
Sancton
North Cliffe
South Cliffe
North Newbald
South Newbald
High Hunsley
Little Weighton
Skidby
Cottingham
Rowley
Hotham
North Cave
Everthorpe
Riplingham
West End
South Cave
Eppleworth
Willerby
Kirk Ella
West Ella
Anlaby
Welhambridge
Bursea
Hive
Sandholme
Newport
Scalby
Eastrington
Brantingham
Ellerker
Swanland
A166
A614
A164
A1079
A1035
A1034
A63
B1248
B1246
B1230
YORKSHIRE WOLDS WAY
207
216
217
199
200
1 mile 2 3 miles
0 1 2 3 4 5 km

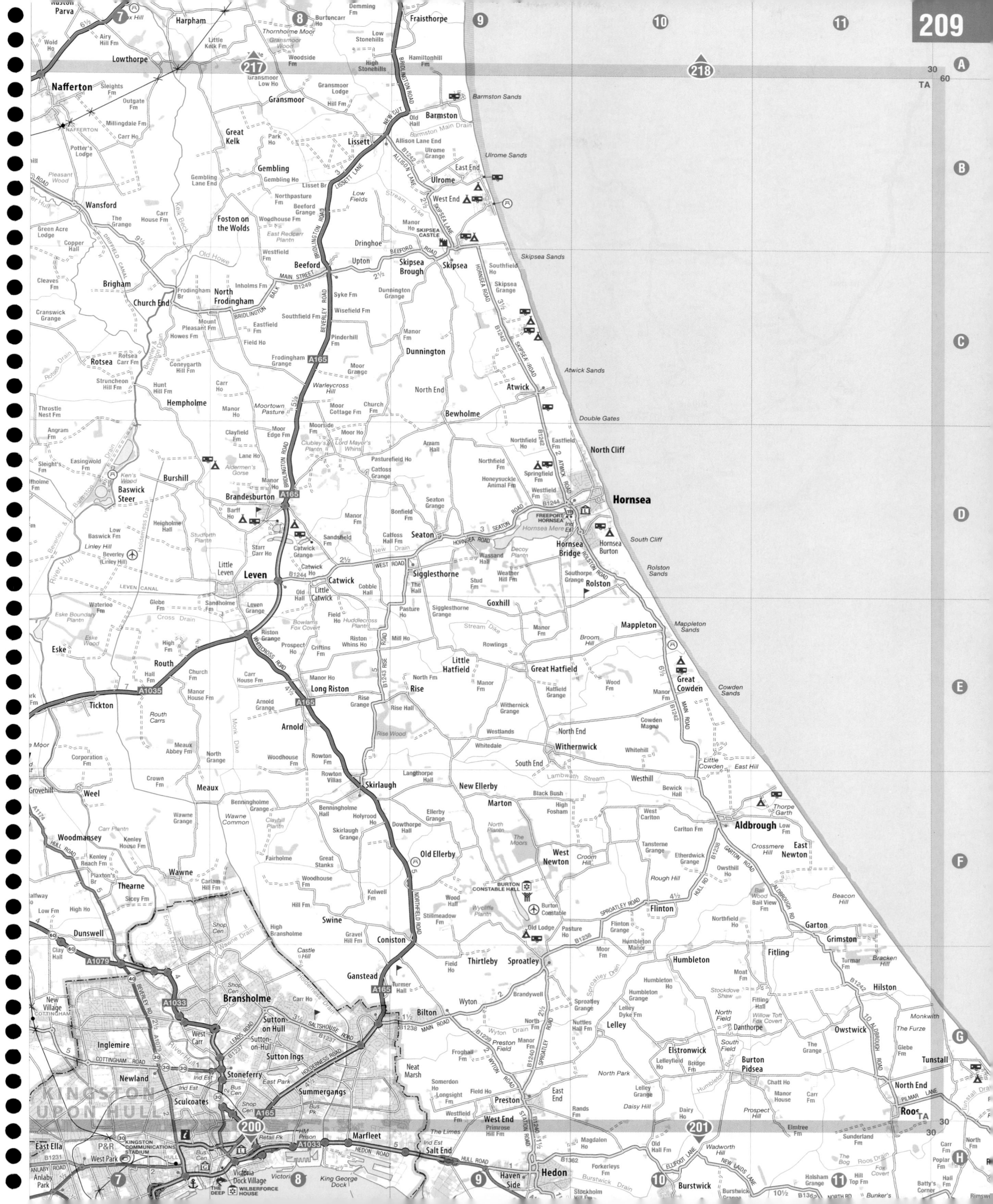

209
Harpham
Fraisthorpe
Lowthorpe
Nafferton
Gransmoor
Barmston
Barmston Sands
Great Kelk
Lissett
Gembling
Ulrome
Ulrome Sands
West End
Wansford
Foston on the Wolds
Skipsea
Skipsea Brough
Skipsea Sands
Dringhoe
Beeford
Upton
Brigham
Church End
North Frodingham
Dunnington
Rotsea
Atwick
Atwick Sands
North End
Hempholme
Bewholme
Double Gates
North Cliff
Burshill
Baswick Steer
Brandesburton
Hornsea
Hornsea Mere
Hornsea Bridge
Hornsea Burton
South Cliff
Seaton
Leven
Little Leven
Catwick
Little Catwick
Sigglesthorne
Rolston
Rolston Sands
Goxhill
Mappleton
Mappleton Sands
Eske
Routh
Little Hatfield
Great Hatfield
Great Cowden
Cowden Sands
Tickton
Long Riston
Rise
Arnold
Withernwick
North End
South End
Skirlaugh
New Ellerby
Marton
Meaux
Weel
Aldbrough
East Newton
Woodmansey
Old Ellerby
West Newton
Thearne
Wawne
Flinton
Garton
Grimston
Dunswell
Swine
Coniston
Fitling
Thirtleby
Sproatley
Humbleton
Hilston
Ganstead
Bransholme
Bilton
Wyton
Lelley
Danthorpe
Owstwick
Tunstall
Inglemire
Sutton-on-Hull
Sutton Ings
Stoneferry
Elstronwick
Burton Pidsea
Newland
Summergangs
Sculcoates
Preston
North End
Roos
Kingston upon Hull
Marfleet
Salt End
Hedon
Haven Side
East Ella
West Park
Anlaby Park
Victoria Dock Village
Burstwick
A165
A1035
A1033
A1079
B1242
B1244
B1249
B1238
B1240
217
218
200
201
A
B
C
D
E
F
G
H
7
8
9
10
11
TA
30
60

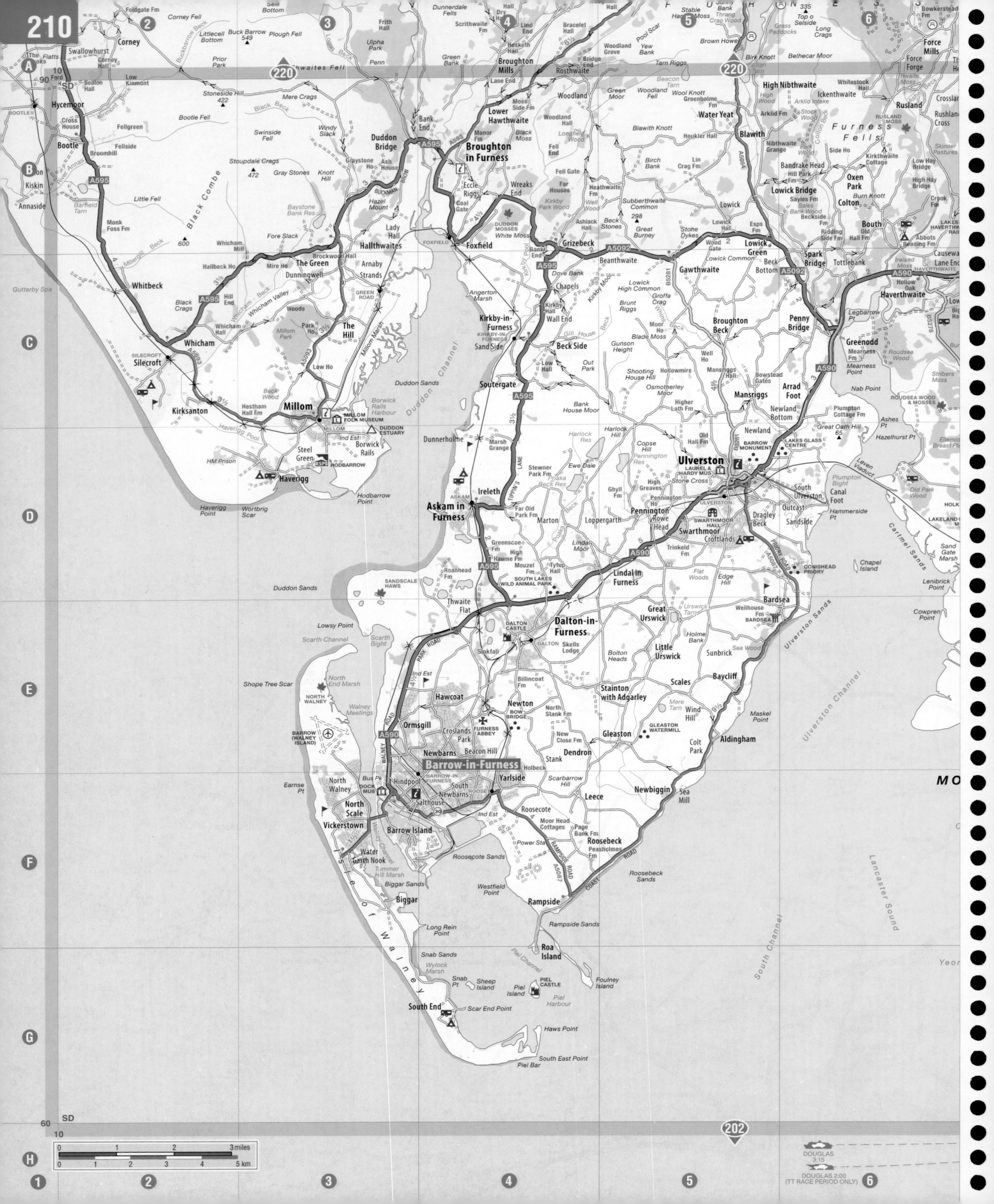
Corney
Bootle
Hycemoor
Whitbeck
Whicham
Silecroft
Kirksanton
Millom
Haverigg
Steel Green
Borwick Rails
Hodbarrow Point
Haverigg Point
Black Combe
Duddon Bridge
Broughton in Furness
Broughton Mills
Lower Hawthwaite
Foxfield
Grizebeck
Hallthwaites
The Green
The Hill
Kirkby-in-Furness
Sand Side
Beck Side
Soutergate
Askam in Furness
Ireleth
Dunnerholme
Marsh Grange
Duddon Sands
Duddon Channel
Lindal in Furness
Dalton-in-Furness
Ulverston
Swarthmoor
Pennington
Bardsea
Great Urswick
Little Urswick
Baycliff
Aldingham
Gleaston
Dendron
Stainton with Adgarley
Newton
Hawcoat
Ormsgill
Barrow-in-Furness
Yarlside
Roosebeck
Rampside
Roa Island
Piel Island
Piel Castle
Foulney Island
North Walney
North Scale
Vickerstown
Biggar
South End
Isle of Walney
Walney Channel
Barrow Island
Leece
Newbiggin
Sea Mill
Gawthwaite
Broughton Beck
Penny Bridge
Greenodd
Arrad Foot
Mansriggs
Newland
Lowick
Lowick Bridge
Lowick Green
Spark Bridge
Colton
Oxen Park
Rusland
Blawith
Water Yeat
High Nibthwaite
Haverthwaite
Furness Fells
Ulverston Sands
Ulverston Channel
South Channel
Lancaster Sound
Cartmel Sands
Chapel Island
Conishead Priory
Canal Foot
Scarth Channel
Lowsy Point
Shope Tree Scar
Earnse Pt
Long Rein Point
Snab Sands
Scar End Point
Haws Point
South East Point
Piel Bar
Roosebeck Sands
Rampside Sands
Westfield Point
Roosecote Sands
A595
A590
A5092
A5093
A5087
A5084
B5281
220
202
SD
60
10
90
0 1 2 3 miles
0 1 2 3 4 5 km
DOUGLAS 3:15
DOUGLAS 2:00 (TT RACE PERIOD ONLY)
A B C D E F G H
1 2 3 4 5 6

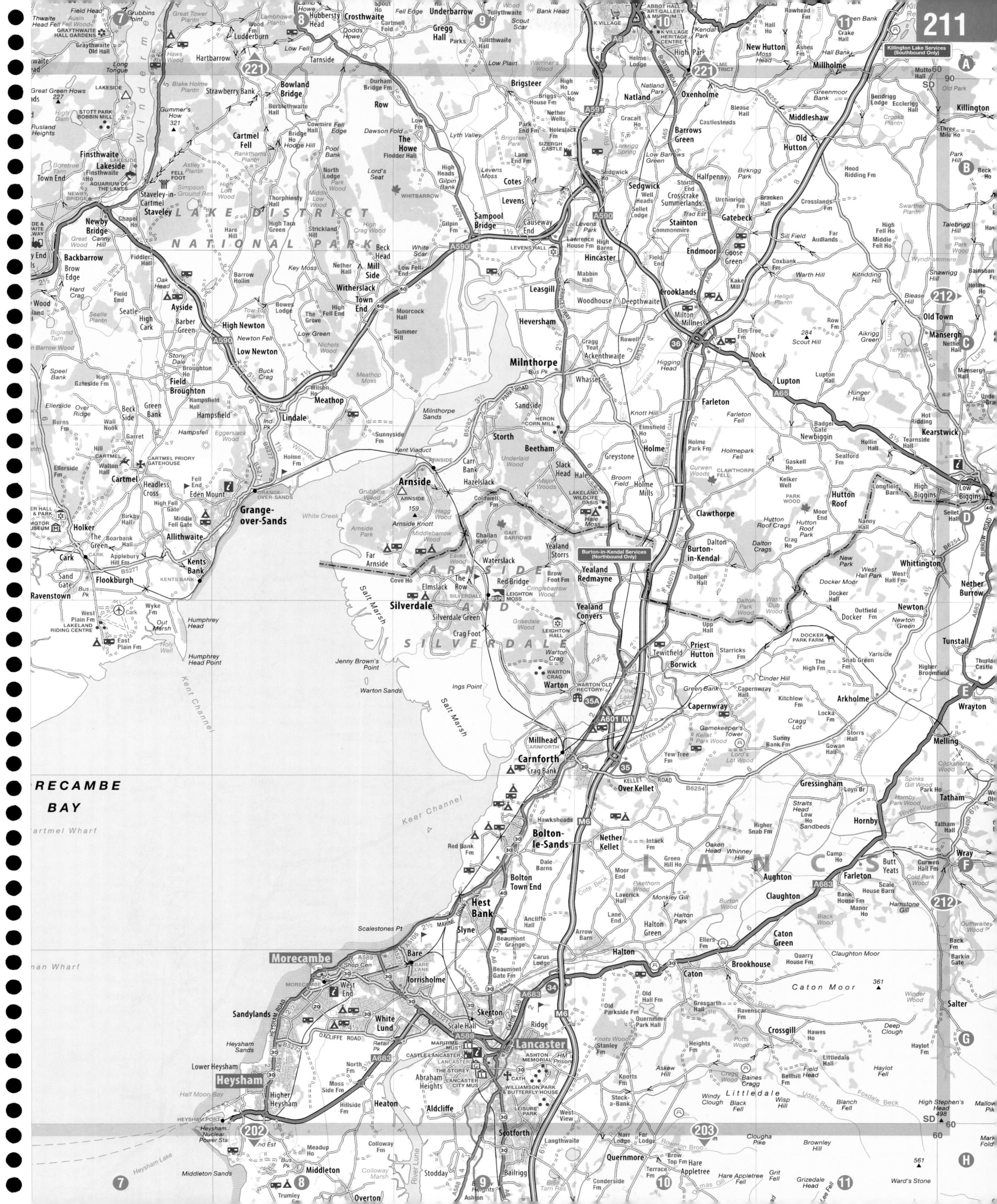

Killington Lake Services (Southbound Only)
Burton-in-Kendal Services (Northbound Only)
LAKE DISTRICT NATIONAL PARK
ARNSIDE AND SILVERDALE
MORECAMBE BAY
Kent Channel
Keer Channel
Morecambe
Heysham
Lancaster
Grange-over-Sands
Arnside
Silverdale
Carnforth
Milnthorpe
Kendal
Natland
Oxenholme
Sedgwick
Levens
Beetham
Burton-in-Kendal
Holme
Warton
Bolton-le-Sands
Hest Bank
Kirkby Lonsdale
Whittington
Arkholme
Melling
Hornby
Caton
Halton
Lupton
Kearstwick
Killington
Cartmel
Flookburgh
Allithwaite
Kents Bank
Newby Bridge
Lakeside
Staveley-in-Cartmel
Lindale
Meathop
Witherslack
Crosthwaite
Underbarrow
Brigsteer
Crooklands
Endmoor
Gatebeck
Stainton
Priest Hutton
Borwick
Capernwray
Over Kellet
Nether Kellet
Slyne
Torrisholme
Scotforth
Aldcliffe
Heaton
Middleton
Quernmore
Caton Moor
Littledale

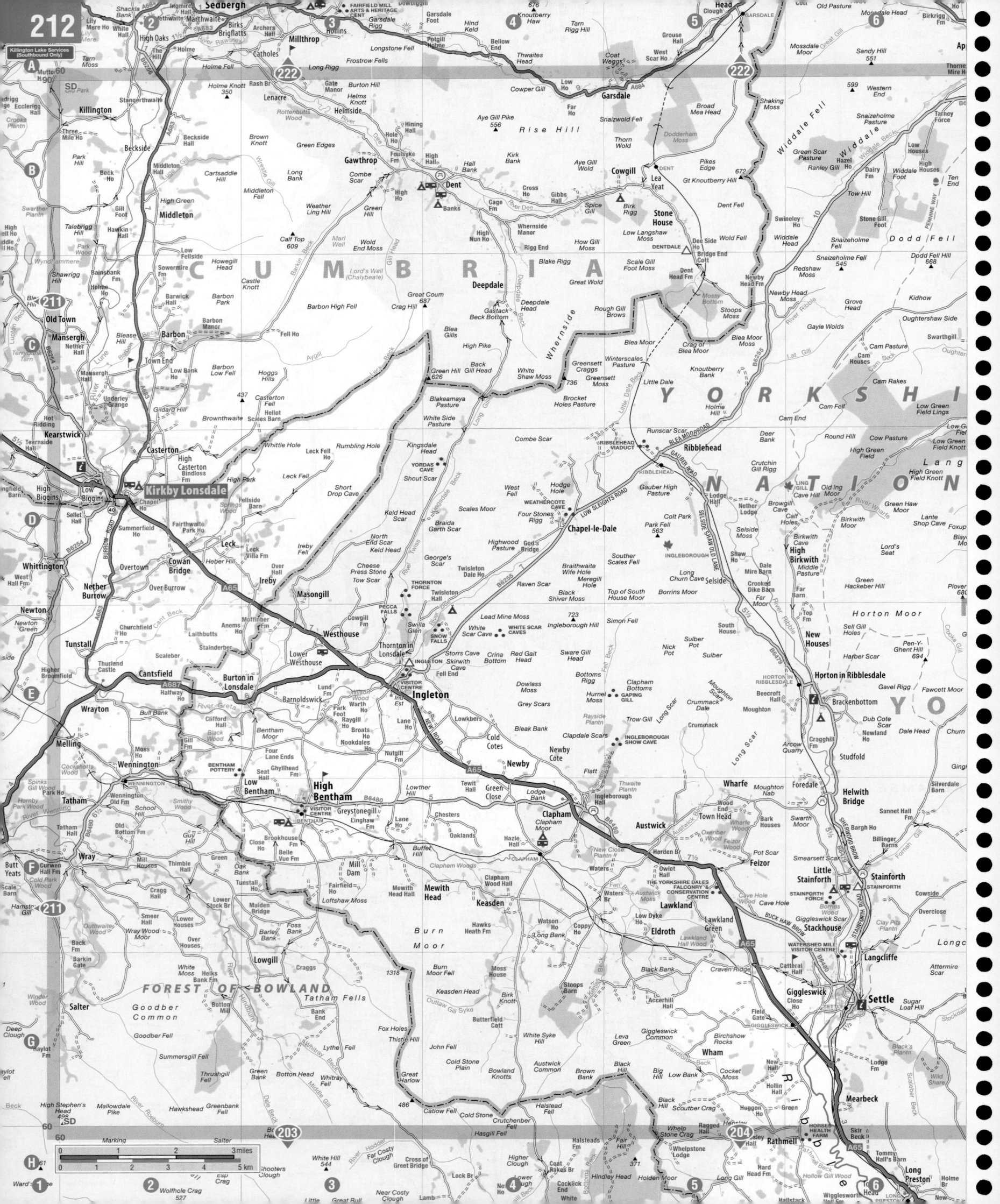
Killington Lake Services (Southbound Only)
Sedbergh
Millthrop
Killington
Middleton
Gawthrop
Dent
Cowgill
Lea Yeat
Stone House
Garsdale
Deepdale
Barbon
Old Town
Mansergh
Casterton
Kirkby Lonsdale
Kearstwick
Biggins
Whittington
Nether Burrow
Tunstall
Cantsfield
Burton in Lonsdale
Leck
Cowan Bridge
Ireby
Masongill
Westhouse
Thornton in Lonsdale
Ingleton
Chapel-le-Dale
Ribblehead
Selside
Horton in Ribblesdale
Brackenbottom
Newby
Clapham
Austwick
Lawkland
Eldroth
Keasden
Mewith Head
High Bentham
Low Bentham
Wennington
Melling
Wrayton
Tatham
Wray
Lowgill
Salter
Wharfe
Feizor
Helwith Bridge
Little Stainforth
Stainforth
Stackhouse
Langcliffe
Giggleswick
Settle
Mearbeck
Rathmell
Long Preston
Studfold
C U M B R I A
Y O R K S H I
N A T I O N
FOREST OF BOWLAND
Rise Hill
Whernside
Dodd Fell
Widdale Fell
Horton Moor
Burn Moor
Tatham Fells
Goodber Common
Great Coum 687
Calf Top 609
Ingleborough Hill 723
Penyghent Hill 694
Dodd Fell Hill 668
Snaizeholme Fell 545
Sandy Hill 551
Green Hill 626
Park Fell 563
RIBBLEHEAD VIADUCT
WHITE SCAR CAVES
INGLEBOROUGH SHOW CAVE
GAPING GILL
THORNTON FORCE
PECCA FALLS
SNOW FALLS
YORDAS CAVE
WEATHERCOTE CAVE
THE YORKSHIRE DALES FALCONRY & CONSERVATION CENTRE
WATERSHED MILL VISITOR CENTRE
STAINFORTH FORCE
HORSES HEALTH FARM
BENTHAM POTTERY
FAIRFIELD MILL ARTS & HERITAGE CENT
A65
A683
A684
A687
B6255
B6254
B6480
B6479
B6480
LOW SLEIGHTS ROAD
BLEA MOOR ROAD
GAUBER ROAD
SELSIDE SHAW OLD LANE
NEW ROAD
BUCK HAW BROW
SHERWOOD BROW
STAINFORTH ROAD
BURROW ROAD
PENNINE WAY
River Dee
River Lune
River Greta
River Wenning
River Ribble
River Hindburn
River Roeburn
River Twiss
River Doe
River Wharfe
222
211
203
204
0 1 2 3 miles
0 1 2 3 4 5 km

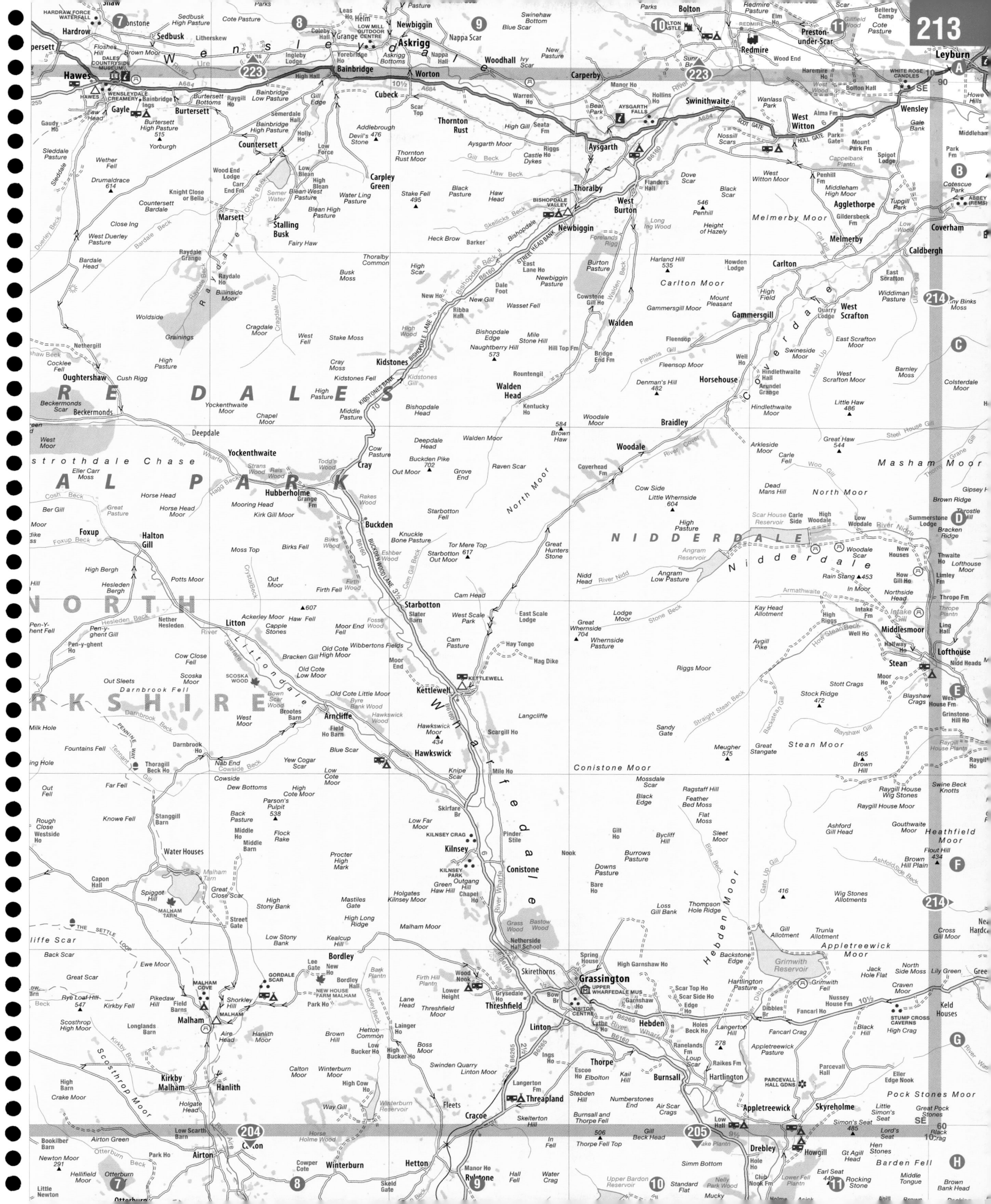
HARDRAW FORCE WATERFALL
Hardrow
Sedbusk
Sedbusk High Pasture
Litherskew
Cote Pasture
Leas Ho
Helm
Coleby Hall
LOW MILL OUTDOOR CENTRE
Grange
Newbiggin
Askrigg
Nappa Scar
Swineshaw Bottom
Blue Scar
Bolton
Redmire Pasture
Elm Ho
Redmire
Preston-under-Scar
Bellerby Camp
Cote Pasture
Leyburn
W e n s l e y d a l e
Flosher Hill
DALES COUNTRYSIDE MUSEUM
Brown Moor
Ingleby Lodge
Yorebridge Ho
Askrigg Bottoms
Nappa Hall
Woodhall
Ivy Scar
New Pasture
Wood End
Harmire Ho
WHITE ROSE CANDLES
Hawes
High Hall
Bainbridge
Worton
Carperby
Manor Ho
Hollins Ho
Bolton Hall
West Wood
Howe Hills
WENSLEYDALE CREAMERY
Bainbridge Ings
Burtersett Bottoms
Raygill Ho
Bainbridge Low Pasture
Gill Edge
Cubeck
Warren Ho
Swinithwaite
Wanlass Park
Wensley
Gayle
Burtersett
Semerdale Hall
Scar Top
Bear Park
AYSGARTH FALLS
Alma Fm
West Witton
Gale Bank
Gaudy Ho
Eaw Head
Burtersett High Pasture
Bainbridge High Pasture
Holly Ho
Addlebrough 476
Devil's Stone
Thornton Rust
High Gill
Seata Fm
Nossill Scars
Park Gate
Mount Park Fm
Middleham
Yorburgh
Countersett
Low Force
Aysgarth Moor
Riggs Ho
Aysgarth
Capplebank Plantn
Spigot Lodge
Park Fm
Sleddale Pasture
Wether Fell
Thornton Rust Moor
Castle Dykes
Drumaldrace 614
Wood End Lodge
Carr End Fm
Low Blean
High Blean
Carpley Green
Haw Beck
Penhill Fm
Cotescue Park
Semer Water
Blean West Pasture
Knight Close or Bella
Water Ling Pasture
Stake Fell 495
Black Pasture
Haw Head
Thoralby
Flanders Hall
Dove Scar
Black Scar
West Witton Moor
Middleham High Moor
Agglethorpe
Tupgill Park
ABBEY (REMS)
Countersett Bardale
Marsett
Blean High Pasture
BISHOPDALE VALLEY
West Burton
546 Penhill
Gildersbeck Fm
Close Ing
Stalling Busk
Newbiggin
Long Ing Wood
Height of Hazely
Melmerby Moor
Low Wood
Coverham
West Duerley Pasture
Fairy Haw
Heck Brow
Barker
Melmerby
Raydale Grange
Thoralby Common
Forelands Rigg
Caldbergh
Bardale Head
Raydale Ho
High Scar
East Lane Ho
Burton Pasture
Harland Hill 535
Howden Lodge
Carlton
Busk Moss
Newbiggin Pasture
Carlton Moor
East Scrafton
Billinside Moor
New Ho
Dale Foot
Cowstone Gill Ho
Widdiman Pasture
New Gill
Wasset Fell
Mount Pleasant
High Field
Gammersgill Moor
Gammersgill
Quarry Lodge
West Scrafton
Woldside
Ribba Hall
Walden
Cragdale Moor
High Wood
Bishopdale Edge
Mile Stone Hill
Grainings
West Fell
Stake Moss
Naughtberry Hill 573
Hill Top Fm
Fleensop
East Scrafton Moor
Nethergill
Bridge End Fm
Swineside Moor
Well Ho
Cocklee Fell
High Pasture
Cray Moss
Kidstones
Fleensop Moor
Hindlethwaite Hall
West Scrafton Moor
Barnley Moss
Oughtershaw
Cush Rigg
Kidstones Fell
Rountengill
Horsehouse
Colsterdale Moor
Denman's Hill 482
Arundel Grange
R E D A L E S
Walden Head
Beckermonds Scar
Beckermonds
Yockenthwaite Moor
High Pasture
Middle Pasture
Bishopdale Head
Kentucky Ho
Hindlethwaite Moor
Little Haw 486
Chapel Moor
Woodale Moor
Braidley
Deepdale
584 Brown Haw
West Moor
Deepdale Head
Walden Moor
Great Haw 544
Cow Pasture
Woodale
Arkleside Moor
Carle Fell
strothdale Chase
Yockenthwaite
Buckden Pike 702
Masham Moor
Eller Carr Moss
Strans Wood
Reis Wood
Todd's Wood
Cray
Out Moor
Grove End
Raven Scar
Coverhead Fm
A L P A R K
Dead Mans Hill
North Moor
Cow Side
Brown Ridge
Horse Head
Hubberholme
Little Whernside 604
Gipsey H
Ber Gill
Great Pasture
Horse Head Moor
Mooring Head
Grange Fm
Rakes Wood
Starbotton Fell
Scar House Reservoir
Carle Side
High Woodale
Low Woodale
Summerstone Lodge
Bracken Ridge
Kirk Gill Moor
Buckden
High Pasture
Foxup
Halton Gill
Knuckle Bone Pasture
N I D D E R D A L E
Tor Mere Top
Great Hunters Stone
Angram Reservoir
Woodale Scar
New Houses
Thwaite Ho
Moss Top
Birks Fell
Birks Wood
Starbotton Out Moor 617
Nidderdale
Lofthouse Moor
High Bergh
Eshber Wood
Rain Stang 453
How Gill Ho
Limley Fm
Hesleden Bergh
Potts Moor
Out Moor
Nidd Head
Angram Low Pasture
In Moor
Firth Fell
Firth Wood
Northside Head
Cam Head
Armathwaite Gill
Thorpe Fm
Thorpe Plantn
N O R T H
Starbotton
Kay Head Allotment
Intake Fm
Pen-Y-ghent Fell
Nether Hesleden
Ackerley Moor
Haw Fell
607
Slater Barn
West Scale Park
East Scale Lodge
Lodge Moor
High Riggs
Middlesmoor
Ling Hall
Litton
Capple Stones
Moor End Fell
Fosse Wood
Great Whernside 704
Pen-y-ghent Gill
Whernside Pasture
Aygill Pike
Well Ho
Pen-y-ghent Ho
Wibbertons Fields
Cam Pasture
Hay Tonge
Halfway Ho
Lofthouse
Cow Close Fell
Bracken Gill
Old Cote High Moor
Hag Dike
Riggs Moor
Stean
Nidd Heads
Scoska Moor
Old Cote Low Moor
Moor End
SCOSKA WOOD
KETTLEWELL
Stott Crags
Moor Ho
Out Sleets
Darnbrook Fell
Littondale
Old Cote Little Moor
Kettlewell
Stock Ridge 472
Blayshaw Crags
West House Fm
RKSHIRE
Brown Scar Wood
Byre Bank Wood
Brootes Barn
Arncliffe
Hawkswick Wood
Langcliffe
Grinstone Hill Ho
Milk Hole
West Moor
Field Ho Barn
Hawkswick Moor 434
Scargill Ho
Sandy Gate
Wharfedale
Fountains Fell
Darnbrook Ho
Blue Scar
Hawkswick
Meugher 575
Great Stangate
Stean Moor
465 Brown Hill
Raygill House Plantn
Raygill Ho
ing Hole
Thoragill Beck Ho
Yew Cogar Scar
Nab End
Knipe Scar
Mile Ho
Conistone Moor
PENNINE WAY
Cowside
Low Cote Moor
Mossdale Scar
Ragstaff Hill
Swine Beck Knotts
Out Fell
Far Fell
Dew Bottoms
High Cote Moor
Black Edge
Feather Bed Moss
Raygill House Wig Stones
Parson's Pulpit 538
Skirfare Br
Raygill House Moor
Rough Close Westside Ho
Knowe Fell
Stanggill Barn
Back Pasture
Low Far Moor
Flat Moss
Ashford Gill Head
Gouthwaite Moor
Heathfield Moor
Middle Ho
Flock Rake
KILNSEY CRAG
Gill Ho
Bycliff Hill
Sleet Moor
Middle Barn
Kilnsey
Pinder Stile
Water Houses
Procter High Mark
Nook
Burrows Pasture
Flout Hill 434
Malham Tarn
KILNSEY PARK
Conistone
Downs Pasture
Brown Hill Plain
Capon Hall
Great Close Scar
Outgang Hill
Green Haw Hill
Chapel Ho
Bare Ho
Spiggot Hill
High Stony Bank
Mastiles Gate
Holgates Kilnsey Moor
416
Hebden Moor
Loss Gill Bank
Thompson Hole Ridge
Wig Stones Allotments
MALHAM TARN
THE SETTLE LOOP
Street Gate
High Long Ridge
Malham Moor
Grass Wood
Bastow Wood
Gill Allotment
Trunla Allotment
Cross Gill Moor
liffe Scar
Low Stony Bank
Kealcup Hill
Netherside Hall School
Appletreewick Moor
Back Scar
Ewe Moor
Bordley
Spring House
High Garnshaw Ho
Backstone Edge
Grimwith Reservoir
Jack Hole Flat
North Side Moss
Lily Green
Great Scar
MALHAM COVE
GORDALE SCAR
Lee Gate
New Ho
Bark Plantn
Firth Hill Plantn
Wood Nook
Skirethorns
Grassington
Hartlington Pasture
Grimwith Fell
Craven Moor
Rye Loaf Hill 547
Kirkby Fell
Pikedaw Hill
Field Barns
Shorkley Hill
Bordley Hall
NEW HOUSE FARM MALHAM
Park Ho
Lane Head
Lower Height
Grysedale Ho
UPPER WHARFEDALE MUS
Scar Top Ho
Scar Side Ho
Garnshaw Ho
Nussey House Fm
Threshfield
Bow Br
Edge Ho
Dibbles Br
Fancarl Ho
Keld Houses
Malham
MALHAM
Longlands Barn
Threshfield Moor
VISITOR CENTRE
STUMP CROSS CAVERNS
Scosthrop High Moor
Aire Head
Hanlith Moor
Brown Hill
Hetton Common
Lainger Ho
Boss Moor
Linton
Lythe Ho
Hebden
Holes Beck Ho
Langerton Hill
Black Hill
High Crag
Fancarl Crag
Scosthrop Moor
Low Bucker Ho
High Bucker Ho
Ings Ho
278
Ranelands Fm
Loup Scar
Appletreewick Pasture
Kirkby Malham
Hanlith
Calton Moor
Winterburn Moor
Swinden Quarry
Linton Moor
Thorpe
Raikes Fm
Parcevall Hall
Eller Nook
High Barn
Crake Moor
High Cow Ho
Escoe Ho
Elbolton
Kail Hill
Burnsall
Hartlington
PARCEVALL HALL GDNS
Pock Stones Moor
Holgate Head
Way Gill
Winterburn Reservoir
Fleets
Langerton Fm
Threapland
Stebden Hill
Numberstones End
Air Scar Crags
Appletreewick
Skyreholme
Little Simon's Seat
Great Pock Stones
Low Scarth Barn
Cracoe
Skelterton Hill
Burnsall and Thorpe Fell
Simon's Seat 485
Lord's Seat
Black Crag
Bookilber Barn
Airton Green
Horse Holme Wood
In Fell
506
Thorpe Fell Top
Gill Beck Head
Low Hall
Hen Stones
Otterburn Beck
Park Ho
Airton
Calton
Drebley
Howgill
Gt Agill Head
Barden Fell
Newton Moor 291
Cowper Cote
Winterburn
Hetton
Manor Ho
Simm Bottom
Hole Ho
Earl Seat 449
Middle Tongue
Hellifield Moor
Otterburn
Rylstone
Hall Fell
Water Crag
Upper Barden Reservoir
Standard Flat
Nelly Park Wood
Club Nook Fm
Lower Fell Plantn
Rocking Stone
Brown Bank Head
Little Newton
Skeld Gate
Mucky
Otterburn
223
204
205
214

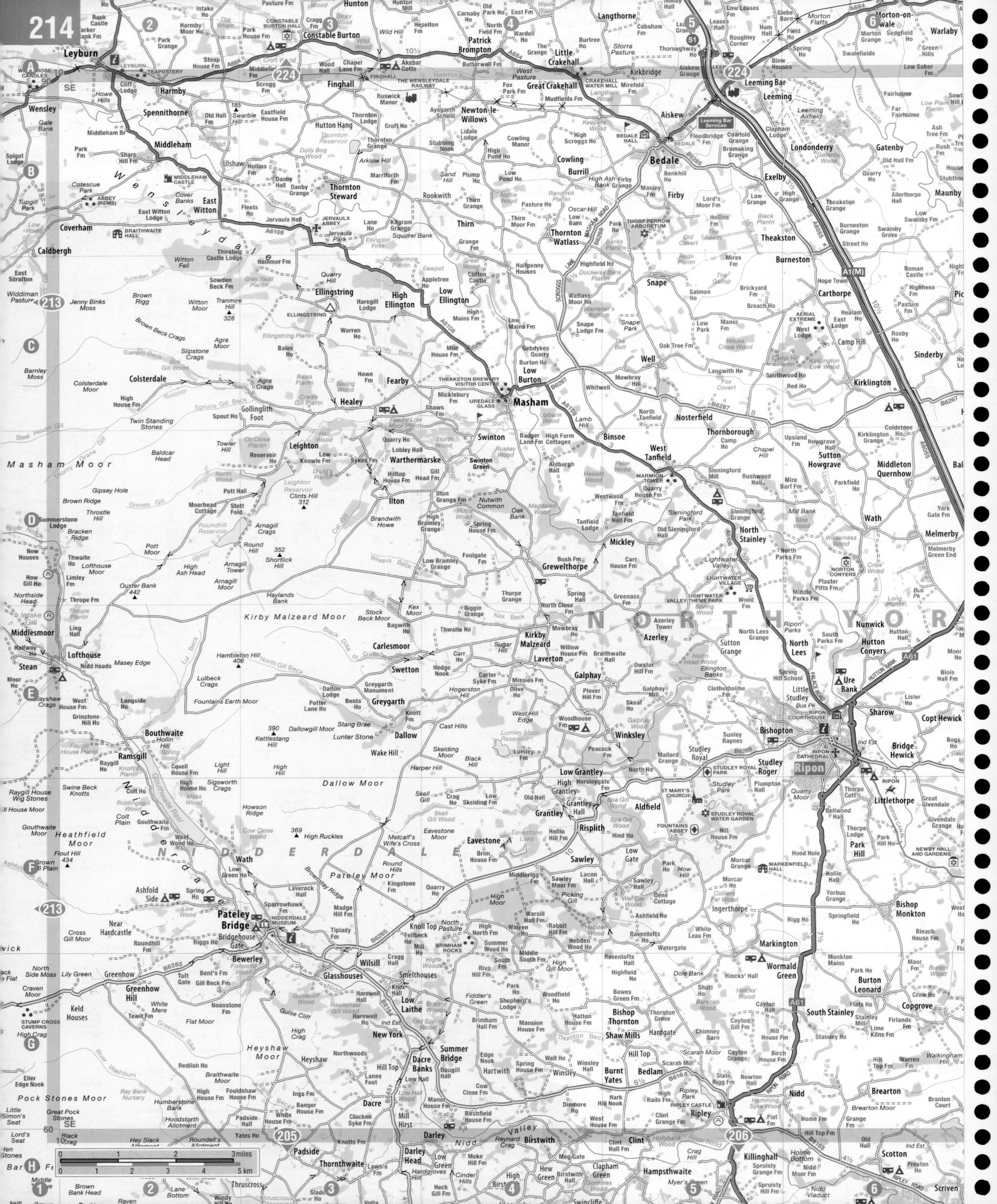

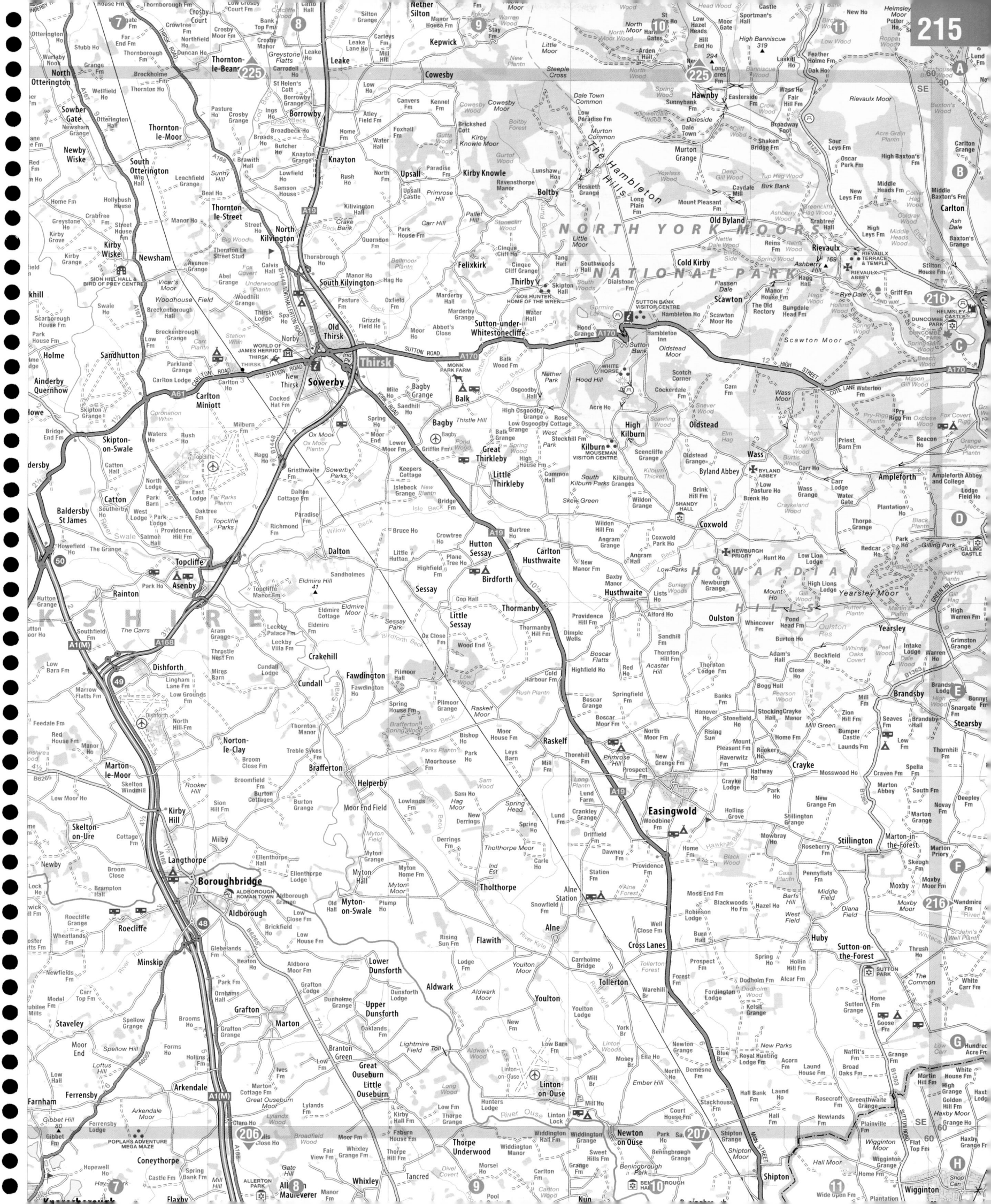
NORTH YORK MOORS
NATIONAL PARK
HOWARDIAN HILLS
The Hambleton Hills
Nether Silton
Kepwick
Cowesby
Hawnby
Rievaulx Moor
Thornton-le-Beans
North Otterington
Leake
Borrowby
Thornton-le-Moor
Knayton
Upsall
Kirby Knowle
Boltby
Murton Grange
South Otterington
Newby Wiske
Thornton-le-Street
North Kilvington
Old Byland
Carlton
Rievaulx
Kirby Wiske
Newsham
Felixkirk
Thirlby
Cold Kirby
South Kilvington
Scawton
Sutton-under-Whitestonecliffe
Sutton Bank Visitor Centre
Helmsley Castle
Duncombe Park
Scawton Moor
Old Thirsk
Thirsk
Sowerby
Sandhutton
Holme
Ainderby Quernhow
Carlton Miniott
Balk
Bagby
World of James Herriot
Bagby Grange
Oldstead
High Kilburn
Kilburn
Wass
Byland Abbey
Ampleforth
Ampleforth Abbey and College
Skipton-on-Swale
Great Thirkleby
Little Thirkleby
Catton
Baldersby St James
Coxwold
Newburgh Priory
Dalton
Hutton Sessay
Carlton Husthwaite
Birdforth
Sessay
Topcliffe
Asenby
Rainton
Husthwaite
Thormanby
Little Sessay
Oulston
Yearsley Moor
Yearsley
Dishforth
Crakehill
Fawdington
Cundall
Brandsby
Stearsby
Norton-le-Clay
Raskelf
Crayke
Marton-le-Moor
Brafferton
Helperby
Easingwold
Kirby Hill
Stillington
Marton-in-the-Forest
Langthorpe
Boroughbridge
Aldborough
Tholthorpe
Myton-on-Swale
Alne
Roecliffe
Flawith
Cross Lanes
Huby
Sutton-on-the-Forest
Minskip
Lower Dunsforth
Tollerton
Aldwark
Grafton
Upper Dunsforth
Marton
Youlton
Staveley
Great Ouseburn
Little Ouseburn
Linton-on-Ouse
Arkendale
Ferrensby
Farnham
Newton on Ouse
Coneythorpe
Thorpe Underwood
Whixley
Tancred
Shipton
Wigginton
Poplars Adventure Mega Maze
Allerton Park
River Swale
River Ouse
A1(M)
A19
A61
A168
A170
B1448
B1363
B1257
B6265
225
206
207
216
50
49
48

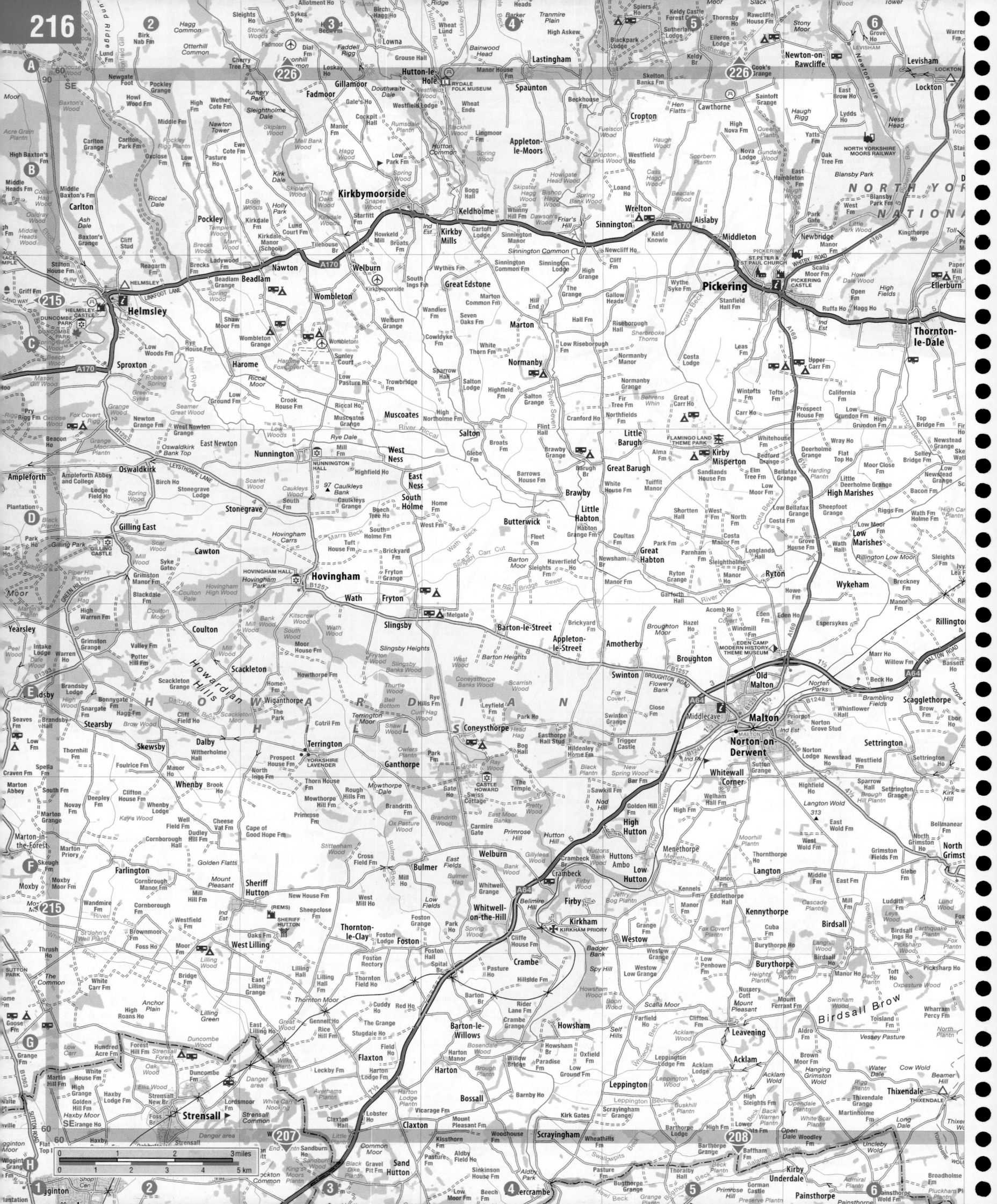
Helmsley
Kirkbymoorside
Pickering
Malton
Norton-on-Derwent
Old Malton
Thornton-le-Dale
Hovingham
Terrington
Sheriff Hutton
Strensall
Lastingham
Hutton-le-Hole
Gillamoor
Fadmoor
Spaunton
Cropton
Appleton-le-Moors
Levisham
Lockton
Newton-on-Rawcliffe
Cawthorne
Wrelton
Aislaby
Middleton
Sinnington
Keldholme
Kirkby Mills
Nawton
Beadlam
Welburn
Wombleton
Great Edstone
Marton
Normanby
Salton
Harome
Sproxton
Carlton
Pockley
Nunnington
West Ness
East Ness
South Holme
Muscoates
Little Barugh
Great Barugh
Kirby Misperton
Brawby
Little Habton
Great Habton
Butterwick
Ryton
Wykeham
Rillington
Oswaldkirk
Ampleforth
Stonegrave
Gilling East
Cawton
Wath
Fryton
Slingsby
Barton-le-Street
Appleton-le-Street
Amotherby
Swinton
Broughton
Coulton
Yearsley
Scackleton
Coneysthorpe
Ganthorpe
Stearsby
Dalby
Skewsby
Whenby
Brandsby
Farlington
Marton-in-the-Forest
Moxby
West Lilling
Thornton-le-Clay
Foston
Bulmer
Welburn
Whitwell-on-the-Hill
Crambe
Firby
Kirkham
Westow
High Hutton
Huttons Ambo
Low Hutton
Menethorpe
Langton
Kennythorpe
Birdsall
Burythorpe
Settrington
Scagglethorpe
North Grimston
Leavening
Acklam
Howsham
Barton-le-Willows
Harton
Bossall
Flaxton
Claxton
Sand Hutton
Leppington
Scrayingham
Thixendale
Kirby Underdale
Painsthorpe
Whitewall Corner
Middlecave
HOWARDIAN HILLS
NORTH YORK MOORS NATIONAL PARK
Birdsall Brow
RYEDALE FOLK MUSEUM
NORTH YORKSHIRE MOORS RAILWAY
FLAMINGO LAND THEME PARK
EDEN CAMP MODERN HISTORY THEME MUSEUM
CASTLE HOWARD
KIRKHAM PRIORY
HOVINGHAM HALL
NUNNINGTON HALL
GILLING CASTLE
HELMSLEY CASTLE
PICKERING CASTLE
DUNCOMBE PARK
A170
A169
A64
B1257
B1363
B1248
B1258
226
215
207
208
0 1 2 3 miles
0 1 2 3 4 5 km

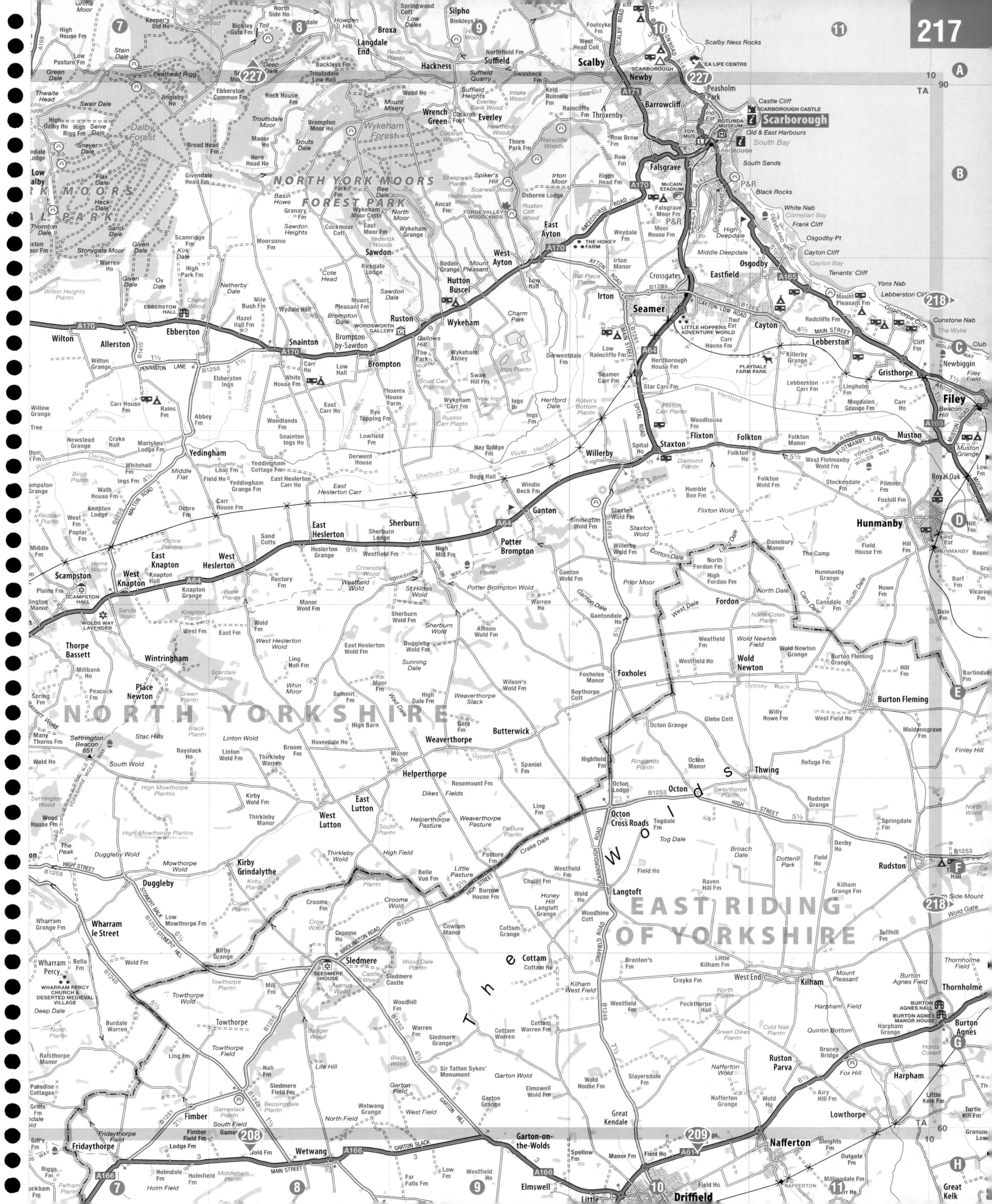

Scalby
Newby
Scarborough
Castle Cliff
Scarborough Castle
Rotunda Museum
Old & East Harbours
South Bay
South Sands
Scalby Ness Rocks
Sea Life Centre
Peasholm Park
Barrowcliff
Falsgrave
Throxenby
Seamer
Crossgates
Eastfield
Osgodby
Cayton
Lebberston
Gristhorpe
Filey
Muston
Hunmanby
Folkton
Flixton
Staxton
Willerby
Ganton
Potter Brompton
Sherburn
East Heslerton
West Heslerton
East Knapton
West Knapton
Scampston
Yedingham
Wilton
Allerston
Ebberston
Snainton
Brompton
Brompton-by-Sawdon
Wykeham
Hutton Buscel
West Ayton
East Ayton
Irton
Ruston
Sawdon
Hackness
Suffield
Broxa
Langdale End
Silpho
Everley
Wrench Green
Langtoft
Foxholes
Fordon
Wold Newton
Burton Fleming
Thwing
Octon
Octon Cross Roads
Rudston
Kilham
Thornholme
Burton Agnes
Harpham
Lowthorpe
Ruston Parva
Nafferton
Driffield
Garton-on-the-Wolds
Wetwang
Fimber
Fridaythorpe
Sledmere
Cottam
Towthorpe
Wharram Percy
Wharram le Street
Duggleby
Kirby Grindalythe
West Lutton
East Lutton
Helperthorpe
Weaverthorpe
Butterwick
Wintringham
Thorpe Bassett
Place Newton
North York Moors Forest Park
Dalby Forest
Wykeham Forest
NORTH YORKSHIRE
EAST RIDING OF YORKSHIRE
The Wolds
Yorkshire Wolds Way
A170
A171
A165
A64
A166
A614
B1253
B1249
B1251
B1252
B1261
A1039
227
218
208
209

NORTH
SEA
FILEY
BAY
BRIDLINGTON
BAY
EAST RIDING
OF YORKSHIRE
Yons Nab
Lebberston Cliff
217
Gristhorpe Cliff
Cunstone Nab
The Wyke
Cliff Fm
Club Pt
Newbiggin
North Cliff
Gristhorpe
Filey Field
Filey Brigg
Brigg End
Filey Sands
Carr Ho
Filey
Beacon Hill
A165
Muston
Muston Grange
Muston Sands
Lowfield Fm
Hunmanby Sands
Royal Oak
Pilmoor Fm
Primrose Valley
Foxhill Fm
Hunmanby Gap
Airy Hill Fm
Hunmanby Moor
Ind Est
Moor Fm
Reighton Sands
Rosedale Fm
Moor Ho
Reighton Gap
Graffitoe Fm
Moor Fm
Speeton Sands
Barf Fm
Howe Fm
Vicarage Fm
Reighton
Speeton Hills
Speeton Cliffs
Dale Fm
Speeton
Buckton Cliffs
Speeton Moor
Reighton Field
Speeton Grange
Buckton Hall
Bempton Cliffs
Scale Nab
Cat Nab
Gull Nook
Standard Hill
Bempton Grange
Wandale Fm
Hill Fm
Bartindale Fm
Speeton
Field Greenlands Fm
Wasters Plantn
Buckton
Dykes Plantn
Thornwick Bay
High Huntow Fm
Bempton
Dane's Dyke
North Cliff
Burton Fleming
Grindale Field
North Dale
North Landing
Cradle Head
North Moor
Stottle Bank Nook
Maidensgrave Fm
Newsham Field
Butterwicks Fm
Selwicks Bay
Flatmere Plantn
Flamborough Head
Finley Hill
Grindale
High Barn
Flamborough Head Lighthouse
High Stacks
Fox Covert Plantn
East Leys Fm
North Mount
Lynhams
The Crofts
Charlestone Fm
Field Ho
Flamborough
Old Fall Plantn
Beacon Fm
Highcliffe Manor
Danes Dyke Fm
Beacon Hill
South Landing
North Wood
High Easton Fm
Ind Est
Sewerby
Sewerby Hall & Garden
Springdale Fm
Binsdale Fm
East Crags Wood
Sewerby Rocks
Boynton
Eastfield Fm
Bondsville Model Village
B1253
Priory
Ruds
West Law Wood
Fish Ponds Wood
Wandale Fm
Bayle Mu
Old Town
Thorpe Hall
Carr Plantn
North Sands
Sands Wood
Bridlington
South Side Mount
Temple Fm
Carnaby Temple
Hallowkiln Wood
High Wood
West Hill
Old Penny Memories
217
The Spa
Wold Gate
Ind Est
Bessingby
Hilderthorpe
Tuffhill Fm
Haisthorpe Field
Carnaby
P&R
Thornholme Field
Haisthorpe
A614
Wilsthorpe
Burton Agnes Field
Thornholme
Ind Est
Park Rose Bird of Prey Centre
Carnaby Moor
Burton Agnes Hall
Burton Agnes Manor House
Brackendale Fm
Harpham Grange
Burton Agnes
Oak Wood Fm
Auburn Fm
Hords Covert
Burton Agnes Stud Fm
A165
Fraisthorpe Sands
Demming Fm
Harpham
Burtoncarr Ho
Fraisthorpe
Thornholme Moor
Gransmoor Wood
Low Stonehills
Little Kelk Fm
Turtle Hill Fm
Woodside Fm
High Stonehills
Hamiltonhill Fm
Gransmoor Low Ho
Gransmoor Lodge
209
Barmston Sands
Barmston
Barmston Main Drain
Great Kelk
Park Ho
Lissett
Allison Lane End
TA
10
30
90
60
0 1 2 3 miles
0 1 2 3 4 5 km
A B C D E F G H
1 2 3 4 5 6

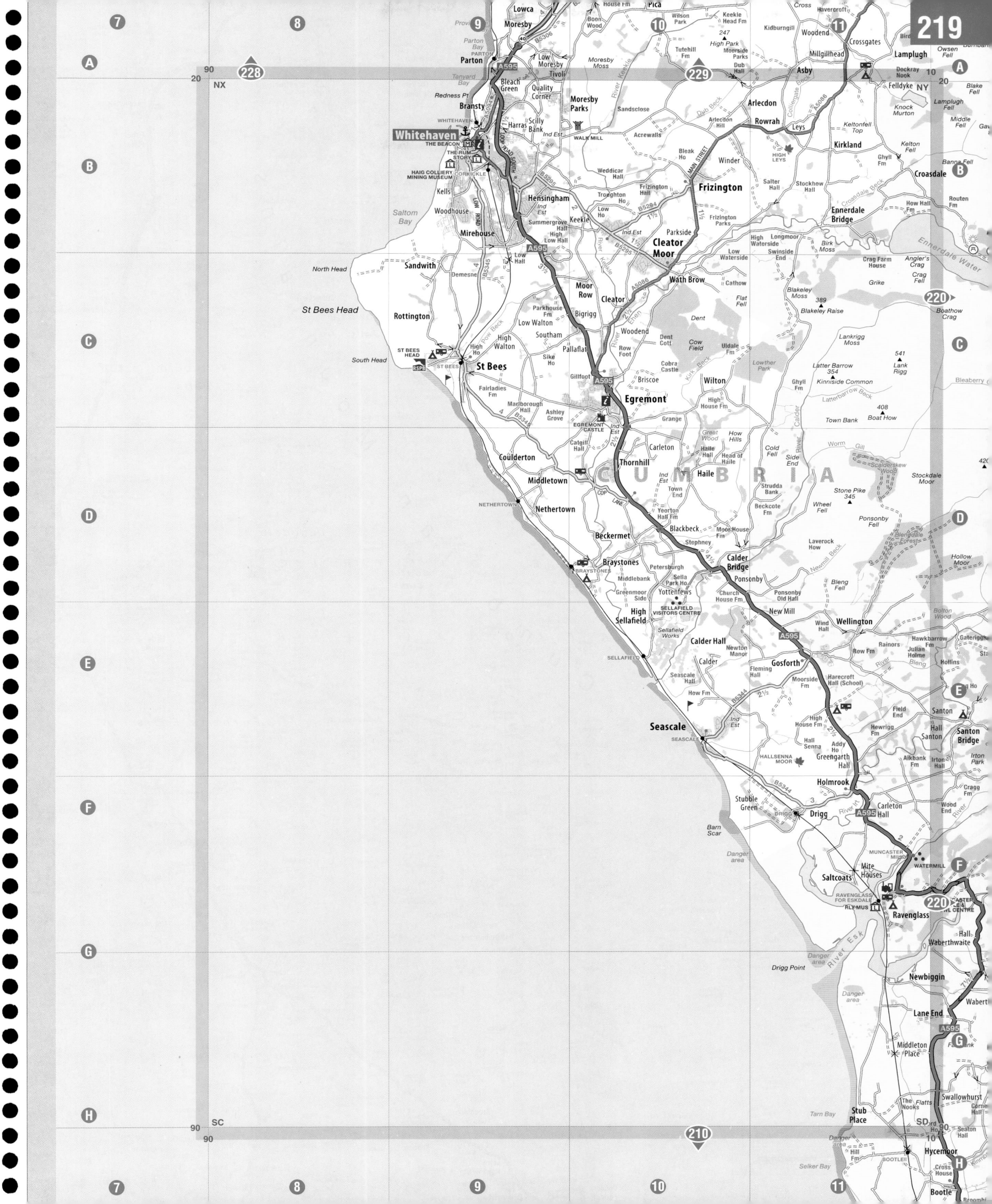
Lowca
Moresby
Parton
Pica
Whitehaven
THE BEACON
THE RUM STORY
HAIG COLLIERY MINING MUSEUM
Bransty
Redness Pt
Bleach Green
Harras
Scilly Bank
Moresby Parks
Walk Mill
Sandsclose
Acrewalls
Arlecdon
Rowrah
Asby
Lamplugh
Kirkland
Croasdale
Frizington
Winder
Hensingham
Kells
Woodhouse
Saltom Bay
Mirehouse
Keekle
Cleator Moor
Parkside
Wath Brow
Cleator
Moor Row
Bigrigg
Ennerdale Bridge
Ennerdale Water
North Head
Sandwith
St Bees Head
Rottington
South Head
St Bees
Egremont
EGREMONT CASTLE
Woodend
Wilton
Briscoe
Lankrigg Moss
Kinniside Common
Boat How
Thornhill
Carleton
Haile
C U M B R I A
Coulderton
Middletown
Nethertown
Beckermet
Blackbeck
Braystones
Calder Bridge
Ponsonby
Yottenfews
SELLAFIELD VISITORS CENTRE
High Sellafield
New Mill
Wellington
Calder Hall
Gosforth
Seascale
Stubble Green
Drigg
Holmrook
Carleton Hall
Saltcoats
Mite Houses
Ravenglass
RAVENGLASS FOR ESKDALE RLY MUS
Muncaster Mill
Waberthwaite
Drigg Point
River Esk
Newbiggin
Lane End
Middleton Place
Stub Place
Hycemoor
Bootle
Selker Bay
Tarn Bay
Santon Bridge
Santon
A595
A5086
B5345
B5344
B5295
228
229
220
210
NX
NY
SC
SD

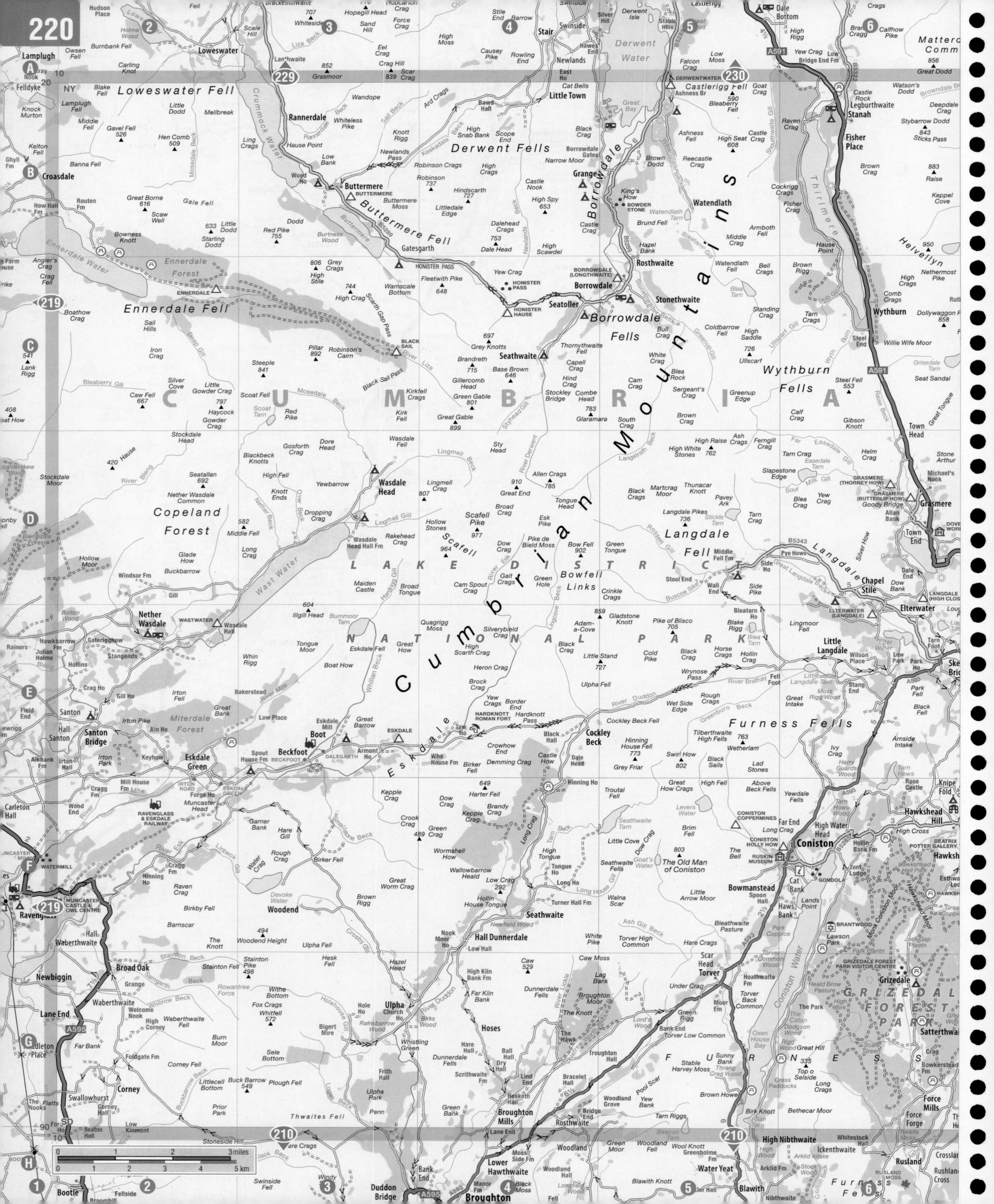

Lamplugh
Loweswater
Loweswater Fell
Crummock Water
Rannerdale
Derwent Fells
Little Town
Newlands
Stair
Derwent Water
Castlerigg Fell
Legburthwaite
Stanah
Fisher Place
Croasdale
Buttermere
Buttermere Fell
Gatesgarth
Grange
Borrowdale
Watendlath
Rosthwaite
Stonethwaite
Seatoller
Borrowdale Fells
Ennerdale Forest
Ennerdale Water
Ennerdale Fell
Wythburn
Thirlmere
Helvellyn
Seathwaite
Wythburn Fells
CUMBRIA
Cumbrian Mountains
Great Gable
899
Scafell Pike
977
Scafell
964
Wasdale Head
Copeland Forest
Langdale Fell
Grasmere
Chapel Stile
Elterwater
LAKE DISTRICT NATIONAL PARK
Bowfell Links
Nether Wasdale
Wast Water
Little Langdale
Santon Bridge
Miterdale Forest
Boot
Beckfoot
Eskdale Green
Eskdale
Cockley Beck
Furness Fells
Coniston
The Old Man of Coniston
803
Hawkshead Hill
Bowmanstead
Seathwaite
Hall Dunnerdale
Woodend
Ravenglass
Waberthwaite
Broad Oak
Newbiggin
Lane End
Ulpha
Hoses
Torver
Coniston Water
GRIZEDALE FOREST PARK
Grizedale
Satterthwaite
Corney
Broughton Mills
Rosthwaite
Water Yeat
High Nibthwaite
Force Mills
Rusland
Blawith
Lower Hawthwaite
Duddon Bridge
Broughton
Bootle
Swallowhurst
Woodland
229
230
219
210
0 1 2 3 miles
0 1 2 3 4 5 km

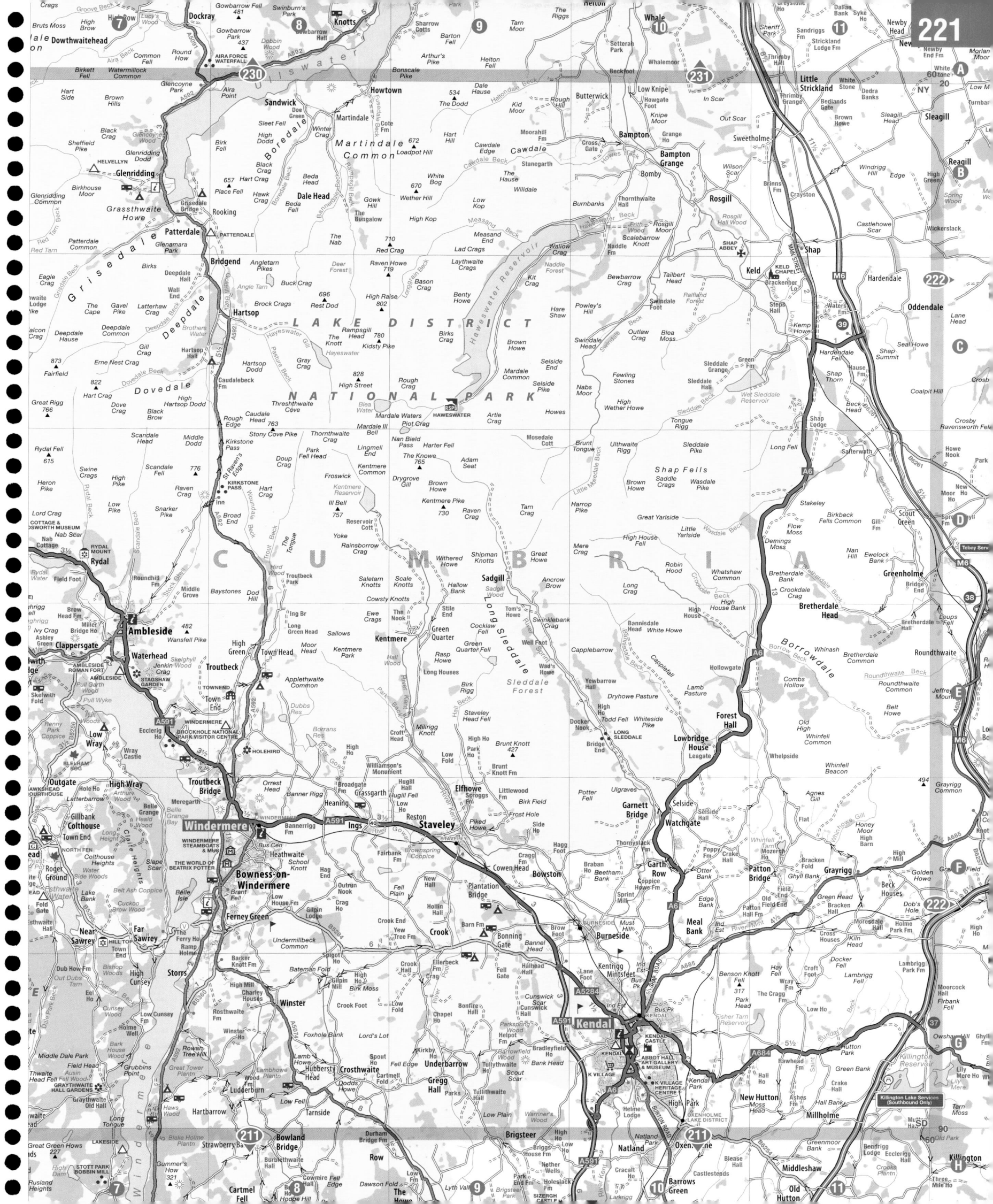

Dockray
Knotts
Ullswater
230
231
Howtown
Sandwick
Martindale
Martindale Common
Boredale
Glenridding
Helvellyn
Patterdale
Grisedale
Bridgend
Hartsop
Deepdale
Dovedale
Bampton
Bampton Grange
Bomby
Rosgill
Shap
Keld
Shap Abbey
Haweswater Reservoir
Haweswater
Lake District National Park
Mardale Common
Shap Fells
Oddendale
Hardendale
Whale
Little Strickland
Sleagill
Reagill
Cumbria
Rydal
Ambleside
Clappersgate
Waterhead
Troutbeck
Kirkstone Pass
Kentmere
Sadgill
Long Sleddale
Sleddale Forest
Green Quarter
Staveley
Ings
Windermere
Bowness-on-Windermere
Troutbeck Bridge
Ferney Green
Far Sawrey
Near Sawrey
Storrs
Crook
Burneside
Kendal
Natland
Oxenholme
Garnett Bridge
Selside
Watchgate
Garth Row
Meal Bank
Patton Bridge
Grayrigg
Greenholme
Bretherdale Head
Borrowdale
Roundthwaite
Forest Hall
Lowbridge House
Crosthwaite
Underbarrow
Gregg Hall
Winster
Bowland Bridge
Brigsteer
Middleshaw
Millholme
New Hutton
Killington
Killington Lake Services (Southbound Only)
Tebay Services
222
211
M6
A6
A591
A592
A684
A685
A5284

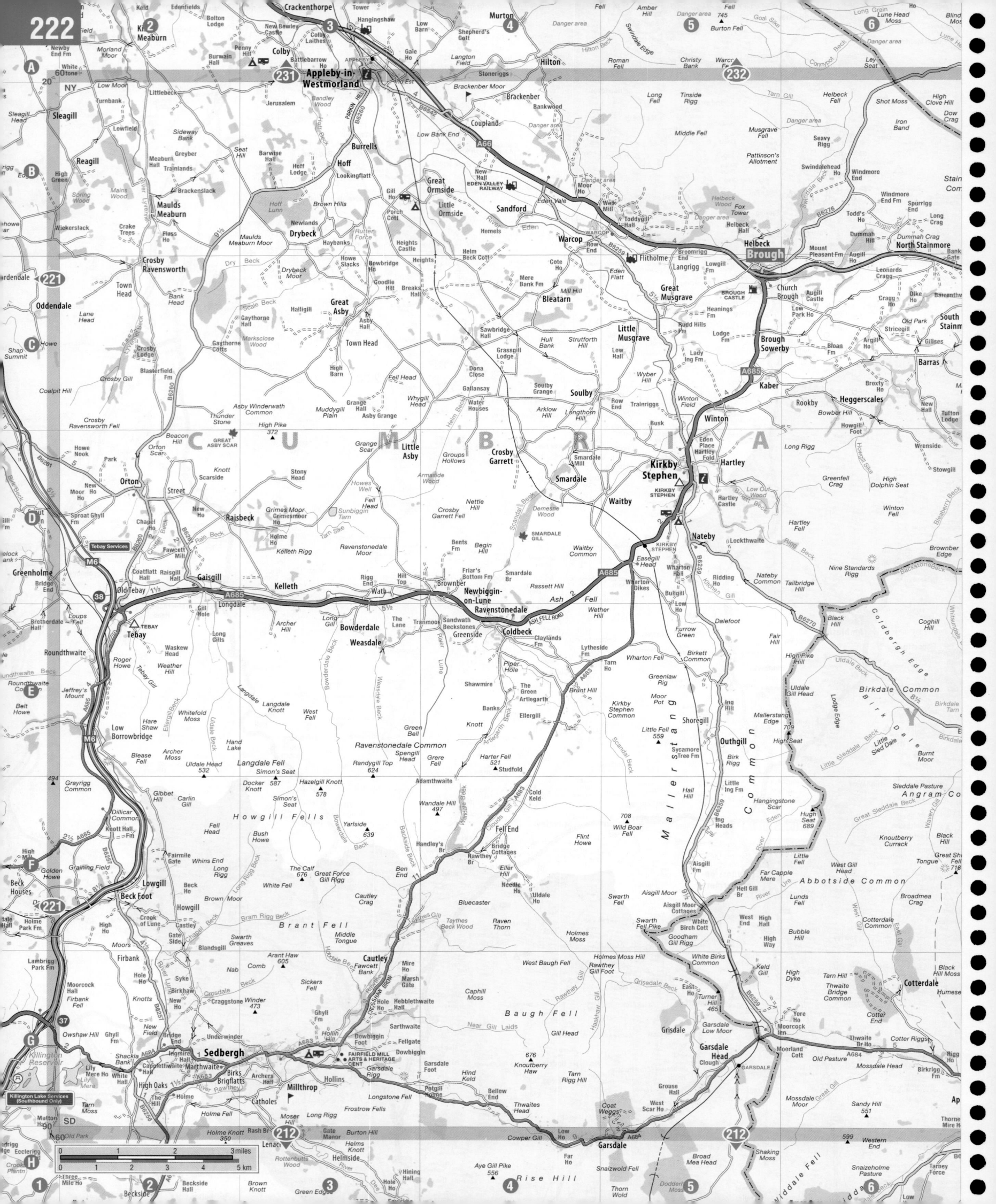
Crackenthorpe
Hangingshaw
Murton
Hilton
Appleby-in-Westmorland
Colby
Colby Laithes
Battlebarrow
New Bewley Castle
Penny Hill
Burwain Hall
Morland Moor
Newby End Fm
White Stone
Kings Meaburn
Bolton Lodge
Edenfields
Keld
Low Barn
Gale Ho
Shepherd's Cott
Langton Field
Stoneriggs
Brackenber Moor
Brackenber
Bankwood
Coupland
Low Bank End
Jerusalem
Bandley Wood
Littlebeck
Low Moor
Turnbank
Sleagill
Sleagill Head
Lowfield
Sideway Bank
Greyber
Seat Hill
Barwise Hall
Hoff Lodge
Burrells
Hoff
Lookingflatt
Reagill
Meaburn Hall
Trainlands
High Green
Brackenslack
Spring Wood
Mains Wood
Maulds Meaburn
Hoff Lunn
Brown Hills
Newlands
Drybeck
Gill Ho
Great Ormside
Little Ormside
Porch Cott
New Hall
EDEN VALLEY RAILWAY
Sandford
Eden Vale
Moor Ho
Walk Mill
Toddygill Hall
Wickerslack
Crake Trees
Flass Ho
Maulds Meaburn Moor
Haybanks
Rutter Force
Heights Castle
Hemels
River Eden
Warcop
Row End
Flitholme
Broomrigg End
Langrigg
Helbeck Wood
Fox Tower
Helbeck Hall
Helbeck
Brough
Mount Pleasant Fm
Augill Ho
Dummah Hill
Dummah Crag
North Stainmore
Crosby Ravensworth
Dry Beck
Drybeck Moor
Howe Slacks
Bowbridge Ho
Goodlie Hill
Heights
Helm Beck Cott
Cote Ho
Mere Bank Fm
Mill Hill
Eden Flatt
Bleatarn
Great Musgrave
Lowgill Fm
BROUGH CASTLE
Church Brough
Augill Castle
Leonards Cragg
Cragg Ho
Dike Ho
Town Head
Bank Head
Scale Beck
Breaks Hall
Great Asby
Halligill
Asby Hall
Gaythorne Hall
Oddendale
Lane Head
Heanings Fm
Rudd Hills Fm
Low Park Ho
Old Park
Stricegill
South Stainmore
Sawbridge Hall
Hull Bank
Strutforth Hill
Little Musgrave
Lodge Fm
Brough Sowerby
Bloan Fm
Argill Ho
Gillses
Barras
Shap Summit
Howe
Crosby Lodge
Gaythorne Cotts
Marksclose Wood
Town Head
Grassgill Lodge
Low Hall
Lady Ing Fm
Blasterfield Fm
High Barn
Dona Close
Crosby Gill
Fell Head
Gallansay
Soulby Grange
Soulby
Wyber Hill
A685
Kaber
Broxty Ho
Coalpit Hill
Whygill Head
Grange Hall
Asby Grange
Muddygill Plain
Water Houses
Arklow Hill
Longthorn Hill
Row End
Trainriggs
Winton Field
Winton
Rookby
Heggerscales
Bowber Hill
Howgill Foot
New Hall
Tufton Lodge
Asby Winderwath Common
High Pike 372
Thunder Stone
Crosby Ravensworth Fell
Beacon Hill
GREAT ASBY SCAR
C U M B R I A
Grange Scar
Little Asby
Groups Hollows
Crosby Garrett
Busk
Eden Place
Hartley Fold
Hartley
Long Rigg
Wrenside
Howe Nook
Orton Scar
Park
Knott
Scarside
Stony Head
Armaside Wood
Smardale Mill
Smardale
Kirkby Stephen
KIRKBY STEPHEN
Greenfell Crag
High Dolphin Seat
Stowgill
Orton
New Ho
Moor Ho
Street
Howes Well
Fell Head
Nettle Hill
Crosby Garrett Fell
Demesne Wood
Waitby
Low Out Wood
Hartley Castle
Winton Fell
Sproat Ghyll Fm
Chapel Ho
New Ho
Raisbeck
Grimes Moor
Grimesmoor
Sunbiggin Tarn
Tarn Sike
Holme Ho
Kelleth Rigg
SMARDALE GILL
Nateby
Lockthwaite
Hartley Fell
Tebay Services
Fawcett Mill
Ravenstonedale Moor
Bents Fm
Begin Hill
Waitby Common
KIRKBY STEPHEN
Easegill Head
Wharton Hall
Nine Standards Rigg
Brownber Edge
Greenholme
Bridge End
M6
Coatflatt Raisgill Hall
Gaisgill
Old Tebay
Kelleth
Rigg End
Wath
Hill Top
Brownber
Friar's Bottom Fm
Smardale Br
Rassett Hill
Newbiggin-on-Lune
Ravenstonedale
Ash Fell
Wharton Dikes
Bullgill
Ridding Ho
Nateby Common
Tailbridge Hill
Backstone Beck
Kitchen Gill
Loups Fell
Bretherdale Hall
Gill Hole
Longdale
A685
Tebay
TEBAY
Archer Hill
Long Gill
Bowderdale
The Lane
Tranmoor
Sandwath Beckstones
Greenside
Coldbeck
ASH FELL ROAD
Claylands Fm
Wether Hill
Low Ho
Dalefoot
B6270
Black Hill
Coldbergh Edge
Coghill Hill
Roundthwaite
Roger Howe
Waskew Head
Long Gills
Weasdale
Furrow Green
Fair Hill
Lytheside Fm
Tarn Ho
Wharton Fell
Birkett Common
High Pike Hill
Uldale Beck
Jeffrey's Mount
Weather Hill
Tebay Gill
Piper Hole
Shawmire
The Green
Artlegarth
A683
Brant Hill
Greenlaw Rig
Moor Pot
Kirkby Stephen Common
Uldale Gill Head
Birkdale Common
Belt Howe
Ellergill Beck
Whitefold Moss
Langdale
Langdale Knott
West Fell
Banks
Ellergill
Ing Hill
Lodge Edge
Birk Dale
Birkdale Tarn
Hare Shaw
Low Borrowbridge
Green Bell
Knott
Little Fell 559
Shoregill
Mallerstang Edge
709
High Seat
Hand Lake
Ravenstonedale Common
Spengill Head
Grere Fell
Outhgill
Sycamore Tree Fm
Little Sleddale Beck
Little Sled Dale
Burnt Moor
Blease Fell
Archer Moss
Uldale Head 532
Langdale Fell
Simon's Seat 587
Randygill Top 624
Harter Fell 521
Studfold
Birk Rigg
494
Grayrigg Common
Docker Knott
Hazelgill Knott 578
Adamthwaite
Cold Keld
Hall Hill
Little Ing Fm
Sleddale Pasture
Angram Common
Gibbet Hill
Carlin Gill
Simon's Seat
Wandale Hill 497
Hangingstone Scar
Hugh Seat 689
Great Sleddale Beck
Dillicar Common
Knott Hall Fm
Howgill Fells
Yarlside 639
708
Wild Boar Fell
Ing Heads
Mallerstang
Common
Knoutberry Currack
Black Hill
Fell Head
Bush Howe
Fell End
Bridge Cottages
Flint Howe
Great Shunner Fell 716
Tongue
Handley's Br
Rawthey Br
Fairmile Gate
Whins End
Graining Field
Long Rigg
The Calf 676
Great Force Gill Rigg
Ben End
Eller Hill
Little Fell
West Gill Head
Far Capple Mere
Abbotside Common
Golden Howe
Beck Houses
Lowgill
Beck Ho
White Fell
Needle Ho
Uldale Ho
Swarth Fell
Aisgill Moor
Hell Gill Br
River Ure
Lunds Fell
Broadmea Crag
Beck Foot
Howgill
Brown Moor
Long Rigg Beck
Cautley Crag
Bluecaster
Aisgill Moor Cottages
Aisgill Fm
Holme Park Fm
Crook of Lune
Castley
High Ho
Bram Rigg Beck
Brant Fell
Taythes Gill
Taythes Beck Wood
Raven Thorn
Swarth Fell Pike
West Birch Cott
West End
High Hall
Bubble Hill
Cotterdale Common
Moors
Firbank
Side
Swarth Greaves
Middle Tongue
Holmes Moss
Goodham Gill Rigg
High Way
Blandsgill
Arant Haw 605
Holmes Moss Hill
West Baugh Fell
Rawthey Gill Foot
White Birks Common
Lambrigg Park Fm
Hole Ho
Syke
Nab
Comb
Cautley
Fawcett Bank
Mire Ho
Marsh Gate
Keld Gill
High Dyke
Tarn Hill
Thwaite Bridge Common
Black Hill Moss
Cotterdale
Humesett
Moorcock Hall
Firbank Fell
Knotts
Birkhaw
Crosdale
Craggstone
Winder 473
Sickers Fell
Caphill Moss
Grisedale Beck
East Ho
Turner Hill 465
B6259
Ghyll Fm
Hole Ho
Hebblethwaite Hall
CROSSDAW BROW
Baugh Fell
Near Gill Laids
Cotter End
Yore Ho
Moorcock Inn
Owshaw Hill
Ghyll Fm
New Field
Bridge End
Underwinder
Hollin Hill
Dowbiggin Foot
Sarthwaite
Fellgate
Dowbiggin
Gill Head
Grisdale
Garsdale Low Moor
Moorland Cott
Thwaite Br Ho
Cotter Riggs
Killington Reservoir
Shackla Bank
Ingmire Hall
Sedbergh
Marthwaite
Birks
Brigflatts
FAIRFIELD MILL ARTS & HERITAGE CENT
Garsdale Rigg
Garsdale Foot
Hind Keld
676
Knoutberry Haw
Tarn Rigg Hill
Garsdale Head
Clough
GARSDALE
A684
Old Pasture
Mossdale Head
Birkrigg Fm
Lily Mere Ho
White Hall
Capplethwaite Hall
Lily Mere
High Oaks
Archers Hall
Millthrop
Hollins
Potgill Ho
Bellow End
Grouse Hall
Killington Lake Services (Southbound Only)
Tarn Moss
The Hill
Holme
Catholes
Longstone Fell
Thwaites Head
Coat Weggs
Scar Ho
Mossdale Moor
Sandy Hill 551
Holme Fell
Moser Hill
Long Rigg
Frostrow Fells
Mutton Hill
Old Park
Holme Knott 350
Rash Br
Gate Manor
Burton Hill
Cowper Gill
Low Ho
Garsdale
Thorne Mire Ho
599
Western End
Lenacre
Helms Knott
Helmside
Far Ho
Broad Mea Head
Shaking Moss
Snaizeholme Pasture
Tarney Force
Ecclerigg
Crook of Plantn
Rottenbutts Wood
Hining Hall
Aye Gill Pike 556
Rise Hill
Snaizwold Fell
Widdale Fell
Three Mile Ho
Beckside
Beckside Hall
Brown Knott
Green Edge
Hole Ho
Thorn Wold
Dodderham Moss
0 1 2 3 miles
0 1 2 3 4 5 km

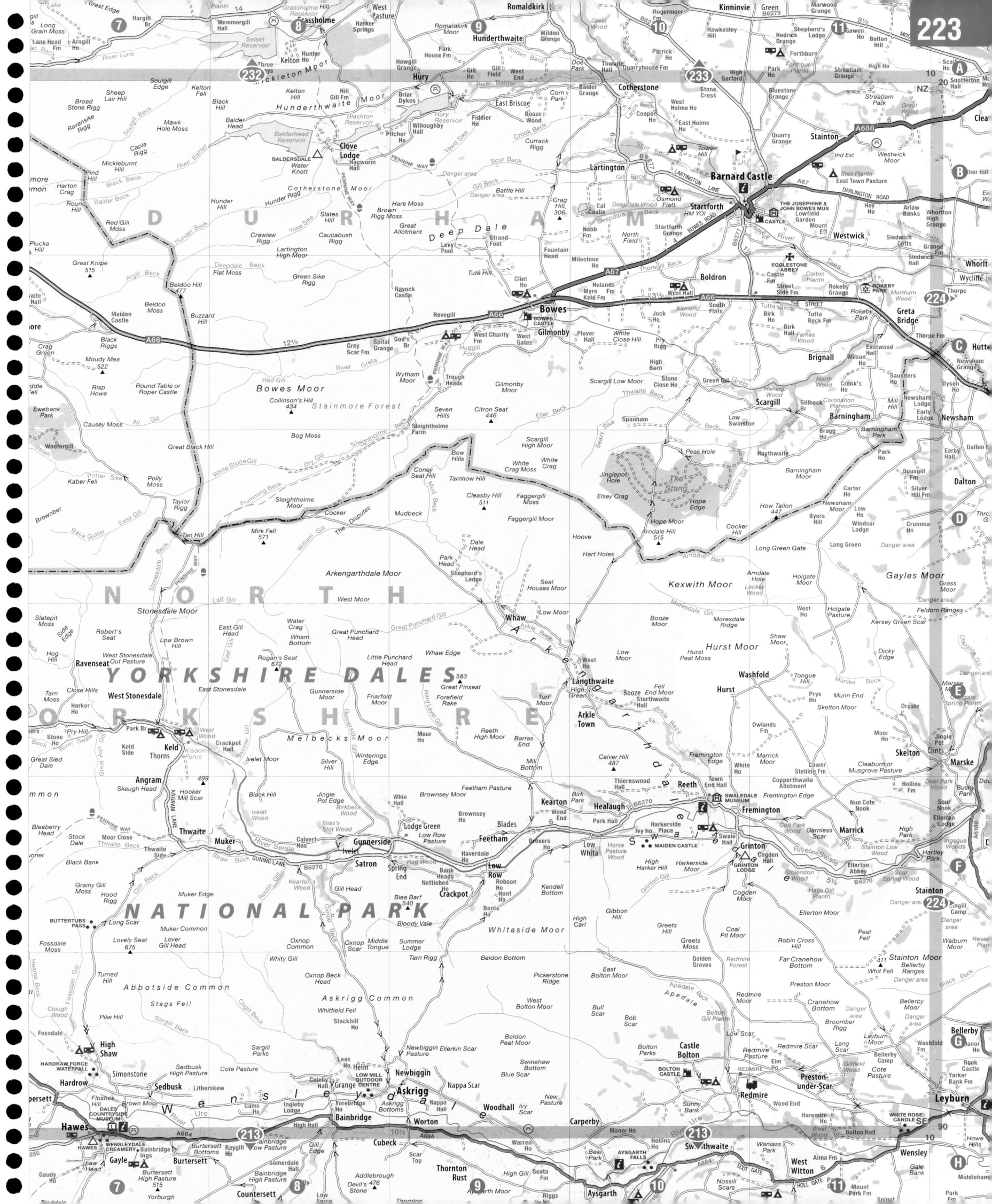
Grassholme
West Pasture
Romaldkirk
Kinninvie
Hunderthwaite
Selset Reservoir
Grassholme Reservoir
Wemmergill Hall
Long Grain Moss
Lune Head Fm
Arngill Ho
Kelton Ho
Hunter Ho
Three Pikes
Mickleton Moor
Hury
Cotherstone
Barnard Castle
Startforth
Lartington
Hunderthwaite Moor
Blackton Reservoir
Hury Reservoir
Balderhead Reservoir
Clove Lodge
BALDERSDALE
Hagworm Hall
PENNINE WAY
Cotherstone Moor
Hunder Rigg
Deep Dale
D U R H A M
Bowes
BOWES CASTLE
Gilmonby
A66
A67
A688
Boldron
Startforth
Westwick
THE JOSEPHINE & JOHN BOWES MUS
CASTLE
EGGLESTONE ABBEY
ROKEBY PARK
Greta Bridge
Stainton
Bowes Moor
Stainmore Forest
Brignall
Scargill
Barningham
Newsham
Dalton
Bog Moss
Sleightholme Farm
The Stang
Hope Moor
Arndale Hill 515
How Tallon 447
Kexwith Moor
Gayles Moor
Tan Hill
Mirk Fell 571
Arkengarthdale Moor
N O R T H
Stonesdale Moor
West Moor
Whaw
Arkle Beck
Langthwaite
Arkle Town
Hurst Moor
Washfold
Hurst
Ravenseat
YORKSHIRE DALES
West Stonesdale
Keld
Thorns
Kisdon Force
Angram
Melbecks Moor
Calver Hill 487
Reeth
Healaugh
Fremington
SWALEDALE MUSEUM
Grinton
GRINTON LODGE
Marrick
Marske
Skelton
MAIDEN CASTLE
Thwaite
Muker
Gunnerside
Ivelet
Satron
Feetham
Low Row
Crackpot
River Swale
B6270
NATIONAL PARK
BUTTERTUBS PASS
Lovely Seat 675
Whitaside Moor
Ellerton Moor
Stainton Moor
Abbotside Common
Askrigg Common
Stags Fell
High Shaw
HARDRAW FORCE WATERFALL
Simonstone
Hardraw
Sedbusk
Newbiggin
Askrigg
Nappa Scar
Woodhall
Carperby
Castle Bolton
BOLTON CASTLE
Redmire
Preston-under-Scar
Leyburn
Wensleydale
River Ure
Hawes
DALES COUNTRYSIDE MUSEUM
WENSLEYDALE CREAMERY
Gayle
Burtersett
Bainbridge
Worton
Cubeck
Thornton Rust
AYSGARTH FALLS
Aysgarth
Swinithwaite
West Witton
Wensley
Countersett
A684
WHITE ROSE CANDLE
Bolton Hall
7
8
9
10
11
232
233
213
224
A
B
C
D
E
F
G
H
NZ
SE

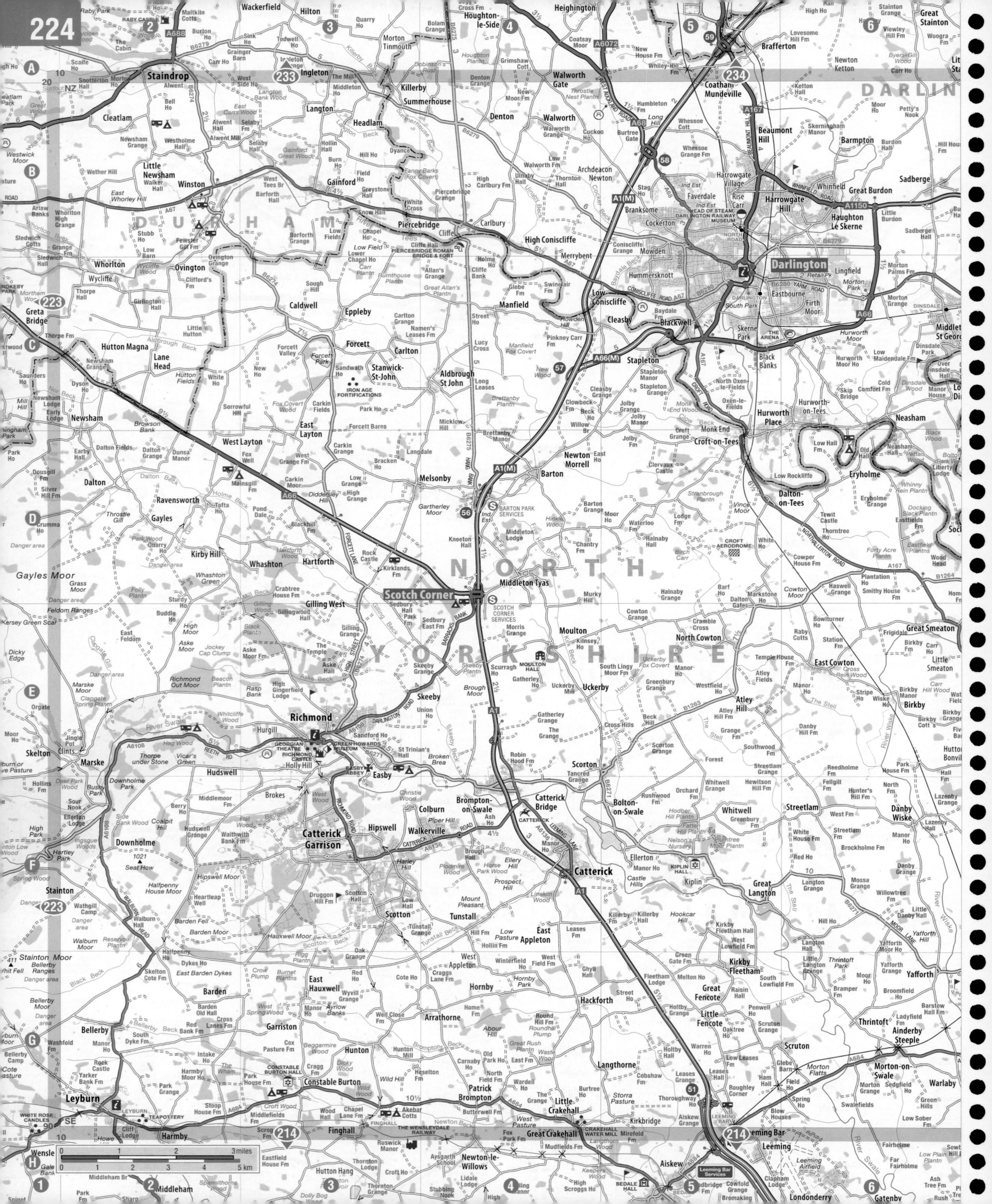
Staindrop
Ingleton
Killerby
Summerhouse
Headlam
Langton
Gainford
Winston
Cleatlam
Little Newsham
Piercebridge
Walworth
Walworth Gate
Denton
Heighington
Houghton-le-Side
High Coniscliffe
Merrybent
Low Coniscliffe
Manfield
Coatham Mundeville
Beaumont Hill
Barmpton
Harrowgate Hill
Harrowgate Village
Great Burdon
Sadberge
Haughton Le Skerne
Darlington
Cockerton
Mowden
Hummersknott
Blackwell
Cleasby
Stapleton
Eastbourne
Firth Moor
Lingfield
Skerne Park
Hurworth Place
Hurworth-on-Tees
Neasham
Croft-on-Tees
Dalton-on-Tees
Eryholme
Whorlton
Wycliffe
Ovington
Greta Bridge
Hutton Magna
Lane Head
Caldwell
Eppleby
Forcett
Carlton
Stanwick-St-John
Aldbrough St John
East Layton
West Layton
Newsham
Dalton
Ravensworth
Gayles
Kirby Hill
Whashton
Hartforth
Melsonby
Barton
Newton Morrell
Scotch Corner
Middleton Tyas
Gilling West
Moulton
North Cowton
East Cowton
Great Smeaton
Little Smeaton
Birkby
Atley Hill
Uckerby
Skeeby
Richmond
Marske
Hudswell
Easby
Brompton-on-Swale
Catterick Bridge
Scorton
Bolton-on-Swale
Streetlam
Whitwell
Danby Wiske
Colburn
Hipswell
Walkerville
Catterick Garrison
Catterick
Downholme
Scotton
Tunstall
East Appleton
Great Langton
Kiplin
Kirkby Fleetham
Great Fencote
Little Fencote
Yafforth
Thrintoft
Ainderby Steeple
Scruton
Morton-on-Swale
Warlaby
Hackforth
Hornby
Arrathorne
East Hauxwell
Garriston
Barden
Bellerby
Hunton
Langthorne
Constable Burton
Patrick Brompton
Little Crakehall
Great Crakehall
Leyburn
Harmby
Finghall
Newton-le-Willows
Aiskew
Leeming Bar
Leeming
Londonderry
Middleham
Wensley
Skelton
Stainton
D U R H A M
N O R T H
Y O R K S H I R E
DARLIN
A1(M)
A66(M)
A66
A67
A1
A684
A6108
A6136
A167
B6275
B6274
B6271
B1263
0 1 2 3 miles
0 1 2 3 4 5 km

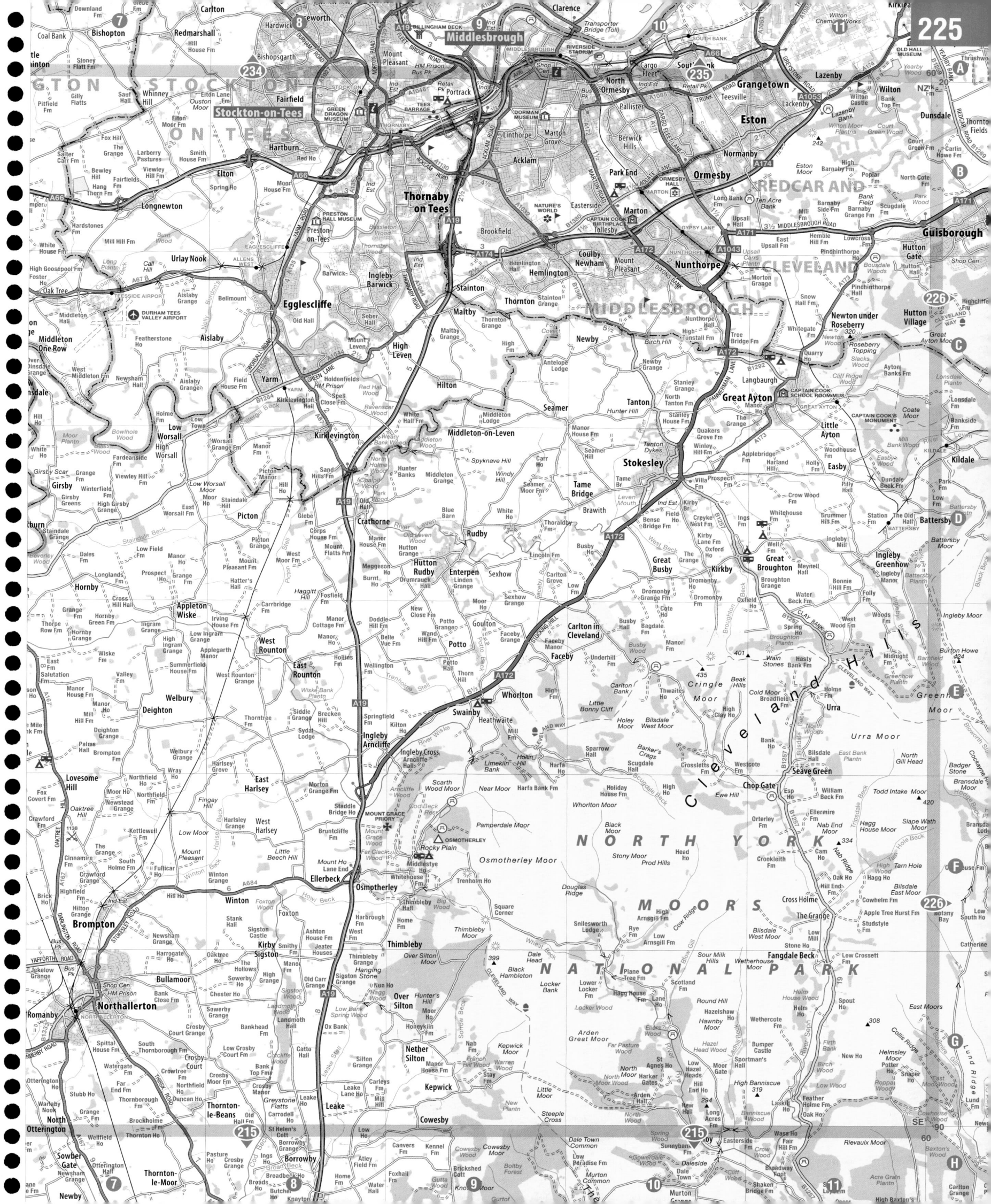

225
Middlesbrough
Stockton-on-Tees
STOCKTON ON TEES
REDCAR AND CLEVELAND
MIDDLESBROUGH
Thornaby on Tees
Billingham Beck
Transporter Bridge (Toll)
Riverside Stadium
Dorman Museum
Green Dragon Museum
Tees Barrage
Preston Hall Museum
Captain Cook Birthplace
Captain Cook Schoolroom Mus
Captain Cook's Monument
Nature's World
Mount Grace Priory
HM Prison
Durham Tees Valley Airport
Teesside Airport
Downland Fm
Carlton
Bishopton
Redmarshall
Coal Bank
Hardwick
Norton
Bishopsgarth
Clarence
Grangetown
South Bank
Lazenby
Wilton
Eston
Dunsdale
Normanby
Ormesby
Fairfield
Whinney Hill
Elton
Hartburn
Longnewton
Urlay Nook
Egglescliffe
Eaglescliffe
Preston-on-Tees
Ingleby Barwick
Stainton
Maltby
Thornton
Hemlington
Coulby Newham
Nunthorpe
Marton
Park End
Acklam
Linthorpe
Brookfield
Tollesby
Guisborough
Hutton Gate
Newton under Roseberry
Roseberry Topping
Hutton Village
Great Ayton
Little Ayton
Kildale
Easby
Battersby
Ingleby Greenhow
Middleton One Row
Aislaby
Yarm
High Leven
Kirklevington
Hilton
Newby
Seamer
Tanton
Langbaurgh
Stokesley
Middleton-on-Leven
Low Worsall
High Worsall
Girsby
Picton
Crathorne
Rudby
Hutton Rudby
Enterpen
Sexhow
Tame Bridge
Great Busby
Kirkby
Great Broughton
Hornby
Appleton Wiske
West Rounton
East Rounton
Potto
Carlton in Cleveland
Faceby
Whorlton
Swainby
Welbury
Deighton
Ingleby Arncliffe
Ingleby Cross
Lovesome Hill
East Harlsey
West Harlsey
Ellerbeck
Osmotherley
Winton
Brompton
Thimbleby
Kirby Sigston
Northallerton
Bullamoor
Over Silton
Nether Silton
Kepwick
Cowesby
Leake
Thornton-le-Beans
Thornton-le-Moor
North Otterington
Romanby
Sowber Gate
Newby
Borrowby
Cleveland Hills
Cringle Moor
Urra Moor
Urra
Chop Gate
Seave Green
Fangdale Beck
Osmotherley Moor
NORTH YORK MOORS NATIONAL PARK
Cleveland Way
A19
A66
A172
A174
A171
A173
A684
A167
A1044
B1257
B1365
B1380
B1264
234
235
215
226

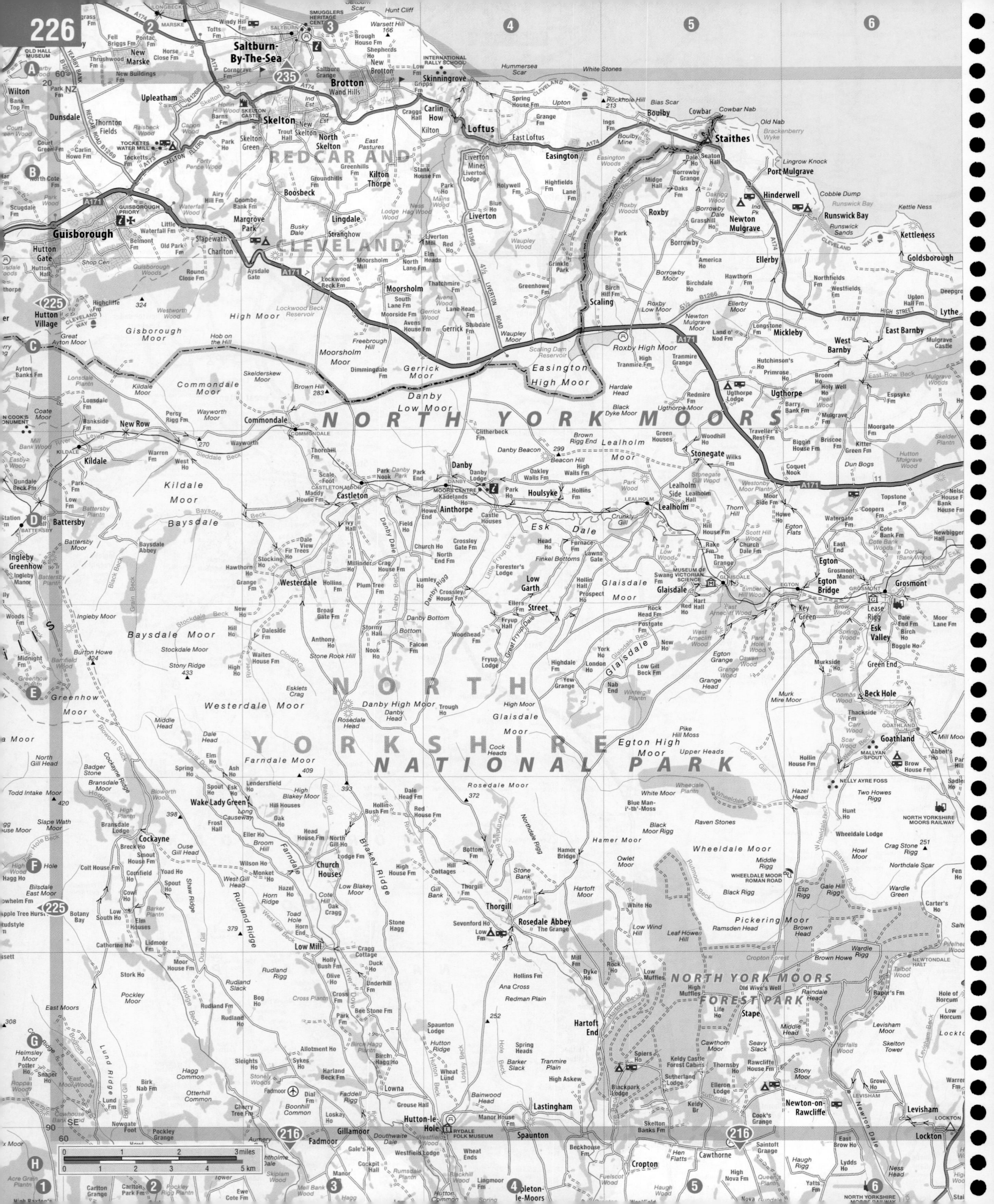

Saltburn-By-The-Sea
Skinningrove
Brotton
Loftus
Carlin How
Boulby
Staithes
Easington
Skelton
North Skelton
Upleatham
Guisborough
Hutton Gate
Hutton Village
Margrove Park
Lingdale
Boosbeck
Kilton Thorpe
Liverton
Moorsholm
Port Mulgrave
Hinderwell
Runswick Bay
Kettleness
Goldsborough
Lythe
East Barnby
West Barnby
Mickleby
Ellerby
Newton Mulgrave
Roxby
Scaling
REDCAR AND CLEVELAND
High Moor
Gisborough Moor
Moorsholm Moor
Gerrick Moor
Easington High Moor
Roxby High Moor
Danby Low Moor
Commondale Moor
Commondale
NORTH YORK MOORS
Ugthorpe
Lealholm
Lealholm Moor
Stonegate
Danby
Danby Beacon
Castleton
Ainthorpe
Houlsyke
Kildale
Kildale Moor
Baysdale
Battersby
Ingleby Greenhow
New Row
Westerdale
Esk Dale
Glaisdale
Glaisdale Moor
Egton
Egton Bridge
Grosmont
Esk Valley
Goathland
Beck Hole
Baysdale Moor
Westerdale Moor
Danby High Moor
Glaisdale Moor
Egton High Moor
NORTH YORKSHIRE NATIONAL PARK
Farndale Moor
Rosedale Moor
Wake Lady Green
Cockayne
Church Houses
Thorgill
Rosedale Abbey
Low Mill
Hartoft End
Lastingham
Hutton-le-Hole
Gillamoor
Fadmoor
Spaunton
Cropton
Cawthorne
Newton-on-Rawcliffe
Levisham
Lockton
Stape
Pickering Moor
Wheeldale Moor
NORTH YORK MOORS FOREST PARK
NORTH YORKSHIRE MOORS RAILWAY
RYEDALE FOLK MUSEUM
A171
A174
A173
B1366
B1266
225
235
216
0 1 2 3 miles
0 1 2 3 4 5 km

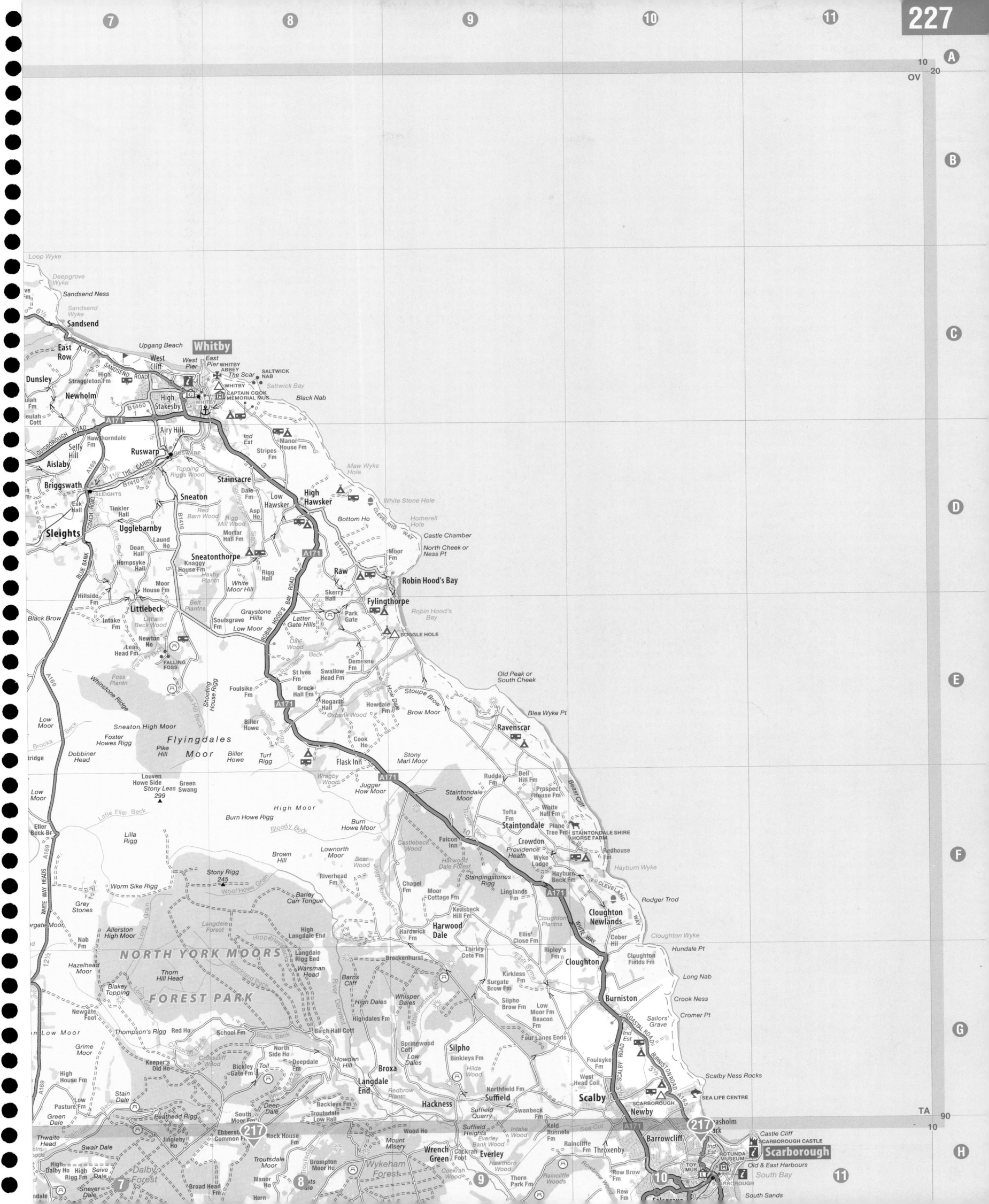

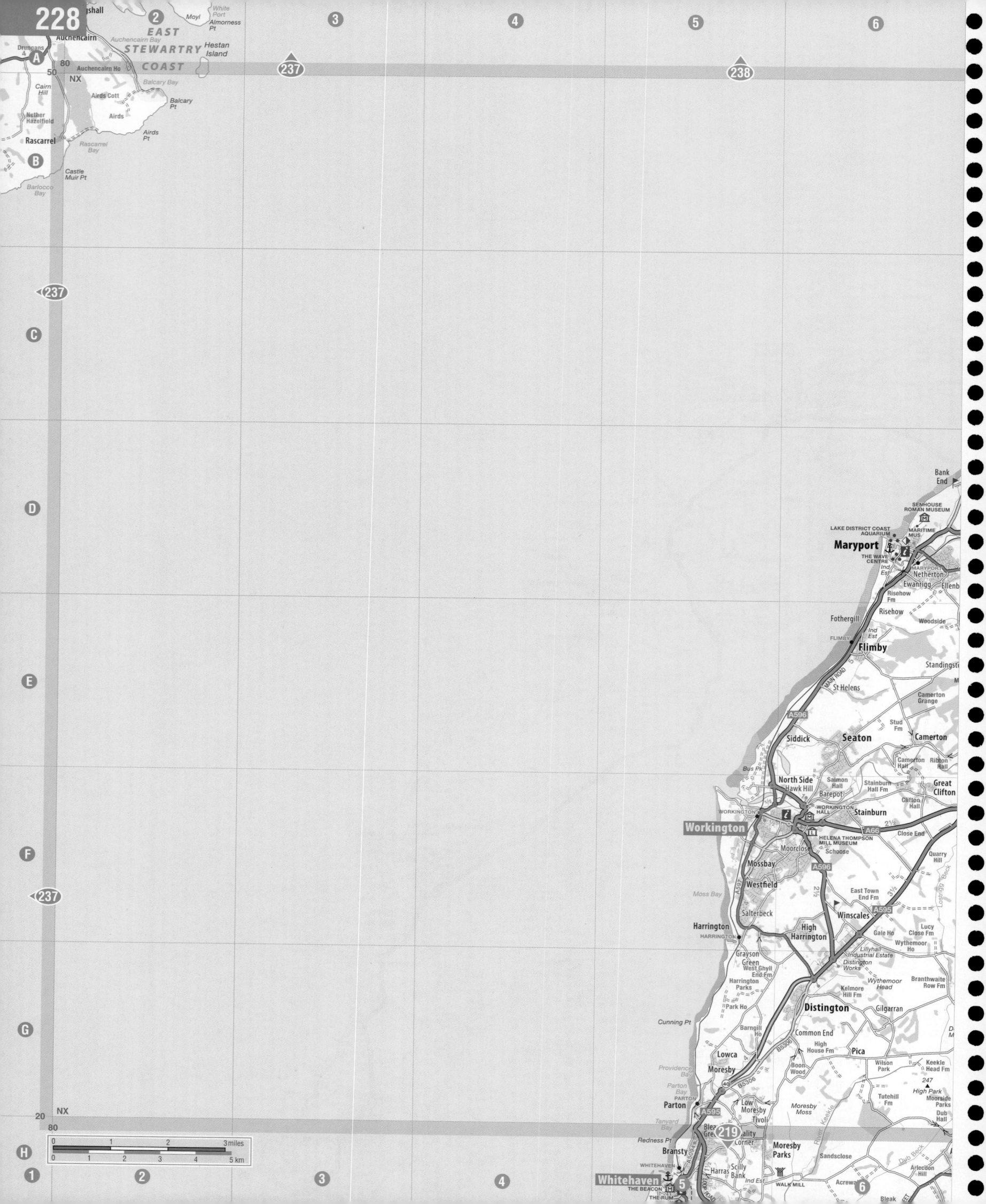

EAST
STEWARTRY

COAST

Drungans

Cairn
Hill

Nether
Hazelfield

Rascarrel

Castle
Muir Pt

Barlocco
Bay

Auchencairn

Auchencairn Ho

NX

Auchencairn Bay

Balcary Bay

Airds Cott

Balcary
Pt

Airds

Airds
Pt

Rascarrel
Bay

shall

Moyl

White
Port
Almorness
Pt

Hestan
Island

237

238

237

237

Bank
End

SENHOUSE
ROMAN MUSEUM

LAKE DISTRICT COAST
AQUARIUM

MARITIME
MUS

Maryport

THE WAVE
CENTRE

MARYPORT
Ind
Est

Netherton

Ewanrigg

Ellenb

Risehow
Fm

Risehow

Woodside

Fothergill

Ind
Est

FLIMBY

Flimby

Standingste

St Helens

MAIN ROAD

Camerton
Grange

A596

Stud
Fm

Siddick

Seaton

Camerton

Camerton
Hall

Ribton
Hall

North Side
Hawk Hill

Salmon
Hall

Stainburn
Hall Fm

Great
Clifton

Barepot

Clifton
Hall

Bus Pk

WORKINGTON
HALL

Stainburn

Workington

A66

Close End

HELENA THOMPSON
MILL MUSEUM

Schoose

Quarry
Hill

Moorclose

Mossbay

A596

Westfield

East Town
End Fm

A597

A595

Moss Bay

Winscales

Salterbeck

Gale Ho

Lucy
Close Fm

Harrington

High
Harrington

Wythemoor
Ho

HARRINGTON

Lillyhall
Industrial Estate

Grayson
Green

West Ghyll
End Fm

Distington
Works

Branthwaite
Row Fm

Harrington
Parks

Wythemoor
Head

Kelmore
Hill Fm

Park Ho

Distington

Gilgarran

Cunning Pt

Barngill
Ho

Common End

High
House Fm

Pica

Lowca

Boon
Wood

Wilson
Park

Keekle
Head Fm

Moresby

247

High Park

Providence
Bay

Parton
Bay

PARTON

Low
Moresby

Moresby
Moss

Tivoli

Moorside
Parks

Dub
Hall

Parton

A595

Moresby
Moss

Tutehill
Fm

Tanyard
Bay

Redness Pt

Ble

Gre

219

ality
Corner

Moresby
Parks

Sandsclose

Branstv

WHITEHAVEN

THE BEACON

Whitehaven

THE RUM

Harras
Bank

Scilly
Bank

Ind Est

WALK MILL

Acrewa

Arlecdon
Hill

Bleak

0  1  2  3 miles
0  1  2  3  4  5 km

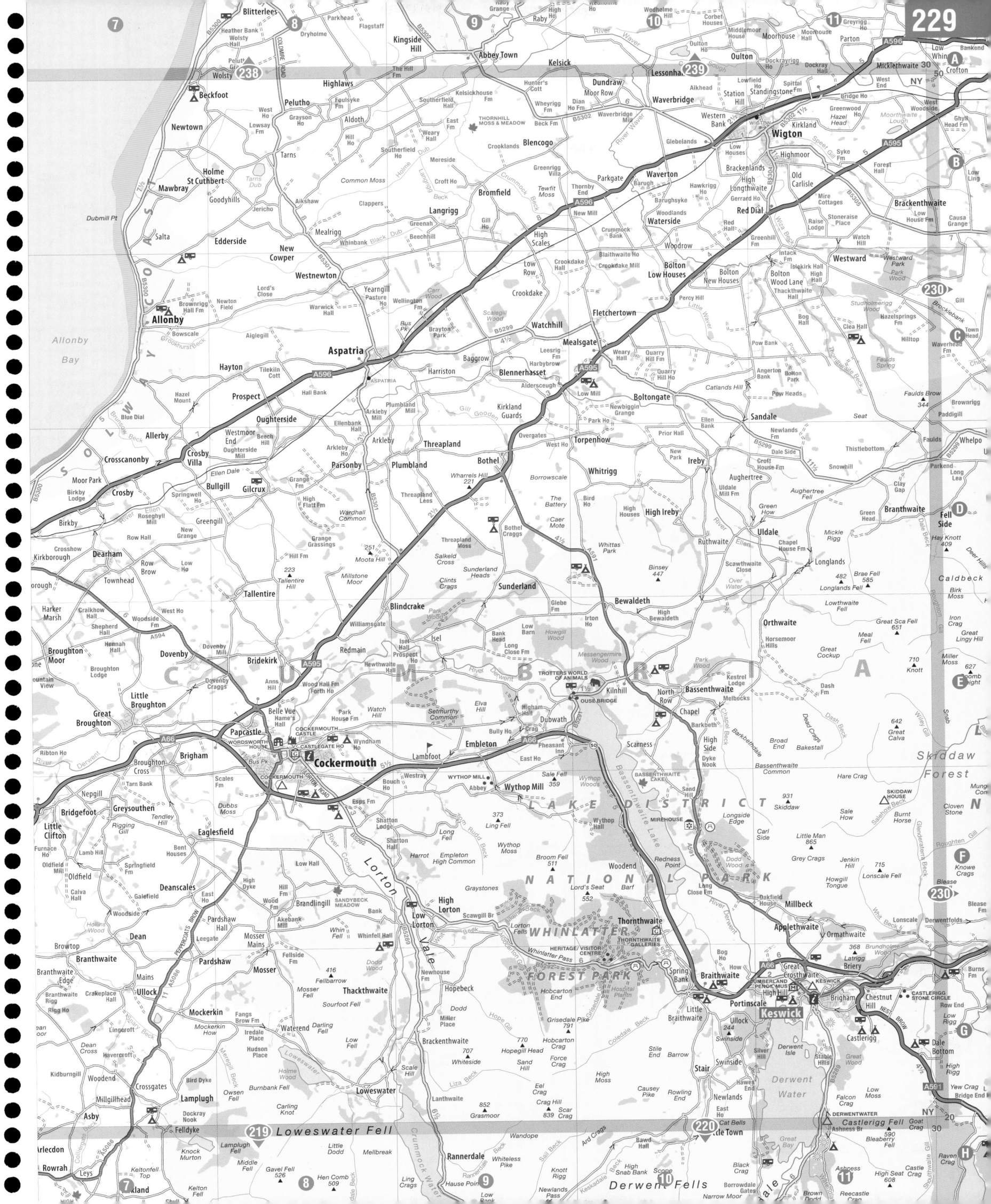

Blitterlees
Heather Bank
Wolsty Hall
Parkhead
Flagstaff
Dryholme
Kingside Hill
Raby Grange
High Ho
Raby
Wedholme Hill
Corbet Houses
Greyrigg Ho
Middlemoor House
Moorhouse
Moorhouse Hall
Parton
Abbey Town
Oulton Ho
Oulton
Low Whinnow
Bankend
Micklethwaite
Crofton
Wolsty
Kelsick
Lessonhall
The Hill Fm
Highlaws
Dundraw
Moor Row
Hunter's Cott
Dockrayrigg Ho
Dockray Hall
Spittal Fm
Beckfoot
Pelutho
Kelsickhouse Fm
Southerfield Hall
Lowfield Ho
Station Hill
Standingstone
Alkhead
Whey rigg Fm
Dian Ho Fm
Bridge Ho
Greenwood Ho
Moorthwaite Lough
West End
Woodside
Ghyll Head Fm
Newtown
Foulsyke Fm
Grayson Ho
West Ho
Lowsay Fm
Aldoth
Hill Ho
Weary Hall
East Fm
Thornhill Moss & Meadow
Beck Fm
Waverbridge Mill
Waverbridge
Western Bank
Wigton
Kirkland
Hazel Head
Glebelands
Tarns
Southerfield Ho
Crooklands
Blencogo
Low Houses
Highmoor
Syke Fm
Forest Hall
Holme St Cuthbert
Mawbray
Goodyhills
Jericho
Tarns Dub
Common Moss
Mereside
Croft Ho
Greenrigg Villa
Parkgate
Waverton
Barugh
Brackenlands
High Longthwaite
Old Carlisle
Low Ling
Tewfit Moss
Thornby End
Hawkrigg Ho
Gerrard Ho
Mire Cottages
Brackenthwaite
Dubmill Pt
Clappers
Aikshaw
Bromfield
Barugh Syke
Red Dial
Low House Fm
Causa Grange
Langrigg
Greenah
Gill Ho
New Mill
Woodlands
Waterside
Stoneraise Place
Raise Lodge
Salta
Mealrigg
Beechhill
High Scales
Crummock Bank
Red Hall
Watch Hill
Greenhill Fm
Edderside
Whinbank
New Cowper
Blaithwaite Ho
Woodrow
Intack Fm
Islekirk Hall
Westward
Westward Park
Park Wood
Low Row
Crookdake Hall
Crookdake Mill
Bolton Low Houses
Bolton New Houses
Bolton Wood Lane
High Hall
Westnewton
Lord's Close
Yearngill Pasture Ho
Carr Wood
Thackthwaite Hall
Crookdake
Percy Hill
Studholmerigg Wood
Allonby
Brownrigg Hall Fm
Newton Field
Warwick Hall
Wellington Fm
Bus Pk
Brayton Park
Scalegill Wood
Watchhill
Fletchertown
Bog Hall
Hazelsprings Fm
Clea Hall
Town Head
Hilltop
Bowscale
Crookhurst Beck
Aiglegill
Allonby Bay
Aspatria
Mealsgate
Leesrig Fm
Harbybrow
Weary Hall
Quarry Hill Fm
Quarry Hill Ho
Pow Bank
Faulds Spring
Waverhead Fm
Baggrow
Hayton
Tilekiln Cott
Harriston
Blennerhasset
Angerton Bank
Bolton Park
Aldersceugh
Low Mill
Catlands Hill
Prospect
Hazel Mount
Hall Bank
Kirkland Guards
Newbiggin Grange
Boltongate
Pow Heads
Faulds Brow
344
Brownrigg
Paddigill
Blue Dial
Oughterside
Ellenbank Hall
Arkleby Mill
Plumbland Mill
Park Ho
Ellen Bank
Sandale
Seat
Allerby
Westmoor End
Beech Hill
Oughterside Mill
Arkleby
Threapland
Overgates
West Ho
Torpenhow
Prior Hall
Newlands Fm
Thistlebottom
Faulds
Whelpo
Crosby Villa
Crosscanonby
Arkleby Ho
Parsonby
Plumbland
Bothel
Wharrels Hill
221
Borrowscale
Whitrigg
New Park
Ireby
Dale Side
Croft House Fm
Snowhill
Parkend
Long Lea
Moor Park
Ellen Dale
Grange Fm
Gilcrux
Bullgill
Crosby
Birkby Lodge
Springwell Ho
High Flatt Fm
Threapland Lees
The Battery
Bird Ho
Aughertree
Uldale Mill Fm
Aughertree Fell
Clay Gap
Birkby
Roseghyll Mill
Greengill
Wardhall Common
High Houses
High Ireby
Green How
Green Head
Branthwaite
Fell Side
Caer Mote
Bothel Craggs
New Grange
Row Hall
Crosshow
Grange Grassings
Threapland Moss
Whittas Park
Ruthwaite
Uldale
Chapel House Fm
Mickle Rigg
Hay Knott
409
Kirkborough
Dearham
251
Moota Hill
Salkeld Cross
Binsey
447
Scawthwaite Close
Longlands
482
Brae Fell
585
Caldbeck
Deer Hills
Row Brow
Low Ho
Hill Fm
223
Tallentire Hill
Millstone Moor
Sunderland Heads
Clints Crags
Sunderland
Over Water
Longlands Fell
Birk Moss
Townhead
Tallentire
Blindcrake
Glebe Fm
Bewaldeth
High Bewaldeth
Lowthwaite Fell
Harker Marsh
Craikhow Hall
West Ho
Woodside Fm
Park Wood
Irton Ho
Orthwaite
Iron Crag
Shepherd Hall
Williamsgate
Low Barn
Howgill Wood
Horsemoor Hills
Great Sca Fell
651
Meal Fell
Great Lingy Hill
Broughton Moor
Hennah Hall
Dovenby
Dovenby Mill
Bridekirk
Redmain
Isel
Isel Hall
Bank Head
Long Close Fm
Great Cockup
Miller Moss
Broughton Lodge
Prospect Ho
Hewthwaite Hall
Messengermire Wood
Park Wood
710
Knott
627
Coomb Height
Dovenby Craggs
Anns Hill
Wood Hall Fm
Forth Ho
Trotters World of Animals
Kilnhill
Kestrel Lodge
Dash Fm
Little Broughton
Belle Vue
Hame's Hall
Park House Fm
Watch Hill
Elva Hill
Ouse Bridge
North Row
Bassenthwaite
Melbecks
Great Broughton
Setmurthy Common
Higham Hall
Dubwath
Chapel
Barkbeth
Dead Crags
642
Great Calva
Cockermouth Castle
Wyndham Ho
Bully Ho
Crag
Ribton Ho
Papcastle
Wordsworth House
Castlegate Ho
Lambfoot
Embleton
Pheasant Inn
Scarness
High Side
Broad End
Bakestall
Skiddaw Forest
Brigham
Broughton Cross
Cockermouth
Bus Pk
East Ho
Dyke Nook
Bassenthwaite Common
Wythop Mill
Westray
Sale Fell
359
Wythop Woods
Bassenthwaite Lake
Hare Crag
Tarn Bank
Scales Fm
Bouch Ho
Abbey
Sand Hill
Skiddaw House
Nepgill
Bridgefoot
Greysouthen
Dubbs Moss
Esps Fm
Lake District
931
Skiddaw
Sale How
Cloven Stone
Tendley Hill
Shatton Lodge
373
Ling Fell
Wythop Hall
Mirehouse
Longside Edge
Burnt Horse
Little Clifton
Rigging Gill
Eaglesfield
Shatton Hall
Long Fell
Wythop Moss
Carl Side
Little Man
865
Furnace Ho
Lamb Hill
Bent Houses
Harrot
Empleton High Common
Broom Fell
511
Redness Point
Dodd Wood
Grey Crags
Jenkin Hill
715
Lonscale Fell
Oldfield Mill
Oldfield
Springfield Fm
Low Hall
Lorton
Woodend
Howgill Tongue
Knowe Crags
Calva Hall
Galefield
Deanscales
High Dyke
Hill Ho
Graystones
National Park
Lord's Seat
552
Barf
Long Close Fm
Oakfield House
Millbeck
Blease
Wood Fm
East Ho
Brandlingill
Sandybeck Meadow
High Lorton
Woodside
Pardshaw Hall
Akebank Mill
Bank
Low Lorton
Scawgill Br
Lorton Fells
Whinlatter
Thornthwaite
Thornthwaite Galleries
Applethwaite
Lonscale
Derwentfolds
Hollins Wood
Dean
Leegate
Mosser Mains
Whin Fell
Whinfell Hall
Heritage/Visitor Centre
Ormathwaite
368
Latrigg
Brundholme Wood
Browtop
Branthwaite
Pardshaw
Fellside Fm
Dodd Wood
Whinlatter Pass
Bog Ho
Briery
Burns Fm
Branthwaite Edge
Mains
Mosser
416
Fellbarrow
Newhouse Fm
Hopebeck
Forest Park
Hobcarton End
Hospital Plantn
Spring Bank
Braithwaite
Great Crosthwaite
Cumberland Pencil Museum
Keswick
Castlerigg Stone Circle
Chestnut Hill
Branthwaite Rigg
Crakeplace Hall
Ullock
Mosser Fell
Thackthwaite
Sourfoot Fell
High Hill
Portinscale
Brigham
Row End
Rigg Ho
Mockerkin
Fangs Brow Fm
Dodd
Miller Place
Little Braithwaite
Low Rigg
Mockerkin How
Darling Fell
Grisedale Pike
791
Ullock
244
Swinside
Lingcroft
Waterend
Iredale Place
Low Fell
Brackenthwaite
770
Hopegill Head
Hobcarton Crag
Castlerigg
Dale Bottom
Dean Cross
Havercroft
Hudson Place
Loweswater
707
Whiteside
Sand Hill
Force Crag
Stile End
Barrow
Derwent Isle
Stable Hills
Great Wood
High Rigg
Kidburngill
Woodend
Holme Wood
Scale Hill
High Moss
Swinside
Stair
Bird Dyke
Burnbank Fell
Liza Beck
Hawes End
Derwent Water
Crossgates
Owsen Fell
Loweswater
Lanthwaite
Eel Crag
Causey Pike
Rowling End
Newlands
Yew Crag
Bridge End
Millgillhead
Lamplugh
Carling Knot
852
Grasmoor
Crag Hill
839
Scar Crag
East Ho
Falcon Crag
Low Moss
Asby
Dockray Nook
Derwentwater
Cat Bells
Castlerigg Fell
Goat Crag
Felldyke
Loweswater Fell
Little Town
Ashness Br
590
Bleaberry Fell
Arlecdon
Lamplugh Fell
Little Dodd
Mellbreak
Wandope
Bawd Hall
Great Bay
Knock Murton
Middle Fell
Whiteless Pike
Ard Crags
Rowrah
Keltonfell Top
Gavel Fell
526
Hen Comb
509
Rannerdale
Knott Rigg
High Snab Bank
Scope End
Black Crag
Ashness
Raven Crag
Leys
Ling Crags
Hause Point
Newlands Pass
Derwent Fells
Borrowdale Gates
High Seat
608
Castle Crag
Kirkland
Kelton Fell
Low Bank
Narrow Moor
Brown Dodd
Reecastle Crag
Solway Coast
Cumbria
Lake District National Park
Whinlatter Forest Park
238
239
230
219
220
NY

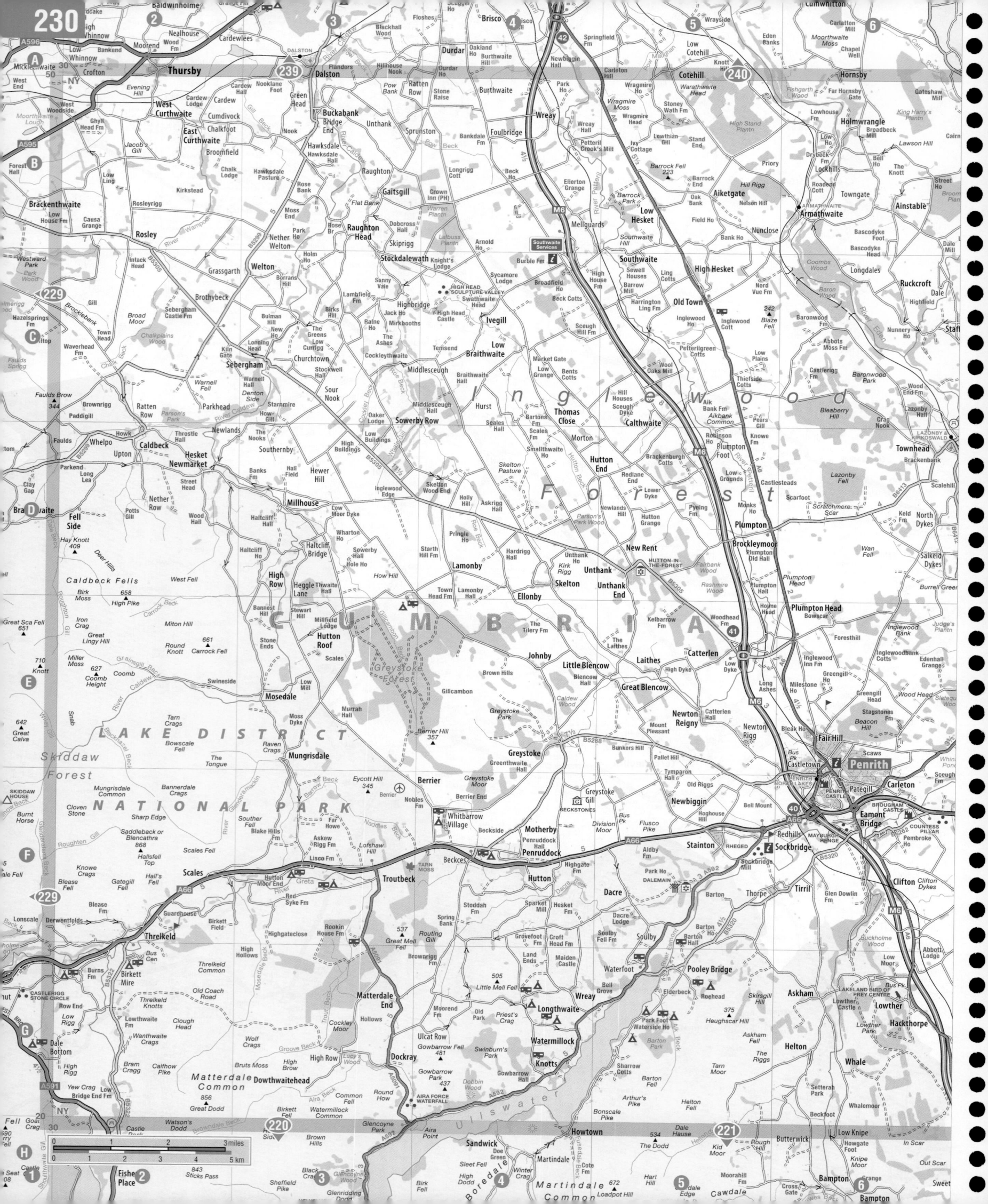

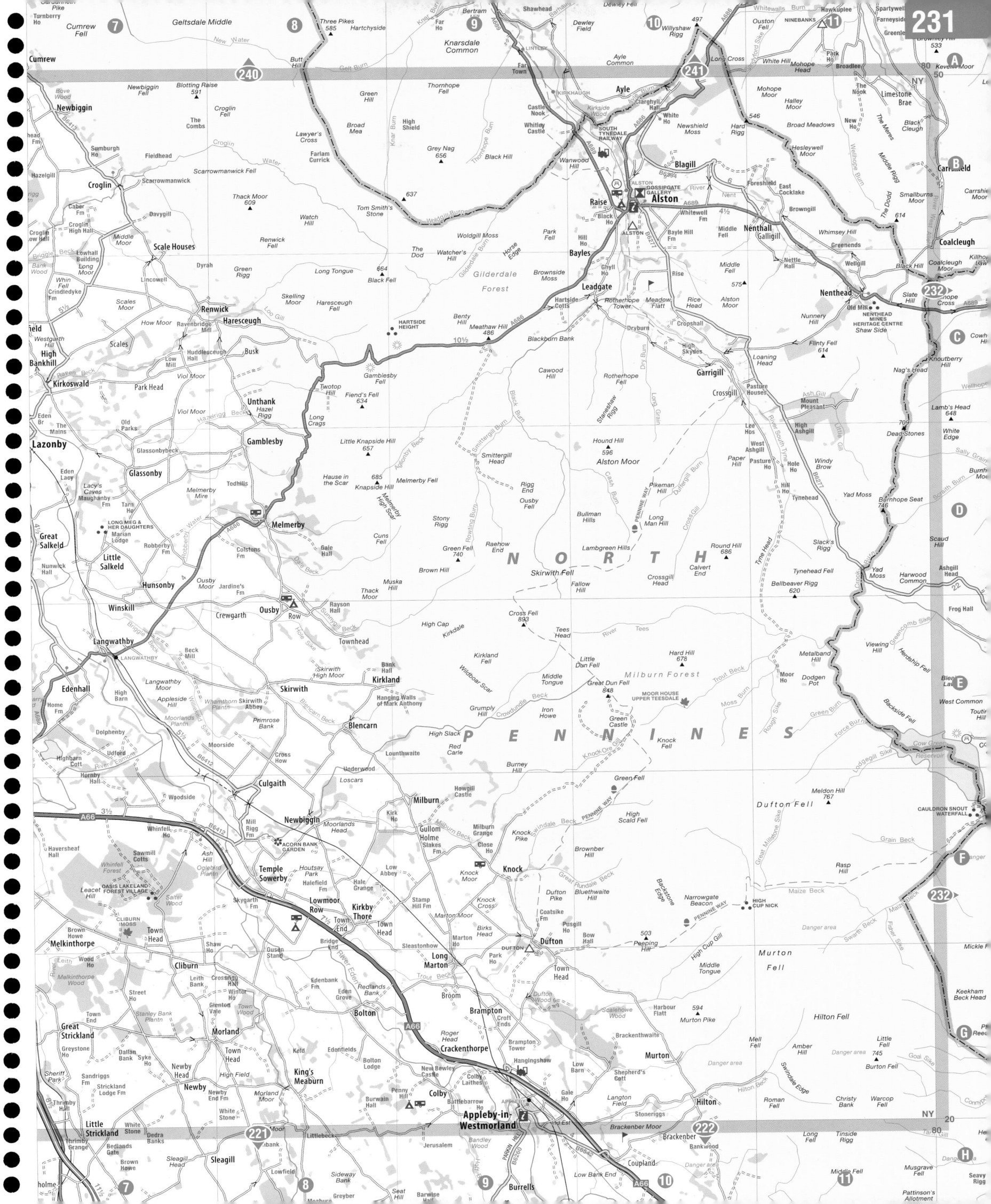
Cumrew Fell
Geltsdale Middle
Three Pikes 585
Hartchyside
Knarsdale Common
Shawhead
Dewley Fell
Willyshaw Rigg
Ouston Fell
Ninebanks
Hawkuplee
Spartywell
Cumrew
Butt Hill
Far Town
Ayle Common
Long Cross
White Hill
Mohope Head
Broadlee
Kevelin Moor
Newbiggin Fell
Blotting Raise 591
Croglin Fell
Green Hill
Thornhope Fell
Kirkhaugh
Ayle
Mohope Moor
Halley Moor
Limestone Brae
Newbiggin
The Combs
Broad Mea
High Shield
Castle Nook
Whitley Castle
Kirkside Wood
Claryhill Hall
White Ho
Newshield Moss
Hard Rigg
Broad Meadows
Black Cleugh
South Tynedale Railway
Lawyer's Cross
Farlam Currick
Grey Nag 656
Black Hill
Wanwood Hill
Blagill
Hesleywell Moor
Middle Rigg
Carrshield
Sumburgh Ho
Fieldhead
Scarrowmanwick Fell
Scarrowmanwick
Hazelgill
Croglin
Thack Moor 609
Tom Smith's Stone
Gossipgate Gallery
Alston
Raise
Foreshield
East Cocklake
Smallburns Moor
Carrshield Moor
Caber Fm
Croglin High Hall
Croglin Low Hall
Davygill
Watch Hill
Woldgill Moss
Park Fell
Hill Ho
Black Ho
Whitewell Fm
Middle Fell
Nenthall
Galligill
Browngill
The Dodd 614
Whimsey Hill
Coalcleugh
Middle Moor
Scale Houses
Renwick Fell
The Dod
Watcher's Hill
Horse Edge
Bayles
Bayle Hill Fm
Greenends
Nettle Hall
Wellgill
Black Hill
Coalcleugh Moor
Lowhall Building
Long Moor
Whin Fell
Crindledyke Fm
Dyrah
Lincowell
Green Rigg
Long Tongue
664 Black Fell
Gilderdale Forest
Brownside Moss
Ghyll Ho
Leadgate
Rise
Middle Fell
575
Nenthead
Slate Hill
Scales Moor
Renwick
Skelling Moor
Haresceugh Fell
Hartside Cotts
Rotherhope Tower
Meadow Flatt
Rice Head
Alston Moor
Nunnery Hill
Nenthead Mines Heritage Centre
Shaw Side
How Moor
Ravenbridge Mill
Haresceugh
Hartside Height
Benty Hill
Meathaw Hill 486
Dryburn
Cropshall
Westgarth Hill
Scales
Blackburn Bank
High Skydes
Flinty Fell 614
High Bankhill
Huddlesceugh Hall
Busk
Low Mill
Viol Moor
Gamblesby Fell
Cawood Hill
Rotherhope Fell
Garrigill
Loaning Head
Nag's Head
Knoutberry Hill
Kirkoswald
Park Head
Twotop Hill
Fiend's Fell 634
Crossgill
Pasture Houses
Ash Gill
Mount Pleasant
Unthank
Hazel Rigg
Long Crags
Staneshaw Rigg
Lamb's Head 648
Eden Br
The Mains
Old Parks
Viol Moor
Lee Hos
High Ashgill
Dead Stones 709
White Edge
Lazonby
Glassonbybeck
Gamblesby
Little Knapside Hill 657
Smittergill Head
Hound Hill 596
Alston Moor
West Ashgill
Paper Hill
Pasture Ho
Hole Ho
Windy Brow
Eden Lacy
Glassonby
Hause in the Scar
685 Knapside Hill
Melmerby Fell
Melmerby High Scar
Rigg End
Pikeman Hill
Hill Ho
Tynehead
Yad Moss
Burnhope Seat 746
Lacy's Caves
Maughanby Fm
Todhills
Melmerby Mire
Tarn Ho
Ousby Fell
Bullman Hills
Long Man Hill
Long Meg & Her Daughters
Marian Lodge
Melmerby
Stony Rigg
Great Salkeld
Robberby Fm
Colstons Fm
Gale Hall
Cuns Fell
Green Fell 740
Raehow End
Lambgreen Hills
Round Hill 686
Slack's Rigg
Scaud Hill
Little Salkeld
Nunwick Hall
North Pennines
Brown Hill
Skirwith Fell
Calvert End
Tynehead Fell
Yad Moss
Harwood Common
Ashgill Head
Hunsonby
Ousby Moor
Jardine's Fm
Muska Hill
Thack Moor
Fallow Hill
Crossgill Head
Bellbeaver Rigg 620
Winskill
Crewgarth
Ousby
Row
Rayson Hall
Frog Hall
Cross Fell 893
High Cap
Kirkdale
Tees Head
River Tees
Viewing Hill
Langwathby
Townhead
Beck Mill
Kirkland Fell
Little Dun Fell
Hard Hill 678
Metalband Hill
Herdship Fell
Skirwith High Moor
Bank Hall
Kirkland
Milburn Forest
Moor Ho
Dodgen Pot
Edenhall
High Barn
Langwathby Moor
Appleside Hill
Skirwith Abbey
Skirwith
Hanging Walls of Mark Anthony
Wildboar Scar
Middle Tongue
Great Dun Fell 848
Moor House Upper Teesdale
West Common
Home Fm
Primrose Bank
Blencarn
Grumply Hill
Iron Howe
Green Castle
Backside Fell
Dolphenby
Udford
High Slack
Red Carle
Knock Fell
Highbarn Cott
Hornby Hall
Moorside
Cross How
Lounthwaite
Burney Hill
Cow Green Reservoir
Underwood
Loscars
Culgaith
Green Fell
Howgill Castle
Milburn
Meldon Hill 767
Dufton Fell
Cauldron Snout Waterfall
Woodside
Newbiggin
Moorlands Head
Kirk Ho
Gullom Holme
Slakes Fm
Milburn Grange
Knock Pike
High Scald Fell
Whinfell Ho
Haversheaf Hall
Sawmill Cotts
Whinfell Forest
Ash Hill
Oglebird Plantn
Mill Rigg Fm
Acorn Bank Garden
Close Ho
Brownber Hill
Grain Beck
Temple Sowerby
Houtsay Park
Halefield Fm
Low Abbey
Knock Moor
Knock
Rasp Hill
Leacet Hill
Oasis Lakeland Forest Village
Salter Wood
Hale Grange
Dufton Pike
Bluethwaite Hill
Backstone Edge
Maize Beck
Skygarth Fm
Lowmoor Row
Kirkby Thore
Stamp Hill Fm
Knock Cross
Narrowgate Beacon
High Cup Nick
Cliburn Moss
Marton Moor
Coatsike Fm
Town End
Town Head
Town Head
Birks Head
Pusgill Ho
Danger area
Brown Howe
Melkinthorpe
Shaw Ho
Ousen Stand
Bridge End
Marton Ho
Sleastonhow
Dufton
Bow Hall
503 Peeping Hill
High Cup Gill
Mickle Fell
Wood Ho
Cliburn
Park Ho
Long Marton
Town Head
Middle Tongue
Murton Fell
Melkinthorpe Wood
Leith Bank
Crossrigg Hall
Winter Ho
Edenbank Fm
Eden Grove
Redlands Bank
Trout Beck
Broom
Dufton Wood
Keekham Beck Head
Street Ho
Glenton Vale
Town Wood
Stanley Bank Plantn
Bolton
Brampton
Croft Ends
Scalehowe Wood
Harbour Flatt
594 Murton Pike
Hilton Fell
Town End
Great Strickland
Morland
Roger Head
Brackenthwaite
Greystone Ho
Dallan Bank
Syke Ho
Town Head
Keld
Edenfields
Crackenthorpe
Brampton Tower
Murton
Mell Fell
Amber Hill
Danger area
Little Fell 745
Burton Fell
Newby Head
High Field
Bolton Lodge
King's Meaburn
Hangingshaw
Low Barn
Shepherd's Cott
Sheriff Park
Sandriggs Fm
Strickland Lodge Fm
Newby
Newby End Fm
New Bewley Castle
Colby Laithes
Danger area
Thrimby Hall
Morland Moor
Penny Hill
Colby
Burwain Hall
Battlebarrow Ho
Gale Ho
Langton Field
Hilton
Roman Fell
Christy Bank
Warcop Fell
Little Strickland
White Stone
Dedra Banks
Appleby-in-Westmorland
Stoneriggs
Thrimby Grange
Moor
Littlebeck
Brackenber Moor
Brackenber
Bankwood
Long Fell
Tinside Rigg
Bedlands Gate
Brown Howe
Sleagill Head
Sleagill
Jerusalem
Bandley Wood
Coupland
Lowfield
Sideway Bank
Low Bank End
Middle Fell
Musgrave Fell
Seavy Rigg
Greyber
Seat Hill
Barwise Hall
Burrells
Pattinson's Allotment
A66
A686
A689
B6412
B6277
B6260
B6542
Pennine Way
240
241
232
221
222
NY
50
80
20

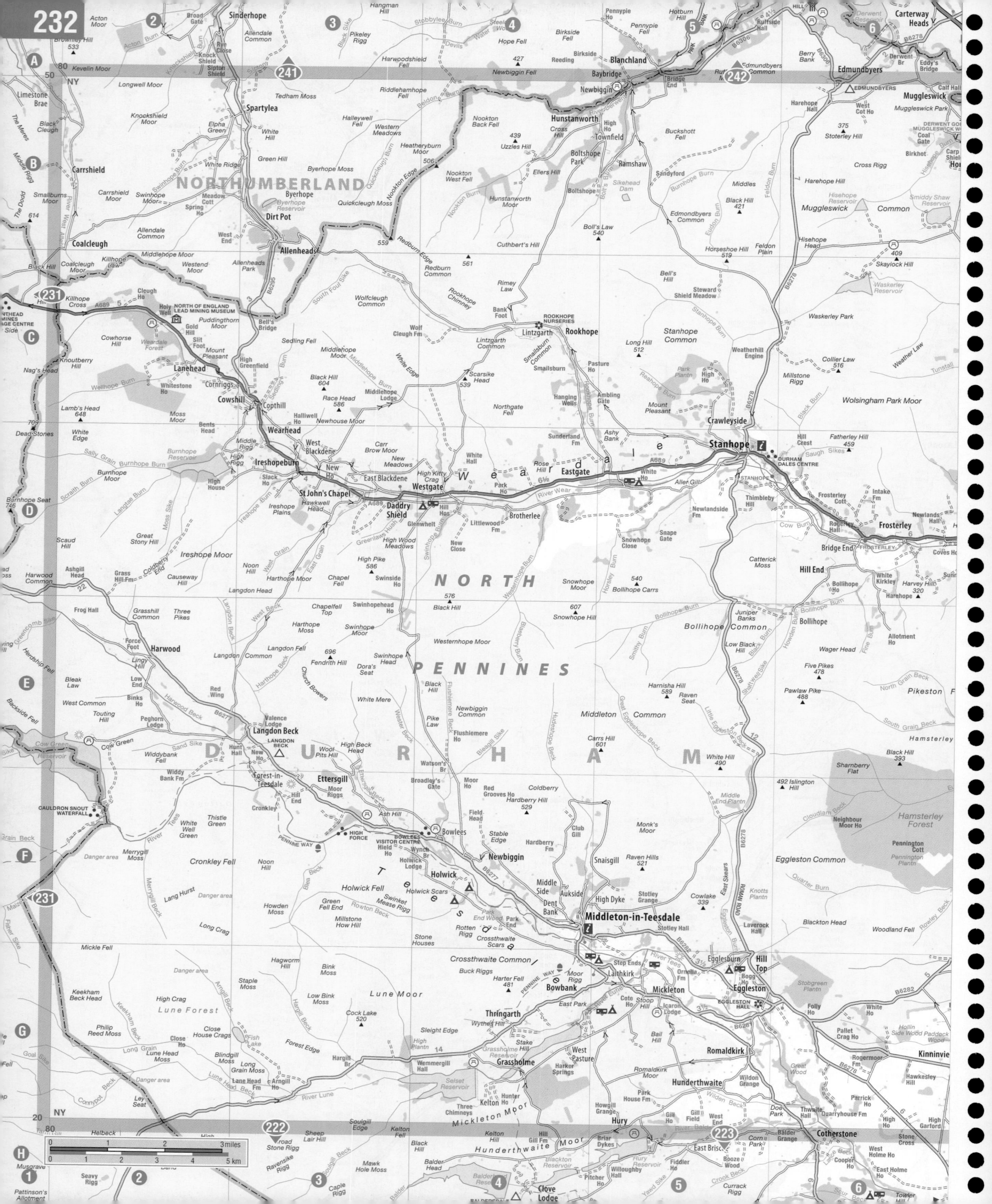

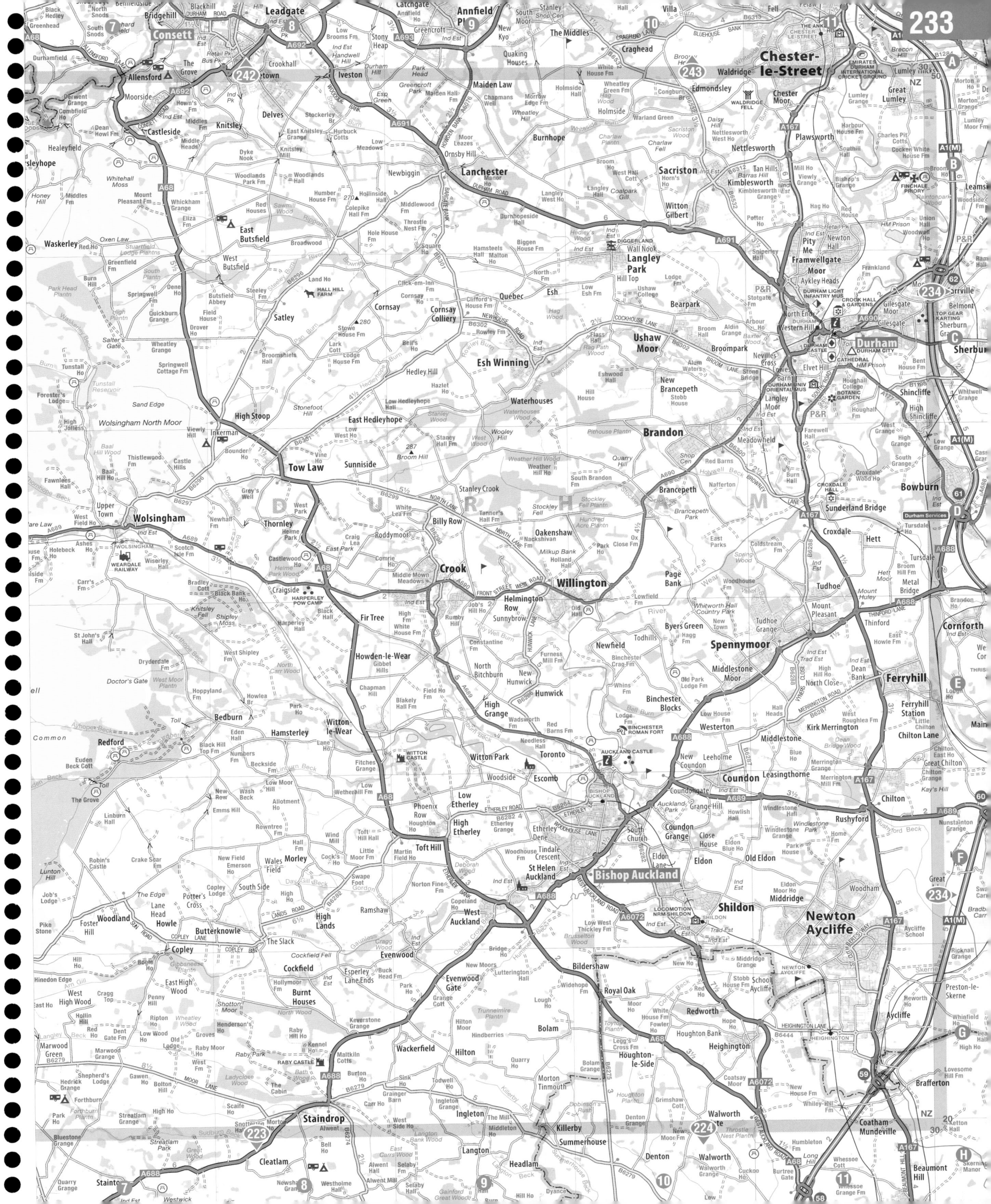

Consett
Leadgate
Annfield Plain
Chester-le-Street
Great Lumley
Allensford
Iveston
Lanchester
Sacriston
Kimblesworth
Plawsworth
Nettlesworth
Castleside
Knitsley
Delves
Burnhope
Esh
Langley Park
Quebec
Cornsay
Cornsay Colliery
Satley
Ushaw Moor
Bearpark
Durham
Esh Winning
Waterhouses
Brandon
Brancepeth
Shincliffe
High Stoop
Tow Law
Sunniside
Wolsingham
Thornley
Stanley Crook
Billy Row
Crook
Willington
Oakenshaw
Bowburn
Sunderland Bridge
Croxdale
Hett
Tudhoe
Spennymoor
Ferryhill
Cornforth
Fir Tree
Howden-le-Wear
Hunwick
High Grange
Witton-le-Wear
Hamsterley
Bedburn
Redford
Witton Park
Toronto
Escomb
Coundon
Leasingthorne
Chilton
Rushyford
Westerton
Kirk Merrington
Middlestone
Etherley Dene
St Helen Auckland
Bishop Auckland
Shildon
Eldon
Newton Aycliffe
West Auckland
Toft Hill
Morley
Copley
Butterknowle
Woodland
Cockfield
Evenwood
Evenwood Gate
Bildershaw
Royal Oak
Redworth
Heighington
Aycliffe
Houghton-le-Side
Hilton
Wackerfield
Staindrop
Killerby
Summerhouse
Walworth
Denton
Coatham Mundeville
Brafferton
Headlam
Langton
Cleatlam
Gainford
Bolam
DURHAM

243
Houghton-Le-Spring
Seaham
Bournmoor
Newbottle
Sunniside
Fence Houses
Great Lumley
Colliery Row
Chilton Moor
Hetton Downs
Great Eppleton
Hetton-le-Hole
Murton
Seaton
Northlea
Burdon
Old Burdon
Dalton-le-Dale
Cold Hesledon
Dawdon
Parkside
Deneside
Featherbed Rocks
Liddle Stack
Nose's Pt
Chourdon Pt
Hawthorn Hive
Hawthorn
Beacon Hill
Shippersea Bay
Shot Rock
White Lea
Fox Holes
Horden Pt
East Rainton
Middle Rainton
West Rainton
Leamside
Low Moorsley
High Moorsley
Easington Lane
Elemore Vale
South Hetton
Hetton-le-Hill
Pittington
Carrville
Belmont
Gilesgate
Sherburn
Sherburn Hill
Littletown
Hallgarth
Haswell
Haswell Plough
Easington
Easington Colliery
Little Thorpe
Peterlee
Horden
Blackhall Colliery
Shotton Colliery
Shotton
Castle Eden
Hesleden
High Hesleden
Blackhall Rocks
Crimdon Park
Shincliffe
High Shincliffe
Shadforth
Ludworth
Running Waters
Thornley
Old Cassop
Cassop
Wheatley Hill
Wingate
Old Wingate
Station Town
Hutton Henry
Bowburn
Old Quarrington
Quarrington Hill
Kelloe
Coxhoe
Deaf Hill
Trimdon Colliery
Trimdon Grange
Trimdon
Cornforth
West Cornforth
Ferryhill
Ferryhill Station
Chilton Lane
Mainsforth
Bishop Middleham
Fishburn
Butterwick
Sedgefield
Embleton
Bradbury
Mordon
Chilton
Sheraton
South Wingate
Hart
Hart Station
High Throston
Elwick
Dalton Piercy
West Park
Hartlepool
Middleton
The Headland
Seaton Carew
Rift House
Owton Manor
Brierton
Greatham
Graythorp
Newton Bewley
Wolviston
Billingham
Cowpen Bewley
Haverton Hill
Port Clarence
Wynyard Village
Thorpe Larches
Grindon
Foxton
Shotton
Stillington
Old Stillington
Whitton
Thorpe Thewles
Carlton
Redmarshall
Bishopton
Great Stainton
Little Stainton
Elstob
Preston-le-Skerne
Aycliffe
Brafferton
Newton Ketton
Norton
Roseworth
Hardwick
Bishopsgarth
Fairfield
Stockton-on-Tees
Middlesbrough
Portrack
North Ormesby
South Bank
Teesville
Pallister
Marton Grove
Linthorpe
Berwick Hills
Hartburn
Whinney Hill
Teesmouth
Seal Sands
Hartlepool Bay
Seaton Sands
North Sands
Parton Rocks
DURHAM
HARTLEPOOL
TYNE AND WEAR
DARLINGTON
STOCKTON-ON-TEES
233
224
225
0 1 2 3 miles
0 1 2 3 4 5 km

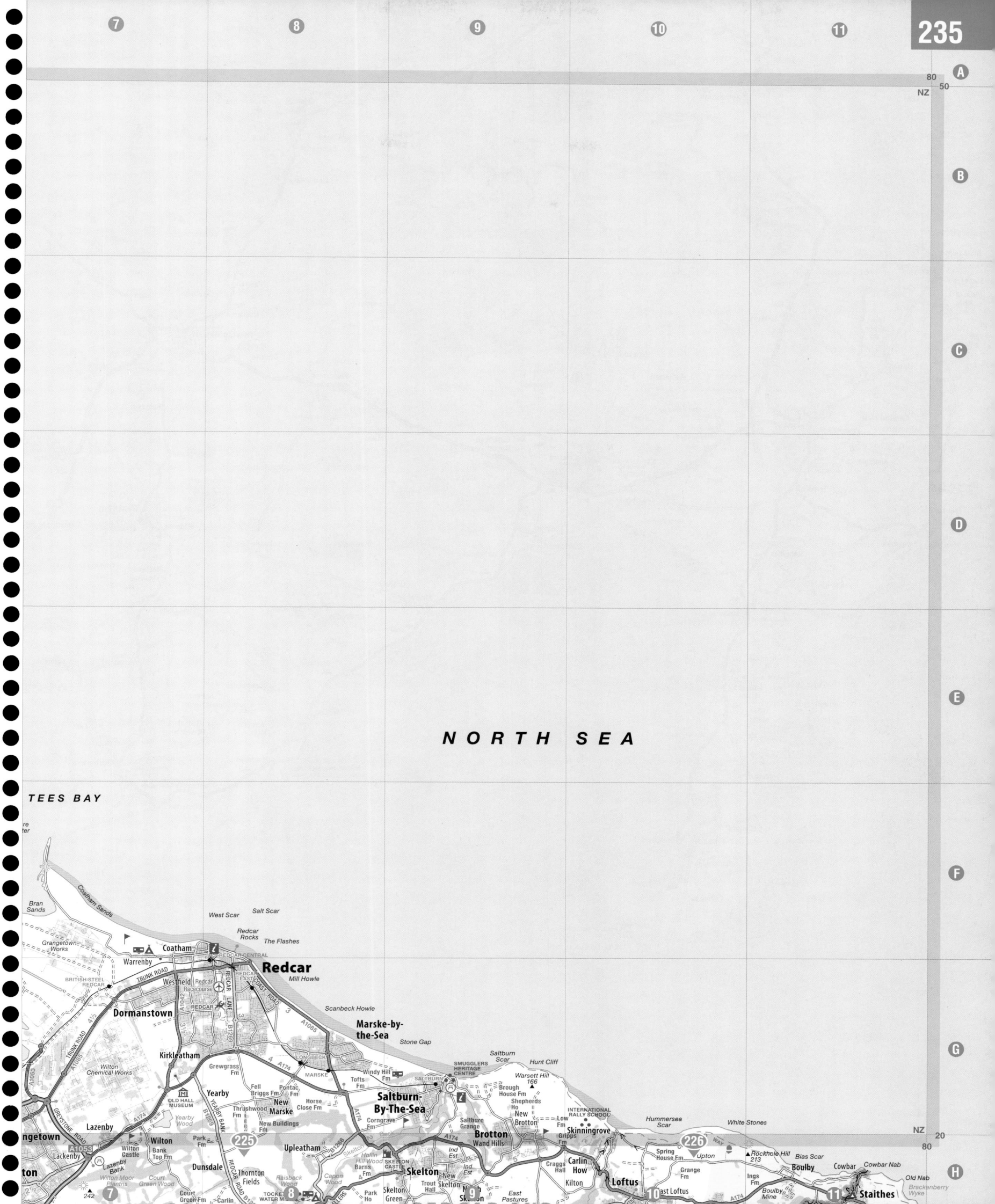

7      8      9      10      11

A
80
50
NZ

B

C

D

E

*NORTH SEA*

*TEES BAY*

F

Bran
Sands

Coatham Sands

West Scar    Salt Scar

Redcar
Rocks   The Flashes

Grangetown
Works

Coatham

**Redcar**

Warrenby

Mill Howle

BRITISH STEEL
REDCAR

Westfield

Redcar
Racecourse

TRUNK ROAD

**Dormanstown**

REDCAR

A1042

Scanbeck Howle

**Marske-by-
the-Sea**

Stone Gap

G

**Kirkleatham**

Wilton
Chemical Works

Grewgrass
Fm

A174

MARSKE

LONGBECK

Windy Hill
Fm

Tofts
Fm

SMUGGLERS
HERITAGE
CENTRE

Saltburn
Scar

Hunt Cliff

Warsett Hill
166

Fell
Briggs Fm

Horse
Close Fm

**Yearby**

OLD HALL
MUSEUM

Pontac
Fm

Thrushwood
Fm

**New
Marske**

**Saltburn-
By-The-Sea**

Brough
House Fm

Shepherds
Ho

Yearby
Wood

New Buildings

Corngrave
Fm

Saltburn
Grange

New
Brotton

Low
Fm

INTERNATIONAL
RALLY SCHOOL

**Skinningrove**

Hummersea
Scar

White Stones

**Lazenby**

YEARBY BANK

**Brotton**

Wand Hills

Gripps
Fm

NZ
20
80

ngetown

**Wilton**

Park
Fm

225

**Upleatham**

A174

A1053

Lackenby

Lazenby
Bank

Wilton
Castle

Bank
Top Fm

**Dunsdale**

Thornton
Fields

Raisbeck
Wood

Capon
Wood

Hollin
Hill Wood

SKELTON
CASTLE

Barns

**Skelton**

New
Skelton

Ind
Est

Ind
Est

**Carlin
How**

Kilton

226

Spring
House Fm

Upton

Rockhole Hill
213

**Loftus**

Bias Scar

Grange
Fm

Boulby
Mine

**Boulby**

**Cowbar**

Old Nab

Cowbar Nab

Brackenberry
Wyke

H

242

Court
Green Wood

Skelton
Green

Carlin

Court
Green Fm

Trout
Hall

Park
Ho

Skelton

East
Pastures

Craggs
Hall

East Loftus

A174

WAY

Ings
Fm

**Staithes**

7      8      9      10      11

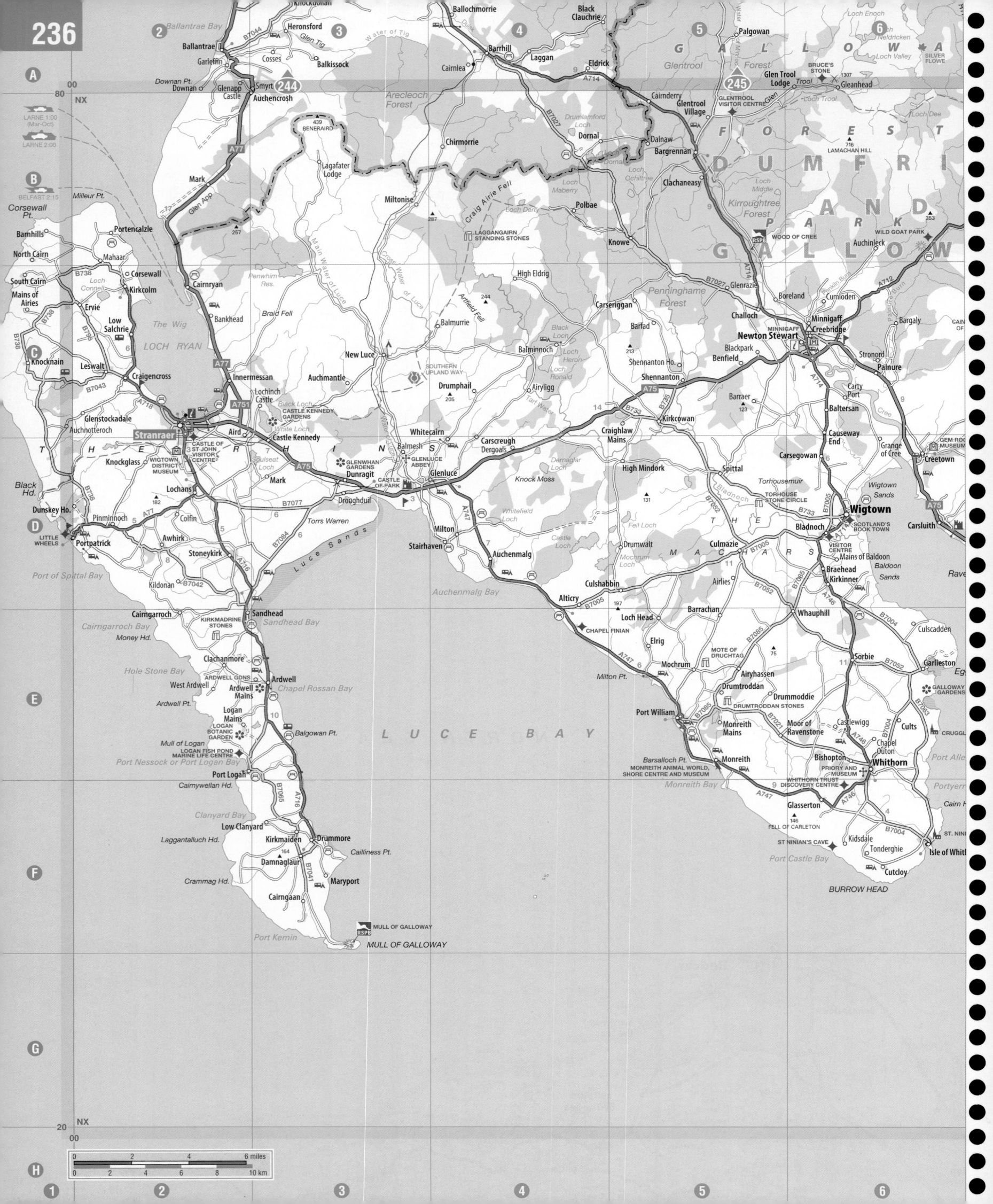

Ballantrae Bay
Ballantrae
Garleffin
Heronsford
Glen Tig
Cosses
Balkissock
Water of Tig
Ballochmorrie
Barrhill
Cairnlea
Laggan
Black Clauchrie
Eldrick
A714
Palgowan
Glentrool
Glen Trool Lodge
Bruce's Stone
Gleanhead
Loch Trool
Loch Enoch
Loch Valley
Silver Flowe
Downan Pt.
Downan
Glenapp Castle
Smyrt
Auchencrosh
244
245
Arecleoch Forest
Cairnderry
Glentrool Village
Glentrool Visitor Centre
Loch Dee
LARNE 1:00 (Mar-Oct)
LARNE 2:00
BELFAST 2:15
NX
80
00
439 BENERAIRD
Chirmorrie
Drumlamford Loch
Dornal
Dalnaw
Bargrennan
F O R E S T
716 LAMACHAN HILL
D U M F R I
A77
Mark
Glen App
Lagafater Lodge
Milleur Pt.
Corsewall Pt.
Miltonise
Craig Airie Fell
Loch Maberry
Loch Ochiltree
Clachaneasy
Loch Middle
Kirroughtree Forest
P A R K
353
A N D
Polbae
Loch Derry
Laggangairn Standing Stones
287
257
Barnhills
Portencalzie
North Cairn
Mahaar
Corsewall
Kirkcolm
South Cairn
Mains of Airies
Ervie
Loch Connell
B738
B798
Low Salchrie
Cairnryan
Penwhirn Res.
Main Water of Luce
Cross Water of Luce
Wood of Cree
Wild Goat Park
Knowe
Auchinleck
G A L L O W
High Eldrig
Penninghame Forest
B7027
Glenrazie
A714
Boreland
Cumloden
A712
Bankhead
Braid Fell
244
Arrfield Fell
Carseriggan
Challoch
Barfad
Minnigaff
Creebridge
Newton Stewart
Bargaly
The Wig
LOCH RYAN
Balmurrie
Black Loch
Knocknain
Leswalt
New Luce
Balminnoch
213
Blackpark
Benfield
Shennanton Ho.
Stronord
Palnure
Craigencross
Innermessan
Auchmantle
Southern Upland Way
Loch Heron
Loch Ronald
Shennanton
Drumphail
205
Airyligg
Tarf Water
A75
Barraer
123
Carty Port
B7043
A718
Lochinch Castle
Black Loch
Castle Kennedy Gardens
White Loch
A751
Baltersan
Glenstockadale
Auchnotteroch
Stranraer
Castle of St John Visitor Centre
Aird
Castle Kennedy
Whitecairn
Carscreugh
Dergoals
B733
Craighlaw Mains
Kirkcowan
Causeway End
Carsegowan
Grange of Cree
Creetown
Gem Rock Museum
T H E R H I N S
Knockglass
Wigtown District Museum
Soulseat Loch
Mark
Balmesh
Glenwhan Gardens
Glenluce Abbey
Dunragit
Castle of Park
Glenluce
Dernaglar Loch
Knock Moss
High Mindork
Spittal
Torhousemuir
Torhouse Stone Circle
Bladnoch
B733
B7052
B7005
Wigtown
Wigtown Sands
Black Hd.
Lochans
182
Colfin
B7077
Droughduil
Whitefield Loch
131
Fell Loch
Scotland's Book Town
Carsluith
Dunskey Ho.
Pinminnoch
A77
Torrs Warren
Milton
Little Wheels
Portpatrick
Awhirk
B7084
Luce Sands
Stairhaven
Castle Loch
Drumwalt
Culmazie
Visitor Centre
Mains of Baldoon
Baldoon Sands
T H E M A C H A R S
Stoneykirk
A716
Auchenmalg
Mochrum Loch
Braehead
Kirkinner
Port of Spittal Bay
Kildonan
B7042
Auchenmalg Bay
Culshabbin
Airlies
B7052
B7085
Cairngarroch
Sandhead
Kirkmadrine Stones
Sandhead Bay
Alticry
B7005
197
Loch Head
Barrachan
Whauphill
A746
B7004
Culscadden
Cairngarroch Bay
Money Hd.
Chapel Finian
Elrig
Mote of Druchtag
75
Sorbie
Garlieston
B7052
Hole Stone Bay
Clachanmore
Ardwell Gdns
West Ardwell
Ardwell
Ardwell Mains
Chapel Rossan Bay
Milton Pt.
A747
Mochrum
Airyhassen
Drumtroddan
Drummoddie
Drumtroddan Stones
Galloway House Gardens
Ardwell Pt.
Logan Mains
Logan Botanic Garden
Balgowan Pt.
L U C E B A Y
Port William
Monreith Mains
Moor of Ravenstone
Castlewigg
Cults
B7063
Mull of Logan
Logan Fish Pond Marine Life Centre
Port Nessock or Port Logan Bay
Chapel Outon
Barsalloch Pt.
Monreith
Monreith Animal World, Shore Centre and Museum
Bishopton
Priory and Museum
Whithorn
Port Logan
Cairnywellan Hd.
B7065
Monreith Bay
Whithorn Trust Discovery Centre
Portyerrock
Clanyard Bay
Low Clanyard
Glasserton
146
Fell of Carleton
B7004
Laggantalluch Hd.
Kirkmaiden
Drummore
164
Damnaglaur
Cailliness Pt.
St Ninian's Cave
Kidsdale
Tonderghie
Isle of Whithorn
Port Castle Bay
Crammag Hd.
B7041
Maryport
Cutcloy
Burrow Head
Cairngaan
Mull of Galloway
RSPB
Port Kemin
MULL OF GALLOWAY
20
NX
00
0 2 4 6 miles
0 2 4 6 8 10 km
A B C D E F G H
1 2 3 4 5 6

Earlstoun
Millquarter
Duchrae
Sundaywell
Milton
Dunscore
Throughgate
Burnhead
ELLISLAND FARM
Auchencairn
Duncow
St John's Town of Dalry
Drumbuie
Garroch
Bogue
Corriedoo Forest
Clatteringshaws Forest
Glenlee
Mid Garrary
New Galloway
Balmaclellan
Blackcraig
Knocklearn
Gibbshill
Newtonairds
Drumpark
Holywood
Irongray
Newbridge
Gallaberry
Killylung
Kirkton
Amisfield
Tinwald
Heathhall
Locharbriggs
Craigencallie Ho.
Craignell
CLATTERINGSHAWS FOREST WILDLIFE CENTRE
Kenmure
BLOWPLAIN OPEN FARM
Ironmacannie
Craig
Corsock
Margreig
Glenkiln
Glen
Shawhead
Terregles Banks
Lincluden
Dumfries
Maxwelltown
Cargenbridge
Collin
RAIDERS ROAD FOREST DRIVE
Bennan Forest
Cairn Edward Hill
Merkland
Crofts
Brooklands
Brae
Lochfoot
Crocketford or Ninemile Bar
Glenlair
Drumrash
Airds of Kells
Mossdale
Parton
Redcroft
Kirkpatrick Durham
Springholm
Milton
Beeswing
Islesteps
Mabie Forest
Mabie
Kingholm Quay
Kelton
Lochar Moss
Horseholm
FELL OF FLEET
KEN-DEE MARSHES
Old Bridge of Urr
DRUMCOLTRAN TOWER
Glencaple
Kirkconnell
Bankend
NATIONAL MUS OF COSTUME
New Abbey
SWEETHEART ABBEY
NEW ABBEY CORN MILL
Shearington
CAERLAVEROCK CASTLE
Bowhouse
WILDFOWL AND WETLAND CENTRE
Crossmichael
Hardgate
Haugh of Urr
Kirkgunzeon
Congeith
Fleet Forest
Craig
Clarebrand
Townhead of Greenlaw
Clints of Dromore
Dromore
Laurieston
Laurieston Forest
Glenlochar
Overton
LONG FELL
THREAVE CASTLE
Leaths
Castle Douglas
OLD BUITTLE TOWER
Barhill
Dalbeattie
Boreland of Southwick
CRIFFELL
Drumburn
Culcronchie
Mark
KELTON MAINS OPEN FARM
THREAVE GARDENS
Bridge of Dee
Rhonehouse or Kelton Hill
Gelston
Glengap Forest
Glengap
BENGRAY
Carsethorn
Kirkbean
ARBIGLAND GARDENS
Glen
Pulcree
Fleuchlang
Ringford
Dalbeattie Forest
Drumstinchall
Caulkerbush
Prestonmill
Anwoth
MILL ON THE FLEET
Gatehouse of Fleet
CARDONESS CASTLE
Valleyfield
Airieland
Palnackie
Barnbarroch
Mainsriddle
JOHN PAUL JONES COTTAGE MUSEUM
MERSEHEAD
CARSLUITH CASTLE
CAIRNHARROW
Lagganmullan
Girthon
GALLOWAY HYDRO VISITOR CENTRE
Twynholm
Tongland
BROUGHTON HOUSE AND GARDEN
BENGAIRN
ORCHARDTON TOWER
Kippford or Scaur
MOTE OF MARK
Sandyhills
Colvend
Rockcliffe
Portling
Southerness
Southerness Pt.
CAIRNHOLY CAIRNS
Barholm
Sandgreen
Rainton
Barharrow
Whinnieliggate
Auchenleck
ROUGH ISLAND
Rough I.
Castlehill Pt.
Mersehead Sands
Ravenshall Pt.
Fleet Bay
Ringdoo Pt.
STEWARTRY MUSEUM
Kirkcudbright
Craigshall
Culnaightrie
Auchencairn
EAST STEWARTRY COAST
Auchencairn Bay
Hestan I.
Carrick
Knockbrex
Islands of Fleet
St Mary's Isle
Bombie
Kirkcarswell
Auchencairn Ho
Balcary Pt.
Kirkandrews
Chapelton Row
Borgue
Mill Hall
Mutehill
Dundrennan
Rascarrel
Rascarrel Bay
WIGTOWN BAY
Borness
Kirkcudbright Bay
The Lake
Townhead
Orroland
DUNDRENNAN ABBEY
Graplin
Ross
Netherlaw
Port Mary
Balmae
Borness Pt.
Abbey Hd.
Little Ross
SOLWAY FIRTH
NITH ESTUARY
MARYPORT MARITIME MUSEUM
Maryport
Flimby
Siddick
Seaton
North Side
Workington
Stainburn
HELENA THOMPSON MUS
Westfield
Mossbay
Winscales
Harrington
High Harrington
Distington
Lowca
Pica
Moresby
Parton
Bransty
THE RUM STORY
WALK MILL
Whitehaven
HAIG COLLIERY MINING MUSEUM
Frizington
Hensingham
Mirehouse
Saltom Bay

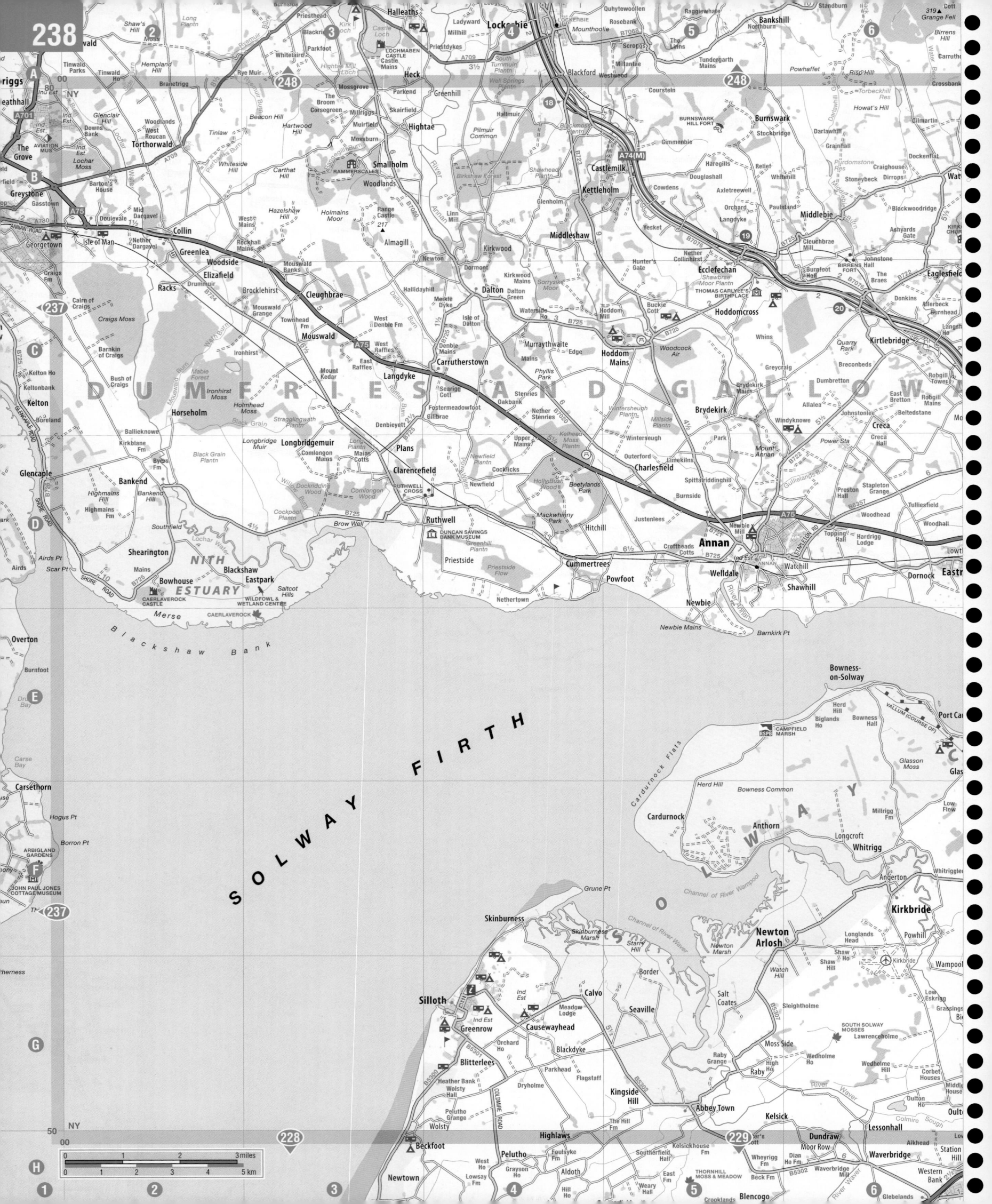

Lockerbie
Halleaths
Lochmaben Castle
Castle Loch
Priestdykes
Heck
Hightae
Smallholm
Rammerscales
Woodlands
Torthorwald
Tinwald
Hempland Hill
Rye Muir
Beacon Hill
Hartwood Hill
Whiteside Hill
Carthat Hill
Collin
Georgetown
Isle of Man
Greenlea
Woodside
Elizafield
Racks
Cleughbrae
Mouswald
Almagill
Range Castle
Holmains Moor
Hazelshaw Hill
Dalton
Newton
Dormont
Kirkwood
Middleshaw
Kettleholm
Castlemilk
Blackford
Burnswark Hill Fort
Burnswark
Bankshill
Ecclefechan
Thomas Carlyle's Birthplace
Hoddomcross
Hoddom Mains
Middlebie
Kirtlebridge
Eaglesfield
Carrutherstown
Langdyke
Murraythwaite
Phyllis Park
Brydekirk
Creca
Dumfries and Galloway
Horseholm
Ironhirst Moss
Holmhead Moss
Longbridgemuir
Bankend
Plans
Clarencefield
Ruthwell
Duncan Savings Bank Museum
Ruthwell Cross
Priestside
Cummertrees
Powfoot
Charlesfield
Annan
Welldale
Watchill
Shawhill
Newbie
Newbie Mains
Barnkirk Pt
Dornock
Kelton
Glencaple
Shearington
Blackshaw
Bowhouse
Eastpark
Caerlaverock Castle
Wildfowl & Wetland Centre
Caerlaverock
Nith Estuary
Merse
Blackshaw Bank
Overton
Carsethorn
Arbigland Gardens
John Paul Jones Cottage Museum
Hogus Pt
Borron Pt
Solway Firth
Bowness-on-Solway
Campfield Marsh
Vallum (course of)
Port Carlisle
Glasson Moss
Cardurnock
Cardurnock Flats
Bowness Common
Herd Hill
Anthorn
Whitrigg
Longcroft
Angerton
Kirkbride
Solway
Grune Pt
Skinburness
Skinburness Marsh
Newton Arlosh
Silloth
Greenrow
Causewayhead
Calvo
Seaville
Blitterlees
Blackdyke
Salt Coates
South Solway Mosses
Lawrenceholme
Kingside Hill
Abbey Town
Kelsick
Dundraw
Beckfoot
Highlaws
Pelutho
Waverbridge
Lessonhall
Aldoth
Newtown
Blencogo
Thornhill Moss & Meadow
A75
A74(M)
A709
A701
B725
B724
B7020
B723
B7076
B722
B6357
B5300
B5301
B5302
B5307
248
237
228
229
0 1 2 3 miles
0 1 2 3 4 5 km

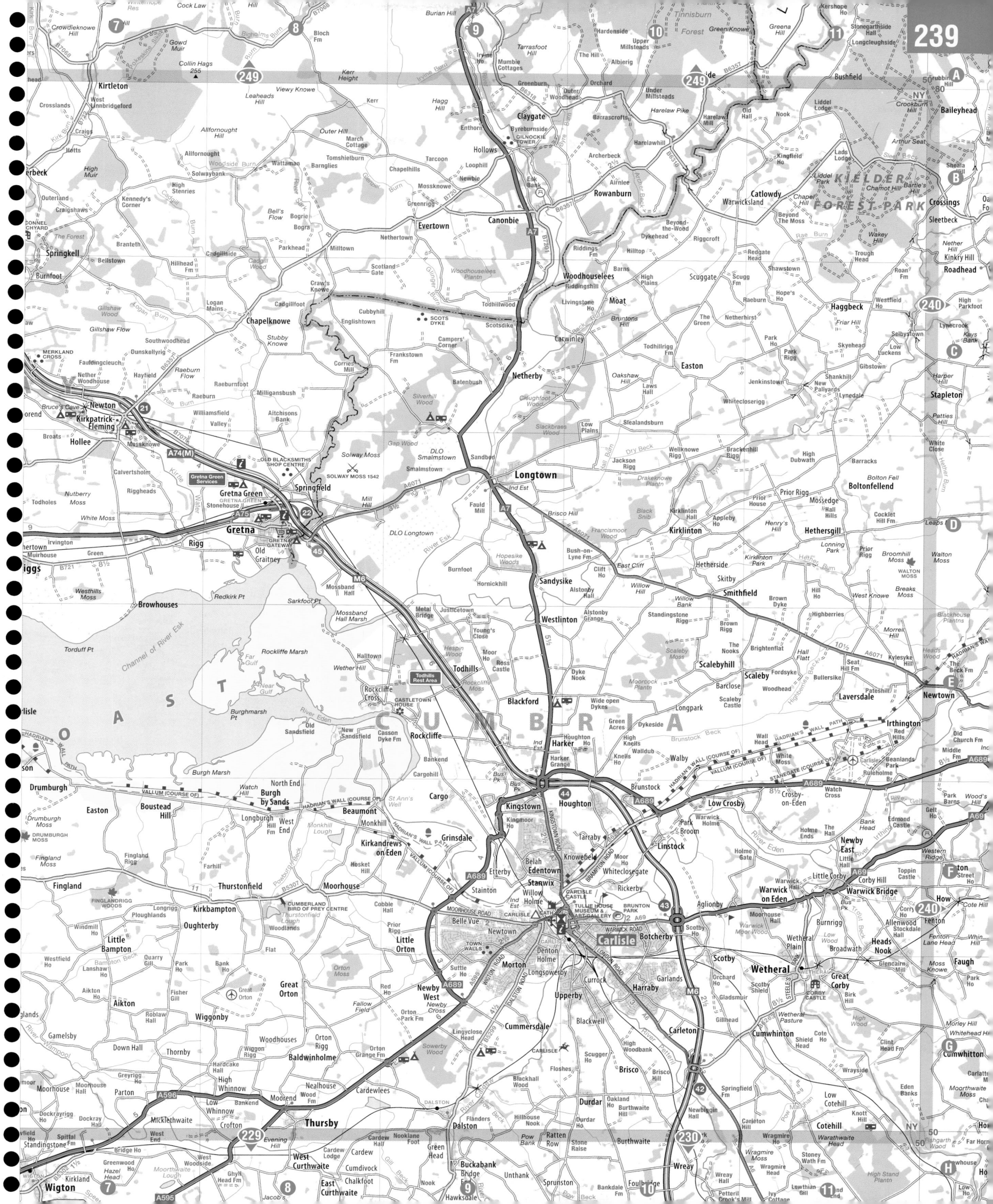

Cock Law
Crowdieknowe Hill
Gowd Muir
Bloch Fm
Burian Hill
Tinnisburn Forest
Hardenside
Upper Millsteads
Greena Hill
Kershope Ho
Stonegarthside Hall
Longcleughside
Collin Hags 255
249
Kerr Height
Terrasfoot Hill
Irvine Ho
Mumbie Cottages
The Hill
Albierig
Bushfield
Kirtleton
Viewy Knowe
Crosslands
West Linnbridgeford
Leaheads Hill
Kerr
Hagg Hill
Greenburn
Outer Woodhead
Orchard
Under Millsteads
Harelaw Pike
Old Hall
Nook
Liddel Lodge
Crookburn Hill
Baileyhead
Craigs
Allfornought Hill
Outer Hill
March Cottage
Enthorn
Claygate
Byreburnside
GILNOCKIE TOWER
Barrascrofts
Harelaw Mill
Arthur Seat
Hotts
Allfornought
Tomshielburn
Barnglies
Tarcoon
Hollows
Harelawhill
Kingfield Ho
Lads Lodge
Sheala Hill
High Muir
Wattaman
Solwaybank
Chapelhills
Loophill
Archerbeck
Airnlee
KIELDER FOREST PARK
Liddel Park
Chamot Hill
Bartie's Hill
Newbie
Esk Bank
Mossknowe
Rowanburn
Catlowdy
Warwicksland
Chapel Hill
Crossings
Outerland
High Stenries
Kennedy's Corner
Greenrigg
Craigshaws
Bell's Flow
Bogrie
Canonbie
Beyond The Moss
Sleetbeck
CONNEL CHYARD
Bogra
Evertown
Beyond-the-Wood
Dykehead
Riggcroft
The Forest
Nethertown
Wakey Hill
Branteth
Parkhead
Milltown
Riddings Fm
Hilltop
Redgate Head
Nether Hill
Kinkry Hill
Springkell
Cadgillside
Trough Head
Beltstown
Hillhead Fm
Cadgill Wood
Scotland Gate
Woodhouselees Plantn
Barns
Shawstown
Roan Fm
Roadhead
Burnfoot
Woodhouselees
Riddingshill
High Plains
Scuggate
Scugg Fm
Craw's Knowe
Hope's Ho
Moat
Raeburn
Westfield Ho
Haggbeck
240
High Parkfoot
Logan Mains
Cadgillfoot
Todhillwood
Livingstone Ho
Gillshaw Wood
Cubbyhill
SCOTS DYKE
Bruntons Hill
The Green
Netherhirst
Friar Hill
Chapelknowe
Englishtown
Scotsdike
Gillshaw Flow
Stubby Knowe
Selbystown
Lynecrook
Southwoodhead
Campers' Corner
Carwinley
Kays Bank
Park Ho
Skyehead
Low Luckens
MERKLAND CROSS
Dunskellyrig
Frankstown Fm
Todhillrigg Fm
Park Rigg
Fauldingcleuch
Hayfield
Corries Mill
Easton
Gibstown
Nether Woodhouse
Raeburn Flow
Batenbush
Oakshaw Hill
Jenkinstown
Shankhill
Harper Hill
Raeburnfoot
Netherby
Laws Hall
New Pallyards
Lynedale
Stapleton
Newton
Raeburn
Milligansbush
Silverhill Wood
Cleughfoot Wood
Bruce's Cave
Williamsfield
Aitchisons Bank
Whitecloserigg
Patties Hill
Kirkpatrick-Fleming
Valley
Low Plains
Slealandsburn
Broats
Hollee
Mossknowe
A74(M)
Slackbraes Wood
Gap Wood
DLO Smalmstown
Dry Beck
White Close
OLD BLACKSMITHS SHOP CENTRE
Solway Moss
Sandbed
Wellknowe Rigg
Brackenhill Rigg
High Dubwath
Jackson Rigg
Barracks
Calvertsholm
Smalmstown
Longtown
Gretna Green Services
Riggheads
SOLWAY MOSS 1542
Drakeknowe Plantn
Bolton Fell
Boltonfellend
Nutberry Moss
Gretna Green
Springfield
Ind Est
GRETNA GREEN
Prior Rigg
Mossedge
Todholes
Stonehouse
Mill Hill
Fauld Mill
Prior House
Hall Hills
Black Snib
Brisco Hill
Kirklinton Hall
Cocklet Hill Fm
White Moss
Appleby Ho
Henry's Hill
Leaps
Gretna
DLO Longtown
Francismoor Wood
Kirklinton
Hethersgill
Irvington
Rigg
GRETNA GATEWAY
Lonning Park
Muirhouse
Green
Old Graitney
Hopesike Woods
Bush-on-Lyne Fm
Prior Rigg
Broomhill Moss
Walton Moss
Hetherside
Kirklinton Park
WALTON MOSS
Burnfoot
Cliff Ho
East Cliff
Westhills Moss
Skitby
Hornickhill
Sandysike
Mossband Hall
Willow Hill
Hill Ho
Breaks Moss
Alstonby Hall
Smithfield
Redkirk Pt
Sarkfoot Pt
Brown Dyke
West Knowe
Browhouses
Mossband Hall Marsh
Metal Bridge
Justicetown
Willow Bank
Alstonby Grange
Standingstone Rigg
Highberries
Westlinton
Blackhouse Plantns
Young's Close
Brown Rigg
Morreil Hill
Torduff Pt
Channel of River Esk
Rockliffe Marsh
Hespin Wood
Moor Ho
Scaleby Moss
The Nooks
Brightenflat
Hall Flatt
Heads Wood
Halltown
Ross Castle
Kylesyke Hill
Todhills
Seat Hill Fm
Far Gulf
Wether Hill
Scalebyhill
Dyke Nook
The Beck Fm
Todhills Rest Area
Moorcock Plantn
Scaleby
Fordsyke
Bullersike
Near Gulf
Rockcliffe Moss
Barclose
Woodhead
Pateshill
Newtown
Rockcliffe Cross
Laversdale
Blackford
Wide open Dykes
Scaleby Castle
CASTLETOWN HOUSE
Longpark
Burghmarsh Pt
River Eden
CUMBRIA
Green Acres
Dykeside
Irthington
Old Sandsfield
New Sandsfield
Casson Dyke Fm
Rockcliffe
Brunstock Beck
Red Hills
Old Church Fm
Houghton Ho
Harker
Ind Est
High Knells
Wall Head
HADRIAN'S WALL PATH
Middle Fm
Walldub
Bankend
Knells Ho
Walby
White Moss
Beanlands Park
Burgh Marsh
Harker Grange
VALLUM (COURSE OF)
STANEGATE (COURSE OF)
Ruleholme Br
Cargohill
North End
Drumburgh
Watch Hill
Burgh by Sands
Brunstock
A689
Crosby-on-Eden
Watch Cross
Park Barns
Wood's Hill
Easton
Boustead Hill
Beaumont
St Ann's Well
Cargo
Kingstown
Houghton
Low Crosby
Gelt Ho
Drumburgh Moss
Longburgh
West End
Kingmoor Ho
Tarraby
Park Broom
Warwick Holme
Edmond Castle
DRUMBURGH MOSS
Monkhill
Monkhill Lough
Hill Fm
Holme Ends
The Hall
Bank Head
Fingland Moss
Fingland Rigg
Kirkandrews on Eden
Grinsdale
Linstock
Newby East
Hosket Hill
Knowefield
Moor Ho
Holme Gate
Little Hall
Western Ridge
Farhill
Belah
Edenstown
Whiteclosegate
Fingland
Thurstonfield
Moorhouse
Etterby
Stanwix
Little Corby
Toppin Castle
Corby Hill
Stainton
Rickerby
CARLISLE CASTLE
Willow Holme
Warwick on Eden
Warwick Bridge
Kirkbampton
Ploughlands
CUMBERLAND BIRD OF PREY CENTRE
Thurstonfield Lough
Cobbie Hall
Longrigg
FINGLANDRIGG WOODS
MOORHOUSE ROAD
CARLISLE
TULLIE HOUSE MUSEUM & ART GALLERY
BRUNTON PARK
Aglionby
Moorhouse Hall
Corry Hill
Allenwood
Stockdale Hall
Oughterby
Windmill Ho
Woodlands
Belle Vue
Newtown
WARWICK ROAD
Scotby Ho
Burnrigg
Fenton
Fenton Lane Head
Little Bampton
Prior Rigg
Little Orton
Carlisle
Botcherby
Warwick Moor Wood
Wetheral Plain
Low Wood
Broadwath
Heads Nook
TOWN WALLS
Denton Holme
Westfield Ho
Bampton Beck
Quarry Gill
Flat
Scotby
Glencairn Mill
Faugh
Lanshaw Ho
Park Ho
Bank Ho
Morton
Longsowerby
Garlands
Wetheral
Moss Knowe
Orton Moss
Suttle Ho
Currock
Orchard Ho
Great Corby
Park Ho
Aikton Ho
Fisher Gill
Great Orton
Great Orton
Red Ho
Newby West
Harraby
Scotby Shield
CORBY CASTLE
Aikton
Roblaw Hall
Fallow Field
Newby Cross
Upperby
Gladsmuir
Birk Hill
Wiggonby
Orton Park Fm
Wetheral Pasture
Blackwell
Gillhead
High Wood
Morley Hill
Gamelsby
Woodhouses
Orton Rigg
Lingyclose Head
Cummersdale
Carleton
Cumwhinton
Cote Ho
Whitehead Hill
Down Hall
Thornby
Wiggon Rigg
Baldwinholme
Orton Grange Fm
Sowerby Wood
Shield Head
Clint Head Fm
Cumwhitton
Scugger Ho
High Woodbank
Wrayside
Greyrigg Ho
Broadrake Hall
Floshes
Brisco
Brisco Hill
Moorhouse
Moorhouse Hall
Parton
High Whinnow
Nealhouse
Cardewlees
Blackhall Wood
Springfield Fm
Eden Banks
Moorthwaite Moss
A596
Low Whinnow
Bankend
Moorend
Wood Fm
DALSTON
Durdar
Oakland Ho
Burthwaite Hill
Low Cotehill
Dockrayrigg Ho
Micklethwaite
Dockray Hall
Thursby
Flanders
Hillhouse Nook
Durdar Ho
Newbiggin Hill
Carleton Hill
Knott Hill
Cotehill
Standingstone
Spittal Fm
West End
Crofton
229
Evening Hill
Dalston
Cardew Hall
Nooklane Foot
Pow Bank
Ratten Row
Stone Raise
Burthwaite
230
Wragmire Ho
Warathwaite Head
Bridge Ho
Greenwood Ho
Hazel Head
West Woodside
Moorthwaite Lough
West Curthwaite
Cardew Lodge
Cardew
Green Head
Wragmire Moss
Stoney Wath Fm
Wigton
Kirkland
Ghyll Head Fm
Cumdivock
Buckabank
Bridge
Unthank
Sprunston
Wreay
Wreay Hall
Wragmire Head
High Stand Plantn
East Curthwaite
Chalkfoot
Nook
Bankdale Fm
Foulbridge
Lowthian Gill
A595
Jacob's
Hawksdale
Bow Beck
Petteril Crook's Mill
Ivy Cottage

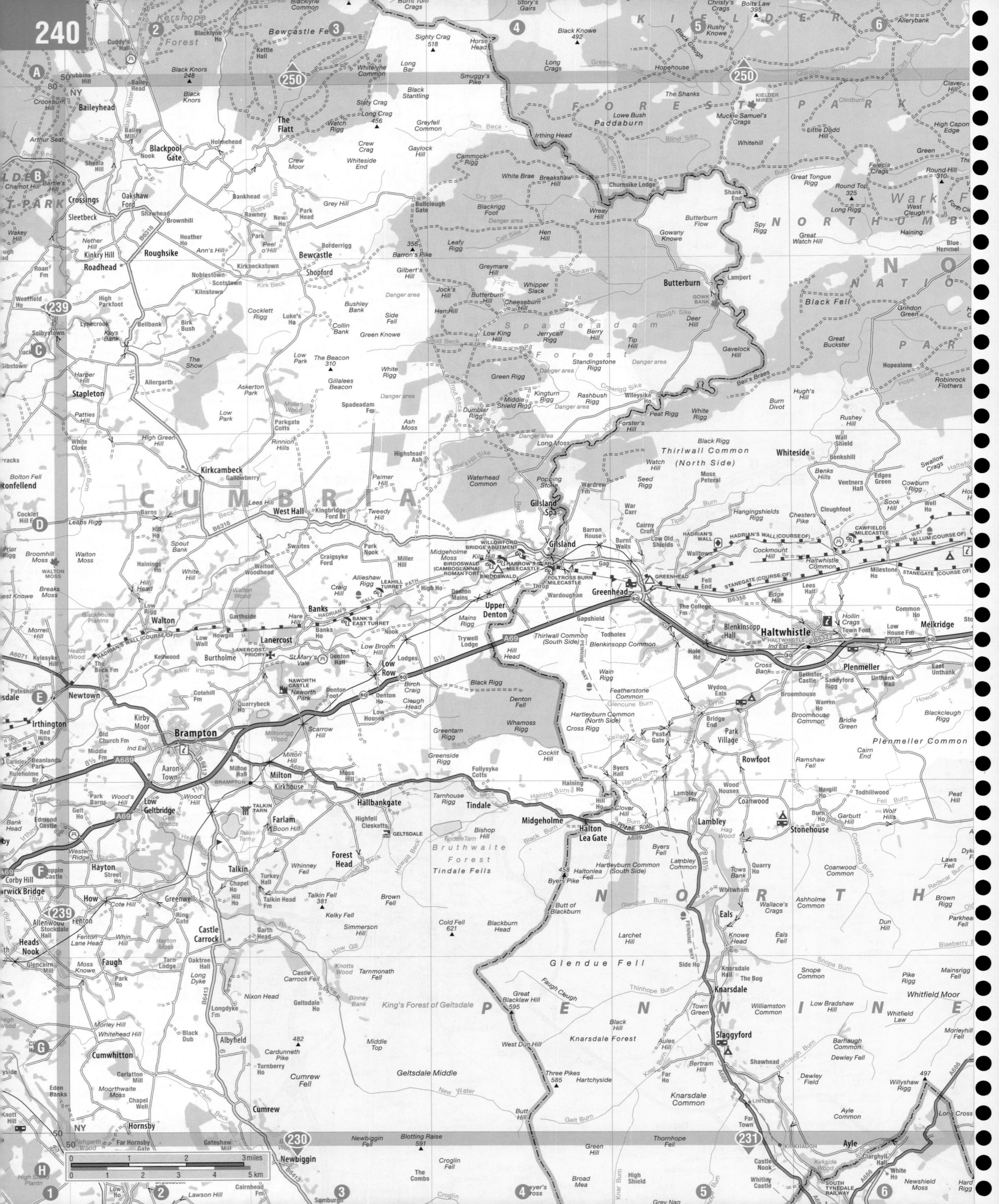
Kershope Forest
Bewcastle Fell
Blacklyne Ho
Kettle Hall
Cuddy's Hall
Black Knors 248
Black Knors
Bailey Head
Baileyhead
Crookburn Hill
Arthur Seat
Blackpool Gate
Holmehead
Nook
Sheala Hill
Chamot Hill
Bartie's Hill
Crossings
Oakshaw Ford
Sleetbeck
Shawhead
Brownhill
Wakey Hill
Nether Hill
Kinkry Hill
Roughsike
Heather Ho
Ann's Hill
Roadhead
Roan Fm
Westfield Ho
High Parkfoot
Lynecrook
Selbystown
Kays Bank
Bellbank
Birk Bush
Harper Hill
Stapleton
Allergarth
The Show
Patties Hill
White Close
High Green Hill
Kirkcambeck
Gallowberry
Bolton Fell
Cockleit Hill Fm
Leaps Rigg
CUMBRIA
Barns
Lees Hill
West Hall
Kingbridge Ford Br
Tweedy Hill
Spout Bank
Broomhill Moss
Walton Moss
Hainings Ho
White Hill
Walton Woodhead
Breaks Moss
Walton
Garthside
Hare Hill
Morrell Hill
Howgill
Low Wall
Lanercost
Lanercost Priory
Burtholme
Kellwood
St Mary's Vale
Denton Hall
Kylesyke Hill
The Beck Fm
Newtown
Irthington
Cotehill Fm
Naworth Castle
Naworth Park
Quarrybeck Ho
Kirby Moor
Brampton
Old Church Fm
Middle Fm
Beanlands Park
Ruleholme Br
Aaron's Town
Milton
Milton Hall
Kirkhouse
Moss Hill
Park Barns
Wood's Hill
Low Geltbridge
Gelt Ho
Edmond Castle
Bank Head
Talkin Tarn
Farlam
Boon Hill
Hallbankgate
Highfield
Cleskettle
Geltsdale
Forest Head
Western Ridge
Hayton
Corby Hill
Warwick Bridge
How
Talkin
Chapel Ho
Turkey Hall
Talkin Head Fm
Talkin Fell 381
Kelky Fell
Brown Fell
Simmerson Hill
Greenwell
Cote Hill
Ring Gate
Fenton
Allenwood
Stockdale Hall
Heads Nook
Fenton Lane Head
Whin Hill
Hayton Moss
Castle Carrock
Garth Head
River Gelt
Faugh
Moss Knowe
Tarn Lodge
Oaktree Hall
Long Dyke
Castle Carrock Fell
Knotts Wood
Tarnmonath Fell
Park Ho
Nixon Head
Geltsdale Ho
Binney Bank
King's Forest of Geltsdale
Longdyke Fm
Morley Hill
Whitehead Hill
Black Dub
Albyfield
Cumwhitton
482
Cardunneth Pike
Turnberry Ho
Middle Top
Carlatton Mill
Moorthwaite Moss
Chapel Well
Cumrew Fell
Geltsdale Middle
Cumrew
Eden Banks
Hornsby
Far Hornsby Gate
Gateshaw Mill
Newbiggin
Newbiggin Fell
Blotting Raise 591
Croglin Fell
The Combs
Cairnhead Fm
Lawson Hill
Sumburgh
Burnt Tom Crags
Sighty Crag 518
Horse Head
Long Bar
Whitelyne Common
Smuggy's Pike
Black Stantling
Slaty Crag
Long Crag 456
Watch Rigg
The Flatt
Greyfell Common
Tarn Beck
Crew Crag
Crew Moor
Gaylock Hill
Whiteside End
Bankhead
Rawney
Bothrigg
Park Head
New Ho
Grey Hill
Bullcleugh Gate
Park
Peel o'Hill
Borderrigg
Bewcastle
Kirkbeckstown
Noblestown
Scotstown
Kilnstown
Kirk Beck
Shopford
356 Barron's Pike
Gilbert's Hill
Cockleit Rigg
Luke's Ho
Bushley Bank
Collin Bank
Side Fell
Green Knowe
Low Park
The Beacon 310
Gillalees Beacon
White Rigg
Askerton Park
Spadeadam Fm
Low Park
Parkgate Cotts
Rinnion Hills
Ash Moss
Highstead Ash
Palmer Hill
Waterhead Common
Story's Gairs
Black Knowe 492
Long Crags
Hopehouse
Cammock Rigg
White Brae
Breakshaw Hill
Irthing Head
Blackrigg Foot
Leafy Rigg
Hen Hill
Greymare Hill
Jock's Hill
Butterburn Hill
Whipper Slack
Cheeseburn Hill
Low King Hill
Jerrycalf Rigg
Berry Hill
Spadeadam Forest
Green Rigg
Standingstone Rigg
Middle Shield Rigg
Kingturn Rigg
Rashbush Rigg
Dumblar Rigg
Long Moss
Popping Stone
Gilsland Spa
Wardrew Fm
KIELDER FOREST PARK
Lowe Bush
Paddaburn
The Shanks
Kielder Mires
Muckle Samuel's Crags
Whitehill
Churnsike Lodge
Wreay Hill
Gowany Knowe
Butterburn Flow
Butterburn
Lampert
Deer Hill
Tip Hill
Gavelock Hill
Bell's Braes
Wileysike Ho
Peat Rigg
White Rigg
Forster's Hill
Christy's Crags
Bolts Law 395
Rushy Knowe
Black Cleugh
Allerybank
Claver Hill
High Capon Edge
Little Dodd Hill
Green
Felecia Crags
Round Hill 310
Great Tongue Rigg
Round Top 325
Shank End
Long Rigg
Wark Forest
West Cleugh
Spy Rigg
Haining
Great Watch Hill
Blue Hemmel
NORTHUMBERLAND NATIONAL PARK
Black Fell
Grindon Green
Great Buckster
Hopealone
Robinrock Flothers
Hugh's Hill
Burn Divot
Rushey Hill
Black Rigg
Thirlwall Common (North Side)
Whiteside
Wall Shield
Benkshill
Watch Hill
Seed Rigg
Moss Peteral
Benks Hills
Ventners Hall
Edges Green
Cowburn Rigg
Swallow Crags
War Carr
Hangingshields Rigg
Chesters Pike
Cleughfoot
Sook Hill
Well Ho
Cairny Croft
Barron House
Burnt Walls
Low Old Shields
Hadrian's Wall
Walltown
Cockmount Hill
Haltwhistle Common
Cawfields Milecastle
Milestone Ho
Stanegate (course of)
Gilsland
Willowford Bridge Abutment
Harrow's Scar Milecastle
Birdoswald (Camboglanna) Roman Fort
Poltross Burn Milecastle
Midgeholme Moss
Kiln Hill
Gap
Greenhead
Fell End
Lees Hall
Edge Hill
Thropp
Wardoughan
Denton Mains
Upper Denton
Park Nook
Miller Hill
Allieshaw Rigg
Leahill Turret
High Ho
Craig Hill
Craigsyke Ford
Swaites
Banks
Bank's East Turret
Banks Ho
Nook
Mains Rigg
Trywell Lodge
Low Broom Hill
Lodges
Low Row
Birch Craig
Denton Foot
Denton Ho
Cleugh Head
Low Houses
Black Rigg
Denton Fell
Scarrow Hill
Greentarn Rigg
Greenside Rigg
Whamoss Rigg
Cocklit Hill
Follysyke Cotts
Tarnhouse Rigg
Tindale
Midgeholme
Bishop Hill
Bruthwaite Forest
Tindale Fells
Halton Lea Gate
Gapshield
Thirlwall Common (South Side)
Todholes
Blenkinsopp Common
Hill Head
Wain Rigg
Featherstone Common
Hartleyburn Common (North Side)
Cross Rigg
Peat Gate
Byers Hall
Haining Ho
Hill Ho
Clover Hill
The College Fm
Blenkinsopp Hall
Haltwhistle
Hole Ho
Cross Bank
Bellister Castle
Sandyford Rigg
Unthank Hall
Plenmeller
East Unthank
Hollin Crags
Town Foot
Low House Fm
Melkridge
Common Ho
Wydon Eals
Broomhouse
Warren Ho
Broomhouse Common
Bridle Green
Blackcleugh Rigg
Bridge End
Park Village
Plenmeller Common
Rowfoot
Ramshaw Fell
Cairn End
Wood Houses
Lambley Fm
Coanwood
Hargill Ho
Todhillwood
Peat Hill
Lambley
Hag Wood
Burn Ho
Garbutt Hill
Wolf Hills
Stonehouse
Byers Fell
Lambley Common
Hartleyburn Common (South Side)
458 Byers Pike
Haltonlea Fell
Butt of Blackburn
Tows Bank
Quarry Ho
Coanwood Common
Laws Fell
Whitwham
Wallace's Crags
Ashholme Common
Brown Rigg
Eals
Cold Fell 621
Blackburn Head
Larchet Hill
Knowe Head
Eals Fell
Dun Hill
Glendue Fell
Side Ho
Knarsdale Hall
The Bog
Snope Common
Pike Rigg
Mainsrigg Fell
Great Blacklaw Hill 595
Knarsdale
Whitfield Moor
Town Green
Williamston Common
Low Bradshaw Hill
Whitfield Law
PENNINE
Black Hill
Knarsdale Forest
Aules Hill
Slaggyford
Barhaugh Common
Dewley Fell
Morleyhill Fell
West Dun Hill
Three Pikes 585
Hartchyside
Bertram Hill
Far Ho
Shawhead
Dewley Field
Willyshaw Rigg
497
Knarsdale Common
Butt Hill
Ayle Common
Far Town
Long Cross
Thornhope Fell
Green Hill
Castle Nook
Ayle
Clarghyll Hall
Kirkside Wood
White Ho
Whitley Castle
South Tynedale Railway
Newshield Moss
High Shield
Broad Mea
Grey Nag
250
239
230
231
0 1 2 3 miles
0 1 2 3 4 5 km

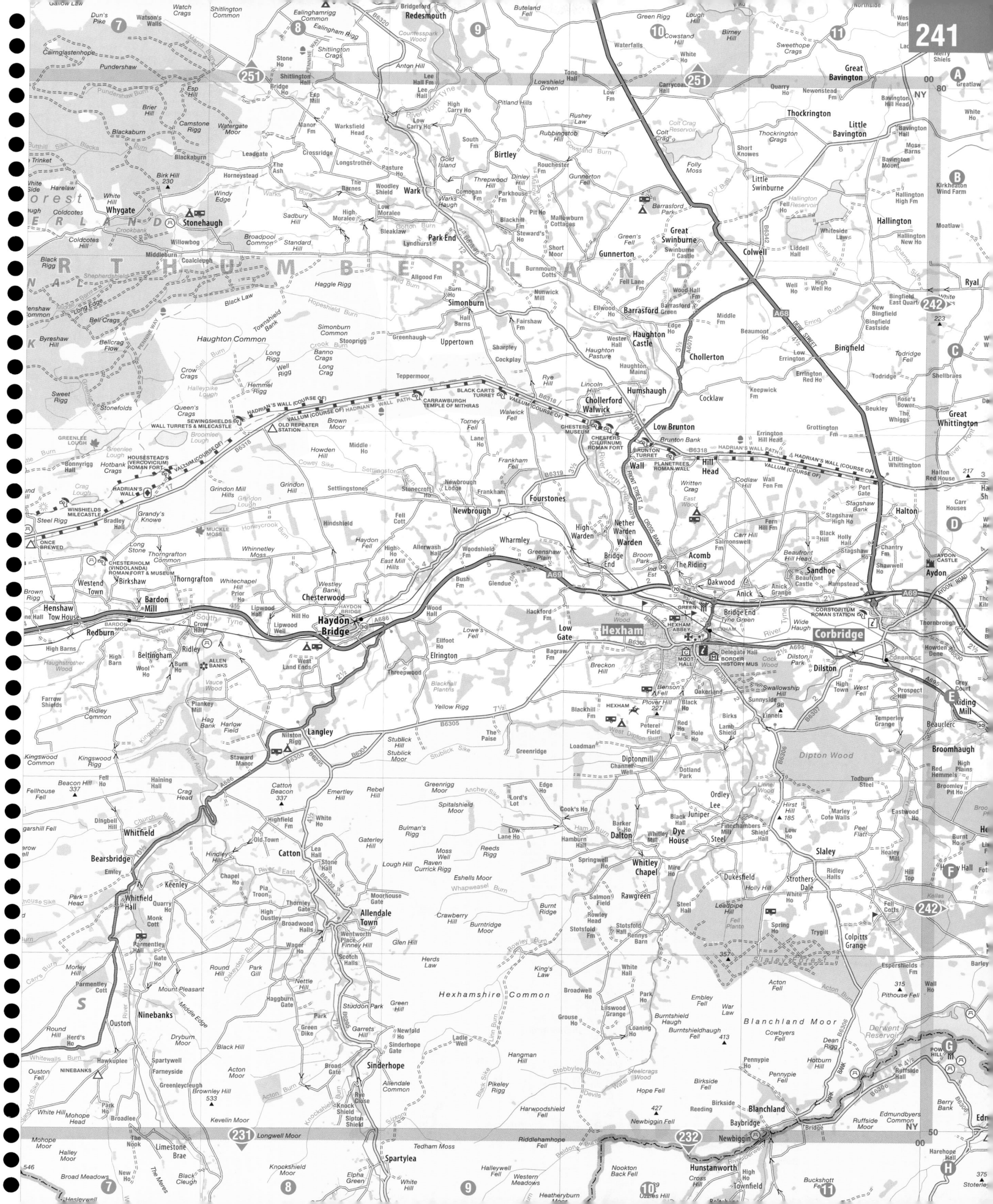

241
Redesmouth
Great Bavington
Thockrington
Little Bavington
Stonehaugh
Whygate
Birtley
Wark
Park End
Gunnerton
Great Swinburne
Colwell
Hallington
Ryal
Simonburn
Barrasford
Haughton Castle
Chollerton
Bingfield
Humshaugh
Chollerford
Walwick
Low Brunton
Great Whittington
Wall
Hill Head
Newbrough
Fourstones
Halton
Acomb
Sandhoe
Aydon
Haydon Bridge
Hexham
Corbridge
Dilston
Bardon Mill
Henshaw
Redburn
Chesterwood
Beltingham
Ridley
Langley
Elrington
Low Gate
Riding Mill
Broomhaugh
Whitfield
Catton
Allendale Town
Dalton
Dye House
Whitley Chapel
Slaley
Ninebanks
Sinderhope
Blanchland
Baybridge
Hunstanworth
Spartylea
N O R T H U M B E R L A N D
Hexhamshire Common
Blanchland Moor
Dipton Wood
Slaley Forest
HADRIAN'S WALL (COURSE OF)
VALLUM (COURSE OF)
HOUSESTEAD'S (VERCOVICIUM) ROMAN FORT
CHESTERHOLM (VINDOLANDA) ROMAN FORT & MUSEUM
CHESTERS (CILURNUM) ROMAN FORT
CORSTOPITUM ROMAN STATION
CARRAWBURGH TEMPLE OF MITHRAS
BORDER HISTORY MUS
HEXHAM ABBEY
A68
A69
A686
A695
B6318
B6319
B6305
B6306
231
232
242
251

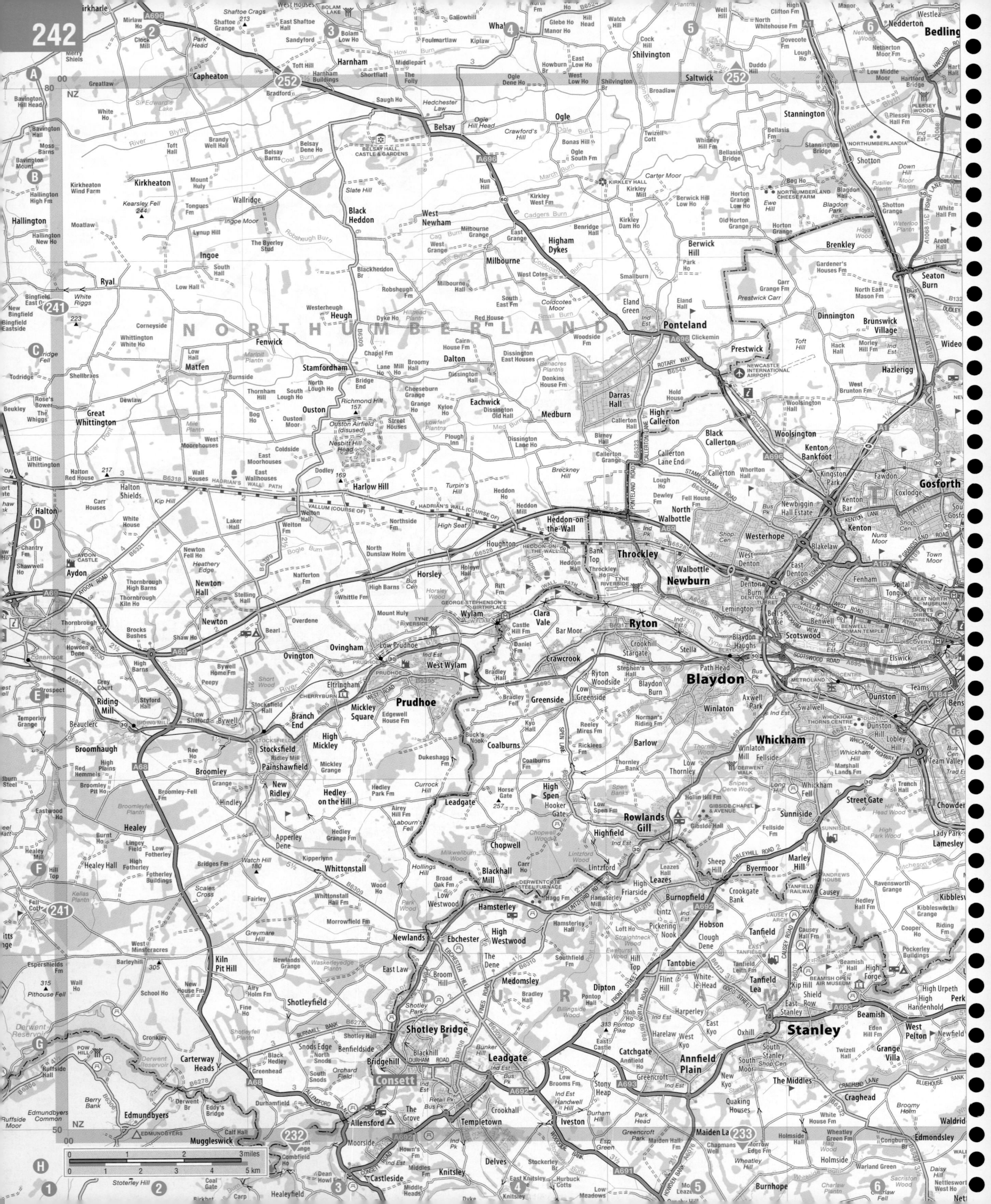
NORTHUMBERLAND
DURHAM
Capheaton
Belsay
Ogle
Shilvington
Saltwick
Stannington
Shotton
Kirkheaton
Black Heddon
West Newham
Higham Dykes
Berwick Hill
Brenkley
Seaton Burn
Hallington
Ingoe
Milbourne
Ryal
Heugh
Ponteland
Prestwick
Dinnington
Brunswick Village
Fenwick
Matfen
Stamfordham
Dalton
Hazlerigg
Great Whittington
Ouston
Eachwick
Medburn
Darras Hall
High Callerton
Black Callerton
Woolsington
Kenton Bankfoot
Gosforth
Harlow Hill
Halton
North Walbottle
Westerhope
Kenton
Aydon
Horsley
Heddon-on-the-Wall
Throckley
Newburn
Newton Hall
Newton
Wylam
Clara Vale
Ryton
Ovington
Ovingham
West Wylam
Blaydon
Scotswood
Riding Mill
Prudhoe
Mickley Square
Branch End
Stocksfield
Bywell
Broomhaugh
High Mickley
Coalburns
Greenside
Winlaton
Whickham
Dunston
Broomley
Painshawfield
New Ridley
Hedley on the Hill
Leadgate
High Spen
Rowlands Gill
Barlow
Street Gate
Sunniside
Healey
Chopwell
Highfield
Blackhall Mill
Lintzford
Byermoor
Marley Hill
Whittonstall
Hamsterley
Burnopfield
Newlands
Ebchester
High Westwood
Hobson
Tanfield
Kiln Pit Hill
Medomsley
Dipton
Tanfield Lea
Stanley
Shotley Bridge
Consett
Leadgate
Catchgate
Annfield Plain
Carterway Heads
Edmundbyers
Muggleswick
Allensford
Templetown
Iveston
Craghead
Castleside
Knitsley
Delves
Burnhope
0 1 2 3 miles
0 1 2 3 4 5 km

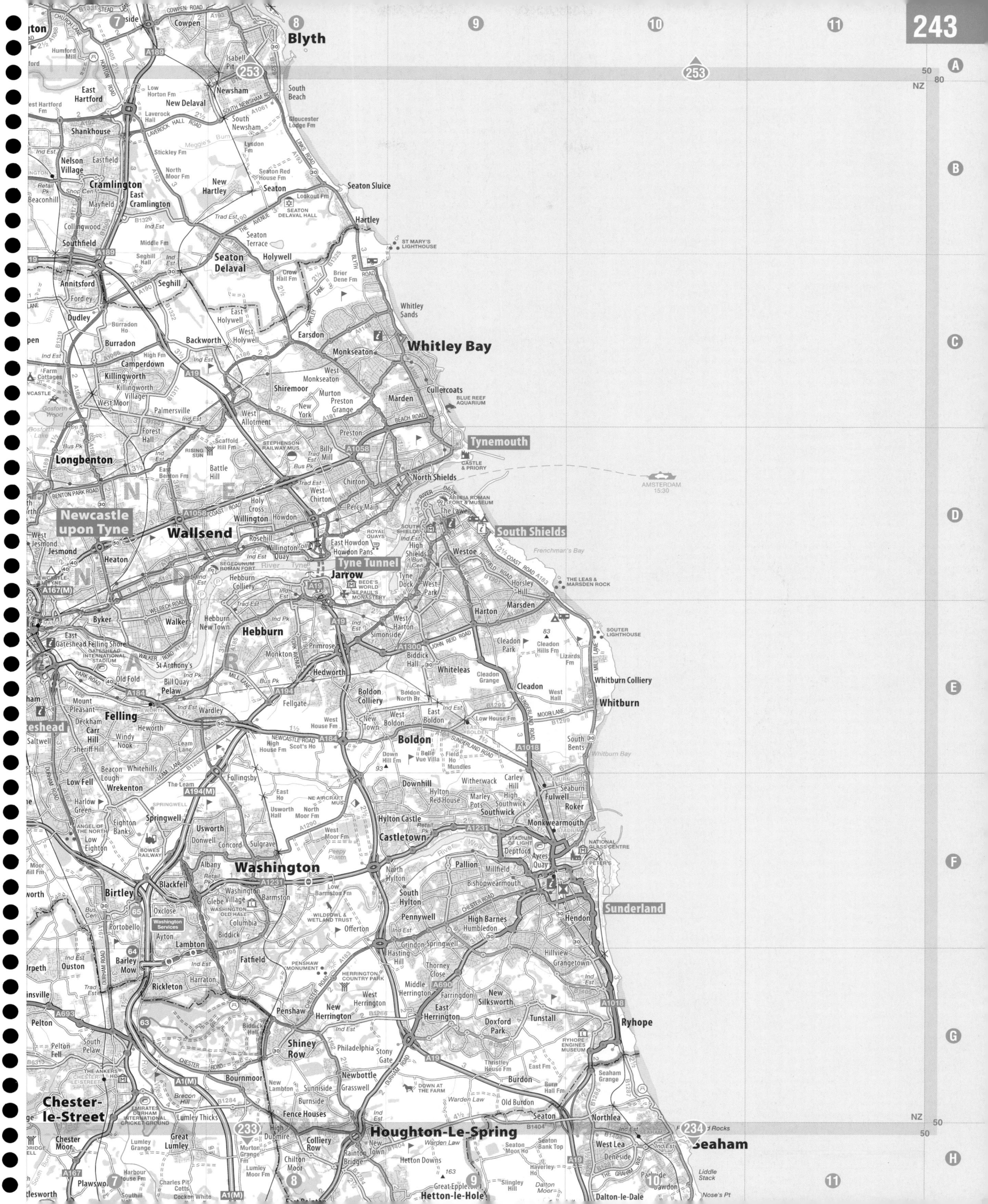

7
8
9
10
11
A
B
C
D
E
F
G
H
253
234
233
NZ
50
80
Blyth
Cowpen
Isabella Pit
Newsham
New Delaval
South Beach
South Newsham
Gloucester Lodge Fm
East Hartford
Shankhouse
Nelson Village
Cramlington
East Cramlington
Mayfield
Collingwood
Southfield
Annitsford
Fordley
Dudley
Burradon
Camperdown
Killingworth
Killingworth Village
West Moor
Palmersville
Forest Hall
Longbenton
Newcastle upon Tyne
Wallsend
Jesmond
Heaton
Byker
Walker
Felling
Heworth
Windy Nook
Low Fell
Wrekenton
Springwell
Usworth
Washington
Birtley
Blackfell
Oxclose
Portobello
Ayton
Lambton
Barley Mow
Rickleton
Ouston
Pelton
Chester-le-Street
Great Lumley
Lumley Thicks
Bournmoor
New Hartley
Seaton
Seaton Sluice
Hartley
Seaton Delaval
Seaton Terrace
Holywell
Seghill
Backworth
East Holywell
West Holywell
Earsdon
Whitley Sands
Whitley Bay
Monkseaton
West Monkseaton
Shiremoor
Murton
Preston Grange
New York
West Allotment
Marden
Cullercoats
Blue Reef Aquarium
Preston
Billy Mill
Battle Hill
Tynemouth
Castle & Priory
North Shields
Chirton
West Chirton
Percy Main
Howdon
Willington
Holy Cross
Rosehill
Willington Quay
Amsterdam 15:30
St Mary's Lighthouse
South Shields
The Lawe
Arbeia Roman Fort & Museum
Westoe
Frenchman's Bay
Tyne Tunnel
Jarrow
Hebburn
Hebburn Colliery
Hebburn New Town
Tyne Dock
West Park
Horsley Hill
Marsden
Harton
West Harton
Simonside
The Leas & Marsden Rock
Souter Lighthouse
Primrose
Monkton
Hedworth
Biddick Hall
Whiteleas
Cleadon Park
Cleadon Hills Fm
Cleadon
Whitburn Colliery
Whitburn
Boldon Colliery
Fellgate
Boldon
East Boldon
West Boldon
New Town
Downhill
Witherwack
Carley Hill
Seaburn
Fulwell
Roker
Monkwearmouth
South Bents
Whitburn Bay
Hylton Castle
Castletown
Marley Pots
Southwick
Pallion
Millfield
Bishopwearmouth
Deptford
Ayres Quay
National Glass Centre
St Peter's
Sunderland
Hendon
High Barnes
Humbledon
South Hylton
Pennywell
Grindon
Springwell
North Hylton
Offerton
Wildfowl & Wetland Trust
Hastings Hill
Thorney Close
Hillview
Grangetown
Middle Herrington
Farringdon
New Silksworth
Tunstall
East Herrington
Doxford Park
Ryhope
Ryhope Engines Museum
Penshaw
Penshaw Monument
Herrington Country Park
West Herrington
New Herrington
Shiney Row
Philadelphia
Stony Gate
Newbottle
Grasswell
Sunniside
Burnside
Fence Houses
Houghton-Le-Spring
Fatfield
Harraton
Biddick
Columbia
Glebe Village
Washington Village
Barmston
Washington Old Hall
Albany
Donwell
Concord
Sulgrave
Burdon
Seaton
Seaham Grange
Northlea
Seaham
West Lea
Deneside
Dalton-le-Dale
Hetton-le-Hole
Hetton Downs
New Town
Rainton Bridge
Chilton Moor
Colliery Row
Dubmire
Murton Grange
Great Eppleton
Warden Law
Old Burdon
Lumley Grange
Chester Moor
Plawsworth
Boldon
Low Barmston Fm
Usworth Hall
Follingsby
Wardley
Bill Quay
Pelaw
Old Fold
Gateshead
Deckham
Carr Hill
Sheriff Hill
Beacon Lough
Whitehills
Harlow Green
Eighton Banks
Low Eighton
A189
A19
A1058
A184
A194(M)
A1231
A1018
A690
A167(M)
A1(M)
A693
A1300
A183

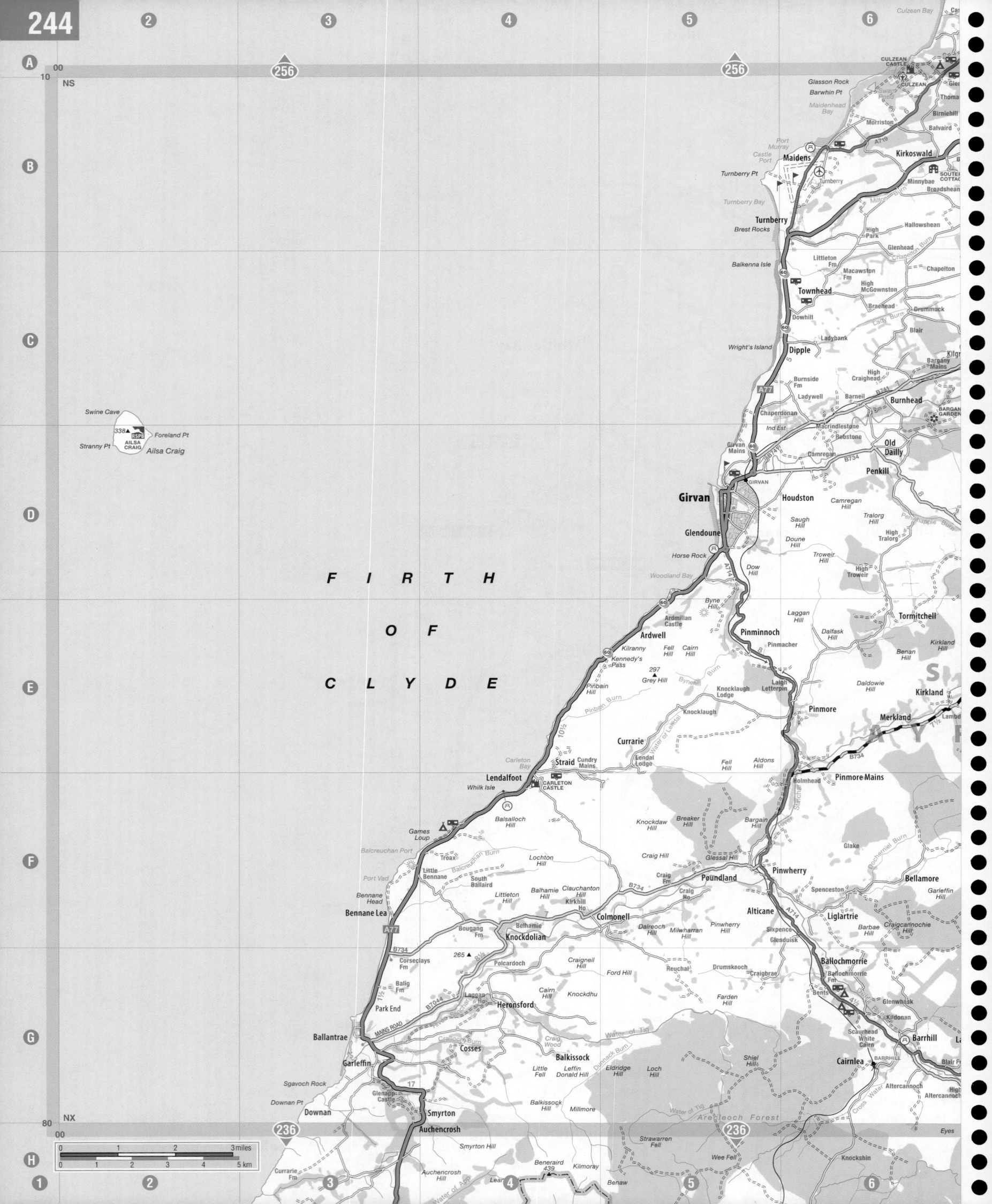

FIRTH

OF

CLYDE

Ailsa Craig
Swine Cave
338▲
RSPB AILSA CRAIG
Stranny Pt
Foreland Pt

Culzean Bay
CULZEAN CASTLE
CULZEAN
Glasson Rock
Barwhin Pt
Maidenhead Bay
Morriston
Birniehill
Balvaird
Port Murray
Castle Port
Maidens
Turnberry Pt
Turnberry
Kirkoswald
SOUTER COTTAGE
Minnybae
Broadsheanmuir
Turnberry
Brest Rocks
High Park
Hallowshean
Glenhead
Balkenna Isle
Littleton Fm
Macawston Fm
Chapelton
Townhead
High McGownston
Braehead
Druminuck
Dowhill
Ladybank
Blair
Wright's Island
Dipple
High Craighead
Kilgr
Bargany Mains
Burnside Fm
Ladywell
Barneil
Burnhead
BARGANY GARDEN
Chaperdonan
Ind Est
Macrindlestone
Bebston
Girvan Mains
Camregan
Old Dailly
GIRVAN
Penkill
Girvan
Houdston
Camregan Hill
Tralorg Hill
Penwhapple
Glendoune
Saugh Hill
Doune Hill
High Tralorg
Horse Rock
Dow Hill
Troweir Hill
High Troweir
Woodland Bay
Byne Hill
Laggan Hill
Tormitchell
Ardmillan Castle
Dalfask Hill
Kirkland Hill
Ardwell
Pinminnoch
Benan Hill
Kilranny
Fell Hill
Cairn Hill
Pinmacher
Kennedy's Pass
297▲
Grey Hill
Bynehill Burn
Knocklaugh Lodge
Laigh Letterpin
Daldowie Hill
Kirkland
Pinbain
Pinbain Burn
Water of Lendal
Knocklaugh
Pinmore
Merkland
Lambd
Currarie
Fell Hill
Aldons Hill
Carleton Bay
Straid
Cundry Mains
Lendal Lodge
Pinmore Mains
Holmhead
Lendalfoot
CARLETON CASTLE
Whilk Isle
Bargain Hill
Balsalloch Hill
Knockdaw Hill
Breaker Hill
Glake
Games Loup
Balcreuchan Port
Troax
Lochton Hill
Craig Hill
Glessal Hill
Pinwherry
Bellamore
Port Vad
Little Bennane
South Ballaird
Balhamie Hill
Clauchanton Hill
Kirkhill Ho
Craig Fm
Craig Ho
Poundland
Spenceston
Garleffin Fm
Bennane Head
Littleton Hill
B734
Alticane
Liglartrie
Bennane Lea
Colmonell
Dalreoch Hill
Milwharran Hill
Pinwherry Hill
Sixpence
Craigcannochie
A77
Bougang Fm
Bethamie Fm
Gleneduisk
Barbae Fm
Knockdolian
265▲
Polcardoch
Dalreoch
Ballochmorrie
B734
Corseclays Fm
Polcardoch
Craigneil Hill
Ford Hill
Reuchat
Drumskeoch
Craigbrae
Ballochmorrie Fm
Balig Fm
Cairn Hill
Knockdhu
Farden Hill
Bents
Glenwhask
Park End
Laggan Ho
Heronsford
Kildonan
B7044
Craig Wood
Scaurhead White Cairn
Barrhill
Ballantrae
Cosses
Balkissock
Water of Tig
Shiel Hill
Cairnlea
BARRHILL
Garleffin
Little Fell
Leffin Donald Hill
Eldridge Hill
Loch Hill
La
Blair H
Sgavoch Rock
Downan Pt
17
Glenapp Castle
Balkissock Hill
Millmore
Water of Tig
Arecleoch Forest
High Altercannoch
Altercannoch
Downan
Smyrton
Auchencrosh
Smyrton Hill
Strawarren Fell
Wee Fell
Eyes
NX
Currarie Fm
Auchencrosh Hill
Beneraird 439
Kilmoray
Benaw
Knockshin
Water of App
Lear

A719
A77
B741
A714
B734
B7044
256

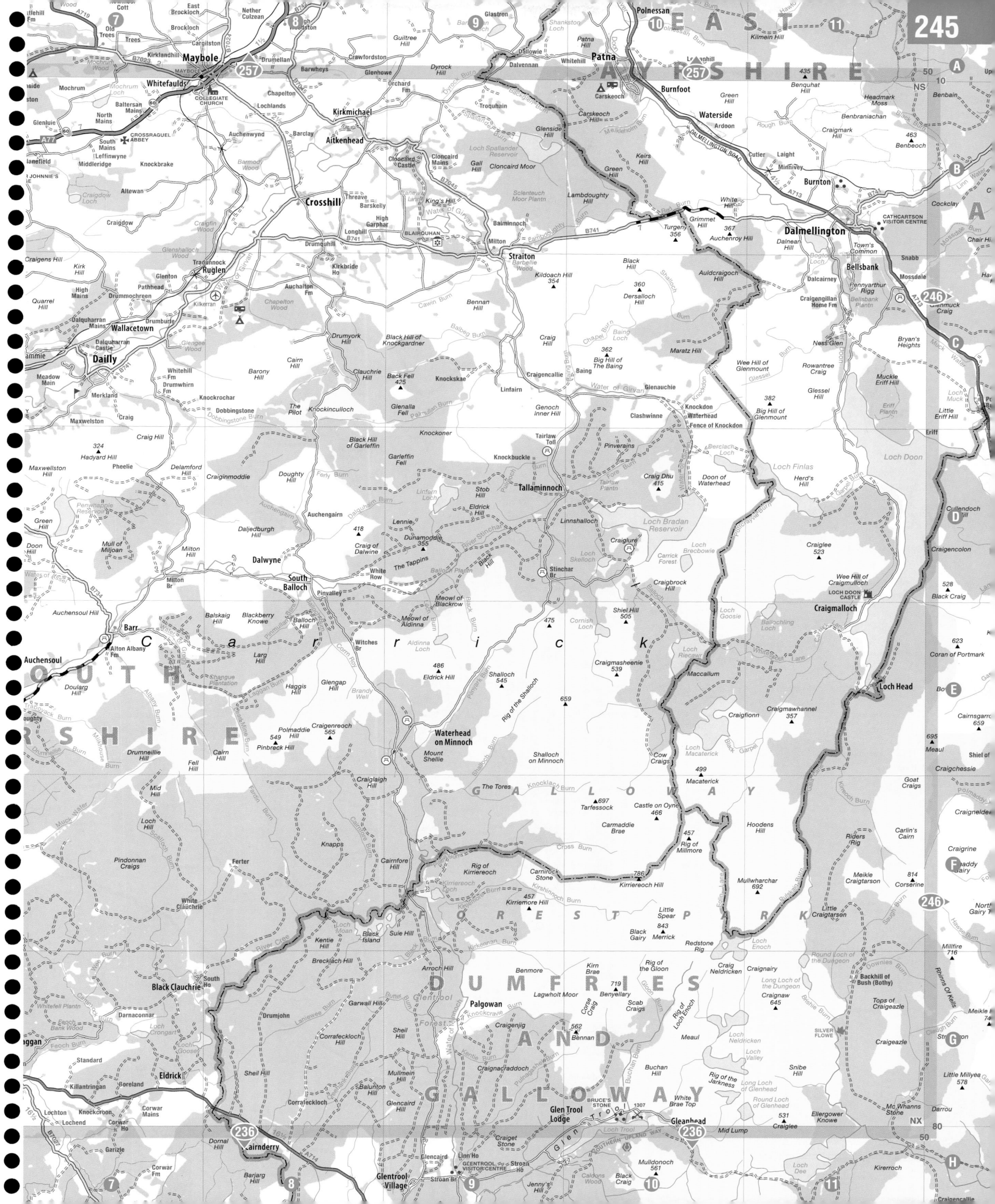
EAST AYRSHIRE
SOUTH AYRSHIRE
Carrick
GALLOWAY FOREST PARK
DUMFRIES AND GALLOWAY
Maybole
Whitefaulds
Kirkoswald
Crosshill
Kirkmichael
Aitkenhead
Straiton
Patna
Dalmellington
Burnfoot
Waterside
Burnton
Bellsbank
Daily
Wallacetown
Ruglen
Tradunnock
Barr
Tallaminnoch
South Balloch
Dalwyne
Pinvalley
Waterhead on Minnoch
Palgowan
Glen Trool Lodge
Glentrool Village
Eldrick
Black Clauchrie
Cairnderry
Craigmalloch
Loch Head
Gleanhead
Loch Doon
Loch Bradan Reservoir
Loch Spallander Reservoir
Loch Trool
LOCH DOON CASTLE
BLAIRQUHAN
CROSSRAGUEL ABBEY
COLLEGIATE CHURCH
CATHCARTSON VISITOR CENTRE
GLENTROOL VISITOR CENTRE
BRUCE'S STONE
SILVER FLOWE
SOUTHERN UPLAND WAY
Glen Trool
Water of Girvan
River Stinchar
Shalloch on Minnoch
Tarfessock 697
Kirriereoch Hill 786
Merrick 843
Mullwharchar 692
Corserine 814
Craiglee 523
Benyellary 719
Mulldonach 561
Lamachan
Bennan 562
Craignaw 645
Cairnsgarroch 659
Meaul 695
Coran of Portmark 623
Craigmasheenie 539
Polmaddie Hill 549
Craigenreoch 565
Shalloch 545
Eldrick Hill 486
Shiel Hill 505
Kildoach Hill 354
Dersalloch Hill 360
Big Hill of The Baing 362
Big Hill of Glenmount 382
Turgeny 356
Auchenroy Hill 367
Benquhat Hill 435
Benbeoch 463
Craig Dhu 415
Back Fell 425
Craig of Dalwine 418
Dunamoddie 355
Hadyard Hill 324
Craigmawhannel 357
Macaterick 499
Castle on Oyne 466
Rig of Millmore 457
Kirriemore Hill 457
Black Craig 528
Millfire 716
Little Millyea 578
Craiglee 531
Rhinns Of Kells
B741
B7023
B7045
B734
B7024
B7027
A77
A713
A714
DALMELLINGTON ROAD
257
236
246
NS
NX
50
10
80
A
B
C
D
E
F
G
H
7
8
9
10
11

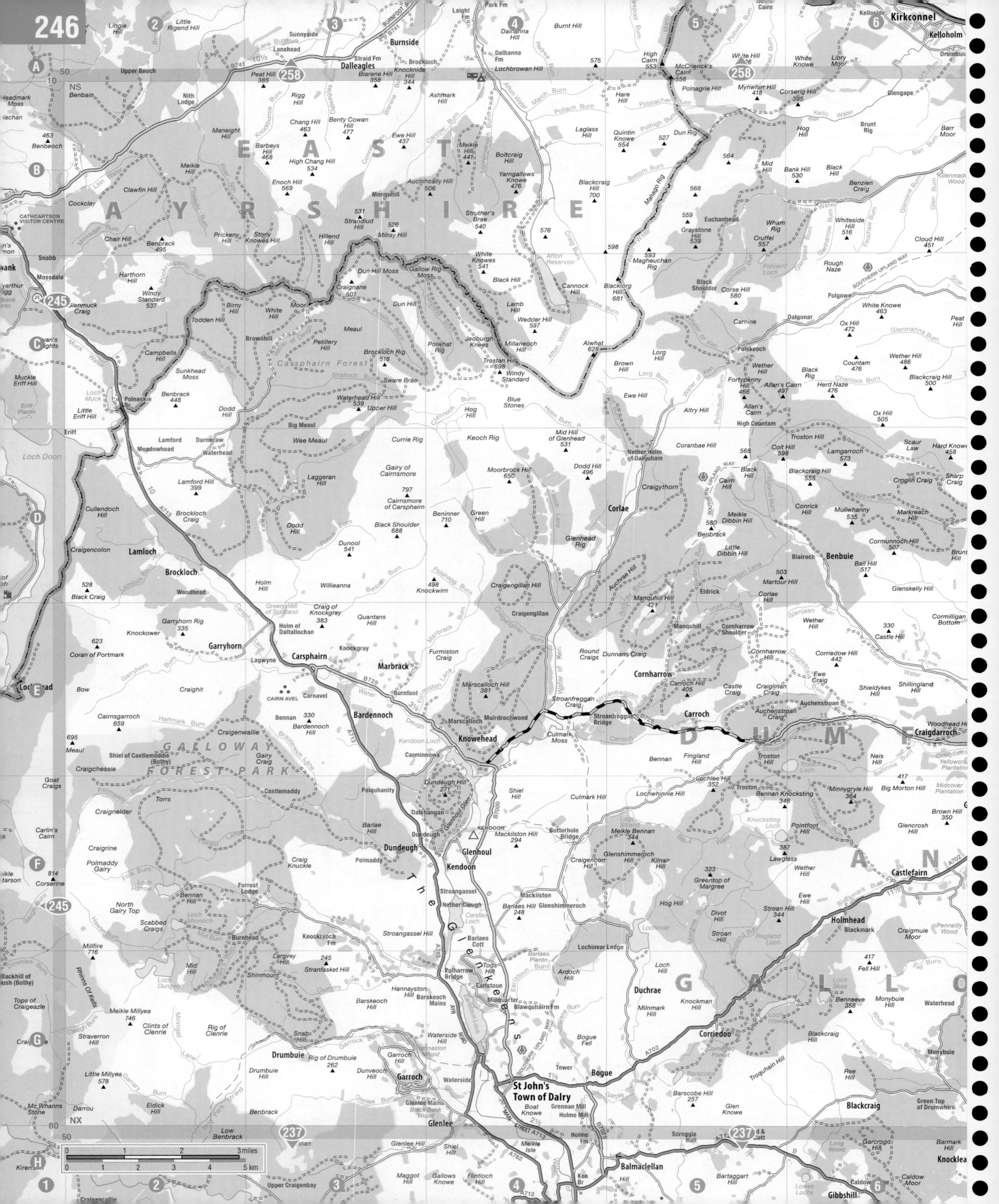

E A S T
A Y R S H I R E
G A L L O W A Y
F O R E S T P A R K
D U M F
G A L L O
A N
258
245
237
Kirkconnel
Kelloholm
Dalleagles
Burnside
Lanehead
Sunnyside
Upper Beoch
Straid Fm
Blarene Hill 358
Knocknide Hill 344
Brockloch
Laight Fm
Park Fm
Dalhanna Hill
Dalhanna Fm
Lochbrowan Hill
Burnt Hill
High Cairn 553
McCrierick's Cairn 556
White Hill 536
Polnagrie Hill
Mynwhir Hill 418
Corserig Hill 395
Glengape
White Knowe
Libry Moor
Lingie Hill
Little Rigend Hill
Peat Hill 385
Rigg Hill
Nith Lodge
Benbain
Headmark Moss
Ashmark Hill
Hare Hill
Chang Hill 463
Benty Cowan Hill 477
Ewe Hill 437
Maneight Hill
Barbeys Hill 468
Benbeoch 463
High Chang Hill 534
Meikle Hill 441
Boltcraig Hill
Laglass Hill
Quintin Knowe 554
Dun Rig
Hog Hill
Brunt Rig
Barr Moor
Enoch Hill 569
Auchincally Hill 506
Monquhill
Yarngallows Knowe 476
Blackcraig Hill 700
Mid Hill
Bank Hill 530
Black Hill
Benzien Craig
Clawfin Hill
Cockclay
Meikle Hill
CATHCARTSON VISITOR CENTRE
Strandlud Hill 531
Milray Hill 526
Struther's Brae 540
Euchanhead
Graystone Hill 539
Wham Rig
Cruffel 557
Whiteside Hill 516
Cloud Hill 451
Chair Hill
Benbrack 495
Prickeny Hill
Stony Knowes Hill
Hillend Hill
Afton Reservoir
Magheuchan Rig 593
Snabb
Mossdale
Harthorn Hill
Windy Standard 537
Dun Hill Moss
Gallow Rig Moss
White Knowes 541
Black Hill
Cannock Hill
Blacklorg Hill 681
Black Shoulder
Corse Hill 580
Rough Naze
SOUTHERN UPLAND WAY
Polgown
Glenmuck Craig
Craignane 501
Birny Hill
White Hill
Moor
Dun Hill
Lamb Hill
Wedder Hill 597
Dalgonar
Carnine
White Knowe 463
Ox Hill 472
Peat Hill
Todden Hill
Brownhill
Meaul
Petillery Hill
Carsphairn Forest
Brockloch Rig 518
Polwhat Rig
Jedburgh Knees
Millaneoch Hill
Alwhat 628
Polskeoch
Campbells Hill
Sunkhead Moss
Trostan Hill 698
Windy Standard
Sware Brae
Lorg Hill
Brown Hill
Wether Hill
Countam 476
Wether Hill 486
Muckle Eriff Hill
Loch Muck
Polnaskie Br
Benbrack 448
Waterhead Hill 539
Upper Hill
Blue Stones
Ewe Hill
Fortypenny Hill 466
Allan's Cairn 497
Black Rig
Herd Naze 476
Blackcraig Hill 500
Little Eriff Hill
Dodd Hill
Hog Hill
Allan's Cairn
Altry Hill
High Countam
Ox Hill 505
Eriff
Big Meaul
Lamford
Darnscaw
Meadowhead
Waterhead
Wee Meaul
Currie Rig
Keoch Rig
Mid Hill of Glenhead 531
Coranbae Hill
Troston Hill
Scaur Law
Hard Knowe 458
Loch Doon
Gairy of Cairnsmore
Moorbrock Hill 650
Dodd Hill 496
Nether Holm of Dalquhain
Colt Hill 598
Lamgarroch 573
Blackcraig Hill 555
Sharp Craig
Croglin Craig
Lamford Hill 399
Laggeran Hill
Cairnsmore of Carsphairn 797
Craigythorn
Black Hill
Cairn Hill
Cullendoch Hill
Brockloch Craig
Corlae
Conrick Hill
Mullwhanny 535
Markreach Hill
Dodd Hill
Black Shoulder 688
Beninner 710
Green Hill
Meikle Dibbin Hill
Craigencolon
Benbrack 580
Cormunnoch Hill 507
Lamloch
Dunool 541
Glenhead Rig
Little Dibbin Hill
Blairoch
Benbuie
Ball Hill 517
Brockloch
Woodhead
Holm Hill
Willieanna
Knockwirn 498
Craigengillan Hill
Auchrae Hill
Martour Hill 503
Eldrick
Corlae Hill
Glenskelly Hill
Black Craig 528
Green Well of Scotland
Craig of Knockgray 383
Quantans Hill
Craigengillan
Manquhill Hill 421
Manquhill
Cornharrow Shoulder
Wether Hill
Castle Hill 330
Cormilligan Bottom
Garryhorn Rig 335
Knockower
Holm of Daltallochan
Coran of Portmark 623
Garryhorn
Carsphairn
Knockgray
Marbrack
Furmiston Craig
Round Craigs
Dunnans Craig
Cornharrow Hill
Corriedow Hill 442
Lagwyne
Cornharrow
Ewe Craig
Bow
Craighit
CAIRN AVEL
Carnavel
Burnfoot
Marscalloch Hill 381
Castle Craig
Craiglinan Craig
Shieldykes Hill
Shillingland Hill
Carroch Hill 405
Stroanfreggan Craig
Stroanfreggan Bridge
Carroch
Auchenstroan
Auchenstroan Craig
Woodhead
Cairnsgarroch 659
Bennan
Bardennoch Hill 330
Bardennoch
Marscalloch
Muirdrochwood
Craigdarroch
Meaul 695
Craigenwallie
Culmark Moss
Knowehead
Shiel of Castlemaddie (Bothy)
Gairy Craig
Kendoon Loch
Carminnows
Bennan
Fingland Hill
Troston Hill
Neis Hill
Craigchessie
Castlemaddy
Dundeugh Hill 271
Shiel Hill
Culmark Hill
Lochlee Hill 352
Lochwhinnie Hill
Troston
Bennan Knocksting 346
Minnygryle Hill 364
Big Morton Hill 417
Midcover Plantation
Goat Craigs
Torrs
Polquhanity
Craignelder
Dalshangan
Barlae Hill
Dundeugh
KENDOON
Mackilston Hill 294
Butterhole Bridge
Meikle Bennan 344
Knocksting Loch
Pointfoot Hill
Glencrosh Hill
Brown Hill 350
Carlin's Cairn
Craigrine
Dundeugh
Glenhoul
Glenshimmeroch Hill
Kilnair Hill
Lawglass 387
Polmaddy Gairy
Polmaddy
Craig Knuckle
Kendoon
Craigencorr Hill
Greentop of Margree 323
Wether Hill
Castlefairn
Corserine 814
Forrest Lodge
The Glenkens
Stroangassel
Nether Cleugh
Mackilston
Glenshimmeroch
Barlaes Hill 248
Ewe Hill
Hog Hill
Divot Hill
Stroan Hill 344
Holmhead
Blackmark
Craigmuie Moor
Penneilly Wood
North Gairy Top
Bennan Hill
Loch Minnoch
Scabbed Craigs
Burnhead
Knockreoch Fm
Stroangassel Hill
Barlaes Cott
Lochinvar
Lochinvar Lodge
Stroan Hill
Regland Loch
Millfire 716
Largvey Hill
Stranfasket Hill 245
Tods Hill
Barlaes Plantn
Loch Hill
Fell Hill 417
Mid Hill
Shinmount
Polharrow Bridge
Earlstoun
Ardoch Hill
Duchrae
Loch Dungeon
Hannayston Hill
Barskeoch Mains
Millquarter
Blawquhain Fm
Milnmark Hill
Knockman Hill
Loch Skae
Benneeve 358
Monybuie Hill
Waterhead
Rhinns Of Kells
Backhill of Bush (Bothy)
Tops of Craigeazle
Meikle Millyea 746
Clints of Clenrie
Rig of Clenrie
Barskeoch Hill
Earlstoun Loch
Snab Hill
Waterside Hill
Bogue Fell
Corriedoo
Corriedoo Forest
Blackcraig Hill
Monybuie
Staverron Hill
Drumbuie
Rig of Drumbuie 262
Garroch Hill
Garroch
Waterside
Tower
Bogue
Barscobe Loch
Troquhain Hill
Ree Hill
Little Millyea 578
Drumbuie Hill
Dunveoch Hill
St John's Town of Dalry
Boat Knowe
Grennan Mill
Holme Mill
Barscobe Hill 257
Glen Knowe
Blackcraig
Green Top of Drumwhirn
Mc Whanns Stone
Darrou
Eldrick Hill
Benbrack
Glenlee Mains
Black Bank Wood
Glenlee
Low Benbrack
MAIN STREET A713
Holme Fm
Scroggie Hall
Long Wood
Garcrogo Hill
Barmark Hill
Knocklea
Glenlee Hill
Shiel Hill
Meikle Isle
Ken Br
Balmaclellan
Kirkland
Maggot Hill
Gallows Knowe
Flintloch Hill
Upper Craigenbay
Hill
Bartaggart Hill
Lowes Loch
Caldow Moor
Gibbshill
Craigencallie
0 1 2 3 miles
0 1 2 3 4 5 km

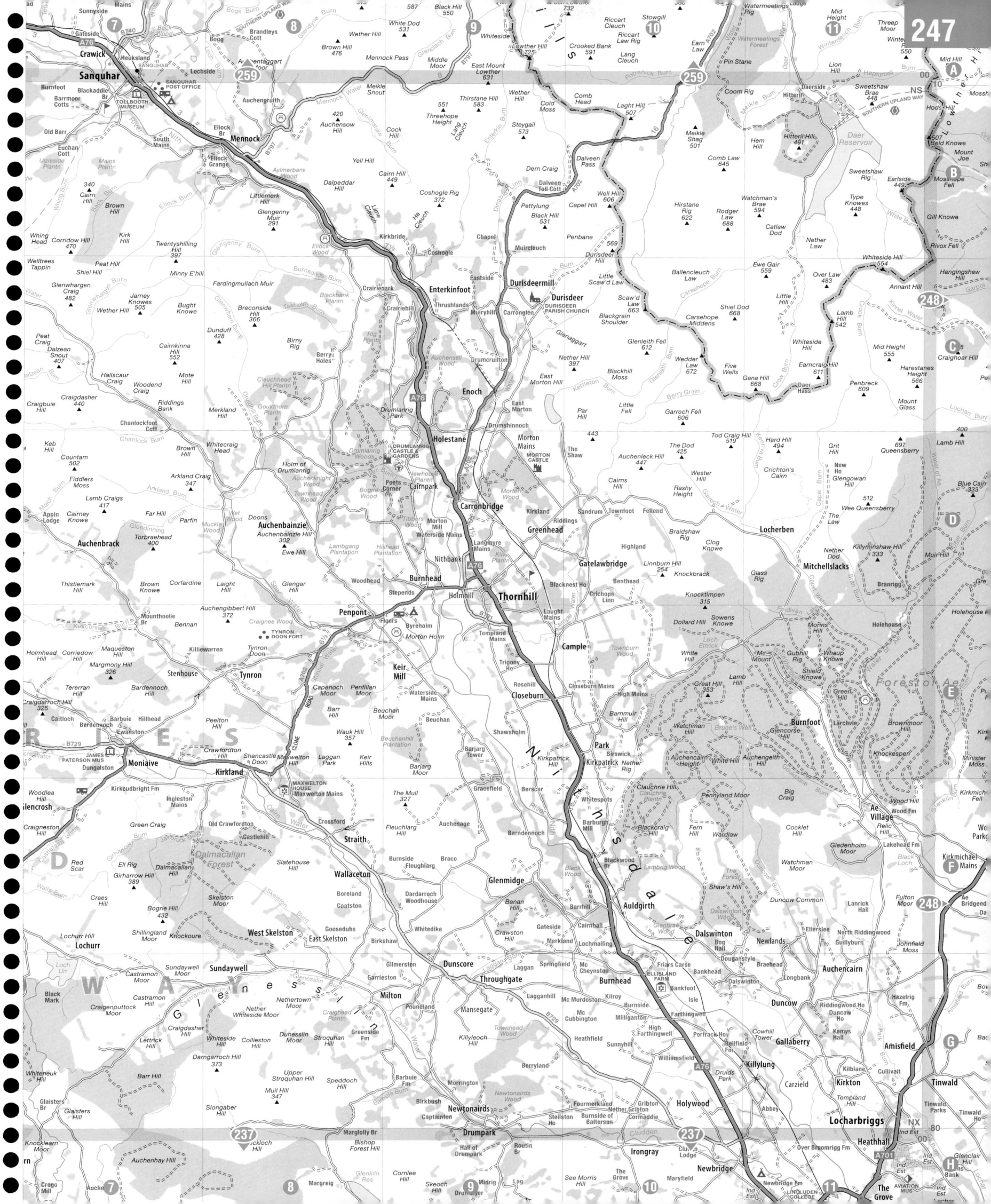
Sanquhar
Crawick
Mennock
Kirkbride
Enterkinfoot
Durisdeermill
Durisdeer
Enoch
Holestane
Carronbridge
Greenhead
Thornhill
Burnhead
Penpont
Tynron
Keir Mill
Camplle
Closeburn
Auchenbainzie
Auchenbrack
Moniaive
Kirkland
Straith
Wallaceton
Glenmidge
Auldgirth
Dalswinton
Dunscore
Throughgate
Milton
Newtonairds
Drumpark
Irongray
Holywood
Newbridge
Locharbriggs
Heathhall
Tinwald
Amisfield
Auchencairn
Killylung
Gallaberry
Duncow
Burnfoot
Locherben
Mitchellslacks
Ae Village
Sundaywell
Lochurr
West Skelston
Nithsdale
Glenesslin
Forest of Ae
Dalveen Pass
Daer Reservoir
A76
A702
A701
B729
259
248
237

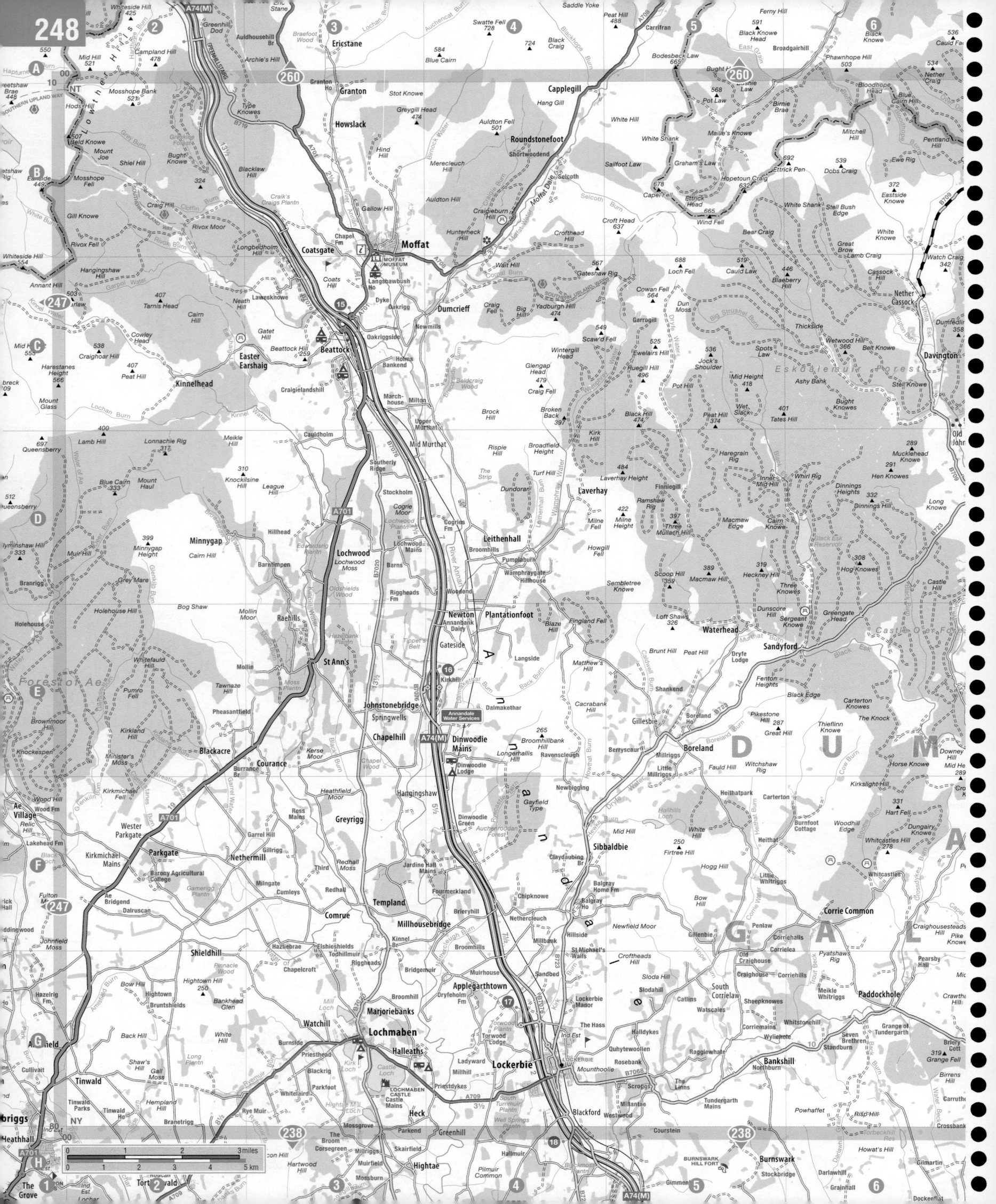

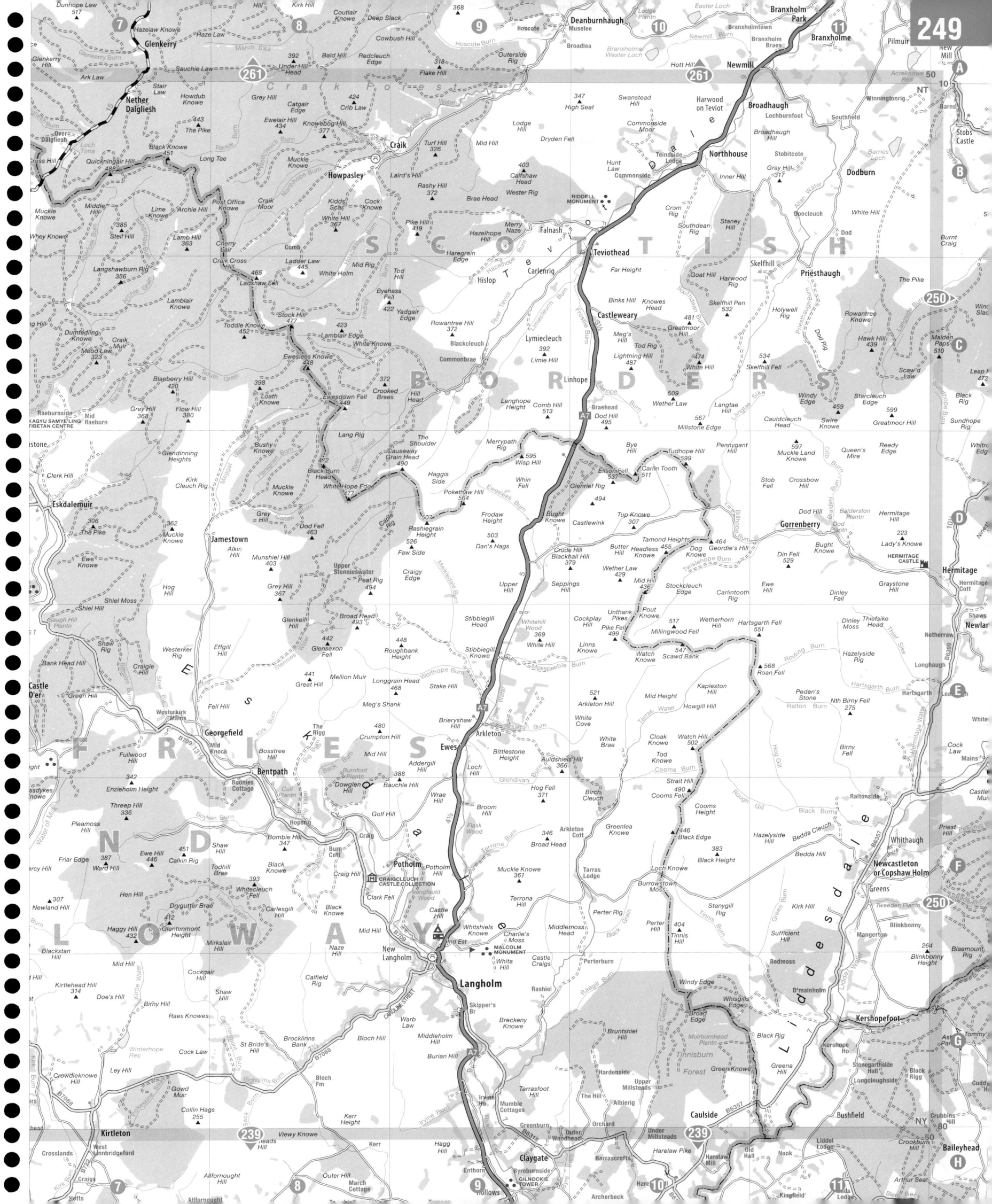

Dunhope Law
517
Hazelaw Knowe
Glenkerry
Haze Law
Coutlair Knowe
Deep Slack
Cowbush Hill
Kirk Hill
368
Deanburnhaugh
Muselee
Hoscote
Lodge Plantn
Easter Loch
Branxholm Park
Branxholmtown
Branxholm Braes
Branxholme
Pilmuir
New Mill
Glenkerry Hill
Sauchie Law
Ark Law
392
Under Hill Head
Bald Hill
Redcleuch Edge
318
Flake Hill
Outerside Rig
Hoscote Burn
Broadlea
Branxholme Wester Loch
Newmill
Hott Hill
Newmill
261
Craik Forest
Stair Law
Nether Dalgliesh
Howdub Knowe
Grey Hill
Catgair Edge
424
Crib Law
347
High Seat
Swanstead Hill
Harwood on Teviot
Broadhaugh
Lochburnfoot
Winningtonrig
Southfield
Barns
Stobs Castle
443
The Pike
Ewelair Hill
434
Knowebog Hill
377
Lodge Hill
Dryden Fell
Commonside Moor
Broadhaugh Hill
Over Dalgliesh
Black Knowe
451
Quickningair Hill
488
Long Tae
Muckle Knowe
Craik
Turf Hill
326
Mid Hill
Teindside Lodge
Northhouse
Stobitcote
Barnes Loch
Cross Hill
Howpasley
Laird's Hill
403
Calfshaw Head
Hunt Law
Commonside
Inner Hill
Gray Hill
317
Dodburn
Rashy Hill
372
Wester Rig
Brae Head
RIDDELL MONUMENT
Crom Rig
Muckle Knowe
Middle Hill
Lime Knowe
Archie Hill
Post Office Knowe
Craik Moor
Kidds Scar
Cock Knowe
White Hill
367
Staney Hill
Doecleuch
White Hill
385
Stell Hill
Whey Knowe
Lamb Hill
363
Cherry Lair
Comb
Pike Hill
419
Merry Naze
Hazelhope Hill
Falnash
Southdean Rig
Dod
Burnt Craig
SCOTTISH BORDERS
Teviothead
Craik Cross Hill
Ladder Law
445
Mid Rig
Haregrain Edge
Skelfhill
Langshawburn Rig
356
465
Ladshaw Fell
White Holm
Tod Hill
Hislop
Carlenrig
Far Height
Goat Hill
Harwood Rig
Priesthaugh
The Pike
Lamblair Knowe
Byehass Fell
422
Yadgair Edge
Binks Hill
Knowes Head
Skelfhill Pen
532
Holywell Rig
250
Stock Hill
477
Castleweary
481
Greatmoor Hill
Rowantree Knowe
Dumfedling Knowe
Craik Muir
Toddle Knowe
452
423
Lamblair Edge
Rowantree Hill
372
Blackcleuch
Lymiecleuch
Meg's Hill
Tod Rig
Dod Rig
Hawk Hill
439
Maiden Paps
510
Mood Law
323
White Knowe
Eweslees Knowe
448
Commonbrae
392
Limie Hill
Lightning Hill
487
474
White Hill
534
Skelfhill Fell
Scaw'd Law
Leap Hill
472
Blaeberry Hill
420
398
Loath Knowe
372
Crooked Knowe
Hill Head
Linhope
509
Wether Law
Langtae Hill
Windy Edge
Starcleuch Edge
Black Rig
Raeburnside
Mid Raeburn
KAGYU SAMYE LING TIBETAN CENTRE
Grey Hill
368
Flow Hill
380
Ewesdown Fell
449
Langhope Height
Comb Hill
513
Braehead
Dod Hill
495
567
Millstone Edge
Cauldcleuch Head
459
Swire Knowe
599
Greatmoor Hill
Sandhope Rig
Lang Rig
The Shoulder
Merrypath Rig
595
Wisp Hill
Bye Hill
Tudhope Hill
599
Pennygant Hill
597
Muckle Land Knowe
Queen's Mire
Reedy Edge
Glendinning Heights
Bushy Knowe
Causeway Grain Head
490
Carlin Tooth
511
Elfson Fell
537
Clerk Hill
Kirk Cleuch Rig
472
Black Burn Head
Haggis Side
Whin Fell
Glenrief Rig
Stob Fell
Crossbow Hill
Muckle Knowe
White Hope Edge
477
Pokethaw Hill
564
494
Eskdalemuir
Grey Hill
Frodaw Height
Bught Knowe
Castlewink
Tup Knowe
307
Dod Hill
Balderston Plantn
Hermitage Hill
306
The Pike
362
Muckle Knowe
Dod Fell
463
507
Rashiegrain Height
Gorrenberry
223
Lady's Knowe
Jamestown
Caple Rig
503
Dan's Hags
Tamond Heights
464
Geordie's Hill
Alkin Hill
526
Faw Side
Crude Hill
Blackhall Hill
379
Butter Hill
455
Headless Knowe
Dog Knowe
Bught Knowe
HERMITAGE CASTLE
Hermitage
Ewe Knowe
Munshiel Hill
403
Upper Stennieswater
Din Fell
529
Wether Law
429
Craigy Edge
Peat Rig
494
Grey Hill
367
Upper Hill
Seppings Hill
Mid Hill
436
Stockcleuch Edge
Carlintooth Rig
Ewe Hill
Dinley Fell
Graystone Hill
Hermitage Cott
Hog Hill
Shiel Moss
Shiel Hill
Glenkell Hill
Broad Head
493
Stibbiegill Head
Whitehill Wood
369
White Hill
Cockplay Hill
Unthank Pikes
Pout Knowe
517
Millingwood Fell
Wetherhorn Hill
Hartsgarth Fell
551
Dinley Moss
Thiefsike Head
Netherraw
Shaws
Newlar
Saugh Hill Plantn
442
Glensaxon Fell
448
Roughbank Height
Stibbiegill Knowe
Pike Fell
499
Linns Knowe
Watch Knowe
547
Scawd Bank
Routing Burn
Hazelyside Rig
Longhaugh
Shaw Rig
Westerker Rig
Effgill Hill
Bank Head Hill
Craigie Hill
Mellion Muir
441
Great Hill
Longgrain Head
468
Stake Hill
568
Roan Fell
Castle O'er
Green Hill
Kapleston Hill
Mid Height
Howgill Hill
Peden's Stone
Nth Birny Fell
275
Hartsgarth
Meg's Shank
521
Arkleton Hill
Fell Hill
Westerkirk Mains
The Rigg
480
Crumpton Hill
Brieryshaw Hill
A7
White Cove
Georgefield
Arkleton
Cleak Knowe
Watch Hill
502
White Brae
Birny Fell
Cock Law
FRIES
Fullwood Hill
Mid Knock
Bosstree Hill
Mid Hill
Ewes
Bittlestone Height
Auldshiels Hill
366
Tod Knowe
Cooms Burn
Bentpath
Addergill Hill
Loch Hill
Glendivan
342
Enzieholm Height
Boonies Cottage
Dowglen Hill
388
Bauchie Hill
Hog Fell
371
Birch Cleuch
Strait Hill
490
Cooms Fell
Raltonside
Threep Hill
336
Wrae Hill
Broom Hill
Golf Hill
Cooms Height
Black Burn
Hopsrig
Flask Wood
Greenlea Knowe
Bedda Cleuch
Priest Hill
Pleamoss Hill
Shaw Hill
Bombie Hill
347
Craig
346
Broad Head
Arkleton Cott
446
Black Edge
Hazelyside Hill
Whithaugh
Friar Edge
387
Ward Hill
Ewe Hill
446
451
Calkin Rig
Burn Cott
Potholm
Potholm Hill
383
Black Height
Bedda Hill
Newcastleton or Copshaw Holm
Todhill Brae
Black Knowe
Craig Hill
CRAIGCLEUCH CASTLE COLLECTION
Muckle Knowe
361
Tarras Lodge
Loch Knowe
393
Whitecleuch Fell
Greens
Hen Hill
Langfauld Wood
Clark Fell
Terrona Hill
Burrowstown Moss
307
Newland Hill
Drygutter Brae
Carlesgill Hill
Black Knowe
Castle Hill
Perter Rig
Stanygill Rig
Kirk Hill
250
412
Glentenmont Height
Haggy Hill
432
Whitshiels Knowe
Charlie's Moss
Middlemoss Head
Perter Hill
404
Tinnis Hill
Sufficient Hill
Blinkbonny
Mangerton
Mid Hill
Mirkslair Hill
Naze Hill
New Langholm
MALCOLM MONUMENT
Whita Hill
Castle Craigs
Perterburn
264
Blinkbonny Height
Blaemount Rig
Blackstan Hill
Redmoss
Mid Hill
Cockgair Hill
Calfield Rig
Langholm
Rashiel
Windy Edge
D'mainholm
Kirtlehead Hill
314
Doe's Hill
Shaw Hill
Skipper's Br
Whisgills Edge
Birny Hill
Raes Knowes
Warb Law
Breckeny Knowe
Bruntshiel Hill
Broad Edge
Kershopefoot
Winterhope Res
Cock Law
St Bride's Hill
Brocklinns Bank
Bloch Hill
Middleholm Hill
Burian Hill
Muirburnhead Plantn
Black Rig
Kershope Ho
Tinnisburn Forest
Green Knowe
Greena Hill
Stonegarthside Hall
Ley Hill
Crowdieknowe Hill
Hardenside
Upper Millsteads
Longcleughside
Black Rigg
Bloch Fm
Gowd Muir
Tarrasfoot Hill
The Hill
Albierig
Collin Hags
255
Irvine Ho
Mumbie Cottages
Caulside
Bushfield
Kerr Height
Greenburn
Orchard
Outer Woodhead
Under Millsteads
Kirtleton
239
Viewy Knowe
Kerr
Hagg Hill
Claygate
Barrascrofts
Harelaw Pike
Harelaw Mill
Old Hall
Nook
Liddel Lodge
Crookburn Hill
Baileyhead
Crosslands
West Linnbridgeford
Craigs
Hatts
Allfornought Hill
Outer Hill
March Cottage
Enthorn
Byreburnside
GILNOCKIE TOWER
Hollows
Hare
Archerbeck
Kingfield
Baids Lodge
Arthur Seat

Bonchester Bridge
Bonchester Hill
Hobkirk
Cleuch Head
Mackside
Chesters
Southdean
Southdean Lodge
Falside
Roughlee
Edgerston Rig
Stonedge
Stobs Castle
Cogsmill
Berryfell Fm
Berryfell Hill
Pike Fell 400
Shankend Fm
Shankend Hill
Langburnshiels
Wauchope Common
Templehall Hill
Harwood Moss
Wyndburgh Hill 507
Wauchope Forest
Hardlee Flow
Dun Knowe
Peden's Cleuch
Millmoor Rig
Tamshiel Rig
Scaw'd Law
Green Law
Burns
Carter Fell 556
Catcleuch Shin
Black Cleuch
Whitelee
Lumsdon Law
Ramshope Lodge
Catcleugh
Catcleugh Reservoir
REDESMIRE FRAY 1575
Arks Edge
Leap Hill
Fairwood Fell
Knock Hills
Hophills Nob 359
Philip Law 414
Ephope Law
Lamblair Edge
Deerlee Knowe
Huntford
Bught Knowe
Hareshaw Knowe
Lethem
Steele Knowe
Crink Law
Charlie's Knowe
Highlee Hill
Weasel Hill
Wolfhee Hill 393
Cribs Hole
Crag Bank
CRAGBANK WOOD
Hell's Hole
Black Hill
Brockie Law
Sim's Knowe
Burnt Craig
Brown's Hill
The Pike
Windy Slack
Maiden Paps 510
Leap Hill 472
Sandy Edge
Black Rig
Whitrope Cottages
Sundhope Rig
Whitrope Edge
Greatmoor Hill
Reedy Edge
White Knowe
Stitchel Hill 318
Whitropefoot
Bell Hill
Riccarton Junction
Outer Knowe Head 415
Kiln Knowe
Lime Kiln Edge
Fanna Hill 514
Wigg Knowe
Dog Knowe
Note o' the Gate
Rushy Rig
Whitegrain Fell
Lamblair Hill 498
Mid Hill
Coopercleuch Knowe
Singdean
East Hill
Coomb Edge
Dod Fell
Needs Law 444
Wheelrig Head 448
Hartshorn Pike 545
Haggie Knowe
Scrathy Holes
Dun Tae
Knox Knowe 500
Limestone Knowe 551
Upper Stony Holes
Grey Mares Knowe 516
KIELDERHEAD
Kielderhead Moor
White Crags
Girdle Fell
Cross Cleugh
WHITELEE MOOR
Redesdale Forest
Chattlehope Crag
Ellis Crag 497
Cairn Cleugh
The Cheviots
Craigy Knowe
Heather Knowe
Peel Fell 602
West Kielder Moor
Mid Fell
Scaup Pikes
KIELDER
Kielder Head
Woody Crags
Wool Meath
Woolmeath Edge
Long Crag
East Kielder Moor
Blakehope Nick
Blackman's Law
Street Head
Berrymoor Edge 459
Caddroun Rig
Saughtree Fell
Liddesdale
Rushy Knowe
Myredykes Plantn
Hob Knowe
Windy Knowe
Thorlieshope Pike 360
Saughtree
Thorlieshope
Thorlieshope Heights
Deadwater
Wirchet
Deadwater Fell 569
Greyhound Law
Scaup
Bran's Walls
Ewe Hill
Ridge End Burn
Wether Lair
Smallhope Rigg
FOREST PARK
Ravenshill Moor
Bells Moor
Three Pikes
Hogswood Moor
Monk Side 513
Round Law
Emblehope Moor
Hermitage
HERMITAGE CASTLE
Lady's Knowe 223
Ninestane Rig
Blackwood Hill
Shiel Knowe
Arnton Fell
Bught Knowe
Burnmouth Fm
Yarrow Knowe 295
Foulmire Heights
SCOTTISH BORDERS
Graystone Hill
Hermitage Cott
Shaws
Newlands
Netherraw
Larriston
Larriston Rigg
Larriston Burn
Hirst Craig
403
Loch Knowe
Crag Head
Black Fell
Kielder
Butteryhaugh
KIELDER CASTLE VISITOR CENTRE
Mount Common
Greys Pike 445
Wainhope
Hawk Knowe
Burn Grange
Harper Crag
The Steele
Steele Road
Steeleroad-end
Hewisbridge Cott
Rain's Hill
Longhaugh
Leahaugh
Larriston Fells 512
Buckside Knowe
Bewshaugh
Cat Cairn
Devil's Lapful
Gowanburn
Millstone Crag
Earl's Seat
The Dodd 353
Dinlabyre
Whitehaugh
Kirndean
Black Knowe
Bellingburn
Bellingburn Head
Rabbit Crag
Highfield
Cock Law
Mains
Ewe Knowe
Hobb's Flow
Coal Grain
Buck Fell
The Cross
Old Castleton
Castleton Muir
Harden Moss
Flight Moss
Watch Knowe
Wilson's Pike
Akenshawburn
Ferny Knowe
Wellhaugh
Pope's Hill
Hawkhope
Priest Hill
Harden Hill
Scotch Knowe
Dinmontlair Knowe
The Forks
Rushy Knowe
Wind Hill
Kielder Water
Hawkhope Hill
Green Eyes Crags
Whithaugh
Newcastleton or Copshaw Holm
Stell Knowe
Newcastleton Forest
Black Knowe
Caplestone Fell
Eliott's Pike
Lazy Knowe
Greenside
KIELDER WATER BIRDS OF PREY CENTRE
Scald Pike
Bullcrag Edge
Kateshaw Hill
TOWER KNOWE VISITOR CENTRE
Yarrow
Yarrow Moor
Falstone
Stannersburn
Stokoe
Long Knowe
Kershopehead
Glendhu Hill 514
Dove Crags
High Long Ho
Lishaw Rigg
Muckle Knowe
Rough Pike
Stower Hill
Low Cranecleugh
White Side
Ridge End
River North Tyne
Blinkbonny
Blinkbonny Height 264
Blaemount Rig
English Kershope
Geordy's Pike
Long Rigg
Robbie's Rigg
Black Hill
Will's Knowe
Broomy Hill
Broomylinn
Jock's Pike
Drove Rigg
Dings Rigg
Smalesmouth
CUMBRIA
Skelton Pike
Reamy Rigg
Beckhead Crag
Stot Crags
Gill Pike
The Rigg
Byreshield Hill
Kyloe Crags
Archy's Rigg
Roughside Moor
Black Crags
Kershopefoot
Ash Park
Tommy's Fell
Kershope Forest
Blacklyne Common
Christianbury Crag 487
Burnt Tom Crags
Story's Gairs
Long Crags
Christy's Crags
Bolts Law 395
Rushy Knowe
Alleryank
Black Rigg
Blacklyne Ho
Bewcastle Fells
Sighty Crag 518
Horse Head
Black Knowe 492
Black Cleugh
Cuddy's Hall
Kettle Hall
Whitelyne Common
Long Bar
Smuggy's Pike
Long Crags
Hopehouse
Black Knors 248
Black Knors
Black Stantling
The Shanks
KIELDER MIRES
Clintburn
Claver Hill
Crubbins Hill
Bailey Head
The Flatt
Slaty Crag
Long Crag 456
Watch Rigg
Greyfell Common
Tarn Beck
Lowe Bush
Paddaburn
Muckle Samuel's Crags
Little Dodd Hill
High Capon Edge
Crookburn
Holmehead
Nook
Gate
Crew Crag
Gaylock Hill
Irthing Head
Whitehill
Green
0 1 2 3 miles
0 1 2 3 4 5 km
A68
B6399
B6357
A6088
262
249
240

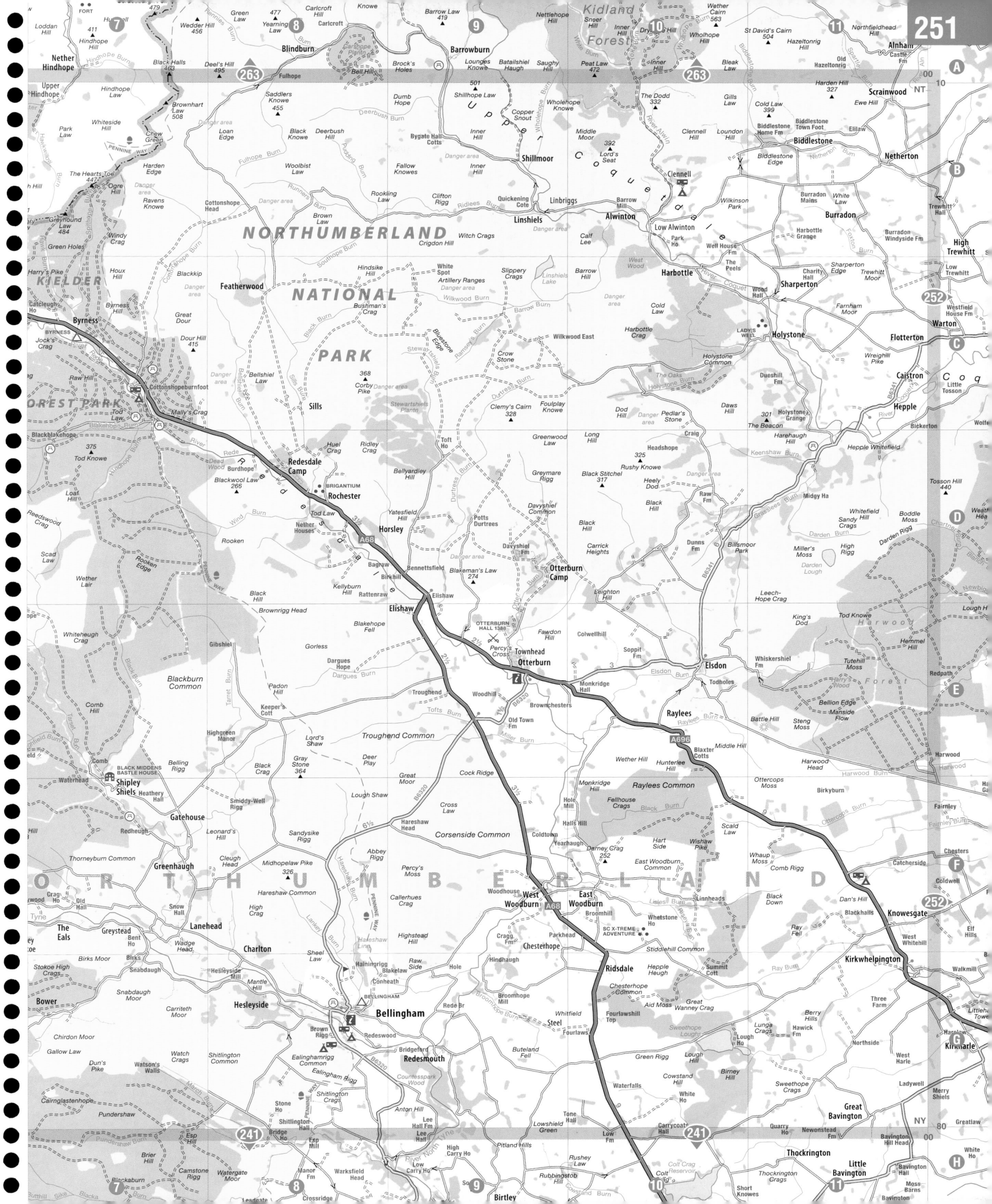
Kidland Forest
Nether Hindhope
Upper Hindhope
Blindburn
Barrowburn
Fulhope
Carlcroft
Barrow Law 419
Wedder Hill 456
Yearning Law 477
Black Halls 463
Deel's Hill 495
Hindhope Law
Brownhart Law 508
Saddlers Knowe 455
Shillhope Law 501
Upper Coquetdale
Shillmoor
Lord's Seat 392
Clennell
Alwinton
Low Alwinton
Linbriggs
Linshiels
Barrow Mill
Biddlestone
Netherton
Burradon
Alnham
Scrainwood
Harbottle
Sharperton
Holystone
Flotterton
Warton
Caistron
Hepple
NORTHUMBERLAND NATIONAL PARK
KIELDER FOREST PARK
Byrness
Cottonshopeburnfoot
Featherwood
Sills
Redesdale Camp
Rochester
Horsley
Elishaw
Otterburn Camp
Otterburn
Elsdon
Raylees
Raylees Common
Troughend Common
Corsenside Common
Blackburn Common
Shipley Shiels
Gatehouse
Greenhaugh
West Woodburn
East Woodburn
Ridsdale
Lanehead
Charlton
Hesleyside
Bellingham
Redesmouth
Bower
The Eals
Knowesgate
Kirkwhelpington
Kirkharle
Great Bavington
Little Bavington
Thockrington
Birtley
NORTHUMBERLAND
Harwood Forest
Redesdale
Otterburn Hall 1388
A68
A696
B6320
B6341
252
263
241

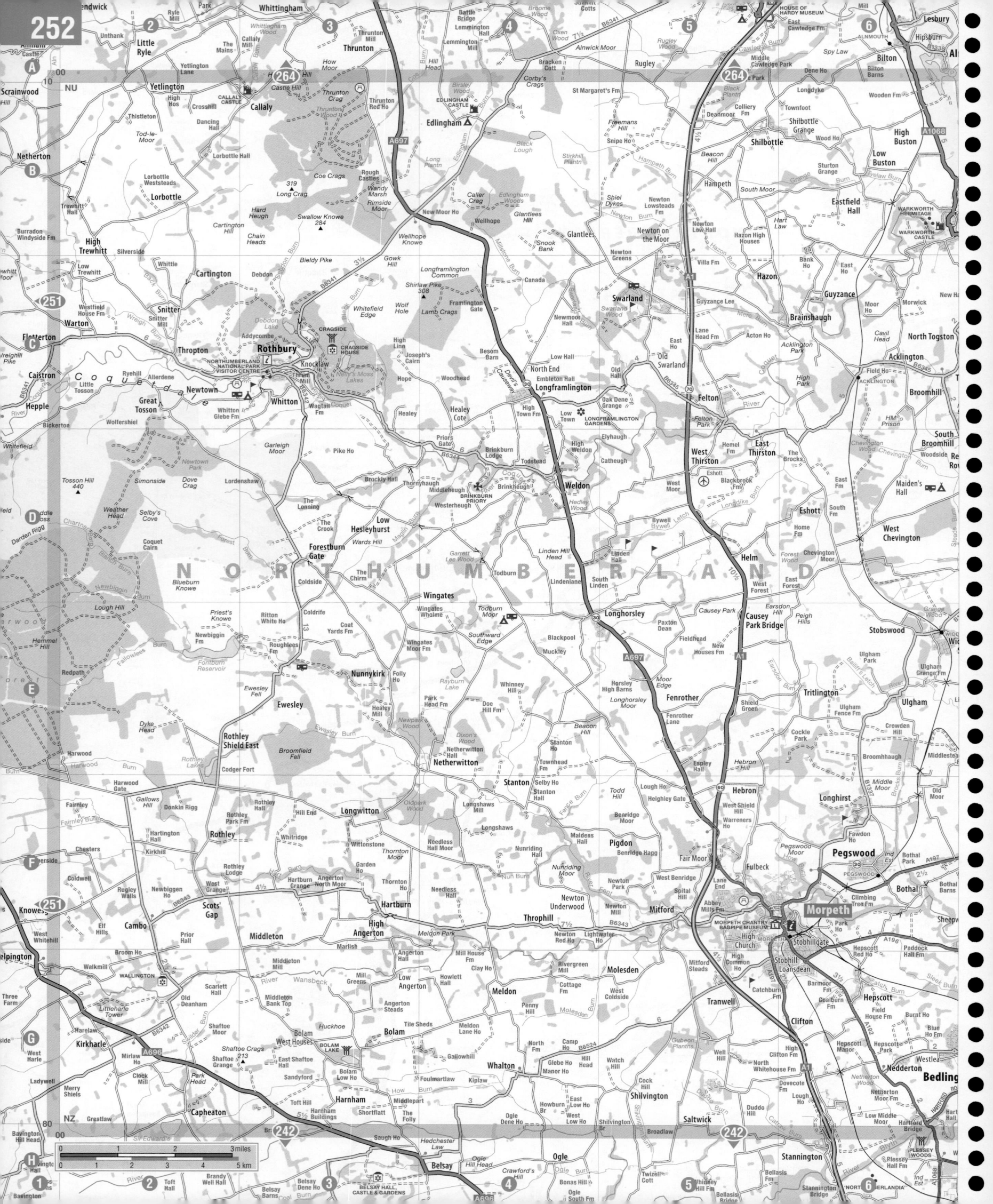

Whittingham
Battle Bridge
Lemmington Hall
Lemmington Mill
Broome Wood
Cotts
House of Hardy Museum
East Cawledge Fm
Mill
Lesbury
Unthank
Little Ryle
Ryle Mill
Whittingham Wood
Callaly Mill
The Mains
Thrunton Mill
Thrunton
Hill Head
Oxen Wood
B6341
Alnwick Moor
Bracken Cott
Rugley Wood
Rugley
Cawledge Burn
Middle Cawledge Park
Alnmouth
Spy Law
Hipsburn
B1338
Bilton
Bilton Barns
Dene Ho
Alnwick
Castle
264
Yetlington Lane
How Moor
Hill
Corby's Crags
Park
Scrainwood
NU
Yetlington
High Hos
Crosshill
Callaly Castle
Callaly
Castle Hill
Thrunton Crag
Thrunton Wood
Thrunton Red Ho
Birsley Wood
Edlingham Castle
Edlingham
St Margaret's Fm
Black Plantn
Colliery Fm
Deanmoor
Longdyke
Townfoot
Wooden Fm
Thistleton
Dancing Hall
Tod-le-Moor
Netherton
Lorbottle Hall
Lorbottle Weststeads
Lorbottle
Coe Crags
319 Long Crag
Rough Castles
Wandy Marsh
Rimside Moor
A697
Black Lough
Long Plantn
Freemans Hill
Snipe Ho
Stirkhill Plantn
Hampeth Burn
Beacon Hill
Hampeth
Shilbottle
Shilbottle Grange
Wood Ho
High Buston
Low Buston
Sturton Grange
South Moor
Grange Burn
Tyelaw Burn
A1068
Trewhitt Hall
High Trewhitt
Burradon Windyside Fm
Hard Heugh
Cartington Hill
Chain Heads
Swallow Knowe 284
Caller Crag
Edlingham Woods
New Moor Ho
Wellhope
Glantlees Hill
Shiel Dykes
Newton Lowsteads Fm
Newton Burn
Newton on the Moor
Newton Low Hall
Hazon High Houses
Hart Law
Eastfield Hall
Warkworth Hermitage
Warkworth Castle
Silverside
Low Trewhitt
Whittle
Cartington
Debdon
Bieldy Pike
Wellhope Knowe
Gowk Hill
Glantlees
Snook Bank
Newton Greens
Hazon Burn
Villa Fm
Bank Ho
East Ho
Hazon
Longframlington Common
Shirlaw Pike 308
Canada
Swarland
Guyzance
Guyzance Lee
Moor Ho
Morwick
New Ha
251
Westfield House Fm
Snitter
Snitter Mill
Warton
Wreigh Burn
Debdon Lake
Addycombe
Whitefield Edge
Wolf Hole
Lamb Crags
Framlington Gate
Newmoor Hall
Swarland Wood
Brainshaugh
Lane Head Fm
Acton Ho
Cavil Head
North Togston
Flotterton
Thropton
Rothbury
Cragside
Cragside House
High Linn
Joseph's Cairn
Besom Barn
Low Hall
East Ho
Old Swarland
Acklington Park
Acklington
Field Ho
Caistron
Little Tosson
Coquetdale
Ryehill
Allerdene
Northumberland National Park Visitor Centre
Knocklaw
Thrum Mill
Nelly's Moss Lakes
Hope
Woodhead
Devil's Causeway
North End
Embleton Hall
Longframlington
Old Hall
B6345
Felton
High Park
Broomhill
Hepple
Great Tosson
Newtown
Whitton
Whitton Glebe Fm
Wagtail Fm
Healey
Healey Cote
High Town Fm
Low Town
Longframlington Gardens
Oak Dene Grange
Felton Park
River Coquet
HM Prison
Bickerton
Wolfershiel
Garleigh Moor
Priors Gate
Brinkburn Lodge
Todstead
High Weldon
Elyhaugh
Catheugh
West Thirston
Hemel Fm
East Thirston
The Brocks
Chevington Wood
South Broomhill
Woodside
Whitefield
Newtown Park
Pike Ho
Brockly Hall
Thornyhaugh
Middleheugh
Brinkburn Priory
Brinkheugh
Weldon
West Moor
Eshott
Blackbrook Fm
Longdike Burn
East Fm
Maiden's Hall
Tosson Hill 440
Simonside
Dove Crag
Lordenshaw
Westerheugh
Hedley Wood
Eshott
South Fm
Weather Head
Selby's Cove
The Lonning
The Crook
Low Hesleyhurst
Wards Hill
Bywell
Bywell Letch
Home Fm
West Chevington
Darden Rigg
Chartners
Coquet Cairn
Forestburn Gate
Garrett Lee Wood
Linden Hill Head
Linden Hall
Helm
Forest Wood
Chevington Moor
Blueburn Knowe
Coldside
The Chirm
Todburn
Lindenlane
South Linden
West Forest
East Forest
N O R T H U M B E R L A N D
Newbiggin Burn
Lough Hill
Wingates
Coldrife
Priest's Knowe
Ritton White Ho
Coat Yards Fm
Wingates Wholme
Todburn Moor
Longhorsley
Paxton Dean
Causey Park
Causey Park Bridge
Earsdon Hill
Peigh Hills
Stobswood
Hemmel Hill
Newbiggin Fm
Roughlees Fm
Wingates Moor Fm
Southward Edge
Blackpool
Fieldhead
New Houses Fm
Muckley
Ulgham Park
Ulgham Grange Fm
Fallowlees Burn
Fontburn Reservoir
Redpath
Nunnykirk
Folly Ho
Rayburn Lake
Whinney Hill
Horsley High Barns
Moor Edge
Earsdon Burn
Tritlington
Ewesley Fell
Ewesley
Healey Mill
Park Head Fm
Doe Hill Fm
Longhorsley Moor
Fenrother
Shield Green
Ulgham Fence Fm
Ulgham
Newpark Wood
Fenrother Lane
Crowden Hill
Dyke Head
Ewesley Burn
Rothley Shield East
Broomfield Fell
Dixon's Wood
Netherwitton Hall
Netherwitton
Beacon Hill
Stanton Ho
Cockle Park
Broomhaugh
Middlestead
Harwood
Harwood Burn
Rothley Lakes
Codger Fort
Townhead Fm
Espley Hall
Hebron Fm
Harwood Gate
Stanton
Selby Ho
Stanton Hall
Lough Ho
Heighley Gate
Hebron
Middle Moor
Old Moor
Gallows Hill
Donkin Rigg
Rothley Hall
Longwitton
Oldpark Wood
Longshaws Mill
Todd Hill
Fence Burn
West Shield Hill
Warreners Ho
Longhirst
Fairnley
Fairnley Burn
Rothley Park Fm
Hill End
Longshaws
Benridge Moor
Fawdon Ho
Hartington Hall
Rothley
Whitridge
Wittonstone
Needless Hall Moor
Maidens Hall
Pigdon
Pegswood Moor
Pegswood
Chesters
Kirkhill
Thornton Moor
Nunriding Hall
Benridge Hagg
Fair Moor
Fulbeck
Bothal Park
A197
Fenwickside
Rothley Lodge
Garden Ho
Nunriding Moor
Pegswood
Coldwell
West Grange
Hartburn Grange
Angerton North Moor
Thornton Ho
Nun Burn
Newton Park
West Benridge
Lane End
Bothal
Bothal Barns
Rugley Walls
Newbiggen Ho
Needless Hall
Spital Hill
Climbing Tree Fm
Knowesgate
Scots' Gap
B6343
Hartburn
Newton Underwood
Newton Mill
Mitford
Abbey Mills Fm
Morpeth
Elf Hills
Cambo
Prior Hall
Middleton
High Angerton
Throphill
Morpeth Chantry Bagpipe Museum
Park Ho
Sheepwash
West Whitehill
Meldon Park
Newton Red Ho
Lightwater Ho
High Church
Stobhillgate
Hepscott Red Ho
Paddock Hall Fm
Kirkwhelpington
Broom Ho
Marlish
Angerton Hall
Mill House Fm
Clay Ho
Rivergreen Mill
Molesden
Mitford Steads
High Common Ho
Stobhill
Loansdean
Walkmill
Wallington
Middleton Mill
Howlett Hall
Barmoor Fm
Coalburn Fm
Sleek Burn
Three Farm
Scarlett Hall
Old Deanham
River Wansbeck
Middleton Bank Top
Mill Greens
Low Angerton
Meldon
Cottage Fm
West Coldside
Catchburn Fm
Tranwell
Hepscott
Littleharle Tower
Angerton Steads
Penny Hill
Moleseden Burn
Field House Fm
Burnt Ho
Harelaw
Shaftoe Moor
Huckhoe
Tile Sheds
Meldon Lane Ho
Clifton
Blue Ho Fm
Kirkharle
B6342
West Houses
Bolam
Bolam Lake
Gallowhill
North Fm
Camp Ho
B6524
Gubeon Plantns
Hepscott Manor
Hepscott Park
Westlea
West Harle
Mirlaw Ho
A696
Shaftoe Crags 213
Shaftoe Grange
East Shaftoe Hall
Glebe Ho
Manor Ho
Hill Head
Watch Hill
Well Hill
High Clifton Fm
North Whitehouse Fm
Nedderton
Clock Mill
Park Head
Bolam Low Ho
Whalton
Netherton Wood
Bedlington
Ladywell
Merry Shiels
Sandyford
Foulmartlaw
Kiplaw
Cock Hill
Dovecote Fm
Netherton Moor Fm
Harnham
Middlepart
Shilvington
Lough Ho
Toft Hill
How Burn
East Low Ho
Howburn Br
Duddo Hill
Low Middle Moor
Capheaton
Greatlaw
Harnham Buildings
Shortflatt
The Folly
Ogle Dene Ho
West Low Ho
Shilvington Br
Saltwick
Hartford Bridge
NZ
Bavington Hill Head
Broadlaw
242
Saugh Ho
Hedchester Law
Ogle Hill Head
Ogle
Ogle Burn
Stannington
Plessey Woods
Plessey Hall Fm
Bavington Hall
Belsay
Crawford's Hill
River Blyth
Toft Hall
Brandy Well Hall
Belsay Dene Ho
Belsay Hall Castle & Gardens
Twizell Cott
Bonas Hill
Whinney Hill Fm
Bellasis Fm
Bellasis Bridge
Stannington Bridge
Northumberlandia
Ind Est
Bavington
Belsay Barns
Coal Burn
Ogle South Fm
A696
0 1 2 3 miles
0 1 2 3 4 5 km

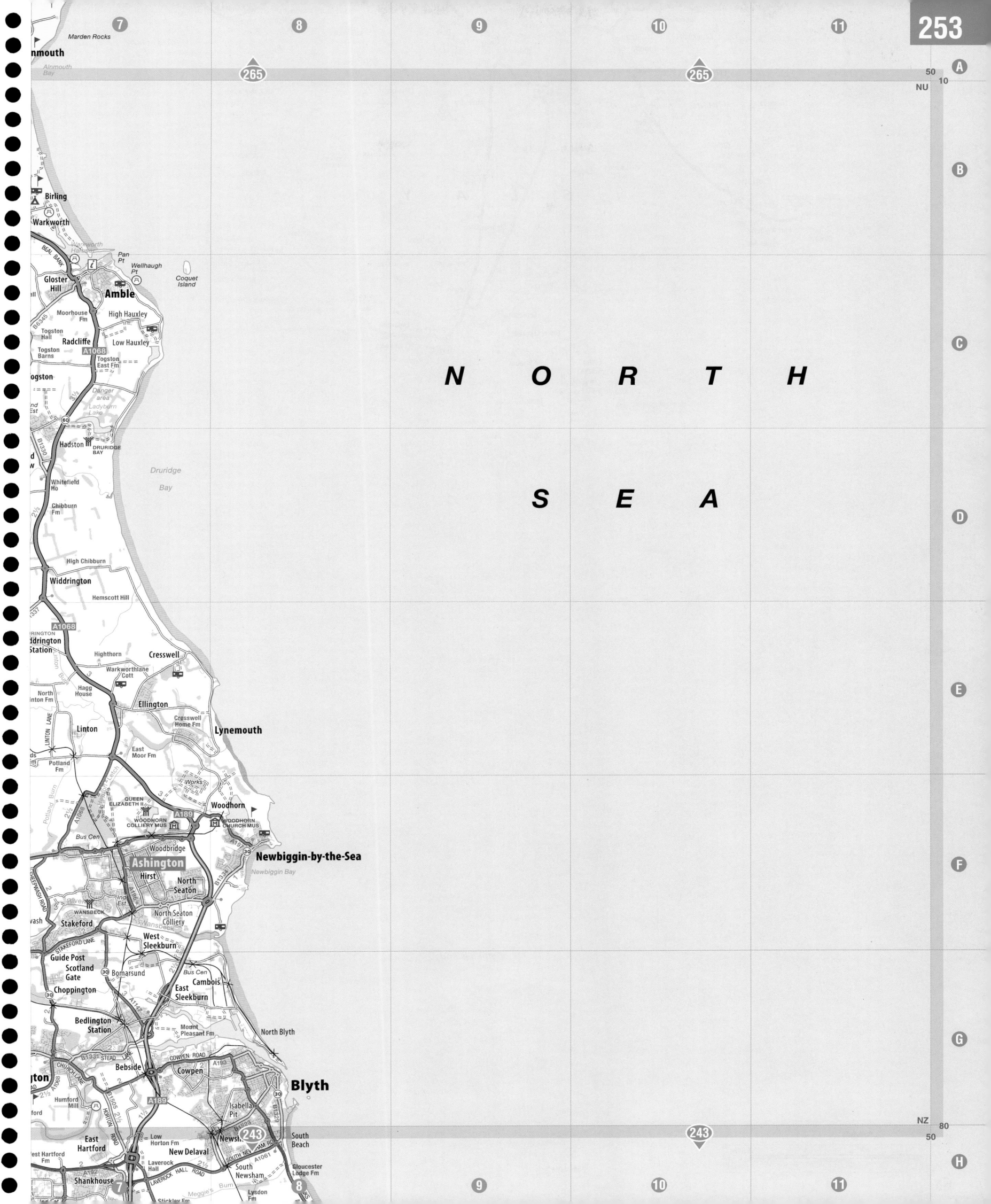
Marden Rocks
Alnmouth Bay
265
Birling
Warkworth
Warkworth Harbour
Pan Pt
Wellhaugh Pt
Coquet Island
Gloster Hill
Amble
High Hauxley
Moorhouse Fm
Togston Hall
Radcliffe
Low Hauxley
Togston Barns
A1068
Togston East Fm
Danger area
Ladyburn Lake
Hadston
DRURIDGE BAY
Druridge Bay
Whitefield Ho
Chibburn Fm
High Chibburn
Widdrington
Hemscott Hill
A1068
Highthorn
Cresswell
Warkworthlane Cott
Hagg House
Ellington
Cresswell Home Fm
Lynemouth
Linton
East Moor Fm
Potland Fm
Works
QUEEN ELIZABETH II
Woodhorn
A189
WOODHORN COLLIERY MUS
WOODHORN CHURCH MUS
Bus Cen
Woodbridge
Newbiggin-by-the-Sea
Newbiggin Bay
Ashington
Hirst
North Seaton
WANSBECK
North Seaton Colliery
Stakeford
West Sleekburn
STAKEFORD LANE
Guide Post
Scotland Gate
Bomarsund
Bus Cen
Cambois
Choppington
East Sleekburn
Bedlington Station
Mount Pleasant Fm
North Blyth
COWPEN ROAD
Bebside
Cowpen
Blyth
Humford Mill
A189
Isabella Pit
East Hartford
Low Horton Fm
New Delaval
South Beach
243
Laverock Hall
South Newsham
Gloucester Lodge Fm
Shankhouse
Lysdon Fm
NORTH SEA
NU
NZ
7
8
9
10
11
A
B
C
D
E
F
G
H

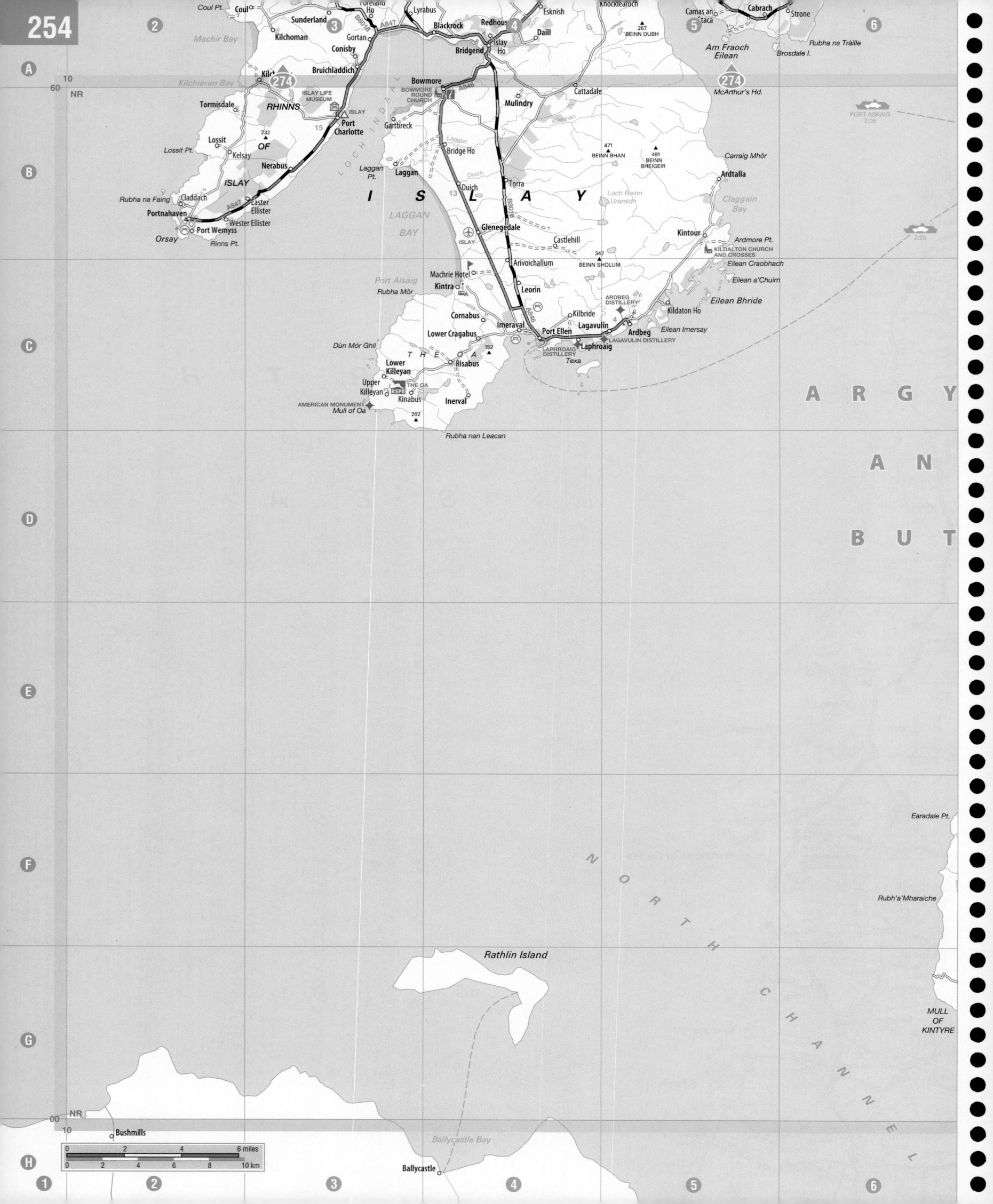

ISLAY
RHINNS OF ISLAY
THE OA
Bowmore
Port Charlotte
Bridgend
Port Ellen
Portnahaven
Port Wemyss
Lagavulin
Ardbeg
Laphroaig
Kilchoman
Bruichladdich
Sunderland
Gortan
Conisby
Blackrock
Redhouse
Islay Ho
Eskn ish
Daill
Lyrabus
Coul
Coul Pt.
Machir Bay
Kilchiaran Bay
Tormisdale
Lossit
Lossit Pt.
Kelsay
Nerabus
Claddach
Rubha na Faing
Easter Ellister
Wester Ellister
Orsay
Rinns Pt.
ISLAY LIFE MUSEUM
BOWMORE ROUND CHURCH
Gartbreck
LOCH INDAAL
Laggan
Laggan Pt.
Bridge Ho
Duich
LAGGAN BAY
Glenegedale
Torra
Mulindry
Cattadale
Castlehill
Arivoichallum
Leorin
Machrie Hotel
Kintra
Port Alsaig
Rubha Mòr
Cornabus
Imeraval
Lower Cragabus
Kilbride
Dùn Mór Ghil
Lower Killeyan
Upper Killeyan
Risabus
Kinabus
Inerval
AMERICAN MONUMENT
Mull of Oa
Rubha nan Leacan
LAPHROAIG DISTILLERY
LAGAVULIN DISTILLERY
ARDBEG DISTILLERY
Texa
Kildaton Ho
Eilean Imersay
Eilean Bhride
Eilean a'Chuirn
Eilean Craobhach
KILDALTON CHURCH AND CROSSES
Ardmore Pt.
Kintour
Claggain Bay
Ardtalla
Carraig Mhór
Loch Beinn Uraraidh
BEINN BHAN 471
BEINN BHEIGEIR 491
BEINN SHOLUM 347
BEINN DUBH 267
Knocklearoch
Am Fraoch Eilean
McArthur's Hd.
Camas an Staca
Cabrach
Strone
Rubha na Tràille
Brosdale I.
PORT ASKAIG 2:05
2:20
ARGYLL AND BUTE
NORTH CHANNEL
Rathlin Island
Ballycastle Bay
Ballycastle
Bushmills
Earadale Pt.
Rubh'a'Mharaiche
MULL OF KINTYRE
0 2 4 6 miles
0 2 4 6 8 10 km

FIRTH OF CLYDE
Isle of Arran
NORTH AYRSHIRE
Brodick
Merkland
Glenrosa
Strathwhillan
North Corriegills
South Corriegills
Margnaheglish
Blairbeg
Lamlash
Cordon
Gortonallister
Holy Island
Pillar Rock Pt
Kingscross
Sandbraes
Whiting Bay
North Kiscadale
South Kiscadale
Largymore
Largymeanoch
Largybeg
Dippin
Kildonan
Levencorroch
Auchenhew
Pladda
Sound of Pladda
Bennan Head
Saltcoats
ARDROSSAN 0:55
BRODICK 0:55
Culzean Bay
CULZEAN CASTLE
Maidenhead Bay
Morriston
Glasson Rock
Barwhin Pt
Broad Craig
255
266
244

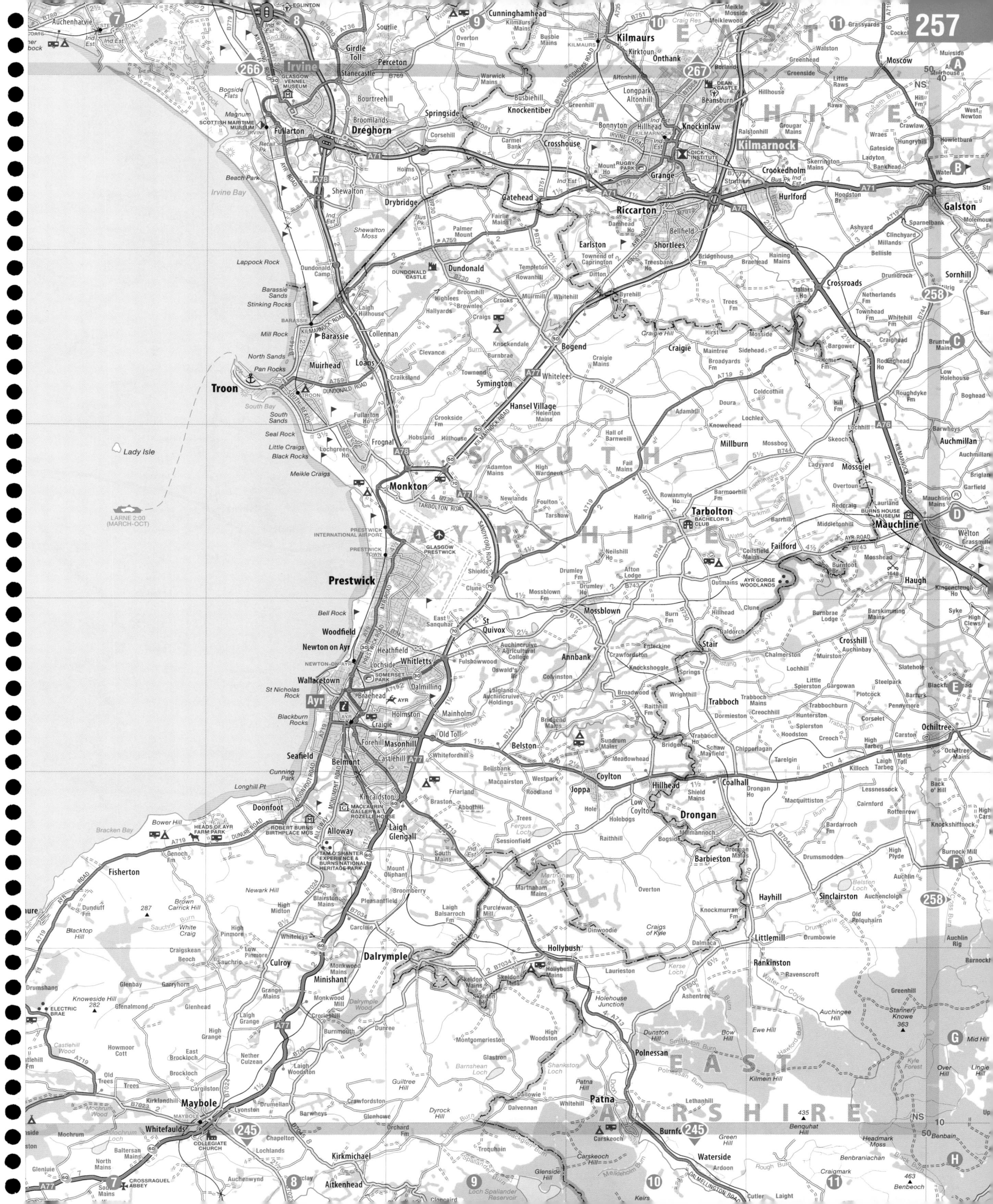
EAST AYRSHIRE
SOUTH AYRSHIRE
Irvine
Kilmarnock
Kilmaurs
Cunninghamhead
Dreghorn
Fullarton
Springside
Knockentiber
Crosshouse
Riccarton
Hurlford
Galston
Gatehead
Drybridge
Dundonald
DUNDONALD CASTLE
Irvine Bay
Barassie
Troon
Loans
Muirhead
Symington
Bogend
Craigie
Crossroads
Sornhill
Lady Isle
Monkton
Prestwick
GLASGOW PRESTWICK
Tarbolton
Mauchline
Failford
Mossgiel
Auchmillan
Mossblown
St Quivox
Annbank
Stair
Newton on Ayr
Whitletts
Ayr
Wallacetown
Holmston
Belston
Coylton
Drongan
Ochiltree
Alloway
Doonfoot
Laigh Glengall
Dalrymple
Hollybush
Maybole
Patna
Polnessan
Minishant
Culroy
Kirkmichael
Whitefaulds
Auchenharvie
Eglinton
Girdle Toll
Perceton
Stanecastle
Onthank
Moscow
Fisherton
Sinclairston
Hayhill
Littlemill
Rankinston
Barbieston
Waterside
Burnfoot
Aitkenhead
LARNE 2:00 (MARCH-OCT)

Sneddon Law
Thrashy Knowe
Pley Moss
Braidley Moss
Mossmulloch
Caldermill
Laigh Crewburn
Hall of Kype
Kype Fm
Little Kype East

Cowans Law
Muirside
Long Green
Burnfoot Fm
Calder Moss
Hookhead
Midlinbank
Hazliebank
High Dyke
Little Kype West

Polbaith
Knockshaw
Braidley
Coldwakning
Hallfield
Gilmourton
High Hazliebank
Newmains
Kype Lodge
Kypewater

Muirhouse
Alton
High Bowhill
Wallacegill Muir
Mount Stobieside
Westertoun
West Dykehead Fm
Coats
Middle Rig
Kype Res

Crawlaw
West Newton
Loudoun Mains
West Heads
Foulpapple
Templehill
Gamesland
Harelea Hill
Drumboy Fm
A71
Syde Fm
High Dykes
Willochsheuch Moss
Martinside

Wraes
Gateside
Howietburn
Cronan
East Heads
Loudoun Hill 316
Rench Fm
Torfoot Fm
North Halls
Feeshie Moss
Rough Moss
Dunside Res

Newmilns
Darvel
Bransfield Fm
Gorsebraehead
WINDY WIZEN
Lochgate
Peelhill
Berry Moss
Harting Rig
Dunside Rig
Logan Res

Greenholm
Lanfine Home Fm
High Greenbank Fm
High Newton
Cairnsaigh
Overhouse
Laigh Plewland
High Plewland
Auchengilloch 462
Grouse Hill
Logan Fm

Galston
Stonyhall
Windyhill
Auchenbart
King's Moss
Mill Rig
Glengavel Reservoir
Dungavel 457
Goodbush Hill 475
Spirebush Hill 469
Nutberry Hill 522

Sparnebank
Molemount Fm
Changue Fm
Tulloch Hill 300
Brow Hill
Mule Hill
Main Castle
Anderside Hill
Black Loch Moss
Bankend Rig
Regal Hill
Starpet Rig 451
Priesthill Height 493

Clinchyard
Millands
Sornhill
Milrig
Eastfield Fm
Greenfield
Distinkhorn 386
Twopenny Knowe
Bibblon Hill 431
Dippal Rig
Head of Greenock Water
Hare Craig

Whitehill Fm
Cairnhill
West Burnhead
Langside
Mean Muir
Logan Moss
Avon Head
Little Hartmidden
Meanlour Hill
Middlefield Law 466
Priesthill
Sclanor Hill

Craig
Rodinghead Ho
Bruntwood Mains
Brown's Muir
Flacket Hill
Grange Muir
Wedder Hill 434
Hart Hill
Burnt Hill
Greenock Bridge
Black Hill
Ponesk Burn

Low Holehouse
Roughdyke Fm
Boghead
Meadowhead
Crotthead
Auchmannoch
Knockdon
Reppoch Knowe
Craigs Hill
Stony Hill
Dun Rig
Upper Hall
Lightshaw
Glenbuck

Auchmillan
Barwheys
South Auchenbrain
Barboigh
Weitshaw Muir
Blackside
Pepper Knowe
Auchenlongford Hill
Heath Cottage
Aikencleugh
Netherwood
Laigh Hall
Tardoes
Earl Hill

Auchmillanhill
Blackbriggs
Oxenshaw
Weitshaw
Wealth of Waters
Meath Hill
Limmerhaugh Muir
Greenock Mains
Marchouse Hill
Burnfoot Moor
Muirkirk
Crossflatt
Brack Hill

Mauchline
Brigland
Garfield
Redgate
Sorn Mains
Tincorn Hill
River Ayr
Nethershield
B743
Smallburn
A70
Auldhouseburn
Hawk Hill

Mauchline Mains
Welton
Grassmillees
Catrine Mains
Sorn
SORN CASTLE
Blindburn
Daldilling
Dalgalie
Upper Heilar
High Wood
Midwellwood Fm
Kames
Wee Hill

Haugh
Kingencleuch Ho
Catrine
Whiteflat
Barrshouse
Logan
Gilmilnscroft
SMALLBURN ROAD
The Steel
Little Cairn Table
Douglas

Barskimming Mains
Syke
High Clews
Brackenhill
Kensley
Bogend
B705
Roundshaw Fm
Airds Moss
Boghead Lane
Boghead Burn
Wood Hill
Cairn Hill
Proscribe Burn
Cairn Table 593

Slatehole
Drumfork
Little Heateth
Meikle Heateth
Glensham Rock Fm
Common
Commondyke Fm
Cronberry
Dalfad Moss
Knockbreck
Whiteyards
Wardlaw Hill 497
Fingland Hill 462

Steele
Barturk
Pennymore
Blackfauldhead
Treeshill
Townhead
Darnlaw
Knowe
Knagshill
Back Rogerton
Auchinleck
BOSWELL MUSEUM & MAUSOLEUM
Dykes
Lugar
Wallaceton
MUIRKIRK ROAD
Panbreck Hill
Mid Hill

Ochiltree
High Carston
Crosshill
Barmickhill
Glaisnock
Dornal Moss
Glenmuir
Low Moss
Glenmuir Water
Stony Hill 562

Ochiltree Mains
Thirdpart
Cumnock
KIER HARDIE STATUE
Netherthird
Craigens
Borland Mains
Avisyard Hill 330
Roughhill Moss
Glenmuir Water
Connor Hill
Drummond's Knowe
White Hill 480

Back o' Hill
Grimgrew
Orchardton
Barshare
Little Auchengibbert
Crosslar
Garleffan Fm
Dornal Moss
Glenmuir
Benalt 382
Black Hill 431
East Forediban Hill
Nether Black Law
Black Law

Laigh Tarbeg
Mote Toll
Horsecleugh Fm
Greenside
High Burnside
Borland
Crawford Hill
Airds Hill
Edge Hill 345
Whiteholm
Shiel Rig
Auchtitench 467
Earl Hill
Finglan

Skares
SKARES
Garlaff
Mossback
Calton Fm
Cairnscadden Hill 314
High Polquheys
Millstone Knowe
Clocklowie Hill 442
Dennigall Hill

High Pk
Auchlin
DOON VALLEY RARE BREEDS CENTRE
Black Loch
Carnivan Hill 324
White Knowe
Benston Fm
Lochhill
Rottenyard
Polquheys
Roughside
Craigdullyeart Hill
Crook Brae 385
Over Guelt
Guelt Water
Niviston Hill 460
Lethans Hill
Halfmerk Hill 453
Todholes Hill 481

Auchencloigh
Auchlin Rig
Burnockhead
High Mount 365
Carsgailoch Hill
Hall of Auchincross
Foremouth
Woodend
Connel Park
West Polquhirter
Over Cairn
Corsencon 475
Corsencon
Glenwharrie
Kirkland

Greenhill
Stannery Knowe 363
Mid Hill
Little Rigend Hill
Dalgin
Hungry Hill
Bankglen
North Boig
New Cumnock
Mansfield
Mansfield Mains
East Polquhirter
Meikle Westland
A76
Laigh Cairn
Lagrae
Todholes
Guffock Hill

Over Hill
Lingie Hill
Sunnyside
Lanehead
Pathhead
West Polguhirter
High Cairn
Nether Cairn
Rigg Fm
Glen Hall
Kirkland Plantn

Kyle Forest
Burnside
Dalleagles
Straid Fm
Blarene Hill
Brockloch Knocknide Hill 368
Ashmark Hill
Dalhanna Hill
Burnt Hill
High Cairn 553
McCricrick's Cairn 556
White Hill 406
Kelloside
Kirkconnel
Kelloholm

Upper Beoch
Benbain
Peat Hill 385
Chang Hill 463
Ewe Hill 437
Meikle Hill 441
Lochbrowan Hill 344
Quintin Knowe 554
Dun 527
Hare Hill
Polnagrie Hill 418
Corsrig Hill 395
Hog Hill
Brunt Rig
Barr Moor

Scale:
0 1 2 3 miles
0 1 2 3 4 5 km

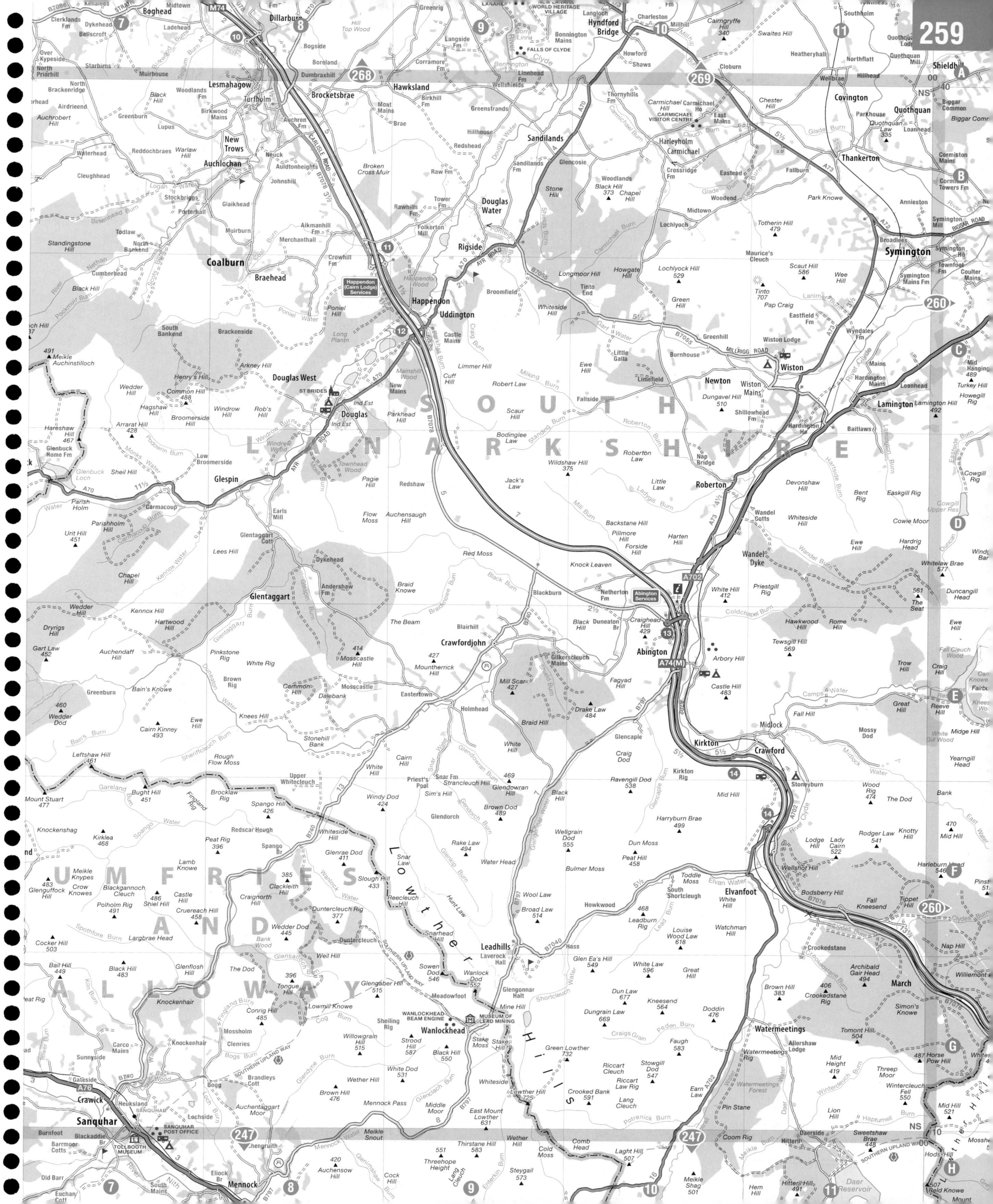
SOUTH LANARKSHIRE
DUMFRIES AND GALLOWAY
Lowther Hills
Boghead
Dillarburn
Lesmahagow
Turfholm
New Trows
Auchlochan
Hawksland
Brocketsbrae
Coalburn
Braehead
Douglas Water
Rigside
Happendon
Happendon (Cairn Lodge) Services
Uddington
Douglas West
Douglas
St Brides
Glespin
Carmacoup
Glentaggart
Crawfordjohn
Abington
Abington Services
Kirkton
Crawford
Midlock
Elvanfoot
Leadhills
Wanlockhead
Wanlockhead Beam Engine
Museum of Lead Mining
Sanquhar
Sanquhar Post Office
Tolbooth Museum
Crawick
Mennock
Hyndford Bridge
Falls of Clyde
World Heritage Village
Sandilands
Carmichael
Carmichael Visitor Centre
Harleyholm
Thankerton
Covington
Quothquan
Symington
Wiston
Newton
Lamington
Roberton
Wandel Dyke
Watermeetings
March
Tinto 707
Green Lowther 732
Southern Upland Way
Carlisle Road
Ayr Road
Biggar Road
Millrigg Road
A70
A73
A74(M)
A702
A72
A76
B7078
B7055
B7040
B797
B740
B7076
M74
268
269
260
247
NS
River Clyde
Daer Reservoir

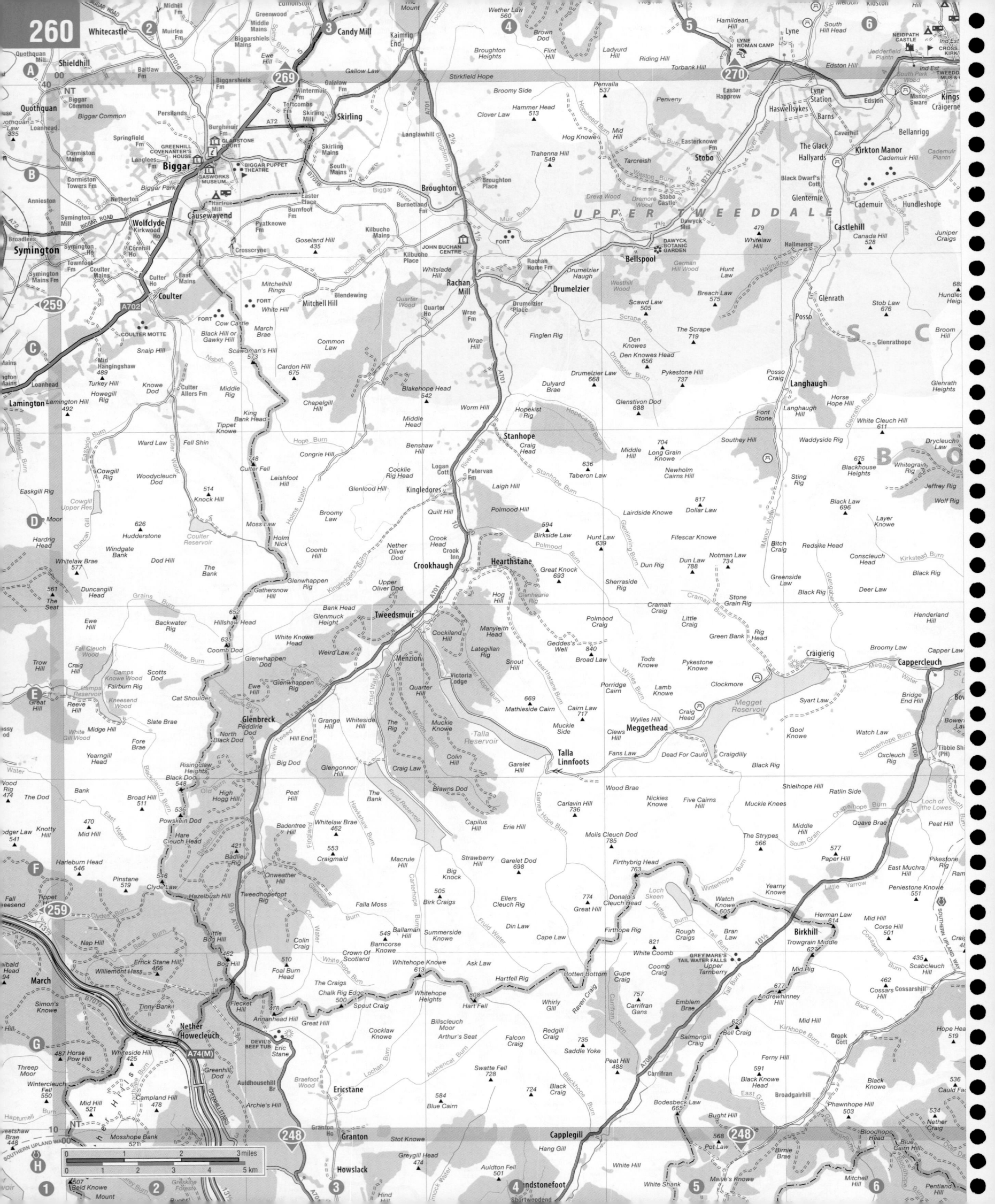
Whitecastle
Midhill Fm
Muirlea Fm
Greenwood
Middle Mains
Biggarshiels Mains
Candy Mill
Kaimrig End
The Mount
Wether Law 560
Brown Dod
Flint Hill
Broughton Heights
Ladyurd Hill
Riding Hill
Hamildean Hill
Lyne
LYNE ROMAN CAMP
South Hill Head
NEIDPATH CASTLE
Quothquan Mill
Shieldhill
Baitlaw Fm
Ewe Hill
Gallow Law
Stirkfield Hope
Torbank Hill
Edston Hill
Biggarshiels Fm
Galalaw Fm
Wintermuir Fm
Toftcombs Fm
Skirling Mill
Skirling
Broomy Side
Penvalla 537
Easter Happrew
Lyne Station
Haswellsykes
Edston
Manor Sware
Kings
Craigerne
Quothquan
Biggar Common
Biggar Common
Quothquan Law 335
Loanhead
Persilands
Burghmuir Fm
GLADSTONE COURT
GREENHILL COVENANTER'S HOUSE
Clover Law
Hammer Head 513
Penveny
Barns
Cavehill
Bellanrigg
Springfield Fm
Langlawhill
Hog Knowe
Mid Hill
Easterknowe Fm
The Glack
Kirkton Manor
Cademuir Hill
Cademuir Plantn
Cormiston Mains
Langlees Fm
Biggar
BIGGAR PUPPET THEATRE
GASWORKS MUSEUM
Skirling Mains
South Mains
Trahenna Hill 549
Tarcreish
Stobo
Hallyards
Cormiston Towers Fm
Biggar Park
Broughton
Broughton Place
Weston Burn
Black Dwarf's Cott
Glenternie
Annieston
Netherton
Hartree Mill
Causewayend
Easter Place
Burnetland Fm
Burnfoot Fm
Biggar Water
Dreva Wood
Dramore Wood
Stobo Castle
Cademuir
Hundleshope
Symington Mill
BIGGAR ROAD
Wolfclyde
Kirkwood Ho
Pyatknowe Fm
UPPER TWEEDDALE
Dawyck Mill
Castlehill
Broadlees
Symington
Symington Ho
Cornhill Ho
Goseland Hill 435
Kilbucho Mains
JOHN BUCHAN CENTRE
FORT
479 Whitelaw Hill
Hallmanor
Canada Hill 528
Juniper Craigs
DAWYCK BOTANIC GARDEN
Bellspool
Crosscryne
Townfoot Fm
Coulter Mains
Kilbucho Place
Rachan Home Fm
German Hill Wood
Symington Mains Fm
Culter Ho
East Mains
Whitslade Hill
Drumelzier Haugh
Hunt Law
Mitchelhill Rings
Rachan Mill
Drumelzier
Westhill Wood
Coulter
Mitchell Hill
Blendewing
Breach Law 575
Glenrath
Stob Law 676
Quarter Wood
Quarter Ho
Scawd Law 505
Drumelzier Place
Wrae Fm
COULTER MOTTE
Cow Castle
White Hill
Black Hill or Gawky Hill
March Brae
Scrape Burn
Posso
Glenrathope
Broom Hill
Common Law
The Scrape 719
Wrae Hill
Finglen Rig
Den Knowes
Snaip Hill
Mid Hangingshaw 489
Scawdman's Hill 573
Nisbet Burn
Den Knowes Head 656
Turkey Hill
Cardon Hill 675
Drumelzier Law 668
Pykestone Hill 737
Posso Craig
Lamington
Loanhead
Knowe Dod
Culter Allers Fm
Howegill Rig
Middle Rig
Dulyard Brae
Langhaugh
Glenrath Heights
Lamington Hill 492
Chapelgill Hill
Blakehope Head 542
Glenstivon Dod 688
Horse Hope Hill
King Bank Head
Worm Hill
Hopekist Rig
Langhaugh Hill
Tippet Knowe
Middle Head
Font Stone
White Cleuch Hill 611
Ward Law
Fell Shin
Hope Burn
Stanhope
Craig Head
Middle Hill
704 Long Grain Knowe
Southey Hill
Waddyside Rig
Drycleuch Law
Congrie Hill
Benshaw Hill
Cowgill Rig
Woodycleuch Dod
748 Culter Fell
Leishfoot Hill
Cocklie Rig Head
Logan Cott
Paterван Fm
636 Taberon Law
Newholm Cairns Hill
675 Blackhouse Heights
Whitegrain Rig
Sting Rig
Laigh Hill
Jeffrey Rig
Easkgill Rig
Cowgill Upper Res
514 Knock Hill
Glenlood Hill
Kingledores
817 Dollar Law
Black Law 696
Wolf Rig
Quilt Hill
Polmood Hill
Lairdside Knowe
Layer Knowe
626 Hudderstone
Moss Law
Broomy Law
594 Birkside Law
Hunt Law 639
Fifescar Knowe
Hardrig Head
Coulter Reservoir
Holm Nick
Crook Head
Nether Oliver Dod
Crook Inn
Bitch Craig
Redsike Head
Windgate Bank
Dod Hill
Coomb Hill
Polmood Burn
Notman Law 734
Conscleuch Head
Whitelaw Brae 577
The Bank
Crookhaugh
Hearthstone
Great Knock 693
Dun Law 788
Dun Rig
Kirkstead Burn
Black Rig
Greenside Law
Duncangill Head
Glenwhappen Rig
Upper Oliver Dod
Sherraside Rig
Deer Law
561 The Seat
Grains Burn
Gathersnow Hill
Hog Hill
Stone Grain Rig
Black Rig
Ewe Hill
Backwater Rig
652 Hillshaw Head
Bank Head
Glenmuck Height
Tweedsmuir
Manyleith Head
Polmood Craig
Cramalt Craig
Little Craig
Rig Head
Henderland Hill
White Knowe Head
Cockiland Hill
Lategillan Rig
Green Bank
Fall Cleuch Wood
635 Coomb Dod
Weird Law
Geddes's Well
840 Broad Law
Broomy Law
Capper Law
Trow Hill
Craig Hill
Whitelaw Burn
Glenwhappen Dod
Menzion
Snout Hill
Tods Knowe
Pykestone Knowe
Craigierig
Cappercleuch
Scotts Dod
Camps Knowe Wood
Hallow Burn
Victoria Lodge
Porridge Cairn
Clockmore
Megget Water
Fairburn Rig
Cat Shoulder
Ewe Hill
Glenwhappen Rig
Quarter Hill
669 Mathieside Cairn
Lamb Knowe
Megget Reservoir
Syart Law
Bridge End Hill
Reeve Hill
Kneesend Wood
Great Hill
Cairn Law 717
Craig Head
Wylies Hill
Meggethead
Slate Brae
Glenbreck
Peddirie Dod
Grange Hill
Whiteside Hill
The Rig
Muckle Knowe
Talla Reservoir
Muckle Side
Clews Hill
Gool Knowe
Watch Law
Bowerhope Law
White Gill Wood
Midge Hill
North Black Dod
Hill End
Talla Linnfoots
Fans Law
Dead For Cauld
Craigdilly
Summerhope Burn
Oxcleuch Rig
Tibbie Shiels (PH)
Fore Brae
Yearngill Head
Big Dod
Glengonnor Hill
Craig Law
Colin Hill
Garelet Hill
Black Rig
Risingclaw Heights
Black Dod 548
Wood Rig 474
The Dod
Bank
High Hogg Hill
Broad Hill 511
Peat Hill
The Bank
Fruid Reservoir
Brawns Dod
Wood Brae
Carlavin Hill 736
Nickies Knowe
Five Cairns Hill
Muckle Knees
Shielhope Hill
Ratlin Side
Loch of the Lowes
536 Powskein Dod
470 Mid Hill
Hare Cleuch Head
Whitelaw Brae 462
Badentree Hill
Capilus Hill
Erie Hill
Middle Hill
Chapelhope Burn
Quave Brae
Peat Hill
Lodger Law 541
Knotty Hill
421 Badlieu Rig
553 Craigmaid
Macrule Hill
Strawberry Hill
Garelet Dod 698
Molls Cleuch Dod 785
The Strypes 566
577 Paper Hill
Harleburn Head 546
Pinstane 519
Clyde Law
Onweather Hill
Tweedhopefoot Rig
Big Knock
Firthybrig Head 763
East Muchra Hill
Pikestone Rig
546
Hazelbush Hill
505 Birk Craigs
Ellers Cleuch Rig
774 Great Hill
Donald's Cleuch Head
Loch Skeen
Yearny Knowe
Peniestone Knowe 551
Fall Moss
Watch Knowe 605
Herman Law 614
Birkhill
Tippet Knowe
Clydes Burn
Little Bog Hill
549 Barncorse Knowe
Ballaman Hill
Summerside Knowe
Din Law
Firthope Rig
Rough Craigs
Bran Law
Mid Hill
Corse Hill 501
Nap Hill
Colin Craig
Crown Of Scotland
Cape Law
821 White Coomb
Trowgrain Middle 627
Errick Stane Hill
462 Bog Hill
510 Foal Burn Head
Whitehope Knowe 613
Ask Law
GREY MARE'S TAIL WATER FALLS
Upper Tarnberry
Coomb Craig
435 Scabcleuch Hill
Williemont Hass
466
Hartfell Rig
Rotten Bottom
Gupe Craig
Mid Rig
March
The Craigs
Chalk Rig Edge 500
Whitehope Heights
808 Hart Fell
Whirly Gill
Raven Craig
757 Carrifran Gans
Emblem Brae
677 Andrewhinney Hill
462 Cossars Hill
Cossarshill
Simon's Knowe
Tinny Bank
Flecket Hill
478 Annanhead Hill
Spout Craig
Great Hill
Billscleuch Moor
Arthur's Seat
Redgill Craig
Mid Hill
Nether Howecleuch
DEVIL'S BEEF TUB
Eric Stane
Cocklaw Knowe
Falcon Craig
735 Saddle Yoke
623 Bell Craig
Salmongill Craig
Crook Cott
Hope Head 519
487 Horse Pow Hill
Whiteside Hill 425
A74(M)
Peat Hill 488
Ferny Hill
Threep Moor
Greenhill Dod
Swatte Fell 728
Carrifran
591 Black Knowe Head
Black Knowe
Wintercleuch Fell 550
Auldhousehill Br
Braefoot Wood
Ericstane
724
Black Craig
Broadgairhill
536 Cauld Face
Mid Hill 521
Campland Hill 478
Archie's Hill
584 Blue Cairn
Bodesbeck Law 665
Phawnhope Hill 503
534 Nether Craig
Hapturnell
Bught Hill
Mosshope Bank 521
Granton Ho
Granton
Stot Knowe
Capplegill
568 Pot Law
Bloodhope Head
Blue Cairn Hill
Hang Gill
Greygill Head 474
Birnie Brae
SOUTHERN UPLAND WAY
Howslack
Auldton Fell 501
White Hill
507 Beld Knowe Mount
Greskine Forest
Hind Hill
Shortwoodend
White Shank
Mailie's Knowe
Mitchell Hill
Pentland Hill
0 1 2 3 miles
0 1 2 3 4 5 km
NT 00 40
NT 10
A B C D E F G H
1 2 3 4 5 6
259 269 270 248
A702 A701 A72 A708 A74(M) B7016 B712 B7076

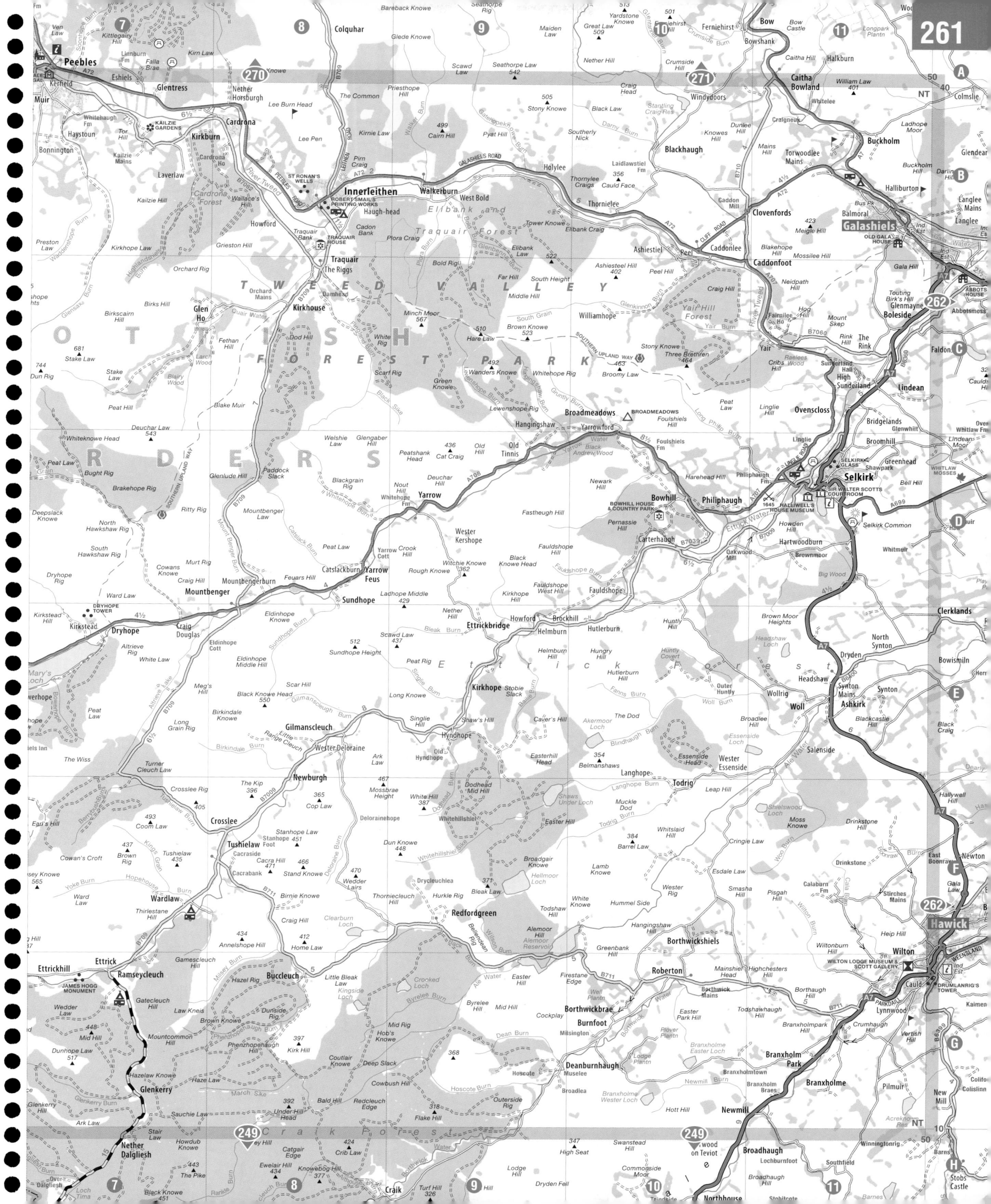
Peebles
Kerfield
Eshiels
Glentress
Cardrona
Kirkburn
Kailzie Gardens
Haystoun
Bonnington
Laverlaw
Cardrona Forest
Kailzie Hill
Nether Horsburgh
Lee Burn Head
Lee Pen
Colquhar
Glede Knowe
Bareback Knowe
Maiden Law
Great Law
Nether Hill
Fernieherst
Bow
Bow Castle
Bowshank
Caitha Hill
Halkburn
Caitha Bowland
William Law
Colmslie
Windydoors
Crumside Hill
Craig Head
Black Law
Stantling Craig Res
Priesthope Hill
The Common
Seathorpe Law
Scawd Law
Stony Knowe
Kirnie Law
Cairn Hill
Pyat Hill
Southerly Nick
Dunlee Hill
Knowes Hill
Blackhaugh
Mains Hill
Torwoodlee Mains
Buckholm
Ladhope Moor
Glendearg
Galashiels Road
Holylee
Laidlawstiel Fm
Cauld Face
Thornylee Craigs
Thornielee
Walkerburn
Innerleithen
St Ronan's Wells
Robert Smail's Printing Works
Haugh-head
West Bold
Elibank and Traquair Forest
Traquair House
Traquair
The Riggs
Cadon Bank
Plora Craig
Caddon Mill
Clovenfords
Galashiels
Old Gala House
Balmoral
Buckholm Hill
Halliburton
Langlee
Tower Knowe
Elibank Craig
Elibank Law
Ashiestiel
Peel
Caddonlee
Caddonfoot
Blakehope Hill
Mossilee Hill
Meigle Hill
Gala Hill
Tweed Valley Forest Park
Scottish Borders
Bold Rig
Far Hill
South Height
Middle Hill
Ashiesteel Hill
Peel Hill
Craig Hill
Yair Hill Forest
Neidpath Hill
Touting Birk's Hill
Glenmayne
Boleside
Abbotsford House
Abbotsmoss
Orchard Rig
Orchard Mains
Damhead
Kirkhouse
Glen Ho
Birks Hill
Birkscairn Hill
Minch Moor
Hare Law
Brown Knowe
South Grain
Williamhope
Southern Upland Way
Stony Knowe
Three Brethren
Yair
Fairnilee Ho
Hog Hill
Mount Skep
Rink Hill
The Rink
Faldonside
Fethan Hill
Dod Hill
White Rig
Stake Law
Dun Rig
Scarf Rig
Wanders Knowe
Green Knowe
Whitehope Rig
Broomy Law
Cribs Hill
Sunderland Hall
High Sunderland
Lindean
Lewenshope Rig
Broadmeadows
Hangingshaw
Yarrowford
Peat Law
Linglie Hill
Ovenscloss
Foulshiels Hill
Bridgelands
Glenwhilt
Peat Hill
Blake Muir
Deuchar Law
Whiteknowe Head
Welshie Law
Glengaber Hill
Peatshank Head
Cat Craig
Old Hill
Old Tinnis
Black Andrew Wood
Foulshiels Fm
Linglie
Broomhill
Greenhead
Selkirk
Selkirk Glass
Shawpark
Bell Hill
Whitlaw Mosses
Peat Law
Bught Rig
Brakehope Rig
Glenlude Hill
Paddock Slack
Blackgrain Rig
Nout Hill
Whitehope Fm
Deuchar Hill
Yarrow
Newark Hill
Bowhill House & Country Park
Bowhill
Harehead Hill
Philiphaugh
Halliwell's House Museum
Sir Walter Scott's Courtroom
Deepslack Knowe
North Hawkshaw Rig
South Hawkshaw Rig
Ritty Rig
Mountbenger Law
Fastheugh Hill
Pernassie Hill
Carterhaugh
Howden Hill
Hartwoodburn
Brownmoor
Selkirk Common
Wester Kershope
Fauldshope Hill
Yarrow Cott
Crook Hill
Witchie Knowe
Black Knowe Head
Oakwood Mill
Big Wood
Dryhope Rig
Cowans Knowe
Murt Rig
Craig Hill
Peat Law
Catslackburn
Yarrow Feus
Rough Knowe
Fauldshope West Hill
Fauldshope
Ward Law
Dryhope Tower
Mountbenger
Mountbengerburn
Feuars Hill
Sundhope
Ladhope Middle
Kirkhope Hill
Clerklands
Kirkstead Hill
Kirkstead
Dryhope
Craig Douglas
Eldinhope Cott
Eldinhope Knowe
Nether Hill
Ettrickbridge
Howford
Brockhill
Helmburn
Hutlerburn
Huntly Hill
Brown Moor Heights
North Synton
Altrieve Rig
White Law
Eldinhope Middle Hill
Scawd Law
Sundhope Height
Peat Rig
Helmburn Hill
Hungry Hill
Hutlerburn Hill
Headshaw Loch
Dryden
Bowismiln
Meg's Hill
Scar Hill
Black Knowe Head
Long Knowe
Ettrick Forest
Kirkhope
Stobie Slack
Outer Huntly
Wollrig
Headshaw
Synton Mains
Synton
Ashkirk
Woll
Peat Law
Birkindale Knowe
Long Grain Rig
Gilmanscleuch
Singlie Hill
Shaw's Hill
Caver's Hill
Akermoor Loch
The Dod
Broadlee Hill
Blackcastle Hill
Black Craig
The Wiss
Little Range Cleuch
Wester Deloraine
Hyndhope
Old Hyndhope
Ark Law
Easterhill Head
Belmanshaws
Essenside Loch
Essenside Head
Wester Essenside
Salenside
Turner Cleuch Law
Crosslee Rig
The Kip
Newburgh
Mossbrae Height
Cop Law
White Hill
Dodhead Mid Hill
Langhope
Todrig
Leap Hill
Hallywell Hill
Earl's Hill
Coom Law
Crosslee
Deloraineshope
Whitehillshiel
Shaws Under Loch
Muckle Dod
Shielswood Loch
Moss Knowe
Drinkstone Hill
Tushielaw
Stanhope Law
Stanhope Foot
Easter Hill
Whitslaid Hill
Barrel Law
Cringie Law
Cowan's Croft
Brown Rig
Tushielaw
Cracrbank
Cacra Hill
Stand Knowe
Dun Knowe
Drinkstone
East Boonraw
Newton
Wedder Lairs
Broadgair Knowe
Lamb Knowe
Esdale Law
Gala Law
Ward Law
Wardlaw
Drycleuchlea
Thorniecleuch Hill
Hurkle Rig
Bleak Law
Hellmoor Loch
Wester Rig
Smasha Hill
Pisgah Hill
Calaburn Fm
Stirches Mains
Hawick
Thirlestane Hill
Birnie Knowe
Craig Hill
Clearburn Loch
Redfordgreen
Todshaw Hill
White Knowe
Hummel Side
Hangingshaw Hill
Heip Hill
Wiltonburn Hill
Wilton
Wilton Lodge Museum & Scott Gallery
Annelshope Hill
Home Law
Alemoor Hill
Alemoor Reservoir
Greenbank Hill
Borthwickshiels
Ettrick
Ettrickhill
Ramseycleuch
James Hogg Monument
Gamescleuch Hill
Buccleuch
Little Bleak Law
Crooked Loch
Kingside Loch
Easter Hill
Firestane Edge
Roberton
Mainshiel Head
Highchesters Hill
Cauld
Drumlanrig's Tower
Gatecleuch Hill
Hazel Rig
Law Kneis
Brown Knowe
Dunside Rig
Byrelee Hill
Mid Hill
Cockplay
Borthwickbrae
Burnfoot
Milsington
Well Plantn
Borthwick Mains
Easter Park Hill
Todshawhaugh Hill
Borthaugh Hill
Lynnwood
Kaimend
Wedder Law
Mid Hill
Mountcommon Hill
Phenzhopehaugh Hill
Kirk Hill
Mid Rig
Hob's Knowe
Dean Burn
Plover Plantn
Branxholme Easter Loch
Branxholmpark Hill
Crumhaugh Hill
Vertish Hill
Dunhope Law
Hazelaw Knowe
Haze Law
Coutlair Knowe
Deep Slack
Hoscote
Deanburnhaugh
Muselee
Lodge Plantn
Branxholm Park
Branxholmtown
Branxholme
Glenkerry
Glenkerry Hill
Ark Law
Sauchie Law
Under Hill Head
Bald Hill
Cowbush Hill
Redcleuch Edge
Outerside Rig
Flake Hill
Broadlea
Branxholme Wester Loch
Hott Hill
Newmill
Pilmuir
New Mill
Colislinn
Stair Law
Nether Dalgliesh
Howdub Knowe
Catgair Edge
Crib Law
Craik Forest
High Seat
Swanstead Hill
Hawkwood on Teviot
Acreknowe Res
Winningtonrig
Barns
Ewelair Hill
Knowebog Hill
The Pike
Black Knowe
Craik
Turf Hill
Lodge Hill
Dryden Fell
Commonside Moor
Broadhaugh
Lochburnfoot
Broadhaugh Hill
Southfield
Stobs Castle
Northhouse
Loch Tima
Dalgliesh
Teindside
Stobitcote

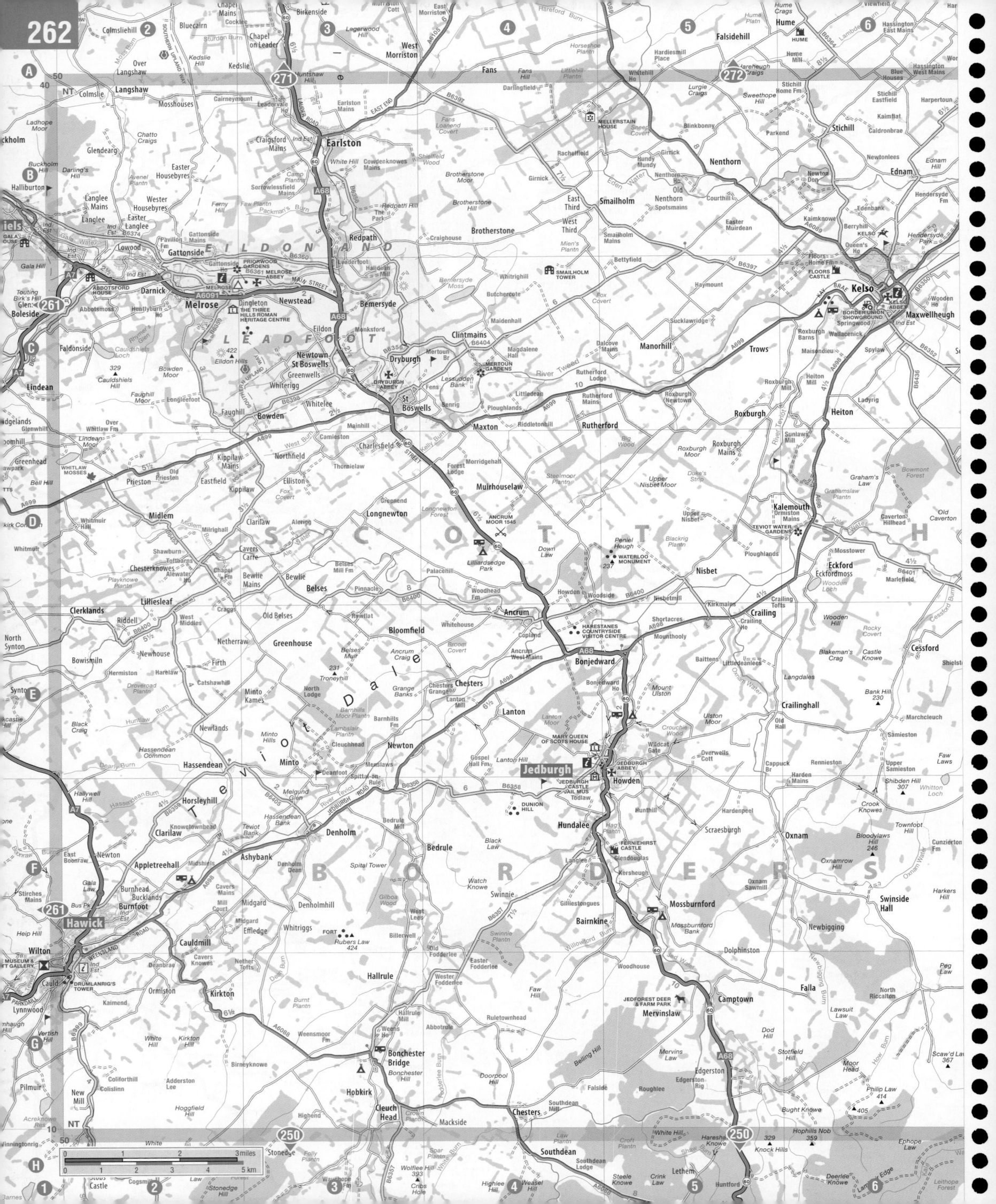

Colmsliehill
Bluecairn
Chapel Mains
Cockleе
Chapel on Leader
Birkenside
Legerwood Hill
West Morriston
Fans
Falsidehill
Hume
Over Langshaw
Kedslie
271
272
Huntshaw Hill
Whitehill Ho
Colmslie
Langshaw
Mosshouses
Cairneymount
Leadervale Ho
Earlston Mains
Darlingfield
Lurgie Craigs
Sweethope Hill
Stichill Home Fm
Stichill Eastfield
Harpertoun
Ladhope Moor
Chatto Craigs
Craigsford Mains
Earlston
MELLERSTAIN HOUSE
Blinkbonny
Parkend
Stichill
Kaimflat
Caldronbrae
Glendearg
Buckholm Hill
Darling's Hill
Easter Housebyres
Cowdenknowes Mains
Shielfield Wood
Rachelfield
Hundy Mundy
Girrick
Nenthorn
Newtonlees
Ednam
Halliburton
Langlee Mains
Wester Housebyres
Camp Plantn
Sorrowlessfield Mains
Brotherstone Moor
Girnick
Nenthorn Ho
Old Nenthorn Spotsmains
Smailholm
Newton Don
Hendersyde Fm
Langlee
Easter Langlee
Redpath Hill
Brotherstone Hill
East Third
West Third
Edenbank
Easter Muirdean
Kaimknowe
Berryhill
Redpath
Craighouse
Brotherstone
Smailholm Mains
KELSO
Hendersyde Park
Gala Hill
Gattonside
EILDON AND
Lowood
Leaderfoot
Haldean Mill
Bettyfield
PRIORWOOD GARDENS
MELROSE ABBEY
Whitrighill
SMAILHOLM TOWER
FLOORS CASTLE
Kelso
ABBOTSFORD HOUSE
Darnick
Melrose
Newstead
Bemersyde Moss
Butchercote
Haymount
Fox Covert
Boleside
261
Abbotsmoss
Huntlyburn Ho
Dingleton
THE THREE HILLS ROMAN HERITAGE CENTRE
Bemersyde
Maidenhall
Sucklawridge
BORDER UNION SHOWGROUND
Springwood
Maxwellheugh
Eildon
Monksford
Clintmains
Dalcove Mains
Manorhill
Roxburgh Barns
Wallacenick
Faldonside
Cauldshiels Loch
LEADFOOT
Eildon Hills
Newtown St Boswells
Dryburgh
Mertoun Br
Magdalene Hall
MERTOUN GARDENS
River Tweed
Trows
Maisondieu
Spylaw
Lindean
Cauldshiels Hill
Bowden Moor
Greenwells
Whiterigg
DRYBURGH ABBEY
Lessudden Bank
Rutherford Lodge
Heiton Mill
Roxburgh Mill
Faughill Moor
Longleefoot
Fens
Littledean
Rutherford Mains
Roxburgh Newtown
Ladyrig
Faughill
Bowden
Whitelee
St Boswells
Benrig
Ploughlands
Roxburgh
Heiton
Over Whitlaw Fm
Mainhill
Maxton
Riddletonhill
Rutherford
Lindean Moor
Camieston
Charlesfield
Sunlaws Mill
Northfield
Big Wood
Roxburgh Moor
Roxburgh Mains
Bowmont Forest
WHITLAW MOSSES
Kippilaw Mains
Thornielaw
Forest Lodge
Morridgehall
Steelmoor Plantn
Duke's Strip
Graham's Law
Greenhead
Bell Hill
Prieston
Old Prieston
Eastfield
Elliston
Upper Nisbet Moor
Kippilaw
Fox Covert
Muirhouselaw
Grahamslaw Plantn
Longnewton
Longnewton Forest
Greenend
Kalemouth
Ormiston Mains
Old Caverton
Caverton Hillhead
Midlem
Whitmuir Hall
Clarilaw
Alerigg
ANCRUM MOOR 1545
Upper Nisbet
TEVIOT WATER GARDENS
Milrighall
SCOTTISH
Shawburn
Toftbarns
Cavers Carre
Lilliardsedge Park
Down Law
Peniel Heugh
WATERLOO MONUMENT
Blackrig Plantn
Ploughlands
Mosstower
Eckford
Eckfordmoss
Marlefield
Chesterknowes
Alewater Ho
Chapel Fm
Bewlie Mains
Bewlie
Belses Mill Fm
Palacehill
Nisbet
Wooden Loch
Playknowe Plantn
Belses
Pinnacle
Woodhead Fm
Howden
Woodside
Nisbetmill
Kirkmains
Crailing Tofts
Clerklands
Lilliesleaf
Riddell
Craggs
West Middles
Old Belses
Rawflat
Ancrum
Whitehouse
Shortacres
Crailing
Crailing Ho
Wooden Hill
Rocky Covert
North Synton
Netherraw
Greenhouse
Bloomfield
Copland
HARESTANES COUNTRYSIDE VISITOR CENTRE
Mounthooly
Newhouse
Belses Muir
Ancrum Craig
Broom Covert
Ancrum West Mains
Bonjedward
Baittens
Littledeanlees
Blakeman's Crag
Castle Knowe
Cessford
Bowismiln
Hermiston
Harelaw
Firth
Troneyhill
Chesters Grange
Chesters
Bonjedward Ho
Mount Ulston
Langdales
Bank Hill
Catshawhill
Droveroad Plantn
Minto Kames
North Lodge
Grange Banks
Lanton Mill
Teviot Dale
Crailinghall
Black Craig
Huntlaw
Barnhills Moor Plantn
Barnhills Fm
Lanton
Lanton Moor
Ulston Moor
Old Hall
Marchcleuch
Newlands
Minto Hills
Lambslair Plantn
Cleuchhead
Newton
MARY QUEEN OF SCOTS HOUSE
Crouchie Wood
Wildcat Gate
Samieston
Hassendean Common
Gospel Hall Fm
Lanton Hill
Overwells Cott
Faw Laws
Hassendean
Minto
Menslaws
Jedburgh
JEDBURGH ABBEY
Cappuck Br
Rennieston
Upper Samieston
Deanfoot
Spittal-on-Rule
Howden
Harden Mains
Shibden Hill
Whitton Loch
Hallywell Hill
Horsleyhill
Melgund Glen
River Teviot
JEDBURGH CASTLE JAIL MUS
Todlaw
DUNION HILL
Crook Knowes
Clarilaw
Knowetownhead
Teviot Bank
Hassendean Bank
Denholm
Bedrule Mill
Hunthill
Hardenpeel
Hundalee
Scraesburgh
Oxnam
Townfoot Hill
Bloodylaws Hill
Cunzierton Fm
Newton
East Boonraw
Appletreehall
Midshiels
Ashybank
Denholm Dean
Bedrule
Black Law
Hag Plantn
FERNIEHIRST CASTLE
Glendouglas
Langlee
Kersheugh
Oxnamrow Hill
BORDERS
Gala Law
Burnhead
Bucklands
Cavers Mains
Spital Tower
Watch Knowe
Swinnie
Oxnam Sawmill
Harkers Hill
Stirches Mains
Burnfoot
Mill Court
Midgard
Denholmhill
Gilboa Wood
Gilliestongues
Mossburnford
Swinside Hall
Bus Pk
Hawick
Midgard
Effledge
Whitriggs
FORT
Rubers Law
West Lees
Bairnkine
Mossburnford Bank
Newbigging
Help Hill
Cauldmill
Billerwell
Swinnie Plantn
Willowford Burn
Dolphinston
Wilton
Cavers Knowes
Nether Tofts
Old Fodderlee
Easter Fodderlee
MUSEUM & ART GALLERY
Deanbrae
Hallrule
Woodhouse
Peg Law
Cauld
DRUMLANRIG'S TOWER
Ormiston
Kirkton
Wester Fodderlee
Faw Hill
Falla
North Riccalton
Lynnwood
Kaimend
Burnt Plantn
JEDFOREST DEER & FARM PARK
Mervinslaw
Camptown
Hallrule Mill
Ruletownhead
Lawsuit Law
Vertish Hill
White Hill
Kirkton Hill
Weensmoor Fm
Weens Ho
Abbotrule
Dod Hill
Bonchester Bridge
Belling Hill
Mervins Law
Stotfield Hill
Moor Head
Scaw'd Law
Bonchester Hill
Edgerston
Birneyknowe
Colliforthill
Adderston Lee
Doorpool Hill
Edgerston Rig
Pilmuir
Colislinn
Hobkirk
Falside
Roughlee
Philip Law
New Mill
Hoggfield Hill
Cleuch Head
Crown Plantn
Mackside
Chesters
Southdean Mill
Bught Knowe
Acreknowe Res
Highend
250
White Hill
Hopehills Nob
Law Plantn
Croft Plantn
Harestane Knowe
Knock Hills
Ephope Law
Stonedge
Folly Plantn
Southdean
Shaw Burn
Spar Plantn
Southdean Lodge
Wolfiee Hill
Lethem
Steele Knowe
Crink Law
Stobs Castle
Cogsmill
Stonedge Hill
Cribs Hole
Highlee Hill
Weasel Hill
Huntford
Deerlee Knowe
Leithope Forest
0 1 2 3 miles
0 1 2 3 4 5 km

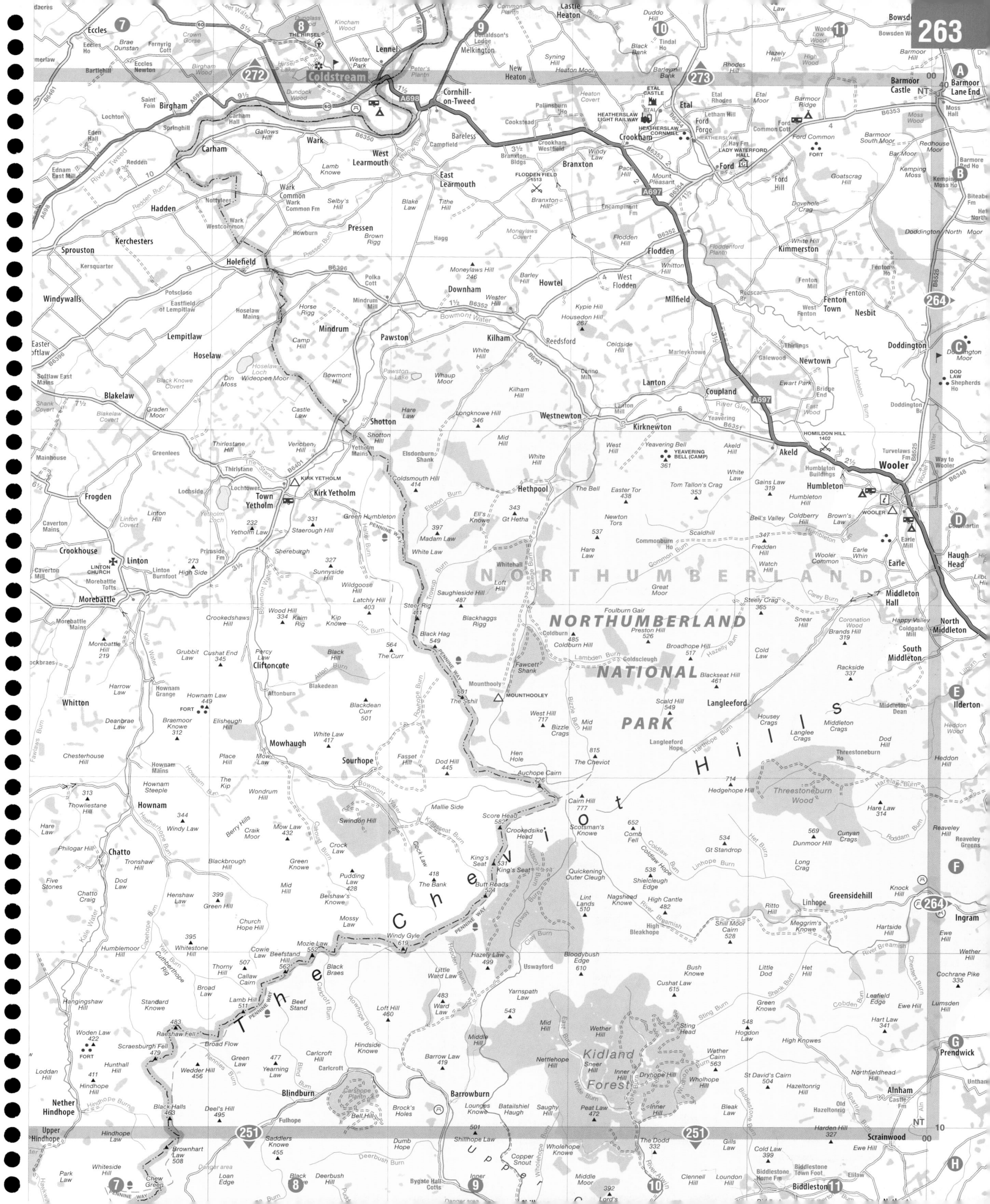

Eccles
Eccles Ho
Brae Dunstan
Fernyrig Cott
Crown Gorse
Dunglass Wood
THE HIRSEL
Kincham Wood
Lennel
Donaldson's Lodge
Melkington
Castle Heaton
Duddo Hill
Tindal Ho
Black Bank
Law
Hazely Law
Low Wood
High Wood
Bowsden
Bowsden Wood
Barmoor Hill
Bartlehill
Eccles Newton
Birgham Wood
Hirsel Lake
Coldstream
Wester Park
Peter's Plantn
New Heaton
Heaton Moor
Syning Hill
Barleymill Bank
Rhodes Hill
272
273
Barmoor Castle
Barmoor Lane End
Saint Foin
Birgham
Lochton
Dundock Wood
Cornhill-on-Tweed
A698
Heaton Covert
ETAL CASTLE
Etal
Etal Rhodes
Etal Moor
Barmoor Ridge
Moss Wood
Moss Hall
Eden Hall
Springhill
Carham Hall
Gallows Hill
Pallinsburn Ho
HEATHERSLAW LIGHT RAILWAY
HEATHERSLAW CORNMILL
Letham Hill
Ford Forge
Ford Cott
Common Cott
Ford Common
Barmoor South Moor
Redhouse Moor
Ednam East Mill
River Tweed
Redden
Carham
Wark
Bareless
Campfield
Cookstead
Crookham Westfield
Crookham
Lady Waterford Hall
Ford
Bar Moor
Barmoor Red Ho
Lamb Knowe
West Learmouth
Branxton Bldgs
Windy Law
Branxton
Flodden Field 1513
Pace Hill
Mount Pleasant
Kemping Moss
Goatscrag Hill
Kemping Moss Ho
Ford Hill
Biteabout Fm
Hadden
Nottylees
Wark Common
Wark Common Fm
Selby's Hill
East Learmouth
Blake Law
Tithe Hill
Branxton Hill
Encampment Fm
A697
Dovehole Crag
Kerchesters
Wark Westcommon
Pressen
Brown Rigg
Howburn
Hagg
Moneylaws Covert
Flodden Hill
Floddenford Plantn
White Hill
Kimmerston
Doddington North Moor
Sprouston
Holefield
Kersquarter
Moneylaws Hill 246
Barley Hill
Howtel
West Flodden
Flodden
Whitton Hill
Fenton Ho
Fenton Mill
Polka Cott
Downham
Milfield
Redscar Br
Fenton
Fenton Town
West Fenton
Nesbit
264
Windywalls
Potsclose
Eastfield of Lempitlaw
Horse Rigg
Mindrum Mill
Wester Hill
Kypie Hill
Housedon Hill 267
Hoselaw Mains
Mindrum
Bowmont Water
Easter Softlaw
Lempitlaw
Camp Hill
Pawston
Kilham
Reedsford
Coldside Hill
Marleyknowe
Thirlings
Galewood
Newtown
Doddington
Doddington Moor
Hoselaw
Hoselaw Loch
Wideopen Moor
White Hill
Pawston Lake
Whaup Moor
Canno Mill
Lanton
Ewart Park
Bridge End
Dod Law
Shepherds Ho
Softlaw East Mains
Black Knowe Covert
Din Moss
Bowmont Hill
Kilham Hill
Coupland
Blakelaw
Shank Covert
Blakelaw Covert
Graden Moor
Castle Law
Hare Law
Longknowe Hill 346
Westnewton
Lanton Mill
Kirknewton
River Glen
Yeavering
East Wood
Doddington Br
Shotton
Mainhouse
Greenlees
Thirlestane Hill
Verchen Hill
Shotton Hill
Yetholm Mains
Elsdonburn Shank
Mid Hill
West Hill
Yeavering Bell
YEAVERING BELL (CAMP) 361
Akeld Hill
Akeld
HOMILDON HILL 1402
Turvelaws Fm
Way to Wooler
Wooler
White Hill
Thirlestane
KIRK YETHOLM
Coldsmouth Hill 414
The Bell
Easter Tor 438
Tom Tallon's Crag 353
White Law
Gains Law 319
Humbleton Buildings
Humbleton
Frogden
Lochside
Lochtower
Town Yetholm
Kirk Yetholm
Hethpool
Humbleton Hill
WOOLER
Linton Hill
Linton Covert
Yetholm Loch
Green Humbleton
343 Gt Hetha
Ell's Knowe
Newton Tors
Scaldhill
Bell's Valley
Coldberry Hill
Brown's Law
Caverton Mains
232 Yetholm Law
331 Staerough Hill
PENNINE WAY
397 Madam Law
537
Commonburn Ho
347
Fredden Hill
Earle Mill
Crookhouse
Primside Fm
Shereburgh
White Law
Hare Law
Wooler Common
Earle Whin
Haugh Head
Linton
LINTON CHURCH
273 High Side
Linton Burnfoot
327 Sunnyside Hill
Whitehall
NORTHUMBERLAND
Watch Hill
Earle
Caverton Mill
Morebattle Tofts
Wildgoose Hill
Loft Hill
Saughieside Hill 487
Great Moor
Middleton Hall
Morebattle
Latchly Hill 403
Steer Rig 411
Foulburn Gair
Steely Crag 365
Morebattle Mains
Wood Hill 334
Kaim Rig
Crookedshaws Hill
Kip Knowe
Blackhaggs Rigg
NORTHUMBERLAND
Preston Hill 526
Snear Hill
Coronation Wood
Brands Hill 319
Happy Valley
Coldgate Mill
North Middleton
Morebattle Hill 219
Black Hag 549
Coldburn
485 Coldburn Hill
Broadhope Hill 517
South Middleton
Grubbit Law
Cushat End 345
Percy Law
Cliftoncote
Black Hill
564 The Curr
Lambden Burn
Goldscleugh
NATIONAL
Cold Law
Rackside 337
Blakedean
Fawcett Shank
Blackseat Hill 461
Harrow Law
Hownam Grange
Attonburn
Mounthooly
MOUNTHOOLY
Whitton
Hownam Law 449
FORT
Blackdean Curr 501
681 The Schil
Scald Hill 549
Langleeford
Middleton Dean
Ilderton
Deanbrae Law
Braemoor Knowe 312
Elisheugh Hill
West Hill 717
Bizzle Crags
Mid Hill
PARK
Housey Crags
Middleton Crags
Hedgeley Wood
White Law 417
Mowhaugh
Langleeford Hope
Langlee Crags
Dod Hill
Chesterhouse Hill
Place Hill
Mow Law
Sourhope
Fasset Hill
Dod Hill 445
Hen Hole
815 The Cheviot
Threestoneburn Ho
Heddon Hill
Hownam Mains
The Kip
Auchope Cairn 726
714 Hedgehope Hill
Hownam Steeple
Wondrum Hill
Threestoneburn Wood
313 Thowliestane Hill
Hownam
Mallie Side
Cairn Hill 777
Hare Law 314
The Cheviot Hills
344 Windy Law
Berry Hills
Craik Moor
Mow Law 432
Swindon Hill
Score Head 582
Crookedsike Head
Scotsman's Knowe
652 Comb Fell
569 Dunmoor Hill
Cunyan Crags
Reaveley Hill
Reaveley Greens
Hare Law
Philogar Hill
Chatto
Tronshaw Hill
Blackbrough Hill
Crock Law
Cock Law
King's Seat
531 King's Seat
534 Gt Standrop
Five Stones
Dod Law
Green Knowe
Pudding Law 428
418 The Bank
Quickening Outer Cleugh
538 Shielcleugh Edge
Long Crag
Chatto Craig
Mid Hill
Butt Roads 524
Linhope Burn
Knock Hill
Greensidehill
Henshaw Law
399 Green Hill
Belshaw's Knowe
Lint Lands 510
Nagshead Knowe
High Cantle 482
Ritto Hill
Linhope
Ingram
Church Hope Hill
Mossy Law
Windy Gyle 619
High Bleakhope
Shill Moor Cairn 528
Meggrim's Knowe
Hartside Hill
Ewe Hill
395 Whitestone Hill
Cowie Law
Mozie Law 552
Beefstand Hill 562
Black Braes
Hazely Law 499
Uswayford
Bloodybush Edge 610
Humblemoor Hill
Cuthberthope Rig
Thorny Hill
507 Callaw Cairn
Little Ward Law
Bush Knowe
Little Dod
Het Hill
Wether Hill
Cochrane Pike 335
Broad Law
Cushat Law 615
Hangingshaw Hill
Standard Knowe
Lamb Hill 511
Beef Stand
483 Ward Law
Yarnspath Law
Green Knowe
Leafield Edge
Lumsden Hill
Loft Hill 460
543
Ewe Hill
483
Raeshaw Fell
Woden Law 422
Mid Hill
Wether Hill
Sting Head
548 Hogdon Law
Hart Law 341
Scraesburgh Fell 479
Broad Flow
Carlcroft Hill
Hindside Knowe
Middle Hill
Kidland Forest
Wether Cairn 563
High Knowes
Prendwick
Loddan Hill
Hunthall Hill
Wedder Hill 456
Green Law
477 Yearning Law
Carlcroft
Barrow Law 419
Nettlehope Hill
Sneer Hill
Inner Hill
Dryhope Hill
Wholhope Hill
St David's Cairn 504
Northfieldhead Hill
411 Hindhope Hill
Blindburn
Barrowburn
Hazeltonrig Hill
Alnham
Nether Hindhope
Black Halls 463
Deel's Hill 495
Brock's Holes
Lounges Knowe
Batailshiel Haugh
Saughy Hill
Peat Law 472
Inner Hill
Bleak Law
Old Hazeltonrig
Alnham Castle Fm
Fulhope
Bell Hill
Upper Hindhope
Hindhope Law
251
501
Shillhope Law
Harden Hill 327
Scrainwood
Brownhart Law 508
Saddlers Knowe 455
Dumb Hope
Wholehope Knowe
The Dodd 332
Gills Law
Cold Law 399
Ewe Hill
Whiteside Hill
Deerbush Burn
Copper Snout
Upper Coquetdale
Biddlestone Home Fm
Biddlestone Town Foot
Eilaw
Park Law
Chew Green
Loan Edge
Deerbush Hill
Bygate Hall Cotts
Middle Moor
Clennell Hill
Loundon Hill
Biddlestone
392 Lord's
Danger area

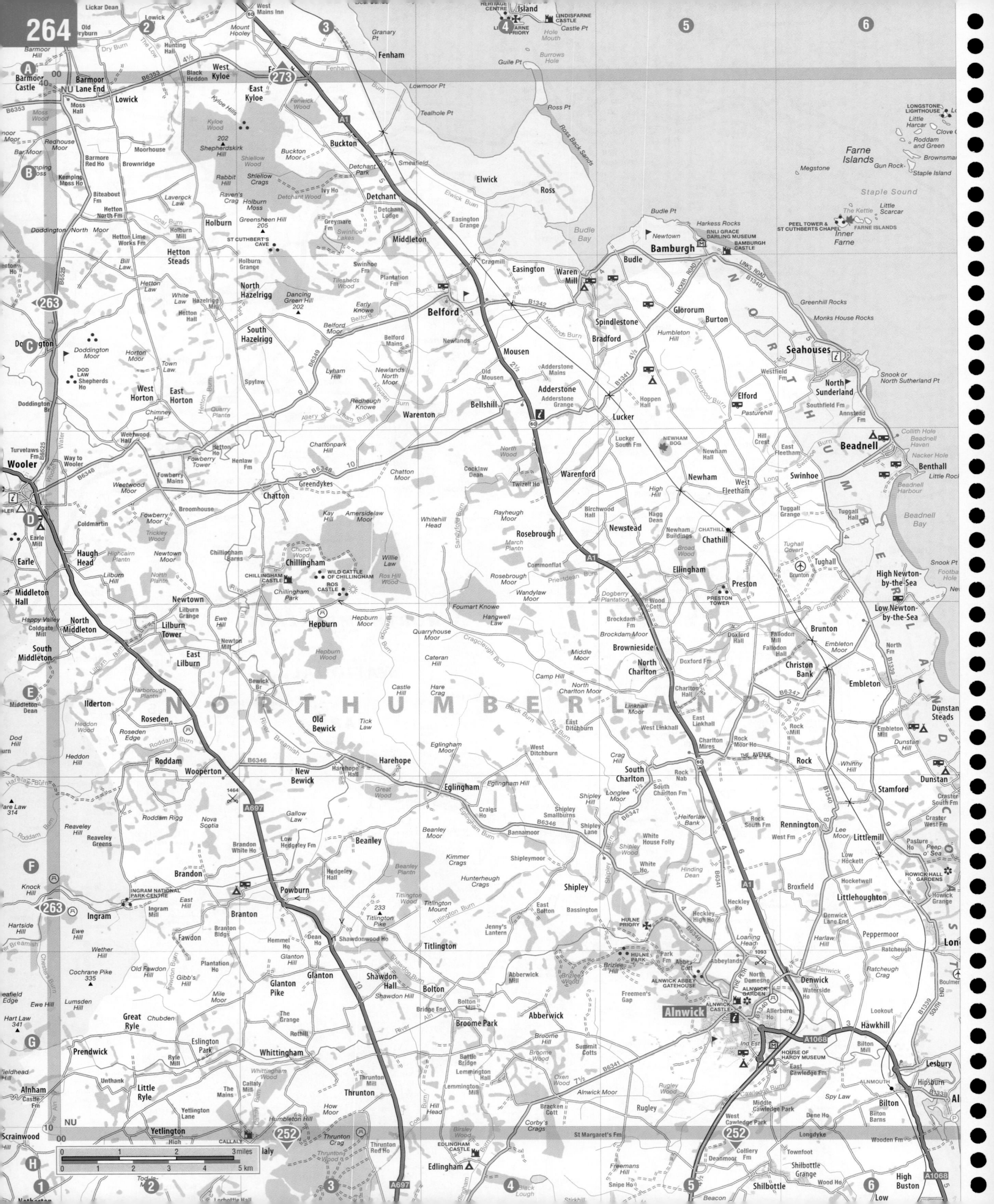

Lickar Dean
Lowick
West Mains Inn
Island
LINDISFARNE CASTLE
Castle Pt
Old Bryburn
Mount Hooley
Granary Pt
Hole Mouth
Barmoor Hill
Hunting Hall
Fenham
Burrows Hole
Guile Pt
Barmoor Castle
Barmoor Lane End
Black Heddon
West Kyloe
East Kyloe
Lowmoor Pt
Lowick
Moss Hall
Fenwick Wood
Tealhole Pt
Ross Pt
Kyloe Hills
Kyloe Wood
Shepherdskirk Hill
Redhouse Moor
Moorhouse
Buckton Moor
Buckton
Ross Back Sands
LONGSTONE LIGHTHOUSE
Little Harcar
Clove C
Roddam and Green
Farne Islands
Gun Rock
Brownsman
Staple Island
Megstone
Barmore Red Ho
Brownridge
Shiellow Wood
Smeafield
Detchant Park
Elwick
Ross
Kemping Moss Ho
Rabbit Hill
Shiellow Crags
Ivy Ho
Staple Sound
Biteabout Fm
Raven's Crag
Laverock Law
Holburn Moss
Detchant Wood
Detchant
Elwick Burn
The Kettle
Little Scarcar
Hetton North Fm
Coal Burn
Holburn
Greensheen Hill
Greymare Fm
Detchant Lodge
Easington Grange
Budle Pt
Harkess Rocks
PEEL TOWER & ST CUTHBERTS CHAPEL
FARNE ISLANDS
Doddington North Moor
Hetton Lime Works Fm
Holburn Mill
ST CUTHBERT'S CAVE
Swinhoe Lakes
Middleton
Budle Bay
Newtown
RNLI GRACE DARLING MUSEUM
BAMBURGH CASTLE
Inner Farne
Hetton Steads
Holburn Grange
Swinhoe Fm
Cragmill
Easington
Bamburgh
Budle
LINKS ROAD
Bill Law
Tileshed Wood
Plantation Fm
Waren Mill
LUCKER ROAD
Hetton Law
North Hazelrigg
White Law
Hazelrigg Mill
Dancing Green Hill
Early Knowe
Belford
B1342
Glororum
Greenhill Rocks
Hetton Hall
Belford Moor
Spindlestone
Burton
Monks House Rocks
Doddington
Doddington Moor
South Hazelrigg
Newlands
Mousen
Bradford
Humbleton Hill
Seahouses
Horton Moor
DOD LAW
Shepherds Ho
Town Law
Lyham Hill
Belford Mains
Newlands North Moor
Adderstone Mains
Westfield Fm
Old Mousen
Snook or North Sutherland Pt
North Sunderland
Spylaw
Adderstone
Crackerpool Burn
Elford
Hoppen Hall
Southfield Fm
Doddington Br
West Horton
East Horton
Redheugh Knowe
Bellshill
Adderstone Grange
Pasturehill
Annstead Fm
Chimney Hill
Quarry Plantn
Warenton
Lucker
Collith Hole
Beadnell Haven
Weetwood Hall
Hill Crest
East Fleetham
Beadnell
Turvelaws Fm
Lucker South Fm
NEWHAM BOG
Newham Hall
Nacker Hole
Hetton Ho
Chattonpark Hill
North Wood
Wooler
Way to Wooler
Fowberry Tower
Henlaw Fm
Cocklaw Dean
Warenford
Newham
Swinhoe
Benthall
Little Rock
Fowberry Mains
Chatton Moor
West Fleetham
Long Nanny
Weetwood Moor
Greendykes
Twizell Ho
High Hill
Beadnell Harbour
Chatton
Broomhouse
Birchwood Hall
Tuggall Grange
Tuggall Hall
Beadnell Bay
Fowberry Moor
Kay Hill
Amersidelaw Moor
Whitehill Head
Rayheugh Moor
Hagg Dean
Earle Mill
Coldmartin
Trickley Wood
Sandyford Burn
Rosebrough
Newstead
Newham Buildings
CHATHILL
Chathill
Tughall Covert
Newtown Moor
Chillingham Barns
Church Wood
March Plantn
Broad Wood
Tughall
Snook Pt
Football Hole
Haugh Head
Highcairn Plantn
Chillingham
Willie Law
Commonflat
Ellingham
Brunton
High Newton-by-the-Sea
Earle
Lilburn Hill
North Plantn
CHILLINGHAM CASTLE
WILD CATTLE OF CHILLINGHAM
Ros Hill Wood
Rosebrough Moor
Priestdean Burn
Middleton Hall
ROS CASTLE
Chillingham Park
Wandylaw Moor
Dogberry Plantation
Wood Cott
Preston
PRESTON TOWER
Newtown
Foumart Knowe
Low Newton-by-the-Sea
Lilburn Grange
Hepburn
Hangwell Law
Brockdam Fm
Happy Valley
Coldgate Mill
North Middleton
Lilburn Tower
Ewe Hill
Hepburn Moor
Brockdam Moor
Doxford Hall
Fallodon Mill
Brunton
Embleton Moor
Quarryhouse Moor
Cragcleugh Burn
Fallodon Hall
North Fm
Newton Mill
Hepburn Wood
Cateran Hill
Middle Moor
Brownieside
South Middleton
East Lilburn
North Charlton
Doxford Fm
Christon Bank
Camp Hill
North Charlton Moor
Charlton Hall
B6347
Embleton
Bewick Br
Castle Hill
Hare Crag
Harehope Burn
Middleton Dean
Ilderton
Harborough Plantn
Linkhall Moor
Embleton Burn
Dunstan Steads
N O R T H U M B E R L A N D
Roseden
Old Bewick
Tick Law
Black Burn
East Ditchburn
East Linkhall
Rock Mill
Embleton Fm
Heddon Wood
Roseden Edge
Roddam Burn
River Breamish
West Linkhall
Charlton Mires
Rock Moor Ho
Dunstan Hill
Dod Hill
Eglingham Moor
Red Burn
Heddon Hill
West Ditchburn
Crag Hill
THE AVENUE
Rock
Whinny Hill
Roddam
B6346
Harehope Hall
Harehope
South Charlton
Rock Nab
Dunstan
Harelaw Burn
Wooperton
New Bewick
Eglingham Hill
South Charlton Fm
Stamford
Craster South Fm
Great Wood
Eglingham
Longlee Moor
Shipley Hill
B1340
Hare Law
Gallow Law
Craigs Ho
Shipley Smallburns
Heiferlaw Bank
Rock South Fm
Rennington
Craster West Fm
Roddam Rigg
Nova Scotia
Bannamoor
Shipley Lane
Reaveley Hill
Reaveley Greens
Low Hedgeley Fm
Beanley Moor
Eglingham Burn
White House Folly
Lee Moor
Littlemill
Brandon White Ho
Beanley
Shipley Wood
West Fm
Pasture Hill
Peep o' Sea
Kimmer Crags
Low Hockett
Beanley Plantn
Shipleymoor
White Ho
Hinding Dean
Brandon
Hedgeley Hall
Hunterheugh Crags
Hocketwell
HOWICK HALL GARDENS
Knock Hill
INGRAM NATIONAL PARK CENTRE
Powburn
Shipley
Broxfield
Littlehoughton
East Hill
Titlington Wood
Titlington Mount
Titlington Burn
East Bolton
Howick Grange
Ingram
Ingram Mill
Branton
Bassington
Heckley Ho
Hartside Hill
Branton Bldgs
Titlington Pike
Shawdonwood Ho
Heckley High Ho
Denwick Lane End
Peppermoor
Ewe Hill
Fawdon
Hemmel Ho
Dean Ho
Jenny's Lantern
HULNE PRIORY
Harlaw Hill
Loaning Head
Wether Hill
Glanton Hill
Titlington
Ratcheugh
Breamish
Plantation Ho
HULNE PARK
Park Fm
Abbey Cott
Abbeylands
Cochrane Pike
Old Fawdon Hill
Gibb's Hill
Glanton
Shawdon Hall
Abberwick Mill
Brizlee Hill
Brizlee Wood
North Demesne
Denwick
Ratcheugh Crag
Fawdon Burn
Glanton Pike
Bolton
Shawdon Hill
ALNWICK ABBEY GATEHOUSE
ALNWICK GARDEN
Waterside Ho
Mile Moor
Freemen's Gap
Lumsden Hill
Chesters Burn
Ewe Hill
Bridge End
Bolton Mill
THE PETH
ALNWICK CASTLE
Allerburn Ho
Lookout
Great Ryle
Chubden
The Grange
Broome Park
Abberwick
Alnwick
Hawkhill
Hart Law
Rothill
River Aln
Broome Hill
Summit Cotts
A1068
Prendwick
Eslington Park
Ryle Mill
Whittingham
Battle Bridge
Broome Wood
Ind Est
HOUSE OF HARDY MUSEUM
Bilton Mill
Lemmington Hall
East Cawledge Fm
Lesbury
Fieldhead Hill
Unthank
Whittingham Wood
The Mains
Callaly Mill
Thrunton Mill
Oxen Wood
Alnwick Moor
Rugley Wood
ALNMOUTH
Hipsburn
Alnham
Little Ryle
Thrunton
Lemmington Mill
Bracken Cott
Cawledge Burn
Spy Law
Bilton
Castle Fm
Yetlington Lane
How Moor
Hill Head
Corby's Crags
Rugley
Middle Cawledge Park
Bilton Barns
Dene Ho
Humbleton Hill
West Cawledge Park
Scrainwood
Yetlington
CALLALY
Thrunton Crag
Birsley Wood
St Margaret's Fm
Longdyke
Wooden Fm
Thrunton Red Ho
EDLINGHAM CASTLE
Colliery Fm
Townfoot
Thrunton Wood
Edlingham
Freemans Hill
Deanmoor
Shilbottle Grange
High Buston
Snipe Ho
Shilbottle
Wood Ho
Black Lough
Beacon
Low
0 1 2 3 miles
0 1 2 3 4 5 km

N O R T H

S E A

Embleton
Bay

Castle Pt
DUNSTANBURGH
CASTLE
Queen
Margaret's Cove

Craster

Cullernose Pt

Howick

Rumbling Kern

Red
Stead
Howick
Haven

Sugar Sands

Low
Stead
Howdiemont Sands

ghoughton

Red Ends

Boulmer

Boulmer
Haven

Field
Ho

Seaton Pt

Marden Rocks

nmouth

Alnmouth
Bay

ongstone

Car

wton Pt

FIRTH OF CLYDE
INVERCLYDE
CLYDE-MUIRSHIEL REGIONAL PARK
NORTH AYRSHIRE
Island of Bute
Great Cumbrae Island
Little Cumbrae Island
Inverkip
Wemyss Bay
Skelmorlie
Upper Skelmorlie
Meigle
Routenburn
Largs
Fairlie
Millport
Portencross
Ardneil
West Kilbride
Seamill
Ardrossan
Saltcoats
Stevenston
Kilwinning
Irvine
Dalry
Kilbirnie
Beith
Lochwinnoch
Glengarnock
Longbar
Innellan
Toward
Castle Toward
Craigmore
Montford
Ascog
Kerrycroy
Scoulag
Piperhall
Kingarth
Kilchattan Bay
Meikle Kilchattan Butts
Garvock
Shielhill
Chapelhill
Dykesmains
Drakemyre
Gifffordland
Dalgarven
Girdle Toll
Dreghorn
BRODICK 0:55
0:35
0:10
276
275
255
256
257
NS
0 1 2 3 miles
0 1 2 3 4 5 km

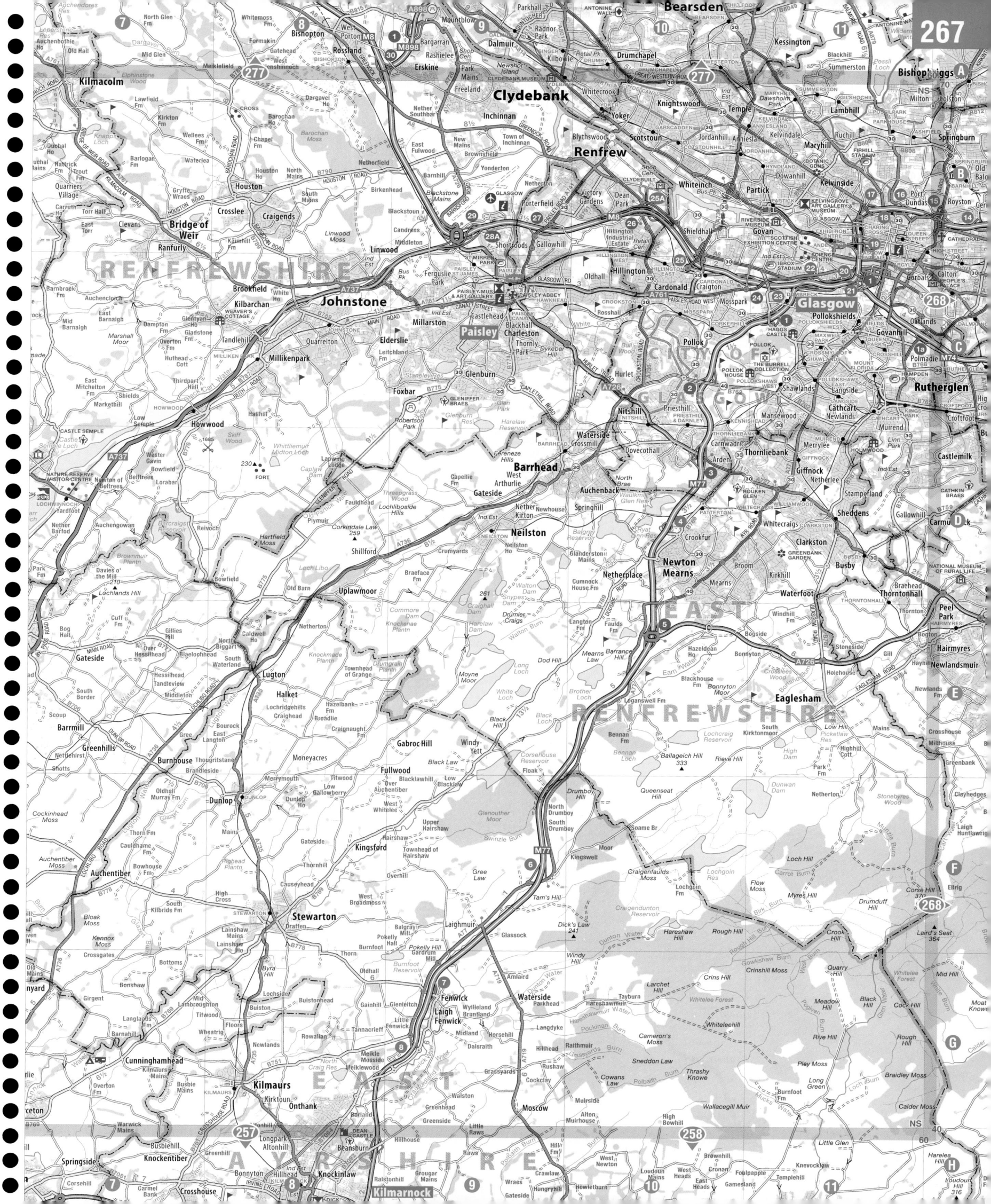
Bearsden
Clydebank
Renfrew
Paisley
Glasgow
Johnstone
RENFREWSHIRE
CITY OF GLASGOW
EAST RENFREWSHIRE
EAST AYRSHIRE
Rutherglen
Barrhead
Neilston
Newton Mearns
Eaglesham
Stewarton
Kilmaurs
Kilmarnock
Kilmacolm
Bridge of Weir
Houston
Erskine
Dalmuir
Drumchapel
Bishopbriggs
Lugton
Dunlop
Fenwick
Uplawmoor
Howwood
Kilbarchan
Elderslie
Busby
Clarkston
Giffnock
Thornliebank
Pollokshields
Govan
Partick
Knightswood
Scotstoun
Yoker
Bishopton
Linwood
Waterfoot
Carmunnock
Cunninghamhead
Knockentiber
Crosshouse
Springside
277
268
257
258

NORTH LANARKSHIRE
CITY OF GLASGOW
SOUTH LANARKSHIRE
Cadder
Jellyhill
Lenzie
Millersneuk
Auchinloch
Bridgend
Moodiesburn
Mollinsburn
Chryston
Muirhead
Bishopbriggs
Lumloch
Auchinairn
Balornock
Springburn
Barmulloch
Stepps
Garnkirk
Gartcosh
Millerston
Provanmill
Hogganfield
Riddrie
Royston
Germiston
Garthamlock
Craigend
Ruchazie
Easterhouse
Queenslie
Cranhill
Carntyne
Haghill
Greenfield
Springboig
Barlanark
Bridgeton
Calton
Shettleston
Barrachnie
Garrowhill
Baillieston
Parkhead
Braidfauld
Fullarton
Mount Vernon
Dalmarnock
Oatlands
Govanhill
Polmadie
Rutherglen
Carmyle
Broomhouse
Birkenshaw
Tannochside
Viewpark
Coatbridge
Langloan
Dundyvan
Old Monkland
Kirkshaw
Shawhead
Rosehall
Bargeddie
Airdrie
Coatdyke
Greenend
Cairnhill
Carnbroe
Calderbank
Chapelhall
Glenboig
Glenmavis
Gartsherrie
Riggend
Wattston
Stand
Plains
Caldercruix
Longriggend
Salsburgh
Newhouse
Holytown
New Stevenston
Mossend
Bellshill
Uddingston
Bothwell
Newton
Cambuslang
Flemington
Burnside
Castlemilk
Carmunnock
Westburn
Eastfield
Croftfoot
Blantyre
High Blantyre
Stonefield
Hamilton
Burnbank
Udston
Motherwell
Craigneuk
Wishaw
Newarthill
Cleland
Newmains
Coltness
Cambusnethan
Overtown
Netherton
Waterloo
Bogside
Law
Larkhall
Millheugh
Quarter
Limekilnburn
Ferniegair
Allanton
Dalserf
Rosebank
Ashgill
Stonehouse
Glassford
Strathaven
Sandford
Chapelton
Blackwood
Kirkmuirhill
Boghead
Auchenheath
Lesmahagow
Dillarbun
Crossford
Hazelbank
East Kilbride
Thorntonhall
Peel Park
College Milton
Calderwood
Saint Leonards
Hairmyres
Newlandsmuir
The Murray
Kelvin
Whitehills
Nerston
Auldhouse
Carnduff
Caldermill
Gilmourton
Stobieside
Whitelaw
Glasgow
Lanarkshire
0 1 2 3 miles
0 1 2 3 4 5 km

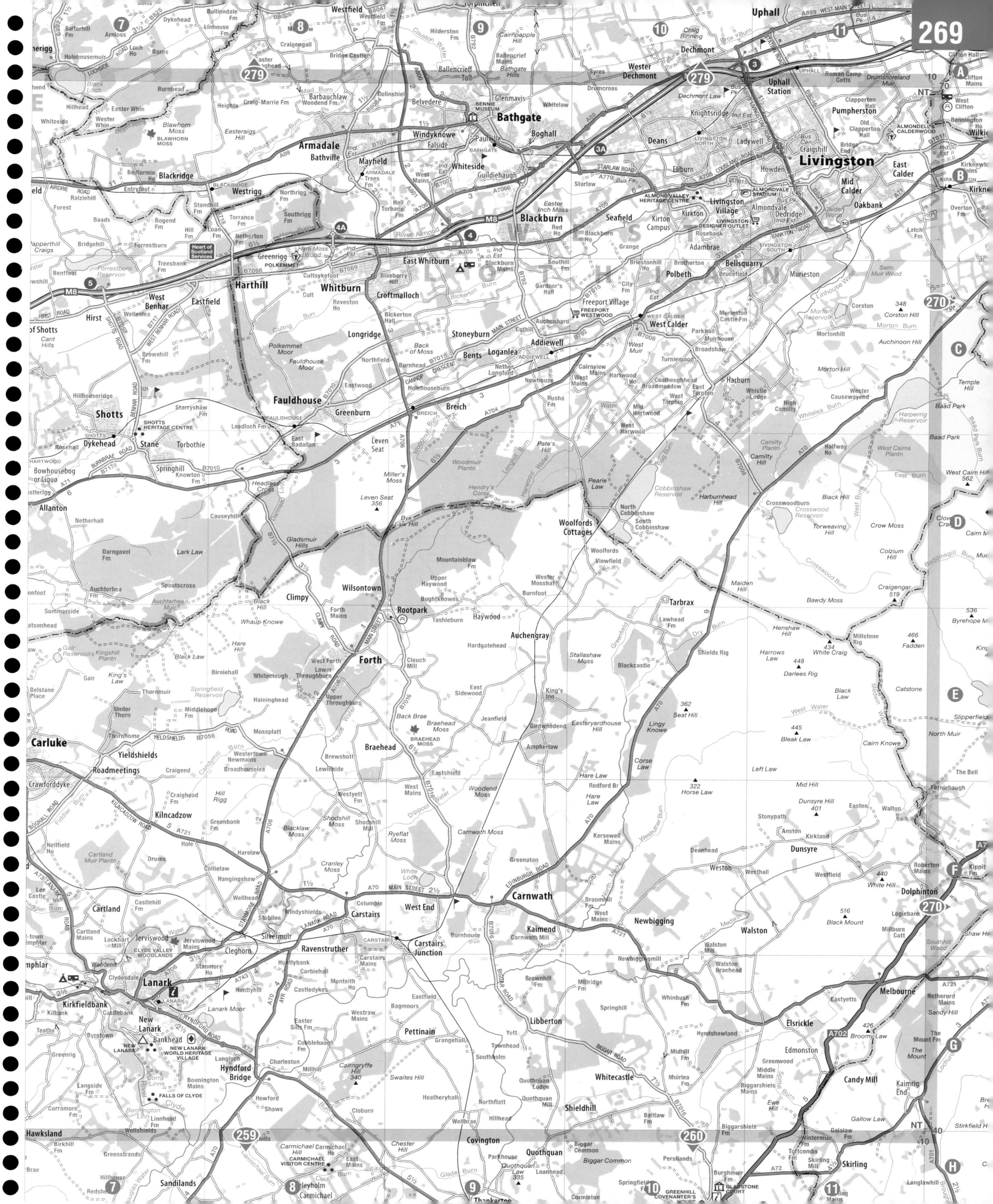
279
270
259
260
Westfield
Uphall
Dechmont
Wester Dechmont
Uphall Station
Bathgate
Armadale
Bathville
Mayfield
Windyknowe
Boghall
Deans
Ladywell
Livingston
East Calder
Mid Calder
Oakbank
Pumpherston
Blackridge
Westrigg
Blackburn
Seafield
Livingston Village
Kirkton Campus
Adambrae
Bellsquarry
Polbeth
Murieston
East Whitburn
Whitburn
Harthill
Eastfield
West Benhar
Hirst
Croftmalloch
Longridge
Stoneyburn
Bents
Loganlea
Addiewell
West Calder
Freeport Village
Fauldhouse
Greenburn
Breich
Shotts
Dykehead
Stane
Torbothie
Allanton
Woolfords Cottages
Wilsontown
Climpy
Rootpark
Haywood
Auchengray
Tarbrax
Forth
Carluke
Yieldshields
Roadmeetings
Kilncadzow
Braehead
Carnwath
Kaimend
Carstairs
Carstairs Junction
Ravenstruther
West End
Newbigging
Walston
Dunsyre
Dolphinton
Cartland
Lanark
New Lanark
Kirkfieldbank
Hyndford Bridge
Pettinain
Libberton
Whitecastle
Shieldhill
Covington
Quothquan
Elsrickle
Melbourne
Candy Mill
Skirling
Sandilands
Hawksland
Carmichael
Thankerton
LOTHIAN

270
Ratho Station
Ratho
Hermiston
Juniper Green
Currie
Balerno
Kirknewton
Wilkieston
Bonnington
Burnwynd
Sighthill
Morningside
Craiglockhart
Colinton
Liberton
Fairmilehead
Gilmerton
Dalkeith
Eskbank
Newbattle
Loanhead
Bilston
Straiton
Bonnyrigg and Lasswade
Roslin
Rosewell
Newtongrange
Gorebridge
Carrington
Temple
Penicuik
Silverburn
Nine Mile Burn
Carlops
Leadburn
Howgate
Auchendinny
Milton Bridge
Woodhouselee
Easter Howgate
West Linton
Romannobridge
Mountain Cross
Dolphinton
Blyth Bridge
Kirkurd
Melbourne
Drochil
Eddleston
Peebles
Kings Muir
Hallyne
Lyne
Cardrona
Kirkburn
Colquhar
Whim Farm
Cowdenburn
Waterheads
Halmyre Mains
Damside
PENTLAND HILLS REGIONAL PARK
Pentland Hills
SCOTTISH BORDERS
MIDLOTHIAN
TWEED VALLEY FOREST PARK
Moorfoot
EDINBURGH
CITY OF
280
269
260
261
0 1 2 3 miles
0 1 2 3 4 5 km

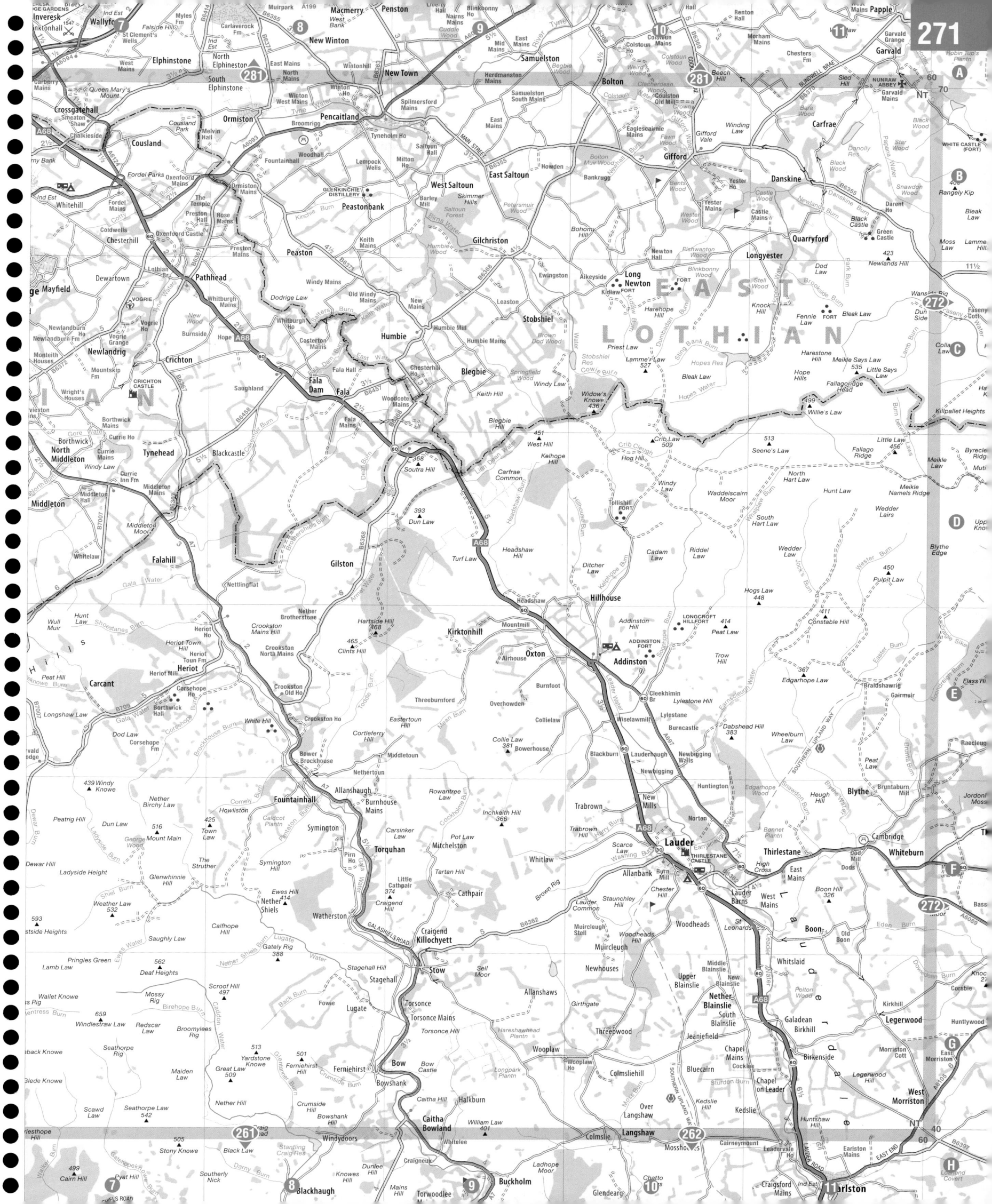
Inveresk
Wallyford
Macmerry
Penston
Pencaitland
Samuelston
Bolton
Garvald
Papple
Elphinstone
New Winton
New Town
Crossgatehall
Cousland
Ormiston
Gifford
Danskine
Carfrae
East Saltoun
West Saltoun
Peastonbank
Gilchriston
Quarryford
Longyester
Long Newton
Peaston
Pathhead
Mayfield
Dewartown
Chesterhill
Whitehill
Newlandrig
Crichton
Humbie
Stobshiel
Blegbie
Fala Dam
Fala
EAST
LOTHIAN
Tynehead
North Middleton
Middleton
Falahill
Gilston
Hillhouse
Kirktonhill
Oxton
Addinston
Heriot
Carcant
Fountainhall
Allanshaugh
Torquhan
Lauder
Thirlestane
Blythe
Whiteburn
Cambridge
Stow
Killochyett
Watherston
Lugate
Bow
Caitha Bowland
Langshaw
Legerwood
West Morriston
Boon
Buckholm
Blackhaugh
Earlston
Kedslie
Upper Blainslie
Nether Blainslie
Colmslie
Colmsliehill
Bluecairn
A68
A7
A6093
B6355
B6368
B6362
281
272
261
262
A
B
C
D
E
F
G
H
7
8
9
10
11
NT
60
70
40

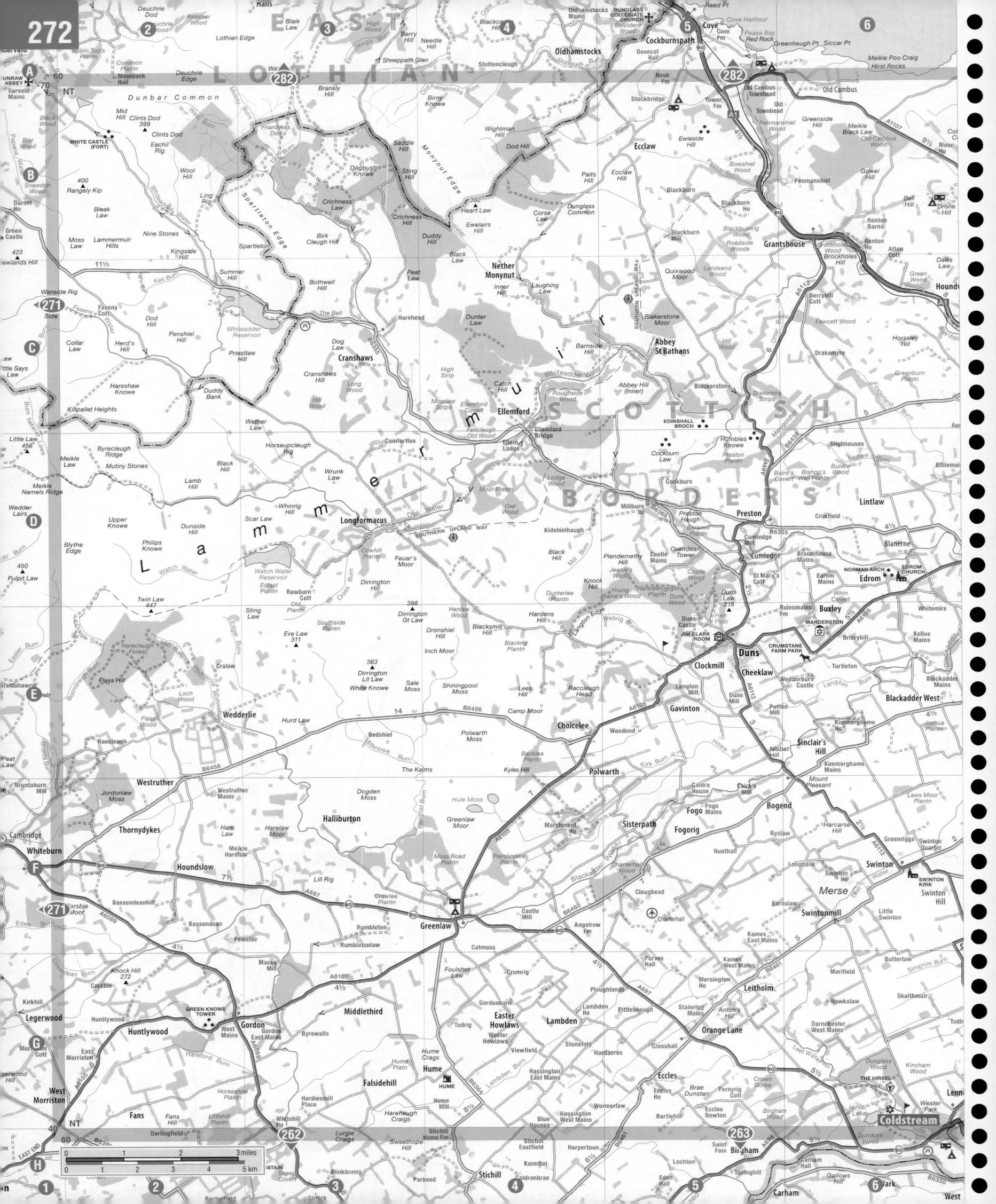

EAST LOTHIAN
SCOTTISH BORDERS
Lammermuir
Dunbar Common
Lammermuir Hills
Merse
Cockburnspath
Cove
Oldhamstocks
Old Cambus
Ecclaw
Grantshouse
Penmanshiel
Nether Monynut
Abbey St Bathans
Cranshaws
Ellemford
Longformacus
Preston
Lintlaw
Cumledge
Edrom
Buxley
Duns
Clockmill
Cheeklaw
Blackadder West
Gavinton
Choicelee
Sinclair's Hill
Wedderlie
Westruther
Polwarth
Fogo
Fogorig
Bogend
Sisterpath
Halliburton
Thornydykes
Whiteburn
Houndslow
Swinton
Swintonmill
Greenlaw
Leitholm
Orange Lane
Middlethird
Easter Howlaws
Lambden
Gordon
Huntlywood
Legerwood
Hume
Falsidehill
Eccles
Fans
West Morriston
Coldstream
Birgham
Stichill
Whiteadder Reservoir
Watch Water Reservoir
Twin Law 447
Southern Upland Way
Spartleton Edge
Monynut Edge
Langton Edge
A1
A697
A6105
A6112
A6089
B6355
B6456
B6461
B6364
271
282
262
263
0 1 2 3 miles
0 1 2 3 4 5 km

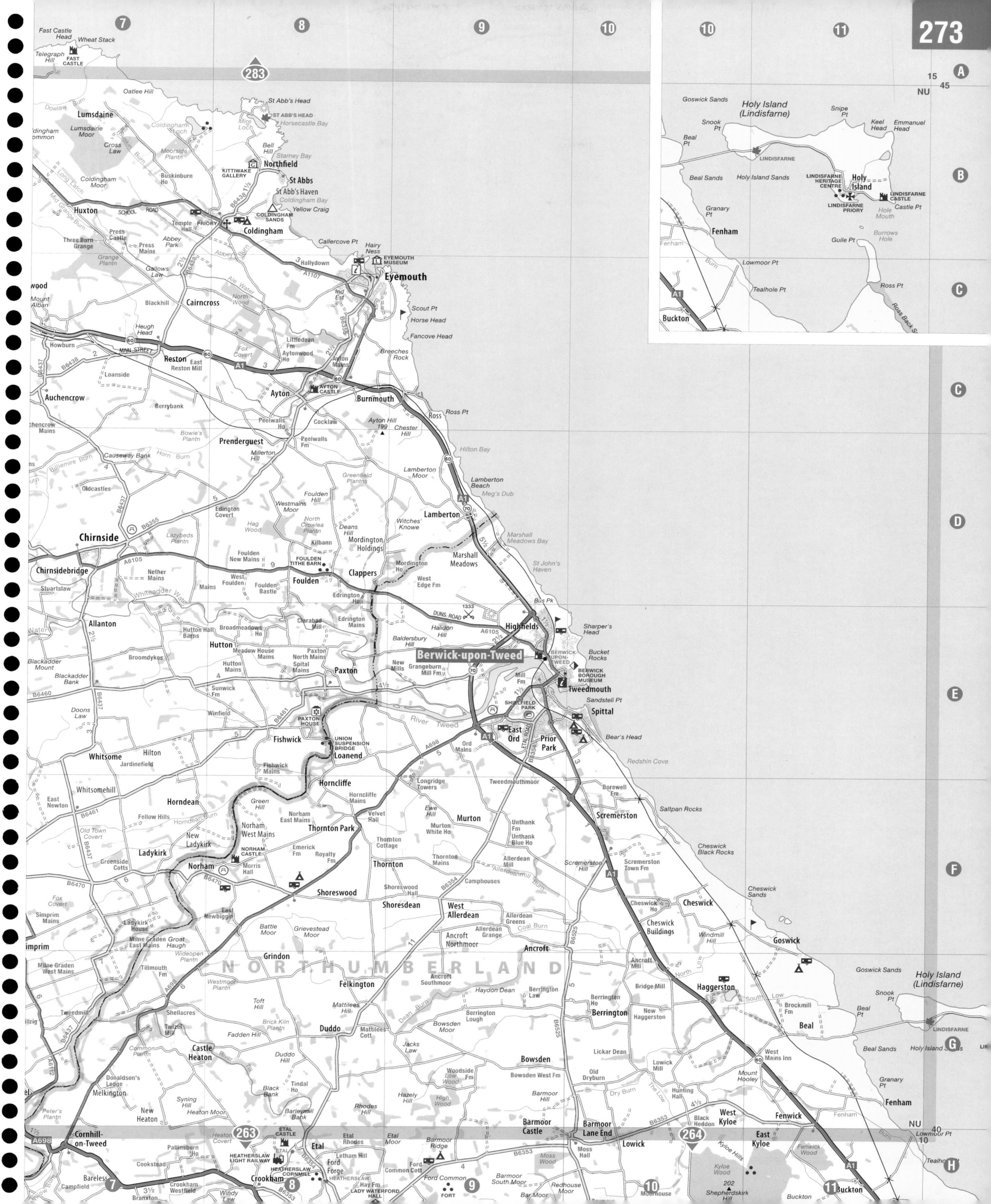

273
283
263
264
Fast Castle Head
Wheat Stack
Telegraph Hill
FAST CASTLE
Oatlee Hill
Lumsdaine
Lumsdaine Moor
Coldingham Loch
Cross Law
Moorside Plantn
St Abb's Head
ST ABB'S HEAD
Horsecastle Bay
Mire Loch
Bell Hill
Starney Bay
KITTIWAKE GALLERY
Northfield
St Abbs
St Abb's Haven
Coldingham Bay
Yellow Craig
COLDINGHAM SANDS
Buskinburn Ho
Coldingham Moor
Huxton
SCHOOL ROAD
Temple Hall
PRIORY
Coldingham
Three Burn Grange
Press Castle
Press Mains
Abbey Park
Grange Plantn
Gallows Law
Callercove Pt
Hairy Ness
EYEMOUTH MUSEUM
Hallydown
Eyemouth
Blackhill
Cairncross
Ale Water
North Wood
Ind Est
Scout Pt
Horse Head
Fancove Head
Heugh Head
Howburn
MAIN STREET
Reston
East Reston Mill
Fox Covert
Littledean Fm
Aytonwood Ho
Ayton Mains
Breeches Rock
Loanside
Auchencrow
AYTON CASTLE
Ayton
Burnmouth
Ross
Ross Pt
Berrybank
Peelwalls Ho
Cocklaw
Ayton Hill 199
Chester Hill
Prenderguest
Peelwalls Fm
Hilton Bay
Bowie's Plantn
Causeway Bank
Horn Burn
Millerton Hill
Billiemire Burn
Greenfield Plantns
Lamberton Moor
Lamberton Beach
Meg's Dub
Oldcastles
Foulden Hill
Westmains Moor
Lamberton
Edington Covert
Witches' Knowe
Hag Wood
North Crowlea Plantn
Deans Hill
Chirnside
Lazybeds Plantn
Kilbann
Mordington Holdings
Marshall Meadows Bay
Marshall Meadows
Foulden New Mains
FOULDEN TITHE BARN
Clappers
Mordington Ho
St John's Haven
Chirnsidebridge
Nether Mains
West Foulden
Foulden Bastle
Foulden
West Edge Fm
Stuartslaw
Whiteadder Water
Mains
Edrington Ho
Bus Pk
Allanton
Hutton Hall Barns
Broadmeadows Ho
Clarabad Mill
Edrington Mains
DUNS ROAD
1333
Highfields
Halidon Hill
Sharper's Head
Baldersbury Hill
Blackadder Mount
Broomdykes
Hutton
Meadow House Mains
Paxton North Mains
Spital Mains
Berwick-upon-Tweed
BERWICK-UPON-TWEED
Bucket Rocks
Hutton Mains
Paxton
New Mills
Grangeburn Mill Fm
BERWICK BOROUGH MUSEUM
Blackadder Bank
Sunwick Fm
Mill Fm
Tweedmouth
Sandstell Pt
Doons Law
Winfield
PAXTON HOUSE
SHIELFIELD PARK
Spittal
River Tweed
East Ord
Prior Park
Bear's Head
Fishwick
UNION SUSPENSION BRIDGE
Loanend
Ord Mains
ETAL ROAD
Hilton
Whitsome
Jardinefield
Redshin Cove
Fishwick Mains
Horncliffe
Longridge Towers
Tweedmouthmoor
Whitsomehill
Borewell Fm
East Newton
Horndean
Green Hill
Horncliffe Mains
Saltpan Rocks
Fellow Hills
Norham East Mains
Velvet Hall
Ewe Hill
Murton
Scremerston
Horndean Burn
Norham West Mains
Thornton Park
Murton White Ho
Unthank Fm
Unthank Blue Ho
Old Town Covert
New Ladykirk
Thornton Cottage
Cheswick Black Rocks
Ladykirk
NORHAM CASTLE
Emerick Fm
Royalty Fm
Thornton Mains
Allerdean Mill
Scremerston Hill
Scremerston Town Fm
Greenside Cotts
Norham
Morris Hall
Thornton
Allerdeanmill Burn
Camphouses
Shoreswood
Shoreswood Hall
Cheswick Sands
Fox Covert
East Newbiggin
Shoresdean
West Allerdean
Cheswick Ho
Cheswick
Simprim Mains
Ladykirk House
Battle Moor
Grievestead Moor
Allerdean Greens
Coal Burn
Cheswick Buildings
Windmill Hill
Goswick
Milne Graden East Mains
Groat Haugh
Allerdean Grange
Ancroft Northmoor
Ancroft
Wideopen Plantn
Grindon
NORTHUMBERLAND
Milne Graden West Mains
Tillmouth Fm
Ancroft Mill
Goswick Sands
Westmoor Plantn
Ancroft Southmoor
Felkington
Haydon Dean
Berrington Law
Bridge Mill
Haggerston
Holy Island (Lindisfarne)
Toft Hill
Berrington Ho
Snook Pt
Tweedmill
Shellacres
Mattilees Hill
Dean Burn
Berrington Lough
Berrington
New Haggerston
Brockmill Fm
Beal Pt
Beal
LINDISFARNE
Brick Kiln Plantn
Twizel Mill
Fadden Hill
Duddo
Mattilees Cott
Bowsden Moor
Castle Heaton
Common Plantn
River Till
Duddo Hill
Jacks Law
Lickar Dean
Beal Sands
Holy Island Sands
West Mains Inn
Bowsden
Lowick Mill
Donaldson's Lodge
Woodside Fm
Low Wood
Bowsden West Fm
Old Dryburn
Mount Hooley
Melkington
Tindal Ho
Black Bank
Dry Burn
The Low
Hunting Hall
Granary Pt
Syning Hill
Hazely Hill
High Wood
Barmoor Hill
New Heaton
Heaton Moor
Rhodes Hill
Barleymill Bank
Fenham
Peter's Plantn
Barmoor Castle
Barmoor Lane End
West Kyloe
Black Heddon
Fenwick
Cornhill-on-Tweed
Heaton Covert
ETAL CASTLE
Etal Rhodes
Etal Moor
Barmoor Ridge
Lowick
East Kyloe
Lowmoor Pt
Pallinsburn Ho
Etal
Letham Hill
Moss Wood
Moss Hall
Kyloe Hills
Fenwick Wood
Cookstead
HEATHERSLAW LIGHT RAILWAY
HEATHERSLAW CORNMILL
Ford
Ford Forge
Common Cott
Ford Cott
Kyloe Wood
Tealhowe Pt
Bareless
Campfield
Crookham Westfield
Crookham
HEATHERSLAW
Hay Fm
LADY WATERFORD HALL
Ford Common
FORT
Barmoor South Moor
Redhouse Moor
Bar Moor
Moorhouse
202
Shepherdskirk Hill
Buckton
Branxton
Windy Law
Goswick Sands
Holy Island (Lindisfarne)
Snipe Pt
Keel Head
Emmanuel Head
Snook Pt
Beal Pt
LINDISFARNE
Beal Sands
Holy Island Sands
LINDISFARNE HERITAGE CENTRE
Holy Island
LINDISFARNE CASTLE
LINDISFARNE PRIORY
Castle Pt
Granary Pt
Hole Mouth
Fenham
Burrows Hole
Guile Pt
Lowmoor Pt
Ross Pt
Tealhole Pt
Ross Back Sands
Buckton
NU

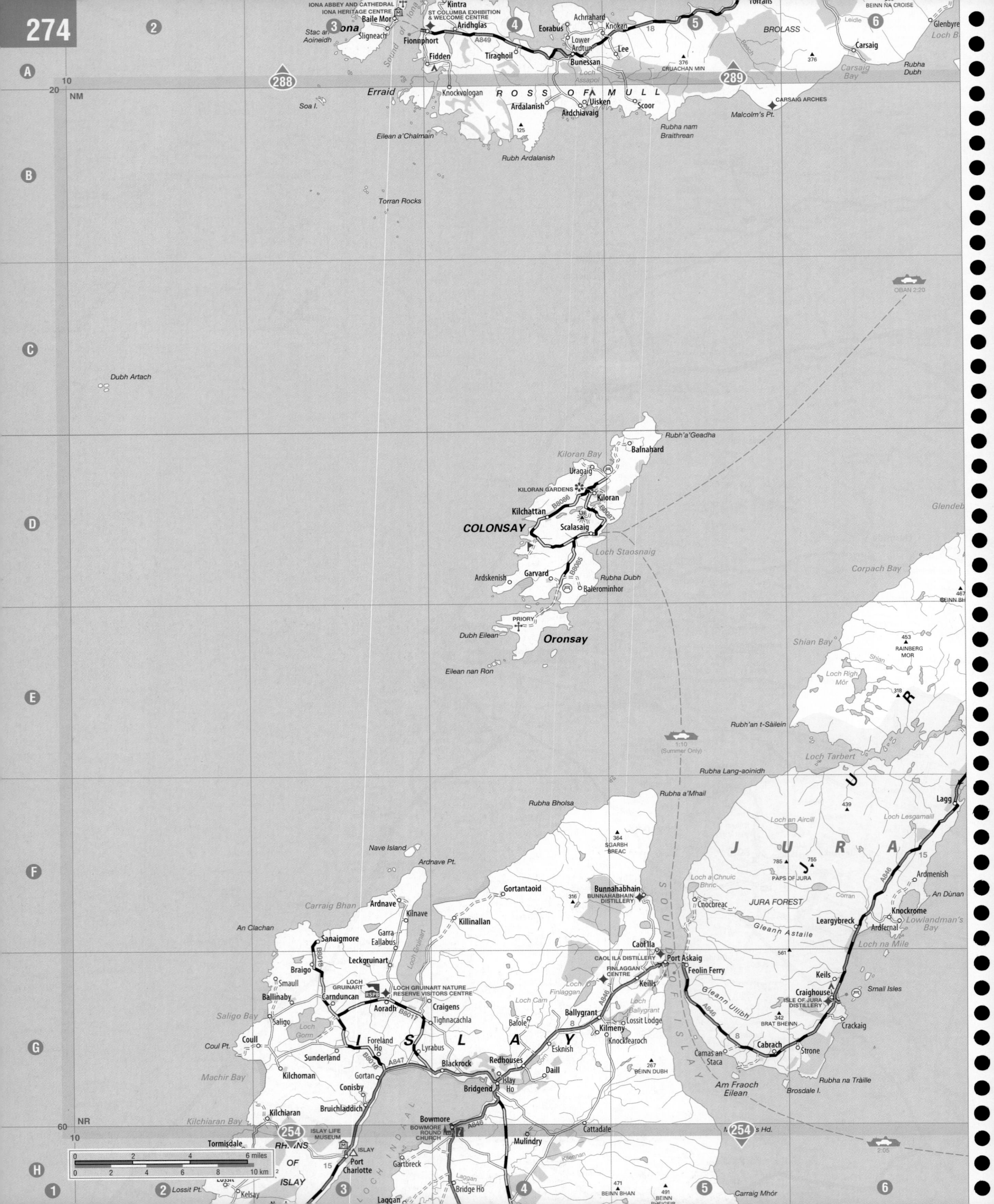
IONA ABBEY AND CATHEDRAL
IONA HERITAGE CENTRE
Baile Mor
Stac an Aoineidh
Sligneach
Kintra
ST COLUMBA EXHIBITION & WELCOME CENTRE
Aridhglas
Fionnphort
A849
Fidden
Tiraghoil
Eorabus
Achnahard
Knokan
Lower Ardtun
Lee
Bunessan
Loch Assapol
CRUACHAN MIN
BROLASS
BEINN NA CROISE
Leidle
Glenbyre
Carsaig
Carsaig Bay
Rubha Dubh
Erraid
Knockvologan
ROSS OF MULL
Soa I.
Ardalanish
Uisken
Ardchiavaig
Scoor
CARSAIG ARCHES
Malcolm's Pt.
Rubha nam Braithrean
Eilean a'Chalmain
Rubh Ardalanish
Torran Rocks
OBAN 2:20
Dubh Artach
Rubh'a'Geadha
Kiloran Bay
Balnahard
Uragaig
KILORAN GARDENS
Kiloran
Kilchattan
B8086
B8087
Scalasaig
COLONSAY
Loch Staosnaig
Ardskenish
Garvard
B8085
Rubha Dubh
Balerominhor
Glendeb
Corpach Bay
BEINN BH
PRIORY
Dubh Eilean
Oronsay
Eilean nan Ron
Shian Bay
RAINBERG MOR
Loch Righ Mòr
Rubh'an t-Sàilein
1:10 (Summer Only)
Loch Tarbert
Rubha Lang-aoinidh
Rubha a'Mhail
Rubha Bholsa
Lagg
Loch an Aircill
Loch Lesgamaill
SGARBH BREAC
Nave Island
Ardnave Pt.
JURA
PAPS OF JURA
Loch a Chnuic Bhric
Cnocbreac
JURA FOREST
Corran
Ardmenish
An Dùnan
A846
Gortantaoid
Bunnahabhain
BUNNAHABHAIN DISTILLERY
Carraig Bhan
Ardnave
Kilnave
Killinallan
SOUND OF ISLAY
Gleann Astaile
Leargybreck
Knockrome
Ardfernal
Lowlandman's Bay
Loch na Mile
An Clachan
Sanaigmore
Garra Eallabus
Loch Gruinart
Caol Ila
CAOL ILA DISTILLERY
Port Askaig
Feolin Ferry
FINLAGGAN CENTRE
Braigo
Leckgruinart
Smaull
LOCH GRUINART
LOCH GRUINART NATURE RESERVE VISITORS CENTRE
RSPB
Keills
Loch Finlaggan
Gleann Ullibh
Keils
Craighouse
ISLE OF JURA DISTILLERY
Small Isles
Ballinaby
Carnduncan
Aoradh
Craigens
Loch Cam
Ballygrant
Loch Ballygrant
Lossit Lodge
B8017
Tighnacachla
Saligo Bay
Saligo
Loch Gorm
Balole
Kilmeny
BRAT BHEINN
Crackaig
ISLAY
Foreland Ho
Lyrabus
Knocklearoch
Coull
Coul Pt.
Sunderland
A847
Blackrock
Redhouses
Esknish
Cabrach
Strone
Camas an Staca
Kilchoman
Gortan
Daill
BEINN DUBH
Rubha na Tràille
Machir Bay
Conisby
Bridgend
Islay Ho
Am Fraoch Eilean
Brosdale I.
Kilchiaran
Bruichladdich
LOCH INDAAL
Kilchiaran Bay
Bowmore
BOWMORE ROUND CHURCH
A846
Cattadale
Tormisdale
RHINNS OF ISLAY
ISLAY LIFE MUSEUM
ISLAY
Port Charlotte
Mulindry
Gartbreck
Kilennan
Laggan
Bridge Ho
Lossit Pt.
Kelsay
Laggan
BEINN BHAN
Carraig Mhór
2:05
0 2 4 6 miles
0 2 4 6 8 10 km
NM
NR
288
289
254

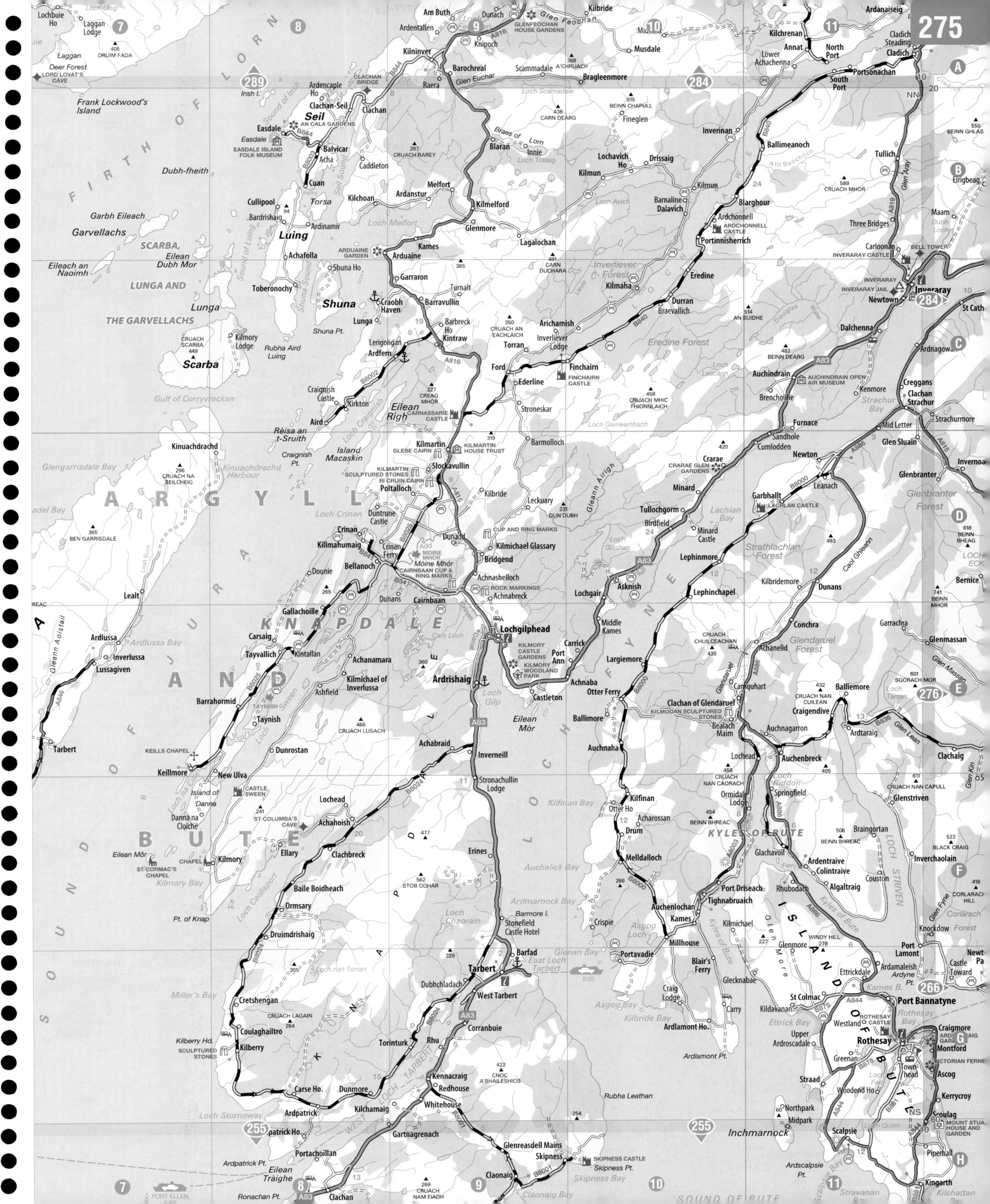
Lochgilphead
Inveraray
Tarbert
Rothesay
Port Bannatyne
Ardrishaig
FIRTH OF LORN
SOUND OF JURA
KNAPDALE
ARGYLL AND BUTE
LOCH FYNE
KYLES OF BUTE
ISLAND OF BUTE
Luing
Seil
Shuna
Scarba
Lunga
Garvellachs
Inchmarnock
Kilmartin
Crinan
Kilmelford
Minard
Furnace
Strachur
Tighnabruaich
Portavadie
Kennacraig
Skipness
Claonaig
Lochgair
Otter Ferry
Kilfinan
Colintraive
289
284
276
266
255

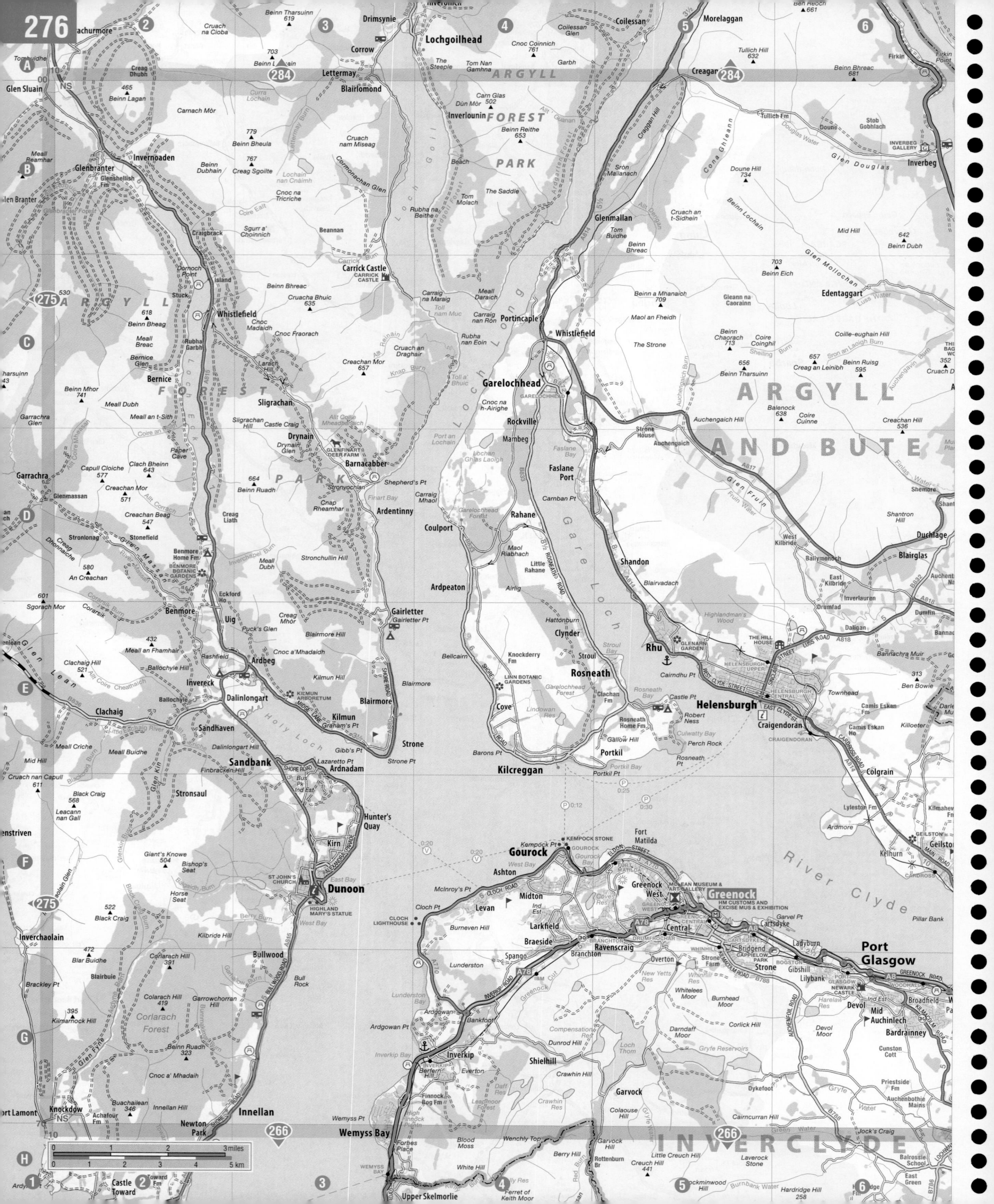
A
B
C
D
E
F
G
H
1
2
3
4
5
6
284
275
266
ARGYLL
FOREST
PARK
ARGYLL
AND BUTE
INVERCLYDE
River Clyde
Holy Loch
Loch Long
Gare Loch
Loch Eck
Loch Goil
Lochgoilhead
Drimsynie
Corrow
Lettermay
Blairlomond
Carrick Castle
Coilessan
Morelaggan
Creagan
Inverbeg
Glen Douglas
Glenmallan
Edentaggart
Portincaple
Whistlefield
Garelochhead
Rockville
Mambeg
Faslane Port
Rahane
Shandon
Clynder
Rosneath
Rhu
Helensburgh
Craigendoran
Colgrain
Kilcreggan
Cove
Portkil
Gourock
Ashton
Greenock
Port Glasgow
Ravenscraig
Braeside
Larkfield
Levan
Inverkip
Wemyss Bay
Dunoon
Kirn
Hunter's Quay
Sandbank
Ardnadam
Kilmun
Strone
Blairmore
Ardentinny
Gairletter
Barnacabber
Drynain
Sligrachan
Invernoaden
Glenbranter
Whistlefield
Benmore
Uig
Ardbeg
Invereck
Dalinlongart
Clachaig
Sandhaven
Stronsaul
Innellan
Bullwood
Knockdow
Newton Park
Castle Toward
Inverchaolain
Glen Sluain
Garrachra
Bernice
Colarach Forest
Shielhill
Garvock
Skelmorlie
Upper Skelmorlie
Devol
Mid Auchinlech
Bardrainney
Broadfield
Strone
Gibshill
Lilybank
Ladyburn
Cartsdyke
Overton
Midton
Spango
Branchton
Greenock West
Central
Kempock Stone
Fort Matilda
Cloch Lighthouse
Cloch Pt
Lunderston
Ardgowan
Bankfoot
Everton
Dunrod Hill
Crawhin Hill
Cairncurran Hill
Auchenbothie Mains
Gryfe Reservoirs
Loch Thom
0 1 2 3 miles
0 1 2 3 4 5 km

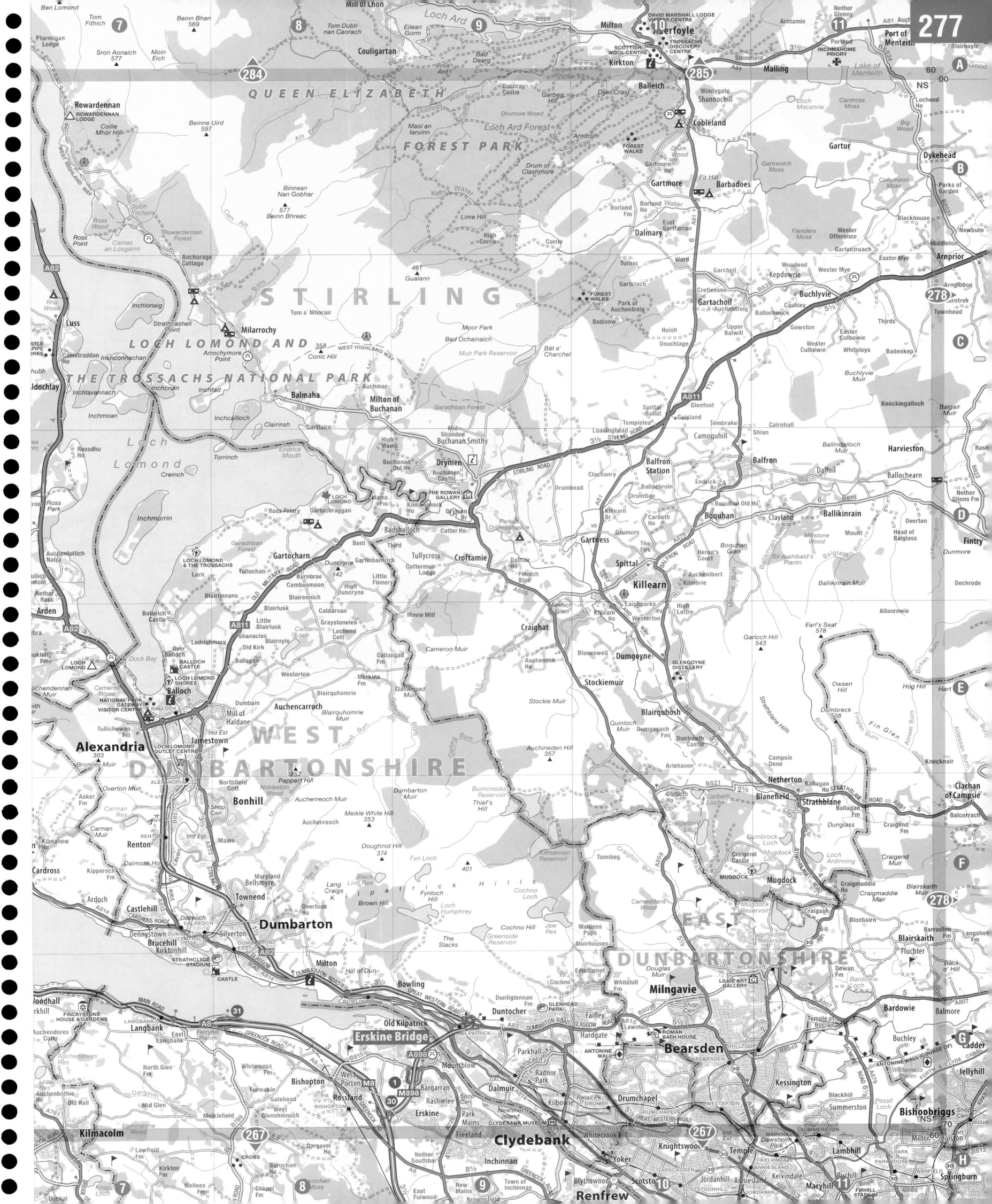
Ben Lomond
Aberfoyle
Port of Menteith
Lake of Menteith
Milton
Kirkton
Malling
Couligartan
Loch Ard
Rowardennan
QUEEN ELIZABETH FOREST PARK
Loch Ard Forest
Balleich
Cobleland
Gartmore
Barbadoes
Gartur
Dykehead
Dalmary
Arnprior
Kepdowrie
Buchlyvie
Gartachoil
STIRLING
LOCH LOMOND AND THE TROSSACHS NATIONAL PARK
Luss
Milarrochy
Balmaha
Milton of Buchanan
Inchmurrin
Loch Lomond
Drymen
Balfron Station
Balfron
Ballikinrain
Fintry
Boquhan
Gartness
Spittal
Killearn
Croftamie
Gartocharn
Badshalloch
Tullycross
Craighat
Dumgoyne
Stockiemuir
Blairquhosh
Balloch
Alexandria
Jamestown
WEST DUNBARTONSHIRE
Bonhill
Renton
Cardross
Dumbarton
Castlehill
Kilpatrick Hills
Netherton
Blanefield
Strathblane
Mugdock
EAST DUNBARTONSHIRE
Milngavie
Bearsden
Bowling
Milton
Old Kilpatrick
Erskine Bridge
Duntocher
Clydebank
Dalmuir
Erskine
Bishopton
Langbank
Kilmacolm
Drumchapel
Knightswood
Yoker
Renfrew
Kessington
Bardowie
Bishopbriggs
Lambhill
Maryhill
Springburn
Clachan of Campsie
Harvieston
Arden
Duck Bay
Dennystown
Brucehill
Silverton
Townend
Inchinnan
Scotstoun
Jordanhill

Doune
Deanston
Dunblane
Thornhill
Ruskie
Boquhapple
Blair Drummond
Flanders Moss
Dykehead
Bridge of Allan
Sunnylaw
Badgergate
Blairlogie
Menstrie
Causeway-head
Blair Drummond Moss
Arnprior
Kippen
Cauldhame
Glentirranmuir
Old Leckie
Gargunnock
Raploch
Cambuskenneth
Riverside
Stirling
Cambusbarron
Torbrex
Braehead
Fallin
Gargunnock Hills
Carleatheran 485
Lees Hill 411
Broomridge
St Ninians
Bannockburn
STIRLING
Harviestoun
Stronend 511
Fintry Hills
Culcreuch Castle
Touchadam Muir
Earlsburn Reservoirs
North Third Reservoir
Stirling Services
Craigend
Plean
Fintry
Easter Cringate
Cairnoch Hill 413
Craigengelt Hill
Loch Coulter Reservoir
Torwood
Dungoil 424
Campsie Muir
Carron Valley Reservoir
Muirmill
Carron Bridge
Dunipace
Denny
Campsie Fells
Meikle Bin 570
Little Bin
Kilsyth Hills
Tomtain 453
Garrel Hill 459
Lecket Hill 547
Birkenburn Reservoir
Fankerton
Stoneywood
Head of Muir
Bankhead
Bonnybridge
Dennyloanhead
Clachan of Campsie
Cort-ma Law 531
EAST DUNBARTONSHIRE
Kilsyth Hills
Banknock
Longcroft
Haggs
Castlecary
Balgrochan
Lennoxtown
Queenzieburn
Kilsyth
Banton
Colzium House
High Bonnybridge
Greenhill
FALKIRK
Milton of Campsie
Auchenreoch
Twechar
Croy
Dullatur
Cumbernauld Village
Abronhill
Old Inns Services
Birdston
Kirkintilloch
Balloch
Cumbernauld
Jawcraig
Torrance
Westfield
Condorrat
Luggiebank
Blairskaith
Bardowie
Balmore
Lenzie
Cadder
Jellyhill
Bishopbriggs
Auchinloch
Mollinsburn
Bridgend
Moodiesburn
Chryston
NORTH LANARKSHIRE
Riggend
Wattston
Greengairs
Longriggend
Lumloch
Muirhead
Stand
Glenboig
Marnock
Garnkirk
Springburn
Caldercruix
0 1 2 3 miles
0 1 2 3 4 5 km

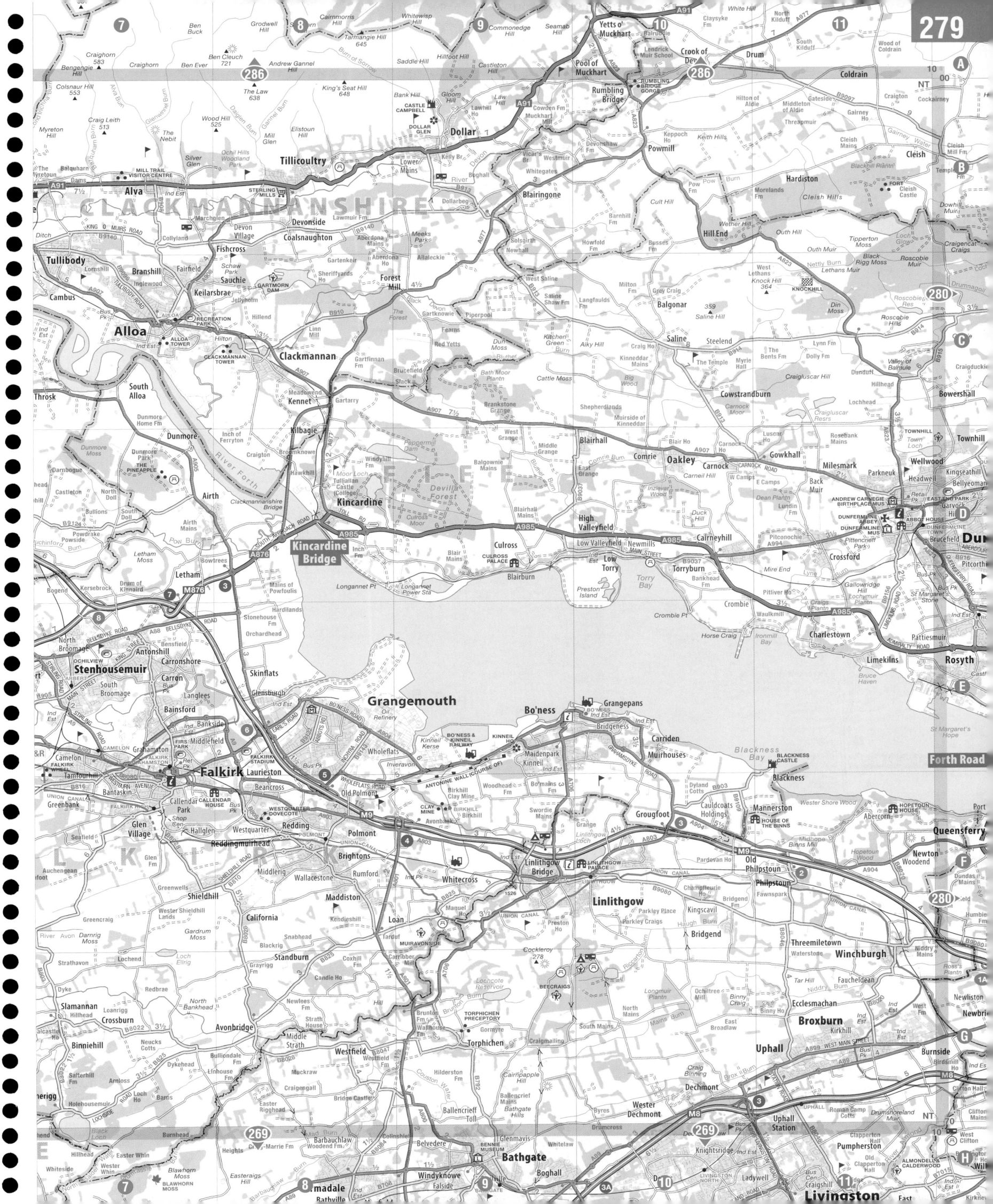
Ben Buck
Grodwell Hill
Cairnmorris Hill
Whitewisp Hill
Commonedge Hill
Seamab Hill
Yetts o' Muckhart
White Hill
Claysyke Fm
North Kilduff
Craighorn 583
Ben Cleuch 721
Tarmangie Hill 645
South Kilduff
Wood of Coldrain
Bengengie Hill
Craighorn
Ben Ever
Andrew Gannel Hill
Saddle Hill
Hillfoot Hill
Castleton Hill
Pool of Muckhart
Crook of Devon
Drum
Coldrain
286
Colsnaur Hill 553
The Law 638
King's Seat Hill 648
Bank Hill
Gloom Hill
Law Hill
Rumbling Bridge
Castle Campbell
Dollar Glen
Dollar
Craig Leith 513
Myreton Hill
The Nebit
Wood Hill 525
Mill Glen
Elistoun Hill
Cowden Fm
Muckhart Mill
Hilton of Aldie
Middleton of Aldie
Gateside
Craigton
Gairney Ho
Cockairney
Threapmuir
Keppoch Ho
Keith Hills
Cleish Mains
Cleish
Powmill
Devonshaw Fm
Silver Glen
Ochil Hills Woodland Park
Tillicoultry
Lower Mains
Kelly Br
Vicar's Br
Westmuir
Whitegates
Boghall
Mill Trail Visitor Centre
Alva
Sterling Mills
Blairingone
Hardiston
Morelands Fm
Cleish Hills
Cleish Castle
CLACKMANNANSHIRE
Dollarbeg
Marchglen
Devonside
Lawmuir Fm
Cult Hill
Barnhill Fm
Devon Village
Coalsnaughton
Aberdona Mains
Meeks Park
Solsgirth
Newhall
Howfold Fm
Busses Fm
Hill End
Wether Hill
Outh Hill
Tipperton Moss
Craigencat Craigs
Tullibody
Fishcross
Allaleckie
Outh Muir
Lornshill
Branshill
Fairfield
Schaw Park
Sauchie
Gartmorn Dam
Gartenkeir
Sheriffyards Ho
Forest Mill
West Saline
Saline Shaw Fm
Milton Fm
Grey Craig
West Lethans
Knock Hill 364
Knockhill
Black Rigg Moss
Roscobie Muir
Lethans Muir
Cambus
Keilarsbrae
Jellyholm
Langfaulds Fm
Balgonar
Saline Hill 359
Din Moss
Roscobie Res
280
Alloa
Recreation Park
Hillend
Linn Mill
Gartknowie
Piperpool
Roscobie Hills
Alloa Tower
Hilton
Clackmannan Tower
Clackmannan
Fearns
Red Yetts
Dun Moss
Kitchen Green
Alky Hill
Craig Ho
Saline
Steelend
Lynn Fm
Kinneddar Mains
The Temple
Myrie Hall
The Bents Fm
Dolly Fm
Valley of Balmule
Gartfinnan Fm
Brucefield
Slack
Bath Moor Plantn
Cattle Moss
Big Wood
Craigluscar Hill
Dunduff
Hillhead
Bowershall
South Alloa
Throsk
Meadowend
Kennet
Gartarry
Brankstone Grange
Shepherdlands
Muirside of Kinneddar
Cowstrandburn
Carnock Moor
Lochhead
Dunmore Home Fm
Inch of Ferryton
Kilbagie
Peppermill Dam
West Grange
Blairhall
Craigluscar Resrs
Rosebank Mains
Townhill
Dunmore Moss
Dunmore
Dunmore Park
The Pineapple
River Forth
Craigton
Broomknowe
Windyhill Fm
Middle Grange
Balgownie Mains
Comrie
Oakley
Blair Ho
Carnock
Gowkhall
Luscar Ho
Milesmark
Parkneuk
Wellwood
Headwell
Kingseathill
Bellyeoman
FIFE
Darnbogue
Hawkhill
Moor Loch
Tulliallan Castle (College)
Devilla Forest
East Grange
Carneil Hill
W Camps
E Camps
Back Muir
Castleton
North Doll
Airth
Clackmannanshire Bridge
Kincardine
Inzievar Wood
Dean Plantn
Lundin Fm
Andrew Carnegie Birthplace Mus
East End Park
Garvock
Bullions
South Doll
Culross Moor
Blairhall Mains
High Valleyfield
Duck Hill
Dunfermline Abbey
Dunfermline Mus
Abbot House
Airth Mains
Powdrake
Powside
Kincardine Bridge
Culross
Culross Palace
Low Valleyfield
Newmills
Cairneyhill
Pitconochie
Pittencrieff Park
Brucefield
Letham Moss
Bowtrees
Inch Fm
Blair Mains
Low Torry
Torryburn
Crossford
Mire End
Pitcorthie
Letham
Bogend
Kersebrock
Drum of Kinnaird
Mains of Powfoulis
Longannet Pt
Longannet Power Sta
Blairburn
Preston Island
Torry Bay
Bankhead Fm
Gallowridge Hill
Lochmuir Plantn
St Margaret's Stone
Hardilands
Crombie
Pitliver Ho
Craigs Plantn
North Broomage
Stonehouse Fm
Orchardhead
Crombie Pt
Waulkmill
Charlestown
Pattiesmuir
Antonshill
Bensfield
Horse Craig
Ironmill Bay
Limekilns
Rosyth
Ochilview
Stenhousemuir
Carronshore
Skinflats
Bruce Haven
Carron
South Broomage
Langlees
Glensburgh
Grangemouth
Grangepans
Bainsford
Oil Refinery
Bo'ness
Bridgeness
Carriden
Bankside
Firs Park
Middlefield
Grahamston
Falkirk Stadium
Wholeflats
Bo'ness & Kinneil Railway
Kinneil Ho
Kinneil Kerse
Maidenpark
Kinneil
Muirhouses
Blackness Bay
Blackness Castle
Blackness
St Margaret's Hope
Forth Road
Camelon
Falkirk Wheel
Tamfourhill
Falkirk
Laurieston
Inveravon
Antonine Wall (course of)
Beancross
Old Polmont
Woodhead Fm
Bo'mains Fm
Dyland Cotts
Bantaskin
Greenbank
Callendar Park
Callendar House
Westquarter Dovecote
Birkhill Clay Mine
Birkhill
Swordie Mains
Cauldcoats Holdings
Mannerston
House of the Binns
Wester Shore Wood
Hopetoun House
Abercorn
Port
Seafield
Glen Village
Hallglen
Westquarter
Redding
Avonbank
Grange
Linlithgow Loch
Grougfoot
Queensferry
Midhope
Binns Mill
Reddingmuirhead
Polmont
Newton
Woodend
Hopetoun Wood
Glen Fm
Brightons
Linlithgow Bridge
Linlithgow Palace
Pardovan Ho
Old Philpstoun
Auchengean
Middlerig
Wallacestone
Rumford
Whitecross
Philpstoun
Fawnspark
Dundas Mains
Greenwells
Shieldhill
Maddiston
Linlithgow
Champfleurie Ho
Bridgend Fm
Wester Shieldhill Lands
California
Manuel Ho
Parkley Place
Parkley Craigs
Kingscavil
Kendieshill
Loan
Preston Ho
Greencraig
Gardrum Moss
Snabhead
Tarduf
Muiravonside
Bridgend
Threemiletown
Darnrig Moss
Blackrig
Cockleroy 278
Waterstone
Winchburgh
Strathavon
Lochend
Loch Elrig
Standburn
Coxhill Fm
Carribber Mill
Niddry Mains
Grayrigg Fm
Candie Ho
Lochcote Reservoir
Beecraigs
Longmuir Plantn
Ochiltree Mill
Tar Hill
Faucheldean
Dyke
Redbrae
Binny Craig
Binny Ho
Newliston
Slamannan
Loanrigg
North Bankhead
Newlees Fm
Brunton Fm
Torphichen Preceptory
North Mains
Ecclesmachan
Newbridge
Hillhead
Crossburn
Avonbridge
Strath House
Walhouse
Gormyre
South Mains
East Broadlaw
Broxburn
Kirkhill
Binniehill
Neucks Cotts
Middle Strath
Torphichen
Craigmailing
Uphall
Burnside
Westfield
Bullionslade Fm
Dykehead
Linhouse Fm
Muckraw
Hilderston Fm
Cairnpapple Hill
Craig Binning
Dechmont
Birdsmill Ho
Clifton Hall
Sattenhill Fm
Arnloss
Loch Ho
Barns
Craigengall
Ballencrief Mains
Bathgate Hills
Holehousemuir
Easter Rigghead
Bridge Castle
Ballencrieff Toll
Byres
Wester Dechmont
Uphall Station
Roman Camp Cotts
Drumshoreland Muir
Clifton Mains
Burnhead
Mid Burn
Barbauchlaw Woodend Fm
Colinshiel
Glenmavis
Bennie Museum
Whitelaw
Drumcross
Clapperton Hall
Pumpherston
West Clifton
269
Hillhead
Easter Whin
Wester Whin
Whiteside
Blawhorn Moss
Heights
Easteraigs Hill
Belvedere
Bathgate
Boghall
Knightsridge
Old Clapperton Hall
Almondell & Calderwood
Windyknowe
Falside
Ladywell
Craigshill
Livingston North
Livingston
Armadale
Bathville

Loch Leven
Leslie
Glenrothes
Markinch
Milton of Balgonie
Balcurvie
Windygates
Scotlandwell
Auchmuirbridge
Kinglassie
Coaltown of Balgonie
Stenton
Thornton
Gairney Bank
Ballingry
Lochore
Crosshill
Woodend
Auchterderran
Bowhill
Jamphlars
Cluny
FIFE REGIONAL PARK
Kelty
Glencraig
Cardenden
Dundonald
Chapel
Dunnikier
Gallatown
Dysart
West Wemyss
Coaltown of Wemyss
East Wemyss
Lochgelly
Lumphinnans
Cowdenbeath
Lassodie
Templehall
Hayfield
Pathhead
Kirkcaldy
Port Brae
Linktown
F I F E
Auchtertool
Kingseat
Hill of Beath
Townhill
Wellwood
Kingseathill
Crossgates
Donibristle
Fordell
Halbeath
Dunfermline
Balmule
Kinghorn
Pettycur
Burntisland
Aberdour
Hillend
Dalgety Bay
Rosyth
Inverkeithing
North Queensferry
FIRTH OF FORTH
Inchkeith
Inchcolm
Forth Road Bridge
Queensferry
Dalmeny
Newbigging
Kirkliston
Cramond
Barnton
Silverknowes
Granton
Newhaven
Leith
Edinburgh
Portobello
Musselburgh
Joppa
Duddingston
Corstorphine
Murrayfield
Gogar
Ratho Station
Ratho
Sighthill
Gorgie
Morningside
Craiglockhart
Colinton
Liberton
Gilmerton
Danderhall
Millerhill
Newcraighall
Whitecraig
Fairmilehead
Currie
Juniper Green
Burnwynd
E D I N B U R G H
C I T Y O F

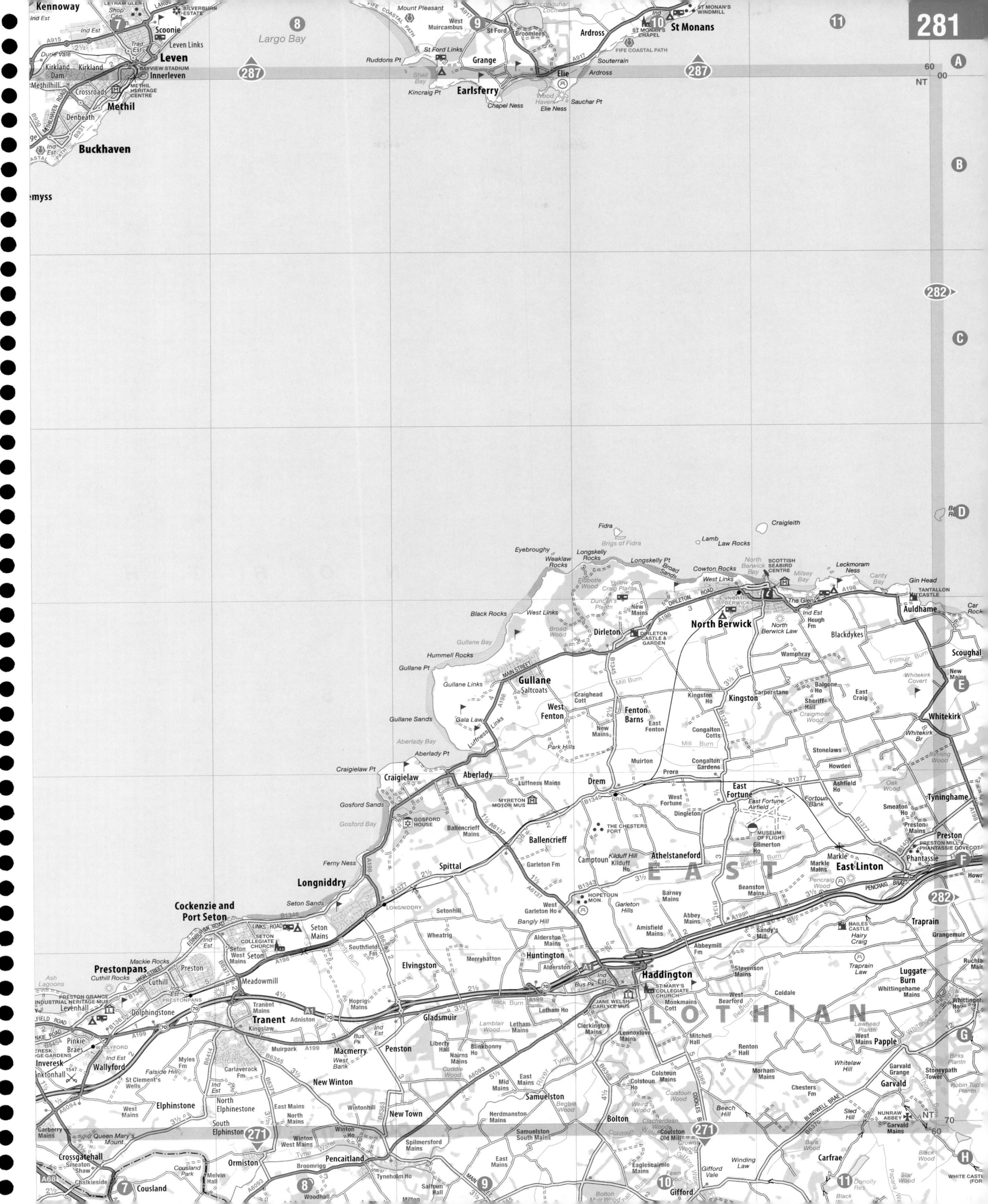

Kennoway
7
Ind Est
Scoonie
Leven Links
Leven
BAYVIEW STADIUM
Innerleven
Kirkland Dam
Kirkland
Crossroads
Methil
METHIL HERITAGE CENTRE
Denbeath
Buckhaven
emyss

Largo Bay
8
Mount Pleasant
West Muircambus
9
St Ford
Broomlees
FIFE COASTAL PATH
ST MONAN'S WINDMILL
Ardross
ST MONAN'S CHAPEL
10
St Monans
11
Grange
St Ford Links
Ruddons Pt
A917
Elie
Ardross
Souterrain
FIFE COASTAL PATH
Shell Bay
Earlsferry
Kincraig Pt
Chapel Ness
Elie Ness
Sauchar Pt
Wood Haven

287
287
60
00
NT

A
B

282

C

Fidra
Craigleith
D
Brigs of Fidra
Lamb
Eyebroughy
Longskelly Rocks
Law Rocks
Weaklaw Rocks
Longskelly Pt
Broad Sands
Cowton Rocks
North Berwick Bay
SCOTTISH SEABIRD CENTRE
Milsey Bay
Leckmoram Ness
Gin Head
Canty Bay
Elbottle Wood
Yellow Craig Plantn
New Mains
West Links
North Berwick
The Glen
TANTALLON CASTLE
Car Rock
Black Rocks
West Links
Duncan Plantn
DIRLETON ROAD
North Berwick Law
Ind Est Heugh Fm
Auldhame
Broad Wood
Dirleton
DIRLETON CASTLE & GARDEN
Wamphray
Blackdykes
Pilmuir Burn
Scoughal
Hummell Rocks
B1345
Kingston Ho
Carperstane
Balgone Ho
Whitekirk Covert
New Mains
Gullane Pt
Craighead Cott
Kingston
Sheriff Hall
East Craig
E
Gullane Links
Gullane
Saltcoats
West Fenton
Fenton Barns
Congalton Cotts
Craigmoor Wood
Whitekirk
Whitekirk Br
Gullane Sands
Gala Law
Luffness Links
New Mains
East Fenton
Congalton Gardens
Stonelaws
Shining Wood
Aberlady Bay
Park Hills
Muirton
Prora
Howden
Aberlady Pt
Drem
Oak Wood
Craigielaw Pt
Luffness Mains
DREM
West Fortune
East Fortune
Ashfield Ho
Tyninghame
Craigielaw
Aberlady
B1345
East Fortune Airfield
Fortune Bank
Smeaton Ho
A198
Gosford Sands
MYRETON MOTOR MUS
B1377
MUSEUM OF FLIGHT
Preston Mains
Preston
GOSFORD HOUSE
THE CHESTERS FORT
Gilmerton Ho
PRESTON MILL & PHANTASSIE DOVECOT
Gosford Bay
Ballencrieff Mains
Ballencrieff
Markle
Phantassie
Ferny Ness
Garleton Fm
Camptoun
Kilduff Hill
Athelstaneford
Markle Mains
East Linton
EAST
Howr
Longniddry
Spittal
Kilduff Ho
Pencraig Wood
PENCRAIG BRAE
282
Cockenzie and Port Seton
Seton Sands
Longniddry
Setonhill
West Garleton Ho
HOPETOUN MON
Garleton Hills
Barney Mains
Beanston Mains
NT
Traprain
Grangemuir
LINKS ROAD
B1348
Bangly Hill
Amisfield Mains
Sandy's Mill
Seton Mains
Wheatrig
Alderston Mains
Abbeymill Fm
HAILES CASTLE
Hairy Craig
Ruchla Mait
Mackie Rocks
SETON COLLEGIATE CHURCH
Southfield Fm
Abbey Mains
Traprain Law
Luggate Burn
Prestonpans
Preston
Seton West Mains
Elvingston
Merryhatton
Huntington
A1
Whittingehame Mains
Cuthill Rocks
A198
Alderston
Bus Pk
Haddington
Stevenson Mains
Coldale
Whittinge Ho
PRESTON GRANGE INDUSTRIAL HERITAGE MUS
Meadowmill
A1
ST MARY'S COLLEGIATE CHURCH
West Bearford
Whittingehame
LOTHIAN
Levenhall
Dolphingstone
Hoprig Mains
Gladsmuir
Back Burn
Letham Ho
JANE WELSH CARLYLE MUS
Monkmains Cott
West Mains
Papple
Inveresk
Pinkie Braes
Tranent
Adniston
Kingslaw
Penston
Liberty Hall
Lamblair Wood
Letham Mains
Clerkington Mains
Mitchell Hall
Renton Hall
Whitelaw Hill
Stoneypath Tower
Wallyford
Muirpark
Macmerry
West Bank
Nairns Mains
Blinkbonny Ho
Lennoxlove Mains
Morham Mains
Garvald Grange
Robin Tup's Plantn
West Mains
Elphinstone
North Elphinstone
East Mains
New Town
Cuddie Wood
A6093
East Mains
Samuelston
Colstoun Ho
Chesters Wood
Garvald
Birks Plantn
Carberry Mains
South Elphinstone
271
Winton Ho
Spilmersford Mains
Herdmanston Mains
Samuelston South Mains
Colstoun Old Mill
Beech Wood
Sled Hill
271
NT
70
60
Crossgatehall
7
Cousland
Cousland Park
Ormiston
Pencaitland
8
Broomrigg
Winton West Mains
9
East Mains
10
Bolton
Clacherdean
Winding Law
NUNRAW ABBEY
Garvald Mains
Black Wood
Chalkieside
Melvin Hall
Tynehome Mains
Milton
Gifford
Eaglescairnie Mains
Gifford Vale
Carfrae
WHITE CASTLE (FOR)
Star Wood
11
Danolly Res

287
North Ness
ISLE OF MAY
Isle of May
South Ness
NT
281
Bass Rock
N O R T H
S E A
Gin Head
TANTALLON CASTLE
Auldhame
Car Rocks
Scoughall
Scoughall Rocks
New Mains
Peffer Sands
Ravensheugh Sands
Frances Craig
Whitekirk
Whitekirk Br
Tyninghame Links
Tyne Sands
Tyninghame
Preston
PRESTON MILL & PHANTASSIE DOVECOT
Knowes
Heckies Hole
Hedderwick Hill
JOHN MUIR
Belhaven Bay
Belhaven
Long Craigs
Scart Rock
Meikle Spiker
Dunbar
BELHAVEN ROAD
JOHN MUIR BIRTHPLACE
West Barns
A1087
A199
A198
A1
EDINBURGH RD
Broxburn
Mill Stone Neuk
White Sands
Barns Ness
East Barns
Hedderwick
Howmuir
South Belton
Old Belton
Biel Water
Bielhill
Bielmill
Traprain
Grangemuir
Wester Broomhouse
Little Pinkerton
Meikle Pinkerton
Dunbar Cement Works
Spott
Spott Fm
Doon Hill
Spott West Mains
Pinkerton Hill
Pitcox
B6370
Meikleraig Wood
Ruchlaw Mains
Luggate Burn
Stenton
Spott Mill
THE CHESTERS (FORT)
Brunt Hill
The Brunt
Thurston Manor
Chapel Pt
Skateraw Harbour
Torness Pt
Long Craig
Thorntonloch Power Sta
Skateraw
Crowhill
Thorntonloch
Innerwick
Thurston Mains
Thurston Mains Burn
Whittingehame Ho
Ruchlaw West Mains
Pressmennan Wood
Highside Hill
Old Branxton
Deuchrie Dod
Rammer Wood
Halls
Birks Plantn
Stoneypath Tower
Robin Tup's Plantn
Lothian Edge
Blaik Law
E A S T
L O T H I A N
High Wood
Berry Hill
Needle Hill
Blackcastle Hill
Oldhamstocks Mains
DUNGLASS COLLEGIATE CHURCH
Belvidere Wood
Oldhamstocks
Bilsdean Creek
Reed Pt
Cove
Cove Harbour
Cove Fm
Pease Bay
Red Rock
Greenheugh Pt
Siccar Pt
Cockburnspath
Dovecot Hall
Sheeppath Glen
Stottencleugh
Common Plantn
Moorcock Hall
Deuchrie Edge
Watch Law
Meikle Poo Craig
Hirst Rocks
Dunbar Common
272
Bransly Hill
Birny Knowe
Neuk Fm
Stockbridge
Tower Fm
Old Cambus Townhead
Old Cambus
Old Townhead
Penmanshiel Wood
Greenside Hill
Meikle Black Law
A1107
WHITE CASTLE (FORT)
Saddle Hill
Wightman Hill
Ecclaw
0 1 2 3 miles
0 1 2 3 4 5 km

7   8   9   10   11

A   B   C   D   E   F   G   H

10
NT 00

Lumsdaine

Fast Castle
Head   Wheat Stack

Telegraph
Hill   FAST
CASTLE

NT 70
10

Oatlee Hill

273   St Abb's Head

273

ST ABB'S HEAD

Horsecastle Bay

Dowlaw   Burn

Lumsdaine

dingham
ommon   Lumsdaine
Moor   Coldingham
Loch

Cross
Law   Moorside

Bell
Hill

7   8   9   10   11

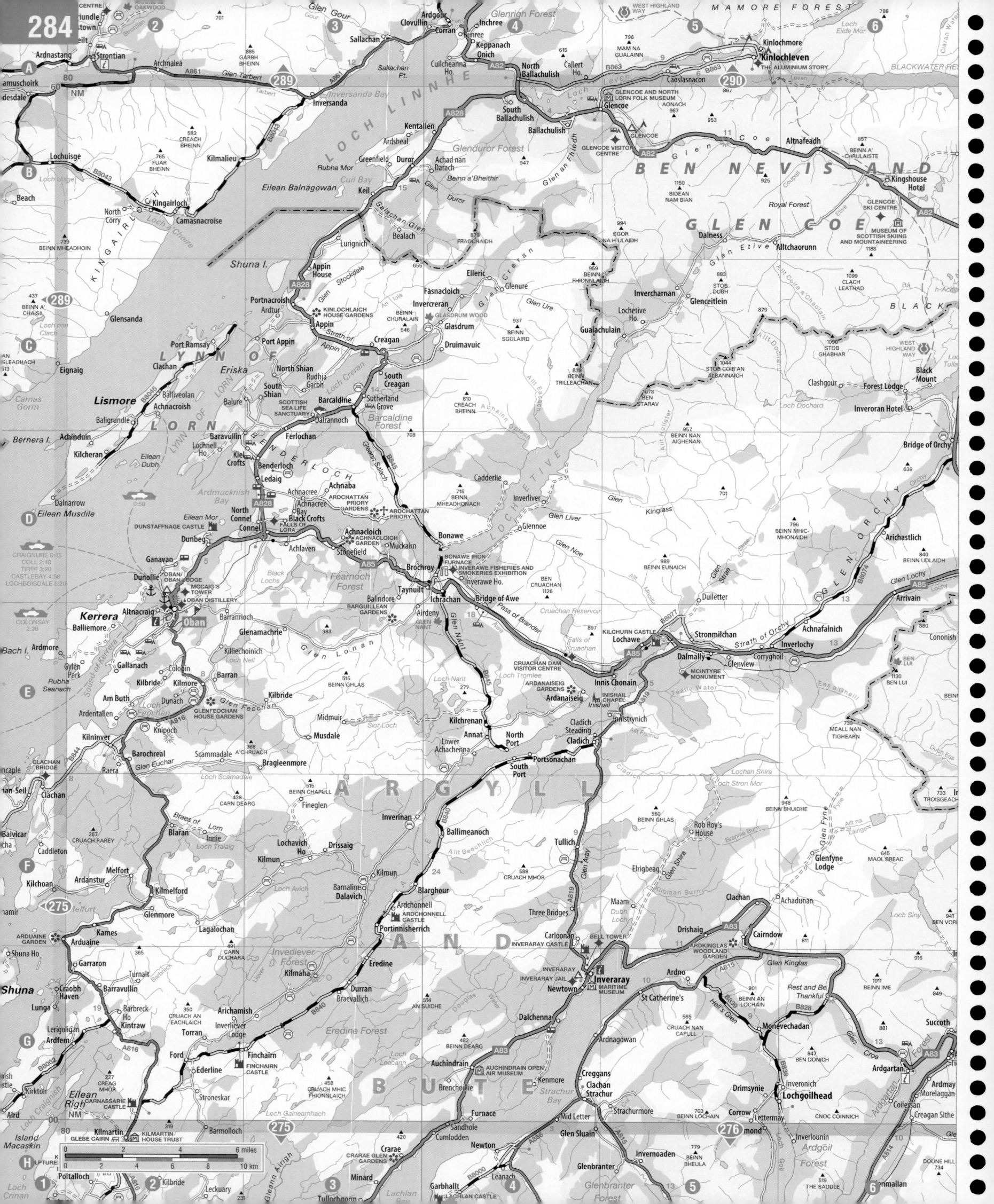

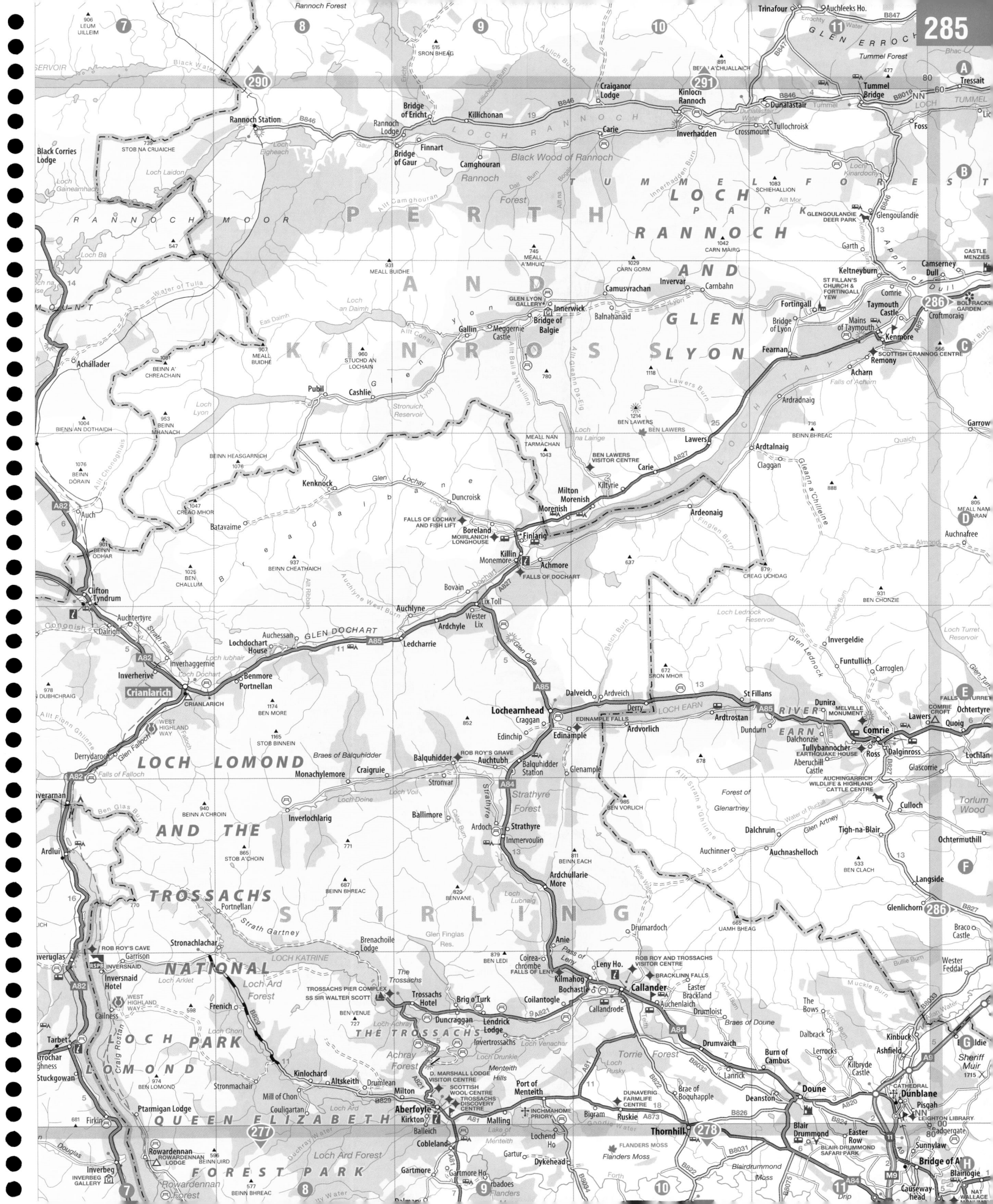
Rannoch Forest
Trinafour
Auchleeks Ho.
GLEN ERROCHTY
Tummel Forest
LEUM UILLEIM
SRON BHEAG
Black Water
290
291
Bridge of Ericht
Killichonan
Craiganor Lodge
Kinloch Rannoch
Dunalastair
Tummel Bridge
Tressait
LOCH TUMMEL
Rannoch Station
Bridge of Gaur
Finnart
Camghouran
Carie
Inverhadden
Crossmount
Tullochroisk
Foss
LOCH RANNOCH
Loch Eigheach
STOB NA CRUAICHE
Black Corries Lodge
Loch Laidon
Black Wood of Rannoch
Rannoch Forest
TUMMEL FOREST
LOCH RANNOCH AND GLEN LYON
SCHIEHALLION
GLENGOULANDIE DEER PARK
Glengoulandie
RANNOCH MOOR
PERTH AND KINROSS
CARN MAIRG
Garth
CASTLE MENZIES
Camserney
Dull
Keltneyburn
MEALL BUIDHE
MEALL A'MHUIC
CARN GORM
Camusvrachan
Invervar
Carnbahn
ST FILLAN'S CHURCH & FORTINGALL YEW
Fortingall
Comrie
Taymouth Castle
286
BOLFRACKS GARDEN
Croftmoraig
GLEN LYON GALLERY
Innerwick
Bridge of Balgie
Balnahanaid
Gallin
Meggernie Castle
Bridge of Lyon
Mains of Taymouth
Kenmore
Fearnan
SCOTTISH CRANNOG CENTRE
Remony
Acharn
Falls of Acharn
Water of Tulla
Achallader
BEINN A' CHREACHAIN
STUCHD AN LOCHAIN
Pubil
Cashlie
Glen Lyon
Stronuich Reservoir
Ardradnaig
Loch Lyon
BEINN MHANACH
BIENN AN DOTHAIDH
BEN LAWERS
Lawers
LOCH TAY
BEINN HEASGARNICH
MEALL NAN TARMACHAN
BEN LAWERS VISITOR CENTRE
Carie
Kiltyrie
Ardtalnaig
Claggan
BEINN DÒRAIN
Kenknock
Glen Lochay
Duncroisk
Milton Morenish
Morenish
Ardeonaig
Auch
CREAG MHOR
Batavaime
Breadalbane
FALLS OF LOCHAY AND FISH LIFT
Boreland
MOIRLANICH LONGHOUSE
Finlarig
Killin
Monemore
Achmore
FALLS OF DOCHART
BEINN ODHAR
BEN CHALLUM
BEINN CHEATHAICH
CREAG UCHDAG
Auchnafree
MEALL NAM ARAN
BEN CHONZIE
Clifton
Tyndrum
Auchtertyre
Dalrigh
Strath Fillan
Bovain
Auchlyne
Ardchyle
Lix Toll
Wester Lix
Loch Lednock Reservoir
Glen Lednock
Invergeldie
Funtullich
Carroglen
Loch Turret Reservoir
Lochdochart House
Auchessan
GLEN DOCHART
Ledcharrie
Inverhaggernie
Inverherive
Benmore
Portnellan
Crianlarich
BEN MORE
Glen Ogle
SRON MHOR
Dalveich
Ardveich
Derry
LOCH EARN
St Fillans
Ardtrostan
RIVER EARN
Dunira
MELVILLE MONUMENT
Comrie
Lawers
Ochtertyre
Quoig
Lochearnhead
Craggan
EDINAMPLE FALLS
Edinample
Ardvorlich
Dundurn
Dalchonzie
Tullybannocher
EARTHQUAKE HOUSE
Ross
Dalginross
Aberuchill Castle
Lochlane
Glascorrie
STOB BINNEIN
WEST HIGHLAND WAY
Derrydaroch
Glen Falloch
LOCH LOMOND
Braes of Balquhidder
Balquhidder
ROB ROY'S GRAVE
Auchtubh
Balquhidder Station
Glenample
Monachylemore
Craigruie
Stronvar
Falls of Falloch
Loch Doine
Loch Voil
Strathyre Forest
BEN VORLICH
Forest of Glenartney
AUCHINGARRICH WILDLIFE & HIGHLAND CATTLE CENTRE
Culloch
Torlum Wood
Inverarnan
BEINN A' CHROIN
Inverlochlarig
Ballimore
Ardoch
Strathyre
Immervoulin
Dalchruin
Glen Artney
Tigh-na-Blair
Ochtermuthill
AND THE
Ardlui
STOB A'CHOIN
BEINN EACH
Auchinner
Auchnashelloch
BEN CLACH
Langside
BEINN BHREAC
BENVANE
Ardchullarie More
Loch Lubnaig
TROSSACHS
STIRLING
Portnellan
Strath Gartney
Drumardoch
UAMH BHEAG
Glenlichorn
Braco Castle
Stronachlachar
Brenachoile Lodge
Glen Finglas Res.
Anie
Pass of Leny
ROB ROY'S CAVE
Garrison
RSPB INVERSNAID
LOCH KATRINE
BEN LEDI
Coireachrombe
FALLS OF LENY
Leny Ho.
ROB ROY AND TROSSACHS VISITOR CENTRE
BRACKLINN FALLS
Wester Feddal
Inversnaid Hotel
NATIONAL
Loch Arklet
Loch Ard Forest
The Trossachs
TROSSACHS PIER COMPLEX
SS SIR WALTER SCOTT
Trossachs Hotel
Brig o'Turk
Kilmahog
Bochastle
Callander
Easter Brackland
Auchenlaich
Callandrode
Drumloist
Braes of Doune
Coilantogle
Frenich
Duncraggan
Lendrick Lodge
BEN VENUE
Cailness
LOCH PARK
THE TROSSACHS
Invertrossachs
Loch Venachar
Drumvaich
The Bows
Dalbrack
Kinbuck
Ashfield
Sheriff Muir
Tarbet
Arrochar
Craig Rostan
Loch Chon
Achray Forest
Loch Drunkie
Torrie Forest
Loch Rusky
Lerrocks
Burn of Cambus
Kilbryde Castle
Stuckgowan
LOMOND
BEN LOMOND
Kinlochard
Altskeith
Drumlean
D. MARSHALL LODGE VISITOR CENTRE
Menteith Hills
Lanrick
Stronmachair
Mill of Chon
Milton
SCOTTISH WOOL CENTRE
TROSSACHS DISCOVERY CENTRE
Port of Menteith
DUNAVERIG FARMLIFE CENTRE
Brae of Boquhapple
Deanston
Doune
CATHEDRAL
Dunblane
Pisgah
Ptarmigan Lodge
Couligartan
Loch Ard
Aberfoyle
Kirkton
INCHMAHOME PRIORY
Bigram
Ruskie
Thornhill
278
LEIGHTON LIBRARY
Firkin
QUEEN ELIZABETH
277
Balleich
Lake of Menteith
Malling
Lochend Ho
Blair Drummond
BLAIR DRUMMOND SAFARI PARK
Easter Row
Gadgergate
Sunnylaw
Douglas
Rowardennan
ROWARDENNAN LODGE
BEINN UIRD
Cobleland
Gartur
FLANDERS MOSS
Flanders Moss
Bridge of Allan
Inverbeg
INVERBEG GALLERY
FOREST PARK
Loch Ard Forest
Gartmore
Gartmore Ho
Dykehead
Blairdrummond Moss
Causewayhead
Blairlogie
BEINN BHREAC
Rowardennan Forest
Flanders
Forth
NAT WALLACE

Blair Atholl Distillery
Tulach Hill
Lettoch
Aldclune
Fincastle Ho.
Killiecrankie
Killiecrankie Visitor Centre
Bonskeid House
Tenandry
Atholl Country Collection
841 Ben Vrackie
Dalnavaid
Tarvie
Straloch
Glen Brerachan
Enochdhu
Dalnaglar Castle
Meikle Forter
Folda
Lair
744 Mount Blair
Glenmarkie Lodge
Glenhead Farm
Glenisla
Backwater Res.
Longdrum
Brewlands Bridge
Freuchies
Ashintully Castle
Loch Bhac
Loch
Balavoulin
Queen's View
Tressait
Tummel Bridge
Tummel
Loch Tummel
Queen's View Centre
Falls of Tummel
Moulin
Pitlochry
Kinnaird
Edradour Distillery
Milton of Edradour
Balmore
Linn of Tummel
Loch Faskally
Hydro-Electric Visitor Centre
Scottish Plant Collectors Garden
Blair Atholl Distillery Visitor Centre
641 Creag Dhubh
Kirkmichael
Middle Balnald
Blacklunans
520 Cairn Gibbs
Kirkton of Glenisla
Bellaty
497 Creigh Hill
Balintore
Foss
Lick
Tummel Forest
Farragon Hill
Loch Derculich
Loch Broom
534 Meall Reamhar
Knock of Balmyle
Forest of Alyth
Dykends
Milton of Dalcapon
Ballintuim
Peel Farm
Bridgend of Lintrathen
Balduff Hill
Reekie Linn Waterfall
Bridge of Craigisla
Loch of Lintrathen
Glengoulandie
Strathtay
Ballechin
Edradynate
Grandtully
Tulliemet
561 Creag nam Mial
Netherton
Milton of Drimmie
Tullymurdoch
Auchrannie
Cluny House Gardens
Tombui
Little Ballinluig
Ballinluig
Logierait
Balnaguard
Blackcraig Forest
Forest of Clunie
Bridge of Cally
Bamff
Castle Menzies
St Mary's Church
Weem
Balmacneil
Loch Ordie
Loch Benachally
Cochrage Muir
Shanzie
Camserney
Dull
Aberfeldy Distillery & Dewar's World of Whisky
Aberfeldy
Wade's Bridge
Kindallachan
Riemore
Tullyfergus
Pitcrocknie
Ruthven
Alyth
New Alyth
Comrie
Taymouth Castle
Bolfracks Garden
Falls of Moness
Kincraigie
Guay
Dowally
509 Deuchary Hill
Middleton
Craighall
Courthill
Westfields of Rattray
Lornty
Croftmoraig
Urlar
Loch Skiach
Riechip
Balharry
Dalguise
Craigvinean Forest
Butterstone
Kenmore
Loch Kennard
Dalmarnock
Forneth
Achalader
Blairgowrie
Kinloch
Rattray
Leitfie
Meigle Museum
Remony
Scottish Crannog Centre
River Tay
Scottish Horse Regimental Mus
Loch of Lowes
Loch of Lowes Nature Reserve
Concraigie
Loch of Clunie
Loch of Drumellie
Muirton of Ardblair
Rosemount
Kinloch
Meigle
Loch Hoil
Glen Cochill
Cath
Dunkeld
Little Dunkeld
Birnam
Clunie
Craigie
Wester Essendy
Kirkton of Lethendy
Longleys
Arthurstone
Scotston
Waterfall
Ballinlick
The Hermitage
Inver
Snaigow House
West Myreriggs
Ardler
Newbigging
690 Meall Dearg
Trochry
Spittalfield
Keillor
Kirkton
Garrow
Delvine
Caputh
Coupar Angus
Hill of Keillor
Turrerich
Glen Quaich
Loch Freuchie
Cablea
Strathbraan
Obney Hills
Meikle Obney
Gellyburn
Muir of Thorn
Murthly
Meikleour
Beech Hedge
Kinclaven
Markethill
Kettins
Hallyburton House
Campmuir
Ardoch
Ballathie
Woodside
Burrelton
Leys
Pitcur
Lundie
Glenquaich Lodge
Amulree
Upper Obney
Balquharn
Waterloo
Cargill
805 Meall nam Fuaran
Corrymuckloch
Perth and Kinross
Whitefield
Bankfoot
Airntully
Littleton
Auchnafree
Almond
Little Glenshee
623 Meall nan Caoraich
Milton Burn
Tullybelton
Liqueur Centre
West Tofts
Stanley
Saucher
Collace
King's Seat
377
Wolfhill
Loanhead
Dunsinnan
Kinrossie
Kirkton of Collace
Knapp
Abernyte
Sidlaw
Newton
Logiealmond Lodge
Logiealmond
Guildtown
St Martins
Newmiln
Bandirran
Rossie
931 Ben Chonzie
Glen Almond
Sma' Glen
Chapelhill
Harrietfield
Downhill
Stormontfield
Balbeggie
Ballindean
648 Meall Tarsuinn
Moneydie
Luncarty
Perth
Loch Turret Reservoir
Shaggie Burn
Glenalmond Ho.
Buchanty
Glenalmond College
Redgorton
Braes of the Carse
Kinnaird
Craigdallie
Inchture
Westown
Rait
Drummick
Pitcairngreen
Caithness Glass
Scone Palace
East Bonhard
Carroglen
Glen Turret
Falls of Turret
Comrie Croft
Ochtertyre
Monzie
Monzie Castle
Hosh
350
Fowlis Wester
Standing Stones
Methven
Keillour
Craigend
Almondbank
Huntingtower
Lochty
Perth Mart Visitor Centre
Scone
Murrayshall
288 Pole Hill
Kilspindie
Grange
Lawers
Quoig
Gilmerton
Burnside
Braegrum
Tibbermore
Huntingtower Castle
Muirton
Tulloch
Museum & Art Gallery
Gannochy
Fergusson Gallery
Kinfauns Forest
Myreside
Megginch Castle Gardens
Errol Station
Comrie
Ross
Dalginross
Glenturret Distillery
Crieff
Tomaknock
Milton of Cultoquhey
Keillour Forest
Pow Water
Balgowan
Letham
Broxden Services
Cherrybank
Perth
Branklyn Garden
Balthayock
Kinfauns
Glendoick
Errol
Carse of Gowrie
Firth of Tay
Lochlane
Glascorrie
Crieff Visitors' Centre
Stuart Crystal Visitor Centre
Pittachar
Madderty
Findo Gask
Bell's Cherrybank Gardens
Craigie
Friarton
Walnut Grove
Elcho
Glencarse
Fairways Heavy Horse Centre
Carthagena Bank
Auchingarrich Wildlife & Highland Cattle Centre
The Balloch
Concraig
Mains of Innerpeffray
Chapelhill
St David's
Clathy
Milltown of Aberdalgie
Aberdalgie
Tarsappie
Rhynd
Inchyra
Leetown
Chapelhill
St Madoes
Port Allen
Ballinbreich
Culloch
Torlum Wood
Drummond Castle Gardens
Innerpeffray Library
Kirkton
Dupplin Castle
Craigend
Mugdrum I.
Laing Museum
Newburgh
Higham
Glenduckie
Old Church & Tower
Muthill
Lawhill
Forteviot
Forgandenny
Bridge of Earn
Easter Rhynd
Dunbog
Ochtermuthill
Machany Water
Milton of Machany
Kinkell Bridge
Strathearn
Ardargie House Hotel
Kintillo
Abernethy
Round Tower
Lindores
Grange of Lindores
Lindores Loch
Strathallan Castle
Aberuthven
Glenearn
Dron
Aberargie
Glenfoot
Drumness
Middleton
Tullibardine
Tullibardine Chapel
Dunning
Newton of Pitcairns
Rossie Ochill
Pitmedden Forest
Colzie
Newhill
Monimail
Collessie
Langside
Auchterarder
Milton
Heritage Centre
Glentarkie
Auchtermuchty
Kinloch
Giffordtown
Garrick
Murton
Pathstruie
Newton of Balcanquhal
Glenfarg Res.
Path of Condie
Dunshalt
Braco Castle
Ardoch Roman Camp
Blackhall Roman Camps
Gleneagles Hotel
Gleneagles
Glenfarg
Arngask
Strathmiglo
Charlottetown
Howe of Fife
Bullie Burn
Wester Feddal
Braco
Strathallan
Blackford
Gleneagles House
Coulshill
Glen Eagles
Common of Dunning
Middle Rigg
Duncrievie
Newhill
Gateside
Nether Urquhart
Kilgour
Falkland Palace
Greenloaning
Tullibardine Distillery
Braes of Ogilvie
485 Steel's Knowe
497 Innerdouny Hill
Burnside
Fife
Falkland
Newton of Falkland
Dam of Quoiggs
Kinbuck
Athron Hall
Middleton
West Lomond
522
Lomond Hills
Wester Gospetry
Falkland
Freuchie
Balhaldie
Ashfield
Glendevon Resvrs.
543
Glen Devon
Glendevon
Craigow
Upper Tillyrie
Glassie
Glenlomond
Wester Balgedie
Michael Bruce's Cottage
Regional Park
Muirhead
Dalqueich
Burleigh Castle
Milnathort
Sheriff Muir 1715
611
Castlehill Reservoir
Burnfoot
Carnbo
Kinross Services
Loch Leven
Easter Balgedie
Kinnesswood
Pitkevy
Kirkforthar Feus
Cathedral
Dunblane
Pisgah
Library
Blairdenon Hill
721 Ben Cleuch
Pool o' Muckhart
Yetts o' Muckhart
Lochleven Castle
Kinross House
Kinross
Scotlandwell
Auchmuirbridge
Cadham
Leslie
Glenrothes
Drum
Coldrain
St Serf's Island
Gairney Bank
Badgerrate
Castle Campbell
Dollar Glen
King's Seat Hill
Rumbling Bridge
Rumbling Bridge Gorge
Crook of Devon
Vane Farm Nature Centre
RSPB
Vane Farm
Kinglassie
Stenton
Thornton
Tillicoultry
Dollar
Pow mill
Cleish
Ballingry
Benarty Hill
Dogton Stone
Alva
Tullibody
National Wallace Monument
Fishcross
Sterling Mills
Devonside
Blairingone
Hardiston
Cleish Hills
Hill End
Lochran
Lochore
Woodend
Auchterderran
Crosshill
Cluny
0 2 4 6 miles
0 2 4 6 8 10 km
A9
A85
A822
A827
A826
A823
A824
A91
A912
A913
A923
A924
A926
A93
A94
A984
A90
A977
M90
B8019
B8063
B8062
B934
B935
B9112
B996
B947
B953
B954
B951
B950
B898
B846
B827
B8033
B9141
B9097
B919
B920
B936
B937
B921
B922
279
280
285
291
292

Glenmoy
Redheugh
Auchnacree
Kirkton of Menmuir
Tigerton
Balrownie
Newtonmill
Logie Pert
Craigo
Lochside
St Cyrus
Milton Ness
Easter Lednathie
Glenogil
Deuchar
Fern
Mains of Balhall
Balnamoon
Lochty
Bellieshill
Little Brechin
Keithock
Muirton of Ballochy
North Craigo
Logie
Morphie
Pathhead
Glenquiech
Ogil
Noranside
Careston
West Muir
Trinity
Hillside
Maritings
CAPTAIN SCOTT & DR. WILSON CAIRN
Horniehaugh
CAT LAW
Dykehead
Brechin
BRECHIN CASTLE CENTRE
HOUSE OF DUN
Kirkhill
ANGUS
STRATHMORE
Pearsie
Cortachy
Memus
Careston Castle
PICTAVIA
CATHEDRAL & ROUND TOWER
CALEDONIAN RAILWAY
Dun
Montrose
Balloch
Inverquharity
Tannadice
Cadger Path
South Esk
Aldbar Castle
Bridge of Dun
Montrose Basin
MUSEUM AND ART GALLERY
Scurdie Ness
WILLIAM LAMB MEMORIAL STUDIO
MILE HILL
Murthill
Shielhill
Finavon
Oathlaw
Netherton
Mains of Melgund
Middle Drums
Kinnaird Castle
Barnhead
MONTROSE BASIN VISITOR CENTRE
Inchbraoch
Ferryden
Kirkton of Kingoldrum
Northmuir
Kinnordy
Crosston
ABERLEMNO SCULPTURED STONES
Aberlemno
Farnell
Bonnyton
Maryton
Kirkton of Craig
Long Craig
Fishtown of Usan
LOCH OF KINNORDY NATURE RESERVE
Kirriemuir
BARRIE'S BIRTHPLACE
Carse Gray
Pitkennedy
Montreathmont Forest
Montreathmont Moor
Carcary
Dunninald
Rossie Moor
Westerton
Boddin Pt.
Westmuir
Maryton
Mosside
Blackgate
Turin
GATEWAY TO THE GLENS MUS
Lunanhead
RESTENNETH PRIORY
Rescobie
Dubton
Bolshan
Renmure
Braehead of Lunan
Kirkton of Airlie
Mains of Ballindarg
Padanaram
Forfar
FORFAR LOCH
Reswallie
Balgavies
Glasterlaw
Lunan
Craigton
Roundyhill
METEFFAN GALL & MUS
Burnside
Milldens
Guthrie
Kinnell
LUNAN BAY
Redcastle
Airlie
Drumgley
Kingsmuir
Pitmuies
Friockheim
Boysack
Inverkeilor
Ruthven House
EASSIE SCULPTURED STONE
Leys of Cossans
ST ORLAND'S STONE
Dean Water
Dunnichen
Letham
HOUSE OF PITMUIES GARDEN
Lunan Water
Lang Craig
Ethie Mains
GLAMIS CASTLE
Caldhame
Lownie Moor
Bowriefauld
Idvies
Chapelton
Inchock
Red Head
Douglastown
Craichie
Leysmill
Cauldcots
Ethie Castle
Glamis
Castleton
Thornton
Kirkton
Lour
Tulloes
Cononsyth
Drunkendub
Charleston
ANGUS FOLK MUSEUM
Foffarty
Mosston
Colliston
Letham Grange
Balkeerie
Kirkinch
Eassie
Milton
Gateside
Inverarity
Whigstreet
Kirkbuddo
Greystone
Redford
Boysack
St Vigeans
Auchmithie
Meg's Craig
Marywell
Wester Denoon
ARK HILL
Nether Handwick
Gallowfauld
Carmyllie
Woodville Feus
ST VIGEANS MUSEUM
Hayshead
Newtyle
HILLS
Hayhillock
Carrot
Denhead of Arbilot
Cliffburn
The Deil's Heid
ARBROATH ABBEY
Arbroath
CROMBIE
Arbirlot
Coldstream
Husbandtown
Kirkton of Monikie
Fauldiehill
Easter Knox
Elliot
SIGNAL TOWER MUSEUM
Bonnyton
Balkemback
Tealing
Todhill
Monikie
Balmirmer
Kirkton of Auchterhouse
Newbigging
Craigton
Kirkton
Salmond's Muir
Auchterhouse
North Dronley
Leoch
Muir of Pert
Inveraldie
East March
Wellbank
CARLUNGIE SOUTERRAIN
Muirdrum
Hatton
Bucklerheads
East Haven
Dronley
Bridgefoot
Burnside of Duntrune
Drumsturdy
Newbigging
Clayholes
BARRY MILL
Panbride
Muirhead
Birkhill
CLATTO
Kellas
Barry
Fowlis
CAMPERDOWN AND TEMPLETON WOODS
SOUTERRAIN ARDESTIE
Mains of Ardestie
Carnoustie
Fintry
Downfield
Baldovie
CARNOUSTIE
Liff
Douglas & Angus
Barry Links
Denhead of Gray
DUNDEE
VERDANT WORKS
Craigie
West Ferry
Monifieth
Benvie
Lochee
MILLS OBSERVATORY
MUS AND ART GALL
BROUGHTY CASTLE
Barnhill
Priory
Stannergate
Broughty Ferry
BROUGHTY CASTLE MUSEUM
Buddon Ness
Invergowrie
Dundee
FRIGATE UNICORN
Tay Bridge
Longforgan
DISCOVERY POINT
Tayport
Castle Huntly
Kingoodie
UNIVERSITY BOTANIC GARDENS
DUNDEE
Newport-on-Tay
Scotscraig
TENTSMUIR
Woodhaven
Shanwell
Tay Rail Bridge
Wormit
Fetterdale
Tentsmuir Forest
OF TAY
Balmerino
BALMERINO ABBEY
Kirkton
Bottomcraig
Pickletillem
Coultra
Gauldry
Rhynd
Hazelton Walls
Kilmany
Lucklawhill
Carrick
Creich
Leuchars
LEUCHARS NORMAN CHURCH
Rathillet
Logie
Balmullo
Brunton
Milton
Eden Mouth
Luthrie
Muirhead
Guardbridge
EDEN ESTUARY CENTRE
ST ANDREWS BAY
Dairsie or Osnaburgh
Kincaple
ST ANDREWS
ST ANDREWS AQUARIUM
Moonzie
BRITISH GOLF MUS
St Andrews
Lindifferon
Kilmaron Castle
Foodieash
CATH & ST RULE'S TOWER
MOUNT HILL
Strathkinness
Clatto
Newpark
Fernie
DOUGLAS BADER GARDENS FOR THE DISABLED
Cupar
Kemback
Brownhills
Buddo Ness
Letham
Blebocraigs
Balone
ST ANDREWS BOTANIC GARDEN
Boarhills
Babbet Ness
CRAIGTOUN
Bow of Fife
Cupar Muir
Denhead
Prior Muir
SCOTTISH DEER CENTRE
HILL OF TARVIT MANSIONHOUSE
Pitscottie
Kingsbarns
Cambo Ness
CAMBO GARDENS
Carr Brigs
Bridgend
Cameron Res.
Stravithie
Tullybothy Craigs
Springfield
Ceres
Baldinnie
Dunino
FIFE FOLK MUSEUM
Balcomie
Craighead
SCOTSTARVIT TOWER
Craigrothie
Beleybridge
Ladybank
Peat Inn
Wormiston
Chance Inn
Fife Ness
Pitlessie
Cults
Struthers
Falfield
Radernie
Kingsmuir
CRAIL TOLBOOTH
Kingskettle
Balmalcolm
Lathones
Lochty
SCOTLAND'S SECRET BUNKER
Burnturk
Kettlehill
Kame
Woodside
New Gilston
Crail
CRAIL MUSEUM AND HERITAGE CENTRE
Largoward
Carnbee
Pitcorthie
West Ness
Montrave
Pitkierie
Rameldry Mill Bank
Wester Newburn
Lathallan Mill
KELLIE CASTLE AND GARDEN
Kilrenny
FIFE COASTAL PATH
PRAYTIS FARM PARK
SCOTLAND'S LARDER
Arncroach
Newton of Balcormo
Grangemuir
Langdyke
Kirkton of Largo
Anstruther Easter
SCOTTISH FISHERIES MUSEUM
Baintown
Drumeldrie
Colinsburgh
Star
Lundin Links
Abercrombie
Pittenweem
Anstruther Wester
Kennoway
Bonnybank
ROBINSON CRUSOE STATUE
Balchrystie
Kilconquhar
ST FILLAN'S CAVE
Markinch
Scoonie
Lower Largo
ST MONAN'S WINDMILL
BALGONIE CASTLE
Balcurvie
SILVERBURN ESTATE
Ardross
St Monans
ST MONAN'S CHURCH
LETHAM GLEN
Leven
Largo Bay
Milton of Balgonie
Windygates
Innerleven
Ruddons Pt.
Grange
Elie
Isle of May
Coaltown of Balgonie
Methil
Earlsferry
Sauchar Pt.
Chapel Ness
Buckhaven
MUSEUM
FIFE COASTAL PATH
East Wemyss
Coaltown of Wemyss
292
293
281
282
NO
80
60
00

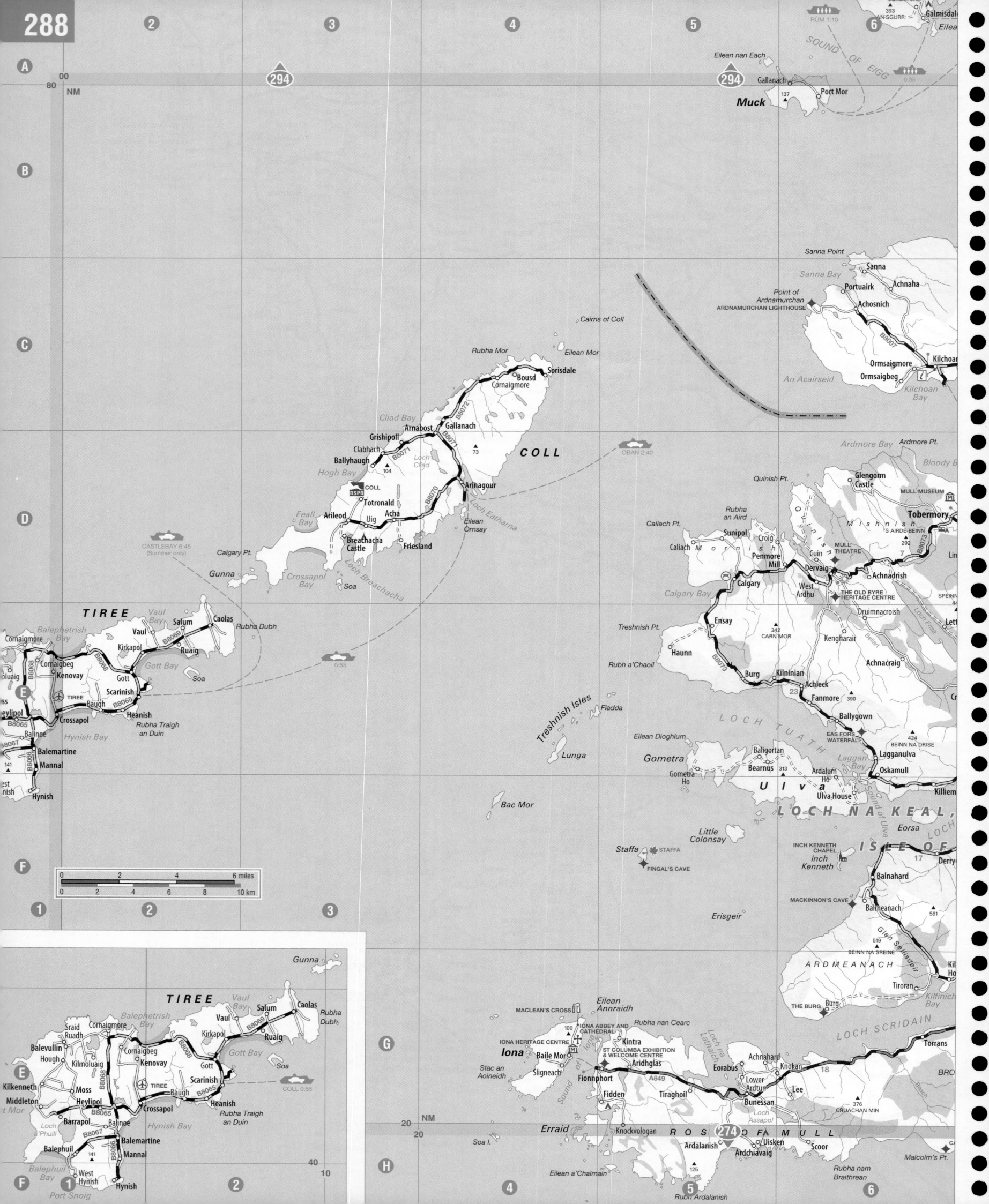
Muck
Gallanach
Port Mor
Eilean nan Each
SOUND OF EIGG
Galmisdale
COLL
Sorisdale
Bousd
Cornaigmore
Rubha Mor
Eilean Mor
Cairns of Coll
Arnabost
Gallanach
Grishipoll
Clabhach
Ballyhaugh
Cliad Bay
Hogh Bay
Loch Cliad
Arinagour
Totronald
Arileod
Uig
Acha
Feall Bay
Breachacha Castle
Friesland
Eilean Ornsay
Loch Eatharna
Loch Breachacha
Crossapol Bay
Soa
Calgary Pt.
Gunna
CASTLEBAY 6:45 (Summer only)
OBAN 2:40
TIREE
Vaul Bay
Salum
Caolas
Rubha Dubh
Vaul
Kirkapol
Ruaig
Cornaigmore
Balephetrish Bay
Cornaigbeg
Kenovay
Gott Bay
Gott
Scarinish
Baugh
Heanish
Crossapol
Balinoe
Hynish Bay
Balemartine
Mannal
Hynish
Rubha Traigh an Duin
Sanna Point
Sanna
Sanna Bay
Portuairk
Achnaha
Achosnich
Point of Ardnamurchan
ARDNAMURCHAN LIGHTHOUSE
Ormsaigmore
Ormsaigbeg
Kilchoan
Kilchoan Bay
An Acairseid
Ardmore Bay
Ardmore Pt.
Bloody Bay
Quinish Pt.
Glengorm Castle
MULL MUSEUM
Tobermory
Rubha an Aird
Caliach Pt.
Sunipol
Croig
Caliach
Mornish
Mishnish
Penmore Mill
MULL THEATRE
Cuin
Dervaig
Achnadrish
Calgary
Calgary Bay
West Ardhu
THE OLD BYRE HERITAGE CENTRE
Druimnacroish
Treshnish Pt.
Ensay
CARN MOR
Kengharair
Haunn
Rubh a'Chaoil
Achnacraig
Burg
Kilninian
Achleck
Fanmore
Treshnish Isles
Fladda
Ballygown
LOCH TUATH
EAS FORS WATERFALL
BEINN NA DRISE
Eilean Dioghlum
Lunga
Gometra
Gometra Ho
Baligortan
Bearnus
Ardalum Ho
Laggan Bay
Lagganulva
Oskamull
Ulva
Ulva House
Bac Mor
LOCH NA KEAL
Eorsa
Little Colonsay
Staffa
STAFFA
FINGAL'S CAVE
INCH KENNETH CHAPEL
Inch Kenneth
ISLE OF
Balnahard
MACKINNON'S CAVE
Balmeanach
Erisgeir
Glen Seilisdeir
BEINN NA SREINE
ARDMEANACH
Tiroran
THE BURG
Burg
Kilfinichen Bay
LOCH SCRIDAIN
Torrans
Eilean Annraidh
MACLEAN'S CROSS
IONA ABBEY AND CATHEDRAL
Rubha nan Cearc
IONA HERITAGE CENTRE
Iona
Baile Mor
Kintra
ST COLUMBA EXHIBITION & WELCOME CENTRE
Loch na Lathaich
Achnahard
Stac an Aoineidh
Sligneach
Sound of Iona
Aridhglas
Eorabus
Lower Ardtun
Knokan
Fionnphort
Fidden
Tiraghoil
Lee
Bunessan
Loch Assapol
CRUACHAN MIN
Erraid
Knockvologan
ROSS OF MULL
Soa I.
Ardalanish
Uisken
Ardchiavaig
Scoor
Malcolm's Pt.
Eilean a'Chalmain
Rubha nam Braithrean
Rubh Ardalanish
RUM 1:10
AN SGURR
Balevullin
Sraid Ruadh
Hough
Kilmoluaig
Kilkenneth
Moss
Middleton
Heylipol
Barrapol
Loch a'Phuill
Balephuil
Balephuil Bay
West Hynish
Port Snoig
COLL 0:55
0 2 4 6 miles
0 2 4 6 8 10 km

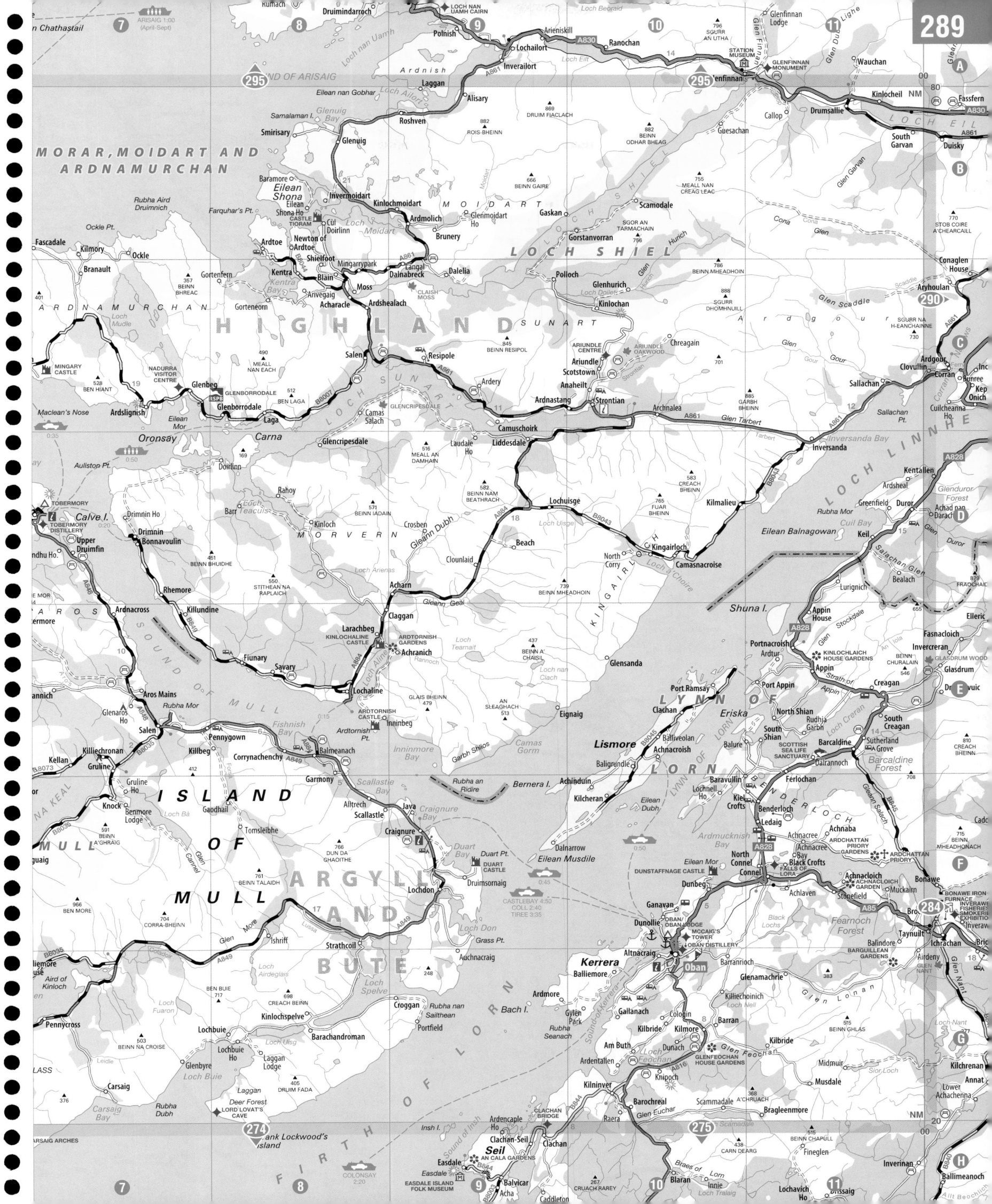

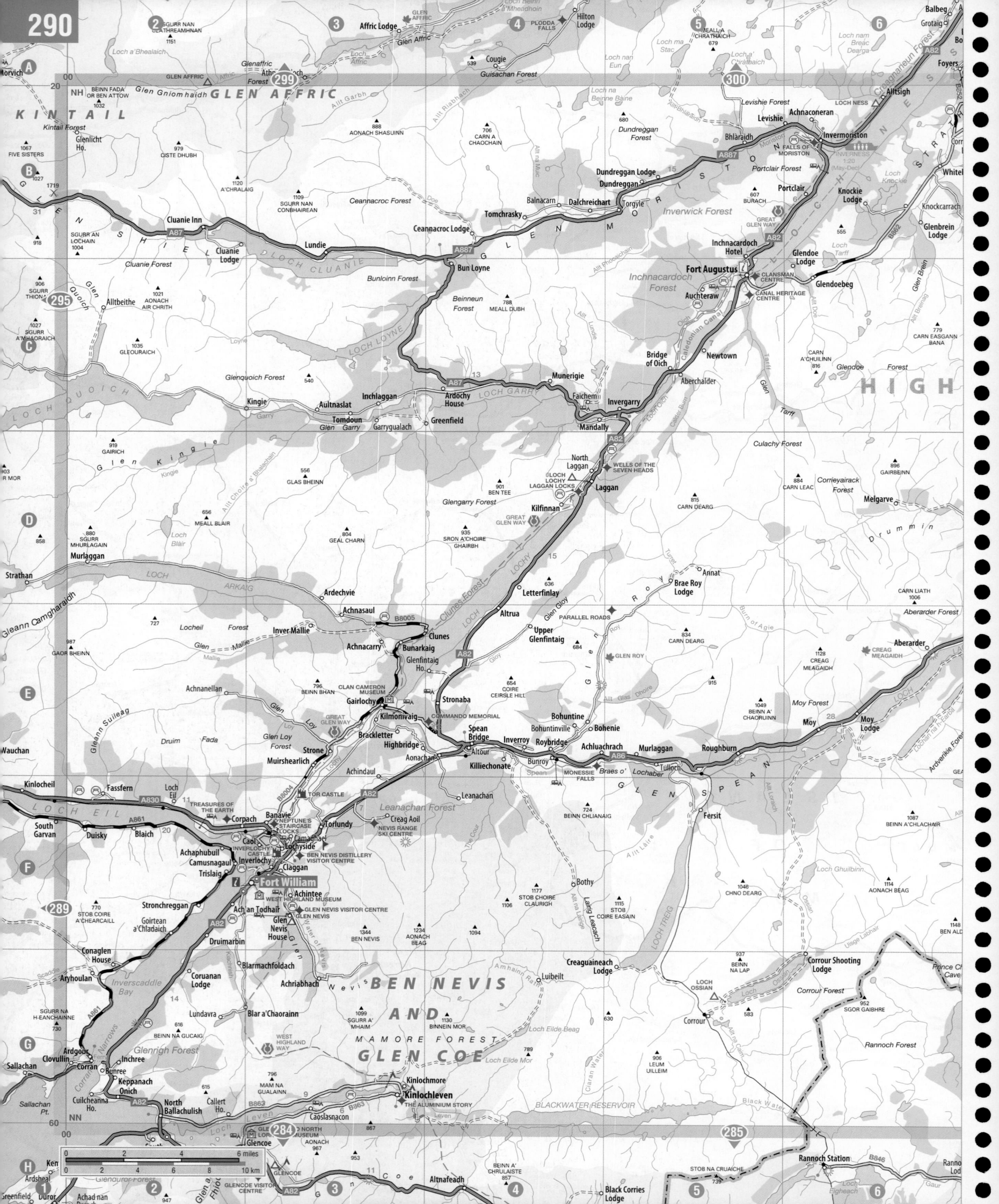

Affric Lodge
Glen Affric
Plodda Falls
Hilton Lodge
Balbeg
Grotaig
Loch a'Bhealaich
Cougie
Guisachan Forest
Loch ma Stac
Loch nan Eun
Loch nam Breac Dearga
Foyers
A82
Glen Affric
Glenaffric Forest
299
300
GLEN AFFRIC
KINTAIL
Kintail Forest
Glenlicht Ho.
1067 FIVE SISTERS
1032 BEINN FADA OR BEN ATTOW
979 CISTE DHUBH
888 AONACH SHASUINN
706 CARN A' CHAOCHAIN
680
Dundreggan Forest
Levishie Forest
Levishie
Achnaconeran
Alltsigh
LOCH NESS
Invermoriston
Bhlaraidh
FALLS OF MORISTON
A887
Portclair Forest
Dundreggan Lodge
Dundreggan
Portclair
Knockie Lodge
Knockcarrach
Whitel
1120 A'CHRALAIG
1109 SGURR NAN CONBHAIREAN
Ceannacroc Forest
Balnacarn
Dalchreichart
Torgyle
Tomchrasky
607 BURACH
GREAT GLEN WAY
Inverwick Forest
Glenbrein Lodge
Cluanie Inn
A87
Ceannacroc Lodge
Lundie
Cluanie Lodge
LOCH CLUANIE
A887
GLEN MORISTON
Inchnacardoch Hotel
Glendoe Lodge
918
1004 SGURR AN LOCHAIN
Cluanie Forest
Bun Loyne
Bunloinn Forest
Fort Augustus
CLANSMAN CENTRE
CANAL HERITAGE CENTRE
Glendoebeg
906 SGURR THIONA
295
Glen Quoich
Alltbeithe
1021 AONACH AIR CHRITH
Beinneun Forest
788 MEALL DUBH
Inchnacardoch Forest
Auchteraw
779 CARN EASGANN BANA
1027 SGURR A'MHAORAICH
1035 GLEOURAICH
LOCH LOYNE
Bridge of Oich
Newtown
Caledonian Canal
CARN A'CHUILINN 816
Glendoe Forest
HIGH
Glenquoich Forest
540
A87
Munerigie
Aberchalder
LOCH QUOICH
Kingie
Aultnaslat
Inchlaggan
Ardochy House
LOCH GARRY
Faichem
Invergarry
Tomdoun
Glen Garry
Garrygualach
Greenfield
Mandally
919 GAIRICH
Glen Kingie
556 GLAS BHEINN
A82
North Laggan
WELLS OF THE SEVEN HEADS
Culachy Forest
896 GAIRBEINN
884 CARN LEAC
Corrieyairack Forest
LOCH LOCHY
LAGGAN LOCKS
Laggan
901 BEN TEE
815 CARN DEARG
Melgarve
656 MEALL BLAIR
Glengarry Forest
Kilfinnan
GREAT GLEN WAY
Drummin
880 SGURR MHURLAGAIN
858
804 GEAL CHARN
935 SRON A'CHOIRE GHAIRBH
Murlaggan
Strathan
LOCH ARKAIG
Ardechvie
636
Letterfinlay
Annat
Brae Roy Lodge
Glen Roy
CARN LIATH 1006
Gleann Camgharaidh
Achnasaul
B8005
Clunes Forest
Altrua
Glen Gloy
PARALLEL ROADS
Aberarder Forest
727
Locheil Forest
Inver Mallie
Clunes
Upper Glenfintaig
834 CARN DEARG
Burn of Agie
Aberarder
987 GAOR BHEINN
Glen Mallie
Achnacarry
Bunarkaig
Glenfintaig Ho.
A82
684
GLEN ROY
1128 CREAG MEAGAIDH
CREAG MEAGAIDH
915
Achnanellan
796 BEINN BHAN
CLAN CAMERON MUSEUM
654 COIRE CEIRSLE HILL
Gairlochy
Stronaba
Moy Forest
1049 BEINN A' CHAORUINN
Glen Loy
GREAT GLEN WAY
Kilmonivaig
COMMANDO MEMORIAL
Bohuntine
Bohuntinville
Bohenie
Moy
Moy Lodge
Gleann Suileag
Druim Fada
Glen Loy Forest
Brackletter
Highbridge
Spean Bridge
Inverroy
Roybridge
Achluachrach
Murlaggan
Roughburn
Wauchan
Strone
Aonachan
Altour
A86
Muirshearlich
Achindaul
Killiechonate
Bunroy
Braes o' Lochaber
Tulloch
MONESSIE FALLS
GLEN SPEAN
Kinlocheil
Fassfern
Loch Eil
TREASURES OF THE EARTH
TOR CASTLE
Leanachan
A830
A82
B8004
LOCH EIL
A861
Corpach
Banavie
NEPTUNE'S STAIRCASE LOCKS
Torlundy
Leanachan Forest
Creag Aoil
NEVIS RANGE SKI CENTRE
724 BEINN CHLIANAIG
Fersit
1087 BEINN A'CHLACHAIR
South Garvan
Duisky
Blaich
Caol
INVERLOCHY CASTLE
Camaghael
Lochyside
Achaphubuil
Camusnagaul
Inverlochy
BEN NEVIS DISTILLERY VISITOR CENTRE
Claggan
Trislaig
Fort William
Achintee
WEST HIGHLAND MUSEUM
Bothy
Loch Ghuilbinn
289
770 STOB COIRE A'CHEARCAILL
Stronchreggan
Ach'an Todhair
GLEN NEVIS VISITOR CENTRE
GLEN NEVIS
1177 STOB CHOIRE CLAURIGH
1106
1115 STOB COIRE EASAIN
1046 CHNO DEARG
1114 AONACH BEAG
Goirtean a'Chladaich
A82
Glen Nevis House
1344 BEN NEVIS
1234 AONACH BEAG
1094
Lairig Leacach
LOCH TREIG
1148 BEN ALD
Druimarbin
Water of Nevis
Conaglen House
Blarmachfoldach
Creaguaineach Lodge
937 BEINN NA LAP
Corrour Shooting Lodge
Aryhoulan
Inverscaddle Bay
Coruanan Lodge
Achriabhach
BEN NEVIS
Luibeilt
LOCH OSSIAN
Corrour Forest
SGURR NA H-EANCHAINNE 730
Lundavra
Blar a'Chaorainn
1099 SGURR A' MHAIM
AND
1130 BINNEIN MOR
630
Corrour
583
952 SGOR GAIBHRE
A861
Corran Narrows
616 BEINN NA GUCAIG
WEST HIGHLAND WAY
MAMORE FOREST
Loch Eilde Beag
Ardgour
Clovullin
Corran
Inchree
Glenrigh Forest
GLEN COE
789
Loch Eilde Mor
906 LEUM UILLEIM
Rannoch Forest
Sallachan
Bunree
Keppanach
Onich
796 MAM NA GUALAINN
Kinlochmore
Cuilcheanna Ho.
A82
North Ballachulish
615
Callert Ho.
B863
Kinlochleven
THE ALUMINIUM STORY
BLACKWATER RESERVOIR
Black Water
Sallachan Pt.
Caolasnacon
NN
00
60
Loch Leven
Glencoe
284
GLENCOE NORTH LORN MUSEUM
AONACH 967
953
867
285
BEINN A' CHRULAISTE 857
STOB NA CRUAICHE 739
Rannoch Station
B846
0 2 4 6 miles
0 2 4 6 8 10 km
GLENCOE
GLENCOE VISITOR CENTRE
Altnafeadh
Black Corries Lodge
Ardsheal
Duror
Achad nan
947
A82
Loch Eigheach

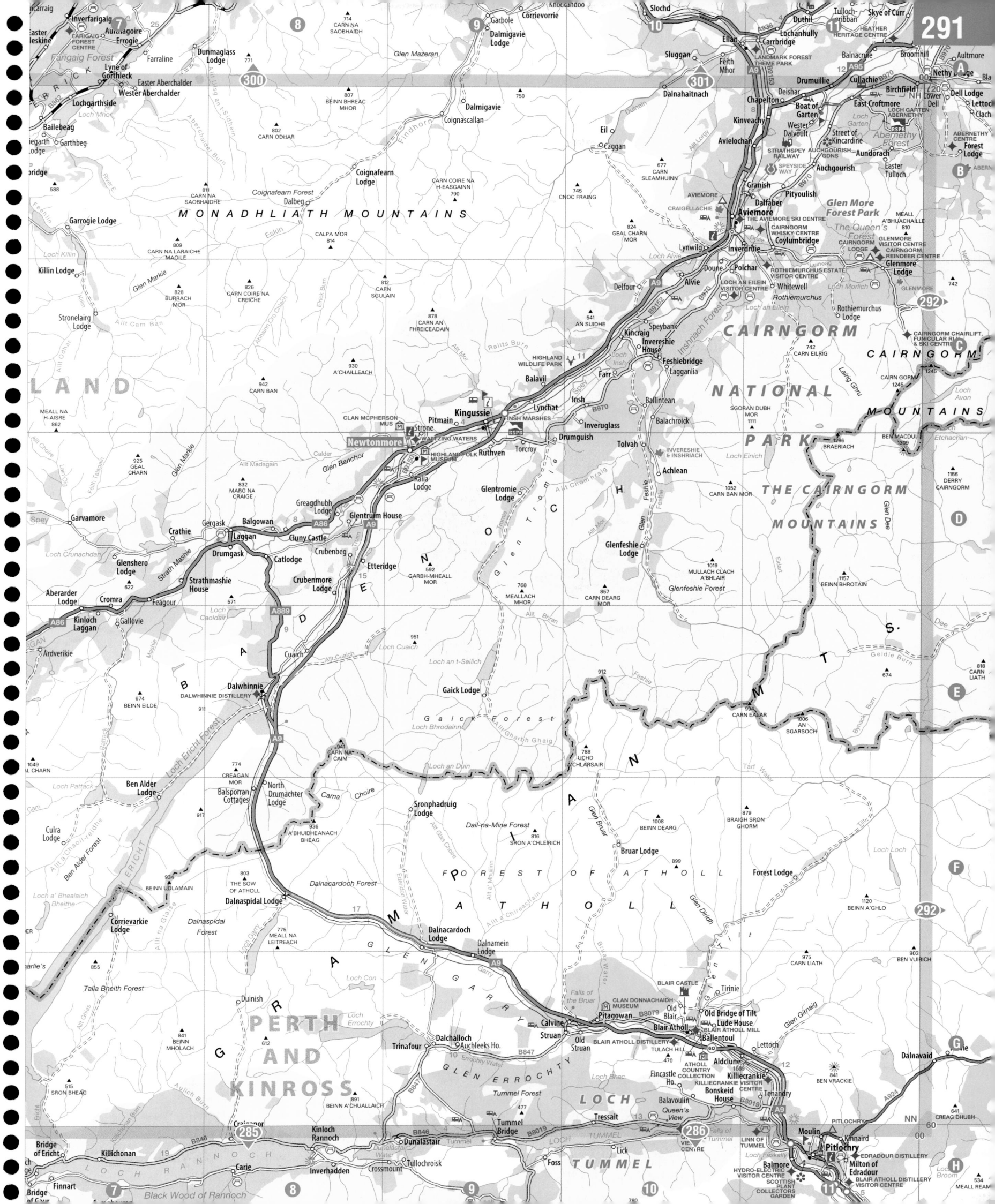

MONADHLIATH MOUNTAINS
CAIRNGORM NATIONAL PARK
CAIRNGORM MOUNTAINS
THE CAIRNGORM MOUNTAINS
BADENOCH
FOREST OF ATHOLL
GRAMPIAN MOUNTAINS
PERTH AND KINROSS
GLEN GARRY
GLEN ERROCHTY
LOCH TUMMEL
LOCH RANNOCH
Inverfarigaig
Farigaig Forest
Lyne of Gorthleck
Easter Aberchalder
Wester Aberchalder
Lochgarthside
Dunmaglass Lodge
Farraline
Garrogie Lodge
Killin Lodge
Stronelairg Lodge
Coignafearn Lodge
Coignafearn Forest
Dalbeg
Dalmigavie Lodge
Dalmigavie
Coignascallan
Corrievorrie
Garbole
Glen Mazeran
Slochd
Duthil
Tulloch-gribban
Skye of Curr
Lochanhully
Carrbridge
Ellan
Sluggan
Feith Mhor
Dalnahaitnach
Drumuillie
Cullachie
Balnacruie
Broomhill
Nethy Bridge
Dell Lodge
Deishar
Chapelton
Boat of Garten
Birchfield
East Croftmore
Kinveachy
Avielochan
Wester Dalvoult
Street of Kincardine
Aundorach
Auchgourish
Eastern Tulloch
Abernethy Forest
Granish
Dalfaber
Pityoulish
Aviemore
Coylumbridge
Glen More Forest Park
The Queen's Forest
Glenmore Lodge
Lynwilg
Inverdruie
Doune
Polchar
Alvie
Delfour
Whitewell
Rothiemurchus
Rothiemurchus Lodge
Kincraig
Speybank
Invereshie House
Inshriach Forest
Feshiebridge
Lagganlia
Farr
Insh
Balavil
Lynchat
Inveruglass
Ballintean
Balachroick
Kingussie
Pitmain
Strone
Newtonmore
Ruthven
Torcroy
Drumguish
Tolvah
Achlean
Ralia Lodge
Glentromie Lodge
Glen Tromie
Glenfeshie Lodge
Glenfeshie Forest
Glen Feshie
Greagdhubh Lodge
Glentruim House
Garvamore
Crathie
Gergask
Balgowan
Laggan
Cluny Castle
Drumgask
Catlodge
Crubenbeg
Etteridge
Glenshero Lodge
Strathmashie House
Crubenmore Lodge
Aberarder Lodge
Cromra
Feagour
Kinloch Laggan
Gallovie
Ardverikie
Cuaich
Loch Cuaich
Loch an t-Seilich
Gaick Lodge
Gaick Forest
Dalwhinnie
Dalwhinnie Distillery
Loch Ericht Forest
Ben Alder Lodge
Balsporran Cottages
North Drumachter Lodge
Sronphadruig Lodge
Dail-na-Mine Forest
Bruar Lodge
Forest Lodge
Culra Lodge
Ben Alder Forest
Dalnacardoch Forest
Dalnaspidal Lodge
Dalnaspidal Forest
Corrievarkie Lodge
Dalnacardoch Lodge
Dalnamein Lodge
Talla Bheith Forest
Duinish
Blair Castle
Clan Donnachaidh Museum
Calvine
Pitagowan
Struan
Old Struan
Old Blair
Blair Atholl
Old Bridge of Tilt
Lude House
Tirinie
Ballentoul
Blair Atholl Distillery
Aldclune
Killiecrankie
Bonskeid House
Fincastle Ho.
Lettoch
Tenandry
Balavoulin
Dalnavaid
Trinafour
Dalchalloch
Auchleeks Ho.
Tummel Forest
Tummel Bridge
Tressait
Queen's View
Craiganour
Kinloch Rannoch
Dunalastair
Bridge of Ericht
Killichonan
Carie
Inverhadden
Crossmount
Tullochroisk
Foss
Lick
Finnart
Black Wood of Rannoch
Moulin
Kinnaird
Pitlochry
Edradour Distillery
Milton of Edradour
Balmore
A9
A86
A889
A95
A938
A924
B847
B846
B8019
B8079
B970
B9152
B9153
B9150
300
301
285
286
292

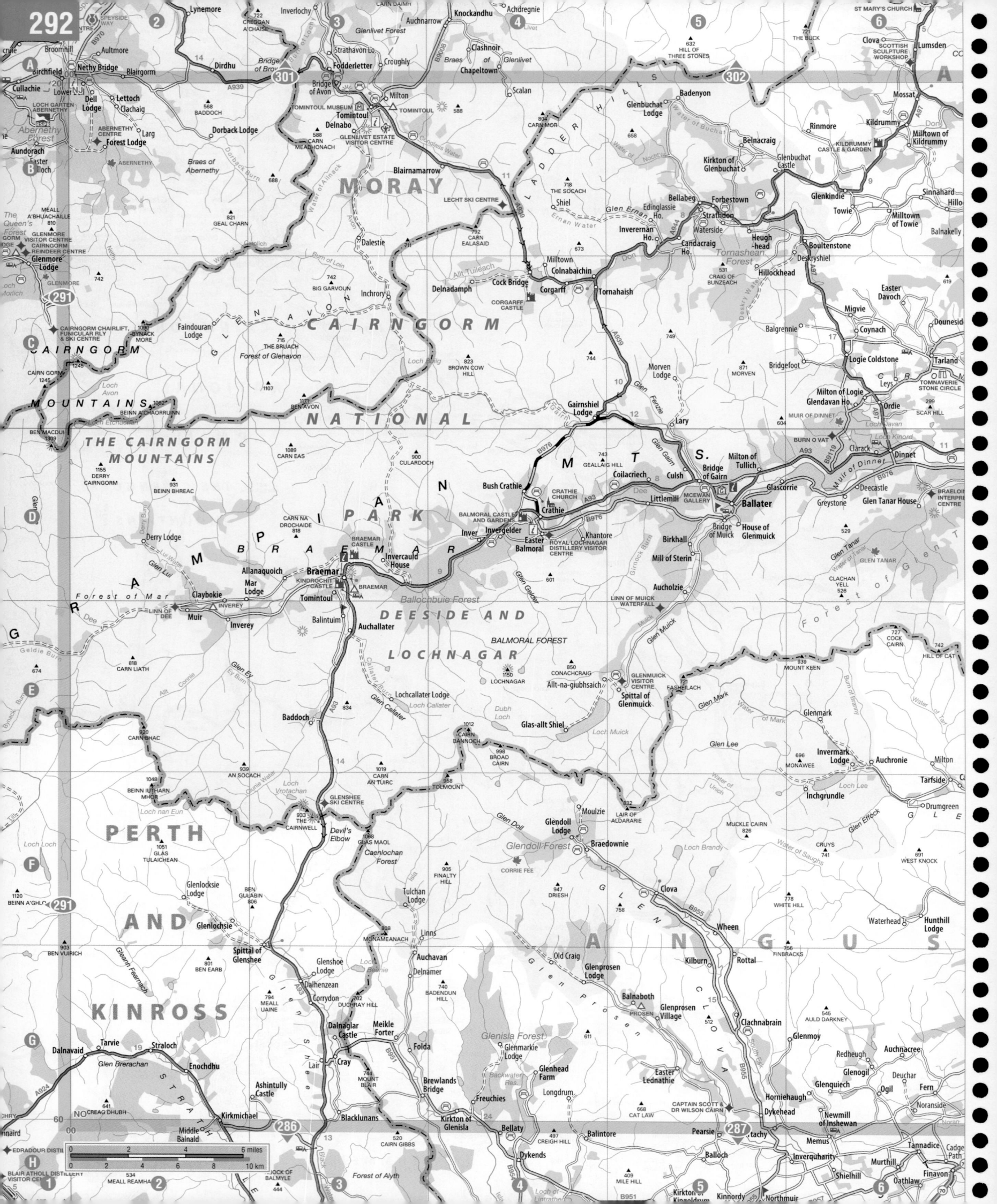

Lynemore
SPEYSIDE WAY
722 CREGGAN A'CHAISE
Inverlochy
Auchnarrow
Knockandhu
Achdregnie
Livet
ST MARY'S CHURCH
THE BUCK
632 HILL OF THREE STONES
Clova
SCOTTISH SCULPTURE WORKSHOP
Lumsden
Broomhill
Aultmore
Nethy Bridge
Blairgorm
Dirdhu
Bridge of Brown
Strathavon Lo.
Fodderletter
Croughly
Glenlivet Forest
Clashnoir
Braes of Glenlivet
Chapeltown
Scalan
Birchfield
Cullachie
Lower
Dell Lodge
Lettoch
Clachaig
LOCH GARTEN ABERNETHY
RSPB
Abernethy Forest
568 BADDOCH
Bridge of Avon
Milton
TOMINTOUL MUSEUM
Tomintoul
TOMINTOUL
588
Delnabo
GLENLIVET ESTATE VISITOR CENTRE
588 CARN MEADHONACH
Conglass Water
ABERNETHY CENTRE
Larg
Forest Lodge
Dorback Lodge
Aundorach
Easter Tulloch
ABERNETHY
Braes of Abernethy
Dorback Burn
688
Water of Ailnack
MORAY
Blairnamarrow
804 CARN MOR
Glenbuchat Lodge
Badenyon
Water of Buchat
658
LADDER HILLS
Rinmore
Mossat
Kildrummy
Milltown of Kildrummy
KILDRUMMY CASTLE & GARDEN
Belnacraig
Kirkton of Glenbuchat
Glenbuchat Castle
Glenkindie
Towie
Sinnahard
Milltown of Towie
Balnakelly
718 THE SOCACH
Shiel
LECHT SKI CENTRE
Glen Ernan
Ernan Water
Edinglassie Ho.
Bellabeg
Forbestown
Strathdon
Waterside
Inverernan Ho.
Candacraig Ho.
Heugh-head
Boultenstone
Deskryshiel
Hillockhead
Tornashean Forest
531 CRAIG OF BUNZEACH
MEALL A'BHUACHAILLE 810
The Queen's Forest
GLENMORE VISITOR CENTRE
CAIRNGORM REINDEER CENTRE
Glenmore Lodge
GLENMORE
742
821 GEAL CHARN
Dalestie
792 CARN EALASAID
673
Milltown
Colnabaichin
Allt Tuileach
Cock Bridge
Corgarff
Tornahaish
CORGARFF CASTLE
Delnadamph
742 BIG GARVOUN
Inchrory
Burn of Loin
CAIRNGORM CHAIRLIFT, FUNICULAR RLY & SKI CENTRE
1090 BYNACK MORE
Faindouran Lodge
GLEN AVON
CAIRNGORM
715 THE BRUACH
Forest of Glenavon
Loch Builg
923 BROWN COW HILL
744
749
Morven Lodge
871 MORVEN
Easter Davoch
Migvie
Coynach
Douneside
Balgrennie
Bridgefoot
Logie Coldstone
Tarland
Leys
TOMNAVERIE STONE CIRCLE
Milton of Logie
Glendavan Ho.
Ordie
299 SCAR HILL
MUIR OF DINNET
CAIRNGORM
CAIRN GORM 1245
Loch Avon
1107
MOUNTAINS
1082 BEINN A'CHAORRUINN
1171 BEN AVON
Loch Etchachan
NATIONAL
Gairnshiel Lodge
Glen Fenzie
Lary
604
Loch Davan
BURN O VAT
Clarack
Loch Kinord
Dinnet
Muir of Dinnet
BEN MACDUI 1309
THE CAIRNGORM MOUNTAINS
1089 CARN EAS
900 CULARDOCH
743 GEALLAIG HILL
Glen Gairn
MTS.
Bridge of Gairn
Milton of Tullich
Culsh
Coilacriech
1155 DERRY CAIRNGORM
931 BEINN BHREAC
Bush Crathie
CRATHIE CHURCH
Crathie
Littlemill
MCEWAN GALLERY
Ballater
Glascorrie
Deecastle
Greystone
Glen Tanar House
BRAELOIN INTERPRETIVE CENTRE
CARN NA DROCHAIDE 818
PARK
BALMORAL CASTLE AND GARDENS
Inver
Invergelder
Easter Balmoral
ROYAL LOCHNAGAR DISTILLERY VISITOR CENTRE
Khantore
Birkhall
Bridge of Muick
House of Glenmuick
529
Derry Lodge
BRAEMAR CASTLE
Invercauld House
Mill of Sterin
Glen Tanar
GLEN TANAR
Glen Lui
GRAMPIAN
BRAEMAR
Allanaquoich
Braemar
601
Aucholzie
CLACHAN YELL 526
Forest of Mar
Claybokie
Mar Lodge
KINDROCHIT CASTLE
Tomintoul
INVEREY
LINN OF DEE
Muir
Inverey
Ballochbuie Forest
LINN OF MUICK WATERFALL
Forest of Glen Tanar
Balintuim
Auchallater
DEESIDE AND LOCHNAGAR
BALMORAL FOREST
Glen Muick
727 COCK CAIRN
742 HILL OF CAT
Geldie Burn
674
818 CARN LIATH
Glen Ey
LOCHNAGAR
1150 LOCHNAGAR
850 CONACHCRAIG
Allt-na-giubhsaich
GLENMUICK VISITOR CENTRE
Spittal of Glenmuick
939 MOUNT KEEN
FASHEILACH
Glen Mark
Lochcallater Lodge
Loch Callater
Glen Callater
834
Baddoch
Dubh Loch
Glas-allt Shiel
Loch Muick
Glenmark
920 CARN BHAC
1012 CAIRN BANNOCH
998 BROAD CAIRN
Glen Lee
696 MONAWEE
Invermark Lodge
Auchronie
Milton
Tarfside
Loch Lee
Inchgrundle
939 AN SOCACH
1019 CARN AN TUIRC
958 TOLMOUNT
1048 BEINN IUTHARN MHOR
Loch Vrotachan
GLENSHEE SKI CENTRE
Drumgreen
Loch nan Eun
933 THE CAIRNWELL
Devil's Elbow
832 LAIR OF ALDARARIE
Glen Doll
Glendoll Lodge
Moulzie
MUCKLE CAIRN 826
Glen Effock
PERTH
1051 GLAS TULAICHEAN
1068 GLAS MAOL
Caenlochan Forest
Glendoll Forest
Braedownie
Loch Brandy
Water of Saughs
CRUYS 741
691 WEST KNOCK
Loch Loch
905 FINALTY HILL
CORRIE FEE
1120 BEINN A'GHLO
Glenlocksie Lodge
BEN GULABIN 806
Tulchan Lodge
947 DRIESH
Clova
778 WHITE HILL
AND
Glenlochsie
758
GLEN CLOVA
Wheen
Waterhead
Hunthill Lodge
903 BEN VUIRICH
Spittal of Glenshee
898 MONAMEANACH
Linns
ANGUS
Gleann Fearnach
801 BEN EARB
Glenshee Lodge
Auchavan
Old Craig
Kilburn
Rottal
756 FINBRACKS
Delnamer
Glenprosen Lodge
Dalhenzean
740 BADENDUN HILL
Glen Prosen
794 MEALL UAINE
Corrydon
702 DUCHRAY HILL
Balnaboth
PROSEN
Glenprosen Village
545 AULD DARKNEY
KINROSS
Dalnaglar Castle
Meikle Forter
Glenisla Forest
512
Clachnabrain
611
Glenmoy
Dalnavaid
Tarvie
Straloch
Glenmarkie Lodge
Redheugh
Auchnacree
Folda
Glen Brerachan
Enochdhu
Lair
Cray
744 MOUNT BLAIR
Glenhead Farm
Glenogil
Easter Lednathie
Deuchar
Brewlands Bridge
Backwater Res.
Glenquiech
Ogil
Fern
STRATH
Ashintully Castle
Longdrum
Hornieheaugh
641 CREAG DHUBH
Freuchies
668 CAT LAW
CAPTAIN SCOTT & DR WILSON CAIRN
Dykehead
Noranside
Newmill of Inshewan
Kirkmichael
Blacklunans
Kirkton of Glenisla
Middle Balnald
Bellaty
497 CREIGH HILL
Balintore
Pearsie
Memus
EDRADOUR DISTILLERY
520 CAIRN GIBBS
Dykends
Balloch
Inverquharity
Tannadice
Cadger Path
Murthill
BLAIR ATHOLL DISTILLERY VISITOR CENTRE
534 MEALL REAMHAR
HILL OF BALMYLE 444
Forest of Alyth
409 MILE HILL
Kirkton of Kingoldrum
Kinnordy
Northmuir
Shielhill
Oathlaw
Finavon
0 2 4 6 miles
0 2 4 6 8 10 km

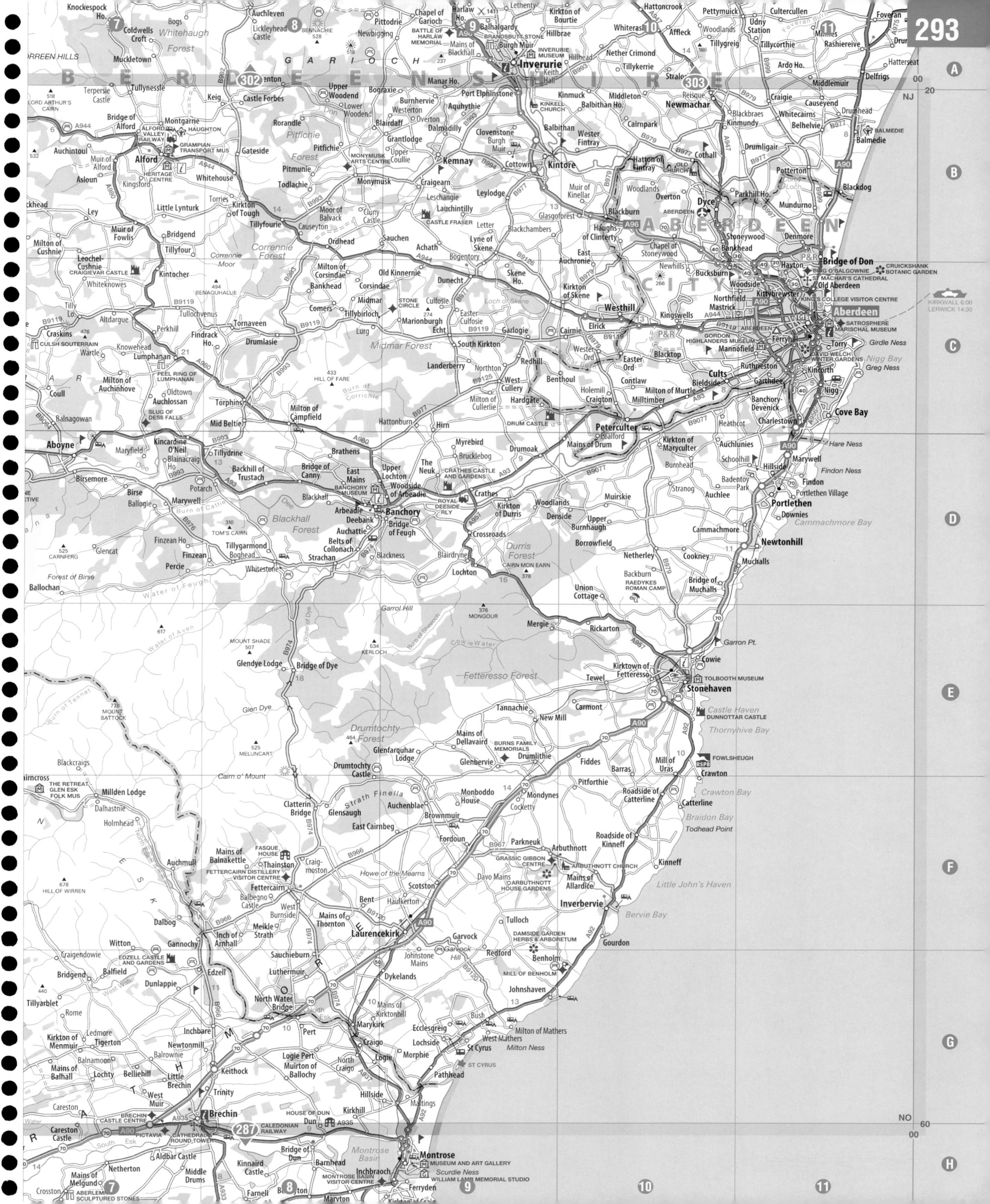
ABERDEENSHIRE
ABERDEEN CITY
Aberdeen
Inverurie
Kintore
Dyce
Westhill
Alford
Kemnay
Newmachar
Balmedie
Bridge of Don
Old Aberdeen
Torry
Cults
Peterculter
Banchory
Aboyne
Torphins
Portlethen
Newtonhill
Stonehaven
Laurencekirk
Inverbervie
Montrose
Brechin
Edzell
Fettercairn
St Cyrus
Marykirk
Cove Bay
Muchalls
Catterline
Gourdon
Johnshaven
Bridge of Dye
Strachan
Crathes
Drumoak
Echt
Monymusk
Midmar Forest
Durris Forest
Fetteresso Forest
Drumtochty Forest
Blackhall Forest
Pitfichie Forest
Corrennie Forest
Whitehaugh Forest
Forest of Birse
Water of Feugh
Howe of the Mearns
Strath Finella
Cairn o' Mount
Glen Dye
Garrol Hill
Nigg Bay
Girdle Ness
Greg Ness
Findon Ness
Cammachmore Bay
Garron Pt.
Castle Haven
Thornyhive Bay
Crawton Bay
Braidon Bay
Todhead Point
Little John's Haven
Bervie Bay
Milton Ness
Montrose Basin
Scurdie Ness
CASTLE FRASER
DRUM CASTLE
CRATHES CASTLE AND GARDENS
DUNNOTTAR CASTLE
FOWLSHEUGH
TOLBOOTH MUSEUM
ARBUTHNOTT CHURCH
GRASSIC GIBBON CENTRE
FETTERCAIRN DISTILLERY VISITOR CENTRE
FASQUE HOUSE
EDZELL CASTLE AND GARDENS
BRECHIN CASTLE CENTRE
PICTAVIA
CALEDONIAN RAILWAY
HOUSE OF DUN
MUSEUM AND ART GALLERY
WILLIAM LAMB MEMORIAL STUDIO
MONTROSE BASIN VISITOR CENTRE
ABERLEMNO SCULPTURED STONES
GRAMPIAN TRANSPORT MUS
ALFORD VALLEY RAILWAY
CRAIGIEVAR CASTLE
PEEL RING OF LUMPHANAN
BANCHORY MUSEUM
ROYAL DEESIDE RLY
SATROSPHERE
MARISCHAL MUSEUM
KING'S COLLEGE VISITOR CENTRE
ST MACHAR'S CATHEDRAL
CRUICKSHANK BOTANIC GARDEN
DAVID WELCH WINTER GARDENS
GORDON HIGHLANDERS MUSEUM
INVERURIE MUSEUM
BATTLE OF HARLAW MEMORIAL
KIRKWALL 6:00
LERWICK 14:30
A90
A96
A93
A944
A980
A957
A92
A935
B974
B966
B9077
302
303
287
NJ
NO

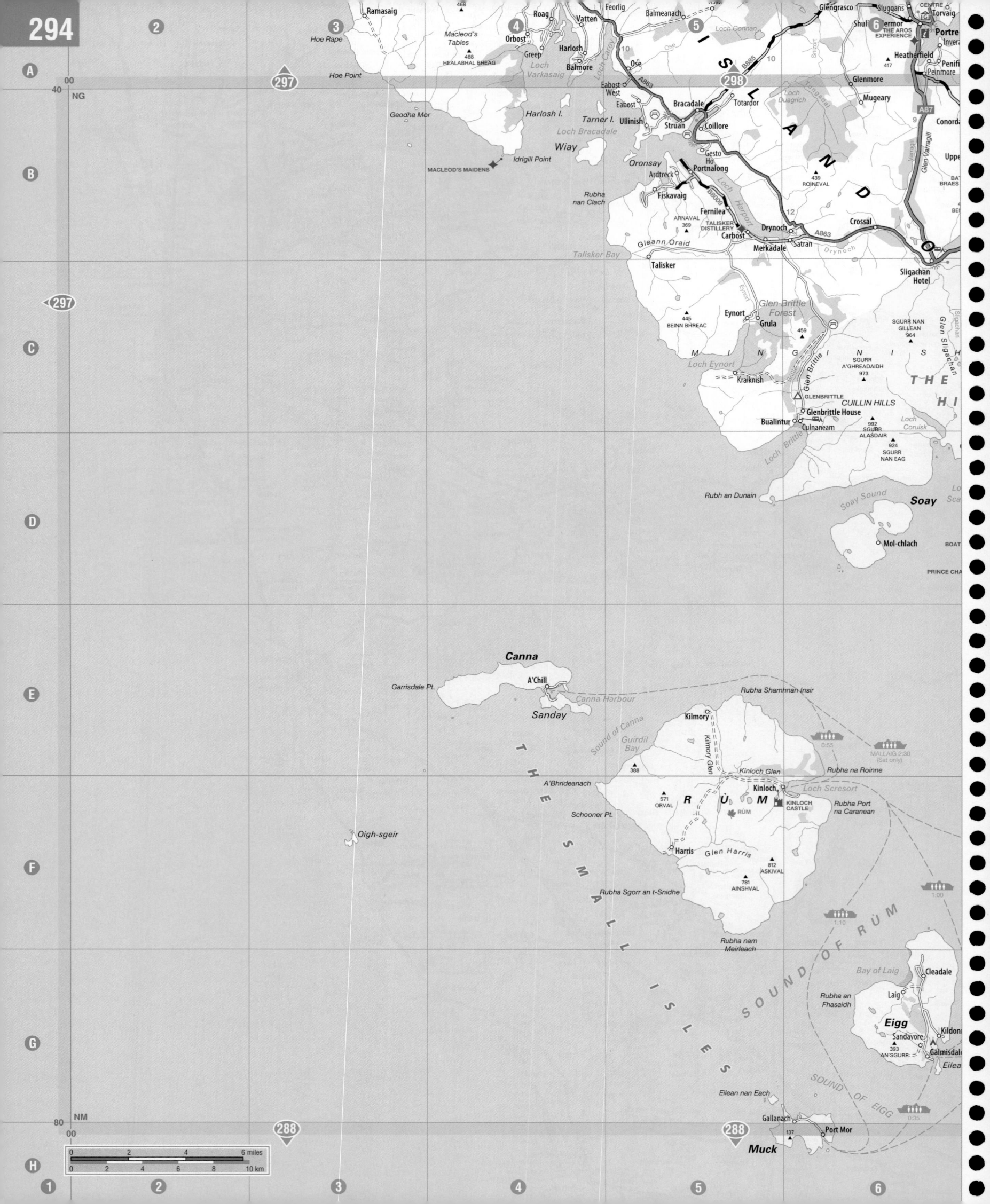

Ramasaig
Roag
Feorlig
Vatten
Balmeanach
Loch Connan
Glengrasco
Sluggans
CENTRE
Torvaig

Hoe Rape
Macleod's Tables
Orbost
Harlosh
Greep
Balmore
HEALABHAL BHEAG

Hoe Point
NG
Eabost West
Ose
A863

Geodha Mor
Harlosh I.
Tarner I.
Ullinish
Struan
Bracadale
Totardor
Coillore

Wiay
MACLEOD'S MAIDENS
Idrigill Point
Oronsay
Gesto Ho
Portnalong
Ardtreck
ROINEVAL

Rubha nan Clach
Fiskavaig
Fernilea
Loch Harport
ARNAVAL
TALISKER DISTILLERY
Carbost
Drynoch
Crossal

Talisker Bay
Gleann Oraid
Satran
Merkadale
Drynoch
A863

Talisker
Sligachan Hotel

Glen Brittle Forest
BEINN BHREAC
Eynort
Grula
SGURR NAN GILLEAN
964

Loch Eynort
Kraiknish
SGURR A'GHREADAIDH
973
THE HI

GLENBRITTLE
CUILLIN HILLS
Glenbrittle House
SGURR ALASDAIR
992

Bualintur
Culnaneam
SGURR NAN EAG
924

Rubh an Dunain
Soay Sound
Soay

Mol-chlach
BOAT

PRINCE CHA

Canna
A'Chill

Garrisdale Pt.
Canna Harbour

Sanday
Kilmory

Sound of Canna
Guirdil Bay
Kilmory Glen
Rubha Shamhnan Insir
MALLAIG 2:30 (Sat only)

A'Bhrideanach
388
Kinloch Glen
Kinloch
Loch Scresort
Rubha na Roinne

ORVAL
571
RÚM
KINLOCH CASTLE
Rubha Port na Caranean

Oigh-sgeir
Schooner Pt.
Harris
Glen Harris
ASKIVAL
812

Rubha Sgorr an t-Snidhe
AINSHVAL
781

Rubha nam Meirleach

Bay of Laig
Cleadale

Rubha an Fhasaidh
Laig

Eilean nan Each
Eigg
Sandavore
AN-SGURR
393
Galmisdale

Gallanach
Port Mor
137

Muck

0  2  4  6 miles
0  2  4  6  8  10 km

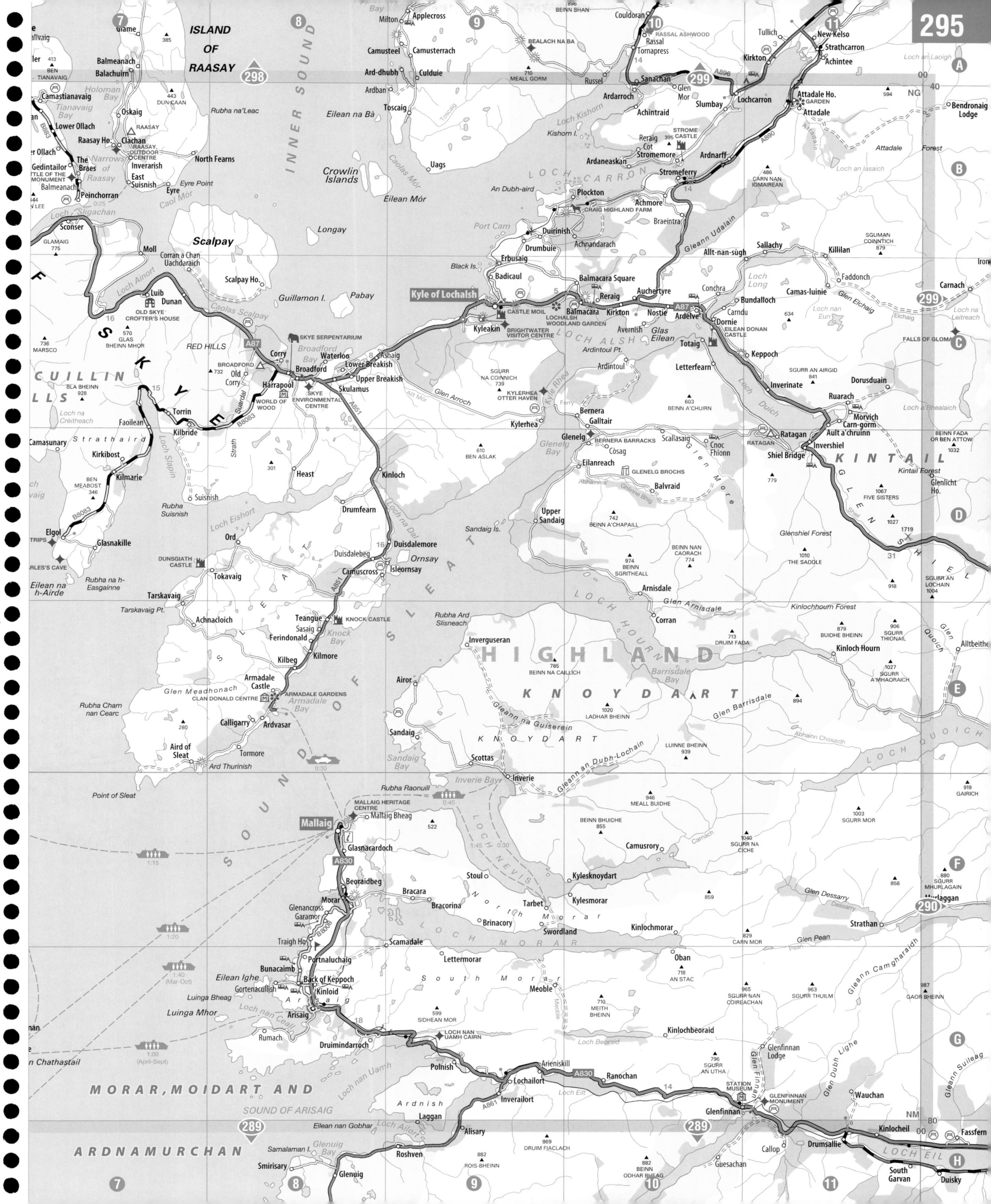

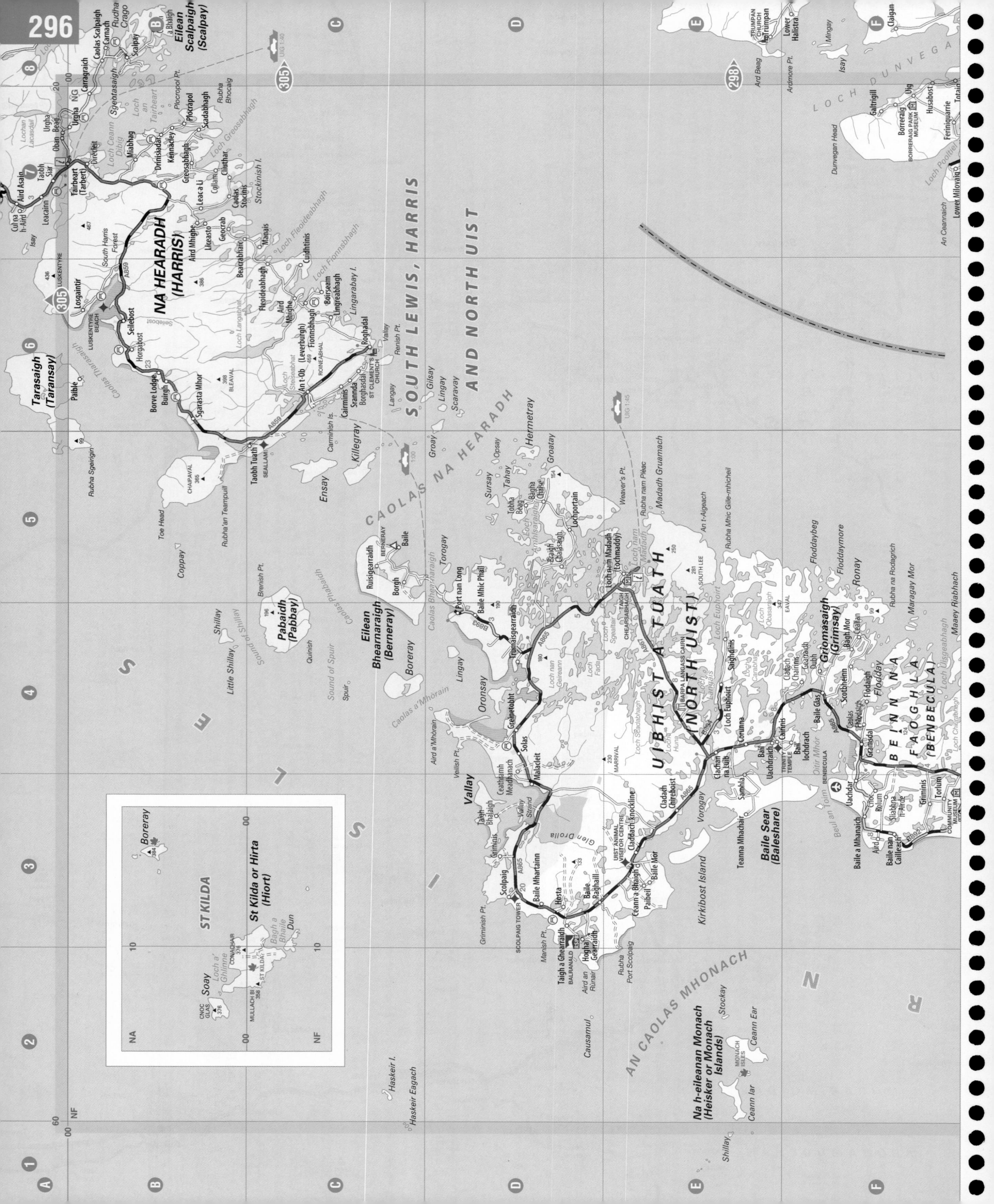

NA HEARADH (HARRIS)
SOUTH LEWIS, HARRIS
AND NORTH UIST
UIBHIST A TUATH (NORTH UIST)
BEINN NA FAOGHLA (BENBECULA)
CAOLAS NA HEARADH
AN CAOLAS MHONACH
LOCH DUNVEGA
Tarasaigh (Taransay)
Eilean Scalpaigh (Scalpay)
Eilean Bhearnaraigh (Berneray)
Pabaidh (Pabbay)
Baile Sear (Baleshare)
Griomasaigh (Grimsay)
Na h-eileanan Monach (Heisker or Monach Islands)
ST KILDA
St Kilda or Hirta (Hiort)
Boreray
Soay
Tairbeart (Tarbert)
An t-Ob (Leverburgh)
Loch nam Madadh (Lochmaddy)
Taobh Tuath
Roghadal
Seilebost
Losgaintir
Borve Lodge
Sgarasta Mhor
Cladach Chireboist
Claddach-Knockline
Baile a Mhanaich
Uachdar
Lochportain
Baile Mhic Phail
Port nan Long
Greinetobht
Solas
Malacleit
Scolpaig
Hosta
Baile Mhartainn
Vallay
Taigh a Ghearraidh
Kirkibost Island
Haskeir I.
Haskeir Eagach
Causamul
Stockay
Shillay
Ensay
Killegray
Coppay
Little Shillay
Sound of Spuir
Lingay
Oronsay
Torogay
Hermetray
Groatay
Ronay
Floddaymore
Isay
Mingay
A859
A865
A867
B893
305
298

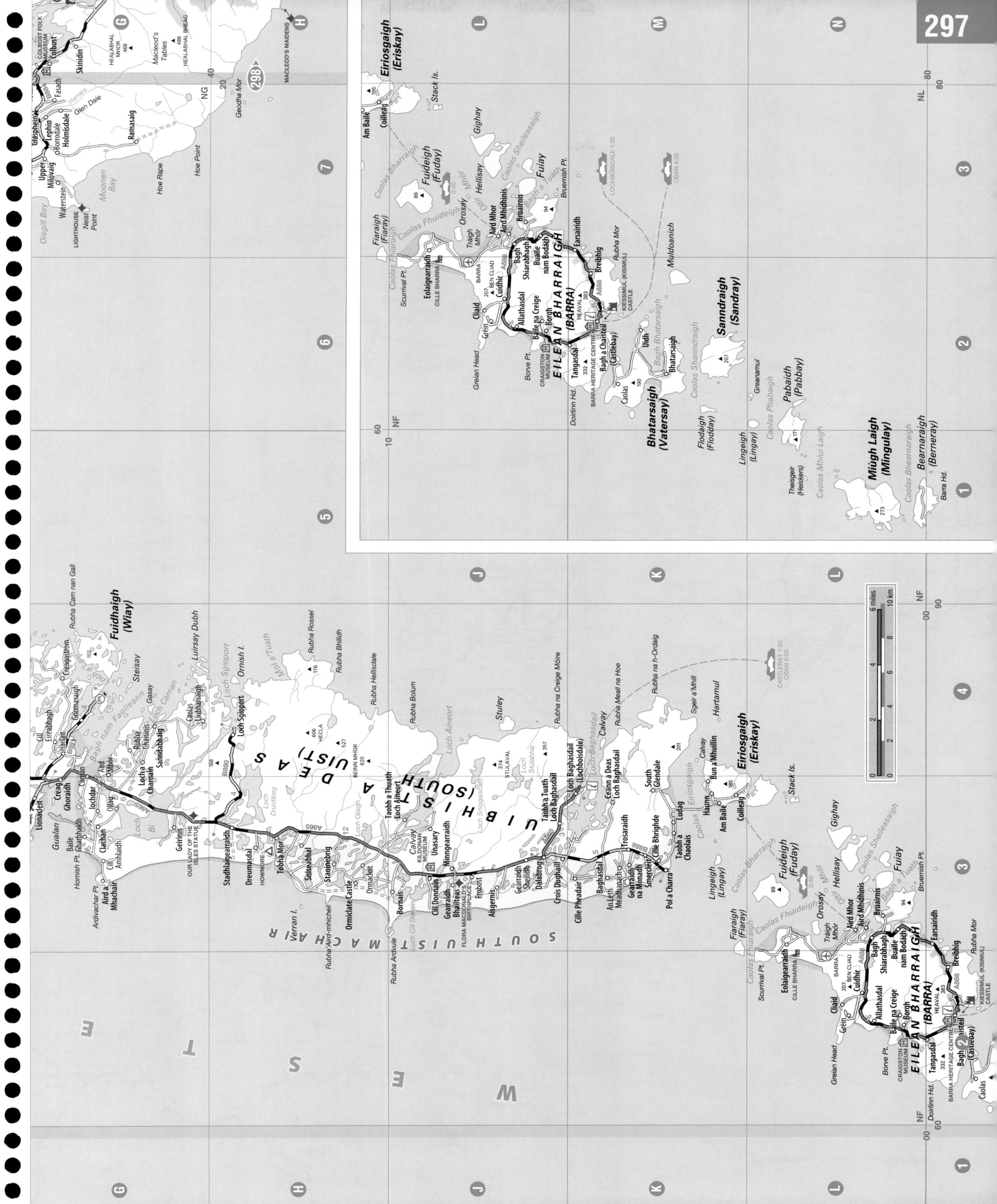

**Grid references (top):** G H (38, 40, NG, 20) L M N

**Northern section (Barra area, top right):**
Eiriosgaigh (Eriskay), Am Baile, Coilleag, Stack Is., Caolas Bharraigh, Fuideigh (Fuday), Gighay, Caolas Shelleasaigh, Hellisay, Fuiay, Bagh a Tuath, Bruarnish Pt., Fiaraigh (Fiaray), Scurrival Pt., Traigh Mhor, Orosay, Aird Mhor, Aird Mhidhinis, Bruairnis, Muldoanich, Eolaigearraidh, Cliad, Grein, BEN CLIAD, Cuidhir, Allathasdal, Baile na Creige, Borgh, Bagh, Sharabhagh, Buaile nam Bodach, Earsairidh, Rubha Mor, Rubha (Kisimul), Breibhig, KIESSIMUL (KISIMUL) CASTLE, EILEAN BHARRAIGH (BARRA), HEAVAL, LOOCHBOISDALE 1:30, OBAN 4:50, Grein Head, Borve Pt., CRAGSTON MUSEUM, Tangasdal, BARRA HERITAGE CENTRE, Bagh a Chaisteil (Castlebay), Dorlinn Hd., Uidh, Caolas, Bhatarsaigh, Caolas Shannndraigh, Sanndraigh (Sandray), Bhatarsaigh (Vatersay), Flodaigh (Flodday), Lingeigh (Lingay), Pabaidh (Pabbay), Caolas Phabaigh, Greanamul, Caolas Mhiui Laigh, Theisgeir (Heiskers), Miugh Laigh (Mingulay), Bearnaraigh (Berneray), Caolas Bhearnaraigh, Barra Hd.

**Grid numbers:** 7, 6 (NF, 60, 10), 5, NL 80, 3, 2, 1

**Southern/western section (South Uist and Barra):**
Fuidhaigh (Wiay), Rubha Cam nan Gall, Creagastrom, Cill Eireabhagh, Flodaigh, Grimsaigh, Steisay, Gasay, Luirsay Dubh, Caolas a Charnain, Ornish I., Rubha Rossel, Rubha Bhilich, Mol a Tuath, Rubha Hellisdale, Rubha Bolum, Stuley, Rubha na Creige Moire, Calvay, Rubha Meall na Hoe, Rubha h-Ordaig, Sgeir a'Mhill, Hartamul, CASTLEBAY 1:30, OBAN 5:20, Eiriosgaigh (Eriskay), Stack Is.

Lionacleit, Gualan, Hornish Pt., Cill Amhlaidh, Aird a'Mhachair, Ardivachar Pt., Rubha 'Aird-mhichel, Verran I., Ormidale Castle, OUR LADY OF THE ISLES STATUE, Stadhlaigearraidh, Dreumasdal, Tobha Mor, HOWMORE, Snaiseabhal, Staoinebrig, Bornais, Cill Donain, Gearraidh Bhailteas, FLORA MACDONALD'S BIRTHPLACE, Kilphedir, Asgernis, Gearraidh Sheilidh, Dalabrog, Crois Dughaill, Cille Pheadair, Pol a Charra, Smeircleit, Ludag, Cille Bhrighde, Taobh a Chaolais, Baghasdail, Trosaraidh, Gearraidh na Monadh, An Leth Meadhanach, Pol a Charra

UIBHIST A DEAS (SOUTH UIST) / A MACHAIR, BEINN MHOR, HECLA, STULAVAL, Loch Druidibeag, Loch Olaigh, Loch Shogasdail, Loch Aineort, Loch Eiport, Loch Sgioport, Loch Bi, Loch Cill Domain, Loch Baghasdail (Lochboisdale), Ceann a Deas, Loch Baghasdail, South Glendale, Haun, Am Baile, Coilleag, Bun a'Mhuilinn, Caolas Eiriosgaigh, Calvay

A865, A888, B890, B891, Calvay KILDONAN MUSEUM, Unasary, Mingearraidh, Taobh a Thuath Loch Aineort, Taobh a Tuath, Loch Stulabhal

Fuideigh (Fuday), Lingeigh (Lingay), Fiaraigh (Fiaray), Caolas Fhuideigh, Orosay, Hellisay, Caolas Shelleasaigh, Gighay, Fuiay, Bagh a Tuath, Bruarnish Pt., Traigh Mhor, Aird Mhor, Aird Mhidhinis, Bruairnis, Earsairidh

EILEAN BHARRAIGH (BARRA), HEAVAL, KIESSIMUL (KISIMUL) CASTLE, Bagh a Chaisteil (Castlebay), Tangasdal, CRAGSTON MUSEUM, BARRA HERITAGE CENTRE, Grein Head, Borve Pt., Dorlinn Hd., Caolas, Eolaigearraidh, CILLE BHARRA, BEN CLIAD, Cuidhir, Cliad, Grein, Allathasdal, Baile na Creige, Borgh, Bagh, Sharabhagh, Buaile nam Bodach, Breibhig, Rubha Mor

**Scale bar:** 6 miles / 10 km

**Grid references (bottom):** G H J K L, E T S W E (NF 90, 00, NF, 00), 4, 3, 2, 1

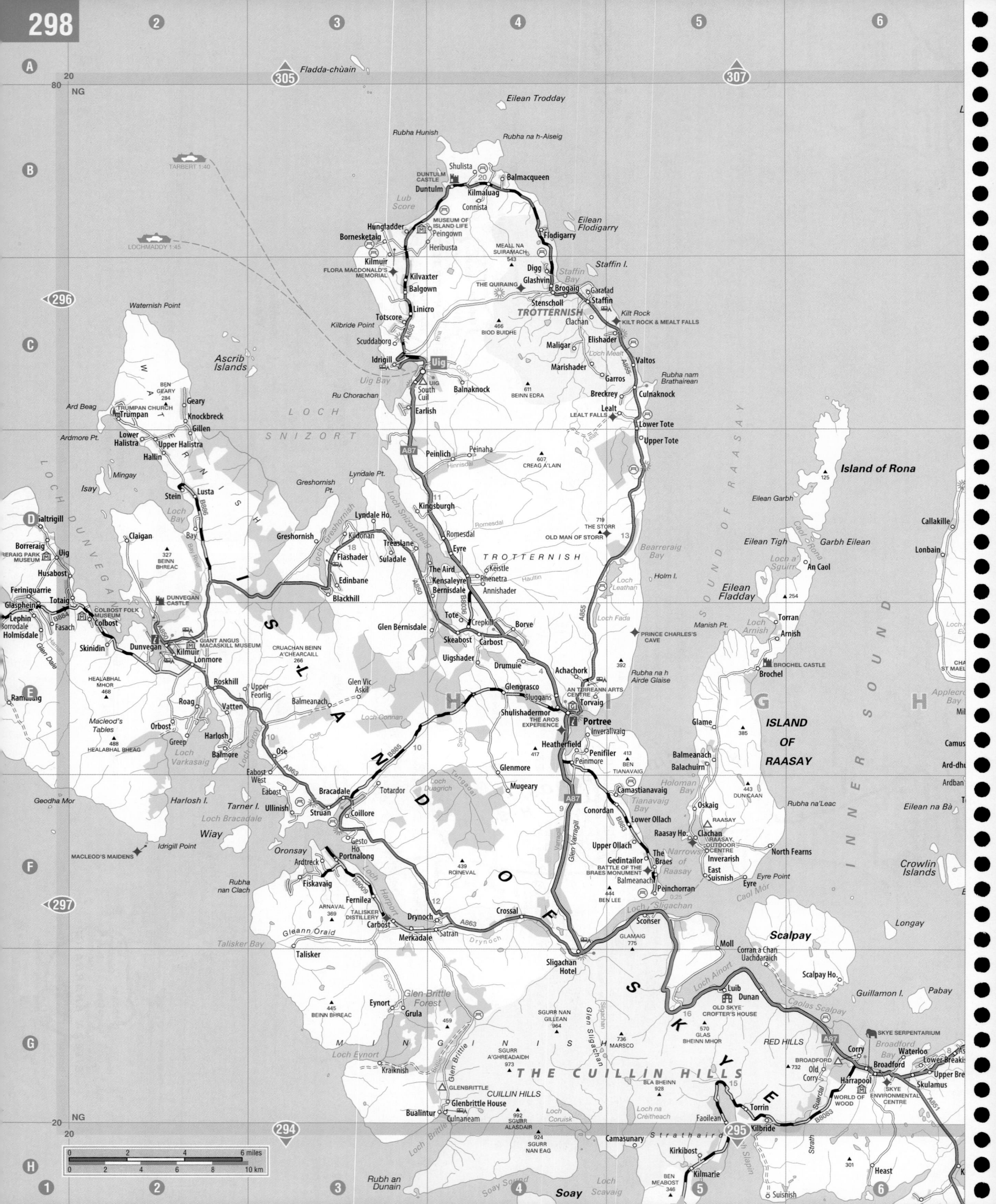298
Fladda-chùain
Eilean Trodday
Rubha Hunish
Rubha na h-Aiseig
TARBERT 1:40
LOCHMADDY 1:45
Shulista
Duntulm Castle
Duntulm
Balmacqueen
Kilmaluag
Connista
Lub Score
Eilean Flodigarry
Hungladder
Museum of Island Life
Peingown
Borneskeitaig
Flodigarry
Heribusta
Kilmuir
Meall na Suiramach 543
Flora MacDonald's Memorial
Digg
Staffin Bay
Staffin I.
Kilvaxter
Glashvin
The Quiraing
Brogaig
Garafad
Staffin
Balgown
Stenscholl
Trotternish
Waternish Point
Linicro
Kilt Rock
Kilt Rock & Mealt Falls
Totscore
466 Biod Buidhe
Clachan
Kilbride Point
Scuddaborg
Maligar
Elishader
Loch Mealt
Ascrib Islands
Idrigill
Uig
Valtos
Marishader
Uig Bay
South Cuil
Balnaknock
611 Beinn Edra
Garros
Rubha nam Brathairean
Ru Chorachan
Breckrey
Culnaknock
Ben Geary 284
Geary
Ard Beag
Trumpan Church
Trumpan
Knockbreck
Earlish
Lealt
Lealt Falls
Loch Snizort
Gillen
Lower Tote
Ardmore Pt.
Lower Halistra
Upper Halistra
Upper Tote
Hallin
A87
Peinlich
Peinaha
Hinnisdal
607 Creag a'Lain
Mingay
Island of Rona
Isay
Lyndale Pt.
Greshornish Pt.
Stein
Lusta
Waternish
Eilean Garbh
Kingsburgh
Loch Bay
Galtrigill
Lyndale Ho.
Romesdal
719 The Storr
Old Man of Storr
Claigan
Greshornish
Kildonan
Romesdal
Eilean Tigh
Garbh Eilean
Callakille
Borreraig
Borreraig Park Museum
Uig
327 Beinn Bhreac
Treaslane
Flashader
Suladale
Eyre
Trotternish
Bearreraig Bay
Loch a' Sguirr
An Caol
Lonbain
Husabost
The Aird
Keistle
Rhenetra
Holm I.
Edinbane
Kensaleyre
Bernisdale
Annishader
Haultin
Loch Leathan
Eilean Fladday
Feriniquarrie
Dunvegan Castle
Blackhill
Totaig
254
Glasphein
Colbost Folk Museum
Tote
Torran
Lephin
Colbost
Glen Bernisdale
Crepkill
Borve
Loch Fada
Manish Pt.
Borrodale
Fasach
Skeabost
Carbost
Prince Charles's Cave
Loch Arnish
Arnish
Holmisdale
Giant Angus MacAskill Museum
Skinidin
Dunvegan
Kilmuir
Cruachan Beinn a'Chearcaill 266
Uigshader
Glen Dale
Lonmore
Drumuie
392
Brochel Castle
Brochel
Healabhal Mhor 468
Achachork
Rubha na h Airde Glaise
Roskhill
Upper Feorlig
Glen Vic Askil
Glengrasco
An Tuireann Arts Centre
Ramasaig
Torvaig
Roag
Balmeanach
Sluggans
Vatten
Shulishadermor
The Aros Experience
Portree
Glame
Island of Raasay
Macleod's Tables
Orbost
Loch Connan
Inveralivaig
385
Healabhal Bheag 488
Greep
Harlosh
Loch Varkasaig
Ose
Heatherfield
417
Penifiler
Peinmore
413 Ben Tianavaig
Balmeanach
Balachuirn
Balmore
Glenmore
Eabost West
Mugeary
Holoman Bay
443 Dun Caan
Geodha Mor
Harlosh I.
Tarner I.
Eabost
Loch Duagrich
Camastianavaig
Tianavaig Bay
Ullinish
Bracadale
Totardor
Oskaig
Rubha na'Leac
Eilean na Bà
Loch Bracadale
Struan
Coillore
Conordan
Raasay
Lower Ollach
Wiay
Raasay Ho.
Clachan
Raasay Outdoor Centre
Macleod's Maidens
Idrigill Point
Gesto Ho
Upper Ollach
The Braes
Narrows of Raasay
North Fearns
Oronsay
Portnalong
Glen Varragill
Inverarish
Ardtreck
Gedintailor
Battle of the Braes Monument
Crowlin Islands
Rubha nan Clach
Fiskavaig
439 Roineval
Balmeanach
East Suisnish
Eyre Point
Eyre
Fernilea
Loch Harport
444 Ben Lee
Peinchorran
Caol Mòr
Arnaval 369
Talisker Distillery
Crossal
Loch Sligachan
Drynoch
Sconser
Longay
Carbost
Scalpay
Talisker Bay
Gleann Oraid
Merkadale
Satran
Drynoch
Glamaig 775
Moll
Corran a Chan Uachdaraich
Talisker
Sligachan Hotel
Scalpay Ho.
Loch Ainort
Luib
Dunan
Guillamon I.
Pabay
Glen-Brittle Forest
445 Beinn Bhreac
Eynort
Sgurr nan Gillean 964
Old Skye Crofter's House
Grula
459
570 Glas Bheinn Mhor
Caolas Scalpay
Skye Serpentarium
736 Marsco
Red Hills
Broadford Bay
Loch Eynort
Sgurr a'Ghreadaidh 973
Glen Sligachan
Corry
Waterloo
Lower Breakish
Kraiknish
The Cuillin Hills
Broadford
Upper Breakish
732
Old Corry
Harrapool
Glenbrittle
Bla Bheinn 928
Skulamus
Cuillin Hills
Skye Environmental Centre
World of Wood
Glenbrittle House
Loch Coruisk
Loch na Creitheach
Torrin
Bualintur
Culnaneam
992 Sgurr Alasdair
Faoilean
Kilbride
924 Sgurr nan Eag
Camasunary
Strathaird
Loch Brittle
Kirkibost
Strath Suardal
301
Heast
Ben Meabost 346
Kilmarie
Loch Slapin
Rubh an Dunain
Soay Sound
Soay
Loch Scavaig
Suisnish
Isle of Skye
Loch Dunvegan
Sound of Raasay
Inner Sound
0 2 4 6 miles
0 2 4 6 8 10 km

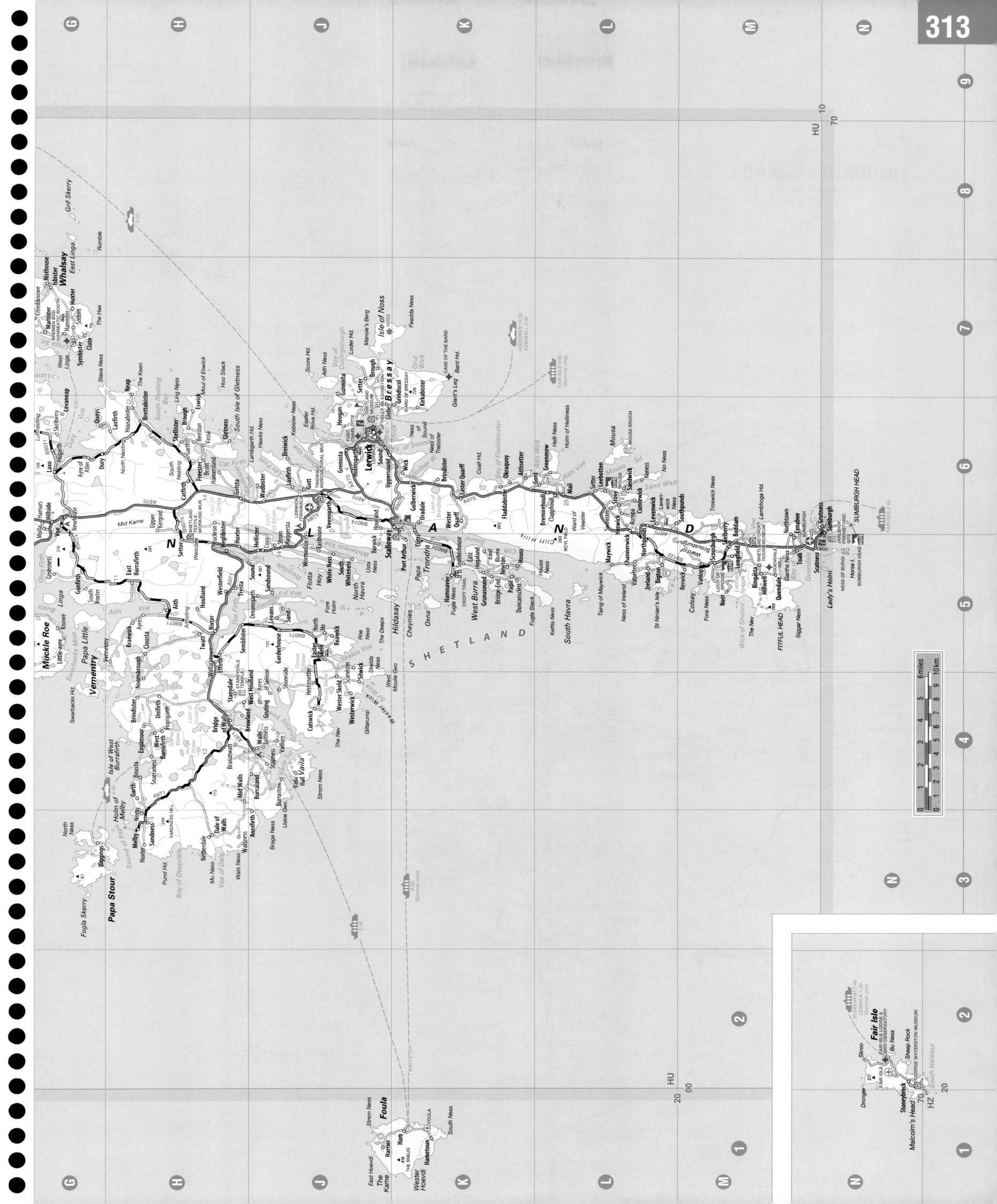
SHETLAND
Lerwick
Bressay
Isle of Noss
Whalsay
Mousa
Scalloway
Trondra
West Burra
South Havra
Papa Stour
Vementry
Muckle Roe
Papa Little
Vaila
Foula
Fair Isle
SUMBURGH HEAD
FITFUL HEAD
Sumburgh
Sandwick
Levenwick
Aith
Walls
Voe
Tingwall
Gott
Girlsta
Quendale
Lady's Holm
Hildasay
Oxna
Cliff Hills
Mid Kame
CAVE OF THE BARD
MOUSA BROCH
GEORGE WATERSTON MUSEUM
0 1 2 3 4 5 6 miles
0 1 2 3 4 5 6 7 8 9 10 km

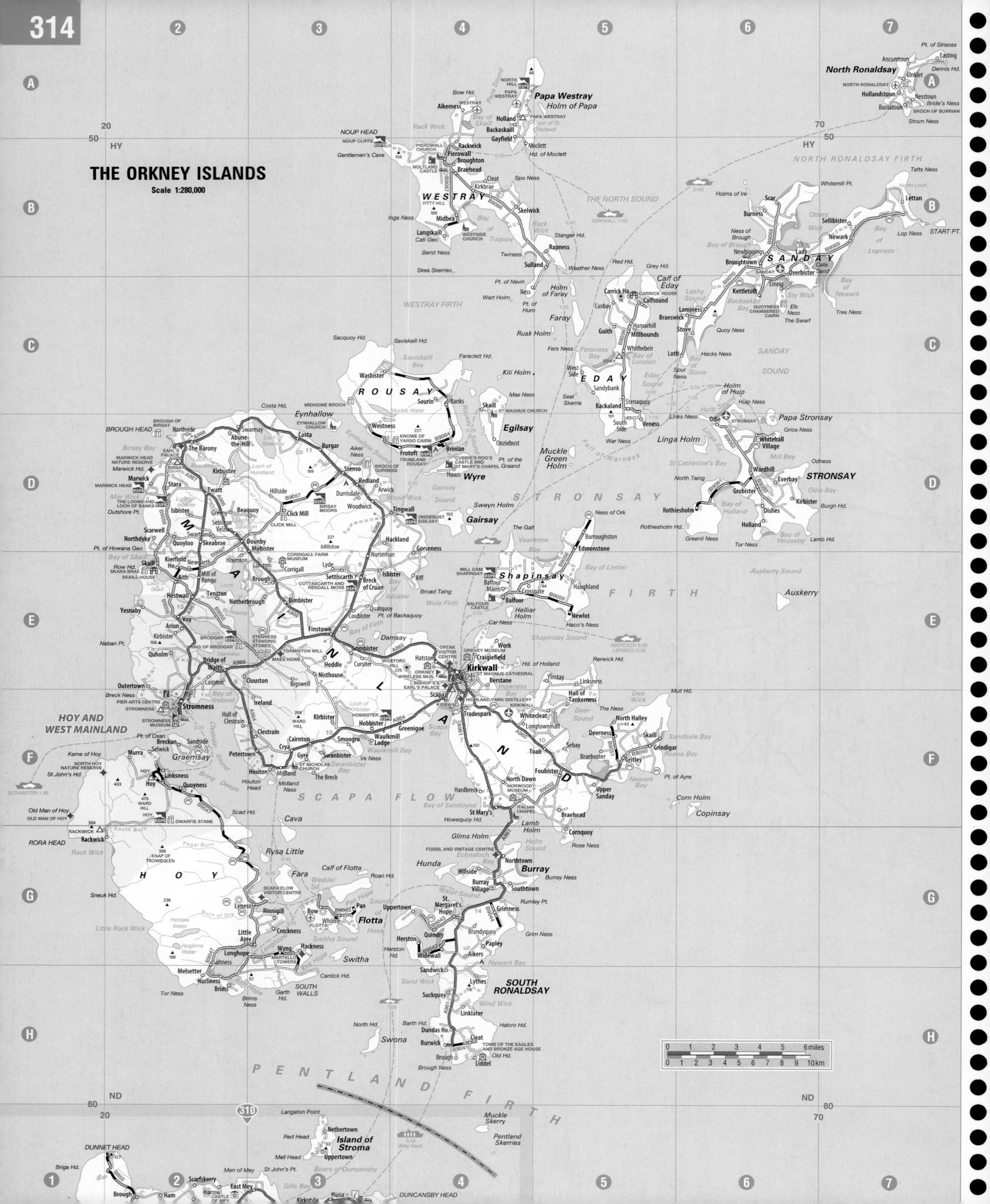

# THE ORKNEY ISLANDS
### Scale 1:280,000

**North Ronaldsay**

**Papa Westray**
Holm of Papa

**WESTRAY**

**SANDAY**

NORTH RONALDSAY FIRTH

THE NORTH SOUND

**EDAY**
Calf of Eday

**Faray**

WESTRAY FIRTH

**ROUSAY**

Eynhallow

**Egilsay**
**Wyre**

**Papa Stronsay**

**STRONSAY**

SANDAY SOUND

**Gairsay**

STRONSAY FIRTH

**Shapinsay**

**M A I N L A N D**

**KIRKWALL**

FIRTH

Auskerry

**HOY AND WEST MAINLAND**

Stromness

Graemsay

SCAPA FLOW

**I S L A N D**

Copinsay

**HOY**

Flotta

Fara

Hunda

**Burray**

Lamb Holm

Holm Sound

South Walls

Swona

**SOUTH RONALDSAY**

PENTLAND FIRTH

Island of Stroma

DUNNET HEAD

Muckle Skerry

Pentland Skerries

DUNCANSBY HEAD

**310**

0  1  2  3  4  5  6 miles
0  1  2  3  4  5  6  7  8  9  10km

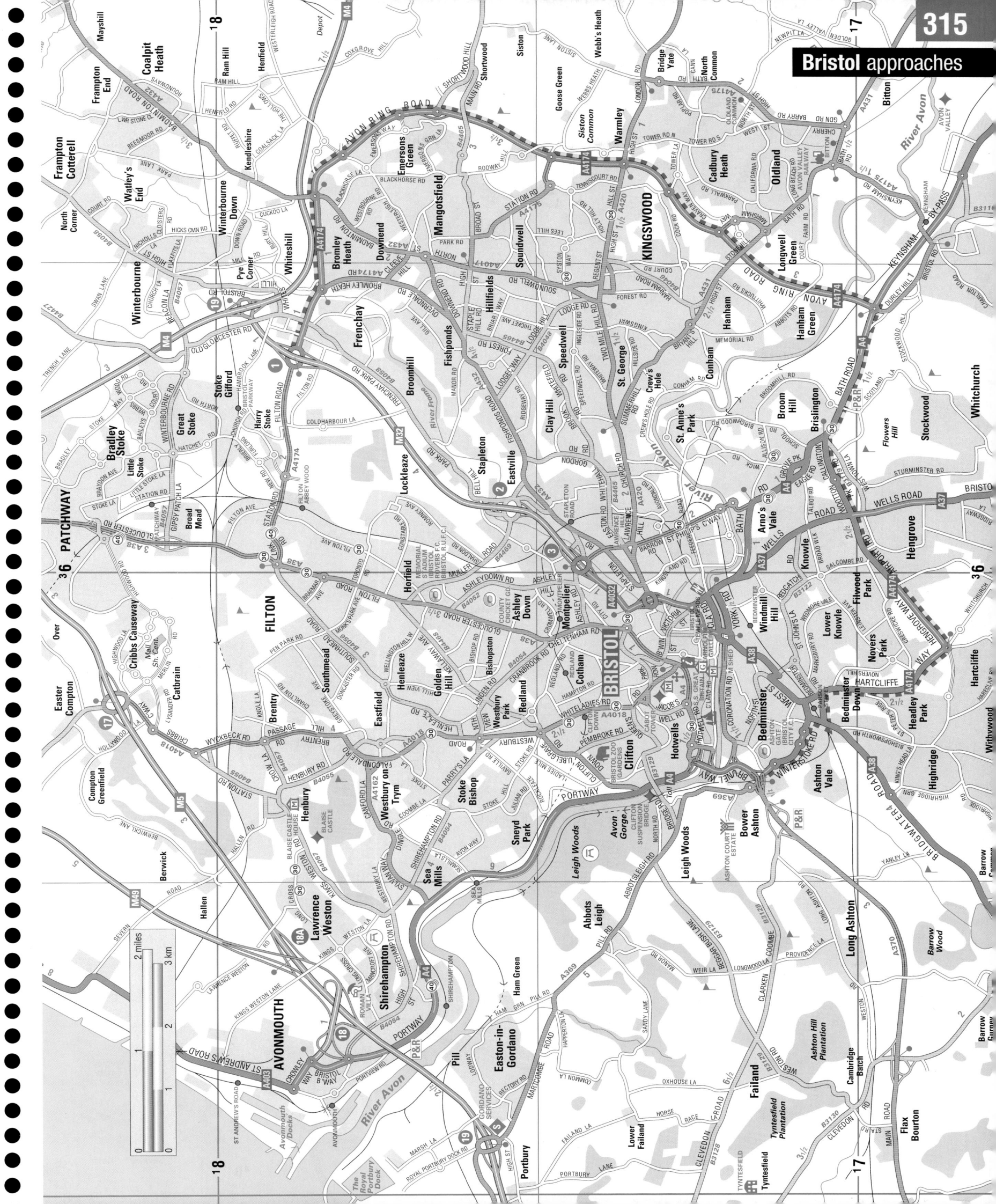
BRISTOL
Frampton Cotterell
Frampton End
Coalpit Heath
Mayshill
Winterbourne
Winterbourne Down
Watley's End
Kendleshire
Whiteshill
Pye Corner
North Corner
PATCHWAY
Bradley Stoke
Little Stoke
Stoke Gifford
Great Stoke
Harry Stoke
Broad Mead
FILTON
Over
Easter Compton
Cribbs Causeway
Catbrain
Compton Greenfield
Brentry
Southmead
Henleaze
Horfield
Lockleaze
Frenchay
Broomhill
Downend
Bromley Heath
Emersons Green
Mangotsfield
Shortwood
Siston
Webb's Heath
Goose Green
Siston Common
Warmley
Bridge Yate
North Common
Cadbury Heath
Oldland
Bitton
KINGSWOOD
Soundwell
Hillfields
Fishponds
Staple Hill
Speedwell
St. George
Crew's Hole
Conham
Hanham
Hanham Green
Longwell Green
Clay Hill
Stapleton
Eastville
Ashley Down
Montpelier
Bishopston
Golden Hill
Redland
Cotham
Eastfield
Westbury Park
Westbury on Trym
Henbury
Stoke Bishop
Sneyd Park
Clifton
Hotwells
Bedminster
Windmill Hill
Arno's Vale
St. Anne's Park
Broom Hill
Brislington
Knowle
Lower Knowle
Filwood Park
Novers Park
Hengrove
Stockwood
Whitchurch
Flowers Hill
Bedminster Down
Headley Park
Hartcliffe
Highridge
Ashton Vale
Withywood
Bower Ashton
Leigh Woods
Avon Gorge
Abbots Leigh
Long Ashton
Ashton Hill Plantation
Barrow Wood
Sea Mills
Shirehampton
Lawrence Weston
AVONMOUTH
Avonmouth Docks
Hallen
Berwick
Pill
Ham Green
Easton-in-Gordano
Portbury
Lower Failand
Failand
Tyntesfield
Tyntesfield Plantation
Cambridge Batch
Flax Bourton
The Royal Portbury Dock
River Avon
River Frome
AVON RING ROAD
KEYNSHAM BY-PASS
BATH ROAD
WELLS ROAD
PORTWAY
2 miles
3 km

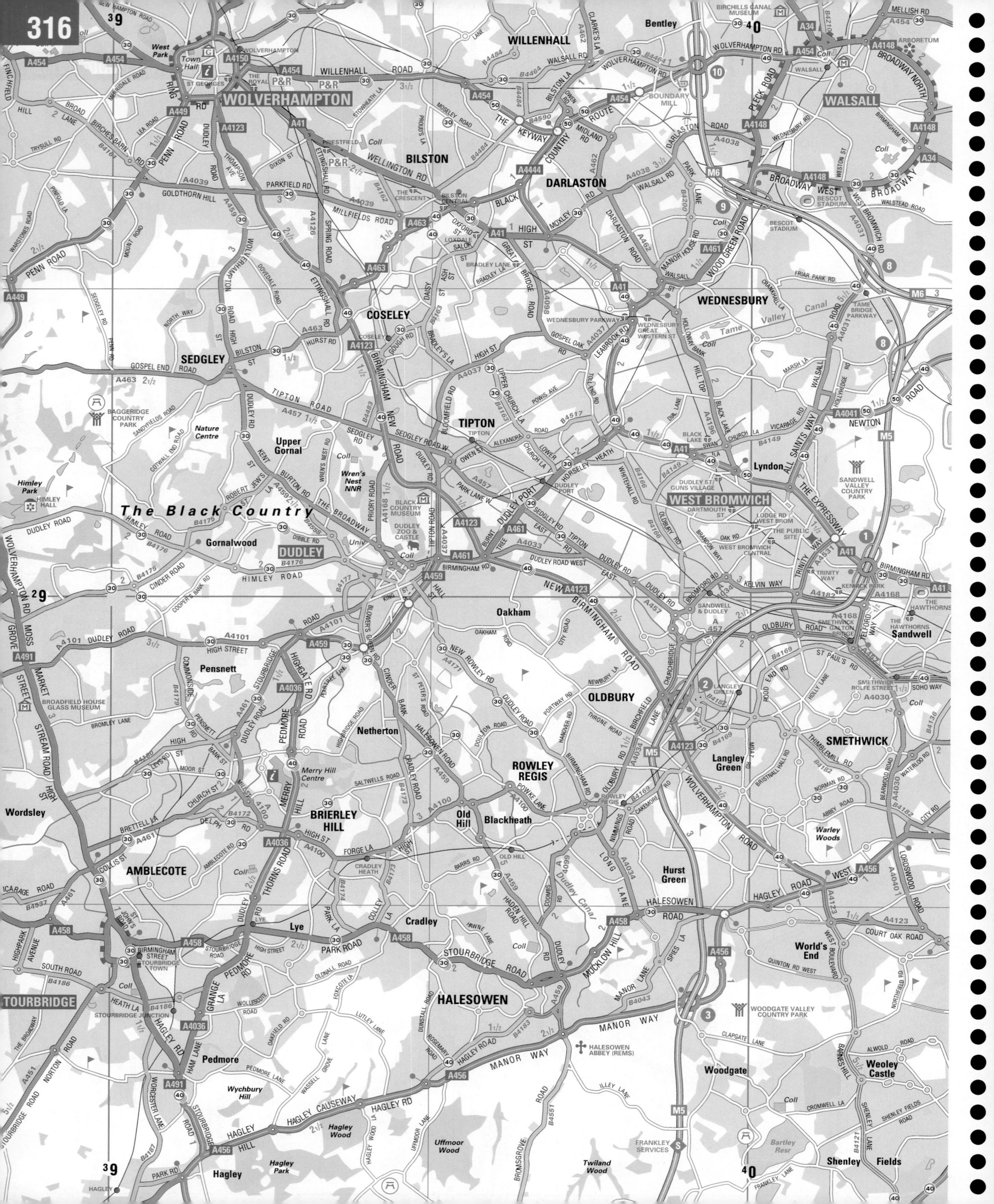

WOLVERHAMPTON
WILLENHALL
Bentley
WALSALL
BILSTON
DARLASTON
WEDNESBURY
COSELEY
SEDGLEY
TIPTON
Upper Gornal
Gornalwood
DUDLEY
WEST BROMWICH
Lyndon
NEWTON
Sandwell
Oakham
OLDBURY
Netherton
Pensnett
ROWLEY REGIS
Langley Green
SMETHWICK
Wordsley
BRIERLEY HILL
Old Hill
Blackheath
AMBLECOTE
Hurst Green
Warley Woods
Lye
Cradley
World's End
TOURBRIDGE
HALESOWEN
Pedmore
Woodgate
Weoley Castle
Wychbury Hill
Hagley Wood
Uffmoor Wood
Twiland Wood
Hagley
Hagley Park
Shenley Fields
The Black Country
BAGGERIDGE COUNTRY PARK
Nature Centre
Himley Park
HIMLEY HALL
Wren's Nest NNR
BLACK COUNTRY MUSEUM
DUDLEY ZOO & CASTLE
Merry Hill Centre
BROADFIELD HOUSE GLASS MUSEUM
SANDWELL VALLEY COUNTRY PARK
BESCOT STADIUM
BIRCHILLS CANAL MUSEUM
ARBORETUM
BOUNDARY MILL
WOODGATE VALLEY COUNTRY PARK
HALESOWEN ABBEY (REMS)
FRANKLEY SERVICES
Bartley Resr
Tame Valley Canal
Dudley Canal
THE HAWTHORNS

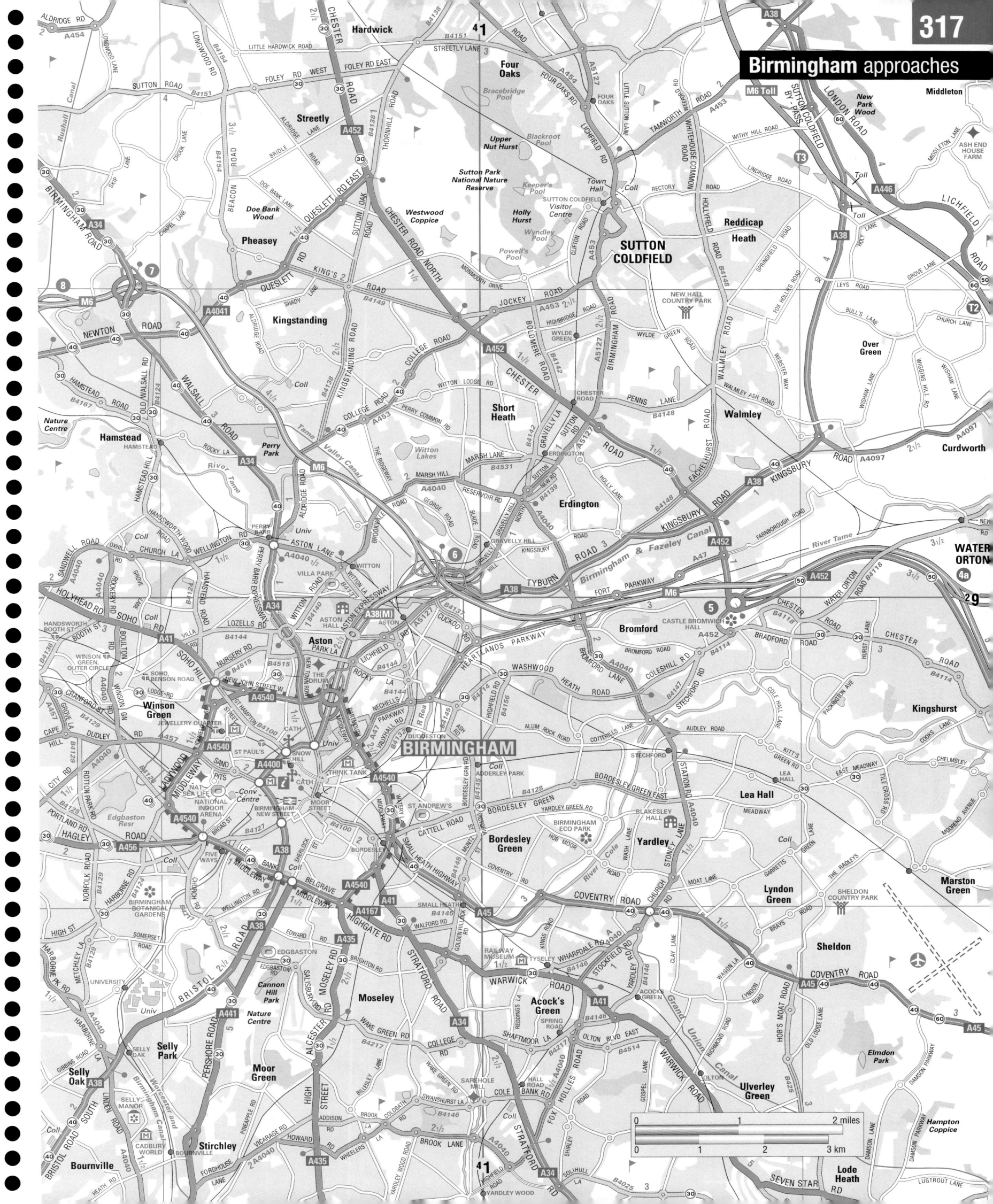
Hardwick
Four Oaks
Streetly
Sutton Park National Nature Reserve
Pheasey
SUTTON COLDFIELD
Reddicap Heath
Middleton
Kingstanding
Over Green
Short Heath
Walmley
Curdworth
Hamstead
Perry Park
Erdington
WATER ORTON
Aston
Bromford
Kingshurst
Winson Green
BIRMINGHAM
Lea Hall
Bordesley Green
Yardley
Marston Green
Lyndon Green
Sheldon
Moseley
Acock's Green
Selly Park
Selly Oak
Moor Green
Ulverley Green
Elmdon Park
Stirchley
Bournville
Hampton Coppice
Lode Heath
0 1 2 miles
0 1 2 3 km

CARDIFF
(CAERDYDD)
CAERPHILLY
(CAERFFILI)
Church Village
Taff Vale
Groes-wen
Watford
Caerphilly Common
The Warren
Van
Coed Parc-y-Van
Rudry
Coed Craig Ruperra
Garth
Coed Coesau-Whips
Llwyncelyn
Park Wood
Nantgarw
Coed y Gedrys
Thornhill
Cefn Mably Woods
Michaelston-y-Fedw
Glan-y-llyn
Gwaelod-y-garth
Grath Hill
Taff's Well
(Ffynnon-Taf)
Coed-y-Wenallt
Castleton
Soar
Garth Wood
Tongwynlais
Lisvane
(Llys Faen)
Began
Pentyrch
Llanishen
Llanedeyrn
Blacktown
Marshfield
Llanishen Reservoir
Morganstown
Pantmawr
Pentwyn
Rhiwbina
St. Mellons
(Llaneirwg)
Radyr
Forest Farm
Llanrumney
Cyncoed
Birchgrove
Peterstone Wentlooge
(Llanbedr Gwynllŵg)
Whitchurch
Trowbridge
Heath
Llandaff North
Rumney
(Rhymni)
Roath Park
Pwll-Mawr
Newton
Gabalfa
Maindy
Llandaff
(Llandaf)
Fairwater
Pontacanna
Cathays
Roath
St Fagans
(Sain Ffagan)
St Brides-super-Ely
(Llansanffraid-ar-Elai)
St Fagans National History Museum
Canton
Tremorfa
Splott
Ely
(Tre-lai)
St George's
Michaelston-super-Ely
Riverside
Millennium Stadium
Caerau
Drope
Saltmead
Cardiff Central
Culverhouse Cross
Downs
Grangetown
Butetown
Leckwith
Wales Millennium Centre
National Assembly
St Nicholas
(Sain Nicolas)
Tinkinswood Burial Chamber
Twyn-yr-odyn
Techniquest
Cardiff Bay Visitor Centre
Wallston
Wenvoe
(Gwenfo)
St Lythans
Michaelston-le-Pit
Llandough
Cardiff Bay Barrage
Cardiff Gate Services
Cardiff West Services
Cardiff Castle
Cathays National Museum Cardiff
Llandaff Cathedral
Cardiff Arms Park
Cardiff City
River Taff
River Ely
Rhymney River
The Lake
Bute E Dock
Roath Dock
Alexandra Dock
M4
A48(M)
A470
A4232
A48
A4119
A4054
A469
A4161
A4160
A4050
A4055
A4234
0 1 2 miles
0 1 2 3 km
18
31
32

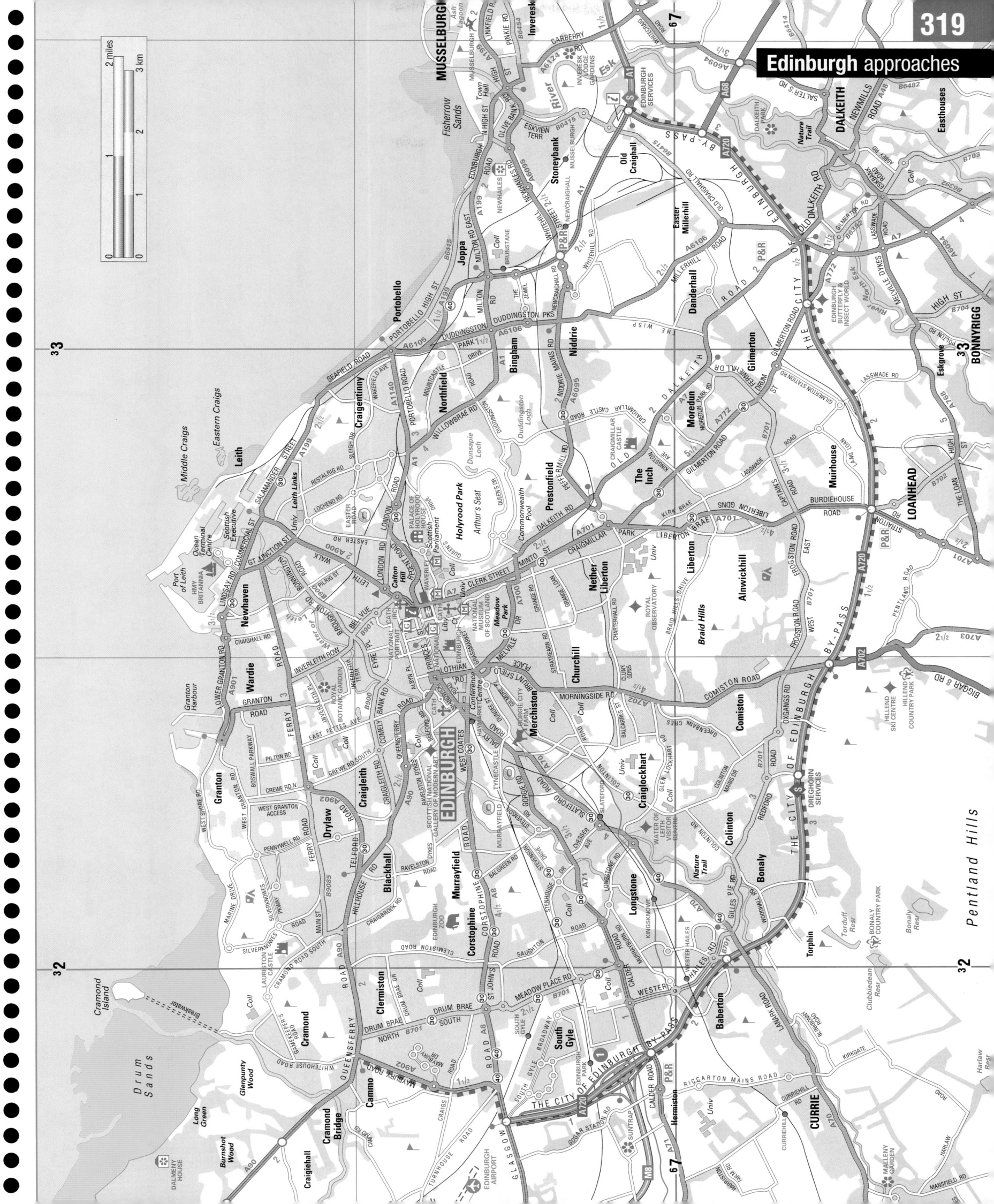
EDINBURGH
Leith
Musselburgh
Dalkeith
Bonnyrigg
Loanhead
Currie
Newhaven
Granton
Wardie
Portobello
Joppa
Craigentinny
Northfield
Bingham
Niddrie
Stoneybank
Danderhall
Gilmerton
Moredun
The Inch
Prestonfield
Liberton
Nether Liberton
Alnwickhill
Muirhouse
Comiston
Colinton
Bonaly
Longstone
Craiglockhart
Merchiston
Churchill
Craigleith
Drylaw
Blackhall
Murrayfield
Corstophine
Clermiston
Cramond
Cammo
Cramond Bridge
Craigiehall
South Gyle
Baberton
Hermiston
Eskgrove
Easthouses
Holyrood Park
Arthur's Seat
Braid Hills
Pentland Hills
Drum Sands
Cramond Island
Middle Craigs
Eastern Craigs
Fisherrow Sands
Edinburgh Airport
Edinburgh Zoo
THE CITY OF EDINBURGH BY-PASS

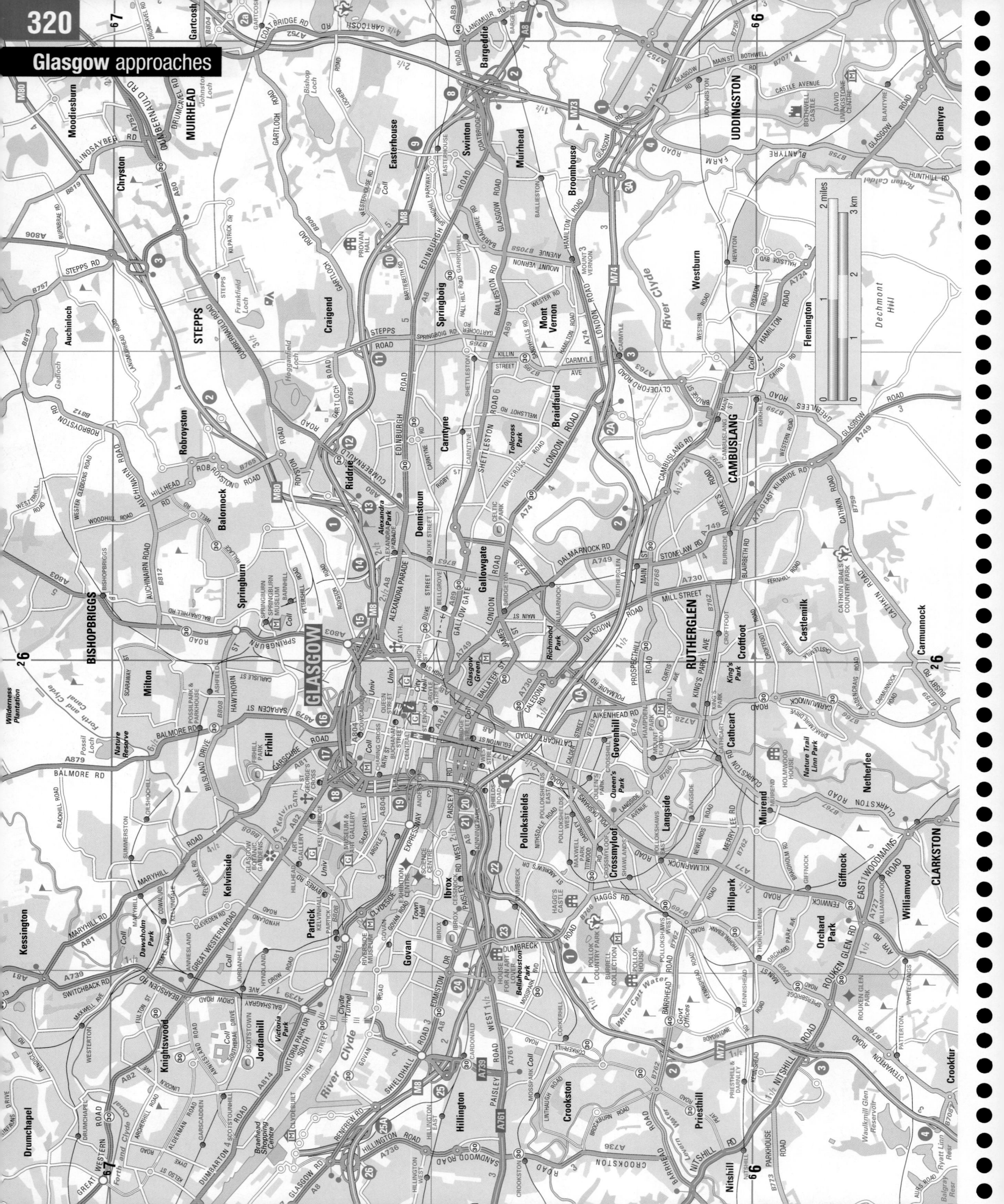
GLASGOW
Drumchapel
Kessington
Wilderness Plantation
BISHOPBRIGGS
Auchinloch
Moodiesburn
Chryston
MUIRHEAD
Gartcosh
STEPPS
Robroyston
Balornock
Springburn
Milton
Firhill
Knightswood
Kelvinside
Jordanhill
Partick
Govan
Ibrox
Hillington
Crookston
Pollokshields
Crossmyloof
Govanhill
Langside
Priesthill
Nitshill
Hillpark
Cathcart
Muirend
Orchard Park
Giffnock
Netherlee
Williamwood
CLARKSTON
Crookfur
Carmunnock
Castlemilk
Croftfoot
RUTHERGLEN
CAMBUSLANG
Flemington
Westburn
UDDINGSTON
Blantyre
Broomhouse
Mont Vernon
Braidfauld
Tollcross Park
Gallowgate
Dennistoun
Riddrie
Craigend
Carntyne
Springboig
Easterhouse
Swinton
Bargeddie
Muirhead
River Clyde
Dechmont Hill
0 1 2 miles
0 1 2 3 km

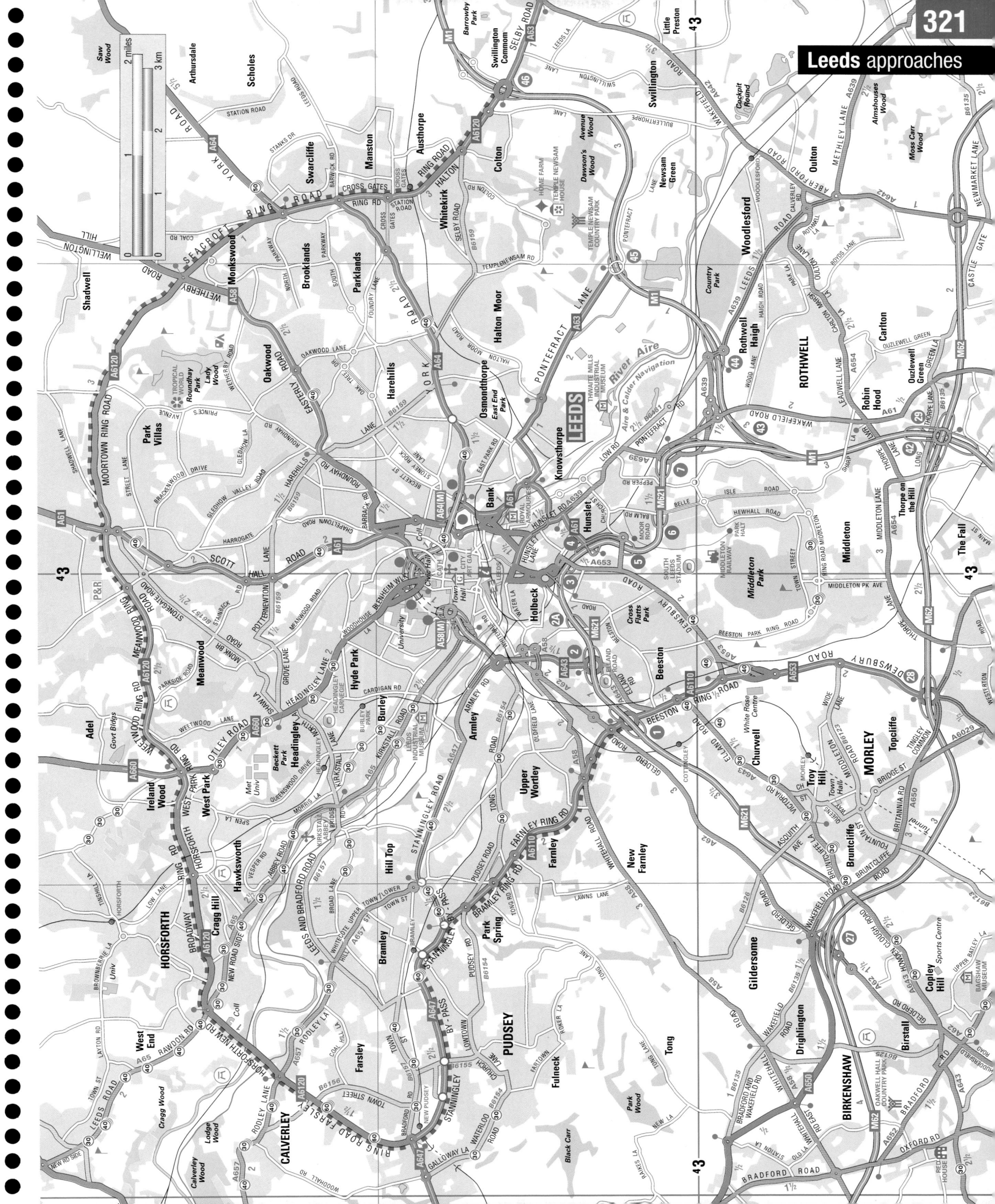

BUSHEY
OXHEY
Bushey Heath
Elstree
Arkley
Barnet Gate
Underhill
EAST BARNET
Totteridge
Whetstone
Osidge
Stanmore Common
Brockley Hill
Edgware Bury
LONDON GATEWAY SERVICES
South Oxhey
Oxhey Woods
Stirling Corner
Apex Corner
Woodside Park
North Finchley
Colney Hatch
FINCHLEY
Church End
West Finchley
Mill Hill
Mill Hill East
Five Ways Corner
EDGWARE
Canons Park
Little Stanmore
STANMORE
Hatch End
Harrow Weald
Headstone Lane
Headstone
Belmont
Burnt Oak
Grahame Park
HENDON
Henley's Corner
Muswell Hill
Coldfall Wood
Fortis Green
East Finchley
Highgate Wood
Queen's Wood
Temple Fortune
Hampstead Garden Suburb
Golders Green
Highgate
PINNER
Eastcote Village
North Harrow
HARROW
Civic Centre
Wealdstone
Queensbury
Colindale
KENTON
Kingsbury
Greenhill
West Harrow
Eastcote
West Hendon
Brent Cross Shopping Centre
Brent Cross
Staples Corner
Brent Reservoir (Welsh Harp)
Barn Hill
Preston Road
Northwick Park
Harrow on the Hill
Ruislip Manor
Rayners Lane
Roxeth
North Wembley
Wembley Park
Child's Hill
Golders Hill Park
Hampstead Heath
Parliament Hill
Dartmouth Park
Gospel Oak
HAMPSTEAD
South Harrow
South Ruislip
Sudbury
WEMBLEY
Neasden Circle
Neasden
Dollis Hill
Gladstone Park
Cricklewood
WILLESDEN
Belsize Park
Swiss Cottage
West Hampstead
Polish War Memorial
NORTHOLT
Target Rdbt
Stonebridge Park
Stonebridge
Harlesden
Brondesbury
Kilburn
Primrose Hill
Perivale
Alperton
Kensal Rise
St. John's Wood
Regents Park
White Hart Rdbt
GREENFORD
Greenford Rdbt
Hangar Lane
Park Royal
Maida Vale
Yeading
Old Oak Common
Wormwood Scrubs Park
Marylebone Flyover
MARYLEBONE
West Acton
Gipsy Corner
Westbourne Park
EALING
Ossie
East

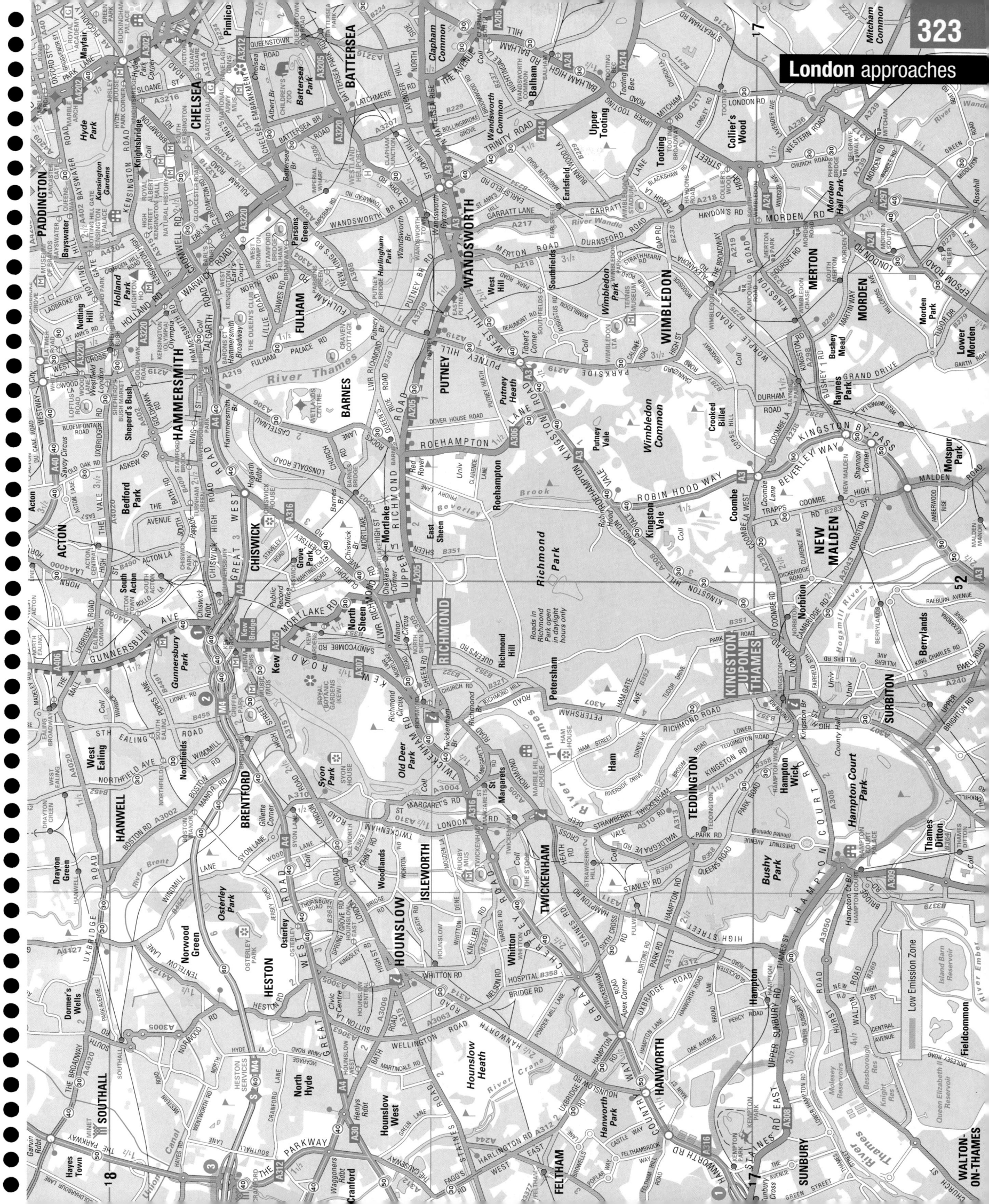
PADDINGTON
Bayswater
Notting Hill
Holland Park
Kensington Gardens
Hyde Park
Knightsbridge
CHELSEA
Pimlico
BATTERSEA
Battersea Park
Clapham Common
Balham
Upper Tooting
Tooting
Collier's Wood
Mitcham Common
Earlsfield
Wandsworth Common
WANDSWORTH
Parsons Green
FULHAM
HAMMERSMITH
Shepherd's Bush
ACTON
Bedford Park
CHISWICK
South Acton
BARNES
PUTNEY
Putney Heath
Southfields
WIMBLEDON
Wimbledon Park
Wimbledon Common
MERTON
MORDEN
Morden Park
Lower Morden
Raynes Park
Motspur Park
NEW MALDEN
Coombe
Kingston Vale
Roehampton
East Sheen
Mortlake
Richmond Park
RICHMOND
Richmond Hill
Petersham
Kew
Royal Botanic Gardens (Kew)
Gunnersbury Park
West Ealing
HANWELL
Northfields
BRENTFORD
Syon Park
Old Deer Park
Ham
KINGSTON UPON THAMES
Norbiton
Berrylands
SURBITON
TEDDINGTON
Hampton Wick
Hampton Court Park
Bushy Park
Thames Ditton
TWICKENHAM
St Margarets
ISLEWORTH
Woodlands
HOUNSLOW
Osterley
HESTON
Norwood Green
Drayton Green
Dormer's Wells
SOUTHALL
North Hyde
Hounslow West
Hounslow Heath
Whitton
HANWORTH
Hanworth Park
Hampton
FELTHAM
SUNBURY
WALTON-ON-THAMES
Fieldcommon
Hayes Town
Cranford
River Thames
River Wandle
River Brent
River Crane
Low Emission Zone
Roads in Richmond Park open in daylight hours only

Cockfosters
Oakwood
Grange Park
Bush Hill Park
Ponders End
Sewardstonebury
LOUGHTON
SOUTHGATE
Winchmore Hill
CHINGFORD
Osidge
Grovelands Park
Friday Hill
Buckhurst Hill
CHIGWELL
Palmers Green
Lower Edmonton
Woodford Wells
Arnos Grove
Pymmes Park
Chingford Hatch
Grange Hill
FRIERN BARNET
EDMONTON
Highams Park
WOODFORD
Colney Hatch
Bowes Park
Hale End
Woodford Bridge
WOOD GREEN
Woodford Green
Higham Hill
Noel Park
Clayhall
Fulwell Cross
TOTTENHAM
Muswell Hill
Alexandra Park
West Green
Tottenham Hale
WALTHAMSTOW
Snaresbrook
Barkingside
Fortis Green
Redbridge
Newbury Park
Gants Hill
HORNSEY
Crouch End
Harringay
South Tottenham
WANSTEAD
Seven Kings
Highgate
Stamford Hill
Upper Clapton
Valentines Park
Wanstead Park
Cranbrook
Hampstead
Finsbury Park
Archway
Leytonstone
STOKE NEWINGTON
Clapton
Dartmouth Park
Lea Bridge
LEYTON
Hackney Marsh
Wanstead Flats
Heath
Parliament Hill
ILFORD
HAMPSTEAD
Gospel Oak
Tufnell Park
Manor Park
Belsize Park
Kentish Town
Shacklewell
Clapton Park
Temple Mills
Loxford
Highbury
Little Ilford
Fair Cross
Forest Gate
Canonbury
HACKNEY
STRATFORD
Swiss Cottage
Plashet
BARKING
Dalston
Upton
West Ham Park
Primrose Hill
CAMDEN TOWN
Victoria Park
ISLINGTON
WEST HAM
Upton Park
Old Ford
Wallend
Regents Park
SHOREDITCH
BETHNAL GREEN
BOW
EAST HAM
Plaistow
FINSBURY
Bromley
Spitalfields
MARYLEBONE
Holborn
Stepney
Beckton
NORTH CIRCULAR ROAD

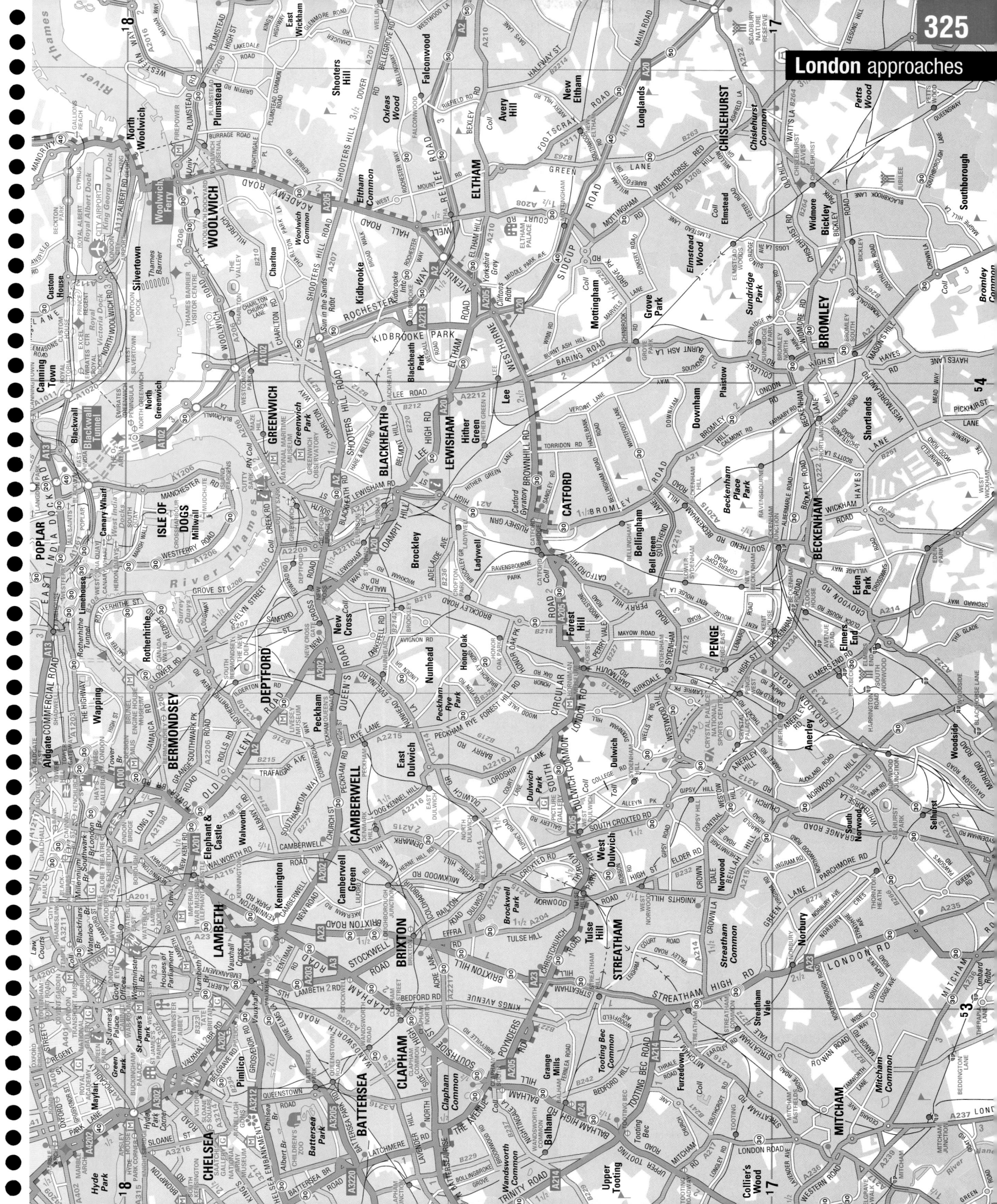
POPLAR
Canning Town
Custom House
Hyde Park
Mayfair
Aldgate
Wapping
Limehouse
Canary Wharf
Blackwall
Silvertown
North Woolwich
ISLE OF DOGS
Millwall
Rotherhithe
BERMONDSEY
CHELSEA
LAMBETH
Elephant & Castle
Pimlico
WOOLWICH
Plumstead
DEPTFORD
GREENWICH
Charlton
Kennington
Walworth
Peckham
New Cross
CAMBERWELL
BATTERSEA
CLAPHAM
BRIXTON
East Dulwich
Nunhead
Brockley
BLACKHEATH
Kidbrooke
Shooters Hill
Eltham Common
Falconwood
LEWISHAM
Hither Green
ELTHAM
Lee
Ladywell
Honor Oak
Avery Hill
Balham
Grange Mills
Forest Hill
CATFORD
New Eltham
Upper Tooting
Tulse Hill
West Dulwich
Dulwich
STREATHAM
Mottingham
Bellingham
Bell Green
Grove Park
Longlands
Furzedown
Streatham Common
Norwood
PENGE
Downham
Plaistow
Elmstead Wood
Beckenham Place Park
CHISLEHURST
Collier's Wood
Streatham Vale
Sundridge Park
Chislehurst Common
Norbury
Anerley
BECKENHAM
BROMLEY
Widmore
Bickley
MITCHAM
South Norwood
Elmers End
Eden Park
Shortlands
Petts Wood
Mitcham Common
Selhurst
Woodside
Southborough
Bromley Common

3 **4**   4 **0**

**CROSBY**

Great Crosby

Melling

**KIRKBY**

Kirkby Park

Westvale

**AINTREE**

**LITHERLAND**

Waterloo

Aintree Race Course

Knowsley

Seaforth

Fazakerley

Croxteth

**BOOTLE**

Walton

**West Derby**

Stockbridge Village

New Brighton

Anfield

**WALLASEY**

Newsham Park

**HUYTON-WITH-ROBY**

Roby

Broad Green

**BIRKENHEAD**

Edge Hill

Wavertree

Childwall

Oxton

Tranmere

**LIVERPOOL**

Toxteth

Sefton Park

Woolton

Aigburth

Allerton

Dingle

Otterspool

**BEBINGTON**

Port Sunlight

Spital

**River Mersey**

**GARSTON**

Hunt's Cross

**SPEKE**

Brimstage

Bromborough

Eastham Ferry

**LIVERPOOL AIRPORT**

| 0 | | 1 | | 2 miles |
| 0 | 1 | 2 | 3 km |

3 **3**   3 **4**

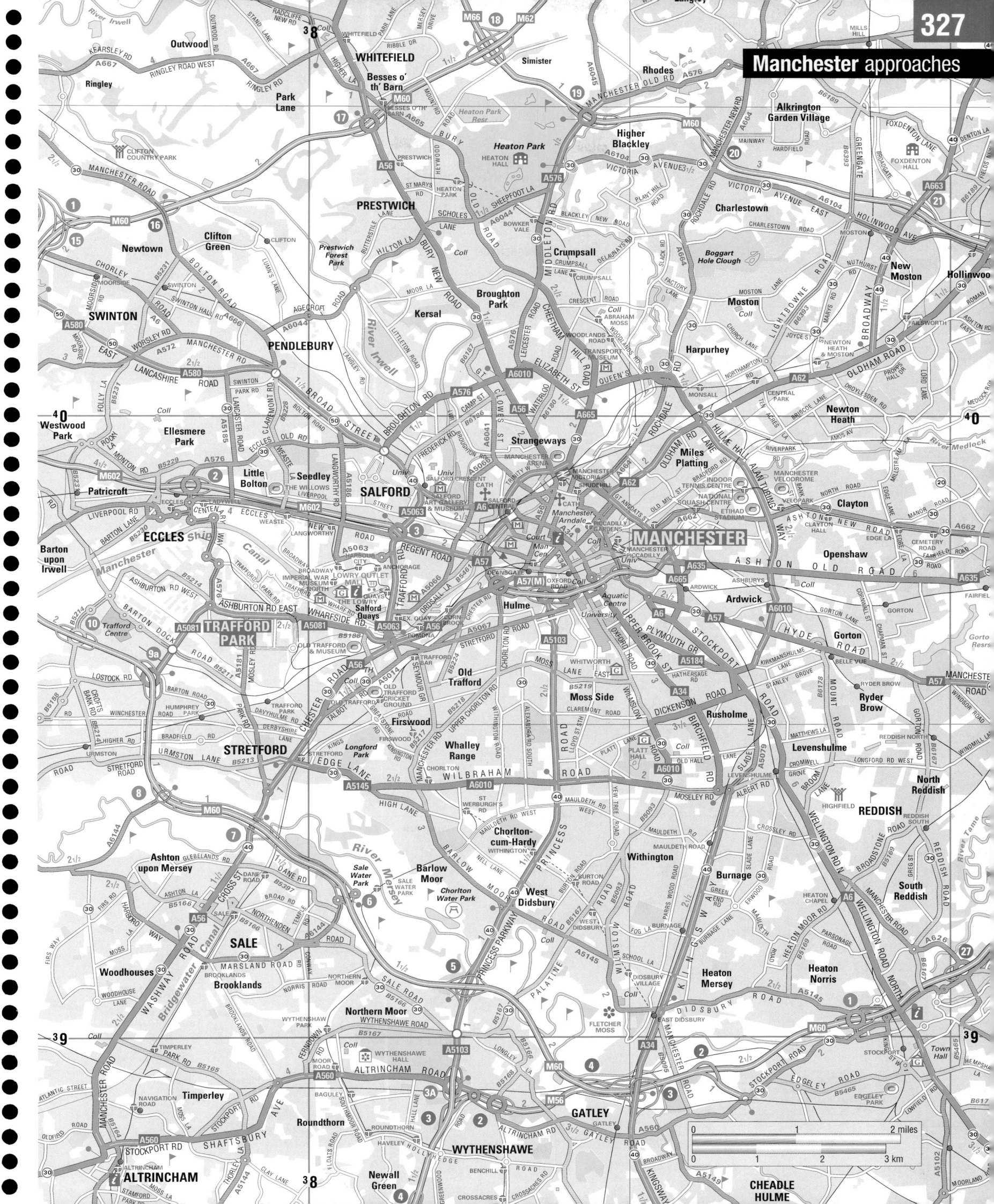
MANCHESTER
SALFORD
TRAFFORD PARK
STRETFORD
SALE
ECCLES
SWINTON
PENDLEBURY
PRESTWICH
WHITEFIELD
REDDISH
ALTRINCHAM
WYTHENSHAWE
GATLEY
CHEADLE HULME
Heaton Park
Chorlton-cum-Hardy
Withington
Levenshulme
Rusholme
Moss Side
Hulme
Ardwick
Gorton
Openshaw
Clayton
Harpurhey
Moston
Crumpsall
Cheetham
Timperley
Brooklands
Northern Moor
Didsbury
West Didsbury
Heaton Mersey
Heaton Norris
Stretford

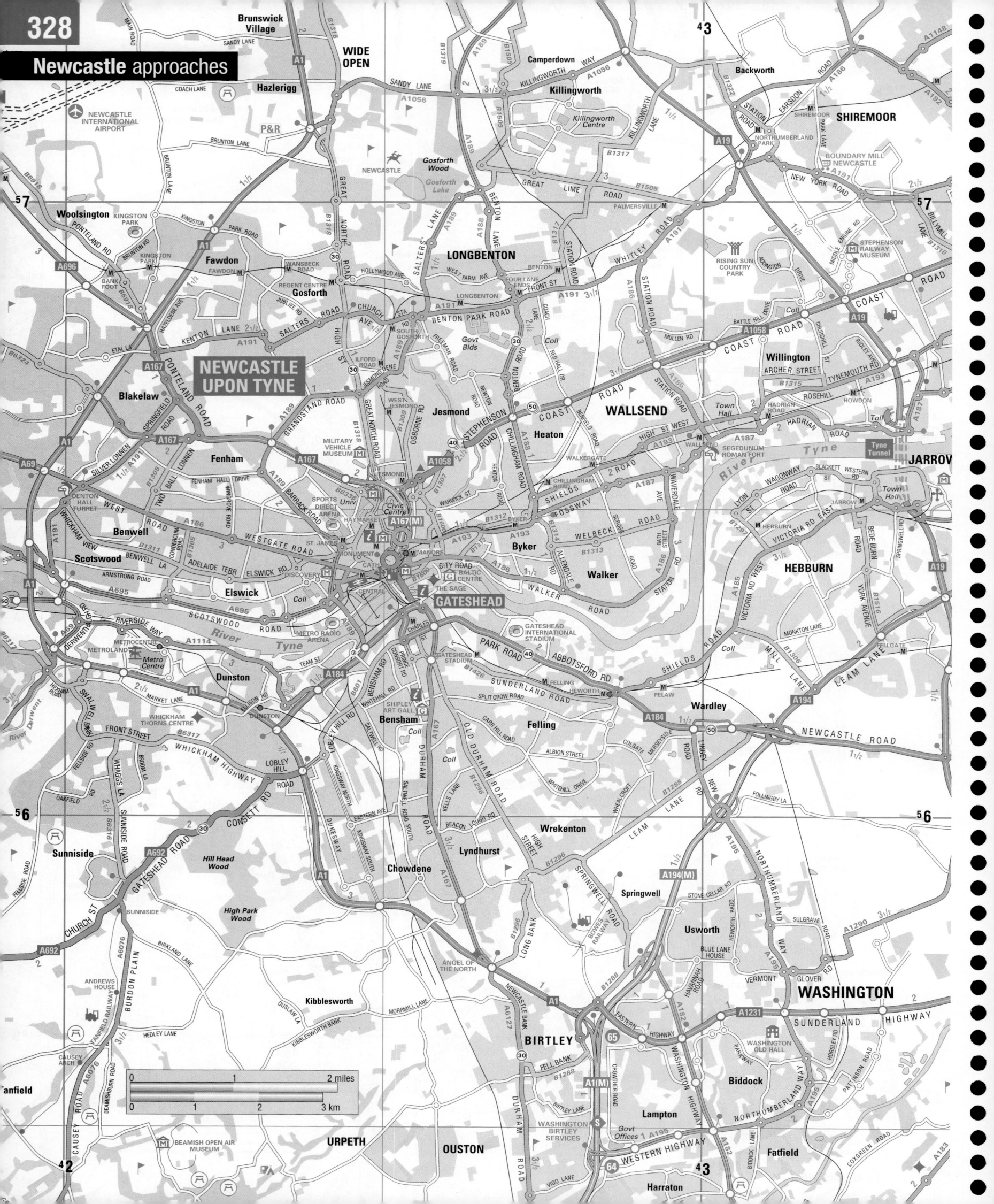

NEWCASTLE UPON TYNE
GATESHEAD
WALLSEND
WASHINGTON
JARROW
HEBBURN
SHIREMOOR
LONGBENTON
BIRTLEY
Brunswick Village
WIDE OPEN
Hazlerigg
NEWCASTLE INTERNATIONAL AIRPORT
Camperdown
Killingworth
Backworth
Woolsington
Fawdon
Gosforth
Blakelaw
Fenham
Jesmond
Heaton
Benwell
Scotswood
Elswick
Byker
Walker
Dunston
Felling
Bensham
Wardley
Willington
Wrekenton
Lyndhurst
Chowdene
Sunniside
Springwell
Usworth
Kibblesworth
Biddock
Lampton
Fatfield
URPETH
OUSTON
Harraton
Gosforth Wood
Gosforth Lake
Hill Head Wood
High Park Wood
River Tyne
Tyne Tunnel
GATESHEAD INTERNATIONAL STADIUM
METRO RADIO ARENA
METROCENTRE
RISING SUN COUNTRY PARK
STEPHENSON RAILWAY MUSEUM
SEGEDUNUM ROMAN FORT
BEAMISH OPEN AIR MUSEUM
WASHINGTON OLD HALL
ANGEL OF THE NORTH
WASHINGTON BIRTLEY SERVICES
BOUNDARY MILL NEWCASTLE
0 1 2 miles
0 1 2 3 km

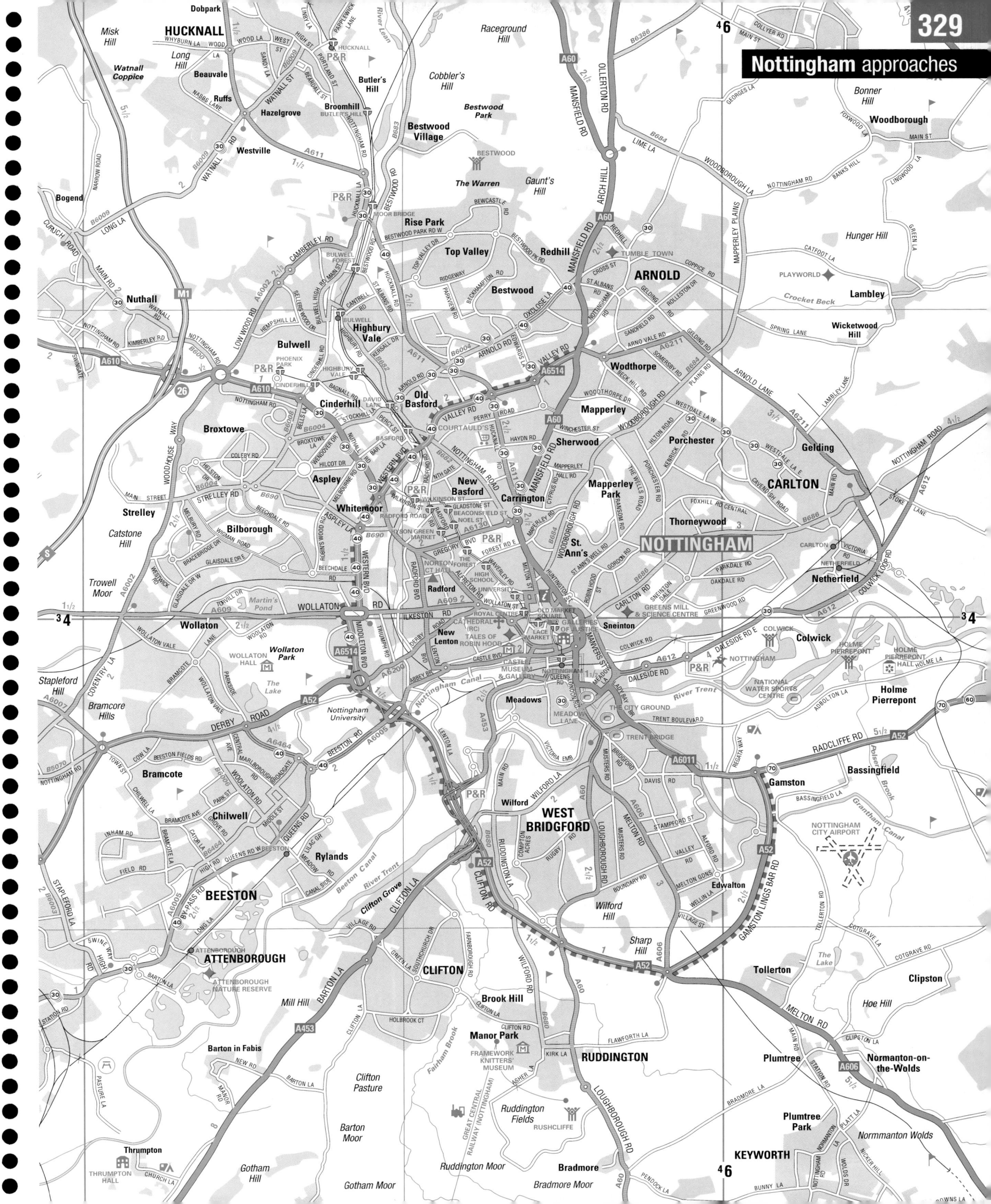
HUCKNALL
ARNOLD
NOTTINGHAM
CARLTON
WEST BRIDGFORD
BEESTON
CLIFTON
RUDDINGTON
KEYWORTH
ATTENBOROUGH
Bulwell
Wollaton
Mapperley
Sherwood
Gedling
Netherfield
Colwick
Gamston
Bramcote
Chilwell
Nuthall
Bestwood Village
Woodborough
Lambley
Tollerton
Plumtree
Normanton-on-the-Wolds
Nottingham University
Nottingham Canal
River Trent

Wharncliffe Wood
GRENOSIDE
ECCLESFIELD
Dropping Well
Kimberworth Park
Greasbrough
Eastwood
Dalton
Whinney Hill
Oughtibridge
Bradgate
Masbrough
ROTHERHAM
Clifton
Dalton Parva
Sunnyside
Dalton Magna
Shiregreen
Blackburn
Kimberworth
Beeley Wood
Birley Edge
Parson Cross
Concord Park
Jordan
Worrall
Broom
Herringthorpe
Brecks
Listerdale
Wickersley
Birley Carr
Pismire Hill
Wincobank
Wadsley Bridge
Longley Estate
Tinsley
Canklow
Moorgate
Wadsley
Firth Park
Shirecliffe
Carbrook
HILLSBOROUGH
Owlerton
Fir Vale
Grimesthorpe
Whiston
Loxley
Parkwood Springs
Pitsmoor
Brightside
Brinsworth
Morthen
Knowle Top
Malinbridge
Walkley
Greenland
Guilthwaite
Upper Whiston
Burngreave
Attercliffe
SHEFFIELD CITY
Tinsley Park
Catcliffe
Steel Bank
Crookes
Crookesmoor
Darnall
Treeton
Brampton en le Morthen
Ulley
Tapton Hill
SHEFFIELD
Manor Park
Sandygate
Handsworth
Dore House Industrial Estate
Aughton
Ranmoor
Greystones
Sheffield Park
Sharrow
Manor Estate
Orgreave
Woodhouse Mill
Fence
Fulwood
Lowfield
Arbourthorne
Richmond
Brincliffe
Woodhouse
Swallownest
Aston
Ecclesall
Nether Edge
Heeley
Intake
Carter Knowle
Newfield Green
Hollins End
Normanton Spring
Meersbrook
Gleadless
Hackenthorpe
Beighton
Parkhead
Millhouses
Hemsworth
Frecheville
Drakehouse
Wales
Gleadless Valley
Birley
Sothall
Whirlow
Norton Woodseats
Backmoor
Abbeydale
Meadow Head
Highlane
Moorhole
Waterthorpe
Rother Valley Lake
Lightwood
Owlthorpe
Dore
Beauchief
Norton
Ridgeway
Holbrook
Westfield
Norwood
Greenhill
Jordanthorpe
Plumbley
Halfway
Killamarsh
Woodall
Abbeydale Park
Lowedges
Ridgeway Moor
Totley Rise
Ford
Upperthorpe
Totley Bents
River Rivelin
River Rother
River Don
River Sheaf
Limb Brook
The Moss
Sheffield to Keadby Canal
Ulley Reservoir
Ecclesall Wood
Ridgeway Cottage Industry Centre
Magna Science Adventure Centre
Sheffield Services
Botanical Gardens
Heeley City Farm
Bishop's House
Meadowhall Ctr.
M1
M18
A57
A61
A630
A631
A6102
A6135
A618
A621
A625
A6109
A6178

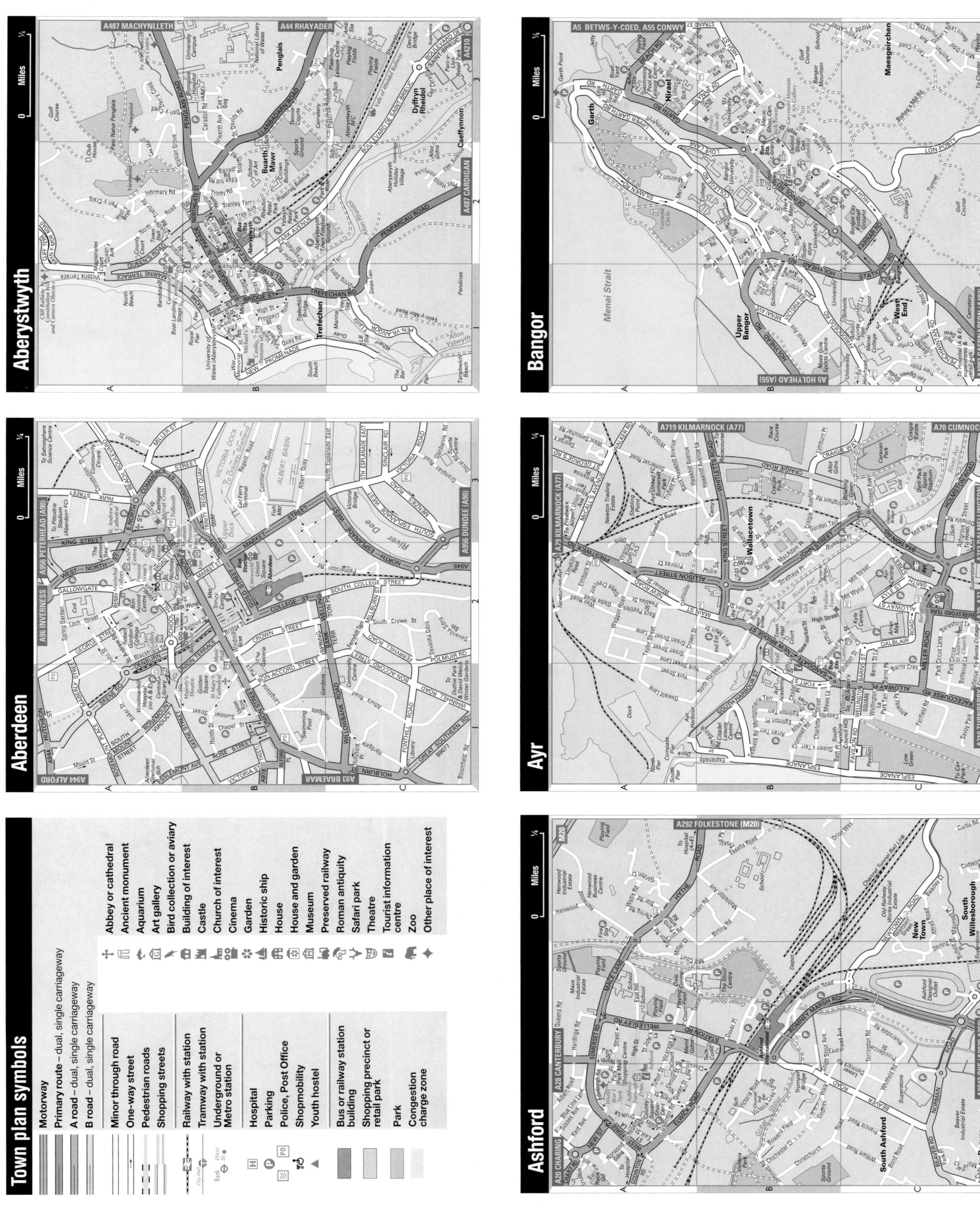

## Town plan symbols

- Motorway
- Primary route – dual, single carriageway
- A road – dual, single carriageway
- B road – dual, single carriageway

- Minor through road
- One-way street
- Pedestrian roads
- Shopping streets

- Railway with station
- Tramway with station

- Underground or Metro station

- Hospital
- Parking
- Police, Post Office
- Shopmobility
- Youth hostel

- Bus or railway station building
- Shopping precinct or retail park
- Park
- Congestion charge zone

- Abbey or cathedral
- Ancient monument
- Aquarium
- Art gallery
- Bird collection or aviary
- Building of interest
- Castle
- Church of interest
- Cinema
- Garden
- Historic ship
- House
- House and garden
- Museum
- Preserved railway
- Roman antiquity
- Safari park
- Theatre
- Tourist information centre
- Zoo
- Other place of interest

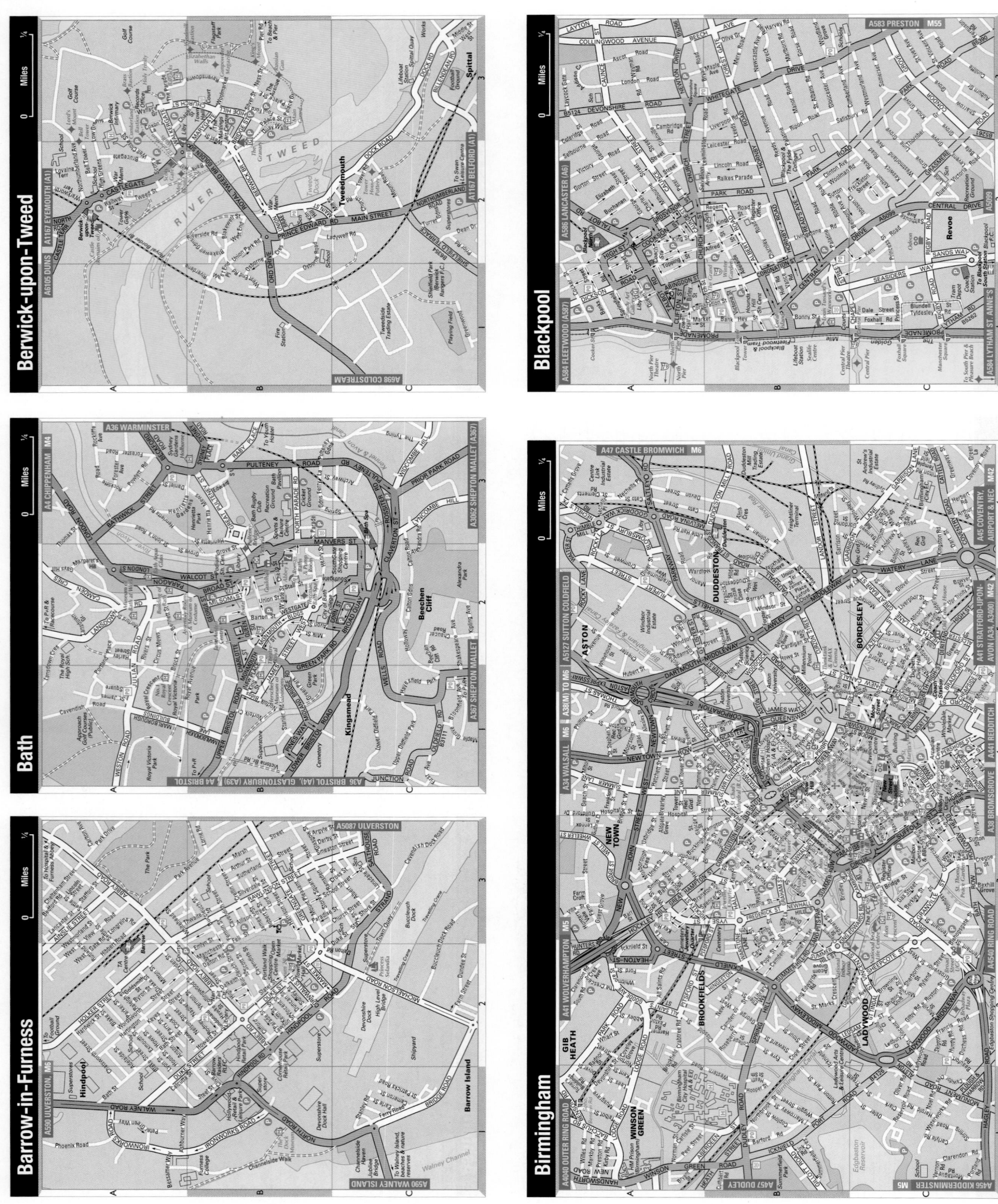
Berwick-upon-Tweed
Blackpool
Bath
Barrow-in-Furness
Birmingham

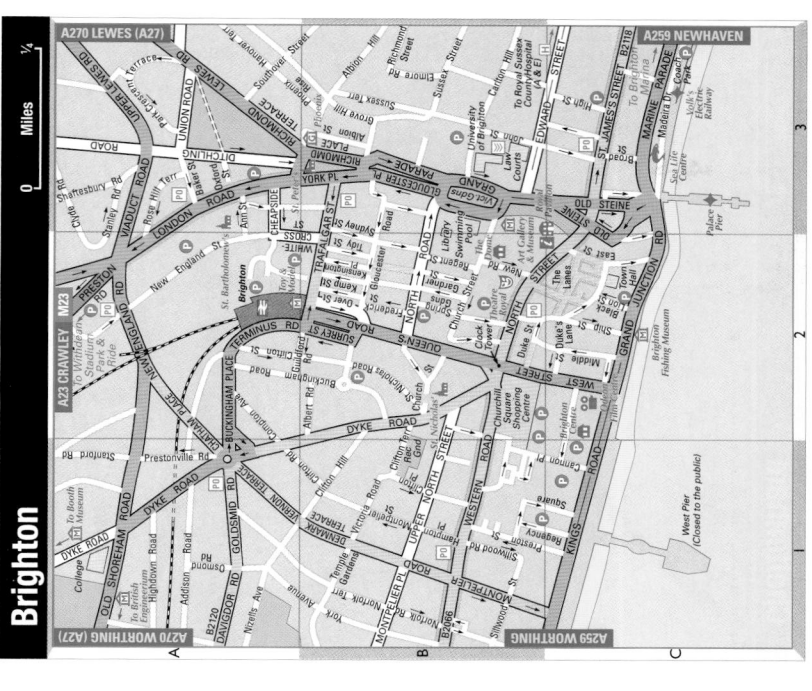
Brighton
A270 LEWES (A27)
A259 NEWHAVEN
A23 CRAWLEY
M23
A270 WORTHING (A27)
A259 WORTHING
Miles

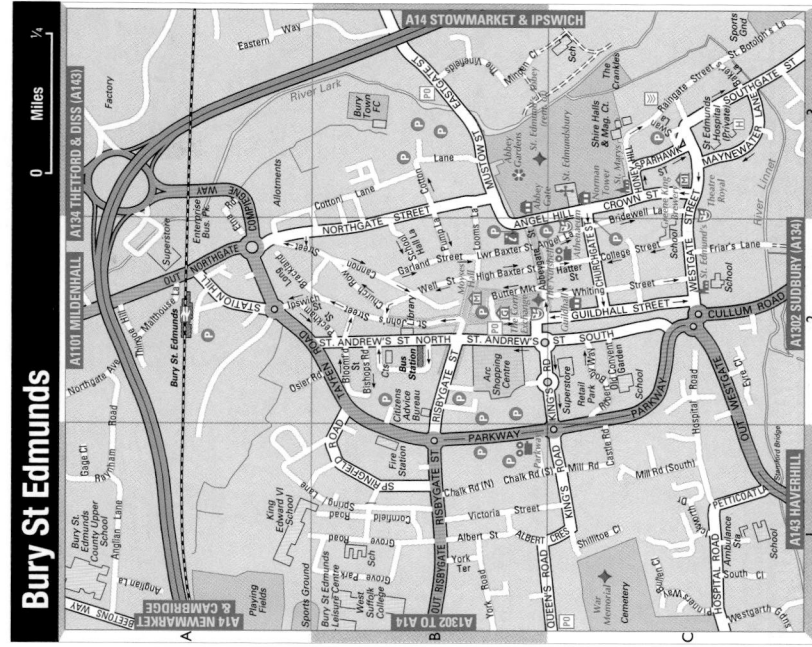
Bury St Edmunds
A14 STOWMARKET & IPSWICH
A134 THETFORD & DISS (A143)
A1101 MILDENHALL
A1302 SUDBURY (A134)
A143 HAVERHILL
A14 NEWMARKET & CAMBRIDGE
A1302 TO A14
Miles

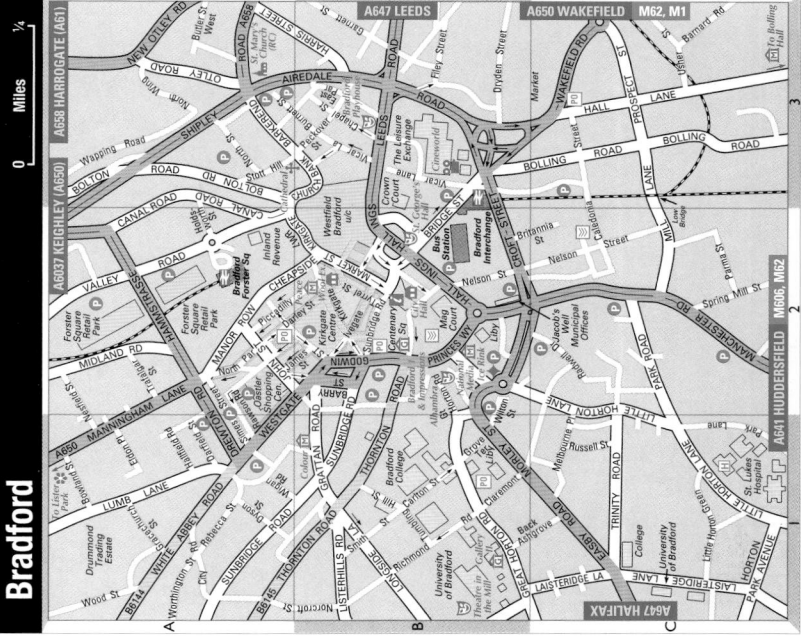
Bradford
A658 HARROGATE (A61)
A647 LEEDS
A650 WAKEFIELD
M62, M1
A6037 KEIGHLEY (A650)
M606, M62
A641 HUDDERSFIELD
A647 HALIFAX
Miles

Bristol
A432 MANGOTSFIELD
A420 CHIPPENHAM
A4032 TO M32 & M4
A38 TO M5
A4018 TO M5
A4 BATH
A37 SHEPTON MALLET
A38 TAUNTON
A370 WESTON-SUPER-MARE
A4 AVONMOUTH & M5
CLIFTON
Miles

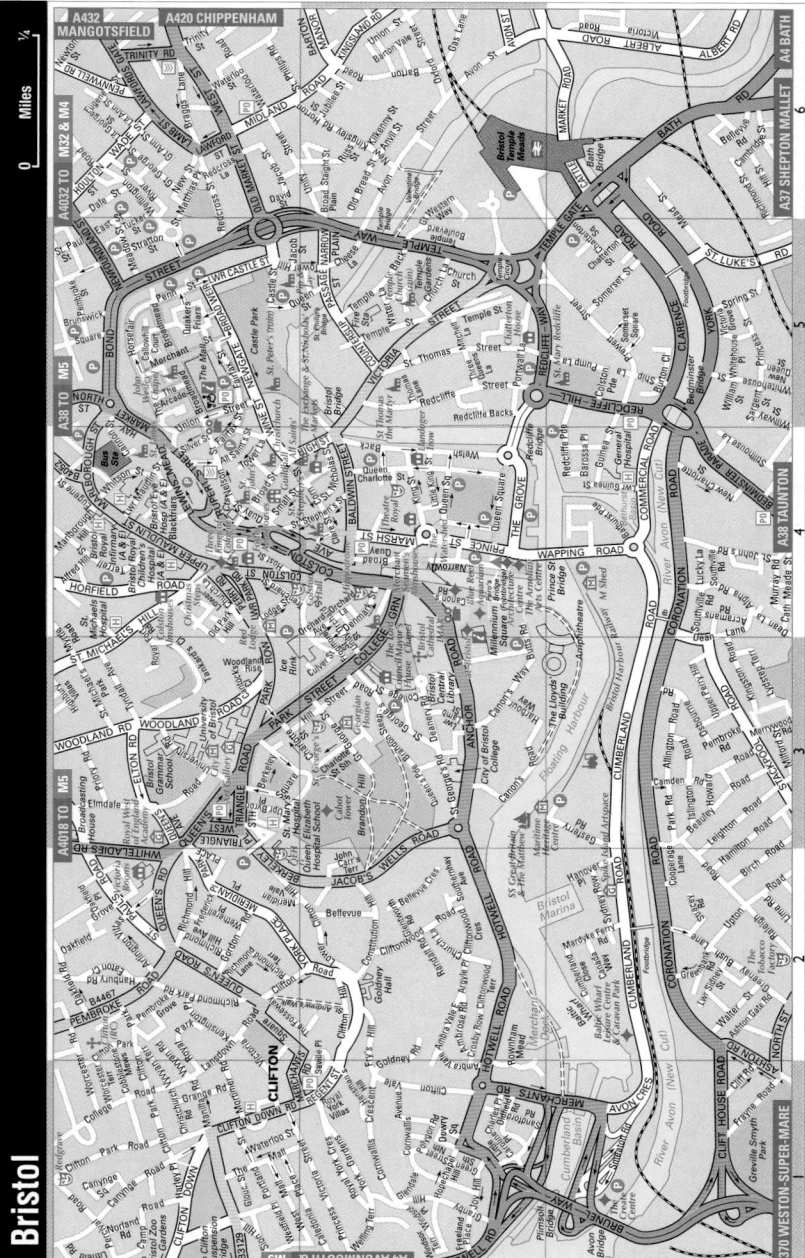
Bournemouth
A338 RINGWOOD
A35 CHRISTCHURCH
A347 FERNDOWN
A338 POOLE (A35)
Poole Bay
Miles

Cambridge
Canterbury
Cardiff / Caerdydd
Carlisle
Chelmsford
Cheltenham

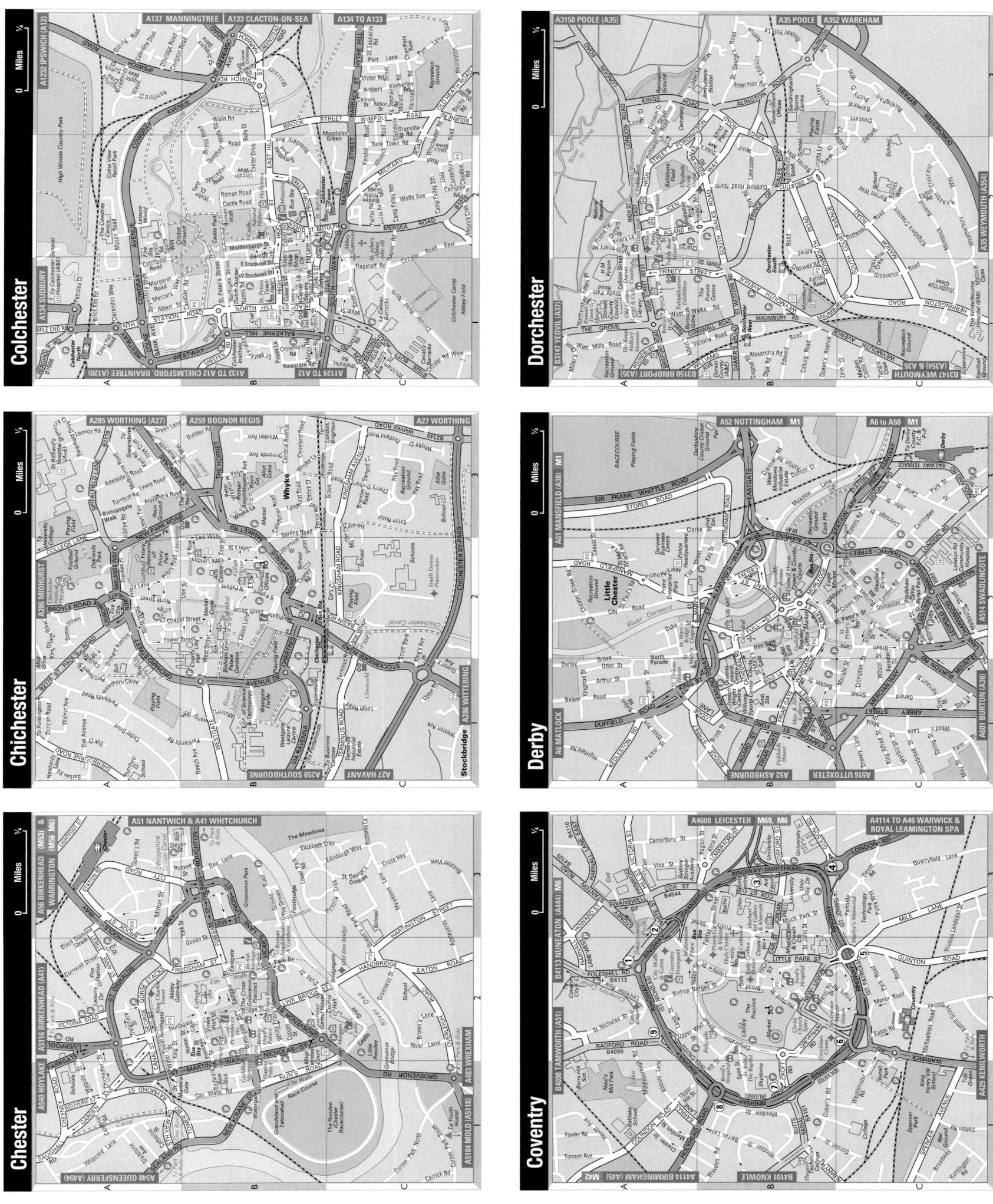
Colchester
A137 MANNINGTREE
A133 CLACTON-ON-SEA
A134 TO A133
A1232 IPSWICH (A12)
A134 SUDBURY
A133 TO A12 CHELMSFORD, BRAINTREE (A120)
A1124 TO A12
Dorchester
A3150 POOLE (A35)
A35 POOLE
A352 WAREHAM
B3147 YEOVIL (A37)
B3150 BRIDPORT (A35)
B3147 WEYMOUTH
A35 WEYMOUTH (A354)
Chichester
A285 WORTHING (A27)
A259 BOGNOR REGIS
A27 WORTHING
A286 MIDHURST
A286 WITTERING
A259 SOUTHBOURNE
A27 HAVANT
Derby
A52 NOTTINGHAM
M1
A6 to A50
A61 MANSFIELD (A38)
A6 MATLOCK
A52 ASHBOURNE
A516 UTTOXETER
A514 SWADLINCOTE
A601 BURTON (A38)
Chester
A51 NANTWICH & A41 WHITCHURCH
A56 BIRKENHEAD (M53) & WARRINGTON (M56 M6)
A5116 BIRKENHEAD (A41)
A540 HOYLAKE
A548 QUEENSFERRY (A494)
A5104 MOLD (A5118)
A483 WREXHAM
Coventry
A4600 LEICESTER M69, M6
A4114 TO A46 WARWICK & ROYAL LEAMINGTON SPA
B4113 NUNEATON (A444) M6
B4098 TAMWORTH (A51)
A4114 BIRMINGHAM (A45) M42
B4101 KNOWLE
A429 KENILWORTH
Miles
0
¼

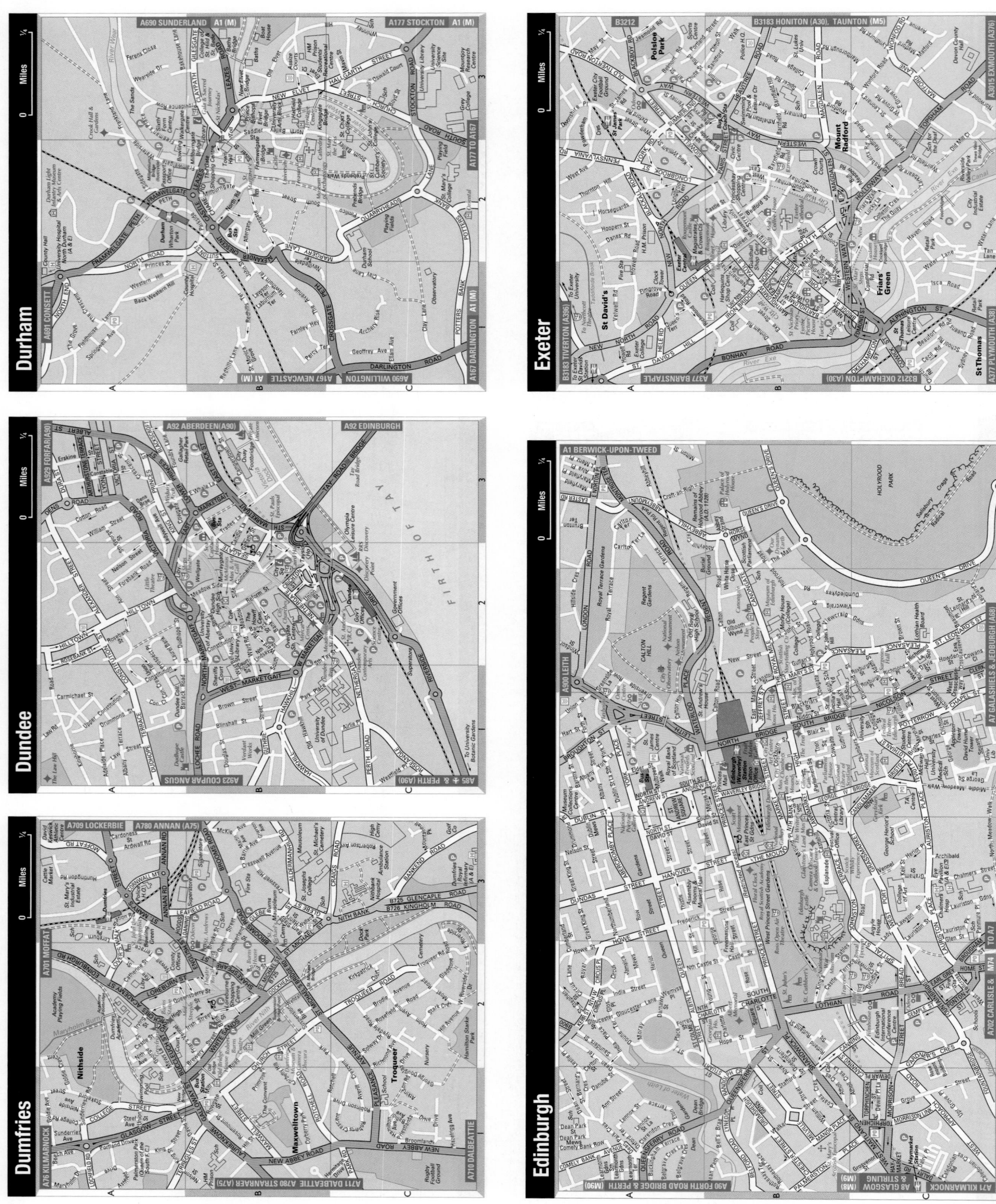
Dumfries
A76 KILMARNOCK
A701 MOFFAT
A710 DALBEATTIE
Dundee
A929 FORFAR(A90)
A92 EDINBURGH
FIRTH OF TAY
Durham
A691 CONSETT
A167 DARLINGTON A1 (M)
A177 TO A167
Edinburgh
A900 LEITH
A702 CARLISLE & M74
TO A7
A7 GALASHIELS & JEDBURGH (A68)
HOLYROOD PARK
Exeter
B3183 TIVERTON (A396)
A377 PLYMOUTH (A38)
A3015 EXMOUTH (A376)

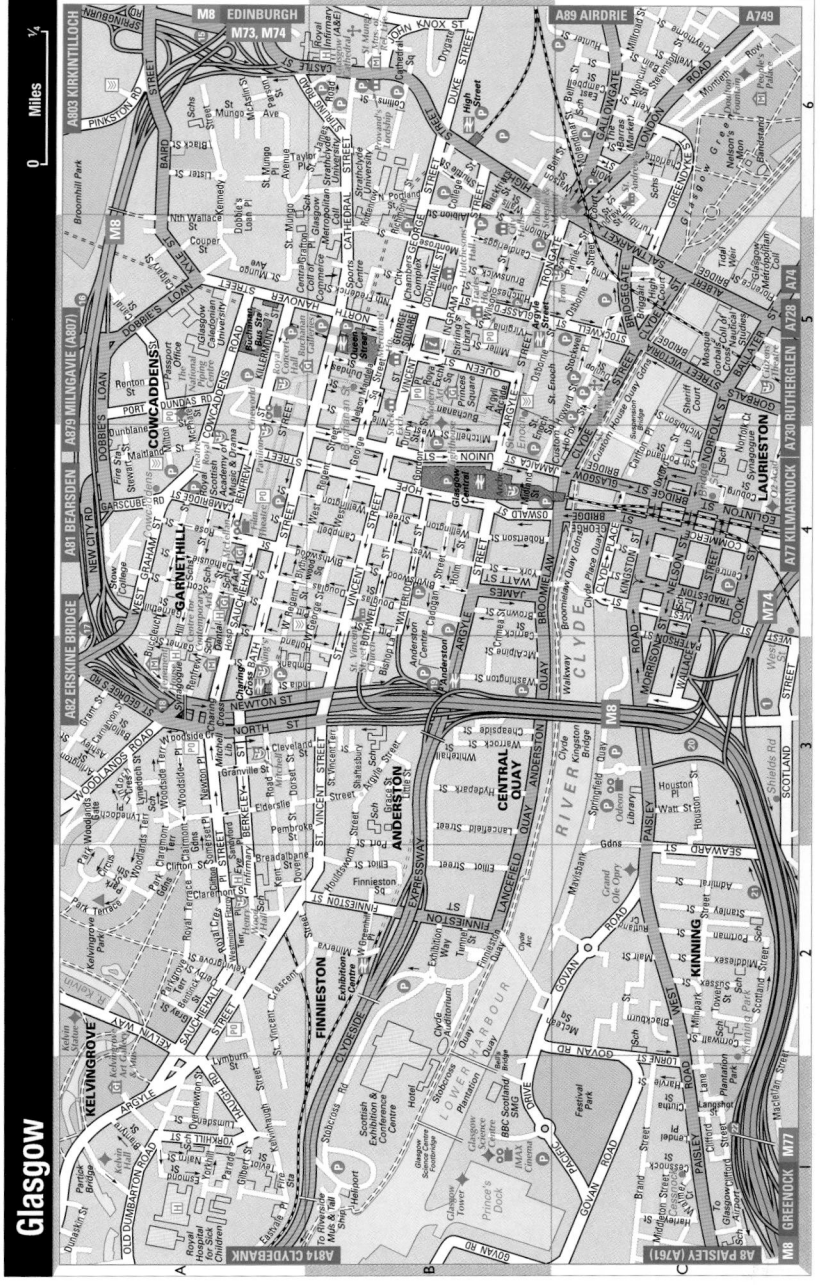
Fort William
0 Miles ¼
A82 INVERNESS
A82 CRIANLARICH
Inverlochy
Loch Linnhe
River Lochy
An Aird
Camusnagaul Ferry (Foot Passengers Only)
Am Breun Chamas
Cow Hill

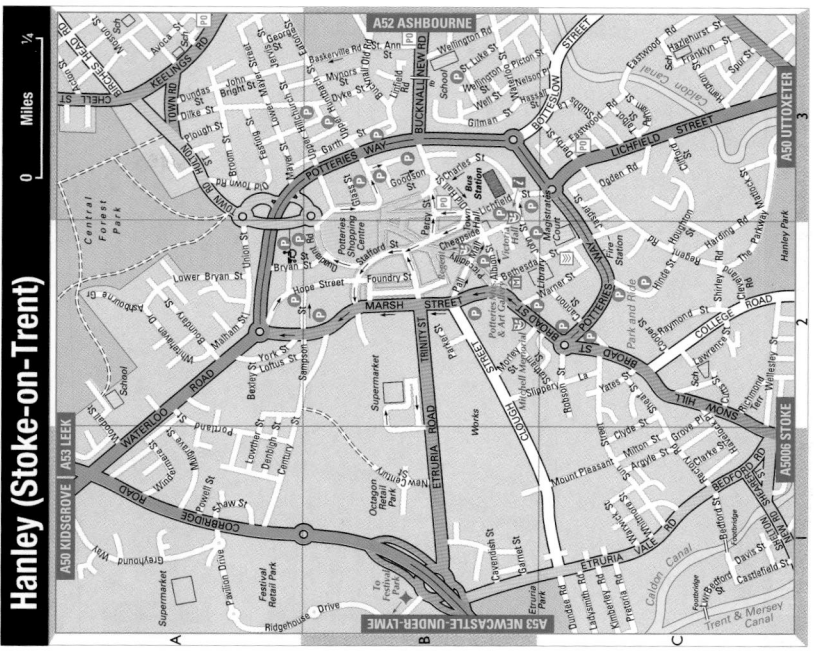
Glasgow
0 Miles ¼
A82 ERSKINE BRIDGE
A81 BEARSDEN
A879 MILNGAVIE (A807)
A803 KIRKINTILLOCH
M8 EDINBURGH
M73, M74
A89 AIRDRIE
A749
A74
A728
A730 RUTHERGLEN
A77 KILMARNOCK
M74
M77
M8 GREENOCK
A8 PAISLEY (A761)
A814 CLYDEBANK
KELVINGROVE
GARNETHILL
COWCADDENS
FINNIESTON
ANDERSTON
CENTRAL QUAY
KINNING
LAURIESTON
RIVER CLYDE

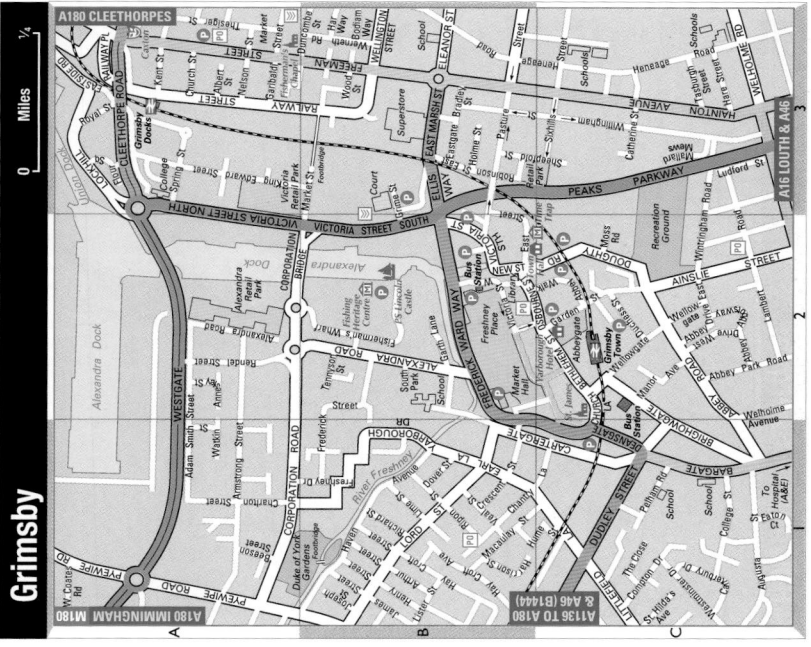
Gloucester
0 Miles ¼
A38 CHELTENHAM (A40) & M5
A4302 TO A38
A430 TO A38 BRISTOL M5
A417 ROSS-ON-WYE (A40)
Gloucester
Cathedral
Kingsholm Rugby Football Ground
St. Oswald's Trading Estate
River Severn
The Park

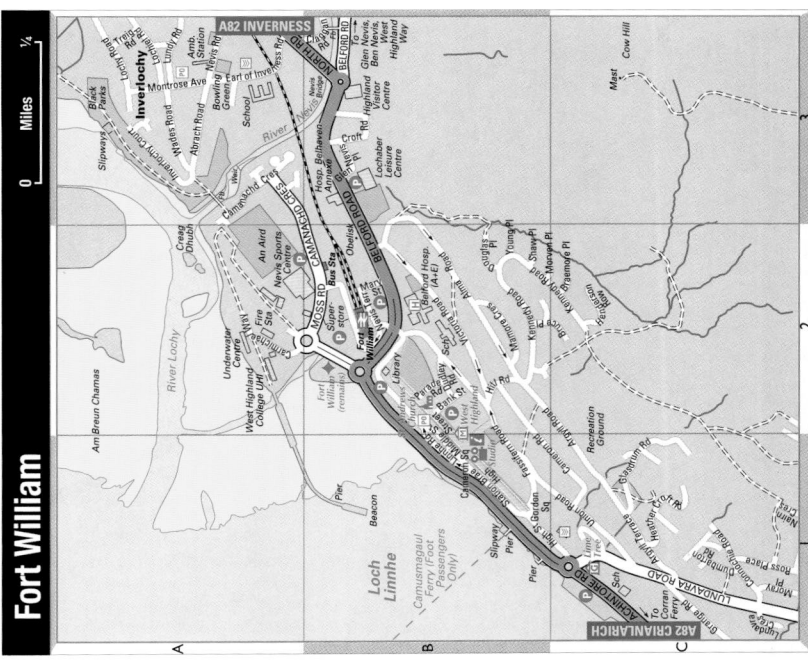
Grimsby
0 Miles ¼
A180 CLEETHORPES
A180 IMMINGHAM M180
A1136 TO A180 & A46 (B1444)
A16 LOUTH & A46
Alexandra Dock
Grimsby Docks
WESTGATE
PEAKS PARKWAY

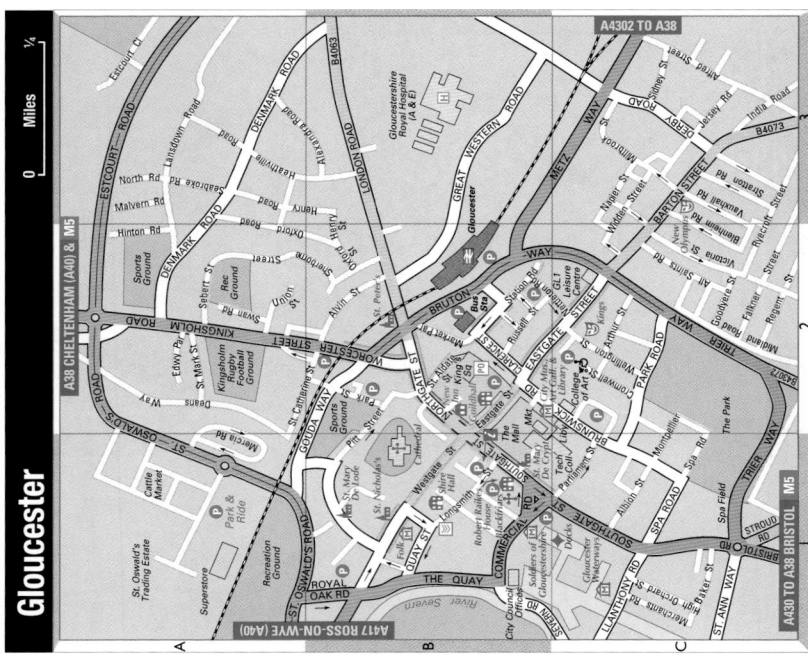
Hanley (Stoke-on-Trent)
0 Miles ¼
A50 KIDSGROVE
A53 LEEK
A52 ASHBOURNE
A50 UTTOXETER
A5006 STOKE
A53 NEWCASTLE-UNDER-LYME
Central Forest Park
Hanley Park
Festival Retail Park

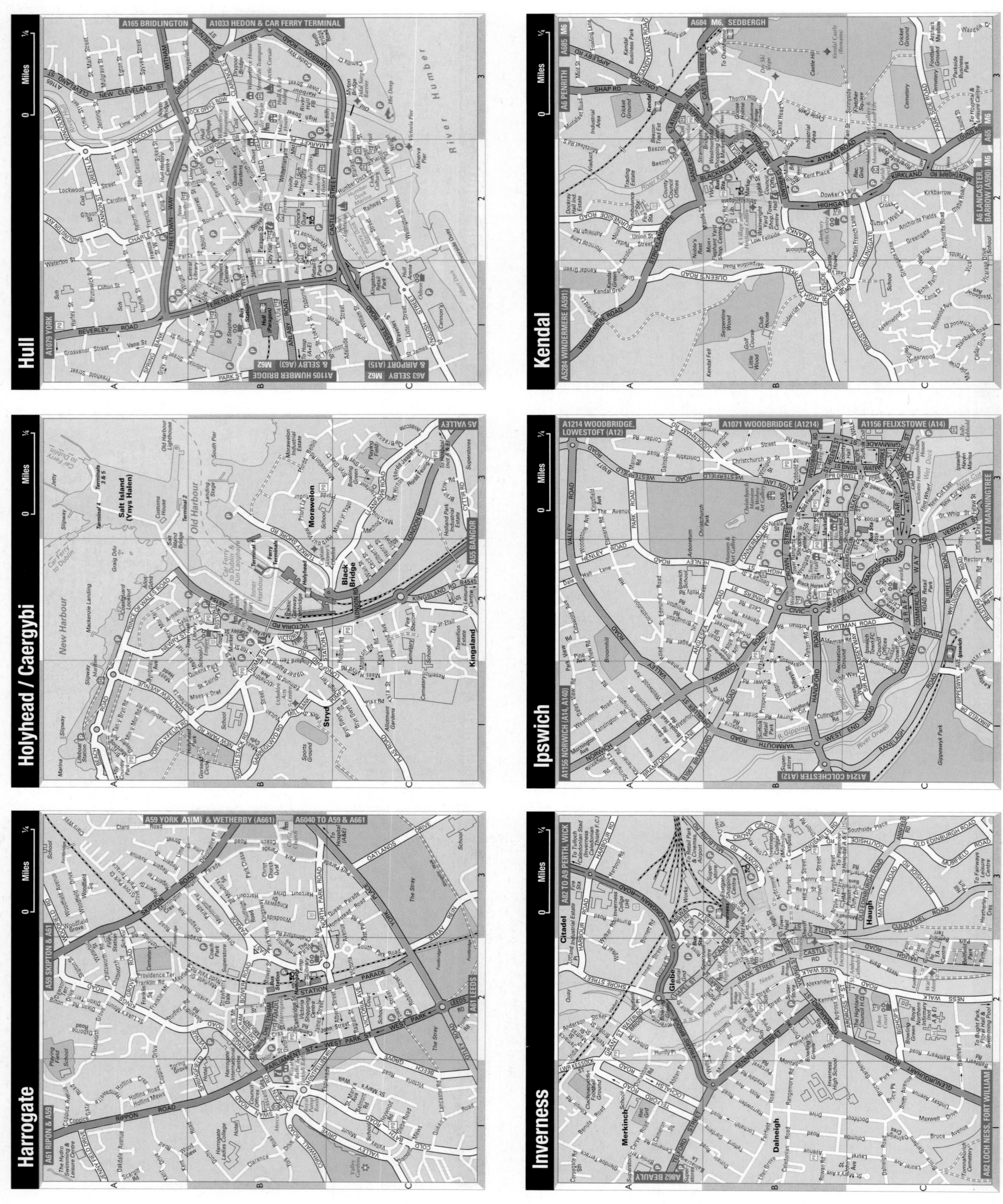
Hull
Kendal
Holyhead / Caergybi
Ipswich
Harrogate
Inverness
A165 BRIDLINGTON
A1033 HEDON & CAR FERRY TERMINAL
A1079 YORK
A1105 HUMBER BRIDGE & SELBY (A63) M62
A63 SELBY M62 & AIRPORT (A15)
A684 M6, SEDBERGH
A6 PENRITH A685 M6
A5284 WINDERMERE (A591)
A6 LANCASTER, BARROW (A590)
A65 M6
A5 VALLEY
A55 BANGOR
A1214 WOODBRIDGE, LOWESTOFT (A12)
A1071 WOODBRIDGE (A1214)
A1156 FELIXSTOWE (A14)
A137 MANNINGTREE
A1156 NORWICH (A14, A140)
A1214 COLCHESTER (A12)
A59 YORK A1(M) & WETHERBY (A661)
A6040 TO A59 & A661
A59 SKIPTON & A61
A61 LEEDS
A61 RIPON & A59
A82 TO A9 PERTH, WICK
A82 LOCH NESS, FORT WILLIAM
A862 BEAULY
Miles

King's Lynn
0 Miles ¼
A1078 TO A148 & HUNSTANTON (A149)
A148 FAKENHAM & A149 (A1076)
A148 WISBECH (A47) & SPALDING (A17)
A149 SWAFFHAM (A47) & DOWNHAM MKT (A10)
North End
Highgate
West Lynn
South Lynn

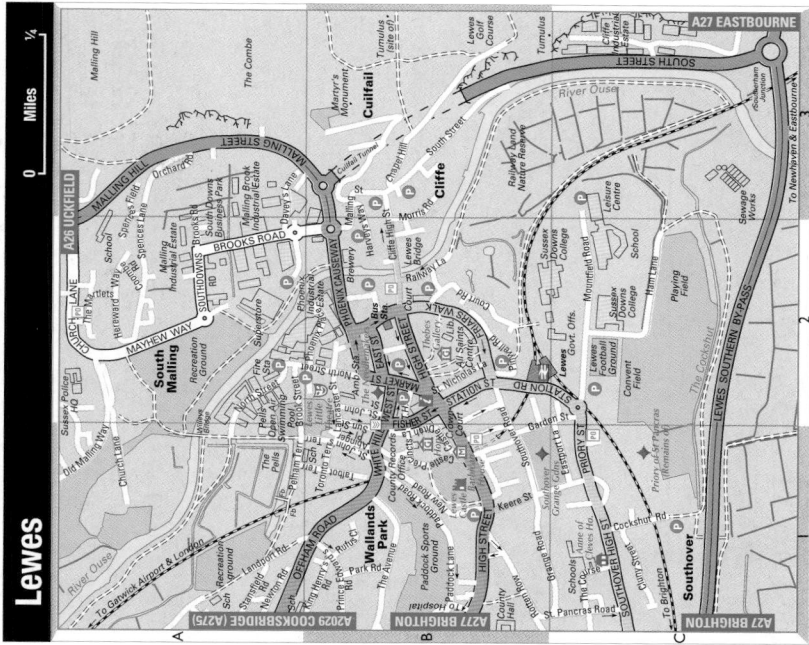
Leeds
0 Miles ¼
A660 SKIPTON (A65)
A58 WETHERBY
A61 HARROGATE
A64 YORK
A65 SKIPTON
A647 BRADFORD
A62 HUDDERSFIELD & M62
A643 DEWSBURY (A653) & M621
A653 DEWSBURY & (M621, M1, M62)
A639 to M621, (M1)
City Centre Loop Road
A61 to M621
A63 to M1
LITTLE WOODHOUSE
MABGATE
QUARRY HILL
RICHMOND HILL
NEW WORTLEY
GRANARY WHARF
WAREHOUSE HILL
STEANDER
CROWN POINT
CAMP FIELD
CAVALIER HILL

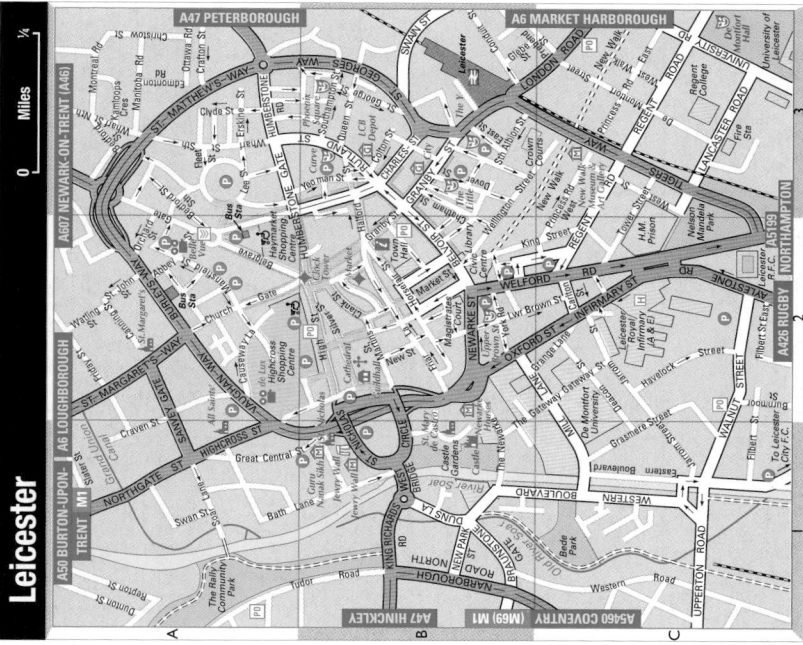
Lancaster
0 Miles ¼
A6 CARNFORTH
A683 KIRKBY LONSDALE & M6
A589 MORECAMBE
A588 TO A585
A6 GARSTANG & M6
Newton
Ridge
Freehold
Moorlands
Abraham Heights
The Greaves
Golgotha

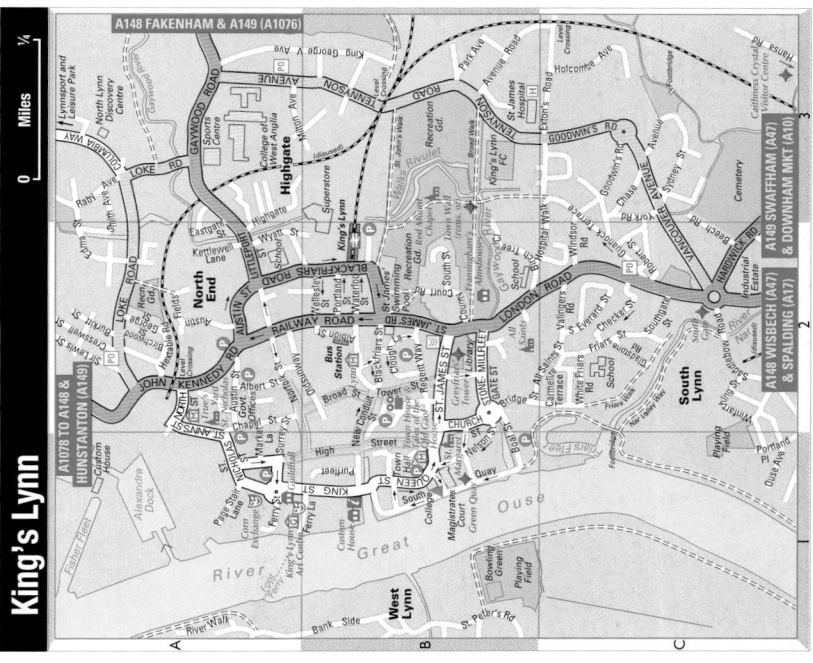
Leicester
0 Miles ¼
A50 BURTON-UPON-TRENT M1
A6 LOUGHBOROUGH
A607 NEWARK-ON-TRENT (A46)
A47 PETERBOROUGH
A6 MARKET HARBOROUGH
A47 HINCKLEY
A5460 COVENTRY (M69) M1
A426 RUGBY
A5199 NORTHAMPTON

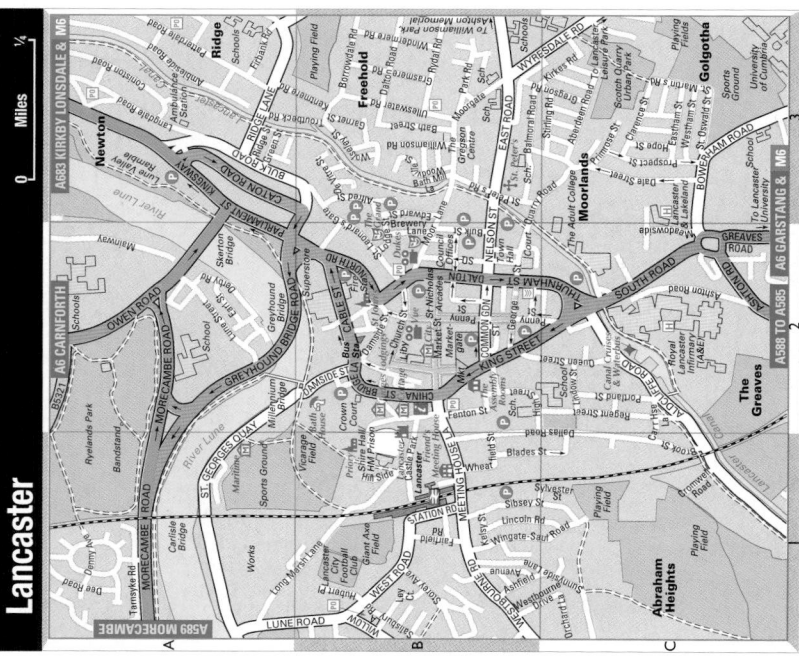
Lewes
0 Miles ¼
A26 UCKFIELD
A2029 COOKSBRIDGE (A275)
A277 BRIGHTON
A27 BRIGHTON
A27 EASTBOURNE
South Malling
Wallands Park
Cuilfail
Cliffe
Southover

2
3
4
B
C
D
E
F
5
ST. JOHN'S WOOD
Lord's Cricket Ground (M.C.C. & Middlesex C.C.C.)
REGENT'S PARK
LISSON GREEN
PADDINGTON
Paddington Basin
Marylebone
REGENT'S PARK
SOMERS TOWN
Euston
St. Pancras International
King's Cross
BLOOMSBURY
FITZROVIA
SOHO
MAYFAIR
ST. JAMES'S
HYDE PARK
KENSINGTON GARDENS
The Long Water
THE SERPENTINE
GREEN PARK
ST. JAMES'S PARK
Buckingham Palace Gardens
KNIGHTSBRIDGE
BROMPTON
WESTMINSTER
PIMLICO
Victoria
Victoria Coach Station
Charing Cross
Speakers Corner
Marble Arch
Wellington Arch
Royal Albert Hall
Natural History Museum
Science Museum
Victoria & Albert Museum
Westminster Abbey
Tate Britain
Duke of York's Headquarters
Chelsea Barracks

HOXTON
FINSBURY
SHOREDITCH
CLERKENWELL
HOLBORN
THE CITY
SOUTHWARK
SOUTH BANK
NEWINGTON
LAMBETH
BERMONDSEY
RIVER
THAMES
PENTONVILLE ROAD
CITY ROAD
OLD STREET
CLERKENWELL ROAD
HOLBORN
HOLBORN VIADUCT
NEWGATE STREET
LONDON WALL
CHEAPSIDE
FLEET STREET
STRAND
ALDWYCH
VICTORIA EMBANKMENT
QUEEN VICTORIA STREET
UPPER THAMES STREET
LOWER THAMES STREET
EASTCHEAP
LEADENHALL STREET
FENCHURCH STREET
CORNHILL
BISHOPSGATE
COMMERCIAL STREET
WHITECHAPEL HIGH ST
TOWER HILL
SOUTHWARK STREET
UNION STREET
BOROUGH HIGH STREET
TOOLEY STREET
WATERLOO ROAD
BLACKFRIARS ROAD
WESTMINSTER BRIDGE ROAD
KENNINGTON ROAD
NEW KENT ROAD
OLD KENT ROAD
WALWORTH ROAD
TOWER BRIDGE ROAD
Waterloo
London Bridge
Blackfriars
Cannon Street
Liverpool Street
Fenchurch Street
Elephant & Castle
Farringdon
The Barbican
St Paul's Cathedral
The Tower of London
Tate Modern
Imperial War Museum
Lambeth Palace
Miles
0
½
5
6
7
8
B
C
D
E
F

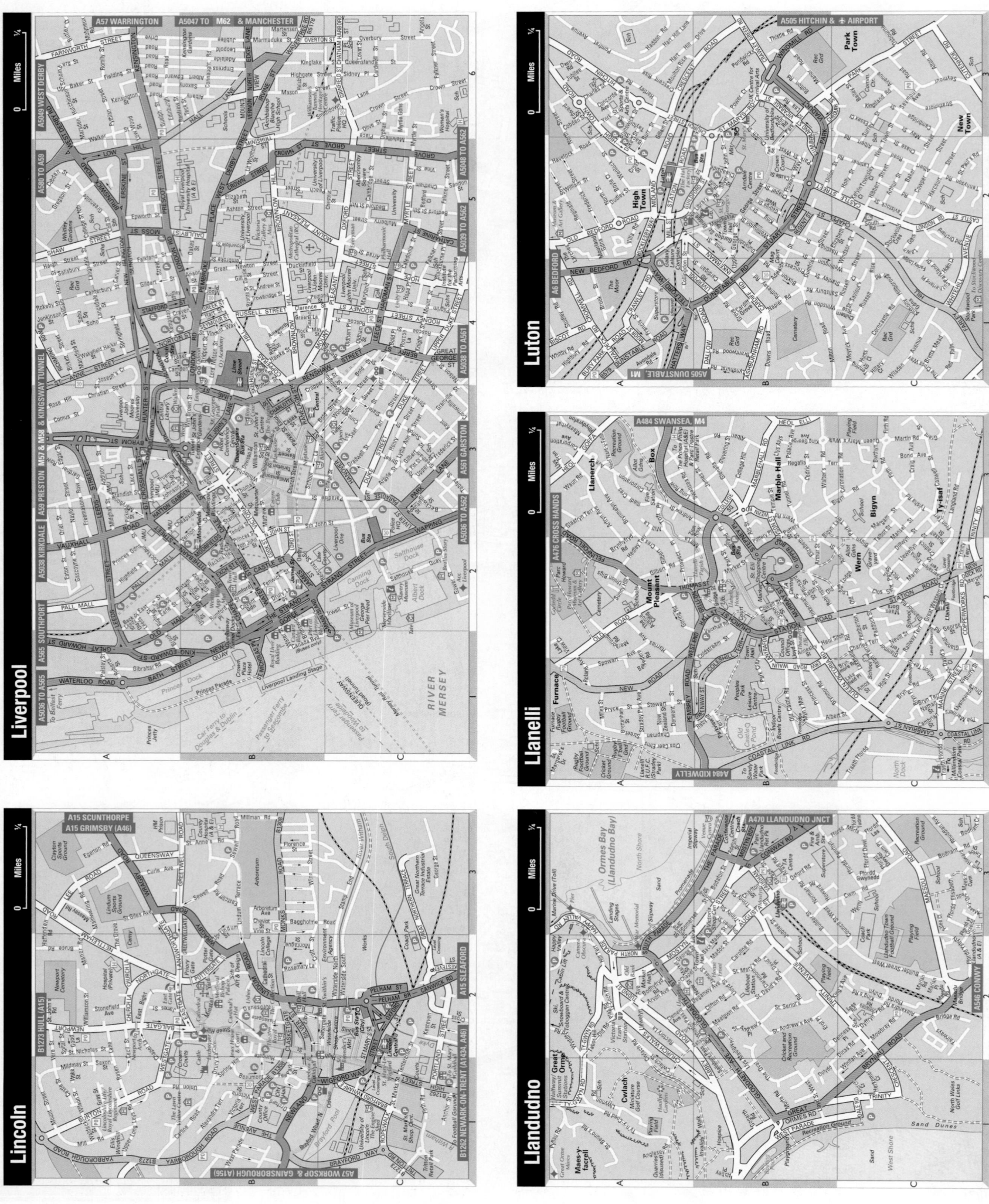
Lincoln
B1273 HULL (A15)
A15 SCUNTHORPE
A15 GRIMSBY (A46)
A57 WORKSOP & GAINSBOROUGH (A156)
B1262 NEWARK-ON-TRENT (A1434, A46)
A15 SLEAFORD
Liverpool
A5036 TO A565
A565 SOUTHPORT
A5038 KIRKDALE
A59 PRESTON M57 & M58 & KINGSWAY TUNNEL
A580 TO A59
A5049 WEST DERBY
A57 WARRINGTON
A5047 TO M62 & MANCHESTER
A5036 TO A562
A561 GARSTON
A5038 TO A561
A5039 TO A562
A5048 TO A562
RIVER MERSEY
Llandudno
A470 LLANDUDNO JNCT
A546 CONWY
Ormes Bay (Llandudno Bay)
Llanelli
A476 CROSS HANDS
A484 SWANSEA, M4
A484 KIDWELLY
Luton
A6 BEDFORD
A505 DUNSTABLE, M1
A505 HITCHIN & AIRPORT

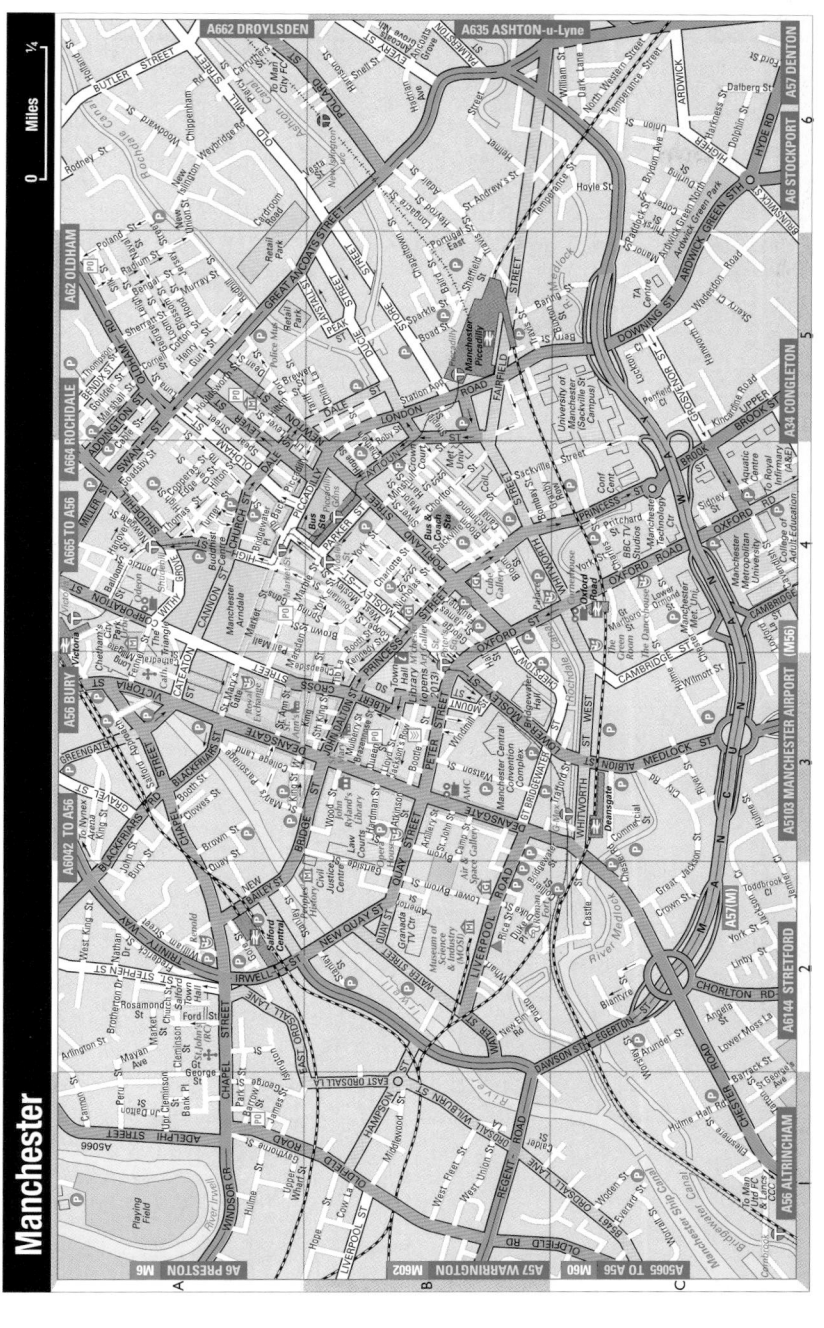
Manchester
Miles
A662 DROYLSDEN
A635 ASHTON-u-Lyne
A57 DENTON
A6 STOCKPORT
A34 CONGLETON
A5103 MANCHESTER AIRPORT
A6144 STRETFORD
A56 ALTRINCHAM
A6 PRESTON M6
A57 WARRINGTON M602
A5065 TO A56 M60
A62 OLDHAM
A664 ROCHDALE
A665 TO A56
A56 BURY
A6042 TO A56

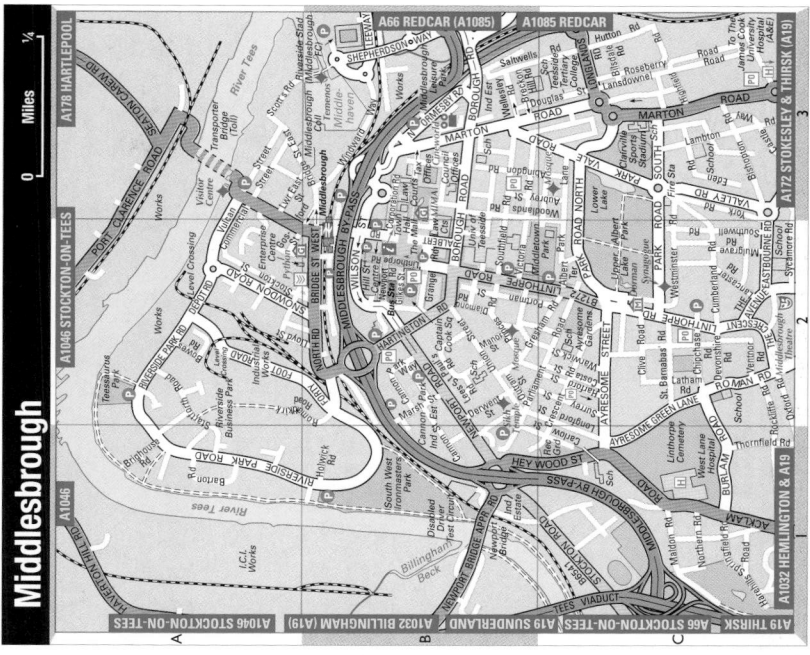
Middlesbrough
Miles
A66 REDCAR (A1085)
A1085 REDCAR
A178 HARTLEPOOL
A1046 STOCKTON-ON-TEES
A1046
A172 STOKESLEY & THIRSK (A19)
A1032 HEMLINGTON & A19
A19 THIRSK
River Tees

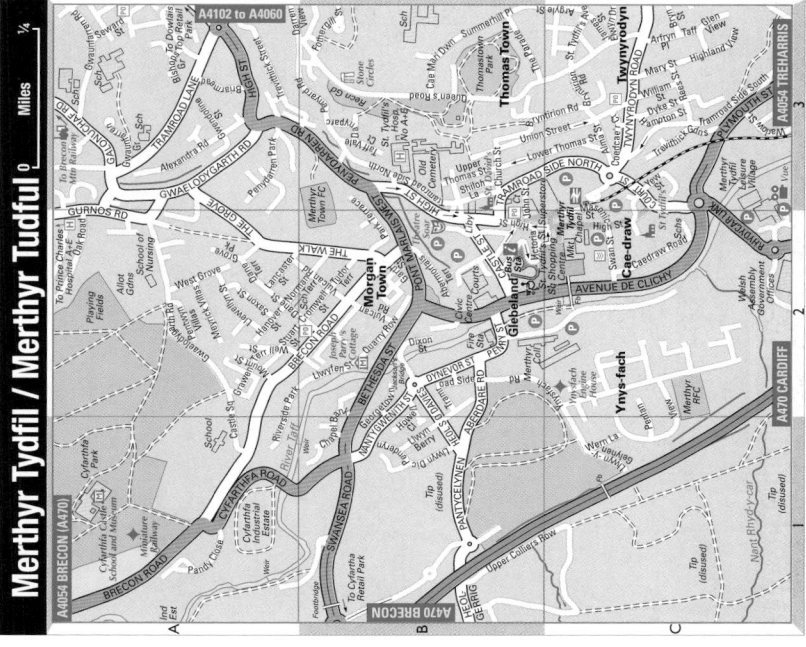
Merthyr Tydfil / Merthyr Tudful
Miles
A4102 to A4060
A4054 TREHARRIS
A470 CARDIFF
A4054 BRECON (A470)
A470 BRECON
Thomas Town
Twynyrodyn
Morgan Town
Georgetown
Cae-draw
Ynys-fach

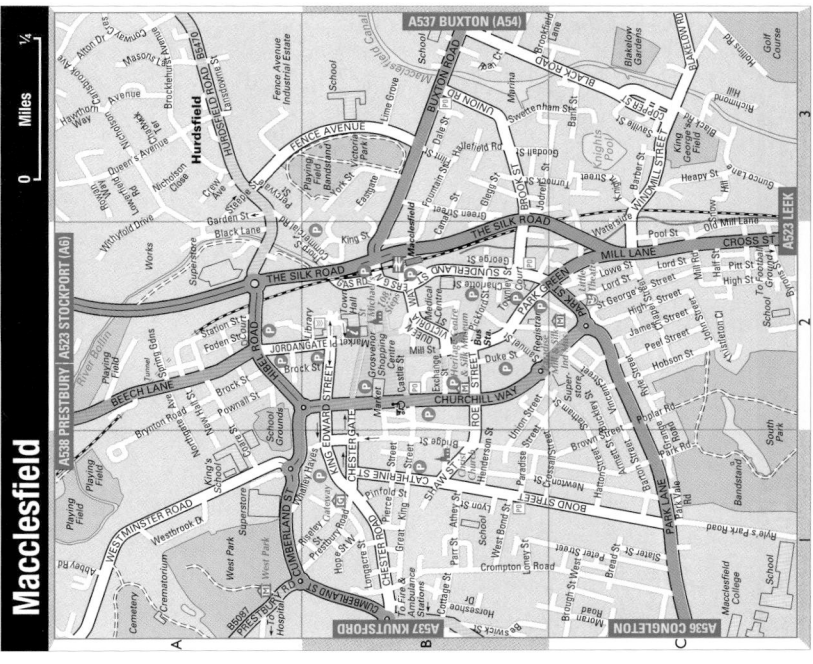
Macclesfield
Miles
A537 BUXTON (A54)
A523 LEEK
A536 CONGLETON
A537 KNUTSFORD
A538 PRESTBURY
A523 STOCKPORT (A6)
Hurdsfield

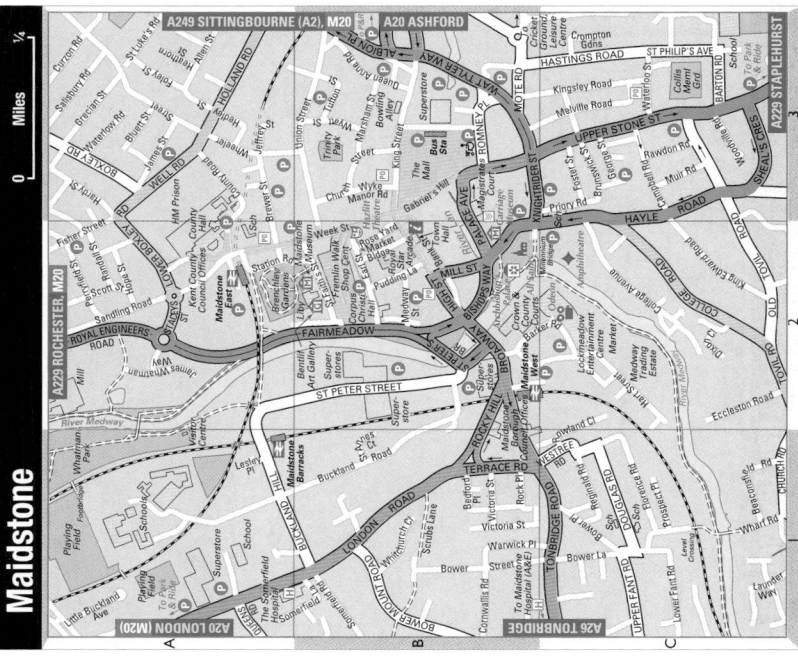
Maidstone
Miles
A249 SITTINGBOURNE (A2), M20
A20 ASHFORD
A229 STAPLEHURST
A26 TONBRIDGE
A20 LONDON (M20)
A229 ROCHESTER, M20
River Medway

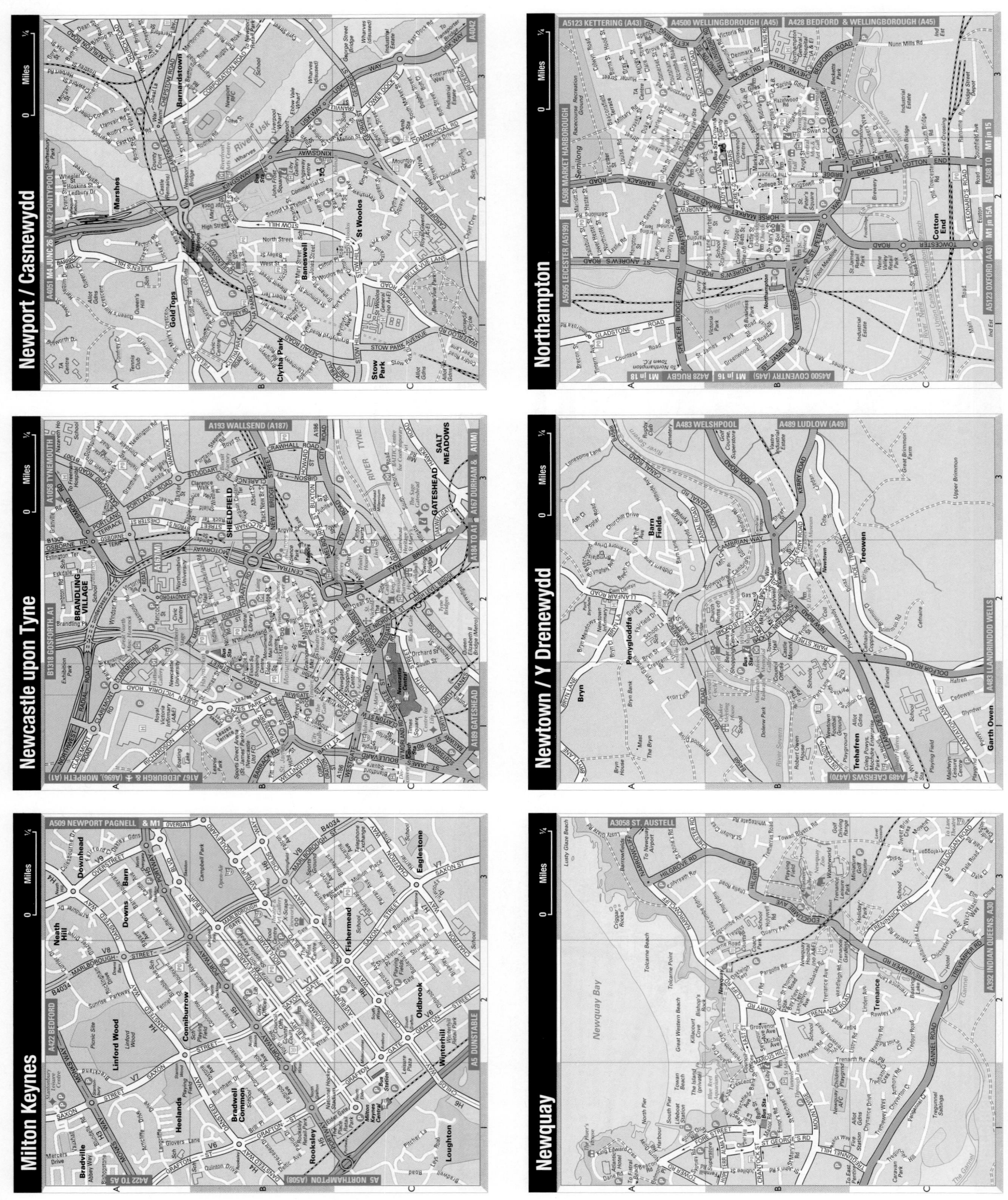
Milton Keynes
0 Miles ¼
A422 BEDFORD
A509 NEWPORT PAGNELL & M1
A5 NORTHAMPTON (A508)
A5 DUNSTABLE
Newcastle upon Tyne
0 Miles ¼
B1318 GOSFORTH, A1
A1058 TYNEMOUTH
A193 WALLSEND (A187)
A189 GATESHEAD
A184 TO A1
A167 DURHAM & A1(M)
Newport / Casnewydd
0 Miles ¼
A4051 M4 JUNC 26
A4042 PONTYPOOL
A4042
Newquay
0 Miles ¼
Newquay Bay
A3058 ST. AUSTELL
A392 INDIAN QUEENS, A30
Newtown / Y Drenewydd
0 Miles ¼
A483 WELSHPOOL
A489 LUDLOW (A49)
A489 CAERSWS (A470)
A483 LLANDRINDOD WELLS
Northampton
0 Miles ¼
A5095 LEICESTER (A5199)
A508 MARKET HARBOROUGH
A5123 KETTERING (A43)
A4500 WELLINGBOROUGH (A45)
A428 BEDFORD & WELLINGBOROUGH (A45)
A5123 OXFORD (A43)
M1 jn 15A
A508 TO M1 jn 15
A4500 COVENTRY (A45)
M1 jn 16
A428 RUGBY
M1 jn 18

**Norwich** page 142 • **Nottingham** page 153 • **Oban** page 289 • **Oxford** page 83 • **Perth** page 286 • **Peterborough** page 138

**345**

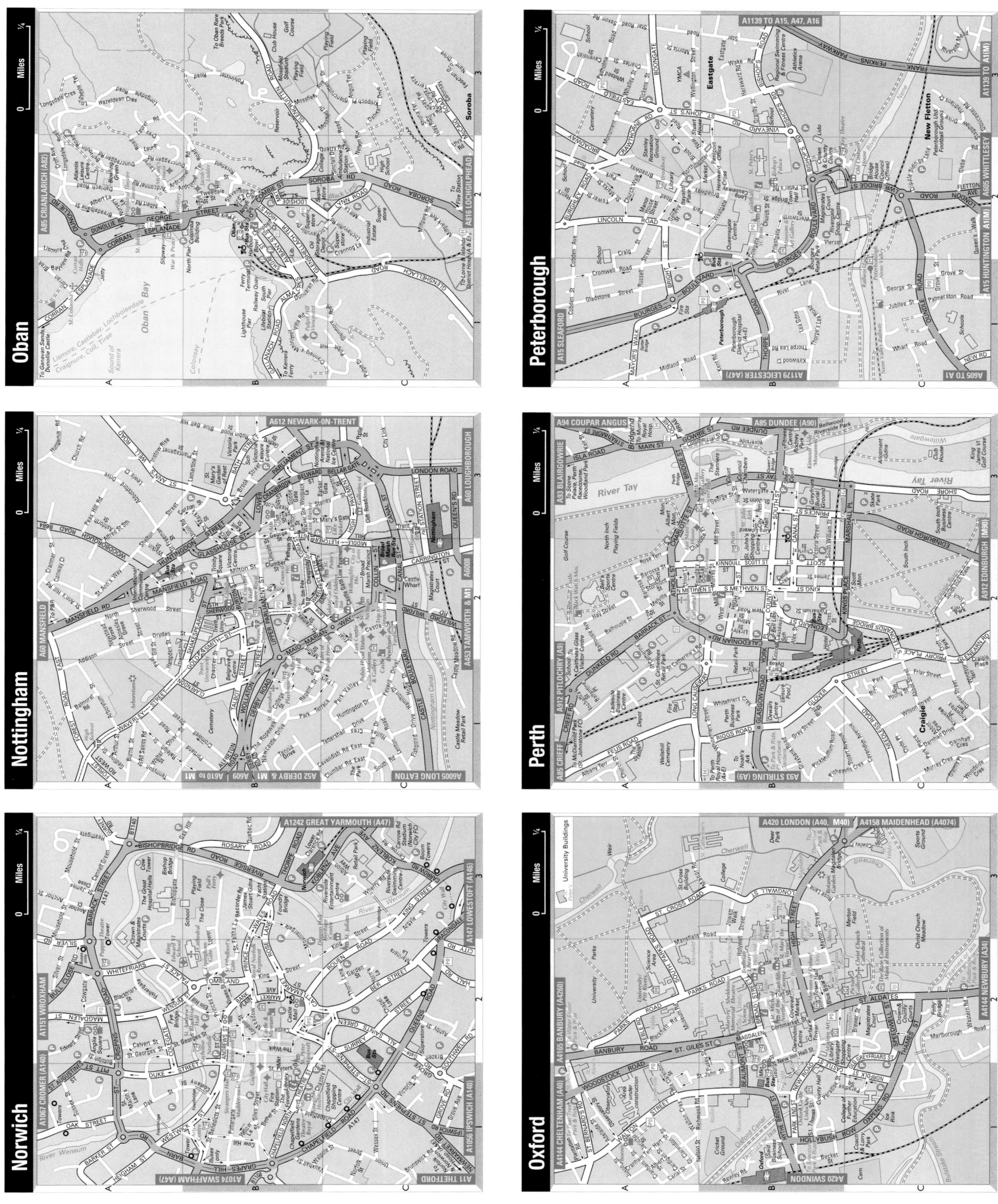

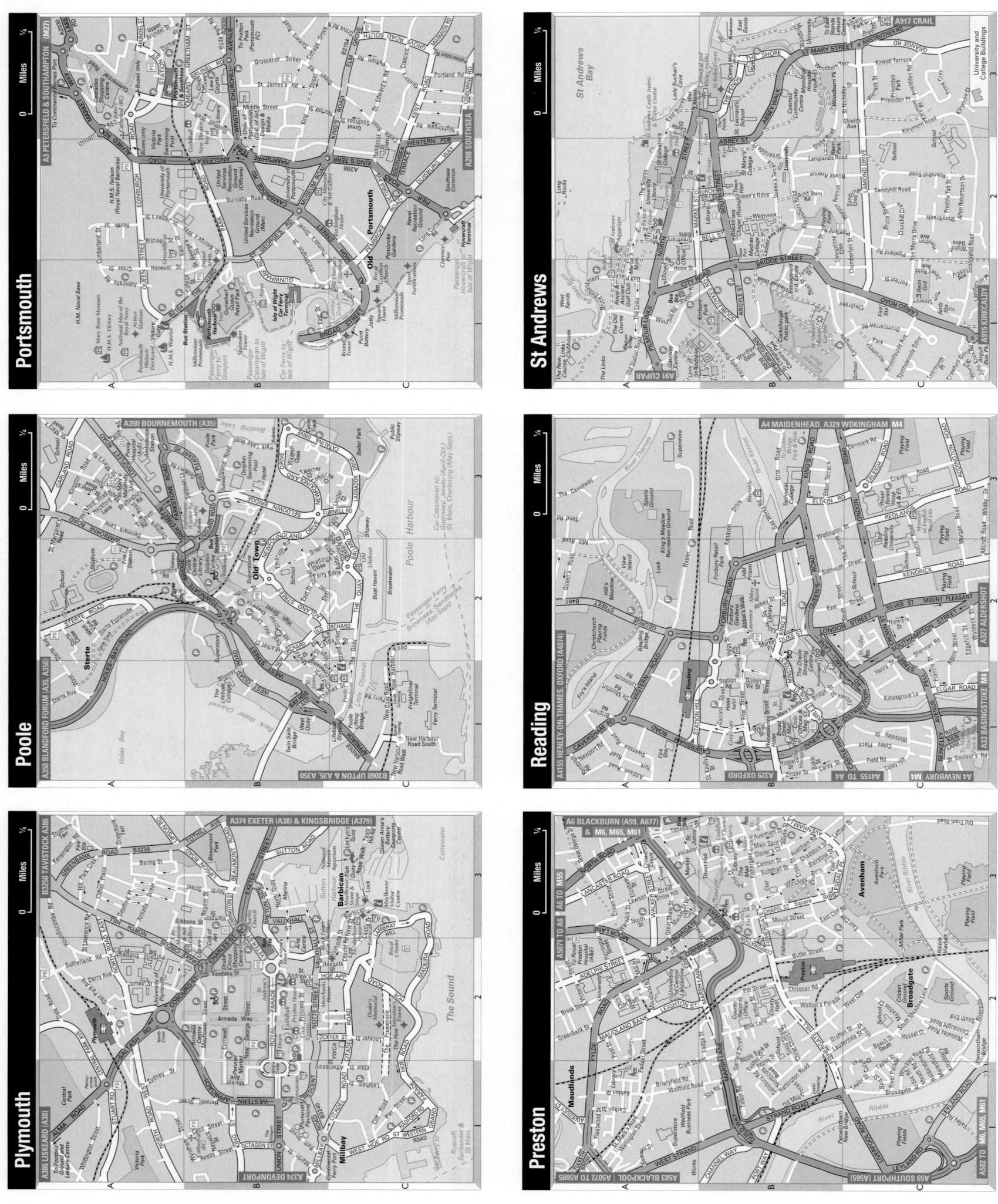
Portsmouth
St Andrews
Poole
Reading
Plymouth
Preston

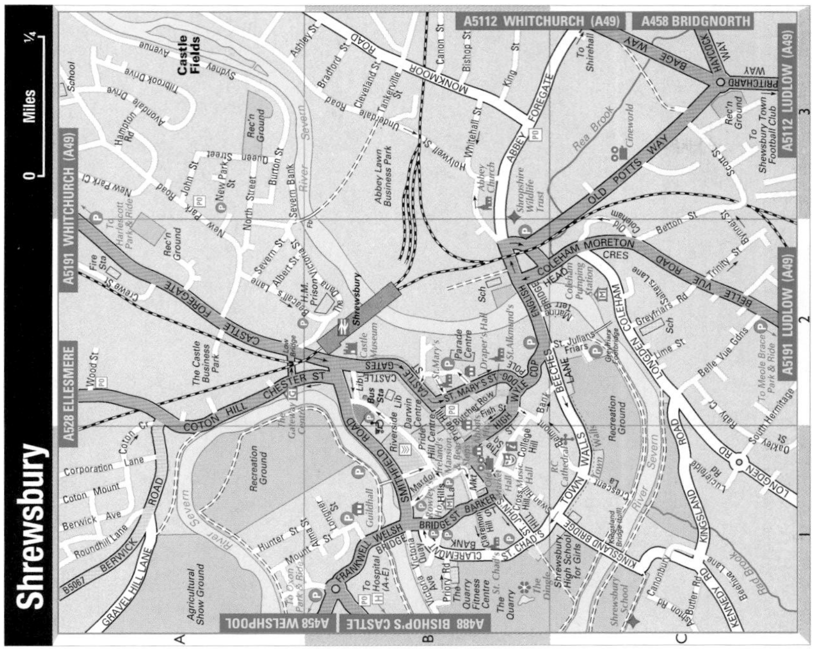

## Shrewsbury

## Southampton
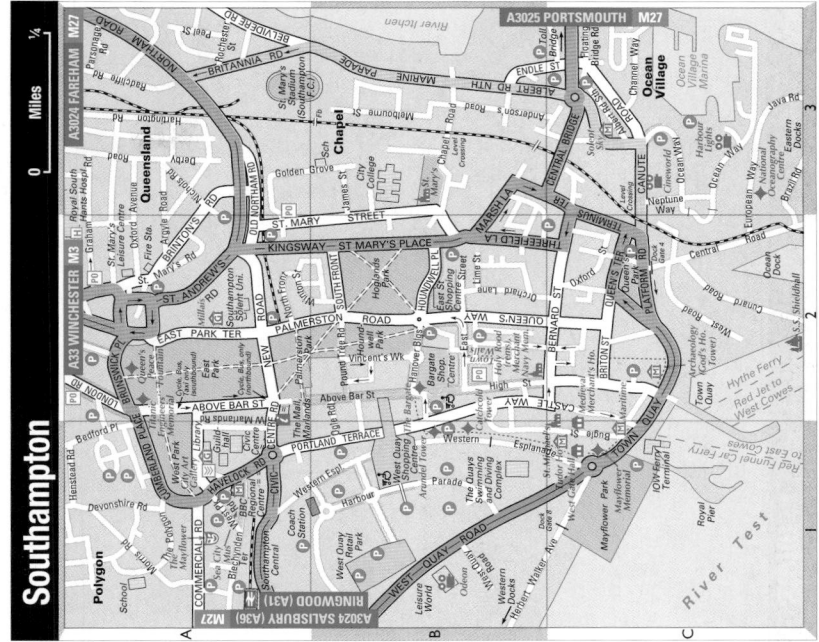

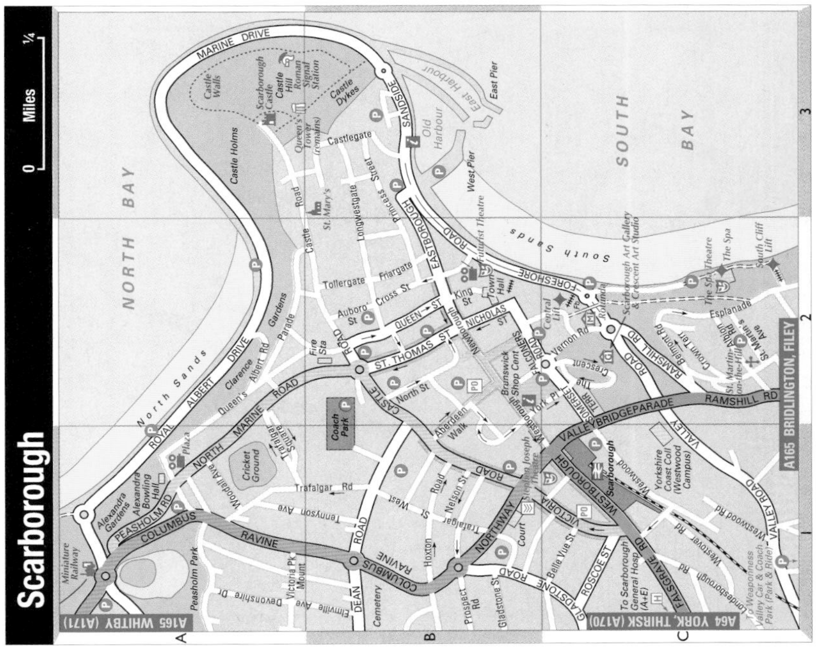

## Scarborough

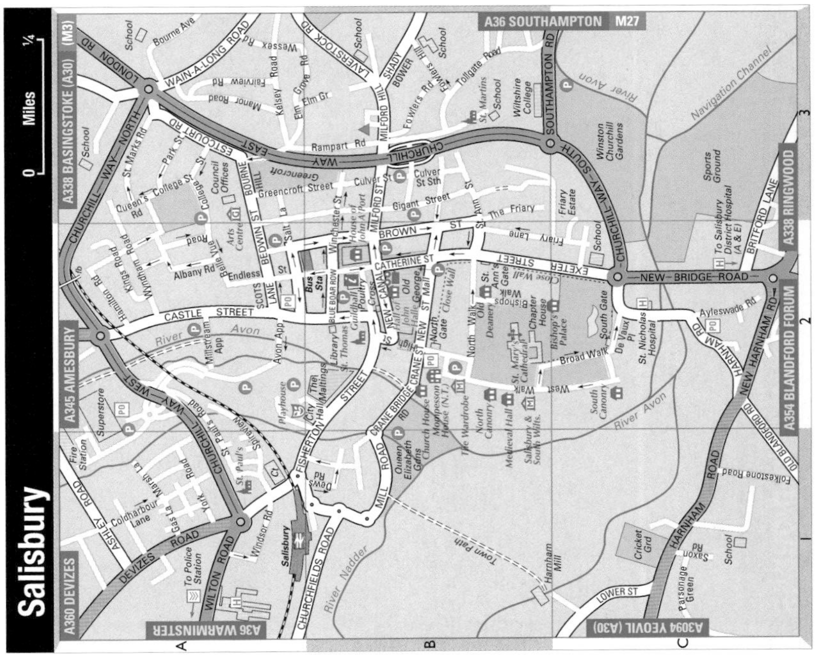

## Sheffield
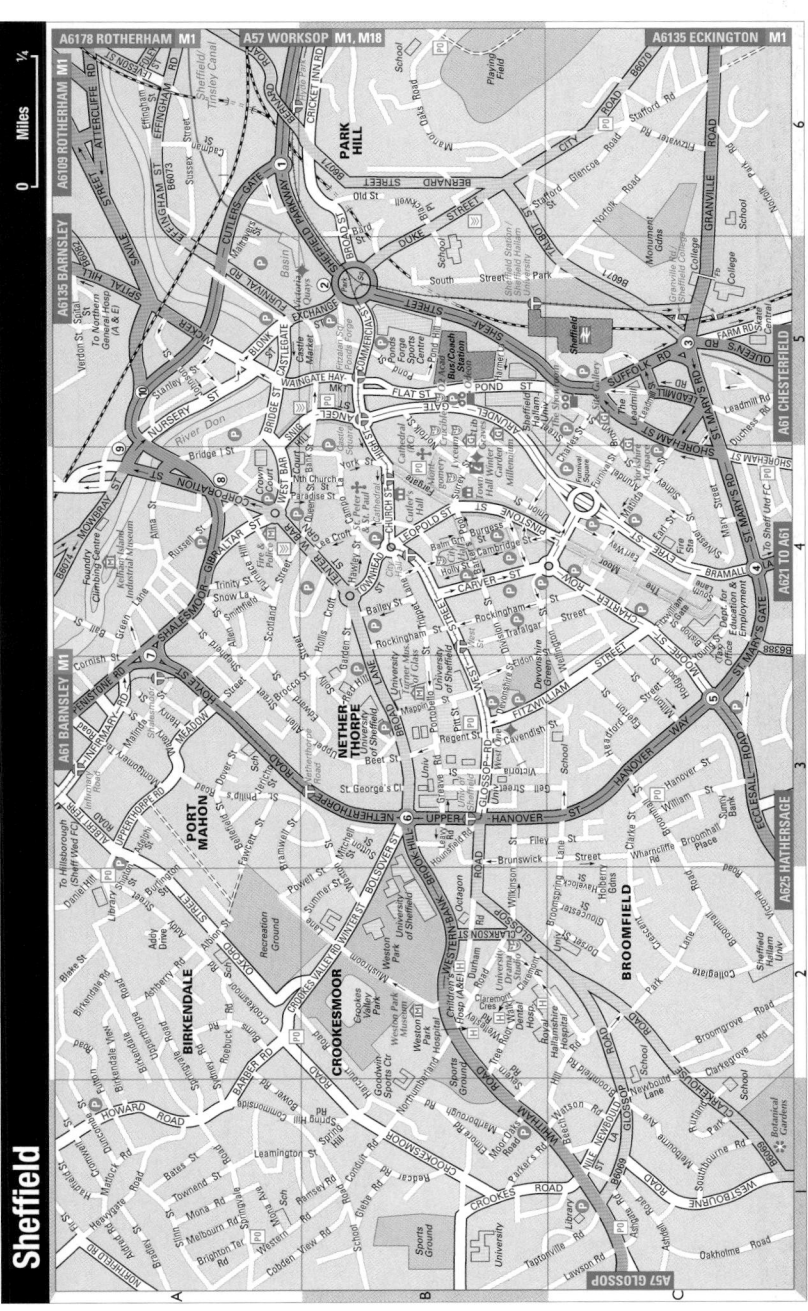

## Salisbury

# 348

**Southend** page 69 • **Stirling** page 278 • **Stoke** page 168 • **Stratford-upon-Avon** page 118 • **Sunderland** page 243 • **Swansea** page 56

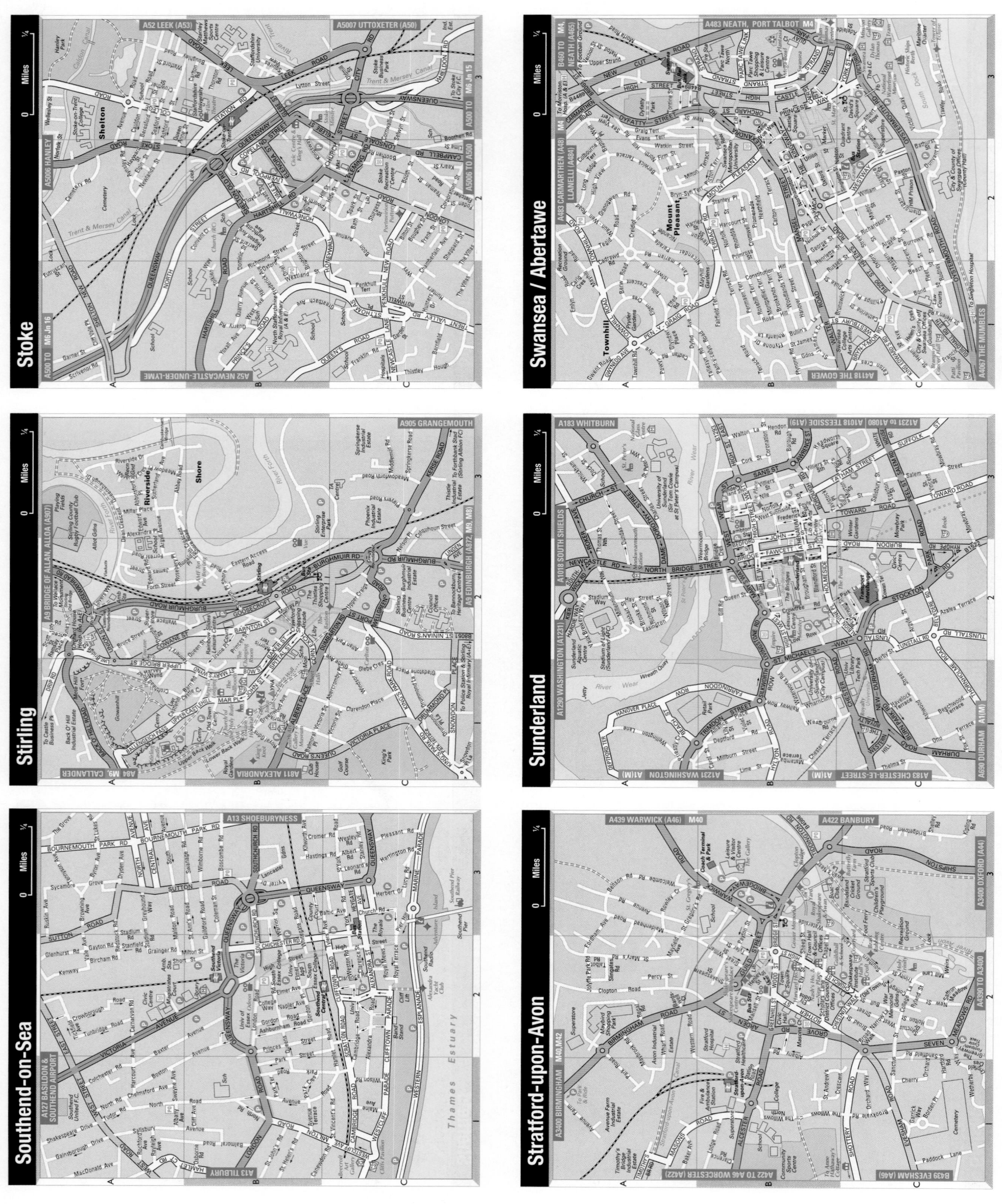

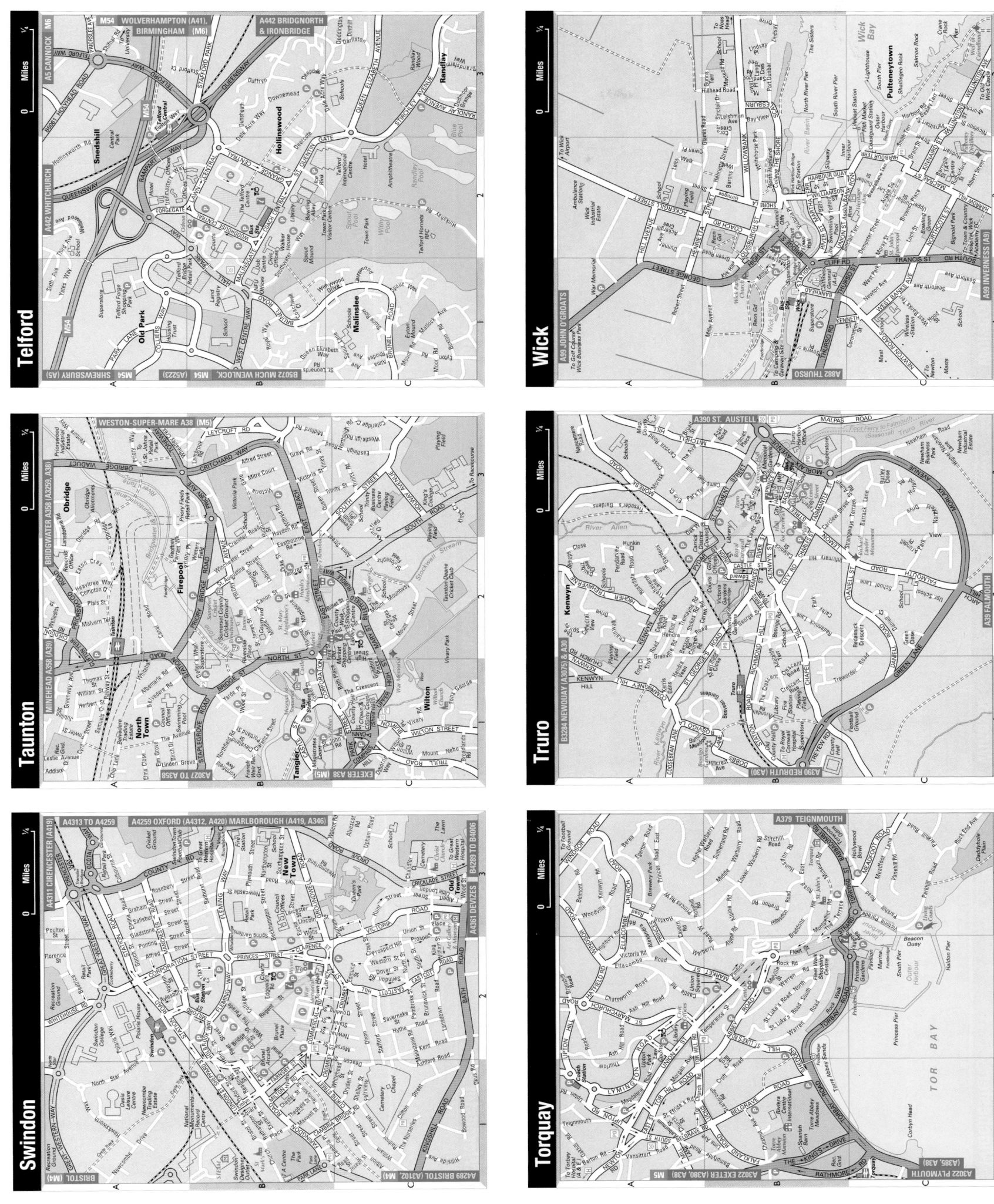
Swindon
Taunton
Telford
Torquay
Truro
Wick
A4311 CIRENCESTER (A419)
A4361 DEVIZES
B4289 TO B4006
MINEHEAD A358 (A39)
BRIDGWATER A358 (A3259, A38)
A442 WHITCHURCH
A5 CANNOCK
B3284 NEWQUAY (A3075) & A30
A39 FALMOUTH
A99 JOHN O'GROATS
A99 INVERNESS (A9)
TOR BAY

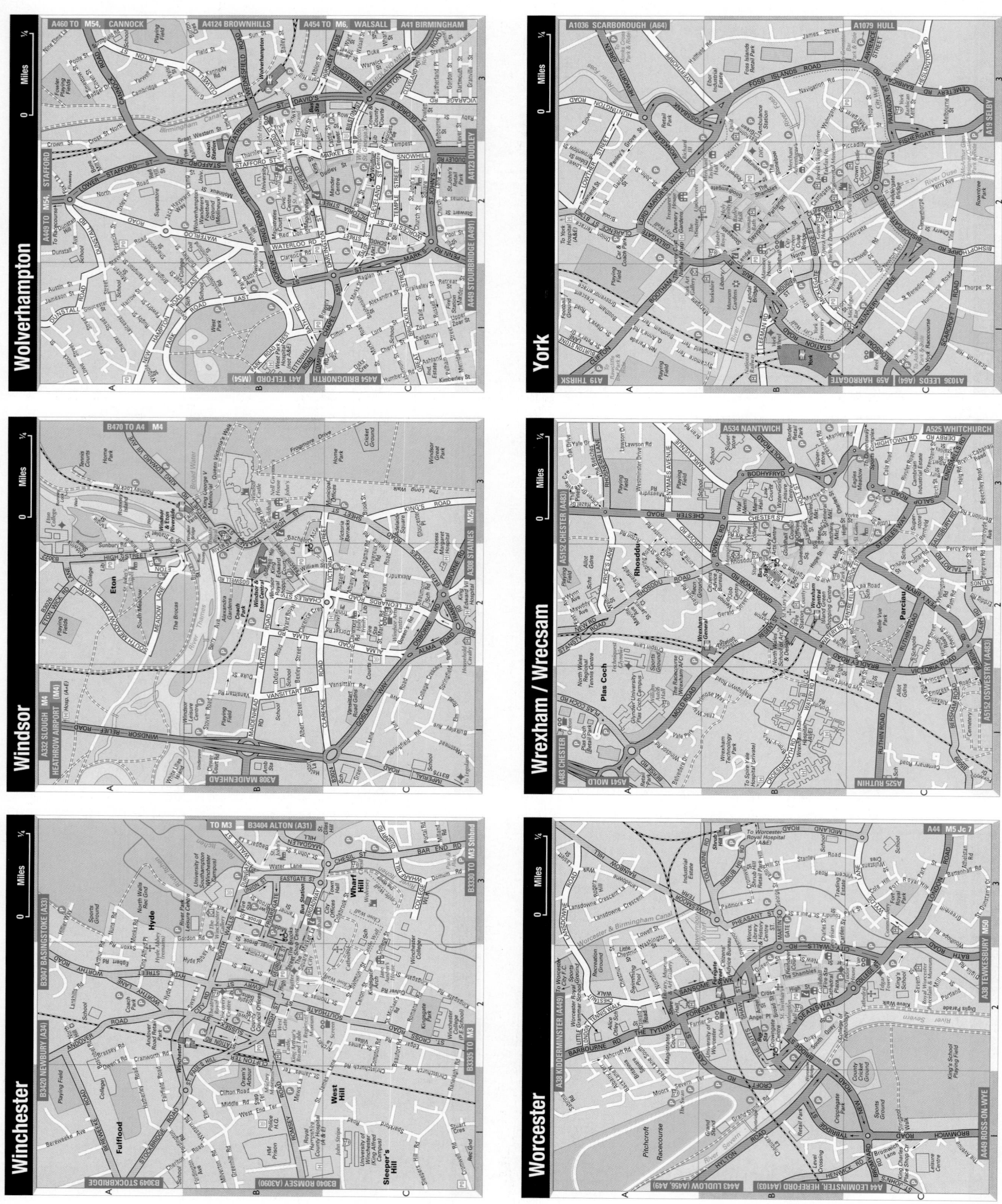
Winchester
0 Miles ¼
Windsor
0 Miles ¼
Wolverhampton
0 Miles ¼
Worcester
0 Miles ¼
Wrexham / Wrecsam
0 Miles ¼
York
0 Miles ¼

## Town plan indexes

Metcalfe St . . . . . . . . C1
Milbourne St . . . . . . . . B1
Myddleton St . . . . . . . . B3
Nelson St . . . . . . . . C1
Norfolk St . . . . . . . . C1
Old Town Hall . . . . . . . . A2
Oswald St . . . . . . . . C3
Peter St . . . . . . . . A2
Petteril St . . . . . . . . B3
Police Station . . . . . . . . A2
Portland Pl . . . . . . . . B2
Portland Sq . . . . . . . . B2
Post Office . . . . . A2/B2/B3/C1/C3
Princess St . . . . . . . . C2
Pugin St . . . . . . . . B1
Red Bank Terr . . . . . . . . C2
Regent St . . . . . . . . C3
Richardson St . . . . . . . . C1
Rickerby Park . . . . . . . . A3
Rickergate . . . . . . . . A2
River St . . . . . . . . B3
Rome St . . . . . . . . C2
Rydal St . . . . . . . . B3
St Cuthbert's . . . . . . . . B2
St Cuthbert's La . . . . . . . . B2
St James' Park . . . . . . . . C1
St James' Rd . . . . . . . . C1
St Nicholas St . . . . . . . . C3
Sands Ctr . . . . . . . . A2
Scotch St . . . . . . . . A2
Shaddongate . . . . . . . . B1
Sheffield St . . . . . . . . B1
South Henry St . . . . . . . . B3
South John St . . . . . . . . C2
South St . . . . . . . . B3
Spencer St . . . . . . . . B2
Sports Ctr . . . . . . . . A2
Strand Rd . . . . . . . . A2
Swimming Baths . . . . . . . . B2
Sybil St . . . . . . . . B3
Tait St . . . . . . . . B2
Thomas St . . . . . . . . B1
Thomson St . . . . . . . . C3
Trafalgar St . . . . . . . . C1
Tullie Ho Museum . . . . . . . . A1
Tyne St . . . . . . . . C3
University of Cumbria . . B3
Viaduct Estate Rd . . . . . . . . B1
Victoria Pl . . . . . . . . A2
Victoria Viaduct . . . . . . . . B2
Vue . . . . . . . . B2
Warwick Rd . . . . . . . . B2
Warwick Sq . . . . . . . . B3
Water St . . . . . . . . B2
West Walls . . . . . . . . B1
Westmorland St . . . . . . . . C1


**Chelmsford** 334


Ambulance Station . . . B1
Anchor St . . . . . . . . C1
Anglia Ruskin Univ . . . . A3
Arbour La . . . . . . . . A3
Baddow Rd . . . . . . . B2/C3
Baker St . . . . . . . . C1
Barrack Sq . . . . . . . . B2
Bellmead . . . . . . . . B2
Bishop Hall La . . . . . . . . A2
Bishop Rd . . . . . . . . A2
Bond St . . . . . . . . B2
Boswells Dr . . . . . . . . B3
Boudicca Mews . . . . . . . . C2
Bouverie Rd . . . . . . . . C2
Bradford St . . . . . . . . C1
Braemar Ave . . . . . . . . C1
Brook St . . . . . . . . A2
Broomfield Rd . . . . . . . . A1
Burns Cres . . . . . . . . C2
Bus Station . . . . . . . . B1
Can Bridge Way . . . . . . . . B2
Cedar Ave . . . . . . . . A1
Cedar Ave West . . . . . . . . A1
Cemetery . . . . . . . . A1
Cemetery . . . . . . . . A2
Cemetery . . . . . . . . C1
Central Park . . . . . . . . B1
Chelmsford . . . . . . . . B2
Chelmsford . . . . . . . . A1
Chichester Dr . . . . . . . . A3
Chinery Cl . . . . . . . . A3
Cinema . . . . . . . . B2
Civic Ctr . . . . . . . . A1
Civic Theatre . . . . . . . . B1
College . . . . . . . . C1
Cottage Pl . . . . . . . . A2
County Cricket Ground . . . . . . . . B2
County Hall . . . . . . . . B2
Coval Ave . . . . . . . . B1
Coval La . . . . . . . . B1
Coval Wells . . . . . . . . B1
Crown Court . . . . . . . . B2
Duke St . . . . . . . . B2
Elm Rd . . . . . . . . C1
Elms Dr . . . . . . . . A1
Essex Record Office, The . . . . . . . . B3
Fairfield Rd . . . . . . . . B1
Falcons Mead . . . . . . . . B1
George St . . . . . . . . C2
Glebe Rd . . . . . . . . A1
Godfrey's Mews . . . . . . . . C2
Goldlay Ave . . . . . . . . C3
Goldlay Rd . . . . . . . . C2
Grove Rd . . . . . . . . C2
HM Prison . . . . . . . . A3
Hall St . . . . . . . . C2
Hamlet Rd . . . . . . . . C2
Hart St . . . . . . . . C1
Henry Rd . . . . . . . . A2
High Bridge Rd . . . . . . . . B2
High Chelmer Sh Ctr . . B2
High St . . . . . . . . B2
Hill Cres . . . . . . . . B3
Hill Rd Sth . . . . . . . . B3
Hill Rd . . . . . . . . B3
Hillview Rd . . . . . . . . A3
Hoffmans Way . . . . . . . . A2
Hospital . . . . . . . . B2
Lady La . . . . . . . . C2
Langdale Gdns . . . . . . . . C3
Legg St . . . . . . . . B2
Library . . . . . . . . B2
Library . . . . . . . . C2
Lionfield Terr . . . . . . . . A3
Lower Anchor St . . . . . . . . C1
Lynmouth Ave . . . . . . . . C2
Lynmouth Gdns . . . . . . . . C3
Magistrates Court . . . . B2
Maltese Rd . . . . . . . . A1
Manor Rd . . . . . . . . C2
Marconi Rd . . . . . . . . A2
Market . . . . . . . . B2
Market Rd . . . . . . . . B2
Marlborough Rd . . . . . . . . C1
Meadows Sh Ctr, The . . B2
Meadowside . . . . . . . . A3
Mews Ct . . . . . . . . C2
Mildmay Rd . . . . . . . . C2
Moulsham Dr . . . . . . . . C2
Moulsham Mill . . . . . . . . C3
Moulsham St . . . . . C1/C2
Navigation Rd . . . . . . . . B3
New London Rd . . . . B2/C1
New St . . . . . . . . A2/B2
New Writtle St . . . . . . . . C1
Nursery Rd . . . . . . . . C2
Orchard St . . . . . . . . C2
Park Rd . . . . . . . . B1
Parker Rd . . . . . . . . C2
Parklands Dr . . . . . . . . A3
Parkway . . . . . . A1/B1/B2
Police Station . . . . . . . . A2
Post Office . . . . A3/B2/C2
Primrose Hill . . . . . . . . A1
Prykes Dr . . . . . . . . B1
Queen St . . . . . . . . C1
Queen's Rd . . . . . . . . B3
Railway St . . . . . . . . A1
Rainsford Rd . . . . . . . . A1
Ransomes Way . . . . . . . . A2
Rectory La . . . . . . . . A2
Regina Rd . . . . . . . . A2
Riverside Ice & L Ctr . . B2
Riverside Retail Park . . A3
Rosebery Rd . . . . . . . . C2
Rothesay Ave . . . . . . . . C1
St John's Rd . . . . . . . . C2
Sandringham Pl . . . . . . . . B3
Seymour St . . . . . . . . B1
Shrublands Cl . . . . . . . . B3
Southborough Rd . . . . . . . . C1
Springfield Basin . . . . B3
Springfield Rd . . A3/B2/B3
Stapleford Cl . . . . . . . . C1
Swiss Ave . . . . . . . . A1
Telford Pl . . . . . . . . A3
The Meades . . . . . . . . B1
Tindal St . . . . . . . . B2
Townfield St . . . . . . . . A1
Trinity Rd . . . . . . . . B3
University . . . . . . . . B1
Upper Bridge Rd . . . . . . . . C1
Upper Roman Rd . . . . . . . . C2
Van Dieman's Rd . . . . . . . . C3
Viaduct Rd . . . . . . . . B1
Vicarage Rd . . . . . . . . C1
Victoria Rd . . . . . . . . A2
Victoria Rd South . . . . B2
Vincents Rd . . . . . . . . C2
Waterloo La . . . . . . . . B2
Weight Rd . . . . . . . . B3
Westfield Ave . . . . . . . . A1
Wharf Rd . . . . . . . . B3
Writtle Rd . . . . . . . . C1
YMCA . . . . . . . . A2
York Rd . . . . . . . . C1


**Cheltenham** 334


Albert Rd . . . . . . . . A3
Albion St . . . . . . . . B3
All Saints Rd . . . . . . . . B3
Ambrose St . . . . . . . . B2
Andover Rd . . . . . . . . C1
Art Gallery & Mus . . . B2
Axiom Ctr . . . . . . . . B3
Back Montpellier Terr . C2
Bandstand . . . . . . . . C2
Bath Pde . . . . . . . . B2
Bath Rd . . . . . . . . C2
Bays Hill Rd . . . . . . . . C1
Beechwood Pl Sh Ctr . B3
Bennington St . . . . . . . . B2
Berkeley St . . . . . . . . B3
Brewery . . . . . . . . A2
Brunswick St South . . A2
Bus Station . . . . . . . . B2
CAB . . . . . . . . B2
Carlton St . . . . . . . . B3
Central Cross Road . . . A3
Cheltenham College . . C2
Cheltenham FC . . . . . . . . A3
Cheltenham General (A&E) . . . . . . . . C3
Christchurch Rd . . . . . . . . B1
Cineworld . . . . . . . . A2
Clarence Rd . . . . . . . . A2
Clarence Sq . . . . . . . . A2
Clarence St . . . . . . . . B2
Cleeveland St . . . . . . . . A1
Coach Park . . . . . . . . A2
College Baths Road . . . C3
College Rd . . . . . . . . C2
Colletts Dr . . . . . . . . A1
Corpus St . . . . . . . . C3
Devonshire St . . . . . . . . A2
Douro Rd . . . . . . . . B1
Duke St . . . . . . . . B3
Dunalley Pde . . . . . . . . A2
Dunalley St . . . . . . . . A2
Everyman . . . . . . . . B2
Evesham Rd . . . . . . . . A3
Fairview Rd . . . . . . . . B3
Fairview St . . . . . . . . B3
Fire Station . . . . . . . . C3
Folly La . . . . . . . . A2
Gloucester Rd . . . . . . . . A1
Grosvenor St . . . . . . . . B3
Grove St . . . . . . . . A1
Gustav Holst . . . . . . . . A3
Hanover St . . . . . . . . A2
Hatherley St . . . . . . . . C1
Henrietta St . . . . . . . . A2
Hewlett Rd . . . . . . . . B3
High St . . . . . . . . B2/B3
Hudson St . . . . . . . . A2
Imperial Gdns . . . . . . . . C2
Imperial La . . . . . . . . B2
Imperial Sq . . . . . . . . C2
Information Ctr . . . . . . . . B2
Keynsham Rd . . . . . . . . C3
King St . . . . . . . . A2
Knapp Rd . . . . . . . . B2
Ladies College . . . . . . . . B2
Lansdown Cr . . . . . . . . C1
Lansdown Rd . . . . . . . . C1
Leighton Rd . . . . . . . . B3
London Rd . . . . . . . . C3
Lypiatt Rd . . . . . . . . C1
Malvern Rd . . . . . . . . B1
Manser St . . . . . . . . A2
Market St . . . . . . . . A1
Marle Hill Pde . . . . . . . . A2
Marle Hill Rd . . . . . . . . A2
Millbrook St . . . . . . . . A1
Milsom St . . . . . . . . A2
Montpellier Gdns . . . . . . . . C2
Montpellier Gr . . . . . . . . C2
Montpellier Pde . . . . . . . . C2
Montpellier Spa Rd . . . C2
Montpellier St . . . . . . . . C1
Montpellier Terr . . . . . . . . C2
Montpellier Walk . . . . . . . . C2
New St . . . . . . . . B2
North Pl . . . . . . . . B2
Old Bath Rd . . . . . . . . C3
Oriel Rd . . . . . . . . B2
Overton Park Rd . . . . . . . . B1
Overton Rd . . . . . . . . B1
Oxford St . . . . . . . . C3
Parabola Rd . . . . . . . . B1
Park Pl . . . . . . . . C1
Park St . . . . . . . . A1
Pittville Circus . . . . . . . . A3
Pittville Cr . . . . . . . . A3
Pittville Lawn . . . . . . . . A3
Playhouse . . . . . . . . B2
Police Station . . . . . B1/C1
Portland St . . . . . . . . B3
Post Office . . . . . . . . B2/C2
Prestbury Rd . . . . . . . . A3
Prince's Rd . . . . . . . . C1
Priory St . . . . . . . . B3
Promenade . . . . . . . . B2
Queen St . . . . . . . . A1
Recreation Ground . . . A2
Regent Arcade . . . . . . . . B2
Regent St . . . . . . . . B2
Rodney Rd . . . . . . . . B2
Royal Cr . . . . . . . . B2
Royal Wells Rd . . . . . . . . B2
St George's Pl . . . . . . . . B2
St Georges Rd . . . . . . . . B1
St Gregory's . . . . . . . . B2
St James St . . . . . . . . B3
St John's Ave . . . . . . . . B3
St Luke's Rd . . . . . . . . C2
St Margarets Rd . . . . . . . . A2
St Mary's . . . . . . . . B2
St Matthew's . . . . . . . . B2
St Paul's La . . . . . . . . A2
St Paul's Rd . . . . . . . . A2
St Paul's St . . . . . . . . A2
St Stephen's Rd . . . . . . . . C1
Sandford Lido . . . . . . . . C3
Sandford Mill Road . . . C3
Sandford Park . . . . . . . . C3
Sandford Rd . . . . . . . . C2
Selkirk St . . . . . . . . A3
Sherborne Pl . . . . . . . . B3
Sherborne St . . . . . . . . B3
Suffolk Pde . . . . . . . . C2
Suffolk Rd . . . . . . . . C1
Suffolk Sq . . . . . . . . C1
Sun St . . . . . . . . A1
Swindon Rd . . . . . . . . B2
Sydenham Villas Rd . . . C3
Tewkesbury Rd . . . . . . . . A1
The Courtyard . . . . . . . . B1
Thirlstaine Rd . . . . . . . . C2
Tivoli Rd . . . . . . . . C1
Tivoli St . . . . . . . . C1
Town Hall & Theatre . . B2
Townsend St . . . . . . . . A1
Trafalgar St . . . . . . . . C2
Union St . . . . . . . . B3
Univ of Gloucestershire (Francis Cl Hall) . . . . . A2
Univ of Gloucestershire (Hardwick) . . . . . . . . A1
Victoria Pl . . . . . . . . B3
Victoria St . . . . . . . . A2
Vittoria Walk . . . . . . . . C2
Wel Pl . . . . . . . . B2
Wellesley Rd . . . . . . . . A2
Wellington Rd . . . . . . . . A3
Wellington Sq . . . . . . . . A3
Wellington St . . . . . . . . B2
West Drive . . . . . . . . A3
Western Rd . . . . . . . . B1
Winchcombe St . . . . . . . . B3


**Chester** 335


Abbey Gateway . . . . . . . . A2
Appleyards La . . . . . . . . C3
Bedward Row . . . . . . . . B1
Beeston View . . . . . . . . C3
Bishop Lloyd's Pal . . . B2
Black Diamond St . . . . . . . . A2
Bottoms La . . . . . . . . C3
Boughton . . . . . . . . B3
Bouverie St . . . . . . . . A1
Bridge St . . . . . . . . B2
Bridgegate . . . . . . . . C2
British Heritage Ctr . . B2
Brook St . . . . . . . . A3
Brown's La . . . . . . . . C2
Bus Station . . . . . . . . B2
Cambrian Rd . . . . . . . . A1
Canal St . . . . . . . . A2
Carrick Rd . . . . . . . . C1
Castle . . . . . . . . C2
Castle Dr . . . . . . . . C2
Cathedral . . . . . . . . B2
Catherine St . . . . . . . . A1
Chester . . . . . . . . A3
Cheyney Rd . . . . . . . . A1
Chichester St . . . . . . . . A1
City Rd . . . . . . . . A3
City Walls . . . . . . . . B1/B2
City Walls Rd . . . . . . . . B1
Cornwall St . . . . . . . . A2
County Hall . . . . . . . . C2
Cross Hey . . . . . . . . C3
Cuppin St . . . . . . . . B2
Curzon Park North . . . . C1
Curzon Park South . . . . C1
Dee Basin . . . . . . . . A1
Dee La . . . . . . . . B3
Delamere St . . . . . . . . A2
Dewa Roman Experience . . . . . . . . B2
Duke St . . . . . . . . B2
Eastgate . . . . . . . . B2
Eastgate St . . . . . . . . B2
Eaton Rd . . . . . . . . C2
Edinburgh Way . . . . . . . . C3
Elizabeth Cr . . . . . . . . B3
Fire Station . . . . . . . . A2
Foregate St . . . . . . . . B2
Frodsham St . . . . . . . . B2
Gamul House . . . . . . . . B2
Garden La . . . . . . . . A1
Gateway Theatre . . . . . . . . B2
George St . . . . . . . . A2
Gladstone Ave . . . . . . . . A1
God's Providence House . . . . . . . . B2
Gorse Stacks . . . . . . . . A2
Greenway St . . . . . . . . C2
Grosvenor Bridge . . . . . . . . C1
Grosvenor Museum . . . B2
Grosvenor Park . . . . . . . . B3
Grosvenor Precinct . . . B2
Grosvenor Rd . . . . . . . . C1
Grosvenor St . . . . . . . . B2
Groves Rd . . . . . . . . B3
Guildhall Museum . . . . B1
Handbridge . . . . . . . . C2
Hartington St . . . . . . . . C3
Hoole Way . . . . . . . . A2
Hunter St . . . . . . . . B2
Information Ctr . . . . . . . . B2
King Charles' Tower . . . . . . . . A2
King St . . . . . . . . A2
Leisure Ctr . . . . . . . . A2
Library . . . . . . . . B2
Lightfoot St . . . . . . . . A3
Little Roodee . . . . . . . . C2
Liverpool Rd . . . . . . . . A2
Love St . . . . . . . . B3
Lower Bridge St . . . . . . . . B2
Lower Park Rd . . . . . . . . B3
Lyon St . . . . . . . . A2
Magistrates Court . . . . B2
Meadows La . . . . . . . . C3
Military Museum . . . . . . . . C2
Milton St . . . . . . . . A3
New Crane St . . . . . . . . B1
Nicholas St . . . . . . . . B2
Northgate . . . . . . . . A2
Northgate St . . . . . . . . A2
Nun's Rd . . . . . . . . B1
Old Dee Bridge . . . . . . . . C2
Overleigh Rd . . . . . . . . C2
Park St . . . . . . . . B2
Police Station . . . . . . . . B2
Post Office . . . . . . . . A2/A3/B2/C2
Princess St . . . . . . . . B2
Queen St . . . . . . . . B2
Queen's Park Rd . . . . . . . . C3
Queen's Rd . . . . . . . . A3
Race Course . . . . . . . . B1
Raymond St . . . . . . . . A1
River La . . . . . . . . C2
Roman Amphitheatre & Gardens . . . . . . . . B2
Roodee, The (Chester Racecourse) . . . . . . . . B1
Russell St . . . . . . . . A3
St Anne St . . . . . . . . A2
St George's Cr . . . . . . . . C3
St Martin's Gate . . . . . . . . A1
St Martin's Way . . . . . . . . B1
St Oswalds Way . . . . . . . . A2
Saughall Rd . . . . . . . . A1
Sealand Rd . . . . . . . . A1
South View Rd . . . . . . . . A1
Stanley Palace . . . . . . . . B1
Station Rd . . . . . . . . A3
Steven St . . . . . . . . A3
The Bars . . . . . . . . B3
The Cross . . . . . . . . B2
The Groves . . . . . . . . B3
The Meadows . . . . . . . . B3
Tower Rd . . . . . . . . B1
Town Hall . . . . . . . . B2
Union St . . . . . . . . B3
Vicar's La . . . . . . . . B2
Victoria Cr . . . . . . . . C3
Victoria Rd . . . . . . . . A2
Walpole St . . . . . . . . A1
Water Tower St . . . . . . . . A1
Watergate . . . . . . . . B1
Watergate St . . . . . . . . B2
Whipcord La . . . . . . . . A1
White Friars . . . . . . . . B2
York St . . . . . . . . B3


**Chichester** 335


Adelaide Rd . . . . . . . . A3
Alexandra Rd . . . . . . . . A3
Arts Ctr . . . . . . . . B2
Ave de Chartres . . . B1/B2
Barlow Rd . . . . . . . . A1
Basin Rd . . . . . . . . C2
Beech Ave . . . . . . . . B1
Bishops Pal Gardens . . B2
Bishopsgate Walk . . . . A3
Bramber Rd . . . . . . . . C3
Broyle Rd . . . . . . . . A2
Bus Station . . . . . . . . B2
Caledonian Rd . . . . . . . . B3
Cambrai Ave . . . . . . . . B3
Canal Wharf . . . . . . . . C2
Canon La . . . . . . . . B2
Cathedral . . . . . . . . B2
Cavendish St . . . . . . . . A1
Cawley Rd . . . . . . . . B2
Cedar Dr . . . . . . . . A1
Chapel St . . . . . . . . A2
Cherry Orchard Rd . . . . C3
Chichester By-Pass . . . . . . . . C2/C3
Chichester Cinema . . . B3
Chichester Festival Theatre . . . . . . . . A2
Chichester . . . . . . . . B2
Churchside . . . . . . . . A2
Cineworld . . . . . . . . C1
City Walls . . . . . . . . B2
Cleveland Rd . . . . . . . . B3
College La . . . . . . . . A2
College of Science & Technology . . . . . . . . B1
Cory Close . . . . . . . . C2
Council Offices . . . . . . . . B2
County Hall . . . . . . . . B2
Courts . . . . . . . . B2
District . . . . . . . . B2
Duncan Rd . . . . . . . . A1
Durnford Cl . . . . . . . . A1
East Pallant . . . . . . . . B2
East Row . . . . . . . . B2
East St . . . . . . . . B2
East Walls . . . . . . . . B3
Eastland Rd . . . . . . . . C3
Ettrick Cl . . . . . . . . B3
Ettrick Rd . . . . . . . . B3
Exton Rd . . . . . . . . C3
Fire Station . . . . . . . . A2
Football Ground . . . . . . . . A2
Franklin Pl . . . . . . . . A2
Friary (Remains of) . . . A2
Garland Cl . . . . . . . . C3
Green La . . . . . . . . A3
Grove Rd . . . . . . . . C3
Guilden Rd . . . . . . . . B3
Guildhall . . . . . . . . A2
Hawthorn Cl . . . . . . . . A1
Hay Rd . . . . . . . . C3
Henty Gdns . . . . . . . . B1
Herald Dr . . . . . . . . C3
Information Ctr . . . . . . . . B2
John's St . . . . . . . . B2
Joys Croft . . . . . . . . A3
Jubilee Pk . . . . . . . . A3
Jubilee Rd . . . . . . . . A3
Juxon Cl . . . . . . . . B1
Kent Rd . . . . . . . . A3
King George Gdns . . . . A2
King's Ave . . . . . . . . C2
Kingsham Ave . . . . . . . . C3
Kingsham Rd . . . . . . . . C2
Laburnum Gr . . . . . . . . B3
Leigh Rd . . . . . . . . C1
Lennox Rd . . . . . . . . A3
Lewis Rd . . . . . . . . A3
Library . . . . . . . . B2
Lion St . . . . . . . . B2
Litten Terr . . . . . . . . A3
Little London . . . . . . . . B2
Lyndhurst Rd . . . . . . . . B3
Market . . . . . . . . B3
Market Ave . . . . . . . . B2
Market Cross . . . . . . . . B2
Market Rd . . . . . . . . B3
Martlet Cl . . . . . . . . C2
Melbourne Rd . . . . . . . . A3
Mount La . . . . . . . . B1
New Park Rd . . . . . . . . A3
Newlands La . . . . . . . . A1
North Pallant . . . . . . . . B2
North St . . . . . . . . A2
North Walls . . . . . . . . A2
Northgate . . . . . . . . A2
Oak Ave . . . . . . . . A1
Oak Cl . . . . . . . . A1
Oaklands Park . . . . . . . . A2
Oaklands Way . . . . . . . . A2
Orchard Ave . . . . . . . . A1
Orchard St . . . . . . . . A1
Ormonde Ave . . . . . . . . B3
Pallant House . . . . . . . . B2
Parchment St . . . . . . . . A1
Parklands Rd . . . . . A1/B1
Peter Weston Pl . . . . . . . . B3
Police Station . . . . . . . . C2
Post Office . . . . A1/B2/B3
Priory La . . . . . . . . A2
Priory Park . . . . . . . . A2
Priory Rd . . . . . . . . A2
Queen's Ave . . . . . . . . C1
Riverside . . . . . . . . A3
Roman Amphitheatre . B3
St Cyriacs . . . . . . . . A2
St Pancras . . . . . . . . A3
St Paul's Rd . . . . . . . . A2
St Richard's Hospital (A+E) . . . . . . . . A3
Shamrock Cl . . . . . . . . A3
Sherbourne Rd . . . . . . . . A1
Somerstown . . . . . . . . A2
South Bank . . . . . . . . C2
South Downs Planetarium . . . . . . . . C2
South Pallant . . . . . . . . B2
South St . . . . . . . . B2
Southgate . . . . . . . . B2
Spitalfield La . . . . . . . . A3
Stirling Rd . . . . . . . . B3
Stockbridge Rd . . . C1/C2
Swanfield Dr . . . . . . . . A3
Terminus Ind Est . . . . . C1
Terminus Rd . . . . . . . . C1
The Hornet . . . . . . . . B3
The Litten . . . . . . . . A3
Tower St . . . . . . . . A2
Tozer Way . . . . . . . . A3
Turnbull Rd . . . . . . . . A3
Upton Rd . . . . . . . . C1
Velyn Ave . . . . . . . . B3
Via Ravenna . . . . . . . . B1
Walnut Ave . . . . . . . . A1
West St . . . . . . . . B2
Westgate . . . . . . . . B1
Westgate Fields . . . . . . . . B1
Westgate Leisure Ctr . . B1
Weston Ave . . . . . . . . C1
Whyke Cl . . . . . . . . C3
Whyke La . . . . . . . . B3
Whyke Rd . . . . . . . . C3
Winden Ave . . . . . . . . B3


**Colchester** 335


Abbey Gateway . . . . . . . . C2
Albert St . . . . . . . . A1
Albion Grove . . . . . . . . C2
Alexandra Rd . . . . . . . . C1
Artillery St . . . . . . . . C3
Arts Ctr . . . . . . . . B1
Balkerne Hill . . . . . . . . B1
Barrack St . . . . . . . . C3
Beaconsfield Rd . . . . . . . . C1
Beche Rd . . . . . . . . C3
Bergholt Rd . . . . . . . . A1
Bourne Rd . . . . . . . . C3
Brick Kiln Rd . . . . . . . . A1
Bristol Rd . . . . . . . . B2
Broadlands Way . . . . . . . . A3
Brook St . . . . . . . . B3
Bury Cl . . . . . . . . B2
Bus Sta . . . . . . . . B2
Butt Rd . . . . . . . . C1
Camp Folley North . . . . C2
Camp Folley South . . . . C2
Campion Rd . . . . . . . . C2
Cannon St . . . . . . . . C3
Canterbury Rd . . . . . . . . C2
Castle . . . . . . . . B2
Castle Park . . . . . . . . B2
Castle Rd . . . . . . . . B2
Catchpool Rd . . . . . . . . A1
Causton Rd . . . . . . . . B1
Cavalry Barracks . . . . . . . . C1
Chandlers Row . . . . . . . . C3
Circular Rd East . . . . . . . . C2
Circular Rd North . . . . . . . . C1
Circular Rd West . . . . . . . . C1
Clarendon Way . . . . . . . . A1
Claudius Rd . . . . . . . . C2
Colchester Camp Abbey Field . . . . . . . . C1
Colchester Institute . . . B1
Colchester . . . . . . . . A1
Colchester Town . . . . . . . . C2
Colne Bank Ave . . . . . . . . A1
Colne View Retail Park A2
Compton Rd . . . . . . . . A3
Cowdray Ave . . . . . A1/A2
Cowdray Ctr, The . . . . A2
Crouch St . . . . . . . . B1
Crowhurst Rd . . . . . . . . B1
Culver Square Sh Ctr . B1
Culver St East . . . . . . . . B2
Culver St West . . . . . . . . B1
Dilbridge Rd . . . . . . . . A3
East Hill . . . . . . . . B2
East St . . . . . . . . B3
East Stockwell St . . . . . . . . B1
Eld La . . . . . . . . B1
Essex Hall Rd . . . . . . . . A1
Exeter Dr . . . . . . . . B2
Fairfax Rd . . . . . . . . C2
Fire Station . . . . . . . . A2
Flagstaff Rd . . . . . . . . C1
George St . . . . . . . . B2
Gladstone Rd . . . . . . . . C2
Golden Noble Hill . . . . . . . . C2
Goring Rd . . . . . . . . A3
Granville Rd . . . . . . . . C3
Greenstead Rd . . . . . . . . B3
Guildford Rd . . . . . . . . B2
Harsnett Rd . . . . . . . . C3
Harwich Rd . . . . . . . . B3
Head St . . . . . . . . B1
High St . . . . . . . . B1/B2
High Woods Ctry Park . A2
Hollytrees . . . . . . . . B2
Hythe Hill . . . . . . . . C3
Information Ctr . . . . . . . . B2
Ipswich Rd . . . . . . . . A3
Jarmin Rd . . . . . . . . A2
Kendall Rd . . . . . . . . C2
Kimberley Rd . . . . . . . . C3
King Stephen Rd . . . . . . . . C3
Le Cateau Barracks . . . C1
Leisure World . . . . . . . . A2
Library . . . . . . . . B1
Lincoln Way . . . . . . . . B2
Lion Walk Sh Ctr . . . . . . . . B1
Lisle Rd . . . . . . . . C2
Lucas Rd . . . . . . . . C2
Magdalen Green . . . . . . . . C3
Magdalen St . . . . . . . . C2
Maidenburgh St . . . . . . . . B2
Maldon Rd . . . . . . . . C1
Manor Rd . . . . . . . . B1
Margaret Rd . . . . . . . . A1
Mason Rd . . . . . . . . A2
Mercers Way . . . . . . . . A1
Mercury . . . . . . . . B1
Mersea Rd . . . . . . . . C2
Meyrick Cr . . . . . . . . C2
Mile End Rd . . . . . . . . A1
Military Rd . . . . . . . . C2
Mill St . . . . . . . . C2
Minories . . . . . . . . B2
Moorside . . . . . . . . B3
Morant Rd . . . . . . . . C3
Napier Rd . . . . . . . . C2
Natural History . . . . . . . . B2
New Town Rd . . . . . . . . C2
Norfolk Cr . . . . . . . . A3
North Hill . . . . . . . . B1
North Station Rd . . . . . A1
Northgate St . . . . . . . . B1
Nunns Rd . . . . . . . . B1
Odeon . . . . . . . . B1
Old Coach Rd . . . . . . . . B3
Old Heath Rd . . . . . . . . C3
Osborne St . . . . . . . . B2
Petrolea Cl . . . . . . . . A1
Police Station . . . . . . . . C1
Popes La . . . . . . . . B1
Port La . . . . . . . . C3
Post Office . . . . B1/B2/C2
Priory St . . . . . . . . B2
Queen St . . . . . . . . B2
Rawstorn Rd . . . . . . . . B1
Rebon St . . . . . . . . C3
Recreation Rd . . . . . . . . C3
Ripple Way . . . . . . . . A3
Roman Rd . . . . . . . . B2
Roman Wall . . . . . . . . B2
Romford Cl . . . . . . . . A3
Rosebery Ave . . . . . . . . B2
St Andrews Ave . . . . . . . . B3
St Andrews Gdns . . . . . . . . B3
St Botolph St . . . . . . . . B2
St Botolphs . . . . . . . . B2
St John's Abbey (site of) . . . . . . . . C2
St John's St . . . . . . . . B1
St Johns Walk Sh Ctr . B1
St Leonards Rd . . . . . . . . C3
St Marys Fields . . . . . . . . B1
St Peters . . . . . . . . B1
St Peter's St . . . . . . . . B1
Salisbury Ave . . . . . . . . C1
Serpentine Walk . . . . . . . . A1
Sheepen Pl . . . . . . . . B1
Sheepen Rd . . . . . . . . B1
Sir Isaac's Walk . . . . . . . . B1
Smythies Ave . . . . . . . . B2
South St . . . . . . . . C1
South Way . . . . . . . . C1
Sports Way . . . . . . . . A2
Suffolk Cl . . . . . . . . A3
Town Hall . . . . . . . . B1
Valentine Dr . . . . . . . . A3
Victor Rd . . . . . . . . C3
Wakefield Cl . . . . . . . . B2
Wellesley Rd . . . . . . . . C1
Wells Rd . . . . . . . . B2/B3
West St . . . . . . . . C1
West Stockwell St . . . . . . . . B1
Weston Rd . . . . . . . . C3
Westway . . . . . . . . A1
Wickham Rd . . . . . . . . C1
Wimpole Rd . . . . . . . . C3
Winchester Rd . . . . . . . . C2
Winnock Rd . . . . . . . . C2
Wolfe Ave . . . . . . . . C2
Worcester Rd . . . . . . . . B2


**Coventry** 335


Abbots La . . . . . . . . A1
Albany Rd . . . . . . . . B1
Alma St . . . . . . . . B3
Art Faculty . . . . . . . . B3
Asthill Grove . . . . . . . . C2
Bablake School . . . . . . . . A1
Barras La . . . . . . A1/B1
Barrs Hill School . . . . . . . . A1
Belgrade . . . . . . . . B2
Bishop Burges St . . . . . . . . A2
Bond's Hospital . . . . . . . . B1
Broad Gate . . . . . . . . B2
Broadway . . . . . . . . C1
Bus Station . . . . . . . . A3
Butts Radial . . . . . . . . B1
Canal Basin . . . . . . . . A2
Canterbury St . . . . . . . . A3
Cathedral . . . . . . . . B3
Chester St . . . . . . . . A1
Cheylesmore Manor House . . . . . . . . B2
Christ Church Spire . . B2
City Walls & Gates . . . A2
Corporation St . . . . . . . . B2
Council House . . . . . . . . B2
Coundon Rd . . . . . . . . A1
Coventry Station . . . . . . . . C2
Coventry Transport Museum . . . . . . . . A2
Cox St . . . . . . . . A3
Croft Rd . . . . . . . . B1
Dalton Rd . . . . . . . . C1
Deasy Rd . . . . . . . . C3
Earl St . . . . . . . . B2
Eaton Rd . . . . . . . . C2
Fairfax St . . . . . . . . B2
Foleshill Rd . . . . . . . . A2
Ford's Hospital . . . . . . . . B2
Fowler Rd . . . . . . . . A1
Friars Rd . . . . . . . . C2
Gordon St . . . . . . . . C1
Gosford St . . . . . . . . B3
Greyfriars Green . . . . . . . . B2
Greyfriars Rd . . . . . . . . B2
Gulson Rd . . . . . . . . B3
Hales St . . . . . . . . A2
Harnall Lane East . . . . . . . . A3
Harnall Lane West . . . . . . . . A2
Herbert Art Gallery & Museum . . . . . . . . B3
Hertford St . . . . . . . . B2
Hewitt Ave . . . . . . . . A1
High St . . . . . . . . B2
Hill St . . . . . . . . B1
Holy Trinity . . . . . . . . B2
Holyhead Rd . . . . . . . . A1
Howard St . . . . . . . . A3
Huntingdon Rd . . . . . . . . C1
Information Ctr . . . . . . . . B2
Jordan Well . . . . . . . . B3
King Henry VIII School C1
Lady Godiva Statue . . B2
Lamb St . . . . . . . . A2
Leicester Row . . . . . . . . A2
Library . . . . . . . . B2
Little Park St . . . . . . . . B2
London Rd . . . . . . . . C3
Lower Ford St . . . . . . . . B3
Magistrates & Crown Courts . . . . . . . . B2
Manor House Drive . . . B2
Manor Rd . . . . . . . . C2
Market . . . . . . . . B2
Martyr's Memorial . . . C2
Meadow St . . . . . . . . B1
Meriden St . . . . . . . . A1
Michaelmas Rd . . . . . . . . C2
Middleborough Rd . . . . A1
Mile La . . . . . . . . C3
Millennium Place . . . . . . . . A2
Much Park St . . . . . . . . B3
Naul's Mill Park . . . . . . . . A1
New Union . . . . . . . . B2
Park Rd . . . . . . . . C2
Parkside . . . . . . . . C3
Post Office . . . . . . . . B2
Primrose Hill St . . . . . . . . A3
Priory Gardens & Visitor Ctr . . . . . . . . B2
Priory St . . . . . . . . B3
Puma Way . . . . . . . . C3
Quarryfield La . . . . . . . . C3
Queen's Rd . . . . . . . . B1
Quinton Rd . . . . . . . . C2
Radford Rd . . . . . . . . A2
Raglan St . . . . . . . . B3
Retail Park . . . . . . . . C1
Ringway (Hill Cross) . . A1
Ringway (Queens) . . . . B1
Ringway (Rudge) . . . . . B1
Ringway (St Johns) . . . B3
Ringway (St Nicholas) . A2
Ringway (St Patricks) . C2
Ringway (Swanswell) . A2
Ringway (Whitefriars) B3
St John St . . . . . . . . B2
St John The Baptist . . B2
St Nicholas St . . . . . . . . A2
Skydome . . . . . . . . B1
Spencer Ave . . . . . . . . C1
Spencer Park . . . . . . . . C1
Spon St . . . . . . . . B1
Sports Ctr . . . . . . . . B3
Stoney Rd . . . . . . . . C2
Stoney Stanton Rd . . . . A3
Swanswell Pool . . . . . . . . A3
Sydney Stringer Acad . A3
Technical College . . . . . B1
Technology Park . . . . . . . . C3
The Precinct . . . . . . . . B2
Theatre . . . . . . . . B1
Thomas Landsdail St . . C2
Tomson Ave . . . . . . . . A1
Top Green . . . . . . . . C1
Trinity St . . . . . . . . B2
University . . . . . . . . B3
University Sports Ctr . B3
Upper Hill St . . . . . . . . A1
Upper Well St . . . . . . . . A2
Victoria St . . . . . . . . A3
Vine St . . . . . . . . A3
Warwick Rd . . . . . . . . C2
Waveley Rd . . . . . . . . B1
Westminster Rd . . . . . . . . C1
White St . . . . . . . . A3
Windsor St . . . . . . . . B1


**Derby** 335


Abbey St . . . . . . . . C1
Agard St . . . . . . . . B1
Albert St . . . . . . . . B2
Albion St . . . . . . . . B2
Ambulance Station . . . . B1
Arthur St . . . . . . . . A1
Ashlyn Rd . . . . . . . . B3
Assembly Rooms . . . . . . . . B2
Babington La . . . . . . . . C2
Becket St . . . . . . . . B1
Belper Rd . . . . . . . . A1
Bold La . . . . . . . . B1
Bradshaw Way . . . . . . . . C2
Bradshaw Way Ret Pk . C2
Bridge St . . . . . . . . B1
Brook St . . . . . . . . B1
Burrows Walk . . . . . . . . C2
Burton Rd . . . . . . . . C1
Bus Station . . . . . . . . B2
Caesar St . . . . . . . . A2
Canal St . . . . . . . . C3
Carrington St . . . . . . . . C3
Cathedral . . . . . . . . B2
Cathedral Rd . . . . . . . . B1
Charnwood St . . . . . . . . C2
Chester Green Rd . . . . . A2
City Rd . . . . . . . . A2
Clarke St . . . . . . . . A3
Cock Pitt . . . . . . . . B3
Council House . . . . . . . . B2
Courts . . . . . . . . B1
Cranmer Rd . . . . . . . . B3
Crompton St . . . . . . . . C1
Crown & County Courts . . . . . . . . B2
Crown Walk . . . . . . . . C2
Curzon St . . . . . . . . B1
Darley Grove . . . . . . . . A1
Derby . . . . . . . . C3
Derbyshire County Cricket Ground . . . . . . . . B3
Derwent Business Ctr . A2
Derwent St . . . . . . . . B2
Devonshire Walk . . . . . . . . C2
Drewry La . . . . . . . . C1
Duffield Rd . . . . . . . . A1
Duke St . . . . . . . . A2
Dunton Cl . . . . . . . . B3
Eagle Market . . . . . . . . C2
Eastgate . . . . . . . . B3
East St . . . . . . . . B2
Exeter St . . . . . . . . B2
Farm St . . . . . . . . C1
Ford St . . . . . . . . B1
Forester St . . . . . . . . C1
Fox St . . . . . . . . A2
Friar Gate . . . . . . . . B1
Friary St . . . . . . . . B1
Full St . . . . . . . . B2
Gerard St . . . . . . . . C1
Gower St . . . . . . . . C2
Green La . . . . . . . . C2
Grey St . . . . . . . . C1
Guildhall . . . . . . . . B2
Harcourt St . . . . . . . . C1
Highfield Rd . . . . . . . . A1
Hill La . . . . . . . . C2
Information Ctr . . . . . . . . B2
Iron Gate . . . . . . . . B2
John St . . . . . . . . C3
Joseph Wright Ctr . . . . B1
Kedleston Rd . . . . . . . . A1
Key St . . . . . . . . B2
King Alfred St . . . . . . . . C1
King St . . . . . . . . A1
Kingston St . . . . . . . . A1
Lara Croft Way . . . . . . . . C2
Leopold St . . . . . . . . C2
Library . . . . . . . . B1
Liversage St . . . . . . . . C3
Lodge La . . . . . . . . B1
London Rd . . . . . . . . C2
London Rd Community Hospital . . . . . . . . C2
Macklin St . . . . . . . . C1
Mansfield Rd . . . . . . . . A2
Market . . . . . . . . B2
Market Pl . . . . . . . . B2
May St . . . . . . . . C1
Meadow La . . . . . . . . B3
Melbourne St . . . . . . . . C2
Mercian Way . . . . . . . . C1
Midland Rd . . . . . . . . C3
Monk St . . . . . . . . C1
Morledge . . . . . . . . B2
Mount St . . . . . . . . C1
Mus & Art Gallery . . . . B1
Noble St . . . . . . . . C3
North Parade . . . . . . . . A1
North St . . . . . . . . A1
Nottingham Rd . . . . . . . . B3
Osmaston Rd . . . . . . . . C2
Otter St . . . . . . . . A1
Park St . . . . . . . . C3
Parker St . . . . . . . . A1
Pickfords House . . . . . . . . B1
Playhouse . . . . . . . . C2
Police HQ . . . . . . . . A2
Police Station . . . . . . . . B2
Post Office . . . . A1/A2/B1/B2/C2/C3
Prime Enterprise Park A2
Pride Parkway . . . . . . . . C3
Prime Parkway . . . . . . . . A2
Queens Leisure Ctr . . . B1
Racecourse . . . . . . . . A3
Railway Terr . . . . . . . . C3
Register Office . . . . . . . . B2
Sacheverel St . . . . . . . . C2
Sadler Gate . . . . . . . . B1
St Alkmund's Way . B1/B2
St Helens House . . . . . . . . A1
St Mary's . . . . . . . . A1
St Mary's Bridge . . . . . . . . A2
St Mary's Bridge Chapel . . . . . . . . A2
St Mary's Gate . . . . . . . . B1
St Paul's Rd . . . . . . . . A2
St Peter's . . . . . . . . C2
St Peter's St . . . . . . . . C2
Siddals Rd . . . . . . . . C3
Silk Mill . . . . . . . . B2
Sir Frank Whittle Rd . . A3
Spa La . . . . . . . . C1
Spring St . . . . . . . . C1
Stafford St . . . . . . . . B1
Station Approach . . . . . . . . C3
Stockbrook St . . . . . . . . C1
Stores Rd . . . . . . . . A3
Traffic St . . . . . . . . C2
Wardwick . . . . . . . . B1
Werburgh St . . . . . . . . C1
West Ave . . . . . . . . A1
Westfield Ctr . . . . . . . . B2
West Meadows Ind Est B3
Wharf Rd . . . . . . . . A2
Wilmot St . . . . . . . . C2
Wilson St . . . . . . . . C1
Wood's La . . . . . . . . C1


**Dorchester** 335


Ackerman Rd . . . . . . . . B3
Acland Rd . . . . . . . . A2
Albert Rd . . . . . . . . A1
Alexandra Rd . . . . . . . . B1
Alfred Place . . . . . . . . B3
Alfred Rd . . . . . . . . B2
Alington Ave . . . . . . . . B3
Alington Rd . . . . . . . . B3
Ambulance Station . . . B3
Ashley Rd . . . . . . . . B1
Balmoral Cres . . . . . . . . C3
Barnes Way . . . . . . . B2/C2
Borough Gdns . . . . . . . . A1
Bridport Rd . . . . . . . . A1
Buckingham Way . . . . . . . . C3
Caters Place . . . . . . . . A1
Cemetery . . . . . . . A3/C1
Charles St . . . . . . . . A2
Coburg Rd . . . . . . . . B1
Colliton St . . . . . . . . A1
Cornwall Rd . . . . . . . . A1
Cromwell Rd . . . . . . . . B1
Culliford Rd . . . . . . . . B2
Culliford Rd North . . . . B2
Dagmar Rd . . . . . . . . B1
Damer's Rd . . . . . . . . B1
Diggory Cres . . . . . . . . C2
Dinosaur Museum . . . . . A2
Dorchester Bypass . . . C2
Dorchester South Station . . . . . . . . B1
Dorchester West Station . . . . . . . . B1

Dorset County Council Offices A1
Dorset County (A+E) H B1
Dorset County Mus A1
Duchy Close C3
Duke's Ave B2
Durngate St A2
Durnover Court A3
Eddison Ave B3
Edward Rd B1
Egdon Rd C2
Elizabeth Frink Statue ✦ B2
Farfrae Cres B2
Forum Ctr, The B1
Friary Hill A2
Friary Lane A2
Frome Terr A2
Garland Cres C3
Glyde Path Rd A1
Government Offices B3
Gt Western Rd B1
Grosvenor Cres C1
Grosvenor Rd C1
HM Prison A1
Herringston Rd C1
High St East A2
High St Fordington A2
High Street West A1
Holloway Rd A2
Icen Way A2
Keep Military Museum, The A1
Kings Rd A3/B3
Kingsbere Cres C2
Lancaster Rd B2
Library A1
Lime Cl C1
Linden Ave B2
London Cl A3
London Rd A2/A3
Lubbecke Way A3
Lucetta La B2
Maiden Castle Rd C1
Manor Rd C2
Maumbury Rd B1
Maumbury Rings B1
Mellstock Ave C2
Mill St A3
Miller's Cl A1
Mistover Cl C1
Monmouth Rd B1/B2
Nature Reserve A2
North Sq A2
Northernhay A1
Old Crown Court & Cells A1
Olga Rd B1
Orchard St A2
Police Station B1
Post Office A1/B1
Pound Lane A2
Poundbury Rd A1
Prince of Wales Rd B2
Prince's St A1
Queen's Ave B1
Roman Town House A1
Roman Wall A1
Rothesay Rd C2
St George's Rd B3
Salisbury Field A2
Sandringham Sports Ctr B3
Shaston Cres C2
Smokey Hole La B3
South Court Ave C1
South St B1
South Walks Rd B2
Superstore C3
Teddy Bear House A1
Temple Cl C1
Terracotta Warriors & Teddy Bear Mus A2
The Grove A1
Town Hall A2
Town Pump ✦ A2
Trinity St A1
Tutankhamun Ex A1
Victoria Rd B1
Weatherbury Way C2
Wellbridge Cl C1
West Mills Rd A1
West Walks Rd A1
Weymouth Ave C1
Williams Ave B1
Winterbourne (BMI) H C1
Wollaston Rd A2
York Rd B2

## Dumfries 336

Academy St A2
Aldermanhill Rd B3
Ambulance Station C3
Annan Rd A3
Ardwall Rd A3
Ashfield Dr A1
Atkinson Rd C1
Averill Cres C1
Balliol Ave C1
Bank St B2
Bankend Rd C3
Barn Slaps B3
Barrie Ave B3
Beech Ave A1
Bowling Green A3
Brewery St B2
Brodie Ave C2
Brooke St B2
Broomlands Dr C1
Brooms Rd B3
Buccleuch St A2
Burns House B2
Burns Mausoleum B3
Burns St B2
Burns Statue ✦ A2
Bus Station B1
Cardoness St A3
Castle St A2
Catherine St A2
Cattle Market A3
Cemetery B3
Cemetery C2
Church Cres A2
Church St B2
College Rd A1
College St A1
Corbelly Hill B1
Convent, The B1
Corberry Park B1
Cornwall Mt A3
County Offices A2
Court A2
Craigs Rd C3
Cresswell Ave B3
Cresswell Hill B3
Cumberland St B3
David Keswick Athletic Ctr A3
David St B1
Dock Park C3
Dockhead B2
Dumfries ≥ A3
Dumfries Academy A2
Dumfries Museum & Camera Obscura B2
Dumfries Royal Infirmary (A&E) H C3
East Riverside Dr C3
Edinburgh Rd A2
English St B2
Fire Station B3
Friar's Vennel A2
Galloway St B1
George Douglas Dr C1
George St A2
Gladstone Rd C2
Glasgow St A1
Glebe St B3
Glencaple Rd C3
Goldie Ave A1
Goldie Cres A1
Golf Course C3
Greyfriars A2
Grierson Ave B3
HM Prison B1
Hamilton Ave C1
Hamilton Starke Park C2
Hazelrigg Ave C1
Henry St B3
Hermitage Dr C1
High Cemetery C3
High St A2
Hill Ave C2
Hill St B1
Holm Ave C2
Hoods Loaning A3
Howgate St B1
Huntingdon Rd A3
Information Ctr B2
Irish St B2
Irving St A2
King St A1
Kingholm Rd C3
Kirkpatrick Ct C2
Laurieknowe B1
Leafield Rd B3
Library A2
Lochfield Rd A1
Loreburn Pk A3
Loreburn St A2
Loreburne Sh Ctr B2
Lover's Walk A2
Martin Ave B3
Maryholm Dr A1
Mausoleum B3
Maxwell St B1
McKie Ave B3
Mews La A2
Mid Steeple ✦ B2
Mill Green B2
Mill Rd B1
Moat Rd C2
Moffat Rd A3
Mountainhall Pk C3
Nelson St B1
New Abbey Rd B1/C1
New Bridge B1
Newall Terr A2
Nith Ave A2
Nith Bank C3
Nithbank Hospital H C3
Nithside Ave A1
Odeon B2
Old Bridge B1
Old Bridge House B1
Palmerston Park (Queen of the South FC) A1
Park Rd C1
Pleasance Ave C1
Police HQ A3
Police Station A2
Portland Dr A1
Post Office A2/B1/B2/B3/B3
Priestlands Dr C1
Primrose St B1
Queen St B3
Queensberry St A2
Rae St A2
Richmond Ave C2
Robert Burns Ctr B2
Roberts Cres C1
Robertson Ave C3
Robinson Dr C1
Rosefield Rd C2
Rosemount St B1
Rotchell Park C1
Rotchell Rd B1
Rugby Football Gd C1
Ryedale Rd C2
St Andrews B2
St John the Evangelist A2
St Josephs College B3
St Mary's Ind Est A3
St Mary's St A3
St Michael St B2
St Michael's B2
St Michael's Bridge B2
St Michael's Bridge Rd B2
St Michael's Cemetery B3
Shakespeare St B2
Solway Dr C2
Stakeford St A1
Stark Cres C2
Station Rd A3
Steel Ave A1
Sunderries Ave A1
Sunderries Rd A1
Suspension Brae B2
Swimming Pool A1
Terregles St B1
Theatre Royal B2
Troqueer Rd C2
Union St A1
Wallace St B3
Welldale B2
West Riverside Dr C2
White Sands B2

## Dundee 336

Adelaide Pl A1
Airlie Pl C1
Albany Terr A1
Albert St A3
Alexander St A2
Ann St A2
Arthurstone Terr A3
Bank St B2
Barrack Rd A1
Barrack St B2
Bell St B2
Blackscroft A3
Blinshall St B1
Brown St B1
Bus Station B3
Caird Hall B2
Camperdown St B3
Candle La B3
Carmichael St A1
City Churches B2
City Quay B3
City Sq B2
Commercial St B2
Constable St A3
Constitution Ct A1
Constitution Cres A1
Constitution St A1/B2
Cotton Rd A3
Courthouse Sq B1
Cowgate A3
Crescent St A3
Crichton St B2
Dens Brae A3
Dens Rd A3
Discovery Point ✦ C2
Douglas St B1
Drummond St A1
Dudhope Castle A1
Dudhope St A2
Dudhope Terr A1
Dundee ≥ C2
Dundee College A1
Dundee Contemporary Arts ✦ C2
Dundee High School B2
Dundee Repertory C2
Dura St A3
East Dock St B3
East Whale La B3
East Marketgait B3
Erskine St A3
Euclid Cr B2
Forebank Rd A2
Foundry La A3
Frigate Unicorn B3
Gallagher Retail Park B3
Gellatly St B3
Government Offices C2
Guthrie St B1
Hawkhill B1
Hilltown A2
Howff Cemetery, The B2
Information Ctr B2
King St A3
Kinghorne Rd A1
Ladywell Ave A3
Laurel Bank A2
Law Hill, The ✦ A1
Law Rd A1
Law St A1
Library A2
Little Theatre A2
Lochee Rd B1
Lower Princes St A3
Lyon St A3
McManus Museum & Art Gallery B2
Meadow Side B2
Meadowside St Pauls B2
Mercat Cross ✦ B2
Murraygate B2
Nelson St A2
Nethergate B2/C1
North Marketgait B2
North Lindsay St B2
Old Hawkhill B1
Olympia Leisure Ctr C3
Overgate Shopping Ctr B2
Park Pl B1
Perth Rd C1
Police Station A2/B1
Post Office B2
Princes St A3
Prospect Pl A2
Reform St B2
Riverside Dr C2
Roseangle C1
Rosebank St A2
RRS Discovery C2
St Andrew's C2
St Pauls Episcopal B3
Science Ctr ✦ C2
Seagate B2
Sheriffs Court B1
South George St A2
South Marketgait B3
South Tay St B2
South Ward Rd B2
Steps A2
Tay Road Bridge ✦ C3
Tayside House B2
Trades La B3
Union St B2
Union Terr A1
University Library B2
University of Abertay B2
University of Dundee B1
Upper Constitution St A1
Verdant Works ✦ B1
Victoria Dock B3
Victoria Rd A2
Victoria St A3
West Marketgait B1/B2
Ward Rd B1
Wellgate B2
West Bell St B1
Westfield Pl C1
William St A3
Wishart Arch ✦ A3

## Durham 336

Alexander Cr B2
Allergate B2
Archery Rise C1
Assize Courts B3
Back Western Hill A1
Bakehouse La A3
Baths B3
Baths Bridge B3
Boat House B3
Bowling A2
Boyd St C3
Bus Station B2
Castle B2
Castle Chare B2
Cathedral B2
Church St C3
Clay La C1
Claypath B3
College of St Hild & St Bede B3
County Hall A1
County Hospital H B1
Crook Hall & Gardens ✦ A3
Crossgate B2
Crossgate Peth C1
Darlington Rd C1
Durham ≥ A2
Durham Light Infantry Mus & Arts Ctr A2
Durham School C2
Ellam Ave C1
Elvet Bridge B3
Elvet Court B3
Farnley Hey B1
Ferens Cl A3
Fieldhouse La A1
Flass St B1
Framwelgate A2
Framwelgate Bridge B2
Framwelgate Peth A2
Framwelgate Waterside A2
Frankland La A3
Freeman's Pl A3
Gala & Sacred Journey B3
Gate Sh Ctr, The B2
Geoffrey Ave C1
Gilesgate B3
Grey College C3
Hallgarth St C3
Hatfield College B3
Hawthorn Terr B1
Heritage Ctr B3
HM Prison B3
Information Ctr B3
John St B1
Kingsgate Bridge B3
Laburnum Terr B1
Lawson Terr B1
Leazes Rd B2/B3
Library B2
Margery La B2
Mavin St C3
Millburngate B2
Millburngate Bridge B2
Millennium Bridge (foot/cycle) A2
Mountjoy Research Ctr C3
Mus of Archaeology B2
Nevilledale Terr B1
New Elvet B3
New Elvet Bridge B3
North Bailey B3
North End A1
North Rd A1/B2
Observatory C1
Old Elvet B3
Oriental Museum C2
Oswald Court C3
Parkside B2
Passport Office A2
Percy Terr B1
Pimlico C2
Police Station B3
Post Office A1/B2
Potters Bank C1/C2
Prebends Bridge C2
Prebends Walk C2
Prince Bishops Sh Ctr B3
Princes St A1
Providence Row A3
Quarryheads La C2
Redhills La B1
Redhills Terr B1
Saddler St B3
St Chad's College C3
St Cuthbert's Society C2
St John's College C2
St Margaret's B2
St Mary The Less C2
St Mary's College C2
St Monica Grove B1
St Nicholas' B3
St Oswald's C3
Sidegate A2
Silver St B2
Add Sixth Form Ctr (Durham Gilesgate) A3
South Bailey C2
South Rd C3
South St B2
Springwell Ave A1
Stockton Rd C3
Students' Rec Ctr B3
Sutton St B2
The Avenue B1
The Crescent A1
The Grove A1
The Sands A3
Town Hall B2
Treasury Museum B2
University ✦ B2
University Arts Block B3
University Library C3
Univ Science Site C3
Walkergate Ctr A3
Wearside Dr A3
Western Hill A1
Wharton Park A2
Whinney Hill C3

## Edinburgh 336

Abbey Strand B6
Abbeyhill B6
Abbeyhill Cr B6
Abbeymount A6
Abercromby Pl A3
Adam St C5
Albany La A4
Albany St A4
Albert Memorial ✦ B2
Albyn Pl A2
Alva Pl A6
Alva St B1
Ann St A1
Appleton Tower C4
Archibald Pl C3
Argyle House C3
Assembly Rooms & Musical Hall A3
Atholl Cr B1
Atholl Crescent La C1
Bank St B4
Barony St A4
Beaumont Pl C5
Belford Rd B1
Belgrave Cr A1
Belgrave Crescent La A1
Bell's Brae B1
Blackfriars St B4
Blair St B4
Bread St C2
Bristo Pl C4
Bristo St C4
Brougham St C2
Broughton St A4
Brown St C5
Brunton Terr A6
Buckingham Terr A1
Burial Ground A6
Bus Station A4
Caledonian Cr C1
Caledonian Rd C1
Calton Hill A4
Calton Hill A5
Calton Rd B4
Camera Obscura & Outlook Tower B3
Candlemaker Row C4
Canning St B2
Canongate B5
Canongate B5
Carlton St A1
Carlton Terr A6
Carlton Terrace La A6
Castle St B2
Castle Terr B2
Castlehill B3
Central Library B4
Chalmers Hospital H C3
Chalmers St C3
Chambers St C4
Chapel St C4
Charles St C4
Charlotte Sq B2
Chester St B1
Circus La A2
Circus Pl A2
City Art Ctr B4
City Chambers B4
City Observatory ✦ A5
Clarendon Cr A1
Clerk St C5
Coates Cr B1
Cockburn St B4
College of Art C3
Comely Bank Ave A1
Comely Bank Row A1
Cornwall St C2
Cowans Cl C5
Cowgate B4
Cranston St B5
Crichton St C4
Croft-An-Righ A6
Cumberland St A2
Dalry Pl C1
Dalry Rd C1
Danube St A1
Darnawy St A2
David Hume Tower C4
Davie St C5
Dean Bridge A1
Dean Gdns A1
Dean Park Cr A1
Dean Park Mews A1
Dean Park St A1
Dean Path B1
Dean St A1
Dean Terr A1
Dewar Pl C1
Dewar Place La C1
Doune Terr A2
Drummond Pl A3
Drummond St C5
Drumsheugh Gdns B1
Dublin Mews A3
Dublin St A4
Dublin Street La South A4
Dumbiedykes Rd B5
Dundas St A3
Earl Grey St C2
East Crosscauseway C5
East Market St B4
East Norton Pl A6
East Princes St Gdns B3
Easter Rd A6
Edinburgh (Waverley) ≥ B4
Edinburgh Castle B3
Edinburgh Dungeon ✦ B4
Edinburgh International Conference Ctr C2
Elder St A4
Esplanade B3
Eton Terr A1
Eye Pavilion H C3
Festival Office B3
Festival Theatre Edinburgh C4
Filmhouse C2
Fire Station C2
Floral Clock ✦ B3
Forres St A2
Forth St A4
Fountainbridge C2
Frederick St A3
Freemasons' Hall B3
Fruit Market B4
Gardner's Cr C2
George Heriot's School C3
George IV Bridge B4
George Sq C4
George Sq La C4
George St B3
Georgian House B2
Gladstone's Land B3
Glen St C3
Gloucester La A2
Gloucester Pl A2
Gloucester St A2
Graham St C3
Grassmarket C3
Great King St A3
Great Stuart B1
Greenside La A5
Greenside Row A5
Greyfriars Kirk C4
Grindlay St C2
Grosvenor St C1
Grove St C1
Gullan's Cl B5
Guthrie St B4
Hanover St A3
Hart St A4
Haymarket C1
Haymarket Station ≥ C1
Heriot Pl C3
Heriot Row A2
High School Yard B5
High St B4
Hill Pl C5
Hill St A2
Hillside Cr A5
Holyrood Park C6
Holyrood Rd B5
Home St C2
Hope St B2
Horse Wynd B6
Howden St C5
Howe St A2
India Pl A2
India St A2
Infirmary St B4
Information Ctr B4
Jamaica Mews A2
Jeffrey St B4
John Knox House B4
Johnston Terr C3
Keir St C3
Kerr St A2
King's Stables Rd B2
Lady Lawson St C3
Lauriston Gdns C3
Lauriston Park C3
Lauriston Pl C3
Lauriston St C3
Lawnmarket B3
Learmonth Gdns A1
Learmonth Terr A1
Leith St A4
Lennox St A1
Lennox St La A1
Leslie Pl A2
London Rd A5
Lothian Health Board C5
Lothian Rd B2
Lothian St C4
Lower Menz Pl A6
Lynedoch Pl B1
Manor Pl B1
Market St B4
Marshall St C4
Maryfield A6
Maryfield Pl A6
McEwan Hall C4
Medical School C4
Melville St B1
Meuse La B4
Middle Meadow Walk C4
Milton St A6
Montrose Terr A6
Moray House (college) B5
Moray Place A2
Morrison Link C1
Morrison St C1
Mound Pl B3
Multrees Walk A4
Mus Collections Ctr A4
Mus of Childhood B5
Mus of Edinburgh B5
Mus on the Mound B4
National Gallery B3
National Library of Scotland B4
National Monument ✦ A5
National Museum of Scotland C4
National Portrait Gallery B4
National Records Scotland A4
Nelson Monument ✦ A5
Nelson St A3
New St B5
Nicolson Sq C4
Nicolson St C4
Niddry St B4
North Bridge B4
North Meadow Walk C3
North Bank St B3
North Castle St A2
North Charlotte St A2
North St Andrew St A4
North St David St A3
North West Circus Pl A2
Northumberland St A3
Odeon C2
Old Royal High School A5
Old Tolbooth Wynd B5
Omni Ctr ✦ A4
Our Dynamic Earth ✦ B6
Oxford Terr A1
Pal of Holyrood Ho B6
Palmerston Pl B1
Panmure Pl C3
Parliament House B4
Parliament Sq B4
People's Story, The B5
Playhouse Theatre A4
Pleasance C5
Police Station A3
Ponton St C2
Post Office A3/A4/B5/C1/C2/C4/C5
Potterrow C4
Princes Mall B4
Princes St B3
Queen St A2
Queen Street Gdns A3
Queen's Dr B6/C6
Queensferry Rd A1
Queensferry St B1
Queensferry Street La B2
Radical Rd C6
Randolph Cr B1
Regent Gdns A5
Regent Rd B5
Regent Rd Park A6
Regent Terr A5
Remains of Holyrood Abbey (AD 1128) A6
Richmond La C5
Richmond Pl C5
Rose St B2
Rosemount Bldgs C1
Ross Open Air Theatre B3
Rothesay Pl B1
Rothesay Terr B1
Roxburgh Pl C5
Roxburgh St C5
Royal Bank of Scotland A4
Royal Circus A2
Royal Lyceum C2
Royal Scottish Acad B3
Royal Terr A5
Royal Terrace Gdns A5
Rutland Sq B2
Rutland St B2
St Andrew Sq A3
St Andrew's House A4
St Bernard's Cr A1
St Cecilia's Hall B4
St Colme St A2
St Cuthbert's B2
St Giles' ✝ B4
St James Ctr A4
St John St B5
St John's B2
St John's Hill B5
St Leonard's Hill C5
St Leonard's La C5
St Leonard's St C5
St Mary's (RC) A4
St Mary's Scottish Episcopal ✝ B1
St Mary's St B5
St Stephen St A2
Salisbury Crags C6
Saunders St A2
Scotch Whisky Experience ✦ B3
Scott Monument ✦ B4
Scottish Parliament B6
Scottish Storytelling Ctr ✦ B5
Semple St C2
Shandwick Pl B2
South Bridge B4
South Charlotte St B2
South College St C4
South Learmonth Gdns A1
South St Andrew St A4
South St David St A3
Spittal St C2
Stafford St B1
Student Ctr C4
Surgeons' Hall C5
TA Ctr C4
Tattoo Office B4
Teviot Pl C4
The Mall B6
The Mound B3
The Royal Mile B5
The Writer's Mus B4
Thistle St A3
Torphichen Pl C1
Torphichen St C1
Traverse Theatre B2
Tron Sq B4
Tron, The ✦ B4
Union St A4
University C4
University Library C4
Upper Grove Pl C1
Usher Hall C2
Vennel C3
Victoria St B3
Viewcraig Gdns B5
Viewcraig St B5
VUE A4
Walker St B1
Waterloo Pl A4
Waverley Bridge B4
Wemyss Pl A2
West Approach Rd C1
West Crosscauseway C5
West Maitland St C1
West of Nicholson St C4
West Port C3
West Princes St Gdns B3
West Richmond St C5
West Tollcross C2
White Horse Cl B5
William St B1
Windsor St A5
York La A4
York Pl A4
Young St B2

## Exeter 336

Alphington St C1
Athelstan Rd B3
Bampfylde St B2
Barnardo Rd C3
Barnfield Hill B3
Barnfield Rd B2/B3
Barnfield Theatre B2
Bartholomew St East B1
Bartholomew St West B1
Bear St B2
Beaufort Rd C1
Bedford St B2
Belgrave Rd A3
Belmont Rd A3
Blackall Rd A2
Blackboy Rd A3
Bonhay Rd B1
Bull Meadow Rd C2
Bus & Coach Sta B3
Castle St B2
Cecil Rd C1
Cheeke St A3
Church Rd C1
Chute St A3
City Industrial Estate C2
City Wall B1/B2
Civic Ctr B2
Clifton Rd B3
Clifton St B3
Clock Tower A1
College Rd B3
Colleton Cr C2
Commercial Rd C1
Coombe St B2
Cowick St C1
Crown Courts B2
Custom House C2
Danes' Rd A2
Denmark Rd B3
Devon County Hall C3
Devonshire Pl A3
Dinham Rd B1
East Grove Rd C3
Edmund St C1
Elmgrove Rd A1
Exe St B1
Exeter Cathedral ✝ B2
Exeter Central Sta ≥ A1
Exeter City Football Ground A3
Exeter College A1
Exeter Picture Ho B1
Fire Station A1
Fore St B1
Friars Walk C2
Guildhall B2
Guildhall Shopping Ctr B2
Harlequins Sh Ctr B1
Haven Rd C2
Heavitree Rd B3
Hele Rd A1
High St B2
HM Prison A2
Holloway St C2
Hoopern St A2
Horseguards A2
Howell Rd A1
Information Ctr B3
Iron Bridge B1
Isca Rd C1
Jesmond Rd A3
King William St A2
King St B1
Larkbeare Rd C2
Leisure Ctr C1
Library B2
Longbrook St A2
Longbrook Terr A2
Lower North St B1
Lucky La C2
Lyndhurst Rd C3
Magdalen Rd B3
Magdalen St B2
Magistrates & Crown Courts A2
Market B2
Market St B2
Marlborough Rd C3
Mary Arches St B1
Matford Ave C3
Matford La C3
Matford Rd C3
May St A3
Mol's Coffee House B2
New Theatre C2
New Bridge St B1
New North Rd A1/A2
North St B1
Northernhay St B1
Norwood Ave C3
Odeon A3
Okehampton St C1
Old Mill Cl C2
Old Tiverton Rd A3
Oxford Rd A3
Paris St B2
Parr St A3
Paul St B1
Pennsylvania Rd A2
Police HQ B3
Portland Street A3
Post Office A3/B1/B3/C1
Powderham Cr A3
Preston St B1
Princesshay Sh Ctr B2
Queen St A1
Queens Rd C1
Queen's Terr A1
Radford Rd C2
Richmond Rd A1
Roberts Rd C2
Rougemont Castle A2
Rougemont House ✦ B2
Royal Albert Memorial Museum B2
St David's Hill A1
St James' Pk Sta ≥ A3
St James' Rd A3
St Leonard's Rd C3
St Lukes University B3
St Mary Steps C1
St Nicholas Priory B1
St Thomas Station ≥ C1
Sandford Walk B3
School for the Deaf C2
School Rd C1
Sidwell St A2
Smythen St B1
South St B2
Southernhay East B2
Southernhay West B2
Spacex Gallery B1
Spicer Rd B3
Sports Ctr A3
Summerland St A3
Swimming Pool & L Ctr B3
Sydney Rd C1
Tan La C2
The Quay C2
Thornton Hill A2
Topsham Rd C3
Tucker's Hall B1
Tudor St B1
Velwell Rd A1
Verney St A3
Water La C1/C2
Weirfield Rd C2
Well St A3
West Ave A2
West Grove Rd C3
Western Way A3/B1/B2
Wonford Rd B3/C3
York Rd A2

## Fort William 337

Abrach Rd A3
Achintore Rd C1
Alma Rd B2
Am Breun Chamas A2
Ambulance Station A3
An Aird A2
Argyll Rd C1
Argyll Terr C1
Bank St B2
Belford Hospital H B2
Belford Rd B2/B3
Black Parks A3
Braemore Pl C2
Bruce Pl C2
Bus Station B2
Camanachd Cr A3/B2
Cameron Rd C1
Cameron Sq B1
Carmichael Way A2
Claggan Rd B3
Connochie Rd C1
Cow Hill C3
Creag Dhubh A2
Croft Rd B3
Douglas Pl B2
Dudley Rd B2
Dumbarton Rd C1
Earl of Inverness Rd A3
Fassifern Rd B1
Fire Station A2
Fort William ≥ B2
Fort William (Remains) ✦ B2
Glasdrum Rd C1
Glen Nevis Pl B3
Gordon Sq B1
Grange Rd C1
Heather Croft Rd C1
Henderson Row C2
High St B1
Highland Visitor Ctr B3
Hill Rd B2
Hospital Belhaven Annexe B3
Information Ctr A3
Inverlochy Ct A3
Kennedy Rd B2/C2
Library B2
Lime Tree Gallery ✦ C1
Linnhe Rd B1
Lochaber Leisure Ctr B3
Lochiel Rd A3
Lochy Rd A3
Lundavra Cres C1
Lundavra Rd C1

Lundy Rd A3
Mamore Cr B2
Mary St B2
Middle St B1
Montrose Ave A3
Moray Pl C1
Morven Pl C2
Moss Rd B2
Nairn Cres C1
Nevis Bridge B3
Nevis Rd A3
Nevis Sports Ctr A2
Nevis Terr B2
North Rd B3
Obelisk B2
Parade Rd B2
Police Station A3/C1
Post Office A3/B2
Ross Pl C1
St Andrews B2
Shaw Pl B2
Station Brae B1
Studio B1
Treig Rd A3
Underwater Ctr A2
Union Rd C1
Victoria Rd B2
Wades Rd A3
West Highland B2
West Highland College UHI A2
Young Pl B2

## Glasgow 337

Admiral St C2
Albert Bridge C5
Albion St B5
Anderston B3
Anderston Ctr B3
Anderston Quay B3
Arches B4
Argyle St A1/A2/B3/B4/B5
Argyle Street B5
Argyll Arcade B5
Arlington St A3
Arts Ctr B3
Ashley St A3
Bain St C6
Baird St A6
Baliol St A3
Ballater St C5
Barras, The (Market) C6
Bath St A3
BBC Scotland/SMG B1
Bell St C6
Bell's Bridge B1
Bentinck St A2
Berkeley St A3
Bishop La B3
Black St A6
Blackburn St C2
Blackfriars St B6
Blantyre St A1
Blythswood Sq A4
Blythswood St B4
Bothwell St B4
Brand St C1
Breadalbane St A2
Bridge St C4
Bridge St C4
Bridgegate C5
Briggait C5
Broomhill Park A6
Broomielaw B4
Broomielaw Quay Gdns B3
Brown St B4
Brunswick St B5
Buccleuch St A3
Buchanan Bus Station A5
Buchanan Galleries A5
Buchanan St B5
Buchanan St B5
Cadogan St B4
Caledonian University A5
Calgary St A5
Cambridge St A4
Canal St A5
Candleriggs B5
Carlton Pl C4
Carnarvon St A3
Carrick St B4
Castle St B6
Cathedral Sq B6
Cathedral St B5
Central College of Commerce B5
Ctr for Contemporary Arts A4
Centre St C4
Cessnock C1
Cessnock St C1
Charing Cross A3
Charlotte St C6
Cheapside St B3
Cineworld A5
Citizens' Theatre C5
City Chambers Complex B5
City Halls B5
Clairmont Gdns A2
Claremont St A2
Claremont Terr A2
Claythorne St C6
Cleveland St A3
Clifford La C1
Clifford St C1
Clifton Pl A2
Clifton St A2
Clutha St C1
Clyde Arc B2
Clyde Auditorium B2
Clyde Pl C4
Clyde Place Quay C4
Clyde St C5
Clyde Walkway C3
Clydeside Expressway B2
Coburg St C4
Cochrane St B5
College of Nautical Studies C5
College St B6
Collins St B6
Commerce St C4
Cook St C4
Cornwall St C2
Couper St A5
Cowcaddens A4
Cowcaddens Rd A4
Crimea St B3
Custom House C4
Custom Ho Quay Gdns C4
Dalhousie St A4
Dental Hospital A4
Derby St A2
Dobbie's Loan A4/A5
Dobbie's Loan Pl A5
Dorset St A3
Douglas St B4
Doulton Fountain C6
Dover St A2
Drury St B4
Drygate B6
Duke St B6
Dunaskin St A1
Dunblane St A4
Dundas St B5
Dunlop St C5
East Campbell St C6
Eastvale Pl A1
Eglinton St C4
Elderslie St A3
Elliot St B2
Elmbank St A3
Esmond St A1
Exhibition Ctr B2
Exhibition Way B2
Eye Infirmary A2
Festival Park C1
Film Theatre A4
Finnieston Quay B2
Finnieston Sq B2
Finnieston St B2
Fitzroy Pl A2
Florence St C5
Fox St C5
Gallowgate C6
Garnet St A3
Garnethill St A4
Garscube Rd A4
George Sq B5
George St B5
George V Bridge C4
Gilbert St A1
Glasgow Bridge C4
Glasgow Cathedral B6
Glasgow Central B4
Glasgow Green C6
Glasgow Metropolitan College B5/C5
Glasgow Tower B1
Glasgow Science Ctr B1
Glasgow Science Ctr Footbridge B1
Glassford St B5
Glebe St A6
Gorbals Cross C5
Gorbals St C5
Gordon St B4
Govan Rd B1/C1/C2
Grace St B3
Grand Ole Opry C2
Grafton Pl A5
Grant St A3
Granville St A3
Gray St A2
Greendyke St C6
Harley St C1
Harvie St C1
Haugh Rd A1
Heliport B1
Henry Wood Hall A2
High Court C5
High St B6
High Street B6
Hill St A3
Holland St A3
Holm St B4
Hope St A5
Houldsworth St B2
Houston Pl C3
Houston St C3
Howard St C5
Hunter St C6
Hutcheson St B5
Hutchesons Hall B5
Hydepark St B3
Imax Cinema B1
India St A3
Information Ctr B5
Ingram St B5
Jamaica St B4
James Watt St B4
John Knox St B6
John St B5
Kelvin Hall A1
Kelvin Statue A2
Kelvin Way A2
Kelvingrove Art Gallery & Museum A1
Kelvingrove Park A2
Kelvingrove St A2
Kelvinhaugh St A1
Kennedy St A6
Kent Rd A2
Killermont St A5
King St B5
King's A3
Kingston Bridge C3
Kingston St C4
Kinning Park C2
Kyle St A5
Lancefield Quay B2
Lancefield St B3
Langshot St C1
Lendel Pl C1
Lighthouse B4
Lister St A6
Little St B3
London Rd C6
Lorne St C1
Lower Harbour B1
Lumsden St A1
Lymburn St A1
Lyndoch Cr A3
Lynedoch Pl A3
Lynedoch St A3
Maclellan St C1
Mair St C2
Maitland St A4
Mavisbank Gdns C2
Mcalpine St B3
Mcaslin St A6
McLean Sq C2
McLellan Gallery A4
McPhater St A4
Merchants' House B5
Middlesex St C2
Middleton St C1
Midland St B4
Miller St B5
Millroad St C6
Milnpark St C2
Milton St A4
Minerva St B2
Mitchell Library A3
Mitchell St West B4
Mitchell Theatre A3
Modern Art Gallery B5
Moir St C6
Molendinar St C6
Moncur St C6
Montieth Row C6
Montrose St B5
Morrison St C3
Mosque C5
Nairn St A1
Nelson Mandela Sq B5
Nelson St C4
Nelson's Monument C6
New City Rd A4
Newton St A3
Newton Pl A3
Nicholson St C4
Nile St B5
Norfolk Court C4
Norfolk St C4
North Frederick St B5
North Hanover St B5
North Portland St B6
North St A3
North Wallace St A5
O2 Academy C4
Odeon C3
Old Dumbarton Rd A1
Osborne St B5/C5
Oswald St B4
Overnewton St A1
Oxford St C4
Pacific Dr B1
Paisley Rd C3
Paisley Rd West C1
Park Circus A2
Park Gdns A2
Park St South A2
Park Terr A2
Parkgrove Terr A2
Parnie St C5
Parson St A6
Partick Bridge A1
Passport Office A5
Pavilion Theatre A4
Pembroke St A3
People's Palace C6
Pinkston Rd A6
Piping Ctr, The National A5
Pitt St A4/B4
Plantation Park C1
Plantation Quay B1
Police Sta A4/A6/B5
Port Dundas Rd A5
Port St B2
Portman St C2
Prince's Dock B1
Princes Sq B5
Provand's Lordship B6
Queen St B5
Queen Street B5
Renfrew St A3/A4
Renton St A5
Richmond St B5
Robertson St B4
Rose St A4
Rottenrow B5
Royal Concert Hall A5
Royal Cr A2
Royal Exchange Sq B5
Royal Highland Fusiliers Museum A3
Royal Hospital For Sick Children A1
Royal Infirmary B6
Royal Scottish Academy of Music & Drama A4
Royal Terr A2
Rutland Cr C2
St Kent St C6
St Andrew's (RC) C5
St Andrew's C6
St Andrew's St C5
St Enoch B5
St Enoch Shopping Ctr B5
St Enoch Sq B4
St George's Rd A3
St James Rd B6
St Mungo Ave A5/A6
St Mungo Museum of Religious Life B6
St Mungo Pl A6
St Vincent Cr A2
St Vincent Pl B5
St Vincent St B3/B4
St Vincent Street Church B4
St Vincent Terr B3
Saltmarket C5
Sandyford Pl A3
Sauchiehall St A2/A4
School of Art A4
Scotland St C2
Scott St A4
Scottish Exhibition & Conference Ctr B1
Seaward St C2
Shaftesbury St B3
Sheriff Court C5
Shields Rd C3
Shuttle St B6
Somerset Pl A2
South Portland St C4
Springburn Rd A6
Springfield Quay C3
Stanley St C2
Stevenson St C6
Stewart St A4
Stirling Rd B6
Stirling's Library B5
Stobcross Quay B1
Stobcross Rd B1
Stock Exchange B5
Stockwell Pl C5
Stockwell St B5
Stow College A4
Strathclyde University B6
Sussex St C2
Synagogues A3/C4
Taylor Pl A6
Tenement House A3
Teviot St A1
Theatre Royal A4
Tolbooth Steeple & Mercat Cross C6
Tower St C2
Trades House B5
Tradeston St C4
Transport Museum A1
Tron C5
Trongate B5
Tunnel St B2
Turnbull St C5
Union St B4
Victoria Bridge C5
Virginia St B5
West Greenhill Pl B2
West Regent St A4
Wallace St C3
Walls St B6
Walmer Cr C1
Warrock St B3
Washington St B3
Waterloo St B4
Watson St B6
Watt St C3
Wellington St B4
West Campbell St B4
West George St B4
West Graham St A4
West Regent St B4
West St C4
West St C4
Westminster Terr A2
Whitehall St B3
Wilson St B5
Woodlands Gate A3
Woodlands Rd A3
Woodlands Terr A2
Woodside Cr A3
Woodside Pl A3
Woodside Terr A3
York St B4
Yorkhill Pde A1
Yorkhill St A1

## Gloucester 337

Albion St C1
Alexandra Rd B3
Alfred St C3
All Saints Rd C2
Alvin St B2
Arthur St C2
Baker St C1
Barton St C2
Blackfriars B1
Blenheim Rd C2
Bristol Rd C1
Brunswick Rd C2
Bruton Way B2
Bus Station B2
Cattle Market A1
City Council Offices B1
City Mus, Art Gall & Library B2
Clarence St B2
College of Art C2
Commercial Rd B1
Cromwell St C2
Deans Way A2
Denmark Rd A3
Derby Rd C3
Docks C1
Eastgate St B2
Edwy Pde A2
Estcourt Cl A3
Estcourt Rd A3
Falkner St C2
Folk Museum B1
GL1 Leisure Ctr C2
Gloucester Cath B1
Gloucester Station B2
Gloucestershire Royal Hospital (A&E) B3
Gloucester Waterways C1
Goodyere St C2
Gouda Way A1
Great Western Rd B3
Guildhall B2
Heathville Rd A3
Henry Rd B3
Henry St B2
High Orchard St C1
Hinton Rd A2
India Rd C3
Information Ctr B1
Jersey Rd C3
King's C2
King's Sq B2
Kingsholm Rd A2
Kingsholm Rugby Football Ground A2
Lansdown Rd A3
Library C2
Llanthony Rd C1
London Rd B3
Longsmith St B1
Malvern Rd A3
Market Pde B2
Merchants Rd C1
Mercia Rd A1
Metz Way C3
Midland Rd C2
Millbrook St C3
Market B2
Montpellier C1
Napier St C3
Nettleton Rd C2
New Inn B2
New Olympus C3
North Rd A3
Northgate St B2
Oxford Rd A2
Oxford St B2
Pk & Ride Gloucester A1
Park Rd C2
Park St B2
Parliament St C1
Pitt St B1
Police Station B1
Post Office B2
Quay St B1
Recreation Gd A1/A2
Regent St C2
Robert Raikes Ho B1
Royal Oak Rd B1
Russell St B2
Ryecroft St C2
St Aldate St B2
St Ann Way C1
St Catherine St A2
St Mark St A2
St Mary De Crypt B1
St Mary De Lode B1
St Nicholas's B1
St Oswald's Rd A1
St Oswald's Trading Estate A1
St Peter's B2
Seabroke Rd A3
Sebert St A2
Severn Rd C1
Sherborne St B2
Shire Hall B1
Sidney St C3
Soldiers of Gloucestershire B1
Southgate St B1/C1
Spa Field C1
Spa Rd C1
Sports Ground A2/B2
Station Rd B2
Stratton Rd C3
Stroud Rd C1
Superstore A1
Swan Rd A2
Technical College C1
The Mall B1
The Park C2
The Quay B1
Trier Way C1/C2
Union St A2
Vauxhall Rd C3
Victoria St C2
Wellington St C2
Westgate St B1
Widden St C2
Worcester St B2

## Grimsby 337

Abbey Drive East C2
Abbey Drive West C2
Abbey Park Rd C2
Abbey Rd C2
Abbey Walk C2
Abbeygate Sh Ctr C2
Abbotsway C2
Adam Smith St A1/A2
Ainslie St C2
Albert St A3
Alexandra Dock A2/B2
Alexandra Retail Park A2
Alexandra Rd A2/B2
Annesley St A2
Armstrong St A1
Arthur St B1
Augusta St C1
Bargate C1
Beeson St A1
Bethlehem St C2
Bodiam Way B3
Bradley St B3
Brighowgate C1/C2
Bus Station B2/C2
Canterbury Dr C1
Cartergate B1/C1
Catherine St C3
Caxton A3
Chantry La B1
Charlton St A1
Church La C2
Church St A3
Cleethorpe Rd A3
College A3
College St C1
Compton Dr C1
Corporation Bridge A2
Corporation Rd A1
Court B3
Crescent St B1
Deansgate C1
Doughty Rd C2
Dover St B1
Duchess St C2
Dudley St C1
Duke of York Gardens B1
Duncombe St B3
Earl La B1
East Marsh St B3
East St B2
Eastgate B3
Eastside Rd A3
Eaton Ct C1
Eleanor St B3
Ellis Way B3
Fisherman's Chapel A3
Fisherman's Wharf B2
Fishing Heritage Ctr B2
Flour Sq A3
Frederick St B1
Frederick Ward Way B2
Freeman St A3/B3
Freshney Dr B1
Freshney Pl B2
Garden St C2
Garibaldi St A3
Garth La B2
Grime St B3
Grimsby Docks Sta A3
Grimsby Town Sta C2
Hainton Ave C3
Har Way B3
Hare St C3
Harrison St B1
Haven Ave B1
Hay Croft Ave B1
Hay Croft St B1
Heneage Rd B3/C3
Henry St B1
Holme St B3
Hume St C1
James St B1
Joseph St B1
Kent St A3
King Edward St A3
Lambert Rd C2
Library B2
Lime St B1
Lister St B1
Littlefield La C1
Lockhill A3
Lord St B1
Ludford St C3
Macaulay St B1
Mallard Mews C3
Manor Ave C2
Market A3
Market Hall B2
Market St B3
Moss Rd C2
Nelson St A3
New St B2
Osbourne St B2
Pasture St B3
Peaks Parkway C3
Pelham Rd C1
Police Station A3
Post Office B1/B2/C2
PS Lincoln Castle B2
Pyewipe Rd A1
Railway Pl A3
Railway St A3
Recreation Ground C2
Rendel St A2
Retail Park B3
Richard St B1
Ripon St B1
Robinson St East B3
Royal St A3
St Hilda's Ave C1
St James C2
Sheepfold St B3/C3
Sixhills St C3
South Park B2
Spring St A3
Superstore B3
Tasburgh St C3
Tennyson St B2
The Close C1
Thesiger St A3
Time Trap C2
Town Hall B2
Veal St B1
Victoria Retail Park A3
Victoria St North A2
Victoria St South B2
Victoria St West B2
Watkin St A1
Welholme Ave C2
Welholme Rd C3
Wellington St B3
Wellowgate C2
Werneth Rd B3
West Coates Rd A1
Westgate A2
Westminster Dr C1
Willingham St C3
Wintringham Rd C2
Wood St B3
Yarborough Dr B1
Yarborough Hotel C2

## Hanley 337

Acton St A3
Albion St B2
Argyle St C1
Ashbourne Gr A2
Avoca St A3
Baskerville Rd B3
Bedford Rd C1
Bedford St C1
Bethesda St B2
Bexley St A2
Birches Head Rd A3
Botteslow St C3
Boundary St A2
Broad St C2
Broom St A3
Bryan St A2
Bucknall New Rd B3
Bucknall Old Rd B3
Bus Station B3
Cannon St C2
Castlefield St C1
Cavendish St B1
Central Forest Pk A2
Charles St B3
Cheapside B2
Chell St A3
Clarke St C1
Cleveland Rd C2
Clifford St C3
Clough St B2
Clyde St C1
College Rd C2
Cooper St C2
Corbridge Rd A1
Cutts St C2
Davis St C1
Denbigh St A1
Derby St C3
Dilke St A3
Dundas St A3
Dundee Rd C1
Dyke St B3
Eastwood Rd C3
Eaton St A3
Etruria Park B1
Etruria Rd B1
Etruria Vale Rd C1
Festing St A3
Festival Retail Park A1
Fire Station C2
Foundry St B2
Franklyn St C3
Garnet St B1
Garth St B3
George St A3
Gilman St B3
Glass St B3
Goodson St B3
Greyhound Way A1
Grove Pl C1
Hampton St C3
Hanley Park C2
Harding Rd C2
Hassall St B3
Havelock Pl C1
Hazlehurst St C3
Hinde St C2
Hope St B2
Houghton St C2
Hulton St A3
Information Ctr B3
Jasper St C2
Jervis St A3
John Bright St A3
John St B2
Keelings Rd A3
Kimberley Rd C1
Ladysmith Rd C1
Lawrence St C2
Leek Rd C3
Library C2
Lichfield St C3
Linfield Rd B3
Loftus St A2
Lower Bedford St C1
Lower Bryan St A2
Lower Mayer St A3
Lowther St A1
Magistrates Court C2
Malham St A2
Marsh St B2
Matlock St C3
Mayer St A3
Milton St C1
Mitchell Memorial Theatre B2
Morley St B2
Moston St A3
Mount Pleasant C1
Mulgrave St A1
Mynors St B3
Nelson Pl B3
New Century St B1
Octagon Retail Park B1
Ogden Rd C3
Old Hall St B3
Old Town Rd A3
Pall Mall B2
Palmerston St C3
Park and Ride C2
Parker St B2
Pavilion Dr A1
Pelham St C3
Percy St B2
Piccadilly B2
Picton St B3
Plough St A3
Police Station C2
Portland St A1
Post Office A3/B3/C3
Potteries Museum & Art Gallery B2
Potteries Sh Ctr B2
Potteries Way C2
Powell St A1
Pretoria Rd C1
Quadrant Rd B2
Ranelagh St C2
Raymond St C2
Rectory Rd C1
Regent Rd C2
Regent Theatre B2
Richmond Terr C2
Ridgehouse Dr A1
Robson St C2
St Ann St B3
St Luke St B3
Sampson St B2
Shaw St A1
Sheaf St C2
Shearer St C1
Shelton New Rd C1
Shirley Rd C2
Slippery La B2
Snow Hill C2
Spur St C3
Stafford St B2
Statham St B2
Stubbs La C3
Sun St C1
Supermarket A1/B2
Talbot St C3
The Parkway C2
Town Hall B2
Town Rd A3
Trinity St B2
Union St A2
Upper Hillchurch St A3
Upper Huntbach St B3
Victoria Hall Theatre B3
Warner St C2
Warwick St C1
Waterloo Rd A1
Waterloo St B3
Well St B3
Wellesley St C2
Wellington Rd B3
Wellington St B3
Whitehaven Dr A2
Whitmore St C1
Windermere St A1
Woodall St A1
Yates St C2
York St A2

## Harrogate 338

Albert St C2
Alexandra Rd B2
Arthington Ave B2
Ashfield Rd A2
Back Cheltenham Mount B2
Beech Grove C1
Belmont Rd C1
Bilton Dr A2
Bower Rd B2
Bower St B2
Bus Station B2
Cambridge Rd B2
Cambridge St B2
Cemetery A2
Chatsworth Pl A2
Chatsworth Grove A2
Chatsworth Rd A2
Chelmsford Rd B3
Cheltenham Cr B2
Cheltenham Mt B2
Cheltenham Pde B2
Christ Church B3
Christ Church Oval B3
Chudleigh Rd B3
Clarence Dr B1
Claro Rd A3
Claro Way A3
Coach Park B2
Coach Rd B3
Cold Bath Rd C1
Commercial St B2
Coppice Ave A1
Coppice Dr A1
Coppice Gate A1
Cornwall Rd B1
Council Offices B1
Court C3
Crescent Gdns B1
Crescent Rd B1
Dawson Terr A2
Devonshire Pl B3
Diamond Mews C1
Dixon Rd A2
Dixon Terr A2
Dragon Ave B3
Dragon Parade B2
Dragon Rd B2
Duchy Rd B1
East Parade B2
East Park Rd C3
Esplanade B1
Fire Station A2
Franklin Mount A2
Franklin Rd B2
Franklin Square A2
Glebe Rd C1
Grove Park Ct A3
Grove Park Terr A3
Grove Rd A2
Hampswaite Rd A1
Harcourt Dr B3
Harcourt Rd B3
Harrogate B2
Harrogate Int Ctr B1
Harrogate Ladies Coll B1
Harrogate Theatre B2
Heywood Rd C1
Hollins Cr A1
Hollins Mews A1
Hollins Rd A1
Homestead Rd C3
Hydro Leisure Ctr, The A1
Information Ctr B1
James St B2
Jenny Field Dr A1
John St B2
Kent Dr A1
Kent Rd A1
Kings Rd A2
Kingsway B3
Kingsway Dr B3
Lancaster Rd C1
Leeds Rd C2
Lime Grove B3
Lime St A3
Mayfield Grove B2
Mayfield Pl A2
Mercer B1
Montpellier Hill B1
Mornington Cr A3
Mornington Terr B3
Mowbray Sq B3
North Park Rd B3
Nydd Vale Rd B2
Oakdale Ave A1
Oatlands Dr C3
Odeon B2
Osborne Rd A2
Otley Rd C2
Oxford St B2
Park Chase B3
Park Parade B3
Park View B2
Parliament St B1
Police Station B3
Post Office B2/C1
Providence Terr A2
Queen Parade C3
Queen's Rd C1
Raglan St C2
Regent Ave A3
Regent Grove A3
Regent Parade A3
Regent St A3
Regent Terr A3
Rippon Rd A1
Robert St C2
Royal Baths & Turkish Baths B1
Royal Pump Room B1
St Luke's Mount A2
St Mary's Ave C1
St Mary's Walk C1
Scargill Rd A1
Skipton Rd A3
Skipton St A2
Slingsby Walk C3
South Park Rd C2
Spring Grove A1
Springfield Ave B1
Station Ave B2
Station Parade B2
Strawberry Dale B2
Stray Rein C3
Studley Rd A2
Superstore B2
Swan Rd B1
The Parade B2
The Stray C2/C3
Tower St C2
Trinity Rd C2
Union St B2
Valley Dr C1
Valley Gardens C1
Valley Mount C1
Victoria Ave C2
Victoria Rd C1
Victoria Shopping Ctr B2
Waterloo St A2
West Park C2
West Park St C2
Wood View A1
Woodfield Ave A3
Woodfield Dr A3
Woodfield Grove A3
Woodfield Rd A3
Woodfield Square A3
Woodside B3
York Pl C3
York Rd B1

## Holyhead *Caergybi* 338

Armenia St A2
Arthur St C2
Beach Rd A1
Boston St B2
Bowling Green C3
Bryn Erw Rd C3
Bryn Glas Cl C3
Bryn Glas Rd C3
Bryn Gwyn Rd C1
Bryn Marchog A1
Bryn Mor Terr A2
Bryngoleu Ave A1
Cae Braenar C3
Cambria St B1
Captain Skinner's Obelisk B2
Cecil St C2
Celtic Gateway Footbridge B2
Cemetery C1/C2
Cleveland Ave C2
Coastguard Lookout A2
Court B2
Customs House A3
Cybi Pl A2
Cyttir Rd C3
Edmund St B1
Empire B2
Ferry Terminals B2
Ffordd Beibio B3
Ffordd Feurig C3
Ffordd Hirnos C3
Ffordd Jasper C3
Ffordd Tudur B3
Fire Station C2
Garreglwyd Rd B1
Gilbert St C2
Gorsedd Circle B1
Gwelfor Ave A1
Harbour View B3
Henry St C2
High Terr C1
Hill St B2
Holborn Rd C2
Holland Park Ind Est C3
Holyhead Park B1
Holyhead Station B2
Information Ctr B2
King's Rd C2
Kingsland Rd C2
Lewascote C3
Library B2
Lifeboat Station A1
Llanfawr Cl C3
Llanfawr Rd C3
Lligwy St C2
Lon Deg C3
London Rd C3
Longford Rd B1
Longford Terr B1
Maes Cybi B1
Maes Hedd A1
Maes-Hyfryd Rd C1
Maes-y-Dref B1
Maes-yr-Haf A2/B1
Maes-yr-Ysgol C3
Marchog C3
Marina A1
Maritime Museum A1

Market B2
Market St B2
Mill Bank B1
Min-y-Mor Rd A1
Morawelon Ind Est B3
Morawelon Rd B3
Moreton Rd C1
New Park Rd B1
Newry St A2
Old Harbour Lighthouse A3
Plas Rd C1
Police Station B2
Porth-y-Felin Rd A1
Post Office A1/B1/B2/B3/C2/C3
Prince of Wales Rd A2
Priory La B3
Pump St C1
Queens Park B1
Reseifion Rd C1
Rock St B1
Roman Fort B2
St Cybi St B2
St Cybi's Church B2
St Seiriol's Cl B1
Salt Island Bridge A2
Seabourne Rd A1
South Stack Rd B1
Sports Ground B1
Stanley St B2
Station St B2
Tan-y-Bryn Rd A1
Tan-yr-Efail C2
Tara St C1
Thomas St B1
Town Hall A2
Treseifion Estate C2
Turkey Shore Rd B2
Ucheldre Arts Ctr B1
Ucheldre Ave B1
Upper Baptist St B1
Victoria Rd B2
Victoria Terr B2
Vulcan St B1
Walthew Ave A1
Walthew La A1
Wian St C2


## Hull 338


Adelaide St C1
Albert Dock C1
Albion St B2
Alfred Gelder St B2
Anlaby Rd B1
Arctic Corsair B3
Beverley Rd A1
Blanket Row C2
Bond St B2
Bridlington Ave A2
Brook St B1
Brunswick Ave A1
Bus Station B1
Camilla Cl C3
Cannon St A2
Cannon's C1
Caroline St A2
Carr La B2
Castle St C2
Central Library B1
Charles St A2
Citadel Way B3
City Hall B2
City Hall Theatre B2
Clarence St B3
Cleveland St A3
Clifton St A1
Club Culture C2
Colonial St B1
Court B2
Deep, The C3
Dock Office Row B3
Dock St B2
Dinostar C2
Drypool Bridge B3
Egton St A3
English St C1
Ferens Gallery B2
Ferensway B1
Francis St A2
Francis St West A2
Freehold St A1
Freetown Way A2
Fruit Theatre C2
Garrison Rd B3
George St B2
Gibson St A2
Great Thornton St B1
Great Union St A3
Green La A2
Grey St A1
Grimston St B2
Grosvenor St A1
Guildhall B2
Guildhall Rd B2
Hands-on History B2
Harley St A1
Hessle Rd C1
High St B3
Holy Trinity B2
Hull & East Riding Museum B3
Hull Arena C1
Hull College B3
Hull History Ctr A2
Hull (Paragon) Sta B1
Hull Truck Theatre B1
Humber Dock Marina C2
Humber Dock St C2
Humber St C2
Hyperion St A3
Information Ctr B2
Jameson St B1
Jarratt St B2
Jenning St A3
King Billy Statue C2
King Edward St B2
King St A2
Kingston Retail Park C1
Kingston St C2
Liddell St A1
Lime St A3
Lister St C1
Lockwood St A2
Maister House B3
Maritime Museum B2
Market B2
Market Place B2
Minerva Pier C2
Mulgrave St A3
Myton Bridge C3
Myton St B1
NAPA (Northern Acad of Performing Arts) B1
Nelson St C2
New Cleveland St A3
New George St A2
New Theatre A2
Norfolk St A1
North Bridge A3
North St B1
Odeon C1
Old Harbour C3
Osborne St B1
Paragon St B2
Park St B1
Percy St A2
Pier St C2
Police Station B2
Post Office A1/B1/B2
Porter St C1
Portland St B1
Posterngate B2
Prince's Quay B2
Prospect Ctr B1
Prospect St B1
Queen's Gdns B2
Railway Dock Marina C2
Railway St C2
Real B1
Red Gallery B1
Reform St A2
Retail Park B1
River Hull Footbridge B3
Riverside Quay C2
Roper St B2
St James St C1
St Luke's St B1
St Mark St A3
St Mary the Virgin B3
St Stephens Sh Ctr B1
Scott St A2
South Bridge Rd B3
Spring Bank A1
Spring St B1
Spurn Lightship C2
Spyvee St A3
Streetlife Transport Museum B3
Sykes St A2
Tidal Surge Barrier C3
Tower St B3
Trinity House B2
University B2
Vane St A1
Victoria Pier C2
Waterhouse La B2
Waterloo St A1
Waverley St C1
Wellington St C2
Wellington St West C2
West St B1
Whitefriargate B2
Wilberforce Dr B2
Wilberforce House B3
Wilberforce Monument B3
William St C1
Wincolmlee A3
Witham A3
Wright St A1


## Inverness 338


Abban St A1
Academy St B2
Alexander Pl B2
Anderson St A2
Annfield Rd C3
Ardconnel St B3
Ardconnel Terr B3
Ardross Pl B2
Ardross St B2
Argyle St B3
Argyle Terr B3
Attadale Rd B1
Ballifeary La C2
Ballifeary Rd C1/C2
Balnacraig La A1
Balnain House B2
Balnain St B2
Bank St B2
Bellfield Park C2
Bellfield Terr C3
Benula Rd A1
Birnie Terr A1
Bishop's Rd C2
Bowling Green A2
Bowling Green B2
Bowling Green C2
Bridge St B2
Brown St A2
Bruce Ave C1
Bruce Gdns C1
Bruce Pk C1
Burial Ground A2
Burnett Rd A3
Bus Station B3
Caledonian Rd B1
Cameron Rd A1
Cameron Sq A1
Carse Rd A1
Carsegate Rd Sth A1
Castle Garrison Encounter B2
Castle Rd B2
Castle St B3
Celt St B2
Chapel St A2
Charles St B3
Church St B2
Clachnacuddin Football Ground A1
Columba Rd B1/C1
Crown Ave B3
Crown Circus B3
Crown Dr B3
Crown Rd B3
Crown St B3
Culduthel Rd C3
Dalneigh Cres C1
Dalneigh Rd C1
Denny St B3
Dochfour Dr B1/C1
Douglas Row B2
Duffy Dr C3
Dunabban Rd A1
Dunain Rd B1
Duncraig St B2
Eastgate Shopping Ctr B3
Eden Court C2
Fairfield Rd B1
Falcon Sq B3
Fire Station A3
Fraser St B2
Fraser St C2
Friars' Bridge A2
Friars' La B2
Friars' St A2
George St A2
Gilbert St A2
Glebe St A2
Glendoe Terr A1
Glenurquhart Rd C1
Gordon Terr B3
Gordonville Rd C2
Grant St A2
Greig St B2
HM Prison B3
Harbour Rd A3
Harrowden Rd B1
Haugh Rd C2
Heatherley Cres C3
High St B3
Highland Council HQ, The C2
Hill Park C3
Hill St B3
Huntly Pl A2
Huntly St B2
India St A2
Industrial Estate A3
Information Ctr B2
Innes St A2
Inverness B3
Inverness College (Midmills Campus) B3
Inverness College UHI A3
Inverness High School B1
Inverness Museum B2
Jamaica St A2
Kenneth St B2
Kilmuir Rd A1
King St B2
Kingsmills Rd B3
Laurel Ave B1/C1
Library A3
Lilac Gr B1
Lindsay Ave C1
Lochalsh Rd A1/B1
Longman Rd A3
Lotland Pl A2
Lower Kessock St A1
Madras St A2
Market Hall B3
Maxwell Dr C1
Mayfield Rd C3
Millburn Rd B3
Mitchell's La C3
Montague Row B2
Muirfield Rd C3
Muirtown St B1
Nelson St A2
Ness Bank C2
Ness Bridge B2
Ness Walk B2/C2
Old Edinburgh Rd C3
Old High Church B2
Park Rd C1
Paton St C2
Perceval Rd B1
Planefield Rd B2
Police Station A3
Porterfield Bank C3
Porterfield Rd C3
Portland Pl A2
Post Office A2/B1/B2/B3
Queen St B2
Queensgate B2
Railway Terr A3
Rangemore Rd B1
Reay St B3
Riverside St A2
Rose St A2
Ross Ave B1
Rowan Rd B1
Royal Northern Infirmary C2
St Andrew's Cath C2
St Columba B2
St John's Ave C1
St Mary's Ave C1
Sheriff Court B3
Shore St A2
Smith Ave C1
Southside Pl C3
Southside Rd C3
Spectrum Ctr B2
Strothers La B3
Superstore B2
TA Ctr C2
Telford Gdns B1
Telford Rd A1
Telford St A1
Tomnahurich Cemetery C1
Tomnahurich St B2
Town Hall B3
Union Rd B3
Union St B3
Walker Pl A2
Walker Rd A3
War Memorial C2
Waterloo Bridge A2
Wells St B1
Young St B2


## Ipswich 338


Alderman Rd B2
All Saints' Rd A1
Alpe St B2
Ancaster Rd C1
Ancient House B3
Anglesea Rd B2
Ann St B2
Arboretum A2
Austin St C2
Belstead Rd C2
Berners St B2
Bibb Way B1
Birkfield Dr C1
Black Horse La B2
Bolton La B3
Bond St C3
Bowthorpe Cl B2
Bramford La A1
Bramford Rd A1
Bridge St C2
Brookfield Rd A1
Brooks Hall Rd A1
Broomhill A2
Broomhill Rd A1
Broughton Rd A2
Bulwer Rd B1
Burrell Rd C2
Butter Market B2
Butter Market Ctr B3
Carr St B3
Cecil Rd B2
Cecilia St C2
Chancery Rd C2
Charles St B2
Chevallier St A1
Christchurch Mansion & Wolsey Art Gallery B3
Christchurch Park A3
Christchurch St B3
Cineworld C2
Civic Ctr B2
Civic Dr B2
Clarkson St B1
Cobbold St B3
Commercial Rd C2
Constable Rd A3
Constantine Rd C1
Constitution Hill A2
Corder Rd A3
Corn Exchange B2
Cotswold Ave A2
Council Offices C2
County Hall B3
Crown Court C2
Crown St B2
Cullingham Rd B1
Cumberland St B2
Curriers La B2
Dale Hall La A2
Dales View Rd A1
Dalton Rd B2
Dillwyn St B1
Elliot St B1
Elm St B2
Elsmere Rd A3
Falcon St C2
Felaw St C3
Flint Wharf C3
Fonnereau Rd B2
Fore St C3
Foundation St C3
Franciscan Way C2
Friars St C2
Gainsborough Rd A3
Gatacre Rd B1
Geneva Rd B2
Gippeswyk Ave C1
Gippeswyk Park C1
Grafton Way C2
Graham Rd A1
Grimwade St C3
Great Whip St C3
Handford Cut B1
Handford Rd B1
Henley Rd A2
Hervey St B3
High St B2
Holly Rd A2
Information Ctr B3
Ipswich Haven Marina C3
Ipswich School A2
Ipswich Station C2
Ipswich Town FC (Portman Road) C2
Ivry St A2
Kensington Rd A1
Kesteven Rd C1
Key St C3
Kingsfield Ave A3
Kitchener Rd A1
Magistrates Court B2
Little's Cr C2
London Rd B1
Low Brook St C3
Lower Orwell St C3
Luther Rd C2
Manor Rd A3
Mornington Ave A1
Mus & Art Gallery B2
Museum St B2
Neale St B3
New Cardinal St C2
New Cut East C3
New Cut West C3
New Wolsey B2
Newson St B2
Norwich Rd A1/B1
Oban St B2
Old Customs House C3
Old Foundry Rd B3
Old Merchant's Ho C3
Orford St B2
Paget Rd A2
Park Rd A3
Park View Rd A2
Peter's St C2
Philip Rd C2
Pine Ave A2
Pine View Rd A2
Police Station B2
Portman Rd B2
Portman Walk C1
Post Office B2/B3
Princes St C2
Prospect St B1
Queen St B2
Ranelagh Rd C1
Recreation Ground B1
Rectory Rd C2
Regent Theatre B3
Retail Park C1
Richmond Rd A1
Rope Walk C3
Rose La C2
Russell Rd C2
St Edmund's Rd A2
St George's St B2
St Helen's St B3
Samuel Rd B3
Sherrington Rd A1
Silent St C2
Sir Alf Ramsey Way C1
Sirdar Rd B1
Soane St B3
Springfield La A1
Star La C3
Stevenson Rd B1
Suffolk College C3
Suffolk Retail Park B1
Superstore B1
Surrey Rd B1
Tacket St C3
Tavern St B3
The Avenue A3
Tolly Cobbold Mus C3
Tower Ramparts B2
Tower Ramparts Shopping Ctr B2
Tower St B3
Town Hall B2
Tuddenham Rd A3
Upper Brook St B3
Upper Orwell St B3
Valley Rd A2
Vermont Cr B3
Vermont Rd B3
Vernon St C3
Warrington Rd A2
Waterloo Rd A1
Waterworks St C3
Wellington St B1
West End Rd B1
Westerfield Rd A3
Westgate St B2
Westholme Rd A1
Westwood Ave A1
Willoughby Rd C2
Withipoll St B3
Woodbridge Rd B3
Woodstone Ave A3
Yarmouth Rd B1


## Kendal 338


Abbot Hall Art Gallery & Museum of Lakeland Life C2
Ambulance Station A2
Anchorite Fields C2
Anchorite Rd C2
Ann St A3
Appleby Rd A3
Archers Meadow C3
Ashleigh Rd A2
Aynam Rd B2
Bankfield Rd B1
Beast Banks B2
Beezon Fields A2
Beezon Rd A2
Beezon Trad Est A3
Belmont B2
Birchwood Cl C1
Blackhall Rd B2
Brewery Arts Ctr B2
Bridge St B2
Brigsteer Rd C1
Burneside Rd A2
Bus Station B2
Buttery Well La C2
Canal Head North B3
Captain French La C2
Caroline St A2
Castle Hill B3
Castle Howe B2
Castle Rd B3
Castle St A3/B3
Cedar Gr C1
Council Offices B2
County Council Offices A2
Cricket Ground A3
Cricket Ground C3
Cross La C2
Dockray Hall Ind Est A2
Dowker's La B2
Dry Ski Slope B3
East View B1
Echo Barn Hill C1
Elephant Yard Sh Ctr B2
Fairfield La A1
Finkle St B2
Fire Station A2
Fletcher Square C3
Football Ground C3
Fowling La A3
Gillinggate C2
Glebe Rd C2
Golf Course B1
Goose Holme B3
Gooseholme Bridge B3
Green St A1
Greengate C2
Greengate La C1/C2
Greenside B1
Greenwood C1
Gulfs Rd B2
High Tenterfell B1
Highgate B2
Hillswood Ave C1
Horncop La A2
Information Ctr B2
K Village and Heritage Ctr B2
Kendal Business Park A3
Kendal Castle (Remains) B3
Kendal Fell B1
Kendal Green A1
Kendal A3
Kendal Station A3
Kent Pl B2
Kirkbarrow C2
Kirkland C2
Library B2
Library Rd B2
Little Aynam B3
Little Wood B1
Long Cl C1
Longpool A3
Lound Rd C3
Lound St C3
Low Fellside B2
Lowther St B2
Maple Dr C1
Market Pl B2
Maude St B2
Miller Bridge B2
Milnthorpe Rd C2
Mint St A3
Mintsfeet Rd A3
Mintsfeet Rd South A2
New Rd B2
Noble's Rest B2
Parish Church C2
Park Side Rd C3
Parkside Bsns Park C3
Parr St B3
Police Station A2
Post Office A3/B2/C2
Quaker Tapestry B2
Queen's Rd B1
Riverside Walk C2
Rydal Mount A2
Sandes Ave A2
Sandgate A3
Sandylands Rd A3
Serpentine Rd B1
Serpentine Wood B1
Shap Rd A3
South Rd C2
Stainbank Rd C1
Station Rd A3
Stramongate B2
Stramongate Bridge B2
Stricklandgate A2/B2
Sunnyside C3
Thorny Hills B3
Town Hall B2
Undercliff Rd B1
Underwood C1
Union St A2
Vicar's Fields C2
Vicarage Dr C1/C2
Wainwright Yd Sh Ctr B2
Wasdale Cl C3
Well Ings C2
Westmorland Shopping Ctr & Market Hall B2
Westwood Ave C1
Wildman St A3
Windermere Rd A1
YHA B2
YWCA B2


## King's Lynn 339


Albert St A2
Albion St B2
All Saints B2
All Saints St B2
Austin Fields A2
Austin St A2
Avenue Rd B3
Bank Side B1
Beech Rd C2
Birch Tree Cl B2
Birchwood St A2
Blackfriars Rd B2
Blackfriars St B2
Boal St B1
Bridge St B2
Broad St B2
Broad Walk B3
Burkitt St A2
Bus Station A2
Carmelite Terr C2
Chapel St A2
Chase Ave C3
Checker St C2
Church St B2
Clough La B2
Coburg St B2
College of West Anglia A3
Columbia Way A3
Corn Exchange A1
County Court Rd B2
Cresswell St A2
Custom House A1
Eastgate St A2
Edma St A2
Exton's Rd C3
Ferry La B1
Ferry St A1
Framingham's Almshouses B2
Friars St C2
Friars Walk C2
Gaywood Rd A3
George St A2
Gladstone Rd C2
Goodwin's Rd C3
Green Quay B1
Greyfriars' Tower B2
Guildhall A1
Hansa Rd C3
Hardwick Rd C2
Hextable Rd A2
High St B1
Holcombe Ave C3
Hospital Walk C2
Information Ctr B1
John Kennedy Rd A2
Kettlewell Lane A2
King George V Ave B3
King's Lynn Art Ctr A1
King's Lynn FC B3
King's Lynn Station B2
King St B1
Library B2
Littleport St A2
Loke Rd A2
London Rd B2
Lynn Museum B2
Majestic B2
Magistrates Court B1
Market La A1
Millfleet B2
Milton Ave A3
Nar Valley Walk C2
Nelson St B1
New Conduit St B2
Norfolk St A2
North Lynn Discovery Ctr A3
North St A2
Oldsunway B2
Ouse Ave C1
Page Stair Lane A1
Park Ave B3
Police Station B2
Portland Pl C1
Portland St B2
Post Office A3/C2
Purfleet B1
Queen St B1
Raby Ave A3
Railway Rd A2
Red Mount Chapel B3
Regent Way B2
River Walk A1
Robert St C2
Saddlebow Rd C2
St Ann's St A1
St James' Rd B2
St James' Swimming Pool B2
St James St B2
St John's Walk B3
St Margaret's B1
St Nicholas A2
St Nicholas St A1
St Peter's Rd B1
Sir Lewis St A2
Smith Ave A3
South Everard St C2
South Gate C2
South Quay B1
South St B2
Southgate St C2
Stonegate St B2
Surrey St A1
Sydney St C3
Tennyson Ave B3
Tennyson Rd B3
Tower St B2
Town Hall B1
Town Ho & Tales of The Old Gaol Ho B1
Town Wall (Remains) B3
True's Yard Mus A2
Valingers Rd C2
Vancouver Ave C2
Waterloo St B2
Wellesley St B2
White Friars Rd C2
Windsor Rd C2
Winfarthing St C2
Wyatt St A2
York Rd C3


## Lancaster 339


Aberdeen Rd C3
Adult College, The C3
Aldcliffe Rd C2
Alfred St B3
Ambleside Rd A3
Ambulance Sta A3
Ashfield Ave B1
Ashton Rd C2
Assembly Rooms B2
Balmoral Rd B3
Bath House B2
Bath Mill La B3
Bath St B3
Blades St B1
Borrowdale Rd B3
Bowerham Rd C3
Brewery La B2
Bridge La B2
Brook St C1
Bulk Rd A3
Bulk St B2
Bus Station B2
Cable St B2
Canal Cruises & Waterbus C2
Carlisle Bridge A1
Carr House La C2
Castle B1
Castle Park B1
Caton Rd A3
China St B2
Church St B2
City Museum B2
Clarence St C3
Common Gdn St B2
Coniston Rd A3
Cottage Museum B2
Council Offices B2
Court B2
Cromwell Rd C2
Crown Court B1
Dale St C3
Dallas Rd B1/C1
Dalton Rd B3
Dalton Sq B2
Damside St B2
De Vitre St B3
Dee Rd A1
Denny Ave A1
Derby Rd A2
Dukes B2
Earl St A2
East Rd B3
Eastham St C3
Edward St B3
Fairfield Rd B1
Fenton St B2
Firbank Rd A3
Fire Station B2
Friend's Meeting Ho B1
Garnet St B3
George St B2
Giant Axe Field B1
Grand, The B2
Grasmere Rd B3
Greaves Rd C2
Green St A3
Gregson Ctr, The B3
Gregson Rd C3
Greyhound Bridge A2
Greyhound Bridge Rd A2
High St B2
Hill Side B1
Hope St C3
Hubert Pl B1
Information Ctr B2
Judges Lodgings B2
Kelsy St B1
Kentmere Rd B3
King St B2
Kingsway A3
Kirkes Rd C3
Lancaster & Lakeland C3
Lancaster City Football Club B1
Lancaster Station B1
Langdale Rd A3
Ley Ct B1
Library B2
Lincoln Rd B1
Lindow St C2
Lodge St B2
Long Marsh La B1
Lune Rd A1
Lune St A2
Lune Valley Ramble A3
Mainway A2
Maritime Museum A1
Market St B2
Marketgate Sh Ctr B2
Meadowside C2
Meeting House La B1
Millennium Bridge A2
Moor La B2
Moorgate B3
Morecambe Rd A1/A2
Nelson St B2
North Rd B2
Orchard La C1
Owen Rd A2
Park Rd B3
Parliament St A3
Patterdale Rd A3
Penny St B2
Police Station B2
Portland St C2
Post Office A3/B1/B2/B3/C3
Primrose St C3
Priory B1
Prospect St C3
Quarry Rd B3
Queen St C2
Regent St C2
Ridge La A3
Ridge St A3
Royal Lancaster Infirmary (A&E) C2
Rydal Rd B3
Ryelands Park A1
St Georges Quay A1
St John's B2
St Leonard's Gate B2
St Martin's Rd C3
St Nicholas Arcades Shopping Ctr B2
St Oswald St C3
St Peter's B3
St Peter's Rd B3
Salisbury Rd B1
Scotch Quarry Urban Park C3
Shire Hall/HM Prison B1
Sibsey St B1
Skerton Bridge A2
South Rd C2
Station Rd B1
Stirling Rd C3
Storey Ave B1
Sunnyside La C1
Sylvester St C1
Tarnsyke Rd A1
Thurnham St C2
Town Hall B2
Troutbeck Rd B3
Ulleswater Rd B3
University of Cumbria C3
Vicarage Field B1
Vue B2
West Rd B1
Westbourne Dr C1
Westbourne Rd B1
Westham St C3
Wheatfield St B1
Williamson Rd B3
Willow La B1
Windermere Rd B3
Wingate-Saul Rd B1
Wolseley St B3
Woodville St B3
Wyresdale Rd C3


## Leeds 339


Aire St B3
Aireside Ctr B2
Albion Pl B4
Albion St B4
Albion Way B1
Alma St A6
Arcades B4
Armley Rd B1
Back Burley Lodge Rd A1
Back Hyde Terr A2
Back Row C3
Bath Rd C3
Beckett St A6
Bedford St B3
Belgrave St A4
Belle View Rd A2
Benson St A5
Black Bull St C5
Blenheim Walk A3
Boar La B4
Bond St B4
Bow St C5
Bowman La C4
Brewery C4
Bridge St A5/B5
Briggate B4
Bruce Gdns C1
Burley Rd A1
Burley St B1
Burmantofs St B6
Bus & Coach Station B5
Butterly St C4
Butts Cr B4
Brewery Wharf C5
Byron St A5
Call La B4
Calverley St A3/B3
Canal St B1
Canal Wharf C3
Carlisle Rd C5
Cavendish Rd A1
Cavendish St A2
Chadwick St C5
Cherry Pl A6
Cherry Row A5
City Museum A4
City Pal of Varieties B4
City Sq B3
Civic Hall A3
Clarence Road C5
Clarendon Rd A2
Clarendon Way A3
Clark La C6
Clay Pit La A4
Cloberry St A2
Clyde Approach C1
Clyde Gdns C1
Coleman St C2
Commercial St B4
Concord St A5
Cookridge St A4
Copley Hill C1
Corn Exchange B4
Cromer Terr A2
Cromwell St A5
Cross Catherine St B6
Cross Green La C6
Cross Stamford St A5
Crown & County Courts A3
Crown Point Bridge C5
Crown Point Retail Pk C4
Crown Point Rd C4
David St C3
Dent St C6
Derwent Pl C3
Dial St C6
Dock St C4
Dolly La A6
Domestic St C2
Duke St B5
Duncan St B4
Dyer St B5
East Field St B6
East Pde B3
East St C5
Eastgate B5
Easy Rd C6
Edward St B4
Ellerby La C6
Ellerby Rd C6
Fenton St A3
Fire Station B2
Fish St B4
Flax Pl B5
Gelderd Rd C1
George St B4
Globe Rd C2
Gloucester Cr B1
Gower St A5
Grafton St A4
Grand Theatre B4
Granville Rd A6
Great George St A3
Great Wilson St C4
Greek St B3
Green La C1
Hanover Ave A2
Hanover La A2
Hanover Sq A2
Hanover Way A2
Harewood St B4
Harrison St B4
Haslewood Cl B6
Haslewood Drive B6
High Court B5
Holbeck La C2

Holdforth Cl C1
Holdforth Gdns B1
Holdforth Gr C1
Holdforth Pl C1
Holy Trinity B4
Hope Rd A5
Hunslet La C4
Hunslet Rd C4
Hyde Terr A2
Infirmary St B3
Information Ctr B3
Ingram Row C3
Junction St C4
Kelso Gdns A2
Kelso Rd A2
Kelso St A2
Kendal La A2
Kendell St C4
Kidacre St C4
King Edward St B4
King St B3
Kippax Pl C6
Kirkgate B4
Kirkgate Market B4
Kirkstall Rd A1
Kitson St C6
Lady La B4
Lands La B4
Lavender Walk B6
Leeds Art Gallery B3
Leeds Bridge C4
Leeds Coll of Music B5
Leeds General Infirmary (A&E) A3
Leeds Metropolitan University A3/A4
Leeds Museum Discovery Ctr C5
Leeds Shopping Plaza B4
Leeds Station B3
Leeds University A3
Library B3
Lincoln Green Rd A6
Lincoln Rd A6
Lindsey Gdns A6
Lindsey Rd A6
Lisbon St B3
Little Queen St B3
Long Close La C6
Lord St C2
Lovell Park A4
Lovell Park Rd A4
Lovell Rd A5
Lower Brunswick St A5
Mabgate A5
Macauly St A5
Magistrates Court A3
Manor Rd C3
Mark La B4
Marlborough St B2
Marsh La B5
Marshall St C3
Meadow La C4
Meadow Rd C4
Melbourne St A5
Merrion Ctr A4
Merrion St A4
Merrion Way A4
Mill St B5
Millennium Sq A3
Mount Preston St A2
Mushroom St A5
Neville St C4
New Briggate A4/B4
New Market St B4
New Station St B4
New York Rd A5
New York St B5
Nile St A5
Nippet La A6
North St A4
Northern St B3
Oak Rd B1
Oxford Pl B3
Oxford Row A3
Park Cross St B3
Park La A2
Park Pl B3
Park Row B4
Park Sq B3
Park Sq East B3
Park Sq West B3
Park St B3
Police Station B5
Pontefract La B6
Portland Cr A3
Portland Way A3
Post Office B4/B5
Project Space Leeds C2
Quarry House (NHS/DSS Headquarters) B5
Quebec St B3
Queen St B3
Railway St B5
Rectory St A6
Regent St A5
Richmond St C5
Rigton Approach B6
Rigton Dr B6
Rillbank La A1
Rosebank Rd A1
Royal Armouries C5
Russell St B3
Rutland St B2
St Anne's Cath (RC) A4
St Anne's St B4
St James' Hospital A6
St Johns Ctr B4
St John's Rd A2
St Mary's St B5
St Pauls St B3
St Peter's B5
Saxton La B5
Sayner La C5
Shakespeare Ave A6
Shannon St B6
Sheepscar St South A5
Siddall St C3
Skinner La A5
South Pde B3
Sovereign St C4
Spence La C2
Springfield Mount A2
Springwell Ct C2
Springwell Rd C2
Springwell St C2
Stoney Rock La A6
Studio Rd A1
Sutton St C2
Sweet St C3
Sweet St West C3
Swinegate B4
Templar St B5
The Calls B5
The Close B6
The Core B4
The Drive B6
The Garth B5
The Headrow B3/B4
The Lane B5
The Light B4
The Parade B6
Thoresby Pl A3
Torre Rd A6
Town Hall A3
Union Pl C3
Union St B5
Upper Accomodation Rd B6
Upper Basinghall St B4
Vicar La B4
Victoria Bridge C4
Victoria Quarter B4
Victoria Rd C4
Vue B4
Wade La A4
Washington St A1
Water La C3
Waterloo Rd C4
Wellington Rd B2/C1
Wellington St B3
West St B2
West Yorkshire Playhouse B5
Westfield Rd A1
Westgate B3
Whitehall Rd B3/C2
Whitelock St A5
Willis St C6
Willow Approach A1
Willow Ave A1
Willow Terrace Rd A3
Wintoun St A5
Woodhouse La A3/A4
Woodsley Rd A1
York Pl B3
York Rd B6
Yorkshire TV Studios A1

## Leicester 339

Abbey St A2
All Saints' A1
Aylestone Rd C2
Bath La A1
Bede Park C1
Bedford St A3
Bedford St South A3
Belgrave Gate A2
Belle Vue A2
Belvoir St B2
Braunstone Gate B1
Burleys Way A2
Burnmoor St C2
Bus Station A2
Canning St A2
Carlton St C2
Castle B1
Castle Gardens B1
Cathedral B2
Causeway La A2
Charles St B3
Chatham St B2
Christow St A3
Church Gate A2
City Gallery B3
Civic Ctr B2
Clank St B2
Clock Tower B2
Clyde St A3
Colton St B3
Conduit St B3
Crafton St A3
Craven St A1
Crown Courts B3
Curve B3
De Lux A2
De Montfort Hall C3
De Montfort St C3
De Montfort Univ C1
Deacon St C2
Dover St B3
Duns La B1
Dunton St A1
East St B3
Eastern Boulevard C1
Edmonton Rd A3
Erskine St A3
Filbert St C1
Filbert St East C2
Fire Station C3
Fleet St A3
Friar La B2
Friday St A2
Gateway St C2
Glebe St B3
Granby St B3
Grange La C2
Grasmere St C1
Great Central St A1
Guildhall B2
Guru Nanak Sikh Museum B1
Halford St B2
Havelock St C2
Haymarket Sh Ctr A2
High St A2
Highcross St A1
Highcross Sh Ctr A2
HM Prison C2
Horsefair St B2
Humberstone Gate B2
Humberstone Rd A3
Infirmary St C2
Information Ctr B2
Jarrom St C2
Jewry Wall B1
Kamloops Cr A3
King Richards Rd B1
King St B2
Lancaster Rd C3
LCB Depot B3
Lee St A3
Leicester RFC C2
Leicester Royal Infirmary (A&E) C2
Leicester Station B3
Library B2
Little Theatre, The B3
London Rd C3
Lower Brown St B2
Magistrates Court B2
Manitoba Rd A3
Mansfield St A2
Market B2
Market St B2
Mill La C2
Montreal Rd A3
Narborough Rd North B1
Nelson Mandela Park C2
New Park St B1
New St B2
New Walk C3
New Walk Museum & Art Gallery C3
Newarke Houses B2
Newarke St B2
Northgate St A1
Orchard St A2
Ottawa Rd A3
Oxford St C2
Upper Brown St B2
Phoenix Square B3
Police Station A3
Post Office A1/B2/C2/C3
Prebend St C3
Princess Rd East C3
Princess Rd West C3
Queen St B3
Regent College C3
Regent Rd C2/C3
Repton St A1
Rutland St B3
St George St B3
St Georges Way B3
St John St A2
St Margaret's A2
St Margaret's Way A2
St Martins B2
St Mary de Castro B1
St Matthew's Way A3
St Nicholas B1
St Nicholas Circle B1
Sanvey Gate A2
Silver St B2
Slater St A1
Soar La A1
South Albion St B3
Southampton St B3
Swain St B3
Swan St A1
The Gateway C2
The Newarke B1
The Rally Com Park A2
Tigers Way C3
Tower St C3
Town Hall B2
Tudor Rd B1
University of Leicester C3
University Rd C3
Upperton Rd C1
Vaughan Way A2
Walnut St C2
Watling St A2
Welford Rd B2
Wellington St B2
West Bridge B1
West St C3
West Walk C3
Western Boulevard C1
Western Rd C1
Wharf St North A3
Wharf St South A3
Y' Theatre, The B3
Yeoman St B3
York Rd B2

## Lewes 339

Abinger Pl B1
All Saints Ctr B2
Ambulance Station B2
Anne of Cleves Ho C1
Barbican Ho Mus B1
Brewery B2
Brook St A2
Brooks Rd A2
Bus Station B2
Castle Ditch La B1
Castle Precincts B1
Chapel Hill B3
Church La A1/A2
Cliffe High St B2
Cliffe Industrial Estate C3
Cluny St C1
Cockshut Rd C1
Convent Field C2
Coombe Rd A2
County Hall B1
County Records Office B1
Court B2
Court Rd B2
Crown Court B2
Cuilfail Tunnel B3
Davey's La A3
East St B2
Eastport La C2
Fire Station A2
Fisher St B2
Friars Walk B2
Garden St B1
Government Offices C2
Grange Rd B1
Ham La C2
Harveys Way B2
Hereward Way A2
High St B1/B2
Hop Gallery B2
Information Ctr B2
Keere St B1
King Henry's Rd B1
Lancaster St B2
Landport Rd A1
Leisure Ctr C3
Lewes Bridge B2
Lewes Castle B1
Lewes Football Gd C2
Lewes Golf Course B3
Lewes Southern By-Pass C2
Lewes Station B2
Library B2
Malling Ind Est A2
Malling Brook Ind Est A3
Malling Hill A3
Malling St A3/B3
Market St B2
Martyr's Monument B3
Mayhew Way A2
Morris Rd B3
Mountfield Rd C2
New Rd B1
Newton Rd A1
North St A2/B2
Offham Rd B1
Old Malling Way A1
Orchard Rd A3
Paddock La B1
Paddock Rd B1
Paddock Sports Gd B1
Park Rd B1
Pelham Terr A1
Pells Open Air Swimming Pool A1
Phoenix Causeway B2
Phoenix Ind Est B2
Phoenix Pl B2
Pinwell Rd B2
Police Station B1
Post Office A2/B1/B2/C1
Prince Edward's Rd B1
Priory St C1
Priory of St Pancras (remains of) C1
Railway La B2
Railway Land Nature Reserve B3
Rotten Row B1
Rufus Cl B1
St Pancras Rd C1
St John St B2
St John's Terr B1
St Nicholas La B2
Sewage Works C3
South Downs Bsns Pk A3
South St B3/C3
Southdowns Rd A2
Southerham Junction C3
Southover Grange Gdns B1
Southover High St C1
Southover Rd B1
Spences Field A3
Spences La A2
Stansfield Rd A1
Station Rd B2
Station St B2
Sun St B1
Sussex Downs College C2
Sussex Police HQ A2
Talbot Terr B1
The Avenue B1
The Course C1
The Martlets A2
The Needlemakers B2
The Pells A1
Thebes Gallery B2
Toronto Terr B1
Town Hall B2
West St B2
White Hill B1
Willeys Bridge A1

## Lincoln 342

Alexandra Terr B1
Anchor St C1
Arboretum B3
Arboretum Ave B3
Baggholme Rd B3
Bailgate A2
Beaumont Fee B1
Brayford Way C1
Brayford Wharf East C1
Brayford Wharf North B1
Bruce Rd A2
Burton Rd A1
Bus Station (City) C2
Canwick Rd C2
Cardinal's Hat B2
Carline Rd B1
Castle B1
Castle St A1
Cathedral B2
Cathedral St B2
Cecil St A2
Chapel La A2
Cheviot St B3
Church La A2
City Hall B1
Clasketgate B2
Clayton Sports Gd A3
Coach Park C2
Collection, The B2
County Hospl (A&E) B3
County Office B1
Courts C1
Croft St B2
Cross St C2
Crown Courts B1
Curle Ave A3
Danesgate B2
Drill Hall B2
Drury La B1
East Bight A2
East Gate A2
Eastcliff Rd B3
Eastgate B2
Egerton Rd A3
Ellis Windmill A1
Engine Shed, The C1
Environment Agency C2
Exchequer Gate B2
Firth Rd C1
Flaxengate B2
Florence St B3
George St C3
Good La A2
Gray St A1
Great Northern Terr C3
Great Northern Terrace Industrial Estate C3
Greetwell Rd B3
Greetwellgate B3
Haffenden Rd A2
High St B2/C1
HM Prison A3
Hospital (Private) A2
Hungate B2
James St A2
Jews House & Ct B2
Kesteven St C2
Langworthgate A2
Lawn Visitor Ctr, The B1
Lee Rd A3
Library B2
Lincoln College B2
Lincoln Central Sta C2
Lincolnshire Life/Royal Lincolnshire Regiment Museum A1
Lindum Rd B2
Lindum Sports Ground A3
Lindum Terr B3
Mainwaring Rd A3
Manor Rd A2
Market C2
Massey Rd A3
Medieval Bishop's Palace B2
Mildmay St A1
Mill Rd A1
Millman Rd B3
Minster Yard B2
Monks Rd B3
Montague St B2
Mount St A1
Nettleham Rd A2
Newland B1
Newport A2
Newport Arch A2
Newport Cemetery A2
Northgate A2
Odeon C1
Orchard St B1
Oxford St C2
Park St B1
Pelham Bridge C2
Pelham St C2
Police Station B1
Portland St C2
Post Office A1/A2/B1/B3/C2
Potter Gate B2
Priory Gate B2
Queensway A3
Rasen La A1
Ropewalk C1
Rosemary La B2
St Anne's Rd B3
St Benedict's C1
St Giles Ave A3
St John's Rd A2
St Marks St C1
St Mark's Sh Ctr C1
St Mary-Le-Wigford C1
St Mary's St C2
St Nicholas St A2
St Swithin's B2
Saltergate C1
Saxon St A1
Sch of Art & Design B2
Sewell Rd B3
Silver St B2
Sincil St C2
Spital St A2
Spring Hill B1
Stamp End C3
Steep Hill B2
Stonebow & Guildhall C2
Stonefield Ave A2
Tentercroft St C1
The Avenue B1
The Grove A3
Theatre Royal B2
Tritton Retail Park C1
Tritton Rd C1
Union Rd B1
University of Lincoln C1
Upper Lindum St B3
Upper Long Leys Rd A1
Usher B2
Vere St A2
Victoria St B1
Victoria Terr B1
Vine St B3
Wake St A1
Waldeck St A1
Waterside Sh Ctr C2
Waterside North C2
Waterside South C2
West Pde B1
Westgate A2
Wigford Way C1
Williamson St A2
Wilson St A1
Winn St B3
Wragby Rd A3
Yarborough Rd A1

## Liverpool 342

Abercromby Sq C5
Acc Liverpool C2
Addison St A3
Adelaide Rd B6
Ainsworth St B4
Albany Rd B6
Albert Dock C2
Albert Edward Rd B6
Angela St C6
Anson St B4
Archbishop Blanche High School B6
Argyle St C3
Arrad St C4
Ashton St B5
Audley St A4
Back Leeds St A2
Basnett St B3
Bath St A1
Beatles Story C2
Beckwith St C3
Bedford Close C5
Bedford St North C5
Bedford St South C5
Benson St C4
Berry St C4
Birkett St A4
Bixteth St B2
Blackburne Place C4
Bluecoat B3
Bold Place C4
Bold St C4
Bolton St B3
Bridport St B4
Bronte St B4
Brook St A1
Brownlow Hill B4/B5
Brownlow St B5
Brunswick Rd A5
Brunswick St B1
Bus Station C2
Butler Cr A6
Byrom St A3
Caledonia St C4
Cambridge St C5
Camden St A4
Canada Blvd B1
Canning Dock C2
Canterbury St A4
Cardwell St C6
Carver St A4
Cases St B3
Castle St B2
Catherine St C5
Cavern Club B3
Central Library A3
Central Station B3
Chapel St B2
Charlotte St B3
Chatham Place C6
Chatham St C5
Cheapside B2
Chestnut St C5
Christian St A3
Church St B3
Churchill Way North A3
Churchill Way South B3
Clarence St B4
Coach Station A4
Cobden St A5
Cockspur St A2
College St C3
College St North A5
College St South A5
Colquitt St C4
Comus St A3
Concert St C3
Connaught Rd B6
Cook St B2
Copperas Hill B4
Cornwallis St C3
Covent Garden B2
Craven St A4
Cropper St B3
Crown St B5/C6
Cumberland St B2
Cunard Building B1
Dale St B2
Dansie St B4
Daulby St B5
Dawson St B3
Derby Sq B2
Drury La B2
Duckinfield St B4
Duke St C3
Earle St A2
East St A2
Eaton St A2
Edgar St A3
Edge La B6
Edinburgh Rd A6
Edmund St B2
Elizabeth St B5
Elliot St B3
Empire Theatre B4
Empress Rd B6
Epworth St A5
Erskine St A5
Everyman Theatre C5
Exchange St East B2
Fact Ctr, The C4
Falkland St A5
Falkner St C5/C6
Farnworth St A6
Fenwick St B2
Fielding St A6
Fleet St C3
Fraser St A4
Freemasons Row A2
Gardner Row A3
Gascoyne St A2
George Pier Head C1
George St B2
Gibraltar Road A1
Gilbert St C3
Gildart St A4
Gill St B4
Goree B2
Gower St C2
Gradwell St C3
Great Crosshall St A3
Great George St C4
Great Howard St A1
Great Newton St B4
Greek St B4
Green La B4
Greenside A5
Greetham St C3
Gregson St A5
Grenville St C3
Grinfield St C6
Grove St C5
Guelph St A6
Hackins Hey B2
Haigh St A4
Hall La B6
Hanover St B3
Harbord St C6
Hardman St C4
Harker St A4
Hart St B4
Hatton Garden A2
Hawke St B4
Helsby St B6
Henry St C3
HM Customs & Excise National Museum C2
Highfield St A2
Highgate St B6
Hilbre St B4
Hope Place C4
Hope St C4
Houghton St B3
Hunter St A3
Hutchinson St A6
Information Ctr C2
Institute For The Performing Arts C4
Irvine St B6
Irwell St B2
Islington A4
James St B2
James St Station B2
Jenkinson St A4
Johnson St A3
Jubilee Drive B6
Kempston St A4
Kensington A6
Kensington Gdns B6
Kensington St A6
Kent St C3
King Edward St A1
Kinglake St B6
Knight St C4
Lace St A3
Langsdale St A4
Law Courts C2
Leece St C4
Leeds St A2
Leopold Rd B6
Lime St B3
Lime St Station B4
Little Woolton St B5
Liver St C2
Liverpool John Moores University A3/B4/C4
Liverpool Landing Stage B1
Liverpool One C2
London Rd A4/B4
Lord Nelson St B4
Lord St B2
Lovat St C6
Low Hill A5
Low Wood St A6
Lydia Ann St C3
Mansfield St A4
Marmaduke St B6
Marsden St A6
Martensen St B6
Marybone A3
Maryland St C4
Mason St B6
Mathew St B2
May St B4
Melville Place C6
Merseyside Maritime Museum C2
Metquarter B3
Metropolitan Cathedral (RC) B5
Midghall St A2
Molyneux Rd A6
Moor Place B4
Moorfields B2
Moorfields Station B2
Moss St A5
Mount Pleasant B4/B5
Mount St C4
Mount Vernon B6
Mulberry St C5
Municipal Buildings B2
Mus of Liverpool C2
Myrtle Gdns C6
Myrtle St C5
Naylor St A2
Nelson St C4
Neptune Theatre B3
New Islington A4
New Quay B1
Newington St C3
North John St B2
North St A3
North View B6
Norton St A4
Oakes St B5
O2 Academy
Odeon B4
Old Hall St A1
Old Leeds St A2
Oldham Place C4
Oldham St C4
Olive St C6
Open Eye Gallery C3
Oriel St A2
Ormond St B2
Orphan St C6
Overbury St C6
Overton St B6
Oxford St C5
Paisley St A1
Pall Mall A2
Paradise St C3
Park La C3
Parker St B3
Parr St C3
Peach St B5
Pembroke Place B4
Pembroke St B5
Philharmonic Hall C5
Pickop St A2
Pilgrim St C4
Pitt St C3
Playhouse Theatre B3
Pleasant St B4
Police HQ C2
Police Station A4/B4
Pomona St B4
Port of Liverpool Building B2
Post Office A2/A4/A5/A6/B2/B3/B4/C4
Pownall St C2
Prescot St A5
Preston St B3
Princes Dock A1
Princes Gdns A2
Princes Jetty A1
Princes Pde B1
Princes St B2
Pythian St A6
Queen Sq Bus Station B3
Queensland St C6
Queensway Tunnel (Docks exit) B1
Queensway Tunnel (Entrance) B3
Radio City B2
Ranelagh St B3
Redcross St B2
Renfrew St B6
Renshaw St B4
Richmond Row A4
Richmond St B3
Rigby St A2
Roberts St A1
Rock St B4
Rodney St C4
Rokeby St A4
Romily St A6
Roscoe La C4
Roscoe St C4
Rose Hill A3
Royal Court Theatre B3
Royal Liver Building B1
Royal Liverpool Hospital (A&E) B5
Royal Mail St B4
Rumford Place B2
Rumford St B2
Russell St B4
St Andrew St B4
St Anne St A4
St Georges Hall B3
St John's Ctr B3
St John's Gdns B3
St John's La B3
St Joseph's Cr A4
St Minishull St B5
St Nicholas Place B1
St Paul's Sq A2
St Vincent Way B4
Salisbury St A4
Salthouse Dock C2
Salthouse Quay C2
Sandon St C5
Saxony Rd B6
Schomberg St A6
School La B2
Seel St C3
Seymour St B4
Shaw St A5
Sidney Place C6
Sir Thomas St B3
Skelhorne St B4
Slater St C3
Slavery Museum C2
Smithdown La B6
Soho Sq A4
Soho St A4
South John St B2
Springfield A4
Stafford St A4
Standish St A3
Stanley St B2
Strand St C2
Suffolk St C3
Tabley St C3
Tarleton St B3
Tate Gallery C2
Teck St B6
Temple St B2
The Beacon B3
The Strand B2
Tithebarn St B2
Town Hall B2
Traffic Police HQ C6
Trowbridge St B4
Trueman St A3
Union St B2
Unity Theatre C4
University C5
University of Liverpool B5
Upper Duke St C4
Upper Frederick St C3
Upper Baker St A6
Vauxhall Rd A2
Vernon St B2
Victoria Gallery & Museum B5
Victoria St B2
Vine St C5
Wakefield St A4
Walker Art Gallery A3
Walker St A6
Wapping C2
Water St B1/B2
Waterloo Rd A1
Wavertree Rd B6
West Derby Rd A6
West Derby St B5
Whitechapel B3
Western Approaches War Museum B2
Whitley Gdns A5
William Brown St B3
William Henry St A4
Williamson Sq B3
Williamson St B3
Williamson's Tunnels Heritage Ctr C6
Women's Hospital C6
Wood St B3
World Museum, Liverpool A3
York St C3

## Llandudno 342

Abbey Pl B1
Abbey Rd B1
Adelphi St B3
Alexandra Rd C2
Anglesey Rd A1
Argyll Rd B3
Arvon Ave A2
Atlee Cl C3
Augusta St B3
Back Madoc St B2
Bodafon St B3
Bodhyfryd Rd A2
Bodnant Cr C3
Bodnant Rd C3
Bridge Rd C2
Bryniau Rd C1
Builder St B3
Builder St West C2
Cabin Lift A2
Camera Obscura A3
Caroline Rd B2
Chapel St A2
Charlton St B3
Church Cr C1
Church Walks A2
Claremont Rd B2
Clement Ave A2
Clifton Rd B2
Clonmel St B3
Coach Station B3
Conway Rd B3
Council St West C3
Cricket and Rec Gd B2
Cwlach Rd A2
Cwlach St A1
Cwm Howard La C3
Cwm Pl C3
Cwm Rd C3
Dale Rd C1
Deganwy Ave B2
Denness Pl C2
Dinas Rd C2
Dolydd B1
Erol Pl B2
Ewloe Dr C3
Fairways C2
Ffordd Dewi C3
Ffordd Dulyn C2
Ffordd Dwyfor C3
Ffordd Elisabeth C3
Ffordd Gwynedd C3
Ffordd Las C3
Ffordd Morfa C3
Ffordd Penrhyn C3
Ffordd Tudno C3
Ffordd yr Orsedd C3
Ffordd Ysbyty C2
Fire & Ambulance Sta B3
Garage St B3
George St A2
Gloddaeth Ave B1
Gloddaeth St B2
Gogarth Rd B1
Great Orme Mines A1
Great Ormes Rd B1
Happy Valley A2
Happy Valley Rd A3
Haulfre Gardens A1
Herkomer Cr C1
Hill Terr A2
Home Front Mus B2
Hospice B1
Howard Rd B3
Information Ctr B2
Invalids' Walk B1
James St B2
Jubilee St B3
King's Ave C2
King's Rd C2
Knowles Rd C2
Lees Rd C2
Library B2
Lifeboat Station B2
Llandudno A2
Llandudno (A&E) C2
Llandudno Station B3
Llandudno Town Football Ground C2
Llewelyn Ave A2
Lloyd St West B1
Lloyd St B2
Llwynon Rd A1
Llys Maelgwn B1
Madoc St B2
Maelgwn Rd B2
Maesdu Bridge C2
Maesdu Rd C2/C3
Maes-y-Cwm C3
Maes-y-Orsedd C3
Marian Pl C2
Marian Rd C2
Marine Drive (Toll) A3

Market Hall A2
Market St A2
Miniature Golf Course A1
Morfa Rd B1
Mostyn B3
Mostyn Broadway B3
Mostyn St B3
Mowbray Rd C2
New St A2
Norman Rd B3
North Parade A2
North Wales Golf Links C1
Old Bank Gallery A2
Old Rd A2
Oxford Rd B3
Parc Llandudno Ret Pk B3
Pier A3
Plas Rd A2
Police Station B3
Post Office B3/C2
Promenade A3
Pyllau Rd A1
Rectory La A2
Rhuddlan Ave C3
St Andrew's Ave B2
St Andrew's Pl B2
St Beuno's Rd A1
St David's Pl B2
St David's Rd B2
St George's Pl A3
St Mary's Rd B2
St Seriol's Rd B2
Salisbury Pass B1
Salisbury Rd B2
Somerset St B3
South Parade A2
Stephen St B3
TA Ctr B3
Tabor Hill A2
The Oval B1
The Parade B3
Town Hall B2
Trinity Ave B1
Trinity Cres C1
Trinity Sq B3
Tudno St A2
Ty-Coch Rd A2
Ty-Gwyn Rd A1/A2
Ty'n-y-Coed Rd A1
Vaughan St B3
Victoria Shopping Ctr B3
Victoria Tram Station A2
War Memorial A2
Werny Wylan C3
West Parade B1
Whiston Pass A2
Winllan Ave C2
Wyddfyd Rd A2
York Rd A2

## Llanelli 342

Alban Rd B3
Albert St B1
Als St B3
Amos St C1
Andrew St A3
Ann St C2
Annesley St B2
Arfryn Ave A3
Arthur St B2
Belvedere Rd A1
Bigyn La B3
Bigyn Park Terr C3
Bigyn Rd C3
Bond Ave C3
Brettenham St A1
Bridge St B2
Bryn Pl C1
Bryn Rd C1
Bryn Terr C1
Brynhyfryd Rd A2
Brynmelyn Ave A3
Brynmor Rd B1
Bryn-More Rd C1
Burry St C1
Bus Station B2
Caersalem Terr C2
Cambrian St C1
Caswell St C3
Cedric St B3
Cemetery A2
Chapman St A1
Charles Terr C2
Church St B2
Clos Caer Elms A1
Clos Sant Paul C2
Coastal Link Rd B1/C1
Coldstream St B2
Coleshill Terr B1
College Hill B3
College Sq B3
Copperworks Rd C2
Coronation Rd C3
Corporation Ave A3
Council Offices B2
Court B2
Cowell St B2
Cradock St C2
Craig Ave C3
Cricket Ground A1
Derwent St A1
Dillwyn St C2
Druce St C1
Elizabeth St B2
Emma St C2
Erw Rd B1
Felinfoel Rd A2
Fire Station A3
Firth Rd C3
Fron Terr C3
Furnace Rugby Football Ground A1
Gelli-On B2
George St C2
Gilbert Cres A2
Gilbert Rd A2
Glanmor Rd C2
Glanmor Terr C2
Glasfryn Terr A3
Glenalla Rd B3
Glevering St B3
Goring Rd A2
Gorsedd Circle A2
Grant St C3
Graveyard C2
Great Western Cl C2
Greenway St B1
Hall St B2
Harries Ave A2
Hedley Terr A2
Heol Elli B3
Heol Goffa A3
Heol Nant-y-Felin A3
Heol Siloh B2
Hick St C2
High St C1
Indoor Bowls Ctr B1
Inkerman St B2
Island Pl B2
James St B3
John St B2
King George Ave B3
Lake View Cl A2
Lakefield Pl C1
Lakefield Rd C1
Langland Rd C3
Leisure Ctr B1
Library B2
Llanelli House B2
Llanelli Parish Church B2
Llanelli RUFC (Stradey Park) A1
Llanelli Station C2
Llewellyn St C2
Lliedi Cres A3
Lloyd St B2
Llys Alys B3
Llys Fran A3
Llysnewedd C1
Long Row A3
Maes Gors C2
Maesyrhaf A3
Mansel St C3
Marblehall Rd B3
Marborough Rd A2
Margam St C3
Marged St C2
Marine St C1
Market B2
Market St B2
Marsh St C2
Martin Rd C3
Miles St A1
Mill La A3/B2
Mincing La B2
Murray St B2
Myn y Mor B1
Nathan St C1
Nelson Terr C1
Nevill St C2
New Dock Rd C2
New Rd A1
New Zealand St A1
Old Lodge C2
Old Rd A2
Paddock St C2
Palace Ave B3
Parc Howard A2
Parc Howard Museum & Art Gallery A2
Park Cres B1
Park St B2
Parkview Terr B1
Pemberton St C2
Pembrey Rd A1
Peoples Park B1
Police Station B2
Post Office A1/A2/B2/C1/C2
Pottery Pl B3
Pottery St B3
Princess St B1
Prospect Pl A2
Pryce St A1
Queen Mary's Walk C3
Queen Victoria Rd C1
Raby St B1
Railway Terr C2
Ralph St B2
Ralph Terr C1
Regalia Terr B3
Rhydyrafon A3
Richard St B2
Robinson St B2
Roland Ave A1
Russell St C3
St David's Cl C1
St Elli Shopping Ctr B2
St Margaret's Dr A1
Spowart Ave A1
Station Rd B2/C2
Stepney Pl B2
Stepney St B2
Stewart St A1
Stradey Park Ave A1
Sunny Hill A2
Swansea Rd A3
TA Ctr B2
Talbot St C3
Temple St B3
The Avenue Cilfig A2
The Mariners C1
Theatr Elli B2
Thomas St A2
Toft Pl A3
Town Hall B2
Traeth Ffordd C1
Trinity Rd C3
Trinity Terr C2
Tunnel Rd B3
Tyisha Rd C3
Union Blgs A2
Upper Robinson St B2
Vauxhall Rd B2
Walter's Rd B3
Waun Lanyrafon B2
Waun Rd A3
Wern Rd B3
West End A2
Y Bwthyn C3
Zion Row B3

## London 340

Abbey Orchard St E4
Abbey St E8
Abchurch La D7
Abingdon St E5
Achilles Way D3
Acton St B5
Addington St E5
Air St D4
Albany St B3
Albemarle St D4
Albert Embankment F5
Alberta St F6
Aldenham St A4
Alderney St F3
Aldersgate St C7
Aldford St D3
Aldgate C8
Aldgate High St C8
Aldwych C5
Allsop Pl B2
Alscot Rd E8
Amwell St B6
Andrew Borde St C4
Angel A6
Appold St C8
Argyle Sq B5
Argyle St B5
Argyll St C4
Arnold Circus B8
Artillery La C8
Artillery Row E4
Ashbridge St B2
Association of Photographers Gallery B7
Baker St B2
Baker St B2
Balaclava Rd F8
Balcombe St B2
Baldwin's Gdns C6
Balfour St F7
Baltic St B7
Bank C7
Bank Museum C7
Bank of England C7
Bankside D7
Bankside Gallery D6
Banner St B7
Barbican C7
Barbican Gallery C7
Basil St E2
Bastwick St B7
Bateman's Row B8
Bath St B7
Bath Terr E7
Bayley St C4
Baylis Rd E6
Bayswater Rd D2
Beak St D4
Beauchamp Pl E2
Bedford Row C5
Bedford Sq C4
Bedford St D5
Bedford Way B4
Beech St C7
Belgrave Pl E3
Belgrave Rd F4
Belgrave Sq E3
Bell La C8
Belvedere Rd E5
Berkeley Sq D3
Berkeley St D3
Bermondsey St E8
Bernard St B5
Berners Pl C4
Berners St C4
Berwick St C4
Bessborough St F4
Bethnal Green Rd B8
Bevenden St B7
Bevis Marks C8
BFI London IMAX Cinema D6
Bidborough St B5
Binney St C3
Birdcage Walk E4
Bishopsgate C8
Black Prince Rd F5
Blackfriars D6
Blackfriars Bridge D6
Blackfriars Rd E6
Blandford St C2
Blomfield St C7
Bloomsbury St C4
Bloomsbury Way C5
Bolton St D3
Bond St C3
Borough E7
Borough High St E7
Borough Rd E7
Boswell St C5
Bourne St F3
Bow St C5
Bowling Green La B6
Brad St D6
Brandon St F7
Bressenden Pl E4
Brewer St D4
Brick St D3
Bridge St E5
Britain at War D8
Britannia Walk B7
British Library B4
British Museum C5
Britton St B6
Broad Sanctuary E4
Broadley St C2
Broadway E4
Brompton Rd E2
Brompton Sq E2
Brook Dr F6
Brook St D3
Brown St C2
Brunswick Pl B7
Brunswick Sq B5
Brushfield St C8
Bruton St D3
Bryanston St C2
Buckingham Gate E4
Buckingham Palace E4
Buckingham Palace Rd F3
Bunhill Row B7
Byward St D8
Cabinet War Rooms & Churchill Museum E4
Cadogan La E3
Cadogan Pl E2
Cadogan Sq F2
Cadogan St F2
Cale St F2
Caledonian Rd A5
Calshot St A5
Calthorpe St B5
Calvert Ave B8
Cambridge Circus C4
Cambridge Sq C2
Cambridge St F3
Camomile St C8
Cannon St D7
Cannon St D7
Capland St B1
Carey St C5
Carlisle La E5
Carlisle Pl E4
Carlton House Terr D4
Carmelite St D6
Carnaby St C4
Carter La C6
Carthusian St C7
Cartwright Gdns B5
Castle Baynard St D6
Cavendish Pl C3
Cavendish Sq C3
Caxton Hall E4
Caxton St E4
Central St B7
Chalton St B4
Chancery Lane C6
Chapel St C2
Chapel St E3
Charing Cross D5
Charing Cross Rd C4
Charles II St D4
Charles Sq B7
Charles St D3
Charlotte Rd B8
Charlotte St C4
Chart St B7
Charterhouse Sq C6
Charterhouse St C6
Chatham St F7
Cheapside C7
Chenies St C4
Chesham St F3
Chester Sq F3
Chester Way F6
Chesterfield Hill D3
Cheval Pl E2
Chiltern St C3
Chiswell St C7
Church St B2
City Garden Row A6
City Rd B7
City Thameslink C6
City University, The B6
Claremont Sq A6
Clarendon St F3
Clarges St D3
Clerkenwell Cl B6
Clerkenwell Green B6
Clerkenwell Rd B6
Cleveland St C4
Clifford St D4
Clink Prison Mus D7
Cliveden Pl F3
Clock Museum C7
Club Row B8
Cockspur St D4
Coleman St C7
Columbia Rd B8
Commercial Rd C9
Commercial St C8
Compton St B6
Conduit St D3
Congreve St F8
Connaught Sq C2
Connaught St C2
Constitution Hill E3
Copperfield St E6
Coptic St C5
Cornhill C7
Cornwall Rd D6
Coronet St B8
County St E7
Courtauld Gallery D5
Courtenay St F6
Covent Garden D5
Covent Garden D5
Cowcross St C6
Cowper St B7
Crampton St F7
Cranbourn St D4
Craven St D5
Crawford Pl C2
Crawford St C2
Creechurch La C8
Cricket Museum B1
Cromer St B5
Cromwell Rd F1
Crosby Row E7
Crucifix La E8
Cumberland Gate D2
Cumberland St F3
Cumberland Terr A3
Cuming Mus F7
Curtain Rd B8
Curzon St D3
Dante Rd F6
D'arblay St C4
Davies St C3
Dean St C4
Deluxe Gallery B8
Denbigh Pl F4
Denmark St C4
Dering St C3
Devonshire St C3
Diana, Princess of Wales Memorial Garden D1
Diana, Princess of Wales Memorial Walk E4
Dingley Rd B7
Dorset St C2
Doughty St B5
Douglas St F4
Dover St D3
Downing St E5
Draycott Avenue F2
Draycott Pl F2
Druid St E8
Drummond St B4
Drury La C5
Drysdale St B8
Duchess St C3
Dufferin St B7
Duke of Wellington Pl E3
Duke St C3/D3
Duke St Hill D7
Duke's Pl C8
Duncannon St D5
Dunton Rd F8
East Rd B7
East St F7
Eastcastle St C4
Eastcheap D8
Eastman Dental Hospital B5
Eaton Gate F3
Eaton Pl E3
Eaton Sq E3
Eaton Terr F3
Ebury Bridge F3
Ebury Bridge Rd F3
Eccleston Bridge F3
Eccleston Sq F3
Eccleston St E3
Edgware Rd C2
Edgware Rd C2
Egerton Gdns E2
Eldon St C7
Elephant & Castle F7
Elephant and Castle E6
Elephant Rd F7
Elizabeth Bridge F3
Elizabeth St F3
Elm Tree Rd B1
Elystan Pl F2
Elystan St F2
Embankment D5
Endell St C5
Endsleigh Pl B4
Enid St E8
Ennismore Gdns E2
Erasmus St F4
Euston B4
Euston Rd B4
Euston Square B4
Evelina Children's Hospital E5
Eversholt St A4
Exhibition Rd E1
Exmouth Market B6
Fair St E8
Falmouth Rd E7
Fann St B7
Farringdon C6
Farringdon Rd C6
Farringdon St C6
Featherstone St B7
Fenchurch St D8
Fenchurch St D8
Fetter La C6
Finsbury Circus C7
Finsbury Pavement C7
Finsbury Sq B7
Fitzalan St F6
Fitzmaurice Pl D3
Fleet St C6
Fleming Lab. Mus C1
Floral St D5
Florence Nightingale Museum E5
Folgate St C8
Fore St C7
Foster La C7
Francis St F4
Frazier St E6
Freemason's Hall C5
Friday St C7
Fulham Rd F1
Gainsford St E8
Garden Row E6
Gee St B7
Geological Mus E1
George Row E9
George St C2
Gerrard St D4
Gibson Rd F5
Giltspur St C6
Glasshouse St D4
Glasshouse Walk F5
Gloucester Pl C2
Gloucester Sq C1
Gloucester St F4
Golden Hinde D7
Golden La B7
Golden Sq D4
Goodge St C4
Goodge St C4
Gordon Hospital F4
Gordon Sq B4
Goswell Rd B6
Gough St B5
Goulston St C8
Gower St B4
Gracechurch St D7
Grafton Way B4
Graham Terr F3
Grange Rd E8
Grange Walk E8
Gray's Inn Rd B5
Great College St E5
Great Cumberland Pl C2
Great Dover St E7
Great Eastern St B8
Great Guildford St D7
Great Marlborough St C4
Great Ormond St B5
Great Ormond Street Children's Hospital B5
Great Percy St B5
Great Peter St E4
Great Portland St B3
Great Portland St C3
Great Queen St C5
Great Russell St C4
Great Scotland Yd D5
Great Smith St E4
Great Suffolk St D6/E6
Great Titchfield St C4
Great Tower St D8
Great Windmill St D4
Greek St C4
Green Park D4
Green St D3
Greencoat Pl F4
Gresham St C7
Greville St B5/C6
Greycoat Hosp Sch E4
Greycoat Pl E4
Grosvenor Cres E3
Grosvenor Gdns E3
Grosvenor Pl E3
Grosvenor Sq D3
Grosvenor St D3
Grove End Rd B1
Guards Museum and Chapel E4
Guildhall Art Gallery C7
Guilford St B5
Guy's Hospital D7
Haberdasher St B7
Hackney Rd B8
Half Moon St D3
Halkin St E3
Hall PL B1
Hall St B6
Hallam St C3
Hamilton CL B1
Hampstead Rd B4
Hanover Sq C3
Hans Cres E2
Hans Rd E2
Hanway St C4
Hardwick St B6
Harewood Ave B2
Harley St C3
Harper Rd E7
Harrington Rd F1
Harrison St B5
Harrowby St C2
Hasker St F2
Hastings St B5
Hatfields D6
Hayles St F6
Haymarket D4
Hayne St C6
Hay's Galleria D8
Hay's Mews D3
Hayward Gallery D5
Helmet Row B7
Herbrand St B5
Hercules Rd E5
Hertford St D3
Heygate St F7
High Holborn C5
Hill St D3
HMS Belfast D8
Hobart Pl E3
Holborn C5
Holborn C6
Holborn Viaduct C6
Holland St D6
Holmes Mus B2
Holywell La B8
Horse Guards' Rd D4
Horseferry Rd F4
Houndsditch C8
Houses of Parliament E5
Howland St C4
Hoxton Sq B8
Hoxton St B8
Hugh St F3
Hunter St B5
Hunterian Mus C5
Hyde Park D2
Hyde Park Cnr E3
Hyde Park Cres C2
Hyde Park St C2
Imperial Coll London E1
Imperial College Rd E1
Imperial War Mus E6
Inner Circle B3
Institute of Archaeology (London Univ) B3
Ironmonger Row B7
Jacob St E9
Jamaica Rd E8
James St C3
James St D5
Jermyn St D4
Jockey's Fields C5
John Carpenter St D6
John Fisher St D9
John Islip St F4
John St B5
Johnathan St F5
Judd St B5
Kennings Way F6
Kennington F6
Kennington La F6
Kennington Park Rd F6
Kennington Rd E6/F6
Kensington Gardens D1
Kensington Gore E1
Kensington Rd E1
Keyworth St E6
King Charles St E5
King St D5
King William St C7
Kingley St C4
King's Cross A5
King's Cross Rd B5
King's Cross St Pancras A5
King's Rd F2
Kingsland Rd B8
Kingsway C5
Kinnerton St E3
Kipling St E7
Knightsbridge E2
Lamb St C8
Lambeth Bridge F5
Lambeth High St F5
Lambeth North E6
Lambeth Palace E5
Lambeth Palace Rd E5
Lambeth Rd E6
Lambeth Walk F5
Lamb's Conduit St C5
Lancaster Gate D1
Lancaster Pl D5
Lancaster St E6
Lancaster Terr D1
Langham Pl C3
Lant St E7
Leadenhall St C8
Leake St E5
Leather La C6
Leathermarket St E8
Leicester Sq D4
Leicester St D4
Leonard St B7
Leroy St E8
Lever St B7
Lexington St D4
Lidlington Pl A4
Lime St D8
Lincoln's Inn Fields C5
Lindsey St C6
Lisle St D4
Lisson Gr B1
Lisson St C2
Liverpool St C8
Liverpool St C8
Lloyd Baker St B6
Lloyd Sq B6
Lodge Rd B2
Lollard St F6
Lombard St C7
London Aquarium E5
London Bridge D7
London Bridge Hospital D7
London City Hall D8
London Dungeon D7
London Film Mus E5
London Guildhall Univ C7
London Rd E6
London St C1
London Transport Museum D5
London Wall C7
London-Eye E5
Long Acre D5
Long La C6
Long La E7
Longford St B3
Lord's Cricket Gd (MCC & Middlesex CCC) B1
Lower Belgrave St E3
Lower Grosvenor Pl E3
Lower Marsh E6
Lower Sloane St F3
Lower Thames St D7
Lowndes St E3
Ludgate Circus C6
Ludgate Hill C6
Luxborough St C3
Lyall St E3
Macclesfield Rd B7
Madame Tussaud's B3
Maddox St D3
Malet St C4
Maltby St E8
Manchester Sq C3
Manchester St C3
Manciple St E7
Mandela Way F8
Mandeville Pl C3
Mansell St D8
Mansion House C7
Mansion House D7
Maple St C4
Marble Arch C2
Marble Arch D2
Marchmont St B5
Margaret St C4
Margery St B6
Mark La D8
Marlborough Rd D4
Marshall St C4
Marshalsea Rd E7
Marsham St E4
Marylebone B2
Marylebone High St C3
Marylebone La C3
Marylebone Rd B3/C2
Marylebone St C3
Mecklenburgh Sq B5
Middle Temple La C6
Middlesex St (Petticoat La) C8
Midland Rd A4
Millbank F5
Milner St F2
Minories C8
Monck St E4
Monkton St F6
Monmouth St C5
Montagu Pl C2
Montagu Sq C2
Montagu St C5
Montague Pl C4
Montpelier St E2
Montpelier Walk E2
Monument D7
Monument St D7
Monument, The D7
Moor La C7
Moorfields C7
Moorfields Eye Hospital B7
Moorgate C7
Moorgate C7
Moreland St B6
Morley St E6
Mortimer St C4
Mossop St F2
Mount Pleasant B6
Mount St D3
Murray Gr A7
Mus of Gdn History E5
Museum of London C7
Museum St C5
Myddelton Sq B6
Myddelton St B6
National Film Theatre D5
National Gallery D4
National Hospital B5
National Portrait Gallery D4
Natural History Museum E1
Neal St C5
Nelson's Column D5
Neville St F1
New Bond St C3/D3
New Bridge St C6
New Cavendish St C3
New Change C7
New Fetter La C6
New Inn Yard B8
New Kent Rd F7
New North Rd A7
New Oxford St C4
New Scotland Yard E4
New Sq C5
Newburn St F5
Newgate St C6
Newington Butts F6
Newington Cswy E7
Newton St C5
Nile St B7
Noble St C7
Noel St C4
Norfolk Cres C2
Norfolk Sq C1
North Audley St D3
North Carriage Dr E2
North Cres C4
North Ride D2
North Row D3
North Wharf Rd C1
Northampton Sq B6
Northington St B5
Northumberland Ave D5
Norton Folgate C8
Nottingham Pl C3
Old Bailey C6
Old Broad St C7
Old Brompton Rd F1
Old Compton St C4
Old County Hall E5
Old Gloucester St C5
Old Jamaica Rd E9
Old Kent Rd F8
Old King Edward St C7
Old Marylebone Rd C2
Old Montague St C9
Old Nichol St B8
Old Paradise St F5
Old Spitalfields Mkt C8
Old St B7
Old St B7
Old Vic E6
Onslow Gdns F1
Onslow Sq F1
Ontario St E6
Open Air Theatre B3
Operating Theatre Museum D7
Orange St D4
Orchard St C3
Ossulston St A4
Outer Circle B2
Ovington Sq E2
Oxford Circus C4
Oxford St C3/C4
Paddington C1
Paddington Green Hospital C1
Paddington St C3
Page's Walk E8
Palace St E4
Pall Mall D4
Pall Mall East D4
Pancras Rd A5
Panton St D4
Paris Gdn D6
Park Cres B3
Park La D3
Park Rd B2
Park St D3
Park St D7
Parker St C5
Parliament Sq E5
Parliament St E5
Paternoster Sq C6
Paul St B7
Pear Tree St B6
Pelham Cres F2
Pelham St F1
Penfold St C2
Penton Pl F6
Penton Rise B5
Penton St A6
Pentonville Rd A5/A6
Percival St B6
Petticoat La (Middlesex St) C8
Petty France E4
Phoenix Pl B5
Phoenix Rd A4
Photo Gallery D4
Piccadilly D3
Piccadilly Circus D4
Pilgrimage St E7
Pimlico F4
Pimlico Rd F3
Pitfield St B8
Pollock's Toy Mus C4
Polygon Rd A4
Pont St E2
Porchester Pl C2
Portland Pl C3
Portman Mews C3
Portman Sq C3
Portman St C2
Portugal St C5
Poultry C7
Praed St C1
Primrose St C8
Prince Consort Rd E1
Prince's Gdns E1
Princes St C7
Procter St C5
Provost St B7
Quaker St B8
Queen Anne St C3
Queen Elizabeth Hall D5
Queen Elizabeth St E8
Queen Sq B5
Queen St D7
Queen Street Pl D7
Queen Victoria St D6
Queens Gallery E4
Queensberry Pl F1
Quilter St B9
Radnor St B7
Rathbone Pl C4
Rawlings St F2
Rawstorne St B6
Red Lion Sq C5
Red Lion St C5
Redchurch St B8
Redcross Way D7
Reedworth St F6
Regency St F4
Regent Sq B5
Regent St C4
Regent's Park B3
Richmond Terr E5
Ridgmount St C4
Riley Rd E8
Rivington St B8
Robert St B3
Rochester Row F4
Rockingham St E7
Rodney Rd F7
Rolls Rd F8
Ropemaker St C7
Rosebery Ave B6
Rossmore Rd B2
Rothsay St E8
Rotten Row E2
Roupell St D6
Royal Acad of Arts D4
Royal Academy of Dramatic Art B4
Royal Acad of Music B3
Royal Albert Hall E1
Royal Brompton Hospital F1, F2
Royal Coll of Nursing C3
Royal Coll of Surgeons C5
Royal Festival Hall D5
Royal London Hosital for Integrated Medicine C5
Royal Marsden Hospital F1
Royal National Theatre D6
Royal National Throat, Nose and Ear Hospital B5
Royal Opera House D5
Rushworth St E6
Russell Sq B4
Russell Square B5
Rutland Gate E2
Sackville St D4
Sadlers Wells B6
Saffron Hill C6
St Alban's St D4
St Andrew St C6
St Barnabas St F3
St Bartholomew's Hospital C6
St Botolph St C8
St Bride St C6
St George's Dr F4
St George's Rd E6
St George's Sq F4
St Giles High St C4
St James's Palace D4
St James's Park E4
St James's St D4
St John St B6
St John's Wood Rd B1
St Margaret St E5
St Mark's Hosp B6
St Martin's La D5
St Martin's Le Grand C7
St Mary Axe C8
St Mary's Hosp C1
St Pancras Int A5
St Paul's C7
St Paul's Cath C7
St Paul's Churchyard C6
St Thomas' Hosp E5
St Thomas St D7
Sale Pl C2
Sancroft St F5
Savile Row D4
Savoy Pl D5
Savoy St D5
School of Hygiene & Tropical Medicine C4
Science Mus E1
Scrutton St B8
Sekforde St B6
Serpentine Gallery E1
Serpentine Rd D2
Seven Dials C5
Seward St B6

Seymour Pl C2
Seymour St C2
Shad Thames D8/E8
Shaftesbury Ave D4
Shakespeare's Globe Theatre 🎭 D7
Shepherd Market D3
Sherwood St D4
Shoe La C6
Shoreditch High St B8
Shoreditch High St ⊖ B8
Shorts Gdns C5
Shouldham St C2
Sidmouth St B5
Silk St C7
Sir John Soane's Museum 🏛 C5
Skinner St B6
Sloane Ave F2
Sloane Sq F2
Sloane Square ⊖ F3
Sloane St E2
Snow Hill C6
Soho Sq C4
Somerset House 🏛 D5
South Audley St D3
South Carriage Dr E2
South Eaton Pl F3
South Kensington ⊖ F1
South Molton St C3
South Parade F1
South Pl C7
South St D3
South Terr F2
South Wharf Rd C1
Southampton Row C5
Southampton St D5
Southwark ⊖ D6
Southwark Bridge D7
Southwark Bridge Rd D7
Southwark Cath ✝ D7
Southwark Park Rd F8
Southwark St D7
Spa Rd E8
Speakers' Corner D2
Spencer St B6
Spital Sq C8
Spring St C1
Stamford St D6
Stanhope St B4
Stanhope Terr D1
Stephenson Way B4
Stock Exchange C6
Stoney St D7
Strand C5
Strathearn Pl D2
Stratton St D3
Sumner St D6
Sussex Gdns C1
Sussex Pl C1
Sussex Sq D1
Sussex St F3
Sutton's Way B7
Swan St E7
Swanfield St B8
Swinton St B5
Sydney Pl F1
Sydney St F2
Tabard St E7
Tabernacle St B7
Tachbrook St F4
Tanner St E8
Tate Britain 🏛 F5
Tate Modern 🏛 D7
Tavistock Pl B5
Tavistock Sq B4
Tea & Coffee Mus 🏛 D7
Temple ⊖ D6
Temple Ave D6
Temple Pl D5
Terminus Pl E3
Thayer St C3
The Barbican Centre for Arts C7
The Cut E6
The Mall E4
Theobald's Rd C5
Thorney St F5
Threadneedle St C7
Throgmorton St C7
Thurloe Pl F1
Thurloe Sq F2
Tonbridge St B5
Tooley St D8
Torrington Pl B4
Tothill St E4
Tottenham Court Rd B4
Tottenham Ct Rd ⊖ C4
Tottenham St C4
Tower Bridge ✦ D8
Tower Bridge App D8
Tower Bridge Rd E8
Tower Hill D8
Tower Hill ⊖ D8
Tower of London, The 🏰 D8
Toynbee St C8
Trafalgar Square D4
Trinity Sq D8
Trinity St E7
Trocadero Centre D4
Tudor St D6
Turin St B9
Turnmill St C6
Tyers St F5
Ufford St E6
Union St D6
Univ Coll Hospl H B4
University of London C4
Univ of Westminster C3
University St B4
Upper Belgrave St E3
Upper Berkeley St C2
Upper Brook St D3
Upper Grosvenor St D3
Upper Ground D6
Upper Montague St C2
Upper St Martin's La D5
Upper Thames St D7
Upper Wimpole St C3
Upper Woburn Pl B4
Vauxhall Bridge Rd F4
Vauxhall St F5
Vere St C3
Vernon Pl C5
Vestry St B7
Victoria ≹⊖ E3
Victoria and Albert Mus 🏛 E1
Victoria Coach Station F3
Victoria Embankment D5
Victoria Pl Sh Ctr F3
Victoria St E4
Villiers St D5
Vincent Sq F4
Vinopolis City of Wine 🏛 D7
Virginia Rd B8
Wakley St B6
Walbrook C7
Walcot Sq F6
Wallace Collection 🏛 C3
Walnut Tree Walk F6
Walton St F2
Walworth Rd F7
Wardour St C4/D4
Warner St B6
Warren St ⊖ B4
Warren St B4
Warwick Sq F4
Warwick Way F3
Waterloo ≹⊖ E6
Waterloo Bridge D5
Waterloo East ≹ D6
Waterloo Rd E6
Watling St C7
Webber St E6
Welbeck St C3
Wellington Arch ✦ E3
Wellington Mus 🏛 E3
Wellington Rd B2
Wellington Row B9
Wells St C4
Wenlock St A7
Wentworth St C8
West Carriage Dr D2
West Smithfield C6
West Sq E6
Westbourne St D1
Westbourne Terr C1
Westminster ⊖ E5
Westminster Abbey ✝ E5
Westminster Bridge E5
Westminster Bridge Rd E6
Westminster Cathedral (RC) ✝ E4
Westminster City Hall E4
Westminster Hall 🏛 E5
Weston St E7
Weymouth St C3
Wharf Rd A7
Wharton St B5
Whitcomb St D4
White Cube 🏛 B8
White Lion Hill D6
White Lion St A6
Whitechapel Rd C9
Whitecross St B7
Whitefriars St C6
Whitehall D5
Whitehall Pl D5
Wigmore Hall C3
Wigmore St C3
William IV St D5
Willow Walk F8
Wilmington Sq B6
Wilson St C7
Wilton Cres E3
Wilton Rd F4
Wimpole St C3
Winchester St F3
Wincott St F6
Windmill Walk D6
Woburn Pl B5
Woburn Sq B4
Wood St C7
Woodbridge St B6
Wootton St D6
Wormwood St C8
Worship St B7
Wren St B5
Wynyatt St B6
York Rd E5
York St C2
York Terrace East B3
York Terrace West B3
York Way A5


## Luton 342


Adelaide St B1
Albert Rd C2
Alma St B2
Alton Rd C3
Anthony Gdns C1
Arndale Ctr B2
Arthur St C2
Ashburnham Rd B1
Ashton Rd C2
Avondale Rd A1
Back St A2
Bailey St C3
Baker St C2
Biscot Rd A1
Bolton Rd B3
Boyle Cl A2
Brantwood Rd B1
Bretts Mead C1
Bridge St B2
Brook St A1
Brunswick St A3
Burr St A3
Bury Park Rd A1
Bute St B2
Buxton Rd B2
Cambridge St C3
Cardiff Grove B1
Cardiff Rd B1
Cardigan St A2
Castle St B2/C2
Chapel St C2
Charles St A3
Chase St C2
Cheapside B2
Chequer St C3
Chiltern Rise C1
Church St B2/B3
Cinema 🎦 A2
Cobden St A3
Collingdon St A1
Community Ctr C3
Concorde Ave A3
Corncastle Rd C1
Cowper St C2
Crawley Green Rd B3
Crawley Rd A1
Crescent Rise A3
Crescent Rd A3
Cromwell Rd A1
Cross St A2
Crown Court B2
Cumberland St B2
Cutenhoe Rd C3
Dallow Rd B1
Downs Rd B1
Dudley St A2
Duke St A2
Dumfries St B1
Dunstable Place B2
Dunstable Rd A1/B1
Edward St A3
Elizabeth St C2
Essex Cl C3
Farley Hill C1
Farley Lodge C1
Flowers Way B2
Francis St A1
Frederick St A2
Galaxy L Complex A2
George St B2
George St West B2
Gillam St A3
Gordon St B2
Grove Rd B1
Guildford St A2
Haddon Rd A3
Harcourt St C2
Hart Hill Drive A3
Hart Hill Lane A3
Hartley Rd A3
Hastings St B2
Hat Factory, The 🎭 B2
Hatters Way A1
Havelock Rd A2
Hibbert St C2
High Town Rd A3
Highbury Rd A1
Hightown Community Sports & Arts Ctr A3
Hillary Cres C1
Hillborough Rd C1
Hitchin Rd A3
Holly St C2
Holm C1
Hucklesby Way A2
Hunts Cl C1
Information Ctr ℹ B2
Inkerman St A2
John St B2
Jubilee St A3
Kelvin Cl C2
King St B2
Kingsland Rd C3
Latimer Rd C2
Lawn Gdns C2
Lea Rd B3
Library B2
Library Rd B2
Liverpool Rd B1
London Rd C2
Luton Station ≹ A2
Lyndhurst Rd B1
Magistrates Court B2
Manchester St B2
Manor Rd B3
May St C3
Meyrick Ave C1
Midland Rd A2
Mill St A2
Milton Rd B1
Moor St A1
Moor, The A1
Moorland Gdns A2
Moulton Rise A3
Museum & Art Gallery 🏛🏛 A2
Napier Rd B1
New Bedford Rd A1
New Town St C2
North St A3
Old Bedford Rd A2
Old Orchard C2
Osbourne Rd C3
Oxen Rd A3
Park Sq B2
Park St B3/C3
Park St West B2
Park Viaduct B3
Parkland Drive C1
Police Station 🚓 B1
Pomfret Ave A3
Pondwicks Rd B3
Post Office [PO] A1/A2/B2/C3
Power Court B3
Princess St B1
Red Rails C1
Regent St B2
Reginald St A2
Rothesay Rd B1
Russell Rise C1
Russell St C1
St Ann's Rd B3
St George's 🎭 B2
St Mary's ⛪ B3
St Marys Rd B3
St Paul's Rd C2
St Saviour's Cres C1
Salisbury Rd B1
Seymour Ave C3
Seymour Rd C3
Silver St B2
South Rd C2
Stanley St B1
Station Rd A2
Stockwood Cres C2
Stockwood Park C1
Strathmore Ave C2
Stuart St B2
Studley Rd A1
Surrey St C3
Sutherland Place C1
Tavistock St C2
Taylor St A3
Telford Way A1
Tennyson Rd C2
Tenzing Grove C1
The Cross Way C1
The Larches A2
Thistle Rd B3
Town Hall B2
Townsley Cl C2
UK Ctr for Carnival Arts ✦ B3
Union St B2
Univ of Bedfordshire B3
Upper George St B2
Vicarage St B3
Villa Rd A2
Waldeck Rd A1
Wellington St B1/B2
Wenlock St A2
Whitby Rd A1
Whitehill Ave C1
William St A2
Wilsden Ave C1
Windmill Rd B3
Windsor St C2
Winsdon Rd B1
York St A3


## Macclesfield 343


108 Steps B2
Abbey Rd A1
Alton Dr A3
Armett St C1
Athey St B1
Bank St C3
Barber St C3
Barton St C1
Beech La A2
Beswick St B1
Black La A2
Black Rd C3
Blakelow Gardens C3
Blakelow Rd C3
Bond St B1/C1
Bread St C1
Bridge St B1
Brock St A2
Brocklehurst Ave A3
Brook St B3
Brookfield La B3
Brough St West C1
Brown St C1
Brynton Rd A2
Buckley St C2
Bus Station B2
Buxton Rd B3
Byrons St C2
Canal St B3
Carlsbrook Ave A3
Castle St B2
Catherine St B1
Cemetery A1
Chadwick Terr A3
Chapel St C2
Charlotte St B2
Chester Rd B1
Chestergate B1
Christ Church ⛪ B1
Churchill Way B2
Coare St A1
Commercial Rd B2
Conway Cres A3
Copper St C3
Cottage St B1
Court A2
Court B2
Crematorium A1
Crew Ave A3
Crompton Rd B1/C1
Cross St C2
Crossall St C1
Cumberland St A1/B1
Dale St B3
Duke St B2
Eastgate B3
Exchange St B2
Fence Ave B3
Fence Ave Ind Est A3
Flint St B3
Foden St A2
Fountain St B3
Gateway Gallery ✦ B1
Garden St A3
Gas Rd B2
George St B2
Glegg St B3
Golf Course C3
Goodall St B3
Grange Rd C1
Great King St B1
Green St B3
Grosvenor Sh Ctr B2
Gunco La C3
Half St C2
Hallefield Rd B3
Hatton St C1
Hawthorn Way A3
Heapy St C3
Henderson St B1
Heritage Ctr & Silk Museum 🏛 B2
Hibel Rd A2
High St C2
Hobson St C2
Hollins Rd C3
Hope St West B1
Horseshoe Dr B1
Hurdsfield Rd A3
Information Ctr ℹ B2
James St C2
Jodrell St B3
John St C2
Jordangate A2
King Edward St B2
King George's Field C3
King St B2
King's School A1
Knight Pool C3
Knight St C3
Lansdowne St A3
Library B2
Lime Gr B3
Little Theatre 🎭 C2
Loney St B1
Longacre St B1
Lord St C2
Lowe St C2
Lowerfield Rd A3
Lyon St B1
Macclesfield College C1
Macclesfield Sta ≹ B2
Marina B3
Market B2
Market Pl B2
Masons La A3
Mill La C2
Mill Rd C2
Mill St B2
Moran Rd C1
New Hall St A2
Newton St C1
Nicholson Ave A3
Nicholson Cl A3
Northgate Ave A2
Old Mill La C2
Paradise Mill 🏛 C2
Paradise St B1
Park Green B2
Park La C1
Park Rd C1
Park St C2
Park Vale Rd C1
Parr St B1
Peel St C2
Percyvale St A3
Peter St C1
Pickford St B2
Pierce St B1
Pinfold St B1
Pitt St C2
Police Station 🚓 B2
Pool St C2
Poplar Rd C2
Post Office [PO] B1/B2/B3
Pownall St A2
Prestbury Rd A1/B1
Queen Victoria St B2
Queen's Ave A3
Registrar B2
Richmond Hill C3
Riseley St B1
Roan Ct B3
Roe St B2
Rowan Way A3
Ryle St C2
Ryle's Park Rd C1
St George's St C2
St Michael's ⛪ B2
Samuel St B2
Saville St C3
Shaw St B1
Slater St C1
Snow Hill C3
South Park C1
Spring Gdns A2
Statham St C2
Station St A2
Steeple St A3
Sunderland St B2
Superstore A1/A2/C2
Swettenham St B3
The Silk Rd A2/B2
Thistleton Cl C2
Thorp St B2
Town Hall B2
Townley St B2
Turnock St C3
Union Rd B3
Union St B2
Victoria Park B3
Vincent St C2
Waters Green B2
Waterside C2
West Bond St B1
West Park A1
West Park Museum 🏛 A1
Westbrook Dr A1
Westminster Rd A1
Whalley Hayes B1
Windmill St C3
Withyfold Dr A2
York St B3


## Maidstone 343


Albion Pl B3
All Saints ⛪ B2
Allen St A3
Amphitheatre ✦ C2
Archbishop's Pal 🏛 B2
Bank St B2
Barker Rd C2
Barton Rd C3
Beaconsfield Rd C1
Bedford Pl B1
Bentlif Art Gallery 🏛 B2
Bishops Way B2
Bluett St A3
Bower La C1
Bower Mount Rd B1
Bower Pl C1
Bower St B1
Bowling Alley B3
Boxley Rd A3
Brenchley Gardens A2
Brewer St A3
Broadway B2
Brunswick St C3
Buckland Hill A1
Buckland Rd B1
Bus Station B3
Campbell Rd C3
Carriage Museum 🏛 B2
Church Rd C1
Church St B3
Cinema 🎦 C2
College Ave C2
College Rd C2
Collis Memorial Gdn C3
Cornwallis Rd B1
Corpus Christi Hall B2
County Hall A2
County Rd A3
Crompton Gdns C3
Crown & County Courts B2
Curzon Rd A3
Dixon Cl C2
Douglas Rd C1
Earl St B2
Eccleston Rd C2
Fairmeadow B2
Fisher St A2
Florence Rd C1
Foley St A3
Foster St C3
Fremlin Walk Sh Ctr B2
Gabriel's Hill B3
George St C3
Grecian St A3
Hardy St A3
Hart St C2
Hastings Rd C3
Hayle Rd C3
Hazlitt Theatre 🎭 B2
Heathorn St A3
Hedley St A3
High St B2
HM Prison A3
Holland Rd A3
Hope St A2
Information Ctr ℹ B2
James St A3
James Whatman Way A2
Jeffrey St A3
Kent County Council Offices A2
King Edward Rd C2
King St B3
Kingsley Rd C3
Knightrider St B3
Launder Way C1
Lesley Pl A1
Library B2
Little Buckland Ave A1
Lockmeadow Leisure Complex C2
London Rd B1
Lower Boxley Rd A2
Lower Fant Rd C1
Magistrates Court B3
Maidstone Barracks Station ≹ A1
Maidstone Borough Council Offices B1
Maidstone East Sta ≹ A2
Maidstone Museum 🏛 B2
Maidstone West Sta ≹ B2
Market C2
Market Buildings B2
Marsham St B3
Medway St B2
Medway Trading Est C2
Melville Rd C3
Mill St B2
Millennium Bridge C2
Mote Rd B3
Muir Rd C3
Old Tovil Rd C2
Palace Ave B3
Perryfield St A2
Police Station 🚓 B3
Post Office [PO] A2/B2/B3/C3
Priory Rd C3
Prospect Pl C1
Pudding La B2
Queen Anne Rd B3
Queens Rd A1
Randall St A2
Rawdon Rd C3
Reginald Rd C1
Rock Pl B1
Rocky Hill B1
Romney Pl B3
Rose Yard B2
Rowland Cl C1
Royal Engineers' Rd A2
Royal Star Arcade B2
St Annes Ct B1
St Faith's St B2
St Luke's Rd A3
St Peter's Br B2
St Peter St B2
St Philip's Ave C3
Salisbury Rd A3
Sandling Rd A2
Scott St A2
Scrubs La B1
Sheal's Cres C3
Somerfield La B1
Somerfield Rd B1
Staceys St A2
Station Rd A2
Superstore A1/B2/B3
Terrace Rd B1
The Mall B3
The Somerfield Hospital H A1
Tonbridge Rd C1
Tovil Rd C2
Town Hall B2
Trinity Park B3
Tufton St B3
Union St B3
Upper Fant Rd C1
Upper Stone St C3
Victoria St B1
Visitor Ctr A1
Warwick Pl B1
Wat Tyler Way B3
Waterloo St C3
Waterlow Rd A3
Week St B2
Well Rd A3
Westree Rd C1
Wharf Rd C1
Whatman Park A1
Wheeler St A3
Whitchurch Cl B1
Woodville Rd C3
Wyatt St B3
Wyke Manor Rd B3


## Manchester 343


Adair St B6
Addington St A5
Adelphi St A1
Air & Space Gallery 🏛 B2
Albert Sq B3
Albion St C3
AMC Great Northern 🎦 B3
Ancoats Gr B6
Ancoats Gr North B6
Angela St C2
Aquatic Ctr C4
Ardwick Green Park C5
Ardwick Green North C5
Ardwick Green South C5
Arlington St A2
Artillery St B3
Arundel St C2
Atherton St B2
Atkinson St B3
Aytoun St B4
Back Piccadilly A4
Baird St B5
Balloon St A4
Bank Pl A1
Baring St B5
Barrack St C1
Barrow St A1
BBC TV Studios C4
Bendix St A5
Bengal St A5
Berry St C5
Blackfriars Rd A3
Blackfriars St A3
Blantyre St C2
Bloom St B4
Blossom St A5
Boad St B5
Bombay St B4
Booth St A3
Booth St B4
Bootle St B3
Brazennose St B3
Brewer St A5
Bridge St A3
Bridgewater Hall B3
Bridgewater Pl A4
Bridgewater St B2
Brook St C4
Brotherton Dr A2
Brown St A3
Brown St B4
Brunswick St C6
Brydon Ave C6
Buddhist Ctr A4
Bury St A2
Bus & Coach Station B4
Bus Station B4
Butler St A6
Buxton St C5
Byrom St B3
Cable St A5
Calder St B1
Cambridge St C3/C4
Camp St B3
Canal St B4
Cannon St A1
Cannon St A4
Cardroom Rd A6
Carruthers St A6
Castle St C2
Cateaton St A3
Cathedral ✝ A3
Cathedral St A3
Cavendish St C4
Chapel St A1/A3
Chapeltown St B5
Charles St C4
Charlotte St B4
Chatham St B4
Cheapside A3
Chepstow St B3
Chester Rd C1/C2
Chester St C4
Chetham's (Dept Store) A3
China La B5
Chippenham Rd A6
Chorlton Rd C2
Chorlton St B4
Church St A2
Church St A4
City Park A4
City Rd C3
Civil Justice Ctr B2
Cleminson St A2
Clowes St A3
College Land A3
Coll of Adult Ed C4
Collier St B2
Commercial St C3
Conference Ctr C4
Cooper St B4
Copperas St A4
Cornbrook 🚊 C1
Cornell St A5
Cornerhouse 🎦 C4
Corporation St A4
Cotter St C6
Cotton St A5
Cow La B1
Cross St B3
Crown Court B4
Crown St C2
Cube Gallery 🏛 B4
Dalberg St C6
Dale St A4/B5
Dancehouse, The 🎭 C4
Dantzic St A4
Dark La C6
Dawson St C2
Dean St A5
Deansgate A3/B3
Deansgate Station ≹ C3
Dolphin St C6
Downing St C5
Ducie St B5
Duke Pl B2
Duke St B2
Durling St C6
East Ordsall La A2/B1
Edge St A4
Egerton St C2
Ellesmere St C1
Everard St C1
Every St B6
Fairfield St B5
Faulkner St B4
Fennel St A3
Ford St A2
Ford St C6
Fountain St B4
Frederick St A2
Gartside St B2
Gaythorne St A1
George Leigh St A5
George St A1
George St B4
G-Mex 🚊 C3
Goadsby St A4
Gore St A2
Goulden St A5
Granada TV Ctr B2
Granby Row B4
Gravel St A3
Great Ancoats St A5
Great Bridgewater St B3
Great George St A1
Great Jackson St C2
Great Marlborough St C4
Greengate A3
Green Room, The 🎭 C4
Grosvenor St C5
Gun St A5
Hadrian Ave B6
Hall St B3
Hampson St B1
Hanover St A4
Hanworth Cl C5
Hardman St B3
Harkness St C6
Harrison St B6
Hart St B4
Helmet St B6
Henry St A5
Heyrod St B6
High St A4
Higher Ardwick C6
Hilton St A4/A5
Holland St A6
Hood St A5
Hope St B1
Hope St B4
Houldsworth St A5
Hoyle St C6
Hulme Hall Rd C1
Hulme St A1
Hulme St C3
Hyde Rd C6
Information Ctr ℹ B3
Irwell St A2
Islington St A2
Jackson Cr C2
Jackson's Row B3
James St A1
Jenner Cl C2
Jersey St A5
John Dalton St A1
John Dalton St B3
John Ryland's Library 🏛 B3
John St A2
Kennedy St B3
Kincardine Rd C5
King St A3
King St West A3
Law Courts B3
Laystall St B5
Lever St A5
Library B3
Linby St C2
Little Lever St A4
Liverpool Rd B2
Liverpool St B1
Lloyd St B3
Lockton Cl C5
London Rd B5
Long Millgate A3
Longacre St B6
Loom St A5
Lower Byrom St B2
Lower Mosley St B3
Lower Moss La C2
Lower Ormond St C4
Loxford La C4
Luna St A5
Major St B4
Manchester Arndale A4
Manchester Art Gallery 🏛 B4
Manchester Central Convension Complex B3
Manchester Metropolitan University B4/C4
Manchester Piccadilly Station ≹ B5
Manchester Technology Ctr C4
Mancunian Way C3
Manor St C5
Marble St A4
Market St A2
Market St A4
Market St 🚊 A4
Marsden St A3
Marshall St A5
Mayan Ave A2
Medlock St C3
Middlewood St B1
Miller St A4
Minshull St B4
Mosley St A4
Mosley St 🚊 B4
Mount St B3
Mulberry St B3
Murray St A5
Museum of Science & Industry (MOSI) 🏛 B2
Nathan Dr A2
Naval St A5
New Bailey St A2
New Elm Rd B2
New Islington A6
New Quay St B2
New Union St A6
Newgate St A4
Newton St A5
Nicholas St B4
North Western St C6
Oak St A4
Odeon 🎦 A4
Old Mill St A6
Oldfield Rd A1/C1
Oldham Rd A5
Oldham St A4
Opera House 🎭 B3
Ordsall La C1
Oxford Rd C4
Oxford Rd ≹ C4
Oxford St B4
Paddock St C6
Palace Theatre 🎭 B4
Pall Mall A3
Palmerston St B6
Park St A1
Parker St B4
Peak St B5
Penfield Cl C5
Peoples' History Museum 🏛 B2
Peru St A1
Peter St B3
Piccadilly A4
Piccadilly 🚊 B5
Piccadilly Gdns 🚊 B4
Piercy St A6
Poland St A5
Police Museum 🏛 A5
Police Station 🚓 B3/B5
Pollard St B6
Port St A5
Portland St B4
Portugal St East B5
Post Office [PO] A1/A4/A5/B3
Potato Wharf B2
Princess St B3/C4
Pritchard St C4
Quay St A2
Quay St B2
Queen St B3
Radium St A5
Redhill St A5
Regent Rd B1
Renold Theatre 🎭 A2
Retail Park A5
Rice St B2
Richmond St B4
River St C3
Roby St B5
Rodney St A6
Roman Fort 🏛 B2
Rosamond St A2
Royal Exchange 🎭 A3
Sackville St B4
St Andrew's St B6
St Ann St A3
St Ann's ⛪ A3
St George's Ave C1
St James St B4
St John St B3
St John's Cath (RC) ✝ A2
St Mary's ⛪ B3
St Mary's Gate A3
St Mary's Parsonage A3
St Peter's Sq 🚊 B3
St Stephen St A2
Salford Approach A3
Salford Central ≹ A2
Sheffield St B5
Shepley St B5
Sherratt St A5
Shudehill A4
Shudehill 🚊 A4
Sidney St C4
Silk St A5
Silver St B4
Skerry Cl C5
Snell St B6
South King St B3
Sparkle St B5
Spear St A4
Spring Gdns A4
Stanley St A2/B2
Station Approach B5
Store St B5
Swan St A4
Tariff St B5
Tatton St C1
Temperance St B6/C6
The Triangle A4
Thirsk St C6
Thomas St A4
Thompson St A5
Tib La B3
Tib St A4

Merthyr Tydfil • Middlesbrough • Milton Keynes • Newcastle upon Tyne • Newport • Newquay • Newtown 361


Town Hall (Manchester) . . . . . . . B3
Town Hall (Salford) . . . A2
Trafford St . . . . . . . . . C3
Travis St . . . . . . . . . . . B5
Trinity Way . . . . . . . . . A2
Turner St . . . . . . . . . . A4
Union St . . . . . . . . . . . C6
University of Manchester (Sackville Street Campus) . . . . . C5
Upper Brook St . . . . . . . C5
Upper Cleminson St . . A1
Upper Wharf St . . . . . . A1
Urbis Museum . . . . . . . A4
Vesta St . . . . . . . . . . . B6
Victoria . . . . . . . . . . . A4
Victoria Station . . . . . . A4
Victoria St . . . . . . . . . A3
Wadesdon Rd . . . . . . . C5
Water St . . . . . . . . . . . B2
Watson St . . . . . . . . . . B3
West Fleet St . . . . . . . . B1
West King St . . . . . . . . A2
West Mosley St . . . . . . B4
West Union St . . . . . . . B1
Weybridge Rd . . . . . . . A6
Whitworth St . . . . . . . . B4
Whitworth St West . . . C3
Wilburn St . . . . . . . . . . B1
William St . . . . . . . . . . A2
William St . . . . . . . . . . C6
Wilmott St . . . . . . . . . . C3
Windmill St . . . . . . . . . B3
Windsor Cr . . . . . . . . . A1
Withy Gr . . . . . . . . . . . A4
Woden St . . . . . . . . . . . C1
Wood St . . . . . . . . . . . . B3
Woodward St . . . . . . . . A6
Worrall St . . . . . . . . . . C1
Worsley St . . . . . . . . . . C2
York St . . . . . . . . . . . . B4
York St . . . . . . . . . . . . C2
York St . . . . . . . . . . . . C4

## Merthyr Tydfil
*Merthyr Tudful* 343

Aberdare Rd . . . . . . . . B2
Abermorlais Terr . . . . . B2
Alexandra Rd . . . . . . . A3
Alma St . . . . . . . . . . . . C3
Arfryn Pl . . . . . . . . . . . C3
Argyle St . . . . . . . . . . . C3
Avenue De Clichy . . . . C2
Bethesda St . . . . . . . . . B2
Bishops Gr . . . . . . . . . . A3
Brecon Rd . . . . . . . A1/B2
Briarmead . . . . . . . . . . A3
Bryn St . . . . . . . . . . . . C3
Bryntirion Rd . . . . B3/C3
Bus Station . . . . . . . . . B2
Caedraw Rd . . . . . . . . . C2
Cae Mari Dwn . . . . . . . B3
Castle Sq . . . . . . . . . . . A1
Castle St . . . . . . . . . . . . B2
Chapel . . . . . . . . . . . . . C2
Chapel Bank . . . . . . . . . B1
Church St . . . . . . . . . . . B3
Civic Ctr . . . . . . . . . . . . B2
Coedcae'r Ct . . . . . . . . C3
Court . . . . . . . . . . . . . . B3
Courts . . . . . . . . . . . . . B2
Court St . . . . . . . . . . . . C3
Cromwell St . . . . . . . . . B2
Cyfarthfa Castle School and Museum . . . . . A1
Cyfarthfa Ind Est . . . . . A1
Cyfarthfa Park . . . . . . . A1
Cyfarthfa Rd . . . . . . . . A1
Dane St . . . . . . . . . . . . A2
Dane Terr . . . . . . . . . . . A2
Danyparc . . . . . . . . . . . B3
Darren View . . . . . . . . A3
Dixon St . . . . . . . . . . . . B2
Dyke St . . . . . . . . . . . . C3
Dynevor St . . . . . . . . . . B2
Elwyn Dr . . . . . . . . . . . C3
Fire Station . . . . . . . . . B2
Fothergill St . . . . . . . . B3
Galonuchaf Rd . . . . . . A3
Garth St . . . . . . . . . . . . B2
Georgetown . . . . . . . . . B2
Grawen Terr . . . . . . . . . A2
Grove Pk . . . . . . . . . . . A2
Gurnos Rd . . . . . . . . . . A2
Gwaelodygarth Rd A2/A3
Gwaunfarren Gr . . . . . . A3
Gwaunfarren Rd . . . . . A3
Gwendoline St . . . . . . . A3
Hampton St . . . . . . . . . C3
Hanover St . . . . . . . . . . A2
Heol S O Davies . . . . . . B1
Heol-Gerrig . . . . . . . . . B1
Highland View . . . . . . . C3
High St . . . . A3/B2/B3/C2
Howell Cl . . . . . . . . . . . B1
Information Ctr . . . . . . B2
Jackson's Bridge . . . . . B2
James St . . . . . . . . . . . C3
John St . . . . . . . . . . . . B3
Joseph Parry's Cott . . . B2
Lancaster St . . . . . . . . A2
Library . . . . . . . . . . . . . B2
Llewellyn St . . . . . . . . A2
Llwyfen St . . . . . . . . . . B2
Llwyn Berry . . . . . . . . . B1
Llwyn Dic Penderyn . . . B1
Llwyn-y-Gelynen . . . . . C1
Lower Thomas St . . . . . B3
Market . . . . . . . . . . . . . C2
Mary St . . . . . . . . . . . . C3
Masonic St . . . . . . . . . . C2
Merthyr RFC . . . . . . . . . C2
Merthyr College . . . . . . B2
Merthyr Town FC . . . . . B3
Merthyr Tydfil Leisure Village . . . . . . . . . . C3
Merthyr Tydfil Sta . . . . C3
Meyrick Villas . . . . . . . A2
Miniature Railway ✦ . . A1
Mount St . . . . . . . . . . . A2
Nantygwenith St . . . . . B1
Norman Terr . . . . . . . . B2
Oak Rd . . . . . . . . . . . . . A2
Old Cemetery . . . . . . . B3
Pandy Cl . . . . . . . . . . . . A1
Pantycelynen . . . . . . . . B1
Park Terr . . . . . . . . . . . B2
Penlan View . . . . . . . . . C2
Penry St . . . . . . . . . . . . B2
Pentwyn Villas . . . . . . . A2
Penyard Rd . . . . . . . . . B3
Penydarren Park . . . . . A3
Penydarren Rd . . . . . . . B3
Plymouth St . . . . . . . . . C3
Police Station . . . . . . . C2
Pont Marlais West . . . . B2
Post Office . . . . . A3/B2/C3
Quarry Row . . . . . . . . . B2
Queen's Rd . . . . . . . . . B3
Rees St . . . . . . . . . . . . C3
Rhydycar Link . . . . . . . C2
Riverside Park . . . . . . . A1
St David's . . . . . . . . . . B3
St Tydfil's . . . . . . . . . . C2
St Tydfil's Ave . . . . . . . C3
St Tydfil's Hospital (No A+E) . . . . . . . . . . B3
St Tydfil's Sq Sh Ctr . . C2
Saxon St . . . . . . . . . . . A2
School of Nursing . . . . A2
Seward St . . . . . . . . . . A3
Shiloh La . . . . . . . . . . . B3
Stone Circles . . . . . . . . B3
Stuart St . . . . . . . . . . . A2
Summerhill Pl . . . . . . . B3
Superstore . . . . . . . . . B3
Swan St . . . . . . . . . . . . C2
Swansea Rd . . . . . . . . . B1
Taff Glen View . . . . . . . C3
Taff Vale Ct . . . . . . . . . B3
Theatre Soar . . . . . . . . B2
The Grove . . . . . . . . . . A2
The Parade . . . . . . . . . B3
The Walk . . . . . . . . . . . B2
Thomastown Park . . . . B3
Tramroad La . . . . . . . . A3
Tramroad Side . . . . . . . B2
Tramroad Side North . . B3
Tramroad Side South . C3
Trevithick Gdns . . . . . . C3
Trevithick St . . . . . . . . A3
Tudor Terr . . . . . . . . . . B2
Twynyrodyn Rd . . . . . . C3
Union St . . . . . . . . . . . . B3
Upper Colliers Row . . . B1
Upper Thomas St . . . . . B3
Victoria St . . . . . . . . . . B2
Vue . . . . . . . . . . . . . . . C3
Vulcan Rd . . . . . . . . . . B2
Warlow St . . . . . . . . . . C3
Well St . . . . . . . . . . . . . A2
Welsh Assembly Government Offices . C2
Wern La . . . . . . . . . . . . C1
West Gr . . . . . . . . . . . . A2
William St . . . . . . . . . . C3
Yew St . . . . . . . . . . . . . C3
Ynysfach Engine Ho ✦ C2
Ynysfach Rd . . . . . . . . C2

## Middlesbrough 343

Abingdon Rd . . . . . . . . C3
Acklam Rd . . . . . . . . . . C1
Albert Park . . . . . . . . . C2
Albert Rd . . . . . . . . . . . B2
Albert Terr . . . . . . . . . . C2
Aubrey St . . . . . . . . . . . C3
Ayresome Gdns . . . . . . C2
Ayresome Green La . . . C1
Ayresome St . . . . . . . . . C2
Barton Rd . . . . . . . . . . . A1
Bilsdale Rd . . . . . . . . . . C3
Bishopton Rd . . . . . . . . C3
Borough Rd . . . . . . . B2/B3
Bowes Rd . . . . . . . . . . . A2
Breckon Hill Rd . . . . . . B3
Bridge St East . . . . . . . B3
Bridge St West . . . . . . . B2
Brighouse Rd . . . . . . . . A1
Burlam Rd . . . . . . . . . . C1
Bus Station . . . . . . . . . B2
Cannon Park . . . . . . . . B1
Cannon Park Way . . . . . B2
Cannon St . . . . . . . . . . B1
Captain Cook Sq . . . . . B2
Carlow St . . . . . . . . . . . C1
Castle Way . . . . . . . . . . C3
Chipchase Rd . . . . . . . . C2
Cineworld . . . . . . . . . . B3
Clairville Sports Stadium . . . . . . . . . . . . C3
Cleveland Ctr . . . . . . . . B2
Clive Rd . . . . . . . . . . . . C2
Commercial St . . . . . . . A2
Corporation Rd . . . . . . B2
Costa St . . . . . . . . . . . . C2
Council Offices . . . . . . B3
Crescent Rd . . . . . . . . . C2
Cumberland Rd . . . . . . C2
Depot Rd . . . . . . . . . . . A2
Derwent St . . . . . . . . . . B2
Devonshire Rd . . . . . . . C2
Diamond Rd . . . . . . . . . B2
Disabled Driver Test Circuit . . . . . . . . . . . . B1
Dorman Museum . . . . . C2
Douglas St . . . . . . . . . . B3
Eastbourne Rd . . . . . . . C2
Eden Rd . . . . . . . . . . . . C3
Enterprise Ctr . . . . . . . A2
Forty Foot Rd . . . . . . . A2
Gilkes St . . . . . . . . . . . B2
Gosford St . . . . . . . . . . A2
Grange Rd . . . . . . . . . . B2
Gresham Rd . . . . . . . . . B2
Harehills Rd . . . . . . . . . C1
Harford St . . . . . . . . . . C2
Hartington Rd . . . . . . . . B2
Haverton Hill Rd . . . . . A1
Hey Wood St . . . . . . . . . B1
Highfield Rd . . . . . . . . . C3
Hill St Ctr . . . . . . . . . . B2
Holwick Rd . . . . . . . . . . B1
Hutton Rd . . . . . . . . . . . C3
ICI Works . . . . . . . . . . . A1
Information Ctr . . . . . . B2
Lambton Rd . . . . . . . . . C3
Lancaster Rd . . . . . . . . C2
Lansdowne Rd . . . . . . . C3
Latham Rd . . . . . . . . . . C2
Law Courts . . . . . . . B2/B3
Lees Rd . . . . . . . . . . . . B2
Leeway . . . . . . . . . . . . . B3
Linthorpe Cemetery . . . C1
Linthorpe Rd . . . . . . . . B2
Lloyd St . . . . . . . . . . . . B2
Longford St . . . . . . . . . . C2
Longlands Rd . . . . . . . . C3
Lower East St . . . . . . . . A3
Lower Lake . . . . . . . . . . C3
Maldon Rd . . . . . . . . . . C1
Manor St . . . . . . . . . . . B2
Marsh St . . . . . . . . . . . . B2
Marton Rd . . . . . . . . . . B3
Middlehaven . . . . . . . . . B3
Middlesbrough By-Pass . . . . . . . . B2/C1
Middlesbrough Coll . . . B3
Middlesbrough L Park . B3
Middlesbrough Sta . . . B2
Middlesbrough Theatre . . . . . . . . . . . C2
Middletown Park . . . . . C2
MIMA . . . . . . . . . . . . . . B3
Mosque ✦ . . . . . . . . . . B2
Mosque ✦ . . . . . . . . . . C3
Mulgrave Rd . . . . . . . . . C2
North Ormesby Rd . . . . B3
Newport Bridge . . . . . . B1
Newport Bridge Approach Rd . . . . . . . B1
Newport Rd . . . . . . . . . B2
North Rd . . . . . . . . . . . B2
Northern Rd . . . . . . . . . C1
Outram St . . . . . . . . . . . B2
Oxford Rd . . . . . . . . . . . C2
Park La . . . . . . . . . . . . . C2
Park Rd North . . . . . . . C2
Park Rd South . . . . . . . C2
Park Vale Rd . . . . . . . . C3
Parliament Rd . . . . . . . B1
Police Station . . . . . . . A2
Port Clarence Rd . . . . . A3
Portman St . . . . . . . . . . B2
Post Office . . . . . B2/B3/C1/C2/C3
Princes Rd . . . . . . . . . . B2
Python . . . . . . . . . . . . . A2
Riverside Bsns Park . . . A2
Riverside Park Rd . . . . A1
Riverside Stadium (Middlesbrough FC) . B3
Rockliffe Rd . . . . . . . . . C2
Romaldkirk Rd . . . . . . . B1
Roman Rd . . . . . . . . . . . C2
Roseberry Rd . . . . . . . . C3
St Barnabas' Rd . . . . . . C2
St Paul's Rd . . . . . . . . . B2
Saltwells Rd . . . . . . . . . B3
Scott's Rd . . . . . . . . . . . A3
Seaton Carew Rd . . . . . A3
Shepherdson Way . . . . B3
Sikh Temple ✦ . . . . . . . B2
Snowdon Rd . . . . . . . . . A2
South West Ironmasters Park . . . . . B1
Southfield Rd . . . . . . . . B2
Southwell Rd . . . . . . . . C2
Springfield Rd . . . . . . . C1
Startforth Rd . . . . . . . . A2
Stockton Rd . . . . . . . . . C1
Stockton St . . . . . . . . . . A2
Surrey St . . . . . . . . . . . C2
Sycamore Rd . . . . . . . . C2
Synagogue ✦ . . . . . . . . C2
Tax Offices . . . . . . . . . B3
Tees Viaduct . . . . . . . . C1
Teessaurus Park . . . . . A2
Teesside Tertiary Coll C3
Temenos ✦ . . . . . . . . . B3
The Avenue . . . . . . . . . C2
The Crescent . . . . . . . . C2
Thornfield Rd . . . . . . . C1
Town Hall . . . . . . . . . . . B2
Transporter Bridge (Toll) . . . . . . . . . . . . A3
Union St . . . . . . . . . . . . B2
University of Teesside . B2
Upper Lake . . . . . . . . . C2
Valley Rd . . . . . . . . . . . C3
Ventnor Rd . . . . . . . . . C2
Victoria Rd . . . . . . . . . B2
Visitor Ctr ✦ . . . . . . . . A3
Vulcan St . . . . . . . . . . . A2
Warwick St . . . . . . . . . C2
Wellesley Rd . . . . . . . . B3
West Lane Hospital . . . C1
Westminster Rd . . . . . . C2
Wilson St . . . . . . . . . . . B2
Windward Way . . . . . . . B3
Woodlands Rd . . . . . . . B2
York Rd . . . . . . . . . . . . C3

## Milton Keynes 344

Abbey Way . . . . . . . . . . A1
Arbrook Ave . . . . . . . . . B1
Armourer Dr . . . . . . . . . A3
Arncliffe Dr . . . . . . . . . A1
Avebury . . . . . . . . . . . . C2
Avebury Blvd . . . . . . . . C2
Bankfield . . . . . . . . . . . B3
Bayard Ave . . . . . . . . . . A2
Belvedere . . . . . . . . . . . A2
Bishopstone . . . . . . . . . A1
Blundells Rd . . . . . . . . . A1
Boycott Ave . . . . . . . . . C2
Bradwell Comm Blvd . . B1
Bradwell Rd . . . . . . . . . C1
Bramble Ave . . . . . . . . . A2
Brearley Ave . . . . . . . . C2
Breckland . . . . . . . . . . . A1
Brill Place . . . . . . . . . . B1
Burnham Dr . . . . . . . . . B1
Bus Station . . . . . . . . . C1
Campbell Park . . . . . . . B3
Cantle Ave . . . . . . . . . . A3
Central Milton Keynes Shopping Area . . . . . B2
Century Ave . . . . . . . . . C2
Chaffron Way . . . . . . . . C3
Childs Way . . . . . . . . . . C1
Christ the Cornerstone . . . . . . . B2
Cineworld . . . . . . . . . . B2
Civic Offices . . . . . . . . B2
Cleavers Ave . . . . . . . . B2
Colesbourne Dr . . . . . . A3
Conniburrow Blvd . . . . B2
County Court . . . . . . . . B2
Currier Dr . . . . . . . . . . A2
Dansteed Way . A2/A3/B1
Deltic Ave . . . . . . . . . . B1
Downs Barn . . . . . . . . . A2
Downs Barn Blvd . . . . A3
Eaglestone . . . . . . . . . . C3
Eelbrook Ave . . . . . . . . B1
Elder Gate . . . . . . . . . . B1
Evans Gate . . . . . . . . . . C2
Fairford Cr . . . . . . . . . . A3
Falcon Ave . . . . . . . . . . B3
Fennel Dr . . . . . . . . . . . A2
Fishermead Blvd . . . . . C3
Food Ctr . . . . . . . . . . . . B3
Fulwoods Dr . . . . . . . . C3
Glazier Dr . . . . . . . . . . . A2
Glovers La . . . . . . . . . . A1
Grafton Gate . . . . . . . . C1
Grafton St . . . . . . . A1/C2
Gurnards Ave . . . . . . . . B3
Harrier Dr . . . . . . . . . . C3
Ibstone Ave . . . . . . . . . B1
Langcliffe Dr . . . . . . . . A1
Leisure Plaza . . . . . . . . C1
Leys Rd . . . . . . . . . . . . . C1
Library . . . . . . . . . . . . . B2
Linford Wood . . . . . . . . A2
Marlborough Gate . . . . B3
Marlborough St . . A2/B3
Mercers Dr . . . . . . . . . . A1
Midsummer . . . . . . . . . C2
Midsummer Blvd . . . . . B2
Milton Keynes Central . . . . . . . . . . . C1
Monks Way . . . . . . . . . . A1
Mullen Ave . . . . . . . . . . A3
Mullion Pl . . . . . . . . . . . C3
National Hockey Stadium . . . . . . . . . . . B1
Neath Hill . . . . . . . . . . . A3
North Elder . . . . . . . . . C1
North Grafton . . . . . . . B1
North Overgate . . . . . . A3
North Row . . . . . . . . . . B2
North Saxon . . . . . . . . . B2
North Secklow . . . . . . . B2
North Skeldon . . . . . . . A3
North Witan . . . . . . . . . B1
Oakley Gdns . . . . . . . . . A3
Oldbrook Blvd . . . . . . . C2
Open-Air Theatre . . . . B3
Overgate . . . . . . . . . . . . A3
Overstreet . . . . . . . . . . A3
Patriot Dr . . . . . . . . . . . B1
Pencarrow Pl . . . . . . . . B3
Penryn Ave . . . . . . . . . . B3
Perran Ave . . . . . . . . . . C3
Pitcher La . . . . . . . . . . . C1
Place Retail Park, The . C1
Point Ctr, The . . . . . . . B2
Police Station . . . . . . . B2
Portway . . . . . . . . . . . . B2
Post Office . . . . . A2/B2/C3
Precedent Dr . . . . . . . . B1
Quinton Dr . . . . . . . . . . B1
Ramsons Ave . . . . . . . . B2
Rockingham Dr . . . . . . A2
Rooksley . . . . . . . . . . . B1
Rooksley Retail Park . . C1
Saxon Gate . . . . . . . . . B2
Saxon St . . . . . . . . A1/C3
Secklow Gate . . . . . . . B2
Shackleton Pl . . . . . . . C2
Silbury Blvd . . . . . . . . . B2
Skeldon . . . . . . . . . . . . A3
South Grafton . . . . . . . C2
South Row . . . . . . . . . . C2
South Saxon . . . . . . . . . C2
South Secklow . . . . . . . B3
South Witan . . . . . . . . . C2
Springfield . . . . . . . . . . B3
Stanton Wood . . . . . . . A1
Stantonbury . . . . . . . . A1
Stantonbury L Ctr ✦ . . A1
Strudwick Dr . . . . . . . . C2
Sunrise Parkway . . . . . A2
Telephone Exchange . . C3
The Boundary . . . . . . . C3
Theatre & Art Gallery . . . . . . . . . . . B3
Tolcarne Ave . . . . . . . . C3
Towan Ave . . . . . . . . . . C3
Trueman Pl . . . . . . . . . . C2
Vauxhall . . . . . . . . . . . . A1
Winterhill Retail Park . C2
Witan Gate . . . . . . . . . . B2
X-Scape . . . . . . . . . . . . B3

## Newcastle upon Tyne 344

Albert St . . . . . . . . . . . B3
Argyle St . . . . . . . . . . . B3
Back New Bridge St . . . B3
BALTIC Ctr for Contemporary Art . . . C3
Barker St . . . . . . . . . . . A3
Barrack Rd . . . . . . . . . . B1
Bath La . . . . . . . . . . . . . B1
Bell's Court . . . . . . . . . B2
Bessie Surtees Ho ✦ . . C2
Bigg Market . . . . . . . . . C2
Biscuit Factory . . . . . . B3
Black Gate . . . . . . . . . . C2
Blackett St . . . . . . . . . . B2
Blandford Sq . . . . . . . . C1
Boating Lake . . . . . . . . A1
Boyd St . . . . . . . . . . . . . B3
Brandling Park . . . . . . . A2
Bus Station . . . . . . . . . B2
Buxton St . . . . . . . . . . . B3
Byron St . . . . . . . . . . . . A3
Camden St . . . . . . . . . . B2
Castle Keep . . . . . . . . . C2
Central . . . . . . . . . . . . . C1
Central Library . . . . . . . B2
Central Motorway . . . . B2
Chester St . . . . . . . . . . . A3
City Hall . . . . . . . . . . . . B2
City Rd . . . . . . . . . . B3/C3
City Walls ✦ . . . . . . . . C1
Civic Ctr . . . . . . . . . . . . A2
Claremont Rd . . . . . . . . A1
Clarence St . . . . . . . . . . B3
Clarence Walk . . . . . . . B3
Clayton St . . . . . . . . C1/B1
Clayton St West . . . . . . C1
Coach Station . . . . . . . C1
College St . . . . . . . . . . . B2
Collingwood St . . . . . . C2
Copland Terr . . . . . . . . B3
Coppice Way . . . . . . . . B3
Corporation St . . . . . . . B1
Courts . . . . . . . . . . . . . . C3
Crawhall Rd . . . . . . . . . B3
Dean St . . . . . . . . . . . . . C2
Discovery . . . . . . . . . . . C1
Dinsdale Pl . . . . . . . . . . A3
Dinsdale Rd . . . . . . . . . A3
Doncaster Rd . . . . . . . . A3
Durant Rd . . . . . . . . . . . B2
Eldon Sq . . . . . . . . . . . . B1
Eldon Sq Shopping Ctr B3
Ellison Pl . . . . . . . . . . . B2
Empire . . . . . . . . . . . . . B1
Eskdale Terr . . . . . . . . . A2
Eslington Terr . . . . . . . A2
Exhibition Park . . . . . . A1
Falconar St . . . . . . . . . . B3
Fenkle St . . . . . . . . . . . . C1
Forth Banks . . . . . . . . . C1
Forth St . . . . . . . . . . . . C1
Gallowgate . . . . . . . . . . B1
Gateshead Heritage @ St Mary's ✦ . . . . . . . C3
Gateshead Millennium Bridge . . . . . . . . . . . . C3
Gibson St . . . . . . . . . . . B3
Goldspink La . . . . . . . . A3
Grainger Market . . . . . B2
Grainger St . . . . . . . . . B2
Grantham Rd . . . . . . . . A3
Granville Rd . . . . . . . . . A3
Great North Mus:Hancock . . . . . . . A2
Grey St . . . . . . . . . . . . . B2
Groat Market . . . . . . . . C2
Guildhall . . . . . . . . . . . C2
Hancock St . . . . . . . . . . A2
Hanover St . . . . . . . . . . C2
Hatton Gallery . . . . . . . A1
Hawks Rd . . . . . . . . . . . C3
Haymarket . . . . . . . . . . B2
Heber St . . . . . . . . . . . . B1
Helmsley Rd . . . . . . . . . A3
High Bridge . . . . . . . . . B2
High Level Bridge . . . . C2
Hillgate . . . . . . . . . . . . C3
Howard St . . . . . . . . . . B3
Hutton Terr . . . . . . . . . A3
Information Ctr . . . . . . C3
Jesmond . . . . . . . . . . . A2
Jesmond Rd . . . . . . A2/A3
John Dobson St . . . . . . B2
John George Joicey Museum . . . . . . . . . . . C2
Jubilee Rd . . . . . . . . . . . B3
Kelvin Gr . . . . . . . . . . . A3
Kensington Terr . . . . . . A2
Laing Gallery . . . . . . . . B2
Lambton Rd . . . . . . . . . A2
Leazes Cr . . . . . . . . . . . B1
Leazes La . . . . . . . . . . . B1
Leazes Park . . . . . . . . . B1
Leazes Park Rd . . . . . . B1
Leazes Terr . . . . . . . . . B1
Live . . . . . . . . . . . . . . . C2
Low Friar St . . . . . . . . . C1
Manor Chare . . . . . . . . C2
Manors . . . . . . . . . . . . . B2
Manors Station . . . . . . B2
Market St . . . . . . . . . . . B2
Melbourne St . . . . . . . . B2
Mill Rd . . . . . . . . . . . . . C3
Mill Volvo Tyne . . . . . . C1
Monument . . . . . . . . . . B2
Monument Mall Sh Ctr B2
Morpeth St . . . . . . . . . . A2
Mosley St . . . . . . . . . . . C2
Napier St . . . . . . . . . . . A3
Nazareth House . . . . . . A3
New Bridge St . . . . B2/B3
Newcastle Central Station . . . . . . . . . . . . C1
Newcastle University . A1
Newgate Shopping Ctr C1
Newgate St . . . . . . . . . . B1
Newington Rd . . . . . . . A3
Northern Stage Theatre . . . . . . . . . . . A2
Northumberland Rd . . . B2
Northumberland St . . . B2
Northumbria Univ . . . . A2
Northwest Radial Rd . . A1
O2 Academy ✦ . . . . . . C1
Oakwellgate . . . . . . . . . C3
Orchard St . . . . . . . . . . C2
Osborne Rd . . . . . . . . . A2
Osborne Terr . . . . . . . . A3
Pandon . . . . . . . . . . . . . C3
Pandon Bank . . . . . . . . B3
Park Terr . . . . . . . . . . . A1
Percy St . . . . . . . . . . . . B1
Pilgrim St . . . . . . . . . . . B2
Pipewellgate . . . . . . . . C2
Pitt St . . . . . . . . . . . . . . B1
Plummer Tower . . . . . . A2
Police Station . . . . . . . B2
Portland Rd . . . . . . A3/B3
Portland Terr . . . . . . . . A3
Post Office . . . . . . . A3/B1/B2/B3
Pottery La . . . . . . . . . . . C1
Prudhoe Pl . . . . . . . . . . B1
Prudhoe St . . . . . . . . . . B1
Quayside . . . . . . . . . . . . C2
Queen Elizabeth II Bridge . . . . . . . . . . . . C2
Queen Victoria Rd . . . . A1
Richardson Rd . . . . . . . A1
Ridley Pl . . . . . . . . . . . . B2
Rock Terr . . . . . . . . . . . B3
Rosedale Terr . . . . . . . . A3
Royal Victoria Infirmary . . . . . . . . . . . A1
Sage Gateshead, The ✦ . . . . . . . . . . . . . C3
St Andrew's St . . . . . . . B1
St James . . . . . . . . . . . . B1
St James' Blvd . . . . . . . C1
Sports Direct Arena (St James' Park) (Newcastle Utd FC) . . B1
St Mary's (RC) † . . . . . C1
St Mary's Place . . . . . . B2
St Nicholas † . . . . . . . . C2
St Nicholas St . . . . . . . C2
St Thomas' St . . . . . . . B1
Sandyford Rd . . . . A2/A3
Science Park . . . . . . . . B2
Shield St . . . . . . . . . . . . B3
Shieldfield . . . . . . . . . . B3
Simpson Terr . . . . . . . . B3
South Shore Rd . . . . . . C3
South St . . . . . . . . . . . . C1
Starbeck Ave . . . . . . . . A3
Stepney Rd . . . . . . . . . . B3
Stoddart St . . . . . . . . . . B3
Stowell St . . . . . . . . . . . B1
Strawberry Pl . . . . . . . . B1
Swing Bridge . . . . . . . . C2
Temple St . . . . . . . . . . . C1
Terrace Pl . . . . . . . . . . . B1
The Close . . . . . . . . . . . C2
The Gate ✦ . . . . . . . . . B1
The Side . . . . . . . . . . . . C2
Theatre Royal . . . . . . . B2
Times Sq . . . . . . . . . . . . C1
Tower St . . . . . . . . . . . . B3
Trinity House . . . . . . . . C2
Tyne Bridge . . . . . . . . . C2
Tyne Bridges ✦ . . . . . . C2
Tyneside . . . . . . . . . . . . B2
Victoria Sq . . . . . . . . . . A2
Warwick St . . . . . . . . . . A3
Waterloo St . . . . . . . . . C1
Wellington St . . . . . . . . B1
Westgate Rd . . . . . C1/C2
Windsor Terr . . . . . . . . A2
Worswick St . . . . . . . . . B2
Wretham Pl . . . . . . . . . B3

## Newport
*Casnewydd* 344

Albert Terr . . . . . . . . . . B1
Allt-yr-Yn Ave . . . . . . . A1
Alma St . . . . . . . . . . . . C2
Ambulance Station . . . C3
Bailey St . . . . . . . . . . . B2
Barrack Hill . . . . . . . . . A2
Bath St . . . . . . . . . . . . . A3
Bedford Rd . . . . . . . . . B3
Belle Vue La . . . . . . . . . C1
Belle Vue Park . . . . . . . C1
Bishop St . . . . . . . . . . . A3
Blewitt St . . . . . . . . . . . B1
Bolt Cl . . . . . . . . . . . . . C3
Bolt St . . . . . . . . . . . . . C3
Bond St . . . . . . . . . . . . . A2
Bosworth Dr . . . . . . . . A1
Bridge St . . . . . . . . . . . B1
Bristol St . . . . . . . . . . . A3
Bryngwyn Rd . . . . . . . . B1
Brynhyfryd Ave . . . . . . C1
Brynhyfryd Rd . . . . . . . C1
Bus Station . . . . . . . . . B2
Caerau Cres . . . . . . . . . C1
Caerau Rd . . . . . . . . . . B1
Caerleon Rd . . . . . . . . . A3
Capel Cres . . . . . . . . . . C2
Cardiff Rd . . . . . . . . . . . C2
Caroline St . . . . . . . . . . B3
Castle (Remains) . . . . . A2
Cedar Rd . . . . . . . . . . . . B3
Charles St . . . . . . . . . . . B2
Charlotte Dr . . . . . . . . . C2
Chepstow Rd . . . . . . . . A3
Church Rd . . . . . . . . . . A3
City Cinema . . . . . . . . . B1
Civic Ctr . . . . . . . . . . . . B1
Clarence Pl . . . . . . . . . . A2
Clifton Pl . . . . . . . . . . . B1
Clifton Rd . . . . . . . . . . . C1
Clyffard Cres . . . . . . . . B1
Clytha Park Rd . . . . . . B1
Clytha Sq . . . . . . . . . . . C2
Coldra Rd . . . . . . . . . . . C1
Collier St . . . . . . . . . . . A3
Colne St . . . . . . . . . . . . B3
Comfrey Cl . . . . . . . . . . A1
Commercial Rd . . . . . . C3
Commercial St . . . . . . . B2
Corelli St . . . . . . . . . . . A3
Corn St . . . . . . . . . . . . . B2
Corporation Rd . . . . . . B3
Coulson Cl . . . . . . . . . . C2
County Court . . . . . . . . A2
Courts . . . . . . . . . . . . . . A1
Courts . . . . . . . . . . . . . . B1
Crawford St . . . . . . . . . A3
Cyril St . . . . . . . . . . . . . B3
Dean St . . . . . . . . . . . . . A3
Devon Pl . . . . . . . . . . . . B1
Dewsland Park Rd . . . . C2
Dolman . . . . . . . . . . . . B2
Dolphin St . . . . . . . . . . C3
East Dock Rd . . . . . . . . C3
East St . . . . . . . . . . . . . B1
East Usk Rd . . . . . . . . . A3
Ebbw Vale Wharf . . . . . B3
Emlyn St . . . . . . . . . . . . B2
Enterprise Way . . . . . . C3
Eton Rd . . . . . . . . . . . . . B3
Evans St . . . . . . . . . . . . A2
Factory Rd . . . . . . . . . . A2
Fields Rd . . . . . . . . . . . . B1
Francis Dr . . . . . . . . . . . C2
Frederick St . . . . . . . . . C3
Friars Rd . . . . . . . . . . . . C1
Gaer La . . . . . . . . . . . . . C1
George St . . . . . . . . . . . C3
George Street Bridge . C3
Godfrey Rd . . . . . . . . . . B1
Gold Tops . . . . . . . . . . . B1
Gore St . . . . . . . . . . . . . A3
Gorsedd Circle . . . . . . C1
Grafton Rd . . . . . . . . . . A3
Graham St . . . . . . . . . . B1
Granville St . . . . . . . . . C3
Harlequin Dr . . . . . . . . A1
Harrow Rd . . . . . . . . . . B3
Herbert Rd . . . . . . . . . . A3
Herbert Walk . . . . . . . . C2
Hereford St . . . . . . . . . A3
High St . . . . . . . . . . . . . B2
Hill St . . . . . . . . . . . . . . B2
Hoskins St . . . . . . . . . . A2
Information Ctr . . . . . . B2
Ivor Sq . . . . . . . . . . . . . B2
John Frost Sq . . . . . . . . B2
Jones St . . . . . . . . . . . . B1
Junction Rd . . . . . . . . . A3
Keynshaw Ave . . . . . . . C2
King St . . . . . . . . . . . . . C2
Kingsway . . . . . . . . . . . B2
Kingsway Ctr . . . . . . . . B2
Ledbury Dr . . . . . . . . . . A2
Library . . . . . . . . . . . . . A3
Library, Museum & Art Gallery . . . . . . . . B2
Liverpool Wharf . . . . . . B3
Llanthewy Rd . . . . . . . B1
Llanvair Rd . . . . . . . . . A3
Locke St . . . . . . . . . . . . A2
Lower Dock St . . . . . . . C3
Lucas St . . . . . . . . . . . . A2
Manchester St . . . . . . . A3
Market . . . . . . . . . . . . . B2
Marlborough Rd . . . . . B3
Mellon St . . . . . . . . . . . C3
Mill St . . . . . . . . . . . . . . A2
Morgan St . . . . . . . . . . A3
Mountjoy Rd . . . . . . . . C2
Newport Bridge . . . . . . A2
Newport Ctr . . . . . . . . . B2
Newport RFC . . . . . . . . B3
Newport Station . . . . . B2
North St . . . . . . . . . . . . B2
Oakfield Rd . . . . . . . . . B1
Park Sq . . . . . . . . . . . . . C2
Police Station . . . . A3/C2
Post Office . . . . . B1/B2/C1/C3
Power St . . . . . . . . . . . . A1
Prince St . . . . . . . . . . . . A3
Pugsley St . . . . . . . . . . . A2
Queen St . . . . . . . . . . . . C2
Queen's Cl . . . . . . . . . . A1
Queen's Hill . . . . . . . . . A1
Queen's Hill Cres . . . . A1
Queensway . . . . . . . . . . B2
Railway St . . . . . . . . . . B2
Riverfront Arts Ctr . . . . . . . . . . B2
Riverside . . . . . . . . . . . A3
Rodney Rd . . . . . . . . . . B2
Royal Gwent (A+E) . . . C2
Rudry St . . . . . . . . . . . . A3
Rugby Rd . . . . . . . . . . . B3
Ruperra La . . . . . . . . . . C3
Ruperra St . . . . . . . . . . C3
St Edmund St . . . . . . . . B1
St Mark's Cres . . . . . . . A1
St Mary St . . . . . . . . . . B1
St Vincent Rd . . . . . . . A3
St Woolos † . . . . . . . . . C2
St Woolos General (no A+E) . . . . . . . . . . C1
St Woolos Rd . . . . . . . . B1
School La . . . . . . . . . . . B2
Serpentine Rd . . . . . . . B1
Shaftesbury Park . . . . . A2
Sheaf La . . . . . . . . . . . . A3
Skinner St . . . . . . . . . . B2
Sorrel Dr . . . . . . . . . . . A1
South Market St . . . . . C3
Spencer Rd . . . . . . . . . B1
Stow Hill . . . . . . B2/C1/C2
Stow Park Ave . . . . . . . C1
Stow Park Dr . . . . . . . . C1
TA Ctr . . . . . . . . . . . . . . A1
Talbot St . . . . . . . . . . . . B2
Tennis Club . . . . . . . . . A1
Tregare St . . . . . . . . . . A3
Trostrey St . . . . . . . . . . A3
Tunnel Terr . . . . . . . . . B1
Turner St . . . . . . . . . . . A3
Upper Dock St . . . . . . . B2
Usk St . . . . . . . . . . . . . . A3
Usk Way . . . . . . . . . B3/C3
Victoria Cr . . . . . . . . . . B1
War Memorial . . . . . . . A3
Waterloo Rd . . . . . . . . . C1
West St . . . . . . . . . . . . . B1
Wharves . . . . . . . . . . . . B2
Wheeler St . . . . . . . . . . A2
Whitby Pl . . . . . . . . . . . A3
Windsor Terr . . . . . . . . B1
York Pl . . . . . . . . . . . . . C1

## Newquay 344

Agar Rd . . . . . . . . . . . . B2
Alma Pl . . . . . . . . . . . . . B1
Ambulance Station . . . B2
Anthony Rd . . . . . . . . . C1
Atlantic Hotel . . . . . . . A1
Bank St . . . . . . . . . . . . . B1
Barrowfields . . . . . . . . A3
Bay View Terr . . . . . . . B2
Beachfield Ave . . . . . . . B1
Beach Rd . . . . . . . . . . . B1
Beacon Rd . . . . . . . . . . A1
Belmont Pl . . . . . . . . . . A1
Berry Rd . . . . . . . . . . . . B2
Blue Reef Aquarium . . . . . . . . . B1
Boating Lake . . . . . . . . C2
Bus Station . . . . . . . . . B1
Chapel Hill . . . . . . . . . . B1
Chester Rd . . . . . . . . . . A3
Cheviot Rd . . . . . . C1/C2
Chichester Cres . . . . . . C2
Chynance Dr . . . . . . . . C1
Chyverton Cl . . . . . . . . C1
Cliff Rd . . . . . . . . . . . . . B2
Coach Park . . . . . . . . . . B2
Colvreath Rd . . . . . . . . A3
Council Ofices . . . . . . . B1
Crantock St . . . . . . . . . B1
Criggar Rocks . . . . . . . A3
Dale Cl . . . . . . . . . . . . . C3
Dale Rd . . . . . . . . . . . . . C3
Dane Rd . . . . . . . . . . . . A1
East St . . . . . . . . . . . . . B2
Edgcumbe Ave . . . . . . . B3
Edgcumbe Gdns . . . . . . B3
Eliot Gdns . . . . . . . . . . B3
Elm Cl . . . . . . . . . . . . . . C3
Ennor's Rd . . . . . . . . . . B1
Fernhill Rd . . . . . . . . . . B1
Fire Station . . . . . . . . . B1
Fore St . . . . . . . . . . . . . B1
Gannel Rd . . . . . . . . . . C2
Golf Driving Range . . . B3
Gover La . . . . . . . . . . . . B1
Great Western Beach . A2
Grosvenor Ave . . . . . . . B2
Harbour . . . . . . . . . . . . A1
Hawkins Rd . . . . . . . . . C2
Headleigh Rd . . . . . . . . B2
Hilgrove Rd . . . . . . A3/B3
Holywell Rd . . . . . . . . . B3
Hope Terr . . . . . . . . . . . B1
Huer's House, The . . . . A1
Information Ctr . . . . . . B1
Island Cres . . . . . . . . . . B2
Jubilee St . . . . . . . . . . . B1
Kew Cl . . . . . . . . . . . . . C3
Killacourt Cove . . . . . . A2
King Edward Cres . . . . A1
Lanhenvor Ave . . . . . . . B2
Library . . . . . . . . . . . . . B1
Lifeboat Station . . . . . A1
Linden Ave . . . . . . . . . . C2
Listry Rd . . . . . . . . . . . . C2
Lusty Glaze Beach . . . . A3
Lusty Glaze Rd . . . . . . A3
Manor Rd . . . . . . . . . . . B1
Marcus Hill . . . . . . . . . B2
Mayfield Rd . . . . . . . . . C2
Meadowside . . . . . . . . . C3
Mellanvrane La . . . . . . C2
Michell Ave . . . . . . . . . B2
Miniature Golf Course C3
Miniature Railway ✦ . . B3
Mount Wise . . . . . . . . . B1
Mowhay Cl . . . . . . . . . . C3
Narrowcliff . . . . . . . . . . A3
Newquay . . . . . . . . . . . B2
Newquay Hospital (no A&E) . . . . . . . . . . B2
Newquay Town Football Ground . . . . B1
Newquay Zoo . . . . . . . . B3
North Pier . . . . . . . . . . A1
North Quay Hill . . . . . . A1
Oakleigh Terr . . . . . . . B2
Pargolla Rd . . . . . . . . . B2
Pendragon Cres . . . . . . C3
Pengannel Cl . . . . . . . . C1
Penina Ave . . . . . . . . . . C3
Police Sta & Courts . . . B2
Post Office . . . . . . . B1/B2
Quarry Park Rd . . . . . . B3
Rawley La . . . . . . . . . . . C2
Reeds Way . . . . . . . . . . B1
Robartes Rd . . . . . . . . . B2
St Anne's Rd . . . . . . . . A3
St Aubyn Cres . . . . . . . B3
St George's Rd . . . . . . . B1
St John's Rd . . . . . . . . . B1
St Mary's Rd . . . . . . . . B1
St Michael's . . . . . . . . . B1
St Michael's Rd . . . . . . B1
St Thomas' Rd . . . . . . . B2
Seymour Ave . . . . . . . . B2
South Pier . . . . . . . . . . A1
South Quay Hill . . . . . . A1
Sweet Briar Cres . . . . . C3
Sydney Rd . . . . . . . . . . A1
The Crescent . . . . . . . . B1
Tolcarne Beach . . . . . . A2
Tolcarne Point . . . . . . . A2
Tolcarne Rd . . . . . . . . . B2
Tor Rd . . . . . . . . . . . . . . B2
Towan Beach . . . . . . . . A1
Towan Blystra Rd . . . . B3
Tower Rd . . . . . . . . . . . A1
Trebarwith Cres . . . . . B2
Tredour Rd . . . . . . . . . C2
Treforda Rd . . . . . . . . . C3
Tregoss Rd . . . . . . . . . . B3
Tregunnel Hill . . . . B1/C1
Tregunnel Saltings . . . C1
Trelawney Rd . . . . . . . . B2
Treloggan La . . . . . . . . C3
Treloggan Rd . . . . . . . . C3
Trembath Cres . . . . . . . C1
Trenance Ave . . . . . . . . B2
Trenance Gardens . . . . B2
Trenance La . . . . . . . . . C2
Trenance Leisure Park B3
Trenance Rd . . . . . . . . . B2
Trenarth Rd . . . . . . . . . B2
Treninnick Hill . . . . . . . C3
Tretherras Rd . . . . . . . . B3
Trethewey Way . . . . . . C1
Trevemper Rd . . . . . . . C2
Tunnels Through Time . . . . . . . . . . . . . B1
Ulalia Rd . . . . . . . . . . . B3
Vivian Cl . . . . . . . . . . . . B2
Waterworld . . . . . . . . . B3
Whitegate Rd . . . . . . . . B3
Wych Hazel Way . . . . . C3

## Newtown
*Y Drenewydd* 344

Ash Cl . . . . . . . . . . . . . . A3
Back La . . . . . . . . . . . . . B2
Baptist Chapel . . . . . . . B2
Barn La . . . . . . . . . . . . . A2
Bear Lanes Sh Ctr . . . . B2
Beech Cl . . . . . . . . . . . . A2
Beechwood Dr . . . . . . . A2
Brimmon Cl . . . . . . . . . C2
Brimmon Rd . . . . . . . . . C2
Broad St . . . . . . . . . . . . B2
Bryn Bank . . . . . . . . . . . A1
Bryn Cl . . . . . . . . . . . . . A2
Bryn Gdns . . . . . . . . . . A1
Bryn House . . . . . . . . . A1
Bryn La . . . . . . . . . . A1/A2
Bryn Meadows . . . . . . . A2
Bryn St . . . . . . . . . . . . . A2
Brynglais Ave . . . . . . . . A2
Brynglais Cl . . . . . . . . . A2
Bus Station . . . . . . . . . B2
Byrnwood Dr . . . . . . . . A1
Cambrian Bridge . . . . . B3
Cambrian Gdns . . . . . . B2
Cambrian Way . . . . . . . B2
Canal Rd . . . . . . . . . . . . A3
Castle Mound . . . . . . . . B2
Cedewain . . . . . . . . . . . C1
Cefnaire . . . . . . . . . . . . C2
Cefnaire Coppice . . . . . C2
Ceiriog . . . . . . . . . . . . . C2
Cemetery . . . . . . . . . . . A3
Church (Remains of) . . B2
Churchill Dr . . . . . . . . . A3
Cledan . . . . . . . . . . . . . B3
Colwyn . . . . . . . . . . . . . B3
Commercial St . . . . . . . A2
Council Offices . . . . . . B1
Crescent St . . . . . . . . . A1
Cwm Llanfair . . . . . . . . A2
Davies Memorial Gallery . . . . . . . . . . . B2
Dinas . . . . . . . . . . . . . . B2
Dolafon Rd . . . . . . . . . . B3
Dolerw Park . . . . . . . . . B1
Dolfor Rd . . . . . . . . . . . C1
Eirianell . . . . . . . . . . . . C1
Fairfield Dr . . . . . . . . . . A2
Ffordd Croesawdy . . . . B2
Fire Station . . . . . . . . . C1
Frankwell St . . . . . . . . A2
Frolic St . . . . . . . . . . . . B2
Fron La . . . . . . . . . . . . . A1
Garden La . . . . . . . . . . A2
Gas St . . . . . . . . . . . . . B2
Glyndŵr . . . . . . . . . . . . C1
Golwgydre La . . . . . . . . B2
Gorsedd Circle . . . . . . B1
Great Brimmon Farm . C3
Hafren . . . . . . . . . . . . . C1
Halfpenny Bridge . . . . B2
High St . . . . . . . . . . . . . B2
Hillside Ave . . . . . . . . . A3
Hoel Treowen . . . . . . . C2
Information Ctr . . . . . . B2
Kerry Rd . . . . . . . . . . . . B3
Ladywell Shopping Ctr B2
Library . . . . . . . . . . . . . B1
Llanfair Rd . . . . . . . . . . A2
Llanidloes Rd . . . . . . . . C1
Llys Ifor . . . . . . . . . . . . A2
Lon Cerddyn . . . . . . . . B1
Lonesome La . . . . . . . . A3
Long Bridge . . . . . . . . . A2
Lon Helyg . . . . . . . . . . . C1
Lower Canal Rd . . . . . . B3
Maldwyn Leisure Ctr . C1
Market . . . . . . . . . . . . . B2
Market St . . . . . . . . . . . B2
Milford Rd . . . . . . . . . . B1
Mill Cl . . . . . . . . . . . . . B2
Miniature Railway ✦ . . B1
Mwyn Fynydd . . . . . . . A3
New Church St . . . . . . B2
New Rd . . . . . . . . . . . . B2
Newtown Football Gd . B1
Newtown Infirmary . . A2
Newtown Station . . . . B2
Oak Tree Ave . . . . . . . . A3
Old Kerry Rd . . . . . . . . B2
Oldbarn La . . . . . . . . . . A2
Park Cl . . . . . . . . . . . . . B1
Parklands . . . . . . . . . . . B1
Park La . . . . . . . . . . . . . B1
Park St . . . . . . . . . . . . . B2
Pavillion Ct . . . . . . . . . C1
Plantation La . . . . . . . C1
Police Station . . . . . . . B1
Pont Brynfedw . . . . . . A2
Pool Rd . . . . . . . . . . . . B3
Poplar Rd . . . . . . . . . . . A3
Post Office . . . . . . . B2/C1
Powys . . . . . . . . . . . . . . C1
Powys Theatre . . . . . . . A2
Pryce Jones Stores & Museum . . . . . . . . . . . B2
Quaker Meeting Ho . . B1

Regent B2
Robert Owen House B1
Robert Owen Mus B2
Rugby Club A3
St David's A2
School La A2
Sheaf St B2
Short Bridge St B2
Stone St B2
Sycamore Dr A2
Textile Museum A2
The Bryn A1
The Park B1
Town Hall B2
Union St A2
Upper Brimmon C3
Vastre Industrial Est B3
War Memorial B2
WHSmith Museum B2
Wynfields C1
Y Ffrydd A3

### Northampton 344

78 Derngate B3
Abington Sq B3
Abington St B3
Alcombe St A3
All Saints' B2
Ambush St B1
Angel St B2
Arundel St A2
Ash St A2
Auctioneers Way C2
Bailiff St A2
Barrack Rd A2
Beaconsfield Terr A3
Becketts Park C3
Bedford Rd B3
Billing Rd B3
Brecon St A1
Brewery C2
Bridge St C2
Bridge St Depot C3
Broad St B2
Burns St A3
Bus Station A2
Campbell St A2
Castle (Site of) B2
Castle St B2
Cattle Market Rd C2
Central Museum & Art Gallery B2
Charles St A3
Cheyne Walk B3
Church La A2
Clare St A3
Cloutsham St A3
College St B2
Colwyn Rd A3
Cotton End C2
Countess Rd A1
County Hall B2
Court A2
Craven St A3
Crown & County Courts B3
Denmark Rd B3
Derngate B3
Derngate & Royal Theatres B3
Doddridge Church B2
Duke St A3
Dunster St A3
Earl St A3
Euston Rd C2
Fire Station A3
Foot Meadow B2
Gladstone Rd A1
Gold St B2
Grafton St A2
Gray St A3
Green St B1
Greenwood Rd B1
Greyfriars B2
Grosvenor Ctr B2
Grove Rd A3
Guildhall B2
Hampton St A2
Harding Terr A2
Hazelwood Rd B3
Herbert St B2
Hervey St A3
Hester St A2
Holy Sepulchre A2
Hood St A3
Horse Market B2
Hunter St A3
Information Ctr B1
Kettering Rd A3
Kingswell St B2
Lady's La B2
Leicester St A2
Leslie Rd A2
Library B3
Lorne Rd A2
Lorry Park A1
Louise Rd A2
Lower Harding St A2
Lower Hester St A2
Lower Mounts B3
Lower Priory St A2
Main Rd C1
Marefair B2
Market Sq B2
Marlboro Rd B1
Marriott St A2
Military Rd A3
Nene Valley Retail Pk C1
New South Bridge Rd C2
Northampton General Hospital (A&E) B3
Northampton Sta B1
Northcote St A2
Nunn Mills Rd C3
Old Towcester Rd C2
Overstone Rd A3
Peacock Pl B2
Pembroke Rd A1
Penn Court C2
Police Station B3
Post Office A1/A2/B3/C2
Quorn Way A2
Ransome Rd C3
Regent Sq A2
Robert St A2
St Andrew's Rd B1
St Andrew's St A2
St Edmund's Rd B3
St George's St A2
St Giles B3
St Giles St B3
St Giles' Terr B3
St James' Mill Rd B1
St James' Mill Rd East C1
St James Park Rd B1
St James Retail Park C1
St James Rd B1
St Leonard's Rd C2
St Mary's St B2
St Michael's Rd A3
St Peter's B2
St Peter's Sq Sh Prec B2
St Peter's Way B2
Salisbury St A2
Scarletwell St B2
Semilong Rd A2
Sheep St B2
Sol Central (L Ctr) B2
Somerset St A3
South Bridge C2
Southfield Ave C2
Spencer Bridge Rd A1
Spencer Rd A3
Spring Gdns B3
Spring La B2
Swan St B3
TA Ctr A3
Tanner St B2
The Drapery B2
The Ridings B3
Tintern Ave A1
Towcester Rd C2
Upper Bath St B2
Upper Mounts A2
Victoria Park A1
Victoria Promenade B2
Victoria Rd B3
Victoria St A2
Wellingborough Rd B3
West Bridge B1
York Rd B3

### Norwich 345

Albion Way C3
All Saints Green C2
Anchor Cl A3
Anchor St A3
Anglia Sq A2
Argyle St C3
Arts Ctr B1
Ashby St C2
Assembly House B1
Bank Plain B2
Barker St A1
Barn Rd A1
Barrack St A3
Ber St C2
Bethel St B1
Bishop Bridge A3
Bishopbridge Rd A3
Bishopgate A3
Blackfriars St A2
Botolph St A2
Bracondale C3
Brazen Gate C2
Bridewell B2
Brunswick Rd C1
Bull Close Rd A2
Bus Station C2
Calvert St A2
Cannell Green A3
Carrow Rd C3
Castle Mall B2
Castle Meadow B2
Castle & Museum B2
Cathedral B2
Cattlemarket St B2
Chantry Rd C1
Chapel Loke C2
Chapelfield East B1
Chapelfield Gdns B1
Chapelfield North B1
Chapelfield Rd B1
Chapelfield Sh Ctr C1
City Hall B1
City Rd C2
City Wall C1/C3
Colegate A2
Coslany St B1
Cow Hill B1
Cow Tower A3
Cowgate A2
Crown & Magistrates Courts A2
Dragon Hall Heritage Ctr C3
Duke St A1
Edward St A2
Elm Hill B2
Erpingham Gate B2
Fire Station B1
Fishergate A2
Foundry Bridge B3
Fye Bridge A2
Garden St C2
Gas Hill B3
Grapes Hill B1
Great Hospl Halls, The A3
Grove Ave C1
Grove Rd C1
Guildhall B1
Gurney Rd A3
Hall Rd C2
Heathgate A3
Heigham St A1
Horn's La C2
Information Ctr B1
Ipswich Rd C1
James Stuart Gdns B3
King Edward VI School B2
King St B2
King St C3
Koblenz Ave C3
Library B1
London St B2
Lower Clarence Rd B3
Lower Cl B3
Maddermarket B1
Magdalen St A2
Mariners La C2
Market B2
Market Ave B2
Mountergate B3
Mousehold St A3
Newmarket Rd C1
Norfolk Gallery B2
Norfolk St C1
Norwich City FC C3
Norwich Station B3
Oak St A1
Palace St A2
Pitt St A1
Playhouse B2
Post Office A2/B2/C2
Pottergate B1
Prince of Wales Rd B2
Princes St B2
Pull's Ferry B3
Puppet Theatre A2
Quebec Rd B3
Queen St B2
Queens Rd C2
Recorder Rd B3
Retail Park C3
Riverside Entertainment Ctr C3
Riverside Swimming Ctr C3
Riverside Rd B3
Rosary Rd B3
Rose La B2
Rouen Rd C2
Royal Norfolk Regiment Museum B2
St Andrew's & Blackfriars Hall B2
St Andrews St B2
St Augustines St A1
St Benedicts St B1
St Ethelbert's Gate B2
St Faiths La B3
St Georges St A2
St Giles St B1
St James Cl A3
St Julians C2
St Martin's La A1
St Peter Mancroft B2
St Peters St B1
St Stephens Rd C1
St Stephens St C1
Silver Rd A2
Silver St A2
Southwell Rd C2
Strangers Hall B1
Superstore C2
Surrey St C2
Sussex St A1
The Close B3
The Forum B1
The Walk B2
Theatre Royal B1
Theatre St B1
Thorn La C2
Thorpe Rd B3
Tombland B2
Union St C1
Vauxhall St B1
Victoria St C1
Walpole St B1
Wensum St A2
Wessex St C1
Westwick St A1
Wherry Rd C3
Whitefriars A2
Willow La B1
Yacht Station B3

### Nottingham 345

Abbotsford Dr A3
Addison St A1
Albert Hall B1
Alfred St South B3
Alfreton Rd B1
All Saints Rd A1
Annesley Gr A2
Arboretum A1
Arboretum St A1
Arthur St A1
Arts Theatre B3
Ashforth St A3
Balmoral Rd A1
Barker Gate B3
Bath St B3
Belgrave Ctr B1
Bellar Gate B3
Belward St B3
Blue Bell Hill Rd B3
Brewhouse Yard C2
Broad Marsh Bus Sta C2
Broad Marsh Precinct C2
Broad St B3
Brook St B3
Burns St A1
Burton St B2
Bus Station A2
Canal St C2
Carlton St B3
Carrington St C2
Castle Blvd C1
Castle C2
Castle Gate C2
Castle Mdw Retail Pk C1
Castle Meadow Rd C2
Castle Museum & Gallery C2
Castle Rd C2
Castle Wharf C2
Cavendish Rd East C1
Cemetery B1
Chaucer St B1
Cheapside B2
Church Rd A3
City Link C3
City of Caves C2
Clarendon St B1
Cliff Rd C3
Clumber Rd East C1
Clumber St B2
College St B1
Collin St C2
Conway Cl A2
Council House B2
Court B2
Cranbrook St B3
Cranmer St A2
Cromwell St B1
Curzon St B3
Derby Rd B1
Dryden St A2
Fishpond Dr C1
Fletcher Gate B3
Forest Rd East A1
Forest Rd West A1
Friar La C2
Galleries of Justice C3
Gedling Gr A1
Gedling St B3
George St B3
Gill St A2
Glasshouse St B2
Goldsmith St B2
Goose Gate B3
Great Freeman St A2
Guildhall B2
Hamilton Dr C1
Hampden St A1
Heathcote St B3
High Pavement C3
High School A1
Holles Cr C1
Hope Dr C1
Hungerhill Rd A3
Huntingdon Dr C1
Huntingdon St A2
Information Ctr B2
Instow Rise A3
International Com Ctr A2
Kent St B3
King St B2
Lace Ctr, The C2
Lace Market C3
Lace Mkt Theatre C3
Lamartine St B3
Lenton Rd C1
Lewis Cl A3
Lincoln St B2
London Rd C3
Long Row B2
Low Pavement C2
Lower Parliament St B3
Magistrates Court C2
Maid Marian Way B2
Mansfield Rd A2/B2
Middle Hill C2
Milton St B2
Mount St B2
National Ice Ctr C3
Newcastle Dr B1
Newstead Gr A2
North Sherwood St A2
Nottingham Arena C3
Nottingham Station C3
Old Market Square B2
Oliver St A1
Park Dr C1
Park Row C1
Park Terr B1
Park Valley C1
Peas Hill Rd A3
Peel St A1
Pelham St B2
Peveril Dr C1
Plantagenet St A3
Playhouse Theatre B1
Plumptre St C3
Police Station B2
Poplar St C3
Portland Rd B1
Post Office B2
Queen's Rd C3
Raleigh St A1
Regent St B1
Rick St B3
Robin Hood Statue C2
Robin Hood St B3
Royal Ctr B2
Royal Children Inn C2
Royal Concert Hall B2
St Ann's Hill Rd A2
St Ann's Way A2
St Ann's Well Rd A3
St Barnabas B1
St James' St B2
St Mark's St B3
St Mary's Gdn of Rest B3
St Mary's Gate B3
St Nicholas C2
St Peter's C2
St Peter's Gate B2
Salutation Inn C2
Shakespeare St B2
Shelton St A2
South Pde B2
South Rd C1
South Sherwood St B2
Station St C3
Station Street C3
Stoney St B3
Talbot St B1
Tales of Robin Hood C2
Tattershall Dr C1
Tennis Dr B1
Tennyson St A1
The Park C1
The Ropewalk B1
Theatre Royal B2
Trent St C3
Trent University A2/B2
Trent University B2
Trinity Square Sh Ctr B2
Trip To Jerusalem Inn C2
Union Rd B3
Upper Parliament St B2
Victoria Ctr B2
Victoria Leisure Ctr B3
Victoria Park B3
Victoria St B2
Walter St A1
Warser Gate B3
Watkin St A2
Waverley St A1
Wheeler Gate B2
Wilford Rd C2
Wilford St C2
Willoughby House C2
Wollaton St B1
Woodborough Rd A2
Woolpack La B3
York St A2

### Oban 345

Aird's Cres B2
Albany St B2
Albert La A2
Albert Rd A2
Alma Cres B1
Ambulance Station C2
Angus Terr C3
Ardconnel Rd A2
Ardconnel Terr B2
Argyll Sq B2
Argyll St B2
Atlantis Leisure Ctr A2
Bayview Rd A1
Benvoulin Rd A2
Bowling Green A2
Breadalbane St A2
Bus Station B2
Campbell St B2
College B2
Colonsay Terr C3
Columba Building B2
Combie St B2
Corran Brae A1
Corran Esplanade A1/A2
Corran Halls A2
Court B2
Crannaig-a-Mhinisteir B1
Crannog La C2
Croft Ave A2
Dalintart Dr C3
Dalriach Rd A2
Distillery B2
Drummore Rd C2
Duncraggan Rd A2
Dunollie Rd A2
Dunuaran Rd B1
Feochan Gr C3
Ferry Terminal B1
Gallanach Rd B1
George St A2
Glencruitten Dr C3
Glencruitten Rd B3
Glenmore Rd C1
Glenshellach Rd C1
Glenshellach Terr B2
Harbour Bowl B2
Hazeldean Cres A3
High St B2
Highland Theatre Cinema A2
Hill St B2
Industrial Estate C2
Information Ctr B2
Islay Rd C3
Jacob's Ladder B2
Jura Rd C3
Knipoch Pl C3
Laurel Cres A2
Laurel Rd A2/A3
Library B1
Lifeboat Station B1
Lighthouse Pier B1
Lismore Cres A2
Lochavullin Dr B2
Lochavullin Rd C2
Lochside St B2
Longsdale Cres A3
Longsdale Rd A2/A3
Longsdale Terr A3
Lunga Rd C3
Lynn Rd C2
Market St B2
McCaig Rd C3
McCaig's Tower A2
Mill La C2
Miller Rd C2
Millpark Ave C2
Millpark Rd C2
Mossfield Ave B3
Mossfield Dr B3
Mossfield Stadium B3
Nant Dr C3
Nelson Rd C2
North Pier B2
Nursery La A2
Oban B2
Police Station B2
Polvinister Rd B3
Post Office A2/B2
Pulpit Dr C1
Pulpit Hill C1
Pulpit Hill Viewpoint B1
Quarry Rd C2
Queen's Park Pl B2
Railway Quay B1
Rockfield Rd B2
St Columba's A1
St John's A2
Scalpay Terr C3
Shore St B1
Shuna Terr C3
Sinclair Dr C2
Soroba Rd B2/C2
South Pier B2
Stevenson St B2
Tweedale St B2
Ulva Rd C2
Villa Rd B1
War & Peace A2

### Oxford 345

Adelaide St A1
Albert St A1
All Souls (Coll) B2
Ashmolean Mus B2
Balliol (Coll) B2
Banbury Rd A2
Bate Collection of Musical Instruments C2
Beaumont St B1
Becket St B1
Blackhall Rd A2
Blue Boar St B2
Bodleian Library B2
Botanic Garden B3
Brasenose (Coll) B2
Brewer St C2
Broad St B2
Burton-Taylor Theatre B2
Bus Station B1
Canal St A1
Cardigan St A1
Carfax Tower B2
Castle B1
Castle St B1
Catte St B2
Cemetery C1
Christ Church (Coll) B2
Christ Church Cath C2
Christ Church Mdw C2
Clarendon Ctr B2
Coach & Lorry Park C1
College B3
Coll of Further Ed C1
Cornmarket St B2
Corpus Christi (Coll) B2
County Hall B1
Covered Market B2
Cowley Pl C3
Cranham St A1
Cranham Terr A1
Cricket Ground B1
Crown & County Courts C2
Deer Park B3
Exeter (Coll) B2
Folly Bridge C2
George St B1
Great Clarendon St A1
Hart St A1
Hertford (Coll) B2
High St B3
Hollybush Row B1
Holywell St B2
Hythe Bridge St B1
Ice Rink C1
Information Ctr B2
Jericho St A1
Jesus (Coll) B2
Jowett Walk B3
Juxon St A1
Keble (Coll) A2
Keble Rd A2
Library B2
Linacre (Coll) A3
Lincoln (Coll) B2
Little Clarendon St A1
Longwall St B3
Magdalen (Coll) B3
Magdalen Bridge B3
Magdalen St B2
Magistrate's Court C2
Manchester (Coll) B2
Manor Rd B3
Mansfield (Coll) A2
Mansfield Rd A3
Market B1
Marlborough Rd C2
Martyrs' Memorial B2
Merton Field B3
Merton (Coll) B3
Merton St B2
Mus of Modern Art B2
Museum of Oxford B2
Museum Rd A2
New College (Coll) B3
New Inn Hall St B2
New Rd B1
New Theatre B2
Norfolk St C1
Nuffield (Coll) B1
Observatory A1
Observatory St A1
Odeon B1/B2
Old Fire Station B1
Old Greyfriars St C2
Oriel (Coll) B2
Oxford Station B1
Oxford Story, The B2
Oxford University Research Ctrs A1
Oxpens Rd C1
Paradise Sq C1
Paradise St B1
Park End St B1
Parks Rd A2/B2
Pembroke (Coll) C2
Phoenix A1
Picture Gallery C2
Plantation Rd A1
Playhouse B2
Police Station C2
Post Office A1/B2
Pusey St B1
Queen's La B3
Queen's (Coll) B3
Radcliffe Camera B2
Rewley Rd B1
Richmond Rd A1
Rose La B3
Ruskin (Coll) B1
Saïd Business School B1
St Aldates C2
St Anne's (Coll) A1
St Antony's (Coll) A1
St Bernard's Rd A1
St Catherine's (Coll) B3
St Cross Building A3
St Cross Rd A3
St Edmund Hall (Coll) B3
St Giles St A2
St Hilda's (Coll) C3
St John St B2
St John's (Coll) B2
St Mary the Virgin B2
St Michael at the Northgate B2
St Peter's (Coll) B1
St Thomas St B1
Science Area A2
Science Museum B2
Sheldonian Theatre B2
Somerville (Coll) A1
South Parks Rd A2
Speedwell St C2
Sports Ground C3
Thames St C2
Town Hall B2
Trinity (Coll) B2
Turl St B2
University Coll (Coll) B3
Univ Mus & Pitt Rivers Mus A2
University Parks A2
Wadham (Coll) B2
Walton Cr A1
Walton St A1
Western Rd C2
Westgate Sh Ctr B2
Woodstock Rd A1
Worcester (Coll) B1

### Perth 345

A K Bell Library B2
Abbot Cres C1
Abbot St C1
Albany Terr A1
Albert Monument A3
Alexandra St B2
Atholl St A2
Balhousie Ave A2
Balhousie Castle Black Watch Museum A2
Balhousie St A2
Ballantine Pl A1
Barossa Pl A2
Barossa St A2
Barrack St A2
Bell's Sports Ctr A2
Bellwood B3
Blair St B1
Burn Park C1
Bus Station B2
Caledonian Rd B2
Canal Cres B2
Canal St B3
Cavendish Ave C1
Charles St B2
Charlotte Pl A2
Charlotte St A3
Church St A1
City Hall B3
Club House C3
Clyde Pl C1
Commercial St A3
Concert Hall B3
Council Chambers B3
County Pl B2
Court B3
Craigie Pl C2
Crieff Rd A1
Croft Park C2
Cross St B2
Darnhall Cres C1
Darnhall Dr C1
Dewars Ctr B1
Dundee Rd B3
Dunkeld Rd A1
Earl's Dykes B1
Edinburgh Rd C3
Elibank St B1
Fair Maid's House A3
Fergusson B3
Feus Rd A1
Fire Station A1
Fitness Ctr B1
Foundary La A2
Friar St C1
George St B3
Glamis Pl C1
Glasgow Rd B1
Glenearn Rd C2
Glover St B1/C1
Golf Course A2
Gowrie St A3
Gray St B1
Graybank Rd B1
Greyfriars Burial Grnd B3
Hay St A2
High St B2/B3
Hotel B3
Inchaffray St A1
Industrial/Retail Park B1
Information Ctr B2
Isla Rd A3
James St B2
Keir St A3
King Edward St B3
King James VI Golf Course C3
King St B2
Kings Pl C2
Kinnoull Causeway B2
Kinnoull Aisle 'Monument' B3
Kinnoull St B2
Knowelea Pl C1
Knowelea Terr C1
Ladeside Business Ctr A1
Leisure Pool B1
Leonard St B2
Lickley St B2
Lochie Brae A3
Long Causeway A1
Low St A2
Main St A3
Marshall Pl C3
Melville St A2
Mill St B3
Milne St B2
Murray Cres C1
Murray St B2
Needless Rd C1
New Rd B2
North Inch A3
North Methven St A2
Park Pl C1
Perth B2
Perth Bridge A3
Perth Business Park B1
Perth Museum & Art Gallery B3
Perth Station C2
Pickletulllum Rd B1
Pitheavlis Cres C1
Playhouse B2
Police Station A2
Pomarium St B2
Post Office A3/B2/C2
Princes St B3
Priory Pl C2
Queen St C1
Queen's Bridge B3
Riggs Rd B1
Riverside B3
Riverside Park B3
Rodney Park B3
Rose Terr A2
St Catherines Ret Pk A1
St Catherine's Rd A1/A2
St John St B3
St John's Kirk B3
St John's Shopping Ctr B2
St Leonards Bridge C2
St Ninians Cathedral A2
Scott Monument C2
Scott St B2
Sheriff Court B3
Shore Rd C3
Skate Park C3
South Inch C2
South Inch Bsns Ctr C3
South Inch Park C2
South Inch View C2
South Methven St B2
South St B3
South William St B2
Stormont St A2
Strathmore St A3
Stuart Ave C1
Tay St B3
The Stables A1
The Stanners B3
Union La A2
Victoria St B2
Watergate B3
Wellshill Cemetery A1
West Bridge St A3
West Mill St B2
Whitefriers Cres B1
Whitefriers St B1
Wilson St C1
Windsor Terr C1
Woodside Cres C1
York Pl B2
Young St C1

### Peterborough 345

Athletics Arena B3
Bishop's Palace B2
Bishop's Rd B2/B3
Boongate A3
Bourges Boulevard A1
Bourges Retail Pk B1/B2
Bridge House (Council Offices) C2
Bridge St B2
Bright St A1
Broadway A2
Broadway A2
Brook St A2
Burghley Rd A2
Bus Station B2
Cavendish St A3
Charles St A3
Church St B2
Church Walk A2
Cobden Ave A1
Cobden St A1
Cowgate B2
Craig St A2
Crawthorne Rd A2
Cripple Sidings La C2
Cromwell Rd A1
Dickens St A3
Eastfield Rd A3
Eastgate B3
Fire Station A1
Fletton Ave C2
Frank Perkins Parkway C3
Geneva St A2
George St C1
Gladstone St A1
Glebe Rd C2
Gloucester Rd C3
Granby St B3
Grove St C1
Guildhall B2
Hadrians Ct C3
Henry St A2
Hereward Cross (Sh) B2
Hereward Rd B3
Information Ctr B2
Jubilee St C1
Key Theatre C2
Kent Rd B1
Kirkwood Cl B1
Lea Gdns B1
Library A2
Lincoln Rd A2
London Rd C2
Long Causeway B2
Lower Bridge St C2
Magistrates Court B2
Manor House St A2
Mayor's Walk A1
Midland Rd A1
Monument St A2
Morris St A3
Mus & Art Gallery B2
Nene Valley Railway C1
New Rd A2
New Rd C1
Northminster A2
Old Customs House C2
Oundle Rd C1
Padholme Rd A3
Palmerston Rd C1
Park Rd A2
Passport Office B2
Peterborough District Hospital (A+E) B1
Peterborough Sta B1
Peterborough Nene Valley C1
Peterborough United FC C2
Police Station B2
Post Office A3/B1/B2/B3/C1
Priestgate B2
Queen's Walk C2
Queensgate Ctr B2
Railworld C1
Regional Swimming & Fitness Ctr B3
River La B1
Rivergate Sh Ctr B2
Riverside Mead C3
Russell St A1
St John's B2
St John's St A3
St Marks St A2
St Peter's B2
St Peter's Rd B2
Saxon Rd A3
Spital Bridge A1
Stagshaw Dr C3
Star Rd B3
Thorpe Lea Rd B1
Thorpe Rd B1
Thorpe's Lea Rd B1
Tower St A2
Town Hall B2
Viersen Platz B2
Vineyard Rd B3
Wake Rd B3
Wellington St A3
Wentworth St B2
Westgate B2
Whalley St A3
Wharf Rd C1
Whitsed St A3
YMCA A3

### Plymouth 346

Alma Rd A1
Anstis St B1
Armada Ctr B2
Armada St A3
Armada Way B2
Arts Ctr B2
Athenaeum B1
Athenaeum St C1
Barbican C3
Barbican C3
Baring St A3
Bath St B1
Beaumont Park B3
Beaumont Rd B3
Black Friars Gin Distillery C2
Breton Side B3
Bus Station B2
Castle St C3
Cathedral (RC) B1
Cecil St B1
Central Park A1
Central Park Ave A2
Charles Church B3
Charles Cross B3
Charles St B2
City Museum & Art Gallery B2
Citadel Rd C2
Citadel Rd East C2
Civic Ctr B2
Cliff Rd C1
Clifton Pl A3
Cobourg St A2
College of Art B2
Continental Ferry Port B1
Cornwall St B2
Dale Rd A2
Deptford Pl A3
Derry Ave A2
Derry's Cross B1
Drake Circus B2
Drake Cir Sh Ctr B2
Drake's Memorial C2
Drum B2
Eastlake St B2
Ebrington St B3
Elizabethan House C3
Elliot St C1
Endsleigh Pl A2

Poole • Portsmouth • Preston • Reading • St Andrews • Salisbury • Scarborough • Sheffield 363


Exeter St B3
Fire Station A3
Fish Quay C3
Gibbons St A3
Glen Park Ave A2
Grand Pde C1
Great Western Rd C1
Greenbank Rd A3
Greenbank Terr A3
Guildhall B2
Hampton St B3
Harwell St B1
Hill Park Cr A3
Hoe Approach B2
Hoe Rd C2
Hoegate St C2
Houndiscombe Rd A2
Information Ctr C3
James St A2
Kensington Rd A3
King St B1
Lambhay Hill C3
Leigham St C1
Library B2
Lipson Rd A3/B3
Lockyer St C2
Lockyers Quay C3
Madeira Rd C2
Marina B3
Market Ave B1
Martin St B1
Mayflower Stone & Steps C3
Mayflower St B2
Mayflower Visitor Ctr C3
Merchants House B2
Millbay Rd B1
National Marine Aquarium C3
Neswick St B1
New George St B2
New St C3
North Cross A2
North Hill A3
North Quay B2
North Rd East A2
North Rd West A1
North St B3
Notte St B2
Octagon St B1
Pannier Market B1
Pennycomequick A1
Pier St C1
Plymouth Pavilions B1
Plymouth Station A2
Police Station B3
Portland Sq A2
Post Office A1/B1/B2
Princess St B2
Prysten House B2
Queen Anne's Battery Seasports Ctr C3
Radford Rd C1
Regent St B3
Rope Walk C3
Royal Citadel C2
Royal Pde B2
St Andrew's B2
St Andrew's Cross B2
St Andrew's St B2
St Lawrence Rd A2
Saltash Rd A2
Smeaton's Tower C2
Southern Terr A3
Southside St C2
Stuart Rd A1
Sutherland Rd A2
Sutton Rd B3
Sydney St A1
Teats Hill Rd C3
The Crescent B1
The Hoe C2
The Octagon B1
The Promenade C2
Tothill Ave B3
Union St B1
Univ of Plymouth A2
Vauxhall St B2/3
Victoria Park A1
West Hoe Rd C1
Western Approach B1
Whittington St A1
Wyndham St B1
YMCA B2
YWCA C2

## Poole 346

Ambulance Station A3
Baiater Gdns C2
Baiter Park C3
Ballard Cl C2
Ballard Rd C2
Bay Hog La B1
Bridge Approach C1
Bus Station B2
Castle St B2
Catalina Dr B3
Chapel La B2
Church St B1
Cinnamon La B1
Colborne Cl B3
Dear Hay La B2
Denmark La A3
Denmark Rd A3
East St B2
Elizabeth Rd A3
Emerson Rd B2
Ferry Rd C1
Ferry Terminal C1
Fire Station A2
Freightliner Terminal C1
Furnell Rd B3
Garland Rd A3
Green Rd B2
Heckford La A3
Heckford Rd A3
High St B2
High St North A3
Hill St B2
Holes Bay Rd A1
Hospital (A+E) A3
Information Ctr C2
Kingland Rd B3
Kingston Rd A3
Labrador Dr C3
Lagland St B2
Lander Cl C3
Old Lifeboat C2
Lighthouse – Poole Ctr for the Arts B3
Longfleet Rd A3
Maple Rd A3
Market Cl B2
Market St B2
Mount Pleasant Rd B3
New Harbour Rd C1
New Harbour Rd South C1
New Harbour Rd West C1
New Orchard B1
New Quay Rd C1
New St B2
Newfoundland Dr B2
North St B2
Old Orchard B2
Parish Rd A3
Park Lake Rd B3
Parkstone Rd A3
Perry Gdns B2
Pitwines Cl B2
Police Station A2
Poole Central Library B2
Poole Lifting Bridge C1
Poole Park B2
Poole Station A2
Poole Waterfront Museum C1
Post Office A2/B2
St John's Rd A3
St Margaret's Rd A2
St Mary's Maternity Unit A3
St Mary's Rd A3
Seldown Bridge B3
Seldown La B3
Seldown Rd B3
Serpentine Rd A2
Shaftesbury Rd A3
Skinner St B2
Slipway B1
Stanley Rd C2
Sterte Ave A2
Sterte Ave West A1
Sterte Cl A2
Sterte Esplanade A2
Sterte Rd A2
Strand St C2
Swimming Pool B3
Taverner Cl B3
Thames St B1
The Lifeboat College B2
The Quay C2
Towngate Bridge B2
Vallis Cl C3
Waldren Cl B3
West Quay B1
West Quay Rd B1
West St B1
West View Rd A2
Whatleigh Cl B2
Wimborne Rd A3

## Portsmouth 346

Action Stations C1
Admiralty Rd A1
Alfred Rd A2
Anglesea Rd B2
Arundel St B3
Aspex B1
Bishop St A2
Broad St C1
Buckingham House C2
Burnaby Rd B2
Bus Station B1
Camber Dock C1
Cambridge Rd B2
Car Ferry to Isle of Wight B1
Cascades Sh Ctr A3
Castle Rd C3
City Museum & Art Gallery B2
Civic Offices B3
Clarence Pier C2
College St B1
Commercial Rd A3
Cottage Gr B3
Cross St A1
Cumberland St A2
Duisburg Way C2
Durham St A3
East St B1
Edinburgh Rd A2
Elm Gr C3
Great Southsea St C3
Green Rd B3
Greetham St B3
Grosvenor St B3
Groundlings A2
Grove Rd North C3
Grove Rd South C3
Guildhall B3
Guildhall Walk B3
Gunwharf Quays Retail Park B1
Gunwharf Rd B1
Hambrook St C2
Hampshire Terr B2
Hanover St A1
High St C2
HM Naval Base A1
HMS Nelson (Royal Naval Barracks) A2
HMS Victory A1
HMS Warrior A1
Hovercraft Terminal C2
Hyde Park Rd B3
Information Ctr A1/B3
Isambard Brunel Rd B3
Isle of Wight Car Ferry Terminal B1
Kent Rd C3
Kent St A2
King St B3
King's Rd C3
King's Terr C2
Lake Rd A3
Law Courts B3
Library B3
Long Curtain Rd C2
Market Way A3
Marmion Rd C3
Mary Rose Museum A1
Middle St B3
Millennium Prom B1/C1
Museum Rd B2
National Museum of the Royal Navy A1
Naval Recreation Gd C2
Nightingale Rd C3
Norfolk St B3
North St A2
Osborne Rd C3
Park Rd B2
Passenger Catamaran to Isle of Wight B1
Passenger Ferry to Gosport B1
Pelham Rd C3
Pembroke Gdns C2
Pier Rd C2
Point Battery C1
Police Station B3
Portsmouth & Southsea A3
Portsmouth Harbour B1
Portsmouth Historic Dockyard A1
Post Office A2/A3/B1/B3/C3
Queen St A1
Queen's Cr C3
Round Tower C1
Royal Garrison Church C1
St Edward's Rd C3
St George's Rd B2
St George's Sq B1
St George's Way B2
St James's Rd B3
St James's St A2
St John's Cath (RC) A3
St Thomas's Cath C1
St Thomas's St B2
Somers Rd B3
Southsea Common C2
Southsea Terr C2
Spinnaker Tower B1
Square Tower C1
Station St A3
Swimming Pool A2
The Hard B1
Town Fortifications C1
Unicorn Rd A2
United Services Recreation Ground B2
University of Portsmouth A2/B2
University of Portsmouth – College of Art, Design and Media B3
Upper Arundel St A3
Victoria Ave C2
Victoria Park A2
Victory Gate A1
Vue B1
Warblington St B1
Western Pde C2
White Hart Rd C1
Winston Churchill Ave B3

## Preston 346

Adelphi St A2
Anchor Ct B3
Aqueduct St A1
Ardee Rd C1
Arthur St B2
Ashton St A1
Avenham La B3
Avenham Park C3
Avenham Rd B3
Avenham St B3
Bairstow St B3
Balderstone Rd C1
Beamont Dr A1
Beech St South C2
Bird St C1
Bow La B2
Brierfield Rd A1
Broadgate C1
Brook St A2
Bus Station A3
Butler St B2
Cannon St B3
Carlton St A1
Chaddock St B3
Channel Way B1
Chapel St B3
Christ Church St B2
Christian Rd B2
Cold Bath St A2
Coleman Ct C1
Connaught Rd C2
Corn Exchange B3
Corporation St A2/B2
County Hall B2
County Records Office B2
Court A3
Court B3
Cricket Ground C2
Croft St A1
Cross St B3
Crown Court A3
Crown St A3
East Cliff C3
East Cliff Rd B3
Edward St A3
Elizabeth St A3
Euston St B1
Fishergate B2/B3
Fishergate Hill B2
Fishergate Sh Ctr B2
Fitzroy St B1
Fleetwood St A1
Friargate A3
Fylde Rd A1/A2
Gerrard St B2
Glover's Ct B3
Good St B2
Grafton St B2
Great George St A3
Great Shaw St A3
Greenbank St A2
Guild Way B1
Guildhall & Charter B3
Guildhall St B3
Harrington St A2
Harris Museum B3
Hartington Rd B1
Hasset Cl C2
Heatley St B2
Hind St C2
Information Ctr B3
Kilruddery Rd C1
Lancaster Rd A3/B3
Latham St B3
Lauderdale St C2
Lawson St A3
Leighton St A2
Leyland Rd C1
Library A1
Library B3
Liverpool Rd C1
Lodge St B2
Lune St B3
Main Sprit West B3
Maresfield Rd C1
Market St West A3
Marsh La B1/B2
Maudland Bank A2
Maudland Rd A2
Meadow Ct C2
Meath Rd C1
Mill Hill A2
Miller Arcade B3
Miller Park C3
Moor La A3
Mount St B3
North Rd A3
North St A3
Northcote Rd B1
Old Milestones B1
Old Tram Rd C3
Pedder St A1/A2
Peel St A2
Penwortham Bridge C2
Penwortham New Bridge C1
Pitt St B2
Playhouse A3
Police Station A3
Port Way B1
Post Office B3
Preston Station B2
Ribble Bank St B2
Ribble Viaduct C2
Ribblesdale Pl B3
Ringway B3
River Parade C1
Riverside C2
St Georges B3
St Georges Sh Ctr B3
St Johns B3
St Johns Shopping Centre A3
St Mark's Rd A1
St Walburges A1
Salisbury Rd B1
Sessions House B3
Snow Hill A3
South End C2
South Meadow La C2
Spa Rd B1
Sports Ground C2
Strand Rd B1
Syke St B3
Talbot Rd B1
Taylor St C1
Tithebarn St A3
Town Hall B3
Tulketh Brow A1
University of Central Lancashire A2
Valley Rd C1
Victoria St A2
Walker St A3
Walton's Parade B2
Warwick St A3
Wellfield Bsns Park A1
Wellfield Rd A1
Wellington St A1
West Cliff C2
West Strand A1
Winckley Rd C1
Winckley Square B3
Wolseley Rd C2

## Reading 346

Abbey Ruins B2
Abbey Sq B2
Abbey St B2
Abbot's Walk B2
Acacia Rd C2
Addington Rd C3
Addison Rd A1
Allcroft Rd C3
Alpine St C2
Baker St B1
Berkeley Ave C1
Bridge St B1
Brigham Rd A1
Broad St B1
Broad Street Mall B1
Carey St B1
Castle Hill C1
Castle St B1
Caversham Rd A1
Christchurch Playing Fields A2
Civic Offices & Magistrate's Court B1
Coley Hill C1
Coley Pl C1
Craven Rd C3
Crown St C2
De Montfort Rd A1
Denmark Rd C3
Duke St B2
East St B2
Edgehill St C2
Eldon Rd B3
Eldon Terr B3
Elgar Rd C1
Erleigh Rd C3
Field Rd C1
Fire Station A1
Fobney St B1
Forbury Gdns B2
Forbury Retail Park B2
Forbury Rd B2
Francis St C1
Friar St B1
Garrard St B1
Gas Works Rd B3
George St A2
Great Knollys St B1
Greyfriars B1
Gun St B1
Henry St C1
Hexagon Theatre, The B1
Hill's Meadow A2
HM Prison B2
Howard St B1
Information Ctr B1
Inner Distribution Rd B1
Katesgrove La C1
Kenavon Dr B2
Kendrick Rd C2
King's Meadow Recreation Ground A2
King's Rd B2
Library B2
London Rd C3
London St B2
Lynmouth Rd A1
Market Pl B2
Mill La B2
Mill Rd A2
Minster St B1
Morgan Rd C3
Mount Pleasant C2
Museum of English Rural Life C3
Napier Rd A2
Newark St C2
Newport Rd A1
Old Reading Univ C3
Oracle Sh Ctr, The B1
Orts Rd B3
Pell St C1
Queen Victoria St B1
Queen's Rd A2
Queen's Rd B2
Police Station B1
Post Office B2
Randolph Rd A1
Reading Bridge A2
Reading Station A1
Redlands Rd C3
Renaissance Hotel B1
Riverside Museum B3
Rose Kiln La C1
Royal Berks Hospital (A & E) C3
St Giles C2
St Laurence B2
St Mary's B1
St Mary's Butts B1
St Saviour's Rd C1
Send Rd A3
Sherman Rd C2
Sidmouth St B2
Silver St C2
South St B2
Southampton St C2
Station Hill A1
Station Rd B1
Superstore A3
Swansea Rd A1
Technical College B3
The Causeway A3
The Grove B2
Valpy St B2
Vastern Rd A1
Vue B2
Waldeck St C2
Watlington St B3
West St B1
Whitby Dr C3
Wolseley St C1
York Rd A1
Zinzan St B1

## St Andrews 346

Abbey St B2
Abbey Walk B3
Abbotsford Cres A1
Albany Pk C3
Allan Robertson Dr C2
Ambulance Station C1
Anstruther Rd C3
Argyle St B1
Argyll Business Park C1
Auld Burn Rd B2
Bassaguard Ind Est B1
Bell St B2
Blackfriars Chapel (Ruins) B2
Boase Ave B2
Braid Cres C3
Brewster Pl C3
Bridge St B1
British Golf Mus A1
Broomfaulds Ave C1
Bruce Embankment A1
Bruce St C2
Bus Station A1
Byre B2
Canongate C1
Cathedral and Priory (Ruins) B3
Cemetery B3
Chamberlain St C1
Church St B2
Churchill Cres C2
City Rd A1
Claybraes C1
Cockshaugh Public Park B1
Cosmos Com Ctr B3
Council Office A2
Crawford Gdns C1
Doubledykes Rd B1
Drumcarrow Rd C1
East Sands B3
East Scores A3
Fire Station C1
Forrest St C1
Fraser Ave C1
Freddie Tait St C2
Gateway Ctr A1
Glebe Rd B2
Golf Pl A1
Grange Rd C3
Greenside Pl B2
Greyfriars Gdns A2
Hamilton Ave C2
Hepburn Gdns B1
Holy Trinity B2
Horseleys Park C1
Information Ctr B2
Irvine Cres C3
James Robb Ave C1
James St B1
John Knox Rd C1
Kennedy Gdns B1
Kilrymont Cl C3
Kilrymont Pl C3
Kilrymont Rd C3
Kinburn Park B1
Kinkell Terr C3
Kinnesburn Rd B2
Ladebraes Walk B2
Lady Buchan's Cave A3
Lamberton Pl C1
Lamond Dr C2
Langlands Rd B2
Largo Rd C1
Learmonth Pl C1
Library B2
Links Clubhouse A1
Links, The A1
Livingstone Cres B2
Long Rocks A2
Madras College B2
Market St A2
Martyr's Monument A1
Memorial Hospital (No A+E) B3
Murray Pk A2
Murray Pl A2
Nelson St B2
New Course, The A1
New Picture House A2
North Castle St A3
North St A2
Old Course, The A1
Old Station Rd A1
Pends, The B3
Pilmour Links A1
Pipeland Rd B2/C2
Police Station A2
Post Office B2
Preservation Trust B3
Priestden Pk C3
Priestden Pl C3
Priestden Rd C3
Queen's Gdns B2
Queen's Terr B2
Roundhill Rd C2
Royal & Ancient Golf Club A1
St Andrews B1
St Andrews Aquarium A2
St Andrews Botanic Garden B1
St Andrews Castle (Ruins) & Visitor Ctr A2
St Leonard's School B3
St Mary St B3
St Mary's College B2
St Nicholas St C3
St Rules Tower B3
St Salvator's College A2
Sandyhill Cres C2
Sandyhill Rd C2
Scooniehill Rd C2
Shields Ave C3
Shoolbraids C2
Sloan St B1
South St B2
Spottiswoode Gdns C1
Station Rd A1
Swilcen Bridge A1
The Scores A2
The Shore B3
Tom Morris Dr C2
Tom Stewart La C1
Town Hall B2
Union St A2
University Chapel A2
University Library A2
Univ of St Andrews A1
Viaduct Walk B1
War Memorial A3
Wardlaw Gdns B1
Warrack St C3
Watson Ave B2
West Port B2
West Sands A1
Westview B2
Windmill Rd A1
Winram Pl C1
Wishart Gdns C2
Woodburn Pk B3
Woodburn Pl B3
Woodburn Terr B3
Younger Hall A2

## Salisbury 347

Albany Rd A2
Arts Ctr A3
Ashley Rd A1
Avon Approach A2
Ayleswade Rd C2
Bedwin St A2
Belle Vue A2
Bishop's Palace C2
Bishops Walk B2
Blue Boar Row B2
Bourne Ave A3
Bourne Hill A3
Britford La C2
Broad Walk C2
Brown St B2
Bus Station B2
Castle St A2
Catherine St B2
Chapter House B2
Church House B2
Churchfields Rd B1
Churchill Way East B3
Churchill Way North A3
Churchill Way South C2
Churchill Way West A1
City Hall B2
Close Wall B2
Coldharbour La A1
College St A3
Council Offices A3
Court A1
Crane Bridge Rd B2
Crane St B2
Cricket Ground C1
Culver St South B3
De Vaux Pl C2
Devizes Rd A1
Dews Rd B1
Elm Grove B3
Elm Grove Rd A3
Endless St A2
Estcourt Rd A3
Exeter St C2
Fairview Rd A3
Fire Station A1
Fisherton St A1
Folkestone Rd C1
Fowlers Hill B3
Fowlers Rd B3
Friary Estate C3
Friary La B2
Gas La A1
Gigant St B3
Greencroft B3
Greencroft St A3
Guildhall B2
Hall of John Halle B2
Hamilton Rd A2
Harnham Mill B1
Harnham Rd C1/C2
High St B2
Hospital A1
Ho of John A'Port B2
Information Ctr B2
Kelsey Rd A3
King's Rd A2
Laverstock Rd B3
Library B2
London Rd A3
Lower St C1
Maltings, The B2
Manor Rd A3
Marsh La A1
Medieval Hall B2
Milford Hill B3
Milford St B3
Mill Rd B1
Millstream Approach A2
Mompesson House (NT) B2
New Bridge Rd C2
New Canal B2
New Harnham Rd C2
New St B2
North Canonry B2
North Gate B2
North Walk B2
Old George Hall B2
Old Blandford Rd C1
Old Deanery B2
Park St A3
Parsonage Green C1
Playhouse Theatre A2
Post Office A2/B2/C2
Poultry Cross B2
Queen Elizabeth Gdns B1
Queen's Rd A3
Rampart Rd B3
St Ann's Gate B2
St Ann St B2
St Marks Rd A3
St Martins B3
St Mary's Cathedral B2
St Nicholas Hospital C2
St Paul's A1
St Paul's Rd A1
St Thomas B2
Salisbury & South Wiltshire Museum B2
Salisbury General Hospital (A&E) C2
Salisbury Station A1
Salt La A3
Saxon Rd C1
Scots La A2
Shady Bower B3
South Canonry C2
South Gate C2
Southampton Rd B2
Spire View A1
Sports Ground C3
The Friary B3
Tollgate Rd B3
Town Path B1
Wain-a-Long Rd A3
Wardrobe, The B2
Wessex Rd A3
West Walk C2
Wilton Rd A1
Wiltshire College B3
Winchester St B3
Windsor Rd A1
Winston Churchill Gdns C3
Wyndham Rd A2
YHA B3
York Rd A1

## Scarborough 347

Aberdeen Walk B2
Albert Rd A2
Albion Rd C2
Alexandra Bowling Hall A1
Alexandra Gardens A1
Auborough St B2
Belle Vue St C1
Belmont Rd C2
Brunswick Sh Ctr B2
Castle Dykes B3
Castlegate B3
Castle Holms A3
Castle Hill A3
Castle Rd B2
Castle Walls A3
Cemetery B1
Central Lift C2
Clarence Gardens A2
Coach Park B1
Columbus Ravine A1
Court B1
Cricket Ground A1
Cross St B2
Crown Terr C2
Dean Rd B1
Devonshire Dr A1
East Harbour B3
East Pier B3
Eastborough B2
Elmville Ave B1
Esplanade C2
Falconers Rd B2
Falsgrave Rd C1
Fire Station B2
Foreshore Rd B2
Friargate B2
Futurist Theatre B2
Gladstone Rd B1
Gladstone St B1
Hoxton Rd B1
Information Ctr B2/B3
King St B2
Londesborough Rd C1
Longwestgate B3
Marine Dr A3
Miniature Railway A1
Nelson St B1
Newborough B2
Nicolas St B2
North Marine Rd A1
North St B2
Northway B1
Old Harbour B3
Peasholm Park A1
Peasholm Rd A1
Plaza A1
Police Station B1
Post Office B2/C1
Princess St B3
Prospect Rd B1
Queen St B2
Queen's Parade A2
Queen's Tower (Remains) A3
Ramshill Rd C2
Roman Signal Sta A3
Roscoe St C1
Rotunda Museum C2
Royal Albert Dr A2
St Martin-on-the-Hill C2
St Martin's Ave C2
St Mary's B3
St Thomas St B2
Sandside B3
Scarborough Art Gallery and Crescent Art Studio C2
Scarborough Castle A3
Scarborough C1
Somerset Terr C2
South Cliff Lift C2
Spa, The C2
Spa Theatre, The C2
Stephen Joseph Theatre B1
Tennyson Ave B1
The Crescent C2
Tollergate B2
Town Hall B2
Trafalgar Rd B1
Trafalgar Square A1
Trafalgar St West B1
Valley Bridge Parade C2
Valley Rd C1
Vernon Rd C2
Victoria Park Mount A1
Victoria Rd B1
West Pier B3
Westborough C1
Westover Rd C1
Westwood C1
Woodall Ave A1
York Pl B2
Yorkshire Coast College (Westwood Campus) C1

## Sheffield 347

Addy Dr A2
Addy St A2
Adelphi St A3
Albert Terrace Rd A3
Albion St A2
Aldred Rd A1
Allen St A4
Alma St A4
Angel St B5
Arundel Gate B5
Arundel St C4
Ashberry Rd A2
Ashdell Rd C1
Ashgate Rd C1
Athletics Ctr B2
Attercliffe Rd A6
Bailey St B4
Ball St A4
Balm Green B4
Bank St B4
Barber Rd A2
Bard St B5
Barker's Pool B4
Bates St A1
Beech Hill Rd C1
Beet St B3
Bellefield St A3
Bernard Rd A6
Bernard St B6
Birkendale A2
Birkendale Rd A2
Birkendale View A1
Bishop St C4
Blackwell Pl B6
Blake St A2
Blonk St A5
Bolsover St B2
Botanical Gdns C1
Bower Rd A1
Bradley St A1
Bramall La C4
Bramwell St A3
Bridge St A4/A5
Brighton Terrace Rd A1
Broad La B3
Broad St B6
Brocco St A3
Brook Hill B3
Broomfield Rd C1
Broomgrove Rd C2
Broomhall Pl C3
Broomhall Rd C2
Broomhall St C3
Broomspring La C2
Brown St C5
Brunswick St B3
Burgess St B4
Burlington St A2
Burns Rd A2
Bus/Coach Station B5
Cadman St A6
Cambridge St B4
Campo La B4
Carver St B4
Castle Market B5
Castle Square B5
Castlegate A5
Cathedral (RC) B4
Cathedral B4
Cavendish St B3
Charles St C4
Charter Row C4
Children's Hospital (A&E) B2
Church St B4
City Hall B4
City Hall B4
City Rd C6
Claremont Cr B2
Claremont Pl B2
Clarke St C3
Clarkegrove Rd C2
Clarkehouse Rd C1
Clarkson St B2
Cobden View Rd A1
Collegiate Cr C2
Commercial St B5
Commonside A1
Conduit Rd B1
Cornish St A3
Corporation St A4
Court B4
Cricket Inn Rd B6
Cromwell St A1
Crookes Rd B1
Crookes Valley Park B2
Crookes Valley Rd B2
Crookesmoor Rd A2
Crown Court A4
Crucible Theatre B5
Cutlers Gate A6
Cutler's Hall B4
Daniel Hill A2
Dental Hospital B2
Dept for Education & Employment C4
Devonshire Green B3
Devonshire St B3
Division St B4
Dorset St C2
Dover St A3
Duchess Rd C5
Duke St B5
Duncombe St A1
Durham Rd B2
Earl St C4
Earl Way C4
Ecclesall Rd C3
Edward St B3
Effingham Rd A6
Effingham St A6
Egerton St C3
Eldon St B3
Elmore Rd B1
Exchange St B5

Eyre St C4
Fargate B4
Farm Rd C5
Fawcett St A3
Filey St B3
Fire & Police Mus A4
Fire Station C4
Fir St A1
Fitzalan Sq/ Ponds Forge B5
Fitzwater Rd C6
Fitzwilliam Gate C4
Fitzwilliam St B3
Flat St B5
Foley St A6
Foundry Climbing Ctr A4
Fulton Rd A1
Furnace Hill A4
Furnival Rd A5
Furnival Sq C4
Furnival St C4
Garden St B3
Gell St B3
Gibraltar St A4
Glebe Rd B1
Glencoe Rd C6
Glossop Rd B2/B3/C1
Gloucester St C2
Granville Rd C6
Granville Rd/ Sheffield College C5
Graves Gallery B5
Greave Rd B3
Green La A4
Hadfield St A1
Hanover St C3
Hanover Way C3
Harcourt Rd B1
Harmer La B5
Havelock St C2
Hawley St B4
Haymarket B5
Headford St C3
Heavygate Rd A1
Henry St A3
High St B4
Hodgson St C3
Holberry Gdns C2
Hollis Croft B4
Holly St B4
Hounsfield Rd B3
Howard Rd A1
Hoyle St A3
Hyde Park A6
Infirmary Rd A3
Infirmary Rd A3
Information Ctr B4
Jericho St A3
Johnson St A5
Kelham Island Industrial Museum A4
Lawson Rd C1
Leadmill Rd C5
Leadmill St C5
Leadmill, The C5
Leamington St A1
Leavy Rd B3
Lee Croft B4
Leopold St B4
Leveson St A6
Library A2
Library B5
Library C1
Lyceum Theatre B5
Malinda St A3
Maltravers St A5
Manor Oaks Rd B6
Mappin St B3
Marlborough Rd B1
Mary St C4
Matilda St C4
Matlock Rd A1
Meadow St A3
Melbourn Rd A1
Melbourne Ave C1
Millennium Galleries B5
Milton St C3
Mitchell St B3
Mona Ave A1
Mona Rd A1
Montgomery Terr Rd A3
Montgomery Theatre B4
Monument Gdns C6
Moor Oaks Rd B1
Moore St C3
Mowbray St A4
Mushroom La B2
Netherthorpe Rd B3
Netherthorpe Rd B3
Newbould La C1
Nile St C1
Norfolk Park Rd C6
Norfolk Rd C6
Norfolk St B4
North Church St B4
Northfield Rd A1
Northumberland Rd B1
Nursery St A5
O2 Academy B5
Oakholme Rd C1
Octagon B2
Odeon B5
Old St B6
Oxford St A2
Paradise St B4
Park La C2
Park Sq B5
Parker's Rd B1
Pearson Building (Univ) C2
Penistone Rd A3
Pinstone St B4
Pitt St B3
Police Station A4/B5
Pond Hill B5
Pond St B5
Ponds Forge Sports Ctr B5
Portobello St B3
Post Office A1/A2/B3/B4/B5/B6/C1/C3/C4/C6
Powell St A2
Queen St B4
Queen's Rd C5
Ramsey Rd B1
Red Hill B3
Redcar Rd B1
Regent St B3
Rockingham St B4
Roebuck Rd A2
Royal Hallamshire Hospital C2
Russell St A4
Rutland Park C1
St George's Cl B3
St Mary's Gate C3
St Mary's Rd C4/C5
St Peter & St Paul Cathedral B4
St Philip's Rd A3
Savile St A5
School Rd B1
Scotland St A4
Severn Rd B1
Shalesmoor A4
Shalesmoor A3
Sheaf St B5
Sheffield Hallam Univ B5
Sheffield Ice Sports Ctr – Skate Central C5
Sheffield Parkway A6
Sheffield Station ≋ C5
Sheffield Sta/ Sheffield Hallam University B5
Sheffield University B2
Shepherd St A3
Shipton St A2
Shoreham St C4
Showroom, The C5
Shrewsbury Rd C5
Sidney St C4
Site Gallery C5
Slinn St A1
Smithfield A4
Snig Hill A5
Snow La A4
Solly St B3
Southbourne Rd C1
South La C4
South Street Park B5
Spital Hill A5
Spital St A5
Spring Hill B1
Spring Hill Rd B1
Springvale Rd A1
Stafford Rd C6
Stafford St B6
Stanley St A5
Suffolk Rd C5
Summer St B2
Sunny Bank C3
Surrey St B4
Sussex St A6
Sutton St B3
Sydney Rd A2
Sylvester St C4
Talbot St B5
Taptonville Rd B1
Tax Office C4
Tenter St B4
The Moor C4
Town Hall B4
Townend St A1
Townhead St B4
Trafalgar St B4
Tree Root Walk B2
Trinity St A4
Trippet La B4
Turner Mus of Glass B3
Union St B4
Univ Drama Studio B2
Univ of Sheffield B3
Upper Allen St A3
Upper Hanover St B3
Upperthorpe Rd A2/A3
Verdon St A5
Victoria Quays ✦ B5
Victoria Rd C2
Victoria St B3
Waingate B5
Watery St A3
Watson Rd C1
Wellesley Rd B2
Wellington St C3
West Bar A4
West Bar Green A4
West One B3
West St B3
West St B4
Westbourne Rd C1
Western Bank B2
Western Rd A1
Weston Park B2
Weston Park Hospl B2
Weston Park Mus B2
Weston St B2
Wharncliffe Rd C3
Whitham Rd B1
Wicker A5
Wilkinson St B2
William St C3
Winter Garden ✦ B4
Winter St B2
York St B4
Yorkshire Artspace C5
Young St C4

## Shrewsbury 347

Abbey Church B3
Abbey Foregate B3
Abbey Lawn Bsns Park B3
Abbots House B2
Agricultural Show Gd A1
Albert St A2
Alma St B1
Ashley St A3
Ashton Rd C1
Avondale Dr A3
Bage Way C3
Barker St B1
Beacall's La A2
Beeches La C2
Beehive La C1
Belle Vue Gdns C2
Belle Vue Rd C2
Belmont Bank C1
Berwick Ave A1
Berwick Rd A1
Betton St C2
Bishop St B3
Bradford St B3
Bridge St B1
Bus Station B2
Butcher Row B2
Burton St A3
Butler Rd C1
Bynner St C2
Canon St B3
Canonbury C1
Castle Bsns Park, The A2
Castle Foregate A2
Castle Gates B2
Castle Museum B2
Castle St B2
Cathedral (RC) C1
Chester St A2
Cineworld C3
Claremont Bank B1
Claremont Hill B1
Cleveland St B3
Coleham Head B2
Coleham Pumping Station C2
College Hill B1
Corporation La A1
Coton Cres A1
Coton Hill A2
Coton Mount A1
Crescent La C1
Crewe St A2
Cross Hill B1
Darwin Ctr B2
Dingle, The B1
Dogpole B2
Draper's Hall B2
English Bridge B2
Fish St B2
Frankwell B1
Gateway Ctr, The A2
Gravel Hill La A1
Greyfriars Rd C2
Guildhall B1
Hampton Rd A3
Haycock Way C3
HM Prison B2
High St B1
Hills La B1
Holywell St B3
Hunter St A1
Information Ctr B1
Ireland's Mansion & Bear Steps B1
John St A3
Kennedy Rd C1
King St B3
Kingsland Bridge C1
Kingsland Bridge (toll) C1
Kingsland Rd C1
Library B2
Lime St C2
Longden Coleham C2
Longden Rd C1
Longner St B1
Luciefelde Rd C1
Mardol B1
Market B1
Marine Terr C2
Monkmoor Rd B3
Moreton Cr C2
Mount St A1
Music Hall B1
New Park Cl A3
New Park Rd A2
New Park St A3
North St A2
Oakley St C1
Old Coleham C2
Old Market Hall B1
Old Potts Way C3
Parade Ctr B2
Police Station B1
Post Office A2/B1/B2/B3
Pride Hill B1
Pride Hill Ctr B1
Priory Rd B1
Pritchard Way C3
Queen St A2
Raby Cr C2
Rad Brook C1
Rea Brook C3
Riverside B1
Roundhill La A1
Rowley's House B1
St Alkmund's B2
St Chad's B1
St Chad's Terr B1
St John's Hill B1
St Julians Friars C2
St Mary's B2
St Mary's St B2
Salters La C2
Scott St C3
Severn Bank A3
Severn St A2
Shrewsbury ≋ B2
Shrewsbury High School for Girls C1
Shrewsbury School ✦ C1
Shropshire Wildlife Trust ✦ B3
Smithfield Rd B1
South Hermitage C1
Swan Hill B1
Sydney Ave A3
Tankerville St B3
The Dana B2
The Quarry B1
The Square B1
Tilbrook Dr A3
Town Walls C1
Trinity St C2
Underdale Rd B3
Victoria Ave B1
Victoria Quay B1
Victoria St B2
Welsh Bridge B1
Whitehall St B3
Wood St A2
Wyle Cop B2

## Southampton 347

Above Bar St A2
Albert Rd North B3
Albert Rd South C3
Anderson's Rd B3
Archaeology Mus (God's Ho Tower) C2
Argyle Rd A2
Arundel Tower ✦ B1
Bargate, The ✦ B2
Bargate Shopping Ctr B2
BBC Regional Ctr A1
Bedford Pl A1
Belvidere Rd A3
Bernard St C2
Blechynden Terr A1
Brazil Rd C3
Brinton's Rd A2
Britannia Rd A3
Briton St C2
Brunswick Pl A2
Bugle St C1
Canute Rd C3
Castle Way C2
Catchcold Tower ✦ B1
Central Bridge C3
Central Rd C2
Channel Way C3
Chapel Rd B3
Cineworld C3
City Art Gallery A1
City College B3
Civic Ctr A1
Civic Ctr Rd A1
Coach Station B1
Commercial Rd A1
Cumberland Pl A1
Cunard Rd C2
Derby Rd A3
Devonshire Rd A1
Dock Gate 4 C2
Dock Gate 8 B1
East Park A2
East Park Terr A2
East St B2
East St Shopping Ctr B2
Endle St B3
European Way C2
Fire Station A2
Floating Bridge Rd C3
Golden Gr A3
Graham Rd A2
Guildhall A1
Hanover Bldgs B2
Harbour Lights C3
Harbour Pde B1
Hartington Rd A3
Havelock Rd A1
Henstead Rd A1
Herbert Walker Ave B1
High St B2
Hoglands Park B2
Holy Rood (Rems), Merchant Navy Memorial B2
Houndwell Park B2
Houndwell Pl B2
Hythe Ferry C2
Information Ctr A1
Isle of Wight Ferry Terminal C1
James St B3
Java Rd C2
Kingsway A2
Leisure World B1
Library A1
Lime St B2
London Rd A2
Marine Pde B3
Maritime C1
Marsh La B2
Mayflower Meml ✦ C1
Mayflower Park C1
Mayflower Theatre, The A1
Medieval Merchant's House C1
Melbourne St B3
Millais A2
Morris Rd A1
National Oceanography Ctr ✦ C3
Neptune Way C3
New Rd A2
Nichols Rd A3
North Front A2
Northam Rd A3
Ocean Dock C2
Ocean Village Marina C3
Ocean Way C3
Odeon B1
Ogle Rd B1
Old Northam Rd A2
Orchard La B2
Oxford Ave A2
Oxford St C2
Palmerston Park A2
Palmerston Rd A2
Parsonage Rd A3
Peel St A3
Platform Rd C2
Police Station A1
Portland Terr B1
Post Office A2/A3/B2
Pound Tree Rd B2
Quays Swimming & Diving Complex, The B1
Queen's Park C2
Queen's Peace Fountain ✦ A2
Queen's Terr C2
Queen's Way B2
Radcliffe Rd A3
Rochester St A3
Royal Pier C1
Royal South Hants Hospital A2
St Andrew's Rd A2
St Mary St A2
St Mary's B3
St Mary's Leisure Ctr A2
St Mary's Pl B2
St Mary's Rd A2
St Mary's Stadium (Southampton FC) A3
St Michael's C1
Solent Sky C3
South Front B2
Southampton Central Station ≋ A1
Southampton Solent University A2
SS Shieldhall C2
Terminus Terr C2
The Mall, Marlands A1
The Polygon A1
Threefield La B2
Titanic Engineers' Memorial ✦ A2
Town Quay C1
Town Walls B2
Tudor House C1
Vincent's Walk B2
West Gate Hall C1
West Marlands Rd A1
West Park A1
West Park Rd A1
West Quay Rd B1
West Quay Retail Park B1
West Quay Sh Ctr B1
West Rd C2
Western Esplanade B1
Winton St A2

## Southend-on-Sea 348

Adventure Island ✦ C3
Albany Ave A1
Albert Rd C3
Alexandra Rd C2
Alexandra St C2
Alexandra Yacht Club ✦ C2
Ashburnham Rd B2
Ave Rd B1
Avenue Terr B1
Balmoral Rd B1
Baltic Ave B3
Baxter Ave A2/B2
Beecroft Art Gallery C1
Bircham Rd A2
Boscombe Rd B3
Boston Ave A1/B2
Bournemouth Park Rd A3
Browning Ave A3
Bus Station C3
Byron Ave A3
Cambridge Rd C1/C2
Canewdon Rd B1
Carnarvon Rd A2
Central Ave A3
Chelmsford Ave A1
Chichester Rd B2
Church Rd C3
Civic Ctr A2
Clarence Rd C2
Clarence St C2
Cliff Ave B1
Cliffs Pavilion C1
Clifftown Parade C2
Clifftown Rd C2
Colchester Rd A1
College Way B2
Coleman St B3
County Court B3
Cromer Rd B3
Crowborough Rd A2
Dryden Ave A3
East St A2
Elmer App B2
Elmer Ave B2
Gainsborough Dr A1
Gayton Rd A2
Glenhurst Rd A2
Gordon Pl B2
Gordon Rd B2
Grainger Rd A2
Greyhound Way A3
Guildford Rd B3
Hamlet Ct Rd B1
Hamlet Rd C1
Harcourt Ave A1
Hartington Rd C3
Hastings Rd B3
Herbert Gr C3
Heygate Ave C3
High St B2/C2
Information Ctr C3
Kenway A2
Kilworth Ave B3
Lancaster Gdns B3
Library B2
London Rd B1
Lucy Rd C3
MacDonald Ave A1
Magistrates Court A2
Maldon Rd A2
Maine Ave C1
Marine Rd C1
Marine Parade C3
Milton Rd B1
Milton St B2
Napier Ave B2
North Ave A3
North Rd A1/B1
Odeon B2
Osborne Rd B1
Park Cres B1
Park Rd B1
Park St B1
Park Terr B1
Pier Hill C3
Pleasant Rd C3
Police Station A2
Post Office B2/B3
Princes St B2
Queens Rd B2
Queensway B2/B3/C3
Rayleigh Ave A1
Redstock Rd A2
Rochford Ave A1
Royal Mews C2
Royal Terr C2
Royals Sh Ctr, The C3
Ruskin Ave A3
St Ann's Rd B3
St Helen's Rd B1
St John's Rd B1
St Leonard's Rd C3
St Lukes Rd A3
St Vincent's Rd C1
Salisbury Ave A1/B1
Scratton Rd C2
Shakespeare Dr A1
Short St A2
South Ave A3
Southchurch Rd B3
South Essex College B2
Southend Central ≋ B2
Southend Pier Railway C3
Southend Radio C2
Southend United FC A1
Southend Victoria ≋ B2
Stadium Rd A2
Stanfield Rd A2
Stanley Rd C3
Sutton Rd A3/B3
Swanage Rd B3
Sweyne Ave A1
Sycamore Gr A3
Tennyson Ave A3
The Grove A3
Tickfield Ave A2
Tudor Rd A1
Tunbridge Rd A2
Tylers Ave B3
Tyrrel Dr B3
Univ of Essex B2/C2
Vale Ave A2
Victoria Ave A2
Victoria Sh Ctr, The B2
Warrior Sq B3
Wesley Rd C3
West Rd A1
West St A1
Westcliff Ave C1
Westcliff Parade C1
Western Esplanade C1
Weston Rd C2
Whitegate Rd B3
Wilson Rd C1
Wimborne Rd B3
York Rd C3

## Stirling 348

Abbey Rd A3
Abbotsford Pl A3
Abercromby Pl C1
Albert Halls B1
Albert Pl B1
Alexandra Pl A3
Allan Park C2
Ambulance Station A2
AMF Ten Pin Bowling ✦ B2
Argyll Ave A3
Argyll's Lodging ✦ B1
Back O' Hill Ind Est A1
Back O' Hill Rd A1
Baker St B2
Ballengeich Pass A1
Balmoral Pl B1
Barn Rd B1
Barnton St B2
Bow St B1
Bruce St A2
Burghmuir Ind Est C2
Burghmuir Rd A2/B2/C2
Bus Station B2
Cambuskenneth Bridge A3
Carlton C2
Castle Ct B1
Causewayhead Rd A2
Cemetery A1
Church of the Holy Rude B1
Clarendon Pl C1
Club House B1
Colquhoun St C3
Corn Exchange B2
Council Offices C2
Court B2
Cowane A2
Cowane St A2
Cowane's Hospital B1
Crawford Sh Arc B2
Crofthead Rd A1
Dean Cres A3
Douglas St A2
Drip Rd A1
Drummond La C1
Drummond Pl C1
Drummond Pl La C1
Dumbarton Rd C2
Eastern Access Rd B2
Edward Ave A3
Edward Rd A2
Forrest Rd A2
Fort A1
Forth Cres B2
Forth St A2
Gladstone Pl C1
Glebe Ave C1
Glebe Cres C1
Golf Course C1
Goosecroft Rd B2
Gowanhill A1
Greenwood Ave B1
Harvey Wynd A1
Information Ctr B1
Irvine Pl B2
James St A2
John St B1
Kerse Rd C3
King's Knot ✦ B1
King's Park C1
King's Park Rd C1
Laurencecroft Rd A2
Leisure Pool B2
Library B2
Linden Ave C2
Lovers Wk A2
Lower Back Walk B1
Lower Bridge St A2
Lower Castlehill A1
Mar Pl B1
Meadow Pl A3
Meadowforth Rd C3
Middlemuir Rd C3
Millar Pl A3
Morris Terr B2
Mote Hill A1
Murray Pl B2
Nelson Pl C2
Old Town Cemetery B1
Old Town Jail ✦ B1
Orchard House Hospital (No A+E) A2
Park Terr C1
Phoenix Industrial Est C3
Players Rd C3
Port St C2
Princes St B2
Queen St B2
Queen's Rd B1
Queenshaugh Dr A3
Rainbow Slides B2
Ramsay Pl A2
Riverside Dr A3
Ronald Pl A1
Rosebery Pl A2
Royal Gardens B1
Royal Gdns B1
St Mary's Wynd B1
St Ninian's Rd C2
Scott St A2
Seaforth Pl B2
Shore Rd B2
Smith Art Gallery & Museum B1
Snowdon Pl C1
Snowdon Pl La C1
Spittal St B2
Springkerse Ind Est C3
Springkerse Rd C3
Stirling Business Ctr C2
Stirling Castle A1
Stirling County Rugby Football Club A3
Stirling Enterprise Pk B3
Stirling Old Bridge A2
Stirling Station ≋ B2
Superstore A2
Sutherland Ave A3
TA Ctr C3
Tannery La A2
The Bastion ✦ C2
The Changing Room B1
Thistle Industrial Est C3
Thistles Sh Ctr, The B2
Tollbooth, The ✦ B1
Town Wall B1
Union St A2
Upper Back Walk B1
Upper Bridge St A1
Upper Castlehill B1
Upper Craigs C2
Victoria Pl C1
Victoria Rd B1
Victoria Sq B1/C1
Vue B2
Wallace St A2
Waverley Cres A3
Wellgreen Rd C2
Windsor Pl C1
YHA B1

## Stoke 348

Ashford St A3
Avenue Rd A3
Aynsley Rd A2
Barnfield C1
Bath St C2
Beresford St A3
Bilton St C2
Boon Ave C2
Booth St C2
Boothen Rd C2/C3
Boughey St C2
Boughley Rd B3
Brighton St B1
Campbell Rd C2
Carlton Rd B3
Cauldon Rd A3
Cemetery A2
Cemetery Rd A2
Chamberlain Ave C1
Church (RC) B2
Church St C2
City Rd C3
Civic Ctr & King's Hall B3
Cliff Vale Pk A1
College Rd A3
Convent Cl B2
Copeland St B2
Cornwallis St C3
Corporation St C2
Crowther St A3
Dominic St B1
Elenora St B2
Elgin St B2
Epworth St A3
Etruscan St A1
Film Theatre B3
Fleming Rd C2
Fletcher Rd C2
Floyd St B2
Foden St C2
Frank St C2
Franklin Rd C1
Frederick Ave B1
Garden St C1
Garner St A1
Gerrard St B2
Glebe St B3
Greatbach Ave B1
Hanley Park A3
Harris St B1
Hartshill Rd B1
Hayward St A2
Hide St B2
Higson Ave B2
Hill St B2
Honeywall B2
Hunters Dr C1
Hunters Way C1
Keary St C2
Kingsway B2
Leek Rd B3
Library C2
Lime St C2
Liverpool Rd B2
London Rd C2
Lonsdale St C2
Lovatt St B2
Lytton St B3
Market C2
Newcastle La C1
Newlands St A2
Norfolk St A2
North St A1/B2
North Staffordshire Royal Infirmary (A&E) B1
Northcote Ave B2
Oldmill St C3
Oriel St B1
Oxford St B1
Penkhull New Rd C1
Penkhull St C1
Police Station C2
Portmeirion Pottery ✦ C2
Post Office A3/B1/B3/C1/C2
Prince's Rd B1
Pump St B2
Quarry Ave B1
Quarry Rd B1
Queen Anne St A3
Queen's Rd C1
Queensway A1/B2/C3
Richmond St B1
Rothwell St C1
St Peter's B3
St Thomas Pl C1
Scrivenor Rd A1
Seaford St A3
Selwyn St C3
Shelton New Rd A1
Shelton Old Rd B2
Sheppard St C2
Spark St C2
Spencer Rd B3
Spode St C2
Squires View B3
Staffordshire Univ B3
Stanley Matthews Sports Ctr B3
Station Rd B3
Stoke Business Park C3
Stoke Recreation Ctr C2
Stoke Rd A2
Stoke-on-Trent Coll A3
Stoke-on-Trent Sta ≋ B3
Sturgess St C2
The Villas C1
Thistley Hough C1
Thornton Rd B3
Tolkien Way B1
Trent Valley Rd C1
Vale St B2
Watford St A3
Wellesley St A3
West Ave B1
Westland St B1
Yeaman St C2
Yoxall Ave B1

## Stratford-upon-Avon 348

Albany Rd B1
Alcester Rd B1
Ambulance Station B1
Arden St B1
Avenue Farm A1
Ave Farm Ind Est A1
Avenue Rd A3
Avon Industrial Estate A2
Baker Ave A1
Bandstand C3
Benson Rd A3
Birmingham Rd A2
Boat Club B3
Borden Pl C1
Brass Rubbing Ctr ✦ C2
Bridge St B2
Bridgetown Rd C3
Bridgeway B3
Broad St C2
Broad Walk C2
Brookvale Rd C1
Bull St C2
Bus Station B2
Butterfly Farm ✦ C3
Cemetery C1
Chapel La B2
Cherry Orchard C1
Chestnut Walk B2
Children's Playground C3
Church St C2
Civic Hall B2
Clarence Rd B1
Clopton Bridge ✦ B3
Clopton Rd A2
Coach Terminal & Park B3
College B1
College La C2
College St C2
Community Sports Ctr B1
Council Offices (District) B2
Courtyard C2
Cox's Yard ✦ B3
Cricket Ground C3
Ely Gdns B2
Ely St B2
Evesham Rd C1
Fire Station B1
Foot Ferry C3
Fordham Ave A2
Gallery, The B3
Garrick Way C1
Gower Memorial ✦ B3
Great William St B2
Greenhill St B2
Grove Rd B2
Guild St B2
Guildhall & School B2
Hall's Croft C2
Hartford Rd C1
Harvard House B2
Henley St B2
High St B2
Holton St C2
Holy Trinity C2
Information Ctr B3
Jolyffe Park Rd A2
Kipling Rd C3
Leisure & Visitor Ctr B3
Library B2
Lodge Rd B1
Maidenhead Rd A3
Mansell St B2
Masons Court B2
Masons Rd A1
Maybird Shopping Pk A2
Maybrook Rd A1
Mayfield Ave A2
Meer St B2
Mill La C2
Moat House Hotel B3
Narrow La C2
Nash's Ho & New Pl B2
New St C2
Old Town C2
Orchard Way C1
Paddock La C1
Park Rd A1
Payton St B2
Percy St A2
Police Station B2
Post Office B2/B3
Recreation Ground C2
Regal Road A2
Rother St B2
Rowley Cr A3
Royal Shakespeare & Swan Theatres B3
Ryland St C2
Saffron Meadow C2
St Andrew's Cr B1
St Gregory's A3
St Gregory's Rd A3
St Mary's Rd A2
Sanctus Dr C2
Sanctus St C1
Sandfield Rd C2
Scholars La B2
Seven Meadows Rd C2
Shakespeare Ctr ✦ B2
Shakespeare Institute C2
Shakespeare St B2
Shakespeare's Birthplace ✦ B2
Sheep St B2
Shelley Rd C3
Shipston Rd C3
Shottery Rd C1
Slingates Rd A2
Southern La C2
Station Rd B1
Stratford Healthcare B2
Stratford Hospital B2
Stratford Sports Club B1
Stratford-upon-Avon Station ≋ B1
Swan's Nest La B3
Talbot Rd A2
The Greenway C2
The Willows B1
The Willows North B1
Tiddington Rd B3
Timothy's Bridge Industrial Estate A1
Timothy's Bridge Rd A1
Town Hall & Council Offices B2
Town Sq B2
Trinity St C2
Tyler St B2
War Memorial Gdns B3
Warwick Rd B3
Waterside B3
Welcombe Rd A3
West St C2
Western Rd A2
Wharf Rd A2
Wood St B2

Sunderland • Swansea • Swindon • Taunton • Telford • Torquay • Truro • Wick 365


**Sunderland** 348

Albion Pl C2
Alliance Pl B1
Argyle St C2
Ashwood St C1
Athenaeum St B2
Azalea Terr C2
Beach St A1
Bede Theatre C3
Bedford St B2
Beechwood Terr C1
Belvedere Rd C2
Blandford St B2
Borough Rd B3
Bridge Cr B2
Bridge St B2
Brooke St A2
Brougham St B2
Burdon Rd C2
Burn Park C1
Burn Park Rd C1
Burn Park Tech Park C1
Carol St B1
Charles St A3
Chester Rd C1
Chester Terr B1
Church St A3
Civic Ctr C2
Cork St B3
Coronation St B3
Cowan Terr C2
Crowtree Rd B2
Dame Dorothy St A2
Deptford Rd B1
Deptford Terr A1
Derby St C2
Derwent St C2
Dock St A3
Dundas St A2
Durham Rd C1
Easington St A2
Egerton St C3
Empire B2
Empire Theatre B2
Farringdon Row B1
Fawcett St B2
Fox St C1
Foyle St B3
Frederick St B3
Gill Rd B2
Hanover Pl A1
Havelock Terr C1
Hay St A2
Headworth Sq B3
Hendon Rd B3
High St East B3
High St West B2/B3
Holmeside B2
Hylton Rd B1
Information Ctr B2
John St B3
Kier Hardie Way A2
Lambton St B3
Laura St C3
Lawrence St B3
Leisure Ctr B2
Library & Arts Ctr B3
Lily St B1
Lime St B1
Livingstone Rd B2
Low Row B2
Matamba Terr B1
Millburn St B1
Millennium Way A2
Minster B2
Monkwearmouth Station Museum A2
Mowbray Park C3
Mowbray Rd C3
Murton St C3
National Glass Ctr A3
New Durham Rd C1
Newcastle Rd A2
Nile St B3
Norfolk St B3
North Bridge St A2
Northern Gallery for Contemporary Art B3
Otto Terr C1
Park La C2
Park Lane C2
Park Rd C2
Paul's Rd B3
Peel St C3
Police Station B2
Post Office B2
Priestly Cr A1
Queen St B2
Railway Row B1
Retail Park B1
Richmond St A2
Roker Ave A2
Royalty Theatre C1
Ryhope Rd C2
St Mary's Way B2
St Michael's Way B2
St Peter's A2
St Peter's A2
St Peter's Way A3
St Vincent St C3
Salem Rd C3
Salem St C3
Salisbury St C3
Sans St B3
Silkworth Row B1
Southwick Rd A2
Stadium of Light (Sunderland AFC) A2
Stadium Way A2
Stobart St A2
Stockton Rd C2
Suffolk St C3
Sunderland Aquatic Ctr A2
Sunderland B2
Sunderland Mus B3
Sunderland Station B2
Sunderland St B3
Tatham St C3
Tavistock Pl B3
The Bridges B2
The Place B3
The Royalty C1
Thelma St C1
Thomas St North A2
Thornholme Rd C1
Toward Rd C3
Transport Interchange C2
Trimdon St Way B1
Tunstall Rd C2
University C1
University Library C1
University of Sunderland (City Campus) B1
University of Sunderland (Sir Tom Cowie at St Peter's Campus) A3
Vaux Brewery Way A2
Villiers St B3
Villiers St South B3
Vine Pl C2
Violet St B1
Walton La B3
Waterworks Rd B1
Wearmouth Bridge B2
Wellington La A1
West Sunniside B3
West Wear St B3
Westbourne Rd B1
Western Hill C1
Wharncliffe B1
Whickham St A3
White House Rd C3
Wilson St North A2
Winter Gdns C3
Wreath Quay A1

**Swansea** *Abertawe* 348

Adelaide St C3
Albert Row C3
Alexandra Rd B3
Argyle St C1
Baptist Well Pl A2
Beach St C1
Belle Vue Way B3
Berw Rd A1
Berwick Terr A2
Bond St C1
Brangwyn Concert Hall C1
Bridge St A3
Brookands Terr B1
Brunswick St C1
Bryn-Syfi Terr A2
Bryn-y-Mor Rd C1
Bullins La B1
Burrows Rd C1
Bus/Rail link A3
Bus Station C2
Cadfan Rd A1
Cadrawd Rd A1
Caer St B3
Carig Cr A1
Carlton Terr B2
Carmarthen Rd A3
Castle Square B3
Castle St B3
Catherine St C1
City & County of Swansea Offices (County Hall) C2
City & County of Swansea Offices (Guildhall) C1
Clarence St C2
Colbourne Terr A2
Constitution Hill B1
Court B3
Creidiol Rd A2
Cromwell St B2
Duke St B1
Dunvant Pl C2
Dyfatty Park A3
Dyfatty St A3
Dyfed Ave A1
Dylan Thomas Ctr B3
Dylan Thomas Theatre C3
Eaton Cr C1
Eigen Cr A1
Elfed Rd A1
Emlyn Rd A1
Evans Terr A3
Fairfield Terr B1
Ffynone Dr B1
Ffynone Rd B1
Fire Station B3
Firm St A2
Fleet St C1
Francis St C1
Fullers Row B2
George St B2
Glamorgan St C2
Glyndŵr Pl A1
Graig Terr A3
Grand Theatre C2
Granogwen Rd A2
Guildhall Rd South C1
Gwent Rd A1
Gwynedd Ave A1
Hafod St A3
Hanover St B1
Harcourt St B2
Harries St A2
Heathfield B2
Henrietta St B2
Hewson St B2
High St A3/B3
High View A2
Hill St A2
Historic Ships Berth C3
HM Prison C2
Information Ctr C2
Islwyn Rd A1
King Edward's Rd C1
Law Courts C1
Library B3
Long Ridge A2
Madoc St C2
Mansel St B2
Maritime Quarter C3
Market B3
Mayhill Gdns B1
Mayhill Rd A1
Mega Bowl B3
Milton Terr A2
Mission Gallery C3
Montpellier Terr B1
Morfa Rd A3
Mount Pleasant B2
National Waterfront Museum C3
Nelson St C2
New Cut Rd A3
New St A3
Nicander Pde A2
Nicander Pl A2
Nicholl St B2
Norfolk St B2
North Hill Rd A2
Northampton La B2
Orchard St B3
Oxford St B2
Oystermouth Rd C1
Page St B2
Pant-y-Celyn Rd B1
Parc Tawe Link B3
Parc Tawe North B3
Parc Tawe Sh & L Ctr B3
Patti Pavilion C1
Paxton St C2
Penmaen Terr B1
Pen-y-Graig Rd A1
Phillips Pde C1
Picton Terr B2
Plantasia B3
Police Station B2
Post Office A1/A2/B2/C1
Powys Ave A1
Primrose St B2
Princess Way B3
Promenade B2
Pryder Gdns A1
Quadrant Ctr C2
Quay Park B3
Rhianfa La B1
Rhondda St B2
Richardson St C2
Rodney St C1
Rose Hill B1
Rosehill Terr B1
Russell St B1
St David's Sq C3
St Helen's Ave C1
St Helen's Cr C1
St Helen's Rd C1
St James Gdns B1
St James's Cr B1
St Mary's B3
Sea View Terr A3
Singleton St C2
South Dock C3
Stanley Pl B2
Strand B3
Swansea Castle B3
Swansea Coll Arts Ctr C1
Swansea Metropolitan University B2
Swansea Museum C3
Swansea Station A3
Taliesyn Rd B1
Tan y Marian Rd A1
Tegid Rd A2
Teilo Cr A1
Terrace Rd B1/B2
The Kingsway B2
The LC C3
Tontine St A3
Tower of Eclipse C3
Townhill Rd A1
Tram Museum C3
Trawler Rd C3
Union St B2
Upper Strand A3
Vernon St A3
Victoria Quay C3
Victoria Rd B3
Vincent St C1
Walter Rd B1
Watkin St A2
Waun-Wen Rd A2
Wellington St C2
Westbury St C1
Western St C1
Westway C2
William St C2
Wind St B3
Woodlands Terr B1
YMCA B2
York St C3

**Swindon** 349

Albert St C3
Albion St C1
Alfred St A2
Alvescot Rd C3
Art Gallery & Mus C3
Ashford Rd C1
Aylesbury St A2
Bath Rd C2
Bathampton St B1
Bathurst Rd B3
Beatrice St A2
Beckhampton St B3
Bowood Rd C1
Bristol St B1
Broad St A3
Brunel Arcade B2
Brunel Plaza B2
Brunswick St C2
Bus Station B2
Cambria Bridge Rd B1
Cambria Place B1
Canal Walk B2
Carfax St B2
Carr St B1
Cemetery C1/C3
Chandler Cl C3
Chapel C1
Chester St B1
Christ Church C3
Church Place B1
Cirencester Way A3
Clarence St B2
Clifton St C1
Cockleberry A2
Colbourne A3
Colbourne St A3
College St B2
Commercial Rd B2
Corporation St A2
Council Offices B3
County Rd A3
Courts B2
Cricket Ground A3
Cricklade Street C3
Crombey St B1/C2
Cross St C2
Curtis St B1
Deacon St C1
Designer Outlet (Great Western) B1
Dixon St C2
Dover St C2
Dowling St C2
Drove Rd C3
Dryden St C1
Durham St C3
East St B1
Eastcott Hill C2
Eastcott Rd C2
Edgeware Rd B2
Edmund St C2
Elmina Rd A3
Emlyn Square B1
Euclid St B3
Exeter St B1
Fairview C1
Faringdon Rd B1
Farnsby St B1
Fire Station B3
Fleet St B2
Fleming Way B2/B3
Florence St A2
Gladstone St A3
Gooch St A2
Graham St A3
Great Western Way A1/A2
Groundwell Rd B3
Hawksworth Way A1
Haydon St A2
Henry St B2
Hillside Ave C1
Holbrook Way B2
Hunt St C3
Hydro B1
Hythe Rd C2
Information Ctr B2
Joseph St C1
Kent Rd C2
King William St C2
Kingshill Rd C1
Lansdown Rd C2
Leicester St B3
Library B2
Lincoln St B3
Little London C3
London St B1
Magic Roundabout B3
Maidstone Rd C2
Manchester Rd A3
Maxwell St B1
Milford St B2
Milton Rd B1
Morse St C2
National Monuments Record Ctr B1
Newcastle St B3
Newcombe Drive A1
Newcombe Trading Estate A1
Newhall St C2
North St C2
North Star Ave A1
North Star A1
Northampton St B3
Oasis Leisure Ctr A1
Ocotal Way A3
Okus Rd C1
Old Town C3
Oxford St B1
Park Lane B1
Park Lane B1
Pembroke St C2
Plymouth St B3
Polaris House A2
Polaris Way A2
Police Station B2
Ponting St A2
Post Office B1/B2/C1/C3
Poulton St A3
Princes St B2
Prospect Hill C2
Prospect Place C2
Queen St B2
Queen's Park C3
Radnor St C1
Read St C1
Reading St B1
Regent St B2
Retail Park A2/A3/B3
Rosebery St A3
St Mark's B1
Salisbury St A3
Savernake St C2
Shelley St C1
Sheppard St B1
South St C2
Southampton St B3
Spring Gardens B3
Stafford Street C2
Stanier St C2
Station Road A2
STEAM B1
Swindon College A2
Swindon Rd C2
Swindon Station A2
Swindon Town Football Club A3
TA Ctr B1
Tennyson St B1
The Lawn C3
The Nurseries C1
The Parade B2
The Park B1
Theobald St B1
Town Hall B2
Transfer Bridges A3
Union St C2
Upham Rd C3
Victoria Rd C3
Walcot Rd B3
War Memorial B2
Wells St B3
Western St C2
Westmorland Rd B3
Whalebridge B2
Whitehead St C1
Whitehouse Rd A2
William St C1
Wood St C3
Wyvern Theatre & Arts Ctr B2
York Rd B3

**Taunton** 349

Addison Gr A1
Albemarle Rd A1
Alfred St B3
Alma St C2
Bath Pl C1
Belvedere Rd A1
Billet St B2
Billetfield C2
Birch Gr A1
Brewhouse Theatre B2
Bridge St B1
Bridgwater & Taunton Canal A2
Broadlands Rd C1
Burton Pl C1
Bus Station B1
Canal Rd A2
Cann St C1
Canon St B2
Castle B1
Castle St B1
Cheddon Rd A2
Chip Lane A1
Clarence St B1
Cleveland St B1
Clifton Terr A2
Coleridge Cres C3
Compass Hill C1
Compton Cl A2
Corporation St B1
Council Offices A1
County Walk Sh Ctr C2
Courtyard B2
Cranmer Rd B2
Critchard Way B3
Cyril St A1
Deller's Wharf B1
Duke St B2
East Reach B3
East St B3
Eastbourne Rd B2
Eastleigh Rd C3
Eaton Cres A2
Elm Gr A1
Elms Cl A1
Fons George C1
Fore St B2
Fowler St A1
French Weir Rec Grd B1
Geoffrey Farrant Wk A2
Gray's Almshouses B2
Grays Rd B3
Greenway Ave A1
Guildford Pl C1
Hammet St B2
Haydon Rd B3
Heavitree Way A2
Herbert St A1
High St C2
Holway Ave C3
Hugo St B3
Huish's Almshouses B2
Hurdle Way C2
Information Ctr C2
Jubilee St A1
King's College C3
Kings Cl C3
Laburnum St B2
Lambrook Rd B3
Lansdowne Rd A3
Leslie Ave A1
Leycroft Rd B3
Library C2
Linden Gr A1
Magdalene St B2
Magistrates Court B1
Malvern Terr A2
Market House B2
Mary St C2
Middle St B2
Midford Rd B3
Mitre Court B3
Mount Nebo C1
Mount St C2
Mountway C2
Mus of Somerset B1
North St B2
Northfield Ave B1
Northfield Rd B1
Northleigh Rd C3
Obridge Allotments A3
Obridge Lane A3
Obridge Rd A3
Obridge Viaduct A3
Old Mkt Shopping Ctr C2
Osborne Way C1
Park St C1
Paul St C2
Plais St A2
Playing Field C3
Police Station C1
Portland St B1
Post Office B1/B2/C1
Priorswood Ind Est A3
Priorswood Rd A2
Priory Ave B2
Priory Bridge Rd B2
Priory Fields Retail Pk A3
Priory Park A2
Priory Way A3
Queen St B3
Railway St A1
Records Office A2
Recreation Grd A1
Riverside Place B2
St Augustine St B2
St George's C2
St Georges Sq C2
St James B2
St James St B2
St John's C1
St John's Rd B1
St Josephs Field C3
St Mary Magdalene's B2
Samuels Ct A1
Shire Hall & Law Courts C1
Somerset County Cricket Ground B2
Somerset County Hall C1
Somerset Cricket B2
South Rd C3
South St C3
Staplegrove Rd B1
Station Rd A1
Stephen St B2
Swimming Pool A1
Tancred St B2
Tauntfield Cl C3
Taunton Dean Cricket Club C2
Taunton Station A2
The Avenue A1
The Crescent C1
The Mount C2
Thomas St A1
Toneway A3
Tower St B1
Trevor Smith Pl C3
Trinity Business Ctr C3
Trinity Rd C3
Trinity St B3
Trull Rd C1
Tudor House B2
Upper High St C1
Venture Way A3
Victoria Gate B3
Victoria Park B3
Victoria St B3
Viney St B3
Vivary Park C2
Vivary Rd C1
War Memorial C1
Wellesley St A2
Wheatley Cres A3
Whitehall A1
Wilfred Rd B3
William St A1
Wilton Church C1
Wilton Cl C1
Wilton Gr C1
Wilton St C1
Winchester St B2
Winters Field B2
Wood St B1
Yarde Pl B1

**Telford** 349

Alma Ave C1
Amphitheatre C2
Bowling Alley B2
Brandsfarm Way C3
Brunel Rd B1
Bus Station B2
Buxton Rd C1
Central Park A2
Civic Offices B2
Coach Central B2
Coachwell Cl B1
Colliers Way A1
Courts B2
Dale Acre Way B3
Darliston C3
Deepdale B3
Deercote B2
Dinthill C3
Doddington C3
Dodmoor Grange C3
Downemead B3
Duffryn B3
Dunsheath B3
Euston Way A3
Eyton Mound C1
Eyton Rd C1
Forgegate A2
Grange Central B2
Hall Park Way B1
Hinkshay Rd C2
Hollinsworth Rd A2
Holyhead Rd A3
Housing Trust A1
Ice Rink B2
Information Ctr B2
Ironmasters Way A2
Job Ctr B1
Land Registry B1
Lawn Central B2
Lawnswood C1
Library B2
Malinsgate B1
Matlock Ave C1
Moor Rd C1
Mount Rd C1
NFU Offices B1
Odeon B2
Park Lane A1
Police Station B1
Priorslee Ave A3
Queen Elizabeth Ave C3
Queen Elizabeth Way B1
Queensway A2/B3
Rampart Way A2
Randlay Ave C3
Randlay Wood C3
Rhodes Ave C1
Royal Way B1
St Leonards Rd B1
St Quentin Gate B2
Shifnal Rd A3
Sixth Ave A1
Southwater Way B1
Spout Lane C1
Spout Mound B1
Spout Way C1
Stafford Court B3
Stafford Park B3
Stirchley Ave C3
Stone Row C1
Telford Bridge Ret Pk A1
Telford Central Sta A3
Telford Ctr, The B2
Telford Forge Ret Pk A1
Telford Hornets RFC C2
Telford Int Ctr C2
Telford Way A3
Third Ave A2
Town Park C2
Town Park Visitor Ctr B2
Walker House B2
Wellswood Ave A2
West Ctr Way B1
Withywood Drive C1
Woodhouse Central B2
Yates Way A1

**Torquay** 349

Abbey Rd B2
Alexandra Rd A2
Alpine Rd B3
Ash Hill Rd A2
Babbacombe Rd B3
Bampfylde Rd B1
Barton Rd A1
Beacon Quay C2
Belgrave Rd A1/B1
Belmont Rd A3
Berea Rd A3
Braddons Hill Rd East B3
Brewery Park A3
Bronshill Rd A2
Castle Rd A2
Cavern Rd A3
Central B2
Chatsworth Rd A2
Chestnut Ave B1
Church St A1
Civic Offices A2
Coach Station A1
Corbyn Head C1
Croft Hill B1
Croft Rd B1
Daddyhole Plain C3
East St A1
Egerton Rd A3
Ellacombe Church Rd A3
Ellacombe Rd A2
Falkland Rd B1
Fleet St B2
Fleet Walk Sh Ctr B2
Grafton Rd B3
Haldon Pier C2
Hatfield Rd A2
Highbury Rd A2
Higher Warberry Rd A3
Hillesdon Rd B3
Hollywood Bowl C3
Hoxton Rd A3
Hunsdon Rd B3
Information Ctr B2
Inner Harbour C3
Kenwyn Rd A3
Laburnum St A1
Law Courts A2
Library A2
Lime Ave B1
Living Coasts C3
Lower Warberry Rd B3
Lucius St B1
Lymington Rd A1
Magdalene Rd A1
Marina C2
Market St B2
Meadfoot Lane C3
Meadfoot Rd C3
Melville St B2
Middle Warberry Rd B3
Mill Lane A1
Montpellier Rd B3
Morgan Ave A1
Museum Rd B3
Newton Rd A1
Oakhill Rd A1
Outer Harbour C2
Parkhill Rd C3
Pavilion C2
Pimlico B2
Police Station A1
Post Office A1/B2
Princes Rd A3
Princes Rd East A3
Princes Rd West A3
Princess Gdns C2
Princess Pier C2
Princess Theatre C2
Rathmore Rd B1
Recreation Grd B1
Riviera Ctr Int B1
Rock End Ave C3
Rock Rd B2
Rock Walk B2
Rosehill Rd A3
St Efride's Rd A1
St John's B3
St Luke's Rd B2
St Luke's Rd North B2
St Luke's Rd South B2
St Marychurch Rd A2
Scarborough Rd B1
Shedden Hill B2
South Pier C2
South St A1
Spanish Barn B1
Stitchill Rd B3
Strand B3
Sutherland Rd B3
Teignmouth Rd A1
Temperance St B2
The King's Drive B1
The Terrace B3
Thurlow Rd A1
Tor Bay B1
Tor Church Rd A1
Tor Hill Rd A1
Torbay Rd B2
Torquay Museum B3
Torquay Station C1
Torre Abbey Mansion B1
Torre Abbey Meadows B1
Torre Abbey Sands B1
Torwood Gdns B3
Torwood St C3
Union Square A2
Union St A1
Upton Hill A2
Upton Park A1
Upton Rd A1
Vanehill Rd C3
Vansittart Rd A1
Vaughan Parade C3
Victoria Parade C3
Victoria Rd A2
Warberry Rd West B2
Warren Rd B2
Windsor Rd A2/A3
Woodville Rd A3

**Truro** 349

Adelaide Ter B1
Agar Rd B3
Arch Hill C2
Arundell Pl C2
Avondale Rd B1
Back Quay B3
Barrack La C3
Barton Meadow A1
Benson Rd A2
Bishops Cl A2
Bosvean Gdns B1
Bosvigo Gardens B1
Bosvigo La A1
Bosvigo Rd B2
Broad St A3
Burley Cl C3
Bus Station B3
Calenick St B2
Campfield Hill B3
Carclew St B3
Carew Rd A2
Carey Park B2
Carlyon Rd A2
Carvoza Rd A3
Castle St B2
Cathedral View A2
Chainwalk Dr A2
Chapel Hill B1
Charles St B2
City Hall B3
City Rd B2
Coinage Hall B3
Comprigney Hill A1
Coosebean La A1
Copes Gdns A2
County Hall B1
Courtney Rd A2
Crescent Rd B1
Crescent Rise B1
Daniell Court C2
Daniell Rd C2
Daniell St C2
Daubuz Cl A2
Dobbs La B1
Edward St B2
Eliot Rd A2
Elm Court A3
Enys Cl A1
Enys Rd A1
Fairmantle St B3
Falmouth Rd C2
Ferris Town B2
Fire Station B1
Frances St B2
George St B2
Green Cl C2
Green La C1
Grenville Rd A2
Hall For Cornwall B3
Hendra Rd A2
Hendra Vean A1
High Cross B3
Higher Newham La C3
Higher Trehaverne A2
Hillcrest Ave B1
Hospital B2
Hunkin Cl A2
Hurland Rd C3
Infirmary Hill B2
James Pl B3
Kenwyn Church Rd A1
Kenwyn Hill A1
Kenwyn Rd A2
Kenwyn St B2
Kerris Gdns A1
King St B3
Lemon Quay B3
Lemon St Gallery B3
Library B1/B3
Malpas Rd B3
Market B3
Memorial Gdns B3
Merrifield Close B1
Mitchell Hill A3
Moresk Cl A3
Moresk Rd A3
Morlaix Ave C3
Nancemere Rd A3
Newham Bsns Park C3
Newham Industrial Est C3
Newham Rd C3
Northfield Dr C3
Oak Way A3
Old County Hall B1
Pal's Terr A3
Park View C2
Pendarves Rd A2
Plaza Cinema B3
Police Station B3
Post Office B2/B3
Prince's St B3
Pydar St A2
Quay St B3
Redannick Cres C2
Redannick La B2
Richard Lander Monument C2
Richmond Hill B1
River St B2
Rosedale Rd A2
Royal Cornwall Mus B2
St Aubyn Rd C3
St Clement St B3
St George's Rd A1
School La C2
Station Rd B1
Stokes Rd A2
Strangways Terr C3
Tabernacle St B3
The Avenue A3
The Crescent B1
The Leats B2
The Spires A2
Trehaverne La A2
Tremayne Rd A2
Treseder's Gdns A3
Treworder Rd B1
Treyew Rd B1
Truro Cathedral B3
Truro Harbour Office B3
Truro Station B3
Union St B2
Upper School La C2
Victoria Gdns B2
Waterfall Gdns B2

**Wick** 349

Ackergill Cres A2
Ackergill St A2
Albert St C2
Ambulance Station A2
Argyle Sq C2
Assembly Rooms C2
Bank Row C2
Bankhead B1
Barons Well B2
Barrogill St C2
Bay View B3
Bexley Terr C3
Bignold Park C2
Bowling Green C2
Breadalbane Terr C2
Bridge of Wick B1
Bridge St B2
Brown Pl C2
Burn St B2
Bus Station B1
Caithness General Hospital (A+E) B1
Cliff Rd B1
Coach Rd B2
Coastguard Station C3
Corner Cres B3
Coronation St C1
Council Offices B2
Court B2
Crane Rock C3
Dempster St C2
Dunnet Ave A2
Fire Station B2
Fish Market C3
Francis St C1
George St A1
Girnigoe St B2
Glamis Rd B2
Gowrie Pl B1
Grant St C2
Green Rd B2
Gunns Terr B3
Harbour Quay B2
Harbour Rd C3
Harbour Terr C2
Harrow Hill C2
Henrietta St A2/B2
Heritage Museum C2
High St B2
Hill Ave A2
Hillhead Rd B3
Hood St C1
Huddart St C2
Information Ctr B2
Kenneth St C1
Kinnaird St C2
Kirk Hill B1
Langwell Cres B3
Leishman Ave B3
Leith Walk A2
Library B2
Lifeboat Station C3
Lighthouse C3
Lindsay Dr B3
Lindsay Pl B3
Loch St C2
Louisburgh St B2
Lower Dunbar St C2
Macleay La B1
Macleod Rd B3
MacRae St C2
Martha Terr B2
Miller Ave B1

Miller La B1
Moray St C2
Mowat Pl B3
Murchison St C3
Newton Ave C1
Newton Rd C1
Nicolson St C3
North Highland Coll. B2
North River Pier B3
Northcote St C2
Owen Pl A2
Police Station B1
Port Dunbar B3
Post Office B2/C2
Pulteney Distillery C2
River St B2
Robert St A1
Rutherford St C2
St John's Episcopal C2
Sandigoe Rd B3
Scalesburn B3
Seaforth Ave C1
Shore La B2
Sinclair Dr B3
Sinclair Terr C2
Smith Terr C3
South Pier C3
South Quay C3
South Rd C1
South River Pier B3
Station Rd B1
Swimming Pool B2
TA Ctr C2
Telford St B2
The Shore B2
Thurso Rd B1
Thurso St B1
Town Hall B2
Union St B2
Upper Dunbar St C2
Vansittart St C3
Victoria Pl B2
War Memorial A1
Well of Cairndhuna C3
Wellington Ave C3
Wellington St C3
West Banks Ave C1
West Banks Terr C1
West Park C1
Whitehorse Park B2
Wick Harbour Bridge B2
Wick Industrial Estate A2
Wick Parish Church B1
Wick Station B1
Williamson St B2
Willowbank B2

## Winchester 350

Andover Rd A2
Andover Rd Retail Pk A2
Archery La C2
Arthur Rd B2
Bar End Rd C3
Beaufort Rd C2
Beggar's La B3
Bereweeke Ave A1
Bereweeke Rd A1
Boscobel Rd A2
Brassey Rd A2
Broadway B3
Brooks Sh Ctr, The B3
Bus Station B3
Butter Cross B2
Canon St C2
Castle Wall C2/C3
Castle, King Arthur's Round Table B2
Cathedral C2
Cheriton Rd A1
Chesil St C3
Chesil Theatre C3
Christchurch Rd C1
City Museum B2
City Offices C3
City Rd B2
Clifton Rd B1
Clifton Terr B2
Close Wall C2/C3
Coach Park A2
Colebrook St C3
College St C2
College Walk C3
Compton Rd C2
County Council Offices B2
Cranworth Rd A2
Cromwell Rd C1
Culver Rd C2
Domum Rd C3
Durngate Pl B3
Eastgate St B3
Edgar Rd C2
Egbert Rd A2
Elm Rd B1
Fairfield Rd A1
Fire Station B3
Fordington Ave B1
Fordington Rd A1
Friarsgate B3
Gordon Rd B3
Greenhill Rd B1
Guildhall B3
HM Prison B1
Hatherley Rd A1
High St B2
Hillier Way A3
Hyde Abbey (Remains) A2
Hyde Abbey Rd B2
Hyde Cl A2
Hyde St A2
Information Ctr B3
Jane Austen's Ho C2
Jewry St B2
John Stripe Theatre C1
King Alfred Pl A2
Kingsgate Arch C2
Kingsgate Park C2
Kingsgate Rd C2
Kingsgate St C2
Lankhills Rd A2
Library B2
Lower Brook St B3
Magdalen Hill B3
Market La B2
Mews La B1
Middle Brook St B3
Middle Rd B1
Military Museums B2
Milland Rd C3
Milverton Rd B1
Monks Rd A3
North Hill Cl A2
North Walls B2
North Walls Rec Gnd A3
Nuns Rd A3
Oram's Arbour B1
Owen's Rd A2
Parchment St B2
Park & Ride C3
Park Ave B3
Playing Field A1
Police HQ B1
Police Station B3
Portal Rd C3
Post Office B2/C1
Quarry Rd C3
Ranelagh Rd C1
Regiment Museum B2
River Park Leisure Ctr B3
Romans' Rd C2
Romsey Rd B1
Royal Hampshire County Hospital (A&E) B1
St Cross Rd C2
St George's St B2
St Giles Hill C3
St James' La B1
St James' Terr B1
St James Villas C2
St John's B3
St John's St B3
St Michael's Rd C2
St Paul's Hill B1
St Peter St B2
St Swithun St C2
St Thomas St C2
Saxon Rd A2
School of Art B3
Screen C2
Sleepers Hill Rd C1
Southgate St B2
Sparkford Rd C1
Staple Gdns B2
Station Rd B2
Step Terr B1
Stockbridge Rd A1
Stuart Cres C1
Sussex St B2
Swan Lane B2
Tanner St B3
The Square B2
The Weirs C3
The Winchester Gallery B3
Theatre Royal B2
Tower St B2
Town Hall C3
Union St B3
Univ of Winchester (King Alfred Campus) C1
Upper Brook St B2
Wales St B3
Water Lane B3
West End Terr B1
West Gate A2
Western Rd B1
Wharf Hill C3
Winchester College C2
Winchester Station A2
Wolvesey Castle C3
Worthy Lane A2
Worthy Rd A2

## Windsor 350

Adelaide Sq C3
Albany Rd C2
Albert St B1
Alexandra Gdns B2
Alexandra Rd C2
Alma Rd B2
Ambulance Station B1
Arthur Rd B2
Bachelors Acre B3
Barry Ave B2
Beaumont Rd C2
Bexley St B1
Boat House B2
Brocas St B2
Brook St C3
Bulkeley Ave C1
Castle Hill B3
Charles St B2
Claremont Rd C2
Clarence Cr B2
Clarence Rd B1
Clewer Court Rd B1
Coach Park B2
College Cr C1
Courts C2
Cricket Ground C3
Dagmar Rd C2
Datchet Rd B3
Devereux Rd C2
Dorset Rd C2
Duke St B1
Elm Rd C1
Eton College A3
Eton Ct A2
Eton Sq A2
Eton Wick Rd A2
Fire Station C2
Farm Yard B3
Frances Rd C2
Frogmore Dr B3
Gloucester Pl C3
Goslar Way C1
Goswell Hill B2
Goswell Rd B2
Green La C1
Grove Rd C2
Guildhall B3
Helena Rd C2
Helston La B1
High St A2/B3
Holy Trinity C2
Hospital (Private) C2
Household Cavalry C2
Imperial Rd C1
Information Ctr B2/B3
Keats La A2
King Edward Ct B2
King Edward VII Ave A3
King Edward VII Hospital C2
King George V Meml B3
King's Rd C3
King Stable St A2
Library C2
Maidenhead Rd B1
Meadow La A2
Municipal Offices C3
Nell Gwynne's Ho B3
Osborne Rd C2
Oxford Rd B1
Park St B3
Peascod St B2
Police Station C2
Post Office A2
Princess Margaret Hospital C2
Queen Victoria's Walk B3
Queen's Rd C2
River St B2
Romney Island A3
Romney Lock A3
Romney Lock Rd A3
Russell St C2
St John's B3
St John's Chapel A2
St Leonards Rd C2
St Mark's Rd C2
Sheet St C3
South Meadow A2
South Meadow La A2
Springfield Rd C1
Stovell Rd B1
Sunbury Rd A3
Tangier La A2
Tangier St A3
Temple Rd C2
Thames St B3
The Brocas A2
The Home Park A3/C3
The Long Walk C3
Theatre Royal B3
Trinity Pl C2
Vansittart Rd B1/C1
Vansittart Rd Gdns C1
Victoria Barracks C2
Victoria St C2
Ward Royal B2
Westmead C1
White Lilies Island A1
William St B2
Windsor Arts Ctr C2
Windsor Castle B3
Windsor & Eton Central B2
Windsor & Eton Riverside A3
Windsor Bridge B3
Windsor Great Park C3
Windsor Leisure Ctr B1
Windsor Relief Rd A1
Windsor Royal Sh B2
York Ave C1
York Rd C1

## Wolverhampton 350

Albion St B3
Alexandra St C1
Arena B2
Arts Gallery B2
Ashland St C1
Austin St A1
Badger Dr A3
Bailey St B3
Bath Ave B1
Bath Rd B1
Bell St C2
Berry St B3
Bilston Rd C3
Bilston St C3
Birmingham Canal A3
Bone Mill La A2
Brewery Rd B1
Bright St A1
Burton Cres B3
Bus Station B3
Cambridge St A3
Camp St B2
Cannock Rd A3
Castle St C2
Chapel Ash C1
Cherry St C1
Chester St A1
Church La C2
Church St C2
Civic Ctr B2
Clarence Rd B2
Cleveland St C2
Clifton St C1
Coach Station B2
Compton Rd B1
Corn Hill B3
Coven St A3
Craddock St A1
Cross St North A2
Crown & County Courts C3
Crown St A2
Culwell St B3
Dale St C1
Darlington St C1
Dartmouth St C3
Devon Rd A1
Drummond St B2
Dudley Rd C2
Dudley St B2
Duke St C3
Dunkley St B1
Dunstall Ave A2
Dunstall Hill A2
Dunstall Rd A1/A2
Evans St A1
Fawdry St A1
Field St B3
Fire Station C1
Fiveways A2
Fowler Playing Fields A3
Fox's La A2
Francis St A2
Fryer St B3
Gloucester St A1
Gordon St C3
Graiseley St C1
Grand B3
Granville St C3
Great Brickkiln St C1
Great Hampton St A1
Great Western St A2
Grimstone St B3
Harrow St A1
Hilton St A3
Horseley Fields C3
Humber Rd C1
Jack Hayward Way A2
Jameson St A1
Jenner St C3
Kennedy Rd B3
Kimberley St C1
King St B2
Laburnum St C1
Lansdowne Rd B1
Leicester St A1
Lever St C3
Library C3
Lichfield St B2
Light House B3
Little's La B3
Lock St B3
Lord St C1
Lowe St A1
Lower Stafford St A2
Magistrates Court B2
Mander Ctr C2
Mander St C1
Market St B2
Market C2
Melbourne St C3
Merridale St C1
Middlecross C3
Molineux St B2
Mostyn St A1
New Hampton Rd East A1
Nine Elms La A3
North Rd A2
Oaks Cres C1
Oxley St A2
Paget St A1
Park Ave B1
Park Road East A1
Park Road West B1
Paul St C2
Pelham St C1
Penn Rd C2
Piper's Row C3
Pitt St C2
Police Station C3
Pool St C2
Poole St A3
Post Office A1/A2/B2/B2
Powlett St C3
Queen St B2
Raby St C3
Raglan St C1
Railway Dr B3
Red Hill St A2
Red Lion St B2
Retreat St C1
Ring Rd B2
Rugby St A1
Russell St C1
St Andrew's B1
St David's B3
St George's C3
St George's Pde C2
St James St C3
St John's C2
St John's C2
St John's Retail Park C2
St John's Square C2
St Mark's C1
St Marks Rd C1
St Marks St C1
St Patrick's B2
St Peter's B2
St Peter's B2
Salisbury St C1
Salop St C2
School St C2
Sherwood St A2
Smestow St A3
Snowhill C2
Springfield Rd A3
Stafford St B2
Staveley Rd A1
Steelhouse La C3
Stephenson St C1
Stewart St C2
Sun St B3
Sutherland Pl C3
Tempest St C2
Temple St C2
Tettenhall Rd B1
The Maltings B2
The Royal (Metro) C3
Thomas St C2
Thornley St B2
Tower St C2
University B2
Upper Zoar St C1
Vicarage Rd C3
Victoria St C2
Walpole St A1
Walsall St C3
Ward St C3
Warwick St C3
Water St A3
Waterloo Rd B2
Wednesfield Rd B3
West Pk (not A&E) B1
West Park Swimming Pool B1
Wharf St C3
Whitmore Hill B2
Wolverhampton B3
Wolverhampton St George's (Metro) C2
Wolverhampton Wanderers Football Ground (Molineux) B2
Worcester St C2
Wulfrun Ctr C2
Yarwell Cl A3
York St C3
Zoar St C1

## Worcester 350

Albany Terr A1
Alice Otley School A2
Angel Pl B2
Angel St B2
Ashcroft Rd A2
Athelstan Rd C3
Back Lane North A1
Back Lane South A1
Barbourne Rd A2
Bath Rd C2
Battenhall Rd C3
Bridge St B2
Britannia Sq A1
Broad St B2
Bromwich La C1
Bromwich Rd C1
Bromyard Rd C1
Bus Station B2
Carden St B3
Castle St A2
Cathedral C2
Cathedral Plaza B2
Charles St B3
Chequers La B1
Chestnut St A2
Chestnut Walk A2
Citizens' Advice Bureau B2
City Walls Rd B2
Cole Hill C3
College of Technology B2
College St C2
Commandery C3
County Cricket Gd C1
Cripplegate Park B1
Croft Rd B1
Cromwell St B3
Crowngate Ctr B2
Deansway B2
Diglis Pde C2
Diglis Rd C2
Edgar Tower C2
Farrier St A2
Fire Station B2
Foregate St B2
Foregate Street B2
Fort Royal Hill C3
Fort Royal Park C3
Foundry St B3
Friar St C2
George St B3
Grand Stand Rd B1
Greenhill C3
Greyfriars B2
Guildhall B2
Henwick Rd B1
High St B2
Hill St B3
Huntingdon Hall B2
Hylton Rd B1
Information Ctr B2
King Charles Place Shopping Centre C1
King's School C2
King's School Playing Field C2
Kleve Walk C2
Lansdowne Cr A3
Lansdowne Rd A3
Lansdowne Walk A3
Laslett St A3
Leisure Ctr A3
Library, Museum & Art Gallery A2
Little Chestnut St A2
Little London A2
London Rd C3
Lowell St A3
Lowesmoor B2
Lowesmoor Terr A3
Lowesmoor Wharf A3
Magistrates Court A2
Midland Rd B3
Mill St C2
Moors Severn Terr A1
New Rd C1
New St B2
Northfield St A2
Odeon B2
Padmore St B3
Park St C3
Pheasant St B3
Pitchcroft Racecourse A1
Police Station A2
Portland St C2
Post Office B2
Quay St B2
Queen St B2
Rainbow Hill A3
Recreation Ground A2
Reindeer Court B2
Rogers Hill A3
Sabrina Rd A1
St Dunstan's Cr C3
St John's C1
St Martin's Gate B3
St Oswald's Rd A2
St Paul's St B3
St Swithin's Church B2
St Wulstans Cr C3
Sansome Walk A2
Severn St C2
Shaw St B2
Shire Hall A2
Shrub Hill B3
Shrub Hill Retail Park B3
Shrub Hill Rd B3
Slingpool Walk C1
South Quay B2
Southfield St A2
Sports Ground A2/C1
Stanley Rd B3
Swan, The A1
Swimming Pool A2
Tallow Hill B3
Tennis Walk A2
The Avenue C1
The Butts B2
The Cross B2
The Shambles B2
The Tything A2
Tolladine Rd B3
Tudor House B2
Tybridge St B1
Univ of Worcester B2
Vincent Rd B3
Vue C2
Washington St A3
Woolhope Rd C3
Worcester Bridge B2
Worcester Library & History Ctr B3
Worcester Porcelain Museum C2
Worcester Royal Grammar School A2
Wylds La C3

## Wrexham *Wrecsam* 350

Abbot St B2
Acton Rd A3
Albert St C3
Alexandra Rd C1
Aran Rd A3
Barnfield C3
Bath Rd C2
Beechley Rd C3
Belgrave Rd C2
Belle Vue Park C2
Belle Vue Rd C2
Belvedere Dr A1
Bennion's Rd C3
Berse Rd A1
Bersham Rd C1
Birch St C3
Bodhyfryd B3
Border Retail Park B3
Bradley Rd C2
Bright St B1
Bron-y-Nant B1
Brook St C2
Bryn-y-Cabanau Rd C3
Bury St C3
Bus Station B2
Butchers Market B3
Caia Rd C3
Cambrian Ind Est C3
Caxton Pl B2
Cemetery C1
Centenary Rd C1
Chapel St C2
Charles St B3
Chester Rd A3
Chester St B3
Cilcen Gr A3
Citizens Advice Bureau B2
Cobden Rd B1
Council Offices B3
County A2
Crescent Rd B3
Crispin La A2
Croesnewyth Rd B1
Cross St A2
Cunliffe St A2
Derby Rd C3
Dolydd Rd B1
Duke St B2
Eagles Meadow C3
Earle St C2
East Ave A2
Edward St C2
Egerton St B2
Empress Rd C1
Erddig Rd C2
Fairy Rd C2
Fire Station B2
Foster Rd A3
Foxwood Dr C1
Garden Rd A2
General Market B3
Gerald St B2
Gibson St C1
Glyndŵr University Plas Coch Campus A1
Greenbank St C3
Greenfield A2
Grosvenor Rd B2
Grove Park B3
Grove Park Rd B3
Grove Rd A3
Guildhall B2
Haig Rd C3
Hampden Rd C2
Hazel Gr A3
Henblas St B3
High St B3
Hightown Rd C3
Hill St B2
Holt Rd B3
Holt St B3
Hope St B2
Huntroyde Ave C3
Information Ctr B3
Island Gn Sh Ctr B2
Job Ctr B2
Jubilee Rd B2
King St B2
Kingsmills Rd C3
Lambpit St B3
Law Courts B3
Lawson Cl A3
Lawson Rd A3
Lea Rd C2
Library & Arts Ctr B2
Lilac Way B1
Llys David Lord B1
Lorne St A2
Maesgwyn Rd B1
Maesydre Rd A3
Manley Rd B3
Market St B3
Mawddy Ave A2
Mayville Ave A2
Memorial Gallery B2
Memorial Hall B3
Mold Rd A1
Mount St C3
Neville Cres A3
New Rd A2
North Wales Regional Tennis Ctr A1
North Wales School of Art & Design B2
Oak Dr A3
Park Ave A3
Park St A2
Peel St C1
Pentre Felin C2
Pen y Bryn C2
Penymaes Ave A3
Peoples Market B3
Percy St C2
Plas Coch Retail Park A1
Plas Coch Rd A1
Police Station B3
Poplar Rd C2
Post Office A2/B2/C2/C3
Powell Rd B3
Poyser St C2
Price's La A2
Primose Way B1
Princess St C1
Queen St B3
Queens Sq B2
Regent St B2
Rhosddu Rd A2/B2
Rhosnesni La A3
Rivulet Rd C3
Ruabon Rd C2
Ruthin Rd C1/C2
St Giles C3
St Giles Way C3
St James Ct A2
St Mary's B2
Salisbury Rd C3
Salop Rd C3
Sontley Rd C2
Spring Rd A2
Stanley St C3
Stansty Rd A2
Station Approach B2
Studio B2
Talbot Rd C2
Techniquest Glyndŵr A2
The Beeches A3
The Pines A3
Town Hill C2
Trevor St C2
Trinity St B2
Tuttle St C3
Vale Park A1
Vernon St B2
Vicarage Hill B2
Victoria Rd C2
Walnut St A2
War Memorial B3
Waterworld L Ctr B3
Watery Rd B1/B2
Wellington Rd C2
Westminster Dr A3
William Aston Hall A1
Windsor Rd A1
Wrexham AFC A1
Wrexham Central B2
Wrexham General B2
Wrexham Maelor Hospital (A+E) B1
Wrexham Technology Park B1
Wynn Ave A2
Yale College B3
Yale Gr A3
Yorke St C3

## York 350

Aldwark B2
Ambulance Station B3
Barbican Rd C3
Barley Hall B2
Bishopgate St C2
Bishopthorpe Rd C2
Blossom St C1
Bootham A1
Bootham Cr A1
Bootham Terr A1
Bridge St B2
Brook St A2
Brownlow St A2
Burton Stone La A1
Castle Museum C2
Castlegate B2
Cemetery Rd C2
Cherry St C2
City Screen B2
City Wall A2/B1/C3
Clarence St A2
Clementhorpe C2
Clifford St B2
Clifford's Tower B2
Clifton A1
Coach park A2
Coney St B2
Cromwell Rd C2
Crown Court C2
Davygate B2
Deanery Gdns A2
DIG B2
Ebor Industrial Estate B3
Fairfax House B2
Fishergate C3
Foss Islands Retail Pk B3
Foss Islands Rd B3
Fossbank A3
Garden St A2
George St C3
Gillygate A2
Goodramgate B2
Grand Opera House B2
Grosvenor Terr A1
Guildhall B2
Hallfield Rd A3
Heslington Rd C3
Heworth Green A3
Holy Trinity B2
Hope St C3
Huntington Rd A3
Information Ctr B2
James St B3
Jorvik Viking Ctr B2
Kent St C3
Lawrence St C3
Layerthorpe A3
Leeman Rd B1
Lendal B2
Lendal Bridge B1
Library B1
Longfield Terr A1
Lord Mayor's Walk A2
Lower Eldon St A2
Lowther St A2
Mansion House B2
Margaret St C3
Marygate A1
Melbourne St C3
Merchant Adventurer's Hall B2
Merchant Taylors' Hall B2
Micklegate B1
Micklegate Bar C1
Minster, The A2
Monkgate A2
Moss St C1
Museum Gdns B1
Museum St B1
National Railway Museum B1
Navigation Rd B3
Newton Terr C2
North Pde A1
North St B2
Nunnery La C1
Nunthorpe Rd C1
Ouse Bridge B2
Paragon St C3
Park Gr A3
Park St C1
Parliament St B2
Peasholme Green B3
Penley's Grove St A2
Piccadilly B2
Police Station B2
Post Office B1/B2/C3
Purey Cust Nuffield Hospital, The A2
Queen Anne's Rd A1
Quilt Museum B3
Reel C1
Regimental Mus B2
Richard III Museum A2
Roman Bath B2
Rowntree Park C2
St Andrewgate B2
St Benedict Rd C1
St John St A2
St Olave's Rd A1
St Peter's Gr A1
St Saviourgate B2
Scarcroft Hill C1
Scarcroft Rd C1
Skeldergate C2
Skeldergate Bridge C2
Station Rd B1
Stonegate B2
Sycamore Terr A1
Terry Ave C2
The Shambles B2
The Stonebow B2
Theatre Royal B2
Thorpe St C1
Toft Green B1
Tower St C2
Townend St A2
Treasurer's House A2
Trinity La B1
Undercroft Mus A2
Union Terr A2
Victor St C2
Vine St C2
Walmgate B3
Wellington St C3
York Art Gallery A1
York Barbican C3
York Brewery B2
York Dungeon, The B2
York Station B1

W Isles
Moray
Highland
Aberds
Aberdeen
Perth and Kinross
Angus
Dundee
Argyll and Bute
Stirling
Fife
Glasgow
Edin
E Loth
N Ayrs
Midloth
S Lanark
E Ayrs
Borders
S Ayrs
Dumfries and Galloway
Northumberland
Tyne and Wear
Hartlepool
Redcar and Cleveland
Middlesbrough
Darlington
Stockton-on-Tees
Cumbria
Durham
IoM
North Yorkshire
York
E Yorks
Blackpool
Lancs
W Yorks
N Lincs
NE Lincs
Anglesey
Mers
Gtr Man
S Yorks
Conwy
Flint
Denb
Ches
Derbys
Notts
Lincolnshire
Gwyn
Wrex
Telford
Staffs
Leics
Rutland
Norfolk
Ceredigion
Shrops
W Mid
Powys
Worcs
Warks
Northants
Cambs
Hereford
Bedford
Suffolk
C Beds
Pembs
Carms
Mon
Glos
Bucks
Herts
Essex
Swansea
Cardiff
Bristol
Oxon
W Berks
London
Southend
Medway
Wilts
Hants
Surrey
Kent
Somerset
Soton
W Sus
E Sus
Devon
Dorset
IoW
Ptsmouth
Brighton
Cornwall
Torbay
Bmouth
Poole
Plymouth
Scilly

## Abbreviations used in the index

- Aberdeen **Aberdeen City**
- Aberds **Aberdeenshire**
- Ald **Alderney**
- Anglesey **Isle of Anglesey**
- Angus **Angus**
- Argyll **Argyll and Bute**
- Bath **Bath and North East Somerset**
- Bedford **Bedford**
- Bl Gwent **Blaenau Gwent**
- Blackburn **Blackburn with Darwen**
- Blackpool **Blackpool**
- Bmouth **Bournemouth**
- Borders **Scottish Borders**
- Brack **Bracknell**
- Bridgend **Bridgend**
- Brighton **City of Brighton and Hove**
- Bristol **City and County of Bristol**
- Bucks **Buckinghamshire**
- C Beds **Central Bedfordshire**
- Caerph **Caerphilly**
- Cambs **Cambridgeshire**
- Cardiff **Cardiff**
- Carms **Carmarthenshire**
- Ceredig **Ceredigion**
- Ches E **Cheshire East**
- Ches W **Cheshire West and Chester**
- Clack **Clackmannanshire**
- Conwy **Conwy**
- Corn **Cornwall**
- Cumb **Cumbria**
- Darl **Darlington**
- Denb **Denbighshire**
- Derby **City of Derby**
- Derbys **Derbyshire**
- Devon **Devon**
- Dorset **Dorset**
- Dumfries **Dumfries and Galloway**
- Dundee **Dundee City**
- Durham **Durham**
- E Ayrs **East Ayrshire**
- E Dunb **East Dunbartonshire**
- E Loth **East Lothian**
- E Renf **East Renfrewshire**
- E Sus **East Sussex**
- E Yorks **East Riding of Yorkshire**
- Edin **City of Edinburgh**
- Essex **Essex**
- Falk **Falkirk**
- Fife **Fife**
- Flint **Flintshire**
- Glasgow **City of Glasgow**
- Glos **Gloucestershire**
- Gtr Man **Greater Manchester**
- Gwyn **Gwynedd**
- Halton **Halton**
- Hants **Hampshire**
- Hereford **Herefordshire**
- Herts **Hertfordshire**
- Highld **Highland**
- Hrtlpl **Hartlepool**
- Hull **Hull**
- IoM **Isle of Man**
- IoW **Isle of Wight**
- Invclyd **Inverclyde**
- Kent **Kent**
- Lancs **Lancashire**
- Leicester **City of Leicester**
- Leics **Leicestershire**
- Lincs **Lincolnshire**
- London **Greater London**
- Luton **Luton**
- M Keynes **Milton Keynes**
- M Tydf **Merthyr Tydfil**
- Mbro **Middlesbrough**
- Medway **Medway**
- Mers **Merseyside**
- Midloth **Midlothian**
- Mon **Monmouthshire**
- Moray **Moray**
- N Ayrs **North Ayrshire**
- N Lincs **North Lincolnshire**
- N Lanark **North Lanarkshire**
- N Som **North Somerset**
- N Yorks **North Yorkshire**
- NE Lincs **North East Lincolnshire**
- Neath **Neath Port Talbot**
- Newport **City and County of Newport**
- Norf **Norfolk**
- Northants **Northamptonshire**
- Northumb **Northumberland**
- Nottingham **City of Nottingham**
- Notts **Nottinghamshire**
- Orkney **Orkney**
- Oxon **Oxfordshire**
- Pboro **Peterborough**
- Pembs **Pembrokeshire**
- Perth **Perth and Kinross**
- Plym **Plymouth**
- Poole **Poole**
- Powys **Powys**
- Ptsmth **Portsmouth**
- Reading **Reading**
- Redcar **Redcar and Cleveland**
- Renfs **Renfrewshire**
- Rhondda **Rhondda Cynon Taff**
- Rutland **Rutland**
- S Ayrs **South Ayrshire**
- S Glos **South Gloucestershire**
- S Lanark **South Lanarkshire**
- S Yorks **South Yorkshire**
- Scilly **Scilly**
- Shetland **Shetland**
- Shrops **Shropshire**
- Slough **Slough**
- Som **Somerset**
- Soton **Southampton**
- Staffs **Staffordshire**
- Southend **Southend-on-Sea**
- Stirling **Stirling**
- Stockton **Stockton-on-Tees**
- Stoke **Stoke-on-Trent**
- Suff **Suffolk**
- Sur **Surrey**
- Swansea **Swansea**
- Swindon **Swindon**
- T&W **Tyne and Wear**
- Telford **Telford & Wrekin**
- Thurrock **Thurrock**
- Torbay **Torbay**
- Torf **Torfaen**
- V Glam **The Vale of Glamorgan**
- W Berks **West Berkshire**
- W Dunb **West Dunbartonshire**
- W Isles **Western Isles**
- W Loth **West Lothian**
- W Mid **West Midlands**
- W Sus **West Sussex**
- W Yorks **West Yorkshire**
- Warks **Warwickshire**
- Warr **Warrington**
- Wilts **Wiltshire**
- Windsor **Windsor and Maidenhead**
- Wokingham **Wokingham**
- Worcs **Worcestershire**
- Wrex **Wrexham**
- York **City of York**

# Index to road maps of Britain

## How to use the index

Example **Blatherwycke** Northants **137** D9

- grid square
- page number
- county or unitary authority

## A




**Aaron's Hill** Sur 50 E3
**Aaron's Town** Cumb 240 E2
**Abbas Combe** Som 30 C2
**Abberley** Worcs 116 D5
**Abberton** Essex 89 B8
**Abberton** Worcs 117 G9
**Abberwick** Northumb 264 G4
**Abbess End** Essex 87 C9
**Abbess Roding** Essex 87 C9
**Abbey** Devon 27 E10
**Abbeycwmhir** Powys 113 C11
**Abbey-cwm-hir** Powys 113 C11
**Abbeydale** Glos 80 B5
**Abbeydale** S Yorks 186 E4
**Abbeydale Park** S Yorks 186 E4
**Abbey Dore** Hereford 97 E7
**Abbey Field** Essex 107 G9
**Abbey Gate** Kent 53 B9
**Abbey Green** Shrops 149 C10
**Abbey Green** Staffs 169 D7
**Abbey Hey** Gtr Man 184 B5
**Abbeyhill** Edin 280 G5
**Abbey Hulton** Stoke 168 F6
**Abbey Mead** Sur 66 F4
**Abbey St Bathans** Borders 272 C5
**Abbeystead** Lancs 203 C7
**Abbey Town** Cumb 238 G5
**Abbey Village** Lancs 194 C6
**Abbey Wood** London 68 D3
**Abbots Bickington** Devon 24 E5
**Abbots Bromley** Staffs 151 E11
**Abbotsbury** Dorset 17 D7
**Abbotsford** W Sus 36 C4
**Abbotsham** Devon 24 B6
**Abbotskerswell** Devon 9 B7
**Abbots Langley** Herts 85 E9
**Abbotsleigh** Devon 8 F6
**Abbots Leigh** N Som 60 E4
**Abbotsley** Cambs 122 F4
**Abbot's Meads** Ches W 166 B5
**Abbots Morton** Worcs 117 F10
**Abbots Ripton** Cambs 122 B4
**Abbots Salford** Warks 117 G11
**Abbotstone** Hants 48 G5
**Abbotswood** Hants 32 C5
**Abbotswood** Sur 50 C4
**Abbots Worthy** Hants 48 G3
**Abbotts Ann** Hants 47 E10
**Abcott** Shrops 115 B7
**Abdon** Shrops 131 F11
**Abdy** S Yorks 186 B6
**Aber** Ceredig 93 B9
**Aberaeron** Ceredig 111 E9
**Aberaman** Rhondda 77 E8
**Aberangell** Gwyn 146 G6
**Aber-Arad** Carms 92 D6
**Aberarder** Highld 290 E6
**Aberarder House** Highld 300 G6
**Aberarder Lodge** Highld 291 E7
**Aberargie** Perth 286 F5
**Aberarth** Ceredig 111 E9
**Aberavon** Neath 57 C8
**Aber-banc** Ceredig 93 C7
**Aberbargoed** Caerph 77 E11
**Aberbechan** Powys 130 E2
**Aberbeeg** Bl Gwent 78 E2
**Aberbran** Powys 95 F9
**Abercanaid** M Tydf 77 E9
**Abercarn** Caerph 78 G2
**Abercastle** Pembs 91 E7
**Abercegir** Powys 128 C6
**Aberchalder** Highld 290 C5
**Aberchirder** Aberds 302 D6
**Abercorn** W Loth 279 F11
**Aber Cowarch** Gwyn 147 F7
**Abercraf** Powys 76 C4
**Abercregan** Neath 57 B11
**Abercrombie** Fife 287 G9
**Abercwmboi** Rhondda 77 F8
**Abercych** Pembs 92 C4
**Abercynafon** Powys 77 B9
**Abercynffig / Aberkenfig** Bridgend 57 E11
**Abercynon** Rhondda 77 F9
**Aberdalgie** Perth 286 E4
**Aberdâr / Aberdare** Rhondda 77 E7
**Aberdare / Aberdâr** Rhondda 77 E7
**Aberdaron** Gwyn 144 D3
**Aberdeen** Aberdeen 293 C11
**Aberdesach** Gwyn 162 E6
**Aberdour** Fife 280 D3
**Aberdovey / Aberdyfi** Gwyn 128 D2
**Aberdulais** Neath 76 E3
**Aberdyfi / Aberdovey** Gwyn 128 D2
**Aberedw** Powys 95 B11
**Abereiddy** Pembs 90 E5
**Abererch** Gwyn 145 B7
**Aberfan** M Tydf 77 E9
**Aberfeldy** Perth 286 C2
**Aberffraw** Anglesey 162 B5
**Aberffrwd** Ceredig 112 B3
**Aberffrwd** Mon 78 D5
**Aberford** W Yorks 206 F4
**Aberfoyle** Stirl 285 G9
**Abergarw** Bridgend 58 C2
**Abergarwed** Neath 76 E4
**Abergavenny** Mon 78 C3
**Abergele** Conwy 180 F6
**Aber-Giâr** Carms 93 C10
**Abergorlech** Carms 93 E11
**Abergwaun / Fishguard** Pembs 91 D9
**Abergwesyn** Powys 113 G7
**Abergwili** Carms 93 G8
**Abergwynant** Gwyn 146 F3
**Abergwynfi** Neath 57 B11
**Aber-gwynfi** Neath 57 B11
**Abergwyngregyn** Gwyn 179 G11
**Abergynolwyn** Gwyn 128 B3
**Aber-Hirnant** Gwyn 147 C9
**Aberhosan** Powys 128 D6
**Aberkenfig / Abercynffig** Bridgend 57 E11
**Aberlady** E Loth 281 E9
**Aberlemno** Angus 287 B9
**Aberlerry** Ceredig 128 E2
**Aberllefenni** Gwyn 128 B5
**Aberllydan / Broad Haven** Pembs 72 C5
**Aberllynfi / Three Cocks** Powys 96 D3
**Abermagwr** Ceredig 112 C3
**Abermaw / Barmouth** Gwyn 146 F2
**Abermeurig** Ceredig 111 F11
**Aber miwl / Abermule** Powys 130 E3
**Abermorddu** Flint 166 D4
**Abermule / Aber-miwl** Powys 130 E3
**Abernaint** Powys 148 E2
**Abernant** Carms 92 G6
**Abernant** Powys 130 D3
**Aber-nant** Rhondda 77 E8
**Abernethy** Perth 286 F5
**Abernyte** Perth 286 D6
**Aber-oer** Wrex 166 F3
**Aberogwr / Ogmore by Sea** V Glam 57 F11
**Aberpennar / Mountain Ash** Rhondda 77 F8
**Aberporth** Ceredig 110 G5
**Aber-Rhiwlech** Gwyn 147 E8
**Aberriw / Berriew** Powys 130 C3
**Abersoch** Gwyn 144 D6
**Abersychan** Torf 78 E3
**Abertawe / Swansea** Swansea 56 C6
**Aberteifi / Cardigan** Ceredig 92 B3
**Aberthin** V Glam 58 D4
**Abertillery** Bl Gwent 78 E2
**Abertridwr** Caerph 58 B6
**Abertridwr** Powys 147 F10
**Abertrinant** Gwyn 128 B2
**Abertysswg** Caerph 77 D10
**Aberuchill Castle** Perth 285 E11
**Aberuthven** Perth 286 F3
**Aber-Village** Powys 96 G2
**Aberyscir** Powys 95 F9
**Aberystwyth** Ceredig 111 A11
**Abhainn Suidhe** W Isles 305 H2
**Abingdon** Oxon 83 F7
**Abinger Common** Sur 50 D6
**Abinger Hammer** Sur 50 D5
**Abington** Northants 120 E5
**Abington** S Lnrk 259 E10
**Abington Pigotts** Cambs 104 C6
**Abington Vale** Northants 120 E5
**Abingworth** W Sus 35 D10
**Ab Kettleby** Leics 154 E4
**Ab Lench** Worcs 117 G10
**Ablington** Glos 81 D10
**Ablington** Wilts 47 D7
**Abney** Derbys 185 F11
**Aboyne** Aberds 293 D7
**Abraham Heights** Lancs 211 G9
**Abram** Gtr Man 194 G6
**Abriachan** Highld 300 F5
**Abridge** Essex 87 F7
**Abronhill** N Lnrk 278 F5
**Abshot** Hants 33 F8
**Abson** S Glos 61 E8
**Abthorpe** Northants 102 B2
**Abune-the-Hill** Orkney 314 D2
**Aby** Lincs 190 F6
**Acaster Malbis** York 207 D7
**Acaster Selby** N Yorks 207 E7
**Accrington** Lancs 195 B9
**Acha** Argyll 275 B8
**Acha** Argyll 288 D3
**Achabraid** Argyll 275 E9
**Achachork** Highld 298 E4
**Achadh an Eas** Highld 308 F6
**Achad nan Darach** Highld 284 B4
**Achadunan** Argyll 284 F5
**Achafolla** Argyll 275 B8
**Achagary** Highld 308 D7
**Achaglass** Argyll 255 C8
**Achahoish** Argyll 275 F8
**Achalader** Perth 286 C5
**Achallader** Argyll 285 C7
**Achalone** Highld 310 D5
**Acha Mor** W Isles 304 F5
**Achanalt** Highld 300 C2
**Achanamara** Argyll 275 E8
**Achandunie** Highld 300 B6
**Achanelid** Argyll 275 E11
**Ach'an Todhair** Highld 290 F2
**Achany** Highld 309 J5
**Achaphubuil** Highld 290 F2
**Acharacle** Highld 289 C8
**Acharn** Highld 289 D9
**Acharn** Perth 285 C11
**Acharole** Highld 310 D6
**Acharossan** Argyll 275 F10
**Acharry Muir** Highld 309 K6
**Achath** Aberds 293 B9
**Achavanich** Highld 310 E5
**Achavelgin** Highld 301 D9
**Achavraat** Highld 301 E9
**Achddu** Carms 74 E6
**Achdregnie** Moray 302 G2
**Achduart** Highld 307 J5
**Achentoul** Highld 310 F2
**Achfary** Highld 306 F7
**Achfrish** Highld 309 H5
**Achgarve** Highld 307 K3
**Achiemore** Highld 308 C3
**Achiemore** Highld 310 D2
**A'Chill** Highld 294 E4
**Achiltibuie** Highld 307 J5
**Achina** Highld 308 C7
**Achinahuagh** Highld 308 C5
**Achindaul** Highld 290 E3
**Achindown** Highld 301 E8
**Achinduich** Highld 309 J5
**Achinduin** Argyll 289 F10
**Achingills** Highld 310 C5
**Achininver** Highld 308 C5
**Achintee** Highld 290 F3
**Achintee** Highld 299 E9
**Achintraid** Highld 295 B10
**Achlaven** Argyll 289 F11
**Achlean** Highld 291 D10
**Achleck** Argyll 288 E6
**Achlorachan** Highld 300 D3
**Achluachrach** Highld 290 E4
**Achlyness** Highld 306 D7
**Achmelvich** Highld 307 G5
**Achmore** Highld 295 B10
**Achmore** Stirl 285 D9
**Achnaba** Argyll 275 E10
**Achnaba** Argyll 289 F11
**Achnabat** Highld 300 F5
**Achnabreck** Argyll 275 D9
**Achnacarnin** Highld 306 F5
**Achnacarry** Highld 290 E3
**Achnacloich** Argyll 289 F11
**Achnacloich** Highld 295 E7
**Achnaconeran** Highld 290 B6
**Achnacraig** Argyll 288 E6
**Achnacree** Argyll 289 F11
**Achnacree Bay** Argyll 289 F11
**Achnacroish** Argyll 289 E10
**Achnadrish** Argyll 288 D6
**Achnafalnich** Argyll 284 E6
**Achnagarron** Highld 300 C6
**Achnaha** Highld 288 C6
**Achnahanat** Highld 309 K5
**Achnahannet** Highld 301 G9
**Achnahard** Argyll 288 G5
**Achnairn** Highld 309 H5
**Achnaluachrach** Highld 309 J6
**Achnandarach** Highld 295 B10
**Achnanellan** Highld 290 E2
**Achnasaul** Highld 290 E3
**Achnasheen** Highld 299 D11
**Achnashelloch** Argyll 275 D9
**Achnavast** Highld 310 C4
**Achneigie** Highld 299 B10
**Achormlarie** Highld 309 K6
**Achorn** Highld 310 F5
**Achosnich** Highld 288 C6
**Achranich** Highld 289 E9
**Achreamie** Highld 310 C4
**Achriabhach** Highld 290 G3
**Achriesgill** Highld 306 D7
**Achrimsdale** Highld 311 J3
**Achtoty** Highld 308 C6
**Achurch** Northants 137 G10
**Achuvoldrach** Highld 308 D5
**Achvaich** Highld 309 K7
**Achvarasdal** Highld 310 C3
**Ackenthwaite** Cumb 211 C10
**Ackergill** Highld 310 D7
**Acklam** Mbro 225 B9
**Acklam** N Yorks 216 G5
**Ackleton** Shrops 132 D5
**Acklington** Northumb 252 C6
**Ackton** W Yorks 198 C2
**Ackworth Moor Top** W Yorks 198 D2
**Acle** Norf 161 G8
**Acock's Green** W Mid 134 G2
**Acol** Kent 71 F10
**Acomb** Northumb 241 D10
**Acomb** York 207 C7
**Acre** Gtr Man 196 F2
**Acre** Lancs 195 C9
**Acrefair** Wrex 166 G3
**Acres Nook** Staffs 168 E4
**Acre Street** W Sus 21 B11
**Acton** Ches E 167 E10
**Acton** Dorset 18 F5
**Acton** London 67 C8
**Acton** Shrops 130 G6
**Acton** Staffs 168 G4
**Acton** Suff 107 C7
**Acton** Worcs 116 D6
**Acton** Wrex 166 E4
**Acton Beauchamp** Hereford 116 G3
**Acton Bridge** Ches W 183 F9
**Acton Burnell** Shrops 131 C10
**Acton Green** Hereford 116 G3
**Acton Green** London 67 D8
**Acton Pigott** Shrops 131 C10
**Acton Place** Suff 107 B7
**Acton Reynald** Shrops 149 E10
**Acton Round** Shrops 132 D2
**Acton Scott** Shrops 131 F9
**Acton Trussell** Staffs 151 F8
**Acton Turville** S Glos 61 C10
**Adabroc** W Isles 304 B7
**Adambrae** W Loth 269 A10
**Adam's Green** Dorset 29 F8
**Adbaston** Staffs 150 D5
**Adber** Dorset 29 C9
**Adbolton** Notts 154 B2
**Adderbury** Oxon 101 D9
**Adderley** Shrops 150 B3
**Adderley Green** Stoke 168 G6
**Adderstone** Northumb 264 C4
**Addiewell** W Loth 269 C9
**Addingham** W Yorks 205 D7
**Addingham Moorside** W Yorks 205 D7
**Addington** Bucks 102 F4
**Addington** Corn 6 B5
**Addington** Kent 53 B7
**Addington** London 67 G11
**Addinston** Borders 271 E10
**Addiscombe** London 67 F10
**Addlestone** Sur 66 G5
**Addlestonemoor** Sur 66 F4
**Addlethorpe** Lincs 175 B8
**Adel** W Yorks 205 F11
**Adeney** Telford 150 F4
**Adeyfield** Herts 85 D9
**Adfa** Powys 129 C11
**Adforton** Hereford 115 C8
**Adgestone** IoW 21 D7
**Adisham** Kent 55 C8
**Adlestrop** Glos 100 F4
**Adlingfleet** E Yorks 199 C10
**Adlington** Ches E 184 E6
**Adlington** Lancs 194 E6
**Adlington Park** Lancs 194 E5
**Admaston** Staffs 151 E10
**Admaston** Telford 150 G2
**Admington** Warks 100 B4
**Adpar** Ceredig 92 C6
**Adsborough** Som 28 B3
**Adscombe** Som 43 F7
**Adstock** Bucks 102 E4
**Adstone** Northants 119 G11
**Adswood** Gtr Man 184 D5
**Adversane** W Sus 35 C9
**Advie** Highld 301 F11
**Adwalton** W Yorks 197 B8
**Adwell** Oxon 83 F11
**Adwick le Street** S Yorks 198 F4
**Adwick upon Dearne** S Yorks 198 G3
**Adziel** Aberds 303 D9
**Ae** Dumfries 247 F11
**Ae Village** Dumfries 247 F11
**Affetside** Gtr Man 195 E9
**Affleck** Aberds 303 G8
**Affpuddle** Dorset 18 C2
**Affric Lodge** Highld 299 G11
**Afon Eitha** Wrex 166 F3
**Afon-wen** Flint 181 G10
**Afon Wen** Gwyn 145 B8
**Afton** IoW 20 D2
**Agar Nook** Leics 153 G9
**Agbrigg** W Yorks 197 D10
**Aggborough** Worcs 116 B6
**Agglethorpe** N Yorks 213 B11
**Aglionby** Cumb 239 F10
**Agneash** IoM 192 D5
**Aifft** Denb 165 B10
**Aigburth** Mers 182 D5
**Aiginis** W Isles 304 E6
**Aike** E Yorks 209 D7
**Aikenway** Moray 302 E2
**Aikerness** Orkney 314 A4
**Aikers** Orkney 314 G4
**Aiketgate** Cumb 230 B5
**Aikton** Cumb 239 G7
**Ailby** Lincs 190 F6
**Ailey** Hereford 96 B6
**Ailstone** Warks 118 G4
**Ailsworth** Pboro 138 D2
**Aimes Green** Essex 86 E5
**Ainderby Quernhow** N Yorks 215 C7
**Ainderby Steeple** N Yorks 224 G6
**Aingers Green** Essex 108 G2
**Ainley Top** W Yorks 196 D6
**Ainsdale** Mers 193 E10
**Ainsdale-on-Sea** Mers 193 E9
**Ainstable** Cumb 230 B6
**Ainsworth** Gtr Man 195 E9
**Ainthorpe** N Yorks 226 D4
**Aintree** Mers 182 B5
**Aird** Argyll 275 C8
**Aird** Dumfries 236 C2
**Aird** Highld 299 B7
**Aird** W Isles 296 F3
**Aird** W Isles 304 E7
**Airdachuilinn** Highld 306 E7
**Aird a Mhachair** W Isles 297 G3
**Aird a' Mhulaidh** W Isles 305 G3
**Aird Asaig** W Isles 305 H3
**Aird Dhail** W Isles 304 B6
**Airdens** Highld 309 K6
**Airdeny** Argyll 289 G11
**Aird Mhidhinis** W Isles 297 L3
**Aird Mhighe** W Isles 296 C6
**Aird Mhighe** W Isles 305 J3
**Aird Mhòr** W Isles 297 G4
**Aird Mhor** W Isles 297 L3
**Aird of Sleat** Highld 295 E7
**Airdrie** N Lnrk 268 B5
**Airds of Kells** Dumfries 237 B8
**Aird Thunga** W Isles 304 E6
**Airdtorrisdale** Highld 308 C6
**Aird Uig** W Isles 304 E2
**Airedale** W Yorks 198 B3
**Aire View** N Yorks 204 D5
**Airidh a Bhruaich** W Isles 305 G4
**Airieland** Dumfries 237 D9
**Airinis** W Isles 304 E6
**Airlie** Angus 287 B7
**Airlies** Dumfries 236 D5
**Airmyn** E Yorks 199 B8
**Airntully** Perth 286 D4
**Airor** Highld 295 E9
**Airth** Falk 279 D7
**Airthrey Castle** Stirl 278 B6
**Airton** N Yorks 204 B4
**Airyhassen** Dumfries 236 E5
**Airy Hill** N Yorks 227 D7
**Airyligg** Dumfries 236 C4
**Aisby** Lincs 155 B10
**Aisby** Lincs 188 C5
**Aisgernis** W Isles 297 J3
**Aish** Devon 8 C3
**Aish** Devon 8 D6
**Aisholt** Som 43 F7
**Aiskew** N Yorks 214 B5
**Aislaby** N Yorks 216 B5
**Aislaby** N Yorks 227 D7
**Aislaby** Stockton 225 C8
**Aisthorpe** Lincs 188 E6
**Aith** Orkney 314 E2
**Aith** Shetland 312 D8
**Aith** Shetland 313 H5
**Aithnen** Powys 148 E4
**Aithsetter** Shetland 313 K6
**Aitkenhead** S Ayrs 245 B8
**Aitnoch** Highld 301 F9
**Akeld** Northumb 263 D11
**Akeley** Bucks 102 D4
**Akenham** Suff 108 B2
**Albany** T&W 243 F7
**Albaston** Corn 12 G4
**Alberbury** Shrops 149 G7
**Albert Town** Pembs 72 B6
**Albert Village** Leics 152 F6
**Albourne** W Sus 36 D3
**Albourne Green** W Sus 36 D3
**Albrighton** Shrops 132 C6
**Albrighton** Shrops 149 F9
**Albro Castle** Ceredig 92 B3
**Alburgh** Norf 142 F5
**Albury** Herts 105 G8
**Albury** Sur 50 D5
**Albury End** Herts 105 G8
**Albury Heath** Sur 50 D5
**Albyfield** Cumb 240 G2
**Alby Hill** Norf 160 C3
**Alcaig** Highld 300 D5
**Alcaston** Shrops 131 F9
**Alcester** Dorset 30 C5
**Alcester** Warks 117 F11
**Alcester Lane's End** W Mid 133 G11
**Alciston** E Sus 23 D8
**Alcombe** Som 42 D3
**Alcombe** Wilts 61 F10
**Alconbury** Cambs 122 B3
**Alconbury Weston** Cambs 122 B3
**Aldbar Castle** Angus 287 B9
**Aldborough** Norf 160 C3
**Aldborough** N Yorks 215 F8
**Aldborough Hatch** London 68 B3
**Aldbourne** Wilts 63 D9
**Aldbrough** E Yorks 209 F10
**Aldbrough St John** N Yorks 224 C4
**Aldbury** Herts 85 C7
**Aldcliffe** Lancs 211 G9
**Aldclune** Perth 291 G11
**Aldeburgh** Suff 127 F9
**Aldeby** Norf 143 E8
**Aldenham** Herts 85 F10
**Alderbrook** E Sus 37 B8
**Alderbury** Wilts 31 B11
**Aldercar** Derbys 170 F6
**Alderford** Norf 160 F2
**Alder Forest** Gtr Man 184 B3
**Alderholt** Dorset 31 E10
**Alderley** Glos 80 G3
**Alderley Edge** Ches E 184 F4
**Alderman's Green** W Mid 135 G7
**Aldermaston** W Berks 64 F5
**Aldermaston Soke** W Berks 64 G6
**Aldermaston Wharf** W Berks 64 F6
**Alderminster** Warks 100 B4
**Aldermoor** Soton 32 D5
**Alder Moor** Staffs 152 D4
**Alderney** Poole 18 C6
**Alder Row** Som 45 E9
**Aldersbrook** London 68 B2
**Alder's End** Hereford 98 C2
**Aldersey Green** Ches W 167 D7

Aldershawe Staffs 134 B2
Aldershot Hants 49 C11
Alderton Glos 99 E10
Alderton Northants 102 B5
Alderton Shrops 149 E9
Alderton Suff 108 C6
Alderton Wilts 61 C10
Alderton Fields Glos 99 E10
Alderwasley Derbys 170 E4
Aldfield N Yorks 214 F5
Aldford Ches W 166 D6
Aldgate Rutland 137 C9
Aldham Essex 107 F8
Aldham Suff 107 B10
Aldie Highld 309 L7
Aldingbourne W Sus 22 B6
Aldingham Cumb 210 E5
Aldington Kent 54 F5
Aldington Worcs 99 C11
Aldington Frith Kent 54 F4
Aldivalloch Moray 302 G3
Aldochlay Argyll 277 C7
Aldon Shrops 115 B8
Aldoth Cumb 229 B8
Aldourie Castle Highld 300 F6
Aldreth Cambs 123 C8
Aldridge W Mid 133 C11
Aldringham Suff 127 E8
Aldrington Brighton 36 F3
Aldsworth Glos 81 C11
Aldunie Moray 302 G3
Aldwark Derbys 170 D2
Aldwark N Yorks 215 G9
Aldwarke S Yorks 186 C6
Aldwick W Sus 22 D6
Aldwincle Northants 137 G10
Aldworth W Berks 64 D5
Alehouseburn Aberds 302 C6
Alehousehill Aberds 303 G10
Ale Oak Shrops 130 G4
Alexandria W Dunb 277 F7
Aley Som 43 F7
Aley Green C Beds 85 B9
Alfardisworthy Devon 24 E3
Alfington Devon 15 B8
Alfold Sur 50 G4
Alfold Bars W Sus 50 G4
Alfold Crossways Sur 50 F4
Alford Aberds 293 B7
Alford Lincs 191 F7
Alford Som 44 G6
Alfred's Well Worcs 117 C8
Alfreton Derbys 170 D6
Alfrick Worcs 116 G4
Alfrick Pound Worcs 116 G4
Alfriston E Sus 23 E8
Algakirk Lincs 156 B5
Algaltraig Argyll 275 F11
Algarkirk Lincs 156 B5
Alhampton Som 44 G6
Aline Lodge W Isles 305 G3
Alisary Highld 289 B9
Alkborough N Lincs 199 C11
Alkerton Glos 80 D3
Alkerton Oxon 101 C7
Alkham Kent 55 E9
Alkington Shrops 149 B10
Alkmonton Derbys 152 B3
Alkrington Garden Village Gtr Man 195 G11
Alladale Lodge Highld 309 L4
Allaleigh Devon 8 E6
Allanaquoich Aberds 292 D3
Allanbank Borders 271 F10
Allanbank N Lnrk 268 D6
Allangrange Mains Highld 300 D6
Allanshaugh Borders 271 F8
Allanshaws Borders 271 G9
Allanton Borders 273 E7
Allanton N Lnrk 269 D7
Allanton S Lnrk 268 E4
Allaston Glos 79 E10
Allathasdal W Isles 297 L2
Allbrook Hants 33 C7
All Cannings Wilts 62 G5
Allendale Town Northumb 241 F8
Allen End Warks 134 D3
Allenheads Northumb 232 B3
Allensford Durham 242 G3
Allens Green Herts 87 B7
Allensmore Hereford 97 D9
Allenton Derby 153 C7
Allenwood Cumb 239 F11
Aller Devon 9 B7
Aller Devon 27 F9
Aller Dorset 30 G3
Aller Som 28 B6
Allerby Cumb 229 D7
Allerford Som 27 B11
Allerford Som 42 D2
Aller Park Devon 9 B7
Allerston N Yorks 217 C7
Allerthorpe E Yorks 207 D11
Allerton Mers 182 D6
Allerton W Yorks 205 G8
Allerton Bywater W Yorks 198 B2
Allerton Mauleverer N Yorks 206 B4
Allesley W Mid 134 G6
Allestree Derby 152 B6
Allet Corn 4 F5
Allexton Leics 136 C6
Allgreave Ches E 169 B7
Allhallows Medway 69 D10
Allhallows-on-Sea Medway 69 D10
Alligin Shuas Highld 299 D8
Allimore Green Staffs 151 F7
Allington Kent 53 B8
Allington Lincs 172 G5
Allington Wilts 47 F8
Allington Wilts 61 D11
Allington Wilts 62 G5
Allington Bar Wilts 61 E11
Allithwaite Cumb 211 D7
Alloa Clack 279 C7
Allonby Cumb 229 C7
Allostock Ches W 184 G2
Alloway S Ayrs 257 F8
Allowenshay Som 28 E5
All Saints Devon 28 G4
All Saints South Elmham Suff 142 G6
Allscot Shrops 132 D4
Allscott Telford 150 G2
All Stretton Shrops 131 D9
Allt Carms 75 E9
Alltami Flint 166 B3
Alltbeithe Highld 290 C2
Alltchaorunn Highld 284 B5
Alltforgan Powys 147 E9
Alltmawr Powys 95 B11
Alltnacaillich Highld 308 E4
Allt-na-giubhsaich Aberds 292 E4
Allt na h-Airbhe Highld 307 K6
Allt-nan-sùgh Highld 295 C11
Alltrech Argyll 289 F8
Alltsigh Highld 290 B6
Alltwalis Carms 93 E8
Alltwen Neath 76 E2
Alltyblaca Ceredig 93 B10
Allt-yr-yn Newport 59 B9
Allwood Green Suff 125 C10
Alma Notts 171 E7
Almagill Dumfries 238 B3
Almeley Hereford 114 G6
Almeley Wooton Hereford 114 G6
Almer Dorset 18 B4
Almholme S Yorks 198 F5
Almington Staffs 150 C4
Alminstone Cross Devon 24 C4
Almondbank Perth 286 E4
Almondbury W Yorks 197 D7
Almondsbury S Glos 60 C6
Almondvale W Loth 269 B11
Almshouse Green Essex 106 E5
Alne N Yorks 215 F9
Alne End Warks 118 F2
Alne Hills Warks 118 E2
Alness Highld 300 C6
Alnessferry Highld 300 C6
Alne Station N Yorks 215 F10
Alnham Northumb 263 G11
Alnmouth Northumb 264 G6
Alnwick Northumb 264 G5
Alperton London 67 C7
Alphamstone Essex 107 D7
Alpheton Suff 125 G7
Alphington Devon 14 C4
Alpington Norf 142 C5
Alport Derbys 170 C2
Alport Powys 130 D5
Alpraham Ches E 167 D9
Alresford Essex 107 G11
Alrewas Staffs 152 F3
Alsager Ches E 168 D3
Alsagers Bank Staffs 168 F4
Alscot Bucks 84 E4
Alsop en le Dale Derbys 169 D11
Alston Cumb 231 B10
Alston Devon 28 G4
Alstone Glos 99 E9
Alstone Glos 99 G8
Alstone Som 43 D10
Alstonefield Staffs 169 D10
Alston Sutton Som 44 C2
Alswear Devon 26 C2
Alt Gtr Man 196 G2
Altandhu Highld 307 H4
Altanduin Highld 311 G2
Altarnun Corn 11 E10
Altass Highld 309 J4
Altbough Hereford 97 E10
Altdargue Aberds 293 C7
Alterwall Highld 310 C6
Altham Lancs 203 G11
Alt Hill Gtr Man 196 G2
Althorne Essex 88 F6
Althorpe N Lincs 199 F10
Alticane S Ayrs 244 F6
Alticry Dumfries 236 D4
Altmore Windsor 65 D11
Altnabreac Station Highld 310 E4
Altnacealgach Hotel Highld 307 H7
Altnacraig Argyll 289 G10
Altnafeadh Highld 284 B6
Altnaharra Highld 308 F5
Altofts W Yorks 197 C11
Alton Derbys 170 C5
Alton Hants 49 F8
Alton Staffs 169 G9
Alton Wilts 47 D7
Alton Barnes Wilts 62 G6
Altonhill E Ayrs 257 B10
Alton Pancras Dorset 30 G2
Alton Priors Wilts 62 G6
Altonside Moray 302 D2
Altour Highld 290 E4
Altrincham Gtr Man 184 D3
Altrua Highld 290 E4
Altskeith Stirl 285 G8
Altyre Ho Moray 301 D10
Alum Rock W Mid 134 F2
Alva Clack 279 B7
Alvanley Ches W 183 G7
Alvaston Derby 153 C7
Alvechurch Worcs 117 C10
Alvecote Warks 134 C4
Alvediston Wilts 31 C7
Alveley Shrops 132 G5
Alverdiscott Devon 25 B8
Alverstoke Hants 21 B8
Alverstone IoW 21 D7
Alverthorpe W Yorks 197 C10
Alverton Notts 172 G3
Alves Moray 301 C11
Alvescot Oxon 82 E3
Alveston S Glos 60 B6
Alveston Warks 118 F4
Alveston Down S Glos 60 B6
Alveston Hill Warks 118 G4
Alvie Highld 291 C10
Alvingham Lincs 190 C5
Alvington Glos 79 E10
Alvington Som 29 D8
Alwalton Cambs 138 D2
Alway Newport 59 B10
Alweston Dorset 29 E11
Alwington Devon 24 C6
Alwinton Northumb 251 B10
Alwoodley W Yorks 205 E11
Alwoodley Gates W Yorks 206 E2
Alwoodley Park W Yorks 205 E11
Alyth Perth 286 C6
Amalebra Corn 1 B5
Amalveor Corn 1 B5
Amatnatua Highld 309 K4
Am Baile W Isles 297 K3
Ambaston Derbys 153 C8
Ambergate Derbys 170 E4
Amber Hill Lincs 174 F2
Amberley Glos 80 E5
Amberley Hereford 97 B10
Amberley W Sus 35 E8
Amble Northumb 253 C7
Amblecote W Mid 133 F7
Ambler Thorn W Yorks 196 B5
Ambleside Cumb 221 E7
Ambleston Pembs 91 F10
Ambrosden Oxon 83 B10
Am Buth Argyll 289 G10
Amcotts N Lincs 199 E11
Amen Corner Brack 65 F10
Amersham Bucks 85 F7
Amersham Common Bucks 85 F7
Amersham Old Town Bucks 85 F7
Amersham on the Hill Bucks 85 F7
Amerton Staffs 151 D9
Amesbury Bath 45 B7
Amesbury Wilts 47 E7
Ameysford Dorset 31 G9
Amington Staffs 134 C4
Amisfield Dumfries 247 G11
Amlwch Anglesey 178 C6
Amlwch Port Anglesey 179 C7
Ammanford / Rhydaman Carms 75 C10
Ammerham Som 28 F5
Amod Argyll 255 D8
Amotherby N Yorks 216 E4
Ampfield Hants 32 C6
Ampleforth N Yorks 215 D11
Ampney Crucis Glos 81 E9
Ampney St Mary Glos 81 E9
Ampney St Peter Glos 81 E9
Amport Hants 47 E9
Ampthill C Beds 103 D10
Ampton Suff 125 C7
Amroth Pembs 73 D11
Amulree Perth 286 D2
Amwell Herts 85 C11
Anagach Highld 301 G10
Anaheilt Highld 289 C10
Anancaun Highld 299 C10
An Caol Highld 298 D6
Ancarraig Highld 300 G4
Ancaster Lincs 173 G7
Anchor Shrops 130 G3
Anchorage Park Ptsmth 33 G11
Anchor Corner Norf 141 D10
Anchorsholme Blkpool 202 E2
Anchor Street Norf 160 E6
An Cnoc W Isles 304 E6
Ancoats Gtr Man 184 B5
Ancroft Northumb 273 F9
Ancroft Northmoor Northumb 273 F9
Ancrum Borders 262 E4
Ancton W Sus 35 G7
Ancumtoun Orkney 314 A7
Anderby Lincs 191 F8
Anderby Creek Lincs 191 F8
Andersea Som 43 G10
Andersfield Som 43 G8
Anderson Dorset 18 B3
Anderton Ches W 183 F10
Anderton Corn 7 E8
Anderton Lancs 194 E6
Andertons Mill Lancs 194 E4
Andover Hants 47 D11
Andover Down Hants 47 D11
Andoversford Glos 81 B8
Andreas IoM 192 C5
Andwell Hants 49 C7
Anelog Gwyn 144 D3
Anerley London 67 F10
Anfield Mers 182 C5
Angarrack Corn 2 B3
Angarrick Corn 3 B7
Angelbank Shrops 115 B11
Angersleigh Som 27 D11
Angerton Cumb 238 F6
Angle Pembs 72 E5
An Gleann Ur W Isles 304 E6
Angmering W Sus 35 G9
Angram N Yorks 206 D6
Angram N Yorks 223 F7
Anick Northumb 241 D11
Anie Stirl 285 F9
Ankerdine Hill Worcs 116 F4
Ankerville Highld 301 B8
Anlaby E Yorks 200 B4
Anlaby Park Hull 200 B5
An Leth Meadhanach W Isles 297 K3
Anmer Norf 158 D4
Anmore Hants 33 E11
Annan Dumfries 238 D5
Annaside Cumb 210 B1
Annat Argyll 284 E4
Annat Highld 290 D5
Annat Highld 299 D8
Anna Valley Hants 47 E10
Annbank S Ayrs 257 E10
Annesley Notts 171 E8
Annesley Woodhouse Notts 171 E7
Annfield Plain Durham 242 G5
Anniesland Glasgow 267 B10
Annifirth Shetland 313 J3
Annishader Highld 298 D4
Annis Hill Suff 143 F7
Annitsford T&W 243 C7
Annscroft Shrops 131 B9
Ann's Hill Hants 33 G9
Annwell Place Derbys 152 F6
Ansdell Lancs 193 B10
Ansells End Herts 85 B11
Ansford Som 44 G6
Ansley Warks 134 E5
Ansley Common Warks 134 E6
Anslow Staffs 152 D4
Anslow Gate Staffs 152 D3
Ansteadbrook Sur 50 G2
Anstey Herts 105 E8
Anstey Leics 135 B10
Anstruther Easter Fife 287 G9
Anstruther Wester Fife 287 G9
Ansty Hants 49 E8
Ansty Warks 135 G7
Ansty Wilts 31 B7
Ansty W Sus 36 C3
Ansty Coombe Wilts 31 B7
Ansty Cross Dorset 30 G3
Anthill Common Hants 33 E10
Anthony Corn 7 E7
Anthony's Cross Glos 98 G4
Anthorn Cumb 238 F5
Antingham Norf 160 C5
An t-Ob W Isles 296 C6
Anton's Gowt Lincs 174 F3
Antonshill Falk 279 E7
Antony Corn 7 E7
Antony Passage Corn 7 D8
Antrobus Ches W 183 F10
Anvil Green Kent 54 D6
Anvilles W Berks 63 F10
Anwick Lincs 173 E10
Anwoth Dumfries 237 D7
Aonachan Highld 290 E4
Aoradh Argyll 274 G3
Apedale Staffs 168 F4
Aperfield London 52 B2
Apes Dale Worcs 117 C9
Apes Hall Cambs 139 E11
Apethorpe Northants 137 D10
Apeton Staffs 151 F7
Apley Lincs 189 F10
Apley Forge Shrops 132 D4
Apperknowle Derbys 186 F5
Apperley Glos 99 F7
Apperley Bridge W Yorks 205 F9
Apperley Dene Northumb 242 F3
Appersett N Yorks 223 G7
Appin Argyll 289 E11
Appin House Argyll 289 E11
Appleby N Lincs 200 E3
Appleby-in-Westmorland Cumb 231 G9
Appleby Magna Leics 134 B6
Appleby Parva Leics 134 B6
Applecross Highld 299 E7
Applecross Ho Highld 299 E7
Appledore Devon 27 E9
Appledore Devon 40 G3
Appledore Kent 39 B7
Appledore Heath Kent 54 G3
Appleford Oxon 83 G8
Applegarthtown Dumfries 248 G4
Applehouse Hill Windsor 65 C10
Applemore Hants 32 F5
Appleshaw Hants 47 D10
Applethwaite Cumb 229 F11
Appleton Halton 183 D8
Appleton Oxon 82 E6
Appleton-le-Moors N Yorks 216 B4
Appleton-le-Street N Yorks 216 E4
Appleton Park Warr 183 E10
Appleton Roebuck N Yorks 207 E7
Appleton Thorn Warr 183 E10
Appleton Wiske N Yorks 225 E7
Appletreehall Borders 262 F2
Appletreewick N Yorks 213 G11
Appley IoW 21 C8
Appley Som 27 C9
Appley Bridge Lancs 194 F4
Apse Heath IoW 21 E7
Apsey Green Suff 126 E5
Apsley Herts 85 D9
Apsley End C Beds 104 E2
Apuldram W Sus 22 C4
Aqueduct Telford 132 B3
Aquhythie Aberds 293 B9
Arabella Highld 301 B8
Arbeadie Aberds 293 D8
Arberth / Narberth Pembs 73 C10
Arbirlot Angus 287 C10
Arboll Highld 311 L2
Arborfield Wokingham 65 F9
Arborfield Cross Wokingham 65 F9
Arborfield Garrison Wokingham 65 F9
Arbourthorne S Yorks 186 D5
Arbroath Angus 287 C10
Arbury Cambs 123 E8
Arbuthnott Aberds 293 F9
Archavandra Muir Highld 309 K7
Archdeacon Newton Darl 224 B5
Archenfield Hereford 96 C5
Archiestown Moray 302 E2
Archnalea Highld 289 C10
Arclid Ches E 168 C3
Arclid Green Ches E 168 C3
Ardachu Highld 309 J6
Ardailly Argyll 255 B7
Ardalanish Argyll 274 B4
Ardallie Aberds 303 F10
Ardalum Ho Argyll 288 F6
Ardamaleish Argyll 275 G11
Ardanaiseig Argyll 284 E4
Ardaneaskan Highld 295 B10
Ardanstur Argyll 275 B9
Ardargie House Hotel Perth 286 F4
Ardarroch Highld 295 B10
Ardban Highld 295 B9
Ardbeg Argyll 254 C5
Ardbeg Argyll 276 E3
Ardcharnich Highld 307 L6
Ardchiavaig Argyll 274 B4
Ardchonnell Argyll 275 B10
Ardchronie Highld 309 L6
Ardchuilk Highld 300 F2
Ardchullarie More Stirl 285 F9
Ardchyle Stirl 285 E9
Ardclach Highld 301 E9
Ard-dhubh Highld 299 E7
Arddleen Powys 148 F5
Ardechvie Highld 290 D3
Ardeley Herts 104 F6
Ardelve Highld 295 C10
Arden Argyll 277 E7
Arden E Renf 267 D10
Ardencaple Ho Argyll 275 B8
Ardendrain Highld 300 F5
Arden Park Gtr Man 184 C6
Ardens Grafton Warks 118 G2
Ardentallen Argyll 289 G10
Ardentinny Argyll 276 D3
Ardentraive Argyll 275 F11
Ardeonaig Stirl 285 D10
Ardersier Highld 301 D7
Ardery Highld 289 C9
Ardessie Highld 307 L5
Ardfern Argyll 275 C9
Ardfernal Argyll 274 F6
Ardgartan Argyll 284 G6
Ardgay Highld 309 K5
Ardglassie Aberds 303 C10
Ardgour Highld 290 G2
Ardgye Moray 301 C11
Ardheslaig Highld 299 D7
Ardiecow Moray 302 C5
Ardinamir Argyll 275 B8
Ardindrean Highld 307 L6
Ardingly W Sus 36 B4
Ardington Oxon 64 B2
Ardington Wick Oxon 64 B2
Ardintoul Highld 295 C10
Ardlair Aberds 302 G5
Ardlair Highld 299 B9
Ardlamey Argyll 255 C7
Ardlamont Ho Argyll 275 G10
Ardlawhill Aberds 303 C8
Ardleigh Essex 107 F11
Ardleigh Green London 68 B4
Ardleigh Heath Essex 107 E10
Ardler Perth 286 C6
Ardley Oxon 101 F10
Ardley End Essex 87 C8
Ardlui Argyll 285 F7
Ardlussa Argyll 275 E7
Ardmair Highld 307 K6
Ardmay Argyll 284 G6
Ardmenish Argyll 274 F6
Ardminish Argyll 255 C7
Ardmolich Highld 289 B9
Ardmore Argyll 289 G9
Ardmore Highld 306 D7
Ardmore Highld 309 L7
Ardnacross Argyll 289 E7
Ardnadam Argyll 276 F3
Ardnagowan Argyll 284 G4
Ardnagrask Highld 300 E5
Ardnarff Highld 295 B10
Ardnastang Highld 289 C10
Ardnave Argyll 274 F3
Ardneil N Ayrs 266 F3
Ardno Argyll 284 G5
Ardo Aberds 303 F8
Ardoch Argyll 277 F7
Ardoch Perth 286 D4
Ardoch Stirl 285 F9
Ardochy House Highld 290 C4
Ardo Ho Aberds 303 G9
Ardoyne Aberds 302 G6
Ardpatrick Argyll 275 G8
Ardpatrick Ho Argyll 255 B8
Ardpeaton Argyll 276 D4
Ardradnaig Perth 285 C11
Ardrishaig Argyll 275 E9
Ardross Fife 287 G9
Ardross Highld 300 B6
Ardrossan N Ayrs 266 G4
Ardross Castle Highld 300 B6
Ardshave Highld 309 K7
Ardsheal Highld 289 D11
Ardshealach Highld 289 C8
Ardskenish Argyll 274 D4
Ardsley S Yorks 197 F11
Ardslignish Highld 289 C7
Ardtalla Argyll 254 B5
Ardtalnaig Perth 285 D11
Ardtaraig Argyll 275 E11
Ardtoe Highld 289 B8
Ardtreck Highld 294 B5
Ardtrostan Perth 285 E10
Ardtur Argyll 289 E11
Arduaine Argyll 275 B8
Ardullie Highld 300 C5
Ardvannie Highld 309 L6
Ardvar Highld 306 F6
Ardvasar Highld 295 E8
Ardveich Stirl 285 E10
Ardverikie Highld 291 E7
Ardvorlich Perth 285 E10
Ardwell Dumfries 236 E3
Ardwell Moray 302 F3
Ardwell S Ayrs 244 E5
Ardwell Mains Dumfries 236 E3
Ardwick Gtr Man 184 B5
Areley Kings Worcs 116 C6
Arford Hants 49 F10
Argoed Caerph 77 F11
Argoed Powys 113 E9
Argoed Powys 130 E5
Argoed Shrops 130 G6
Argoed Shrops 148 E6
Argos Hill E Sus 37 B9
Arichamish Argyll 275 C10
Arichastlich Argyll 284 D6
Aridhglas Argyll 288 G5
Arieniskill Highld 295 G9
Arileod Argyll 288 D3
Arinacrinachd Highld 299 D7
Arinagour Argyll 288 D4
Arineckaig Highld 299 E9
Arion Orkney 314 E2
Arisaig Highld 295 G8
Ariundle Highld 289 C10
Arivegaig Highld 289 C8
Arivoichallum Argyll 254 C4
Arkendale N Yorks 215 G7
Arkesden Essex 105 E9
Arkholme Lancs 211 E11
Arkleby Cumb 229 D8
Arkleton Dumfries 249 E9
Arkle Town N Yorks 223 E10
Arkley London 86 F2
Arksey S Yorks 198 F5
Arkwright Town Derbys 186 G6
Arle Glos 99 G8
Arlebrook Glos 80 D4
Arlecdon Cumb 219 B10
Arlescote Warks 101 B7
Arlesey C Beds 104 D3
Arleston Telford 150 G3
Arley Ches E 183 E11
Arley Green Ches E 183 E11
Arlingham Glos 80 C2
Arlington Devon 40 E6
Arlington E Sus 23 D8
Arlington Glos 81 D10
Arlington Beccott Devon 40 E6
Armadale Highld 308 C7
Armadale W Loth 269 B8
Armadale Castle Highld 295 E8
Armathwaite Cumb 230 B6
Armigers Essex 105 F11
Arminghall Norf 142 C5
Armitage Staffs 151 F11
Armitage Bridge W Yorks 196 E6
Armley W Yorks 205 G11
Armscote Warks 100 C4
Armsdale Staffs 150 C5
Armshead Staffs 168 F6
Armston Northants 137 F11
Armthorpe S Yorks 198 F6
Arnabost Argyll 288 D4
Arnaby Cumb 210 C3
Arncliffe N Yorks 213 E8
Arncroach Fife 287 G9
Arndilly Ho Moray 302 E2
Arne Dorset 18 D5
Arnesby Leics 136 E2
Arngask Perth 286 F5
Arnisdale Highld 295 D10
Arnish Highld 298 E5
Arniston Midloth 270 C6
Arnol W Isles 304 D5
Arnold E Yorks 209 E8
Arnold Notts 171 F9
Arno's Vale Bristol 60 E6
Arnprior Stirl 278 C2
Arnside Cumb 211 D9
Aros Mains Argyll 289 E7
Arowry Wrex 149 B9
Arpafeelie Highld 300 D6
Arpinge Kent 55 F7
Arrad Foot Cumb 210 C6
Arram E Yorks 208 E6
Arrathorne N Yorks 224 G4
Arreton IoW 20 D6
Arrington Cambs 122 G6
Arrivain Argyll 284 D6
Arrochar Argyll 284 G6
Arrow Warks 117 F11
Arrowe Hill Mers 182 D3
Arrowfield Top Worcs 117 C10
Arrow Green Hereford 115 F8
Arrunden W Yorks 196 F6
Arscaig Highld 309 H5
Arscott Shrops 131 B8
Arthill Ches E 184 D2
Arthington W Yorks 205 E11
Arthingworth Northants 136 G5
Arthog Gwyn 146 G2
Arthrath Aberds 303 F9
Arthursdale W Yorks 206 F3
Arthurstone Perth 286 C6
Arthurville Highld 309 L7
Artington Sur 50 D3
Artrochie Aberds 303 F10
Arundel W Sus 35 F8
Arwick Orkney 314 D3
Aryhoulan Highld 290 G2
Asby Cumb 229 G7
Ascog Argyll 266 C2
Ascoil Highld 311 H2
Ascot Windsor 66 F2
Ascott Warks 100 E6
Ascott d'Oyley Oxon 82 B4
Ascott Earl Oxon 82 B3
Ascott-under-Wychwood Oxon 82 B4
Asenby N Yorks 215 D7
Asfordby Leics 154 F4
Asfordby Hill Leics 154 F4
Asgarby Lincs 173 F10
Asgarby Lincs 174 B4
Ash Devon 8 F6
Ash Dorset 30 E5
Ash Kent 55 B9
Ash Kent 68 G5
Ash Som 28 C3
Ash Som 29 C7
Ash Sur 49 C11
Ashaig Highld 295 C8
Ashampstead W Berks 64 D5
Ashampstead Green W Berks 64 D5
Ashansworth Hants 48 B2
Ashbank Kent 53 C10
Ash Bank Staffs 168 F6
Ashbeer Som 42 F5
Ashbocking Suff 126 G3
Ashbourne Derbys 169 F11
Ashbrittle Som 27 C9
Ashbrook Shrops 131 E9
Ash Bullayne Devon 26 G3
Ashburnham Forge E Sus 23 B11
Ashburton Devon 8 B5
Ashbury Devon 12 B6
Ashbury Oxon 63 C9
Ashby N Lincs 200 F2
Ashby by Partney Lincs 174 B6
Ashby cum Fenby NE Lincs 201 G9
Ashby de la Launde Lincs 173 D9
Ashby-de-la-Zouch Leics 153 F7
Ashby Folville Leics 154 G4
Ashby Hill NE Lincs 201 G8
Ashby Magna Leics 135 E11
Ashby Parva Leics 135 F10
Ashby Puerorum Lincs 190 G4
Ashby St Ledgers Northants 119 D11
Ashby St Mary Norf 142 C6
Ashchurch Glos 99 E8
Ashcombe Devon 14 F4
Ashcombe Park N Som 59 G10
Ashcott Som 44 F2
Ashcott Corner Som 44 F2
Ashculme Devon 27 E10
Ashdon Essex 105 C11
Ashe Hants 48 D4
Asheldham Essex 89 E7
Ashen Essex 106 C4
Ashendon Bucks 84 C2
Asheridge Bucks 84 E6
Ashey IoW 21 D7
Ashfield Argyll 275 E8
Ashfield Carms 94 F3
Ashfield Hants 32 D5
Ashfield Hereford 97 G11
Ashfield Shrops 148 D6
Ashfield Stirl 285 G11
Ashfield Suff 126 E4
Ashfield Cum Thorpe Suff 126 E4
Ashfield Green Suff 124 F5
Ashfield Green Suff 126 C5
Ashfields Shrops 150 D4
Ashfold Crossways W Sus 36 B2
Ashfold Side N Yorks 214 F2
Ashford Devon 8 F3
Ashford Devon 40 F4
Ashford Hants 31 E10
Ashford Kent 54 E4
Ashford Sur 66 E5
Ashford Bowdler Shrops 115 C10
Ashford Carbonell Shrops 115 C10
Ashford Common Sur 66 E5
Ashford Hill Hants 64 G5
Ashford in the Water Derbys 185 G11
Ashgate Derbys 186 G5
Ashgill S Lnrk 268 F5
Ash Green Sur 50 D2
Ash Green Warks 134 F6
Ashgrove Bath 45 B8
Ash Grove Wrex 166 G5
Ash Hill Devon 14 G4
Ashiestiel Borders 261 B10
Ashill Devon 27 E9
Ashill Norf 141 C7
Ashill Som 28 D4
Ashingdon Essex 88 G5
Ashington Northumb 253 F7
Ashington Poole 18 B6
Ashington Som 29 C9
Ashington W Sus 35 D10
Ashington End Lincs 175 B8
Ashintully Castle Perth 292 G3
Ashkirk Borders 261 E11
Ashlett Hants 33 G7
Ashleworth Glos 98 F6
Ashley Cambs 124 E3
Ashley Ches E 184 E3
Ashley Devon 25 E10
Ashley Dorset 31 G10
Ashley Glos 80 G6
Ashley Hants 19 B11
Ashley Hants 47 G11
Ashley Kent 55 D10
Ashley Northants 136 E5
Ashley Staffs 150 B5
Ashley Wilts 61 F10
Ashley Dale Staffs 150 B5
Ashley Down Bristol 60 D5
Ashley Green Bucks 85 D7
Ashleyhay Derbys 170 E3
Ashley Heath Ches E 184 D3
Ashley Heath Dorset 31 G10
Ashley Heath Staffs 150 B4
Ashley Moor Hereford 115 D9
Ashley Park Sur 66 F6
Ash Magna Shrops 149 B11
Ashmanhaugh Norf 160 E6
Ashmansworth Hants 48 B2
Ashmansworthy Devon 24 D4
Ashmead Green Glos 80 F3
Ashmill Devon 12 B3
Ash Mill Devon 26 C3
Ash Moor Devon 26 D3
Ashmore Dorset 30 D6
Ashmore Green W Berks 64 F4
Ashmore Lake W Mid 133 D9
Ashmore Park W Mid 133 C9
Ashnashellach Lodge Highld 299 E10
Ashopton Derbys 185 D11
Ashorne Warks 118 F6
Ashover Derbys 170 C4
Ashover Hay Derbys 170 C5
Ashow Warks 118 C6
Ash Parva Shrops 149 B11
Ashperton Hereford 98 C2
Ashprington Devon 8 D6
Ash Priors Som 27 B11
Ashreigney Devon 25 E10
Ashridge Court Devon 25 G11
Ash Street Suff 107 B10
Ashtead Sur 51 B7
Ash Thomas Devon 27 E8
Ashton Corn 2 D4
Ashton Hants 33 D9
Ashton Hereford 115 E10
Ashton Invclyd 276 F4
Ashton Northants 102 B5
Ashton Northants 137 F11
Ashton Pboro 138 B2
Ashton Som 44 D2
Ashton Common Wilts 45 B11
Ashton Gate Bristol 60 E5
Ashton Green E Sus 23 C7
Ashton Hayes Ches W 167 B8
Ashton Heath Halton 183 F9
Ashton-in-Makerfield Gtr Man 183 B9
Ashton Keynes Wilts 81 G8
Ashton under Hill Worcs 99 D9
Ashton-under-Lyne Gtr Man 184 B6
Ashton upon Mersey Gtr Man 184 C3
Ashton Vale Bristol 60 E5
Ashurst Hants 32 E4
Ashurst Kent 52 F4
Ashurst Lancs 194 F3
Ashurst W Sus 35 D11
Ashurst Bridge Hants 32 E4
Ashurst Wood W Sus 52 F2
Ashvale Bl Gwent 77 C10
Ash Vale Sur 49 C11
Ashwater Devon 12 B3
Ashwell Devon 14 G3
Ashwell Herts 104 D5
Ashwell Rutland 155 G7
Ashwell Som 28 D5
Ashwell End Herts 104 C5
Ashwellthorpe Norf 142 D2
Ashwick Som 44 D6
Ashwicken Norf 158 F4
Ashwood Staffs 133 F7
Ashybank Borders 262 F2
Askam in Furness Cumb 210 D4
Askern S Yorks 198 E5
Askerswell Dorset 16 C6
Askerton Hill Lincs 172 F4
Askett Bucks 84 D4
Askham Cumb 230 G6
Askham Notts 188 G2
Askham Bryan York 207 D7
Askham Richard York 206 D6
Asknish Argyll 275 D10
Askrigg N Yorks 223 G8
Askwith N Yorks 205 D9
Aslackby Lincs 155 C11
Aslacton Norf 142 E3
Aslockton Notts 154 B4
Asloun Aberds 293 B7
Asney Som 44 F3
Aspall Suff 126 D3
Aspatria Cumb 229 C8
Aspenden Herts 105 F7
Asperton Lincs 156 B5
Aspley Nottingham 171 G8
Aspley Staffs 150 C6
Aspley Guise C Beds 103 D8
Aspley Heath C Beds 103 D8
Aspley Heath Warks 117 C11
Aspull Gtr Man 194 F6
Aspull Common Gtr Man 183 B10
Assater Shetland 312 F4
Asselby E Yorks 199 B8
Asserby Lincs 191 F7
Asserby Turn Lincs 191 F7
Assington Suff 107 D8
Assington Green Suff 124 G5
Assynt Ho Highld 300 C5
Astbury Ches E 168 C4
Astcote Northants 120 G3
Asterby Lincs 190 F3

Asterley Shrops 131 B7
Asterton Shrops 131 E7
Asthall Oxon 82 C3
Asthall Leigh Oxon 82 C4
Astle Ches E 184 G4
Astle Highld 309 K7
Astley Gtr Man 195 G8
Astley Shrops 149 F10
Astley Warks 134 F6
Astley Worcs 116 D5
Astley Abbotts Shrops 132 D4
Astley Bridge Gtr Man 195 E8
Astley Cross Worcs 116 D6
Astley Green Gtr Man 184 B2
Astmoor Halton 183 E8
Aston Ches E 167 F10
Aston Ches W 183 F9
Aston Derbys 152 C3
Aston Derbys 185 E11
Aston Flint 166 B4
Aston Hereford 115 C9
Aston Hereford 115 E9
Aston Herts 104 G5
Aston Oxon 82 E4
Aston Powys 130 E5
Aston Shrops 132 E6
Aston Shrops 149 D10
Aston Staffs 151 E7
Aston Staffs 168 G3
Aston S Yorks 187 D7
Aston Telford 132 B2
Aston W Mid 133 F11
Aston Wokingham 65 C9
Aston Abbotts Bucks 102 G6
Aston Bank Worcs 116 C2
Aston Botterell Shrops 132 G2
Aston-by-Stone Staffs 151 C8
Aston Cantlow Warks 118 F2
Aston Clinton Bucks 84 C5
Aston Crews Hereford 98 G3
Aston Cross Glos 99 E8
Aston End Herts 104 G5
Aston Eyre Shrops 132 E3
Aston Fields Worcs 117 D9
Aston Flamville Leics 135 E9
Aston Ingham Hereford 98 G3
Aston juxta Mondrum Ches E 167 D11
Aston le Walls Northants 119 G9
Aston Magna Glos 100 D3
Aston Munslow Shrops 131 F10
Aston on Carrant Glos 99 E8
Aston on Clun Shrops 131 G7
Aston-on-Trent Derbys 153 D8
Aston Pigott Shrops 130 B6
Aston Rogers Shrops 130 B6
Aston Rowant Oxon 84 F2
Aston Sandford Bucks 84 D3
Aston Somerville Worcs 99 D10
Aston Square Shrops 148 D6
Aston Subedge Glos 100 C2
Aston Tirrold Oxon 64 B5
Aston Upthorpe Oxon 64 B5
Astrop Northants 101 D10
Astrope Herts 84 C5
Astwick C Beds 104 D4
Astwith Derbys 170 C6
Astwood M Keynes 103 B9
Astwood Worcs 117 D8
Astwood Worcs 117 F7
Astwood Bank Worcs 117 E10
Aswarby Lincs 173 G9
Aswardby Lincs 190 G5
Atcham Shrops 131 B10
Atch Lench Worcs 117 G10
Athelhampton Dorset 17 C11
Athelington Suff 126 C4
Athelney Som 28 B4
Athelstaneford E Loth 281 F10
Atherfield Green IoW 20 F5
Atherington Devon 25 C9
Atherington W Sus 35 G8
Athersley North S Yorks 197 F11
Athersley South S Yorks 197 F11
Atherstone Som 28 D5
Atherstone Warks 134 D6
Atherstone on Stour Warks 118 G4
Atherton Gtr Man 195 G7
Athnamulloch Highld 299 G11
Athron Hall Perth 286 G4
Atley Hill N Yorks 224 E5
Atlow Derbys 170 F2
Attadale Highld 295 B11
Attadale Ho Highld 295 B11
Attenborough Notts 153 B10
Atterbury M Keynes 103 D7
Atterby Lincs 189 C7
Attercliffe S Yorks 186 D5
Atterley Shrops 132 D2
Atterton Leics 135 D7
Attleborough Norf 141 D10
Attleborough Warks 135 E7
Attlebridge Norf 160 F2
Attleton Green Suff 124 G4
Atwick E Yorks 209 C9
Atworth Wilts 61 F11
Auberrow Hereford 97 B9
Aubourn Lincs 172 C6
Auch Argyll 285 D7
Auchagallon N Ayrs 255 D9
Auchallater Aberds 292 E3
Auchareoch N Ayrs 255 E10
Aucharnie Aberds 302 E6
Auchattie Aberds 293 D8
Auchavan Angus 292 G3
Auchbreck Moray 302 G2
Auchenback E Renf 267 D10
Auchenbainzie Dumfries 247 D8
Auchenblae Aberds 293 F9
Auchenbrack Dumfries 247 D7
Auchenbreck Argyll 255 C8
Auchenbreck Argyll 275 E11
Auchencairn Dumfries 237 D9
Auchencairn Dumfries 247 G11
Auchencairn N Ayrs 256 D2
Auchencairn Ho Dumfries 237 D10
Auchencar N Ayrs 255 D9
Auchencarroch W Dunb 277 E8
Auchencrosh S Ayrs 236 B3
Auchencrow Borders 273 C7
Auchendinny Midloth 270 C5
Auchengray S Lnrk 269 E9
Auchenhalrig Moray 302 C3
Auchenharvie N Ayrs 266 G5
Auchenheath S Lnrk 268 G6
Auchenhew N Ayrs 256 E2
Auchenlaich Stirl 285 G10
Auchenleck Dumfries 237 D9
Auchenlochan Argyll 275 F10
Auchenmalg Dumfries 236 D4
Auchenreoch E Dunb 278 F3
Auchensoul S Ayrs 245 E7
Auchentibber S Lnrk 268 E3
Auchentiber N Ayrs 267 F7
Auchertyre Highld 295 C10
Auchessan Stirl 285 E8
Auchgourish Highld 291 B11
Auchinairn E Dunb 268 B2
Auchindrain Argyll 284 G4
Auchindrean Highld 307 L6
Auchininna Aberds 302 E6
Auchinleck Dumfries 236 B6
Auchinleck E Ayrs 258 E3
Auchinloch N Lnrk 278 G3
Auchinner Perth 285 F10
Auchinraith S Lnrk 268 D3
Auchinroath Moray 302 D2
Auchinstarry N Lnrk 278 F4
Auchintoul Aberds 293 B7
Auchintoul Highld 309 K5
Auchiries Aberds 303 F10
Auchlee Aberds 293 D10
Auchleeks Ho Perth 291 G9
Auchleven Aberds 302 G6
Auchlinn Aberds 303 D7
Auchlochan S Lnrk 259 B8
Auchlossan Aberds 293 C7
Auchlunachan Highld 307 L6
Auchlunies Aberds 293 D10
Auchlyne Stirl 285 E9
Auchmacoy Aberds 303 F9
Auchmair Moray 302 G3
Auchmantle Dumfries 236 C3
Auchmenzie Aberds 302 G5
Auchmillan E Ayrs 258 D2
Auchmithie Angus 287 C10
Auchmore Highld 300 D4
Auchmuirbridge Fife 286 G6
Auchmull Angus 293 F7
Auchnacraig Argyll 289 G9
Auchnacree Angus 292 G6
Auchnafree Perth 286 D2
Auchnagallin Highld 301 F10
Auchnagarron Argyll 275 E11
Auchnagatt Aberds 303 E9
Auchnaha Argyll 275 E10
Auchnahillin Highld 301 F7
Auchnarrow Moray 302 G2
Auchnashelloch Perth 285 F11
Auchnotteroch Dumfries 236 C1
Aucholzie Aberds 292 D5
Auchrannie Angus 286 B6
Auchroisk Highld 301 G10
Auchronie Angus 292 E6
Auchterarder Perth 286 F3
Auchteraw Highld 290 C5
Auchterderran Fife 280 B4
Auchterhouse Angus 287 D7
Auchtermuchty Fife 286 F6
Auchterneed Highld 300 D4
Auchtertool Fife 280 C4
Auchtertyre Moray 301 D11
Auchtertyre Stirl 285 E7
Auchtubh Stirl 285 E9
Auckengill Highld 310 C7
Auckley S Yorks 199 G7
Audenshaw Gtr Man 184 B6
Audlem Ches E 167 G11
Audley Staffs 168 E3
Audley End Essex 105 D10
Audley End Essex 106 D6
Audley End Norf 142 G2
Audley End Suff 125 G7
Auds Aberds 302 C6
Aughertree Cumb 229 D11
Aughton E Yorks 207 F10
Aughton Lancs 193 F11
Aughton Lancs 211 F10
Aughton S Yorks 187 D7
Aughton Wilts 47 B8
Aughton Park Lancs 194 F2
Aukside Durham 232 F4
Auldearn Highld 301 D9
Aulden Hereford 115 G9
Auldgirth Dumfries 247 F10
Auldhame E Loth 281 E11
Auldhouse S Lnrk 268 E2
Auldtown of Carnoustie Aberds 302 E6
Ault a'chruinn Highld 295 C11
Aultanrynie Highld 308 F3
Aultbea Highld 307 L3
Aultdearg Highld 300 C2
Aultgrishan Highld 307 L2
Aultguish Inn Highld 300 B3
Ault Hucknall Derbys 171 B7
Aultibea Highld 311 G4
Aultiphurst Highld 310 C2
Aultivullin Highld 310 C2
Aultmore Highld 301 G10
Aultmore Moray 302 D4
Aultnagoire Highld 300 G5
Aultnamain Inn Highld 309 L6
Aultnaslat Highld 290 C3
Aulton Aberds 302 G6
Aulton of Atherb Aberds 303 E9
Aultvaich Highld 300 E5
Aunby Lincs 155 G10
Aundorach Highld 291 B11
Aunk Devon 27 G8
Aunsby Lincs 155 B10
Auquhorthies Aberds 303 G8
Aust S Glos 60 B5
Austendike Lincs 156 E5
Austen Fen Lincs 190 C5
Austenwood Bucks 66 B3
Austerfield S Yorks 187 C11
Austerlands Gtr Man 196 F3
Austhorpe W Yorks 206 G3
Austrey Warks 134 B5
Austwick N Yorks 212 F5
Authorpe Lincs 190 E6
Authorpe Row Lincs 191 G8
Avebury Wilts 62 F6
Avebury Trusloe Wilts 62 F5
Aveley Thurrock 68 C5
Avening Glos 80 F5
Avening Green S Glos 80 G2
Averham Notts 172 E3
Avernish Highld 295 C10
Avery Hill London 68 E2
Aveton Gifford Devon 8 F3
Avielochan Highld 291 B11
Aviemore Highld 291 B10
Avington Hants 48 G4
Avington W Berks 63 F11
Avoch Highld 301 D7
Avon Hants 19 B8
Avon Wilts 62 D3
Avonbridge Falk 279 G8
Avoncliff Wilts 45 B10
Avon Dassett Warks 101 B8
Avonmouth Bristol 60 D4
Avonwick Devon 8 D4
Awbridge Hants 32 C4
Awhirk Dumfries 236 D2
Awkley S Glos 60 B5
Awliscombe Devon 27 G10
Awre Glos 80 D2
Awsworth Notts 171 G7
Axbridge Som 44 C2
Axford Hants 48 E6
Axford Wilts 63 F8
Axmansford Hants 64 G5
Axminster Devon 15 B11
Axmouth Devon 15 C11
Axton Flint 181 E10
Axtown Devon 7 B10
Axwell Park T&W 242 E5
Aycliff Kent 55 E10
Aycliffe Durham 233 G11
Aydon Northumb 242 D2
Aykley Heads Durham 233 C11
Aylburton Glos 79 E10
Aylburton Common Glos 79 E10
Ayle Northumb 231 B10
Aylesbeare Devon 14 C6
Aylesbury Bucks 84 C4
Aylesby NE Lincs 201 F8
Aylesford Kent 53 B8
Aylesham Kent 55 C8
Aylestone Leicester 135 C11
Aylestone Hill Hereford 97 C10
Aylestone Park Leicester 135 C11
Aylmerton Norf 160 B3
Aylsham Norf 160 D3
Aylton Hereford 98 D3
Aylworth Glos 100 G2
Aymestrey Hereford 115 D8
Aynho Northants 101 E10
Ayot Green Herts 86 C2
Ayot St Lawrence Herts 85 B11
Ayot St Peter Herts 86 B2
Ayr S Ayrs 257 E8
Ayre of Atler Shetland 313 G6
Ayres Shetland 313 H5
Ayres End Herts 85 C11
Ayres of Selivoe Shetland 313 J4
Ayres Quay T&W 243 F9
Aysgarth N Yorks 213 B10
Ayshford Devon 27 D8
Ayside Cumb 211 C7
Ayston Rutland 137 C7
Aythorpe Roding Essex 87 B9
Ayton Borders 273 C8
Ayton T&W 243 F7
Ayton Castle Borders 273 C8
Aywick Shetland 312 E7
Azerley N Yorks 214 E5

## B

Babbacombe Torbay 9 B8
Babbington Notts 171 G7
Babbinswood Shrops 148 C6
Babbs Green Herts 86 B5
Babcary Som 29 B9
Babel Carms 94 D6
Babel Green Suff 106 B4
Babell Flint 181 G11
Babeny Devon 13 F9
Babingley Norf 158 D3
Babraham Cambs 123 G10
Babworth Notts 187 E11
Bac W Isles 304 D6
Bachau Anglesey 178 E6
Bache Shrops 131 G9
Bacheldre Powys 130 E4
Bachelor's Bump E Sus 38 E4
Bache Mill Shrops 131 F10
Bach-y-gwreiddyn Swansea 75 E10
Backaland Orkney 314 C5
Backaskaill Orkney 314 A4
Backbarrow Cumb 211 C7
Backbower Gtr Man 185 C7
Backburn Aberds 293 D10
Backe Carms 74 B3
Backfolds Aberds 303 D10
Backford Ches W 182 G6
Backford Cross Ches W 182 G5
Backhill Aberds 303 F7
Backhill Aberds 303 F10
Backhill of Clackriach Aberds 303 E9
Backhill of Fortree Aberds 303 E9
Backhill of Trustach Aberds 293 D8
Backies Highld 311 J2
Backlass Highld 310 D6
Backlass Highld 310 E4
Back Muir Fife 279 D11
Back of Keppoch Highld 295 G8
Back o' th' Brook Staffs 169 E9
Back Rogerton E Ayrs 258 E3
Back Street Suff 124 F4
Backwell N Som 60 F3
Backwell Common N Som 60 F3
Backwell Green N Som 60 F3
Backworth T&W 243 C8
Bacon End Essex 87 B10
Baconend Green Essex 87 B10
Bacon's End W Mid 134 F3
Baconsthorpe Norf 160 B2
Bacton Hereford 97 E7
Bacton Norf 160 C6
Bacton Suff 125 D11
Bacton Green Norf 160 C6
Bacton Green Suff 125 D10
Bacup Lancs 195 C11
Badachonacher Highld 300 B6
Badachro Highld 299 B7
Badanloch Lodge Highld 308 F7
Badarach Highld 309 K5
Badavanich Highld 299 D11
Badbea Highld 307 K5
Badbury Swindon 63 C7
Badbury Wick Swindon 63 C7
Badby Northants 119 F11
Badcall Highld 306 D7
Badcaul Highld 307 K5
Baddeley Edge Stoke 168 E6
Baddeley Green Stoke 168 E6
Baddesley Clinton Warks 118 C4
Baddesley Ensor Warks 134 D5
Baddidarach Highld 307 G5
Baddoch Aberds 292 E3
Baddock Highld 301 D7
Baddow Park Essex 88 E2
Badeach Moray 302 F2
Badenscallie Highld 307 J5
Badenscoth Aberds 303 F7
Badentoy Park Aberds 293 D11
Badenyon Aberds 292 B5
Badgall Corn 11 D10
Badgeney Cambs 139 D8
Badger Shrops 132 D5
Badgergate Stirl 278 B5
Badger's Hill Worcs 99 B10
Badger's Mount Kent 68 G3
Badger Street Som 28 D3
Badgeworth Glos 80 B6
Badgworth Som 43 C11
Badharlick Corn 11 D11
Badicaul Highld 295 C9
Badingham Suff 126 D6
Badintagairt Highld 309 H4
Badlesmere Kent 54 C4
Badlipster Highld 310 E6
Badluarach Highld 307 K4
Badminton S Glos 61 C10
Badnaban Highld 307 G5
Badnabay Highld 306 E7
Badnagie Highld 310 F5
Badninish Highld 309 K7
Badrallach Highld 307 K5
Badsey Worcs 99 C11
Badshalloch W Dunb 277 D9
Badshot Lea Sur 49 D11
Badsworth W Yorks 198 E3
Badwell Ash Suff 125 D9
Badwell Green Suff 125 D10
Badworthy Devon 8 C3
Bae Cinmel / Kinmel Bay Conwy 181 E7
Bae Colwyn / Colwyn Bay Conwy 180 F4
Bae Penrhyn / Penrhyn Bay Conwy 180 E4
Baffins Ptsmth 33 G11
Bagber Dorset 30 E3
Bagby N Yorks 215 C9
Bagby Grange N Yorks 215 C9
Bag Enderby Lincs 190 G5
Bagendon Glos 81 D8
Bagginswood Shrops 132 G3
Baggrow Cumb 229 C9
Bàgha Chàise W Isles 296 D5
Bagh a Chaisteil W Isles 297 M2
Bagham Kent 54 C5
Baghasdal W Isles 297 K3
Bagh Mor W Isles 296 F4
Bagh Shiarabhagh W Isles 297 L3
Bagillt Flint 182 F2
Baginton Warks 118 C6
Baglan Neath 57 C8
Bagley Shrops 149 D8
Bagley Som 44 D3
Bagley W Yorks 205 F10
Bagley Green Som 27 D10
Bagley Marsh Shrops 149 D7
Bagmore Hants 49 E7
Bagnall Staffs 168 E6
Bagnor W Berks 64 F3
Bagpath Glos 80 E5
Bagpath Glos 80 G4
Bagshaw Derbys 185 E9
Bagshot Sur 66 G2
Bagshot Wilts 63 F10
Bagshot Heath Sur 66 G2
Bagslate Moor Gtr Man 195 E11
Bagstone S Glos 61 B7
Bagthorpe Norf 158 C5
Bagthorpe Notts 171 E7
Baguley Gtr Man 184 D4
Bagworth Leics 135 B8
Bagwyllydiart Hereford 97 F8
Bagwy Llydiart Hereford 97 F8
Bail Àrd Bhuirgh W Isles 304 C6
Bailbrook Bath 61 F9
Baildon W Yorks 205 F9
Baildon Green W Yorks 205 F8
Baile W Isles 296 C5
Baile Ailein W Isles 304 F4
Baile a Mhanaich W Isles 296 F3
Baile an Truiseil W Isles 304 C5
Bailebeag Highld 291 B7
Baile Boidheach Argyll 275 F8
Baile Gharbhaidh W Isles 297 G3
Baile Glas W Isles 296 F4
Baile Mhartainn W Isles 296 D3
Baile Mhic Phail W Isles 296 D4
Baile Mor Argyll 288 G4
Baile Mor W Isles 296 E3
Baile na Creige W Isles 297 L2
Baile nan Cailleach W Isles 296 F3
Baile Raghaill W Isles 296 D3
Bailey Green Hants 33 B11
Baileyhead Cumb 240 B2
Bailiesward Aberds 302 F4
Bailiff Bridge W Yorks 196 C6
Baillieston Glasgow 268 C3
Bail' Iochdrach W Isles 296 F4
Bailrigg Lancs 202 B5
Bail Uachdraich W Isles 296 E4
Bail' Ur Tholastaidh W Isles 304 D7
Bainbridge N Yorks 223 G8
Bainsford Falk 279 E7
Bainshole Aberds 302 F6
Bainton E Yorks 208 C5
Bainton Oxon 101 F11
Bainton Pboro 137 B11
Baintown Fife 287 G7
Bairnkine Borders 262 F5
Baker's Cross Kent 53 F9
Bakers End Herts 86 B5
Baker's Hill Glos 79 C9
Baker Street Thurrock 68 C6
Baker's Wood Bucks 66 B4
Bakesdown Corn 24 G2
Bakestone Moor Derbys 187 F8
Bakewell Derbys 170 B2
Balachroick Highld 291 C10
Balachuirn Highld 298 E5
Balance Hill Staffs 151 C11
Balavil Highld 291 C9
Balavoulin Perth 291 G10
Bala / Y Bala Gwyn 147 B8
Balbeg Highld 300 F4
Balbeg Highld 300 G4
Balbeggie Perth 286 E5
Balbegno Castle Aberds 293 F8
Balbithan Aberds 293 B9
Balbithan Ho Aberds 293 B10
Balblair Highld 300 E5
Balblair Highld 301 C7
Balblair Highld 309 K5
Balby S Yorks 198 G5
Balcherry Highld 311 L2
Balchladich Highld 306 F5
Balchraggan Highld 300 E5
Balchraggan Highld 300 F5
Balchraggan Highld 300 G5
Balchrick Highld 306 D6
Balchrystie Fife 287 G8
Balcladaich Highld 300 G2
Balcombe W Sus 51 G10
Balcombe Lane W Sus 51 G10
Balcomie Fife 287 F10
Balcraggie Lodge Highld 310 F5
Balcurvie Fife 287 G7
Baldersby N Yorks 215 D7
Baldersby St James N Yorks 215 D7
Balderstone Gtr Man 196 E2
Balderstone Lancs 203 G8
Balderton Ches W 166 C5
Balderton Notts 172 E4
Baldhu Corn 4 G5
Baldingstone Gtr Man 195 E10
Baldinnie Fife 287 F8
Baldock Herts 104 E4
Baldon Row Oxon 83 E9
Baldoon Highld 300 B6
Baldovie Dundee 287 D8
Baldrine IoM 192 D5
Baldslow E Sus 38 E3
Baldwin IoM 192 D4
Baldwinholme Cumb 239 G8
Baldwin's Gate Staffs 168 G3
Baldwins Hill W Sus 51 F11
Bale Norf 159 B10
Balearn Aberds 303 D10
Balemartine Argyll 288 E1
Balephuil Argyll 288 E1
Balerno Edin 270 B3
Balerominhor Argyll 274 D4
Balevullin Argyll 288 E1
Balfield Angus 293 G7
Balfour Orkney 314 E4
Balfour Mains Orkney 314 E4
Balfron Stirl 277 D10
Balfron Station Stirl 277 D10
Balgaveny Aberds 302 E6
Balgavies Angus 287 B9
Balgonar Fife 279 C10
Balgove Aberds 303 F8
Balgowan Highld 291 D8
Balgowan Perth 286 E3
Balgown Highld 298 C3
Balgrennie Aberds 292 C6
Balgrochan E Dunb 278 F2
Balgy Highld 299 D8
Balhaldie Stirl 286 G2
Balhalgardy Aberds 303 G7
Balham London 67 E9
Balhary Perth 286 C6
Baliasta Shetland 312 C8
Baligill Highld 310 C2
Baligortan Argyll 288 E5
Baligrundle Argyll 289 E10
Balindore Argyll 289 F11
Balinoe Argyll 288 E1
Balintore Angus 286 B6
Balintore Highld 301 B8
Balintraid Highld 301 B7
Balintuim Aberds 292 E3
Balk N Yorks 215 C9
Balkeerie Angus 287 C7
Balkemback Angus 287 D7
Balk Field Notts 188 E2
Balkholme E Yorks 199 B9
Balkissock S Ayrs 244 G4
Ball Corn 10 G6
Ball Shrops 148 D6
Ballabeg IoM 192 E3
Ballacannel IoM 192 D5
Ballachraggan Moray 301 E11
Ballachrochin Highld 301 F8
Ballachulish Highld 284 B4
Balladen Lancs 195 C10
Ballajora IoM 192 C5
Ballaleigh IoM 192 D4
Ballamodha IoM 192 E3
Ballantrae S Ayrs 244 G3
Ballaquine IoM 192 D5
Ballard's Ash Wilts 62 C5
Ballards Gore Essex 88 G6
Ballard's Green Warks 134 E5
Ballasalla IoM 192 C4
Ballasalla IoM 192 E3
Ballater Aberds 292 D5
Ballathie Perth 286 D5
Ballaugh IoM 192 C4
Ballaveare IoM 192 E4
Ballcorach Moray 301 G11
Ballechin Perth 286 B3
Balleich Stirl 277 B10
Balleigh Highld 309 L7
Ballencrieff E Loth 281 F9
Ballencrieff Toll W Loth 279 G9
Ballentoul Perth 291 G10
Ball Green Stoke 168 E5
Ball Haye Green Staffs 169 D7
Ballhill Devon 24 C3
Ball Hill Hants 64 G2
Ballidon Derbys 170 E2
Balliekine N Ayrs 255 D9
Balliemore Argyll 275 E11
Balliemore Argyll 289 G10
Ballikinrain Stirl 277 D11
Ballimeanoch Argyll 284 F4
Ballimore Argyll 275 E10
Ballimore Stirl 285 F9
Ballinaby Argyll 274 G3
Ballinbreich Fife 286 E6
Ballindean Perth 286 E6
Ballingdon Suff 107 C7
Ballingdon Bottom Herts 85 C8
Ballinger Bottom Bucks 84 E6
Ballinger Bottom (South) Bucks 84 E6
Ballinger Common Bucks 84 E6
Ballingham Hereford 97 E11
Ballingham Hill Hereford 97 E11
Ballingry Fife 280 B3
Ballinlick Perth 286 C3
Ballinluig Perth 286 B3
Ballintean Highld 291 C10
Ballintuim Perth 286 B5
Balliveolan Argyll 289 E10
Balloch Angus 287 B7
Balloch Highld 301 E7
Balloch N Lnrk 278 G4
Balloch W Dunb 277 E7
Ballochan Aberds 293 D7
Ballochearn Stirl 277 D11
Ballochford Moray 302 F3
Ballochmorrie S Ayrs 244 G6
Ball o'Ditton Halton 183 D7
Ballogie Aberds 293 D7
Balls Cross W Sus 35 B7
Balls Green Essex 107 G11
Balls Green E Sus 52 F3
Balls Green W Sus 35 C10
Ball's Green Glos 80 F5
Balls Hill W Mid 133 E9
Ballygown Argyll 288 E6
Ballygrant Argyll 274 G4
Ballygroggan Argyll 255 F7
Ballyhaugh Argyll 288 D3
Balmacara Highld 295 C10
Balmacara Square Highld 295 C10
Balmaclellan Dumfries 237 B8
Balmacneil Perth 286 B3
Balmacqueen Highld 298 B4
Balmae Dumfries 237 E8
Balmaha Stirl 277 C8
Balmalcolm Fife 287 G7
Balmalloch N Lnrk 278 F4
Balmeanach Argyll 288 F6
Balmeanach Argyll 289 E8
Balmeanach Highld 295 B7
Balmeanach Highld 298 E3
Balmeanach Highld 298 E5
Balmedie Aberds 293 B11
Balmer Shrops 149 C8
Balmer Heath Shrops 149 C8
Balmerino Fife 287 E7
Balmerlawn Hants 32 G4
Balmesh Dumfries 236 D3
Balmichael N Ayrs 255 D10
Balminnoch Dumfries 236 C4
Balmirmer Angus 287 D9
Balmoral Borders 261 B11
Balmore E Dunb 278 G2
Balmore Highld 298 E2
Balmore Highld 300 F3
Balmore Highld 301 E8
Balmore Perth 286 B3
Balmule Fife 280 D4
Balmullo Fife 287 E8
Balmungie Highld 301 D7
Balmurrie Dumfries 236 C4
Balnaboth Angus 292 G5
Balnabreich Moray 302 D3
Balnabruaich Highld 301 C7
Balnabruich Highld 311 G5
Balnacarn Highld 290 B4
Balnacoil Highld 311 H2
Balnacra Highld 299 E9
Balnacruie Highld 301 G9
Balnafoich Highld 300 F6
Balnagall Highld 311 L2
Balnagowan Aberds 293 C7
Balnagrantach Highld 300 F4
Balnaguard Perth 286 B3
Balnahanaid Perth 285 C10
Balnahard Argyll 274 D5
Balnahard Argyll 288 F6
Balnain Highld 300 F4
Balnakeil Highld 308 C3
Balnakelly Aberds 293 B7
Balnaknock Highld 298 C4
Balnamoon Aberds 303 D9
Balnamoon Angus 293 G7
Balnapaling Highld 301 C7
Balne N Yorks 198 D5
Balnoon Corn 2 B2
Balochroy Argyll 255 B8
Balole Argyll 274 G4
Balone Fife 287 F8
Balornock Glasgow 268 B2
Balquharn Perth 286 D4
Balquhidder Stirl 285 E9
Balquhidder Station Stirl 285 E9
Balquhindachy Aberds 303 E8
Balrownie Angus 293 G7
Balsall W Mid 118 B4
Balsall Common W Mid 118 B4
Balsall Heath W Mid 133 G11
Balsall Street W Mid 118 B4
Balsam Cambs 123 G11
Balscote Oxon 101 C7
Balscott Oxon 101 C7
Balsham Cambs 123 G11
Balsporran Cottages Highld 291 F8
Baltasound Shetland 312 C8
Balterley Staffs 168 E3
Balterley Green Staffs 168 E3
Balterley Heath Staffs 168 E2
Baltersan Dumfries 236 C6
Balthangie Aberds 303 D8
Balthayock Perth 286 E5
Baltonsborough Som 44 G4
Balure Argyll 289 E11
Balvaird Highld 300 D5
Balvenie Moray 302 E3
Balvicar Argyll 275 B8
Balvraid Highld 295 D10
Balvraid Highld 301 F8
Balwest Corn 2 C3
Bamber Bridge Lancs 194 B5
Bamber's Green Essex 105 G11
Bamburgh Northumb 264 C5
Bamff Perth 286 B6
Bamford Derbys 186 E2
Bamford Gtr Man 195 E11
Bamfurlong Glos 99 G8
Bamfurlong Gtr Man 194 G5
Bampton Cumb 221 B10
Bampton Devon 27 C7
Bampton Oxon 82 E4
Bampton Grange Cumb 221 B10
Banavie Highld 290 F3
Banbury Oxon 101 C9
Bancffosfelen Carms 75 C7
Banchor Highld 301 E9
Banchory Aberds 293 D8
Banchory-Devenick Aberds 293 C11
Bancycapel Carms 74 B6
Banc-y-Darren Ceredig 128 G3
Bancyfelin Carms 74 B4
Bancyffordd Carms 93 D8
Bandirran Perth 286 D6
Bandonhill London 67 G9
Bandrake Head Cumb 210 B6
Banff Aberds 302 C6
Bangor Gwyn 179 G9
Bangor is y coed / Bangor on Dee Wrex 166 F5
Bangor on Dee / Bangor-is-y-coed Wrex 166 F5
Bangors Corn 11 B10
Bangor Teifi Ceredig 93 C7
Banham Norf 141 F11
Bank Hants 32 F3
Bankend Dumfries 238 D2
Bank End Cumb 210 B3
Bank End Cumb 228 D6
Bank Fold Blkburn 195 C8
Bankfoot Perth 286 D4
Bankglen E Ayrs 258 G4
Bankhead Aberdeen 293 B10
Bankhead Aberds 293 C8
Bankhead Dumfries 236 C2
Bankhead Falk 278 E6
Bankhead S Lnrk 269 G7
Bank Hey Blkburn 203 G9
Bank Houses Lancs 202 C4
Bankland Som 28 B4
Bank Lane Gtr Man 195 D9
Bank Newton N Yorks 204 C4
Banknock Falk 278 F5
Banks Cumb 240 E3
Banks Lancs 193 C11
Banks Orkney 314 C4
Bank's Green Worcs 117 D9
Bankshead Shrops 130 F6
Bankshill Dumfries 248 G5
Bankside Falk 279 E7
Bank Street Worcs 116 E2
Bank Top Gtr Man 195 E8
Bank Top Lancs 194 F4
Bank Top Stoke 168 E5
Bank Top T&W 242 D4
Bank Top W Yorks 196 C6
Bank Top W Yorks 205 F9
Banners Gate W Mid 133 D11
Banningham Norf 160 D4
Banniskirk Ho Highld 310 D5
Banniskirk Mains Highld 310 D5
Bannister Green Essex 106 G3
Bannockburn Stirl 278 C5
Banns Corn 4 F4
Banstead Sur 51 B8
Bantam Grove W Yorks 197 B9
Bantaskin Falk 279 F7
Bantham Devon 8 G3
Banton N Lnrk 278 F5
Banwell N Som 43 B11
Banyard's Green Suff 126 C5
Bapchild Kent 70 G2
Baptist End W Mid 133 F8
Bapton Wilts 46 F3
Barabhas W Isles 304 D5
Barabhas Iarach W Isles 304 D5
Barabhas Uarach W Isles 304 C5
Barachandroman Argyll 289 G8
Baramore Highld 289 B8
Barassie S Ayrs 257 C8
Baravullin Argyll 289 F10
Barbadoes Stirl 277 B11
Barbaraville Highld 301 B7
Barbauchlaw W Loth 269 B8
Barber Booth Derbys 185 E10
Barber Green Cumb 211 C7
Barber's Moor Lancs 194 D3
Barbican Plym 7 E9
Barbieston S Ayrs 257 F10
Barbon Cumb 212 C2
Barbourne Worcs 116 F6
Barbreck Ho Argyll 275 C9
Barbridge Ches E 167 D10
Barbrook Devon 41 D8
Barby Northants 119 C10
Barby Nortoft Northants 119 C11
Barcaldine Argyll 289 E11
Barcelona Corn 6 E4
Barcheston Warks 100 D5
Barclose Cumb 239 E10
Barcombe E Sus 36 E6
Barcombe Cross E Sus 36 D6
Barcroft W Yorks 204 F6
Barden N Yorks 224 G2
Bardennoch Dumfries 246 E3

Barden Park Kent 52 D5
Barden Scale N Yorks 205 B7
Bardfield End Green Essex 106 E2
Bardfield Saling Essex 106 F3
Bardister Shetland 312 F5
Bardnabeinne Highld 309 K7
Bardney Lincs 173 B10
Bardon Leics 153 G8
Bardon Mill Northumb 241 E7
Bardowie E Dunb 277 G11
Bardown E Sus 37 B11
Bardrainney Invclyd 276 G6
Bardrishaig Argyll 275 B8
Bardsea Cumb 210 E6
Bardsey W Yorks 206 E3
Bardsley Gtr Man 196 G2
Bardwell Suff 125 C8
Bare Lancs 211 G9
Bare Ash Som 43 F9
Bareless Northumb 263 B9
Bar End Hants 33 B7
Barepot Cumb 228 F6
Bareppa Corn 3 D7
Barfad Argyll 275 G9
Barfad Dumfries 236 C5
Barford Norf 142 B2
Barford Sur 49 F11
Barford Warks 118 E5
Barford St John Oxon 101 E8
Barford St Martin Wilts 46 G5
Barford St Michael Oxon 101 E8
Barfrestone Kent 55 C9
Bargaly Dumfries 236 C6
Bargarran Renfs 277 G9
Bargate Derbys 170 F5
Bargeddie N Lnrk 268 C4
Bargoed Caerph 77 F10
Bargrennan Dumfries 236 B5
Barham Cambs 122 B2
Barham Kent 55 C8
Barham Suff 126 G2
Barharrow Dumfries 237 D8
Barhill Dumfries 237 C10
Bar Hill Cambs 123 E7
Bar Hill Staffs 168 G3
Barholm Dumfries 237 D7
Barholm Lincs 155 G11
Barkby Leics 136 B2
Barkby Thorpe Leics 136 B2
Barkers Green Shrops 149 D10
Barkers Hill Wilts 30 B6
Barkestone-le-Vale Leics 154 C5
Barkham Wokingham 65 F9
Barking London 68 C2
Barking Suff 125 G11
Barkingside London 68 B2
Barking Tye Suff 125 G11
Barkisland W Yorks 196 D5
Barkla Shop Corn 4 E4
Barkston Lincs 172 G6
Barkston N Yorks 206 F5
Barkston Ash N Yorks 206 F5
Barkway Herts 105 D7
Barlake Som 45 D7
Barlanark Glasgow 268 C3
Barland Powys 114 E5
Barland Common Swansea 56 D5
Barlaston Staffs 151 B7
Barlavington W Sus 35 D7
Barlborough Derbys 187 F7
Barlby N Yorks 207 G8
Barlestone Leics 135 B8
Barley Herts 105 D7
Barley Lancs 204 E2
Barleycroft End Herts 105 F8
Barley End Bucks 85 C7
Barley Green Lancs 204 E2
Barley Mow T&W 243 G7
Barleythorpe Rutland 136 B6
Barling Essex 70 B2
Barlings Lincs 189 G9
Barlow Derbys 186 G4
Barlow N Yorks 198 B6
Barlow T&W 242 E5
Barlow Moor Gtr Man 184 C4
Barmby Moor E Yorks 207 D11
Barmby on the Marsh E Yorks 199 B7
Barmer Norf 158 C6
Barming Heath Kent 53 B8
Barmolloch Argyll 275 D9
Bar Moor T&W 242 E4
Barmoor Castle Northumb 263 B11
Barmoor Lane End Northumb 264 B2
Barmouth / Abermaw Gwyn 146 F2
Barmpton Darl 224 B6
Barmston E Yorks 209 B9
Barmston T&W 243 F8
Barmulloch Glasgow 268 B2
Barnaby Green Suff 127 B9
Barnacabber Argyll 276 D3
Barnack Pboro 137 B11
Barnacle Warks 135 G7
Barnaline Argyll 275 B10
Barnard Castle Durham 223 B11
Barnard Gate Oxon 82 C6
Barnardiston Suff 106 B4
Barnard's Green Worcs 98 B5
Barnardtown Newport 59 B10
Barnbarroch Dumfries 237 D10
Barnbow Carr W Yorks 206 F3
Barnburgh S Yorks 198 G3
Barnby Suff 143 F9
Barnby Dun S Yorks 198 F6
Barnby in the Willows Notts 172 E5
Barnby Moor Notts 187 E11
Barncluith S Lnrk 268 E4
Barndennoch Dumfries 247 F9
Barne Barton Plym 7 D8
Barnehurst London 68 D4
Barnes Cray London 68 D4
Barnes Hall S Yorks 186 B4
Barnes Street Kent 52 D6
Barnet London 86 F2
Barnetby le Wold N Lincs 200 F5
Barnet Gate London 86 F2
Barnettbrook Worcs 117 B7
Barnett Brook Ches E 167 G10
Barney Norf 159 C9
Barnfield Kent 54 D2
Barnfields Hereford 97 C9
Barnfields Staffs 169 D7
Barnham Suff 125 B7
Barnham W Sus 35 G7
Barnham Broom Norf 141 B11
Barnhead Angus 287 B10
Barnhill Ches W 167 E7
Barnhill Dundee 287 D8
Barnhill Moray 301 D11
Barnhills Dumfries 236 B1
Barningham Durham 223 C11
Barningham Suff 125 B9
Barningham Green Norf 160 C2
Barnmoor Green Warks 118 E3
Barnoldby le Beck NE Lincs 201 G8
Barnoldswick Lancs 204 D3
Barnoldswick N Yorks 212 E3
Barns Borders 260 B6
Barnsbury London 67 C10
Barnsdale Rutland 137 B8
Barns Green W Sus 35 B10
Barnside W Yorks 197 F7
Barnsley Glos 81 D9
Barnsley Shrops 132 E5
Barnsley S Yorks 197 F10
Barnsole Kent 55 B9
Barnstaple Devon 40 G5
Barnston Essex 87 B10
Barnston Mers 182 E3
Barnstone Notts 154 B4
Barnt Green Worcs 117 C10
Barnton Ches W 183 F10
Barnton Edin 280 F3
Barnwell Northants 137 G10
Barnwell All Saints Northants 137 G10
Barnwell St Andrew Northants 137 F10
Barnwood Glos 80 B5
Barochreal Argyll 289 G10
Barons Cross Hereford 115 F9
Barr Highld 289 D8
Barr S Ayrs 245 E7
Barr Som 27 C11
Barra Castle Aberds 303 G7
Barrachan Dumfries 236 E5
Barrachnie Glasgow 268 C3
Barrack Aberds 303 E8
Barrack Hill Newport 59 B10
Barraer Dumfries 236 C5
Barraglom W Isles 304 E3
Barrahormid Argyll 275 E8
Barran Argyll 289 G10
Barranrioch Argyll 289 G10
Barrapol Argyll 288 E1
Barras Aberds 293 E10
Barras Cumb 222 C6
Barrasford Northumb 241 C10
Barravullin Argyll 275 C9
Barr Common W Mid 133 D11
Barregarrow IoM 192 D4
Barrets Green Ches E 167 D9
Barrhead E Renf 267 D9
Barrhill S Ayrs 244 G6
Barrington Cambs 105 B7
Barrington Som 28 D5
Barripper Corn 2 B4
Barrmill N Ayrs 267 E7
Barrock Highld 310 B6
Barrock Ho Highld 310 C6
Barrow Glos 99 G7
Barrow Lancs 203 F10
Barrow Rutland 155 F7
Barrow Shrops 132 C3
Barrow Som 44 E5
Barrow Suff 124 E5
Barrow S Yorks 186 B5
Barroway Drove Norf 139 C11
Barrow Bridge Gtr Man 195 E7
Barrowburn Northumb 263 G9
Barrow Burn Northumb 263 G9
Barrowby Lincs 155 B7
Barrowcliff N Yorks 217 B10
Barrow Common N Som 60 F4
Barrowden Rutland 137 C8
Barrowford Lancs 204 F3
Barrow Green Kent 70 G3
Barrow Gurney N Som 60 F4
Barrow Hann N Lincs 200 C5
Barrow Haven N Lincs 200 C5
Barrowhill Kent 54 F6
Barrow Hill Derbys 186 F6
Barrow Hill Dorset 18 B5
Barrow-in-Furness Cumb 210 F4
Barrow Island Cumb 210 F3
Barrowmore Estate Ches W 167 B7
Barrow Nook Lancs 194 G2
Barrows Green Ches E 167 D11
Barrows Green Cumb 211 B10
Barrows Green Notts 171 E7
Barrow's Green Mers 183 D8
Barrow Street Wilts 45 G10
Barrow upon Humber N Lincs 200 C5
Barrow upon Soar Leics 153 F11
Barrow upon Trent Derbys 153 D7
Barrow Vale Bath 60 G6
Barrow Wake Glos 80 B6
Barry Angus 287 D9
Barry V Glam 58 F6
Barry Dock V Glam 58 F6
Barry Island V Glam 58 F6
Barsby Leics 154 G3
Barsham Suff 143 F7
Barshare E Ayrs 258 F3
Barstable Essex 69 B8
Barston W Mid 118 B4
Bartestree Hereford 97 C11
Barthol Chapel Aberds 303 F8
Bartholomew Green Essex 106 G4
Barthomley Ches E 168 E3
Bartington Ches W 183 F10
Bartley Hants 32 E4
Bartley Green W Mid 133 G10
Bartlow Cambs 105 B11
Barton Cambs 123 F8
Barton Ches W 166 E6
Barton Glos 80 B4
Barton Glos 99 F11
Barton IoW 20 D6
Barton Lancs 193 F11
Barton Lancs 202 F6
Barton N Som 43 B11
Barton N Yorks 224 D4
Barton Oxon 83 D9
Barton Torbay 9 B8
Barton Warks 118 G2
Barton Abbey Oxon 101 G9
Barton Bendish Norf 140 B4
Barton Court Hereford 98 C4
Barton End Glos 80 F4
Barton Gate Devon 41 E7
Barton Gate Staffs 152 F3
Barton Green Staffs 152 F3
Barton Hartshorn Bucks 102 E2
Barton Hill Bristol 60 E6
Barton Hill N Yorks 216 G4
Barton in Fabis Notts 153 C10
Barton in the Beans Leics 135 B7
Barton-le-Clay C Beds 103 E11
Barton-le-Street N Yorks 216 E4
Barton-le-Willows N Yorks 216 G4
Barton Mills Suff 124 C4
Barton on Sea Hants 19 C10
Barton on the Heath Warks 100 E5
Barton St David Som 44 G4
Barton Seagrave Northants 121 B7
Bartonsham Hereford 97 D10
Barton Stacey Hants 48 E2
Barton Town Devon 41 E7
Barton Turf Norf 161 E7
Barton Turn Staffs 152 F4
Barton-under-Needwood Staffs 152 F3
Barton-upon-Humber N Lincs 200 C4
Barton Upon Irwell Gtr Man 184 B3
Barton Waterside N Lincs 200 C4
Barugh S Yorks 197 F10
Barugh Green S Yorks 197 F10
Barway Cambs 123 B10
Barwell Leics 135 D8
Barwell London 67 G7
Barwick Devon 25 F9
Barwick Herts 86 B5
Barwick Som 29 E9
Barwick in Elmet W Yorks 206 F3
Baschurch Shrops 149 E8
Bascote Warks 119 E8
Bascote Heath Warks 119 E7
Base Green Suff 125 E10
Basford Shrops 131 F7
Basford Staffs 168 F5
Basford Green Staffs 169 E7
Bashall Eaves Lancs 203 E9
Bashley Hants 19 B10
Bashley Park Hants 19 B10
Basildon Essex 69 B8
Basingstoke Hants 48 C6
Baslow Derbys 186 G3
Bason Bridge Som 43 D10
Bassaleg Newport 59 B9
Bassenthwaite Cumb 229 E10
Bassett Soton 32 D6
Bassett S Yorks 186 E3
Bassett Green Soton 32 D6
Bassingbourn Cambs 104 C6
Bassingfield Notts 154 B2
Bassingham Lincs 172 C6
Bassingthorpe Lincs 155 D9
Bassus Green Herts 104 F6
Basta Shetland 312 D7
Basted Kent 52 B6
Baston Lincs 156 G2
Bastonford Worcs 116 G6
Bastwick Norf 161 F8
Baswich Staffs 151 E8
Baswick Steer E Yorks 209 D7
Batavaime Stirl 285 D8
Batch Som 43 B10
Batchcott Shrops 115 C9
Batchfields Hereford 98 B3
Batchley Worcs 117 D10
Batchworth Herts 85 G9
Batchworth Heath Herts 85 G9
Batcombe Dorset 29 G10
Batcombe Som 45 F7
Bate Heath Ches E 183 F11
Bateman's Green Worcs 117 B11
Bateman's Hill Pembs 73 E8
Batemoor S Yorks 186 E5
Batford Herts 85 B10
Bath Bath 61 F8
Bathampton Bath 61 F9
Bathealton Som 27 C9
Batheaston Bath 61 F9
Bathford Bath 61 F9
Bathgate W Loth 269 B9
Bathley Notts 172 D3
Bathpool Corn 11 G11
Bathpool Som 28 B3
Bath Side Essex 108 E5
Bath Vale Ches E 168 C5
Bathville W Loth 269 B8
Bathway Som 44 C5
Bathwick Bath 61 F9
Batlers Green Herts 85 F11
Batley W Yorks 197 C8
Batley Carr W Yorks 197 C8
Batsford Glos 100 E3
Batson Devon 9 G9
Batsworthy Devon 26 D4
Batten's Green Som 28 D3
Battenton Green Worcs 116 D6
Battersby N Yorks 225 D11
Battersea London 67 D9
Battisborough Cross Devon 7 F11
Battisford Suff 125 G11
Battisford Tye Suff 125 G10
Battle E Sus 38 D2
Battle Powys 95 E10
Battledown Glos 99 G9
Battledown Cross Devon 25 F7
Battlefield Shrops 149 F10
Battle Hill T&W 243 D8
Battlesbridge Essex 88 G3
Battlescombe Glos 80 D6
Battlesden C Beds 103 F9
Battlesea Green Suff 126 B4
Battleton Som 26 B6
Battlies Green Suff 125 E7
Battram Leics 135 B8
Battramsley Hants 20 B2
Battramsley Cross Hants 20 B2
Batt's Corner Hants 49 E10
Battyeford W Yorks 197 C7
Batworthy Devon 13 D10
Bauds of Cullen Moray 302 C4
Baugh Argyll 288 E2
Baughton Worcs 99 C7
Baughurst Hants 48 B5
Baulking Oxon 82 G4
Baumber Lincs 190 G2
Baunton Glos 81 E8
Baverstock Wilts 46 G4
Bawburgh Norf 142 B3
Bawdeswell Norf 159 E10
Bawdrip Som 43 F10
Bawdsey Suff 108 C6
Bawsey Norf 158 F3
Bawtry S Yorks 187 C11
Baxenden Lancs 195 B9
Baxterley Warks 134 D5
Baxter's Green Suff 124 F5
Bay Dorset 30 B4
Bay Highld 298 D2
Baybridge Hants 33 C8
Baybridge Northumb 241 G11
Baycliff Cumb 210 E5
Baydon Wilts 63 D9
Bayford Herts 86 D4
Bayford Som 30 B2
Bay Gate Lancs 203 D11
Bay Horse Lancs 202 C5
Bayles Cumb 231 C10
Bayley's Hill Kent 52 C4
Baylham Suff 126 G2
Baylis Green Worcs 117 C11
Baynard's Green Oxon 101 F10
Baynhall Worcs 99 B7
Baysham Hereford 97 F11
Bayston Hill Shrops 131 B9
Bayswater London 67 C9
Baythorne End Essex 106 C4
Baythorpe Lincs 174 G2
Bayton Worcs 116 C3
Bayton Common Worcs 116 C4
Bay View Kent 70 E4
Bayworth Oxon 83 E8
Beach Highld 289 D9
Beach S Glos 61 E8
Beachampton Bucks 102 D5
Beachamwell Norf 140 B5
Beachans Moray 301 E10
Beacharr Argyll 255 C7
Beachborough Kent 55 F7
Beach Hay Worcs 116 C4
Beachlands E Sus 23 E11
Beachley Glos 79 G9
Beacon Corn 2 B5
Beacon Devon 27 F11
Beacon Devon 28 F2
Beacon Down E Sus 37 C9
Beacon End Essex 107 G9
Beaconhill Northumb 243 B7
Beacon Hill Bath 61 F9
Beacon Hill Bucks 84 G6
Beacon Hill Cumb 210 E4
Beacon Hill Dorset 18 C5
Beacon Hill Essex 88 C5
Beacon Hill Kent 53 G10
Beacon Hill Notts 172 E4
Beacon Hill Suff 108 B4
Beacon Hill Sur 49 F11
Beacon Lough T&W 243 F7
Beacon's Bottom Bucks 84 F3
Beaconsfield Bucks 66 B2
Beaconside Staffs 151 E8
Beacrabhaic W Isles 305 J3
Beadlam N Yorks 216 C3
Beadlow C Beds 104 D2
Beadnell Northumb 264 D6
Beaford Devon 25 E9
Beal Northumb 273 G11
Beal N Yorks 198 B4
Bealach Highld 289 D11
Bealach Maim Argyll 275 E10
Bealbury Corn 7 B7
Beal's Green Kent 53 G9
Bealsmill Corn 12 F3
Beambridge Shrops 131 F10
Beam Bridge Som 27 D10
Beam Hill Staffs 152 D4
Beamhurst Staffs 151 B11
Beamhurst Lane Staffs 151 B11
Beaminster Dorset 29 G7
Beamish Durham 242 G6
Beamond End Bucks 84 F6
Beamsley N Yorks 205 C7
Bean Kent 68 E5
Beanacre Wilts 62 F2
Beancross Falk 279 F8
Beanhill M Keynes 103 D7
Beanley Northumb 264 F3
Beansburn E Ayrs 257 B10
Beanthwaite Cumb 210 C4
Beaquoy Orkney 314 D3
Bear Cross Bmouth 19 B7
Beard Hill Som 44 E6
Beardly Batch Som 44 E6
Beardwood Blkburn 195 B7
Beare Devon 27 G7
Beare Green Sur 51 E7
Bearley Warks 118 E3
Bearley Cross Warks 118 E3
Bearnus Argyll 288 E5
Bearpark Durham 233 C10
Bearsbridge Northumb 241 F7
Bearsden E Dunb 277 G10
Bearsted Kent 53 B9
Bearstone Shrops 150 B4
Bearwood Hereford 115 F7
Bearwood Poole 18 B6
Bearwood W Mid 133 F10
Beasley Staffs 168 F4
Beattock Dumfries 248 C3
Beauchamp Roding Essex 87 C9
Beauchief S Yorks 186 E4
Beauclerc Northumb 242 E2
Beaudesert Warks 118 D3
Beaufort Bl Gwent 77 C11
Beaufort Castle Highld 300 E5
Beaulieu Hants 32 G5
Beaulieu Wood Dorset 30 F2
Beauly Highld 300 E5
Beaumaris Anglesey 179 F10
Beaumont Cumb 239 F8
Beaumont Essex 108 G3
Beaumont Windsor 66 E3
Beaumont Hill Darl 224 B5
Beaumont Leys Leicester 135 B11
Beausale Warks 118 C4
Beauvale Notts 171 F8
Beauworth Hants 33 B9
Beavan's Hill Hereford 98 G3
Beaworthy Devon 12 B5
Beazley End Essex 106 F4
Bebington Mers 182 E4
Bebside Northumb 253 G7
Beccles Suff 143 E8
Becconsall Lancs 194 C2
Beck Bottom Cumb 210 C5
Beck Bottom W Yorks 197 C10
Beckbury Shrops 132 C5
Beckces Cumb 230 F4
Beckenham London 67 F11
Beckermet Cumb 219 D10
Beckermonds N Yorks 213 C7
Beckery Som 44 F3
Beckett End Norf 140 D5
Beckfoot Cumb 220 E3
Beckfoot Cumb 229 B7
Beck Foot Cumb 222 F2
Beck Foot W Yorks 205 F8
Beckford Worcs 99 D9
Beckhampton Wilts 62 F5
Beck Head Cumb 211 C8
Beck Hole N Yorks 226 E6
Beck Houses Cumb 221 F11
Beckingham Lincs 172 E5
Beckingham Notts 188 D3
Beckington Som 45 C10
Beckjay Shrops 115 B7
Beckley E Sus 38 C5
Beckley Hants 19 B10
Beckley Oxon 83 C9
Beckley Furnace E Sus 38 C4
Beck Row Suff 124 B3
Beckside Cumb 212 B2
Beck Side Cumb 210 C4
Beck Side Cumb 211 C7
Beckton London 68 C2
Beckwith N Yorks 205 C11
Beckwithshaw N Yorks 205 C11
Becontree London 68 B3
Bedale N Yorks 214 B5
Bedburn Durham 233 E8
Bedchester Dorset 30 D5
Beddau Rhondda 58 B5
Beddgelert Gwyn 163 F9
Beddingham E Sus 36 F6
Beddington London 67 G10
Beddington Corner London 67 F9
Bedfield Suff 126 D4
Bedford Beds 121 G11
Bedford Gtr Man 183 B11
Bedford Park London 67 D8
Bedgebury Cross Kent 53 G8
Bedgrove Bucks 84 C4
Bedham W Sus 35 C8
Bedhampton Hants 22 B2
Bedingfield Suff 126 D3
Bedingham Green Norf 142 E5
Bedlam N Yorks 214 G5
Bedlam Som 45 D9
Bedlam Street W Sus 36 D3
Bedlar's Green Essex 105 G10
Bedlington Northumb 253 G7
Bedlington Station Northumb 253 G7
Bedlinog M Tydf 77 E9
Bedminster Bristol 60 E5
Bedminster Down Bristol 60 F5
Bedmond Herts 85 E9
Bednall Staffs 151 F9
Bednall Head Staffs 151 F9
Bedrule Borders 262 F4
Bedstone Shrops 115 B7
Bedwas Caerph 59 B7
Bedwell Herts 104 G4
Bedwell Wrex 166 F5
Bedwellty Caerph 77 E11
Bedwellty Pits Bl Gwent 77 D11
Bedwlwyn Wrex 148 B4
Bedworth Warks 135 F7
Bedworth Heath Warks 134 F6
Bedworth Woodlands Warks 134 F6
Bed-y-coedwr Gwyn 146 D4
Beeby Leics 136 B3
Beech Hants 49 F7
Beech Staffs 151 B7
Beechcliff Staffs 151 B7
Beechcliffe W Yorks 205 E7
Beechen Cliff Bath 61 G9
Beech Hill Gtr Man 194 F5
Beech Hill W Berks 65 G7
Beechingstoke Wilts 46 B5
Beech Lanes W Mid 133 F10
Beechwood Halton 183 E8
Beechwood Newport 59 B10
Beechwood W Mid 118 B5
Beechwood W Yorks 206 F2
Beecroft C Beds 103 G10
Beedon W Berks 64 D3
Beedon Hill W Berks 64 D3
Beeford E Yorks 209 C8
Beeley Derbys 170 B3
Beelsby NE Lincs 201 G8
Beenham W Berks 64 F5
Beenham's Heath Windsor 65 D10
Beenham Stocks W Berks 64 F5
Beeny Corn 11 C8
Beer Devon 15 D10
Beer Som 44 G2
Beercrocombe Som 28 C4
Beer Hackett Dorset 29 E9
Beesands Devon 8 G6
Beesby Lincs 191 E7
Beeslack Midloth 270 C4
Beeson Devon 8 G6
Beeston C Beds 104 B3
Beeston Ches W 167 D8
Beeston Norf 159 F8
Beeston Notts 153 B10
Beeston W Yorks 205 G11
Beeston Hill W Yorks 205 G11
Beeston Park Side W Yorks 197 B9
Beeston Regis Norf 177 E11
Beeston Royds W Yorks 205 G11
Beeston St Lawrence Norf 160 E6
Beeswing Dumfries 237 C10
Beetham Cumb 211 D9
Beetham Som 28 E3
Beetley Norf 159 F9
Beffcote Staffs 150 F6
Began Cardiff 59 C8
Begbroke Oxon 83 C7
Begdale Cambs 139 B9
Begelly Pembs 73 D10
Beggar Hill Essex 87 E10
Beggarington Hill W Yorks 197 C9
Beggars Ash Hereford 98 D4
Beggars Bush W Sus 35 F11
Beggar's Bush Powys 114 E5
Beggars Pound V Glam 58 F4
Beggearn Huish Som 42 F4
Beguildy Powys 114 B3
Beighton Norf 143 B7
Beighton S Yorks 186 E6
Beighton Hill Derbys 170 E3
Beili-glas Mon 78 C4
Beitearsaig W Isles 305 G1
Beith N Ayrs 266 E6
Bekesbourne Kent 55 B7
Bekesbourne Hill Kent 55 B7
Belah Cumb 239 F9
Belan Powys 130 C4
Belaugh Norf 160 F5
Belbins Hants 32 C5
Belbroughton Worcs 117 B8
Belchalwell Dorset 30 F3
Belchalwell Street Dorset 30 F3
Belchamp Otten Essex 106 C6
Belchamp St Paul Essex 106 C5
Belchamp Walter Essex 106 C6
Belcher's Bar Leics 135 B8
Belchford Lincs 190 F3
Beleybridge Fife 287 F9
Belfield Gtr Man 196 E2
Belford Northumb 264 C4
Belgrano Conwy 181 F7
Belgrave Ches W 166 C5
Belgrave Leicester 135 B11
Belgrave Staffs 134 C4
Belgravia London 67 D9
Belhaven E Loth 282 F3
Belhelvie Aberds 293 B11
Belhinnie Aberds 302 G4
Bellabeg Aberds 292 B5
Bellamore S Ayrs 244 F6
Bellanoch Argyll 275 D8
Bellanrigg Borders 260 B6
Bellasize E Yorks 199 B10
Bellaty Angus 286 B6
Bell Bar Herts 86 D3
Bell Busk N Yorks 204 B4
Bell Common Essex 86 E6
Belleau Lincs 190 F6
Belle Eau Park Notts 171 D11
Belle Green S Yorks 197 F11
Bellehiglash Moray 301 F11
Belle Isle W Yorks 197 B10
Bell End Worcs 117 B8
Bellerby N Yorks 224 G2
Belle Vale Mers 182 D6
Belle Vale W Mid 133 G9
Bellever Devon 13 F9
Bellevue Worcs 117 C9
Belle Vue Cumb 229 E8
Belle Vue Cumb 239 F9
Belle Vue Gtr Man 184 B5
Belle Vue Shrops 149 G9
Belle Vue S Yorks 198 G5
Belle Vue W Yorks 197 D10
Bellfield E Ayrs 257 B10
Bellfields Sur 50 C3
Bell Green London 67 E11
Bell Green W Mid 135 G7
Bell Heath Worcs 117 B9
Bell Hill Hants 34 C2
Belliehill Angus 293 G7
Bellingdon Bucks 84 D6
Bellingham London 67 E11
Bellingham Northumb 251 G8
Bellmount Norf 157 E10
Belloch Argyll 255 D7
Bellochantuy Argyll 255 D7
Bell o' th' Hill Ches W 167 F8
Bellsbank E Ayrs 245 C11
Bell's Close T&W 242 E5
Bell's Corner Suff 107 D9
Bellshill N Lnrk 268 C4
Bellshill Northumb 264 C4
Bellside N Lnrk 268 D6
Bellsmyre W Dunb 277 F8
Bellspool Borders 260 B5
Bellsquarry W Loth 269 C10
Bells Yew Green E Sus 52 F6
Belluton Bath 60 G6
Bellyeoman Fife 280 D2
Belmaduthy Highld 300 D6
Belmesthorpe Rutland 155 G10
Belmont Blkburn 195 D7
Belmont Durham 234 C2
Belmont E Sus 38 E4
Belmont Harrow 67 G9
Belmont Oxon 63 B11
Belmont S Ayrs 257 E8
Belmont Shetland 312 C7
Belmont Sutton 85 G11
Belnacraig Aberds 292 B5
Belnagarrow Moray 302 E3
Belnie Lincs 156 C5
Belowda Corn 5 C9
Belper Derbys 170 F4
Belper Lane End Derbys 170 F4
Belph Derbys 187 F8
Belsay Northumb 242 B4
Belses Borders 262 D3
Belsford Devon 8 D5
Belsize Herts 85 E8
Belstead Suff 108 C2
Belston S Ayrs 257 E9
Belstone Devon 13 C8
Belstone Corner Devon 13 B8
Belthorn Blkburn 195 C8
Beltinge Kent 71 F7
Beltingham Northumb 241 E7
Beltoft N Lincs 199 F10
Belton Leics 153 E8
Belton Lincs 155 B8
Belton N Lincs 199 F9
Belton Norf 143 C9
Belton in Rutland Rutland 136 C6
Beltring Kent 53 D7
Belts of Collonach Aberds 293 D8
Belvedere London 68 D3
Belvedere W Loth 269 B9
Belvoir Leics 154 C6
Bembridge IoW 21 D8
Bemersyde Borders 262 C3
Bemerton Wilts 46 G6
Bemerton Heath Wilts 46 G6
Bempton E Yorks 218 E3
Benacre Suff 143 G10
Ben Alder Lodge Highld 291 F7
Ben Armine Lodge Highld 309 H7
Benbuie Dumfries 246 D6
Ben Casgro W Isles 304 F6
Benchill Gtr Man 184 D4
Bencombe Glos 80 F3
Benderloch Argyll 289 F11
Bendish Herts 104 G3
Bendronaig Lodge Highld 299 F10
Benenden Kent 53 G10
Benfield Dumfries 236 C5
Benfieldside Durham 242 G3
Bengal Pembs 91 E9
Bengate Norf 160 D6
Bengeo Herts 86 C4
Bengeworth Worcs 99 C10
Bengrove Glos 99 E9
Benhall Glos 99 G8
Benhall Green Suff 127 E7
Benhall Street Suff 127 E7
Benhilton London 67 F9
Benholm Aberds 293 G10
Beningbrough N Yorks 206 B6
Benington Herts 104 G5
Benington Lincs 174 F5
Benington Sea End Lincs 174 F6
Benllech Anglesey 179 E8
Benmore Argyll 276 E2
Benmore Stirl 285 E8
Benmore Lodge Argyll 289 F7
Benmore Lodge Highld 309 H3
Bennacott Corn 11 C11
Bennah Devon 14 E2
Bennan N Ayrs 255 E10
Bennane Lea S Ayrs 244 F3
Bennetland E Yorks 199 B10
Bennetsfield Highld 300 D6
Bennett End Bucks 84 F3
Bennetts End Herts 85 D9
Benniworth Lincs 190 E2
Benover Kent 53 D8
Ben Rhydding W Yorks 205 D8
Bensham T&W 242 E6
Benslie N Ayrs 266 G6
Benson Oxon 83 G10
Benston Shetland 313 H6
Bent Aberds 293 F8
Benter Som 44 D6
Bentfield Bury Essex 105 F9
Bentfield Green Essex 105 F10
Bentgate Gtr Man 196 E2
Bent Gate Lancs 195 C9
Benthall Northumb 264 D6
Benthall Shrops 132 C3
Bentham Glos 80 B6
Benthoul Aberdeen 293 C10
Bentilee Stoke 168 F6
Bentlass Pembs 73 E7
Bentlawnt Shrops 130 C6
Bentley Essex 87 F9
Bentley E Yorks 208 F6
Bentley Hants 49 E9
Bentley Suff 108 D2
Bentley S Yorks 198 F5
Bentley Warks 134 D5
Bentley W Mid 133 D9
Bentley Worcs 117 D9
Bentley Common Warks 134 D5
Bentley Heath Herts 86 F2
Bentley Heath W Mid 118 B3
Bentley Rise S Yorks 198 G5
Benton Devon 41 F7
Benton Green W Mid 118 B5
Bentpath Dumfries 249 E8
Bents W Loth 269 C9
Bents Head W Yorks 205 F7
Bentwichen Devon 41 G8
Bentworth Hants 49 E7
Benvie Dundee 287 D7
Benville Dorset 29 G8
Benwell T&W 242 E6
Benwick Cambs 138 E6
Beobridge Shrops 132 E5
Beoley Worcs 117 D11
Beoraidbeg Highld 295 F8
Bepton W Sus 34 D5
Berden Essex 105 F9
Bere Alston Devon 7 B8
Berechurch Essex 107 G9
Bere Ferrers Devon 7 C9
Berefold Aberds 303 F9
Berepper Corn 2 E5
Bere Regis Dorset 18 C2
Bergh Apton Norf 142 C6
Berghers Hill Bucks 66 B2
Berhill Som 44 F2
Berinsfield Oxon 83 F9
Berkeley Glos 79 F11
Berkeley Heath Glos 79 F11
Berkeley Road Glos 80 E2
Berkeley Towers Ches E 167 E11
Berkhamsted Herts 85 D7
Berkley Som 45 D10
Berkley Down Som 45 D9
Berkley Marsh Som 45 D10
Berkswell W Mid 118 B4
Bermondsey London 67 D10
Bermuda Warks 135 F7
Bernards Heath Herts 85 D11
Bernera Highld 295 C10
Berner's Cross Devon 25 F10
Berner's Hill E Sus 53 G8
Berners Roding Essex 87 D10

Blunt's Green Warks 118 D2
Blurton Stoke 168 G5
Blyborough Lincs 188 C6
Blyford Suff 127 B8
Blymhill Staffs 150 G6
Blymhill Lawns Staffs 150 G6
Blyth Borders 270 F2
Blyth Northumb 253 G8
Blyth Notts 187 D10
Blyth Bridge Borders 270 F2
Blythburgh Suff 127 B9
Blythe Borders 271 F11
Blythe Bridge Staffs 169 G7
Blythe Marsh Staffs 169 G7
Blyth End Warks 134 E4
Blythswood Renfs 267 B10
Blyton Lincs 188 C5
Boarhills Fife 287 F9
Boarhunt Hants 33 F10
Boarsgreave Lancs 195 C10
Boarshead E Sus 52 G4
Boars Hill Oxon 83 E7
Boarstall Bucks 83 C10
Boasley Cross Devon 12 C5
Boath Highld 300 B5
Boat of Garten Highld 291 B11
Bobbing Kent 69 F11
Bobbington Staffs 132 E6
Bobbingworth Essex 87 D8
Bobby Hill Suff 125 C10
Boblainy Highld 300 F4
Bocaddon Corn 6 D3
Bochastle Stirl 285 G10
Bockhanger Kent 54 E4
Bocking Essex 106 G5
Bocking Churchstreet Essex 106 F5
Bocking's Elm Essex 89 B11
Bockleton Worcs 115 E11
Bockmer End Bucks 65 B10
Bocombe Devon 24 C5
Bodantionail Highld 299 B7
Boddam Aberds 303 E11
Boddam Shetland 313 M5
Bodden Som 44 E6
Boddington Glos 99 F7
Bodedern Anglesey 178 E4
Bodellick Corn 10 G5
Bodelva Corn 5 E11
Bodelwyddan Denb 181 F8
Bodenham Hereford 115 G10
Bodenham Wilts 31 B11
Bodenham Bank Hereford 98 E2
Bodenham Moor Hereford 115 G10
Bodermid Gwyn 144 D3
Bodewryd Anglesey 178 C5
Bodfari Denb 181 G9
Bodffordd Anglesey 178 F6
Bodham Norf 177 E10
Bodiam E Sus 38 B3
Bodicote Oxon 101 D9
Bodiechell Aberds 303 E7
Bodieve Corn 10 G5
Bodiggo Corn 5 D10
Bodilly Corn 2 C5
Bodinnick Corn 6 E2
Bodle Street Green E Sus 23 C11
Bodley Devon 41 D7
Bodmin Corn 5 B11
Bodmiscombe Devon 27 F10
Bodney Norf 140 D6
Bodorgan Anglesey 162 B5
Bodsham Kent 54 D6
Boduan Gwyn 144 B6
Boduel Corn 6 C4
Bodwen Corn 5 C10
Bodymoor Heath Warks 134 D4
Bofarnel Corn 6 C2
Bogallan Highld 300 D6
Bogbrae Aberds 303 F10
Bogend Borders 272 F5
Bogend Notts 171 F7
Bogend S Ayrs 257 C9
Bogentory Aberds 293 C9
Boghall Midloth 270 B4
Boghall W Loth 269 B9
Boghead Aberds 293 D8
Boghead S Lnrk 268 G5
Bogmoor Moray 302 C3
Bogniebrae Aberds 302 E5
Bogniebrae Aberds 302 E6
Bognor Regis W Sus 22 D6
Bograxie Aberds 293 B9
Bogs Aberds 302 G5
Bogs Bank Borders 270 E3
Bogside N Lnrk 268 E6
Bogthorn W Yorks 204 F6
Bogton Aberds 302 D6
Bogtown Aberds 302 C5
Bogue Dumfries 246 G4
Bohemia E Sus 38 E4
Bohemia Wilts 32 D2
Bohenie Highld 290 E4
Bohetherick Corn 7 B8
Bohortha Corn 3 C9
Bohuntine Highld 290 E4
Bohuntinville Highld 290 E4
Boirseam W Isles 296 C6
Bojewyan Corn 1 C3
Bokiddick Corn 5 C11
Bolahaul Fm Carms 74 B6
Bolam Durham 233 G9
Bolam Northumb 252 G3
Bolam West Houses Northumb 252 G3
Bolas Heath Telford 150 E3
Bolberry Devon 9 G8
Bold Heath Mers 183 D8
Boldmere W Mid 134 E2
Boldon T&W 243 E9
Boldon Colliery T&W 243 E8
Boldre Hants 20 B2
Boldron Durham 223 C10
Bole Notts 188 D3
Bolehall Staffs 134 C4
Bolehill Derbys 170 E3
Bolehill Derbys 186 G6
Bolehill S Yorks 186 E5
Bole Hill Derbys 186 G4
Bolenowe Corn 2 B5
Boleside Borders 261 C11
Boley Park Staffs 134 B2
Bolham Devon 27 E7
Bolham Notts 188 E2
Bolham Water Devon 27 E11
Bolholt Gtr Man 195 E9
Bolingey Corn 4 E5
Bolitho Corn 2 C5
Bollihope Durham 232 E6
Bollington Ches E 184 F6
Bollington Cross Ches E 184 F6
Bolney W Sus 36 C3
Bolnhurst Beds 121 F11
Bolnore W Sus 36 C4
Bolshan Angus 287 B10
Bolsover Derbys 187 G7
Bolsterstone S Yorks 186 B3
Bolstone Hereford 97 E11
Boltby N Yorks 215 B9
Bolter End Bucks 84 G3
Bolton Cumb 231 G8
Bolton E Loth 281 G10
Bolton E Yorks 207 C11
Bolton Gtr Man 195 F8
Bolton Northumb 264 G4
Bolton W Yorks 205 F9
Bolton Abbey N Yorks 205 C7
Bolton Bridge N Yorks 205 C7
Bolton-by-Bowland Lancs 203 D11
Boltonfellend Cumb 239 D11
Boltongate Cumb 229 C10
Bolton Green Lancs 194 D5
Bolton Houses Lancs 202 G4
Bolton-le-Sands Lancs 211 F9
Bolton Low Houses Cumb 229 C10
Bolton New Houses Cumb 229 C10
Bolton-on-Swale N Yorks 224 F5
Bolton Percy N Yorks 206 E6
Bolton Town End Lancs 211 F9
Bolton upon Dearne S Yorks 198 G3
Bolton Wood Lane Cumb 229 C11
Bolton Woods W Yorks 205 F9
Boltshope Park Durham 232 B4
Bolventor Corn 11 F9
Bomarsund Northumb 253 G7
Bombie Dumfries 237 D9
Bomby Cumb 221 B10
Bomere Heath Shrops 149 F9
Bonaly Edin 270 B4
Bonar Bridge Highld 309 K6
Bonawe Argyll 284 D4
Bonby N Lincs 200 D4
Boncath Pembs 92 D4
Bonchester Bridge Borders 262 G3
Bonchurch IoW 21 F7
Bondend Glos 80 B5
Bond End Staffs 152 F3
Bondleigh Devon 25 G11
Bondman Hays Leics 135 B9
Bonds Lancs 202 E5
Bondstones Devon 25 F9
Bonehill Devon 13 F10
Bonehill Staffs 134 C3
Bo'ness Falk 279 E9
Bonhill W Dunb 277 F7
Boningale Shrops 132 C6
Bonjedward Borders 262 E5
Bonkle N Lnrk 268 D6
Bonnavoulin Highld 289 D7
Bonning Gate Cumb 221 F9
Bonnington Borders 261 B7
Bonnington Edin 270 B2
Bonnington Kent 54 F5
Bonnybank Fife 287 G7
Bonnybridge Falk 278 E6
Bonnykelly Aberds 303 D8
Bonnyrigg and Lasswade Midloth 270 B6
Bonnyton Aberds 302 F6
Bonnyton Angus 287 B10
Bonnyton Angus 287 D7
Bonnyton E Ayrs 257 B10
Bonsall Derbys 170 D3
Bonskeid House Perth 291 G10
Bonson Som 43 E8
Bont Mon 78 B5
Bontddu Gwyn 146 F3
Bont-Dolgadfan Powys 129 C7
Bont Fawr Carms 94 F4
Bont goch / Elerch Ceredig 128 F3
Bonthorpe Lincs 191 G7
Bontnewydd Ceredig 112 D2
Bontnewydd Gwyn 163 D7
Bont-newydd Conwy 181 G8
Bont Newydd Gwyn 146 E5
Bont Newydd Gwyn 164 G2
Bontuchel Denb 165 D9
Bonvilston / Tresimwn V Glam 58 E5
Bon-y-maen Swansea 57 B7
Boode Devon 40 F4
Booker Bucks 84 G4
Bookham Dorset 30 G2
Booleybank Shrops 149 D11
Boon Borders 271 F11
Boon Hill Staffs 168 E4
Boorley Green Hants 33 E8
Boosbeck Redcar 226 B3
Boose's Green Essex 106 E6
Boot Cumb 220 E3
Booth Staffs 151 D10
Booth W Yorks 196 B4
Booth Bank Ches E 184 D2
Booth Bridge Lancs 204 D4
Boothby Graffoe Lincs 173 D7
Boothby Pagnell Lincs 155 C9
Boothen Stoke 168 G5
Boothferry E Yorks 199 B8
Boothgate Derbys 170 F5
Booth Green Ches E 184 E6
Boothroyd W Yorks 197 C8
Boothsdale Ches W 167 B8
Boothstown Gtr Man 195 G8
Boothtown W Yorks 196 B5
Boothville Northants 120 E5
Booth Wood W Yorks 196 D4
Bootle Cumb 210 B2
Bootle Mers 182 B4
Booton Norf 160 E2
Boots Green Ches W 184 G3
Boot Street Suff 108 B4
Booze N Yorks 223 E10
Boquhan Stirl 277 D10
Boquio Corn 2 C5
Boraston Shrops 116 D2
Boraston Dale Shrops 116 C2
Borden Kent 69 G11
Borden W Sus 34 C4
Border Cumb 238 G5
Bordesley W Mid 133 F11
Bordesley Green W Mid 134 F2
Bordlands Borders 270 F3
Bordley N Yorks 213 G8
Bordon Hants 49 F10
Bordon Camp Hants 49 F9
Boreham Essex 88 D3
Boreham Wilts 45 E11
Boreham Street E Sus 23 C11
Borehamwood Herts 85 F11
Boreland Dumfries 236 C5
Boreland Dumfries 248 E5
Boreland Fife 280 C6
Boreland Stirl 285 D9
Boreland of Southwick Dumfries 237 C11
Boreley Worcs 116 D6
Borestone Stirl 278 C5
Borgh W Isles 296 C5
Borgh W Isles 297 L2
Borghasdal W Isles 296 C6
Borghastan W Isles 304 D4
Borgie Highld 308 D6
Borgue Dumfries 237 E8
Borgue Highld 311 G5
Borley Essex 106 C6
Borley Green Essex 106 C6
Borley Green Suff 125 E9
Bornais W Isles 297 J3
Bornesketaig Highld 298 B3
Borness Dumfries 237 E8
Borough Scilly 1 G3
Boroughbridge N Yorks 215 F7
Borough Green Kent 52 B6
Borough Marsh Wokingham 65 D9
Borough Park Staffs 134 B4
Borough Post Som 28 C4
Borras Wrex 166 E4
Borras Head Wrex 166 E5
Borreraig Highld 296 F7
Borrobol Lodge Highld 311 G2
Borrodale Highld 297 G7
Borrohill Aberds 303 D9
Borrowash Derbys 153 C8
Borrowby N Yorks 215 B8
Borrowby N Yorks 226 B5
Borrowdale Cumb 220 C5
Borrowfield Aberds 293 D10
Borrowston Highld 310 E7
Borrowstoun Mains Falk 279 E9
Borstal Medway 69 F8
Borthwick Midloth 271 D7
Borthwickbrae Borders 261 G10
Borthwickshiels Borders 261 F10
Borth / Y Borth Ceredig 128 E2
Borth-y-Gest Gwyn 145 B11
Borve Highld 298 E4
Borve Lodge W Isles 305 J2
Borwick Lancs 211 E10
Borwick Rails Cumb 210 D3
Bosavern Corn 1 C3
Bosbury Hereford 98 C3
Boscadjack Corn 2 C5
Boscastle Corn 11 C8
Boscean Corn 1 C3
Boscombe Bmouth 19 C8
Boscombe Wilts 47 F8
Boscomoor Staffs 151 G8
Boscoppa Corn 5 E10
Boscreege Corn 2 C3
Bosham W Sus 22 C4
Bosham Hoe W Sus 22 C4
Bosherston Pembs 73 G7
Boskednan Corn 1 C4
Boskenna Corn 1 E4
Bosleake Corn 4 G3
Bosley Ches E 168 B6
Boslowick Corn 3 C7
Boslymon Corn 5 C11
Bosoughan Corn 5 C7
Bosporthennis Corn 1 B4
Bossall N Yorks 216 G4
Bossiney Corn 11 D7
Bossingham Kent 54 D6
Bossington Hants 47 G10
Bossington Kent 55 B8
Bossington Som 41 D11
Bostadh W Isles 304 D3
Bostock Green Ches W 167 B11
Boston Lincs 174 G4
Boston Long Hedges Lincs 174 F5
Boston Spa W Yorks 206 D4
Boston West Lincs 174 F3
Boswednack Corn 1 B4
Boswin Corn 2 C5
Boswinger Corn 5 G9
Boswyn Corn 2 B5
Botallack Corn 1 C3
Botany Bay London 86 F3
Botany Bay Mon 79 E8
Botcherby Cumb 239 F10
Botcheston Leics 135 B9
Botesdale Suff 125 B10
Bothal Northumb 252 F6
Bothampstead W Berks 64 D4
Bothamsall Notts 187 G11
Bothel Cumb 229 D9
Bothenhampton Dorset 16 C5
Bothwell S Lnrk 268 D4
Bothy Highld 290 F4
Botley Bucks 85 E7
Botley Hants 33 E8
Botley Oxon 83 D7
Botloe's Green Glos 98 F4
Botolph Claydon Bucks 102 G4
Botolphs W Sus 35 F11
Bottacks Highld 300 C4
Botternell Corn 11 G11
Bottesford Leics 154 B6
Bottesford N Lincs 199 F11
Bottisham Cambs 123 E10
Bottlesford Wilts 46 B6
Bottom Boat W Yorks 197 C11
Bottomcraig Fife 287 E7
Bottom House Staffs 169 E8
Bottomley W Yorks 196 D5
Bottom of Hutton Lancs 194 B3
Bottom o' th' Moor Gtr Man 195 E7
Bottom Pond Kent 53 B11
Bottoms Corn 1 E3
Bottreaux Mill Devon 26 B4
Bottrells Close Bucks 85 G7
Botts Green Warks 134 E4
Botusfleming Corn 7 C8
Botwnnog Gwyn 144 C5
Bough Beech Kent 52 D3
Boughrood Powys 96 D2
Boughrood Brest Powys 96 D2
Boughspring Glos 79 F9
Boughton Ches W 166 B6
Boughton Lincs 173 F10
Boughton Norf 140 C3
Boughton Northants 120 D5
Boughton Notts 171 B11
Boughton Aluph Kent 54 D4
Boughton Corner Kent 54 D4
Boughton Green Kent 53 C9
Boughton Heath Ches W 166 B6
Boughton Lees Kent 54 D4
Boughton Malherbe Kent 53 D11
Boughton Monchelsea Kent 53 C9
Boughton Street Kent 54 B5
Bougton End C Beds 103 D9
Boulby Redcar 226 B5
Bould Oxon 100 G4
Boulden Shrops 131 F10
Boulder Clough W Yorks 196 C4
Bouldnor IoW 20 D3
Bouldon Shrops 131 F10
Boulmer Northumb 265 G7
Boulsdon Glos 98 G4
Boulston Pembs 73 C7
Boultenstone Aberds 292 B6
Boultham Lincs 173 B7
Boultham Moor Lincs 173 B7
Boulton Derbys 153 C7
Boulton Moor Derbys 153 C7
Boundary Leics 152 F6
Boundary Staffs 169 G7
Boundstone Sur 49 E10
Bountis Thorne Devon 24 D5
Bourn Cambs 122 F6
Bournbrook W Mid 133 G10
Bourne Lincs 155 E11
Bourne N Som 44 B3
Bourne End Beds 121 E10
Bourne End Bucks 65 B11
Bourne End C Beds 103 C9
Bourne End Herts 85 D8
Bournemouth Bmouth 19 C7
Bournes Green Glos 80 E6
Bournes Green Sthend 70 B2
Bournes Green Worcs 117 C8
Bourne Vale W Mid 133 D11
Bourne Valley Poole 19 C7
Bournheath Worcs 117 C9
Bournmoor Durham 243 G8
Bournside Glos 99 G8
Bournstream Glos 80 G2
Bournville W Mid 133 G10
Bourton Bucks 102 E4
Bourton Dorset 45 G9
Bourton N Som 59 G11
Bourton Oxon 63 B8
Bourton Shrops 131 D11
Bourton Wilts 62 G4
Bourton on Dunsmore Warks 119 C8
Bourton-on-the-Hill Glos 100 E3
Bourton-on-the-Water Glos 100 G3
Bourtreehill N Ayrs 257 B8
Bousd Argyll 288 C4
Bousta Shetland 313 H4
Boustead Hill Cumb 239 F7
Bouth Cumb 210 B6
Bouthwaite N Yorks 214 E2
Bouts Worcs 117 F10
Bovain Stirl 285 D9
Boveney Bucks 66 D2
Boveridge Dorset 31 E9
Boverton V Glam 58 F3
Bovey Tracey Devon 14 F2
Bovingdon Herts 85 E8
Bovingdon Green Bucks 65 B10
Bovingdon Green Herts 85 E8
Bovinger Essex 87 D8
Bovington Camp Dorset 18 D2
Bow Borders 271 G9
Bow Devon 8 D6
Bow Devon 26 G2
Bow Orkney 314 G3
Bow Oxon 82 G4
Bowbank Durham 232 G4
Bowbeck Suff 125 B8
Bow Brickhill M Keynes 103 E8
Bowbridge Glos 80 E5
Bowbrook Shrops 149 G9
Bow Broom S Yorks 187 B7
Bowburn Durham 234 D2
Bowcombe IoW 20 D5
Bow Common London 67 C11
Bowd Devon 15 C8
Bowden Borders 262 C3
Bowden Devon 8 F6
Bowden Dorset 30 C3
Bowden Hill Wilts 62 F2
Bowdens Som 28 B6
Bowderdale Cumb 222 E3
Bowdon Gtr Man 184 D3
Bower Highld 310 C6
Bower Northumb 251 G7
Bower Ashton Bristol 60 E5
Bowerchalke Wilts 31 C8
Bower Heath Herts 85 B10
Bowerhill Wilts 62 G2
Bower Hinton Som 29 D7
Bowerhope Borders 261 E7
Bower House Tye Suff 107 C9
Bowermadden Highld 310 C6
Bowers Staffs 150 B6
Bowers Gifford Essex 69 B9
Bowershall Fife 279 C11
Bowertower Highld 310 C6
Bowes Durham 223 C9
Bowes Park London 86 G4
Bowgreave Lancs 202 E5
Bowgreen Gtr Man 184 D3
Bowhill Borders 261 D10
Bowhill Fife 280 B4
Bowhouse Dumfries 238 D2
Bowhousebog or Liquo N Lnrk 269 D7
Bowing Park Mers 182 D6
Bowismiln Borders 262 E2
Bowithick Corn 11 E9
Bowker's Green Lancs 194 G2
Bowland Bridge Cumb 211 B8
Bowldown Wilts 62 D2
Bowlee Gtr Man 195 F10
Bowlees Durham 232 F4
Bowler's Town E Sus 38 C6
Bowley Hereford 115 G10
Bowley Lane Hereford 98 C3
Bowley Town Hereford 115 G10
Bowlhead Green Sur 50 F2
Bowling W Dunb 277 G9
Bowling W Yorks 205 G9
Bowling Alley Hants 49 D9
Bowling Bank Wrex 166 F5
Bowling Green Corn 5 D10
Bowling Green Corn 12 G3
Bowling Green Glos 81 E8
Bowling Green Hants 19 B11
Bowling Green Shrops 150 D2
Bowling Green W Mid 133 F8
Bowling Green Worcs 116 G6
Bowlish Som 44 E6
Bowmans Kent 68 E4
Bowmanstead Cumb 220 F6
Bowmore Argyll 254 B4
Bowness-on-Solway Cumb 238 E6
Bowness-on-Windermere Cumb 221 F8
Bow of Fife Fife 287 F7
Bowridge Hill Dorset 30 B4
Bowrie-fauld Angus 287 C9
Bowsden Northumb 273 G9
Bowsey Hill Windsor 65 C10
Bowshank Borders 271 G9
Bowside Lodge Highld 310 C2
Bowston Cumb 221 F9
Bow Street Ceredig 128 G2
Bow Street Norf 141 D10
Bowthorpe Norf 142 B3
Bowyer's Common Hants 34 B3
Box Glos 80 E5
Box Wilts 61 F10
Boxbush Glos 80 C2
Boxbush Glos 98 G3
Box End Beds 103 B10
Boxford Suff 107 C9
Boxford W Berks 64 E2
Boxgrove W Sus 22 B6
Box Hill Sur 51 C7
Box Hill Wilts 61 F10
Boxley Kent 53 B9
Boxmoor Herts 85 D9
Box's Shop Corn 24 G2
Boxted Essex 107 E9
Boxted Suff 124 G6
Boxted Cross Essex 107 E10
Boxted Heath Essex 107 E10
Box Trees W Mid 118 C2
Boxwell Glos 80 G4
Boxworth Cambs 122 E6
Boxworth End Cambs 123 D7
Boyatt Wood Hants 32 C6
Boyden End Suff 124 F4
Boyden Gate Kent 71 F8
Boyland Common Norf 141 G11
Boylestone Derbys 152 B3
Boylestonfield Derbys 152 B3
Boyndie Aberds 302 C6
Boyn Hill Windsor 65 C11
Boynton E Yorks 218 F2
Boysack Angus 287 C9
Boysack Angus 287 C10
Boys Hill Dorset 29 E11
Boys Village V Glam 58 F4
Boythorpe Derbys 186 G5
Boyton Corn 12 C2
Boyton Suff 109 B7
Boyton Wilts 46 F3
Boyton Cross Essex 87 D10
Boyton End Essex 106 E2
Boyton End Suff 106 C4
Bozeat Northants 121 F8
Bozen Green Herts 105 F8
Braaid IoM 192 E4
Braal Castle Highld 310 C5
Brabling Green Suff 126 E5
Brabourne Kent 54 E5
Brabourne Lees Kent 54 E5
Brabster Highld 310 C7
Bracadale Highld 294 B5
Bracara Highld 295 F9
Braceborough Lincs 155 G11
Bracebridge Lincs 173 B7
Bracebridge Heath Lincs 173 B7
Bracebridge Low Fields Lincs 173 B7
Braceby Lincs 155 B10
Bracewell Lancs 204 D3
Bracken Bank W Yorks 204 F6
Brackenber Cumb 222 B4
Brackenbottom N Yorks 212 E6
Brackenfield Derbys 170 D5
Brackenhall W Yorks 197 D7
Bracken Hill W Yorks 197 C7
Brackenlands Cumb 229 B11
Bracken Park W Yorks 206 E3
Brackenthwaite Cumb 229 B11
Brackenthwaite Cumb 229 G9
Brackenthwaite N Yorks 205 C11
Brackla / Bragle Bridgend 58 D2
Bracklamore Aberds 303 D8
Bracklesham W Sus 22 D4
Brackletter Highld 290 E3
Brackley Argyll 255 C8
Brackley Northants 101 D11
Brackloch Highld 307 G6
Bracknell Brack 65 F11
Braco Perth 286 G2
Bracobrae Moray 302 D5
Braco Castle Perth 286 F2
Bracon N Lincs 199 F9
Bracon Ash Norf 142 D3
Braco Park Aberds 303 C9
Bracorina Highld 295 F9
Bradaford Devon 12 C3
Bradbourne Derbys 170 E2
Bradbury Durham 234 F2
Bradda IoM 192 F2
Bradden Northants 102 B2
Braddock Corn 6 C3
Braddocks Hay Staffs 168 D5
Bradeley Stoke 168 E5
Bradeley Green Ches E 167 G8
Bradenham Bucks 84 F4
Bradenham Norf 141 B8
Bradenstoke Wilts 62 D4
Brades Village W Mid 133 E9
Bradfield Devon 27 F9
Bradfield Essex 108 E2
Bradfield Norf 160 C5
Bradfield W Berks 64 E6
Bradfield Combust Suff 125 F7
Bradfield Green Ches E 167 D11
Bradfield Heath Essex 108 F2
Bradfield St Clare Suff 125 F8
Bradfield St George Suff 125 E8
Bradford Corn 11 F8
Bradford Derbys 170 C2
Bradford Devon 24 F6
Bradford Gtr Man 184 B5
Bradford Northumb 264 C5
Bradford W Yorks 205 G9
Bradford Abbas Dorset 29 E9
Bradford Leigh Wilts 61 G10
Bradford-on-Avon Wilts 61 G10
Bradford-on-Tone Som 27 C11
Bradford Peverell Dorset 17 C9
Bradgate S Yorks 186 C6
Bradiford Devon 40 G5
Brading IoW 21 D8
Bradley Derbys 170 F2
Bradley Glos 80 G3
Bradley Hants 48 E6
Bradley NE Lincs 201 F8
Bradley Staffs 151 F7
Bradley W Mid 133 D8
Bradley Wrex 166 E4
Bradley W Yorks 197 C7
Bradley Cross Som 44 C3
Bradley Fold Gtr Man 195 F9
Bradley Green Ches W 167 F8
Bradley Green Glos 80 G2
Bradley Green Som 43 F9
Bradley Green Warks 134 C5
Bradley Green Worcs 117 E9
Bradley in the Moors Staffs 169 G9
Bradley Mills W Yorks 197 D7
Bradley Mount Ches E 184 F6
Bradley Stoke S Glos 60 C6
Bradlow Hereford 98 D4
Bradmore Notts 153 C11
Bradmore W Mid 133 D7
Bradney Shrops 132 D5
Bradney Som 43 F10
Bradninch Devon 27 G8
Bradnock's Marsh W Mid 118 B4
Bradnop Staffs 169 D8
Bradnor Green Hereford 114 F5
Bradpole Dorset 16 C5
Bradshaw Gtr Man 195 E8
Bradshaw Staffs 168 D6
Bradshaw W Yorks 196 E5
Bradshaw W Yorks 205 G7
Bradstone Devon 12 E3
Bradville M Keynes 102 C6
Bradwall Green Ches E 168 C3
Bradway S Yorks 186 E4
Bradwell Derbys 185 E11
Bradwell Devon 40 E3
Bradwell Essex 106 G6
Bradwell M Keynes 102 D6
Bradwell Norf 143 C10
Bradwell Staffs 168 F4
Bradwell Common M Keynes 102 D6
Bradwell Grove Oxon 82 D2
Bradwell Hills Derbys 185 E11
Bradwell on Sea Essex 89 D8
Bradwell Waterside Essex 89 D7
Bradworthy Devon 24 E4
Bradworthy Cross Devon 24 E4
Brae Dumfries 237 B10
Brae Highld 307 L3
Brae Highld 309 J4
Brae Shetland 312 G5
Braeantra Highld 300 B5
Braebuster Orkney 314 F5
Braedownie Angus 292 F4
Braeface Falk 278 E5
Braefield Highld 300 F4
Braefindon Highld 300 D6
Braegrum Perth 286 E4
Braehead Dumfries 236 D6
Braehead Orkney 314 B4
Braehead Orkney 314 F5
Braehead S Ayrs 257 E8
Braehead S Lnrk 259 C8
Braehead S Lnrk 267 D11
Braehead S Lnrk 269 E9
Braehead Stirl 278 C6
Braehead of Lunan Angus 287 B10
Braehoulland Shetland 312 F4
Braehour Highld 310 D4
Braehungie Highld 310 F5
Braeintra Highld 295 B10
Braelangwell Lodge Highld 309 K5
Braemar Aberds 292 D3
Braemore Highld 299 B11
Braemore Highld 310 F4
Brae of Achnahaird Highld 307 H5
Brae of Boquhapple Stirl 285 G10
Braepark Edin 280 F3
Brae Roy Lodge Highld 290 D5
Braeside Invclyd 276 F4
Braes of Enzie Moray 302 D3
Braes of Ullapool Highld 307 K6
Braeswick Orkney 314 C6
Braevallich Argyll 275 C10
Braewick Shetland 312 F4
Braewick Shetland 313 H5
Brafferton Darl 233 G11
Brafferton N Yorks 215 E8
Brafield-on-the-Green Northants 120 F6
Bragar W Isles 304 D4
Bragbury End Herts 104 G5
Bragenham Bucks 103 F8
Bragle / Brackla Bridgend 58 D2
Bragleenmore Argyll 289 G11
Braichmelyn Gwyn 163 B10
Braichyfedw Powys 129 E7
Braid Edin 280 G4
Braides Lancs 202 C4
Braidfauld Glasgow 268 C2
Braidley N Yorks 213 C10
Braids Argyll 255 C8
Braidwood S Lnrk 268 F6
Braigh Chalasaigh W Isles 296 D5
Braigo Argyll 274 G3
Brailsford Derbys 170 G3
Brailsford Green Derbys 170 G3
Braingortan Argyll 275 F11
Brain's Green Glos 79 D11
Brainshaugh Northumb 252 C6
Braintree Essex 106 G5
Braiseworth Suff 126 C2
Braishfield Hants 32 B5
Braiswick Essex 107 F9
Braithwaite Cumb 229 G10
Braithwaite S Yorks 198 E6
Braithwaite W Yorks 204 E6
Braithwell S Yorks 187 C8
Brakefield Green Norf 141 B10
Brakenhill W Yorks 198 D2
Bramber W Sus 35 E11
Bramblecombe Dorset 30 G3
Brambridge Hants 33 C7
Bramcote Notts 153 B10
Bramcote Warks 135 F8
Bramcote Hills Notts 153 B10
Bramcote Mains Warks 135 F8
Bramdean Hants 33 B10
Bramerton Norf 142 C5
Bramfield Herts 86 B3
Bramfield Suff 127 C7
Bramford Suff 108 B2
Bramford W Mid 133 E8
Bramhall Gtr Man 184 D5
Bramhall Moor Gtr Man 184 D6
Bramhall Park Gtr Man 184 D5
Bramham W Yorks 206 E4
Bramhope W Yorks 205 E11
Bramley Derbys 186 F6
Bramley Hants 48 B6
Bramley Sur 50 D4
Bramley S Yorks 187 C7
Bramley W Yorks 205 F10
Bramley Corner Hants 48 B6
Bramley Green Hants 49 B7
Bramley Head N Yorks 205 B8
Bramley Vale Derbys 171 B7
Bramling Kent 55 B8
Brampford Speke Devon 14 B4
Brampton Cambs 122 C4
Brampton Cumb 231 G9
Brampton Cumb 240 E2
Brampton Derbys 186 G5
Brampton Hereford 97 D8
Brampton Lincs 188 F4
Brampton Norf 160 E4
Brampton Suff 143 G8
Brampton S Yorks 198 G2
Brampton Abbotts Hereford 98 F2
Brampton Ash Northants 136 F5
Brampton Bryan Hereford 115 C7
Brampton en le Morthen S Yorks 187 D7
Brampton Park Cambs 122 C4
Brampton Street Suff 143 G8
Bramshall Staffs 151 C11
Bramshaw Hants 32 D3
Bramshill Hants 65 G8
Bramshott Hants 49 G10
Bramwell Som 28 B6
Branatwatt Shetland 313 H4
Branault Highld 289 C7
Branbridges Kent 53 D7
Brancaster Norf 176 E3
Brancaster Staithe Norf 176 E3
Brancepeth Durham 233 D10
Branch End Northumb 242 E3
Branchill Moray 301 D10
Branchton Invclyd 276 F4
Brand End Lincs 174 F5
Branderburgh Moray 302 B2
Brandesburton E Yorks 209 D8
Brandeston Suff 126 E4
Brand Green Glos 98 F4
Brand Green Hereford 98 C5
Brandhill Shrops 115 B8
Brandis Corner Devon 24 G6
Brandish Street Som 42 D2
Brandiston Norf 160 E2
Brandlingill Cumb 229 F8
Brandon Durham 233 D10
Brandon Lincs 172 F6
Brandon Northumb 264 F2
Brandon Suff 140 F5
Brandon Warks 119 B8
Brandon Bank Cambs 140 F2
Brandon Creek Norf 140 E2
Brandon Parva Norf 141 B11
Brandsby N Yorks 215 E11
Brands Hill Windsor 66 D4
Brandwood Shrops 149 D9
Brandwood End W Mid 117 B11
Brandy Carr W Yorks 197 C10
Brandy Hole Essex 88 F4
Brandyquoy Orkney 314 G4
Brandy Wharf Lincs 189 B8
Brane Corn 1 D4
Bran End Essex 106 F3

Broughton Hackett Worcs 117 G8
Broughton in Furness Cumb 210 B4
Broughton Lodges Leics 154 E4
Broughton Mills Cumb 220 G4
Broughton Moor Cumb 228 E6
Broughton Park Gtr Man 195 G10
Broughton Poggs Oxon 82 E2
Broughtown Orkney 314 B6
Broughty Ferry Dundee 287 D8
Brow Edge Cumb 211 C7
Browhouses Dumfries 239 D7
Browland Shetland 313 H4
Brown Bank N Yorks 205 C10
Brownber Cumb 222 D4
Brownbread Street E Sus 23 B11
Brown Candover Hants 48 F5
Brownedge Ches E 168 C3
Brown Edge Lancs 193 E11
Brown Edge Mers 183 C8
Brown Edge Staffs 168 E6
Brownheath Devon 27 D10
Brownheath Shrops 149 D9
Brown Heath Ches W 167 B7
Brown Heath Hants 33 D8
Brownheath Common Worcs 117 E7
Brownhill Aberds 302 E6
Brownhill Aberds 303 E8
Brownhill Blkburn 203 G9
Brownhill Shrops 149 E8
Brownhills Fife 287 F9
Brownhills Shrops 150 B3
Brownhills W Mid 133 B10
Brownieside Northumb 264 E5
Browninghill Green Hants 48 B5
Brown Knowl Ches W 167 E7
Brown Lees Staffs 168 D5
Brownlow Ches E 168 C4
Brownlow Mers 194 G4
Brownlow Fold Gtr Man 195 E8
Brownlow Heath Ches E 168 C4
Brown Moor W Yorks 206 G3
Brownmuir Aberds 293 F9
Brown's Bank Ches E 167 G10
Brown's End Glos 98 E4
Brown's Green W Mid 133 E10
Brownshill Glos 80 E5
Brownshill Green W Mid 134 G6
Brownside Lancs 204 G3
Brownsover Warks 119 B10
Brownston Devon 8 E3
Brown Street Suff 125 E11
Browns Wood M Keynes 103 D8
Browsburn N Lnrk 268 C5
Browston Green Norf 143 C9
Browtop Cumb 229 G7
Broxa N Yorks 227 G8
Broxbourne Herts 86 D5
Broxburn E Loth 282 F3
Broxburn W Loth 279 G11
Broxfield Northumb 264 F6
Broxholme Lincs 188 F6
Broxted Essex 105 F11
Broxton Ches W 167 E7
Broxtowe Nottingham 171 G8
Broxwood Hereford 115 G7
Broyle Side E Sus 23 C7
Brù W Isles 304 D5
Bruairnis W Isles 297 L3
Bruan Highld 310 F7
Bruar Lodge Perth 291 F10
Brucefield Fife 280 D2
Brucehill W Dunb 277 F7
Bruche Warr 183 D10
Brucklebog Aberds 293 D9
Bruera Ches W 166 C6
Bruern Abbey Oxon 100 G5
Bruichladdich Argyll 274 G3
Bruisyard Suff 126 D6
Brumby N Lincs 199 F11
Brunant Powys 130 B5
Brund Staffs 169 C10
Brundall Norf 142 B6
Brundish Norf 143 D7
Brundish Suff 126 D5
Brundish Street Suff 126 C5
Brundon Suff 107 C7
Brunery Highld 289 B9
Brunnion Corn 2 B2
Brunshaw Lancs 204 G3
Brunstane Edin 280 G6
Brunstock Cumb 239 F10
Brunswick Gtr Man 184 B4
Brunswick Park London 86 G3
Brunswick Village T&W 242 C6
Bruntcliffe W Yorks 197 B9
Brunt Hamersland Shetland 313 H6
Brunthwaite W Yorks 205 D7
Bruntingthorpe Leics 136 F2
Brunton Fife 287 E7
Brunton Northumb 264 E6
Brunton Wilts 47 B8
Brushes Gtr Man 185 B7
Brushfield Derbys 185 G11
Brushford Devon 25 F11
Brushford Som 26 B6
Bruton Som 45 G7
Bryans Midloth 270 C6
Bryan's Green Worcs 117 D7
Bryanston Dorset 30 F5
Bryant's Bottom Bucks 84 F5
Brydekirk Dumfries 238 C5
Bryher Scilly 1 G3
Brymbo Conwy 180 G4
Brymbo Wrex 166 E3
Brympton Som 29 D8
Brympton D'Evercy Som 29 D8
Bryn Caerph 77 F11
Bryn Carms 75 E8
Bryn Ches W 183 G10
Bryn Gtr Man 194 G5
Bryn Gwyn 179 G9
Bryn Neath 57 C10
Bryn Powys 130 C3
Bryn Rhondda 76 D6
Bryn Shrops 130 F5
Bryn Swansea 56 C4
Brynafan Ceredig 112 C4
Brynamman Carms 76 C2
Brynawel Caerph 77 G11
Brynberian Pembs 92 D2
Brynbryddan Neath 57 C9
Brynbryddan Neath 57 C9
Bryn Bwbach Gwyn 146 B2
Bryncae Rhondda 58 C3
Bryncae Rhondda 58 C3
Bryn Celyn Anglesey 179 F10
Bryn Celyn Flint 181 F11
Bryncethin Bridgend 58 C2
Bryncethin Bridgend 58 C2
Bryncir Gwyn 163 G7
Bryncoch Bridgend 58 C2
Bryn-coch Neath 57 B8
Bryn Common Flint 166 D3
Bryncroes Gwyn 144 C4
Bryncrug Gwyn 128 C2
Brynderwen Powys 130 D3
Bryndu Carms 75 D8
Bryn Du Anglesey 178 G4
Bryn Dulas Conwy 180 F6
Bryneglwys Denb 165 F10
Bryn Eglwys Gwyn 163 B10
Brynford Flint 181 G11
Bryn Gates Gtr Man 194 G5
Brynglas Newport 59 B10
Bryn-glas Conwy 164 B4
Brynglas Sta Gwyn 128 C2
Bryn Golau Rhondda 58 B3
Bryngwran Anglesey 178 F4
Bryngwyn Ceredig 92 B5
Bryngwyn Mon 78 D5
Bryngwyn Powys 96 B3
Brynhenllan Pembs 91 D10
Bryn-henllan Pembs 91 D10
Brynheulog Bridgend 57 C11
Brynhoffnant Ceredig 110 G6
Bryniau Denb 181 E9
Bryning Lancs 194 B2
Brynithel Bl Gwent 78 E2
Bryn-Iwan Carms 92 E6
Brynllywarch Powys 130 F3
Brynmawr Bl Gwent 77 C11
Bryn-mawr Gwyn 144 C4
Bryn Mawr Powys 148 F5
Brynmenyn Bridgend 58 B2
Brynmill Swansea 56 C6
Brynmorfudd Conwy 164 C4
Bryn Myrddin Carms 93 G8
Brynna Rhondda 58 C3
Bryn-nantllech Conwy 164 B6
Brynnau Gwynion Rhondda 58 C3
Bryn-newydd Denb 165 G11
Bryn Offa Wrex 166 F4
Brynore Shrops 149 B7
Bryn-penarth Powys 130 C2
Bryn Pen-y-lan Wrex 166 G4
Bryn Pydew Conwy 180 F4
Brynrefail Anglesey 179 D7
Brynrefail Gwyn 163 C9
Bryn Rhyd-yr-Arian Conwy 165 B7
Bryn-rhys Conwy 180 F4
Brynsadler Rhondda 58 C4
Bryn Saith Marchog Denb 165 E9
Brynsiencyn Anglesey 163 B7
Bryn Sion Gwyn 147 F7
Brynsworthy Devon 40 G4
Bryn Tanat Powys 148 E4
Brynteg Anglesey 179 E7
Brynteg Ceredig 93 C9
Brynteg Wrex 166 E4
Bryntirion Bridgend 57 E11
Bryn-y-cochin Shrops 149 B7
Bryn-y-gwenin Mon 78 B4
Bryn-y-maen Conwy 180 F4
Bryn-yr-Eos Wrex 166 G3
Bryn-yr-eryr Gwyn 162 F5
Bryn-yr-ogof Denb 165 D11
Buaile nam Bodach W Isles 297 L3
Bualintur Highld 294 C6
Bualnaluib Highld 307 K3
Buarthmeini Gwyn 146 C6
Bubbenhall Warks 119 C7
Bubblewell Glos 80 E5
Bubnell Derbys 186 G2
Bubwith E Yorks 207 F10
Buccleuch Borders 261 G8
Buchanan Smithy Stirl 277 D9
Buchanhaven Aberds 303 E11
Buchan Hill W Sus 51 G9
Buchanty Perth 286 E3
Buchley E Dunb 277 G11
Buchlyvie Stirl 277 C11
Buckabank Cumb 230 B3
Buckbury Worcs 98 E6
Buckden Cambs 122 D3
Buckden N Yorks 213 D8
Buckenham Norf 143 B7
Buckerell Devon 27 G10
Bucket Corner Hants 32 C6
Buckfast Devon 8 B4
Buckfastleigh Devon 8 B4
Buckham Dorset 29 G7
Buckhaven Fife 281 B7
Buck Hill Wilts 62 E3
Buckholm Borders 261 B11
Buckholt Mon 79 B8
Buckhorn Devon 12 B3
Buckhorn Weston Dorset 30 C3
Buckhurst Kent 53 E10
Buckhurst Hill Essex 86 G6
Buckie Moray 302 C4
Buckies Highld 310 C5
Buckingham Bucks 102 E3
Buckland Bucks 84 C5
Buckland Devon 8 G3
Buckland Devon 14 G3
Buckland Glos 99 D11
Buckland Hants 20 B2
Buckland Herts 105 E7
Buckland Kent 55 E10
Buckland Oxon 82 F4
Buckland Sur 51 C8
Buckland Brewer Devon 24 C6
Buckland Common Bucks 84 D6
Buckland Dinham Som 45 C9
Buckland Down Som 45 C8
Buckland End W Mid 134 F2
Buckland Filleigh Devon 25 F7
Buckland in the Moor Devon 13 G10
Buckland Marsh Oxon 82 F4
Buckland Monachorum Devon 7 B9
Buckland Newton Dorset 29 F11
Buckland Ripers Dorset 17 E8
Bucklands Borders 262 F2
Buckland St Mary Som 28 E3
Buckland Valley Kent 55 E10
Bucklandwharf Bucks 84 C5
Bucklebury W Berks 64 E5
Bucklebury Alley W Berks 64 E4
Bucklegate Lincs 156 B6
Buckleigh Devon 24 B6
Bucklerheads Angus 287 D8
Bucklers Hard Hants 20 B4
Bucklesham Suff 108 C4
Buckley / Bwcle Flint 166 C3
Buckley Green Warks 118 D3
Buckley Hill Mers 182 B4
Bucklow Hill Ches E 184 E2
Buckminster Leics 155 E7
Buckmoorend Bucks 84 E4
Bucknall Lincs 173 B11
Bucknall Stoke 168 F6
Bucknell Oxon 101 F11
Bucknell Shrops 115 C7
Buckoak Ches W 183 G8
Buckover S Glos 79 G11
Buckpool Moray 302 C4
Buckpool W Mid 133 F7
Buckridge Worcs 116 C4
Bucksburn Aberdeen 293 C10
Buck's Cross Devon 24 C4
Bucks Green W Sus 50 G5
Buckshaw Village Lancs 194 C5
Bucks Hill Herts 85 E9
Bucks Horn Oak Hants 49 E10
Buckskin Hants 48 C6
Buck's Mills Devon 24 C5
Buckton E Yorks 218 E3
Buckton Hereford 115 C7
Buckton Northumb 264 B3
Buckton Vale Gtr Man 196 G3
Buckworth Cambs 122 B2
Budbrooke Warks 118 D5
Budby Notts 171 B10
Buddgbrake Shetland 312 B8
Buddileigh Staffs 168 F3
Budd's Titson Corn 24 G2
Bude Corn 24 F2
Budge's Shop Corn 6 D6
Budlake Devon 14 B5
Budle Northumb 264 B5
Budleigh Som 27 D11
Budleigh Salterton Devon 15 E7
Budlett's Common E Sus 37 C7
Budock Water Corn 3 C7
Budworth Heath Ches W 183 F11
Buersil Head Gtr Man 196 E2
Buerton Ches E 167 G11
Buffler's Holt Bucks 102 D3
Bufton Leics 135 B8
Bugbrooke Northants 120 F3
Bugford Devon 40 E6
Bughtlin Edin 280 G3
Buglawton Ches E 168 C5
Bugle Corn 5 D10
Bugle Gate Worcs 116 D6
Bugley Dorset 30 C3
Bugley Wilts 45 E11
Bugthorpe E Yorks 207 B11
Building End Essex 105 D8
Buildwas Shrops 132 C2
Builth Road Powys 113 G10
Builth Wells Powys 113 G10
Buirgh W Isles 305 J2
Bulbourne Herts 84 C6
Bulbridge Wilts 46 G5
Bulby Lincs 155 D11
Bulcote Notts 171 G11
Buldoo Highld 310 C3
Bulford Wilts 47 E7
Bulford Camp Wilts 47 E7
Bulkeley Ches E 167 E8
Bulkeley Hall Shrops 168 G2
Bulkington Warks 135 F7
Bulkington Wilts 46 B2
Bulkworthy Devon 24 E5
Bullamoor N Yorks 225 G7
Bull Bay / Porthllechog Anglesey 178 C6
Bullbridge Derbys 170 E5
Bullbrook Brack 65 F11
Bulleign Kent 53 G11
Bullenhill Wilts 45 B11
Bullen's Green Herts 86 D2
Bulley Glos 80 B3
Bullgill Cumb 229 D7
Bull Hill Hants 20 B2
Bullhurst Hill Derbys 170 G3
Bullinghope Hereford 97 D10
Bullington Hants 48 E3
Bullington Lincs 189 F9
Bullo Glos 79 D11
Bullock's Horn Wilts 81 G7
Bullockstone Kent 71 F7
Bulls Cross London 86 F4
Bulls Green Som 45 D8
Bull's Green Herts 86 B3
Bull's Green Norf 143 E8
Bull's Hill Hereford 97 G11
Bullwood Argyll 276 G3
Bullyhole Bottom Mon 79 F7
Bulmer Essex 106 C6
Bulmer N Yorks 216 F3
Bulmer Tye Essex 106 D6
Bulphan Thurrock 68 B6
Bulstrode Herts 85 E8
Bulthy Shrops 148 G6
Bulverhythe E Sus 38 F3
Bulwark Aberds 303 E9
Bulwark Mon 79 G8
Bulwell Nottingham 171 F8
Bulwell Forest Nottingham 171 F8
Bulwick Leics 136 E3
Bulwick Northants 137 E9
Bumble's Green Essex 86 D6
Bumwell Hill Norf 142 E2
Bun Abhainn Eadarra W Isles 305 H3
Bunacaimb Highld 295 G8
Bun a'Mhuillin W Isles 297 K3
Bunarkaig Highld 290 E3
Bunbury Ches E 167 D9
Bunbury Heath Ches E 167 D9
Bunce Common Sur 51 D8
Bunchrew Highld 300 E6
Bundalloch Highld 295 C10
Buness Shetland 312 C8
Bunessan Argyll 288 G5
Bungay Suff 142 F6
Bunkers Hill Gtr Man 184 D6
Bunkers Hill Oxon 83 B7
Bunker's Hill Cambs 139 B8
Bunker's Hill Lincs 174 E3
Bunker's Hill Lincs 189 G7
Bunker's Hill Norf 142 B3
Bunker's Hill Suff 143 C10
Bunloit Highld 300 G5
Bun Loyne Highld 290 C4
Bunnahabhain Argyll 274 F5
Bunny Notts 153 D11
Bunny Hill Notts 153 D11
Bunree Highld 290 G2
Bunroy Highld 290 E4
Bunsley Bank Ches E 167 G11
Bunstead Hants 32 C6
Buntait Highld 300 F3
Buntingford Herts 105 F7
Bunting's Green Essex 106 E6
Bunwell Norf 142 E2
Bunwell Bottom Norf 142 D2
Buoltach Highld 310 F5
Burbage Derbys 185 G8
Burbage Leics 135 E8
Burbage Wilts 63 G8
Burcher Hereford 114 E6
Burchett's Green Windsor 65 C10
Burcombe Wilts 46 G5
Burcot Oxon 83 F9
Burcot Worcs 117 C9
Burcote Shrops 132 D4
Burcott Bucks 84 B4
Burcott Bucks 103 G7
Burcott Som 44 D4
Burdiehouse Edin 270 B5
Burdon T&W 243 G9
Burdonshill V Glam 58 E6
Burdrop Oxon 101 D7
Bures Suff 107 E8
Bures Green Suff 107 D8
Burford Ches E 167 E10
Burford Devon 24 C4
Burford Oxon 82 C3
Burford Shrops 115 D11
Burford Som 44 E5
Burg Argyll 288 E5
Burg Argyll 288 G6
Burgar Orkney 314 D3
Burgate Hants 31 D11
Burgate Suff 125 B11
Burgates Hants 34 B3
Burgedin Powys 148 G4
Burge End Herts 104 E2
Burgess Hill W Sus 36 D4
Burgh Suff 126 G4
Burgh by Sands Cumb 239 F8
Burgh Castle Norf 143 B9
Burghclere Hants 64 G3
Burghclere Common Hants 64 G3
Burgh Common Norf 141 E11
Burghead Moray 301 C11
Burghfield W Berks 65 F7
Burghfield Common W Berks 64 F6
Burghfield Hill W Berks 65 F7
Burgh Heath Sur 51 B8
Burgh Hill E Sus 23 C8
Burgh Hill E Sus 38 B2
Burghill Hereford 97 C9
Burgh le Marsh Lincs 175 B8
Burgh Muir Aberds 293 B9
Burgh Muir Aberds 303 G7
Burgh next Aylsham Norf 160 D4
Burgh on Bain Lincs 190 D2
Burgh St Margaret / Fleggburgh Norf 161 G8
Burgh St Peter Norf 143 E9
Burgh Stubbs Norf 159 C10
Burghwallis S Yorks 198 E4
Burgois Corn 10 G4
Burham Kent 69 G8
Burham Court Kent 69 G8
Buriton Hants 34 C2
Burland Ches E 167 E10
Burlawn Corn 10 G5
Burleigh Brack 65 E11
Burleigh Glos 80 E5
Burlescombe Devon 27 D9
Burleston Dorset 17 C11
Burlestone Devon 8 F6
Burley Hants 32 G2
Burley Rutland 155 G7
Burley Shrops 131 G9
Burley W Yorks 205 G11
Burley Beacon Hants 32 G2
Burleydam Ches E 167 G10
Burley Gate Hereford 97 B11
Burley in Wharfedale W Yorks 205 D9
Burley Lawn Hants 32 G2
Burley Lodge Hants 32 F2
Burley Street Hants 32 G2
Burley Woodhead W Yorks 205 E9
Burlinch Som 28 B3
Burlingham Green Norf 161 G7
Burlingjobb Powys 114 F5
Burlish Park Worcs 116 C6
Burlorne Tregoose Corn 5 B10
Burlow E Sus 23 B9
Burlton Shrops 149 D9
Burmantofts W Yorks 206 G2
Burmarsh Hereford 97 B10
Burmarsh Kent 54 G5
Burmington Warks 100 D5
Burn N Yorks 198 B5
Burnage Gtr Man 184 C5
Burnard's Ho Devon 24 G4
Burnaston Derbys 152 C5
Burnbank S Lnrk 268 D4
Burn Bridge N Yorks 206 C2
Burnby E Yorks 208 D2
Burncross S Yorks 186 B4
Burndell W Sus 35 G7
Burnden Gtr Man 195 F8
Burnedge Gtr Man 196 E2
Burnend Aberds 303 E8
Burneside Cumb 221 F10
Burness Orkney 314 B6
Burneston N Yorks 214 B6
Burnett Bath 61 F7
Burnfoot Borders 261 G10
Burnfoot Borders 262 F2
Burnfoot Dumfries 239 C7
Burnfoot Dumfries 247 E11
Burnfoot E Ayrs 245 B10
Burnfoot N Lnrk 268 B5
Burnfoot Perth 286 G3
Burngreave S Yorks 186 D5
Burnham Bucks 66 C2
Burnham N Lincs 200 D5
Burnham Deepdale Norf 176 E4
Burnham Green Herts 86 B3
Burnham Market Norf 176 E4
Burnham Norton Norf 176 E4
Burnham-on-Crouch Essex 88 F6
Burnham-on-Sea Som 43 D10
Burnham Overy Staithe Norf 176 E4
Burnham Overy Town Norf 176 E4
Burnham Thorpe Norf 176 E5
Burnhead Aberds 293 D10
Burnhead Borders 262 F2
Burnhead Dumfries 247 D9
Burnhead Dumfries 247 G10
Burnhead S Ayrs 244 C6
Burnhervie Aberds 293 B9
Burnhill Green Staffs 132 C5
Burnhope Durham 233 B9
Burnhouse N Ayrs 267 E7
Burnhouse Mains Borders 271 F8
Burniere Corn 10 G5
Burniestrype Moray 302 C3
Burniston N Yorks 227 G10
Burnlee W Yorks 196 F6
Burnley Lancs 204 G2
Burnley Lane Lancs 204 G2
Burnley Wood Lancs 204 G2
Burnmouth Borders 273 C9
Burn Naze Lancs 202 E2
Burn of Cambus Stirl 285 G11
Burnopfield Durham 242 F5
Burnrigg Cumb 239 F11
Burnsall N Yorks 213 G10
Burn's Green Herts 104 G6
Burnside Aberds 303 E8
Burnside Angus 287 B9
Burnside E Ayrs 258 G3
Burnside Fife 286 G5
Burnside Perth 286 E4
Burnside Shetland 312 F4
Burnside S Lnrk 268 C2
Burnside T&W 243 G8
Burnside W Loth 279 G11
Burnside of Duntrune Angus 287 D8
Burnstone Devon 24 C4
Burnswark Dumfries 238 B5
Burnt Ash Glos 80 E5
Burntcommon Sur 50 C4
Burntheath Derbys 152 C4
Burnt Heath Derbys 186 F2
Burnt Heath Essex 107 F11
Burnt Hill W Berks 64 E5
Burnthouse Corn 3 B7
Burnt Houses Durham 233 G8
Burntisland Fife 280 D4
Burnt Mills Essex 88 G2
Burnt Oak E Sus 37 B8
Burnt Oak London 86 G2
Burnton E Ayrs 245 B11
Burnt Tree W Mid 133 E9
Burnturk Fife 287 G7
Burntwood Staffs 133 B11
Burntwood Green Staffs 133 B11
Burntwood Pentre Flint 166 C3
Burnt Yates N Yorks 214 G5
Burnworthy Som 27 D11
Burnwynd Edin 270 B2
Burpham Sur 50 C4
Burpham W Sus 35 F8
Burradon Northumb 251 B11
Burradon T&W 243 C7
Burrafirth Shetland 312 B8
Burraland Shetland 312 F5
Burraland Shetland 313 J4
Burras Corn 2 C5
Burrastow Shetland 313 J4
Burraton Corn 7 D8
Burraton Coombe Corn 7 D8
Burravoe Shetland 312 F7
Burravoe Shetland 312 G5
Burray Village Orkney 314 G4
Burrelldales Aberds 303 F7
Burrells Cumb 222 B3
Burrelton Perth 286 D6
Burridge Devon 28 F4
Burridge Devon 40 F5
Burridge Hants 33 E8
Burrigill Highld 310 F6
Burrill N Yorks 214 B4
Burringham N Lincs 199 F10
Burrington Devon 25 D10
Burrington Hereford 115 C8
Burrington N Som 44 B3
Burrough End Cambs 124 F2
Burrough Green Cambs 124 F2
Burrough on the Hill Leics 154 G5
Burroughs Grove Bucks 65 B11
Burroughston Orkney 314 D5
Burrow Devon 14 B5
Burrow Som 28 C6
Burrow Som 42 E2
Burrowbridge Som 43 G11
Burrow-bridge Som 28 B5
Burrowhill Sur 66 G3
Burrows Cross Sur 50 D5
Burrowsmoor Holt Notts 172 G2
Burrsville Park Essex 89 B11
Burrswood Kent 52 F4
Burry Swansea 56 C3
Burry Green Swansea 56 C3
Burry Port / Porth Tywyn Carms 74 E6
Burscott Devon 24 C4
Burscough Lancs 194 E2
Burscough Bridge Lancs 194 E2
Bursdon Devon 24 D3
Bursea E Yorks 208 G2
Burshill E Yorks 209 D7
Bursledon Hants 33 F7
Burslem Stoke 168 F5
Burstall Suff 107 C11
Burstallhill Suff 107 B11
Burstock Dorset 28 G6
Burston Devon 26 G2
Burston Norf 142 G2
Burston Staffs 151 C8
Burstow Sur 51 E10
Burstwick E Yorks 201 B8
Burtersett N Yorks 213 B7
Burtholme Cumb 240 E2
Burthorpe Suff 124 E5
Burthwaite Cumb 230 B4
Burtle Som 43 E11
Burtle Hill Som 43 E11
Burtoft Lincs 156 B5
Burton Ches W 167 C8
Burton Ches W 182 G4
Burton Dorset 17 C9
Burton Dorset 19 C9
Burton Lincs 189 G7
Burton Northumb 264 C5
Burton Pembs 73 D7
Burton Som 29 E8
Burton Som 43 E7
Burton V Glam 58 F4
Burton Wilts 45 G10
Burton Wilts 61 D10
Burton Wrex 166 D5
Burton Agnes E Yorks 218 G2
Burton Bradstock Dorset 16 D5
Burton Corner Lincs 174 F4
Burton Dassett Warks 119 G7
Burton End Cambs 106 B2
Burton End Essex 105 G10
Burton Ferry Pembs 73 D7
Burton Fleming E Yorks 217 E11
Burton Green Essex 106 F6
Burton Green W Mid 118 B5
Burton Green Wrex 166 D4
Burton Hastings Warks 135 E8
Burton-in-Kendal Cumb 211 D10
Burton in Lonsdale N Yorks 212 E3
Burton Joyce Notts 171 G10
Burton Latimer Northants 121 C8
Burton Lazars Leics 154 F5
Burton-le-Coggles Lincs 155 D9
Burton Leonard N Yorks 214 G6
Burton Manor Staffs 151 E8
Burton on the Wolds Leics 153 E11
Burton Overy Leics 136 D3
Burton Pedwardine Lincs 173 G10
Burton Pidsea E Yorks 209 G10
Burton Salmon N Yorks 198 B3
Burton Stather N Lincs 199 D11
Burton upon Stather N Lincs 199 D11
Burton upon Trent Staffs 152 E5
Burton Westwood Shrops 132 D2
Burtonwood Warr 183 C9
Burwardsley Ches W 167 D8
Burwarton Shrops 132 F2
Burwash E Sus 37 C11
Burwash Common E Sus 37 C10
Burwash Weald E Sus 37 C10
Burwell Cambs 123 D11
Burwell Lincs 190 F5
Burwen Anglesey 178 C6
Burwick Orkney 314 H4
Burwick Shetland 313 J5
Burwood Shrops 131 F9
Burwood Park Sur 66 G6
Bury Cambs 138 G5
Bury Gtr Man 195 E10
Bury Som 26 B6
Bury W Sus 35 E8
Buryas Br Corn 1 D4
Burybank Staffs 151 B7
Bury End Beds 121 G9
Bury End C Beds 104 E2
Bury End Worcs 99 D11
Bury Green Herts 86 E4
Bury Green Herts 105 G8
Bury Hollow W Sus 35 E8
Bury Park Luton 103 G11
Bury St Edmunds Suff 125 E7
Bury's Bank W Berks 64 F3
Burythorpe N Yorks 216 G5
Busbiehill N Ayrs 257 B9
Busbridge Sur 50 E3
Busby E Renf 267 D11
Buscot Oxon 82 F2
Buscott Som 44 F2
Bush Aberds 293 G9
Bush Corn 24 F2
Bush Bank Hereford 115 G9
Bushbury Sur 51 D7
Bushbury W Mid 133 C8
Bushby Leics 136 C3
Bush Crathie Aberds 292 D4
Bush End Essex 87 B9
Bush Estate Norf 161 D8
Bushey Dorset 18 E5
Bushey Herts 85 G10
Bushey Ground Oxon 82 D4
Bushey Heath Herts 85 G11
Bushey Mead London 67 F8
Bushfield Cumb 249 G11
Bush Green Norf 141 D10
Bush Green Norf 142 F4
Bush Green Suff 125 F8
Bush Hill Park London 86 F4
Bushley Worcs 99 E7
Bushley Green Worcs 99 E7
Bushmead Beds 122 E2
Bushmoor Shrops 131 F8
Bushton Wilts 62 D5
Bushy Common Norf 159 G9
Bushy Hill Sur 50 C4
Busk Cumb 231 C8
Busk Gtr Man 196 F2
Buslingthorpe Lincs 189 D9
Bussage Glos 80 E5
Bussex Som 43 F11
Busta Shetland 312 G5
Bustard Green Essex 106 F2
Bustard's Green Norf 142 E3
Bustatoun Orkney 314 A7
Busveal Corn 4 G4
Butcher's Common Norf 160 E6
Butcher's Cross E Sus 37 B9
Butcombe N Som 60 G4
Butetown Cardiff 59 D7
Bute Town Caerph 77 D10
Butlane Head Shrops 149 G8
Butleigh Som 44 G4
Butleigh Wootton Som 44 G4
Butlersbank Shrops 149 E11
Butlers Cross Bucks 85 G7
Butler's Cross Bucks 84 D4
Butler's End Warks 134 G4
Butler's Hill Notts 171 F8
Butlers Marston Warks 118 G6
Butley Suff 127 G7
Butley High Corner Suff 109 B7
Butley Low Corner Suff 109 B7
Butley Town Ches E 184 F6
Butlocks Heath Hants 33 F7
Butter Bank Staffs 151 E7
Butterburn Cumb 240 C5
Buttercrambe N Yorks 207 B10
Butteriss Gate Corn 2 C6
Butterknowle Durham 233 F8
Butterleigh Devon 27 F7
Butterley Derbys 170 C4
Butterley Derbys 170 E6
Buttermere Cumb 220 B3
Buttermere Wilts 63 G10
Butterrow Glos 80 E5
Butters Green Staffs 168 E4
Buttershaw W Yorks 196 B6
Butterstone Perth 286 C4
Butterton Staffs 168 G4
Butterton Staffs 169 D9
Butterwick Cumb 221 B10
Butterwick Durham 234 F3
Butterwick Lincs 174 G5
Butterwick N Yorks 216 D4
Butterwick N Yorks 217 E9
Butteryhaugh Northumb 250 E4
Butt Green Ches E 167 E11
Buttington Powys 130 B5
Butt Lane Staffs 168 E4
Buttonbridge Shrops 116 B4
Button Haugh Green Suff 125 D9
Buttonoak Worcs 116 B5
Button's Green Suff 125 G8
Butts Devon 14 D2
Buttsash Hants 32 F6
Buttsbear Cross Corn 24 G3
Buttsbury Essex 87 F11
Butts Green Essex 105 E9
Butt's Green Essex 88 E3
Butt's Green Hants 32 B4
Buttsole Kent 55 C10
Butt Yeats Lancs 211 F11
Buxhall Suff 125 F10
Buxhall Fen Street Suff 125 F10
Buxley Borders 272 E6
Buxted E Sus 37 C7
Buxton Derbys 185 G9
Buxton Norf 160 E4
Buxworth Derbys 185 E8
Bwcle / Buckley Flint 166 C3
Bwlch Flint 181 G11
Bwlch Powys 96 G2
Bwlch-derwin Gwyn 163 F7
Bwlchgwyn Wrex 166 E3
Bwlch-Llan Ceredig 111 F11
Bwlchnewydd Carms 93 G7
Bwlch-newydd Carms 93 G7
Bwlchtocyn Gwyn 144 D6
Bwlch-y-cibau Powys 148 F3
Bwlch-y-cwm Cardiff 58 C6
Bwlchyddar Powys 148 E3
Bwlch-y-fadfa Ceredig 93 B8
Bwlch-y-ffridd Powys 129 D11
Bwlchygroes Pembs 92 D4
Bwlchyllyn Gwyn 163 D8
Bwlch-y-Plain Powys 114 B4
Bwlch-y-sarnau Powys 113 C10
Bybrook Kent 54 E4
Bycross Hereford 97 C7
Byeastwood Bridgend 58 C2
Byebush Aberds 303 F7
Bye Green Bucks 84 C5
Byerhope Northumb 232 B3
Byermoor T&W 242 F5
Byers Green Durham 233 E10
Byfield Northants 119 G10
Byfleet Sur 66 G5
Byford Hereford 97 C7
Byford Common Hereford 97 C7
Bygrave Herts 104 D5
Byker T&W 243 E7
Byland Abbey N Yorks 215 D10
Bylchau Conwy 165 C7
Byley Ches W 168 B2
Bynea Carms 56 B4
Byram N Yorks 198 B3
Byrness Northumb 251 C7
Bythorn Cambs 121 B11
Byton Hereford 115 E7
Byton Hand Hereford 115 E7
Bywell Northumb 242 E2
Byworth W Sus 35 C7


## C


Cabbacott Devon 24 C6
Cabbage Hill Brack 65 E11
Cabharstadh W Isles 304 F5
Cabin Shrops 130 F6
Cablea Perth 286 D3
Cabourne Lincs 200 G6
Cabrach Argyll 274 G5
Cabrach Moray 302 G3
Cabrich Highld 300 E5
Cabus Lancs 202 D5
Cackle Hill Lincs 157 D7
Cackleshaw W Yorks 204 F6

Church Green Norf 141 E11
Church Gresley Derbys 152 F5
Church Hanborough Oxon 82 C6
Church Hill Ches W 167 C10
Church Hill Pembs 73 C7
Church Hill Staffs 151 G10
Church Hill W Mid 133 D9
Church Hill Worcs 117 D11
Church Hougham Kent 55 E9
Church Houses N Yorks 226 F3
Churchill Devon 28 G4
Churchill Devon 40 E5
Churchill N Som 44 B2
Churchill Oxon 100 G5
Churchill Worcs 117 B7
Churchill Worcs 117 G8
Churchill Green N Som 60 G2
Churchinford Som 28 E2
Church Knowle Dorset 18 E4
Church Laneham Notts 188 F4
Church Langton Leics 136 E4
Church Lawford Warks 119 B8
Church Lawton Ches E 168 D4
Church Leigh Staffs 151 B10
Church Lench Worcs 117 G10
Church Mayfield Staffs 169 G11
Church Minshull Ches E 167 C11
Churchmoor Rough Shrops 131 F8
Church Norton W Sus 22 D5
Church Oakley Hants 48 C5
Churchover Warks 135 G10
Church Preen Shrops 131 D10
Church Pulverbatch Shrops 131 C8
Churchstanton Som 27 E11
Churchstoke Powys 130 E5
Churchstow Devon 8 F4
Church Stowe Northants 120 F2
Church Street Essex 106 C5
Church Street Kent 69 E8
Church Stretton Shrops 131 E9
Churchton Pembs 73 D10
Churchtown Corn 11 F7
Churchtown Cumb 230 C3
Churchtown Derbys 170 C3
Churchtown Devon 24 G3
Churchtown Devon 41 E7
Churchtown IoM 192 C5
Churchtown Lancs 202 E5
Churchtown Mers 193 D11
Churchtown Shrops 130 F5
Churchtown Som 42 F3
Church Town Corn 4 G3
Church Town Leics 153 F7
Church Town N Lincs 199 F9
Church Town Sur 51 C11
Church Village Rhondda 58 B5
Church Warsop Notts 171 B9
Church Westcote Glos 100 G4
Church Whitfield Kent 55 D10
Church Wilne Derbys 153 C8
Churchwood W Sus 35 D8
Churnet Grange Staffs 169 E7
Churnsike Lodge Northumb 240 B5
Churscombe Torbay 9 C7
Churston Ferrers Torbay 9 D8
Churt Sur 49 F11
Churton Ches W 166 D6
Churwell W Yorks 197 B9
Chute Cadley Wilts 47 C10
Chute Standen Wilts 47 C10
Chweffordd Conwy 180 G4
Chwilog Gwyn 145 B8
Chwitffordd / Whitford Flint 181 F10
Chyandour Corn 1 C5
Chyanvounder Corn 2 E5
Chycoose Corn 3 B8
Chynhale Corn 2 C4
Chynoweth Corn 2 C2
Chyvarloe Corn 2 E5
Cicelyford Mon 79 E8
Cilan Uchaf Gwyn 144 E5
Cilau Pembs 91 D8
Cilcain Flint 165 B11
Cilcennin Ceredig 111 E10
Cilcewydd Powys 130 C4
Cilfor Gwyn 146 B2
Cilfrew Neath 76 E3
Cilfynydd Rhondda 77 G9
Cilgerran Pembs 92 C3
Cilgwyn Carms 94 F4
Cilgwyn Ceredig 92 C6
Cilgwyn Gwyn 163 E7
Cilgwyn Pembs 91 D11
Ciliau Aeron Ceredig 111 F9
Cill Amhlaidh W Isles 297 G3
Cill Donnain W Isles 297 J3
Cille Bhrighde W Isles 297 K3
Cill Eireabhagh W Isles 297 G4
Cille Pheadair W Isles 297 K3
Cilmaengwyn Neath 76 D2
Cilmery Powys 113 G10
Cilsan Carms 93 G11
Ciltalgarth Gwyn 164 G5
Ciltwrch Powys 96 C3
Cilybebyll Neath 76 E2
Cil y coed / Caldicot Mon 60 B3
Cilycwm Carms 94 D5
Cimla Neath 57 B9
Cinderford Glos 79 C11
Cinderhill Derbys 170 F5
Cinderhill Nottingham 171 G8
Cinder Hill Gtr Man 195 F9
Cinder Hill Kent 52 D4
Cinder Hill W Mid 133 E8
Cinder Hill W Sus 36 B5
Cinnamon Brow Warr 183 C10
Cippenham Slough 66 C2
Cippyn Pembs 92 B2
Circebost W Isles 304 E3
Cirencester Glos 81 E8
Ciribhig W Isles 304 D3
City London 67 C10
City Powys 130 F4
City V Glam 58 D3
City Dulas Anglesey 179 D7
Clabhach Argyll 288 D3
Clachaig Argyll 276 E2
Clachaig Highld 292 B2
Clachaig N Ayrs 255 E10
Clachan Argyll 255 B8
Clachan Argyll 275 B8
Clachan Argyll 284 F5
Clachan Argyll 289 E10
Clachan Highld 295 B7
Clachan Highld 298 C4
Clachan Highld 307 L6
Clachan W Isles 297 G3
Clachaneasy Dumfries 236 B5
Clachanmore Dumfries 236 E2
Clachan na Luib W Isles 296 E4
Clachan of Campsie E Dunb 278 F2
Clachan of Glendaruel Argyll 275 E10
Clachan-Seil Argyll 275 B8
Clachan Strachur Argyll 284 G4
Clachbreck Argyll 275 F8
Clachnabrain Angus 292 G5
Clachtoll Highld 307 G5
Clackmannan Clack 279 C8
Clackmarras Moray 302 D2
Clacton-on-Sea Essex 89 B11
Cladach N Ayrs 256 B2
Cladach Chairinis W Isles 296 F4
Cladach Chireboist W Isles 296 E3
Claddach Argyll 254 B2
Claddach-knockline W Isles 296 E3
Cladich Argyll 284 E4
Cladich Steading Argyll 284 E4
Cladswell Worcs 117 F10
Claggan Highld 289 E8
Claggan Highld 290 F3
Claggan Perth 285 D11
Claigan Highld 298 D2
Claines Worcs 117 F7
Clandown Bath 45 B7
Clanfield Hants 33 D11
Clanfield Oxon 82 E3
Clanking Bucks 84 D4
Clanville Hants 47 D10
Clanville Som 44 G6
Clanville Wilts 62 D2
Claonaig Argyll 255 B9
Claonel Highld 309 J5
Clapgate Dorset 31 G8
Clapgate Herts 105 G8
Clapham Beds 121 G10
Clapham Devon 14 D3
Clapham London 67 D9
Clapham N Yorks 212 F4
Clapham W Sus 35 F9
Clapham Green Beds 121 G10
Clapham Green N Yorks 205 B10
Clapham Hill Kent 70 G6
Clapham Park London 67 E9
Clap Hill Kent 54 F5
Clapper Corn 10 G6
Clapper Hill Kent 53 F10
Clappers Borders 273 D8
Clappersgate Cumb 221 E7
Clapphoull Shetland 313 L6
Clapton Som 28 F6
Clapton Som 44 C6
Clapton W Berks 63 E11
Clapton in Gordano N Som 60 E3
Clapton-on-the-Hill Glos 81 B11
Clapton Park London 67 B11
Clapworthy Devon 25 C11
Clarach Ceredig 128 G2
Clarack Aberds 292 D6
Clara Vale T&W 242 E4
Clarbeston Pembs 91 G10
Clarbeston Road Pembs 91 G10
Clarborough Notts 188 E2
Clardon Highld 310 C5
Clare Oxon 83 F11
Clare Suff 106 B5
Clarebrand Dumfries 237 C9
Claregate W Mid 133 C7
Claremont Park Sur 66 G6
Claremount W Yorks 196 B5
Clarencefield Dumfries 238 D3
Clarence Park N Som 59 G10
Clarendon Park Leicester 135 C11
Clareston Pembs 73 C7
Clarilaw Borders 262 D3
Clarilaw Borders 262 F2
Clarken Green Hants 48 C5
Clark Green Ches E 184 F6
Clarksfield Gtr Man 196 G2
Clark's Green Sur 51 F7
Clark's Hill Lincs 157 E7
Clarkston E Renf 267 D11
Clarkston N Lnrk 268 B5
Clase Swansea 57 B7
Clashandorran Highld 300 E5
Clashcoig Highld 309 K6
Clasheddy Highld 308 C6
Clashgour Argyll 284 C6
Clashindarroch Aberds 302 F4
Clashmore Highld 306 F5
Clashmore Highld 309 L7
Clashnessie Highld 306 F5
Clashnoir Moray 302 G2
Clate Shetland 313 G7
Clatford Wilts 63 F7
Clatford Oakcuts Hants 47 F10
Clathy Perth 286 F3
Clatt Aberds 302 G5
Clatter Powys 129 E9
Clatterford IoW 20 D5
Clatterford End Essex 87 C10
Clatterford End Essex 87 D9
Clatterford End Essex 87 E8
Clatterin Bridge Aberds 293 F8
Clatto Fife 287 F8
Clatworthy Som 42 G5
Clauchlands N Ayrs 256 C2
Claughton Lancs 202 E6
Claughton Lancs 211 F11
Claughton Mers 182 D4
Clavelshay Som 43 G9
Claverdon Warks 118 E3
Claverham N Som 60 F2
Claverhambury Essex 86 E6
Clavering Essex 105 E9
Claverley Shrops 132 E5
Claverton Bath 61 G9
Claverton Down Bath 61 G9
Clawdd-côch V Glam 58 D5
Clawdd-newydd Denb 165 E9
Clawdd Poncen Denb 165 G9
Clawthorpe Cumb 211 D10
Clawton Devon 12 B3
Claxby Lincs 189 C10
Claxby Lincs 191 G7
Claxby St Andrew Lincs 191 G7
Claxton Norf 142 C6
Claxton N Yorks 216 G3
Claybokie Aberds 292 D2
Claybrooke Magna Leics 135 F9
Claybrooke Parva Leics 135 F9
Clay Common Suff 143 G9
Clay Coton Northants 119 B11
Clay Cross Derbys 170 C5
Claydon Glos 99 E8
Claydon Oxon 119 G9
Claydon Suff 126 G2
Clay End Herts 104 F6
Claygate Dumfries 239 B9
Claygate Kent 52 C6
Claygate Kent 53 E8
Claygate Sur 67 G7
Claygate Cross Kent 52 B6
Clayhall Hants 21 B8
Clayhall London 86 G6
Clayhanger Devon 27 C8
Clayhanger Som 28 E4
Clayhanger W Mid 133 C10
Clayhidon Devon 27 D11
Clayhill E Sus 38 C4
Clayhill Hants 32 F4
Clay Hill Bristol 60 E6
Clay Hill London 86 F4
Clay Hill W Berks 64 E5
Clayhithe Cambs 123 E10
Clayholes Angus 287 D9
Clay Lake Lincs 156 E5
Clayland Stirl 277 D11
Clay Mills Derbys 152 D5
Clayock Highld 310 D5
Claypit Hill Cambs 123 G7
Claypits Devon 27 B7
Claypits Glos 80 D3
Claypits Kent 55 B9
Claypits Suff 140 G4
Claypole Lincs 172 F5
Clays End Bath 61 G8
Claythorpe Lincs 190 F6
Clayton Gtr Man 184 B5
Clayton Staffs 168 G5
Clayton S Yorks 198 F3
Clayton W Sus 36 E3
Clayton W Yorks 205 G8
Clayton Brook Lancs 194 C5
Clayton Green Lancs 194 C5
Clayton Heights W Yorks 205 G8
Clayton-le-Dale Lancs 203 G9
Clayton-le-Moors Lancs 203 G10
Clayton-le-Woods Lancs 194 C5
Clayton West W Yorks 197 E9
Clayworth Notts 188 D2
Cleadale Highld 294 G6
Cleadon T&W 243 E9
Cleadon Park T&W 243 E9
Clearbrook Devon 7 B10
Clearwell Glos 79 D9
Clearwell Newport 59 B9
Clearwood Wilts 45 D10
Cleasby N Yorks 224 C5
Cleat Orkney 314 B4
Cleat Orkney 314 H4
Cleatlam Durham 224 B2
Cleator Cumb 219 C10
Cleator Moor Cumb 219 B10
Cleave Devon 28 G2
Clebrig Highld 308 F5
Cleckheaton W Yorks 197 B7
Cleddon Mon 79 E8
Cleedownton Shrops 131 G11
Cleehill Shrops 115 B11
Cleekhimin N Lnrk 268 D5
Cleemarsh Shrops 131 G11
Clee St Margaret Shrops 131 G11
Cleestanton Shrops 115 B11
Cleethorpes NE Lincs 201 F10
Cleeton St Mary Shrops 116 B2
Cleeve Glos 80 C2
Cleeve N Som 60 F3
Cleeve Oxon 64 C6
Cleeve Hill Glos 99 F9
Cleeve Prior Worcs 99 B11
Cleghorn S Lnrk 269 F8
Clegyrnant Powys 129 B8
Clehonger Hereford 97 D9
Cleirwy / Clyro Powys 96 C4
Cleish Perth 279 B11
Cleland N Lnrk 268 D5
Clements End Glos 79 D9
Clement's End C Beds 85 B8
Clement Street Kent 68 E4
Clench Wilts 63 G7
Clench Common Wilts 63 F7
Clencher's Mill Hereford 98 D4
Clenchwarton Norf 157 E11
Clennell Northumb 251 B10
Clent Worcs 117 B8
Cleobury Mortimer Shrops 116 B3
Cleobury North Shrops 132 F2
Cleongart Argyll 255 D7
Clephanton Highld 301 D8
Clerkenwater Corn 5 B11
Clerkenwell London 67 C10
Clerk Green W Yorks 197 C8
Clerklands Borders 262 E2
Clermiston Edin 280 G3
Clestrain Orkney 314 F3
Cleuch Head Borders 262 G3
Cleughbrae Dumfries 238 C3
Clevancy Wilts 62 D5
Clevans Renfs 267 B7
Clevedon N Som 60 E2
Cleveley Oxon 101 G7
Cleveleys Lancs 202 E2
Cleverton Wilts 62 B3
Clevis Bridgend 57 F10
Clewer Som 44 C2
Clewer Green Windsor 66 D2
Clewer New Town Windsor 66 D3
Clewer Village Windsor 66 D3
Cley next the Sea Norf 177 E8
Cliaid W Isles 297 L2
Cliasmol W Isles 305 H2
Cliburn Cumb 231 G7
Click Mill Orkney 314 D3
Cliddesden Hants 48 D6
Cliff Derbys 185 D8
Cliff Warks 134 D4
Cliffburn Angus 287 C10
Cliffe Lancs 203 G10
Cliffe Medway 69 D8
Cliffe N Yorks 207 G9
Cliffe N Yorks 224 B4
Cliff End E Sus 38 E5
Cliff End W Yorks 196 D6
Cliffe Woods Medway 69 E8
Clifford Devon 24 C4
Clifford Hereford 96 B4
Clifford W Yorks 206 E4
Clifford Chambers Warks 118 G3
Clifford's Mesne Glos 98 G4
Cliffs End Kent 71 G10
Clifftown Sthend 69 B11
Clifton Bristol 60 E5
Clifton C Beds 104 D3
Clifton Ches W 183 F8
Clifton Cumb 230 F6
Clifton Derbys 169 G11
Clifton Devon 40 E5
Clifton Gtr Man 195 G9
Clifton Lancs 202 G5
Clifton Northumb 252 G6
Clifton Nottingham 153 C11
Clifton N Yorks 205 D9
Clifton Oxon 101 E9
Clifton Stirl 285 D7
Clifton S Yorks 186 C6
Clifton S Yorks 187 B8
Clifton Worcs 98 B6
Clifton W Yorks 197 C7
Clifton York 207 C7
Clifton Campville Staffs 152 G5
Cliftoncote Borders 263 E8
Clifton Green Gtr Man 195 G9
Clifton Hampden Oxon 83 F8
Clifton Junction Gtr Man 195 G9
Clifton Manor C Beds 104 D3
Clifton Maybank Dorset 29 E9
Clifton Moor York 207 B7
Clifton Reynes M Keynes 121 G8
Clifton upon Dunsmore Warks 119 B10
Clifton upon Teme Worcs 116 E4
Cliftonville Kent 71 E11
Cliftonville N Lnrk 268 B4
Cliftonville Norf 160 B6
Climping W Sus 35 G8
Climpy S Lnrk 269 D8
Clink Som 45 D9
Clinkham Wood Mers 183 B8
Clint N Yorks 205 B11
Clint Green Norf 159 G10
Clintmains Borders 262 C4
Clints N Yorks 224 E2
Cliobh W Isles 304 E2
Clipiau Gwyn 146 G6
Clippesby Norf 161 G8
Clippings Green Norf 159 G10
Clipsham Rutland 155 F9
Clipston Northants 136 G4
Clipston Notts 154 C2
Clipstone C Beds 103 F8
Clitheroe Lancs 203 E10
Cliuthar W Isles 305 J3
Clive Ches W 167 B11
Clive Shrops 149 E10
Clive Green Ches W 167 C11
Clive Vale E Sus 38 E4
Clivocast Shetland 312 C8
Clixby Lincs 200 G6
Cloatley Wilts 81 G7
Cloatley End Wilts 81 G7
Clocaenog Denb 165 E9
Clochan Aberds 303 E9
Clochan Moray 302 C4
Clock Face Mers 183 C8
Clock House London 67 G9
Clockmill Borders 272 E5
Clock Mills Hereford 96 B5
Cloddiau Powys 130 B4
Cloddymoss Moray 301 D9
Clodock Hereford 96 F6
Cloford Som 45 E8
Cloford Common Som 45 E8
Cloigyn Carms 74 C6
Clola Aberds 303 E10
Clophill C Beds 103 D11
Clopton Northants 137 G11
Clopton Suff 126 G4
Clopton Corner Suff 126 G4
Clopton Green Suff 124 G5
Clopton Green Suff 125 E9
Closeburn Dumfries 247 E9
Close Clark IoM 192 E3
Close House Durham 233 F10
Closworth Som 29 E9
Clothall Herts 104 E5
Clothall Common Herts 104 E5
Clotton Ches W 167 C8
Clotton Common Ches W 167 C8
Cloudesley Bush Warks 135 F9
Clouds Hereford 97 D11
Cloud Side Staffs 168 C6
Clough Gtr Man 196 D2
Clough Gtr Man 196 F2
Clough W Yorks 196 E5
Clough Dene Durham 242 F5
Cloughfold Lancs 195 C10
Clough Foot W Yorks 196 C2
Clough Hall Staffs 168 E4
Clough Head W Yorks 196 C5
Cloughton N Yorks 227 G10
Cloughton Newlands N Yorks 227 F10
Clounlaid Highld 289 D9
Clousta Shetland 313 H5
Clouston Orkney 314 E2
Clova Aberds 302 G4
Clova Angus 292 F5
Clovelly Devon 24 C4
Clove Lodge Durham 223 B8
Clovenfords Borders 261 B10
Clovenstone Aberds 293 B9
Cloves Moray 301 C11
Clovullin Highld 290 G2
Clowance Wood Corn 2 C4
Clow Bridge Lancs 195 B10
Clowne Derbys 187 F7
Clows Top Worcs 116 C4
Cloy Wrex 166 G5
Cluanie Inn Highld 290 B2
Cluanie Lodge Highld 290 B2
Clubmoor Mers 182 C5
Clubworthy Corn 11 C11
Cluddley Telford 150 G2
Clun Shrops 130 G6
Clunbury Shrops 131 G7
Clunderwen Carms 73 B10
Clune Highld 301 D9
Clune Highld 301 G7
Clunes Highld 290 E4
Clungunford Shrops 115 B7
Clunie Aberds 302 D6
Clunie Perth 286 C5
Clunton Shrops 130 G6
Cluny Fife 280 B4
Cluny Castle Aberds 293 B8
Cluny Castle Highld 291 D8
Clutton Bath 44 B6
Clutton Ches W 167 E7
Clutton Hill Bath 44 B6
Clwt-grugoer Conwy 165 C7
Clwt-y-bont Gwyn 163 C9
Clwydyfagwyr M Tydf 77 D8
Clydach Mon 78 C2
Clydach Swansea 75 E11
Clydach Terrace Powys 77 C11
Clydach Vale Rhondda 77 G7
Clydebank W Dunb 277 G9
Clyffe Pypard Wilts 62 D5
Clynder Argyll 276 E4
Clyne Neath 76 E4
Clynelish Highld 311 J2
Clynnog-fawr Gwyn 162 F6
Clyro / Cleirwy Powys 96 C4
Clyst Honiton Devon 14 C5
Clyst Hydon Devon 27 G8
Clyst St George Devon 14 D5
Clyst St Lawrence Devon 27 G8
Clyst St Mary Devon 14 C5
Cnip W Isles 304 E2
Cnoc Amhlaigh W Isles 304 E7
Cnoc an t-Solais W Isles 304 D6
Cnocbreac Argyll 274 F5
Cnoc Fhionn Highld 295 D10
Cnoc Màiri W Isles 304 E6
Cnoc Rolum W Isles 296 F3
Cnwch-coch Ceredig 112 B3
Coachford Aberds 302 E4
Coad's Green Corn 11 F11
Coal Aston Derbys 186 F5
Coal Bank Darl 234 G3
Coalbrookdale Telford 132 C3
Coalbrookvale Bl Gwent 77 D11
Coalburn S Lnrk 259 C8
Coalburns T&W 242 E4
Coalcleugh Northumb 232 B2
Coaley Glos 80 E3
Coaley Peak Glos 80 E3
Coalford Aberds 293 D10
Coalhall E Ayrs 257 F10
Coalhill Essex 88 F3
Coalmoor Telford 132 B3
Coalpit Field Warks 135 F7
Coalpit Heath S Glos 61 C7
Coalpit Hill Staffs 168 E4
Coal Pool W Mid 133 C10
Coalport Telford 132 C3
Coalsnaughton Clack 279 B8
Coaltown of Balgonie Fife 280 B5
Coaltown of Wemyss Fife 280 B6
Coalville Leics 153 G8
Coalway Glos 79 C9
Coanwood Northumb 240 F5
Coarsewell Devon 8 E4
Coat Som 29 C7
Coatbridge N Lnrk 268 C4
Coatdyke N Lnrk 268 C5
Coate Swindon 63 C7
Coate Wilts 62 G4
Coates Cambs 138 D6
Coates Glos 81 E7
Coates Lancs 204 D3
Coates Lincs 188 E6
Coates Midloth 270 C4
Coates Notts 188 E4
Coates W Sus 35 D7
Coatham Redcar 235 F7
Coatham Mundeville Darl 233 G11
Coatsgate Dumfries 248 B3
Cobairdy Aberds 302 E5
Cobbaton Devon 25 B10
Cobbler's Corner Worcs 116 F5
Cobbler's Green Norf 142 E5
Cobbler's Plain Mon 79 E7
Cobbs Warr 183 D10
Cobb's Cross Glos 98 E5
Cobbs Fenn Essex 106 E5
Cobby Syke N Yorks 205 B9
Coberley Glos 81 B7
Cobhall Common Hereford 97 D9
Cobham Kent 69 F7
Cobham Sur 66 G6
Cobleland Stirl 277 B10
Cobler's Green Essex 87 B11
Cobley Dorset 31 C8
Cobley Hill Worcs 117 C10
Cobnash Hereford 115 E9
Cobridge Stoke 168 F5
Cobscot Shrops 150 B3
Coburty Aberds 303 C9
Cockadilly Glos 80 E4
Cock Alley Derbys 186 G6
Cock and End Suff 124 G4
Cockayne N Yorks 226 F2
Cock Bank Wrex 166 F5
Cock Bevington Warks 117 G11
Cock Bridge Aberds 292 C4
Cockburnspath Borders 282 G5
Cock Clarks Essex 88 E4
Cockden Lancs 204 G3
Cockenzie and Port Seton E Loth 281 F8
Cocker Bar Lancs 194 C4
Cockerham Lancs 202 C5
Cockermouth Cumb 229 E8
Cockernhoe Herts 104 G2
Cockernhoe Green Herts 104 G2
Cockersdale W Yorks 197 B8
Cockerton Darl 224 B5
Cockett Swansea 56 C6
Cocketty Aberds 293 F9
Cockfield Durham 233 G8
Cockfield Suff 125 G8
Cockfosters London 86 F3
Cock Gate Hereford 115 D9
Cock Green Essex 87 B11
Cockhill Som 44 G6
Cock Hill N Yorks 206 B6
Cocking W Sus 34 D5
Cocking Causeway W Sus 34 D5
Cockington Torbay 9 C7
Cocklake Som 44 D2
Cocklaw Northumb 241 C10
Cockleford Glos 81 C7
Cockley Beck Cumb 220 E4
Cockley Cley Norf 140 C5
Cockley Hill W Yorks 197 D7
Cock Marling E Sus 38 D5
Cocknowle Dorset 18 E4
Cockpole Green Wokingham 65 C9
Cocks Corn 4 E5
Cocks Green Suff 125 F7
Cockshead Ceredig 112 F2
Cockshoot Hereford 97 D11
Cockshutford Shrops 131 F11
Cockshutt Shrops 132 G4
Cockshutt Shrops 149 D8
Cock Street Kent 53 C9
Cock Street Suff 107 D9
Cockthorpe Norf 177 E7
Cockwells Corn 2 C2
Cockwood Devon 14 E5
Cockwood Som 43 E8
Cockyard Derbys 185 F8
Cockyard Hereford 97 E8
Codda Corn 11 F9
Coddenham Suff 126 G2
Coddenham Green Suff 126 F2
Coddington Ches W 167 D7
Coddington Hereford 98 C4
Coddington Notts 172 E4
Codford St Mary Wilts 46 F3
Codford St Peter Wilts 46 F3
Codicote Herts 86 B2
Codicote Bottom Herts 86 B2
Codmore Bucks 85 E7
Codmore Hill W Sus 35 C9
Codnor Derbys 170 F6
Codnor Breach Derbys 170 F6
Codnor Gate Derbys 170 E6
Codnor Park Derbys 170 E6
Codrington S Glos 61 D8
Codsall Staffs 133 C7
Codsall Wood Staffs 132 B6
Codsend Som 41 F11
Coedcae Bl Gwent 77 D11
Coedcae Torf 78 D3
Coed Cwnwr Mon 78 F6
Coedely Rhondda 58 B4
Coed Eva Torf 78 G3
Coedkernew Newport 59 C9
Coed Llai / Leeswood Flint 166 D3
Coed Mawr Gwyn 179 G9
Coed Morgan Mon 78 C5
Coedpoeth Wrex 166 E3
Coed-Talon Flint 166 D3
Coedway Powys 148 G6
Coed-y-bryn Ceredig 93 C7
Coed-y-caerau Newport 78 G5
Coed-y-fedw Mon 78 D6
Coed y Garth Ceredig 128 E3
Coed y go Shrops 148 D5
Coed-y-paen Mon 78 F4
Coed-y-parc Gwyn 163 B10
Coed-yr-ynys Powys 96 G3
Coed Ystumgwern Gwyn 145 E11
Coed-y-wlad Powys 130 B4
Coelbren Powys 76 C4
Coffee Hall M Keynes 103 D7
Coffinswell Devon 9 B7
Cofton Devon 14 E5
Cofton Common W Mid 117 B10
Cofton Hackett Worcs 117 B10
Cog V Glam 59 F7
Cogan V Glam 59 E7
Cogenhoe Northants 120 E6
Cogges Oxon 82 D5
Coggeshall Essex 106 G6
Coggeshall Hamlet Essex 107 G7
Coggins Mill E Sus 37 B9
Coignafearn Lodge Highld 291 B8
Coignascallan Highld 291 B9
Coig Peighinnean W Isles 304 B7
Coig Peighinnean Bhuirgh W Isles 304 C6
Coilacriech Aberds 292 D5
Coilantogle Stirl 285 G9
Coilessan Argyll 284 G6
Coilleag W Isles 297 K3
Coillemore Highld 300 B6
Coillore Highld 294 B5
Coirea-chrombe Stirl 285 G9
Coisley Hill S Yorks 186 E6
Coity Bridgend 58 C2
Cokenach Herts 105 D7
Cokhay Green Derbys 152 D5
Col W Isles 304 D6
Colaboll Highld 309 H5
Colan Corn 5 C7
Colaton Raleigh Devon 15 D7
Colbost Highld 298 E2
Colburn N Yorks 224 F3
Colby Cumb 231 G9
Colby IoM 192 E3
Colby Norf 160 C4
Colchester Essex 107 F10
Colchester Green Suff 125 F8
Colcot V Glam 58 F6
Cold Ash W Berks 64 F4
Cold Ashby Northants 120 B3
Cold Ash Hill Hants 49 G10
Cold Ashton S Glos 61 E9
Cold Aston Glos 81 B10
Coldbackie Highld 308 D6
Coldbeck Cumb 222 E4
Coldblow London 68 E4
Cold Blow Pembs 73 C10
Cold Brayfield M Keynes 121 G8
Coldbrook Powys 96 D3
Cold Christmas Herts 86 B5
Cold Cotes N Yorks 212 E4
Coldean Brighton 36 F4
Coldeast Devon 14 G2
Coldeaton Derbys 169 D10
Cold Elm Glos 98 E6
Colden W Yorks 196 B3
Colden Common Hants 33 C7
Coldfair Green Suff 127 E8
Coldham Cambs 139 C8
Coldham Staffs 133 B7
Coldham's Common Cambs 123 F9
Cold Hanworth Lincs 189 E8
Coldharbour Corn 4 F5
Coldharbour Devon 27 E9
Coldharbour Dorset 17 E9
Coldharbour Glos 79 E9
Coldharbour Kent 52 C5
Coldharbour London 68 D4
Coldharbour Sur 50 E6
Cold Harbour Dorset 18 D4
Cold Harbour Herts 85 B10
Cold Harbour Kent 69 G11
Cold Harbour Lincs 155 C9
Cold Harbour Oxon 64 D6
Cold Harbour Wilts 45 B11
Cold Harbour Wilts 45 D11
Cold Harbour Windsor 65 D10
Cold Hatton Telford 150 E2
Cold Hatton Heath Telford 150 E2
Cold Hesledon Durham 234 B4
Cold Hiendley W Yorks 197 E11
Cold Higham Northants 120 G3
Coldingham Borders 273 B8
Cold Inn Pembs 73 D10
Cold Kirby N Yorks 215 C10
Coldmeece Staffs 151 C7
Cold Moss Heath Ches E 168 C3
Cold Newton Leics 136 B4
Cold Northcott Corn 11 D10
Cold Norton Essex 88 E4
Coldoch Stirl 278 B3
Cold Overton Leics 154 G6
Coldra Newport 59 B11
Coldrain Perth 286 G4
Coldred Kent 55 D9
Coldridge Devon 25 F11
Cold Row Lancs 202 E3
Coldstream Angus 287 D7
Coldstream Borders 263 B8
Coldvreath Corn 5 D9
Coldwaltham W Sus 35 D8
Cold Well Staffs 151 G11
Coldwells Aberds 303 E11
Coldwells Croft Aberds 302 G5
Cole Som 45 G7
Colebatch Shrops 130 F6
Colebrook Devon 27 F8
Colebrooke Devon 13 B11
Coleburn Moray 302 D2
Coleby Lincs 173 C7
Coleby N Lincs 199 D11
Cole End Essex 105 D11
Cole End Warks 134 F3
Coleford Devon 26 G3
Coleford Glos 79 C9
Coleford Som 45 D7
Coleford Water Som 42 G6
Colegate End Norf 142 F3
Cole Green Herts 86 C3
Cole Green Herts 105 E8
Colehall W Mid 134 F2
Cole Henley Hants 48 C3
Colehill Dorset 31 G8
Coleman Green Herts 85 C11
Coleman's Hatch E Sus 52 G3
Colemere Shrops 149 C8
Colemore Hants 49 G8
Colemore Green Shrops 132 D4
Coleorton Leics 153 F8
Coleorton Moor Leics 153 F8
Cole Park London 67 E7
Colerne Wilts 61 E10
Colesbourne Glos 81 C7
Colesbrook Dorset 30 B4
Cole's Cross Dorset 28 G5
Colesden Beds 122 F2
Coles Green Suff 107 C11
Coles Green Worcs 116 G5
Cole's Green Suff 126 E5
Coleshill Bucks 85 F7
Coleshill Oxon 82 G2
Coleshill Warks 134 F4
Coles Meads Sur 51 C9
Colestocks Devon 27 G9
Colethrop Glos 80 C4
Coley Bath 44 B5
Coley Reading 65 E8
Coley W Yorks 196 B6
Colfin Dumfries 236 D2
Colgate W Sus 51 G8
Colgrain Argyll 276 E6
Colham Green London 66 C5
Colindale London 67 B8
Colinsburgh Fife 287 G8
Colinton Edin 270 B4
Colintraive Argyll 275 F11
Colkirk Norf 159 D8
Collace Perth 286 D6
Collafield Glos 79 C11
Collafirth Shetland 312 G6
Collam W Isles 305 J3
Collamoor Head Corn 11 C9
Collaton Devon 9 G9

Craigshall Dumfries 237 D10
Craigshill W Loth 269 B11
Craigside Durham 233 D8
Craigston Castle Aberds 303 D7
Craigton Aberdeen 293 C10
Craigton Angus 287 B7
Craigton Angus 287 D9
Craigton Glasgow 267 C10
Craigton Highld 300 E6
Craigton Highld 309 H6
Craigton Highld 309 K6
Craigtown Highld 310 D2
Craig-y-don Conwy 180 E3
Craig-y-Duke Swansea 76 E2
Craig-y-nos Powys 76 B4
Craig-y-penrhyn Ceredig 128 E3
Craig-y-Rhacca Caerph 59 B7
Craik Borders 249 B8
Crail Fife 287 G10
Crailing Borders 262 E5
Crailinghall Borders 262 E5
Crakaig Highld 311 H3
Crakehill N Yorks 215 E8
Crakemarsh Staffs 151 B11
Crambe N Yorks 216 G4
Crambeck N Yorks 216 F4
Cramhurst Sur 50 E2
Cramlington Northumb 243 B7
Cramond Edin 280 F3
Cramond Bridge Edin 280 F3
Crampmoor Hants 32 C5
Cranage Ches E 168 B3
Cranberry Staffs 150 B6
Cranborne Dorset 31 E9
Cranbourne Brack 66 E2
Cranbourne Hants 48 C6
Cranbrook Kent 53 F9
Cranbrook London 68 B2
Cranbrook Common Kent 53 F9
Crane Moor S Yorks 197 G10
Crane's Corner Norf 159 G8
Cranfield C Beds 103 C9
Cranford Devon 24 C4
Cranford London 66 D6
Cranford St Andrew Northants 121 B8
Cranford St John Northants 121 B8
Cranham Glos 80 C5
Cranham London 68 B5
Cranhill Glasgow 268 B2
Cranhill Warks 118 G2
Crank Mers 183 B8
Crankwood Gtr Man 194 G6
Crank Wood Gtr Man 194 G6
Cranleigh Sur 50 F5
Cranley Suff 126 C3
Cranley Gardens London 67 B9
Cranmer Green Suff 125 C10
Cranmore IoW 20 D3
Cranmore Som 45 E7
Cranna Aberds 302 D6
Crannich Argyll 289 E7
Crannoch Moray 302 D4
Cranoe Leics 136 D5
Cransford Suff 126 E6
Cranshaws Borders 272 C3
Cranstal IoM 192 B5
Cranswick E Yorks 208 C6
Crantock Corn 4 C5
Cranwell Lincs 173 F8
Cranwich Norf 140 E5
Cranworth Norf 141 C9
Craobh Haven Argyll 275 C8
Crapstone Devon 7 B10
Crarae Argyll 275 D10
Crask Highld 308 C7
Crask Inn Highld 309 G5
Craskins Aberds 293 C7
Crask of Aigas Highld 300 E4
Craster Northumb 265 F7
Craswall Hereford 96 D5
Crateford Shrops 132 F4
Crateford Staffs 133 B8
Cratfield Suff 126 B6
Crathes Aberds 293 D9
Crathie Aberds 292 D4
Crathie Highld 291 D7
Crathorne N Yorks 225 D8
Craven Arms Shrops 131 G8
Crawcrook T&W 242 E4
Crawford Lancs 194 G3
Crawford S Lnrk 259 E11
Crawforddyke S Lnrk 269 F7
Crawfordjohn S Lnrk 259 E9
Crawick Dumfries 259 G7
Crawley Devon 28 F3
Crawley Hants 48 G2
Crawley Oxon 82 C4
Crawley W Sus 51 F9
Crawley Down W Sus 51 F10
Crawley End Essex 105 C8
Crawley Hill Sur 65 G11
Crawleyside Durham 232 C5
Crawshaw W Yorks 197 E8
Crawshawbooth Lancs 195 B10
Crawton Aberds 293 F10
Cray N Yorks 213 D8
Cray Perth 292 G3
Crayford London 68 E4
Crayke N Yorks 215 E11
Craymere Beck Norf 159 C11
Crays Hill Essex 88 G2
Cray's Pond Oxon 64 C6
Crazies Hill Wokingham 65 C9
Creacombe Devon 26 D4
Creagan Argyll 289 E11
Creagan Sithe Argyll 284 G6
Creag Aoil Highld 290 F3
Creagastrom W Isles 297 G4
Creag Ghoraidh W Isles 297 G3
Creaguaineach Lodge Highld 290 G5
Creaksea Essex 88 F6
Creamore Bank Shrops 149 C10
Crean Corn 1 E3
Creaton Northants 120 C4
Creca Dumfries 238 C6
Credenhill Hereford 97 C9
Crediton Devon 26 G4
Creebridge Dumfries 236 C6
Creech Dorset 18 E4
Creech Bottom Dorset 18 E4
Creech Heathfield Som 28 B3
Creech St Michael Som 28 B3
Creed Corn 5 F8
Creediknowe Shetland 312 G7
Creegbrawse Corn 4 G4
Creekmoor Poole 18 C6
Creekmouth London 68 C3
Creeksea Essex 88 F6
Creeting Bottoms Suff 126 F2
Creeting St Mary Suff 125 F11
Creeton Lincs 155 E10
Creetown Dumfries 236 D6
Creggans Argyll 284 G4
Cregneash IoM 192 F2
Creg-ny-Baa IoM 192 D4
Cregrina Powys 114 G2
Creich Fife 287 E7
Creigau Mon 79 F7
Creighton Staffs 151 B11
Creigiau Cardiff 58 C5
Crelly Corn 2 C5
Cremyll Corn 7 E9
Crendell Dorset 31 E9
Crepkill Highld 298 E4
Creslow Bucks 102 G6
Cressage Shrops 131 C11
Cressbrook Derbys 185 G11
Cresselly Pembs 73 D9
Cressex Bucks 84 G4
Cress Green Glos 80 E3
Cressing Essex 106 G5
Cresswell Northumb 253 E7
Cresswell Staffs 151 B9
Cresswell Quay Pembs 73 D9
Creswell Derbys 187 G8
Creswell Staffs 151 D7
Creswell Staffs 151 D8
Creswell Green Staffs 151 G11
Cretingham Suff 126 E4
Cretshengan Argyll 275 G8
Creunant / Crynant Neath 76 E3
Crewe Ches E 168 D2
Crewe Ches W 166 E6
Crewe-by-Farndon Ches W 166 E6
Crewgarth Cumb 231 E8
Crewgreen Powys 148 F6
Crewkerne Som 28 F6
Crews Hill London 86 F4
Crew's Hole Bristol 60 E6
Crewton Derby 153 C7
Crianlarich Stirl 285 E7
Cribbs Causeway S Glos 60 C5
Cribden Side Lancs 195 C9
Cribyn Ceredig 111 G10
Criccieth Gwyn 145 B9
Crich Derbys 170 E5
Crich Carr Derbys 170 E4
Crichie Aberds 303 E9
Crichton Midloth 271 C7
Crick Mon 79 G7
Crick Northants 119 C11
Crickadarn Powys 95 C11
Cricket Hill Hants 65 G10
Cricket Malherbie Som 28 E5
Cricket St Thomas Som 28 F5
Crickham Som 44 D2
Crickheath Shrops 148 E5
Crickheath Wharf Shrops 148 E5
Crickhowell Powys 78 B2
Cricklade Wilts 81 G10
Cricklewood London 67 B8
Crickmery Shrops 150 D3
Crick's Green Hereford 116 G2
Criddlestyle Hants 31 E11
Cridling Stubbs N Yorks 198 C4
Cridmore IoW 20 E5
Crieff Perth 286 E2
Criggan Corn 5 C10
Criggion Powys 148 F5
Crigglestone W Yorks 197 D10
Crimble Gtr Man 195 E11
Crimchard Som 28 F4
Crimdon Park Durham 234 D5
Crimond Aberds 303 D10
Crimonmogate Aberds 303 D10
Crimp Corn 24 D3
Crimplesham Norf 140 C3
Crimscote Warks 100 B4
Crinan Argyll 275 D8
Crinan Ferry Argyll 275 D8
Crindau Newport 59 B10
Crindledyke N Lnrk 268 D6
Cringleford Norf 142 B3
Cringles W Yorks 204 D6
Cringletie Borders 270 G4
Crinow Pembs 73 C10
Cripple Corner Essex 107 E7
Cripplesease Corn 2 B2
Cripplestyle Dorset 31 E9
Cripp's Corner E Sus 38 C3
Crispie Argyll 275 F10
Crist Derbys 185 E8
Critchell's Green Hants 32 B3
Critchill Som 45 D9
Critchmere Sur 49 G11
Crit Hall Kent 53 G9
Crizeley Hereford 97 E8
Croanford Corn 10 G6
Croasdale Cumb 219 B11
Crobeag W Isles 304 F5
Crockenhill Kent 68 F4
Crocker End Oxon 65 B8
Crockerhill Hants 33 F9
Crockerhill W Sus 22 B6
Crockernwell Devon 13 C11
Crockers Devon 40 F5
Crocker's Ash Hereford 79 B8
Crockerton Wilts 45 E11
Crockerton Green Wilts 45 E11
Crocketford or Ninemile Bar Dumfries 237 B10
Crockey Hill York 207 D8
Crockham Heath W Berks 64 G2
Crockham Hill Kent 52 C2
Crockhurst Street Kent 52 E6
Crockleford Heath Essex 107 F10
Crockleford Hill Essex 107 F10
Crockness Orkney 314 G3
Crock Street Som 28 E4
Croesau Bach Shrops 148 D4
Croeserw Neath 57 B11
Croes-goch Pembs 87 E11
Croes-Hywel Mon 78 C4
Croes-lan Ceredig 93 C7
Croes Llanfair Mon 78 D4
Croesor Gwyn 163 G10
Croespenmaen Caerph 77 F11
Croes-wian Flint 181 G10
Croesyceiliog Carms 74 B6
Croesyceiliog Torf 78 F4
Croes-y-mwyalch Torf 78 G4
Croes y pant Mon 78 E4
Croesywaun Gwyn 163 D8
Croft Hereford 115 D9
Croft Leics 135 D10
Croft Lincs 175 C8
Croft Pembs 92 C3
Croft Warr 183 C10
Croftamie Stirl 277 D9
Croftfoot S Lnrk 268 C2
Crofthandy Corn 4 G4
Croftlands Cumb 210 D5
Croftmalloch W Loth 269 C8
Croft Mitchell Corn 2 B5
Croftmoraig Perth 285 C11
Croft of Tillymaud Aberds 303 F11
Crofton Cumb 239 G8
Crofton London 68 F2
Crofton Wilts 63 G9
Crofton W Yorks 197 D11
Croft-on-Tees N Yorks 224 D5
Crofts Dumfries 237 B9
Crofts Bank Gtr Man 184 B3
Crofts of Benachielt Highld 310 F5
Crofts of Haddo Aberds 303 F8
Crofts of Inverthernie Aberds 303 E7
Crofts of Meikle Ardo Aberds 303 E8
Crofty Swansea 56 B4
Croggan Argyll 289 G9
Croglin Cumb 231 B7
Croich Highld 309 K4
Croick Highld 310 D2
Croig Argyll 288 D5
Crois Dughaill W Isles 297 J3
Cromarty Highld 301 C7
Cromasaig Highld 299 C10
Crombie Fife 279 D10
Crombie Castle Aberds 302 D5
Cromblet Aberds 303 F7
Cromdale Highld 301 G10
Cromer Herts 104 F5
Cromer Norf 160 A4
Cromer-Hyde Herts 86 C2
Cromford Derbys 170 D3
Cromhall S Glos 79 G11
Cromhall Common S Glos 61 B7
Cromor W Isles 304 F6
Crompton Fold Gtr Man 196 F2
Cromra Highld 291 D7
Cromwell Notts 172 C3
Cromwell Bottom W Yorks 196 C6
Cronberry E Ayrs 258 E4
Crondall Hants 49 D9
Cronk-y-Voddy IoM 192 D4
Cronton Mers 183 D7
Crook Cumb 221 G9
Crook Devon 27 G11
Crook Durham 233 D9
Crookdake Cumb 229 C9
Crooke Gtr Man 194 F5
Crooked Billet London 67 E8
Crookedholm E Ayrs 257 B11
Crooked Soley Wilts 63 E10
Crooked Withies Dorset 31 F9
Crookes S Yorks 186 D4
Crookesmoor S Yorks 186 D4
Crookfur E Renf 267 D10
Crookgate Bank Durham 242 F5
Crookhall Durham 242 G4
Crookham Northumb 263 B10
Crookham W Berks 64 G4
Crookham Village Hants 49 C9
Crookhaugh Borders 260 D4
Crookhill T&W 242 E5
Crookhouse Borders 263 D7
Crooklands Cumb 211 C10
Crook of Devon Perth 286 G4
Crookston Glasgow 267 C10
Cropredy Oxon 101 B9
Cropston Leics 153 G11
Cropthorne Worcs 99 C9
Cropton N Yorks 216 B5
Cropwell Bishop Notts 154 B3
Cropwell Butler Notts 154 B3
Cros W Isles 304 B7
Crosben Highld 289 D9
Crosbost W Isles 304 F5
Crosby Cumb 229 D7
Crosby IoM 192 E4
Crosby Mers 182 B4
Crosby N Lincs 199 E11
Crosby Court N Yorks 225 G7
Crosby Garrett Cumb 222 D4
Crosby-on-Eden Cumb 239 F11
Crosby Ravensworth Cumb 222 C2
Crosby Villa Cumb 229 D7
Croscombe Som 44 E5
Crosemere Shrops 149 D8
Crosland Edge W Yorks 196 E6
Crosland Hill W Yorks 196 E6
Crosland Moor W Yorks 196 D6
Croslands Park Cumb 210 E4
Cross Devon 40 F3
Cross Devon 40 G6
Cross Shrops 149 B7
Cross Som 44 C2
Crossaig Argyll 255 B9
Crossal Highld 294 B6
Crossapol Argyll 288 E1
Cross Ash Mon 78 B6
Cross-at-Hand Kent 53 D9
Cross Bank Worcs 116 C4
Crossbrae Aberds 302 D6
Crossburn Falk 279 G7
Crossbush W Sus 35 F8
Crosscanonby Cumb 229 D7
Cross Coombe Corn 4 E4
Crosscrake Cumb 211 B10
Crossdale Street Norf 160 B4
Cross End Beds 121 F11
Cross End Essex 107 E7
Cross End M Keynes 103 D8
Crossens Mers 193 D11
Crossflatts W Yorks 205 E8
Crossford Fife 279 D11
Crossford S Lnrk 268 F6
Crossgate Lincs 156 D4
Crossgate Orkney 314 E4
Crossgate Staffs 151 B8
Cross Gate W Sus 35 E8
Crossgatehall E Loth 271 B7
Crossgates Cumb 229 G7
Crossgates Fife 280 D2
Crossgates N Yorks 217 C10
Crossgates Powys 113 E11
Cross Gates W Yorks 205 F7
Cross Gates W Yorks 206 G3
Crossgill Cumb 231 C10
Crossgill Lancs 211 G11
Crossgreen Shrops 149 F9
Cross Green Devon 12 D3
Cross Green Staffs 133 B8
Cross Green Suff 124 G6
Cross Green Suff 125 F7
Cross Green Suff 125 G9
Cross Green Telford 150 G2
Cross Green Warks 119 F7
Cross Green W Yorks 206 G2
Crosshands Carms 92 G3
Cross Hands Carms 75 C9
Cross-hands Carms 92 G3
Cross Hands Pembs 73 C9
Cross Heath Staffs 168 F4
Crosshill E Ayrs 257 E11
Crosshill Fife 280 B3
Crosshill S Ayrs 245 B8
Cross Hill Corn 10 G6
Cross Hill Derbys 170 F6
Cross Hill Glos 79 F9
Cross Hills N Yorks 204 E6
Cross Holme N Yorks 225 F11
Crosshouse E Ayrs 257 B9
Cross Houses Shrops 131 B10
Cross Houses Shrops 132 E3
Crossings Cumb 240 B2
Cross in Hand E Sus 37 C9
Cross in Hand Leics 135 G10
Cross Inn Carms 74 C3
Cross Inn Ceredig 111 E10
Cross Inn Ceredig 111 F7
Cross Inn Rhondda 58 C5
Crosskeys Caerph 78 G2
Cross Keys Kent 52 C4
Cross Keys Wilts 61 E11
Crosskirk Highld 310 B4
Crosslands Cumb 210 B6
Cross Lane Ches E 167 C11
Cross Lane Head Shrops 132 D4
Crosslanes Shrops 148 F6
Cross Lanes Corn 2 E5
Cross Lanes Dorset 30 G3
Cross Lanes N Yorks 215 F10
Cross Lanes Oxon 65 D7
Cross Lanes Wrex 166 F5
Crosslee Borders 261 F8
Crosslee Renfs 267 B8
Crossley Hall W Yorks 205 G8
Cross Llyde Hereford 97 F8
Crossmichael Dumfries 237 C9
Crossmill E Renf 267 D10
Crossmoor Lancs 202 F4
Crossmount Perth 285 B11
Cross Oak Powys 96 G2
Cross of Jackston Aberds 303 F7
Cross o' th' hands Derbys 170 F3
Cross o' th' Hill Ches W 167 F7
Crosspost W Sus 36 C3
Crossroads Aberds 293 D9
Crossroads E Ayrs 257 C11
Crossroads Fife 281 B7
Cross Roads Devon 12 D4
Cross Roads W Yorks 204 F6
Cross Stone Aberds 303 G9
Cross Street Suff 126 B3
Crosston Angus 287 B9
Crosstown Corn 24 D2
Crosstown V Glam 58 F4
Cross Town Ches E 184 F3
Crosswater Sur 49 F11
Crossway Hereford 98 E2
Crossway Mon 78 B6
Crossway Powys 113 F11
Crossway Green Mon 79 G8
Crossway Green Worcs 116 D6
Crossways Dorset 17 D11
Crossways Kent 68 D5
Crossways Mon 96 G6
Crossways S Glos 79 G11
Crossways Sur 49 F11
Crosswell / Ffynnongroes Pembs 92 D2
Crosswood Ceredig 112 C3
Crosthwaite Cumb 221 G8
Croston Lancs 194 D3
Crostwick Norf 160 F5
Crostwight Norf 160 D6
Crothair W Isles 304 E3
Crouch Kent 52 B6
Crouch Kent 54 B5
Crouch End London 67 B9
Crouchers W Sus 22 C4
Croucheston Wilts 31 B9
Crouch Hill Dorset 30 E2
Crouch House Green Kent 52 D2
Croughly Moray 301 G11
Croughton Northants 101 E10
Crovie Aberds 303 C8
Crow Hants 31 G11
Crowan Corn 2 C4
Crowborough E Sus 52 G4
Crowborough Staffs 168 D6
Crowborough Warren E Sus 52 G4
Crowcombe Som 42 F6
Crowcroft Worcs 116 G5
Crowden Derbys 185 B9
Crowden Devon 12 B5
Crowder Park Devon 8 D4
Crowdhill Hants 33 C7
Crowdicote Derbys 169 B10
Crowdleham Kent 52 B5
Crowdon N Yorks 227 F9
Crow Edge S Yorks 197 G7
Crowell Oxon 84 F2
Crowell Hill Oxon 84 F3
Crowfield Northants 102 C2
Crowfield Suff 126 F2
Crowgate Street Norf 160 E6
Crowgreaves Shrops 132 D4
Crow Green Essex 87 F9
Crowhill Gtr Man 184 B6
Crowhill M Keynes 102 D6
Crow Hill Hereford 98 F2
Crowhole Derbys 186 F4
Crowhurst E Sus 38 E3
Crowhurst Sur 51 D11
Crowhurst Lane End Sur 51 D11
Crowland Lincs 156 G4
Crowlas Corn 2 C2
Crowle N Lincs 199 E9
Crowle Worcs 117 F8
Crowle Green Worcs 117 F8
Crowle Hill N Lincs 199 E9
Crowle Park N Lincs 199 E9
Crowmarsh Gifford Oxon 64 B6
Crown Corner Suff 126 C5
Crown East Worcs 116 G6
Crown Nest W Yorks 205 F8
Crownfield Bucks 84 F4
Crownhill Plym 7 D9
Crown Hills Leicester 136 C2
Crownland Suff 125 D10
Crownpits Sur 50 E3
Crownthorpe Norf 141 C11
Crowntown Corn 2 C4
Crown Wood Brack 65 F11
Crows-an-wra Corn 1 D3
Crow's Green Essex 106 F3
Crowshill Norf 141 B8
Crowsley Oxon 65 D8
Crowsnest Shrops 131 C7
Crow's Nest Corn 6 B5
Crowther's Pool Powys 96 B4
Crowthorne Brack 65 G10
Crowton Ches W 183 G9
Crow Wood Halton 183 D8
Croxall Staffs 152 G3
Croxby Lincs 189 B11
Croxby Top Lincs 189 B11
Croxdale Durham 233 D11
Croxden Staffs 151 B11
Croxley Green Herts 85 F9
Croxteth Mers 182 B6
Croxton Cambs 122 E4
Croxton N Lincs 200 E5
Croxton Norf 141 F7
Croxton Norf 159 C9
Croxton Staffs 150 C5
Croxtonbank Staffs 150 C5
Croxton Green Ches E 167 E8
Croxton Kerrial Leics 154 D6
Croy Highld 301 E7
Croy N Lnrk 278 F4
Croyde Devon 40 F2
Croyde Bay Devon 40 F2
Croydon Cambs 104 B6
Croydon London 67 F10
Crozen Hereford 97 B11
Crubenbeg Highld 291 D8
Crubenmore Lodge Highld 291 D8
Cruckmeole Shrops 131 B8
Cruckton Shrops 149 G8
Cruden Bay Aberds 303 F10
Crudgington Telford 150 F2
Crudie Aberds 303 D7
Crudwell Wilts 81 G7
Crug Powys 114 C3
Crugmeer Corn 10 F4
Crugybar Carms 94 D3
Cruise Hill Worcs 117 E10
Crulabhig W Isles 304 E3
Crumlin Caerph 78 F2
Crumplehorn Corn 6 E4
Crumpsall Gtr Man 195 G10
Crumpsbrook Shrops 116 B2
Crumpton Hill Worcs 98 B5
Crundale Kent 54 D5
Crundale Pembs 73 B7
Cruwys Morchard Devon 26 E5
Crux Easton Hants 48 B2
Cruxton Dorset 17 B8
Crwbin Carms 75 C7
Crya Orkney 314 F3
Cryers Hill Bucks 84 F5
Crymlyn Gwyn 179 G10
Crymych Pembs 92 E3
Crynant / Creunant Neath 76 E3
Crynfryn Ceredig 111 E11
Cuaich Highld 291 E8
Cuaig Highld 299 D7
Cuan Argyll 275 B8
Cubbington Warks 118 D6
Cubeck N Yorks 213 B9
Cubert Corn 4 D5
Cubitt Town London 67 D11
Cubley S Yorks 197 G8
Cubley Common Derbys 152 B3
Cublington Bucks 102 G6
Cublington Hereford 97 D8
Cuckfield W Sus 36 B4
Cucklington Som 30 B3
Cuckney Notts 187 G9
Cuckold's Green Suff 143 G9
Cuckold's Green Wilts 46 B3
Cuckoo Green Suff 143 D10
Cuckoo Hill Notts 188 C2
Cuckoo's Corner Hants 49 E8
Cuckoo's Corner Wilts 46 B4
Cuckoo's Knob Wilts 63 G7
Cuckoo Tye Suff 107 C7
Cuckron Shetland 313 H6
Cucumber Corner Norf 143 B7
Cuddesdon Oxon 83 E10
Cuddington Bucks 84 C2
Cuddington Ches W 183 G10
Cuddington Heath Ches W 167 F7
Cuddy Hill Lancs 202 F5
Cudham London 52 B2
Cudlipptown Devon 12 F6
Cudliptown Devon 12 F6
Cudworth Som 28 E5
Cudworth Sur 51 E8
Cudworth S Yorks 197 F11
Cudworth Common S Yorks 197 F11
Cuerden Green Lancs 194 C5
Cuerdley Cross Warr 183 D8
Cufaude Hants 48 B6
Cuffern Pembs 91 G7
Cuffley Herts 86 E4
Cuiashader W Isles 304 C7
Cuidhir W Isles 297 L2
Cuidhtinis W Isles 296 C6
Cuiken Midloth 270 C4
Cuilcheanna Ho Highld 290 G2
Cuin Argyll 288 D6
Culbo Highld 300 C6
Culbokie Highld 300 D6
Culburnie Highld 300 E4
Culcabock Highld 300 E6
Culcairn Highld 300 C6
Culcharry Highld 301 D8
Culcheth Warr 183 B11
Culcronchie Dumfries 237 C7
Cùl Doirlinn Highld 289 B8
Culdrain Aberds 302 F5
Culduie Highld 299 E7
Culeave Highld 309 K5
Culford Suff 124 D6
Culfordheath Suff 125 C7
Culfosie Aberds 293 C9
Culgaith Cumb 231 F8
Culham Oxon 83 F8
Culkein Highld 306 F5
Culkein Drumbeg Highld 306 F6
Culkerton Glos 80 F6
Cullachie Highld 301 G9
Cullen Moray 302 C5
Cullercoats T&W 243 C9
Cullicudden Highld 300 C6
Cullingworth W Yorks 205 F7
Cullipool Argyll 275 B8
Cullivoe Shetland 312 C7
Culloch Perth 285 F11
Culloden Highld 301 E7
Cullompton Devon 27 F8
Culmaily Highld 311 K2
Culmazie Dumfries 236 D5
Culm Davy Devon 27 D10
Culmer Sur 50 F2
Culmers Kent 70 G5
Culmington Shrops 131 G9
Culmore Stirl 278 B3
Culmstock Devon 27 E10
Culnacraig Highld 307 J5
Cul na h-Aird W Isles 305 H3
Culnaightrie Dumfries 237 D9
Culnaknock Highld 298 C5
Culnaneam Highld 294 C6
Culpho Suff 108 B4
Culrain Highld 309 K5
Culra Lodge Highld 291 F7
Culross Fife 279 D9
Culroy S Ayrs 257 G8
Culscadden Dumfries 236 E6
Culsh Aberds 292 D5
Culsh Aberds 303 E8
Culshabbin Dumfries 236 D5
Culswick Shetland 313 J4
Cultercullen Aberds 303 G9
Cults Aberdeen 293 C10
Cults Aberds 302 F5
Cults Dumfries 236 E6
Cults Fife 287 G7
Culverlane Devon 8 C4
Culverstone Green Kent 68 G6
Culverthorpe Lincs 173 G8
Culworth Northants 101 B10
Culzie Lodge Highld 300 B5
Cumberlow Green Herts 104 E6
Cumbernauld N Lnrk 278 G5
Cumbernauld Village N Lnrk 278 F5
Cumber's Bank Wrex 149 B8
Cumberworth Lincs 191 G8
Cumdivock Cumb 230 B2
Cumeragh Village Lancs 203 F7
Cuminestown Aberds 303 D8
Cumledge Borders 272 D5
Cumlewick Shetland 313 L6
Cumlodden Argyll 275 D11
Cumloden Dumfries 236 C6
Cummersdale Cumb 239 G9
Cummerton Aberds 303 C8
Cummertrees Dumfries 238 D4
Cummingston Moray 301 C11
Cumnock E Ayrs 258 E3
Cumnor Oxon 83 E7
Cumnor Hill Oxon 83 D7
Cumrew Cumb 240 G2
Cumwhinton Cumb 239 G10
Cumwhitton Cumb 240 G2
Cundall N Yorks 215 E8
Cundy Cross S Yorks 197 F11
Cundy Hos S Yorks 186 B4
Cunninghamhead N Ayrs 267 G7
Cunnister Shetland 312 D7
Cupar Fife 287 F7
Cupar Muir Fife 287 F7
Cupernham Hants 32 C5
Cupid Green Herts 85 D9
Cupid's Hill Mon 97 F8
Curbar Derbys 186 G3
Curborough Staffs 152 G2
Curbridge Hants 33 E8
Curbridge Oxon 82 D4
Curdridge Hants 33 E8
Curdworth Warks 134 E3
Curgurrell Corn 3 B9
Curin Highld 300 D3
Curland Som 28 D3
Curland Common Som 28 D3
Curlew Green Suff 127 D7
Curling Tye Green Essex 88 D4
Curload Som 28 B4
Currarie S Ayrs 244 E5
Currian Vale Corn 5 D9
Curridge W Berks 64 E3
Currie Edin 270 B3
Currock Cumb 239 G10
Curry Lane Corn 11 C11
Curry Mallet Som 28 C4
Curry Rivel Som 28 B5
Cursiter Orkney 314 E3
Curteis' Corner Kent 53 F11
Curtisden Green Kent 53 E8
Curtisknowle Devon 8 E4
Curtismill Green Essex 87 F8
Cury Corn 2 E5
Cusbay Orkney 314 C5
Cusgarne Corn 4 G5
Cushnie Aberds 303 C7
Cushuish Som 43 G7
Cusop Hereford 96 C4
Custards Hants 32 F3
Custom House London 68 C2
Cusveorth Coombe Corn 4 G5
Cusworth S Yorks 198 G4
Cutcloy Dumfries 236 F6
Cutcombe Som 42 F2
Cutgate Gtr Man 195 E11
Cuthill E Loth 281 G7
Cutiau Gwyn 146 F2
Cutlers Green Essex 105 E11
Cutler's Green Som 44 C5
Cutmadoc Corn 5 C11
Cutmere Corn 6 C6
Cutnall Green Worcs 117 D7
Cutsdean Glos 99 E11
Cutsyke W Yorks 198 C2
Cutteslowe Oxon 83 C8
Cutthorpe Derbys 186 G4
Cuttiford's Door Som 28 E4
Cutts Shetland 313 K6
Cuttybridge Pembs 72 B6
Cuttyhill Aberds 303 D10
Cuxham Oxon 83 F11
Cuxton Medway 69 F8
Cuxwold Lincs 201 G7
Cwm Bl Gwent 77 D11
Cwm Denb 181 F9
Cwm Neath 57 C10
Cwm Powys 129 D11
Cwm Powys 130 E5
Cwm Shrops 114 B6
Cwm Swansea 57 B7
Cwmafan Neath 57 C9
Cwmaman Rhondda 77 F8
Cwmann Carms 93 B11
Cwmavon Torf 78 D3
Cwmbach Carms 75 E7
Cwmbach Carms 92 F5
Cwmbach Powys 96 D3
Cwmbach Rhondda 77 E8
Cwmbâch Rhondda 77 E8
Cwmbach Llechrhyd Powys 113 G10
Cwmbelan Powys 129 G8
Cwmbran Torf 78 G3
Cwmbrwyno Ceredig 128 G4
Cwm-byr Carms 94 E2
Cwm Capel Carms 75 E7
Cwmcarn Caerph 78 G2
Cwmcarvan Mon 79 D7
Cwm-celyn Bl Gwent 78 D2
Cwm-Cewydd Gwyn 147 G7
Cwmcoednerth Ceredig 92 B6
Cwm-cou Ceredig 92 C5
Cwmcrawnon Powys 77 B10
Cwmcych Carms 92 D5
Cwmdare Rhondda 77 E7
Cwm Dows Caerph 78 F2
Cwmdu Carms 94 E2
Cwmdu Powys 96 G3
Cwmdu Swansea 56 C6
Cwmduad Carms 93 E7
Cwm-Dulais Swansea 75 E10
Cwmdwr Carms 94 E4
Cwmerfyn Ceredig 128 G3
Cwmfelin Bridgend 57 D11
Cwmfelin M Tydf 77 E9
Cwmfelin Boeth Carms 73 B11
Cwm felin fach Caerph 77 G11
Cwmfelin Mynach Carms 92 G4
Cwmffrwd Carms 74 B6
Cwm Ffrwd-oer Torf 78 E3
Cwm-Fields Torf 78 E3
Cwm Gelli Caerph 77 F11
Cwmgiedd Powys 76 C3
Cwmgors Neath 76 C2
Cwmgwili Carms 75 C9
Cwmgwrach Neath 76 E5
Cwm Gwyn Swansea 56 C6
Cwm Head Shrops 131 F8
Cwm-hesgen Gwyn 146 D5
Cwmhiraeth Carms 92 D6
Cwm-hwnt Rhondda 76 D6
Cwmifor Carms 94 F3
Cwm Irfon Powys 95 B7
Cwmisfael Carms 75 B7
Cwm-Llinau Powys 128 B6
Cwmllynfell Neath 76 C2
Cwm-mawr Carms 75 C8
Cwm-miles Carms 92 G3
Cwm Nant-gam Bl Gwent 78 C2
Cwmnantyrodyn Caerph 77 F11
Cwmorgan Pembs 92 E5
Cwmparc Rhondda 77 F7
Cwm-parc Rhondda 77 F7
Cwmpengraig Carms 92 D6
Cwm Penmachno Conwy 164 F3
Cwmpennar Rhondda 77 E8
Cwm Plysgog Ceredig 92 C3
Cwmrhos Powys 96 G3
Cwmrhydyceirw Swansea 57 B7
Cwmsychpant Ceredig 93 B9
Cwmsyfiog Caerph 77 E11
Cwmsymlog Ceredig 128 G4
Cwmtillery Bl Gwent 78 D2
Cwm-twrch Isaf Powys 76 C3
Cwm-twrch Uchaf Powys 76 C3
Cwmwdig Water Pembs 90 E6
Cwmwysg Powys 95 F7
Cwm-y-glo Carms 75 C9
Cwm-y-glo Gwyn 163 C8
Cwmynyscoy Torf 78 F3
Cwmyoy Mon 96 G5
Cwmystwyth Ceredig 112 C5
Cwrt Gwyn 128 C3
Cwrt-newydd Ceredig 93 B9
Cwrt-y-cadno Carms 94 C3
Cwrt-y-gollen Powys 78 B2
Cydweli / Kidwelly Carms 74 D6
Cyffordd Llandudno / Llandudno Junction Conwy 180 F3
Cyffylliog Denb 165 D9

Cyfronydd Powys 130 B2
Cymau Flint 166 D3
Cymdda Bridgend 58 C2
Cymer Neath 57 B11
Cymmer Rhondda 77 G8
Cyncoed Cardiff 59 C7
Cynghordy Carms 94 C6
Cynheidre Carms 75 D7
Cynonville Neath 57 B10
Cyntwell Cardiff 58 D6
Cynwyd Denb 165 G9
Cynwyl Elfed Carms 93 F7
Cywarch Gwyn 147 F7

## D

Daccombe Devon 9 B8
Dacre Cumb 230 F5
Dacre N Yorks 214 G3
Dacre Banks N Yorks 214 G3
Daddry Shield Durham 232 D3
Dadford Bucks 102 D3
Dadlington Leics 135 D8
Dafarn Faig Gwyn 163 F7
Dafen Carms 75 E8
Daffy Green Norf 141 B9
Dagdale Staffs 151 C11
Dagenham London 68 C3
Daggons Dorset 31 E10
Daglingworth Glos 81 D7
Dagnall Bucks 85 B7
Dagtail End Worcs 117 E10
Dagworth Suff 125 E10
Dail Beag W Isles 304 D4
Dail bho Dheas W Isles 304 B6
Dail bho Thuath W Isles 304 B6
Daill Argyll 274 G4
Dailly S Ayrs 245 C7
Dail Mor W Isles 304 D4
Dainton Devon 9 B7
Dairsie or Osnaburgh Fife 287 F8
Daisy Green Suff 125 D10
Daisy Green Suff 125 D11
Daisy Hill Gtr Man 195 G7
Daisy Hill W Yorks 197 B9
Daisy Hill W Yorks 205 G8
Daisy Nook Gtr Man 196 G2
Dalabrog W Isles 297 J3
Dalavich Argyll 275 B10
Dalbeattie Dumfries 237 C10
Dalbeg Highld 291 B8
Dalblair E Ayrs 258 F4
Dalbog Angus 293 F7
Dalbrack Stirl 285 G11
Dalbury Derbys 152 C5
Dalby IoM 192 E3
Dalby Lincs 190 G6
Dalby N Yorks 216 E2
Dalchalloch Perth 291 G9
Dalchalm Highld 311 J3
Dalchenna Argyll 284 G4
Dalchirach Moray 301 F11
Dalchonzie Perth 285 E11
Dalchork Highld 309 H5
Dalchreichart Highld 290 B4
Dalchruin Perth 285 F11
Dalderby Lincs 174 B2
Dale Cumb 230 C6
Dale Gtr Man 196 F3
Dale Pembs 72 D4
Dale Shetland 312 G6
Dale Abbey Derbys 153 B8
Dalebank Derbys 170 C5
Dale Bottom Cumb 229 G11
Dale Brow Ches E 184 F6
Dale End Derbys 170 C2
Dale End N Yorks 204 D5
Dale Head Cumb 221 B8
Dale Hill E Sus 53 G7
Dale Hill E Sus 53 G8
Dalelia Highld 289 C9
Dale Moor Derbys 153 B8
Dale of Walls Shetland 313 H3
Dales Brow Gtr Man 195 G9
Dales Green Staffs 168 D5
Daless Highld 301 F8
Dalestie Moray 292 B3
Dalestorth Notts 171 C8
Dalfaber Highld 291 B11
Dalfoil Stirl 277 D11
Dalganachan Highld 310 E4
Dalgarven N Ayrs 266 F5
Dalgety Bay Fife 280 E3
Dalginross Perth 285 E11
Dalguise Perth 286 C3
Dalhalvaig Highld 310 D2
Dalham Suff 124 E4
Dalhastnie Angus 293 F7
Dalhenzean Perth 292 G3
Dalinlongart Argyll 276 E2
Dalkeith Midloth 270 B6
Dallam Warr 183 C9
Dallas Moray 301 D11
Dallas Lodge Moray 301 D11
Dallcharn Highld 308 D6
Dalleagles E Ayrs 258 G3
Dallicott Shrops 132 E5
Dallimores IoW 20 C6
Dallinghoo Suff 126 G5
Dallington E Sus 23 B11
Dallington Northants 120 E4
Dallow N Yorks 214 E3
Dalmadilly Aberds 293 B9
Dalmally Argyll 284 E5
Dalmarnock Glasgow 268 C2
Dalmarnock Perth 286 C3
Dalmary Stirl 277 B10
Dalmellington E Ayrs 245 B11
Dalmeny Edin 280 F2
Dalmigavie Highld 291 B9
Dalmigavie Lodge Highld 301 G7
Dalmilling S Ayrs 257 E9
Dalmore Highld 300 C6
Dalmuir W Dunb 277 G9
Dalnabreck Highld 289 C8
Dalnacardoch Lodge Perth 291 F9
Dalnacroich Highld 300 D3
Dalnaglar Castle Perth 292 G3
Dalnahaitnach Highld 301 G8
Dalnamein Lodge Perth 291 G9
Dalnarrow Argyll 289 F9
Dalnaspidal Lodge Perth 291 F8
Dalnavaid Perth 292 G2
Dalnavie Highld 300 B6
Dalnaw Dumfries 236 B5
Dalnawillan Lodge Highld 310 E4
Dalness Highld 284 B5
Dalnessie Highld 309 H6
Dalphaid Highld 309 H3
Dalqueich Perth 286 G4
Dalrannoch Argyll 289 E11
Dalreavoch Highld 309 J7
Dalriach Highld 301 F10
Dalrigh Stirl 285 E7
Dalry Edin 280 G4
Dalry N Ayrs 266 F5
Dalrymple E Ayrs 257 G9
Dalscote Northants 120 G3
Dalserf S Lnrk 268 E6
Dalshannon N Lnrk 278 G4
Dalston Cumb 239 G9
Dalston London 67 C10
Dalswinton Dumfries 247 F10
Dalton Cumb 211 D10
Dalton Dumfries 238 C4
Dalton Lancs 194 F3
Dalton Northumb 241 F10
Dalton Northumb 242 C4
Dalton N Yorks 215 D8
Dalton N Yorks 224 D2
Dalton S Lnrk 268 D3
Dalton S Yorks 187 C7
Dalton W Yorks 197 D7
Dalton-in-Furness Cumb 210 E4
Dalton-le-Dale Durham 234 B4
Dalton Magna S Yorks 187 C7
Dalton-on-Tees N Yorks 224 D5
Dalton Parva S Yorks 187 C7
Dalton Piercy Hrtlpl 234 E5
Dalveallan Highld 300 F6
Dalveich Stirl 285 E10
Dalvina Lo Highld 308 E6
Dalwey Telford 132 B3
Dalwhinnie Highld 291 E8
Dalwood Devon 28 G3
Dalwyne S Ayrs 245 D8
Damask Green Herts 104 F5
Damems W Yorks 204 F6
Damerham Hants 31 D10
Damery Glos 80 G2
Damgate Norf 143 B8
Damgate Norf 161 F9
Dam Green Norf 141 F11
Damhead Moray 301 D10
Dam Head W Yorks 196 B6
Damhead Holdings Midloth 270 B5
Dam Mill Staffs 133 C7
Damnaglaur Dumfries 236 F3
Dam of Quoiggs Perth 286 G2
Damside Borders 270 F3
Dam Side Lancs 202 D4
Danaway Kent 69 G11
Danbury Essex 88 E3
Danbury Common Essex 88 E3
Danby N Yorks 226 D4
Danby Wiske N Yorks 224 F6
Dan Caerlan Rhondda 58 C5
Dancers Hill Herts 86 F2
Dancing Green Hereford 98 G2
Dandaleith Moray 302 E2
Danderhall Midloth 270 B6
Dandy Corner Suff 125 D11
Danebank Ches E 185 E7
Dane Bank Gtr Man 184 B6
Danebridge Ches E 169 B7
Dane End Herts 104 G6
Danegate E Sus 52 G5
Danehill E Sus 36 B6
Dane in Shaw Ches E 168 C5
Danemoor Green Norf 141 B11
Danesbury Herts 86 B2
Danesfield Bucks 65 C10
Danesford Shrops 132 E4
Daneshill Hants 49 C7
Danesmoor Derbys 170 C6
Danes Moss Ches E 184 G6
Dane Street Kent 54 C5
Daneway Glos 80 E6
Dangerous Corner Gtr Man 195 G7
Dangerous Corner Lancs 194 E4
Daniel's Water Kent 54 E3
Danna na Cloiche Argyll 275 F7
Dannonchapel Corn 10 E6
Danskine E Loth 271 B11
Danthorpe E Yorks 209 G10
Danygraig Caerph 78 G2
Danzey Green Warks 118 D2
Dapple Heath Staffs 151 D10
Darby End W Mid 133 F9
Darby Green Hants 65 G10
Darbys Green Worcs 116 F4
Darby's Hill W Mid 133 F9
Darcy Lever Gtr Man 195 F8
Dardy Powys 78 B2
Darenth Kent 68 E5
Daresbury Halton 183 E9
Daresbury Delph Halton 183 E9
Darfield S Yorks 198 G2
Darfoulds Notts 187 F9
Dargate Kent 70 G5
Dargate Common Kent 70 G5
Darite Corn 6 B5
Darkland Moray 302 C2
Darland Wrex 166 D5
Darlaston W Mid 133 D9
Darlaston Green W Mid 133 D9
Darley N Yorks 205 B10
Darley Shrops 132 D3
Darley Abbey Derby 153 B7
Darley Bridge Derbys 170 C3
Darley Dale Derbys 170 C3
Darleyford Corn 11 G11
Darley Green Warks 118 C3
Darleyhall Herts 104 G2
Darley Head N Yorks 205 B9
Darley Hillside Derbys 170 C3
Darlingscott Warks 100 C4
Darlington Darl 224 C5
Darliston Shrops 149 C11
Darlton Notts 188 G3
Darmsden Suff 125 G11
Darnall S Yorks 186 D5
Darnaway Castle Moray 301 D9
Darnford Staffs 134 B2
Darnhall Ches W 167 C10
Darnhall Mains Borders 270 F4
Darn Hill Gtr Man 195 E10
Darnick Borders 262 C2
Darowen Powys 128 C6
Darra Aberds 303 E7
Darracott Devon 24 D2
Darracott Devon 40 F3
Darras Hall Northumb 242 C5
Darrington W Yorks 198 D3
Darrow Green Norf 142 F5
Darsham Suff 127 D8
Darshill Som 44 E6
Dartford Kent 68 E4
Dartford Crossing Kent 68 D5
Dartington Devon 8 C5
Dartmeet Devon 13 G9
Dartmouth Devon 9 E7
Dartmouth Park London 67 B9
Darton S Yorks 197 F10
Darvel E Ayrs 258 B3
Darvillshill Bucks 84 F4
Darwell Hole E Sus 23 B11
Darwen Blkburn 195 C7
Dassels Herts 105 F7
Datchet Windsor 66 D3
Datchet Common Windsor 66 D3
Datchworth Herts 86 B3
Datchworth Green Herts 86 B3
Daubhill Gtr Man 195 F8
Daugh of Kinermony Moray 302 E2
Dauntsey Wilts 62 C3
Dauntsey Lock Wilts 62 C3
Dava Moray 301 F10
Davenham Ches W 183 G11
Davenport Ches E 168 B4
Davenport Gtr Man 184 D5
Davenport Green Ches E 184 F4
Davenport Green Gtr Man 184 D4
Daventry Northants 119 E11
Davidson's Mains Edin 280 F4
Davidston Highld 301 C7
Davidstow Corn 11 D9
David Street Kent 68 G6
David's Well Powys 113 B11
Davington Dumfries 248 C6
Davington Kent 70 G4
Daviot Aberds 303 G7
Daviot Highld 301 F7
Davis's Town E Sus 23 B8
Davoch of Grange Moray 302 D4
Davo Mains Aberds 293 F9
Davyhulme Gtr Man 184 B3
Daw Cross N Yorks 205 C11
Dawdon Durham 234 B4
Daw End W Mid 133 C10
Dawesgreen Sur 51 D8
Dawker Hill N Yorks 207 F7
Dawley Telford 132 B3
Dawley Bank Telford 132 B3
Dawlish Devon 14 F5
Dawlish Warren Devon 14 F5
Dawn Conwy 180 G5
Daw's Cross Essex 107 E7
Daw's Green Som 27 C11
Daws Heath Essex 69 B10
Dawshill Worcs 116 G6
Daw's House Corn 12 E2
Dawsmere Lincs 157 C8
Daybrook Notts 171 F9
Day Green Ches E 168 D3
Dayhills Staffs 151 C9
Dayhouse Bank Worcs 117 B9
Daylesford Glos 100 F4
Daywall Shrops 148 C5
Ddol Flint 181 G10
Ddôl Cownwy Powys 147 F10
Ddrydwy Anglesey 178 G5
Deacons Hill Herts 85 F11
Deadman's Cross C Beds 104 C2
Deadman's Green Staffs 151 B10
Deadwater Hants 49 F10
Deadwater Northumb 250 D4
Deaf Hill Durham 234 D3
Deal Hall Essex 89 F8
Deal Hall Kent 55 C11
Dean Cumb 229 F7
Dean Devon 8 C4
Dean Devon 40 D6
Dean Devon 40 E4
Dean Devon 41 D8
Dean Dorset 31 D7
Dean Edin 280 G4
Dean Hants 33 D9
Dean Hants 48 G2
Dean Lancs 195 B11
Dean Oxon 100 G6
Dean Som 45 E7
Dean Bank Durham 233 E11
Deanburnhaugh Borders 261 G9
Dean Court Oxon 83 D7
Dean Cross Devon 40 E4
Deane Gtr Man 195 F7
Deane Hants 48 C4
Deanend Dorset 31 D7
Dean Head S Yorks 197 G9
Deanich Lodge Highld 309 L3
Deanland Dorset 31 D7
Deanlane End W Sus 34 E2
Dean Lane Head W Yorks 205 G7
Dean Park Renfs 267 B10
Dean Prior Devon 8 C4
Dean Row Ches E 184 E5
Deans W Loth 269 B10
Deans Bottom Kent 69 G11
Deanscales Cumb 229 F7
Deansgreen Ches E 183 D11
Dean's Green Warks 118 D2
Deanshanger Northants 102 D5
Deans Hill Kent 69 G11
Deanston Stirl 285 G11
Dean Street Kent 53 C8
Dearham Cumb 229 D7
Dearnley Gtr Man 196 D2
Debach Suff 126 G4
Debdale Gtr Man 184 B5
Debden Essex 86 F6
Debden Essex 105 E11
Debden Cross Essex 105 E11
Debden Green Essex 86 F6
Debden Green Essex 105 E11
De Beauvoir Town London 67 C10
Debenham Suff 126 E3
Deblin's Green Worcs 98 B6
Dechmont W Loth 279 G10
Deckham T&W 243 E7
Deddington Oxon 101 E9
Dedham Essex 107 E11
Dedham Heath Essex 107 E11
Dedridge W Loth 269 B11
Dedworth Windsor 66 D2
Deebank Aberds 293 D8
Deecastle Aberds 292 D6
Deene Northants 137 E8
Deenethorpe Northants 137 E9
Deepcar S Yorks 186 B3
Deepclough Derbys 185 B8
Deepcut Sur 50 B2
Deepdale C Beds 104 B4
Deepdale Cumb 212 C4
Deepdale N Yorks 213 D7
Deepdene Sur 51 D7
Deepfields W Mid 133 E8
Deeping Gate Lincs 138 B2
Deeping St James Lincs 138 B3
Deeping St Nicholas Lincs 156 F4
Deepthwaite Cumb 211 C10
Deepweir Mon 60 B3
Deerhill Moray 302 D4
Deerhurst Glos 99 F7
Deerhurst Walton Glos 99 F7
Deerland Pembs 73 C7
Deerness Orkney 314 F5
Deer's Green Essex 105 E9
Deerstones N Yorks 205 C7
Deerton Street Kent 70 G3
Defford Worcs 99 C8
Defynnog Powys 95 F8
Deganwy Conwy 180 F3
Degar V Glam 58 D4
Degibna Corn 2 D5
Deighton N Yorks 225 E7
Deighton W Yorks 197 D7
Deighton York 207 E8
Deiniolen Gwyn 163 C9
Deishar Highld 291 B11
Delabole Corn 11 E7
Delamere Ches W 167 B9
Delfour Highld 291 C10
Delfrigs Aberds 303 G9
Dellieture Highld 301 F10
Dell Lodge Highld 292 B2
Dell Quay W Sus 22 C4
Delly End Oxon 82 C5
Delnabo Moray 292 B3
Delnadamph Aberds 292 C4
Delnamer Angus 292 G3
Delph Gtr Man 196 F3
Delves Durham 233 B8
Delvine Perth 286 C5
Delvin End Essex 106 D5
Dembleby Lincs 155 B10
Demelza Corn 5 C9
Denaby Main S Yorks 187 B7
Denbeath Fife 281 B7
Denbigh Denb 165 B9
Denbury Devon 8 B6
Denby Derbys 170 F5
Denby Bottles Derbys 170 F5
Denby Common Derbys 170 F6
Denby Dale W Yorks 197 F8
Denchworth Oxon 82 G5
Dendron Cumb 210 E4
Denel End C Beds 103 D10
Denend Aberds 302 F6
Dene Park Kent 52 C5
Deneside Durham 234 B4
Denford Northants 121 B9
Denford Staffs 169 E7
Dengie Essex 89 E7
Denham Bucks 66 B4
Denham Bucks 102 G5
Denham Suff 124 E5
Denham Suff 126 C3
Denham Corner Suff 126 C3
Denham End Suff 124 E5
Denham Green Bucks 66 B4
Denham Street Suff 126 C3
Denhead Aberds 303 D9
Denhead Fife 287 F8
Denhead of Arbilot Angus 287 C9
Denhead of Gray Dundee 287 D7
Denholm Borders 262 F3
Denholme W Yorks 205 G7
Denholme Clough W Yorks 205 G7
Denholme Edge W Yorks 205 G7
Denholme Gate W Yorks 205 G7
Denholmhill Borders 262 F3
Denio Gwyn 145 B7
Denmead Hants 33 E11
Denmore Aberdeen 293 B11
Denmoss Aberds 302 E6
Dennington Suff 126 D5
Dennington Corner Suff 126 D5
Dennington Hall Suff 126 D5
Denny Falk 278 E6
Denny Bottom Kent 52 F5
Denny End Cambs 123 D9
Dennyloanhead Falk 278 E6
Denny Lodge Hants 32 F4
Dennystown W Dunb 277 F7
Denshaw Gtr Man 196 E3
Denside Aberds 293 D10
Densole Kent 55 E8
Denston Suff 124 G5
Denstone Staffs 169 G9
Denstroude Kent 70 G6
Dent Cumb 212 B4
Dent Bank Durham 232 F4
Denton Cambs 138 F2
Denton Darl 224 B4
Denton E Sus 23 E7
Denton Gtr Man 184 B6
Denton Kent 55 D8
Denton Kent 69 E7
Denton Lincs 155 C7
Denton Norf 142 F5
Denton Northants 120 F6
Denton N Yorks 205 D8
Denton Oxon 83 E9
Denton Burn T&W 242 D5
Denton Holme Cumb 239 G10
Denton's Green Mers 183 B7
Denver Norf 140 C2
Denvilles Hants 22 B2
Denwick Northumb 264 G6
Deopham Norf 141 C11
Deopham Green Norf 141 D10
Deopham Stalland Norf 141 D10
Depden Suff 124 F5
Depden Green Suff 124 F5
Deppers Bridge Warks 119 F7
Deptford London 67 D11
Deptford T&W 243 F9
Deptford Wilts 46 F4
Derby Derbys 153 B7
Derby Devon 40 G5
Derbyhaven IoM 192 F3
Derbyshire Hill Mers 183 C8
Dereham Norf 159 G9
Dergoals Dumfries 236 D4
Deri Caerph 77 E10
Derriford Plym 7 D9
Derril Devon 24 G4
Derringstone Kent 55 D8
Derrington Shrops 132 E2
Derrington Staffs 151 E7
Derriton Devon 24 G4
Derry Stirl 285 E10
Derrydaroch Stirl 285 E7
Derry Downs London 68 F3
Derry Fields Wilts 81 G8
Derryguaig Argyll 288 F6
Derry Hill Wilts 62 E3
Derry Lodge Aberds 292 D2
Derrythorpe N Lincs 199 F10
Dersingham Norf 158 C3
Dertfords Wilts 45 D10
Dervaig Argyll 288 D6
Derwen Bridgend 58 C2
Derwen Denb 165 E9
Derwenlas Powys 128 D4
Desborough Northants 136 G6
Desford Leics 135 C9
Deskryshiel Aberds 292 B6
Detchant Northumb 264 B3
Detling Kent 53 B9
Deuchar Angus 292 G6
Deuddwr Powys 148 F4
Deuxhill Shrops 132 F3
Devauden Mon 79 F7
Deveral Corn 2 B3
Devil's Bridge / Pontarfynach Ceredig 112 B4
Devitts Green Warks 134 E5
Devizes Wilts 62 G4
Devol Invclyd 276 G6
Devonport Plym 7 E9
Devonside Clack 279 B8
Devon Village Clack 279 B8
Devoran Corn 3 B7
Dewar Borders 270 F6
Dewartown Midloth 271 C7
Dewes Green Essex 105 E9
Dewlands Common Dorset 31 F9
Dewlish Dorset 17 B11
Dewsbury W Yorks 197 C8
Dewsbury Moor W Yorks 197 C8
Dewshall Court Hereford 97 E9
Dhoon IoM 192 D5
Dhoor IoM 192 C5
Dhowin IoM 192 B5
Dhustone Shrops 115 B11
Dial Green W Sus 34 B6
Dial Post W Sus 35 D11
Dibberford Dorset 29 G7
Dibden Hants 32 F6
Dibden Purlieu Hants 32 F6
Dickens Heath W Mid 118 B2
Dickleburgh Norf 142 G3
Dickleburgh Moor Norf 142 G3
Dickon Hills Lincs 174 D6
Didbrook Glos 99 E11
Didcot Oxon 64 B4
Diddington Cambs 122 D3
Diddlebury Shrops 131 F10
Diddywell Devon 25 B7
Didley Hereford 97 E9
Didling W Sus 34 D4
Didlington Norf 140 D5
Didmarton Glos 61 B10
Didsbury Gtr Man 184 C4
Didworthy Devon 8 C3
Diebidale Highld 309 L4
Digbeth W Mid 133 F11
Digby Lincs 173 E9
Digg Highld 298 C4
Diggle Gtr Man 196 F4
Diglis Worcs 116 G6
Digmoor Lancs 194 F3
Digswell Herts 86 B3
Digswell Park Herts 86 C2
Digswell Water Herts 86 C3
Dihewyd Ceredig 111 F9
Dilham Norf 160 D6
Dilhorne Staffs 169 G7
Dillarburn S Lnrk 268 G6
Dill Hall Lancs 195 B8
Dillington Cambs 122 D2
Dillington Som 28 D5
Dilston Northumb 241 E11
Dilton Marsh Wilts 45 D11
Dilwyn Hereford 115 G8
Dimlands V Glam 58 F3
Dimmer Som 44 G6
Dimple Derbys 170 C3
Dimple Gtr Man 195 D8
Dimsdale Staffs 168 F4
Dimson Corn 12 G4
Dinas Carms 92 E5
Dinas Corn 10 G4
Dinas Gwyn 144 B5
Dinas Gwyn 163 D7
Dinas Cross Pembs 91 D10
Dinas Dinlle Gwyn 162 D6
Dinas-Mawddwy Gwyn 147 G7
Dinas Mawr Conwy 164 E4
Dinas Powys V Glam 59 E7
Dinbych y Pysgod / Tenby Pembs 73 E10
Dinckley Lancs 203 F9
Dinder Som 44 E5
Dinedor Hereford 97 D10
Dinedor Cross Hereford 97 D10
Dines Green Worcs 116 F6
Dingestow Mon 79 C7
Dinghurst N Som 44 B2
Dingle Mers 182 D5
Dingleden Kent 53 G10
Dingleton Borders 262 C2
Dingley Northants 136 F5
Dingwall Highld 300 D5
Dinlabyre Borders 250 E2
Dinmael Conwy 165 G8
Dinnet Aberds 292 D6
Dinnington Som 28 E6
Dinnington S Yorks 187 D8
Dinnington T&W 242 C6
Dinorwic Gwyn 163 C9
Dinton Bucks 84 C3
Dinton Wilts 46 G4
Dinwoodie Mains Dumfries 248 E4
Dinworthy Devon 24 D4
Dipford Som 28 C2
Dipley Hants 49 B8
Dippenhall Sur 49 D10
Dippertown Devon 12 E4
Dippin N Ayrs 256 E2
Dipple Devon 24 D4
Dipple Moray 302 D3
Dipple S Ayrs 244 C6
Diptford Devon 8 D4
Dipton Durham 242 G5
Diptonmill Northumb 241 E10
Dirdhu Highld 301 G10
Direcleit W Isles 305 J3
Dirleton E Loth 281 E10
Dirt Pot Northumb 232 B3
Discoed Powys 114 E5
Discove Som 45 G7
Diseworth Leics 153 E9
Dishes Orkney 314 D6
Dishforth N Yorks 215 E7
Dishley Leics 153 E10
Disley Ches E 185 E7
Diss Norf 126 B2
Disserth Powys 113 F10
Distington Cumb 228 G6
Ditchampton Wilts 46 G5
Ditcheat Som 44 F6
Ditchfield Bucks 84 G4
Ditchford Hill Worcs 100 D4
Ditchingham Norf 142 E6
Ditchling E Sus 36 D4
Ditherington Shrops 149 G10
Ditteridge Wilts 61 F10
Dittisham Devon 9 E7
Ditton Halton 183 D7
Ditton Kent 53 B8
Ditton Green Cambs 124 F3
Ditton Priors Shrops 132 F2
Dittons E Sus 23 E10
Divach Highld 300 G4
Divlyn Carms 94 D5
Dixton Glos 99 E9
Dixton Mon 79 C8
Dizzard Corn 11 B9
Dobcross Gtr Man 196 F3
Dobs Hill Flint 166 C4
Dobson's Bridge Shrops 149 C9
Dobwalls Corn 6 C4
Doccombe Devon 13 D11
Dochfour Ho Highld 300 F6
Dochgarroch Highld 300 E6
Dockeney Norf 143 E7
Dockenfield Sur 49 E10
Docker Lancs 211 E11
Docking Norf 158 B5
Docklow Hereford 115 F11
Dockray Cumb 230 G3
Dockroyd W Yorks 204 F6
Doc Penfro / Pembroke Dock Pembs 73 E7
Docton Devon 24 C2
Dodbrooke Devon 8 G4
Dodburn Borders 249 B11
Doddenham Worcs 116 F5
Doddinghurst Essex 87 F9
Doddington Cambs 139 E7
Doddington Kent 54 B2
Doddington Lincs 188 G6
Doddington Northumb 263 C11
Doddington Shrops 116 B2
Doddiscombsleigh Devon 14 D3
Doddshill Norf 158 C3
Doddycross Corn 6 C6
Dodford Northants 120 E2
Dodford Worcs 117 C8
Dodington S Glos 61 C9
Dodington Som 43 E7
Dodleston Ches W 166 C5
Dodmarsh Hereford 97 C11
Dodscott Devon 25 D8
Dods Leigh Staffs 151 C10
Dodworth S Yorks 197 F10
Dodworth Bottom S Yorks 197 G10
Dodworth Green S Yorks 197 G10
Doe Bank W Mid 134 D2
Doe Green Warr 183 D9
Doehole Derbys 170 D5
Doe Lea Derbys 171 B7
Doffcocker Gtr Man 195 E7
Dogdyke Lincs 174 D2
Dog & Gun Mers 182 B5
Dog Hill Gtr Man 196 F3
Dogingtree Estate Staffs 151 G9
Dogley Lane W Yorks 197 E7
Dogmersfield Hants 49 C9
Dogridge Wilts 62 B5
Dogsthorpe Pboro 138 C3
Dog Village Devon 14 B5
Doirlinn Highld 289 D8
Dolanog Powys 147 G11
Dolau Powys 114 D2
Dolau Rhondda 58 C3
Dolbenmaen Gwyn 163 G8
Dole Ceredig 128 F2
Dolemeads Bath 61 G9
Doley Staffs 150 D4
Dolfach Powys 129 C8
Dol-ffanog Gwyn 146 G4
Dolfor Powys 130 F2
Dol-fôr Powys 128 B6
Dolgarrog Conwy 164 B3
Dolgellau Gwyn 146 F4
Dolgerdd Ceredig 111 G8
Dolgoch Gwyn 128 C3
Dolgran Carms 93 E8
Dolhelfa Powys 113 C8
Dolhendre Gwyn 147 C7
Doll Highld 311 J2
Dollar Clack 279 B9
Dolley Green Powys 114 D5
Dollis Hill London 67 B8
Dollwen Ceredig 128 G3
Dolphin Flint 181 G11
Dolphingstone E Loth 281 G7
Dolphinholme Lancs 202 C6
Dolphinston Borders 262 F5
Dolphinton S Lnrk 270 F2
Dolton Devon 25 E9
Dolwen Conwy 180 G5
Dolwen Powys 129 B9
Dolwyd Conwy 180 F4
Dolwyddelan Conwy 164 E2
Dôl-y-Bont Ceredig 128 F2
Dol-y-cannau Powys 96 B3
Dolydd Gwyn 163 D7
Dolyhir Powys 114 F4
Dolymelinau Powys 129 D11
Dolywern Wrex 148 B4
Domewood Sur 51 E10
Domgay Powys 148 F5
Dommett Som 28 E3
Doncaster S Yorks 198 G5
Doncaster Common S Yorks 198 G6
Dones Green Ches W 183 F10
Donhead St Andrew Wilts 30 C6
Donhead St Mary Wilts 30 C6
Donibristle Fife 280 D3
Doniford Som 42 E5
Donington Lincs 156 B4
Donington Shrops 132 C6
Donington Eaudike Lincs 156 B4
Donington le Heath Leics 153 G8
Donington on Bain Lincs 190 E2
Donington South Ing Lincs 156 C4
Donisthorpe Leics 152 G6
Don Johns Essex 106 F6
Donkey Street Kent 54 G6
Donkey Town Sur 66 G2
Donna Nook Lincs 190 B6
Donnington Glos 100 F3
Donnington Hereford 98 E4
Donnington Shrops 131 B11
Donnington Telford 150 G4
Donnington W Berks 64 F3
Donnington W Sus 22 C5
Donnington Wood Telford 150 G4
Donwell T&W 243 F7
Donyatt Som 28 E4
Doomsday Green W Sus 35 B11
Doonfoot S Ayrs 257 F8
Dora's Green Hants 49 D10
Dorback Lodge Highld 292 B2
Dorcan Swindon 63 C7
Dorchester Dorset 17 C9
Dorchester Oxon 83 G9
Dordale Worcs 117 C8
Dordon Warks 134 C5
Dore S Yorks 186 E4
Dores Highld 300 F5
Dorking Sur 51 D7
Dorking Tye Suff 107 D8
Dorley's Corner Suff 127 D7
Dormansland Sur 52 E2
Dormans Park Sur 51 E11
Dormanstown Redcar 235 G7
Dormer's Wells London 66 C6
Dormington Hereford 97 C11
Dormston Worcs 117 F9
Dorn Glos 100 E4
Dornal S Ayrs 236 B4
Dorney Bucks 66 D2
Dorney Reach Bucks 66 D2
Dorn Hill Worcs 100 E3
Dornie Highld 295 C10
Dornoch Highld 309 L7
Dornock Dumfries 238 D6
Dorrery Highld 310 D4
Dorridge W Mid 118 B3
Dorrington Lincs 173 E9
Dorrington Shrops 131 C9
Dorsington Warks 100 B2
Dorstone Hereford 96 C6
Dorton Bucks 83 C11
Dorusduain Highld 295 C11
Doseley Telford 132 B3
Dosmuckeran Highld 300 C2
Dosthill Staffs 134 C4
Dosthill Staffs 134 D4
Dothan Anglesey 178 G5
Dothill Telford 150 G2
Dottery Dorset 16 B5
Doublebois Corn 6 C3
Double Hill Bath 45 B8
Dougarie N Ayrs 255 D9
Doughton Glos 80 G5
Doughton Norf 159 D7
Douglas IoM 192 E4
Douglas S Lnrk 259 C8
Douglas & Angus Dundee 287 D8
Douglastown Angus 287 C8
Douglas Water S Lnrk 259 B9
Douglas West S Lnrk 259 C8
Doulting Som 44 E6
Dounby Orkney 314 D2
Doune Highld 291 C10
Doune Highld 309 J4
Doune Stirl 285 G11
Doune Park Aberds 303 C7
Douneside Aberds 292 C6
Dounie Argyll 275 D8
Dounie Highld 309 K5
Dounie Highld 309 L6
Dounreay Highld 310 C3
Doura N Ayrs 266 G6
Dousland Devon 7 B10
Dovaston Shrops 149 E7
Dovecot Mers 182 C6
Dovecothall Glasgow 267 D10
Dove Green Notts 171 E7
Dove Holes Derbys 185 F9
Dovenby Cumb 229 E7
Dovendale Lincs 190 E4
Dove Point Mers 182 C2
Dover Gtr Man 194 G6
Dover Kent 55 E10
Dovercourt Essex 108 E5
Doverdale Worcs 117 D7
Doverhay Som 41 D11
Doveridge Derbys 152 C2
Doversgreen Sur 51 D9
Dowally Perth 286 C4
Dowanhill Glasgow 267 B11
Dowbridge Lancs 202 G4
Dowdeswell Glos 81 B7
Dowe Hill Norf 161 F10
Dowlais M Tydf 77 D10
Dowlais Top M Tydf 77 D9
Dowland Devon 25 E9
Dowles Worcs 116 B5
Dowlesgreen Wokingham 65 F10
Dowlish Ford Som 28 E5
Dowlish Wake Som 28 E5
Downall Green Gtr Man 194 G5
Down Ampney Glos 81 F10
Downan Moray 301 F11
Downan S Ayrs 244 G3
Downcraig Ferry N Ayrs 266 D3
Downderry Corn 6 E6
Downe London 68 G2
Downend Glos 80 F4
Downend IoW 20 D6
Downend S Glos 60 D6

Downend W Berks 64 D3
Down End Som 43 E10
Downfield Dundee 287 D7
Down Field Cambs 124 C2
Downgate Corn 11 G11
Downgate Corn 12 G3
Down Hall Cumb 239 G7
Downham Essex 88 F2
Downham Lancs 203 E11
Downham London 67 E11
Downham Northumb 263 C9
Downham Market Norf 140 C2
Down Hatherley Glos 99 G7
Downhead Som 29 B9
Downhead Som 45 D7
Downhead Park M Keynes 103 C7
Downhill Corn 5 B7
Downhill Perth 286 D4
Downhill T&W 243 F9
Downholland Cross Lancs 193 F11
Downholme N Yorks 224 F2
Downicary Devon 12 C3
Downies Aberds 293 D11
Downinney Corn 11 C10
Downley Bucks 84 G4
Down Park W Sus 51 F10
Downs V Glam 58 E6
Down St Mary Devon 26 G2
Downside C Beds 103 G10
Downside E Sus 23 E9
Downside N Som 60 F3
Downside Som 44 D6
Downside Sur 50 B6
Downside Sur 51 B7
Down Street E Sus 36 C6
Down Thomas Devon 7 E10
Downton Hants 19 C11
Downton Powys 114 E4
Downton Shrops 149 G10
Downton Wilts 31 C11
Downton on the Rock Hereford 115 C8
Dowsby Lincs 156 D2
Dowsdale Lincs 156 G5
Dowslands Som 28 C2
Dowthwaitehead Cumb 230 G3
Doxey Staffs 151 E8
Doxford Park T&W 243 G9
Doynton S Glos 61 E8
Drabblegate Norf 160 D4
Draethen Newport 59 B8
Draffan S Lnrk 268 F5
Dragley Beck Cumb 210 D5
Dragonby N Lincs 200 E2
Dragons Green W Sus 35 C10
Drakehouse S Yorks 186 E6
Drakeland Corner Devon 7 D11
Drakelow Worcs 132 G6
Drakemyre Aberds 303 F9
Drakemyre N Ayrs 266 E5
Drake's Broughton Worcs 99 B8
Drakes Cross Worcs 117 B11
Drakestone Green Suff 107 B9
Drakewalls Corn 12 G4
Draughton Northants 120 B5
Draughton N Yorks 204 C6
Drawbridge Corn 6 B3
Drax N Yorks 199 B7
Draycot Oxon 83 D10
Draycot Cerne Wilts 62 D2
Draycote Warks 119 C8
Draycot Fitz Payne Wilts 62 G6
Draycot Foliat Swindon 63 D7
Draycott Derbys 153 C8
Draycott Glos 80 E2
Draycott Glos 100 D3
Draycott Shrops 132 E6
Draycott Som 29 C8
Draycott Som 44 C3
Draycott Worcs 99 B7
Draycott in the Clay Staffs 152 D3
Draycott in the Moors Staffs 169 G7
Drayford Devon 26 E3
Drayton Leics 136 E6
Drayton Lincs 156 B4
Drayton Norf 160 G3
Drayton Northants 119 E11
Drayton Oxon 83 G7
Drayton Oxon 101 C8
Drayton Ptsmth 33 F11
Drayton Som 28 C6
Drayton Som 29 D7
Drayton Warks 118 F3
Drayton Worcs 117 B8
Drayton Bassett Staffs 134 C3
Drayton Beauchamp Bucks 84 C6
Drayton Parslow Bucks 102 F6
Drayton St Leonard Oxon 83 F10
Drebley N Yorks 205 B7
Dreemskerry IoM 192 C5
Dreenhill Pembs 72 C6
Drefach Carms 75 C8
Drefach Carms 92 G5
Drefach Carms 93 D7
Dre-fach Carms 75 B11
Dre-fach Ceredig 93 B10
Drefelin Carms 93 D7
Dreggie Highld 301 G10
Dreghorn Edin 270 B4
Dreghorn N Ayrs 257 B9
Dre-gôch Denb 165 B10
Drellingore Kent 55 E8
Drem E Loth 281 F10
Dresden Stoke 168 G6
Dreumasdal W Isles 297 H3
Drewsteignton Devon 13 C10
Driby Lincs 190 G5
Driffield E Yorks 208 B6
Driffield Glos 81 F9
Drift Corn 1 D4
Drigg Cumb 219 F11
Drighlington W Yorks 197 B8
Drimnin Highld 289 D7
Drimnin Ho Highld 289 D7
Drimpton Dorset 28 F6
Drimsynie Argyll 284 G5
Dringhoe E Yorks 209 C9
Dringhouses York 207 D7
Drinisiadar W Isles 305 J3
Drinkstone Suff 125 E9
Drinkstone Green Suff 125 E9
Drishaig Argyll 284 F5
Drissaig Argyll 275 B10
Drive End Dorset 29 F9
Driver's End Herts 86 B2
Drochedlie Aberds 302 C5
Drochil Borders 270 G3
Drointon Staffs 151 D10
Droitwich Spa Worcs 117 E7
Droman Highld 306 D6
Dromore Dumfries 237 C7
Dron Perth 286 F5
Dronfield Derbys 186 F5
Dronfield Woodhouse Derbys 186 F4
Drongan E Ayrs 257 F10
Dronley Angus 287 D7
Droop Dorset 30 F3
Drope Cardiff 58 D6
Dropping Well S Yorks 186 C5
Droughduil Dumfries 236 D3
Droxford Hants 33 D10
Droylsden Gtr Man 184 B6
Drub W Yorks 197 B7
Druggers End Worcs 98 D5
Druid Denb 165 G8
Druidston Pembs 72 B5
Druim Highld 301 D9
Druimarbin Highld 290 F2
Druimavuic Argyll 284 C4
Druimdrishaig Argyll 275 F8
Druimindarroch Highld 295 G8
Druimkinnerras Highld 300 F4
Druimnacroish Argyll 288 E6
Druimsornaig Argyll 289 F9
Druimyeon More Argyll 255 B7
Drum Argyll 275 F10
Drum Edin 270 B6
Drum Perth 286 G4
Drumardoch Stirl 285 F10
Drumbeg Highld 306 F6
Drumblade Aberds 302 E5
Drumblair Aberds 302 E6
Drumbuie Dumfries 246 G3
Drumbuie Highld 295 B9
Drumburgh Cumb 239 F7
Drumburn Dumfries 237 C11
Drumchapel Glasgow 277 G10
Drumchardine Highld 300 E5
Drumchork Highld 307 L3
Drumclog S Lnrk 258 B4
Drumdelgie Aberds 302 E4
Drumderfit Highld 300 D6
Drumdollo Aberds 302 F6
Drumeldrie Fife 287 G8
Drumelzier Borders 260 C4
Drumfearn Highld 295 D8
Drumgask Highld 291 D8
Drumgelloch N Lnrk 268 B5
Drumgley Angus 287 B8
Drumgreen Angus 292 F6
Drumguish Highld 291 D9
Drumhead Aberds 293 B11
Drumin Moray 301 F11
Drumindorsair Highld 300 E4
Drumlasie Aberds 293 C8
Drumlean Stirl 285 G8
Drumlemble Argyll 255 F7
Drumliah Highld 309 K6
Drumligair Aberds 293 B11
Drumlithie Aberds 293 E9
Drumloist Stirl 285 G10
Drummersdale Lancs 193 E11
Drummick Perth 286 E3
Drummoddie Dumfries 236 E5
Drummond Highld 300 C6
Drummore Dumfries 236 F3
Drummuir Moray 302 E3
Drummuir Castle Moray 302 E3
Drumnadrochit Highld 300 G5
Drumnagorrach Moray 302 D5
Drumness Perth 286 F2
Drumoak Aberds 293 D9
Drumore Argyll 255 E8
Drumpark Dumfries 247 G9
Drumpellier N Lnrk 268 B4
Drumphail Dumfries 236 C4
Drumrash Dumfries 237 B8
Drumrunie Highld 307 J6
Drumry W Dunb 277 G10
Drums Aberds 303 G9
Drumsallie Highld 289 B11
Drumsmittal Highld 300 E6
Drumstinchall Dumfries 237 D10
Drumsturdy Angus 287 D8
Drumtochty Castle Aberds 293 F8
Drumtroddan Dumfries 236 E5
Drumuie Highld 298 E4
Drumuillie Highld 301 G9
Drumvaich Stirl 285 G10
Drumwalt Dumfries 236 D5
Drumwhindle Aberds 303 F9
Drunkendub Angus 287 C10
Drury Flint 166 C3
Drurylane Norf 141 C8
Drury Lane Wrex 167 G7
Drury Square Norf 159 F8
Drybeck Cumb 222 B3
Drybridge Moray 302 C4
Drybridge N Ayrs 257 B9
Drybrook Glos 79 B10
Dryburgh Borders 262 C3
Dryden Borders 261 E11
Dry Doddington Lincs 172 F4
Dry Drayton Cambs 123 E7
Dryhill Kent 52 B3
Dry Hill Hants 49 F7
Dryhope Borders 261 E7
Drylaw Edin 280 F4
Drym Corn 2 C4
Drymen Stirl 277 D9
Drymere Norf 140 B5
Drymuir Aberds 303 E9
Drynachan Lodge Highld 301 F8
Drynain Argyll 276 D3
Drynham Wilts 45 B11
Drynie Park Highld 300 D5
Drynoch Highld 294 B6
Dry Sandford Oxon 83 E7
Dryslwyn Carms 93 G11
Dry Street Essex 69 B7
Dryton Shrops 131 B11
Drywells Aberds 302 D6
Duag Bridge Highld 309 K3
Duartbeg Highld 306 F6
Duartmore Bridge Highld 306 F6
Dubbs Cross Devon 12 C3
Dubford Aberds 303 C8
Dubhchladach Argyll 275 G9
Dublin Suff 126 D3
Dubton Angus 287 B9
Dubwath Cumb 229 E9
Duchally Highld 309 H3
Duchlage Argyll 276 D6
Duchrae Dumfries 246 G5
Duck Corner Suff 109 C7
Duck End Beds 103 C11
Duck End Beds 121 G9
Duck End Bucks 102 F5
Duck End Cambs 122 E4
Duck End Essex 105 G10
Duck End Essex 106 E3
Duck End Essex 106 F3
Duckend Green Essex 106 G4
Duckhole S Glos 79 G10
Duckington Ches W 167 E7
Ducklington Oxon 82 D5
Duckmanton Derbys 186 G6
Duck's Cross Beds 122 F2
Ducks Island London 86 F2
Duckswich Worcs 98 D6
Dudbridge Glos 80 E4
Dudden Hill London 67 B8
Duddenhoe End Essex 105 D9
Duddingston Edin 280 G5
Duddington Northants 137 C9
Duddlestone Som 28 C2
Duddleswell E Sus 37 B7
Duddlewick Shrops 132 G3
Duddo Northumb 273 G8
Duddon Ches W 167 C8
Duddon Bridge Cumb 210 B3
Duddon Common Ches W 167 B8
Dudleston Shrops 148 B6
Dudleston Grove Shrops 149 B7
Dudleston Heath (Criftins) Shrops 149 B7
Dudley T&W 243 C7
Dudley W Mid 133 E8
Dudley Hill W Yorks 205 G9
Dudley Port W Mid 133 E9
Dudley's Fields W Mid 133 C9
Dudley Wood W Mid 133 F8
Dudlows Green Warr 183 E10
Dudsbury Dorset 19 B7
Dudswell Herts 85 D7
Dudwells Pembs 91 G8
Duerdon Devon 24 D4
Duffield Derbys 170 G4
Duffieldbank Derbys 170 G5
Duffryn Neath 57 B10
Duffryn Newport 59 B9
Duffryn Shrops 130 G4
Dufftown Moray 302 F3
Duffus Moray 301 C11
Dufton Cumb 231 F9
Duggleby N Yorks 217 F7
Duich Argyll 254 B4
Duiletter Argyll 284 D5
Duinish Perth 291 G8
Duirinish Highld 295 B9
Duisdalebeg Highld 295 D8
Duisdalemore Highld 295 D9
Duisky Highld 290 F2
Duke End Warks 134 F4
Dukesfield Northumb 241 F10
Dukestown Bl Gwent 77 C10
Dukinfield Gtr Man 184 B6
Dulas Anglesey 179 D7
Dulcote Som 44 E5
Dulford Devon 27 F9
Dull Perth 286 C2
Dullatur N Lnrk 278 F4
Dullingham Cambs 124 F2
Dullingham Ley Cambs 124 F2
Dulnain Bridge Highld 301 G9
Duloch Fife 280 D2
Duloe Beds 122 E3
Duloe Corn 6 D4
Dulsie Highld 301 E9
Dulverton Som 26 B6
Dulwich London 67 E10
Dulwich Village London 67 E10
Dumbarton W Dunb 277 F7
Dumbleton Glos 99 D10
Dumcrieff Dumfries 248 C4
Dumfries Dumfries 237 B11
Dumgoyne Stirl 277 E10
Dummer Hants 48 D5
Dumpford W Sus 34 C4
Dumpinghill Devon 24 F6
Dumpling Green Norf 159 G10
Dumplington Gtr Man 184 B3
Dumpton Kent 71 F11
Dun Angus 287 B10
Dunach Argyll 289 G10
Dunadd Argyll 275 D9
Dunain Ho Highld 300 E6
Dunalastair Perth 285 B11
Dunan Highld 295 C7
Dunans Argyll 275 D9
Dunans Argyll 275 D11
Dunball Som 43 E10
Dunbar E Loth 282 F3
Dunbeath Highld 311 G5
Dunbeg Argyll 289 F10
Dunblane Stirl 285 G11
Dunbog Fife 286 F6
Dunbridge Hants 32 B4
Duncansclett Shetland 313 K5
Duncanston Highld 300 D5
Duncanstone Aberds 302 G5
Dun Charlabhaigh W Isles 304 D3
Dunchideock Devon 14 D3
Dunchurch Warks 119 C9
Duncombe Lancs 202 F6
Duncote Northants 120 G3
Duncow Dumfries 247 G11
Duncraggan Stirl 285 G9
Duncrievie Perth 286 G5
Duncroisk Stirl 285 D9
Duncton W Sus 35 D7
Dundas Ho Orkney 314 H4
Dundee Dundee 287 D8
Dundeugh Dumfries 246 F3
Dundon Som 44 G3
Dundonald Fife 280 C4
Dundonald S Ayrs 257 C9
Dundon Hayes Som 44 G3
Dundonnell Highld 307 L5
Dundonnell Hotel Highld 307 L5
Dundonnell House Highld 307 L6
Dundraw Cumb 229 B10
Dundreggan Highld 290 B5
Dundreggan Lodge Highld 290 B5
Dundrennan Dumfries 237 E9
Dundridge Hants 33 D9
Dundry N Som 60 F5
Dundurn Perth 285 E11
Dundyvan N Lnrk 268 C4
Dunecht Aberds 293 C9
Dunfermline Fife 279 D11
Dunfield Glos 81 F10
Dunford Bridge S Yorks 197 G7
Dungate Kent 54 B2
Dunge Wilts 45 C11
Dungeness Kent 39 D9
Dungworth S Yorks 186 D3
Dunham Notts 188 G4
Dunham-on-the-Hill Ches W 183 G7
Dunham on Trent Notts 188 G4
Dunhampstead Worcs 117 E8
Dunhampton Worcs 116 D6
Dunham Town Gtr Man 184 D2
Dunham Woodhouses Gtr Man 184 D2
Dunholme Lincs 189 F8
Dunino Fife 287 F9
Dunipace Falk 278 E6
Dunira Perth 285 E11
Dunkeld Perth 286 C4
Dunkerton Bath 45 B8
Dunkeswell Devon 27 F10
Dunkeswick N Yorks 206 D2
Dunkirk Cambs 139 F10
Dunkirk Ches W 182 G5
Dunkirk Kent 54 B5
Dunkirk Norf 160 D4
Dunkirk Nottingham 153 B11
Dunkirk S Glos 61 B9
Dunkirk Staffs 168 E4
Dunkirk Wilts 62 G3
Dunk's Green Kent 52 C6
Dunlappie Angus 293 G7
Dunley Hants 48 C3
Dunley Worcs 116 D5
Dunlichity Lodge Highld 300 F6
Dunlop E Ayrs 267 F8
Dunmaglass Lodge Highld 300 G5
Dunmere Corn 5 B10
Dunmore Argyll 275 G8
Dunmore Falk 279 D7
Dunmore Highld 300 E5
Dunnerholme Cumb 210 D4
Dunnet Highld 310 B6
Dunnichen Angus 287 C9
Dunnikier Fife 280 C5
Dunninald Angus 287 B11
Dunning Perth 286 F4
Dunnington E Yorks 209 C9
Dunnington Warks 117 G11
Dunnington York 207 C9
Dunningwell Cumb 210 C3
Dunnockshaw Lancs 195 B10
Dunnose IoW 21 F7
Dunnsheath Shrops 149 F9
Dunn Street Kent 54 D3
Dunn Street Kent 69 G9
Dunollie Argyll 289 F10
Dunoon Argyll 276 F3
Dunragit Dumfries 236 D3
Dunrobin Mains Highld 311 J2
Dunrostan Argyll 275 E8
Duns Borders 272 E5
Dunsa Derbys 186 G2
Dunsby Lincs 156 D2
Dunscar Gtr Man 195 E8
Dunscore Dumfries 247 G9
Dunscroft S Yorks 199 F7
Dunsdale Redcar 226 B2
Dunsden Green Oxon 65 D8
Dunsfold Sur 50 F4
Dunsfold Common Sur 50 F4
Dunsfold Green Sur 50 F4
Dunsford Devon 14 D2
Dunsford Sur 50 F4
Dunshalt Fife 286 F6
Dunshillock Aberds 303 E9
Dunsill Notts 171 C7
Dunsinnan Perth 286 D5
Dunskey Ho Dumfries 236 D2
Dunslea Corn 11 G11
Dunsley N Yorks 227 C7
Dunsley Staffs 133 G7
Dunsmore Bucks 84 D5
Dunsmore Warks 119 B10
Dunsop Bridge Lancs 203 C9
Dunstable C Beds 103 G10
Dunstal Staffs 151 D11
Dunstall Staffs 152 E3
Dunstall Common Worcs 99 C7
Dunstall Green Suff 124 E4
Dunstall Hill W Mid 133 C8
Dunstan Northumb 265 F7
Dunstan Steads Northumb 264 E6
Dunster Som 42 E3
Duns Tew Oxon 101 F9
Dunston Derbys 186 G5
Dunston Lincs 173 C9
Dunston Norf 142 C4
Dunston Staffs 151 F8
Dunston T&W 242 E6
Dunstone Devon 7 E11
Dunstone Devon 8 G5
Dunston Heath Staffs 151 F8
Dunston Hill T&W 242 E6
Dunsville S Yorks 198 F6
Dunswell E Yorks 209 F7
Dunsyre S Lnrk 269 F11
Dunterton Devon 12 F3
Dunthrop Oxon 101 F7
Duntisbourne Abbots Glos 81 D7
Duntisbourne Leer Glos 81 D7
Duntisbourne Rouse Glos 81 D7
Duntish Dorset 29 F11
Duntocher W Dunb 277 G9
Dunton Bucks 102 G6
Dunton C Beds 104 C4
Dunton Norf 159 C7
Dunton Bassett Leics 135 E10
Dunton Green Kent 52 B4
Dunton Patch Norf 159 C7
Dunton Wayletts Essex 87 G11
Duntrune Castle Argyll 275 D8
Duntulm Highld 298 B4
Dunure S Ayrs 257 F7
Dunvant / Dynfant Swansea 56 C5
Dunvegan Highld 298 E2
Dunveth Corn 10 G5
Dunwear Som 43 F10
Dunwich Suff 127 C9
Dunwood Staffs 168 D6
Dupplin Castle Perth 286 F4
Durdar Cumb 239 G10
Durgan Corn 3 D7
Durgates E Sus 52 G6
Durham Durham 233 C11
Durisdeer Dumfries 247 C9
Durisdeermill Dumfries 247 C9
Durkar W Yorks 197 D10
Durleigh Som 43 F9
Durleighmarsh W Sus 34 C3
Durley Hants 33 D8
Durley Wilts 63 G8
Durley Street Hants 33 D8
Durlock Kent 55 B9
Durlow Common Hereford 98 D2
Durn Gtr Man 196 D2
Durnamuck Highld 307 K5
Durness Highld 308 C4
Durnfield Som 29 C7
Durno Aberds 303 G7
Durns Town Hants 19 B11
Duror Highld 289 D11
Durran Argyll 275 C10
Durran Highld 310 C5
Durrant Green Kent 53 F11
Durrants Hants 22 B2
Durrington Wilts 47 E7
Durrington W Sus 35 F10
Durrisdale Orkney 314 D3
Dursley Glos 80 F3
Dursley Wilts 45 C11
Dursley Cross Glos 98 G3
Durston Som 28 B3
Durweston Dorset 30 F5
Dury Shetland 313 G6
Duryard Devon 14 C4
Duston Northants 120 E4
Dutch Village Essex 69 C10
Duthil Highld 301 G9
Dutlas Powys 114 B4
Duton Hill Essex 106 F2
Dutson Corn 12 D2
Dutton Ches W 183 F9
Duxford Cambs 105 B9
Duxford Oxon 82 F5
Duxmoor Shrops 115 B8
Dwygyfylchi Conwy 180 F2
Dwyran Anglesey 162 B6
Dwyrhiw Powys 129 C11
Dyce Aberdeen 293 B10
Dyche Som 43 E7
Dye House Northumb 241 F10
Dyer's Common S Glos 60 C5
Dyer's Green Cambs 105 B7
Dyffryn Bridgend 57 C11
Dyffryn Carms 92 G6
Dyffryn Ceredig 110 G5
Dyffryn Pembs 91 D8
Dyffryn Ardudwy Gwyn 145 E11
Dyffryn-bern Ceredig 110 G5
Dyffryn Castell Ceredig 128 G5
Dyffryn Ceidrych Carms 94 F4
Dyffryn Cellwen Neath 76 D5
Dyke Lincs 156 E2
Dyke Moray 301 D9
Dykehead Angus 292 G5
Dykehead N Lnrk 269 D7
Dykehead Stirl 277 B11
Dykelands Aberds 293 G9
Dykends Angus 286 B6
Dykeside Aberds 303 E7
Dykesmains N Ayrs 266 G5
Dylife Powys 129 E7
Dymchurch Kent 39 B9
Dymock Glos 98 E4
Dynfant / Dunvant Swansea 56 C5
Dyrham S Glos 61 D8
Dysart Fife 280 C6
Dyserth Denb 181 F9


## E


Eabost Highld 294 B5
Eabost West Highld 298 E3
Each End Kent 55 B10
Eachway Worcs 117 B9
Eachwick Northumb 242 C4
Eadar Dha Fhadhail W Isles 304 E2
Eagland Hill Lancs 202 D4
Eagle Lincs 172 B5
Eagle Barnsdale Lincs 172 B5
Eagle Moor Lincs 172 B5
Eaglesfield Cumb 229 F7
Eaglesfield Dumfries 238 C6
Eaglesham E Renf 267 E11
Eaglestone M Keynes 103 D7
Eaglethorpe Northants 137 E11
Eagle Tor Derbys 170 C2
Eagley Gtr Man 195 E8
Eairy IoM 192 E3
Eakley Lanes M Keynes 120 G6
Eakring Notts 171 C11
Ealand N Lincs 199 E9
Ealing London 67 C7
Eals Northumb 240 F5
Eamont Bridge Cumb 230 F6
Earby Lancs 204 D3
Earcroft Blkburn 195 C7
Eardington Shrops 132 E4
Eardisland Hereford 115 F8
Eardisley Hereford 96 B6
Eardiston Shrops 149 D7
Eardiston Worcs 116 D3
Earith Cambs 123 C7
Earle Northumb 263 D11
Earlestown Mers 183 B9
Earley Wokingham 65 E9
Earlham Norf 142 B4
Earlish Highld 298 C3
Earls Barton Northants 121 E7
Earls Colne Essex 107 F7
Earl's Common Worcs 117 F9
Earl's Court London 67 D9
Earl's Croome Worcs 99 C7
Earlsdon W Mid 118 B6
Earl's Down E Sus 23 B10
Earlsferry Fife 281 B9
Earlsfield Lincs 155 B8
Earlsfield London 67 E9
Earlsford Aberds 303 F8
Earl's Green Suff 125 D10
Earlsheaton W Yorks 197 C9
Earl Shilton Leics 135 D9
Earlsmill Moray 301 D9
Earl Soham Suff 126 E4
Earl Sterndale Derbys 169 B9
Earlston Borders 262 B3
Earlston E Ayrs 257 B10
Earlstone Common Hants 64 G3
Earl Stoneham Suff 126 F2
Earl Stonham Suff 126 F2
Earlstoun Dumfries 246 G4
Earlswood Mon 79 F7
Earlswood Sur 51 D9
Earlswood Warks 118 C2
Earnley W Sus 22 D4
Earnock S Lnrk 268 E3
Earnshaw Bridge Lancs 194 C4
Earsairidh W Isles 297 M3
Earsdon T&W 243 C8
Earsham Norf 142 F6
Earsham Street Suff 126 B4
Earswick York 207 B8
Eartham W Sus 22 B6
Earthcott Green S Glos 61 B7
Easby N Yorks 224 E3
Easby N Yorks 225 D11
Easdale Argyll 275 B8
Easebourne W Sus 34 C5
Easenhall Warks 119 B9
Eashing Sur 50 E2
Easington Bucks 83 C11
Easington Durham 234 C4
Easington E Yorks 201 D11
Easington Lancs 203 C10
Easington Northumb 264 C4
Easington Oxon 83 F11
Easington Oxon 101 D9
Easington Redcar 226 B4
Easington Colliery Durham 234 C4
Easington Lane T&W 234 B3
Easingwold N Yorks 215 F10
Easole Street Kent 55 C9
Eason's Green E Sus 23 B8
Eassie Angus 287 C7
East Aberthaw V Glam 58 F4
Eastacombe Devon 25 B8
Eastacombe Devon 25 C9
Eastacott Devon 25 C10
East Acton London 67 C8
East Adderbury Oxon 101 D9
East Allington Devon 8 F5
East Amat Highld 309 K4
East Anstey Devon 26 B5
East Anton Hants 47 D11
East Appleton N Yorks 224 F4
East Ardsley W Yorks 197 B10
East Ashling W Sus 22 B4
East Aston Hants 48 D2
East Auchronie Aberds 293 C10
East Ayton N Yorks 217 B9
East Bank Bl Gwent 78 D2
East Barkwith Lincs 189 E11
East Barming Kent 53 C8
East Barnby N Yorks 226 C6
East Barnet London 86 F3
East Barns E Loth 282 F4
East Barsham Norf 159 C8
East Barton Suff 125 D8
East Beach W Sus 22 E5
East Beckham Norf 177 E11
East Bedfont London 66 E5
East Bergholt Suff 107 D11
East Bierley W Yorks 197 B7
East Bilney Norf 159 F9
East Blackdene Durham 232 D3
East Blatchington E Sus 23 E7
East Bloxworth Dorset 18 C3
East Boldon T&W 243 E9
East Boldre Hants 32 G5
East Bonhard Perth 286 E5
Eastbourne Darl 224 C6
Eastbourne E Sus 23 F10
East Bower Som 43 F10
East Brent Som 43 C11
Eastbridge Suff 127 D9
East Bridgford Notts 171 G11
East Briscoe Durham 223 B9
Eastbrook Som 28 C2
Eastbrook V Glam 59 E7
East Buckland Devon 41 G7
East Budleigh Devon 15 E7
Eastburn E Yorks 208 B5
Eastburn W Yorks 204 E6
Eastburn Br W Yorks 204 E6
East Burnham Bucks 66 C3
East Burrafirth Shetland 313 H5
East Burton Dorset 18 D2
Eastbury London 85 G9
Eastbury W Berks 63 D10
East Butsfield Durham 233 B8
East Butterleigh Devon 27 F7
East Butterwick N Lincs 199 F10
Eastby N Yorks 204 C6
East Cairnbeg Aberds 293 F9
East Calder W Loth 269 B11
East Carleton Norf 142 C3
East Carlton Northants 136 F6
East Carlton W Yorks 205 E10
East Chaldon or Chaldon Herring Dorset 17 E11
East Challow Oxon 63 B11
East Charleton Devon 8 G5
East Chelborough Dorset 29 F9
East Chiltington E Sus 36 D5
East Chinnock Som 29 E7
East Chisenbury Wilts 46 C6
East Cholderton Hants 47 D9
Eastchurch Kent 70 E3
East Clandon Sur 50 C5
East Claydon Bucks 102 F4
East Clevedon N Som 60 E2
East Clyne Highld 311 J3
East Clyth Highld 310 F7
East Coker Som 29 E8
Eastcombe Glos 80 E5
East Combe Som 43 G7
East Common N Yorks 207 G8
East Compton Dorset 30 D5
East Compton Som 44 E6
East Cornworthy Devon 8 D6
Eastcote London 66 B6
Eastcote Northants 120 G3
Eastcote W Mid 118 B3
Eastcote Village London 66 B6
Eastcott Corn 24 D3
Eastcott Wilts 46 B4
East Cottingwith E Yorks 207 E10
Eastcotts Beds 103 B11
Eastcourt Wilts 63 G8
Eastcourt Wilts 81 G7
East Cowes IoW 20 B6
East Cowick E Yorks 199 C7
East Cowton N Yorks 224 E6
East Cramlington Northumb 243 B7
East Cranmore Som 45 E7
East Creech Dorset 18 E4
East Croachy Highld 300 G6
East Croftmore Highld 291 B11
East Curthwaite Cumb 230 B2
East Dean E Sus 23 F9
East Dean Glos 98 G3
East Dean Hants 32 B3
East Dean W Sus 34 E6
East Dene S Yorks 186 C6
East Denton T&W 242 D6
East Didsbury Gtr Man 184 C5
Eastdon Devon 14 F5
Eastdown Devon 8 F6
East Down Devon 40 E6
East Drayton Notts 188 F3
East Dulwich London 67 E10
East Dundry N Som 60 F5
East Ella Hull 200 B5
Eastend Essex 86 C6
Eastend Oxon 100 G6
East End Beds 122 F2
East End Bucks 84 B4
East End C Beds 103 C9
East End Dorset 18 B5
East End Essex 89 D8
East End E Yorks 201 B9
East End E Yorks 209 B9
East End E Yorks 209 G9
East End Glos 81 E11
East End Hants 20 B3
East End Hants 33 C11
East End Hants 64 G2
East End Herts 105 F9
East End Kent 53 E11
East End Kent 53 F10
East End Kent 70 E3
East End M Keynes 103 C8
East End N Som 60 E3
East End Oxon 82 C5
East End Oxon 101 D9
East End Oxon 101 E7
East End S Glos 61 E9
East End Som 29 B10
East End Som 44 C5
East End Som 45 D7
East End Suff 108 E2
East End Suff 126 F3
East End Green Herts 86 C3
Easter Aberchalder Highld 291 B7
Easter Ardross Highld 300 B6
Easter Balgedie Perth 286 G5
Easter Balmoral Aberds 292 D4
Easter Boleskine Highld 300 G5
Easter Brackland Stirl 285 G10
Easter Brae Highld 300 C6
Easter Cardno Aberds 303 C9
Easter Compton S Glos 60 C5
Easter Cringate Stirl 278 D4
Easter Culfosie Aberds 293 C9
Easter Davoch Aberds 292 C6
Easter Earshaig Dumfries 248 C2
Easter Ellister Argyll 254 B3
Easter Fearn Highld 309 L6
Easter Galcantray Highld 301 E8
Eastergate W Sus 22 B6
Easterhouse Glasgow 268 B3
Easter Housebyres Borders 262 B2
Easter Howgate Midloth 270 C4
Easter Howlaws Borders 272 G4
Easter Kinkell Highld 300 D5
Easter Knox Angus 287 D9
Easter Langlee Borders 262 B2
Easter Lednathie Angus 292 G5
Easter Milton Highld 301 D9
Easter Moniack Highld 300 E5
Eastern Green W Mid 134 G5
Easter Ord Aberdeen 293 C10
Easter Quarff Shetland 313 K6
Easter Rhynd Perth 286 F5
Easter Row Stirl 278 B5
Easterside Mbro 225 B10
Easter Silverford Aberds 303 C7
Easter Skeld Shetland 313 J5
Easter Softlaw Borders 263 C7
Easterton Wilts 46 C4
Easterton of Lenabo Aberds 303 E10

Easterton Sands Wilts 46 B4
Eastertown Som 43 C10
Eastertown of Auchleuchries Aberds 303 F10
Easter Tulloch Highld 291 B11
Easter Whyntie Aberds 302 C6
East Everleigh Wilts 47 C8
East Ewell Sur 67 G8
East Farleigh Kent 53 C8
East Farndon Northants 136 F4
East Fen Common Cambs 124 C2
East Ferry Lincs 188 B4
Eastfield Borders 262 D2
Eastfield Bristol 60 D5
Eastfield N Lnrk 269 C7
Eastfield N Lnrk 278 G4
Eastfield Northumb 243 B7
Eastfield N Yorks 217 C10
Eastfield Pboro 138 D4
Eastfield S Lnrk 268 C2
Eastfield S Yorks 197 G9
Eastfield Hall Northumb 252 B6
East Fields W Berks 64 F3
East Finchley London 67 B9
East Finglassie Fife 280 B5
East Firsby Lincs 189 D8
East Fleet Dorset 17 E8
East Fortune E Loth 281 F10
East Garforth W Yorks 206 G4
East Garston W Berks 63 D11
Eastgate Durham 232 D5
Eastgate Norf 160 E2
Eastgate Pboro 138 D4
East Gateshead T&W 243 E7
East Ginge Oxon 64 B2
East Gores Essex 107 G7
East Goscote Leics 154 G2
East Grafton Wilts 63 G9
East Grange Moray 301 C10
East Green Hants 49 E9
East Green Suff 124 G3
East Green Suff 127 D8
East Grimstead Wilts 32 B2
East Grinstead W Sus 51 F11
East Guldeford E Sus 38 C6
East Haddon Northants 120 D3
East Hagbourne Oxon 64 B4
Easthall Herts 104 G3
East Halton N Lincs 200 D6
Eastham Mers 182 E5
Eastham Worcs 116 D3
East Ham London 68 C2
Eastham Ferry Mers 182 E5
East Hampnett W Sus 22 B6
Easthampstead Brack 65 F11
Easthampton Hereford 115 E8
East Hanney Oxon 82 G6
East Hanningfield Essex 88 E3
East Hardwick W Yorks 198 D3
East Harling Norf 141 F9
East Harlsey N Yorks 225 F8
East Harnham Wilts 31 B10
East Harptree Bath 44 B5
East Hartford Northumb 243 B7
East Harting W Sus 34 D3
East Hatch Wilts 30 B6
East Hatley Cambs 122 G5
Easthaugh Norf 159 F11
East Hauxwell N Yorks 224 G3
East Haven Angus 287 D9
Eastheath Wokingham 65 F10
East Heckington Lincs 173 G11
East Hedleyhope Durham 233 C9
East Helmsdale Highld 311 H4
East Hendred Oxon 64 B3
East Herringthorpe S Yorks 187 C7
East Herrington T&W 243 G9
East Heslerton N Yorks 217 D8
East Hewish N Som 59 G11
East Hill Kent 68 G5
East Hoathly E Sus 23 B8
East Hogaland Shetland 313 K5
East Holme Dorset 18 D3
East Holton Dorset 18 C5
East Holywell Northumb 243 C8
Easthope Shrops 131 D11
Easthopewood Shrops 131 D11
East Horndon Essex 68 B6
Easthorpe Essex 107 G8
Easthorpe Leics 154 B6
Easthorpe Notts 172 E2
East Horrington Som 44 D5
East Horsley Sur 50 C5
East Horton Northumb 264 C2
Easthouse Shetland 313 J5
Easthouses Midloth 270 B6
East Howdon T&W 243 D8
East Howe Bmouth 19 B7
East Huntspill Som 43 E10
East Hyde C Beds 85 B10
East Ilkerton Devon 41 D8
East Ilsley W Berks 64 C3
Easting Orkney 314 A7
Eastington Devon 26 F2
Eastington Glos 80 D3
Eastington Glos 81 C10
East Keal Lincs 174 C5
East Kennett Wilts 62 F6
East Keswick W Yorks 206 E3
East Kilbride S Lnrk 268 E2
East Kimber Devon 12 B5
East Kingston W Sus 35 G9
East Kirkby Lincs 174 C4
East Knapton N Yorks 217 D7
East Knighton Dorset 18 D2
East Knowstone Devon 26 C4
East Knoyle Wilts 45 G11
East Kyloe Northumb 264 B3
East Kyo Durham 242 G5
East Lambrook Som 28 D6
East Lamington Highld 301 B7
Eastland Gate Hants 33 E11
East Langdon Kent 55 D10
East Langton Leics 136 E4
East Langwell Highld 309 J7
East Lavant W Sus 22 B5
East Lavington W Sus 34 D6
East Law Northumb 242 G3
East Layton N Yorks 224 D3
Eastleach Martin Glos 82 D2
Eastleach Turville Glos 81 D11
East Leake Notts 153 D11
East Learmouth Northumb 263 B9
Eastleigh Devon 25 B7
Eastleigh Hants 32 D6
East Leigh Devon 8 E3
East Leigh Devon 25 F11
East Lexham Norf 159 F7
East Lilburn Northumb 264 E2
Eastling Kent 54 B3
East Linton E Loth 281 F11
East Liss Hants 34 B3
East Lockinge Oxon 64 B2
East Loftus Redcar 226 B4
East Looe Corn 6 E5
East Lound N Lincs 188 B3
East Lulworth Dorset 18 E3
East Lutton N Yorks 217 F8
East Lydeard Som 27 B11
East Lydford Som 44 G5
East Lyng Som 28 B4
East Mains Aberds 293 D8
East Mains Borders 271 F11
East Mains S Lnrk 268 E2
East Malling Kent 53 B8
East Malling Heath Kent 53 B7
East March Angus 287 D8
East Marden W Sus 34 E4
East Markham Notts 188 G2
East Marsh NE Lincs 201 E9
East Martin Hants 31 D9
East Marton N Yorks 204 C4
East Melbury Dorset 30 C5
East Meon Hants 33 C11
East Mere Devon 27 D7
East Mersea Essex 89 C9
East Mey Highld 310 B7
East Molesey Sur 67 F7
Eastmoor Derbys 186 G4
Eastmoor Norf 140 C4
East Moor W Yorks 197 C10
East Moors Cardiff 59 D8
East Morden Dorset 18 B4
East Morton W Yorks 205 E7
East Moulsecoomb Brighton 36 F4
East Ness N Yorks 216 D3
East Newton E Yorks 209 F11
East Newton N Yorks 216 D2
Eastney Ptsmth 21 B9
Eastnor Hereford 98 D4
East Norton Leics 136 C5
East Nynehead Som 27 C11
East Oakley Hants 48 C5
Eastoft N Lincs 199 D10
East Ogwell Devon 14 G2
Eastoke Hants 21 B10
Easton Bristol 60 E6
Easton Cambs 122 C2
Easton Cumb 239 C10
Easton Cumb 239 F7
Easton Devon 8 F3
Easton Devon 13 D10
Easton Dorset 17 G9
Easton Hants 48 G4
Easton IoW 20 D2
Easton Lincs 155 D8
Easton Norf 160 G2
Easton Som 44 D4
Easton Suff 126 F5
Easton W Berks 64 E2
Easton Wilts 61 E11
Easton Grey Wilts 61 B11
Easton in Gordano N Som 60 D4
Easton Maudit Northants 121 F7
Easton on the Hill Northants 137 C10
Easton Royal Wilts 63 G8
Easton Town Som 44 G5
Easton Town Wilts 61 B11
East Orchard Dorset 30 D4
East Ord Northumb 273 E9
Eastover Som 43 F10
East Panson Devon 12 C3
Eastpark Dumfries 238 D2
East Parley Dorset 19 B8
East Peckham Kent 53 D7
East Pennard Som 44 F5
East Perry Cambs 122 D3
East Portholland Corn 5 G9
East Portlemouth Devon 9 G9
East Prawle Devon 9 G10
East Preston W Sus 35 G9
East Pulham Dorset 30 F2
East Putford Devon 24 D5
East Quantoxhead Som 42 E6
East Rainton T&W 234 B2
East Ravendale NE Lincs 190 B2
East Raynham Norf 159 D7
Eastrea Cambs 138 D5
East Rhidorroch Lodge Highld 307 K7
Eastriggs Dumfries 238 D6
East Rigton W Yorks 206 E3
Eastrington E Yorks 199 B9
Eastrip Wilts 61 E10
East Rolstone N Som 59 G11
Eastrop Hants 48 C6
East Rounton N Yorks 225 E8
East Row N Yorks 227 C7
East Rudham Norf 158 D6
East Runton Norf 177 E11
East Ruston Norf 160 D6
Eastry Kent 55 C10
East Saltoun E Loth 271 B9
East Sheen London 67 D8
East Skelston Dumfries 247 F8
East Sleekburn Northumb 253 G7
East Somerton Norf 161 F9
East Stanley Durham 242 G6
East Stockwith Lincs 188 C3
East Stoke Dorset 18 D3
East Stoke Notts 172 F3
East Stoke Som 29 D7
East Stour Dorset 30 C4
East Stour Common Dorset 30 C4
East Stourmouth Kent 71 G9
East Stowford Devon 25 B10
East Stratton Hants 48 F4
East Street Kent 55 B10
East Street Som 44 F4
East Studdal Kent 55 D10
East Suisnish Highld 295 B7
East Taphouse Corn 6 C3
East-the-Water Devon 25 B7
East Third Borders 262 B4
East Thirston Northumb 252 D5
East Tilbury Thurrock 69 D7
East Tisted Hants 49 G8
East Torrington Lincs 189 E10
East Town Som 42 G6
East Town Som 44 E6
East Town Wilts 45 B11
East Trewent Pembs 73 F8
East Tuddenham Norf 159 G11
East Tuelmenna Corn 6 B4
East Tytherley Hants 32 B3
East Tytherton Wilts 62 E3
East Village Devon 26 F4
East Village V Glam 58 E3
Eastville Bristol 60 E6
Eastville Lincs 174 D6
East Wall Shrops 131 E10
East Walton Norf 158 F4
East Water Som 44 C4
East Week Devon 13 C9
Eastwell Leics 154 D5
East Wellow Hants 32 C4
Eastwell Park Kent 54 D4
East Wemyss Fife 280 B6
East Whitburn W Loth 269 B9
Eastwick Herts 86 C6
Eastwick Shetland 312 F5
East Wickham London 68 D3
East Williamston Pembs 73 E9
East Winch Norf 158 F3
East Winterslow Wilts 47 G8
East Wittering W Sus 21 B11
East Witton N Yorks 214 B2
Eastwood Hereford 98 C2
Eastwood Notts 171 F7
Eastwood Sthend 69 B10
Eastwood S Yorks 186 C6
Eastwood W Yorks 196 B3
East Woodburn Northumb 251 F10
Eastwood End Cambs 139 E8
Eastwood Hall Notts 171 F7
East Woodhay Hants 64 G2
East Woodlands Som 45 E9
East Worldham Hants 49 F8
East Worlington Devon 26 E3
East Worthing W Sus 35 G11
East Wretham Norf 141 E8
East Youlstone Devon 24 D3
Eathorpe Warks 119 D7
Eaton Ches E 168 B5
Eaton Ches W 167 C9
Eaton Hereford 115 F10
Eaton Leics 154 D5
Eaton Norf 142 B4
Eaton Notts 188 F2
Eaton Oxon 82 E6
Eaton Shrops 131 F7
Eaton Shrops 131 F10
Eaton Bishop Hereford 97 D8
Eaton Bray C Beds 103 G9
Eaton Constantine Shrops 131 B11
Eaton Ford Cambs 122 E3
Eaton Green C Beds 103 G9
Eaton Hastings Oxon 82 F3
Eaton Mascott Shrops 131 B10
Eaton on Tern Shrops 150 E3
Eaton Socon Cambs 122 F3
Eaton upon Tern Shrops 150 E3
Eau Brink Norf 157 F11
Eau Withington Hereford 97 C10
Eaves Green W Mid 134 G5
Eavestone N Yorks 214 F4
Ebberly Hill Devon 25 D9
Ebberston N Yorks 217 C7
Ebbesbourne Wake Wilts 31 C7
Ebblake Hants 31 F10
Ebbw Vale Bl Gwent 77 D11
Ebchester Durham 242 F4
Ebdon N Som 59 G11
Ebernoe W Sus 35 B7
Ebford Devon 14 D5
Ebley Glos 80 D4
Ebnal Ches W 167 F7
Ebnall Hereford 115 F9
Ebreywood Shrops 149 F10
Ebrington Glos 100 C3
Ecchinswell Hants 48 B4
Ecclaw Borders 272 B5
Ecclefechan Dumfries 238 C5
Eccle Riggs Cumb 210 B4
Eccles Borders 272 G5
Eccles Gtr Man 184 B3
Eccles Kent 69 G8
Ecclesall S Yorks 186 E4
Ecclesfield S Yorks 186 C5
Ecclesgreig Aberds 293 G9
Eccleshall Staffs 150 D6
Eccleshill W Yorks 205 F9
Ecclesmachan W Loth 279 G11
Eccles on Sea Norf 161 D8
Eccles Road Norf 141 E10
Eccleston Ches W 166 C6
Eccleston Lancs 194 D4
Eccleston Mers 183 B7
Eccleston Park Mers 183 C7
Eccliffe Dorset 30 B3
Eccup W Yorks 205 E11
Echt Aberds 293 C9
Eckford Borders 262 D6
Eckfordmoss Borders 262 D6
Eckington Derbys 186 F6
Eckington Worcs 99 C8
Eckington Corner E Sus 23 D8
Ecklands S Yorks 197 G8
Eckworthy Devon 24 D6
Ecton Northants 120 E6
Ecton Staffs 169 D9
Ecton Brook Northants 120 E6
Edale Derbys 185 D10
Edale End Derbys 185 D11
Edbrook Som 43 E8
Edburton W Sus 36 E2
Edderside Cumb 229 B7
Edderton Highld 309 L7
Eddington Kent 71 F7
Eddington W Berks 63 F10
Eddistone Devon 24 C3
Eddleston Borders 270 F4
Eddlewood S Lnrk 268 E4
Edenbridge Kent 52 D2
Edenfield Lancs 195 D9
Edenhall Cumb 231 E7
Edenham Lincs 155 E11
Eden Mount Cumb 211 D8
Eden Park London 67 F11
Edensor Derbys 170 B2
Edentaggart Argyll 276 C6
Edenthorpe S Yorks 198 F6
Edentown Cumb 239 F9
Eden Vale Durham 234 D4
Eden Vale Wilts 45 C11
Ederline Argyll 275 C9
Edern Gwyn 144 B5
Edford Som 45 D7
Edgarley Som 44 F4
Edgbaston W Mid 133 G11
Edgcote Northants 101 B10
Edgcott Bucks 102 G3
Edgcott Som 41 F10
Edgcumbe Corn 2 C6
Edge Glos 80 D4
Edge Shrops 131 B7
Edgebolton Shrops 149 E11
Edge End Glos 79 C9
Edge End Lancs 203 G10
Edgefield Norf 159 C11
Edgefield Street Norf 159 C11
Edge Fold Blkburn 195 D8
Edge Fold Gtr Man 195 F8
Edge Green Ches W 167 E7
Edge Green Gtr Man 183 B9
Edge Green Norf 141 F10
Edgehill Warks 101 B7
Edge Hill Mers 182 C5
Edge Hill Warks 134 D4
Edgeley Gtr Man 184 D5
Edge Mount S Yorks 186 C3
Edgerley Shrops 148 F6
Edgerston Borders 262 G5
Edgerton W Yorks 196 D6
Edgeside Lancs 195 C10
Edgeworth Glos 80 D6
Edginswell Devon 9 B7
Edgiock Worcs 117 E10
Edgmond Telford 150 F4
Edgmond Marsh Telford 150 E4
Edgton Shrops 131 F7
Edgware London 85 G11
Edgwick W Mid 134 G6
Edgworth Blkburn 195 D8
Edham Borders 262 B6
Edial Staffs 133 B11
Edinample Stirl 285 E9
Edinbane Highld 298 D3
Edinburgh Edin 280 G5
Edinchip Stirl 285 E9
Edingale Staffs 152 G4
Edingight Ho Moray 302 D5
Edinglassie Ho Aberds 292 B5
Edingley Notts 171 D11
Edingthorpe Norf 160 C6
Edingthorpe Green Norf 160 C6
Edington Som 43 E11
Edington Wilts 46 C2
Edingworth Som 43 C11
Edintore Moray 302 E4
Edistone Devon 24 C2
Edithmead Som 43 D10
Edith Weston Rutland 137 B8
Edlaston Derbys 169 G11
Edlesborough Bucks 85 B7
Edlingham Northumb 252 B4
Edlington Lincs 190 G2
Edmondsham Dorset 31 E9
Edmondsley Durham 233 B10
Edmondstown Rhondda 77 G8
Edmondthorpe Leics 155 F7
Edmonston S Lnrk 269 G11
Edmonstone Orkney 314 D5
Edmonton Corn 10 G5
Edmonton London 86 G4
Edmundbyers Durham 242 G2
Ednam Borders 262 B6
Ednaston Derbys 170 G2
Edney Common Essex 87 E11
Edradynate Perth 286 B2
Edrom Borders 272 D6
Edstaston Shrops 149 C10
Edstone Warks 118 E3
Edvin Loach Hereford 116 F3
Edwalton Notts 153 B11
Edwardstone Suff 107 C8
Edwardsville M Tydf 77 F9
Edwinsford Carms 94 E2
Edwinstowe Notts 171 B10
Edworth C Beds 104 C4
Edwyn Ralph Hereford 116 F2
Edzell Angus 293 G7
Efail-fôch Neath 57 B9
Efail Isaf Rhondda 58 C5
Efailnewydd Gwyn 145 B7
Efailwen Carms 92 F2
Efenechtyd Denb 165 D10
Effingham Sur 50 C6
Effirth Shetland 313 H5
Efflinch Staffs 152 F3
Efford Devon 26 G5
Efford Plym 7 D10
Egbury Hants 48 C2
Egdon Worcs 117 G8
Egerton Gtr Man 195 E8
Egerton Kent 54 D2
Egerton Forstal Kent 53 D11
Egerton Green Ches E 167 E8
Egford Som 45 D9
Eggbeare Corn 12 D2
Eggborough N Yorks 198 C5
Eggbuckland Plym 7 D10
Eggesford Station Devon 25 E11
Eggington C Beds 103 F9
Egginton Derbys 152 D5
Egginton Common Derbys 152 D5
Egglesburn Durham 232 G5
Egglescliffe Stockton 225 C8
Eggleston Durham 232 G5
Egham Sur 66 E4
Egham Hythe Sur 66 E4
Egham Wick Sur 66 E3
Egleton Rutland 137 B7
Eglingham Northumb 264 F4
Egloshayle Corn 10 G5
Egloskerry Corn 11 D11
Eglwysbach Conwy 180 G4
Eglwys-Brewis V Glam 58 F4
Eglwys Cross Wrex 167 G7
Eglwys Fach Ceredig 128 D3
Eglwyswen Pembs 92 D3
Eglwyswrw Pembs 92 D2
Egmanton Notts 172 B2
Egmere Norf 159 B8
Egremont Cumb 219 C10
Egremont Mers 182 C4
Egton N Yorks 226 D6
Egton Bridge N Yorks 226 D6
Egypt Bucks 66 B3
Egypt Hants 48 E3
Egypt W Berks 64 D2
Egypt W Yorks 205 G7
Eiden Highld 309 J7
Eight Ash Green Essex 107 F8
Eighton Banks T&W 243 F7
Eignaig Highld 289 E9
Eign Hill Hereford 97 D10
Eil Highld 291 B10
Eilanreach Highld 295 D10
Eildon Borders 262 C3
Eileanach Lodge Highld 300 C5
Eilean Anabaich W Isles 305 H4
Eilean Darach Highld 307 L6
Eilean Shona Ho Highld 289 B8
Einacleite W Isles 304 F3
Einsiob / Evenjobb Powys 114 E5
Eisgean W Isles 305 G5
Eisingrug Gwyn 146 C2
Eland Green Northumb 242 C5
Elan Village Powys 113 D8
Elberton S Glos 60 B6
Elborough N Som 43 B11
Elbridge Shrops 149 E7
Elbridge W Sus 22 C6
Elburton Plym 7 E10
Elcho Perth 286 E5
Elcock's Brook Worcs 117 E10
Elcombe Glos 80 F3
Elcombe Swindon 62 C6
Elcot W Berks 63 F11
Eldene Swindon 63 C7
Eldernell Cambs 138 D6
Eldersfield Worcs 98 E6
Elderslie Renfs 267 C8
Elder Street Essex 105 E11
Eldon Durham 233 F10
Eldon Lane Durham 233 F10
Eldrick S Ayrs 245 G7
Eldroth N Yorks 212 F5
Eldwick W Yorks 205 E8
Elemore Vale T&W 234 B3
Elerch / Bont-goch Ceredig 128 F3
Elfhowe Cumb 221 F9
Elford Northumb 264 C5
Elford Staffs 152 G3
Elford Closes Cambs 123 C10
Elgin Moray 302 C2
Elgol Highld 295 D7
Elham Kent 55 E7
Eliburn W Loth 269 B10
Elie Fife 287 G8
Elim Anglesey 178 D5
Eling Hants 32 E5
Eling W Berks 64 D4
Elishader Highld 298 C5
Elishaw Northumb 251 D9
Elizafield Dumfries 238 C2
Elkesley Notts 187 F11
Elkington Northants 120 B2
Elkins Green Essex 87 E10
Elkstone Glos 81 C7
Ellacombe Torbay 9 C8
Ellan Highld 301 G8
Elland W Yorks 196 C6
Elland Lower Edge W Yorks 196 C6
Elland Upper Edge W Yorks 196 C6
Ellary Argyll 275 F8
Ellastone Staffs 169 G10
Ellel Lancs 202 B5
Ellemford Borders 272 C4
Ellenbrook Cumb 228 D6
Ellenbrook Herts 86 D2
Ellenbrook IoM 192 E4
Ellenglaze Corn 4 D5
Ellenhall Staffs 150 D6
Ellen's Green Sur 50 F5
Ellerbeck N Yorks 225 F8
Ellerburn N Yorks 216 C6
Ellerby N Yorks 226 C5
Ellerdine Telford 150 E2
Ellerdine Heath Telford 150 E2
Ellerhayes Devon 27 G7
Elleric Argyll 284 C4
Ellerker E Yorks 200 B2
Ellerton E Yorks 207 F10
Ellerton N Yorks 224 F5
Ellerton Shrops 150 D4
Ellesborough Bucks 84 D4
Ellesmere Shrops 149 C8
Ellesmere Park Gtr Man 184 B3
Ellesmere Port Ches W 182 F6
Ellicombe Som 42 E3
Ellingham Hants 31 F10
Ellingham Norf 143 E7
Ellingham Northumb 264 D5
Ellingstring N Yorks 214 C3
Ellington Cambs 122 C3
Ellington Northumb 253 E7
Ellington Thorpe Cambs 122 C3
Elliot Angus 287 D10
Elliots Green Som 45 D9
Elliot's Town Caerph 77 E10
Ellisfield Hants 48 D6
Elliston Borders 262 D3
Ellistown Leics 153 G8
Ellon Aberds 303 F9
Ellonby Cumb 230 D4
Ellough Suff 143 F8
Elloughton E Yorks 200 B2
Ellwood Glos 79 D9
Elm Cambs 139 B9
Elmbridge Glos 80 B5
Elmbridge Worcs 117 D8
Elm Corner Sur 50 B5
Elm Cross Wilts 62 D6
Elmdon Essex 105 D9
Elmdon W Mid 134 G3
Elmdon Heath W Mid 134 G3
Elmer W Sus 35 G7
Elmers End London 67 F11
Elmers Green Lancs 194 F3
Elmers Marsh W Sus 34 B5
Elmesthorpe Leics 135 D9
Elmfield IoW 21 C8
Elm Hill Dorset 30 B4
Elmhurst Bucks 84 B4
Elmhurst Staffs 152 G2
Elmley Castle Worcs 99 C9
Elmley Lovett Worcs 117 D7
Elmore Glos 80 B3
Elmore Back Glos 80 B3
Elm Park London 68 B4
Elmscott Devon 24 C2
Elmsett Suff 107 B11
Elms Green Hereford 115 F10
Elms Green Worcs 116 D4
Elmslack Lancs 211 D9
Elmstead Essex 107 F11
Elmstead London 68 E2
Elmstead Heath Essex 107 G11
Elmstead Market Essex 107 G11
Elmsted Kent 54 E6
Elmsthorpe Leics 135 D9
Elmstone Kent 71 G9
Elmstone Hardwicke Glos 99 F8
Elmswell E Yorks 208 B5
Elmswell Suff 125 E9
Elmton Derbys 187 G8
Elness Orkney 314 C6
Elphin Highld 307 H7
Elphinstone E Loth 281 G7
Elrick Aberds 293 C10
Elrig Dumfries 236 E5
Elrigbeag Argyll 284 F5
Elrington Northumb 241 E9
Elscar S Yorks 197 G11
Elsdon Hereford 114 G6
Elsdon Northumb 251 E10
Elsecar S Yorks 186 B5
Elsecar S Yorks 197 G11
Elsenham Essex 105 F10
Elsenham Sta Essex 105 F10
Elsfield Oxon 83 C8
Elsham N Lincs 200 E4
Elsing Norf 159 F11
Elslack N Yorks 204 D4
Elson Hants 33 G10
Elson Shrops 149 B7
Elsrickle S Lnrk 269 G11
Elstead Sur 50 E2
Elsted W Sus 34 D4
Elsthorpe Lincs 155 E11
Elstob Durham 234 G2
Elston Devon 26 G3
Elston Notts 172 F3
Elston Wilts 46 E5
Elstone Devon 25 D11
Elstow Beds 103 B11
Elstree Herts 85 F11
Elstronwick E Yorks 209 G10
Elswick Lancs 202 F4
Elswick T&W 242 E6
Elswick Leys Lancs 202 F4
Elsworth Cambs 122 E6
Elterwater Cumb 220 E6
Eltham London 68 E2
Eltisley Cambs 122 F5
Elton Cambs 137 E11
Elton Ches W 183 F7
Elton Derbys 170 C2
Elton Glos 80 C2
Elton Gtr Man 195 E9
Elton Hereford 115 C9
Elton Notts 154 B5
Elton Stockton 225 B8
Elton Green Ches W 183 G7
Elton's Marsh Hereford 97 C9
Eltringham Northumb 242 E3
Elvanfoot S Lnrk 259 F11
Elvaston Derbys 153 C8
Elveden Suff 124 B6
Elvet Hill Durham 233 C11
Elvingston E Loth 281 G9
Elvington Kent 55 C9
Elvington York 207 D9
Elwell Devon 41 G7
Elwell Dorset 17 E9
Elwick Hrtlpl 234 E5
Elwick Northumb 264 B4
Elworth Ches E 168 C2
Elworthy Som 42 G5
Ely Cambs 139 G10
Ely Cardiff 58 D6
Emberton M Keynes 103 B7
Embleton Cumb 229 E9
Embleton Durham 234 F4
Embleton Northumb 264 E6
Embo Highld 311 K2
Emborough Som 44 C6
Embo Street Highld 311 K2
Embsay N Yorks 204 C6
Emerson Park London 68 B4
Emerson's Green S Glos 61 D7
Emerson Valley M Keynes 102 E6
Emery Down Hants 32 F3
Emley W Yorks 197 E8
Emmbrook Wokingham 65 F9
Emmer Green Reading 65 D8
Emmett Carr Derbys 187 F7
Emmington Oxon 84 E2
Emneth Norf 139 B9
Emneth Hungate Norf 139 B10
Emorsgate Norf 157 E10
Empingham Rutland 137 B8
Empshott Hants 49 G9
Empshott Green Hants 49 G8
Emscote Warks 118 D5
Emstrey Shrops 149 G10
Emsworth Hants 22 B2
Enborne W Berks 64 F2
Enborne Row W Berks 64 G2
Enchmarsh Shrops 131 D10
Enderby Leics 135 D10
Endmoor Cumb 211 C10
Endon Staffs 168 E6
Endon Bank Staffs 168 E6
Energlyn Caerph 58 B6
Enfield London 86 F4
Enfield Worcs 117 D10
Enfield Highway London 86 F5
Enfield Lock London 86 F5
Enfield Town London 86 F4
Enfield Wash London 86 F5
Enford Wilts 46 C6
Engamoor Shetland 313 H4
Engedi Anglesey 178 F5
Engine Common S Glos 61 C7
Englefield W Berks 64 E6
Englefield Green Sur 66 E3
Englesea-brook Ches E 168 E3
English Bicknor Glos 79 B9
Englishcombe Bath 61 G8
English Frankton Shrops 149 D9
Engollan Corn 10 G3
Enham Alamein Hants 47 D11
Enis Devon 25 B9
Enisfirth Shetland 312 F5
Enmore Som 43 G8
Enmore Field Hereford 115 E9
Enmore Green Dorset 30 C5
Ennerdale Bridge Cumb 219 B11
Enniscaven Corn 5 D9
Enoch Dumfries 247 C9
Enochdhu Perth 292 G2
Ensay Argyll 288 E5
Ensbury Bmouth 19 B7
Ensbury Park Bmouth 19 C7
Ensdon Shrops 149 F8
Ensis Devon 25 B9
Enslow Oxon 83 B7
Enstone Oxon 101 G7
Enterkinfoot Dumfries 247 C9
Enterpen N Yorks 225 D9
Enton Green Sur 50 E3
Enville Staffs 132 F6
Eolaigearraidh W Isles 297 L3
Eorabus Argyll 288 G5
Eòropaidh W Isles 304 B7
Epney Glos 80 C3
Epperstone Notts 171 F11
Epping Essex 87 E7
Epping Green Essex 86 D6
Epping Green Herts 86 D3
Epping Upland Essex 86 E6
Eppleby N Yorks 224 C3
Eppleworth E Yorks 208 G6
Epsom Sur 67 G8
Epwell Oxon 101 C7
Epworth N Lincs 199 G9
Epworth Turbary N Lincs 199 G9
Erbistock Wrex 166 G5
Erbusaig Highld 295 C9
Erchless Castle Highld 300 E4
Erdington W Mid 134 E2
Eredine Argyll 275 C10
Eriboll Highld 308 D4
Ericstane Dumfries 260 G3
Eridge Green E Sus 52 F5
Erines Argyll 275 F9
Eriswell Suff 124 B4
Erith London 68 D4
Erlestoke Wilts 46 C3
Ermine Lincs 189 G7
Ermington Devon 8 E2
Ernesettle Plym 7 D8
Erpingham Norf 160 C3
Erriottwood Kent 54 B2
Errogie Highld 300 G5
Errol Perth 286 E6
Errol Station Perth 286 E6
Erskine Renfs 277 G9
Erskine Bridge Renfs 277 G9
Ervie Dumfries 236 C2
Erwarton Suff 108 E4
Erwood Powys 95 C11
Eryholme N Yorks 224 D6
Eryrys Denb 166 D2
Escomb Durham 233 E9
Escott Som 42 F5
Escrick N Yorks 207 E8
Esgairdawe Carms 94 C2
Esgairgeiliog Powys 128 B5
Esgyryn Conwy 180 F4
Esh Durham 233 C9
Esher Sur 66 G6
Eshiels Borders 261 B7
Esholt W Yorks 205 E9
Eshott Northumb 252 D6
Eshton N Yorks 204 B4
Esh Winning Durham 233 C9
Eskadale Highld 300 F4
Eskbank Midloth 270 B6
Eskdale Green Cumb 220 E2
Eskdalemuir Dumfries 249 D7
Eske E Yorks 209 E7
Eskham Lincs 190 B5
Eskholme S Yorks 198 D6
Esknish Argyll 274 G4
Esk Valley N Yorks 226 E6
Eslington Park Northumb 264 G2
Esperley Lane Ends Durham 233 G8
Esprick Lancs 202 F4
Essendine Rutland 155 G10
Essendon Herts 86 D3
Essich Highld 300 F6
Essington Staffs 133 C9
Esslemont Aberds 303 G9
Eston Redcar 225 B11
Estover Plym 7 D10
Eswick Shetland 313 H6
Etal Northumb 263 B10
Etchilhampton Wilts 62 G4
Etchingham E Sus 38 B2
Etchinghill Kent 55 F7
Etchinghill Staffs 151 F10
Etchingwood E Sus 37 C8
Etherley Dene Durham 233 F9
Ethie Castle Angus 287 C10
Ethie Mains Angus 287 C10
Etling Green Norf 159 G10
Etloe Glos 79 D11
Eton Windsor 66 D3
Eton Wick Windsor 66 D2
Etruria Stoke 168 F5
Etsell Shrops 131 C7
Etterby Cumb 239 F9
Etteridge Highld 291 D8
Ettersgill Durham 232 F3
Ettiley Heath Ches E 168 C2
Ettingshall W Mid 133 D8

Marden Kent 53 E8
Marden T&W 243 C9
Marden Wilts 46 B5
Marden Ash Essex 87 E9
Marden Beech Kent 53 E8
Marden's Hill E Sus 52 G3
Marden Thorn Kent 53 E9
Mardleybury Herts 86 B3
Mardu Shrops 130 G5
Mardy Mon 78 B4
Mardy Shrops 148 C5
Marefield Leics 136 B4
Mareham le Fen Lincs 174 C3
Mareham on the Hill Lincs 174 B3
Marehay Derbys 170 F5
Marehill W Sus 35 D9
Maresfield E Sus 37 C7
Maresfield Park E Sus 37 C7
Marfleet Hull 200 B6
Marford Wrex 166 D5
Margam Neath 57 D9
Margaret Marsh Dorset 30 D4
Margaret Roding Essex 87 C9
Margaretting Essex 87 E11
Margaretting Tye Essex 87 E11
Margate Kent 71 E11
Margery Sur 51 C9
Margnaheglish N Ayrs 256 C2
Margreig Dumfries 237 B10
Margrove Park Redcar 226 B3
Marham Norf 158 G4
Marhamchurch Corn 24 G2
Marholm Pboro 138 C2
Marian Flint 181 F9
Marian Cwm Denb 181 F9
Mariandyrys Anglesey 179 E10
Marianglas Anglesey 179 E8
Marian-glas Anglesey 179 E8
Mariansleigh Devon 26 C2
Marian y de / South Beach Gwyn 145 C7
Marian y mor / West End Gwyn 145 C7
Marine Town Kent 70 E2
Marionburgh Aberds 293 C9
Marishader Highld 298 C4
Marjoriebanks Dumfries 248 G3
Mark Dumfries 236 D3
Mark Dumfries 237 C7
Mark S Ayrs 236 B2
Mark Som 43 D11
Markbeech Kent 52 E3
Markby Lincs 191 F7
Mark Causeway Som 43 D11
Mark Cross E Sus 23 C7
Mark Cross E Sus 52 G5
Markeaton Derbys 152 B6
Market Bosworth Leics 135 C8
Market Deeping Lincs 138 B2
Market Drayton Shrops 150 C3
Market Harborough Leics 136 F4
Markethill Perth 286 D6
Market Lavington Wilts 46 C4
Market Overton Rutland 155 F7
Market Rasen Lincs 189 D10
Market Stainton Lincs 190 F2
Market Warsop Notts 171 B9
Market Weighton E Yorks 208 E3
Market Weston Suff 125 B9
Markfield Leics 153 G9
Mark Hall North Essex 87 C7
Mark Hall South Essex 87 C7
Markham Caerph 77 E11
Markham Moor Notts 188 G2
Markinch Fife 286 G6
Markington N Yorks 214 F5
Markland Hill Gtr Man 195 F7
Markle E Loth 281 F11
Marksbury Bath 61 G7
Mark's Corner IoW 20 C5
Marks Gate London 87 G7
Marks Tey Essex 107 G8
Markyate Herts 85 B9
Marland Gtr Man 195 E11
Marlas Hereford 97 F8
Marl Bank Worcs 98 C5
Marlborough Wilts 63 F7
Marlbrook Hereford 115 G10
Marlbrook Worcs 117 C9
Marlcliff Warks 117 G11
Marldon Devon 9 C7
Marle Green E Sus 23 B9
Marle Hill Glos 99 G9
Marlesford Suff 126 F6
Marley Kent 55 C7
Marley Kent 55 C10
Marley Green Ches E 167 F9
Marley Heights W Sus 49 G11
Marley Hill T&W 242 F6
Marley Pots T&W 243 F9
Marlingford Norf 142 B2
Mar Lodge Aberds 292 D2
Marloes Pembs 72 D3
Marlow Bucks 65 B10
Marlow Hereford 115 B8
Marlow Bottom Bucks 65 B11
Marlow Common Bucks 65 B10
Marlpit Hill Kent 52 D2
Marlpits E Sus 38 E2
Marlpool Derbys 170 F6
Marnhull Dorset 30 D3
Marnoch Aberds 302 D5
Marnock N Lnrk 268 B4
Marple Gtr Man 185 D7
Marple Bridge Gtr Man 185 D7
Marpleridge Gtr Man 185 D7
Marr S Yorks 198 F4
Marrel Highld 311 H4
Marr Green Wilts 63 G8
Marrick N Yorks 223 F11
Marrister Shetland 313 G7
Marros Carms 74 D2
Marsden T&W 243 E9
Marsden W Yorks 196 E4
Marsden Height Lancs 204 F3
Marsett N Yorks 213 B8
Marsh Bucks 84 D4
Marsh Devon 28 E3
Marsh W Yorks 196 D6
Marsh W Yorks 204 F6
Marshall Meadows Northumb 273 D9
Marshall's Cross Mers 183 C8
Marshall's Elm Som 44 G3
Marshall's Heath Herts 85 B11
Marshalsea Dorset 28 G5
Marshalswick Herts 85 D11
Marsham Norf 160 E3
Marshaw Lancs 203 C7
Marsh Baldon Oxon 83 F9
Marsh Benham W Berks 64 F2
Marshborough Kent 55 B10
Marshbrook Shrops 131 F8
Marshchapel Lincs 190 B5
Marsh Common S Glos 60 C5
Marsh End Worcs 98 D6
Marshfield Newport 59 C9
Marshfield S Glos 61 E9
Marshfield Bank Ches E 167 D11
Marshgate Corn 11 C9
Marsh Gate W Berks 63 F10
Marsh Gibbon Bucks 102 G2
Marsh Green Ches W 183 F8
Marsh Green Devon 14 C6
Marsh Green Gtr Man 194 F5
Marsh Green Kent 52 E2
Marsh Green Staffs 168 D5
Marsh Green Telford 150 G2
Marsh Houses Lancs 202 C5
Marshland St James Norf 139 B10
Marsh Lane Derbys 186 F6
Marsh Lane Glos 79 D9
Marsh Mills Som 43 F7
Marshmoor Herts 86 D2
Marshside Kent 71 F8
Marshside Mers 193 D11
Marsh Side Norf 176 E3
Marsh Street Som 42 E3
Marshwood Dorset 16 B3
Marske N Yorks 224 E2
Marske-by-the-Sea Redcar 235 G8
Marston Ches W 183 F11
Marston Hereford 115 F7
Marston Lincs 172 G5
Marston Oxon 83 D8
Marston Staffs 150 G6
Marston Staffs 151 D8
Marston Warks 119 B8
Marston Warks 134 E4
Marston Wilts 46 B3
Marston Bigot Som 45 E9
Marston Doles Warks 119 F9
Marston Gate Som 45 D9
Marston Green W Mid 134 F3
Marston Hill Glos 81 F10
Marston Jabbett Warks 135 F7
Marston Magna Som 29 C9
Marston Meysey Wilts 81 F10
Marston Montgomery Derbys 152 B2
Marston Moretaine C Beds 103 C9
Marston on Dove Derbys 152 D4
Marston St Lawrence Northants 101 C10
Marston Stannett Hereford 115 F11
Marston Trussell Northants 136 F3
Marstow Hereford 79 B9
Marsworth Bucks 84 C6
Marten Wilts 47 B9
Marthall Ches E 184 F4
Martham Norf 161 F9
Marthwaite Cumb 222 G2
Martin Hants 31 D9
Martin Kent 55 D10
Martin Lincs 173 D10
Martin Lincs 174 B2
Martindale Cumb 221 B8
Martin Dales Lincs 173 C11
Martin Drove End Hants 31 C9
Martinhoe Devon 41 D7
Martinhoe Cross Devon 41 D7
Martin Hussingtree Worcs 117 E7
Martin Mill Kent 55 D10
Martin Moor Lincs 174 C2
Martinscroft Warr 183 D11
Martin's Moss Ches E 168 C4
Martinstown Dorset 17 D8
Martinstown or Winterbourne St Martin Dorset 17 D8
Martlesham Suff 108 B4
Martlesham Heath Suff 108 B4
Martletwy Pembs 73 C8
Martley Worcs 116 E5
Martock Som 29 D7
Marton Ches E 168 B5
Marton Ches W 167 B10
Marton Cumb 210 D4
Marton E Yorks 209 F9
Marton Lincs 188 E4
Marton Mbro 225 B10
Marton N Yorks 215 G8
Marton N Yorks 216 C4
Marton Shrops 130 C5
Marton Shrops 149 E8
Marton Warks 119 D8
Marton Green Ches W 167 B10
Marton Grove Mbro 225 B9
Marton-in-the-Forest N Yorks 215 F11
Marton-le-Moor N Yorks 215 E7
Marton Moor Warks 119 D8
Marton Moss Side Blkpool 202 G2
Martyr's Green Sur 50 B5
Martyr Worthy Hants 48 G4
Marwick Orkney 314 D2
Marwood Devon 40 F4
Marybank Highld 300 D4
Marybank Highld 301 B7
Maryburgh Highld 300 D5
Maryfield Aberds 293 D7
Maryfield Corn 7 D8
Maryhill Glasgow 267 B11
Marykirk Aberds 293 G8
Maryland Mon 79 D8
Marylebone Gtr Man 194 F5
Marypark Moray 301 F11
Maryport Cumb 228 D6
Maryport Dumfries 236 F3
Mary Tavy Devon 12 F6
Maryton Angus 287 B7
Maryton Angus 287 B10
Marywell Aberds 293 D7
Marywell Aberds 293 D11
Marywell Angus 287 C10
Masbrough S Yorks 186 C6
Mascle Bridge Pembs 73 D7
Masham N Yorks 214 C4
Mashbury Essex 87 C11
Masongill N Yorks 212 D3
Masonhill S Ayrs 257 E9
Mastin Moor Derbys 187 F7
Mastrick Aberdeen 293 C10
Matchborough Worcs 117 D11
Matching Essex 87 C8
Matching Green Essex 87 C8
Matching Tye Essex 87 C8
Matfen Northumb 242 C2
Matfield Kent 53 E7
Mathern Mon 79 G8
Mathon Hereford 98 B4
Mathry Pembs 91 E7
Matlaske Norf 160 C3
Matley Gtr Man 185 B7
Matlock Derbys 170 C3
Matlock Bank Derbys 170 C3
Matlock Bath Derbys 170 D3
Matlock Bridge Derbys 170 D3
Matlock Cliff Derbys 170 D4
Matlock Dale Derbys 170 D3
Matshead Lancs 202 E6
Matson Glos 80 B4
Matterdale End Cumb 230 G3
Mattersey Notts 187 D11
Mattersey Thorpe Notts 187 D11
Matthewsgreen Wokingham 65 F10
Mattingley Hants 49 B8
Mattishall Norf 159 G11
Mattishall Burgh Norf 159 G11
Mauchline E Ayrs 257 D11
Maud Aberds 303 E9
Maudlin Corn 5 C11
Maudlin Dorset 28 F5
Maudlin W Sus 22 B5
Maudlin Cross Dorset 28 F5
Maugersbury Glos 100 F4
Maughold IoM 192 C5
Mauld Highld 300 F4
Maulden C Beds 103 D11
Maulds Meaburn Cumb 222 B2
Maunby N Yorks 215 B7
Maund Bryan Hereford 115 G11
Maundown Som 27 B9
Mauricewood Midloth 270 C4
Mautby Norf 161 G9
Mavesyn Ridware Staffs 151 F11
Mavis Enderby Lincs 174 B5
Maviston Highld 301 D9
Mawbray Cumb 229 B7
Mawdesley Lancs 194 E3
Mawdlam Bridgend 57 E10
Mawgan Corn 2 D6
Mawgan Porth Corn 5 B7
Maw Green Ches E 168 D2
Mawla Corn 4 F4
Mawnan Corn 3 D7
Mawnan Smith Corn 3 D7
Mawsley Northants 120 B6
Mawson Green S Yorks 198 D6
Mawthorpe Lincs 191 G7
Maxey Pboro 138 B2
Maxstoke Warks 134 F4
Maxted Street Kent 54 E6
Maxton Borders 262 C4
Maxton Kent 55 E10
Maxwellheugh Borders 262 C6
Maxwelltown Dumfries 237 B11
Maxworthy Corn 11 C11
Mayals Swansea 56 C6
May Bank Staffs 168 F5
Maybole S Ayrs 257 G8
Maybury Sur 50 B4
Maybush Soton 32 E5
Mayer's Green W Mid 133 E10
Mayes Green Sur 50 F6
Mayeston Pembs 73 E8
Mayfair London 67 C9
Mayfield E Sus 37 B9
Mayfield Midloth 271 C7
Mayfield Northumb 243 B7
Mayfield Staffs 169 F11
Mayfield W Loth 269 B8
Mayford Sur 50 B3
Mayhill Swansea 56 C6
May Hill Mon 79 C8
May Hill Village Glos 98 G4
Mayland Essex 88 E6
Maylandsea Essex 88 E6
Maynard's Green E Sus 23 B9
Mayne Ho Moray 302 C2
Mayon Corn 1 D3
Maypole Bromley 68 G3
Maypole Dartford 68 E4
Maypole Kent 71 G7
Maypole Mon 79 B7
Maypole Scilly 1 G4
Maypole Green Essex 107 G9
Maypole Green Norf 143 D8
Maypole Green Suff 125 F8
Maypole Green Suff 126 D5
Mays Green Oxon 65 C8
May's Green N Som 59 G11
May's Green Sur 50 B5
Mayshill S Glos 61 C7
Maythorn S Yorks 197 F7
Maythorne Notts 171 D11
Maywick Shetland 313 L5
Mead Devon 13 G11
Mead Devon 24 D2
Mead End Hants 19 B11
Mead End Hants 33 E11
Mead End Wilts 31 C8
Meadgate Bath 45 B7
Meadle Bucks 84 D4
Meadowbank Ches W 167 B11
Meadowbank Edin 280 G5
Meadowend Essex 106 C4
Meadowfield Durham 233 D10
Meadowfoot N Ayrs 266 F4
Meadow Green Hereford 116 F4
Meadow Hall S Yorks 186 C5
Meadow Head S Yorks 186 E4
Meadowley Shrops 132 E3
Meadowmill E Loth 281 G8
Meadows Nottingham 153 B11
Meadowtown Shrops 130 C6
Meads E Sus 23 F10
Meadside Oxon 83 G9
Mead Vale Sur 51 D9
Meadwell Devon 12 E4
Meaford Staffs 151 B7
Meagill N Yorks 205 B9
Mealabost W Isles 304 E6
Mealabost Bhuirgh W Isles 304 C6
Mealasta W Isles 304 F1
Meal Bank Cumb 221 F10
Meal Hill W Yorks 197 F7
Mealrigg Cumb 229 B8
Mealsgate Cumb 229 C10
Meanwood W Yorks 205 F11
Mearbeck N Yorks 212 G6
Meare Som 44 E3
Meare Green Som 28 B4
Meare Green Som 28 C3
Mearns Bath 45 B7
Mearns E Renf 267 D10
Mears Ashby Northants 120 D6
Measborough Dike S Yorks 197 F11
Measham Leics 152 G6
Meath Green Sur 51 E9
Meathop Cumb 211 C8
Meaux E Yorks 209 F7
Meaver Corn 2 F5
Meavy Devon 7 B10
Medbourne Leics 136 E5
Medbourne M Keynes 102 D6
Medburn Northumb 242 C4
Meddon Devon 24 D3
Meden Vale Notts 171 B9
Medhurst Row Kent 52 D3
Medlam Lincs 174 D4
Medlar Lancs 202 F4
Medlicott Shrops 131 E8
Medlyn Corn 2 C6
Medmenham Bucks 65 C10
Medomsley Durham 242 G4
Medstead Hants 49 F7
Meerbrook Staffs 169 C7
Meer Common Hereford 115 G7
Meer End W Mid 118 C4
Meerhay Dorset 29 G7
Meers Bridge Lincs 191 D7
Meersbrook S Yorks 186 E5
Meesden Herts 105 E8
Meeson Telford 150 E3
Meeson Heath Telford 150 E3
Meeth Devon 25 F8
Meethe Devon 25 C11
Meeting Green Suff 124 F4
Meeting House Hill Norf 160 D6
Meggernie Castle Perth 285 C9
Meggethead Borders 260 E5
Meidrim Carms 92 G5
Meifod Denb 165 D8
Meifod Powys 148 G3
Meigle N Ayrs 266 B3
Meigle Perth 286 C6
Meikle Earnock S Lnrk 268 E4
Meikle Ferry Highld 309 L7
Meikle Forter Angus 292 G3
Meikle Gluich Highld 309 L6
Meikle Obney Perth 286 D4
Meikleour Perth 286 D5
Meikle Pinkerton E Loth 282 F4
Meikle Strath Aberds 293 F8
Meikle Tarty Aberds 303 G9
Meikle Wartle Aberds 303 F7
Meinciau Carms 75 C7
Meir Stoke 168 G6
Meir Heath Staffs 168 G6
Melbourn Cambs 105 C7
Melbourne Derbys 153 D7
Melbourne E Yorks 207 E11
Melbourne S Lnrk 269 G11
Melbury Abbas Dorset 30 D5
Melbury Bubb Dorset 29 F9
Melbury Osmond Dorset 29 F9
Melbury Sampford Dorset 29 F9
Melby Shetland 313 H3
Melchbourne Beds 121 D10
Melcombe Som 43 G9
Melcombe Bingham Dorset 30 G3
Melcombe Regis Dorset 17 E9
Meldon Devon 13 C7
Meldon Northumb 252 G4
Meldreth Cambs 105 B7
Meldrum Ho Aberds 303 G8
Melfort Argyll 275 B9
Melgarve Highld 290 D6
Meliden / Gallt Melyd Denb 181 E9
Melinbyrhedyn Powys 128 D6
Melin Caiach Caerph 77 F10
Melincourt Neath 76 E4
Melincryddan Neath 57 B8
Melinsey Corn 3 B10
Melin-y-coed Conwy 164 C4
Melin-y-ddôl Powys 129 B11
Melin-y-grug Powys 129 B11
Melin-y-Wig Denb 165 F8
Melkington Northumb 273 G7
Melkinthorpe Cumb 231 F7
Melkridge Northumb 240 E6
Melksham Wilts 62 G2
Melksham Forest Wilts 62 G2
Mellangaun Highld 307 L3
Mellangoose Corn 2 D5
Melldalloch Argyll 275 F10
Mell Green W Berks 64 D3
Mellguards Cumb 230 B4
Melling Lancs 211 E11
Melling Mers 193 G11
Mellingey Corn 10 G4
Melling Mount Mers 194 G2
Mellis Suff 126 C2
Mellis Green Suff 125 C11
Mellon Charles Highld 307 K3
Mellon Udrigle Highld 307 K3
Mellor Gtr Man 185 D7
Mellor Lancs 203 G9
Mellor Brook Lancs 203 G8
Mells Som 45 D8
Mells Suff 127 B8
Mells Green Som 45 D8
Melmerby Cumb 231 D8
Melmerby N Yorks 213 B11
Melmerby N Yorks 214 D6
Melon Green Suff 124 F6
Melplash Dorset 16 B5
Melrose Borders 262 C2
Melsetter Orkney 314 H2
Melsonby N Yorks 224 D3
Meltham W Yorks 196 E6
Meltham Mills W Yorks 196 E6
Melton E Yorks 200 B3
Melton Suff 126 G5
Meltonby E Yorks 207 C11
Melton Constable Norf 159 C10
Melton Mowbray Leics 154 F5
Melton Ross N Lincs 200 E5
Melvaig Highld 307 L2
Melverley Shrops 148 F6
Melverley Green Shrops 148 F6
Melvich Highld 310 C2
Membland Devon 7 F11
Membury Devon 28 G3
Memsie Aberds 303 C9
Memus Angus 287 B8
Mena Corn 5 C10
Menabilly Corn 5 E11
Menadarva Corn 4 G2
Menagissey Corn 4 F4
Menai Bridge / Porthaethwy Anglesey 179 G9
Mendham Suff 142 G5
Mendlesham Suff 126 D2
Mendlesham Green Suff 125 E11
Menethorpe N Yorks 216 F5
Mengham Hants 21 B10
Menheniot Corn 6 C5
Menherion Corn 2 B6
Menithwood Worcs 116 D4
Menna Corn 5 E8
Mennock Dumfries 247 B8
Menston W Yorks 205 E9
Menstrie Clack 278 B6
Mentmore Bucks 84 B6
Menzion Borders 260 E3
Meoble Highld 295 G9
Meole Brace Shrops 149 G9
Meols Mers 182 C2
Meon Hants 33 G8
Meonstoke Hants 33 D10
Meopham Kent 68 F6
Meopham Green Kent 68 F6
Meopham Station Kent 68 F6
Mepal Cambs 139 G8
Meppershall C Beds 104 D2
Merbach Hereford 96 B6
Mercaton Derbys 170 G3
Merchant Fields W Yorks 197 B7
Merchiston Edin 280 G4
Mere Ches E 184 E2
Mere Wilts 45 G10
Mere Brow Lancs 194 D2
Mereclough Lancs 204 G3
Mere Green W Mid 134 D2
Mere Green Worcs 117 E9
Merehead Wrex 149 B9
Mere Heath Ches W 183 G11
Meresborough Medway 69 G10
Mereside Blkpool 202 G2
Meretown Staffs 150 E5
Mereworth Kent 53 C7
Mergie Aberds 293 E9
Meriden Herts 85 F10
Meriden W Mid 134 G4
Merkadale Highld 294 B5
Merkland Dumfries 237 B9
Merkland N Ayrs 256 B2
Merkland S Ayrs 244 E6
Merkland Lodge Highld 309 G4
Merle Common Sur 52 D2
Merley Poole 18 B6
Merlin's Bridge Pembs 72 C6
Merlin's Cross Pembs 73 E7
Merridale W Mid 133 D7
Merridge Som 43 G8
Merrie Gardens IoW 21 E7
Merrifield Devon 8 F6
Merrifield Devon 24 G3
Merrington Shrops 149 E9
Merrion Pembs 72 F6
Merriott Dorset 16 B6
Merriott Som 28 E6
Merriottsford Som 28 E6
Merritown Dorset 19 B8
Merrivale Devon 12 F6
Merrivale Hereford 98 G2
Merrow Sur 50 C4
Merrybent Darl 224 C4
Merry Field Hill Dorset 31 G8
Merry Hill Herts 85 G10
Merry Hill W Mid 133 D7
Merryhill Green Wokingham 65 E9
Merrylee E Renf 267 D11
Merry Lees Leics 135 B9
Merrymeet Corn 6 B5
Merry Meeting Corn 11 G7
Merry Oak Soton 32 E6
Mersham Kent 54 F5
Merstham Sur 51 C9
Merston W Sus 22 C5
Merstone IoW 20 E6
Merther Corn 5 G7
Merther Lane Corn 5 G7
Merthyr Carms 93 G7
Merthyr Cynog Powys 95 D9
Merthyr-Dyfan V Glam 58 F6
Merthyr Mawr Bridgend 57 F11
Merthyr Tydfil M Tydf 77 D8
Merthyr Vale M Tydf 77 F9
Merton Devon 25 E8
Merton London 67 E9
Merton Norf 141 D8
Merton Oxon 83 B9
Merton Park London 67 F9
Mervinslaw Borders 262 G5
Meshaw Devon 26 D3
Messing Essex 88 B5
Messingham N Lincs 199 G11
Mesty Croft W Mid 133 E9
Mesur-y-dorth Pembs 87 E11
Metal Bridge Durham 233 E11
Metfield Suff 142 G5
Metherell Corn 7 B8
Metheringham Lincs 173 C9
Methersgate Suff 108 B5
Methil Fife 281 B7
Methilhill Fife 281 B7
Methlem Gwyn 144 C3
Methley W Yorks 197 B11
Methley Junction W Yorks 197 B11
Methley Lanes W Yorks 197 B11
Methlick Aberds 303 F8
Methven Perth 286 E4
Methwold Norf 140 E4
Methwold Hythe Norf 140 E4
Mettingham Suff 143 F7
Metton Norf 160 B3
Mevagissey Corn 5 G10
Mewith Head N Yorks 212 F4
Mexborough S Yorks 187 B7
Mey Highld 310 B6
Meyrick Park Bmouth 19 C7
Meysey Hampton Glos 81 F10
Miabhag W Isles 305 H2
Miabhag W Isles 305 J3
Miabhig W Isles 304 E2
Mial Highld 299 B7
Michaelchurch Hereford 97 F10
Michaelchurch Escley Hereford 96 E6
Michaelchurch on Arrow Powys 114 G4
Michaelston-le-Pit V Glam 59 E7
Michaelston-y-Fedw Newport 59 C8
Michaelstow Corn 11 F7
Michealston-super-Ely Cardiff 58 D6
Michelcombe Devon 8 B3
Micheldever Hants 48 F4
Michelmersh Hants 32 B4
Mickfield Suff 126 E2
Micklebring S Yorks 187 C8
Mickleby N Yorks 226 C6
Micklefield Bucks 84 G5
Micklefield W Yorks 206 G4
Micklefield Green Herts 85 F8
Mickleham Sur 51 C7
Micklehurst Gtr Man 196 G3
Mickleover Derby 152 C6
Micklethwaite Cumb 239 G7
Micklethwaite W Yorks 205 E8
Mickleton Durham 232 G5
Mickleton Glos 100 C3
Mickletown W Yorks 197 B11
Mickle Trafford Ches W 166 B6
Mickley Derbys 186 F4
Mickley N Yorks 214 D5
Mickley Shrops 150 C2
Mickley Green Suff 124 F6
Mickley Square Northumb 242 E3
Midanbury Hants 33 E7
Mid Ardlaw Aberds 303 C9
Mid Auchinleck Invclyd 276 G6
Midbea Orkney 314 B4
Mid Beltie Aberds 293 C8
Mid Calder W Loth 269 B11
Mid Cloch Forbie Aberds 303 D7
Mid Clyth Highld 310 F6
Middle Assendon Oxon 65 B8
Middle Aston Oxon 101 F9
Middle Balnald Perth 286 B4
Middle Barton Oxon 101 F8
Middle Bickenhill W Mid 134 G4
Middlebie Dumfries 238 B6
Middle Bockhampton Dorset 19 B9
Middle Bourne Sur 49 E10
Middle Bridge N Som 60 D3
Middle Burnham Som 43 D10
Middle Cairncake Aberds 303 E8
Middlecave N Yorks 216 E5
Middle Chinnock Som 29 E7
Middle Claydon Bucks 102 F4
Middle Cliff Staffs 169 E8
Middlecliffe S Yorks 198 F2
Middlecott Devon 13 D10
Middlecott Devon 24 F6
Middlecott Devon 26 F3
Middle Crackington Corn 11 B9
Middlecroft Derbys 186 G6
Middle Drums Angus 287 B9
Middle Duntisbourne Glos 81 D7
Middlefield Falk 279 E7
Middleforth Green Lancs 194 B4
Middle Green Bucks 66 C4
Middle Green Som 27 D10
Middle Green Suff 124 D4
Middleham N Yorks 214 B2
Middle Handley Derbys 186 F6
Middle Harling Norf 141 F9
Middle Herrington T&W 243 G9
Middlehill Corn 6 B5
Middlehill Wilts 61 F10
Middle Hill Pembs 73 C7
Middle Hill Staffs 133 B9
Middlehope Shrops 131 F9
Middle Kames Argyll 275 E10
Middle Littleton Worcs 99 B11
Middle Luxton Devon 28 E2
Middle Madeley Staffs 168 F3
Middle Maes-coed Hereford 96 E6
Middlemarsh Dorset 29 F11
Middle Marwood Devon 40 F4
Middle Mayfield Staffs 169 G10
Middle Mill Pembs 87 F11
Middlemoor Devon 12 G5
Middlemuir Aberds 303 D9
Middlemuir Aberds 303 E8
Middlemuir Aberds 303 G9
Middleport Stoke 168 F5
Middle Quarter Kent 53 F11
Middle Rainton T&W 234 B2
Middle Rasen Lincs 189 D9
Middlerig Falk 279 F8
Middle Rigg Perth 286 G4
Middle Rocombe Devon 9 B8
Middlesbrough Mbro 234 G5
Middlesceugh Cumb 230 C4
Middleshaw Cumb 211 B11
Middle Side Durham 232 F4
Middlesmoor N Yorks 213 E11
Middle Stoford Som 27 C11
Middle Stoke Devon 13 G9
Middle Stoke Medway 69 D10
Middle Stoke W Mid 119 B7
Middlestone Durham 233 E11
Middlestone Moor Durham 233 E10
Middle Stoughton Som 44 D2
Middlestown W Yorks 197 D9
Middle Strath W Loth 279 G8
Middle Street Glos 80 E3
Middle Taphouse Corn 6 C3
Middlethird Borders 272 G3
Middlethorpe York 207 D7
Middleton Aberds 293 B10
Middleton Argyll 288 E1
Middleton Cumb 212 B2
Middleton Derbys 169 C11
Middleton Derbys 170 D3
Middleton Essex 107 D7
Middleton Gtr Man 195 F11
Middleton Hants 48 E2
Middleton Hereford 115 D10
Middleton Hrtlpl 234 E6
Middleton IoW 20 D2
Middleton Lancs 202 B4
Middleton Midloth 271 D7
Middleton Norf 158 F3
Middleton Northants 136 F6
Middleton Northumb 252 F3
Middleton Northumb 264 B4
Middleton N Yorks 204 E5
Middleton N Yorks 205 D8
Middleton N Yorks 216 B5
Middleton Perth 286 C5
Middleton Perth 286 F2
Middleton Perth 286 G5
Middleton Shrops 115 B10
Middleton Shrops 130 D5
Middleton Shrops 148 D6
Middleton Suff 127 D8
Middleton Swansea 56 D2
Middleton Warks 134 D3
Middleton W Yorks 197 B10
Middleton Baggot Shrops 132 E2
Middleton Cheney Northants 101 C9
Middleton Green Staffs 151 B9
Middleton Hall Northumb 263 D11
Middleton-in-Teesdale Durham 232 F4
Middleton Junction Gtr Man 195 G11
Middleton Moor Suff 127 D8
Middleton of Rora Aberds 303 E10
Middleton One Row Darl 225 C7
Middleton-on-Leven N Yorks 225 D9
Middleton-on-Sea W Sus 35 G7
Middleton on the Hill Hereford 115 E10
Middleton-on-the-Wolds E Yorks 208 D4
Middleton Place Cumb 219 G11
Middleton Priors Shrops 132 E2
Middleton Quernhow N Yorks 214 D6
Middleton St George Darl 224 C6
Middleton Scriven Shrops 132 F3
Middleton Stoney Oxon 101 G10
Middleton Tyas N Yorks 224 D4
Middletown Cumb 219 D9
Middletown N Som 60 E3
Middletown Powys 148 G6
Middletown Warks 117 E11
Middle Town Scilly 1 F4
Middle Tysoe Warks 100 C6
Middle Wallop Hants 47 F9
Middle Weald M Keynes 102 D5
Middlewich Ches E 167 B11
Middlewick Wilts 61 E11
Middle Wick Glos 80 F2
Middle Winterslow Wilts 47 G8
Middlewood Ches E 184 E6
Middlewood Corn 11 F11
Middlewood S Yorks 186 C4
Middle Woodford Wilts 46 F6
Middlewood Green Suff 125 E11
Middleyard Glos 80 E4
Middlezoy Som 43 G11
Middridge Durham 233 F11
Midelney Som 28 C6

Mountain Street Kent 54 C5
Mountain Water Pembs 91 G8
Mount Ambrose Corn 4 G4
Mount Ballan Mon 60 B3
Mount Batten Plym 7 E9
Mountbenger Borders 261 D8
Mountbengerburn Borders 261 D8
Mountblow W Dunb 277 G9
Mount Bovers Essex 88 G4
Mount Bures Essex 107 E8
Mount Canisp Highld 301 B7
Mount Charles Corn 5 B10
Mount Charles Corn 5 E10
Mount Cowdown Wilts 47 C9
Mount End Essex 87 E7
Mount Ephraim E Sus 23 B7
Mounters Dorset 30 D3
Mountfield E Sus 38 C2
Mountgerald Highld 300 C5
Mount Gould Plym 7 D9
Mount Hawke Corn 4 F4
Mount Hermon Corn 2 F6
Mount Hermon Sur 50 B4
Mount Hill S Glos 61 E7
Mountjoy Corn 5 C7
Mount Lane Devon 12 B3
Mountnessing Essex 87 F10
Mounton Mon 79 G8
Mount Pleasant Bucks 102 E3
Mount Pleasant Ches E 168 D4
Mount Pleasant Corn 5 C10
Mount Pleasant Derbys 152 D6
Mount Pleasant Derbys 152 F5
Mount Pleasant Derbys 170 F4
Mount Pleasant Devon 27 G11
Mount Pleasant Durham 233 E11
Mount Pleasant E Sus 23 E7
Mount Pleasant E Sus 36 D6
Mount Pleasant Flint 182 G2
Mount Pleasant Hants 19 B11
Mount Pleasant Kent 71 F10
Mount Pleasant London 85 G8
Mount Pleasant M Tydf 77 F9
Mount Pleasant Neath 57 B9
Mount Pleasant Norf 141 E9
Mount Pleasant Pembs 73 D8
Mount Pleasant Shrops 149 G9
Mount Pleasant Stockton 234 G4
Mount Pleasant Stoke 168 G5
Mount Pleasant Suff 106 B4
Mount Pleasant T&W 243 E7
Mount Pleasant Warks 135 F7
Mount Pleasant Worcs 99 D10
Mount Pleasant Worcs 117 E10
Mount Pleasant W Yorks 197 C8
Mount Sion Wrex 166 E3
Mount Skippett Oxon 82 B5
Mountsolie Aberds 303 D9
Mountsorrel Leics 153 F11
Mount Sorrel Wilts 31 C8
Mount Tabor W Yorks 196 B5
Mount Vernon Glasgow 268 C3
Mount Wise Corn 7 E9
Mousehill Sur 50 E2
Mousehole Corn 1 D5
Mousen Northumb 264 C4
Mousley End Warks 118 D4
Mouswald Dumfries 238 C3
Mouth Mill Devon 24 B3
Mowbreck Lancs 202 G4
Mow Cop Ches E 168 D5
Mowden Darl 224 B5
Mowden Essex 88 C3
Mowhaugh Borders 263 E8
Mowmacre Hill Leicester 135 B11
Mowshurst Kent 52 D3
Mowsley Leics 136 F2
Moxby N Yorks 215 F11
Moxley W Mid 133 D9
Moy Argyll 255 E8
Moy Highld 290 E6
Moy Highld 301 F7
Moy Hall Highld 301 F7
Moy Ho Moray 301 C10
Moyles Court Hants 31 F11
Moylgrove / Trewyddel Pembs 92 C2
Moy Lodge Highld 290 E6
Muasdale Argyll 255 C7
Muchalls Aberds 293 D11
Much Birch Hereford 97 E10
Much Cowardne Hereford 98 B2
Much Cowarne Hereford 98 B2
Much Dewchurch Hereford 97 E9
Muchelney Som 28 C6
Muchelney Ham Som 28 C6
Much Hadham Herts 86 B5
Much Hoole Lancs 194 C3
Much Hoole Moss Houses Lancs 194 C3
Much Hoole Town Lancs 194 C3
Muchlarnick Corn 6 D4
Much Marcle Hereford 98 E3
Muchrachd Highld 300 F2
Much Wenlock Shrops 132 C2
Muckairn Argyll 289 F11
Muckernich Highld 300 D5
Mucking Thurrock 69 C7
Muckle Breck Shetland 312 G7
Muckleford Dorset 17 C8
Mucklestone Staffs 150 B4
Muckleton Norf 158 B6
Muckleton Shrops 149 E11
Muckletown Aberds 302 G5
Muckley Shrops 132 D2
Muckley Corner Staffs 133 B11
Muckley Cross Shrops 132 D2
Muckton Lincs 190 E5
Muckton Bottom Lincs 190 E5
Mudale Highld 308 F5
Mudd Gtr Man 185 C7
Muddiford Devon 40 F5
Muddlebridge Devon 40 G4
Muddles Green E Sus 23 C8
Mudeford Dorset 19 C9
Mudford Som 29 D9
Mudford Sock Som 29 D9
Mudgley Som 44 D2
Mugdock Stirl 277 F11
Mugeary Highld 294 B6
Mugginton Derbys 170 G3
Muggintonlane End Derbys 170 G3
Muggleswick Durham 232 B6
Mugswell Sur 51 C9
Muie Highld 309 J6
Muir Aberds 292 E2
Muircleugh Borders 271 F10
Muirden Aberds 303 D7
Muirdrum Angus 287 D9
Muiredge Fife 281 B7
Muirend Glasgow 267 C11
Muirhead Angus 287 D7
Muirhead Fife 286 G6
Muirhead Fife 287 F8
Muirhead N Lnrk 268 B3
Muirhead S Ayrs 257 C8
Muirhouse Edin 280 F4
Muirhouse N Lnrk 268 D5
Muirhouselaw Borders 262 D4
Muirhouses Falk 279 E10
Muirkirk E Ayrs 258 D5
Muirmill Stirl 278 E4
Muir of Alford Aberds 293 B7
Muir of Fairburn Highld 300 D4
Muir of Fowlis Aberds 293 B7
Muir of Kinellar Aberds 293 B10
Muir of Miltonduff Moray 301 D11
Muir of Ord Highld 300 D5
Muir of Pert Angus 287 D8
Muirshearlich Highld 290 E3
Muirskie Aberds 293 D10
Muirtack Aberds 303 F9
Muirton Aberds 303 D7
Muirton Highld 301 C7
Muirton Perth 286 E5
Muirton Perth 286 F3
Muirton Mains Highld 300 D4
Muirton of Ardblair Perth 286 C5
Muirton of Ballochy Angus 293 G8
Muiryfold Aberds 303 D7
Muker N Yorks 223 F8
Mulbarton Norf 142 C3
Mulben Moray 302 D3
Mulberry Corn 5 B10
Mulfra Corn 1 C5
Mulindry Argyll 254 B4
Mulla Shetland 313 G6
Mullardoch House Highld 300 F2
Mullenspond Hants 47 D9
Mullion Corn 2 F5
Mullion Cove Corn 2 F5
Mumbles Hill Swansea 56 D6
Mumby Lincs 191 G8
Mumps Gtr Man 196 F2
Mundale Moray 301 D10
Munderfield Row Hereford 116 G2
Munderfield Stocks Hereford 116 G2
Mundesley Norf 160 B6
Mundford Norf 140 E6
Mundham Norf 142 D6
Mundon Essex 88 E5
Mundurno Aberdeen 293 B11
Mundy Bois Kent 54 D2
Munerigie Highld 290 C4
Muness Shetland 312 C8
Mungasdale Highld 307 K4
Mungrisdale Cumb 230 E3
Munlochy Highld 300 D6
Munsary Cottage Highld 310 E6
Munsley Hereford 98 C3
Munslow Shrops 131 F10
Munstone Hereford 97 C10
Murch V Glam 59 E7
Murchington Devon 13 D9
Murcot Worcs 99 C11
Murcott Oxon 83 B9
Murcott Wilts 81 G7
Murdieston Stirl 278 B3
Murdishaw Halton 183 E9
Murieston W Loth 269 C11
Murkle Highld 310 C5
Murlaggan Highld 290 D2
Murlaggan Highld 290 E5
Murra Orkney 314 F2
Murrayfield Edin 280 G4
Murrayshall Perth 286 E5
Murraythwaite Dumfries 238 C4
Murrell Green Hants 49 B8
Murrell's End Glos 98 E4
Murrell's End Glos 98 G5
Murrion Shetland 312 F4
Murrow Cambs 139 B7
Mursley Bucks 102 F6
Murston Kent 70 G2
Murthill Angus 287 B8
Murthly Perth 286 D4
Murton Cumb 231 G10
Murton Durham 234 B3
Murton Northumb 273 F9
Murton Swansea 56 D5
Murton T&W 243 C8
Murton York 207 C8
Murton Grange N Yorks 215 B10
Murtwell Devon 8 D5
Musbury Devon 15 C11
Muscliff Bmouth 19 B7
Muscoates N Yorks 216 C3
Muscott Northants 120 E2
Musdale Argyll 289 G11
Mushroom Green W Mid 133 F8
Musselburgh E Loth 280 G6
Musselwick Pembs 72 D4
Mustard Hyrn Norf 161 F8
Muston Leics 154 B6
Muston N Yorks 217 D11
Mustow Green Worcs 117 C7
Muswell Hill London 86 G3
Mutehill Dumfries 237 E8
Mutford Suff 143 F9
Muthill Perth 286 F2
Mutley Plym 7 D9
Mutterton Devon 27 G8
Mutton Hall E Sus 37 C9
Muxton Telford 150 G4
Mwdwl-eithin Flint 181 F11
Mwynbwll Flint 165 B11
Mybster Highld 310 D5
Myddfai Carms 94 F5
Myddle Shrops 149 E9
Myddlewood Shrops 149 E9
Myddyn-fych Carms 75 C10
Mydroilyn Ceredig 111 F9
Myerscough Lancs 202 F5
Myerscough Smithy Lancs 203 G8
Mylor Bridge Corn 3 B8
Mylor Churchtown Corn 3 B8
Mynachdy Cardiff 59 D7
Mynachdy Rhondda 77 F8
Mynachlog-ddu Pembs 92 E2
Mynd Shrops 115 C7
Myndd Llandegai Gwyn 163 B10
Myndtown Shrops 131 F7
Mynydd Bach Ceredig 112 B4
Mynydd-bach Mon 79 G7
Mynydd-Bach Swansea 57 B7
Mynydd-bach-y-glo Swansea 56 B6
Mynydd Bodafon Anglesey 179 D7
Mynydd Fflint / Flint Mountain Flint 182 G2
Mynydd Gilan Gwyn 144 E5
Mynydd-isa Flint 166 C3
Mynyddislwyn Caerph 77 G11
Mynydd-llan Flint 181 G11
Mynydd Marian Conwy 180 F5
Mynydd Mechell Anglesey 178 D5
Mynyddygarreg Carms 74 D6
Mynytho Gwyn 144 C6
Myrebird Aberds 293 D9
Myrelandhorn Highld 310 D6
Myreside Perth 286 E6
Myrtle Hill Carms 94 E5
Mytchett Sur 49 B11
Mytchett Place Sur 49 C11
Mytholm W Yorks 196 B3
Mytholmes W Yorks 204 F6
Mytholmroyd W Yorks 196 B4
Mythop Lancs 202 G3
Mytice Aberds 302 F4
Myton Warks 118 E6
Myton Hall N Yorks 215 F8
Myton-on-Swale N Yorks 215 F8
Mytton Shrops 149 F8


## N


Naast Highld 307 L3
Nab Hill W Yorks 197 D7
Nab's Head Lancs 194 B6
Naburn York 207 D7
Nab Wood W Yorks 205 F8
Naccolt Kent 54 E4
Nackington Kent 55 C7
Nacton Suff 108 C4
Nadderwater Devon 14 C3
Nafferton E Yorks 209 B7
Na Gearrannan W Isles 304 D3
Nag's Head Glos 80 F5
Naid-y-march Flint 181 F11
Nailbridge Glos 79 B10
Nailsbourne Som 28 B2
Nailsea N Som 60 D3
Nailstone Leics 135 B8
Nailsworth Glos 80 F5
Nailwell Bath 61 G8
Nairn Highld 301 D8
Nalderswood Sur 51 D8
Nance Corn 4 G3
Nanceddan Corn 2 C2
Nancegollan Corn 2 C4
Nancemellin Corn 4 G2
Nancenoy Corn 2 D6
Nancledra Corn 1 B5
Nangreaves Lancs 195 D10
Nanhoron Gwyn 144 C5
Nanhyfer / Nevern Pembs 91 D11
Nannau Gwyn 146 E4
Nannerch Flint 165 B11
Nanpantan Leics 153 F10
Nanpean Corn 5 D9
Nanquidno Corn 1 D3
Nanstallon Corn 5 B10
Nant Carms 74 B6
Nant Denb 165 D11
Nant Alyn Flint 165 B11
Nant-ddu Powys 77 B8
Nanternis Ceredig 111 F7
Nantgaredig Carms 93 G9
Nantgarw Rhondda 58 B6
Nant-glas Powys 113 E9
Nantglyn Denb 165 C8
Nantgwyn Powys 113 B9
Nantithet Corn 2 E5
Nantlle Gwyn 163 E8
Nantmawr Shrops 148 E5
Nant Mawr Flint 166 C3
Nantmel Powys 113 D10
Nantmor Gwyn 163 F10
Nant Peris / Old Llanberis Gwyn 163 D10
Nantserth Powys 113 C9
Nant Uchaf Denb 165 D8
Nantwich Ches E 167 E11
Nant-y-Bai Carms 94 C5
Nant-y-Bwch Bl Gwent 77 C10
Nant-y-cafn Neath 76 D4
Nantycaws Carms 75 B7
Nant y Caws Shrops 148 D5
Nant-y-ceisiad Caerph 59 B8
Nant-y-derry Mon 78 D4
Nant-y-felin Conwy 179 G11
Nant-y-ffin Carms 93 E11
Nantyffyllon Bridgend 57 C11
Nantyglo Bl Gwent 77 C11
Nant-y-gollen Shrops 148 D4
Nant-y-moel Bridgend 76 G6
Nant-y-pandy Conwy 179 G11
Nant-y-Rhiw Conwy 164 D4
Nantyronen Station Ceredig 112 B3
Napchester Kent 55 D10
Naphill Bucks 84 F4
Napleton Worcs 99 B7
Napley Staffs 150 B4
Napley Heath Staffs 150 B4
Nappa N Yorks 204 C3
Nappa Scar N Yorks 223 G9
Napton on the Hill Warks 119 E9
Narberth / Arberth Pembs 73 C10
Narberth Bridge Pembs 73 C10
Narborough Leics 135 D10
Narborough Norf 158 G4
Narfords Som 28 F3
Narkurs Corn 6 D6
Narracott Devon 24 D5
Narrowgate Corner Norf 161 F8
Nasareth Gwyn 163 E7
Naseby Northants 120 B3
Nash Bucks 102 E5
Nash Hereford 114 E6
Nash Kent 55 B9
Nash London 68 G2
Nash Newport 59 C10
Nash Shrops 116 C2
Nash Som 29 E8
Nashend Glos 80 D5
Nash End Worcs 132 G5
Nashes Green Hants 49 D7
Nash Lee Bucks 84 D4
Nash Mills Herts 85 E9
Nash Street E Sus 23 C8
Nash Street Kent 68 F6
Nassington Northants 137 D11
Nastend Glos 80 D3
Nast Hyde Herts 86 D2
Nasty Herts 105 G7
Natcott Devon 24 C3
Nateby Cumb 222 D5
Nateby Lancs 202 E5
Nately Scures Hants 49 C8
Natland Cumb 211 B10
Natton Glos 99 E8
Naughton Suff 107 B10
Naunton Glos 100 G2
Naunton Worcs 99 D7
Naunton Beauchamp Worcs 117 G9
Navant Hill W Sus 34 B6
Navenby Lincs 173 D7
Navestock Heath Essex 87 F8
Navestock Side Essex 87 F9
Navidale Highld 311 H4
Navity Highld 301 C7
Nawton N Yorks 216 C3
Nayland Suff 107 E9
Nazeing Essex 86 D6
Nazeing Gate Essex 86 D6
Nazeing Long Green Essex 86 E6
Nazeing Mead Essex 86 D5
Neacroft Hants 19 B9
Nealhouse Cumb 239 G8
Neal's Green Warks 134 G6
Neames Forstal Kent 54 B5
Neap Shetland 313 H7
Near Hardcastle N Yorks 214 F2
Near Sawrey Cumb 221 F7
Nearton End Bucks 102 F6
Neasden London 67 B8
Neasham Darl 224 C6
Neat Enstone Oxon 101 G7
Neath Abbey Neath 57 B8
Neatham Hants 49 E8
Neath / Castell-nedd Neath 57 B8
Neath Hill M Keynes 103 C7
Neatishead Norf 160 E6
Neat Marsh E Yorks 209 G9
Neaton Norf 141 C8
Nebo Anglesey 179 C7
Nebo Ceredig 111 D10
Nebo Conwy 164 D4
Nebo Gwyn 163 E7
Nebsworth Warks 100 C3
Nechells W Mid 133 F11
Necton Norf 141 B7
Nedd Highld 306 F6
Nedderton Northumb 252 G6
Nedge Hill Som 44 C5
Nedge Hill Telford 132 B4
Nedging Suff 107 B9
Nedging Tye Suff 107 B10
Needham Norf 142 G4
Needham Green Essex 87 B9
Needham Market Suff 125 G11
Needham Street Suff 124 D4
Needingworth Cambs 122 C6
Needwood Staffs 152 E3
Neen Savage Shrops 116 B3
Neen Sollars Shrops 116 C3
Neenton Shrops 132 F2
Nefod Shrops 148 B6
Nefyn Gwyn 162 G4
Neighbourne Som 44 D6
Neight Hill Worcs 117 F8
Neilston E Renf 267 D9
Neinthirion Powys 129 B9
Neithrop Oxon 101 C8
Nelly Andrews Green Powys 130 B5
Nelson Caerph 77 F10
Nelson Lancs 204 F3
Nelson Village Northumb 243 B7
Nemphlar S Lnrk 269 G7
Nempnett Thrubwell N Som 60 G4
Nene Terrace Lincs 138 B4
Nenthall Cumb 231 B11
Nenthead Cumb 231 C11
Nenthorn Borders 262 B5
Neopardy Devon 13 B11
Nepcote W Sus 35 F10
Nepgill Cumb 229 F7
Nep Town W Sus 36 D2
Nerabus Argyll 254 B3
Nercwys Flint 166 C2
Nerston S Lnrk 268 D2
Nesbit Northumb 263 C11
Ness Ches W 182 F4
Ness Orkney 314 C4
Nesscliffe Shrops 149 F7
Nessholt Ches W 182 F4
Nesstoun Orkney 314 A7
Neston Ches W 182 F3
Neston Wilts 61 F11
Netchells Green W Mid 133 F11
Netham Bristol 60 E6
Nethanfoot S Lnrk 268 F6
Nether Alderley Ches E 184 F4
Netheravon Wilts 46 D6
Nether Blainslie Borders 271 G10
Nether Booth Derbys 185 D10
Netherbrae Aberds 303 D7
Netherbrough Orkney 314 E3
Nether Broughton Leics 154 D3
Netherburn S Lnrk 268 F6
Nether Burrow Lancs 212 D2
Nether Burrows Derbys 152 B5
Netherbury Dorset 16 B5
Netherby Cumb 239 C9
Netherby N Yorks 206 D2
Nether Cassock Dumfries 248 C6
Nether Cerne Dorset 17 B9
Nether Chanderhill Derbys 186 G4
Netherclay Som 28 C3
Nether Compton Dorset 29 D9
Nethercote Oxon 101 C9
Nethercote Warks 119 E10
Nethercott Devon 12 B3
Nethercott Devon 40 F3
Nethercott Oxon 101 G9
Nethercott Som 42 G6
Nether Crimond Aberds 303 G8
Netherdale Shetland 313 H3
Nether Dalgliesh Borders 249 B7
Nether Dallachy Moray 302 C3
Nether Edge S Yorks 186 E4
Netherend Glos 79 E9
Nether End Derbys 186 G3
Nether End Leics 154 G4
Nether End W Yorks 197 F8
Nether Exe Devon 26 G6
Netherfield E Sus 38 D2
Netherfield M Keynes 103 D7
Netherfield Notts 171 G10
Nethergate Norf 159 D11
Nether Glasslaw Aberds 303 D8
Nether Hall Leicester 136 B2
Netherhampton Wilts 31 B10
Nether Handley Derbys 186 F6
Nether Handwick Angus 287 C7
Nether Haugh S Yorks 186 B6
Nether Headon Notts 188 F2
Nether Heage Derbys 170 E5
Nether Heyford Northants 120 F3
Nether Hindhope Borders 263 G7
Nether Horsburgh Borders 261 B8
Nether Howecleuch S Lnrk 260 G2
Nether Kellet Lancs 211 F10
Nether Kidston Borders 270 G4
Nether Kinmundy Aberds 303 E10
Nether Kirton E Renf 267 D9
Netherland Green Staffs 152 C2
Nether Langwith Notts 187 G8
Netherlaw Dumfries 237 E9
Netherlay Dorset 28 F6
Nether Leask Aberds 303 F10
Netherlee E Renf 267 D11
Nether Lenshie Aberds 302 E6
Netherley Aberds 293 D10
Netherley Mers 182 D6
Netherley W Yorks 196 E4
Nether Loads Derbys 170 B4
Nethermill Dumfries 248 F2
Nethermills Moray 302 D5
Nether Monynut Borders 272 C4
Nether Moor Derbys 170 B5
Nethermuir Aberds 303 E9
Netherne on-the-Hill Sur 51 B9
Netheroyd Hill W Yorks 196 D6
Nether Padley Derbys 186 F3
Nether Park Aberds 303 D10
Netherplace E Renf 267 D10
Nether Poppleton York 207 B7
Netherraw Borders 262 E3
Nether Row Cumb 230 D2
Nether Savock Aberds 303 E10
Netherseal Derbys 152 G5
Nether Shiels Borders 271 F8
Nether Silton N Yorks 225 G9
Nether Skyborry Shrops 114 C5
Nether St Suff 125 E8
Netherstoke Dorset 29 F8
Nether Stowe Staffs 152 G2
Nether Stowey Som 43 F7
Nether Street Essex 87 C9
Nether Street Herts 86 B6
Netherthird E Ayrs 258 F3
Netherthong W Yorks 196 F6
Netherthorpe Derbys 186 G6
Netherthorpe S Yorks 187 E8
Netherton Aberds 303 E8
Netherton Angus 287 B9
Netherton Ches W 183 F8
Netherton Corn 11 G11
Netherton Cumb 228 D6
Netherton Devon 14 G3
Netherton Glos 81 E11
Netherton Hants 47 B11
Netherton Hereford 97 F10
Netherton Mers 193 G11
Netherton N Lnrk 268 E5
Netherton Northumb 251 B11
Netherton Oxon 82 F6
Netherton Perth 286 B5
Netherton Shrops 132 G4
Netherton Stirl 277 F11
Netherton W Mid 133 F8
Netherton Worcs 99 C9
Netherton W Yorks 196 E6
Netherton W Yorks 197 D9
Netherton of Lonmay Aberds 303 C10
Nethertown Cumb 219 D9
Nethertown Highld 310 B7
Nethertown Lancs 203 F10
Nethertown Staffs 152 F2
Nether Urquhart Fife 286 G5
Nether Wallop Hants 47 F10
Nether Warden Northumb 241 D10
Nether Wasdale Cumb 220 E2
Nether Welton Cumb 230 B3
Nether Westcote Glos 100 G4
Nether Whitacre Warks 134 E4
Nether Winchendon or Lower Winchendon Bucks 84 C2
Netherwitton Northumb 252 E4
Netherwood E Ayrs 258 D5
Nether Worton Oxon 101 E8
Nether Yeadon W Yorks 205 E10
Nethy Bridge Highld 301 G10
Netley Hants 33 F7
Netley Hill Soton 33 E7
Netley Marsh Hants 32 E4
Nettacott Devon 14 B4
Netteswell Essex 87 C7
Nettlebed Oxon 65 B8
Nettlebridge Som 44 D6
Nettlecombe Dorset 16 B6
Nettlecombe IoW 20 F6
Nettleden Herts 85 C8
Nettleham Lincs 189 F8
Nettlestead Kent 53 C7
Nettlestead Suff 107 B11
Nettlestead Green Kent 53 C7
Nettlestone IoW 21 C8
Nettlesworth Durham 233 B11
Nettleton Glos 80 C6
Nettleton Lincs 200 G6
Nettleton Wilts 61 D10
Nettleton Green Wilts 61 D10
Nettleton Hill W Yorks 196 D5
Nettleton Shrub Wilts 61 D10
Nettleton Top Lincs 189 B10
Netton Wilts 46 F6
Neuadd Carms 94 G3
Nevendon Essex 88 G2
Nevern / Nanhyfer Pembs 91 D11
Nevilles Cross Durham 233 C11
New Abbey Dumfries 237 C11
New Aberdour Aberds 303 C8
New Addington London 67 G11
Newall W Yorks 205 D10
Newall Green Gtr Man 184 D4
New Alresford Hants 48 G5
New Alyth Perth 286 C6
Newark Orkney 314 B7
Newark Pboro 138 C4
Newark-on-Trent Notts 172 E3
New Arley Warks 134 F5
New Arram E Yorks 208 E6
Newarthill N Lnrk 268 D5
New Ash Green Kent 68 F6
New Balderton Notts 172 E4
Newball Lincs 189 F9
Newbarn Kent 55 F7
New Barn Kent 68 F6
New Barnet London 86 F3
New Barnetby N Lincs 200 E5
Newbarns Cumb 210 E4
New Barton Northants 121 E7
New Basford Nottingham 171 G9
Newbattle Midloth 270 B6
New Beaupre V Glam 58 E4
New Beckenham London 67 E11
New Bewick Northumb 264 E3
Newbie Dumfries 238 D5
Newbiggin Cumb 210 F5
Newbiggin Cumb 211 D11
Newbiggin Cumb 219 G11
Newbiggin Cumb 230 F5
Newbiggin Cumb 231 B7
Newbiggin Cumb 231 F8
Newbiggin Durham 232 B5
Newbiggin Durham 232 F4
Newbiggin Durham 233 B8
Newbiggin N Yorks 213 B9
Newbiggin N Yorks 223 G9
Newbiggin-by-the-Sea Northumb 253 F8
Newbigging Aberds 303 G7
Newbigging Angus 287 D8
Newbigging Borders 262 F6
Newbigging Edin 280 F2
Newbigging S Lnrk 269 F10
New-bigging Angus 286 C6
Newbiggings Orkney 314 B6
Newbiggin Hall Estate T&W 242 D6
Newbiggin-on-Lune Cumb 222 D4
New Bilton Warks 119 B9
Newbold Derbys 186 G5
Newbold Gtr Man 196 E2
Newbold Leics 136 B5
Newbold Leics 153 F8
Newbold Heath Leics 135 B8
Newbold on Avon Warks 119 B9
Newbold on Stour Warks 100 B4
Newbold Pacey Warks 118 F5
Newbolds W Mid 133 C8
Newbold Verdon Leics 135 C8
New Bolingbroke Lincs 174 D4
New Bolsover Derbys 187 G7
Newborough Pboro 138 B4
Newborough Staffs 152 D2
New Boston Mers 183 B9
New Botley Oxon 83 D7
Newbottle Northants 101 D10
Newbottle T&W 243 G8
New Boultham Lincs 189 G7
Newbourne Suff 108 C5
New Bradwell M Keynes 102 C6
New Brancepeth Durham 233 C10
Newbridge Bath 61 F8
Newbridge Caerph 78 F2
Newbridge Ceredig 111 F10
Newbridge Corn 1 C4
Newbridge Corn 4 G5
Newbridge Corn 7 B7
Newbridge Dumfries 237 B11
Newbridge Edin 280 G2
Newbridge E Sus 52 G3
Newbridge Hants 32 D3
Newbridge IoW 20 D4
Newbridge Lancs 204 F3
Newbridge N Yorks 216 B6
Newbridge Oxon 82 E6
Newbridge Pembs 91 E8
Newbridge Shrops 148 D6
Newbridge W Mid 133 D7
Newbridge Wrex 166 G3
New Bridge Wrex 166 G3
Newbridge Green Worcs 98 D6
Newbridge-on-Usk Mon 78 G5
Newbridge-on-Wye Powys 113 F10
New Brighton Flint 166 B3
New Brighton Mers 182 C4
New Brighton Wrex 166 E3
New Brighton W Sus 22 B3
New Brighton W Yorks 197 B9
New Brighton W Yorks 205 F8
New Brimington Derbys 186 G6
New Brinsley Notts 171 E7
New Brotton Redcar 235 G9
Newbrough Northumb 241 D9
New Broughton Wrex 166 E4
New Buckenham Norf 141 E11
Newbuildings Devon 26 G3
New Buildings Bath 45 B7
New Buildings Dorset 18 E5
Newburgh Aberds 303 D9
Newburgh Aberds 303 G9
Newburgh Borders 261 F8
Newburgh Fife 286 F6
Newburgh Lancs 194 E3
Newburn T&W 242 D5
Newbury Kent 54 B2
Newbury W Berks 64 F3
Newbury Wilts 45 E10
New Bury Gtr Man 195 F8
Newbury Park London 68 B2
Newby Cumb 231 G7
Newby Lancs 204 D2
Newby N Yorks 205 D11
Newby N Yorks 212 E4
Newby N Yorks 215 F7
Newby N Yorks 225 C10
Newby N Yorks 227 G10
Newby Bridge Cumb 211 B7
Newby Cote N Yorks 212 E4
Newby East Cumb 239 F11
Newby Head Cumb 231 G7
New Byth Aberds 303 D8
Newby West Cumb 239 G9
Newby Wiske N Yorks 215 B7
Newcastle Bridgend 58 D2
Newcastle Mon 78 B6
Newcastle Shrops 130 G4
Newcastle Emlyn / Castell Newydd Emlyn Carms 92 C6
Newcastleton or Copshaw Holm Borders 249 F11
Newcastle-under-Lyme Staffs 168 F4
Newcastle upon Tyne T&W 242 E6
New Catton Norf 160 G4
Newchapel Powys 129 G9
Newchapel Staffs 168 E5
Newchapel Sur 51 E11
Newchapel / Capel Newydd Pembs 92 D4
New Charlton London 68 D2
New Cheltenham S Glos 61 E7
New Cheriton Hants 33 B9
Newchurch Bl Gwent 77 C11
Newchurch Carms 93 G7
Newchurch Hereford 115 G7
Newchurch IoW 21 D7
Newchurch Kent 54 G5
Newchurch Lancs 195 C10
Newchurch Mon 79 F7
Newchurch Powys 114 G4
Newchurch Staffs 152 E2
Newchurch in Pendle Lancs 204 F2
New Clipstone Notts 171 C9
New Costessey Norf 160 G3
Newcott Devon 28 F2
New Coundon Durham 233 E10
New Cowper Cumb 229 B8
Newcraighall Edin 280 G6
New Crofton W Yorks 197 D11
New Cross Ceredig 112 B2
New Cross London 67 D11
New Cross Oxon 65 D9
New Cross Som 28 D6
New Cross Gate London 67 D11
New Cumnock E Ayrs 258 G4
New Deer Aberds 303 E8
New Delaval Northumb 243 B7
New Delph Gtr Man 196 F3
New Denham Bucks 66 C4
Newdigate Sur 51 E7
New Downs Corn 1 C3
New Downs Corn 4 E4
New Duston Northants 120 E4

New Earswick York....207 B8
New Eastwood Notts....171 F7
New Edlington S Yorks....187 B8
New Elgin Moray....302 C2
New Ellerby E Yorks....209 F9
Newell Green Brack....65 E11
New Eltham London....68 E2
New End Lincs....190 G2
New End Warks....118 E2
New End Worcs....117 F11
Newenden Kent....38 B4
New England Essex....106 C4
New England Lincs....175 D8
New England Pboro....138 C3
New England Som....28 E4
Newent Glos....98 F4
Newerne Glos....79 E10
New Farnley W Yorks....205 G10
New Ferry Mers....182 D4
Newfield Durham....233 E10
Newfield Durham....242 G6
Newfield Highld....301 B7
Newfield S Yorks....168 E6
New Fletton Pboro....138 D3
Newford Scilly....1 G4
Newfound Hants....48 C5
New Fryston W Yorks....198 B3
Newgale Pembs....90 G6
New Galloway Dumfries....237 B8
Newgarth Orkney....314 E2
Newgate Lancs....194 F4
Newgate Norf....177 E9
Newgate Corner Norf....161 G8
Newgate Street Herts....86 D4
New Gilston Fife....287 G8
New Greens Herts....85 D10
New Grimsby Scilly....1 F3
New Ground Herts....85 C7
Newgrounds Hants....31 E11
Newhailes Edin....280 G6
New Hainford Norf....160 F4
Newhall Ches E....167 F10
Newhall Derbys....152 E5
Newhall Green Warks....134 F5
New Hall Hey Lancs....195 C10
Newhall House Highld....300 C6
Newhall Point Highld....301 C7
Newham Lincs....174 E3
Newham Northumb....264 D5
New Hartley Northumb....243 B8
Newhaven Derbys....169 C11
Newhaven Devon....24 C5
Newhaven Edin....280 F5
Newhaven E Sus....36 G6
New Haw Sur....66 G5
Newhay N Yorks....207 G9
New Headington Oxon....83 D9
New Heaton Northumb....273 G7
New Hedges Pembs....73 E10
New Herrington T&W....243 G8
Newhey Gtr Man....196 E2
Newhills Fife....286 F6
Newhill Perth....286 G5
Newhill S Yorks....186 B6
Newhills Aberdeen....293 C10
New Hinksey Oxon....83 E8
New Ho Durham....232 D3
New Holkham Norf....159 B7
New Holland N Lincs....200 C5
New Holland W Yorks....205 F7
Newholm N Yorks....227 C7
New Horwich Derbys....185 E8
New Houghton Derbys....171 B7
New Houghton Norf....158 D5
Newhouse Borders....262 E2
New Houses Gtr Man....194 G5
New Houses N Yorks....212 E6
New Humberstone Leicester....136 B2
New Hunwick Durham....233 E9
New Hutton Cumb....221 G11
New Hythe Kent....53 B8
Newick E Sus....36 C6
Newingreen Kent....54 F6
Newington Edin....280 G5
Newington Kent....55 F7
Newington Kent....69 G11
Newington Kent....71 F11
Newington London....67 D10
Newington Notts....187 C11
Newington Oxon....83 F10
Newington Shrops....131 G8
Newington Bagpath Glos....80 G4
New Inn Carms....93 D9
New Inn Devon....24 F6
New Inn Mon....79 E7
New Inn Pembs....91 E11
New Inn Torf....78 F4
New Invention Shrops....114 B5
New Invention W Mid....133 C9
New Kelso Highld....299 E9
New Kingston Notts....153 D10
New Kyo Durham....242 G5

New Ladykirk Borders....273 F7
Newland Cumb....210 D6
Newland E Yorks....199 B10
Newland Glos....79 D9
Newland Hull....209 G7
Newland N Yorks....199 C7
Newland Oxon....82 C5
Newland Worcs....98 B5
Newland Bottom Cumb....210 C5
Newland Common Worcs....117 E8
Newland Green Kent....54 D2
Newlandrig Midloth....271 C7
Newlands Borders....250 E2
Newlands Borders....262 E2
Newlands Cumb....229 G10
Newlands Cumb....230 D2
Newlands Derbys....170 F6
Newlands Dumfries....247 F11
Newlands Glasgow....267 C11
Newlands Highld....301 E7
Newlands Moray....302 D3
Newlands Northumb....242 F3
Newlands Notts....171 C9
Newlands Staffs....151 E11
Newlands Corner Sur....50 D4
Newlandsmuir S Lnrk....268 E2
Newlands of Geise Highld....310 C4
Newlands of Tynet Moray....302 C3
Newlands Park Anglesey....178 E3
New Lane Lancs....194 E2
New Lane End Warr....183 B10
New Langholm Dumfries....249 G9
New Leake Lincs....174 D6
New Leeds Aberds....303 D9
Newliston Edin....280 G2
Newliston Fife....280 C5
New Lodge S Yorks....197 F10
New Longton Lancs....194 B4
Newlot Orkney....314 E5
New Luce Dumfries....236 C3
Newlyn Corn....1 D5
Newmachar Aberds....293 B10
Newmains N Lnrk....268 D6
Newman's End Essex....87 C8
Newman's Green Suff....107 C7
Newman's Place Hereford....96 B5
Newmarket Glos....80 F4
Newmarket Suff....124 E2
Newmarket W Isles....304 E6
New Marske Redcar....235 G8
New Marston Oxon....83 D8
New Marton Shrops....148 C6
New Micklefield W Yorks....206 G4
Newmill Borders....261 G11
Newmill Corn....1 C5
Newmill Moray....302 D4
New Mill Aberds....293 E9
New Mill Borders....262 G2
New Mill Corn....1 C5
New Mill Corn....4 F6
New Mill Cumb....219 E11
New Mill Herts....84 C6
New Mill Wilts....63 G7
New Mill W Yorks....197 F7
Newmillerdam W Yorks....197 D10
Newmill of Inshewan Angus....292 G6
Newmills Corn....11 D11
Newmills Fife....279 D10
Newmills Highld....300 C6
New Mills Borders....271 F10
New Mills Ches E....184 E3
New Mills Corn....5 E7
New Mills Derbys....185 D7
New Mills Glos....79 D10
New Mills Powys....129 C11
Newmills of Boyne Aberds....302 D5
Newmiln Perth....286 D5
Newmilns E Ayrs....258 B2
New Milton Hants....19 B10
New Mistley Essex....108 E2
New Moat Pembs....91 F11
New Moston Gtr Man....195 G11
Newnes Shrops....149 C7
Newney Green Essex....87 D11
Newnham Cambs....123 B8
Newnham Glos....79 C11
Newnham Hants....49 C8
Newnham Herts....104 D4
Newnham Kent....54 B3
Newnham Northants....119 F11
Newnham Warks....118 D4
Newnham Bridge Worcs....116 D2
New Ollerton Notts....171 B11
New Oscott W Mid....133 E11
New Pale Ches W....183 G8
New Park Fife....287 F8
New Park N Yorks....205 B11
New Parks Leicester....135 B11
New Passage S Glos....60 B4
New Pitsligo Aberds....303 D8
New Polzeath Corn....10 F4
Newpool Staffs....168 D5
Newport Corn....12 D2
Newport Devon....40 G5
Newport Dorset....18 C3
Newport Essex....105 E10
Newport Gtr Man....208 G3
Newport Gtr Man....79 F11
Newport Highld....311 G3

Newport IoW....20 D6
Newport Newport....59 B10
Newport Norf....161 F10
Newport Som....28 C4
Newport Telford....150 F4
Newport-on-Tay Fife....287 E8
Newport Pagnell M Keynes....103 C7
Newport / Trefdraeth Pembs....91 D11
Newpound Common W Sus....35 B9
Newquay Corn....4 C6
New Quay / Ceinewydd Ceredig....111 F7
New Rackheath Norf....160 G5
New Radnor Powys....114 E4
New Rent Cumb....230 D5
New Ridley Northumb....242 F3
New Road Side N Yorks....204 E5
New Road Side W Yorks....197 B7
New Romney Kent....39 C9
New Rossington S Yorks....187 B10
New Row Ceredig....112 C4
New Row Lancs....203 F8
New Row N Yorks....226 C2
Newsam Green W Yorks....206 G3
New Sarum Wilts....46 G6
New Sawley Derbys....153 C9
Newsbank Ches E....168 B4
New Scarbro W Yorks....205 G10
Newseat Aberds....303 E10
Newseat Aberds....303 F7
Newsells Herts....105 D7
Newsham Lancs....202 F6
Newsham Northumb....243 B8
Newsham N Yorks....215 C7
Newsham N Yorks....224 C2
New Sharlston W Yorks....197 C11
New Skelton Redcar....226 B3
New Smithy Derbys....185 E9
Newsome W Yorks....196 E6
New Southgate London....86 G3
New Springs Gtr Man....194 F6
New Sprowston Norf....160 G4
New Stanton Derbys....153 B9
Newstead Borders....262 C3
Newstead Northumb....264 D5
Newstead Notts....171 E8
Newstead Staffs....168 G5
Newstead W Yorks....197 E11
New Stevenston N Lnrk....268 D5
New Street Kent....68 G6
New Street Staffs....169 E9
Newstreet Lane Shrops....150 B2
New Swanage Dorset....18 E6
New Swannington Leics....153 F8
Newtake Devon....14 G3
New Thirsk N Yorks....215 C8
Newthorpe Notts....171 F7
Newthorpe N Yorks....206 G5
Newthorpe Common Notts....171 F7
New Thundersley Essex....69 B9
Newtoft Lincs....189 D8
Newton Argyll....275 D11
Newton Borders....262 E3
Newton Borders....262 E3
Newton Bridgend....57 F10
Newton Cambs....105 B8
Newton Cambs....157 G8
Newton Cardiff....59 D8
Newton C Beds....104 C4
Newton Ches W....166 B6
Newton Ches W....167 D8
Newton Ches W....183 F8
Newton Ches W....183 G8
Newton Corn....5 C11
Newton Cumb....210 E4
Newton Derbys....170 D6
Newton Dorset....30 E3
Newton Dumfries....239 C7
Newton Dumfries....248 E4
Newton Gtr Man....185 B7
Newton Hereford....96 C5
Newton Hereford....96 G6
Newton Hereford....115 D7
Newton Hereford....115 G10
Newton Highld....301 C11
Newton Highld....301 E7
Newton Highld....306 D7
Newton Highld....310 E7
Newton Lancs....202 F2
Newton Lancs....202 G4
Newton Lancs....203 C9
Newton Lancs....211 G11
Newton Lincs....155 B10
Newton Mers....182 D2
Newton Moray....301 C11
Newton Norf....158 F6
Newton Northants....137 G7
Newton Northumb....242 F2
Newton Notts....171 G11
Newton Perth....286 D2
Newton S Glos....79 G10
Newton Shetland....312 E5
Newton Shetland....313 K5
Newton Shrops....132 D4
Newton Shrops....149 C8
Newton S Lnrk....259 C10
Newton S Lnrk....268 C3
Newton Som....42 F6
Newton Staffs....151 D10
Newton Suff....107 C8
Newton Swansea....56 D6
Newton S Yorks....198 G5

Newton Warks....119 B10
Newton Wilts....32 C2
Newton W Loth....279 F11
Newton W Mid....133 E10
Newton Derbys....185 E2
Newton Devon....26 B3
Newton Dorset....29 G7
Newton Dorset....29 G7
Newton Falk....279 E9
Newton Glos....79 E11
Newton Glos....80 D3
Newton Glos....99 E8
Newton Gtr Man....195 G9
Newton Hants....21 B8
Newton Hants....32 C4
Newton Hants....32 E3
Newton Hants....33 D8
Newton Hants....33 E10
Newton Hants....33 F7
Newton Hants....49 F8
Newton Hants....49 G10
Newton Hants....64 G3
Newton Hereford....97 E10
Newton Hereford....98 C2
Newton Highld....290 C5
Newton IoW....20 D3
Newton Lincs....189 D9
Newton Norf....142 D4
Newton Norf....143 B10
Newton Northumb....252 C2
Newton Northumb....263 C11
Newton Northumb....264 D2
Newton Oxon....65 C9
Newton Poole....18 C6
Newton Powys....130 E2
Newton Rhondda....77 F9
Newton Shrops....132 C2
Newton Shrops....149 C9
Newton Shrops....149 E8
Newton Som....28 E3
Newton Som....43 F9
Newton Staffs....133 C9
Newton Staffs....168 C6
Newton Staffs....169 C9
Newton Wilts....30 B6
Newton Wilts....63 G10
Newton W Mid....133 F11
Newton Worcs....116 F5
Newton Worcs....117 E7
Newtonairds Dumfries....247 G9
Newton Arlosh Cumb....238 F5
Newton Aycliffe Durham....233 G11
Newton Bewley Hrtlpl....234 F5
Newton Blossomville M Keynes....121 G8
Newton Bromswold Northants....121 D9
Newton Burgoland Leics....153 B7
Newton by Toft Lincs....189 D9
Newton Cross Pembs....91 F7
Newton Ferrers Devon....7 F10
Newton Flotman Norf....142 D4
Newtongrange Midloth....270 C6
Newton Green Mon....79 G8
Newton Hall Durham....233 B11
Newton Hall Northumb....242 D2
Newton Harcourt Leics....136 D2
Newton Heath Gtr Man....195 G11
Newtonhill Aberds....293 D11
Newtonhill Highld....300 E5
Newton Hill W Yorks....197 C10
Newton Ho Aberds....302 G6
Newton Hurst Staffs....151 D11
Newton Ketton Darl....234 G2
Newton Kyme N Yorks....206 E5
Newton-le-Willows Mers....183 B9
Newton-le-Willows N Yorks....214 B4
Newton Longville Bucks....102 E6
Newton Mearns E Renf....267 D10
Newtonmill Angus....293 G8
Newtonmore Highld....291 D9
Newton Morrell N Yorks....224 D4
Newton Morrell Oxon....102 F2
Newton Mulgrave N Yorks....226 B5
Newton of Ardtoe Highld....289 B8
Newton of Balcanquhal Perth....286 F5
Newton of Balcormo Fife....287 G9
Newton of Falkland Fife....286 G6
Newton of Mountblairy Aberds....302 D6
Newton of Pitcairns Perth....286 F4
Newton on Ayr S Ayrs....257 E8
Newton on Ouse N Yorks....206 B6
Newton-on-Rawcliffe N Yorks....226 G6
Newton on the Hill Shrops....149 E9
Newton on the Moor Northumb....252 B5
Newton on Trent Lincs....188 G4
Newton Park Argyll....266 B2
Newton Park Mers....183 C9
Newton Peveril Dorset....18 B4
Newton Poppleford Devon....15 D7
Newton Purcell Oxon....102 E2
Newton Regis Warks....134 B5
Newton Reigny Cumb....230 E5
Newton Rigg Cumb....230 E5
Newton St Boswells Borders....262 C3
Newton St Cyres Devon....14 B3
Newton St Faith Norf....160 F4
Newton St Loe Bath....61 G8
Newton St Petrock Devon....24 E6
Newton Solney Derbys....152 D5
Newton Stacey Hants....48 E2
Newton Stewart Dumfries....236 C6
Newton Tony Wilts....47 E8
Newton Tracey Devon....25 B8
Newton under Roseberry Redcar....225 C11
Newton Underwood Northumb....252 F4
Newton upon Derwent E Yorks....207 D10
Newton Valence Hants....49 G8
Newton with Scales Lancs....202 G4
Newton Wood Gtr Man....184 B6
New Totley S Yorks....186 F4
Newton Argyll....284 G4
Newtown Bl Gwent....77 D11
Newtown Bucks....85 E7
Newton Caerph....78 G2
Newtown Cambs....121 D11
Newtown Ches E....184 E6
Newtown Ches E....184 E6
Newtown Ches W....183 F8

Newtown Corn....2 D3
Newtown Corn....11 H1
Newtown Cumb....229 B7
Newtown Cumb....239 F9
Newtown Cumb....240 G2
Newtown Derbys....185 E2
Newtown Devon....26 B3
Newtown Dorset....29 G7
Newtown Falk....279 E9
Newtown Glos....79 E11
Newtown Glos....80 D3
Newtown Glos....99 E8
Newtown Gtr Man....195 G9
Newtown Hants....21 B8
Newtown Hants....32 C4
Newtown Hants....32 E3
Newtown Hants....33 D8
Newtown Hants....33 E10
Newtown Hants....33 F7
Newtown Hants....49 F8
Newtown Hants....49 G10
Newtown Hants....64 G3
Newtown Hereford....97 E10
Newtown Hereford....98 C2
Newtown Highld....290 C5
Newtown IoM....192 E4
Newtown IoW....20 C4
Newtown Mers....183 B7
Newtown Norf....143 B10
Newtown Northumb....252 C2
Newtown Northumb....263 C11
Newtown Northumb....264 D2
Newtown Oxon....65 C9
Newtown Poole....18 C6
Newtown Powys....130 E2
Newtown Rhondda....77 F9
Newtown Shrops....132 C2
Newtown Shrops....149 C9
Newtown Shrops....149 E8
Newtown Som....28 E3
Newtown Som....43 F9
Newtown Staffs....133 C9
Newtown Staffs....168 C6
Newtown Staffs....169 C9
Newtown Wilts....30 B6
Newtown Wilts....63 G10
Newtown W Mid....133 F11
Newtown Worcs....116 F5
Newtown Worcs....117 E7
New Town Bath....45 B9
New Town Bath....60 G5
New Town Dartford....68 E4
New Town Dorset....30 C3
New Town Dorset....30 D6
New Town Dorset....31 D7
New Town Dorset....31 F7
New Town Edin....280 G4
New Town Edin....280 G5
New Town E Loth....281 G8
New Town E Sus....37 C7
New Town Glos....99 E10
New Town Lancs....203 F8
New Town Luton....103 G11
New Town Maidstone....53 B7
New Town Medway....69 G8
New Town Oxon....100 F5
New Town Reading....65 E8
New Town Shetland....312 E6
New Town Som....29 D9
New Town Som....29 D11
New Town Som....44 D3
New Town Soton....33 E7
New Town Swindon....62 C5
New Town T&W....234 B2
New Town T&W....243 E8
New Town W Berks....64 D6
New Town Wilts....46 C6
New Town Wilts....63 E9
New Town W Mid....133 B11
New Town W Mid....133 E9
New Town W Sus....35 B11
New Town W Yorks....198 C3
Newtown-in-St Martin Corn....2 E6
Newtown Linford Leics....135 B10
Newtown St Boswells Borders....262 C3
Newtown Unthank Leics....135 C9
New Tredegar Caerph....77 E10
New Trows S Lnrk....259 B8
Newtyle Angus....286 C6
New Ulva Argyll....275 E8
New Village E Yorks....209 G7
New Village S Yorks....198 F5
New Walsoken Cambs....139 B9
New Waltham NE Lincs....201 G9
New Well Powys....113 B11
New Wells Powys....130 D3
New Whittington Derbys....186 F5
New Wimpole Cambs....104 B6
New Winton E Loth....281 G8
New Woodhouses Shrops....167 G9
New Works Telford....132 B3
New Wortley W Yorks....205 G11
New Yatt Oxon....82 C5
Newyears Green London....66 B5
New York Lincs....174 D2
New York N Yorks....214 G3
New York T&W....243 C8
New Zealand Wilts....62 D4
Nextend Hereford....114 F6
Neyland Pembs....73 D7
Niarbyl IoM....192 E3
Nib Heath Shrops....149 F8
Nibley Glos....79 D11
Nibley S Glos....60 B2
Nibley Green Glos....80 F2
Nicholashayne Devon....27 D10
Nicholaston Swansea....56 D4
Nidd N Yorks....214 G3
Niddrie Edin....280 G5
Niddry W Loth....279 F11
Nigg Aberdeen....293 C11
Nigg Highld....301 B8

Nigg Ferry Highld....301 C7
Nightcott Som....26 B5
Nilig Denb....165 D8
Nimble Nook Gtr Man....196 G2
Nimlet S Glos....61 E8
Nimmer Som....28 E4
Nine Ashes Essex....87 E9
Nine Elms London....67 D9
Nine Elms Swindon....62 B6
Nine Maidens Downs Corn....2 B5
Nine Mile Burn Midloth....270 D3
Nineveh Worcs....116 C3
Nineveh Worcs....116 E2
Ninewells Glos....79 C9
Nine Wells Pembs....90 G5
Ninfield E Sus....38 E2
Ningwood IoW....20 D3
Ningwood Common IoW....20 D3
Ninnes Bridge Corn....2 B2
Nisbet Borders....262 D5
Nisthouse Orkney....314 E3
Nisthouse Shetland....313 G2
Nithbank Dumfries....247 D9
Nitshill Glasgow....267 C10
Noah's Arks Kent....52 B5
Noah's Green Worcs....117 E10
Noak Bridge Essex....87 G11
Noak Hill Essex....87 G11
Noak Hill London....87 G8
Nob End Gtr Man....195 F9
Nobland Green Herts....86 B5
Noblethorpe S Yorks....197 F9
Nobold Shrops....149 G9
Nobottle Northants....120 E3
Nob's Crook Hants....33 C7
Nocton Lincs....173 C9
Nocturom Mers....182 D3
Nodmore W Berks....64 D2
Noel Park London....86 G4
Nogdam End Norf....143 C7
Nog Tow Lancs....202 G6
Noke Oxon....83 C8
Noke Street Medway....69 E8
Nolton Pembs....72 B5
Nolton Haven Pembs....72 B5
No Man's Heath Ches W....167 F8
No Man's Heath Warks....134 B5
Nomansland Devon....26 E4
Nomansland Herts....85 C11
Nomansland Wilts....32 D3
No Man's Land Corn....6 D5
No Man's Land Hants....33 E10
Noneley Shrops....149 D9
Noness Shetland....313 L6
Nonikiln Highld....300 B6
Nonington Kent....55 C9
Nook Cumb....211 C10
Noon Nick W Yorks....205 F8
Noonsbrough Shetland....313 H4
Noonsun Ches E....184 F4
Noonvares Corn....2 C3
Noranside Angus....292 G6
Norbiton London....67 F7
Norbreck Blkpool....202 E2
Norbridge Hereford....98 C4
Norbury Ches E....167 F9
Norbury Derbys....169 G10
Norbury London....67 F10
Norbury Shrops....131 E7
Norbury Staffs....150 E5
Norbury Common Ches E....167 F9
Norbury Junction Staffs....150 E5
Norbury Moor Gtr Man....184 D6
Norby N Yorks....215 C8
Norby Shetland....313 H3
Norchard Worcs....116 D6
Norcote Glos....81 E8
Norcott Brook Ches W....183 E10
Norcross Blkpool....202 E2
Nordelph Norf....139 C11
Nordelph Corner Norf....141 C10
Norden Dorset....18 E4
Norden Gtr Man....195 E11
Norden Heath Dorset....18 E4
Nordley Shrops....132 D3
Norham Northumb....273 F8
Norham West Mains Northumb....273 F8
Nork Sur....51 B8
Norland Town W Yorks....196 C5
Norleaze Wilts....45 C11
Norley Ches W....183 G9
Norley Devon....25 G8
Norley Common Sur....50 E4
Norleywood Hants....20 B3
Norlington E Sus....36 E6
Normacot Stoke....168 G6
Normanby N Lincs....199 D11
Normanby N Yorks....216 C4
Normanby Redcar....225 B10
Normanby-by-Spital Lincs....189 D7
Normanby by Stow Lincs....188 E5
Normanby le Wold Lincs....189 B10
Norman Cross Cambs....138 E3
Normandy Sur....50 C2
Norman Hill Glos....80 F3
Norman's Bay E Sus....23 D11
Norman's Green Devon....27 G9
Normanston Suff....143 E10
Normanton Derby....152 C6
Normanton Leics....172 G4
Normanton Lincs....172 F6
Normanton Notts....172 E2
Normanton Rutland....137 B8
Normanton Wilts....46 E6

Normanton W Yorks....197 C11
Normanton le Heath Leics....153 G7
Normanton on Soar Notts....153 E10
Normanton-on-the-Wolds Notts....154 C2
Normanton on Trent Notts....172 B3
Normanton Spring S Yorks....186 E6
Normanton Turville Leics....135 D9
Normoss Lancs....202 F2
Norney Sur....50 E2
Norr W Yorks....205 F7
Norrington Common Wilts....61 G11
Norris Green Corn....7 B8
Norris Green Mers....182 C5
Norris Hill Leics....152 F6
Norristhorpe W Yorks....197 C8
Norseman Orkney....314 E3
Northacre Norf....141 D9
North Acton London....67 C8
Northall Bucks....103 G9
Northallerton N Yorks....225 G7
Northall Green Norf....159 G9
Northam Devon....24 B6
Northam Soton....32 E6
Northampton Northants....120 E5
North Anston S Yorks....187 E8
North Ascot Brack....66 F2
North Aston Oxon....101 F9
Northaw Herts....86 E3
Northay Devon....28 G5
Northay Som....28 E3
North Ayre Shetland....312 F6
North Baddesley Hants....32 D5
North Ballachulish Highld....290 G2
North Barrow Som....29 B10
North Barsham Norf....159 C8
North Batsom Som....41 G10
Northbeck Lincs....173 G9
North Beer Corn....12 C2
North Benfleet Essex....69 B9
North Bersted W Sus....22 C4
North Berwick E Loth....281 D11
North Bitchburn Durham....233 E9
North Blyth Northumb....253 G8
North Boarhunt Hants....33 E10
North Bockhampton Dorset....19 B9
Northborough Pboro....138 B3
Northbourne Bmouth....19 B7
Northbourne Kent....55 C10
North Bovey Devon....13 E10
North Bradley Wilts....45 C11
North Brentor Devon....12 E5
North Brewham Som....45 F8
Northbrook Dorset....17 C11
Northbrook Hants....48 F4
Northbrook Oxon....101 G9
Northbrook Wilts....46 C4
North Brook End Cambs....104 C5
North Broomage Falk....279 E7
North Buckland Devon....40 E3
North Burlingham Norf....161 G7
North Cadbury Som....29 B10
North Cairn Dumfries....236 B1
North Camp Hants....49 C11
North Carlton Lincs....188 F6
North Carlton Notts....187 E9
North Cave E Yorks....208 G3
North Cerney Glos....81 D8
North Chailey E Sus....36 C5
Northchapel W Sus....35 B7
North Charford Wilts....31 D11
North Charlton Northumb....264 E5
North Cheam London....67 F8
North Cheriton Som....29 B11
Northchurch Herts....85 D7
North Cliff E Yorks....209 D10
North Cliffe E Yorks....208 F3
North Clifton Notts....188 G4
North Close Durham....233 E11
North Cockerington Lincs....190 C5
North Coker Som....29 E8
North Collafirth Shetland....312 E5
North Common S Glos....61 E7
North Common Suff....125 B9
North Connel Argyll....289 F11
North Cornelly Bridgend....57 E10
North Corner Corn....3 F7
North Corner S Glos....61 C7
North Corriegills N Ayrs....256 C2
North Corry Highld....289 D10
North Cotes Lincs....201 G11
Northcott Corn....24 F2
Northcott Devon....12 C2
Northcott Devon....27 F10
Northcott Devon....27 G10
North Country Corn....4 G3
Northcourt Oxon....83 F8
North Court Som....41 F11
North Cove Suff....143 F9

North Cowton N Yorks....224 E5
North Craigo Angus....293 G8
North Crawley M Keynes....103 C8
North Cray London....68 E3
North Creake Norf....159 B7
North Curry Som....28 B4
North Dalton E Yorks....208 C4
North Darley Corn....11 G11
North Dawn Orkney....314 F4
North Deighton N Yorks....206 C3
North Denes Norf....161 G10
Northdown Kent....71 E11
North Dronley Angus....287 D7
North Drumachter Lodge Highld....291 F8
North Duffield N Yorks....207 F9
Northdyke Orkney....314 D2
North Dykes Cumb....230 D6
North Eastling Kent....54 B3
Northedge Derbys....170 B5
North Elham Kent....55 E7
North Elkington Lincs....190 C3
North Elmham Norf....159 E9
North Elmsall W Yorks....198 E3
North Elmshall W Yorks....198 E3
North Elphinstone E Loth....281 G7
Northend Bath....61 F9
Northend Bucks....84 G2
Northend Essex....89 E7
Northend Warks....105 D10
Northend Warks....119 G7
North End Bath....60 G6
North End Beds....103 B9
North End Beds....121 F10
North End Bexley....68 D4
North End Bucks....102 F4
North End Bucks....102 F6
North End Camden....67 B9
North End Cumb....239 F8
North End Devon....27 D10
North End Dorset....30 B4
North End Durham....233 C11
North End Essex....87 B11
North End Essex....106 D5
North End E Yorks....209 C9
North End E Yorks....209 G11
North End Hants....31 D10
North End Hants....33 B9
North End Hants....64 G2
North End Leics....153 F11
North End Lincs....174 G2
North End Lincs....189 B8
North End Lincs....190 C5
North End Lincs....201 G10
North End N Lincs....200 C6
North End Norf....141 D10
North End Northumb....252 C4
North End N Som....60 E2
North End Ptsmth....33 G11
North End Som....28 B3
North End W Sus....81 G8
North End W Sus....35 F10
North End W Sus....35 G8
North End W Sus....51 F11
Northenden Gtr Man....184 C4
Northern Moor Gtr Man....184 C4
North Erradale Highld....307 L2
North Evington Leicester....136 C2
North Ewster N Lincs....199 G10
North Fambridge Essex....88 F5
North Fearns Highld....295 B7
North Featherstone W Yorks....198 C2
North Feltham London....66 E6
North Feorline N Ayrs....255 E10
North Ferriby E Yorks....200 B3
Northfield Aberdeen....293 C11
Northfield Borders....262 D3
Northfield Borders....273 B8
Northfield Edin....280 G5
Northfield Hull....200 B4
Northfield Highld....301 B7
Northfield M Keynes....103 C7
Northfield Northants....137 D7
Northfield Som....43 F9
Northfield W Mid....117 B10
Northfields Lincs....137 B10
Northfields Lincs....137 B10
North Finchley London....86 G3
Northfleet Kent....68 E6
Northfleet Green Kent....68 E6
North Flobbets Aberds....303 F7
North Frodingham E Yorks....209 C8
Northgate Lincs....156 D3
Northgate Som....27 B9
Northgate W Sus....51 F9
North Gluss Shetland....312 F5
North Gorley Hants....31 E11
North Green Norf....141 B10
North Green Norf....142 B7
North Green Suff....126 B6
North Green Suff....126 E6
North Green Suff....127 D7
North Greetwell Lincs....189 G8
North Grimston N Yorks....216 F6
North Halley Orkney....314 F5

Orton Malborne Pboro 138 D3
Orton-on-the-Hill Leics 134 C6
Orton Rigg Cumb 239 G8
Orton Southgate Pboro 138 E2
Orton Waterville Pboro 138 D3
Orton Wistow Pboro 138 D2
Orwell Cambs 123 G7
Osbaldeston Lancs 203 G8
Osbaldeston Green Lancs 203 G8
Osbaldwick York 207 C8
Osbaston Leics 135 C8
Osbaston Shrops 148 E6
Osbaston Telford 149 F11
Osbaston Hollow Leics 135 B8
Osbournby Lincs 155 B11
Oscroft Ches W 167 B8
Ose Highld 298 E3
Osea Island Essex 88 D6
Osehill Green Dorset 29 F11
Osgathorpe Leics 153 F8
Osgodby Lincs 189 C9
Osgodby N Yorks 207 G8
Osgodby N Yorks 217 C11
Osgodby Common N Yorks 207 F8
Osidge London 86 G3
Oskaig Highld 295 B7
Oskamull Argyll 288 E6
Osleston Derbys 152 B4
Osmaston Derby 153 C7
Osmaston Derbys 170 G2
Osmington Dorset 17 E10
Osmington Mills Dorset 17 E10
Osmondthorpe W Yorks 206 G2
Osmotherley N Yorks 225 F9
Osney Oxon 83 D8
Ospisdale Highld 309 L7
Ospringe Kent 70 G4
Ossaborough Devon 40 E3
Ossemsley Hants 19 B10
Osset Spa W Yorks 197 D9
Ossett W Yorks 197 C9
Ossett Street Side W Yorks 197 C9
Ossington Notts 172 C3
Ostend Essex 88 F6
Ostend Norf 161 C7
Osterley London 66 D6
Oswaldkirk N Yorks 216 D2
Oswaldtwistle Lancs 195 B8
Oswestry Shrops 148 D5
Otby Lincs 189 C10
Oteley Shrops 149 C8
Otford Kent 52 B4
Otham Kent 53 C9
Otham Hole Kent 53 C10
Otherton Staffs 151 G8
Othery Som 43 G11
Otley Suff 126 F4
Otley W Yorks 205 D10
Otterbourne Hants 33 C7
Otterburn Northumb 251 E9
Otterburn N Yorks 204 B3
Otterburn Camp Northumb 251 D9
Otterden Place Kent 54 C2
Otter Ferry Argyll 275 E10
Otterford Som 28 E2
Otterham Corn 11 C9
Otterhampton Som 43 E8
Otterham Quay Kent 69 F10
Otterham Station Corn 11 D9
Otter Ho Argyll 275 F10
Ottershaw Sur 66 G4
Otterspool Mers 182 D5
Otterswick Shetland 312 E7
Otterton Devon 15 D7
Otterwood Hants 32 G6
Ottery St Mary Devon 15 B8
Ottinge Kent 55 E7
Ottringham E Yorks 201 C9
Oughterby Cumb 239 F7
Oughtershaw N Yorks 213 C7
Oughterside Cumb 229 C8
Oughtibridge S Yorks 186 C4
Oughtrington Warr 183 D11
Oulston N Yorks 215 E10
Oulton Cumb 238 G6
Oulton Norf 160 D2
Oulton Staffs 150 E5
Oulton Staffs 151 B8
Oulton Suff 143 D10
Oulton W Yorks 197 B11
Oulton Broad Suff 143 E10
Oultoncross Staffs 151 C8
Oulton Grange Staffs 151 B8
Oulton Heath Staffs 151 B8
Oulton Street Norf 160 D3
Oundle Northants 137 F10
Ounsdale Staffs 133 E7
Ousby Cumb 231 E8
Ousdale Highld 311 G4
Ousden Suff 124 F4
Ousefleet E Yorks 199 C10
Ousel Hole W Yorks 205 E8
Ouston Durham 243 G7
Ouston Northumb 241 G7
Ouston Northumb 242 C3
Outcast Cumb 210 D6
Out Elmstead Kent 55 C8
Outer Hope Devon 8 G3
Outertown Orkney 314 E2
Outgate Cumb 221 F7
Outhgill Cumb 222 E5
Outhill Warks 118 D2
Outhills Aberds 303 D10
Outlands Staffs 150 C5
Outlane W Yorks 196 D5
Outlane Moor W Yorks 196 D5
Outlet Village Ches W 182 G6
Outmarsh Wilts 61 G11
Out Newton E Yorks 201 C11
Out Rawcliffe Lancs 202 E4
Outwell Norf 139 C10
Outwick Hants 31 D10
Outwood Gtr Man 195 F9
Outwood Som 28 B4
Outwood Sur 51 D10
Outwood W Yorks 197 C10
Outwoods Leics 153 F8
Outwoods Staffs 150 F5
Outwoods Staffs 152 E4
Outwoods Warks 134 G4
Ouzlewell Green W Yorks 197 B10
Ovenden W Yorks 196 B5
Ovencloss Borders 261 C11
Over Cambs 123 C7
Over Ches W 167 B10
Over Glos 80 B4
Over S Glos 60 C5
Overa Farm Stud Norf 141 F9
Overbister Orkney 314 B6
Over Burrow Lancs 212 D2
Over Burrows Derbys 152 B5
Overbury Worcs 99 D9
Overcombe Dorset 17 E9
Over Compton Dorset 29 D9
Overend W Mid 133 G9
Over End Cambs 137 E11
Over End Derbys 186 G3
Overgreen Derbys 186 G4
Over Green W Mid 134 E3
Over Haddon Derbys 170 B2
Over Hulton Gtr Man 195 F7
Over Kellet Lancs 211 E10
Over Kiddington Oxon 101 G8
Over Knutsford Ches E 184 F3
Over Langshaw Borders 271 G10
Overleigh Som 44 F3
Overley Staffs 152 F3
Overley Green Warks 117 F11
Over Monnow Mon 79 C8
Overmoor Staffs 169 F7
Over Norton Oxon 100 F6
Over Peover Ches E 184 G3
Overpool Ches W 182 F5
Overs Shrops 131 D7
Overscaig Hotel Highld 309 G4
Overseal Derbys 152 F5
Over Silton N Yorks 225 G9
Overslade Warks 119 C9
Oversland Kent 54 B5
Oversley Green Warks 117 F11
Overstone Northants 120 D6
Over Stowey Som 43 F7
Overstrand Norf 160 A4
Over Stratton Som 28 D6
Over Tabley Ches E 184 E2
Overthorpe Northants 101 C9
Overthorpe W Yorks 197 D8
Overton Aberdeen 293 B10
Overton Aberds 293 B9
Overton Ches W 183 F8
Overton Dumfries 237 C11
Overton Glos 80 C2
Overton Hants 48 D4
Overton Invclyd 276 G5
Overton Lancs 202 B4
Overton N Yorks 207 B7
Overton Shrops 115 C10
Overton Staffs 151 B10
Overton Swansea 56 D3
Overton W Yorks 197 D9
Overton Bridge Wrex 166 G5
Overton / Owrtyn Wrex 166 G5
Overtown Lancs 212 D2
Overtown N Lnrk 268 E6
Overtown Swindon 63 D7
Overtown W Yorks 197 D11
Over Town Lancs 195 B11
Over Wallop Hants 47 F9
Over Whitacre Warks 134 E5
Over Worton Oxon 101 F8
Oving Bucks 102 G5
Oving W Sus 22 C6
Ovingdean Brighton 36 G5
Ovingham Northumb 242 E3
Ovington Durham 224 C2
Ovington Essex 106 C5
Ovington Hants 48 G5
Ovington Norf 141 C8
Ovington Northumb 242 E3
Owen's Bank Staffs 152 D4
Ower Hants 32 D4
Owermoigne Dorset 17 D11
Owlbury Shrops 130 E6
Owlcotes Derbys 170 B6
Owl End Cambs 122 B4
Owler Bar Derbys 186 F3
Owlerton S Yorks 186 D4
Owlet W Yorks 205 F9
Owlpen Glos 80 F4
Owl's Green Suff 126 D5
Owlsmoor Brack 65 G11
Owlswick Bucks 84 D3
Owlthorpe S Yorks 186 E6
Owmby Lincs 200 G5
Owmby-by-Spital Lincs 189 D8
Ownham W Berks 64 E2
Owrtyn / Overton Wrex 166 G5
Owslebury Hants 33 C8
Owston Leics 136 B5
Owston S Yorks 198 E5
Owston Ferry N Lincs 199 G10
Owstwick E Yorks 209 G11
Owthorne E Yorks 201 B10
Owthorpe Notts 154 C3
Owton Manor Hrtlpl 234 F5
Oxborough Norf 140 C4
Oxclose S Yorks 186 E6
Oxclose T&W 243 F7
Oxcombe Lincs 190 F4
Oxcroft Derbys 187 G7
Oxcroft Estate Derbys 187 G7
Oxen End Essex 106 F3
Oxenhall Glos 98 F4
Oxenholme Cumb 211 B10
Oxenhope W Yorks 204 F6
Oxen Park Cumb 210 B6
Oxenpill Som 44 E2
Oxenton Glos 99 E9
Oxenwood Wilts 47 B10
Oxford Oxon 83 D8
Oxford Stoke 168 E5
Oxgang E Dunb 278 G3
Oxgangs Edin 270 B4
Oxhey Herts 85 F10
Oxhill Durham 242 G5
Oxhill Warks 100 B6
Oxlease Herts 86 D2
Oxley W Mid 133 C8
Oxley Green Essex 88 C6
Oxley's Green E Sus 37 C11
Oxlode Cambs 139 F9
Oxnam Borders 262 F5
Oxnead Norf 160 E4
Oxshott Sur 66 G6
Oxspring S Yorks 197 G9
Oxted Sur 51 C11
Oxton Borders 271 E9
Oxton Mers 182 D3
Oxton Notts 171 E10
Oxton N Yorks 206 E6
Oxton Rakes Derbys 186 G4
Oxwich Swansea 56 D3
Oxwich Green Swansea 56 D3
Oxwick Norf 159 D8
Oykel Bridge Highld 309 J3
Oyne Aberds 302 G6
Oystermouth Swansea 56 D6
Ozleworth Glos 80 G3


## P


Pabail Iarach W Isles 304 E7
Pabail Uarach W Isles 304 E7
Pabo Conwy 180 F4
Pace Gate N Yorks 205 C8
Pachesham Park Sur 51 B7
Packers Hill Dorset 30 E2
Packington Leics 153 G7
Packmoor Staffs 168 E5
Packmores Warks 118 D5
Packwood W Mid 118 C3
Packwood Gullet W Mid 118 C3
Padanaram Angus 287 B8
Padbury Bucks 102 E4
Paddington London 67 C9
Paddington Warr 183 D10
Paddlesworth Kent 55 F7
Paddlesworth Kent 69 G7
Paddock Kent 54 C3
Paddock W Yorks 196 D6
Paddockhaugh Moray 302 D2
Paddockhill Ches E 184 F4
Paddockhole Dumfries 248 G6
Paddock Wood Kent 53 E7
Paddolgreen Shrops 149 C10
Padfield Derbys 185 B8
Padgate Warr 183 D10
Padham's Green Essex 87 F10
Padiham Lancs 203 G11
Padney Cambs 123 C10
Padog Conwy 164 E4
Padside N Yorks 205 B9
Padside Green N Yorks 205 B9
Padson Devon 13 B7
Padstow Corn 10 F4
Padworth W Berks 64 F6
Padworth Common Hants 64 G6
Paganhill Glos 80 D4
Page Bank Durham 233 D10
Page Moss Mers 182 C6
Page's Green Suff 126 D2
Pagham W Sus 22 D5
Paglesham Churchend Essex 88 G6
Paglesham Eastend Essex 88 G6
Paibeil W Isles 296 E3
Paible W Isles 305 J2
Paignton Torbay 9 C7
Pailton Warks 135 G9
Painleyhill Staffs 151 C10
Painscastle Powys 96 B3
Painshawfield Northumb 242 E3
Pains Hill Sur 52 C2
Painsthorpe E Yorks 208 B2
Painswick Glos 80 D5
Painter's Forstal Kent 54 B3
Painters Green Wrex 167 G8
Painter's Green Herts 86 B3
Painthorpe W Yorks 197 D10
Paintmoor Som 28 F4
Pairc Shiaboist W Isles 304 D4
Paisley Renfs 267 C9
Pakefield Suff 143 E10
Pakenham Suff 125 D8
Pale Gwyn 147 B9
Pale Green Essex 106 C3
Palehouse Common E Sus 23 B7
Palestine Hants 47 E9
Paley Street Windsor 65 D11
Palfrey W Mid 133 D10
Palgowan Dumfries 245 G9
Palgrave Suff 126 B2
Pallaflat Cumb 219 C9
Pallington Dorset 17 C11
Pallion T&W 243 F9
Pallister Mbro 225 B10
Palmarsh Kent 54 G6
Palmer Moor Derbys 152 C2
Palmersbridge Corn 11 F9
Palmers Cross Staffs 133 C7
Palmers Cross Sur 50 E4
Palmer's Flat Glos 79 D9
Palmers Green London 86 G4
Palmer's Green Kent 53 E7
Palmerstown V Glam 58 F6
Palmersville T&W 243 C7
Palmstead Kent 55 D7
Palnackie Dumfries 237 D10
Palnure Dumfries 236 C6
Palterton Derbys 171 B7
Pamber End Hants 48 B6
Pamber Green Hants 48 B6
Pamber Heath Hants 64 G6
Pamington Glos 99 E8
Pamphill Dorset 31 G7
Pampisford Cambs 105 B9
Pan IoW 20 D6
Pan Orkney 314 G3
Panborough Som 44 D3
Panbride Angus 287 D9
Pancakehill Glos 81 C9
Pancrasweek Devon 24 F3
Pancross V Glam 58 F4
Pandy Gwyn 128 C2
Pandy Gwyn 146 F4
Pandy Gwyn 147 D7
Pandy Mon 96 G6
Pandy Powys 129 C8
Pandy Wrex 148 B3
Pandy Wrex 166 G2
Pandy'r Capel Denb 165 E9
Pandy Tudur Conwy 164 C5
Panfield Essex 106 F4
Pangbourne W Berks 64 D6
Panhall Fife 280 C6
Panks Bridge Hereford 98 B2
Pannal N Yorks 206 C2
Pannal Ash N Yorks 205 C11
Pannel's Ash Essex 106 C5
Panpunton Powys 114 C5
Panshanger Herts 86 C3
Pant Denb 166 E2
Pant Flint 181 G10
Pant Gwyn 144 C4
Pant M Tydf 77 D9
Pant Powys 129 C11
Pant Shrops 148 E5
Pant Wrex 166 D5
Pant Wrex 166 F3
Pantasaph Flint 181 F11
Pantdu Neath 57 C9
Panteg Ceredig 111 E9
Panteg Torf 78 F4
Pantersbridge Corn 6 B3
Pant-glas Gwyn 163 F7
Pant-glâs Powys 128 D5
Pant-glas Shrops 148 C5
Pantgwyn Carms 93 F11
Pantgwyn Ceredig 92 B4
Pant-lasau Swansea 57 B7
Pantmawr Cardiff 58 C6
Pant Mawr Powys 129 G7
Panton Lincs 189 F11
Pant-pastynog Denb 165 C8
Pantperthog Gwyn 128 C4
Pantside Caerph 78 F2
Pant-teg Carms 93 F9
Pant-y-Caws Carms 92 F3
Pant-y-crûg Ceredig 112 B3
Pant-y-dwr Powys 113 B9
Pant-y-ffridd Powys 130 C3
Pantyffynnon Carms 75 C10
Pantygasseg Torf 78 F3
Pantymwyn Flint 165 C11
Pant-y-pyllau Bridgend 58 C2
Pant-yr-awel Bridgend 58 B2
Pant-y-Wacco Flint 181 F10
Panxworth Norf 161 G7
Papcastle Cumb 229 E8
Papermill Bank Shrops 149 D11
Papigoe Highld 310 D7
Papil Shetland 313 K5
Papley Northants 138 F2
Papley Orkney 314 G4
Papple E Loth 281 G11
Papplewick Notts 171 E8
Papworth Everard Cambs 122 E5
Papworth St Agnes Cambs 122 E5
Papworth Village Settlement Cambs 122 E5
Par Corn 5 E11
Paradise Glos 80 C5
Paradise Green Hereford 97 B10
Paramoor Corn 5 F9
Paramour Street Kent 71 G9
Parbold Lancs 194 E3
Parbrook Som 44 F5
Parbrook W Sus 35 B9
Parc Gwyn 147 C7
Parc Erissey Corn 4 G3
Parc-hendy Swansea 56 B4
Parchey Som 43 F10
Parciau Anglesey 179 E7
Parcllyn Ceredig 110 G4
Parc Mawr Caerph 77 G10
Parc-Seymour Newport 78 G6
Parc-y-rhôs Carms 93 B11
Pardown Hants 48 D5
Pardshaw Cumb 229 G7
Pardshaw Hall Cumb 229 F8
Parham Suff 126 E6
Park Corn 10 G6
Park Devon 14 B2
Park Dumfries 247 E10
Park Som 44 G3
Park Swindon 63 C7
Park Barn Sur 50 C3
Park Bottom Corn 4 G3
Park Bridge Gtr Man 196 G2
Park Broom Cumb 239 F10
Park Close Lancs 204 E3
Park Corner Bath 45 B9
Park Corner E Sus 23 C8
Park Corner E Sus 52 F4
Park Corner Oxon 65 B7
Park Corner Windsor 65 C11
Parkend Glos 79 D10
Parkend Glos 80 C3
Park End Beds 121 G9
Park End Cambs 123 E11
Park End Mbro 225 B10
Park End Northumb 241 B9
Park End Som 43 G7
Park End Staffs 168 E3
Park End Worcs 116 C5
Parkengear Corn 5 F8
Parker's Corner W Berks 64 E6
Parker's Green Herts 104 F6
Parker's Green Kent 52 D6
Parkeston Essex 108 E4
Parkfield Corn 6 B6
Parkfield S Glos 61 D7
Parkfield W Mid 133 D8
Parkfoot Falk 278 F6
Parkgate Ches E 184 G3
Parkgate Ches W 182 F3
Parkgate Cumb 229 B10
Parkgate Dumfries 248 F2
Parkgate Essex 87 B11
Parkgate Kent 53 G11
Parkgate Sur 51 E8
Parkgate S Yorks 186 B6
Park Gate Dorset 30 F2
Park Gate Hants 33 F8
Park Gate Kent 55 D7
Park Gate Suff 124 F4
Park Gate Worcs 117 C8
Park Gate W Yorks 197 E8
Park Green Essex 105 F9
Parkhall W Dunb 277 G9
Park Hall Shrops 148 C6
Parkham Devon 24 C5
Parkham Ash Devon 24 C5
Parkhead Cumb 230 C2
Parkhead Glasgow 268 C2
Parkhead S Yorks 186 E4
Park Head Cumb 231 C7
Park Head Derbys 170 E5
Park Head W Yorks 197 F8
Parkhill Aberds 303 E10
Parkhill Invclyd 277 G7
Park Hill Glos 79 F9
Park Hill Kent 54 G3
Park Hill Mers 194 G3
Park Hill Notts 171 E11
Park Hill N Yorks 214 F6
Park Hill S Yorks 186 D5
Parkhill Ho Aberds 293 B10
Parkhouse Mon 79 E7
Parkhouse Green Derbys 170 C6
Parkhurst IoW 20 C5
Parklands W Yorks 206 F3
Park Lane Staffs 133 B7
Park Lane Wrex 149 B8
Park Langley London 67 F11
Park Mains Renfs 277 G9
Parkmill Swansea 56 D4
Park Mill W Yorks 197 E9
Parkneuk Aberds 293 F9
Parkneuk Fife 279 D11
Park Royal London 67 C7
Parkside C Beds 103 G10
Parkside Cumb 219 B10
Parkside Durham 234 B4
Parkside N Lnrk 268 D6
Parkside Staffs 151 D8
Parkside Wrex 166 D5
Parkstone Poole 18 C6
Park Street Herts 85 E10
Park Street W Sus 50 G6
Park Town Luton 103 G11
Park Town Oxon 83 D8
Park Village Northumb 240 E5
Park Village W Mid 133 C8
Park Villas W Yorks 206 F2
Parkway Hereford 98 D4
Parkway Som 29 C9
Park Wood Kent 53 C9
Park Wood Medway 69 G10
Parkwood Springs S Yorks 186 D4
Parley Cross Dorset 19 B7
Parley Green Dorset 19 B7
Parliament Heath Suff 107 C9
Parlington W Yorks 206 F4
Parmoor Bucks 65 B9
Parnacott Devon 24 F4
Parney Heath Essex 107 E10
Parr Mers 183 C8
Parracombe Devon 41 E7
Parr Brow Gtr Man 195 G8
Parrog Pembs 91 D10
Parsley Hay Derbys 169 C10
Parslow's Hillock Bucks 84 E4
Parsonage Green Essex 88 D2
Parsonby Cumb 229 D8
Parson Cross S Yorks 186 C5
Parson Drove Cambs 139 B7
Parsons Green London 67 D9
Parson's Heath Essex 107 F10
Partick Glasgow 267 B11
Partington Gtr Man 184 C2
Partney Lincs 174 B6
Parton Cumb 228 G5
Parton Cumb 239 G7
Parton Dumfries 237 B8
Parton Glos 99 G7
Parton Hereford 96 B6
Partridge Green W Sus 35 D11
Partrishow Powys 96 G5
Parwich Derbys 169 E11
Pasford Staffs 132 D6
Passenham Northants 102 D5
Passfield Hants 49 G10
Passingford Bridge Essex 87 F8
Passmores Essex 86 D6
Paston Norf 160 C6
Paston Pboro 138 C3
Paston Green Norf 160 C6
Pasturefields Staffs 151 D9
Patchacott Devon 12 B5
Patcham Brighton 36 F4
Patchetts Green Herts 85 F10
Patching W Sus 35 F9
Patchole Devon 40 E6
Patchway S Glos 60 C6
Pategill Cumb 230 F6
Pateley Bridge N Yorks 214 F3
Paternoster Heath Essex 88 C6
Pathe Som 43 G11
Pather N Lnrk 268 E5
Pathfinder Village Devon 14 C2
Pathhead Aberds 293 G9
Pathhead E Ayrs 258 G4
Pathhead Fife 280 C5
Pathhead Midloth 271 C7
Path Head T&W 242 E5
Pathlow Warks 118 F3
Path of Condie Perth 286 F4
Pathstruie Perth 286 F4
Patient End Herts 105 F8
Patmore Heath Herts 105 F8
Patna E Ayrs 257 G10
Patney Wilts 46 B5
Patrick IoM 192 D3
Patrick Brompton N Yorks 224 G4
Patricroft Gtr Man 184 B3
Patrington E Yorks 201 C10
Patrington Haven E Yorks 201 C10
Patrixbourne Kent 55 B7
Patsford Devon 40 F4
Patterdale Cumb 221 B7
Pattiesmuir Fife 279 E11
Pattingham Staffs 132 D6
Pattishall Northants 120 G3
Pattiswick Essex 106 G6
Patton Shrops 131 E11
Patton Bridge Cumb 221 F11
Paul Corn 1 D5
Paulerspury Northants 102 B4
Paull E Yorks 201 B7
Paul's Green Corn 2 C4
Paulsgrove Ptsmth 33 F10
Paulton Bath 45 B7
Paulville W Loth 269 B9
Pave Lane Telford 150 F5
Pavenham Beds 121 F9
Pawlett Som 43 E10
Pawlett Hill Som 43 E9
Pawston Northumb 263 C9
Paxford Glos 100 D3
Paxton Borders 273 E8
Payden Street Kent 54 C2
Payhembury Devon 27 G9
Paynes Green Sur 50 F6
Paynter's Cross Corn 7 C7
Paynter's Lane End Corn 4 G3
Paythorne Lancs 204 C2
Payton Som 27 C10
Peacehaven E Sus 36 G6
Peacehaven Heights E Sus 36 G6
Peacemarsh Dorset 30 B4
Peak Dale Derbys 185 F9
Peak Forest Derbys 185 F10
Peak Hill Lincs 156 F5
Peakirk Pboro 138 B3
Pean Hill Kent 70 G6
Pear Ash Som 45 G9
Pearsie Angus 287 B7
Pearson's Green Kent 53 E7
Peartree Herts 86 C2
Pear Tree Derby 153 C7
Peartree Green Essex 87 F9
Peartree Green Hereford 97 E11
Peartree Green Soton 32 E6
Peartree Green Sur 50 F3
Peas Acre W Yorks 205 E8
Peasedown St John Bath 45 B8
Peasehill Derbys 170 F6
Peaseland Green Norf 159 F11
Peasemore W Berks 64 D3
Peasenhall Suff 127 D7
Pease Pottage W Sus 51 G9
Peas Hill Cambs 139 D8
Peaslake Sur 50 E5
Peasley Cross Mers 183 C8
Peasmarsh E Sus 38 C5
Peasmarsh Som 28 E4
Peasmarsh Sur 50 D3
Peaston E Loth 271 B8
Peastonbank E Loth 271 B8
Peathill Aberds 303 C9
Peat Inn Fife 287 G8
Peatling Magna Leics 135 E11
Peatling Parva Leics 135 F11
Peaton Shrops 131 G10
Peatonstrand Shrops 131 G10
Peats Corner Suff 126 E3
Pebmarsh Essex 107 E7
Pebsham E Sus 38 F3
Pebworth Worcs 100 B2
Pecket Well W Yorks 196 B3
Peckforton Ches E 167 D8
Peckham London 67 D10
Peckham Bush Kent 53 D7
Peckingell Wilts 62 E2
Pecking Mill Som 44 F6
Peckleton Leics 135 C9
Pedair-ffordd Powys 148 E2
Pedham Norf 160 G6
Pedlars End Essex 87 D8
Pedlar's Rest Shrops 131 G9
Pedlinge Kent 54 F6
Pedmore W Mid 133 G8
Pednor Bottom Bucks 84 E6
Pednormead End Bucks 85 E7
Pedwell Som 44 F2
Peebles Borders 270 G5
Peel Borders 261 B10
Peel IoM 192 D3
Peel Lancs 202 G3
Peel Common Hants 33 G9
Peel Green Gtr Man 184 B2
Peel Hall Gtr Man 184 D4
Peel Hill Lancs 202 G3
Peel Park S Lnrk 268 E2
Peene Kent 55 F7
Peening Quarter Kent 38 B5
Peggs Green Leics 153 F8
Pegsdon C Beds 104 E2
Pegswood Northumb 252 F6
Pegwell Kent 71 G11
Peinaha Highld 298 D4
Peinchorran Highld 295 B7
Peingown Highld 298 B4
Peinlich Highld 298 D4
Peinmore Highld 298 E4
Pelaw T&W 243 E7
Pelcomb Pembs 72 B6
Pelcomb Bridge Pembs 72 B6
Pelcomb Cross Pembs 72 B6
Peldon Essex 89 B7
Pelhamfield IoW 21 C7
Pell Green E Sus 52 G6
Pellon W Yorks 196 B5
Pelsall W Mid 133 C10
Pelsall Wood W Mid 133 C10
Pelton Durham 243 G7
Pelton Fell Durham 243 G7
Pelutho Cumb 229 B8
Pelynt Corn 6 D4
Pemberton Carms 75 E8
Pemberton Gtr Man 194 G5
Pembles Cross Kent 53 D11
Pembre / Pembrey Carms 74 E6
Pembrey / Pembre Carms 74 E6
Pembridge Hereford 115 F7
Pembroke Pembs 73 E7
Pembroke Dock / Doc Penfro Pembs 73 E7
Pembroke Ferry Pembs 73 E7
Pembury Kent 52 E6
Pempwell Corn 12 F3
Penallt Mon 79 C8
Pen-allt Hereford 97 F11
Penally / Penalun Pembs 73 F10
Penalt Hereford 97 F11
Penalun / Penally Pembs 73 F10
Penare Corn 5 G9
Penarlâg / Hawarden Flint 166 B4
Penarron Powys 130 F2
Penarth V Glam 59 E7
Penarth Moors Cardiff 59 E7
Penbeagle Corn 2 B2
Penbedw Flint 165 B11
Pen-bedw Pembs 92 D4
Penberth Corn 1 E4
Penbidwal Mon 96 G6
Penbodlas Gwyn 144 C5
Pen-bont Rhydybeddau Ceredig 128 G3
Penboyr Carms 93 D7
Penbryn Ceredig 110 G5
Pencader Carms 93 D8
Pencaenewydd Gwyn 162 G6
Pencaerau Neath 57 B8
Pen-caer-fenny Swansea 56 B4
Pencaitland E Loth 271 B8
Pencarnisiog Anglesey 178 G5
Pencarreg Carms 93 B10
Pencarrow Corn 11 E8
Penceiliogi Carms 75 E8
Pencelli Powys 95 F11
Pen-clawdd Swansea 56 B4
Pencoed Bridgend 58 C3
Pencombe Hereford 115 G11
Pen-common Powys 76 D6
Pencoyd Hereford 97 F10
Pencoys Corn 2 B5
Pencraig Anglesey 179 F7
Pencraig Hereford 97 G11
Pencraig Powys 147 D10
Pencroesoped Mon 78 D4
Pencuke Corn 11 C9
Pendas Fields W Yorks 206 F3
Pendeen Corn 1 C3
Pendeford W Mid 133 C7
Penderyn Rhondda 77 D7
Pendine / Pentywyn Carms 74 D2
Pendlebury Gtr Man 195 G9
Pendleton Gtr Man 184 B4
Pendleton Lancs 203 F11
Pendock Worcs 98 E5
Pendoggett Corn 10 F6
Pendomer Som 29 E8
Pendoylan V Glam 58 D5
Pendre Bridgend 58 C2
Pendre Gwyn 110 C2
Pendre Powys 95 F10
Pendrift Corn 11 G8
Penegoes Powys 128 C5
Penelewey Corn 4 G6
Penenden Heath Kent 53 B9
Penffordd Pembs 91 G11
Penffordd Lâs / Staylittle Powys 129 E7
Pengam Caerph 77 F11
Penge London 67 E11
Pengegon Corn 2 B5
Pengelly Corn 11 E7
Pengenffordd Powys 96 E3
Pengersick Corn 2 D3
Pen-gilfach Gwyn 163 C9
Pengold Corn 11 C8
Pengorffwysfa Anglesey 179 C7
Pengover Green Corn 6 B5
Pen-groes-oped Mon 78 D4
Penguithal Hereford 97 G10
Pengwern Denb 181 F8
Penhale Corn 2 F5
Penhale Corn 5 D8
Penhale Jakes Corn 2 D4
Penhallick Corn 3 F7
Penhallick Corn 4 G3
Penhallow Corn 4 E5
Penhalurick Corn 2 B6
Penhalvean Corn 2 B6
Penhelig Gwyn 128 D2
Penhill Devon 40 G4
Penhill Swindon 63 B7
Penhow Newport 78 G6
Penhurst E Sus 23 B11
Peniarth Gwyn 128 B2
Penicuik Midloth 270 C4
Peniel Carms 93 G8
Peniel Denb 165 C8
Penifiler Highld 298 E4
Peninver Argyll 255 E8
Penisa'r Waun Gwyn 163 C9
Penistone S Yorks 197 G8
Penjerrick Corn 3 C7
Penketh Warr 183 D9
Penkhull Stoke 168 G5
Penkill S Ayrs 244 D6
Penknap Wilts 45 D11
Penkridge Staffs 151 G8
Pen-lan Swansea 56 B6
Pen-Lan-mabws Pembs 91 F7
Penleigh Wilts 45 C11
Penley Wrex 149 B8
Penllech Gwyn 144 C4
Penllergaer Swansea 56 B6
Penllwyn Caerph 77 F11
Penllwyn Ceredig 128 G3
Penllyn V Glam 58 D3
Pen-llyn Anglesey 178 E4
Pen-lon Anglesey 162 B6
Penmachno Conwy 164 E3
Penmaen Caerph 77 F11
Penmaen Swansea 56 D4
Penmaenan Conwy 180 F2
Penmaenmawr Conwy 180 F2
Penmaenpool Gwyn 146 F3
Penmaen Rhôs Conwy 180 F5
Penmark V Glam 58 F5
Penmarth Corn 2 B6
Penmayne Corn 10 F4
Pen Mill Som 29 D9
Penmon Anglesey 179 E10
Penmore Mill Argyll 288 D6
Penmorfa Ceredig 110 G6
Penmorfa Gwyn 163 G8
Penmynydd Anglesey 179 G8
Penn Bucks 84 G6
Penn W Mid 133 D7
Pennal Gwyn 128 C4
Pennan Aberds 303 C8
Pennance Corn 4 G4
Pennant Ceredig 111 E10
Pennant Conwy 164 D5
Pennant Denb 147 C10
Pennant Denb 165 E8
Pennant Powys 129 D7
Pennant Melangell Powys 147 D10
Pennar Pembs 73 E7
Pennard Swansea 56 D5
Pennar Park Pembs 72 E6
Penn Bottom Bucks 84 G6
Pennerley Shrops 131 D7
Pennington Cumb 210 D5
Pennington Gtr Man 183 B11
Pennington Hants 20 C2
Pennington Green Gtr Man 194 F6
Pennorth Powys 96 F2
Penn Street Bucks 84 F6
Pennsylvania Devon 14 C4
Pennsylvania S Glos 61 E8
Penny Bridge Cumb 210 C6
Pennycross Argyll 289 G7
Pennycross Plym 7 D9
Pennygate Norf 160 E6
Pennygown Argyll 289 E7
Penny Green Derbys 187 F8
Penny Hill Lincs 157 D7
Penny Hill W Yorks 196 D5
Pennylands Lancs 194 F3
Pennymoor Devon 26 E5
Pennypot Kent 54 G6
Penny's Green Norf 142 D3
Pennytinney Corn 10 F6
Pennywell T&W 243 F9
Pen-onn V Glam 58 F5
Penparc Ceredig 92 B4
Penparc Pembs 91 E7
Penparcau Ceredig 111 B11
Penpedairheol Caerph 77 F10

Pen–Pon 403

Penpedairheol Mon 78 E4
Penpergym Mon 78 C4
Penperlleni Mon 78 E4
Penpethy Corn 11 D7
Penpillick Corn 5 D11
Penplas Carms 74 B5
Penpol Corn 3 B8
Penpoll Corn 6 E2
Penponds Corn 2 B4
Penpont Corn 11 G7
Penpont Dumfries 247 E8
Penpont Powys 95 F9
Penprysg Bridgend 58 C3
Penquit Devon 8 E2
Penrallt Gwyn 145 B7
Penrallt Powys 129 F9
Penrherber Carms 92 D5
Penrhiw Caerph 78 G2
Penrhiwceiber Rhondda 77 F8
Pen-Rhiw-fawr Neath 76 C2
Penrhiwgarreg Bl Gwent 78 E2
Penrhiw-llan Ceredig 93 C7
Penrhiw-pal Ceredig 92 B6
Penrhiwtyn Neath 57 B8
Penrhos Anglesey 178 E3
Penrhos Gwyn 144 C6
Penrhos Hereford 114 F6
Penrhôs Mon 78 C6
Penrhos Mon 78 C6
Penrhos Powys 76 C3
Pen-rhos Wrex 166 E3
Penrhosfeilw Anglesey 178 E2
Penrhos-garnedd Gwyn 179 G9
Penrhyd Lastra Anglesey 178 C6
Penrhyn Bay / Bae-Penrhyn Conwy 180 E4
Penrhyn Castle Pembs 92 B2
Penrhyn-coch Ceredig 128 G2
Penrhyndeudraeth Gwyn 146 B2
Penrhynside Conwy 180 E4
Penrhyn side Conwy 180 E4
Penrhys Rhondda 77 F8
Penrice Swansea 56 D3
Penrith Cumb 230 E6
Penrose Corn 10 G3
Penrose Corn 11 F7
Penrose Hill Corn 2 D4
Penruddock Cumb 230 F4
Penryn Corn 3 C7
Pensarn Carms 74 B6
Pensarn Conwy 181 F7
Pen-sarn Gwyn 145 D11
Pen-sarn Gwyn 162 G6
Pensax Worcs 116 D4
Pensby Mers 182 E3
Penselwood Som 45 G9
Pensford Bath 60 G6
Pensham Worcs 99 C8
Penshaw T&W 243 G8
Penshurst Kent 52 E4
Pensilva Corn 6 B5
Pensnett W Mid 133 F8
Penston E Loth 281 G8
Penstone Devon 26 G3
Penstraze Corn 4 F5
Pentewan Corn 5 F10
Pentiken Shrops 130 G4
Pentir Gwyn 163 B9
Pentire Corn 4 C5
Pentirvin Shrops 130 C6
Pentlepoir Pembs 73 D10
Pentlow Essex 106 B6
Pentlow Street Essex 106 B6
Pentney Norf 158 G4
Penton Corner Hants 47 D10
Penton Grafton Hants 47 D10
Penton Mewsey Hants 47 D10
Pentonville London 67 C10
Pentowin Carms 74 B3
Pentraeth Anglesey 179 F8
Pentrapeod Caerph 77 E11
Pentre Carms 75 C8
Pentre Denb 165 D10
Pentre Flint 165 C11
Pentre Flint 166 B4
Pentre Flint 166 C2
Pentre Flint 166 D2
Pentre Powys 129 F11
Pentre Powys 130 B4
Pentre Powys 130 E5
Pentre Powys 147 D11
Pentre Powys 148 G3
Pentre Rhondda 77 F7
Pentre Shrops 148 D4
Pentre Shrops 149 F7
Pentre Wrex 148 B2
Pentre Wrex 166 G3
Pentrebach Carms 94 E6
Pentrebach M Tydf 77 E9
Pentrebach Rhondda 58 B5
Pentrebach Swansea 75 D10
Pentre-bâch Ceredig 93 B11
Pentre-bach Powys 95 E8
Pentrebane Cardiff 58 D6
Pentrebeirdd Powys 148 G3
Pentre Berw Anglesey 179 G7
Pentre-bont Conwy 164 E2
Pentre Broughton Wrex 166 E4
Pentre Bychan Wrex 166 F4
Pentrecagal Carms 92 C6
Pentre-celyn Shrops 148 D4
Pentre-celyn Denb 165 E11
Pentre-Celyn Powys 129 B7
Pentre-chwyth Swansea 57 B7
Pentre Cilgwyn Wrex 148 B4
Pentre-clawdd Shrops 148 C5
Pentre-coed Shrops 149 B7
Pentre-cwrt Carms 93 D7
Pentre Dolau-Honddu Powys 95 C9
Pentredwr Denb 165 F11
Pentre-dwr Swansea 57 B7
Pentrefelin Anglesey 178 C6
Pentrefelin Carms 93 G11
Pentrefelin Ceredig 94 B2
Pentrefelin Conwy 180 G4
Pentrefelin Denb 166 G2
Pentrefelin Gwyn 145 B10
Pentre-Ffwrndan Flint 182 G3
Pentrefoelas Conwy 164 E5
Pentref-y-groes Caerph 77 F11
Pentre-galar Pembs 92 E3
Pentregat Ceredig 111 G7
Pentre-Gwenlais Carms 75 B10
Pentre Gwynfryn Gwyn 145 D11
Pentre Halkyn Flint 182 G2
Pentreheyling Shrops 130 E4
Pentre Hodre Shrops 114 B6
Pentre Isaf Conwy 164 B5
Pentre Llanrhaeadr Denb 165 C9
Pentre Llifior Powys 130 D2
Pentrellwyn Ceredig 93 C8
Pentre-llwyn-llwyd Powys 113 G9
Pentre-llyn Ceredig 112 C2
Pentre-llyn cymmer Conwy 165 E7
Pentre Maelor Wrex 166 F5
Pentre Meyrick V Glam 58 D3
Pentre-newydd Shrops 148 B5
Pentre-Piod Torf 78 E3
Pentre-Poeth Carms 75 E8
Pentre-poeth Newport 59 B9
Pentre'r beirdd Powys 148 G3
Pentre'r Felin Conwy 164 B4
Pentre'r-felin Denb 165 B10
Pentre'r-felin Powys 95 E8
Pentre-rhew Ceredig 112 G3
Pentre-tafarn-y-fedw Conwy 164 C4
Pentre-ty-gwyn Carms 94 D6
Pentreuchaf Gwyn 145 B7
Pentre-uchaf Conwy 180 F5
Pentrich Derbys 170 E5
Pentridge Dorset 31 D8
Pentrisil Pembs 91 E11
Pentwyn Caerph 77 E10
Pentwyn Cardiff 59 C8
Pen-twyn Caerph 78 E2
Pen-twyn Carms 75 C9
Pen-twyn Mon 79 D8
Pen-twyn Torf 78 E3
Pentwyn Berthlwyd Caerph 77 F10
Pentwyn-mawr Caerph 77 F11
Pentwyn / Pendine Carms 74 D2
Pentyrch Cardiff 58 C6
Penuchadre V Glam 57 G11
Pen-Uchar Plwyf Flint 181 G11
Penuwch Ceredig 111 E11
Penwartha Corn 4 E5
Penwartha Coombe Corn 4 E5
Penweathers Corn 4 G6
Penwithick Corn 5 D10
Penwood Hants 64 G2
Penwortham Lane Lancs 194 B4
Penwyllt Powys 76 B5
Pen-y-Ball Top Flint 181 F11
Penybanc Carms 75 C10
Pen-y-banc Carms 93 G8
Pen-y-banc Carms 94 G2
Pen-y-bank Caerph 77 E10
Penybedd Carms 74 E6
Penybont Ceredig 128 F2
Penybont Powys 114 E2
Pen-y-Bont Bl Gwent 78 D2
Pen-y-bont Carms 92 F6
Pen-y-bont Gwyn 128 C4
Pen-y-bont Gwyn 146 D2
Pen-y-bont Powys 148 E4
Pen y Bont ar ogwr / Bridgend Bridgend 58 C2
Penybontfawr Powys 147 E11
Penybryn Caerph 77 F10
Pen-y-Bryn Gwyn 145 B9
Pen-y-bryn Gwyn 146 F3
Pen-y-bryn Pembs 92 C3
Pen-y-bryn Powys 130 C3
Pen-y-Bryn Shrops 148 B6
Pen-y-bryn Wrex 166 G3
Penycae Wrex 166 F3
Pen-y-cae Bridgend 58 C2
Pen-y-cae Neath 57 D9
Pen-y-cae Powys 76 C4
Pen-y-cae-mawr Mon 78 F6
Penycaerau Gwyn 144 D3
Pen-y-cefn Flint 181 F10
Pen-y-clawdd Mon 79 D7
Pen-y-coed Shrops 148 E5
Pen-y-coedcae Rhondda 58 B5
Penycwm Pembs 90 G6
Pen-y-Darren M Tydf 77 D9
Penydre Swansea 75 E11
Pen-y-fai Bridgend 57 E11
Pen-y-fai Carms 75 E7
Pen-y-fan Carms 56 B4
Pen-y-fan Mon 79 D8
Penyfeidr Pembs 91 F7
Pen-y-felin Flint 165 B11
Penyffordd Flint 166 C4
Pen-y-ffordd Denb 181 F8
Pen-y-ffordd Flint 181 E10
Penyffridd Gwyn 163 D8
Pen y Foel Shrops 148 E5
Penygarn Torf 78 E3
Pen-y-garn Carms 93 E11
Pen-y-garn Ceredig 128 F2
Penygarnedd Powys 148 E2
Pen-y-garnedd Anglesey 179 F8
Penygelli Powys 130 E2
Pen-y-gop Conwy 164 G6
Penygraig Rhondda 77 G7
Pen-y-graig Gwyn 144 C3
Penygraigwen Anglesey 178 D6
Penygroes Gwyn 163 E7
Penygroes Pembs 92 D3
Pen-y-groes Carms 75 C9
Pen-y-groeslon Gwyn 144 C4
Pen-y-Gwryd Hotel Gwyn 163 D11
Pen-y-lan Cardiff 59 D7
Pen-y-lan Newport 59 B9
Pen-y-lan V Glam 58 D3
Pen-y-maes Flint 181 F11
Pen-y-Myndd Carms 75 E7
Penymynydd Flint 166 C4
Pen-y-Park Hereford 96 C5
Penyraber Pembs 91 D9
Pen-yr-englyn Rhondda 76 F6
Penyrheol Caerph 58 B6
Penyrheol Swansea 56 B5
Penyrheol Torf 78 F3
Pen-yr-heol Bridgend 58 C2
Pen-yr-heol Mon 78 C6
Pen-yr-Heolgerrig M Tydf 77 D8
Pen-y-rhiw Rhondda 58 B5
Penysarn Anglesey 179 C7
Pen-y-stryt Denb 165 E11
Penywaun Rhondda 77 E7
Pen-y-wern Shrops 114 B6
Penzance Corn 1 C5
Peopleton Worcs 117 G8
Peover Heath Ches E 184 G3
Peper Harow Sur 50 E2
Peppercombe Devon 24 C5
Pepper Hill Som 43 F7
Pepper Hill W Yorks 196 B6
Peppermoor Northumb 264 F6
Pepper's Green Essex 87 C10
Pepperstock C Beds 85 B9
Perceton N Ayrs 267 G7
Percie Aberds 293 D7
Percuil Corn 3 C9
Percyhorner Aberds 303 C9
Percy Main T&W 243 D8
Per-ffordd-llan Flint 181 F10
Perham Down Wilts 47 D9
Periton Som 42 D3
Perivale London 67 C7
Perkhill Aberds 293 C7
Perkinsville Durham 243 G7
Perlethorpe Notts 187 G11
Perranarworthal Corn 3 B7
Perrancoombe Corn 4 E5
Perran Downs Corn 2 C3
Perranporth Corn 4 E5
Perranuthnoe Corn 2 D2
Perranwell Corn 3 B7
Perranwell Corn 4 E5
Perranwell Station Corn 3 B7
Perran Wharf Corn 3 B7
Perranzabuloe Corn 4 E5
Perrott's Brook Glos 81 D8
Perry Devon 26 F5
Perry Kent 55 B9
Perry W Mid 133 E11
Perry Barr W Mid 133 E11
Perry Beeches W Mid 133 E11
Perry Common W Mid 133 E11
Perry Crofts Staffs 134 C4
Perryfields Worcs 117 C8
Perryfoot Derbys 185 E10
Perry Green Essex 106 G6
Perry Green Herts 86 B6
Perry Green Som 43 F9
Perry Green Wilts 62 B3
Perrymead Bath 61 G9
Perrystone Hill Hereford 98 F2
Perry Street Kent 68 E6
Perry Street Som 28 F4
Perrywood Kent 54 B4
Pershall Staffs 150 C6
Pershore Worcs 99 B8
Pert Angus 293 G8
Pertenhall Beds 121 D11
Perth Perth 286 E5
Perthcelyn Rhondda 77 F9
Perthy Shrops 149 C7
Perton Hereford 97 C11
Perton Staffs 133 D7
Pertwood Wilts 45 F11
Pested Kent 54 C4
Peterborough Pboro 138 D3
Peterburn Highld 307 L2
Peterchurch Hereford 96 D6
Peterculter Aberdeen 293 C10
Peterhead Aberds 303 E11
Peterlee Durham 234 C4
Petersburn N Lnrk 268 C5
Petersfield Hants 34 C2
Peter's Finger Devon 12 D3
Peter's Green Herts 85 B10
Petersham London 67 E7
Peters Marland Devon 25 E7
Peterstone Wentlooge Newport 59 C9
Peterston-super-Ely V Glam 58 D5
Peterstow Hereford 97 G11
Peter Tavy Devon 12 F6
Petertown Orkney 314 F3
Peterville Corn 4 E4
Petham Kent 54 C6
Petherwin Gate Corn 11 D11
Petrockstow Devon 25 F8
Petsoe End M Keynes 103 B7
Pett E Sus 38 E5
Pettaugh Suff 126 F3
Pett Bottom Kent 54 E6
Pett Bottom Kent 55 C7
Petteridge Kent 53 E7
Pettinain S Lnrk 269 G9
Pettings Kent 68 G6
Pettistree Suff 126 G5
Pett Level E Sus 38 E5
Petton Devon 27 C8
Petton Shrops 149 D8
Petts Wood London 68 F2
Petty Aberds 303 F7
Pettycur Fife 280 D5
Petty France S Glos 61 B9
Pettymuick Aberds 303 G9
Pettywell Norf 159 E11
Petworth W Sus 35 C7
Pevensey E Sus 23 E10
Pevensey Bay E Sus 23 E11
Peverell Plym 7 D9
Pewsey Wilts 63 G7
Pewsey Wharf Wilts 63 G7
Pewterspear Warr 183 E10
Phantassie E Loth 281 F11
Pharisee Green Essex 106 G2
Pheasants Bucks 65 B9
Pheasant's Hill Bucks 65 B9
Pheasey W Mid 133 D11
Pheonix Green Hants 49 B9
Phepson Worcs 117 F8
Philadelphia T&W 243 G8
Philham Devon 24 C3
Philiphaugh Borders 261 D10
Phillack Corn 2 B3
Philleigh Corn 3 B9
Phillip's Town Caerph 77 E10
Philpot End Essex 87 B10
Philpstoun W Loth 279 F10
Phocle Green Hereford 98 F2
Phoenix Green Hants 49 B9
Phoenix Row Durham 233 F9
Phorp Moray 301 D10
Pibsbury Som 28 B6
Pibwrlwyd Carms 74 B6
Pica Cumb 228 G6
Piccadilly S Yorks 187 B7
Piccadilly Warks 134 D4
Piccadilly Corner Norf 142 F5
Piccotts End Herts 85 D9
Pickburn S Yorks 198 F4
Picken End Worcs 98 C6
Pickering N Yorks 216 C5
Pickering Nook Durham 242 F5
Picket Hill Hants 31 F11
Picket Piece Hants 47 D11
Picket Post Hants 31 F11
Pickford W Mid 134 G5
Pickford Green W Mid 134 G5
Pickhill N Yorks 214 C6
Picklenash Glos 98 F4
Picklescott Shrops 131 D8
Pickles Hill W Yorks 204 F6
Pickletillem Fife 287 E8
Pickley Green Gtr Man 195 G7
Pickmere Ches E 183 F11
Pickney Som 27 B11
Pickstock Telford 150 E4
Pickup Bank Blkburn 195 C8
Pickwell Devon 40 E3
Pickwell Leics 154 G5
Pickwick Wilts 61 E11
Pickwood Scar W Yorks 196 C5
Pickworth Lincs 155 C10
Pickworth Rutland 155 G9
Picton Ches W 182 G6
Picton Flint 181 E10
Picton N Yorks 225 D8
Pict's Hill Som 28 B6
Piddinghoe E Sus 36 G6
Piddington Bucks 84 G4
Piddington Northants 120 G6
Piddington Oxon 83 B10
Piddlehinton Dorset 17 B10
Piddletrenthide Dorset 17 B10
Pidley Cambs 122 B6
Pidney Dorset 30 F2
Piece Corn 2 B5
Piercebridge Darl 224 B4
Piercing Hill Essex 86 F6
Pierowall Orkney 314 B4
Piff's Elm Glos 99 F8
Pigdon Northumb 252 F5
Pightley Som 43 F8
Pig Oak Dorset 31 G8
Pigstye Green Essex 87 D10
Pike End W Yorks 196 D4
Pikehall Derbys 169 D11
Pike Hill Lancs 204 G3
Pike Law W Yorks 196 D4
Pikeshill Hants 32 F3
Pikestye Hereford 97 B10
Pilford Dorset 31 G8
Pilgrims Hatch Essex 87 F9
Pilham Lincs 188 C5
Pilhough Derbys 170 C3
Pill N Som 60 D4
Pill Pembs 72 D6
Pillaton Corn 7 C7
Pillaton Staffs 151 G8
Pillerton Hersey Warks 100 B6
Pillerton Priors Warks 100 B5
Pilleth Powys 114 D5
Pilley Glos 81 B7
Pilley Hants 20 B2
Pilley S Yorks 197 G10
Pilley Bailey Hants 20 B2
Pillgwenlly Newport 59 B10
Pilling Lancs 202 D4
Pilling Lane Lancs 202 D3
Pillmouth Devon 25 C7
Pillowell Glos 79 D10
Pillows Green Glos 98 F5
Pillwell Dorset 30 D3
Pilmuir Borders 261 G11
Pilning S Glos 60 B5
Pilrig Edin 280 F5
Pilsbury Derbys 169 C10
Pilsdon Dorset 16 B4
Pilsgate Pboro 137 B11
Pilsley Derbys 170 C6
Pilsley Derbys 186 G2
Pilsley Green Derbys 170 C6
Pilson Green Norf 161 G7
Piltdown E Sus 36 C6
Pilton Devon 40 G5
Pilton Edin 280 F4
Pilton Northants 137 G10
Pilton Rutland 137 C8
Pilton Som 44 E5
Pilton Green Swansea 56 D2
Piltown Som 44 F5
Pimhole Gtr Man 195 E10
Pimlico Herts 85 D9
Pimlico Lancs 203 E10
Pimlico London 67 D9
Pimlico Northants 102 C2
Pimperne Dorset 29 F9
Pimperne Dorset 30 F6
Pinchbeck Lincs 156 D4
Pinchbeck Bars Lincs 156 D3
Pinchbeck West Lincs 156 E4
Pincheon Green S Yorks 199 D7
Pinckney Green Wilts 61 G10
Pincock Lancs 194 D5
Pineham Kent 55 D10
Pineham M Keynes 103 C7
Pinehurst Swindon 63 B7
Pinfarthings Glos 80 E5
Pinfold Lancs 193 E11
Pinfold Hill S Yorks 197 G9
Pinfoldpond C Beds 103 E8
Pinford End Suff 124 F6
Pinged Carms 74 E6
Pingewood W Berks 65 F7
Pin Green Herts 104 F4
Pinhoe Devon 14 C5
Pinkett's Booth W Mid 134 G5
Pink Green Worcs 117 D11
Pinkie Braes E Loth 281 G7
Pinkney Wilts 61 B11
Pinkneys Green Windsor 65 C11
Pinksmoor Som 27 D10
Pinley W Mid 119 B7
Pinley Green Warks 118 D4
Pin Mill Suff 108 D4
Pinminnoch Dumfries 236 D2
Pinminnoch S Ayrs 244 E5
Pinmore S Ayrs 244 E6
Pinmore Mains S Ayrs 244 E6
Pinnacles Essex 86 D6
Pinner London 66 B6
Pinner Green London 85 G10
Pinnerwood Park London 85 G10
Pin's Green Worcs 98 B6
Pinsley Green Ches E 167 F9
Pinstones Shrops 131 F9
Pinvin Worcs 99 B9
Pinwall Leics 134 C6
Pinwherry S Ayrs 244 F5
Pinxton Derbys 171 E7
Pipe and Lyde Hereford 97 C10
Pipe Aston Hereford 115 C9
Pipe Gate Shrops 168 G2
Pipehill Staffs 133 B11
Pipehouse Bath 45 B9
Piperhall Argyll 266 D2
Piperhill Highld 301 D8
Pipe Ridware Staffs 151 F11
Piper's Ash Ches W 166 B6
Piper's End Worcs 98 E6
Piper's Hill Worcs 117 D9
Piper's Pool Corn 11 E11
Pipewell Northants 136 F6
Pippacott Devon 40 F4
Pippin Street Lancs 194 C5
Pipps Hill Essex 69 B7
Pipsden Kent 53 G9
Pipton Powys 96 D3
Pirbright Sur 50 B2
Pirbright Camp Sur 50 B2
Pirnmill N Ayrs 255 C9
Pirton Herts 104 E2
Pirton Worcs 99 B7
Pisgah Ceredig 112 B3
Pisgah Stirl 285 G11
Pishill Oxon 65 B8
Pishill Bank Oxon 84 G2
Pismire Hill S Yorks 186 C5
Pistyll Gwyn 162 G4
Pit Mon 78 D5
Pitagowan Perth 291 G10
Pitblae Aberds 303 C9
Pitcairngreen Perth 286 E4
Pitcalnie Highld 301 B8
Pitcaple Aberds 303 G7
Pitchcombe Glos 80 D5
Pitchcott Bucks 102 G5
Pitcher's Green Suff 125 F8
Pitchford Shrops 131 C10
Pitch Green Bucks 84 E3
Pitch Place Sur 49 F11
Pitch Place Sur 50 C3
Pitcombe Som 45 G7
Pitcorthie Fife 280 D2
Pitcorthie Fife 287 G9
Pitcot Som 45 D7
Pitcot V Glam 57 G11
Pitcox E Loth 282 F2
Pitcur Perth 286 D6
Pitfancy Aberds 302 E5
Pitfichie Aberds 293 B8
Pitforthie Aberds 293 F10
Pitgair Aberds 303 D7
Pitgrudy Highld 309 K7
Pithmaduthy Highld 301 B7
Pitkennedy Angus 287 B9
Pitkevy Fife 286 G6
Pitkierie Fife 287 G9
Pitlessie Fife 287 G7
Pitlochry Perth 286 B3
Pitmachie Aberds 302 G6
Pitmain Highld 291 C9
Pitmedden Aberds 303 G8
Pitminster Som 28 D2
Pitmuies Angus 287 C9
Pitmunie Aberds 293 B8
Pitney Som 29 B7
Pitrocknie Perth 286 C6
Pitscottie Fife 287 F8
Pitsea Essex 69 B8
Pitses Gtr Man 196 G2
Pitsford Northants 120 D5
Pitsford Hill Som 42 G6
Pitsmoor S Yorks 186 D5
Pitstone Bucks 84 B6
Pitstone Green Bucks 84 B6
Pitstone Hill Bucks 85 C7
Pitt Hants 33 B7
Pittachar Perth 286 E2
Pitt Court Glos 80 F3
Pittendreich Moray 301 C11
Pittentrail Highld 309 J7
Pittenweem Fife 287 G9
Pitteuchar Fife 280 B5
Pittington Durham 234 C2
Pittodrie Aberds 302 G6
Pitton Swansea 56 D2
Pitton Wilts 47 G8
Pitts Hill Stoke 168 E5
Pittswood Kent 52 D6
Pittulie Aberds 303 C9
Pittville Glos 99 G9
Pityme Corn 10 F5
Pity Me Durham 233 B11
Pityoulish Highld 291 B11
Pixey Green Suff 126 B4
Pixham Sur 51 C7
Pixham Worcs 98 B6
Pixley Hereford 98 D3
Pixley Shrops 150 D3
Pizien Well Kent 53 C7
Place Newton N Yorks 217 E7
Plaidy Aberds 303 D7
Plaidy Corn 6 E5
Plain-an-Gwarry Corn 4 G3
Plain Dealings Pembs 73 B9
Plains N Lnrk 268 B5
Plainsfield Som 43 F7
Plain Spot Notts 171 E7
Plain Street Corn 10 F5
Plaish Shrops 131 D10
Plaistow Bromley 68 E2
Plaistow Newham 68 C2
Plaistow W Sus 50 G4
Plaistow Green Essex 106 F6
Plaitford Wilts 32 D3
Plaitford Green Hants 32 C3
Plank Lane Gtr Man 194 G6
Plans Dumfries 238 D3
Plantation Bridge Cumb 221 F9
Plantationfoot Dumfries 248 E4
Plardiwick Staffs 150 E6
Plasau Shrops 149 E7
Plâs Berwyn Denb 165 G11
Plas-canol Gwyn 145 F11
Plas Coch Wrex 166 E4
Plas Dinam Powys 129 F10
Plas Gogerddan Ceredig 128 G2
Plashet London 68 C2
Plashett Carms 74 D3
Plasiolyn Powys 129 C11
Plas Llwyngwern Powys 128 C5
Plas Meredydd Powys 130 D3
Plas Nantyr Wrex 148 B3
Plasnewydd Powys 129 D9
Plaster's Green Bath 60 G4
Plastow Green Hants 64 G4
Plas-yn-Cefn Denb 181 G8
Platt Kent 52 B6
Platt Bridge Gtr Man 194 G6
Platt Lane Shrops 149 B10
Platts Common S Yorks 197 G11
Platt's Heath Kent 53 C11
Plawsworth Durham 233 B11
Plaxtol Kent 52 C6
Playden E Sus 38 C6
Playford Suff 108 B4
Play Hatch Oxon 65 D8
Playing Place Corn 4 G6
Playley Green Glos 98 E5
Plealey Shrops 131 B8
Pleamore Cross Som 27 D10
Plean Stirl 278 D6
Pleasant Valley Pembs 73 D10
Pleasington Blkburn 194 B6
Pleasley Derbys 171 C8
Pleasleyhill Notts 171 C8
Pleck Dorset 30 D3
Pleck Dorset 30 E2
Pleck W Mid 133 D9
Pleckgate Blkburn 203 G9
Pleck or Little Ansty Dorset 30 G3
Pledgdon Green Essex 105 F11
Pledwick W Yorks 197 D10
Plemstall Ches W 183 G7
Plenmeller Northumb 240 E6
Pleshey Essex 87 C11
Plockton Highld 295 B10
Plocrapol W Isles 305 J3
Plot Gate Som 44 G4
Plot Street Som 44 F5
Ploughfield Hereford 97 C7
Plough Hill Warks 134 E6
Plowden Shrops 131 F7
Ploxgreen Shrops 131 C7
Pluckley Kent 54 D2
Pluckley Thorne Kent 54 E2
Plucks Gutter Kent 71 G9
Plumbland Cumb 229 D9
Plumbley S Yorks 186 E6
Plumford Kent 54 B4
Plumley Ches E 184 F2
Plump Hill Glos 79 B11
Plumpton Cumb 230 D5
Plumpton E Sus 36 E5
Plumpton Northants 101 B11
Plumpton End Northants 102 B4
Plumpton Foot Cumb 230 D5
Plumpton Green E Sus 36 D5
Plumpton Head Cumb 230 E6
Plumstead London 68 D3
Plumstead Norf 160 C2
Plumstead Common London 68 D3
Plumstead Green Norf 160 C2
Plumtree Notts 154 C2
Plumtree Green Kent 53 D10
Plumtree Park Notts 154 C2
Plungar Leics 154 C5
Plush Dorset 30 G2
Plusha Corn 11 E11
Plushabridge Corn 12 G2
Plusterwine Glos 79 F9
Plwmp Ceredig 111 G7
Plymouth Plym 7 E9
Plympton Plym 7 D10
Plymstock Plym 7 E10
Plymtree Devon 27 G9
Pobgreen Gtr Man 196 F4
Pochin Houses Caerph 77 E11
Pocket Nook Gtr Man 183 B10
Pockley N Yorks 216 B2
Pocklington E Yorks 208 D2
Pockthorpe Norf 141 D8
Pockthorpe Norf 158 D6
Pockthorpe Norf 159 E10
Pockthorpe Norf 159 F11
Pode Hole Lincs 156 E4
Podimore Som 29 C8
Podington Beds 121 E8
Podmoor Worcs 117 C7
Podmore Norf 159 G9
Podmore Staffs 150 B5
Podsmead Glos 80 B4
Poffley End Oxon 82 C5
Pogmoor S Yorks 197 F10
Point Corn 3 B8
Point Clear Essex 89 C9
Pointon Lincs 156 C2
Pokesdown Bmouth 19 C8
Pol a Charra W Isles 297 K3
Polbae Dumfries 236 B4
Polbain Highld 307 H4
Polbathic Corn 7 D7
Polbeth W Loth 269 C10
Polborder Corn 7 C7
Polbrock Corn 5 B10
Polchar Highld 291 C10
Polebrook Northants 137 F11
Pole Elm Worcs 98 B6
Polegate E Sus 23 D9
Pole Moor W Yorks 196 D5
Poles Highld 309 K7
Polesden Lacey Sur 50 C6
Poleshill Som 27 C9
Pole's Hole Wilts 45 C10
Polesworth Warks 134 C5
Polgear Corn 2 B5
Polgigga Corn 1 E3
Polglass Highld 307 J5
Polgooth Corn 5 E9
Poling W Sus 35 G8
Poling Corner W Sus 35 F8
Polkerris Corn 5 E11
Polla Highld 308 D3
Polladras Corn 2 C4
Pollard Street Norf 160 C6
Pollhill Kent 53 C11
Poll Hill Mers 182 E3
Pollie Highld 309 H7
Pollington E Yorks 198 D6
Polliwilline Argyll 255 G8
Polloch Highld 289 C9
Pollok Glasgow 267 C10
Pollokshields Glasgow 267 C11
Polmadie Glasgow 267 C11
Polmarth Corn 2 B6
Polmassick Corn 5 F9
Polmear Corn 5 E11
Polmont Falk 279 F8
Polmorla Corn 10 G5
Polnessan E Ayrs 257 G10
Polnish Highld 295 G9
Polopit Northants 121 B10
Polpenwith Corn 2 D6
Polpeor Corn 2 B2
Polperro Corn 6 E4
Polruan Corn 6 E2
Polsham Som 44 E4
Polsloe Devon 14 C4
Polstead Suff 107 D9
Polstead Heath Suff 107 C9
Poltalloch Argyll 275 D9
Poltesco Corn 2 F6
Poltimore Devon 14 B5
Polton Midloth 270 C5
Polwarth Borders 272 E4
Polwheveral Corn 2 D6
Polyphant Corn 11 E11
Polzeath Corn 10 F4
Pomeroy Derbys 169 B10
Pomphlett Plym 7 E10
Ponciau Wrex 166 F3
Pond Close Som 27 B10
Ponde Powys 96 D2
Pondersbridge Cambs 138 E5
Ponders End London 86 F5
Pond Park Bucks 85 E7
Pond Street Essex 105 D9
Pondtail Hants 49 C10
Pondwell IoW 21 C8
Poniou Corn 1 B4
Ponjeravah Corn 2 D6
Ponsanooth Corn 3 B7
Ponsford Devon 27 F8
Ponsonby Cumb 219 D11
Ponsongath Corn 3 F7
Ponsworthy Devon 13 G10
Pont Corn 6 E2
Pont Aber Carms 94 G4
Pont Aber-Geirw Gwyn 146 D5
Pontamman Carms 75 C10
Pontantwn Carms 74 C6
Pontardawe Neath 76 E2
Pontarddulais Swansea 75 E9
Pontarfynach / Devils Bridge Ceredig 112 B4
Pont-ar-gothi Carms 93 G10
Pont ar Hydfer Powys 95 F7
Pont-ar-llechau Carms 94 G4
Pontarsais Carms 93 F8
Pontblyddyn Flint 166 C3
Pontbren Araeth Carms 94 G3
Pontbren Llwyd Rhondda 76 D6
Pontcanna Cardiff 59 D7
Pont Cyfyng Conwy 164 D2
Pont Cysyllte Wrex 166 G3
Pontdolgoch Powys 129 E10
Pont Dolydd Prysor Gwyn 146 B4
Pontefract W Yorks 198 C3
Ponteland Northumb 242 C5
Ponterwyd Ceredig 128 G4
Pontesbury Shrops 131 B7
Pontesbury Hill Shrops 131 B7
Pontesford Shrops 131 B8
Pontfadog Wrex 148 B4
Pontfaen Pembs 91 E10
Pont-faen Powys 95 E9
Pont-Faen Shrops 148 B5
Pont Fronwydd Gwyn 146 E6
Pont-garreg Pembs 92 C2
Pontgarreg Ceredig 110 G6
Ponthen Shrops 148 F6
Pont-Henri Carms 75 D7
Ponthir Torf 78 G4
Ponthirwaun Ceredig 92 B5
Pont Hwfa Anglesey 178 E2
Pontiago Pembs 91 D8
Pont iets / Pontyates Carms 75 D7
Pontithel Powys 96 D3
Pontllanfraith Caerph 77 F11
Pontlliw Swansea 75 E10
Pont-Llogel Powys 147 F10
Pontllyfni Gwyn 162 E6
Pontlottyn Caerph 77 D10
Pontneddfechan Powys 76 D6
Pontnewydd Torf 78 F3
Pont-newydd Carms 74 D6
Pont-newydd Flint 165 B11
Pontnewynydd Torf 78 E3
Pont Pen-y-benglog Gwyn 163 C10
Pontrhydfendigaid Ceredig 112 D4
Pont Rhydgaled Powys 128 G6
Pont Rhyd-goch Conwy 163 C11
Pont-Rhyd-sarn Gwyn 147 D7
Pont Rhyd-y-berry Powys 95 D9
Pont Rhyd-y-cyff Bridgend 57 D11
Pontrhydyfen Neath 57 C9
Pont-rhyd-y-groes Ceredig 112 C4
Pontrhydyrun Torf 78 F3
Pont-Rhythallt Gwyn 163 C8
Pontrilas Hereford 97 F7
Pontrobert Powys 148 G2
Pont-rug Gwyn 163 C8
Pont Senni / Sennybridge Powys 95 F8
Ponts Green E Sus 23 B11
Pontshill Hereford 98 G2
Pont-siôn Ceredig 93 B8
Pont Siôn Norton Rhondda 77 G9
Pontsticill M Tydf 77 C9
Pont-Walby Neath 76 D5
Pontwgan Conwy 180 G3
Pontyates / Pont-iets Carms 75 D7
Pontyberem Carms 75 C8
Pont-y-blew Shrops 148 B6
Pontyclun Rhondda 58 C4
Pontycymer Bridgend 76 G6
Pontyglasier Pembs 92 D2
Pont-y-gwaith Rhondda 77 G8
Pontymister Caerph 78 G2
Pontymoel Torf 78 E3
Pont-y-pant Conwy 164 E3
Pont y Pennant Gwyn 147 E8

Pontypool Torf 78 E3
Pontypridd Rhondda 58 B5
Pont yr Afon-Gam Gwyn 164 G2
Pont-yr-hafod Pembs 91 F8
Pont-y-rhyl Bridgend 58 B2
Pont-Ystrad Denb 165 C9
Pont-y-wal Powys 96 D2
Pontywaun Caerph 78 G2
Pooksgreen Hants 32 E5
Pool Corn 4 G3
Pool W Yorks 205 D10
Poolbrook Worcs 98 C5
Poole N Yorks 198 B3
Poole Poole 18 C6
Poole Som 27 C10
Poole Keynes Glos 81 F8
Poolend Staffs 169 D7
Poolestown Dorset 30 D2
Poolewe Highld 307 L3
Pooley Bridge Cumb 230 G5
Pooley Street Norf 141 G11
Poolfold Staffs 168 D5
Poolhead Shrops 149 C9
Pool Head Hereford 115 G11
Pool Hey Lancs 193 D11
Poolhill Glos 98 F4
Poolmill Hereford 97 G11
Pool o' Muckhart Clack 286 G4
Pool Quay Powys 148 G5
Poolsbrook Derbys 186 G6
Poolside Moray 302 E4
Poolstock Gtr Man 194 G5
Pooltown Som 42 F3
Pootings Kent 52 D3
Pope Hill Pembs 72 C6
Pope's Hill Glos 79 C11
Popeswood Brack 65 F10
Popham Devon 41 G8
Popham Hants 48 E5
Poplar London 67 C11
Poplar Grove Lincs 190 B6
Poplars Herts 104 G5
Popley Hants 48 C6
Porchester Nottingham 171 G9
Porchfield IoW 20 C4
Porin Highld 300 D3
Poringland Norf 142 C5
Porkellis Corn 2 C5
Porlock Som 41 D11
Porlockford Som 41 D11
Porlock Weir Som 41 D11
Portachoillan Argyll 255 B8
Port Allen Perth 286 E6
Port Ann Argyll 275 E10
Port Appin Argyll 289 E11
Port Arthur Shetland 313 K5
Portash Wilts 46 G3
Port Askaig Argyll 274 G5
Portavadie Argyll 275 G10
Port Bannatyne Argyll 275 G11
Port Brae Fife 280 C5
Port Bridge Devon 9 D7
Portbury N Som 60 D4
Port Carlisle Cumb 238 E6
Port Charlotte Argyll 254 B3
Portchester Hants 33 F10
Portclair Highld 290 B6
Port Clarence Stockton 234 G5
Port Dinorwic / Y Felinheli Gwyn 163 B8
Port Driseach Argyll 275 F10
Port Dundas Glasgow 267 B11
Porteath Corn 10 F5
Port Edgar Edin 280 F2
Port Ellen Argyll 254 C4
Port Elphinstone Aberds 293 B9
Portencalzie Dumfries 236 B2
Portencross N Ayrs 266 F3
Porterfield Renfs 267 B9
Port Erin IoM 192 F2
Port Erroll Aberds 303 F10
Porter's End Herts 85 B11
Portesham Dorset 17 D8
Portessie Moray 302 C4
Port e Vullen IoM 192 C5
Port-Eynon Swansea 56 D3
Portfield Argyll 289 G9
Portfield Som 28 B6
Portfield W Sus 22 B5
Portfield Gate Pembs 72 B6
Portgate Devon 12 D4
Port Gaverne Corn 10 E6
Port Glasgow Invclyd 276 G6
Portgordon Moray 302 C3
Portgower Highld 311 H4
Porth Corn 4 C6
Porth Rhondda 77 G8
Porthallow Corn 3 E7
Porthallow Corn 6 E4
Porthcawl Bridgend 57 F10
Porth Colmon Gwyn 144 C3
Porthcothan Corn 10 G3
Porthcurno Corn 1 E3
Portheiddy Pembs 90 E6
Port Henderson Highld 299 B7
Porthgain Pembs 90 E6
Porthgwarra Corn 1 E3
Porthhallow Corn 3 E7
Porthill Shrops 149 G9
Porthill Staffs 168 F5
Port Hill Oxon 65 B7
Porthilly Corn 10 F4
Porth Kea Corn 4 G6
Porthkerry V Glam 58 F5
Porthleven Corn 2 D4
Porthllechog / Bull Bay Anglesey 178 C6
Porthloo Scilly 1 G4
Porthmadog Gwyn 145 B11
Porthmeor Corn 1 B4
Porth Navas Corn 3 D7
Porthoustock Corn 3 E8
Porthpean Corn 5 E10
Porthtowan Corn 4 F3
Porth Tywyn / Burry Port Carms 74 E6
Porth-y-felin Anglesey 178 E2
Porthyrhyd Carms 75 B8
Porthyrhyd Carms 94 D4
Porth-y-waen Shrops 148 E5
Portico Mers 183 C7
Portincaple Argyll 276 C4
Portington Devon 12 F4
Portington E Yorks 207 G11
Portinnisherrich Argyll 275 B10
Portinscale Cumb 229 G11
Port Isaac Corn 10 E5
Portishead N Som 60 D3
Portkil Argyll 276 E5
Portknockie Moray 302 C4
Port Lamont Argyll 275 F11
Portland Som 44 F3
Portlethen Aberds 293 D11
Portlethen Village Aberds 293 D11
Portlevorchy Highld 306 D7
Portling Dumfries 237 D10
Port Lion Pembs 73 D7
Portloe Corn 3 B10
Port Logan Dumfries 236 E2
Portlooe Corn 6 E4
Portmahomack Highld 311 L3
Port Mead Swansea 56 B6
Portmeirion Gwyn 145 B11
Portmellon Corn 5 G10
Port Mholair W Isles 304 E7
Port Mor Highld 288 B6
Portmore Hants 20 B2
Port Mulgrave N Yorks 226 B5
Portnacroish Argyll 289 E11
Portnahaven Argyll 254 B2
Portnalong Highld 294 B5
Portnaluchaig Highld 295 G8
Portnancon Highld 308 C4
Port Nan Giùran W Isles 304 E7
Port nan Long W Isles 296 D4
Portnellan Stirl 285 E8
Portnellan Stirl 285 F8
Port Nis W Isles 304 B7
Portobello Edin 280 G6
Portobello T&W 243 F7
Portobello W Mid 133 D9
Portobello W Yorks 197 D10
Port of Menteith Stirl 285 G9
Porton Wilts 47 F7
Portpatrick Dumfries 236 D2
Port Quin Corn 10 E5
Portrack Stockton 225 B9
Port Ramsay Argyll 289 E10
Portreath Corn 4 F3
Portree Highld 298 E4
Port St Mary IoM 192 F3
Portscatho Corn 3 B9
Portsea Ptsmth 33 G10
Portsea Island Ptsmth 33 G11
Portskerra Highld 310 C2
Portskewett Mon 60 B4
Portslade Brighton 36 F3
Portslade-by-Sea Brighton 36 G3
Portslade Village Brighton 36 F3
Portsmouth Ptsmth 21 B9
Portsmouth W Yorks 196 B2
Port Solent Ptsmth 33 F10
Portsonachan Argyll 284 E4
Portsoy Aberds 302 C5
Port Sunlight Mers 182 E4
Port Sutton Bridge Lincs 157 E9
Portswood Soton 32 E6
Port Talbot Neath 57 D9
Porttanachy Moray 302 C3
Port Tennant Swansea 57 C7
Portuairk Highld 288 C6
Portvasgo Highld 308 C5
Portway Dorset 18 D2
Portway Glos 98 E5
Portway Hereford 97 B9
Portway Hereford 97 D9
Portway Som 28 B6
Portway Som 44 F3
Portway W Mid 133 F9
Portway Worcs 117 C11
Port Wemyss Argyll 254 B2
Port William Dumfries 236 E5
Portwood Gtr Man 184 C6
Portwrinkle Corn 7 E7
Posenhall Shrops 132 C3
Poslingford Suff 106 B5
Posso Borders 260 C6
Postbridge Devon 13 F9
Postcombe Oxon 84 F2
Post Green Dorset 18 C5
Postling Kent 54 F6
Postlip Glos 99 F10
Post Mawr / Synod Inn Ceredig 111 G8
Postwick Norf 142 B5
Potarch Aberds 293 D8
Potash Suff 108 D2
Potbridge Hants 49 C8
Pot Common Sur 50 E2
Potholm Dumfries 249 F9
Potmaily Highld 300 F4
Potman's Heath Kent 38 B5
Potsgrove C Beds 103 F9
Potten End Herts 85 D8
Potten Street Kent 71 F9
Potter Brompton N Yorks 217 D9
Pottergate Street Norf 142 E3
Potterhanworth Lincs 173 B9
Potterhanworth Booths Lincs 173 B9
Potter Heigham Norf 161 F8
Potter Hill Leics 154 E4
Potter Hill S Yorks 186 B4
Potterne Wilts 46 B3
Potterne Wick Wilts 46 B4
Potternewton W Yorks 206 F2
Potters Bar Herts 86 E3
Potters Brook Lancs 202 C5
Potters Corner Kent 54 E3
Potter's Cross Staffs 132 G6
Potters Crouch Herts 85 D10
Potter's Forstal Kent 53 D11
Potter's Green E Sus 37 C8
Potter's Green W Mid 135 G7
Pottersheath Herts 86 B2
Potters Hill N Som 60 F4
Potters Marston Leics 135 D9
Potter Somersal Derbys 152 B2
Potterspury Northants 102 C5
Potter Street Essex 87 D7
Potterton Aberds 293 B11
Potterton W Yorks 206 F4
Pottery Field W Yorks 206 G2
Potthorpe Norf 159 E8
Pottington Devon 40 G5
Potto N Yorks 225 E9
Potton C Beds 104 B4
Pott Row Norf 158 E4
Pott Shrigley Ches E 184 F6
Pouchen End Herts 85 D8
Poughill Corn 24 F2
Poughill Devon 26 F5
Poulner Hants 31 F11
Poulshot Wilts 46 B3
Poulton Ches W 166 D5
Poulton Glos 81 E10
Poulton Mers 182 C4
Poulton Mers 182 E4
Poulton-le-Fylde Lancs 202 F2
Pound Som 28 D6
Pound Bank Worcs 98 B5
Pound Bank Worcs 116 C4
Poundbury Dorset 17 C9
Poundffald Swansea 56 C5
Poundfield E Sus 52 G4
Poundford E Sus 37 C9
Poundgate E Sus 37 B7
Poundgreen Wokingham 65 F7
Pound Green E Sus 37 C8
Pound Green Hants 48 B5
Pound Green IoW 20 D2
Pound Green Suff 124 G4
Pound Green Worcs 116 B5
Pound Hill W Sus 51 F9
Poundland S Ayrs 244 F5
Poundon Bucks 102 F2
Poundsbridge Kent 52 E4
Poundsgate Devon 13 G10
Poundstock Corn 11 B10
Pound Street Hants 64 G3
Pounsley E Sus 37 C8
Poverest London 68 F3
Povey Cross Sur 51 E9
Powburn Northumb 264 F3
Powderham Devon 14 E5
Powder Mills Kent 52 D5
Powers Hall End Essex 88 B4
Powerstock Dorset 16 B6
Powfoot Dumfries 238 D4
Pow Green Hereford 98 C4
Powhill Cumb 238 F6
Powick Worcs 116 G6
Powler's Piece Devon 24 D5
Powmill Perth 279 B10
Pownall Park Ches E 184 E4
Powntley Copse Hants 49 E8
Poxwell Dorset 17 E10
Poyle Slough 66 D4
Poynings W Sus 36 E3
Poyntington Dorset 29 D11
Poynton Ches E 184 E6
Poynton Telford 149 F11
Poynton Green Telford 149 F11
Poyntzfield Highld 301 C7
Poyston Pembs 73 B7
Poyston Cross Pembs 73 B7
Poystreet Green Suff 125 F9
Praa Sands Corn 2 D3
Pratling Street Kent 53 B8
Pratt's Bottom London 68 G3
Praze Corn 2 B3
Praze-an-Beeble Corn 2 B4
Predannack Wollas Corn 2 F5
Prees Shrops 149 C11
Preesall Lancs 202 D3
Preesall Park Lancs 202 D3
Prees Green Shrops 149 C11
Preesgweene Shrops 148 B5
Prees Heath Shrops 149 B11
Preeshenlle Shrops 148 C6
Prees Higher Heath Shrops 149 B11
Prees Lower Heath Shrops 149 C11
Prees Wood Shrops 149 C11
Prenbrigog Flint 166 C3
Prendergast Pembs 73 B7
Prendergast Pembs 90 G6
Prenderguest Borders 273 D8
Prendwick Northumb 264 G2
Pren-gwyn Ceredig 93 C8
Prenteg Gwyn 163 G9
Prenton Mers 182 D4
Prescot Mers 183 C7
Prescott Devon 27 E9
Prescott Glos 99 F9
Prescott Shrops 132 G3
Prescott Shrops 149 E8
Presdales Herts 86 C5
Preshome Moray 302 C4
Press Derbys 170 B5
Pressen Northumb 263 B8
Prestatyn Denb 181 E9
Prestbury Ches E 184 F6
Prestbury Glos 99 G9
Presteigne Powys 114 E6
Presthope Shrops 131 D11
Prestleigh Som 44 E6
Prestolee Gtr Man 195 F9
Preston Borders 272 D5
Preston Brighton 36 F4
Preston Devon 14 G3
Preston Dorset 17 E10
Preston E Loth 281 F11
Preston E Loth 281 G7
Preston E Yorks 209 G9
Preston Glos 81 E8
Preston Glos 98 E3
Preston Herts 104 G3
Preston Kent 70 G4
Preston Kent 71 G8
Preston Lancs 194 B4
Preston London 67 B7
Preston Northumb 264 D5
Preston Rutland 137 C7
Preston Shrops 149 G10
Preston Torbay 9 C7
Preston T&W 243 D8
Preston Wilts 62 D4
Preston Wilts 63 E9
Preston Bagot Warks 118 D3
Preston Bissett Bucks 102 F3
Preston Bowyer Som 27 B10
Preston Brockhurst Shrops 149 E10
Preston Brook Halton 183 E9
Preston Candover Hants 48 E6
Preston Capes Northants 119 G11
Preston Crowmarsh Oxon 83 G10
Preston Deanery Northants 120 F5
Prestonfield Edin 280 G5
Preston Fields Warks 118 D3
Preston Grange T&W 243 C8
Preston Green Warks 118 D3
Preston Gubbals Shrops 149 F9
Preston-le-Skerne Durham 234 G2
Preston Marsh Hereford 97 B11
Prestonmill Dumfries 237 D11
Preston Montford Shrops 149 G8
Preston on Stour Warks 118 G4
Preston-on-Tees Stockton 225 B8
Preston on the Hill Halton 183 E9
Preston on Wye Hereford 97 C7
Prestonpans E Loth 281 G7
Preston Pastures Worcs 100 B3
Preston Plucknett Som 29 D8
Preston St Mary Suff 125 G8
Preston-under-Scar N Yorks 223 G11
Preston upon the Weald Moors Telford 150 F3
Preston Wynne Hereford 97 B11
Prestwich Gtr Man 195 G10
Prestwick Northumb 242 C5
Prestwick S Ayrs 257 D9
Prestwold Leics 153 E11
Prestwood Bucks 84 E5
Prestwood Staffs 133 F7
Prestwood Staffs 169 G10
Prey Heath Sur 50 B3
Price Town Bridgend 76 G6
Prickwillow Cambs 139 G11
Priddy Som 44 C4
Pride Park Derbys 153 B7
Priestacott Devon 24 F6
Priestcliffe Derbys 185 G10
Priestcliffe Ditch Derbys 185 G10
Priest Down Bath 60 G6
Priestfield W Mid 133 D8
Priestfield Worcs 98 C6
Priesthaugh Borders 249 C11
Priesthill Glasgow 267 C10
Priesthorpe W Yorks 205 F10
Priest Hutton Lancs 211 E10
Priestley Green W Yorks 196 B6
Prieston Borders 262 D2
Priestside Dumfries 238 D4
Priestthorpe W Yorks 205 F8
Priest Weston Shrops 130 D5
Priestwood Brack 65 F11
Priestwood Kent 69 G7
Priestwood Green Kent 69 G7
Primethorpe Leics 135 E10
Primrose T&W 243 E8
Primrose Corner Norf 160 G6
Primrose Green Norf 159 F11
Primrosehill Herts 85 E9
Primrose Hill Bath 61 F8
Primrose Hill Lancs 193 F11
Primrose Hill London 67 C9
Primrose Hill W Mid 133 F8
Primrose Valley N Yorks 218 D2
Primsland Worcs 117 E8
Prince Hill Ches E 168 G2
Prince Royd W Yorks 196 D6
Princes End W Mid 133 E9
Princes Gate Pembs 73 C10
Prince's Marsh Hants 34 B3
Princes Park Mers 182 D5
Princes Risborough Bucks 84 E4
Princethorpe Warks 119 C8
Princetown Caerph 77 C10
Princetown Devon 13 G7
Prinsted W Sus 22 B3
Printstile Kent 52 E5
Prion Denb 165 C9
Prior Muir Fife 287 F9
Prior Park Northumb 273 E9
Prior Rigg Cumb 239 D11
Priors Frome Hereford 97 D11
Priors Halton Shrops 115 B9
Priors Hardwick Warks 119 F9
Priorslee Telford 150 G4
Priors Marston Warks 119 F9
Prior's Norton Glos 99 G7
Priors Park Glos 99 E7
Priorswood Som 28 B2
Priory Pembs 72 D6
Priory Green Suff 107 C8
Priory Heath Suff 108 C3
Priory Wood Hereford 96 B5
Prisk V Glam 58 D4
Pristacott Devon 25 B8
Priston Bath 61 G7
Pristow Green Norf 142 F2
Prittlewell Sthend 69 B11
Privett Hants 21 B7
Privett Hants 33 B11
Prixford Devon 40 F4
Probus Corn 5 F7
Proncy Highld 309 K7
Prospect Cumb 229 C8
Prospect Village Staffs 151 G10
Prospidnick Corn 2 C4
Provanmill Glasgow 268 B2
Prowse Devon 26 F4
Prudhoe Northumb 242 E3
Prussia Cove Corn 2 D3
Ptarmigan Lodge Stirl 285 G7
Pubil Perth 285 C8
Publow Bath 60 G6
Puckeridge Herts 105 G7
Puckington Som 28 D5
Pucklechurch S Glos 61 D7
Pucknall Hants 32 B5
Puckrup Glos 99 D7
Puckshole Glos 80 D4
Puddaven Devon 8 C5
Puddinglake Ches W 168 B2
Pudding Pie Nook Lancs 202 F6
Puddington Ches W 182 G4
Puddington Devon 26 E4
Puddle Corn 5 D11
Puddlebridge Som 28 E4
Puddledock Hextable 68 E4
Puddledock Norf 141 E11
Puddledock Westerham 52 C3
Puddletown Dorset 17 C11
Pudleigh Som 28 E4
Pudleston Hereford 115 F11
Pudsey W Yorks 196 B2
Pudsey W Yorks 205 G10
Pulborough W Sus 35 D8
Pulcree Dumfries 237 D7
Pule Hill W Yorks 196 B5
Puleston Telford 150 E4
Pulford Ches W 166 D5
Pulham Dorset 30 F2
Pulham Market Norf 142 F3
Pulham St Mary Norf 142 F4
Pullens Green S Glos 79 G10
Pulley Shrops 131 B9
Pullington Kent 53 G10
Pulloxhill C Beds 103 E11
Pulverbatch Shrops 131 C8
Pumpherston W Loth 269 B11
Pumsaint Carms 94 C3
Puncheston / Cas-Mael Pembs 91 F10
Puncknowle Dorset 16 D6
Punnett's Town E Sus 37 C10
Purbrook Hants 33 F11
Purewell Dorset 19 C9
Purfleet Thurrock 68 D5
Puriton Som 43 E10
Purleigh Essex 88 E4
Purley London 67 G10
Purley on Thames W Berks 65 D7
Purlogue Shrops 114 B5
Purlpit Wilts 61 F11
Purls Bridge Cambs 139 F9
Purn N Som 43 B10
Purse Caundle Dorset 29 D11
Purslow Shrops 131 G7
Purston Jaglin W Yorks 198 D2
Purtington Som 28 F5
Purton Glos 79 E11
Purton W Berks 64 D3
Purton Wilts 62 B5
Purton Common Wilts 62 B5
Purton Stoke Wilts 81 G9
Purwell Herts 104 F4
Pury End Northants 102 B4
Pusey Oxon 82 F5
Putley Hereford 98 D2
Putley Common Hereford 98 D2
Putley Green Hereford 98 D3
Putloe Glos 80 D3
Putney London 67 D8
Putney Heath London 67 E8
Putney Vale London 67 E8
Putnoe Beds 121 G11
Putsborough Devon 40 E3
Putson Hereford 97 D10
Puttenham Herts 84 C5
Puttenham Sur 50 D2
Puttock End Essex 106 C6
Puttock's End Essex 87 B9
Putton Dorset 17 E9
Puxey Dorset 30 E3
Puxley Northants 102 C5
Puxton N Som 60 G2
Pwll Carms 75 E7
Pwll Powys 130 C3
Pwll-clai Flint 181 G11
Pwllcrochan Pembs 72 E6
Pwll-glas Denb 165 E10
Pwllgloyw Powys 95 E10
Pwllheli Gwyn 145 B7
Pwll-Mawr Cardiff 59 D8
Pwll-melyn Flint 181 G11
Pwllmeyric Mon 79 G8
Pwll-trap Carms 74 B3
Pwll-y-glaw Neath 57 C9
Pwllypant Caerph 59 B7
Pye Bridge Derbys 170 E6
Pyecombe W Sus 36 E3
Pye Corner Devon 14 B4
Pye Corner Kent 53 D11
Pye Corner Newport 59 B9
Pye Corner S Glos 60 D6
Pye Green Staffs 151 G9
Pye Hill Notts 170 E6
Pyewipe NE Lincs 201 E9
Pyle IoW 20 F5
Pyle Swansea 56 D5
Pylehill Hants 33 D7
Pyle Hill Sur 50 B3
Pyleigh Som 42 G6
Pyle / Y Pîl Bridgend 57 E10
Pylle Som 44 F6
Pymore or Pymoor Cambs 139 F9
Pype Hayes W Mid 134 E2
Pyrford Sur 50 B4
Pyrford Green Sur 50 B4
Pyrford Village Sur 50 B4
Pyrland Som 28 B2
Pyrton Oxon 83 F11
Pytchley Northants 121 C7
Pyworthy Devon 24 G4

## Q

Quabbs Shrops 130 G4
Quabrook E Sus 52 G2
Quadring Lincs 156 C4
Quadring Eaudike Lincs 156 C4
Quags Corner W Sus 34 C5
Quainton Bucks 84 B2
Quaker's Yard M Tydf 77 F9
Quaking Houses Durham 242 G5
Quality Corner Cumb 219 B9
Quarhouse Glos 80 E5
Quarley Hants 47 E9
Quarmby W Yorks 196 D6
Quarndon Derbys 170 G4
Quarndon Common Derbys 170 G4
Quarrelton Renfs 267 C8
Quarrendon Bucks 84 B4
Quarr Hill IoW 21 C7
Quarriers Village Invclyd 267 B7
Quarrington Lincs 173 G9
Quarrington Hill Durham 234 D2
Quarrybank Ches W 167 B8
Quarry Bank W Mid 133 F8
Quarryford E Loth 271 B11
Quarryhead Aberds 303 C9
Quarry Heath Staffs 151 G8
Quarryhill Highld 309 L7
Quarry Hill Staffs 134 C4
Quarrywood Moray 301 C11
Quarter S Lnrk 268 E4
Quartley Devon 27 B7
Quatford Shrops 132 E4
Quatquoy Orkney 314 E3
Quatt Shrops 132 F5
Quebec Durham 233 C9
Quebec W Sus 34 C3
Quedgeley Glos 80 C4
Queen Adelaide Cambs 139 G11
Queenborough Kent 70 E2
Queen Camel Som 29 C9
Queen Charlton Bath 60 F6
Queen Dart Devon 26 D4
Queenhill Worcs 99 D7
Queen Oak Dorset 45 G9
Queen's Bower IoW 21 E7
Queensbury London 67 B7
Queensbury W Yorks 205 G8
Queen's Corner W Sus 34 B5
Queensferry Edin 280 F2
Queensferry Flint 166 B4
Queen's Head Shrops 148 D6
Queenslie Glasgow 268 B3
Queen's Park Beds 103 B10
Queen's Park Blkburn 195 B7
Queen's Park Ches W 166 B6
Queen's Park Essex 87 F11
Queen's Park Northants 120 E5
Queenstown Blkpool 202 F2
Queen Street Kent 53 D7
Queen Street Wilts 62 B4
Queensville Staffs 151 E8
Queenzieburn N Lnrk 278 F3
Quemerford Wilts 62 F4
Quendale Shetland 313 M5
Quendon Essex 105 E10
Queniborough Leics 154 G2
Quenington Glos 81 E10
Quernmore Lancs 202 B6
Queslett W Mid 133 E11
Quethiock Corn 6 C6
Quhamm Shetland 312 G6
Quholm Orkney 314 E2
Quick Gtr Man 196 G3
Quick Edge Gtr Man 196 G3
Quicks Green W Berks 64 D5
Quidenham Norf 141 F10
Quidhampton Hants 48 C4
Quidhampton Wilts 46 G6
Quilquox Aberds 303 F9
Quina Brook Shrops 149 C10
Quinbury End Northants 120 G2
Quindry Orkney 314 G4
Quinton Northants 120 G5
Quinton W Mid 133 G9
Quintrell Downs Corn 5 C7
Quixhill Staffs 169 G10
Quoditch Devon 12 B4
Quoig Perth 286 E2
Quoisley Ches E 167 F8
Quoit Corn 5 C8
Quorndon or Quorn Leics 153 F11
Quothquan S Lnrk 259 B11
Quoyloo Orkney 314 D2
Quoynee Highld 310 D6
Quoyness Orkney 314 F2
Quoys Shetland 312 B8
Quoys Shetland 313 G6

## R

Raasay Ho Highld 295 B7
Rabbit's Cross Kent 53 D9
Rableyheath Herts 86 B2
Raby Cumb 238 G5
Raby Mers 182 F4
Racecourse Suff 108 C3
Racedown Hants 47 E9
Rachan Mill Borders 260 C4
Rachub Gwyn 163 B10
Rack End Oxon 82 E6
Rackenford Devon 26 D5
Rackham W Sus 35 E9
Rackheath Norf 160 G5
Rackley Som 43 C11
Racks Dumfries 238 C2
Rackwick Orkney 314 B4
Rackwick Orkney 314 G2
Radbourne Derbys 152 B5
Radcliffe Gtr Man 195 F9
Radcliffe Northumb 253 C7
Radcliffe on Trent Notts 154 B2
Radclive Bucks 102 E3
Radcot Oxon 82 F3
Raddery Highld 301 D7
Raddington Som 27 B8
Raddon Devon 26 G6
Radernie Fife 287 G8
Radfall Kent 70 G6
Radfield Kent 70 G2
Radford Bath 45 B7
Radford Nottingham 171 G9
Radford Oxon 101 G8
Radford W Mid 134 G6
Radford Worcs 117 F10
Radfordbridge Oxon 101 G8
Radford Semele Warks 118 E6
Radipole Dorset 17 E9
Radlet Som 43 F8
Radlett Herts 85 F11
Radley Oxon 83 F8
Radley Green Essex 87 D10
Radley Park Oxon 83 F8
Radlith Shrops 131 B8
Radmanthwaite Notts 171 C8
Radmoor Shrops 150 E2
Radmore Green Ches E 167 D9
Radmore Wood Staffs 151 D11
Radnage Bucks 84 F3
Radnor Corn 4 G4
Radnor Park W Dunb 277 G9
Radstock Bath 45 C7
Radstone Northants 101 C11
Radway Warks 101 B7
Radway Green Ches E 168 E3
Radwell Beds 121 F10
Radwell Herts 104 D4
Radwinter Essex 106 D2
Radwinter End Essex 106 D2
Radyr Cardiff 58 C6
Raehills Dumfries 248 E3
Raera Argyll 289 G10
Rafborough Hants 49 B11
Rafford Moray 301 D10
Raga Shetland 312 D6
Ragdale Leics 154 F3
Ragdon Shrops 131 E9
Raggalds W Yorks 205 G7
Ragged Appleshaw Hants 47 D10
Raginnis Corn 1 D5
Raglan Mon 78 D6
Ragmere Norf 141 E11
Ragnal Wilts 63 E10
Ragnall Notts 188 G4
Rahane Argyll 276 D4
Rahoy Highld 289 D8
Raigbeg Highld 301 G8
Rails S Yorks 186 D3
Rainbow Hill Worcs 117 F7
Rainford Mers 194 G3
Rainford Junction Mers 194 G3
Rainham London 68 C4
Rainham Medway 69 F10
Rainhill Mers 183 C7
Rainhill Stoops Mers 183 C8
Rainow Ches E 185 F7
Rainowlow Ches E 185 F7
Rain Shore Gtr Man 195 D11
Rainsough Gtr Man 195 G10
Rainton Dumfries 237 D8
Rainton N Yorks 215 D7
Rainton Bridge T&W 234 B2
Rainton Gate Durham 234 B2
Rainworth Notts 171 D9
Raisbeck Cumb 222 D2
Raise Cumb 231 B10
Rait Perth 286 E6
Raithby Lincs 190 E4
Raithby by Spilsby Lincs 174 B5
Rake W Sus 34 B4
Rake Common Hants 34 B3
Rake End Staffs 151 F11
Rake Head Lancs 195 C10
Rakes Dale Staffs 169 G9
Rakeway Staffs 169 G8
Rakewood Gtr Man 196 E2
Raleigh Devon 40 G5
Ralia Lodge Highld 291 D9
Rallt Swansea 56 C4
Ram Carms 93 B11
Ram Alley Wilts 63 G8
Ramasaig Highld 297 G7
Rame Corn 2 C6
Rame Corn 7 F8
Rameldry Mill Bank Fife 287 G7
Ram Hill S Glos 61 D7
Ram Lane Kent 54 D3
Ramnageo Shetland 312 C8
Rampisham Dorset 29 G9
Rampside Cumb 210 F4
Rampton Cambs 123 D8
Rampton Notts 188 F3
Ramsbottom Gtr Man 195 D9
Ramsburn Moray 302 D5
Ramsbury Wilts 63 E9
Ramscraigs Highld 311 G5
Ramsdean Hants 34 C2
Ramsdell Hants 48 B5
Ramsden London 68 F3
Ramsden Oxon 82 B5
Ramsden Worcs 99 B8
Ramsden Bellhouse Essex 88 G2
Ramsden Heath Essex 88 F2
Ramsden Wood W Yorks 196 C2
Ramsey Cambs 138 F5
Ramsey Essex 108 E4
Ramsey IoM 192 C5
Ramseycleuch Borders 261 G7
Ramsey Forty Foot Cambs 138 F6
Ramsey Heights Cambs 138 F5
Ramsey Island Essex 89 D7
Ramsey Mereside Cambs 138 F5
Ramsey St Mary's Cambs 138 F5
Ramsgate Kent 71 G11
Ramsgill N Yorks 214 E2
Ramshaw Durham 232 B5
Ramshaw Durham 233 F8
Ramsholt Suff 108 C6
Ramshorn Staffs 169 F9
Ramsley Devon 13 C8
Ramslye Kent 52 F5
Ramsnest Common Sur 50 G2
Ranais W Isles 304 F6
Ranby Lincs 190 F2
Ranby Notts 187 E11
Rand Lincs 189 F10
Randwick Glos 80 D4
Ranfurly Renfs 267 C7
Rangag Highld 310 E5
Rangemore Staffs 152 E3
Rangeworthy S Glos 61 B7
Rankinston E Ayrs 257 G11
Rank's Green Essex 88 B3
Ranmoor S Yorks 186 D4
Ranmore Common Sur 50 C6
Rannerdale Cumb 220 B3
Rannoch Lodge Perth 285 B9
Rannoch Station Perth 285 B8
Ranochan Highld 295 G10
Ranskill Notts 187 D11
Ranton Staffs 151 E7
Ranton Green Staffs 150 E6
Ranworth Norf 161 G7
Rapkyns W Sus 50 G6
Raploch Stirl 278 C5
Rapness Orkney 314 B5
Rapps Som 28 D4
Rascal Moor E Yorks 208 F2
Rascarrel Dumfries 237 E9
Rashielee Renfs 277 G9
Rashiereive Aberds 303 G9
Rashwood Worcs 117 D8
Raskelf N Yorks 215 E9
Rassal Highld 299 E8
Rassau Bl Gwent 77 C11
Rastrick W Yorks 196 C6
Ratagan Highld 295 D11
Ratby Leics 135 B10

Ratcliff London 67 C11
Ratcliffe Culey Leics 134 D6
Ratcliffe on Soar Leics 153 D9
Ratcliffe on the Wreake Leics 154 G2
Ratford Wilts 62 E3
Ratfyn Wilts 47 E7
Rathen Aberds 303 C10
Rathillet Fife 287 E7
Rathmell N Yorks 204 B2
Ratho Edin 280 G2
Ratho Station Edin 280 G2
Rathven Moray 302 C4
Ratlake Hants 32 C6
Ratley Warks 101 B7
Ratling Kent 55 C8
Ratlinghope Shrops 131 D8
Ratsloe Devon 14 B5
Rattar Highld 310 B6
Ratten Row Cumb 230 B3
Ratten Row Cumb 230 C2
Ratten Row Lancs 202 E4
Ratten Row Norf 157 G10
Rattery Devon 8 C4
Rattlesden Suff 125 F9
Rattray Perth 286 C5
Raughton Cumb 230 B3
Raughton Head Cumb 230 B3
Raunds Northants 121 C9
Ravelston Edin 280 G4
Ravenfield S Yorks 187 B7
Ravenglass Cumb 219 F11
Ravenhead Mers 183 C8
Ravenhills Green Worcs 116 G4
Raveningham Norf 143 D7
Ravenscar N Yorks 227 E9
Ravenscliffe Stoke 168 E4
Ravenscliffe W Yorks 205 F9
Ravenscraig Invclyd 276 F5
Ravensdale IoM 192 C4
Ravensden Beds 121 G11
Ravenseat N Yorks 223 E7
Raven's Green Essex 108 G2
Ravenshall Staffs 168 F3
Ravenshead Notts 171 E9
Ravensmoor Ches E 167 E10
Ravensthorpe Northants 120 C3
Ravensthorpe Pboro 138 C3
Ravensthorpe W Yorks 197 C8
Ravenstone Leics 153 G8
Ravenstone M Keynes 120 G6
Ravenstonedale Cumb 222 E4
Ravenstown Cumb 211 D7
Ravenstruther S Lnrk 269 F8
Ravenswood Village Settlement Wokingham 65 G10
Ravensworth N Yorks 224 D2
Raw N Yorks 227 D8
Rawcliffe E Yorks 199 C7
Rawcliffe York 207 C7
Rawcliffe Bridge E Yorks 199 C7
Rawdon W Yorks 205 F10
Rawdon Carrs W Yorks 205 F10
Rawfolds W Yorks 197 C7
Rawgreen Northumb 241 F10
Raw Green S Yorks 197 F9
Rawmarsh S Yorks 186 B6
Rawnsley Staffs 151 G10
Rawreth Essex 88 G3
Rawreth Shot Essex 88 G3
Rawridge Devon 28 F2
Rawson Green Derbys 170 F5
Rawtenstall Lancs 195 C10
Rawthorpe W Yorks 197 D7
Rawyards N Lnrk 268 B5
Raxton Aberds 303 F8
Raydon Suff 107 D11
Raygill N Yorks 204 D4
Raylees Northumb 251 E10
Rayleigh Essex 88 G4
Rayne Essex 106 G4
Rayners Lane London 66 B6
Raynes Park London 67 F8
Reabrook Shrops 131 C7
Reach Cambs 123 D11
Read Lancs 203 G11
Reader's Corner Essex 88 E2
Reading Reading 65 E8
Readings Glos 79 B10
Reading Street Kent 54 G2
Reading Street Kent 71 F11
Readymoney Corn 6 E2
Ready Token Glos 81 E10
Reagill Cumb 222 B2
Rearquhar Highld 309 K7
Rearsby Leics 154 G3
Reasby Lincs 189 F9
Rease Heath Ches E 167 E10
Reaster Highld 310 C6
Reaulay Highld 299 D7
Reawick Shetland 313 J5
Reawla Corn 2 B4
Reay Highld 310 C3
Rechullin Highld 299 D8
Reculver Kent 71 F8
Red Ball Devon 27 D9
Redberth Pembs 73 E9
Redbourn Herts 85 C10
Redbournbury Herts 85 C10
Redbourne N Lincs 189 B7
Redbourne N Lincs 200 G3
Redbridge Dorset 17 D11
Redbridge London 68 B2
Redbridge Soton 32 E5
Red Bridge Lancs 211 D9
Redbrook Mon 79 C8
Redbrook Wrex 167 G8
Red Bull Ches E 168 D4
Red Bull Staffs 150 B4
Redburn Highld 300 C5
Redburn Highld 301 E9
Redburn Northumb 241 E7
Redcar Redcar 235 G8
Redcastle Angus 287 B10
Redcastle Highld 300 E5
Redcliff Bay N Som 60 D2
Redcroft Dumfries 237 B9
Redcross Worcs 117 C7
Red Dial Cumb 229 B11
Reddicap Heath W Mid 134 D2
Redding Falk 279 F8
Reddingmuirhead Falk 279 F8
Reddish Gtr Man 184 C5
Reddish Warr 183 D11
Redditch Worcs 117 D10
Rede Suff 124 F6
Redenhall Norf 142 G5
Redenham Hants 47 D10
Redesdale Camp Northumb 251 D8
Redesmouth Northumb 251 G9
Redford Aberds 293 F9
Redford Angus 287 C9
Redford Dorset 29 F10
Redford Durham 233 E7
Redford W Sus 34 B5
Redfordgreen Borders 261 F9
Redgorton Perth 286 E4
Redgrave Suff 125 B10
Redheugh Angus 292 G6
Redhill Aberds 293 C9
Redhill Aberds 302 F6
Redhill Herts 104 E6
Redhill Notts 171 F9
Redhill N Som 60 G4
Redhill Shrops 131 B9
Redhill Shrops 150 G4
Redhill Staffs 150 D6
Redhill Sur 51 C9
Redhill Telford 150 G4
Red Hill Bmouth 19 B7
Red Hill Hants 34 E2
Red Hill Hereford 97 D10
Red Hill Kent 53 C7
Red Hill Leics 135 D10
Red Hill Pembs 72 B6
Red Hill Warks 118 F2
Red Hill Worcs 117 G7
Red Hill W Yorks 198 B2
Redhills Cumb 230 F6
Redhills Devon 14 C4
Redhouse Argyll 275 G9
Red House Common E Sus 36 C5
Redhouses Argyll 274 G4
Redisham Suff 143 G8
Red Lake Telford 150 G3
Redland Bristol 60 D5
Redland Orkney 314 D3
Redland End Bucks 84 E4
Redlands Dorset 17 E9
Redlands Som 44 G3
Redlands Swindon 81 G11
Redlane Som 28 E2
Redlingfield Suff 126 C3
Red Lodge Suff 124 C3
Red Lumb Gtr Man 195 D10
Redlynch Som 45 G8
Redlynch Wilts 32 C2
Redmain Cumb 229 E8
Redmarley D'Abitot Glos 98 E5
Redmarshall Stockton 234 G3
Redmile Leics 154 B5
Redmire N Yorks 223 G10
Redmonsford Devon 24 D4
Redmoor Corn 5 C11
Redmoss Aberds 303 F8
Rednal Shrops 149 D7
Rednal W Mid 117 B10
Redpath Borders 262 B3
Red Pits Norf 159 D11
Redpoint Highld 299 C7
Red Post Corn 24 F3
Red Rail Hereford 97 F10
Red Rice Hants 47 E10
Red Rock Gtr Man 194 F5
Red Roses Carms 74 C2
Red Row Northumb 253 D7
Redruth Corn 4 G3
Red Scar Lancs 203 G7
Redscarhead Borders 270 G4
Redstocks Wilts 62 G2
Red Street Staffs 168 E4
Redtye Corn 5 C10
Redvales Gtr Man 195 F10
Red Wharf Bay Anglesey 179 E8
Redwick Newport 60 C2
Redwick S Glos 60 B4
Redwith Shrops 148 E6
Redworth Darl 233 G10
Reed Herts 105 D7
Reed End Herts 104 D6
Reedham Lincs 174 D2
Reedham Norf 143 C8
Reedley Lancs 204 F2
Reedness E Yorks 199 C9
Reed Point Lincs 174 E2
Reeds Beck Lincs 174 B2
Reedsford Northumb 263 C9
Reeds Holme Lancs 195 C10
Reedy Devon 14 D2
Reen Manor Corn 4 E5
Reepham Lincs 189 G8
Reepham Norf 159 E11
Reeth N Yorks 223 F10
Reeves Green W Mid 118 B5
Refail Powys 130 C3
Regaby IoM 192 C5
Regil Bath 60 G4
Regoul Highld 301 D8
Reiff Highld 307 H4
Reigate Sur 51 C9
Reigate Heath Sur 51 C8
Reighton N Yorks 218 D2
Reighton Gap N Yorks 218 D2
Reinigeadal W Isles 305 H4
Reisque Aberds 293 B10
Reiss Highld 310 D7
Rejerrah Corn 4 D5
Releath Corn 2 C5
Relubbus Corn 2 C3
Relugas Moray 301 E9
Remenham Wokingham 65 C9
Remenham Hill Wokingham 65 C9
Remony Perth 285 C11
Rempstone Notts 153 E11
Remusaig Highld 309 J7
Rendcomb Glos 81 D8
Rendham Suff 126 E6
Rendlesham Suff 126 G6
Renfrew Renfs 267 B10
Renhold Beds 121 G11
Renishaw Derbys 186 F6
Renmure Angus 287 B10
Rennington Northumb 264 F6
Renshaw Wood Shrops 132 B6
Renton W Dunb 277 F7
Renwick Cumb 231 C7
Repps Norf 161 F8
Repton Derbys 152 D6
Reraig Highld 295 C10
Reraig Cot Highld 295 B10
Rerwick Shetland 313 M5
Rescassa Corn 5 G9
Rescobie Angus 287 B9
Rescorla Corn 5 D10
Resipole Highld 289 C9
Reskadinnick Corn 4 G2
Resolfen / Resolven Neath 76 E4
Resolis Highld 300 C6
Resolven / Resolfen Neath 76 E4
Restalrig Edin 280 G5
Reston Borders 273 C7
Reston Cumb 221 F9
Restronguet Passage Corn 3 B8
Restrop Wilts 62 B5
Resugga Green Corn 5 D10
Reswallie Angus 287 B9
Retallack Corn 5 B8
Retew Corn 5 D8
Retford Notts 188 E2
Retire Corn 5 C10
Rettendon Essex 88 F3
Rettendon Place Essex 88 F3
Revesby Lincs 174 C3
Revesby Bridge Lincs 174 C4
Revidge Blkburn 195 B7
Rew Devon 9 G9
Rew Devon 13 G11
Rew Dorset 29 F11
Rewe Devon 14 B4
Rew Street IoW 20 C5
Rexon Devon 12 D4
Rexon Cross Devon 12 D4
Reybridge Wilts 62 F2
Reydon Suff 127 B9
Reydon Smear Suff 127 B9
Reymerston Norf 141 B10
Reynalton Pembs 73 D9
Reynoldston Swansea 56 C3
Rezare Corn 12 F3
Rhadyr Mon 78 E5
Rhaeadr Gwy / Rhayader Powys 113 D9
Rhandir Conwy 180 G4
Rhandirmwyn Carms 94 C5
Rhayader / Rhaeadr Gwy Powys 113 D9
Rhedyn Gwyn 144 C5
Rhegreanoch Highld 307 H5
Rhemore Highld 289 D7
Rhencullen IoM 192 C4
Rhenetra Highld 298 D4
Rhes-y-cae Flint 181 G11
Rhewl Denb 165 C10
Rhewl Denb 165 F11
Rhewl Shrops 148 C6
Rhewl Wrex 149 B7
Rhewl-fawr Flint 181 E10
Rhewl-Mostyn Flint 181 E11
Rhian Highld 309 H5
Rhicarn Highld 307 G5
Rhiconich Highld 306 D7
Rhicullen Highld 300 B6
Rhidorroch Ho Highld 307 K6
Rhiews Shrops 150 B2
Rhifail Highld 308 E7
Rhigolter Highld 308 D3
Rhigos Rhondda 76 D6
Rhilochan Highld 309 J7
Rhippinllwyd Ceredig 92 C5
Rhippinllwyd Ceredig 110 G6
Rhiroy Highld 307 L6
Rhitongue Highld 308 D6
Rhivichie Highld 306 D7
Rhiw Gwyn 144 D4
Rhiwabon / Ruabon Wrex 166 G4
Rhiwbebyll Denb 165 B10
Rhiwbina Cardiff 59 C7
Rhiwbryfdir Gwyn 163 F11
Rhiwceiliog Bridgend 58 C3
Rhiwderin Newport 59 B9
Rhiwen Gwyn 163 C9
Rhiwfawr Neath 76 C2
Rhiwinder Rhondda 58 B4
Rhiwlas Gwyn 147 B8
Rhiwlas Gwyn 163 B9
Rhiwlas Powys 148 C3
Rhode Som 43 G9
Rhode Common Kent 54 B5
Rhodes Gtr Man 195 F11
Rhodesia Notts 187 F9
Rhodes Minnis Kent 55 E7
Rhodiad Pembs 90 F5
Rhonadale Argyll 255 D8
Rhondda Rhondda 77 F7
Rhonehouse or Kelton Hill Dumfries 237 D9
Rhoose V Glam 58 F5
Rhos Carms 93 D7
Rhôs Denb 165 C10
Rhôs Neath 76 E2
Rhos Powys 148 F5
Rhosaman Carms 76 C2
Rhosbeirio Anglesey 178 C5
Rhoscefnhir Anglesey 179 F8
Rhoscolyn Anglesey 178 F3
Rhôs Common Powys 148 F5
Rhoscrowther Pembs 72 E6
Rhosddu Wrex 166 E4
Rhos-ddû Gwyn 144 B5
Rhosdylluan Gwyn 147 D7
Rhosesmor Flint 166 B2
Rhosfach Pembs 92 F2
Rhos-fawr Gwyn 145 B7
Rhosgadfan Gwyn 163 D8
Rhosgoch Anglesey 178 D6
Rhosgoch Powys 96 B3
Rhos-goch Powys 96 B3
Rhosgyll Gwyn 163 G7
Rhos Haminiog Ceredig 111 E10
Rhos-hill Pembs 92 C3
Rhoshirwaun Gwyn 144 D3
Rhos Isaf Gwyn 163 D7
Rhoslan Gwyn 163 G7
Rhoslefain Gwyn 110 B2
Rhosllanerchrugog Wrex 166 F3
Rhôs Lligwy Anglesey 179 D7
Rhosmaen Carms 94 G2
Rhosmeirch Anglesey 179 F7
Rhosneigr Anglesey 178 G4
Rhosnesni Wrex 166 E5
Rhôs-on-Sea Conwy 180 E4
Rhosrobin Wrex 166 E4
Rhossili Swansea 56 D2
Rhosson Pembs 90 F4
Rhostrehwfa Anglesey 178 G6
Rhostryfan Gwyn 163 D7
Rhostyllen Wrex 166 F4
Rhoswiel Shrops 148 B5
Rhosybol Anglesey 178 D6
Rhos-y-brithdir Powys 148 E2
Rhosycaerau Pembs 91 D8
Rhosygadair Newydd Ceredig 92 B4
Rhosygadfa Shrops 148 C6
Rhos-y-garth Ceredig 112 C2
Rhosygilwen Pembs 92 C4
Rhos-y-gwaliau Gwyn 147 C8
Rhos-y-llan Gwyn 144 B4
Rhos-y-Madoc Wrex 166 G4
Rhosymedre Wrex 166 G3
Rhos-y-meirch Powys 114 D5
Rhosyn-coch Carms 92 G5
Rhu Argyll 275 G9
Rhu Argyll 276 E5
Rhuallt Denb 181 F9
Rhubodach Argyll 275 F11
Rhuddall Heath Ches W 167 C9
Rhuddlan Ceredig 93 C9
Rhuddlan Denb 181 F8
Rhue Highld 307 K5
Rhulen Powys 96 B2
Rhunahaorine Argyll 255 C8
Rhyd Ceredig 92 C5
Rhyd Gwyn 163 G10
Rhyd Powys 129 C9
Rhydaman / Ammanford Carms 75 C10
Rhydargaeau Carms 93 F8
Rhydcymerau Carms 93 D11
Rhydd Worcs 98 B6
Rhyd-Ddu Gwyn 163 E9
Rhydd Green Worcs 98 B6
Rhydding Neath 57 B8
Rhydfudr Ceredig 111 D11
Rhydgaled Conwy 165 C7
Rhydgaled / Chancery Ceredig 111 B11
Rhydlewis Ceredig 92 B6
Rhydlios Gwyn 144 C3
Rhydlydan Conwy 164 E5
Rhydlydan Powys 129 E11
Rhydmoelddu Powys 113 B11
Rhydness Powys 96 C2
Rhydowen Carms 92 F3
Rhydowen Ceredig 93 B8
Rhyd-Rosser Ceredig 111 D11
Rhydspence Hereford 96 B4
Rhydtalog Flint 166 D2
Rhyd-uchaf Gwyn 147 B8
Rhydwen Gwyn 146 F4
Rhydwyn Anglesey 178 D4
Rhyd-y-Brown Pembs 91 G11
Rhyd-y-clafdy Gwyn 144 B6
Rhydycroesau Powys 148 C4
Rhyd-y-cwm Shrops 130 G3
Rhydyfelin Carms 92 D5
Rhydyfelin Ceredig 111 B11
Rhydyfelin Powys 129 E11
Rhydyfelin Rhondda 58 B5
Rhyd-y-foel Conwy 180 F6
Rhyd-y-fro Neath 76 D2
Rhydygele Pembs 91 G7
Rhyd-y-gwin Swansea 75 E11
Rhyd-y-gwystl Gwyn 145 B8
Rhydymain Gwyn 146 E6
Rhyd-y-meirch Mon 78 D4
Rhyd-y-meudwy Denb 165 E10
Rhydymwyn Flint 166 B2
Rhyd-y-pandy Swansea 75 E11
Rhyd-yr-onen Gwyn 128 C2
Rhyd-y-sarn Gwyn 163 G11
Rhydywrach Carms 73 B11
Rhyl Denb 181 E8
Rhymney Caerph 77 D10
Rhyn Wrex 148 B6
Rhynd Fife 287 E8
Rhynd Perth 286 E5
Rhynie Aberds 302 G4
Rhynie Highld 301 B8
Ribbesford Worcs 116 C5
Ribblehead N Yorks 212 D5
Ribble Head N Yorks 212 D5
Ribbleton Lancs 203 G7
Ribby Lancs 202 G4
Ribchester Lancs 203 F8
Riber Derbys 170 D4
Ribigill Highld 308 D5
Riby Lincs 201 F7
Riby Cross Roads Lincs 201 F7
Riccall N Yorks 207 F8
Riccarton E Ayrs 257 B10
Richards Castle Hereford 115 D9
Richborough Port Kent 71 G10
Richings Park Bucks 66 D4
Richmond London 67 E7
Richmond N Yorks 224 E3
Richmond S Yorks 186 D6
Richmond Hill W Yorks 206 G2
Richmond's Green Essex 106 F2
Rich's Holford Som 42 G6
Rickard's Down Devon 24 B6
Rickarton Aberds 293 E10
Rickerby Cumb 239 F10
Rickerscote Staffs 151 E8
Rickford N Som 44 B3
Rickinghall Suff 125 B10
Rickleton T&W 243 G7
Rickling Essex 105 E9
Rickling Green Essex 105 F10
Rickmansworth Herts 85 G9
Rickney E Sus 23 D10
Riddell Borders 262 E2
Riddings Derbys 170 E6
Riddlecombe Devon 25 E10
Riddlesden W Yorks 205 E7
Riddrie Glasgow 268 B2
Ridgacre W Mid 133 G10
Ridge Bath 44 B5
Ridge Dorset 18 D4
Ridge Hants 32 D4
Ridge Herts 86 E2
Ridge Lancs 211 G9
Ridge Som 28 F3
Ridge Wilts 46 G3
Ridgebourne Powys 113 E11
Ridge Common Hants 34 C2
Ridge Green Sur 51 D10
Ridgehill N Som 60 G4
Ridge Hill Gtr Man 185 B7
Ridge Lane Warks 134 E5
Ridgemarsh Herts 85 G8
Ridge Row Kent 55 E8
Ridgeway Bristol 60 D6
Ridgeway Derbys 170 E5
Ridgeway Derbys 186 E6
Ridgeway Kent 54 E5
Ridgeway Newport 59 B9
Ridgeway Pembs 73 D10
Ridgeway Som 45 D8
Ridgeway Staffs 168 E5
Ridgeway Cross Hereford 98 B4
Ridgeway Moor Derbys 186 E6
Ridgewell Essex 106 C4
Ridgewood E Sus 23 B7
Ridgmont C Beds 103 D9
Ridgway Shrops 131 F7
Ridgway Sur 50 B4
Riding Gate Som 30 B2
Riding Mill Northumb 242 E2
Ridley Kent 68 G6
Ridley Northumb 241 E7
Ridley Stokoe Northumb 250 F6
Ridleywood Wrex 166 E6
Ridlington Norf 160 C6
Ridlington Rutland 136 C6
Ridlington Street Norf 160 C6
Ridsdale Northumb 251 G10
Riechip Perth 286 C4
Riemore Perth 286 C4
Rienachait Highld 306 F5
Rievaulx N Yorks 215 B11
Riff Orkney 314 E4
Riffin Aberds 303 E7
Rifle Green Torf 78 D3
Rift House Hrtlpl 234 E5
Rigg Dumfries 239 D7
Riggend N Lnrk 278 G5
Rigsby Lincs 190 F6
Rigside S Lnrk 259 B9
Riley Green Lancs 194 B6
Rileyhill Staffs 152 F2
Rilla Mill Corn 11 G11
Rillaton Corn 11 G11
Rillington N Yorks 217 E7
Rimac Lincs 191 C7
Rimington Lancs 204 D2
Rimpton Som 29 C10
Rimswell E Yorks 201 B10
Rimswell Valley E Yorks 201 B10
Rinaston Pembs 91 F9
Rindleford Shrops 132 D4
Ringasta Shetland 313 M5
Ringford Dumfries 237 D8
Ringing Hill Leics 153 F9
Ringinglow S Yorks 186 E3
Ringland Newport 59 B11
Ringland Norf 160 G2
Ringles Cross E Sus 37 C7
Ringlestone Kent 53 B9
Ringlestone Kent 53 B11
Ringley Gtr Man 195 F9
Ringmer E Sus 36 E6
Ringmore Devon 8 F3
Ring o' Bells Lancs 194 E3
Ringorm Moray 302 E2
Ring's End Cambs 139 C7
Ringsfield Suff 143 F8
Ringsfield Corner Suff 143 F8
Ringshall Herts 85 C7
Ringshall Suff 125 G10
Ringshall Stocks Suff 125 G10
Ringstead Norf 176 E2
Ringstead Northants 121 B9
Ringtail Green Essex 87 B11
Ringwood Hants 31 F11
Ringwould Kent 55 D11
Rinmore Aberds 292 B6
Rinnigill Orkney 314 G3
Rinsey Corn 2 D3
Rinsey Croft Corn 2 D4
Riof W Isles 304 E3
Ripe E Sus 23 C8
Ripley Derbys 170 E5
Ripley Hants 19 B9
Ripley N Yorks 214 G5
Ripley Sur 50 B5
Riplingham E Yorks 208 G5
Ripon N Yorks 214 E6
Ripper's Cross Kent 54 E3
Rippingale Lincs 155 D11
Ripple Kent 55 D10
Ripple Worcs 99 D7
Ripponden W Yorks 196 D4
Rireavach Highld 307 K5
Risabus Argyll 254 C4
Risbury Hereford 115 G10
Risby E Yorks 208 G6
Risby Lincs 189 C10
Risby Suff 124 D5
Risca Caerph 78 G2
Rise E Yorks 209 E9
Rise Carr Darl 224 B5
Riseden E Sus 52 G6
Riseden Kent 53 F8
Rise End Derbys 170 D3
Risegate Lincs 156 D4
Riseholme Lincs 189 F7
Risehow Cumb 228 E6
Riseley Beds 121 E10
Riseley Wokingham 65 G8
Rise Park London 87 G8
Rise Park Nottingham 171 F9
Rishangles Suff 126 D3
Rishton Lancs 203 G10
Rishworth W Yorks 196 D4
Rising Bridge Lancs 195 B9
Risingbrook Staffs 151 E8
Risinghurst Oxon 83 D9
Rising Sun Corn 12 G3
Risley Derbys 153 B9
Risley Warr 183 C10
Risplith N Yorks 214 F4
Rispond Highld 308 C4
Rivar Wilts 63 G10
Rivenhall Essex 88 B4
Rivenhall End Essex 88 B4
River Kent 55 E9
River W Sus 34 C6
River Bank Cambs 123 D10
Riverhead Kent 52 B4
Rivers' Corner Dorset 30 E3
Riverside Cardiff 59 D7
Riverside Plym 7 D8
Riverside Stirl 278 C6
Riverside Worcs 117 D10
Riverside Docklands Lancs 194 B4
Riverton Devon 40 G6
Riverview Park Kent 69 E7
Rivington Lancs 194 E6
Rixon Dorset 30 E3
Rixton Warr 183 C11
Roach Bridge Lancs 194 B5
Roaches Gtr Man 196 G3
Roachill Devon 26 C4
Roade Northants 120 G5
Road Green Norf 142 E5
Roadhead Cumb 240 C2
Roadmeetings S Lnrk 269 F7
Roadside Highld 310 C5
Roadside of Catterline Aberds 293 F10
Roadside of Kinneff Aberds 293 F10
Roadwater Som 42 F4
Road Weedon Northants 120 F2
Roag Highld 298 E2
Roa Island Cumb 210 G4
Roast Green Essex 105 E9
Roath Cardiff 59 D7
Roath Park Cardiff 59 D7
Roberton Borders 261 G10
Roberton S Lnrk 259 D10
Robertsbridge E Sus 38 C2
Robertstown Moray 302 E2
Robertstown Rhondda 77 E8
Roberttown W Yorks 197 C7
Robeston Back Pembs 73 B9
Robeston Cross Pembs 72 D5
Robeston Wathen Pembs 73 B9
Robeston West Pembs 72 D5
Robhurst Kent 54 G2
Robin Hill Staffs 168 D6
Robin Hood Derbys 186 G2
Robin Hood Lancs 194 E4
Robin Hood W Yorks 197 B10
Robinhood End Essex 106 D4
Robin Hood's Bay N Yorks 227 D9
Robins W Sus 34 B4
Robinson's End Warks 134 E6
Roborough Devon 7 C10
Roborough Devon 25 D9
Rob Roy's House Argyll 284 F5
Robroyston Glasgow 268 B2
Roby Mers 182 C6
Roby Mill Lancs 194 F4
Rocester Staffs 152 B2
Roch Pembs 91 G7
Rochdale Gtr Man 195 E11
Roche Corn 5 C9
Roche Grange Staffs 169 C7
Rochester Medway 69 F8
Rochester Northumb 251 D8
Rochford Essex 88 G5
Rochford Worcs 116 D2
Roch Gate Pembs 91 G7
Rock Caerph 77 F11
Rock Corn 10 F4
Rock Devon 28 G3
Rock Neath 57 C9
Rock Northumb 264 E6
Rock Som 28 C4
Rock Worcs 116 C4
Rock W Sus 35 E10
Rockbeare Devon 14 C6
Rockbourne Hants 31 D10
Rockcliffe Cumb 239 E9
Rockcliffe Dumfries 237 D10
Rockcliffe Flint 182 G3
Rockcliffe Lancs 195 C11
Rockcliffe Cross Cumb 239 E8
Rock End Staffs 168 D5
Rock Ferry Mers 182 D4
Rockfield Highld 311 L3
Rockfield Mon 79 C7
Rockford Devon 41 D9
Rockford Hants 31 F11
Rockgreen Shrops 115 B10
Rockhampton S Glos 79 G11
Rockhead Corn 11 E7
Rockhill Shrops 114 B5
Rockingham Northants 137 E7
Rockland All Saints Norf 141 D9
Rockland St Mary Norf 142 C6
Rockland St Peter Norf 141 D9
Rockley Notts 188 G2
Rockley Wilts 63 E7
Rockley Ford Som 45 C8
Rockness Glos 80 F4
Rockrobin E Sus 52 G6
Rocksavage Halton 183 E8
Rocks Park E Sus 37 C7
Rockstowes Glos 80 F3
Rockville Argyll 276 C4
Rockwell End Bucks 65 B9
Rockwell Green Som 27 C10
Rocky Hill Scilly 1 G4
Rodbaston Staffs 151 G8
Rodborough Glos 80 E4
Rodbourne Swindon 62 C6
Rodbourne Wilts 62 C2
Rodbourne Bottom Wilts 62 C2
Rodbourne Cheney Swindon 62 B6
Rodbridge Corner Essex 107 C7
Rodd Hereford 114 E6
Roddam Northumb 264 E2
Rodden Dorset 17 E8
Rodd Hurst Hereford 114 E6
Roddymoor Durham 233 D9
Rode Som 45 C10
Rodeheath Ches E 168 B5
Rode Heath Ches E 168 D3
Rode Hill Som 45 C10
Roden Telford 149 F11
Rodford S Glos 61 C7
Rodgrove Som 30 C2
Rodhuish Som 42 F4
Rodington Telford 149 G11
Rodington Heath Telford 149 G11
Rodley Glos 80 C2
Rodley W Yorks 205 F10
Rodmarton Glos 80 F6
Rodmell E Sus 36 F6
Rodmer Clough W Yorks 196 B3
Rodmersham Kent 70 G2
Rodmersham Green Kent 70 G2
Rodney Stoke Som 44 C3
Rodsley Derbys 170 G2
Rodway Som 43 F9
Rodway Telford 150 F3
Rodwell Dorset 17 F9
Roebuck Low Gtr Man 196 F3
Roecliffe N Yorks 215 F7
Roe Cross Gtr Man 185 B7
Roedean Brighton 36 G4
Roe End Herts 85 B8
Roe Green Gtr Man 195 G9
Roe Green Herts 86 D2
Roe Green Herts 104 E6
Roehampton London 67 E8
Roe Lee Blkburn 203 G9
Roesound Shetland 312 G5
Roestock Herts 86 D2
Roffey W Sus 51 G7
Rogart Highld 309 J7
Rogart Station Highld 309 J7
Rogate W Sus 34 C4
Roger Ground Cumb 221 F7
Rogerstone Newport 59 B9
Rogerton S Lnrk 268 D2
Roghadal W Isles 296 C6
Rogiet Mon 60 B3
Rogue's Alley Cambs 139 B7
Roke Oxon 83 G10
Rokemarsh Oxon 83 G10
Roker T&W 243 F10
Rollesby Norf 161 F8
Rolleston Leics 136 C4
Rolleston Notts 172 E2
Rolleston S Yorks 186 E5
Rollestone Wilts 46 E5
Rollestone Camp Wilts 46 E5
Rolleston-on-Dove Staffs 152 D4
Rolls Mill Dorset 30 E3
Rolston E Yorks 209 D10
Rolstone N Som 59 G11
Rolvenden Kent 53 G10
Rolvenden Layne Kent 53 G11
Romaldkirk Durham 232 G5
Romanby N Yorks 225 G7
Roman Hill Suff 143 E10
Romannobridge Borders 270 F3
Romansleigh Devon 26 C2
Rome Angus 293 G7
Romesdal Highld 298 D4
Romford Dorset 31 F9
Romford Kent 52 E6
Romford London 68 B4
Romiley Gtr Man 184 C6
Romney Street Kent 68 G4
Rompa Shetland 313 L6
Romsey Hants 32 C5
Romsey Town Cambs 123 F9
Romsley Shrops 132 G5
Romsley Worcs 117 B9
Romsley Hill Worcs 117 B9
Ronachan Ho Argyll 255 B8
Ronague IoM 192 E3
Rondlay Telford 132 B4
Ronkswood Worcs 117 G7
Rood End W Mid 133 F10
Rookby Cumb 222 C6
Rook End Essex 105 E11
Rookhope Durham 232 C4
Rooking Cumb 221 B8
Rookley IoW 20 E6
Rookley Green IoW 20 E6
Rooks Bridge Som 43 C11
Rooksey Green Suff 125 G8
Rooks Hill Kent 52 C5
Rooksmoor Glos 80 E4
Rook's Nest Som 42 G5
Rook Street Wilts 45 G10
Rookwith N Yorks 214 B4
Rookwood W Sus 21 B11
Roos E Yorks 209 G11
Roose Cumb 210 F4
Roosebeck Cumb 210 F5
Roosecote Cumb 210 F4
Roost End Essex 106 C4
Rootham's Green Beds 122 F2
Rooting Street Kent 54 D3
Rootpark S Lnrk 269 E9
Ropley Hants 48 G6
Ropley Dean Hants 48 G6
Ropley Soke Hants 49 G7
Ropsley Lincs 155 C9
Rora Aberds 303 D10
Rorandle Aberds 293 B8
Rorrington Shrops 130 C5
Rosarie Moray 302 E3
Roscroggan Corn 4 G3
Rose Corn 4 E5
Roseacre Kent 53 B9
Roseacre Lancs 202 F4
Rose-an-Grouse Corn 2 B2
Rose Ash Devon 26 C3
Rosebank E Dunb 278 G3
Rosebank S Lnrk 268 F6
Rosebery Midloth 270 D6
Rosebrae Moray 301 C11
Rosebrough Northumb 264 D4
Rosebush Pembs 91 F11
Rosecare Corn 11 B9
Rosedale Herts 86 E4
Rosedale Abbey N Yorks 226 F4
Roseden Northumb 264 E2
Rosedinnick Corn 5 B8
Rosedown Devon 24 C3
Rosefield Highld 301 D8
Rose Green Essex 107 F8
Rose Green Suff 107 C9
Rose Green Suff 107 D8
Rose Green W Sus 22 D6
Rose Grove Lancs 204 G2
Rosehall Highld 309 J4
Rosehall N Lnrk 268 C4
Rosehaugh Mains Highld 300 D6
Rosehearty Aberds 303 C9
Rosehill Blkburn 195 C8
Rosehill Corn 4 E5
Rosehill Corn 5 C10
Rosehill Gtr Man 184 D3
Rosehill London 67 F9
Rosehill Pembs 72 B5
Rosehill Shrops 150 C3
Rosehill T&W 243 D8
Rose Hill Bucks 66 C2
Rose Hill Derbys 153 B7
Rose Hill E Sus 23 B7
Rose Hill Gtr Man 195 F8
Rose Hill Lancs 204 G2
Rose Hill Oxon 83 E8
Rose Hill Suff 108 C3
Rose Hill Sur 51 D7
Roseisle Moray 301 C11
Roseland Corn 6 C5
Roselands E Sus 23 E10
Rosemarket Pembs 73 D7
Rosemarkie Highld 301 D7
Rosemary Lane Devon 27 E11
Rosemelling Corn 5 D10
Rosemergy Corn 1 B4
Rosemount Perth 286 C5
Rosenannon Corn 5 B9
Rosenithon Corn 3 E8
Roser's Cross E Sus 37 C9
Rose Valley Pembs 73 E8
Rosevean Corn 5 D10
Rosevear Corn 2 E5
Roseville W Mid 133 E8

Shirley Derbys 170 G2
Shirley Hants 19 B9
Shirley London 67 F11
Shirley Soton 32 E6
Shirley W Mid 118 B2
Shirley Heath W Mid 118 B2
Shirley holms Hants 19 B11
Shirley Warren Soton 32 E5
Shirl Heath Hereford 115 F8
Shirrell Heath Hants 33 E9
Shirwell Devon 40 F5
Shirwell Cross Devon 40 F5
Shiskine N Ayrs 255 E10
Shitterton Dorset 18 C2
Shobdon Hereford 115 E8
Shobley Hants 31 F11
Shobnall Staffs 152 E4
Shobrooke Devon 26 G5
Shoby Leics 154 F3
Shocklach Ches W 166 F6
Shocklach Green Ches W 166 F6
Shoeburyness Sthend 70 C2
Sholden Kent 55 C11
Sholing Soton 32 E6
Sholing Common Soton 33 E7
Sholver Gtr Man 196 F3
Shootash Hants 32 C4
Shooters Hill London 68 D2
Shootersway Herts 85 D7
Shoot Hill Shrops 149 G8
Shop Corn 10 G3
Shop Corn 24 E2
Shop Devon 24 E5
Shop Corner Suff 108 E4
Shopford Cumb 240 C3
Shopnoller Som 43 G7
Shopp Hill W Sus 34 B6
Shopwyke W Sus 22 B5
Shore Gtr Man 196 D2
Shore W Yorks 196 B2
Shore Bottom Devon 28 G2
Shoreditch London 67 C10
Shoreditch Som 28 C2
Shoregill Cumb 222 E5
Shoreham Kent 68 G4
Shoreham Beach W Sus 36 G2
Shoreham-by-Sea W Sus 36 F2
Shore Mill Highld 301 C7
Shoresdean Northumb 273 F9
Shores Green Oxon 82 D5
Shoreside Shetland 313 J4
Shoreswood Northumb 273 F8
Shoreton Highld 300 C6
Shorley Hants 33 B9
Shorncliffe Camp Kent 55 F7
Shorncote Glos 81 F8
Shorne Kent 69 E7
Shorne Ridgeway Kent 69 E7
Shorne West Kent 69 E7
Shortacombe Devon 12 D6
Shortacross Corn 6 D5
Shortbridge E Sus 37 C7
Short Cross W Mid 133 G9
Shortfield Common Sur 49 E10
Shortgate E Sus 23 B7
Short Green Norf 141 F11
Shorthampton Oxon 100 G6
Shortheath Hants 49 F9
Shortheath Sur 49 E10
Short Heath Derbys 152 G6
Short Heath W Mid 133 C9
Short Heath W Mid 133 E11
Shorthill Shrops 131 B8
Shortlands London 67 F11
Shortlanesend Corn 4 F6
Shortlees E Ayrs 257 B10
Shortmoor Devon 28 G2
Shortmoor Dorset 29 G7
Shorton Torbay 9 C7
Shortroods Renfs 267 B9
Shortstanding Glos 79 C9
Shortstown Beds 103 B11
Short Street Wilts 45 D10
Shortwood Glos 80 F4
Shortwood S Glos 61 D7
Shorwell IoW 20 E5
Shoscombe Bath 45 B8
Shoscombe Vale Bath 45 B8
Shotatton Shrops 149 E7
Shotesham Norf 142 D5
Shotgate Essex 88 G3
Shotley Northants 137 D8
Shotley Suff 108 D4
Shotley Bridge Durham 242 G3
Shotleyfield Northumb 242 G3
Shotley Gate Suff 108 E4
Shottenden Kent 54 C4
Shottermill Sur 49 G11
Shottery Warks 118 G3
Shotteswell Warks 101 B8
Shottisham Suff 108 C6
Shottle Derbys 170 F4
Shottlegate Derbys 170 F4
Shotton Durham 234 D4
Shotton Durham 234 F3
Shotton Flint 166 B4
Shotton Northumb 242 B6
Shotton Northumb 263 C8
Shotton Colliery Durham 234 C3
Shotts N Lnrk 269 C7
Shotwick Ches W 182 G4
Shouldham Norf 140 B3
Shouldham Thorpe Norf 140 B3
Shoulton Worcs 116 F6
Shover's Green E Sus 53 G7
Shraleybrook Staffs 168 F3
Shrawardine Shrops 149 F8
Shrawley Worcs 116 E6
Shreding Green Bucks 66 C4
Shrewley Warks 118 D4
Shrewley Common Warks 118 D4
Shrewsbury Shrops 149 G9
Shrewton Wilts 46 E5
Shripney W Sus 22 C6
Shrivenham Oxon 63 B8
Shropham Norf 141 E9
Shroton or Iwerne Courtney Dorset 30 E5
Shrub End Essex 107 G9
Shrubs Hill Sur 66 F3
Shrutherhill S Lnrk 268 F5
Shucknall Hereford 97 C11
Shudy Camps Cambs 106 C2
Shulishadermor Highld 298 E4
Shulista Highld 298 B4
Shuna Ho Argyll 275 C8
Shurdington Glos 80 B6
Shurlock Row Windsor 65 E10
Shurnock Worcs 117 E10
Shurrery Highld 310 D4
Shurrery Lodge Highld 310 D4
Shurton Som 43 E8
Shustoke Warks 134 E4
Shute Devon 15 B11
Shute Devon 26 G5
Shute End Wilts 31 B11
Shutford Oxon 101 C7
Shut Heath Staffs 151 E7
Shuthonger Glos 99 D7
Shutlanger Northants 120 G4
Shutta Corn 6 E5
Shutt Green Staffs 133 B7
Shuttington Warks 134 B5
Shuttlesfield Kent 55 E7
Shuttlewood Derbys 187 G7
Shuttleworth Gtr Man 195 D10
Shutton Hereford 98 F3
Shwt Bridgend 57 D11
Siabost bho Dheas W Isles 304 D4
Siabost bho Thuath W Isles 304 D4
Siadar W Isles 304 C5
Siadar Iarach W Isles 304 C5
Siadar Uarach W Isles 304 C5
Sibbaldbie Dumfries 248 F4
Sibbertoft Northants 136 G3
Sibdon Carwood Shrops 131 G8
Sibford Ferris Oxon 101 D7
Sibford Gower Oxon 101 D7
Sible Hedingham Essex 106 E5
Sibley's Green Essex 106 F2
Sibsey Lincs 174 E5
Sibsey Fen Side Lincs 174 E4
Sibson Cambs 137 D11
Sibson Leics 135 C7
Sibster Highld 310 D7
Sibthorpe Notts 172 F3
Sibthorpe Notts 188 G2
Sibton Suff 127 D7
Sibton Green Suff 127 C7
Sicklesmere Suff 125 E7
Sicklinghall N Yorks 206 D3
Sid Devon 15 D8
Sidbrook Som 28 B3
Sidbury Devon 15 C8
Sidbury Shrops 132 F3
Sidcot N Som 44 B2
Sidcup London 68 E3
Siddal W Yorks 196 C6
Siddick Cumb 228 E6
Siddington Ches E 184 G4
Siddington Glos 81 F8
Siddington Heath Ches E 184 G4
Sidemoor Worcs 117 C9
Side of the Moor Gtr Man 195 E8
Sidestrand Norf 160 B5
Sideway Stoke 168 G5
Sidford Devon 15 C8
Sidlesham W Sus 22 D5
Sidlesham Common W Sus 22 C5
Sidley E Sus 38 F2
Sidlow Sur 51 D9
Sidmouth Devon 15 D8
Sidway Staffs 150 B5
Sigford Devon 13 G11
Sigglesthorne E Yorks 209 D9
Sighthill Edin 280 G3
Sighthill Glasgow 268 B2
Sigingstone / Tresigin V Glam 58 E3
Signet Oxon 82 C2
Sigwells Som 29 C10
Silchester Hants 64 G6
Sildinis W Isles 305 G4
Sileby Leics 153 F11
Silecroft Cumb 210 C2
Silfield Norf 142 D2
Silford Devon 24 B6
Silian Ceredig 111 G11
Silkstead Hants 32 C6
Silkstone S Yorks 197 F9
Silkstone Common S Yorks 197 G9
Silk Willoughby Lincs 173 G9
Silloth Cumb 238 G4
Sills Northumb 251 C8
Sillyearn Moray 302 D5
Siloh Carms 94 D4
Silpho N Yorks 227 G9
Silsden W Yorks 204 D6
Silsoe C Beds 103 D11
Silton Dorset 30 B3
Silverburn Midloth 270 C4
Silverdale Lancs 211 E9
Silverdale Staffs 168 F4
Silverdale Green Lancs 211 E9
Silver End Essex 88 B4
Silver End W Mid 133 F8
Silvergate Norf 160 D3
Silver Green Norf 142 E5
Silverhill E Sus 38 E3
Silver Hill E Sus 38 B2
Silverhill Park E Sus 38 E4
Silver Knap Som 29 C11
Silverknowes Edin 280 F4
Silverley's Green Suff 126 B5
Silvermuir S Lnrk 269 F9
Silverstone Northants 102 C3
Silver Street Glos 80 E3
Silver Street Kent 69 G11
Silver Street Som 27 C11
Silver Street Som 44 G4
Silver Street Worcs 117 B11
Silverton Devon 27 G7
Silverton W Dunb 277 F8
Silvertonhill S Lnrk 268 E4
Silvertown London 68 D2
Silverwell Corn 4 F4
Silvington Shrops 116 B2
Silwick Shetland 313 J4
Sim Hill S Yorks 197 G9
Simister Gtr Man 195 F10
Simmondley Derbys 185 C8
Simm's Cross Halton 183 D8
Simm's Lane End Mers 194 G4
Simonburn Northumb 241 C9
Simonsbath Som 41 F9
Simonsburrow Devon 27 D10
Simonside T&W 243 E8
Simonstone Lancs 203 G11
Simonstone N Yorks 223 G7
Simprim Borders 272 F6
Simpson M Keynes 103 D7
Simpson Pembs 72 B5
Simpson Cross Pembs 72 B5
Simpson Green W Yorks 205 F9
Sinclair's Hill Borders 272 E6
Sinclairston E Ayrs 257 F11
Sinclairtown Fife 280 C5
Sinderby N Yorks 214 C6
Sinderhope Northumb 241 G8
Sinderland Green Gtr Man 184 C2
Sindlesham Wokingham 65 F9
Sinfin Derby 152 C6
Sinfin Moor Derby 153 C7
Singdean Borders 250 C3
Singleborough Bucks 102 E5
Single Hill Bath 45 B8
Singleton Lancs 202 F3
Singleton W Sus 34 E5
Singlewell Kent 69 E7
Singret Wrex 166 D4
Sinkhurst Green Kent 53 E10
Sinnahard Aberds 292 B6
Sinnington N Yorks 216 B4
Sinton Worcs 116 E6
Sinton Green Worcs 116 E6
Sion Hill Bath 61 F8
Sipson London 66 D5
Sirhowy Bl Gwent 77 C11
Sisland Norf 142 D6
Sissinghurst Kent 53 F9
Sisterpath Borders 272 F5
Siston S Glos 61 D7
Sithney Corn 2 D4
Sithney Common Corn 2 D4
Sithney Green Corn 2 D4
Sittingbourne Kent 70 G2
Six Ashes Staffs 132 F5
Six Bells Bl Gwent 78 E2
Sixhills Lincs 189 D11
Six Hills Leics 154 E2
Sixmile Kent 54 E6
Six Mile Bottom Cambs 123 F11
Sixpenny Handley Dorset 31 D7
Sizewell Suff 127 E9
Skaigh Devon 13 C8
Skail Highld 308 E7
Skaill Orkney 314 C4
Skaill Orkney 314 E2
Skaill Orkney 314 F5
Skares E Ayrs 258 F2
Skateraw E Loth 282 F4
Skaw Shetland 312 B8
Skaw Shetland 312 G7
Skeabost Highld 298 E4
Skeabrae Orkney 314 D2
Skeeby N Yorks 224 E4
Skeete Kent 54 E6
Skeffington Leics 136 C4
Skeffling E Yorks 201 D11
Skegby Notts 171 C7
Skegby Notts 188 G3
Skegness Lincs 175 C9
Skelberry Shetland 313 G6
Skelberry Shetland 313 M5
Skelbo Highld 309 K7
Skelbo Street Highld 309 K7
Skelbrooke S Yorks 198 E4
Skeldyke Lincs 156 B6
Skelfhill Borders 249 C11
Skellingthorpe Lincs 188 G6
Skellister Shetland 313 H6
Skellorn Green Ches E 184 E6
Skellow S Yorks 198 E4
Skelmanthorpe W Yorks 197 E8
Skelmersdale Lancs 194 F3
Skelmonae Aberds 303 F8
Skelmorlie N Ayrs 266 B3
Skelmuir Aberds 303 E9
Skelpick Highld 308 D7
Skelton Cumb 230 D4
Skelton E Yorks 199 B9
Skelton N Yorks 223 E11
Skelton Redcar 226 B3
Skelton York 207 B7
Skelton-on-Ure N Yorks 215 F7
Skelwick Orkney 314 B4
Skelwith Bridge Cumb 220 E6
Skendleby Lincs 174 B6
Skendleby Psalter Lincs 190 G6
Skene Ho Aberds 293 C9
Skenfrith Mon 97 G9
Skerne E Yorks 208 B6
Skerne Park Darl 224 C5
Skeroblingarry Argyll 255 E8
Skerray Highld 308 C6
Skerricha Highld 306 D7
Skerryford Pembs 72 C6
Skerton Lancs 211 G9
Sketchley Leics 135 E8
Sketty Swansea 56 C6
Skewen / Sgiwen Neath 57 B8
Skewes Corn 5 B9
Skewsby N Yorks 216 E2
Skeyton Norf 160 D4
Skeyton Corner Norf 160 D5
Skiag Bridge Highld 307 G7
Skibo Castle Highld 309 L7
Skidbrooke Lincs 190 C6
Skidbrooke North End Lincs 190 B6
Skidby E Yorks 208 G6
Skilgate Som 27 B7
Skillington Lincs 155 D7
Skinburness Cumb 238 F4
Skinflats Falk 279 E8
Skinidin Highld 298 E2
Skinner's Bottom Corn 4 F4
Skinners Green W Berks 64 F2
Skinnet Highld 308 C5
Skinningrove Redcar 226 B4
Skipness Argyll 255 B9
Skippool Lancs 202 E3
Skiprigg Cumb 230 B3
Skipsea E Yorks 209 B9
Skipsea Brough E Yorks 209 C9
Skipton N Yorks 204 C5
Skipton-on-Swale N Yorks 215 D7
Skipwith N Yorks 207 F9
Skirbeck Lincs 174 G4
Skirbeck Quarter Lincs 174 G4
Skirethorns N Yorks 213 G9
Skirlaugh E Yorks 209 F8
Skirling Borders 260 B3
Skirmett Bucks 65 B9
Skirpenbeck E Yorks 207 B10
Skirwith Cumb 231 E8
Skirza Highld 310 C7
Skitby Cumb 239 D10
Skitham Lancs 202 E4
Skittle Green Bucks 84 E3
Skulamus Highld 295 C8
Skullomie Highld 308 C6
Skyborry Green Shrops 114 C5
Skye Green Essex 107 G7
Skye of Curr Highld 301 G9
Skyfog Pembs 90 F6
Skyreholme N Yorks 213 G11
Slack Derbys 170 C4
Slack W Yorks 196 B3
Slack W Yorks 196 D5
Slackcote Gtr Man 196 F3
Slackhall Derbys 185 E9
Slackhead Moray 302 C4
Slack Head Cumb 211 D9
Slackholme End Lincs 191 G8
Slacks of Cairnbanno Aberds 303 E8
Slad Glos 80 D5
Sladbrook Glos 98 F5
Slade Devon 27 F10
Slade Devon 40 D4
Slade Kent 54 C2
Slade Pembs 72 B6
Slade End Oxon 83 G9
Slade Green London 68 D4
Slade Heath Staffs 133 B8
Slade Hooton S Yorks 187 D8
Sladen Green Hants 48 C2
Sladesbridge Corn 10 G6
Slades Green Worcs 99 E7
Slaggyford Northumb 240 G5
Slaidburn Lancs 203 C10
Slaithwaite W Yorks 196 E5
Slaley Derbys 170 D3
Slaley Northumb 241 F11
Slamannan Falk 279 G7
Slape Cross Som 43 F10
Slapewath Redcar 226 B2
Slapton Bucks 103 G8
Slapton Devon 8 G6
Slapton Northants 102 B2
Slateford Edin 280 G4
Slate Haugh Moray 302 C4
Slatepit Dale Derbys 170 B4
Slattocks Gtr Man 195 F11
Slaugham W Sus 36 B3
Slaughterbridge Corn 11 D8
Slaughterford Wilts 61 E10
Slaughter Hill Ches E 168 D2
Slawston Leics 136 E5
Slay Pits S Yorks 199 F7
Sleaford Hants 49 F10
Sleaford Lincs 173 F9
Sleagill Cumb 221 B11
Sleap Shrops 149 D9
Sleapford Telford 150 F2
Sleapshyde Herts 86 D2
Sleastary Highld 309 K6
Slebech Pembs 73 B8
Sledge Green Worcs 98 E6
Sledmere E Yorks 217 G8
Sleeches Cross E Sus 52 G5
Sleepers Hill Hants 33 B7
Sleetbeck Cumb 240 B2
Sleet Moor Derbys 170 E6
Sleight Dorset 18 B5
Sleights N Yorks 227 D7
Slepe Dorset 18 C4
Sliabhna h-Airde W Isles 296 F3
Slickly Highld 310 C6
Sliddery N Ayrs 255 E10
Slideslow Worcs 117 C9
Sligachan Hotel Highld 294 C6
Sligneach Argyll 288 G4
Sligrachan Argyll 276 C3
Slimbridge Glos 80 E2
Slindon Staffs 150 C6
Slindon W Sus 35 F7
Slinfold W Sus 50 G6
Sling Glos 79 D9
Sling Gwyn 163 B10
Slingsby N Yorks 216 E3
Slioch Aberds 302 F5
Slip End C Beds 85 B9
Slip End Herts 104 D5
Slippery Ford W Yorks 204 E6
Slipton Northants 121 B9
Slitting Mill Staffs 151 F10
Slochd Highld 301 G8
Slockavullin Argyll 275 D9
Slogan Moray 302 E3
Sloley Norf 160 E5
Sloncombe Devon 13 D10
Sloothby Lincs 191 G7
Slough Slough 66 D3
Slough Green Som 28 C3
Slough Green W Sus 36 B3
Slough Hill Suff 125 G7
Sluggan Highld 301 G8
Sluggans Highld 298 E4
Slumbay Highld 295 B10
Sly Corner Kent 54 G3
Slyfield Sur 50 C3
Slyne Lancs 211 F9
Smailholm Borders 262 B4
Smallbridge Gtr Man 196 D2
Smallbrook Devon 14 B3
Smallbrook Glos 79 E9
Smallburgh Norf 160 E6
Smallburn Aberds 303 E10
Smallburn E Ayrs 258 D5
Smalldale Derbys 185 E10
Smalldale Derbys 185 F9
Small Dole W Sus 36 E2
Small End Lincs 174 D6
Smalley Derbys 170 G6
Smalley Common Derbys 170 G6
Smalley Green Derbys 170 G6
Smallfield Sur 51 E10
Smallford Herts 85 D11
Small Heath W Mid 134 F2
Smallholm Dumfries 238 B4
Small Hythe Kent 53 G11
Smallmarsh Devon 25 C10
Smallrice Staffs 151 C9
Smallridge Devon 28 G4
Smallshaw Gtr Man 196 G2
Smallthorne Stoke 168 E5
Small Way Som 44 G6
Smallwood Ches E 168 C4
Smallwood Worcs 117 D10
Smallwood Green Suff 125 F8
Smallwood Hey Lancs 202 D3
Smallworth Norf 141 G10
Smannell Hants 47 D11
Smardale Cumb 222 D4
Smarden Kent 53 E11
Smarden Bell Kent 53 E11
Smart's Hill Kent 52 E4
Smaull Argyll 274 G3
Smeatharpe Devon 27 E11
Smeaton Fife 280 C5
Smeeth Kent 54 F5
Smeeton Westerby Leics 136 E3
Smelthouses N Yorks 214 G3
Smercleit W Isles 297 K3
Smerral Highld 310 F5
Smestow Staffs 133 E7
Smethcott Shrops 131 D9
Smethwick W Mid 133 F10
Smethwick Green Ches E 168 C4
Smirisary Highld 289 B8
Smisby Derbys 152 F6
Smite Hill Worcs 117 F7
Smithaleigh Devon 7 D11
Smithbrook W Sus 34 C6
Smith End Green Worcs 116 G5
Smithfield Cumb 239 D10
Smith Green Lancs 202 C5
Smithies S Yorks 197 F11
Smithincott Devon 27 E9
Smithley S Yorks 197 G11
Smith's End Herts 105 D8
Smiths Green Ches E 184 G4
Smith's Green Ches E 168 E3
Smith's Green Essex 105 G11
Smith's Green Essex 106 C3
Smithston Aberds 302 G5
Smithstown Highld 299 B7
Smithton Highld 301 E7
Smithwood Green Suff 125 G8
Smithy Bridge Gtr Man 196 D2
Smithy Gate Flint 181 F11
Smithy Green Ches E 184 G2
Smithy Green Gtr Man 184 D5
Smithy Houses Derbys 170 F5
Smithy Lane Ends Lancs 194 E2
Smock Alley W Sus 35 D9
Smockington Leics 135 F9
Smoky Row Bucks 84 D4
Smoogro Orkney 314 F3
Smug Oak Herts 85 E10
Smyrton S Ayrs 244 G4
Smythe's Green Essex 88 B6
Snagshall E Sus 38 C3
Snaigow House Perth 286 C4
Snailbeach Shrops 131 C7
Snails Hill Som 29 E7
Snailswell Herts 104 E3
Snailwell Cambs 124 D2
Snainton N Yorks 217 C8
Snaisgill Durham 232 F5
Snaith E Yorks 198 C6
Snape N Yorks 214 C5
Snape Suff 127 F7
Snape Green Lancs 193 E11
Snape Hill Derbys 186 F5
Snape Hill S Yorks 198 G2
Snapper Devon 40 G5
Snaresbrook London 67 B11
Snarestone Leics 134 B6
Snarford Lincs 189 E9
Snargate Kent 39 B7
Snarraness Shetland 313 H4
Snatchwood Torf 78 E3
Snave Kent 39 B8
Sneachill Worcs 117 G8
Snead Powys 130 E6
Snead Common Worcs 116 D4
Sneads Green Worcs 117 D7
Sneath Common Norf 142 F3
Sneaton N Yorks 227 D7
Sneatonthorpe N Yorks 227 D8
Snedshill Telford 132 B4
Sneinton Nottingham 153 B11
Snelland Lincs 189 E9
Snelston Derbys 169 G11
Snetterton Norf 141 E9
Snettisham Norf 158 C3
Sneyd Green Stoke 168 F5
Sneyd Park Bristol 60 D5
Snibston Leics 153 G8
Snig's End Glos 98 F5
Snipeshill Kent 70 G2
Sniseabhal W Isles 297 H3
Snitter Northumb 252 C2
Snitterby Lincs 189 C7
Snitterfield Warks 118 F4
Snitterton Derbys 170 C3
Snitton Shrops 115 B11
Snittongate Shrops 115 B11
Snodhill Hereford 96 C6
Snodland Kent 69 G7
Snods Edge Northumb 242 G3
Snowden Hill S Yorks 197 G9
Snowdown Kent 55 C8
Snow End Herts 105 E8
Snow Hill Ches E 167 E10
Snow Hill W Yorks 197 C10
Snow Lea W Yorks 196 D5
Snowshill Glos 99 E11
Snow Street Norf 141 G11
Snydale W Yorks 198 D2
Soake Hants 33 E11
Soar Anglesey 178 G5
Soar Carms 94 F2
Soar Devon 9 G9
Soar Gwyn 146 B2
Soar Powys 95 E9
Soar-y-Mynydd Ceredig 112 G5
Soberton Hants 33 D10
Soberton Heath Hants 33 E10
Sockbridge Cumb 230 F6
Sockburn Darl 224 D6
Sockety Dorset 29 F7
Sodom Denb 181 G9
Sodom Shetland 313 G7
Sodom Wilts 62 C4
Sodylt Bank Shrops 148 B6
Soham Cambs 123 C11
Soham Cotes Cambs 123 B11
Soho London 67 C9
Soho Som 45 D7
Soho W Mid 133 F10
Solas W Isles 296 D4
Soldon Cross Devon 24 E4
Soldridge Hants 49 G7
Sole Street Kent 54 D5
Sole Street Kent 69 F7
Solfach / Solva Pembs 90 G5
Solihull W Mid 118 B2
Solihull Lodge W Mid 117 B11
Sollers Dilwyn Hereford 115 F8
Sollers Hope Hereford 98 E2
Sollom Lancs 194 D3
Solva / Solfach Pembs 90 G5
Somerby Leics 154 G5
Somerby Lincs 200 F5
Somercotes Derbys 170 E6
Somerdale Bath 61 F7
Somerford Ches E 168 B4
Somerford Dorset 19 C9
Somerford Staffs 133 B7
Somerford Keynes Glos 81 G8
Somerley W Sus 22 D4
Somerleyton Suff 143 D9
Somersal Herbert Derbys 152 B2
Somersby Lincs 190 G4
Somersham Cambs 123 B7
Somersham Suff 107 B11
Somers Town London 67 C9
Somers Town Ptsmth 21 B8
Somerton Newport 59 B10
Somerton Oxon 101 F9
Somerton Som 29 B7
Somerton Suff 124 G6
Somerton Hill Som 29 B7
Somerwood Shrops 149 G11
Sompting W Sus 35 G11
Sompting Abbotts W Sus 35 F11
Sonning Wokingham 65 D9
Sonning Common Oxon 65 C8
Sonning Eye Oxon 65 D9
Sontley Wrex 166 F4
Sookholme Notts 171 B8
Sopley Hants 19 B9
Sopwell Herts 85 D11
Sopworth Wilts 61 B10
Sorbie Dumfries 236 E6
Sordale Highld 310 C5
Sorisdale Argyll 288 C4
Sorley Devon 8 F4
Sorn E Ayrs 258 D3
Sornhill E Ayrs 258 C2
Sortat Highld 310 C6
Sotby Lincs 190 F2
Sothall S Yorks 186 E6
Sots Hole Lincs 173 C10
Sotterley Suff 143 G9
Soudley Shrops 131 E9
Soudley Shrops 150 D4
Soughley S Yorks 197 G7
Soughton / Sychdyn Flint 166 B2
Soulbury Bucks 103 F7
Soulby Cumb 222 C4
Soulby Cumb 230 F5
Souldern Oxon 101 E10
Souldrop Beds 121 E9
Sound Ches E 167 F10
Sound Shetland 313 H5
Sound Shetland 313 J6
Sound Heath Ches E 167 F10
Soundwell S Glos 60 D6
Sourhope Borders 263 E8
Sourin Orkney 314 C4
Sourlie N Ayrs 266 G6
Sour Nook Cumb 230 C3
Sourton Devon 12 C6
Soutergate Cumb 210 C4
South Acre Norf 158 G6
South Acton London 67 D7
South Alkham Kent 55 E8
Southall London 66 C6
South Allington Devon 9 G10
South Alloa Falk 279 C7
Southam Cumb 219 C9
Southam Glos 99 F9
Southam Warks 119 E8
South Ambersham W Sus 34 C6
Southampton Soton 32 E6
South Anston S Yorks 187 E8
South Ascot Windsor 66 F2
South Ashford Kent 54 E4
South Auchmachar Aberds 303 E9
Southay Som 28 D6
South Baddesley Hants 20 B3
South Ballachulish Highld 284 B4
South Balloch S Ayrs 245 D8
South Bank Redcar 234 G6
South Bank York 207 C7
South Barrow Som 29 B10
South Beach Northumb 243 B8
South Beach / Marian-y-de Gwyn 145 C7
South Beddington London 67 G9
South Benfleet Essex 69 B9
South Bents T&W 243 E10
South Bersted W Sus 22 C6
South Blainslie Borders 271 G10
South Bockhampton Dorset 19 B9
Southborough Bromley 68 F2
Southborough Kent 52 E5
Southborough Kingston-upon-Thames 67 F7
Southbourne Bmouth 19 C8
Southbourne W Sus 22 B3
South Bramwith S Yorks 198 E6
South Brent Devon 8 D3
South Brewham Som 45 F8
South Bromley London 67 C11
Southbrook Wilts 45 G10
South Broomage Falk 279 E7
South Broomhill Northumb 252 D6
Southburgh Norf 141 C9
South Burlingham Norf 143 B7
Southburn E Yorks 208 C5
South Cadbury Som 29 B10
South Cairn Dumfries 236 C1
South Carlton Lincs 189 F7
South Carlton Notts 187 E9
South Carne Corn 11 E10
South Cave E Yorks 208 G4
South Cerney Glos 81 F8
South Chailey E Sus 36 D5
South Chard Som 28 F4
South Charlton Northumb 264 E5
South Cheriton Som 29 C11
Southchurch Sthend 70 B2
South Church Durham 233 F10
South Cliffe E Yorks 208 F3
South Clifton Notts 188 G4
South Clunes Highld 300 E5
South Cockerington Lincs 190 D5
South Common Devon 28 G4
Southcoombe Oxon 100 F6
South Cornelly Bridgend 57 E10
South Corriegills N Ayrs 256 C2
South Corrielaw Dumfries 248 G5
Southcote Reading 65 E7
Southcott Corn 11 B9
Southcott Devon 24 D6
Southcott Wilts 47 B7
Southcourt Bucks 84 C4
South Cove Suff 143 G9
South Creagan Argyll 289 E11
South Creake Norf 159 B7
Southcrest Worcs 117 D10
South Crosland W Yorks 196 E6
South Croxton Leics 154 G3
South Croydon London 67 G10
South Cuil Highld 298 C3
South Dalton E Yorks 208 D5
South Darenth Kent 68 F5
Southdean Borders 250 B4
Southdene Mers 182 B6
South Denes Norf 143 C10
Southdown Bath 61 G8
Southdown Corn 7 E8
South Down Hants 33 C7
South Down Som 28 E2
South Duffield N Yorks 207 G9
South Dunn Highld 310 D5
South Earlswood Sur 51 D9
Southease E Sus 36 F6
South Elkington Lincs 190 D3
South Elmsall W Yorks 198 E3
South Elphinstone E Loth 281 G7
Southend Argyll 255 G7
Southend Bucks 65 B9
Southend Glos 80 F2
Southend London 67 E11
Southend Oxon 83 E9
Southend W Berks 64 D2
Southend W Berks 64 E5
Southend Wilts 63 E7
South End Beds 103 B10
South End Bucks 103 F7
South End Cumb 210 G4
South End E Yorks 209 E9
South End Hants 31 D10
South-end Herts 86 B6
South End N Lincs 200 C6
South End Norf 141 E9
Southend-on-Sea Sthend 69 B11
Southerhouse Shetland 313 K5
Southerly Devon 12 D6
Southernby Cumb 230 D3
Southern Cross Brighton 36 F3
Southernden Kent 53 D11
Southerndown V Glam 57 G11
Southerness Dumfries 237 D11
Southern Green Herts 104 E6
South Erradale Highld 299 B7
Southery Norf 140 E2
Southey Green Essex 106 E5
South Fambridge Essex 88 F5
South Farnborough Hants 49 C11
South Fawley W Berks 63 C11
South Ferriby N Lincs 200 C3
Southfield Northumb 243 B7
South Field E Yorks 200 B4
South Field Windsor 66 D3
Southfields London 67 E9
Southfields Thurrock 69 C7
Southfleet Kent 68 E6
South Flobbets Aberds 303 F7
Southford IoW 20 F6
South Garth Shetland 312 D7
South Garvan Highld 289 B11
Southgate Ceredig 111 A11
Southgate London 86 G3
Southgate Norf 159 C7
Southgate Norf 160 E2
Southgate Swansea 56 D5
Southgate W Sus 51 F9
South Glendale W Isles 297 K3
South Gluss Shetland 312 F5
South Godstone Sur 51 D11
South Gorley Hants 31 E11
South Gosforth T&W 242 D6
South Green Essex 87 G11
South Green Essex 89 B8
South Green Kent 69 G11
South Green Norf 157 F10
South Green Norf 159 G11
South Green Suff 126 B3
South Gyle Edin 280 G3
South-haa Shetland 312 E5
South Hackney London 67 C11
South Ham Hants 48 C6
South Hampstead London 67 C9
South Hanningfield Essex 88 F2
South Harefield London 66 B5

Sou–Sto 409


South Harrow London 66 B6
South Harting W Sus 34 D3
South Hatfield Herts 86 D2
South Hayling Hants 21 B10
South Hazelrigg Northumb 264 C3
South Heath Bucks 84 E6
South Heath Essex 89 B10
South Heighton E Sus 23 E7
South-heog Shetland 312 E5
South Hetton Durham 234 B3
South Hiendley W Yorks 197 E11
South Hill Corn 12 G2
South Hill N Som 43 B10
South Hill Pembs 72 C4
South Hinksey Oxon 83 E8
South Hole Devon 24 C2
South Holme N Yorks 216 D3
South Holmwood Sur 51 D7
South Hornchurch London 68 C4
South Huish Devon 8 G3
South Hykeham Lincs 172 C6
South Hylton T&W 243 F9
Southill C Beds 104 C3
Southill Dorset 17 E9
Southington Hants 48 D4
South Kelsey Lincs 189 B8
South Kensington London 67 D9
South Kessock Highld 300 E6
South Killingholme N Lincs 201 D7
South Kilvington N Yorks 215 C8
South Kilworth Leics 136 G2
South Kirkby W Yorks 198 E2
South Kirkton Aberds 293 C9
South Kiscadale N Ayrs 256 D2
South Knighton Devon 14 G2
South Knighton Leicester 136 C2
South Kyme Lincs 173 F11
South Lambeth London 67 D10
South Lancing W Sus 35 G11
Southlands Dorset 17 F9
South Lane S Yorks 197 F9
Southleigh Devon 15 C10
South Leigh Oxon 82 D5
South Leverton Notts 188 E3
South Littleton Worcs 99 B11
South Lopham Norf 141 G10
South Luffenham Rutland 137 C8
South Malling E Sus 36 E6
Southmarsh Som 45 G8
South Marston Swindon 63 B7
Southmead Bristol 60 D5
South Merstham Sur 51 C9
South Middleton Northumb 263 E11
South Milford N Yorks 206 G5
South Millbrex Aberds 303 E8
South Milton Devon 8 G4
South Mimms Herts 86 E2
Southminster Essex 89 F7
South Molton Devon 26 B2
Southmoor Oxon 82 F5
South Moor Durham 242 G5
South Moreton Oxon 64 B5
South Mundham W Sus 22 C5
South Muskham Notts 172 D3
South Newbald E Yorks 208 F4
South Newbarns Cumb 210 F4
South Newington Oxon 101 E8
South Newsham Northumb 243 B8
South Newton Wilts 46 G5
South Normanton Derbys 170 D6
South Norwood London 67 F10
South Nutfield Sur 51 D10
South Ockendon Thurrock 68 C5
Southoe Cambs 122 E3
Southolt Suff 126 D3
South Ormsby Lincs 190 F5
Southorpe Pboro 137 C11
South Ossett W Yorks 197 D9
South Otterington N Yorks 215 B7
Southover Dorset 17 C8
Southover E Sus 36 F6
Southover E Sus 37 B11
South Owersby Lincs 189 C9
Southowram W Yorks 196 C6
South Oxhey Herts 85 G10
South Park Sur 51 D8
South Pelaw Durham 243 G7
South Perrott Dorset 29 F7
South Petherton Som 28 D6
South Petherwin Corn 12 E2
South Pickenham Norf 141 C7
South Pill Corn 7 D8
South Pool Devon 8 G5
South Poorton Dorset 16 B6
Southport Mers 193 D10
South Port Argyll 284 E4
Southpunds Shetland 313 L6
South Quilquox Aberds 303 F8
South Radworthy Devon 41 G9
South Rauceby Lincs 173 F8
South Raynham Norf 159 E7
South Reddish Gtr Man 184 C5
Southrepps Norf 160 B5
South Reston Lincs 190 E6
Southrey Lincs 173 B10
Southrop Glos 81 E11
Southrop Oxon 101 E7
Southrope Hants 49 E7
South Ruislip London 66 B6
South Runcton Norf 140 B2
South Scarle Notts 172 C4
Southsea Ptsmth 21 B8
Southsea Wrex 166 E4
South Shian Argyll 289 E11
South Shields T&W 243 D9
South Shore Blkpool 202 G2
South Side Durham 233 F8
South Side Orkney 314 D5
South Somercotes Lincs 190 C6
South Stainley N Yorks 214 G6
South Stainmore Cumb 222 C6
South Stanley Durham 242 G5
South Stifford Thurrock 68 D6
Southstoke Bath 61 G8
South Stoke Oxon 64 C6
South Stoke W Sus 35 F8
South Stour Kent 54 F4
South Street E Sus 36 D5
South Street Kent 54 B5
South Street Kent 68 G6
South Street Kent 69 G10
South Street Kent 70 F6
South Street London 52 B2
South Tawton Devon 13 C9
South Tehidy Corn 4 G3
South Thoresby Lincs 190 F6
South Tidworth Wilts 47 D8
South Tottenham London 67 B10
Southtown Norf 143 B10
Southtown Orkney 314 G4
Southtown Som 28 D4
Southtown Som 44 F5
South Town Devon 14 E5
South Town Hants 49 F7
South Twerton Bath 61 G8
South Ulverston Cumb 210 D6
South View Hants 48 C6
Southville Devon 8 G4
Southville Torf 78 F3
South Voxter Shetland 313 G5
Southwaite Cumb 230 C4
South Walsham Norf 161 G7
Southwark London 67 D10
South Warnborough Hants 49 D8
Southwater W Sus 35 B11
Southwater Street W Sus 35 B11
Southway Plym 7 C9
Southway Som 44 E4
South Weald Essex 87 G9
South Weirs Hants 32 G3
Southwell Dorset 17 G9
Southwell Notts 172 E2
South Weston Oxon 84 F2
South Wheatley Corn 11 C10
South Wheatley Notts 188 D3
South Whiteness Shetland 313 J5
Southwick Hants 33 F10
Southwick Northants 137 E10
Southwick Som 43 D11
Southwick T&W 243 F9
Southwick Wilts 45 B10
Southwick W Sus 36 F2
South Widcombe Bath 44 B5
South Wigston Leics 135 D11
South Willesborough Kent 54 E4
South Willingham Lincs 189 E11
South Wimbledon London 67 E9
South Wingate Durham 234 E4
South Wingfield Derbys 170 D5
South Witham Lincs 155 F8
Southwold Suff 127 B10
South Wonford Devon 24 F5
South Wonston Hants 48 F3
Southwood Derbys 153 E7
Southwood Hants 49 B10
Southwood Norf 143 B7
Southwood Som 44 G5
Southwood Worcs 116 E4
South Woodford London 86 G6
South Woodham Ferrers Essex 88 F4
South Wootton Norf 158 E2
South Wraxall Wilts 61 G10
South Yardley W Mid 134 G2
South Yarrows Highld 310 E7
South Yeo Devon 25 G8
South Zeal Devon 13 C9
Soval Lodge W Isles 304 F5
Sowber Gate N Yorks 215 B7
Sowerby N Yorks 215 C8
Sowerby W Yorks 196 C4
Sowerby Bridge W Yorks 196 C5
Sowerby Row Cumb 230 D3
Sower Carr Lancs 202 E3
Sowley Green Suff 124 G4
Sowood W Yorks 196 D5
Sowood Green W Yorks 196 D5
Sowton Devon 14 C5
Sowton Barton Devon 14 D2
Soyal Highld 309 K5
Soyland Town W Yorks 196 C4
Spacey Houses N Yorks 206 C2
Spa Common Norf 160 C5
Spalding Lincs 156 E4
Spaldington E Yorks 207 G11
Spaldwick Cambs 122 C2
Spalford Notts 172 B4
Spanby Lincs 155 B11
Spango Invclyd 276 G4
Spanish Green Hants 49 B7
Sparham Norf 159 F11
Sparhamhill Norf 159 F11
Spark Bridge Cumb 210 C6
Sparkbrook W Mid 133 G11
Sparkford Som 29 B10
Sparkhill W Mid 133 G11
Sparkwell Devon 7 D11
Sparl Shetland 312 G5
Sparnon Corn 1 E3
Sparnon Gate Corn 4 G3
Sparrow Green Norf 159 G9
Sparrow Hill Som 44 C2
Sparrowpit Derbys 185 E9
Sparrow's Green E Sus 52 G6
Sparsholt Hants 48 G2
Sparsholt Oxon 63 B10
Spartylea Northumb 232 B3
Spath Staffs 151 B11
Spaunton N Yorks 226 G4
Spaxton Som 43 F8
Spean Bridge Highld 290 E4
Spear Hill W Sus 35 D10
Spearywell Hants 32 B4
Speckington Som 29 C9
Speed Gate Kent 68 F5
Speedwell Bristol 60 E6
Speen Bucks 84 F4
Speen W Berks 64 F3
Speeton N Yorks 218 E2
Speke Mers 182 E6
Speldhurst Kent 52 E5
Spellbrook Herts 87 B7
Spelsbury Oxon 101 G7
Spelter Bridgend 57 C11
Spen W Yorks 197 B7
Spencers Wood Wokingham 65 F8
Spen Green Ches E 168 C4
Spennells Worcs 116 C6
Spennithorne N Yorks 214 B2
Spennymoor Durham 233 E11
Spernall Warks 117 E11
Spetchley Worcs 117 G7
Spetisbury Dorset 30 G6
Spexhall Suff 143 G7
Speybank Highld 291 C10
Spey Bay Moray 302 C3
Speybridge Highld 301 G10
Speyview Moray 302 E2
Spillardsford Aberds 303 D10
Spilsby Lincs 174 B6
Spindlestone Northumb 264 C5
Spinkhill Derbys 187 F7
Spinney Hill Northants 120 E5
Spinney Hills Leicester 136 C2
Spinningdale Highld 309 L6
Spion Kop Notts 171 B9
Spirthill Wilts 62 D3
Spital Mers 182 E4
Spital Windsor 66 D3
Spitalbrook Herts 86 D5
Spitalfields London 67 C10
Spitalhill Derbys 169 F11
Spital Hill S Yorks 187 C10
Spital in the Street Lincs 189 D7
Spital Tongues T&W 242 D6
Spithurst E Sus 36 D6
Spittal Dumfries 236 D5
Spittal E Loth 281 F9
Spittal E Yorks 207 C11
Spittal Highld 310 D5
Spittal Northumb 273 E10
Spittal Pembs 91 G9
Spittal Stirl 277 D10
Spittalfield Perth 286 C5
Spittal Houses S Yorks 186 B5
Spittal of Glenmuick Aberds 292 E5
Spittal of Glenshee Perth 292 F3
Spittlegate Lincs 155 C8
Spixworth Norf 160 F4
Splatt Corn 10 F4
Splatt Corn 11 D10
Splatt Devon 25 F10
Splatt Som 43 F8
Splayne's Green E Sus 36 C6
Splott Cardiff 59 D7
Spofforth N Yorks 206 C3
Spondon Derby 153 B8
Spon End W Mid 118 B6
Spon Green Flint 166 C3
Spooner Row Norf 141 D11
Spoonleygate Shrops 132 D6
Sporle Norf 158 G6
Spotland Bridge Gtr Man 195 E11
Spott E Loth 282 F3
Spratton Northants 120 C4
Spreakley Sur 49 E10
Spreyton Devon 13 B9
Spriddlestone Devon 7 E10
Spridlington Lincs 189 E8
Sprig's Alley Oxon 84 F3
Springbank Glos 99 G8
Spring Bank Cumb 229 G10
Springboig Glasgow 268 C3
Springbourne Bmouth 19 C8
Springburn Glasgow 268 B2
Spring Cottage Leics 152 F6
Spring End N Yorks 223 F9
Springfield Argyll 275 F11
Springfield Caerph 77 F11
Springfield Dumfries 239 D8
Springfield Essex 88 D2
Springfield Fife 287 F7
Springfield Gtr Man 194 F5
Springfield Highld 300 C6
Springfield M Keynes 103 D7
Springfield Moray 301 D10
Springfield W Mid 133 D8
Springfield W Mid 133 F9
Springfield W Mid 133 G11
Springfields Stoke 168 G5
Spring Gardens Som 45 D9
Spring Green Lancs 204 E4
Spring Grove London 67 D7
Springhead Gtr Man 196 G3
Springhill E Renf 267 D10
Springhill IoW 20 B6
Springhill N Lnrk 269 D7
Springhill Staffs 133 B11
Springhill Staffs 133 C9
Spring Hill Gtr Man 196 F2
Spring Hill Lancs 195 B8
Spring Hill W Mid 133 D7
Springholm Dumfries 237 C10
Springkell Dumfries 239 B7
Spring Park London 67 F11
Springside N Ayrs 257 B9
Springthorpe Lincs 188 D5
Spring Vale S Yorks 197 G9
Spring Valley IoM 192 E4
Springwell Essex 105 C10
Springwell T&W 243 F7
Springwell T&W 243 F9
Springwells Dumfries 248 E3
Sproatley E Yorks 209 G9
Sproston Green Ches W 168 B2
Sprotbrough S Yorks 198 G4
Sproughton Suff 108 C2
Sprouston Borders 263 B7
Sprowston Norf 160 G4
Sproxton Leics 155 E7
Sproxton N Yorks 216 C2
Sprunston Cumb 230 B3
Spunhill Shrops 149 C8
Spurlands End Bucks 84 F5
Spurstow Ches E 167 D9
Spurtree Shrops 116 D2
Spynie Moray 302 C2
Spyway Dorset 16 C6
Square and Compass Pembs 91 E7
Squires Gate Blkpool 202 G2
Sraid Ruadh Argyll 288 E1
Srannda W Isles 296 C6
Sronphadruig Lodge Perth 291 F9
Stableford Shrops 132 D5
Stableford Staffs 150 B6
Stacey Bank S Yorks 186 C3
Stackhouse N Yorks 212 F6
Stackpole Pembs 73 F7
Stackpole Quay Pembs 73 F7
Stacksford Norf 141 E11
Stacksteads Lancs 195 C10
Stackyard Green Suff 107 B9
Staddiscombe Plym 7 E10
Staddlethorpe E Yorks 199 B10
Staddon Devon 24 C3
Staddon Devon 24 G5
Staden Derbys 185 G9
Stadhampton Oxon 83 F10
Stadhlaigearraidh W Isles 297 H3
Stadmorslow Staffs 168 D5
Staffield Cumb 230 C6
Staffin Highld 298 C4
Stafford Staffs 151 E8
Stafford Park Telford 132 B4
Stafford's Corner Essex 89 B7
Stafford's Green Dorset 29 C10
Stagbatch Hereford 115 F9
Stagden Cross Essex 87 C10
Stagehall Borders 271 G9
Stagsden Beds 103 B9
Stagsden West End Beds 103 B9
Stag's Head Devon 25 B11
Stain Highld 310 C7
Stainburn Cumb 228 F6
Stainburn N Yorks 205 D10
Stainby Lincs 155 E8
Staincliffe W Yorks 197 C8
Staincross S Yorks 197 E10
Staindrop Durham 233 G8
Staines Green Herts 86 C3
Staines-upon-Thames Sur 66 E4
Stainfield Lincs 155 D11
Stainfield Lincs 189 G10
Stainforth N Yorks 212 F6
Stainforth S Yorks 198 E6
Staining Lancs 202 F3
Stainland W Yorks 196 D5
Stainsacre N Yorks 227 D8
Stainsby Derbys 170 B6
Stainsby Lincs 190 G4
Stainton Cumb 211 B10
Stainton Cumb 230 F5
Stainton Cumb 239 F9
Stainton Durham 223 B11
Stainton Mbro 225 C9
Stainton N Yorks 224 F2
Stainton S Yorks 187 C9
Stainton by Langworth Lincs 189 F9
Staintondale N Yorks 227 F9
Stainton le Vale Lincs 189 C11
Stainton with Adgarley Cumb 210 E5
Stair Cumb 229 G10
Stair E Ayrs 257 E10
Stairfoot S Yorks 197 F11
Stairhaven Dumfries 236 D4
Staithes N Yorks 226 B5
Stakeford Northumb 253 F7
Stake Hill Gtr Man 195 F11
Stakenbridge Worcs 117 B7
Stake Pool Lancs 202 D4
Stalbridge Dorset 30 D2
Stalbridge Weston Dorset 30 D2
Stalham Norf 161 D7
Stalham Green Norf 161 E7
Stalisfield Green Kent 54 C3
Stallen Dorset 29 D10
Stallingborough NE Lincs 201 E7
Stalling Busk N Yorks 213 B8
Stallington Staffs 151 B8
Stalmine Lancs 202 D3
Stalmine Moss Side Lancs 202 D3
Stalybridge Gtr Man 185 B7
Stambermill W Mid 133 G8
Stamborough Som 42 F4
Stambourne Essex 106 D4
Stambourne Green Essex 106 D4
Stamford Lincs 137 B10
Stamford Bridge Ches W 167 B7
Stamford Bridge E Yorks 207 B10
Stamfordham Northumb 242 C3
Stamford Hill London 67 B10
Stamperland E Renf 267 D11
Stamshaw Ptsmth 33 G10
Stanah Cumb 220 B6
Stanah Lancs 202 E3
Stanborough Herts 86 C2
Stanbridge C Beds 103 G9
Stanbridge Dorset 31 G8
Stanbridgeford C Beds 103 G9
Stanbrook Essex 106 F2
Stanbrook Worcs 98 B6
Stanbury W Yorks 204 F6
Stand Gtr Man 195 F9
Stand N Lnrk 268 B5
Standburn Falk 279 G8
Standeford Staffs 133 B8
Standen Kent 53 E11
Standen Hall Lancs 203 E10
Standen Street Kent 53 G10
Standerwick Som 45 C10
Standford Hants 49 G10
Standford Bridge Telford 150 E4
Standingstone Cumb 229 B11
Standingstone Cumb 229 E7
Standish Glos 80 D4
Standish Gtr Man 194 E5
Standish Lower Ground Gtr Man 194 F5
Standlake Oxon 82 E5
Standon Hants 32 B6
Standon Herts 105 G7
Standon Staffs 150 B6
Standon Green End Herts 86 B5
Stane N Lnrk 269 D7
Stanecastle N Ayrs 257 B8
Stanfield Norf 159 E8
Stanfield Stoke 168 E5
Stanford C Beds 104 C3
Stanford Kent 54 F6
Stanford Norf 141 E7
Stanford Shrops 148 G6
Stanford Bishop Hereford 116 G3
Stanford Bridge Worcs 116 D4
Stanford Dingley W Berks 64 E5
Stanford End Wokingham 65 G8
Stanford Hills Notts 153 E10
Stanford in the Vale Oxon 82 G4
Stanford-le-Hope Thurrock 69 C7
Stanford on Avon Northants 119 B11
Stanford on Soar Notts 153 E10
Stanford on Teme Worcs 116 D4
Stanford Rivers Essex 87 E8
Stanfree Derbys 187 G7
Stanground Pboro 138 D4
Stanhill Lancs 195 B8
Stanhoe Norf 158 B6
Stanhope Borders 260 D4
Stanhope Durham 232 D5
Stanhope Kent 54 E3
Stanion Northants 137 F8
Stank Cumb 210 E4
Stanklyn Worcs 117 C7
Stanks W Yorks 206 F3
Stanley Derbys 170 G6
Stanley Durham 242 G5
Stanley Lancs 194 F3
Stanley Notts 171 C7
Stanley Perth 286 D5
Stanley Shrops 132 G3
Stanley Shrops 132 G5
Stanley Staffs 168 E6
Stanley Wilts 62 E3
Stanley W Yorks 197 C10
Stanley Common Derbys 170 G6
Stanley Crook Durham 233 D9
Stanley Downton Glos 80 E4
Stanley Ferry W Yorks 197 C11
Stanley Gate Lancs 194 G2
Stanley Green Ches E 184 E5
Stanley Green Poole 18 C6
Stanley Green Shrops 149 B10
Stanley Hill Hereford 98 C3
Stanley Moor Staffs 168 E6
Stanley Pontlarge Glos 99 E9
Stanleytown Rhondda 77 G8
Stanlow Ches W 182 F6
Stanlow Staffs 132 D5
Stanmer Brighton 36 F4
Stanmore Hants 33 B7
Stanmore London 85 G11
Stanmore Shrops 132 E4
Stanmore W Berks 64 D3
Stanner Powys 114 F5
Stannergate Dundee 287 D8
Stannersburn Northumb 250 F6
Stanners Hill Sur 66 G3
Stanningfield Suff 125 F7
Stanningley W Yorks 205 G10
Stannington Northumb 242 B6
Stannington S Yorks 186 D4
Stanpit Dorset 19 C9
Stansbatch Hereford 114 E6
Stansfield Suff 124 G5
Stanshope Staffs 169 E10
Stanstead Suff 106 B6
Stanstead Abbotts Herts 86 C5
Stansted Kent 68 G6
Stansted Airport Essex 105 G11
Stansted Mountfitchet Essex 105 G10
Stanthorne Ches W 167 B11
Stanton Glos 99 E11
Stanton Mon 96 G6
Stanton Northumb 252 F4
Stanton Staffs 169 F10
Stanton Suff 125 C9
Stantonbury M Keynes 102 C6
Stanton by Bridge Derbys 153 D7
Stanton-by-Dale Derbys 153 B9
Stanton Chare Suff 125 C9
Stanton Drew Bath 60 G5
Stanton Fitzwarren Swindon 81 G11
Stanton Gate Notts 153 B9
Stanton Harcourt Oxon 82 D6
Stanton Hill Notts 171 C7
Stanton in Peak Derbys 170 C2
Stanton Lacy Shrops 115 B9
Stanton Lees Derbys 170 C3
Stanton Long Shrops 131 E11
Stanton-on-the-Wolds Notts 154 C2
Stanton Prior Bath 61 G7
Stanton St Bernard Wilts 62 G5
Stanton St John Oxon 83 D9
Stanton St Quintin Wilts 62 D2
Stanton Street Suff 125 D9
Stanton under Bardon Leics 153 G9
Stanton upon Hine Heath Shrops 149 E11
Stanton Wick Bath 60 G6
Stantway Glos 80 C2
Stanwardine in the Fields Shrops 149 E8
Stanwardine in the Wood Shrops 149 D8
Stanway Essex 107 G8
Stanway Glos 99 E11
Stanway Green Essex 107 G9
Stanway Green Suff 126 C4
Stanwell Sur 66 E5
Stanwell Moor Sur 66 E4
Stanwick Northants 121 C9
Stanwick-St-John N Yorks 224 C3
Stanwix Cumb 239 F10
Stanycliffe Gtr Man 195 F11
Stanydale Shetland 313 H4
Staoinebrig W Isles 297 H3
Stape N Yorks 226 G5
Stapehill Dorset 31 G9
Stapeley Ches E 167 F11
Stapenhill Staffs 152 E5
Staple Kent 55 B9
Staple Som 42 E6
Staplecross E Sus 38 C3
Staple Cross Devon 27 C8
Staplefield W Sus 36 B3
Staple Fitzpaine Som 28 D3
Stapleford Cambs 123 G9
Stapleford Herts 86 B4
Stapleford Leics 154 F6
Stapleford Lincs 172 D5
Stapleford Notts 153 B9
Stapleford Wilts 46 F5
Stapleford Abbotts Essex 87 G8
Stapleford Tawney Essex 87 F8
Staplegrove Som 28 B2
Staplehay Som 28 C2
Staple Hill S Glos 61 D7
Staple Hill Worcs 117 C9
Staplehurst Kent 53 E9
Staple Lawns Som 28 D3
Staplers IoW 20 D6
Staples Hill W Sus 35 B8
Staplestreet Kent 70 G5
Stapleton Bristol 60 D6
Stapleton Cumb 240 C2
Stapleton Hereford 114 D6
Stapleton Leics 135 D8
Stapleton N Yorks 198 D4
Stapleton N Yorks 224 C5
Stapleton Shrops 131 C9
Stapleton Som 29 C7
Stapley Som 27 E11
Staploe Beds 122 E2
Staplow Hereford 98 C3
Stapness Shetland 313 J4
Star Fife 287 G7
Star Pembs 92 E4
Star Som 44 B2
Stara Orkney 314 D2
Starbeck N Yorks 206 B2
Starbotton N Yorks 213 E9
Starcross Devon 14 E5
Stareton Warks 118 C6
Stargate T&W 242 E5
Star Hill Mon 79 E7
Starkholmes Derbys 170 D4
Starling Gtr Man 195 E9
Starlings Green Essex 105 E9
Starr's Green E Sus 38 D3
Starston Norf 142 G4
Start Devon 8 G6
Startforth Durham 223 B10
Start Hill Essex 105 G10
Startley Wilts 62 C2
Startop's End Bucks 84 C6
Starveall S Glos 61 B9
Starvecrow Kent 52 D5
Statenborough Kent 55 B10
Statford St Andrew Suff 127 E7
Statham Warr 183 D11
Stathe Som 28 B5
Stathern Leics 154 C5
Station Hill Cumb 229 B11
Station Town Durham 234 D4
Statland Common Norf 141 D10
Staughton Green Cambs 122 D2
Staughton Highway Cambs 122 E2
Staughton Moor Beds 122 E2
Staunton Glos 79 C8
Staunton Glos 98 F5
Staunton in the Vale Notts 172 G4
Staunton on Arrow Hereford 115 E7
Staunton on Wye Hereford 97 B7
Staupes N Yorks 205 B10
Staveley Cumb 211 B7
Staveley Cumb 221 F9
Staveley Derbys 186 G6
Staveley N Yorks 215 G7
Staveley-in-Cartmel Cumb 211 B7
Staverton Devon 8 C5
Staverton Glos 99 G7
Staverton Northants 119 E10
Staverton Wilts 61 G11
Staverton Bridge Glos 99 G7
Stawell Som 43 F11
Stawley Som 27 C9
Staxigoe Highld 310 D7
Staxton N Yorks 217 D10
Staylittle Ceredig 128 F2
Staylittle / Penffordd-Lâs Powys 129 E7
Staynall Lancs 202 E3
Staythorpe Notts 172 E3
Stead W Yorks 205 D8
Steam Mills Glos 79 B10
Stean N Yorks 213 E11
Steanbow Som 44 F5
Stearsby N Yorks 216 E2
Steart Som 29 B9
Steart Som 43 D9
Stebbing Essex 106 G3
Stebbing Green Essex 106 G3
Stechford W Mid 134 F2
Stede Quarter Kent 53 F11
Stedham W Sus 34 C5
Steel Northumb 241 F10
Steel Northumb 251 G9
Steel Bank S Yorks 186 D4
Steel Cross E Sus 52 G4
Steelend Fife 279 C10
Steele Road Borders 250 E2
Steeleroad-end Borders 250 E2
Steel Green Cumb 210 D3
Steel Heath Shrops 149 B10
Steen's Bridge Hereford 115 F10
Steep Hants 34 B2
Steephill IoW 21 F7
Steep Lane W Yorks 196 C4
Steeple Dorset 18 E4
Steeple Essex 88 E6
Steeple Ashton Wilts 46 B2
Steeple Aston Oxon 101 F9
Steeple Barton Oxon 101 G8
Steeple Bumpstead Essex 106 C3
Steeple Claydon Bucks 102 F3
Steeple Gidding Cambs 138 G2
Steeple Langford Wilts 46 F4
Steeple Morden Cambs 104 C5
Steep Marsh Hants 34 B3
Steeraway Telford 132 B3
Steeton W Yorks 204 E6
Stein Highld 298 D2
Steinmanhill Aberds 303 E7
Stella T&W 242 E5
Stelling Minnis Kent 54 D6
Stelvio Newport 59 B9
Stembridge Som 28 C6
Stembridge Swansea 56 C3
Stemster Highld 310 C5
Stemster Ho Highld 310 C5
Stenalees Corn 5 D10
Stenaquoy Orkney 314 C5
Stencoose Corn 4 F4
Stenhill Devon 27 E9
Stenhouse Dumfries 247 E8
Stenhouse Edin 280 G4
Stenhousemuir Falk 279 E7
Stenigot Lincs 190 E3
Stennack Corn 2 B5
Stenness Shetland 312 F4
Stenscholl Highld 298 C4
Stenso Orkney 314 D3
Stenson Derbys 152 D6
Stenton E Loth 282 G2
Stenton Fife 280 B5
Stentwood Devon 27 F10
Stenwith Lincs 154 B6
Stepaside Corn 5 F9
Stepaside Pembs 73 D10
Stepaside Powys 129 F11
Stepping Hill Gtr Man 184 D6
Steppingley C Beds 103 D10
Stepps N Lnrk 268 B3
Sterndale Moor Derbys 169 B10
Sternfield Suff 127 E7
Sterridge Devon 40 D5
Stert Wilts 46 B4
Sterte Poole 18 C6
Stetchworth Cambs 124 F2
Stevenage Herts 104 G4
Steven's Crouch E Sus 38 D2
Stevenston N Ayrs 266 G5
Stevenstone Devon 25 D8
Steventon Hants 48 D4
Steventon Oxon 83 G7
Steventon Shrops 115 C10
Steventon End Essex 105 C11
Stevington Beds 121 G9
Stewards Essex 87 D7
Steward's Green Essex 87 E7
Stewartby Beds 103 C10
Stewarton Argyll 255 F7
Stewarton E Ayrs 267 F8
Stewkley Bucks 103 F7
Stewkley Dean Bucks 102 F6
Stewley Som 28 D4
Stewton Lincs 190 D5
Steyne Cross IoW 21 D8
Steyning W Sus 35 E11
Steynton Pembs 72 D6
Stibb Corn 24 E2
Stibbard Norf 159 D9
Stibb Cross Devon 24 E6
Stibb Green Wilts 63 G8
Stibbington Cambs 137 D11
Stichill Borders 262 B6
Sticker Corn 5 E9
Stickford Lincs 174 D5
Stick Hill Kent 52 E3
Sticklepath Devon 13 C8
Sticklepath Devon 40 G5
Sticklepath Som 28 E4
Sticklepath Som 42 F4
Sticklinch Som 44 F5
Stickling Green Essex 105 E9
Stickney Lincs 174 D4
Stiffkey Norf 177 E7
Stifford's Bridge Hereford 98 B4
Stiff Street Kent 69 G11
Stileway Som 44 E3
Stillingfleet N Yorks 207 E7
Stillington N Yorks 215 F11
Stillington Stockton 234 G3
Stilton Cambs 138 F3
Stinchcombe Glos 80 F2
Stinsford Dorset 17 C10
Stirchley Telford 132 B4
Stirchley W Mid 133 G11
Stirkoke Ho Highld 310 D7
Stirling Aberds 303 E11
Stirling Stirl 278 C5
Stirtloe Cambs 122 D3
Stirton N Yorks 204 C5
Stisted Essex 106 G5
Stitchcombe Wilts 63 F8
Stitchin's Hill Worcs 116 G5
Stithians Corn 2 B6
Stittenham Highld 300 B6
Stivichall W Mid 118 B6
Stixwould Lincs 173 B11
Stoak Ches W 182 G6
Stobhill Northumb 252 G6
Stobhillgate Northumb 252 F6
Stobieside S Lnrk 258 B4
Stobo Borders 260 B5
Stoborough Dorset 18 D4
Stoborough Green Dorset 18 D4
Stobs Castle Borders 250 B2
Stobshiel E Loth 271 C9

Swanside Mers 182 C6
Swanston Edin. 270 B4
Swan Street Essex 107 F7
Swanton Abbott Norf 160 D5
Swanton Hill Norf. 160 D5
Swanton Morley Norf 159 F10
Swanton Novers Norf 159 C10
Swanton Street Kent 53 B11
Swan Village W Mid 133 E9
Swanwick Derbys 170 E6
Swanwick Hants 33 F8
Swanwick Green Ches E 167 F9
Swarby Lincs 173 G8
Swarcliffe W Yorks 206 F3
Swardeston Norf 142 C4
Swarister Shetland 312 E7
Swarkestone Derbys 153 D7
Swarland Northumb 252 C5
Swarraton Hants 48 F5
Swartha W Yorks 205 D7
Swarthmoor Cumb 210 D5
Swartland Orkney 314 D2
Swathwick Derbys 170 B5
Swaton Lincs 156 B2
Swavesey Cambs 123 D7
Sway Hants 19 B11
Swayfield Lincs 155 E9
Swaythling Soton 32 D6
Sweet Green Worcs 116 E2
Sweetham Devon 14 B3
Sweethaws E Sus 37 B8
Sweethay Som 28 C2
Sweetholme Cumb 221 B11
Sweethouse Corn 5 C11
Sweets Corn 11 B9
Sweetshouse Corn 5 C11
Sweffling Suff 126 E6
Swell Som 28 C5
Swelling Hill Hants 49 G7
Swepstone Leics 153 G7
Swerford Oxon 101 E7
Swettenham Ches E 168 B4
Swetton N Yorks 214 E3
Swffryd Caerph 78 F2
Swiftsden E Sus 38 B2
Swift's Green Kent 53 E11
Swilland Suff 126 G3
Swillbrook Lancs 202 G5
Swillington W Yorks 206 G3
Swillington Common W Yorks 206 G3
Swimbridge Devon 25 B10
Swimbridge Newland Devon 40 G6
Swinbrook Oxon 82 C3
Swincliffe N Yorks 205 B10
Swincliffe W Yorks 197 B8
Swincombe Devon 41 E7
Swinden N Yorks 204 C3
Swinderby Lincs 172 C5
Swindon Glos 99 G8
Swindon Staffs 133 E7
Swindon Swindon 63 C7
Swine E Yorks 209 F8
Swinefleet E Yorks 199 C9
Swineford S Glos 61 F7
Swineshead Beds 121 D11
Swineshead Lincs 174 G2
Swineshead Bridge Lincs 174 G2
Swinethorpe Lincs 172 B5
Swiney Highld 310 F6
Swinford Leics 119 B11
Swinford Oxon 82 D6
Swingate Notts 171 G8
Swingbrow Cambs 139 F7
Swingfield Minnis Kent 55 E8
Swingfield Street Kent 55 E8
Swingleton Green Suff 107 B9
Swinhoe Northumb 264 D6
Swinhope Lincs 190 B2
Swining Shetland 312 G6
Swinister Shetland 312 E5
Swinister Shetland 313 L6
Swinithwaite N Yorks 213 B10
Swinmore Common Hereford 98 C3
Swinnie Borders 262 F4
Swinnow Moor W Yorks 205 G10
Swinscoe Staffs 169 F10
Swinside Cumb 229 G10
Swinside Townfoot Borders 262 F6
Swinstead Lincs 155 E10
Swinton Borders 272 F6
Swinton Glasgow 268 C3
Swinton Gtr Man 195 G9
Swinton N Yorks 214 D4
Swinton N Yorks 216 E5
Swinton S Yorks 186 B6
Swinton Bridge S Yorks 187 B7
Swinton Hill Borders 272 F6
Swintonmill Borders 272 F6
Swinton Park Gtr Man 195 G9
Swiss Valley Carms 75 E8
Swithland Leics 153 G10
Swordale Highld 300 C5
Swordale Highld 309 K6
Swordland Highld 295 F9
Swordly Highld 308 C7
Sworton Heath Ches E 183 E11
Swyddffynnon Ceredig 112 D3
Swynnerton Staffs 151 B7
Swyre Dorset 16 D6
Sycamore Devon 28 F3
Sychdyn / Soughton Flint 166 B2
Sychtyn Powys 129 B9
Sydallt Wrex 166 D4
Syde Glos 81 C7
Sydenham London 67 E11
Sydenham Oxon 84 E2
Sydenham Som 43 F10
Sydenham Damerel Devon 12 F4
Syderstone Norf 158 C6
Sydling St Nicholas Dorset 17 B8
Sydmonton Hants 48 B3
Sydney Ches E 168 D2
Syerston Notts 172 F2
Syke Gtr Man 195 D11
Sykehouse S Yorks 198 D6
Sykes Lancs 203 C8
Syleham Suff 126 B4
Sylen Carms 75 D8
Symbister Shetland 313 G7
Symington Borders 271 F8
Symington S Ayrs 257 C9
Symington S Lnrk 259 B11
Symondsbury Dorset 16 C4
Symonds Green Herts 104 F4
Symonds Yat Hereford 79 B9
Synderford Dorset 28 G5
Synod Inn / Post Mawr Ceredig 111 G8
Synton Borders 261 E11
Synton Mains Borders 261 E11
Synwell Glos 80 G3
Syre Highld 308 E6
Syreford Glos 99 G10
Syresham Northants 102 C2
Syster Highld 310 C6
Syston Leics 154 G2
Syston Lincs 172 G6
Sytchampton Worcs 116 D6
Sytch Ho Green Shrops 132 E5
Sytch Lane Telford 150 E2
Sywell Northants 120 D6

## T

Taagan Highld 299 C10
Tabley Hill Ches E 184 F2
Tabor Gwyn 146 F5
Tàbost W Isles 304 B7
Tabost W Isles 305 G5
Tachbrook Mallory Warks 118 E6
Tacker Street Som 42 F4
Tackley Oxon 101 G9
Tacleit W Isles 304 E3
Tacolneston Norf 142 D2
Tadcaster N Yorks 206 E5
Tadden Dorset 31 G7
Taddington Derbys 185 G10
Taddington Glos 99 E11
Taddiport Devon 25 D7
Tadhill Som 45 D7
Tadley Hants 64 G6
Tadley Oxon 64 B4
Tadlow Beds 104 B5
Tadlow C Beds 104 B5
Tadmarton Oxon 101 D7
Tadnoll Dorset 17 D11
Tadwick Bath 61 E8
Tadworth Sur 51 B8
Tafarnau-bach Bl Gwent 77 C10
Tafarn-y-bwlch Pembs 91 E11
Tafarn-y-gelyn Denb 165 C11
Taff Merthyr Garden Village M Tydf 77 F10
Taff's Well Rhondda 58 C6
Tafolwern Powys 129 C7
Tai Conwy 164 C3
Taibach Neath 57 D9
Tai-bach Powys 148 D3
Taigh a Ghearraidh W Isles 296 D3
Taigh Bhalaigh W Isles 296 D3
Tai-mawr Conwy 165 G7
Tai-morfa Gwyn 144 D5
Tain Highld 309 L7
Tain Highld 310 C6
Tai-nant Wrex 166 F3
Tainlon Gwyn 162 E6
Tairbeart W Isles 305 H3
Tai'r-Bull Powys 95 F9
Tairgwaith Neath 76 C2
Tai'r-heol Caerph 77 G10
Tai'r-ysgol Swansea 57 B7
Tai-Ucha Denb 165 D8
Takeley Essex 105 G11
Takeley Street Essex 105 G10
Talacharn / Laugharne Carms 74 C4
Talachddu Powys 95 E11
Talacre Flint 181 E10
Talardd Gwyn 147 D7
Talaton Devon 15 B7
Talbenny Pembs 72 C4
Talbot Green Rhondda 58 C4
Talbot Heath Poole 19 C7
Talbot's End S Glos 80 G2
Talbot Village Poole 19 C7
Talbot Woods Bmouth 19 C7
Tale Devon 27 G9
Talerddig Powys 129 C8
Talgarreg Ceredig 111 G8
Talgarth Powys 96 E3
Talgarth's Well Swansea 56 D2
Talisker Highld 294 B5
Talke Staffs 168 E4
Talke Pits Staffs 168 E4
Talkin Cumb 240 F3
Talladale Highld 299 B9
Talla Linnfoots Borders 260 E4
Tallaminnoch S Ayrs 245 D10
Talland Corn 6 E4
Tallarn Green Wrex 166 G6
Tallentire Cumb 229 D8
Talley Carms 94 E2
Tallington Lincs 137 B11
Talmine Highld 308 C5
Talog Carms 92 F6
Talsarn Carms 94 F5
Tal-sarn Ceredig 111 F10
Talsarnau Gwyn 146 B2
Talskiddy Corn 5 B8
Talwrn Anglesey 179 F7
Talwrn Wrex 166 F3
Tal-y-bont Ceredig 128 F3
Tal-y-Bont Conwy 164 B3
Tal-y-bont Gwyn 145 E11
Tal-y-bont Gwyn 179 G10
Talybont-on-Usk Powys 96 G2
Tal-y-cafn Conwy 180 G3
Tal-y-coed Mon 78 B6
Talygarn Rhondda 58 C4
Talyllyn Powys 96 F2
Tal-y-llyn Gwyn 128 B4
Talysarn Gwyn 163 E7
Tal-y-waenydd Gwyn 163 F11
Talywain Torf 78 E3
Tal-y-wern Powys 128 C6
Tamanabhagh W Isles 304 F2
Tame Bridge N Yorks 225 D10
Tamer Lane End Gtr Man 194 G6
Tamerton Foliot Plym 7 C9
Tame Water Gtr Man 196 F3
Tamfourhill Falk 279 E7
Tamworth Staffs 134 C4
Tamworth Green Lincs 174 G5
Tancred N Yorks 206 B5
Tandem W Yorks 197 D7
Tanden Kent 54 F2
Tandlehill Renfs 267 C8
Tandridge Sur 51 C11
Tanerdy Carms 93 G8
Tanfield Durham 242 F5
Tanfield Lea Durham 242 G5
Tang N Yorks 205 B10
Tangasdal W Isles 297 M2
Tang Hall York 207 C8
Tangiers Pembs 73 B7
Tangley Hants 47 C10
Tanglwst Carms 92 E6
Tangmere W Sus 22 B6
Tangwick Shetland 312 F4
Tangy Argyll 255 E7
Tan Hills Durham 233 B11
Tan Hinon Powys 129 F7
Tanhouse Lancs 194 F3
Tanis Wilts 62 G3
Tankersley S Yorks 197 G10
Tankerton Kent 70 F6
Tanlan Flint 181 E10
Tan-lan Conwy 164 C3
Tan-lan Gwyn 163 G10
Tanlan Banks Flint 181 E10
Tannach Highld 310 E7
Tannachie Aberds 293 E9
Tannadice Angus 287 B8
Tanner's Green Worcs 117 C11
Tannington Suff 126 D4
Tannington Place Suff 126 D4
Tannochside N Lnrk 268 C4
Tan Office Suff 126 E2
Tan Office Green Suff 124 F5
Tansley Derbys 170 D4
Tansley Hill W Mid 133 F9
Tansley Knoll Derbys 170 C4
Tansor Northants 137 E11
Tanterton Lancs 202 G6
Tantobie Durham 242 G5
Tanton N Yorks 225 C10
Tanwood Worcs 117 C8
Tanworth-in-Arden Warks 118 C2
Tan-y-bwlch Gwyn 163 G11
Tanyfron Wrex 166 E3
Tan-y-fron Conwy 165 C7
Tan-y-graig Anglesey 179 F8
Tan-y-graig Gwyn 144 B6
Tanygrisiau Gwyn 163 F11
Tan-y-groes Ceredig 92 B5
Tan-y-mynydd Gwyn 144 C6
Tan-y-pistyll Powys 147 D11
Tan-yr-allt Denb 181 E9
Tan-yr-allt Gwyn 163 E7
Tanyrhydiau Ceredig 112 D4
Tanysgafell Gwyn 163 B10
Taobh a Chaolais W Isles 297 K3
Taobh a' Ghlinne W Isles 305 G5
Taobh a Thuath Loch Aineort W Isles 297 J3
Taobh a Tuath Loch Baghasdail W Isles 297 J3
Taobh Siar W Isles 305 H3
Taobh Tuath W Isles 296 C5
Taplow Bucks 66 C2
Tapnage Hants 33 E9
Tapton Derbys 186 G5
Tapton Hill S Yorks 186 D4
Tarbat Ho Highld 301 B7
Tarbert Argyll 255 B7
Tarbert Argyll 275 E7
Tarbert Argyll 275 G9
Tarbet Argyll 285 G7
Tarbet Highld 295 F9
Tarbet Highld 306 E6
Tarbock Green Mers 183 D7
Tarbolton S Ayrs 257 D10
Tarbrax S Lnrk 269 D10
Tardebigge Worcs 117 D10
Tardy Gate Lancs 194 B4
Tarfside Angus 292 F6
Tarland Aberds 292 C6
Tarleton Lancs 194 C3
Tarleton Moss Lancs 194 C2
Tarlogie Highld 309 L7
Tarlscough Lancs 194 E2
Tarlton Glos 81 F7
Tarn W Yorks 205 F9
Tarnbrook Lancs 203 B7
Tarnock Som 43 C11
Tarns Cumb 229 B8
Tarnside Cumb 221 G8
Tarporley Ches W 167 C9
Tarpots Essex 69 B9
Tarr Som 42 G6
Tarraby Cumb 239 F10
Tarrant Crawford Dorset 30 G6
Tarrant Gunville Dorset 30 E6
Tarrant Hinton Dorset 30 E6
Tarrant Keyneston Dorset 30 G6
Tarrant Launceston Dorset 30 F6
Tarrant Monkton Dorset 30 F6
Tarrant Rawston Dorset 30 F6
Tarrant Rushton Dorset 30 F6
Tarrel Highld 311 L2
Tarring Neville E Sus 36 G6
Tarrington Hereford 98 C2
Tarrington Common Hereford 98 D2
Tarryblake Ho Moray 302 E5
Tarsappie Perth 286 E5
Tarskavaig Highld 295 E7
Tarts Hill Shrops 149 B8
Tarves Aberds 303 F8
Tarvie Highld 300 D4
Tarvie Perth 292 G2
Tarvin Ches W 167 B7
Tarvin Sands Ches W 167 B7
Tasburgh Norf 142 D4
Tasley Shrops 132 E3
Taston Oxon 101 G7
Tat Bank W Mid 133 F9
Tatenhill Staffs 152 E4
Tatenhill Common Staffs 152 E3
Tathall End M Keynes 102 B6
Tatham Lancs 212 F2
Tathwell Lincs 190 E4
Tatling End Bucks 66 B4
Tatsfield Sur 52 B2
Tattenhall Ches W 167 D7
Tattenhoe M Keynes 102 E6
Tatterford Norf 159 D7
Tattersett Norf 158 C6
Tattershall Lincs 174 D2
Tattershall Bridge Lincs 173 D11
Tattershall Thorpe Lincs 174 D2
Tattingstone Suff 108 D2
Tattingstone White Horse Suff 108 D2
Tattle Bank Warks 118 E3
Tatton Dale Ches E 184 E2
Tatworth Som 28 F4
Taunton Gtr Man 196 G2
Taunton Som 28 C2
Taverham Norf 160 G3
Taverners Green Essex 87 B9
Tavernspite Pembs 73 C11
Tavistock Devon 12 G5
Taw Green Devon 13 B9
Tawstock Devon 25 B9
Taxal Derbys 185 F8
Tay Bridge Dundee 287 E8
Tayinloan Argyll 255 C7
Taymouth Castle Perth 285 C11
Taynish Argyll 275 E8
Taynton Glos 98 G4
Taynton Oxon 82 C2
Taynuilt Argyll 284 D4
Tayport Fife 287 E8
Tayvallich Argyll 275 E8
Tea Green Herts 104 G2
Tealby Lincs 189 C11
Tealing Angus 287 D8
Teams T&W 242 E6
Team Valley T&W 242 E6
Teanford Staffs 169 G8
Teangue Highld 295 E8
Teanna Mhachair W Isles 296 E3
Teasley Mead E Sus 52 F4
Tebay Cumb 222 E2
Tebworth C Beds 103 F9
Tedburn St Mary Devon 14 C2
Teddington Glos 99 E9
Teddington London 67 E7
Teddington Hands Worcs 99 E9
Tedsmore Shrops 149 D7
Tedstone Delamere Hereford 116 F3
Tedstone Wafer Hereford 116 F3
Teesville Redcar 225 B10
Teeton Northants 120 C3
Teffont Evias Wilts 46 G3
Teffont Magna Wilts 46 G3
Tegryn Pembs 92 E4
Teigh Rutland 155 F7
Teigncombe Devon 13 D9
Teigngrace Devon 14 G2
Teignmouth Devon 14 G4
Teign Village Devon 14 E2
Telford Telford 132 B3
Telham E Sus 38 E3
Tellisford Som 45 B10
Telscombe E Sus 36 G6
Telscombe Cliffs E Sus 36 G5
Templand Dumfries 248 F3
Temple Corn 11 G8
Temple Glasgow 267 B10
Temple Midloth 270 D6
Temple Wilts 45 E10
Temple Windsor 65 C10
Temple Balsall W Mid 118 B4
Temple Bar Carms 75 B9
Temple Bar Ceredig 111 G10
Temple Bar W Sus 22 B5
Templeborough S Yorks 186 C6
Temple Cloud Bath 44 B6
Templecombe Som 30 C2
Temple Cowley Oxon 83 E8
Temple End Essex 106 C6
Temple End Suff 124 G3
Temple Ewell Kent 55 E9
Temple Fields Essex 87 C7
Temple Grafton Warks 118 G2
Temple Guiting Glos 99 F11
Templehall Fife 280 C5
Temple Herdewyke Warks 119 G7
Temple Hill Kent 68 D5
Temple Hirst N Yorks 198 C6
Templeman's Ash Dorset 28 G6
Temple Normanton Derbys 170 B6
Temple Sowerby Cumb 231 F8
Templeton Devon 26 E5
Templeton Pembs 73 C10
Templeton W Berks 63 F11
Templeton Bridge Devon 26 E5
Templetown Durham 242 G4
Tempsford C Beds 122 G3
Ten Acres W Mid 133 G11
Tenandry Perth 291 G11
Tenbury Wells Worcs 115 D11
Tenby / Dinbych-y-Pysgod Pembs 73 E10
Tencreek Corn 6 E4
Tendring Essex 108 G2
Tendring Green Essex 108 F2
Tendring Heath Essex 108 F2
Ten Mile Bank Norf 140 D2
Tenston Orkney 314 E2
Tenterden Kent 53 G11
Terfyn Conwy 180 F6
Terfyn Gwyn 163 C9
Terhill Som 43 G7
Terling Essex 88 B3
Ternhill Shrops 150 C2
Terpersie Castle Aberds 302 G5
Terras Corn 5 E8
Terregles Banks Dumfries 237 B11
Terrible Down E Sus 23 B7
Terrick Bucks 84 D4
Terriers Bucks 84 G5
Terrington N Yorks 216 E3
Terrington St Clement Norf 157 E10
Terrington St John Norf 157 G10
Terryhorn Aberds 302 F4
Terry's Green Warks 118 C2
Terwick Common W Sus 34 C4
Teston Kent 53 C8
Testwood Hants 32 E5
Tetbury Glos 80 G5
Tetbury Upton Glos 80 F5
Tetchill Shrops 149 C7
Tetchwick Bucks 83 B11
Tetcott Devon 12 B2
Tetford Lincs 190 G4
Tetley N Lincs 199 E9
Tetney Lincs 201 G10
Tetney Lock Lincs 201 G10
Tetsworth Oxon 83 E11
Tettenhall W Mid 133 D7
Tettenhall Wood W Mid 133 D7
Tetworth Cambs 122 G4
Teuchan Aberds 303 F10
Teversal Notts 171 C7
Teversham Cambs 123 F9
Teviothead Borders 249 B10
Tewel Aberds 293 E10
Tewin Herts 86 C3
Tewin Wood Herts 86 B3
Tewitfield Lancs 211 E10
Tewkesbury Glos 99 E7
Teynham Kent 70 G3
Teynham Street Kent 70 G3
Thackley W Yorks 205 F9
Thackley End W Yorks 205 F9
Thackthwaite Cumb 229 G8
Thainston Aberds 293 F8
Thakeham W Sus 35 D10
Thame Oxon 84 D2
Thames Ditton Sur 67 F7
Thames Haven Thurrock 69 C8
Thames Head Glos 81 F7
Thamesmead London 68 C3
Thanington Kent 54 B6
Thankerton S Lnrk 259 B11
Tharston Norf 142 E3
Thatcham W Berks 64 F4
Thatto Heath Mers 183 C8
Thaxted Essex 106 E2
The Aird Highld 298 D4
Theakston N Yorks 214 B6
Thealby N Lincs 199 D11
The Alders Staffs 134 C3
Theale Som 44 D3
Theale W Berks 64 E6
The Arms Norf 141 D7
Thearne E Yorks 209 F7
The Bage Hereford 96 C5
The Balloch Perth 286 F2
The Bank Ches E 168 D4
The Banks Gtr Man 185 D7
The Banks Wilts 62 D4
The Barony Ches E 167 E11
The Barony Orkney 314 D2
The Barton Wilts 62 D5
The Batch S Glos 61 E7
The Beeches Glos 81 E8
The Bell Gtr Man 194 F4
The Bents Staffs 151 C10
Theberton Suff 127 D8
The Blythe Staffs 151 D10
The Bog Shrops 131 D7
The Borough Dorset 30 E2
The Borough London 67 D10
The Bourne Sur 49 E10
The Bourne Worcs 117 F9
The Bows Stirl 285 G11
The Braes Highld 295 B7
The Brampton Staffs 168 F4
The Brand Leics 153 G10
The Bratch Staffs 133 E7
The Breck Orkney 314 F3
The Brents Kent 70 G4
The Bridge Dorset 30 E3
The Broad Hereford 115 E9
The Brook Suff 125 B11
The Brushes Derbys 186 F5
The Bryn Mon 78 D4
The Burf Worcs 116 D6
The Butts Hants 49 F8
The Butts Som 45 D9
The Camp Glos 80 D6
The Camp Herts 85 D11
The Cape Warks 118 D5
The Chart Kent 52 C3
The Chequer Wrex 167 G7
The Chuckery W Mid 133 D10
The City Bucks 84 F3
The Cleaver Hereford 97 F10
The Close W Sus 22 C5
The Colony Oxon 100 D6
The Common Bath 60 G6
The Common Bucks 102 E5
The Common Dorset 30 E3
The Common Shrops 150 D3
The Common Suff 108 B2
The Common Swansea 56 C4
The Common Wilts 47 G8
The Common Wilts 61 G11
The Common Wilts 62 C4
The Common W Sus 51 G7
The Corner Kent 53 E8
The Corner Shrops 131 F8
The Cot Mon 79 F8
The Craigs Highld 309 K4
The Crofts E Yorks 218 E4
The Cronk IoM 192 C4
The Cross Hands Leics 134 C6
The Cwm Mon 79 G7
Theddingworth Leics 136 F3
Theddlethorpe All Saints Lincs 191 D7
Theddlethorpe St Helen Lincs 191 D7
The Dell Suff 143 D9
The Delves W Mid 133 D10
The Den N Ayrs 266 E6
The Dene Durham 242 G4
The Dene Hants 47 C11
The Down Kent 53 F7
The Down Shrops 132 E3
The Downs Sur 50 F3
The Dunks Wrex 166 E4
The Eals Northumb 251 F7
The Eaves Glos 79 D10
The Fall W Yorks 197 B10
The Fence Glos 79 D8
The Flat Glos 80 B3
The Flatt Cumb 240 B3
The Flourish Derbys 153 B8
The Folly Herts 85 C11
The Folly S Glos 61 E8
The Fording Hereford 98 F3
The Forge Hereford 114 F6
The Forstal Kent 54 F4
The Forties Derbys 152 F6
The Four Alls Shrops 150 C3
The Fox Wilts 62 B6
The Foxholes Shrops 132 G2
The Frenches Hants 32 C4
The Frythe Herts 86 C2
The Garths Shetland 312 B8
The Gibb Wilts 61 D10
The Glack Borders 260 B6
The Gore Shrops 131 G11
The Grange Norf 160 E2
The Grange N Yorks 225 F11
The Green Cambs 122 D5
The Green C Beds 85 B8
The Green Cumb 210 C3
The Green Cumb 211 D7
The Green Essex 88 B3
The Green Hants 32 B3
The Green M Keynes 103 C7
The Green Norf 141 C11
The Green Norf 159 B11
The Green Northants 102 C5
The Green Oxon 101 F9
The Green Shrops 130 G6
The Green S Yorks 197 G8
The Green Warks 118 F4
The Green Wilts 45 G11
The Grove Dumfries 237 B11
The Grove Durham 242 G3
The Grove Herts 85 F9
The Grove Shrops 131 B7
The Grove Shrops 131 G8
The Grove Worcs 99 C7
The Gutter Derbys 170 F5
The Gutter Worcs 117 B9
The Hacket S Glos 61 B7
The Hague Derbys 185 C8
The Hall Shetland 312 D8
The Hallands N Lincs 200 C5
The Ham Wilts 45 C11
The Handfords Staffs 151 E7
The Harbour Kent 53 D10
The Haven W Sus 50 G5
The Headland Hrtlpl 234 E6
The Heath Norf 159 D8
The Heath Norf 160 E3
The Heath Norf 160 E4
The Heath Staffs 151 C11
The Heath Suff 108 D2
The Hem Shrops 132 B4
The Hendre Mon 79 C7
The Herberts V Glam 58 E3
The Hermitage Cambs 123 C7
The High Essex 86 C6
The Highlands E Sus 38 F2
The Hill Cumb 210 C3
The Hobbins Shrops 132 E4
The Hollands Staffs 168 D6
The Hollies Notts 172 E4
The Holmes Derbys 153 B7
The Holt Wokingham 65 D10
The Hook Worcs 98 C6
The Hope Shrops 115 B10
The Howe Cumb 211 B9
The Howe IoM 192 F2
The Humbers Telford 150 G3
The Hundred Hereford 115 E10
The Hyde London 67 B8
The Hyde Worcs 98 C6
The Hythe Essex 107 G10
The Inch Edin 280 G5
The Knab Swansea 56 D6
The Knap V Glam 58 F5
The Knapp Hereford 116 G3
The Knapp S Glos 79 G11
The Knowle W Mid 133 F9
The Laches Staffs 133 B8
The Lake Dumfries 237 E8
The Lakes Worcs 116 B5
The Lawe T&W 243 D9
The Lawns E Yorks 208 G6
Thelbridge Barton Devon 26 E3
The Leacon Kent 54 G3
The Leath Shrops 131 F11
The Lee Bucks 84 E6
The Lees Kent 54 C4
The Leigh Glos 99 F7
The Leys Staffs 134 C4
The Lhen IoM 192 B4
The Ling Norf 142 D6
The Lings Norf 141 B10
The Lings S Yorks 199 F7
The Linleys Wilts 61 F11
Thelnetham Suff 125 B10
The Lunt W Mid 133 D9
Thelveton Norf 142 G3
Thelwall Warr 183 D10
The Manor W Sus 22 C4
The Marsh Ches E 168 C4
The Marsh Hereford 115 F9
The Marsh Powys 130 D6
The Marsh Shrops 150 D3
The Marsh Staffs 150 D6
The Marsh Suff 125 B11
The Marsh Suff 126 B2
The Marsh Wilts 62 C5
Themelthorpe Norf 159 E11
The Middles Durham 242 G6
The Mint Hants 34 B3
The Moor Flint 166 B4
The Moor Kent 38 B3
The Moors Hereford 97 E10
The Mount Hants 64 G2
The Mount Reading 65 E8
The Mumbles / Y Mwmbwls Swansea 56 D6
The Murray S Lnrk 268 E2
The Mythe Glos 99 E7
The Nant Wrex 166 E3
The Narth Mon 79 D8
The Neuk Aberds 293 D9
Thenford Northants 101 C10
The Node Herts 104 G4
The Nook Shrops 149 C11
The Nook Shrops 150 E3
The North Mon 79 D8
Theobald's Green Wilts 62 F4
The Oval Bath 61 G8
The Park Glos 99 G8
The Parks S Yorks 198 F6
The Pitts Wilts 31 B9
The Platt Oxon 83 E9
The Pludds Glos 79 B10
The Point Devon 14 E5
The Pole of Itlaw Aberds 302 D6
The Port of Felixstowe Suff 108 E5
The Potteries Stoke 168 F5
The Pound Glos 98 E4
The Quarry Glos 80 F2
The Quarry Shrops 149 G9
The Quarter Kent 53 E11
The Quarter Kent 53 G11
The Rampings Worcs 99 E7
The Rectory Lincs 156 G2
The Reddings Glos 99 G8
Therfield Herts 104 D6
The Rhos Pembs 73 C8
The Rhydd Hereford 97 E9
The Riddle Hereford 115 E9
The Ridge Wilts 61 F11
The Ridges Wokingham 65 G10
The Ridgeway Herts 86 E3
The Riding Northumb 241 D10
The Riggs Borders 261 C8
The Rink Borders 261 C11
The Rise Windsor 66 F2
The Rock Telford 132 B3
The Rocks Kent 53 B8
The Rocks S Glos 61 C8
The Roe Denb 181 G8
The Rookery Herts 85 G10
The Rookery Staffs 168 D5
The Row Lancs 211 D9
The Rowe Staffs 150 B6
The Ryde Herts 86 D2
The Sands Sur 49 D11
The Scarr Glos 98 F4
The Shoe Wilts 61 E10
The Shruggs Staffs 151 C8
The Slack Durham 233 F8
The Slade W Berks 64 F4
The Smeeth Norf 157 G10
The Smithies Shrops 132 D3
The Spa Wilts 62 G2
The Spring Warks 118 C5
The Square Torf 78 F3
The Stocks Kent 38 B6
The Stocks Wilts 62 G2
The Straits Hants 49 F9
The Straits W Mid 133 E8
The Strand Wilts 46 B2
The Swillett Herts 85 F8
The Sydnall Shrops 150 C3
Thetford Lincs 156 F2
Thetford Norf 141 G7
The Thrift Cambs 104 D6
The Throat Wokingham 65 F10
The Toft Staffs 151 F8
The Towans Corn 2 B3
The Town Scilly 1 F3
The Twittocks Glos 99 D7
The Tynings Glos 80 B6
The Vale W Mid 133 G11
The Valley Ches E 167 D11
The Valley Kent 54 C3
The Valley Leics 154 F4
The Valley Pembs 73 D10
The Vauld Hereford 97 B10
The Village Newport 78 G4
The Village Windsor 66 E3
The Village W Mid 133 F7
The Walshes Worcs 116 C6
The Warren Kent 54 E3
The Warren Wilts 63 F8
The Waterwheel Shrops 131 C7
The Weaven Hereford 97 E10
The Wells Sur 67 G7
The Wern Wrex 166 E3
The Willows NE Lincs 201 F8
The Wood Shrops 148 E6
The Wood Shrops 149 D9
The Woodlands Leics 136 D3
The Woodlands Suff 107 C11
The Woodlands Suff 108 D3
The Woods W Mid 133 D10
The Wrangle Bath 44 B4
The Wrythe London 67 F9
The Wyke Shrops 132 B4
The Wymm Hereford 97 B10
Theydon Bois Essex 86 F6
Theydon Garnon Essex 87 F7
Theydon Mount Essex 87 F7
The Yeld Shrops 131 G11
Thicket Mead Bath 45 B7
Thick Hollins W Yorks 196 E6
Thickthorn Hall Norf 142 B3
Thickwood Wilts 61 E10
Thimbleby Lincs 190 G2
Thimbleby N Yorks 225 F9
Thimble End W Mid 134 E2
Thinford Durham 233 E11
Thingley Wilts 61 E11
Thingwall Mers 182 E3
Thirdpart N Ayrs 266 F3
Thirlby N Yorks 215 C9
Thirlestane Borders 271 F11
Thirn N Yorks 214 B4
Thirsk N Yorks 215 C8
Thirtleby E Yorks 209 G9
Thistleton Lancs 202 F4
Thistleton Rutland 155 F8
Thistley Green Essex 88 B2
Thistley Green Suff 124 B3
Thixendale N Yorks 216 G6
Thockrington Northumb 241 B11
Tholomas Drove Cambs 139 B7
Tholthorpe N Yorks 215 F9
Thomas Chapel Pembs 73 D10
Thomas Close Cumb 230 C4
Thomastown Aberds 302 F5
Thomastown Rhondda 58 B4
Thompson Norf 141 D8
Thomshill Moray 302 D2
Thong Kent 69 E7
Thongsbridge W Yorks 196 F6
Thoralby N Yorks 213 B10
Thoresby Notts 187 G10
Thoresthorpe Lincs 191 F7
Thoresway Lincs 189 B11
Thorganby Lincs 190 B2
Thorganby N Yorks 207 E9
Thorgill N Yorks 226 F4
Thorington Suff 127 C8
Thorington Street Suff 107 D10
Thorlby N Yorks 204 C5
Thorley Herts 87 B7
Thorley IoW 20 D3
Thorley Houses Herts 105 G9
Thorley Street Herts 87 B7
Thorley Street IoW 20 D3
Thormanby N Yorks 215 E9
Thorn Devon 13 D9
Thorn Powys 114 E5
Thornaby on Tees Stockton 225 B9
Thornage Norf 159 B11
Thornborough Bucks 102 E4
Thornborough N Yorks 214 D5
Thornbury Devon 24 F6

Thornbury Hereford 116 F2
Thornbury S Glos 79 G10
Thornby W Yorks 205 G9
Thornby Cumb 239 G7
Thornby Northants 120 B3
Thorncliff W Yorks 197 E8
Thorncliffe Staffs 169 D8
Thorncombe Dorset 28 G5
Thorncombe Dorset 30 G5
Thorncombe Street Sur 50 E4
Thorncote Green C Beds 104 B3
Thorncross IoW 20 E4
Thorndon Suff 126 D2
Thorndon Cross Devon 12 C6
Thorne Corn 24 G2
Thorne S Yorks 199 E7
Thorne Coffin Som 29 D8
Thornehillhead Devon 24 D6
Thorne Moor Devon 12 D3
Thornend Wilts 62 D3
Thorner W Yorks 206 E3
Thornes Staffs 133 C11
Thornes W Yorks 197 D10
Thorne St Margaret Som 27 C9
Thorney Bucks 66 D4
Thorney Notts 188 G5
Thorney Pboro 138 C5
Thorney Som 28 C6
Thorney Close T&W 243 G9
Thorney Crofts E Yorks 201 C8
Thorney Green Suff 125 E11
Thorney Hill Hants 19 B9
Thorney Island W Sus 22 C3
Thorney Toll Pboro 138 C6
Thorneywood Notts 171 G9
Thornfalcon Som 28 C3
Thornford Dorset 29 E10
Thorngrafton Northumb 241 D7
Thorngrove Som 43 G11
Thorngumbald E Yorks 201 B8
Thornham Norf 176 E2
Thornham Fold Gtr Man 195 F11
Thornham Magna Suff 126 C2
Thornham Parva Suff 126 C2
Thornhaugh Pboro 137 C11
Thornhill Cardiff 59 C7
Thornhill Cumb 219 D10
Thornhill Derbys 185 E11
Thornhill Dumfries 247 D9
Thornhill Soton 33 E7
Thornhill Stirl 278 B3
Thornhill Torf 78 F3
Thornhill Wilts 62 D5
Thornhill W Yorks 197 D9
Thorn Hill S Yorks 186 C6
Thornhill Edge W Yorks 197 D8
Thornhill Lees W Yorks 197 D8
Thornhill Park Hants 33 E7
Thornhills W Yorks 197 C7
Thornholme E Yorks 218 G2
Thornicombe Dorset 30 G5
Thornielee Borders 261 B10
Thornley Durham 233 D8
Thornley Durham 234 D3
Thornliebank E Renf 267 D10
Thornly Park Renfs 267 C9
Thornroan Aberds 303 F8
Thorns N Yorks 223 E7
Thorns Suff 124 F4
Thornseat S Yorks 186 C2
Thornsett Derbys 185 D8
Thorns Green Ches E 184 E3
Thornthwaite Cumb 229 F10
Thornthwaite N Yorks 205 B9
Thornton Angus 287 C7
Thornton Bucks 102 D5
Thornton E Yorks 207 D11
Thornton Fife 280 B5
Thornton Lancs 202 E2
Thornton Leics 135 B9
Thornton Lincs 174 B2
Thornton Mbro 225 C9
Thornton Mers 193 G10
Thornton Northumb 273 F9
Thornton Pembs 72 D6
Thornton W Yorks 205 G8
Thornton Curtis N Lincs 200 D5
Thorntonhall S Lnrk 267 D11
Thornton Heath London 67 F10
Thornton Hough Mers 182 E4
Thornton in Craven N Yorks 204 D4
Thornton in Lonsdale N Yorks 212 E3
Thornton-le-Beans N Yorks 225 G7
Thornton-le-Clay N Yorks 216 F3
Thornton-le-Dale N Yorks 216 C6
Thornton le Moor Lincs 189 B9
Thornton-le-Moor N Yorks 215 B7
Thornton-le-Moors Ches W 182 G6
Thornton-le-Street N Yorks 215 B8
Thorntonloch E Loth 282 G4
Thornton Park Northumb 273 F8
Thornton Rust N Yorks 213 B9
Thornton Steward N Yorks 214 B3
Thornton Watlass N Yorks 214 B4
Thornwood Common Essex 87 D7
Thornydykes Borders 272 F2
Thoroton Notts 172 G3
Thorp Gtr Man 196 F2
Thorp Arch W Yorks 206 D4
Thorpe Cumb 230 F5
Thorpe Derbys 169 E11
Thorpe E Yorks 208 D5
Thorpe Lincs 191 E7
Thorpe Norf 143 D8
Thorpe Notts 172 F3
Thorpe N Yorks 213 G10
Thorpe Sur 66 F4
Thorpe Abbotts Norf 126 B3
Thorpe Acre Leics 153 E10
Thorpe Arnold Leics 154 E5
Thorpe Audlin W Yorks 198 D3
Thorpe Bassett N Yorks 217 E7
Thorpe Bay Sthend 70 B2
Thorpe by Water Rutland 137 D7
Thorpe Common Suff 108 D5
Thorpe Constantine Staffs 134 B5
Thorpe Culvert Lincs 175 C7
Thorpe Edge W Yorks 205 F9
Thorpe End Norf 160 G5
Thorpe Fendykes Lincs 175 C7
Thorpe Green Essex 108 G3
Thorpe Green Lancs 194 C5
Thorpe Green Suff 125 G8
Thorpe Green Sur 66 F4
Thorpe Hamlet Norf 142 B4
Thorpe Hesley S Yorks 186 B5
Thorpe in Balne S Yorks 198 E5
Thorpe in the Fallows Lincs 188 E6
Thorpe Langton Leics 136 E4
Thorpe Larches Durham 234 F3
Thorpe Latimer Lincs 156 B2
Thorpe Lea Sur 66 E4
Thorpe-le-Soken Essex 108 G3
Thorpe le Street E Yorks 208 E2
Thorpe le Vale Lincs 190 C2
Thorpe Malsor Northants 120 B6
Thorpe Mandeville Northants 101 B10
Thorpe Market Norf 160 B4
Thorpe Marriot Norf 160 F3
Thorpe Morieux Suff 125 G8
Thorpeness Suff 127 F9
Thorpe on the Hill Lincs 172 B6
Thorpe on The Hill W Yorks 197 B10
Thorpe Row Norf 141 B9
Thorpe St Andrew Norf 142 B5
Thorpe St Peter Lincs 175 C7
Thorpe Salvin S Yorks 187 E8
Thorpe Satchville Leics 154 G4
Thorpe Street Suff 125 B10
Thorpe Thewles Stockton 234 G4
Thorpe Tilney Lincs 173 D10
Thorpe Underwood Northants 136 G5
Thorpe Underwood N Yorks 206 B5
Thorpe Waterville Northants 137 G10
Thorpe Willoughby N Yorks 207 G7
Thorpe Wood N Yorks 207 G7
Thorpland Norf 140 B2
Thorrington Essex 89 B9
Thorverton Devon 26 G6
Thoulstone Wilts 45 D10
Thrandeston Suff 126 B2
Thrapston Northants 121 B9
Thrashbush N Lnrk 268 B5
Threapland Cumb 229 D9
Threapland N Yorks 213 G9
Threapwood Ches W 166 F6
Threapwood Staffs 169 G8
Three Ashes Hants 64 G6
Three Ashes Hereford 97 G10
Three Ashes Shrops 115 B7
Three Ashes Som 45 D7
Three Bridges Argyll 284 F4
Three Bridges Lincs 190 D6
Three Bridges W Sus 51 F9
Three Burrows Corn 4 F4
Three Chimneys Kent 53 F10
Three Cocked Hat Norf 143 D8
Three Cocks / Aberllynfi Powys 96 D3
Three Crosses Swansea 56 C5
Three Cups Corner E Sus 37 C10
Three Fingers Wrex 167 G7
Three Gates Dorset 29 F10
Threehammer Common Norf 160 E6
Three Hammers Corn 11 D10
Three Holes Norf 139 C10
Three Holes Cross Corn 10 G6
Threekingham Lincs 155 B11
Three Leg Cross E Sus 53 G7
Three Legged Cross Dorset 31 F9
Threelows Staffs 169 F9
Three Maypoles W Mid 118 B2
Threemile Cross Wokingham 65 F8
Three Mile Cross Wokingham 65 F8
Threemilestone Corn 4 G5
Threemiletown W Loth 279 F11
Three Oaks E Sus 38 E4
Threepwood Borders 271 G10
Three Sisters Denb 165 C9
Threewaters Corn 5 B10
Threlkeld Cumb 230 F2
Threshers Bush Essex 87 D7
Threshfield N Yorks 213 G9
Thrigby Norf 161 G9
Thringarth Durham 232 G4
Thringstone Leics 153 F8
Thrintoft N Yorks 224 G6
Thriplow Cambs 105 B8
Throapham S Yorks 187 D8
Throckenholt Lincs 139 B7
Throcking Herts 104 E6
Throckley T&W 242 D5
Throckmorton Worcs 99 B9
Throop Dorset 18 C2
Throphill Northumb 252 F4
Thropton Northumb 252 C2
Throsk Stirl 279 C7
Througham Glos 80 D6
Throughgate Dumfries 247 G9
Throwleigh Devon 13 C9
Throwley Kent 54 B3
Throwley Forstal Kent 54 C3
Throxenby N Yorks 217 B10
Thrumpton Notts 153 C10
Thrumpton Notts 188 E2
Thrumster Highld 310 E7
Thrunton Northumb 264 G3
Thrupe Som 44 D6
Thrupp Glos 80 E5
Thrupp Oxon 82 F3
Thrupp Oxon 83 B7
Thruscross N Yorks 205 B9
Thrushelton Devon 12 D4
Thrussington Leics 154 F2
Thruxton Hants 47 D9
Thruxton Hereford 97 E8
Thrybergh S Yorks 187 B7
Thulston Derbys 153 C8
Thunder Bridge W Yorks 197 E7
Thundergay N Ayrs 255 C9
Thunder Hill Norf 161 F8
Thunder's Hill E Sus 23 C9
Thundersley Essex 69 B9
Thundridge Herts 86 B5
Thurcaston Leics 153 G11
Thurcroft S Yorks 187 D7
Thurdon Corn 24 E3
Thurgarton Norf 160 C3
Thurgarton Notts 171 F11
Thurgoland S Yorks 197 G9
Thurlaston Leics 135 D10
Thurlaston Warks 119 C9
Thurlbear Som 28 C3
Thurlby Lincs 156 F2
Thurlby Lincs 172 C6
Thurlby Lincs 191 F7
Thurleigh Beds 121 F11
Thurlestone Devon 8 G3
Thurloxton Som 43 G9
Thurlstone S Yorks 197 G8
Thurlton Norf 143 D8
Thurlton Links Norf 143 D8
Thurlwood Ches E 168 D4
Thurmaston Leics 136 B2
Thurnby Leics 136 C2
Thurne Norf 161 F8
Thurnham Kent 53 B10
Thurnham Lancs 202 C5
Thurning Norf 159 D11
Thurning Northants 137 G11
Thurnscoe S Yorks 198 F3
Thurnscoe East S Yorks 198 F3
Thursby Cumb 239 G8
Thursford Norf 159 C9
Thursford Green Norf 159 C9
Thursley Sur 50 F2
Thurso Highld 310 C5
Thurso East Highld 310 C5
Thurstaston Mers 182 E2
Thurston Suff 125 D8
Thurston Clough Gtr Man 196 F3
Thurston End Suff 124 G5
Thurstonfield Cumb 239 F8
Thurstonland W Yorks 197 E7
Thurton Norf 142 C6
Thurvaston Derbys 152 B2
Thurvaston Derbys 152 B4
Thuxton Norf 141 B10
Thwaite N Yorks 223 F7
Thwaite Suff 126 D2
Thwaite Flat Cumb 210 E4
Thwaite Head Cumb 220 G6
Thwaites W Yorks 205 E7
Thwaite St Mary Norf 142 E6
Thwaites Brow W Yorks 205 E7
Thwing E Yorks 217 E11
Tibbermore Perth 286 E4
Tibberton Glos 98 G5
Tibberton Telford 150 E3
Tibberton Worcs 117 F8
Tibenham Norf 142 F2
Tibshelf Derbys 170 C6
Tibshelf Wharf Notts 171 C7
Tibthorpe E Yorks 208 B5
Ticehurst E Sus 53 G7
Tichborne Hants 48 G5
Tickencote Rutland 137 B9
Tickenham N Som 60 E3
Ticket Wood Devon 8 G4
Tickford End M Keynes 103 C7
Tickhill S Yorks 187 C9
Tickleback Row Brack 65 E11
Ticklerton Shrops 131 E9
Tickmorend Glos 80 F4
Ticknall Derbys 153 E7
Tickton E Yorks 209 E7
Tidbury Green W Mid 117 B11
Tidcombe Wilts 47 B9
Tiddington Oxon 83 E11
Tiddington Warks 118 F4
Tidebrook E Sus 37 B10
Tideford Corn 6 D6
Tideford Cross Corn 6 C6
Tidenham Glos 79 F9
Tidenham Chase Glos 79 F9
Tideswell Derbys 185 F11
Tidmarsh W Berks 64 E6
Tidmington Warks 100 D5
Tidnor Hereford 97 D11
Tidpit Hants 31 D9
Tidworth Wilts 47 D8
Tiers Cross Pembs 72 C6
Tiffield Northants 120 G3
Tifty Aberds 303 E7
Tigerton Angus 293 G7
Tigh-na-Blair Perth 285 F11
Tighnabruaich Argyll 275 F10
Tighnacachla Argyll 274 G3
Tighnafiline Highld 307 L3
Tighness Argyll 284 G6
Tigley Devon 8 C5
Tilbrook Cambs 121 D11
Tilbury Thurrock 68 D6
Tilbury Green Essex 106 C4
Tilbury Juxta Clare Essex 106 C5
Tile Cross W Mid 134 F3
Tilegate Green Essex 87 D8
Tile Hill W Mid 118 B5
Tilehouse Green W Mid 118 B3
Tilehurst Reading 65 E7
Tilekiln Green Essex 105 G10
Tiley Dorset 29 F11
Tilford Sur 49 E11
Tilford Common Sur 49 E11
Tilford Reeds Sur 49 E11
Tilgate W Sus 51 G9
Tilgate Forest Row W Sus 51 G9
Tilkey Essex 106 G6
Tilland Corn 6 C6
Tillathrowie Aberds 302 F4
Tillers' Green Glos 98 E3
Tilley Shrops 149 D10
Tilley Green Shrops 149 D10
Tillicoultry Clack 279 B8
Tillietudlem S Lnrk 268 F6
Tillingham Essex 89 E7
Tillington Hereford 97 B9
Tillington Staffs 151 E8
Tillington W Sus 35 C7
Tillington Common Hereford 97 B9
Tillislow Devon 12 C3
Tillworth Devon 28 G4
Tillyarblet Angus 293 G7
Tillybirloch Aberds 293 C8
Tillycorthie Aberds 303 G9
Tilly Down Hants 47 D10
Tillydrine Aberds 293 D8
Tillyfour Aberds 293 B7
Tillyfourie Aberds 293 B8
Tillygarmond Aberds 293 D8
Tillygreig Aberds 303 G8
Tillykerrie Aberds 303 G8
Tilly Lo Aberds 293 C7
Tillynaught Aberds 302 C5
Tilmanstone Kent 55 C10
Tilney All Saints Norf 157 F11
Tilney cum Islington Norf 157 G11
Tilney Fen End Norf 157 G10
Tilney High End Norf 157 F11
Tilney St Lawrence Norf 157 G10
Tilsdown Glos 80 F2
Tilshead Wilts 46 D4
Tilsmore E Sus 37 C9
Tilsop Shrops 116 C2
Tilstock Shrops 149 B10
Tilston Ches W 167 E7
Tilstone Bank Ches W 167 D9
Tilstone Fearnall Ches W 167 C9
Tilsworth C Beds 103 G9
Tilton on the Hill Leics 136 B4
Tilts S Yorks 198 F5
Tiltups End Glos 80 F4
Tilty Essex 105 F11
Timberden Bottom Kent 68 G4
Timberhonger Worcs 117 C8
Timberland Lincs 173 D10
Timbersbrook Ches E 168 C5
Timberscombe Som 42 E3
Timble N Yorks 205 C9
Timbold Hill Kent 54 B2
Timbrelham Corn 12 E3
Timperley Gtr Man 184 D3
Timsbury Bath 45 B7
Timsbury Hants 32 C4
Timsgearraidh W Isles 304 E2
Timworth Suff 125 D7
Timworth Green Suff 125 D7
Tincleton Dorset 17 C11
Tindale Cumb 240 F4
Tindale Crescent Durham 233 F9
Tindon End Essex 106 E2
Tingewick Bucks 102 E3
Tingley W Yorks 197 B9
Tingon Shetland 312 E4
Tingrith C Beds 103 E10
Tingwall Orkney 314 D3
Tinhay Devon 12 E3
Tinkers End Bucks 102 F5
Tinshill W Yorks 205 F11
Tinsley S Yorks 186 C6
Tinsley Green W Sus 51 F9
Tintagel Corn 11 D7
Tintern Parva Mon 79 E8
Tintinhull Som 29 D8
Tintwistle Derbys 185 B8
Tinwald Dumfries 248 G2
Tinwell Rutland 137 B10
Tipner Ptsmth 33 G10
Tippacott Devon 41 D9
Tipper's Hill Warks 134 F5
Tipperty Aberds 302 C6
Tipperty Aberds 303 G9
Tipple Cross Devon 12 D3
Tipps End Norf 139 D10
Tip's Cross Essex 87 E9
Tiptoe Hants 19 B11
Tipton W Mid 133 E8
Tipton Green W Mid 133 E9
Tipton St John Devon 15 C7
Tiptree Essex 88 B5
Tiptree Heath Essex 88 B5
Tirabad Powys 95 C7
Tiraghoil Argyll 288 G5
Tircanol Swansea 57 B7
Tirdeunaw Swansea 57 B7
Tirinie Perth 291 G10
Tirley Glos 98 F6
Tirley Knowle Glos 98 F6
Tiroran Argyll 288 G6
Tirphil Caerph 77 E10
Tirril Cumb 230 F6
Tirryside Highld 309 H5
Tir-y-berth Caerph 77 F11
Tir-y-dail Carms 75 C10
Tisbury Wilts 30 B6
Tisman's Common W Sus 50 G5
Tissington Derbys 169 E11
Titchberry Devon 24 B2
Titchfield Hants 33 F8
Titchfield Common Hants 33 F8
Titchfield Park Hants 33 F8
Titchmarsh Northants 121 B10
Titchwell Norf 176 E3
Titcomb W Berks 63 F11
Tithby Notts 154 B3
Tithebarn Staffs 169 G9
Tithe Barn Hillock Mers 183 B9
Titley Hereford 114 E6
Titlington Northumb 264 F4
Titmore Green Herts 104 F4
Titsey Sur 52 C2
Titson Corn 24 G2
Tittenhurst Windsor 66 F3
Tittensor Staffs 151 B7
Titterhill Shrops 131 G10
Tittle Row Windsor 65 C11
Tittleshall Norf 159 E7
Titton Worcs 116 D6
Titty Hill W Sus 34 B5
Tiverton Ches W 167 C9
Tiverton Devon 27 E7
Tivetshall St Margaret Norf 142 F3
Tivetshall St Mary Norf 142 F3
Tividale W Mid 133 E9
Tivington Som 42 D2
Tivington Knowle Som 42 E2
Tivoli Cumb 228 G5
Tivy Dale S Yorks 197 F9
Tixall Staffs 151 E9
Tixover Rutland 137 C9
Toab Orkney 314 F5
Toab Shetland 313 M5
Toadmoor Derbys 170 E4
Toad Row Suff 143 F10
Tobermory Argyll 289 D7
Toberonochy Argyll 275 C8
Tobha Beag W Isles 296 D5
Tobha Mor W Isles 297 H3
Tobhtarol W Isles 304 E3
Tobson W Isles 304 E3
Toby's Hill Lincs 191 C7
Tocher Aberds 302 F6
Tockenham Wilts 62 D4
Tockenham Wick Wilts 62 C4
Tockholes Blkburn 195 C7
Tockington S Glos 60 B6
Tockwith N Yorks 206 C5
Todber Dorset 30 C4
Todding Hereford 115 B8
Toddington C Beds 103 F10
Toddington Glos 99 E10
Toddington W Sus 35 G8
Toddlehills Aberds 303 E10
Todd's Green Herts 104 F4
Todenham Glos 100 D4
Todhill Angus 287 D8
Todhills Cumb 239 E9
Todhills Durham 233 E10
Todlachie Aberds 293 B8
Todmorden W Yorks 196 C2
Todpool Corn 4 G4
Todrig Borders 261 F10
Todwick S Yorks 187 E7
Toft Cambs 123 F7
Toft Lincs 155 F11
Toft Shetland 312 F6
Toft Warks 119 C9
Toft Hill Durham 233 F9
Toft Hill Lincs 174 C2
Toft Monks Norf 143 E8
Toft next Newton Lincs 189 D8
Toftrees Norf 159 D7
Tofts Highld 310 C7
Toftshaw W Yorks 197 B7
Toftwood Norf 159 G9
Togston Northumb 252 C6
Tokavaig Highld 295 D8
Tokers Green Oxon 65 D8
Tokyngton London 67 C7
Tolastadh a Chaolais W Isles 304 E3
Tolastadh bho Thuath W Isles 304 D7
Tolborough Corn 11 F9
Tolcarne Corn 2 B5
Tolcarne Corn 2 C5
Tolcarne Wartha Corn 2 B5
Toldish Corn 5 D8
Tolgus Mount Corn 4 G3
Tolhurst E Sus 53 G7
Tolladine Worcs 117 F7
Tolland Som 42 G6
Tollard Farnham Dorset 30 D6
Tollard Royal Wilts 30 D6
Toll Bar Mers 183 C7
Toll Bar Rutland 137 B10
Toll Bar S Yorks 198 F5
Tollbar End W Mid 119 B7
Toll End W Mid 133 E9
Tollerford Dorset 17 B7
Toller Fratrum Dorset 17 B7
Toller Porcorum Dorset 17 B7
Tollerton Notts 154 C2
Tollerton N Yorks 215 G10
Toller Whelme Dorset 29 G8
Tollesbury Essex 89 C7
Tollesby Mbro 225 B10
Tolleshunt D'Arcy Essex 88 C6
Tolleshunt Knights Essex 88 C6
Tolleshunt Major Essex 88 C5
Tollie Highld 300 D5
Toll of Birness Aberds 303 F10
Tolm W Isles 304 E6
Tolmers Herts 86 E4
Tolpuddle Dorset 17 C11
Tolskithy Corn 4 G3
Tolvaddon Downs Corn 4 G3
Tolvah Highld 291 D10
Tolworth London 67 F7
Tomaknock Perth 286 E2
Tom an Fhuadain W Isles 305 G5
Tomatin Highld 301 G8
Tombreck Highld 300 F6
Tombui Perth 286 B2
Tomchrasky Highld 290 B4
Tomdoun Highld 290 C3
Tomich Highld 300 B6
Tomich Highld 300 G3
Tomich House Highld 300 E5
Tomintoul Aberds 292 D3
Tomintoul Moray 292 B3
Tomlow Warks 119 E9
Tomnaven Moray 302 F4
Tomnavoulin Moray 302 G2
Tomperrow Corn 4 G5
Tompkin Staffs 168 E6
Tompset's Bank E Sus 52 G2
Tomsleibhe Argyll 289 F8
Tomthorn Derbys 185 F9
Ton Mon 78 F5
Ton Breigam V Glam 58 D3
Tonbridge Kent 52 D5
Tonderghie Dumfries 236 F6
Tondu Bridgend 57 E11
Tone Som 27 C10
Tonedale Som 27 C10
Tone Green Som 27 C11
Tong Kent 53 D10
Tong Shrops 132 B5
Tong W Yorks 205 G10
Tonge Leics 153 E8
Tonge Corner Kent 70 F2
Tonge Fold Gtr Man 195 F8
Tonge Moor Gtr Man 195 E8
Tong Forge Shrops 132 B5
Tong Green Kent 54 C3
Tongham Sur 49 D11
Tongland Dumfries 237 D8
Tong Norton Shrops 132 B5
Tong Park W Yorks 205 F9
Tong Street W Yorks 205 G9
Tongue Highld 308 D5
Tongue End Lincs 156 F3
Tongwell M Keynes 103 C7
Tongwynlais Cardiff 58 C6
Tonmawr Neath 57 B10
Tonnau / Tonnau Neath 57 B9
Tonnau / Tonna Neath 57 B9
Ton-Pentre Rhondda 77 F7
Ton-teg Rhondda 58 B5
Tontine Lancs 194 G4
Tonwell Herts 86 B4
Tonypandy Rhondda 77 G7
Ton-y-pistyll Caerph 77 F11
Tonyrefail Rhondda 58 B4
Toot Baldon Oxon 83 E9
Toothill Hants 32 D5
Toothill Swindon 62 C6
Toothill W Yorks 196 C6
Toot Hill Essex 87 E8
Toot Hill Staffs 169 G9
Tooting Graveney London 67 E9
Topcliffe N Yorks 215 D8
Topcliffe W Yorks 197 B9
Topcroft Norf 142 E5
Topcroft Street Norf 142 E5
Top End Beds 121 E10
Top Green Notts 172 F3
Topham S Yorks 198 D6
Topleigh W Sus 34 D6
Top Lock Gtr Man 194 F6
Top of Hebers Gtr Man 195 F11
Top o' th' Lane Lancs 194 C5
Top o' th' Meadows Gtr Man 196 F3
Toppesfield Essex 106 D4
Toppings Gtr Man 195 E8
Toprow Norf 142 D3
Topsham Devon 14 D5
Top Valley Nottingham 171 F9
Torbeg N Ayrs 255 E10
Torboll Farm Highld 309 K7
Torbothie N Lnrk 269 D7
Torbreck Highld 309 J7
Torbrex Stirl 278 C5
Torbryan Devon 8 B6
Torbush N Lnrk 268 D6
Torcross Devon 8 G6
Torcroy Highld 291 D9
Tore Highld 300 D6
Torfrey Corn 6 E2
Torgyle Highld 290 B5
Torinturk Argyll 275 G9
Torkington Gtr Man 184 D6
Torksey Lincs 188 F4
Torlum W Isles 296 F3
Torlundy Highld 290 F3
Tormarton S Glos 61 D9
Tormisdale Argyll 254 B2
Tormitchell S Ayrs 244 E6
Tormore Highld 295 E8
Tormore N Ayrs 255 D9
Tornagrain Highld 301 E7
Tornahaish Aberds 292 C4
Tornapress Highld 299 E8
Tornaveen Aberds 293 C8
Torness Highld 300 G5
Toronto Durham 233 E9
Torpenhow Cumb 229 D10
Torphichen W Loth 279 G9
Torphin Edin 270 B4
Torphins Aberds 293 C8
Torpoint Corn 7 E8
Torquay Torbay 9 C8
Torquhan Borders 271 F8
Torr Devon 7 E11
Torr Devon 8 C2
Torra Argyll 254 B4
Torran Argyll 275 C9
Torran Highld 298 E5
Torran Highld 301 B7
Torrance E Dunb 278 G2
Torrans Argyll 288 G6
Torranyard N Ayrs 267 G7
Torre Som 42 E4
Torre Torbay 9 C8
Torridon Highld 299 D9
Torridon Ho Highld 299 D8
Torries Aberds 293 B8
Torrin Highld 295 C7
Torrisdale Highld 308 C6
Torrisdale Castle Argyll 255 D8
Torrisdale-Square Argyll 255 D8
Torrish Highld 311 H3
Torrisholme Lancs 211 G9
Torroble Highld 309 J5
Torroy Highld 309 K5
Torrpark Corn 11 D10
Torry Aberdeen 293 C11
Torry Aberds 302 F4
Torryburn Fife 279 D10
Torsonce Borders 271 G9
Torsonce Mains Borders 271 G9
Torterston Aberds 303 E10
Torthorwald Dumfries 238 B2
Tortington W Sus 35 F8
Torton Worcs 116 C6
Tortworth S Glos 80 G2
Torvaig Highld 298 E4
Torver Cumb 220 G5
Torwood Falk 278 E6
Torwoodlee Mains Borders 261 B11
Torworth Notts 187 D11
Tosberry Devon 24 C3
Toscaig Highld 295 B9
Toseland Cambs 122 E4
Tosside N Yorks 203 B11
Tostock Suff 125 E9
Totaig Highld 295 C10
Totaig Highld 298 D2
Totardor Highld 294 B5
Tote Highld 298 E4
Totegan Highld 310 C2
Tote Hill Hants 32 C4
Tote Hill W Sus 34 C5
Totford Hants 48 F5
Totham Hill Essex 88 C5
Totham Plains Essex 88 C5
Tothill Lincs 190 E6
Tot Hill Hants 64 G3
Totland IoW 20 D2
Totley S Yorks 186 F4
Totley Brook S Yorks 186 E4
Totley Rise S Yorks 186 E4
Totmonslow Staffs 151 B9
Totnell Dorset 29 F10
Totnes Devon 8 C6
Totnor Hereford 97 E11
Toton Notts 153 C10
Totronald Argyll 288 D3
Totscore Highld 298 C3
Tottenham London 86 G4
Tottenham Hale London 67 B10
Tottenhill Norf 158 G2
Tottenhill Row Norf 158 G2
Totteridge Bucks 84 G5
Totteridge London 86 G2
Totternhoe C Beds 103 G9
Totteroak S Glos 61 C8
Totterton Shrops 131 F7
Totties W Yorks 197 F7
Tottington Gtr Man 195 E9
Tottington Norf 141 D7
Tottlebank Cumb 210 C6
Tottleworth Lancs 203 G10
Totton Hants 32 E5
Touchen End Windsor 65 D11
Toulston N Yorks 206 E5
Toulton Som 43 G7
Toulvaddie Highld 311 L2
Tournaig Highld 307 L3
Toux Aberds 303 D9
Tovil Kent 53 C9
Towan Corn 10 G3
Towan Cross Corn 4 F4
Toward Argyll 266 B2
Towcester Northants 102 B3
Towednack Corn 1 B5
Towerage Bucks 84 G4
Tower End Norf 158 F3
Tower Hamlets Kent 55 E10
Towerhead N Som 44 B2
Tower Hill Ches E 184 F6
Tower Hill Devon 12 C3
Tower Hill Essex 108 E5
Tower Hill Herts 85 E8
Tower Hill Mers 194 G2
Tower Hill Sur 51 D7
Tower Hill W Mid 133 E11
Tower Hill W Sus 35 B11
Towersey Oxon 84 D2
Tow House Northumb 241 E7
Towie Aberds 292 B6
Towie Aberds 302 G5
Towie Aberds 303 C8
Towiemore Moray 302 E3
Tow Law Durham 233 D8
Town Barton Devon 14 C2
Townend Derbys 185 E9
Townend Staffs 151 B9
Townend W Dunb 277 F8
Town End Bucks 84 F3
Town End Cambs 139 D8
Town End Cumb 211 B7
Town End Cumb 211 C8
Town End Cumb 212 C2
Town End Cumb 220 D6
Town End Cumb 221 E8
Town End Cumb 221 F7
Town End Cumb 231 F8
Town End Derbys 185 F11
Town End E Yorks 207 C10
Town End Mers 183 D7
Town End W Yorks 196 D5
Townfield Durham 232 B5
Town Fields Ches W 167 B10
Towngate Cumb 230 B6
Towngate Lincs 156 G2
Town Green Gtr Man 183 B9
Town Green Lancs 194 F2
Town Green Norf 161 G7
Townhead Argyll 275 G11
Townhead Cumb 229 D7
Townhead Cumb 230 D6
Townhead Cumb 231 E8
Townhead Dumfries 237 E8
Townhead N Lnrk 268 B4
Townhead Northumb 251 E9
Townhead S Ayrs 244 C6
Townhead S Yorks 186 E4
Townhead S Yorks 197 G7
Town Head Cumb 220 D6
Town Head Cumb 221 E8
Town Head Cumb 222 C2
Town Head Cumb 222 C3
Town Head Cumb 231 F7
Town Head Cumb 231 F8
Town Head Cumb 231 G8
Town Head Cumb 231 G9
Town Head Derbys 185 F11
Town Head N Yorks 204 B2
Town Head N Yorks 212 F5
Town Head Staffs 169 F8
Town Head W Yorks 204 D6
Townhead of Greenlaw Dumfries 237 C9
Townhill Fife 280 D2
Townhill Swansea 56 C6
Townhill Park Hants 33 E7
Town Kelloe Durham 234 D3
Townlake Devon 12 G4
Townland Green Kent 54 G2
Town Lane Gtr Man 183 B11
Town Littleworth E Sus 36 D6
Town of Lowton Mers 183 B10
Town Park Telford 132 B3
Town Row E Sus 52 G5
Townsend Bath 44 B5
Townsend Bucks 84 D2
Townsend Devon 25 B10
Townsend Herts 85 D10
Townsend Oxon 63 B11
Townsend Pembs 72 D4
Townsend Som 44 C4
Townsend Stoke 168 F6
Townsend Wilts 46 B3
Townsend Wilts 46 B4
Towns End Hants 48 B5
Towns End Som 30 D2
Town's End Bucks 102 G2
Town's End Dorset 18 B3
Town's End Dorset 18 E5
Town's End Dorset 29 F9
Town's End Som 45 D7
Townsend Fold Lancs 195 C10
Townshend Corn 2 C3
Town Street Glos 98 F6
Townwell S Glos 79 G11
Town Yetholm Borders 263 D8
Towthorpe E Yorks 217 G8

Towthorpe York 207 B8
Towton N Yorks 206 F5
Towyn Conwy 181 F7
Toxteth Mers 182 D5
Toynton All Saints Lincs 174 C5
Toynton Fen Side Lincs 174 C5
Toynton St Peter Lincs 174 C6
Toy's Hill Kent 52 C3
Trabboch E Ayrs 257 E10
Traboe Corn 2 E6
Trabrown Borders 271 F10
Tracebridge Som 27 C9
Tradespark Highld 301 D8
Tradespark Orkney 314 F4
Trafford Park Gtr Man 184 B3
Traigh Ho Highld 295 F8
Trallong Powys 95 F9
Trallwn Rhondda 77 G9
Trallwn Swansea 57 B7
Tramagenna Corn 11 E7
Tram Inn Hereford 97 E9
Tranch Torf 78 E3
Tranent E Loth 281 G8
Tranmere Mers 182 D4
Trantlebeg Highld 310 D2
Trantlemore Highld 310 D2
Tranwell Northumb 252 G5
Trapp Carms 75 B11
Traprain E Loth 281 F11
Trap's Green Warks 118 D2
Trapshill W Berks 63 G11
Traquair Borders 261 C8
Trash Green W Berks 65 F7
Travellers' Rest Carms 74 B5
Trawden Lancs 204 F4
Trawscoed Powys 95 E11
Trawsfynydd Gwyn 146 B4
Trawsnant Ceredig 111 D11
Treadam Mon 78 B5
Treaddow Hereford 97 G10
Treal Corn 2 F6
Trealaw Rhondda 77 G8
Treales Lancs 202 G4
Trearddur Anglesey 178 F3
Treaslane Highld 298 D3
Treath Corn 3 D7
Treator Corn 10 F4
Tre-Aubrey V Glam 58 E4
Trebanog Rhondda 77 G8
Trebanos Neath 76 E2
Trebarber Corn 5 C7
Trebartha Corn 11 F11
Trebarwith Corn 11 D7
Trebarwith Strand Corn 10 D6
Trebeath Corn 11 D11
Tre-Beferad V Glam 58 F3
Trebell Green Corn 5 C11
Treberfydd Powys 96 F2
Trebetherick Corn 10 F4
Trebilcock Corn 5 C9
Treble's Holford Som 43 G7
Tre-boeth Swansea 57 B7
Treborough Som 42 F4
Trebudannon Corn 5 C7
Trebullett Corn 12 F2
Treburgett Corn 11 F7
Treburgie Corn 6 C4
Treburley Corn 12 F3
Treburrick Corn 10 G3
Trebyan Corn 5 C11
Trecastle Powys 95 F7
Trecenydd Caerph 58 B6
Trecott Devon 25 G10
Trecwn Pembs 91 E9
Trecynon Rhondda 77 E7
Tredannick Corn 10 G6
Tredaule Corn 11 E10
Tredavoe Corn 1 D5
Treddiog Pembs 91 F7
Tredegar Bl Gwent 77 D10
Trederwen Powys 148 F5
Tre-derwen Powys 148 F4
Tredethy Corn 11 G7
Tredington Glos 99 F8
Tredington Warks 100 C5
Tredinnick Corn 1 C4
Tredinnick Corn 5 D10
Tredinnick Corn 6 B3
Tredinnick Corn 6 D4
Tredinnick Corn 10 G4
Tredogan V Glam 58 F5
Tredomen Caerph 77 G10
Tredomen Powys 96 E2
Tredown Devon 24 D2
Tredrizzick Corn 10 F5
Tredunnock Mon 78 G5
Tredustan Powys 96 E2
Tredworth Glos 80 B4
Treen Corn 1 B4
Treen Corn 1 E3
Treesmill Corn 5 D11
Treeton S Yorks 186 D6
Trefaes Gwyn 144 C5
Trefanny Hill Corn 6 D4
Trefasser Pembs 91 D7
Trefdraeth Anglesey 178 G6
Trefdraeth / Newport Pembs 91 D11
Trefecca Powys 96 E2
Trefechan Ceredig 111 A11
Trefechan M Tydf 77 D8
Trefechan Wrex 166 F3
Trefeglwys Powys 129 E9
Trefeitha Powys 96 E2
Trefenter Ceredig 112 D2
Treffgarne Pembs 91 G9
Treffynnon Pembs 90 F6
Treffynnon / Holywell Flint 181 F11
Trefgarn Owen Pembs 91 F7
Trefil Bl Gwent 77 C10
Trefilan Ceredig 111 F11
Trefin / Trevine Pembs 90 E6
Treflach Shrops 148 D5
Trefnanney Powys 148 F4
Trefnant Denb 181 G9
Trefonen Shrops 148 D5
Trefor Anglesey 178 E5
Trefor Gwyn 162 F5
Treforda Corn 11 E7
Treforest Rhondda 58 B5
Treforgan Ceredig 92 B4
Tre-Forgan Neath 76 D3
Treforys / Morriston Swansea 57 B7
Trefriw Conwy 164 C3
Trefrize Corn 12 F2
Tref y Clawdd / Knighton Powys 114 C5
Trefynwy / Monmouth Mon 79 C8
Tregada Corn 12 E2
Tregadgwith Corn 1 D4
Tregadillett Corn 12 E2
Tre-gagle Mon 79 D8
Tregaian Anglesey 178 F6
Tregajorran Corn 4 G3
Tregamere Corn 5 C8
Tregardock Corn 10 E6
Tregare Mon 78 C6
Tregarland Corn 6 D5
Tregarlandbridge Corn 6 D4
Tregarne Corn 3 E7
Tregaron Ceredig 112 F3
Tregarrick Mill Corn 6 D4
Tregarth Gwyn 163 B10
Tregath Gwyn 163 B10
Tregatillian Corn 5 C8
Tregatta Corn 11 D7
Tregavarah Corn 1 D4
Tregear Corn 2 E5
Tregeare Corn 11 D10
Tregeiriog Wrex 148 C3
Tregele Anglesey 178 C5
Tregellist Corn 10 F6
Tregeseal Corn 1 C3
Tregew Corn 3 C8
Tre-Gibbon Rhondda 77 E7
Tregidden Corn 3 E7
Treginnis Pembs 90 G4
Treglemais Pembs 90 F6
Tregole Corn 11 B9
Tregolls Corn 2 B6
Tregolwyn / Colwinston V Glam 58 D2
Tregona Corn 5 B7
Tregonce Corn 10 G4
Tregonetha Corn 5 C9
Tregonna Corn 10 G4
Tregonning Corn 5 D7
Tregony Corn 5 G8
Tregoodwell Corn 11 E8
Tregorden Corn 10 G6
Tregorrick Corn 5 E10
Tregoss Corn 5 C9
Tregoyd Powys 96 D4
Tregoyd Mill Powys 96 D3
Tregreenwell Corn 11 E7
Tregrehan Mills Corn 5 E10
Tregroes Ceredig 93 C8
Tregullon Corn 5 C11
Tregunna Corn 10 G5
Tregurrian Corn 5 B7
Tregurtha Downs Corn 2 C2
Tre Gwyr / Gowerton Swansea 56 B5
Tregyddulan Pembs 91 D7
Tregynon Powys 129 D11
Tre-gynwr Carms 74 B6
Trehafod Rhondda 77 G8
Trehafren Powys 129 E11
Trehan Corn 7 D8
Treharris M Tydf 77 F9
Trehemborne Corn 10 G3
Treherbert Rhondda 76 F6
Tre-hill V Glam 58 E5
Trehunist Corn 6 C6
Tre-Ifor Rhondda 77 D7
Trekeivesteps Corn 11 G10
Trekenner Corn 12 F2
Trekenning Corn 5 C8
Treknow Corn 11 D7
Trelales / Laleston Bridgend 57 F11
Trelan Corn 2 F6
Tre-lan Flint 165 B11
Trelash Corn 11 C9
Trelassick Corn 5 E7
Trelawnyd Flint 181 F9
Trelech Carms 92 E5
Treleddyd-fawr Pembs 90 F5
Treleigh Corn 4 G4
Treletert / Letterston Pembs 91 F8
Trelew Corn 3 B8
Trelewis M Tydf 77 F10
Treligga Corn 11 E7
Trelights Corn 10 F5
Trelill Corn 10 F6
Trelion Corn 5 E8
Treliske Corn 4 F6
Trelissick Corn 3 B8
Treliver Corn 5 B9
Trellech Mon 79 D8
Trelleck Grange Mon 79 E7
Trelogan Flint 181 E10
Treloquithack Corn 2 D5
Trelowia Corn 6 D5
Trelowth Corn 5 E9
Trelystan Powys 130 C5
Tremadog Gwyn 163 G9
Tremail Corn 11 D9
Tremain Ceredig 92 B4
Tremaine Corn 11 D10
Tremains Bridgend 58 D2
Tremar Corn 6 B5
Trematon Corn 7 D7
Trematon Castle Corn 7 D8
Tremayne Corn 2 B4
Trembraze Corn 6 B5
Tremedda Corn 1 B5
Tremeirchion Denb 181 G9
Tremethick Cross Corn 1 C4
Tremore Corn 5 C10
Tremorebridge Corn 5 C10
Tremorfa Cardiff 59 D8
Tre-Mostyn Flint 181 F10
Trenance Corn 4 C6
Trenance Corn 5 B7
Trenance Corn 5 C9
Trenance Corn 10 G4
Trenant Corn 6 B4
Trenant Corn 10 G5
Trenarren Corn 5 F10
Trenay Corn 6 B3
Trench Telford 150 G3
Trench Green Oxon 65 D7
Trench Wood Kent 52 D5
Trencreek Corn 4 C6
Trencrom Corn 2 B2
Trendeal Corn 5 E7
Trenear Corn 2 C5
Treneglos Corn 11 D10
Trenerth Corn 2 B4
Trenewan Corn 6 E3
Trengune Corn 11 C9
Trenhorne Corn 11 F11
Treningle Corn 5 B10
Treninnick Corn 4 C6
Trenoon Corn 2 F6
Trenoweth Corn 3 C7
Trent Dorset 29 D9
Trentham Stoke 168 G5
Trentishoe Devon 40 D6
Trentlock Derbys 153 C9
Trent Vale Stoke 168 G5
Trenwheal Corn 2 C4
Treoes V Glam 58 D2
Treopert / Granston Pembs 91 E7
Treorchy / Treorci Rhondda 77 F7
Treorci / Treorchy Rhondda 77 F7
Treowen Caerph 78 F2
Treowen Powys 130 E2
Tre-pit V Glam 58 E2
Trequite Corn 10 F6
Tre'r-ddôl Ceredig 128 E3
Trerhyngyll V Glam 58 D4
Trerise Corn 2 F6
Trer Ilai / Leighton Powys 130 B4
Trerose Corn 3 D7
Trerulefoot Corn 6 D6
Tresaith Ceredig 110 G5
Tresamble Corn 3 B7
Tresarrett Corn 11 G7
Tresavean Corn 2 B6
Tresawle Corn 5 F7
Tresawsen Corn 4 F5
Trescoll Corn 5 C10
Trescott Staffs 132 D6
Trescowe Corn 2 C3
Tresean Corn 4 D5
Tresevern Croft Corn 2 B6
Tresham Glos 80 G3
Tresigin / Sigingstone V Glam 58 E3
Tresillian Corn 5 F7
Tresimwn / Bonvilston V Glam 58 E5
Tresinney Corn 11 E8
Tresinwen Pembs 91 C7
Treskerby Corn 4 G4
Treskillard Corn 2 B5
Treskilling Corn 5 D10
Treskinnick Cross Corn 11 B10
Treslothan Corn 2 B5
Tresmeer Corn 11 D10
Tresowes Green Corn 2 D3
Tresoweshill Corn 2 D4
Tresparrett Corn 11 C8
Tresparrett Posts Corn 11 C8
Tressady Highld 309 J7
Tressait Perth 291 G10
Tresta Shetland 312 D8
Tresta Shetland 313 H5
Treswell Notts 188 F3
Treswithian Corn 4 G2
Treswithian Downs Corn 4 G2
Tre-Taliesin Ceredig 128 E3
Trethellan Water Corn 2 B6
Trethevy Corn 11 D7
Trethewell Corn 3 B9
Trethewey Corn 1 E3
Trethillick Corn 10 F4
Trethomas Caerph 59 B7
Trethosa Corn 5 E8
Trethowel Corn 5 E10
Trethurgy Corn 5 D10
Tretio Pembs 90 F5
Tretire Hereford 97 G10
Tretower Powys 96 G3
Treuddyn Flint 166 D3
Trevadlock Corn 11 F11
Trevail Corn 4 D5
Trevalga Corn 11 D7
Trevalgan Corn 1 A5
Trevalyn Wrex 166 D5
Trevance Corn 10 G4
Trevanger Corn 10 F5
Trevanson Corn 10 G5
Trevarrack Corn 1 C5
Trevarren Corn 5 C8
Trevarrian Corn 4 B6
Trevarrick Corn 5 G9
Trevarth Corn 4 G4
Trevaughan Carms 73 B11
Trevaughan Carms 93 G7
Tre-vaughan Carms 93 G8
Treveal Corn 1 A5
Trevegean Corn 1 D3
Treveighan Corn 11 F7
Trevellas Corn 4 E4
Trevelmond Corn 6 C4
Trevelver Corn 10 G5
Trevemper Corn 4 D6
Treven Corn 11 D7
Trevena Corn 2 D4
Trevenen Corn 2 D5
Trevenen Bal Corn 2 D5
Trevenning Corn 11 F7
Treveor Corn 5 G9
Treverbyn Corn 5 D10
Treverbyn Corn 6 B4
Treverva Corn 3 C7
Trevescan Corn 1 E3
Trevethin Torf 78 E3
Trevia Corn 11 E7
Trevigro Corn 6 B6
Trevilder Corn 10 G6
Trevilla Corn 3 B8
Trevilson Corn 4 D6
Trevine Corn 10 F5
Trevine / Trefin Pembs 90 E6
Treviscoe Corn 5 D8
Treviskey Corn 2 B6
Trevithal Corn 1 D5
Trevoll Corn 4 D6
Trevone Corn 10 F3
Trevor Wrex 166 G3
Trevorrick Corn 10 G4
Trevor Uchaf Denb 166 G2
Trevowah Corn 4 D5
Trew Corn 2 D4
Trewalder Corn 11 E7
Trewarmett Corn 11 D7
Trewartha Corn 2 B2
Trewartha Corn 3 B10
Trewassa Corn 11 D8
Treween Corn 11 E10
Trewellard Corn 1 C3
Trewen Corn 11 E7
Trewen Corn 11 E11
Trewen Mon 79 G7
Trewennack Corn 2 D5
Trewennan Corn 11 E7
Trewern Powys 148 G5
Trewetha Corn 10 E6
Trewethen Corn 10 F6
Trewethern Corn 10 F6
Trewey Corn 1 B5
Trewidland Corn 6 D5
Trewindle Corn 6 C2
Trewint Corn 6 C5
Trewint Corn 11 B9
Trewint Corn 11 E10
Trewithian Corn 3 B9
Trewithick Corn 11 D11
Trewollock Corn 5 G10
Trewoodloe Corn 12 G2
Trewoofe Corn 1 D4
Trewoon Corn 2 F5
Trewoon Corn 5 E9
Treworga Corn 5 G7
Treworgan Common Mon 78 D6
Treworlas Corn 3 B9
Treworld Corn 11 C8
Trewornan Corn 10 G5
Treworrick Corn 6 B4
Treworthal Corn 3 B9
Trewyddel / Moylgrove Pembs 92 C2
Trewyn Devon 24 G4
Tre-wyn Mon 96 G6
Treyarnon Corn 10 G3
Treyford W Sus 34 D4
Trezaise Corn 5 D9
Trezelah Corn 1 C5
Triangle Glos 79 E8
Triangle Staffs 133 B11
Triangle W Yorks 196 C4
Trickett's Cross Dorset 31 G9
Triffleton Pembs 91 G9
Trillacott Corn 11 D11
Trimdon Durham 234 E3
Trimdon Colliery Durham 234 D3
Trimdon Grange Durham 234 D3
Trimingham Norf 160 B5
Trimley Lower Street Suff 108 D5
Trimley St Martin Suff 108 D5
Trimley St Mary Suff 108 D5
Trimpley Worcs 116 B5
Trimsaran Carms 75 E7
Trims Green Herts 87 B7
Trimstone Devon 40 E3
Trinafour Perth 291 G9
Trinant Caerph 78 E2
Tring Herts 84 C6
Tringford Herts 84 C6
Tring Wharf Herts 84 C6
Trinity Angus 293 G8
Trinity Devon 27 F7
Trinity Edin 280 F4
Trinity Fields Staffs 151 D8
Trisant Ceredig 112 B4
Triscombe Som 43 F7
Trislaig Highld 290 F2
Trispen Corn 4 E6
Tritlington Northumb 252 E6
Troan Corn 5 D7
Trochry Perth 286 C3
Trodigal Argyll 255 E7
Troearhiwgwair Bl Gwent 77 D11
Troedrhiwdalar Powys 113 G9
Troedrhiwffenyd Ceredig 93 C8
Troedrhiwfuwch Caerph 77 E10
Troedyraur Ceredig 92 B6
Troedyrhiw M Tydf 77 E9
Trofarth Conwy 180 G5
Trolliloes E Sus 23 C10
Tromode IoM 192 E4
Trondavoe Shetland 312 F5
Troon Corn 2 B5
Troon S Ayrs 257 C8
Trooper's Inn Pembs 73 C7
Trosaraidh W Isles 297 K3
Trossachs Hotel Stirl 285 G9
Troston Suff 125 C7
Trostre Carms 56 B4
Trostrey Common Mon 78 E5
Troswell Corn 11 C11
Trotshill Worcs 117 F7
Trotten Marsh W Sus 34 B4
Trottiscliffe Kent 68 G6
Trotton W Sus 34 C4
Trough Gate Lancs 195 C11
Troutbeck Cumb 221 E8
Troutbeck Cumb 230 F3
Troutbeck Bridge Cumb 221 F8
Troway Derbys 186 F5
Trowbridge Cardiff 59 C8
Trowbridge Wilts 45 B11
Trowell Notts 153 B9
Trow Green Glos 79 D9
Trowle Common Wilts 45 B10
Trowley Bottom Herts 85 C9
Trows Borders 262 C5
Trowse Newton Norf 142 B4
Troydale W Yorks 205 G10
Troy Town Kent 52 D2
Troy Town Kent 54 E5
Troy Town Medway 69 F8
Truas Corn 11 D7
Trub Gtr Man 195 F11
Trudoxhill Som 45 E8
Trueman's Heath Worcs 117 B11
True Street Devon 8 C6
Trull Som 28 C2
Trumaisgearraidh W Isles 296 D4
Trumfleet S Yorks 198 E6
Trumpan Highld 298 C2
Trumpet Hereford 98 D3
Trumpington Cambs 123 F8
Trumpsgreen Sur 66 F3
Trunch Norf 160 C5
Trunnah Lancs 202 E2
Truro Corn 4 G6
Truscott Corn 12 D2
Trusham Devon 14 E3
Trusley Derbys 152 B5
Trussall Corn 2 D5
Trussell Corn 11 D10
Trusthorpe Lincs 191 E8
Truthan Corn 4 E6
Truthwall Corn 2 C2
Trwstllewelyn Powys 130 D3
Tryfil Anglesey 178 E6
Trysull Staffs 133 E7
Trythogga Corn 1 C5
Tubbs Mill Corn 5 G9
Tubney Oxon 82 F6
Tubslake Kent 53 G9
Tuckenhay Devon 8 D6
Tuckermarsh Devon 7 B8
Tuckerton Som 28 B3
Tuckhill Shrops 132 F5
Tuckingmill Corn 4 G3
Tuckingmill Corn 11 F7
Tuckingmill Wilts 30 B6
Tucking Mill Bath 61 G9
Tuckton Bmouth 19 C8
Tuddenham Suff 108 B3
Tuddenham Suff 124 C4
Tuddenham St Martin Suff 108 B3
Tudeley Kent 52 D6
Tudeley Hale Kent 52 D6
Tudhay Devon 28 G4
Tudhoe Durham 233 D11
Tudhoe Grange Durham 233 E11
Tudor Hill W Mid 134 D2
Tudorville Hereford 97 G11
Tudweiliog Gwyn 144 B4
Tuebrook Mers 182 C5
Tuesley Sur 50 E3
Tuesnoad Kent 54 E2
Tuffley Glos 80 C4
Tufnell Park London 67 B9
Tufton Hants 48 D3
Tufton Pembs 91 F10
Tugby Leics 136 C5
Tugford Shrops 131 F11
Tughall Northumb 264 D6
Tulchan Lodge Angus 292 F3
Tullecombe W Sus 34 B4
Tullibardine Perth 286 F3
Tullibody Clack 279 B7
Tullich Argyll 284 F4
Tullich Highld 299 E9
Tullich Highld 300 G6
Tullich Muir Highld 301 B7
Tulliemet Perth 286 B3
Tulloch Aberds 293 F9
Tulloch Aberds 303 F8
Tulloch Highld 290 E5
Tulloch Perth 286 E4
Tulloch Castle Highld 300 C5
Tullochgorm Argyll 275 D10
Tulloch-gribban Highld 301 G9
Tullochroisk Perth 285 B11
Tullochvenus Aberds 293 C7
Tulloes Angus 287 C9
Tullybannocher Perth 285 E11
Tullybelton Perth 286 D4
Tullycross Stirl 277 D9
Tullyfergus Perth 286 C6
Tullymurdoch Perth 286 B5
Tullynessle Aberds 293 B7
Tulse Hill London 67 E10
Tumbler's Green Essex 106 F6
Tumble / Y Tymbl Carms 75 C8
Tumby Lincs 174 D2
Tumby Woodside Lincs 174 D3
Tummel Bridge Perth 285 B11
Tumpy Green Glos 80 E2
Tumpy Lakes Hereford 97 B10
Tunbridge Hill Medway 69 E10
Tunbridge Wells / Royal Tunbridge Wells Kent 52 F5
Tunga W Isles 304 E6
Tungate Norf 160 D5
Tunley Bath 45 B7
Tunley Glos 80 E6
Tunnel Hill Worcs 98 C6
Tunnel Pits N Lincs 199 G8
Tunshill Gtr Man 196 E2
Tunstall E Yorks 209 G12
Tunstall Kent 69 G11
Tunstall Lancs 212 E2
Tunstall Norf 143 B8
Tunstall N Yorks 224 F4
Tunstall Staffs 150 D5
Tunstall Stoke 168 E5
Tunstall Suff 127 G7
Tunstall T&W 243 G9
Tunstead Derbys 185 G10
Tunstead Gtr Man 196 G4
Tunstead Norf 160 E5
Tunworth Hants 49 D7
Tupsley Hereford 97 C10
Tupton Derbys 170 B5
Turbary Common Poole 19 C7
Turfdown Corn 5 B11
Turf Hill Gtr Man 196 E2
Turfholm S Lnrk 259 B8
Turfmoor Devon 28 G3
Turfmoor Shrops 149 F7
Turgis Green Hants 49 B7
Turin Angus 287 B9
Turkdean Glos 81 B10
Turkey Island Hants 33 E9
Turkey Island W Sus 34 D3
Turkey Tump Hereford 97 F10
Tur Langton Leics 136 E4
Turleigh Wilts 61 G10
Turleygreen Shrops 132 F5
Turlin Moor Poole 18 C5
Turmer Hants 31 F10
Turn Lancs 195 D10
Turnalt Argyll 275 C9
Turnastone Hereford 97 D7
Turnberry S Ayrs 244 B6
Turnchapel Plym 7 E9
Turnditch Derbys 170 F3
Turner Green Lancs 203 G8
Turner's Green E Sus 23 B10
Turner's Green E Sus 52 G6
Turner's Green Warks 118 D3
Turner's Green W Berks 64 F4
Turners Hill W Sus 51 F10
Turners Puddle Dorset 18 C2
Turnerwood S Yorks 187 E8
Turnford Herts 86 E5
Turnhouse Edin 280 G3
Turnhurst Stoke 168 E5
Turnstead Milton Derbys 185 E8
Turnworth Dorset 30 F4
Turrerich Perth 286 D2
Turriff Aberds 303 D7
Tursdale Durham 234 D2
Turton Bottoms Blkburn 195 D8
Turves Cambs 138 D6
Turves Green W Mid 117 B10
Turvey Beds 121 G8
Turville Bucks 84 G3
Turville Heath Bucks 84 G2
Turweston Bucks 102 D2
Tushielaw Borders 261 F8
Tutbury Staffs 152 D4
Tutnall Worcs 117 C9
Tutnalls Glos 79 E10
Tutshill Glos 79 G8
Tutt Hill Kent 54 D3
Tuttington Norf 160 D4
Tutts Clump W Berks 64 E5
Tutwell Corn 12 F3
Tuxford Notts 188 G2
Twatt Orkney 314 D2
Twatt Shetland 313 H5
Twechar E Dunb 278 F4
Tweedale Telford 132 C4
Tweeddaleburn Borders 270 E5
Tweedmouth Northumb 273 E9
Tweedsmuir Borders 260 E3
Twelve Heads Corn 4 G5
Twelve Oaks E Sus 37 C11
Twelvewoods Corn 6 B4
Twemlow Green Ches E 168 B3
Twenties Kent 71 F10
Twenty Lincs 156 E3
Twerton Bath 61 G8
Twickenham London 67 E7
Twigworth Glos 98 G6
Twineham W Sus 36 D3
Twineham Green W Sus 36 C3
Twinhoe Bath 45 B8
Twinstead Essex 107 D7
Twinstead Green Essex 106 D6
Twiss Green Warr 183 B11
Twist Devon 28 G3
Twiston Lancs 204 E2
Twitchen Devon 41 G9
Twitchen Shrops 115 B7
Twitchen Mill Devon 41 G9
Twitham Kent 55 B9
Twitton Kent 52 B4
Two Bridges Devon 13 G8
Two Bridges Glos 79 D11
Two Burrows Corn 4 F4
Two Dales Derbys 170 C3
Two Gates Staffs 134 C4
Two Mile Ash M Keynes 102 D6
Two Mile Ash W Sus 35 B10
Two Mile Hill Bristol 60 E6
Two Mile Oak Cross Devon 8 B6
Two Mills Ches W 182 G5
Two Pots Devon 40 E4
Two Waters Herts 85 D9
Twr Anglesey 178 E2
Twycross Leics 134 C6
Twydall Medway 69 F9
Twyford Bucks 102 F3
Twyford Derbys 152 D6
Twyford Dorset 30 D5
Twyford Hants 33 C7
Twyford Leics 154 G4
Twyford Lincs 155 E8
Twyford Norf 159 E10
Twyford Oxon 101 D9
Twyford Shrops 148 D6
Twyford Wokingham 65 D9
Twyford Worcs 99 B10
Twyford Common Hereford 97 D10
Twyn-Allws Mon 78 C3
Twynholm Dumfries 237 D8
Twyning Glos 99 D7
Twyning Green Glos 99 D8
Twynllanan Carms 94 G5
Twynmynydd Carms 75 C11
Twyn Shôn-Ifan Caerph 77 G11
Twynyrodyn M Tydf 77 D9
Twyn-yr-odyn V Glam 58 E6
Twyn-y-Sheriff Mon 78 D6
Twywell Northants 121 B9
Tyberton Hereford 97 D7
Tyburn W Mid 134 E2
Tyby Norf 159 D11
Ty-coch Swansea 56 C6
Tycroes Carms 75 C10
Tycrwyn Powys 148 F2
Tyddewi / St Davids Pembs 90 F5
Tydd Gote Lincs 157 F9
Tydd St Giles Cambs 157 F8
Tydd St Mary Lincs 157 F8
Tyddyn Powys 129 F9
Tyddyn Angharad Denb 165 F9
Tyddyn Dai Anglesey 178 C6
Tyddyn-mawr Gwyn 163 G9
Ty-draw Conwy 164 D5
Ty-draw Swansea 57 C7
Tye Hants 22 C2
Tye Common Essex 87 G11
Tyegate Green Norf 161 G7
Tye Green Essex 87 C10
Tye Green Essex 87 D7
Tye Green Essex 87 F11
Tye Green Essex 105 D11
Tye Green Essex 105 G10
Tye Green Essex 106 G5
Tyersal W Yorks 205 G9
Ty-fry Mon 78 F6
Tyganol V Glam 58 E4
Ty-hen Carms 92 G6
Ty-hen Gwyn 144 C3
Ty-isaf Carms 56 B4
Tyla Mon 78 C2
Tylagwyn Bridgend 58 B2
Tyldesley Gtr Man 195 G7
Tyle Carms 94 F3
Tyle-garw Rhondda 58 C4
Tyler Hill Kent 70 G6
Tylers Causeway Herts 86 D3
Tylers Green Bucks 84 G6
Tyler's Green Essex 87 D8
Tyler's Green Sur 51 C11
Tyler's Hill Bucks 85 E7
Ty Llwyn Bl Gwent 77 D11
Tylorstown Rhondda 77 F8
Tylwch Powys 129 G9
Ty-mawr Anglesey 179 D7
Ty Mawr Carms 93 C10
Ty-mawr Conwy 181 F7
Ty Mawr Cwm Conwy 164 F6
Tynant Rhondda 58 B5
Ty-nant Conwy 165 G7
Ty-nant Gwyn 147 D8
Tyncelyn Ceredig 112 E2
Tyndrum Stirl 285 D7
Tyne Dock T&W 243 D9
Tyneham Dorset 18 E3
Tynehead Midloth 271 D7
Tynemouth T&W 243 D9
Tyne Tunnel T&W 243 D8
Tynewydd Ceredig 92 B4
Tynewydd Neath 76 D4
Tynewydd Rhondda 76 F6
Ty-Newydd Ceredig 111 D10
Tyning Bath 45 B7
Tyninghame E Loth 282 F2
Tyn-lon Gwyn 163 D7
Tynron Dumfries 247 E8
Tyntesfield N Som 60 E4
Tyntetown Rhondda 77 F9
Ty'n-y-bryn Rhondda 58 B4
Tyn-y-celyn Wrex 148 B3
Tyn-y-coed Shrops 148 D4
Ty'n-y-coedcae Caerph 59 B7
Tyn-y-cwm Swansea 75 E10
Tynyfedw Conwy 165 B7
Tyn-y-fedwen Powys 148 C2
Ty'n-y-ffordd Denb 181 G8
Tyn-y-ffridd Powys 148 C2
Ty'n-y-garn Bridgend 57 E11
Tynygongl Anglesey 179 E8
Tynygraig Ceredig 112 D3
Tyn-y-graig Powys 113 G10
Ty'n-y-groes Conwy 180 G3
Ty'n-y-maes Gwyn 163 C10
Tyn-y-pwll Anglesey 178 D6
Ty'n-yr-eithin Ceredig 112 E3
Tynyrwtra Powys 129 F7
Tyrells End C Beds 103 E9
Tyrell's Wood Sur 51 B7
Ty'r-felin-isaf Conwy 164 C5
Ty Rhiw Rhondda 58 C6
Tyrie Aberds 303 C9
Tyringham M Keynes 103 B7
Tyseley W Mid 134 G2
Ty-Sign Caerph 78 G2
Tythecott Devon 24 D6
Tythegston Bridgend 57 F11
Tytherington Ches E 184 F6
Tytherington S Glos 61 B7
Tytherington Som 45 D9
Tytherington Wilts 46 E2
Tytherleigh Devon 28 G4
Tytherton Lucas Wilts 62 E2
Tyttenhanger Herts 85 D11
Ty-uchaf Powys 147 E10
Tywardreath Corn 5 E11
Tywardreath Highway Corn 5 D11
Tywyn Conwy 180 F3
Tywyn Gwyn 110 C2


## U


Uachdar W Isles 296 F3
Uags Highld 295 B9
Ubberley Stoke 168 F6
Ubbeston Green Suff 126 C6
Ubley Bath 44 B4
Uckerby N Yorks 224 E4
Uckfield E Sus 37 C7
Uckinghall Worcs 99 D7
Uckington Glos 99 G8
Uckington Shrops 131 B11
Uddingston S Lnrk 268 C3
Uddington S Lnrk 259 C9
Udimore E Sus 38 D5
Udley N Som 60 G3
Udny Green Aberds 303 G8
Udny Station Aberds 303 G9
Udston S Lnrk 268 D3
Udstonhead S Lnrk 268 F4
Uffcott Wilts 62 D6
Uffculme Devon 27 E9
Uffington Lincs 137 B11
Uffington Oxon 63 B10
Uffington Shrops 149 G10
Ufford Pboro 137 C11
Ufford Suff 126 G5
Ufton Warks 119 E7
Ufton Green W Berks 64 F6
Ufton Nervet W Berks 64 F6
Ugadale Argyll 255 E8
Ugborough Devon 8 D3
Ugford Wilts 46 G5
Uggeshall Suff 143 G8
Ugglebarnby N Yorks 227 D7
Ughill S Yorks 186 C3
Ugley Essex 105 F10
Ugley Green Essex 105 F10
Ugthorpe N Yorks 226 C5
Uidh W Isles 297 M2
Uig Argyll 276 E2
Uig Argyll 288 D3
Uig Highld 296 F7
Uig Highld 298 C3
Uigen W Isles 304 E2
Uigshader Highld 298 E4
Uisken Argyll 274 B4
Ulaw Aberds 303 G9
Ulbster Highld 310 E7
Ulcat Row Cumb 230 G4
Ulceby Lincs 190 G6
Ulceby N Lincs 200 E6
Ulceby Skitter N Lincs 200 E6
Ulcombe Kent 53 D10
Uldale Cumb 229 D10
Uley Glos 80 F3
Ulgham Northumb 252 E6
Ullapool Highld 307 K6
Ullcombe Devon 28 F2
Ullenhall Warks 118 D2
Ullenwood Glos 80 B6
Ulleskelf N Yorks 206 E6
Ullesthorpe Leics 135 F10
Ulley S Yorks 187 D7
Ullingswick Hereford 97 B11
Ullington Worcs 100 B2
Ullinish Highld 294 B5
Ullock Cumb 229 G7
Ullock Cumb 229 G10
Ulnes Walton Lancs 194 D4
Ulpha Cumb 220 G3
Ulrome E Yorks 209 B9
Ulshaw N Yorks 214 B2
Ulsta Shetland 312 E6
Ulva House Argyll 288 F6
Ulverley Green W Mid 134 G2
Ulverston Cumb 210 D5
Ulwell Dorset 18 E6
Umberleigh Devon 25 C10
Unapool Highld 306 F7
Unasary W Isles 297 J3
Under Bank W Yorks 196 F6
Underbarrow Cumb 221 G9
Undercliffe W Yorks 205 G9
Underdale Shrops 149 G10
Underdown Devon 14 D3
Underhill London 86 F3
Underhill Wilts 45 G11
Underhoull Shetland 312 C7
Underling Green Kent 53 D9
Underriver Kent 52 C5
Underriver Ho Kent 52 C5
Under the Wood Kent 71 F8
Under Tofts S Yorks 186 D4
Underton Shrops 132 E3
Underwood Newport 59 B11
Underwood Notts 171 E7
Underwood Pembs 73 C7
Underwood Plym 7 D10
Undley Suff 140 G3
Undy Mon 60 B2
Ungisiadar W Isles 304 F3
Unifirth Shetland 313 H4
Union Cottage Aberds 293 D10
Union Mills IoM 192 E4
Union Street E Sus 53 G8
United Downs Corn 4 G4
Unstone Derbys 186 F5
Unstone Green Derbys 186 F5
Unsworth Gtr Man 195 F10
Unthank Cumb 230 B3
Unthank Cumb 230 D5
Unthank Cumb 231 C8
Unthank Derbys 186 F4
Unthank End Cumb 230 D5
Upavon Wilts 46 C6
Up Cerne Dorset 29 G11
Upchurch Kent 69 F10
Upcott Devon 24 D2
Upcott Devon 25 F9
Upcott Devon 25 F11